BUSINESS LEGISLATIONS

Dr. NIRAJ KUMAR

M.Com. (Bus. Admin.), Ph.D., LL.B.,
A.M.S.P.I., F.M.S. P.I., F.A.I.M.C.,
GOLD MEDALIST, National Awardee and Paul Harris Fellow
Advisor: Columbia Holistic University, California, USA.
Price water house cooper, USA.

Former Head and Director,
Department of Business Administration,
University of Lucknow.

Himalaya Publishing House

MUMBAI • NEW DELHI • NAGPUR • BENGALURU • HYDERABAD • CHENNAI • PUNE
LUCKNOW • AHMEDABAD • ERNAKULAM • BHUBANESWAR • INDORE • KOLKATA • GUWAHATI

First Edition : 2009

Second Revised Edition : 2012

Edition : 2024

Published by : Mrs. Meena Pandey for **Himalaya Publishing House Pvt. Ltd.,**
"Ramdoot", Dr. Bhalerao Marg, Girgaon, **Mumbai - 400 004.**
Phone: 022-23860170/23863863, Fax: 022-23877178
E-mail: himpub@vsnl.com; Website: www.himpub.com

Branch Offices :

New Delhi : "Pooja Apartments", 4-B, Murari Lal Street, Ansari Road, Darya Ganj, New Delhi - 110 002. Phone: 011-23270392, 23278631; Fax: 011-23256286

Nagpur : Kundanlal Chandak Industrial Estate, Ghat Road, Nagpur - 440 018. Phone: 0712-2738731, 3296733; Telefax: 0712-2721215

Bengaluru : No. 16/1 (Old 12/1), 1st Floor, Next to Hotel Highlands, Madhava Nagar, Race Course Road, Bengaluru - 560 001. Phone: 080-32919385; Telefax: 080-22286611

Hyderabad : No. 3-4-184, Lingampally, Besides Raghavendra Swamy Matham, Kachiguda, Hyderabad - 500 027. Phone: 040-27560041, 27550139; Mobile: 09390905282

Chennai : No. 8/2, Madley 2nd Street, Ground Floor, T. Nagar, Chennai - 600 017. Phone: 044-28144004/28144005; Mobile: 09345345051

Pune : First Floor, "Laksha" Apartment, No. 527, Mehunpura, Shaniwarpeth (Near Prabhat Theatre), Pune - 411 030. Phone: 020-24496323/24496333; Mobile: 09370579333

Lucknow : Jai Baba Bhavan, Church Road, Near Manas Complex and Dr. Awasthi Clinic, Aliganj, Lucknow - 226 024 (U.P.). Phone: 0522-2339329, 4068914; Mobile: 09307501550

Ahmedabad : 114, "SHAIL", 1st Floor, Opp. Madhu Sudan House, C.G. Road, Navrang Pura, Ahmedabad - 380 009. Phone: 079-26560126; Mobile: 09377088847

Ernakulam : 39/176 (New No: 60/251) 1st Floor, Karikkamuri Road, Ernakulam, Kochi - 682011, Phone: 0484-2378012, 2378016; Mobile: 09344199799

Bhubaneswar : 5 Station Square, Bhubaneswar - 751 001 (Odisha). Phone: 0674-2532129, Mobile: 09338746007

Indore : Kesardeep Avenue Extension, 73, Narayan Bagh, Flat No. 302, IIIrd Floor, Near Humpty Dumpty School, Indore - 452 007 (M.P.). Mobile: 09301386468

Kolkata : 108/4, Beliaghata Main Road, Near ID Hospital, Opp. SBI Bank, Kolkata - 700 010, Phone: 033-32449649, Mobile: 09883055590, 07439040301

Guwahati : House No. 15, Behind Pragjyotish College, Near Sharma Printing Press, P.O. Bharalumukh, Guwahati - 781009, (Assam). Mobile: 09883055590, 09883055536

DTP by : HPH, Editorial Office, Bhandup (Priyanka M.)

Printed at : Shri Krishna offset Press Delhi-93

Om Asatoma Satgamaya
Tamasoma Jyotirgamaya
Section 1.01 Mrityorma Amritam Gamaya

Let Us Lead From Untruth To Truth
From Darkness To Light
From Mortality To Immortality.

(1-3-28, *Brihadaranyaka Upanishad*)

Article II.

Article III. Gayatri Mantra

Om Bhur, Bhuvah, Suvah
Tat Savitur Verenayam
Bhargo Devasya Dhimahi
Dhiyo Yo Naa Prachodayat

(*Yajurveda* 36-3)

Om, Who is Dearer than Our Breath
Is Self Subsistent.
All Knowledge and All Bless.
We Meditate upon That Adorable Effulgence of the
Respledent Vivifier of the Marcrocosm, Savita,
May He Illumine Our Intellects Unto The Right Path.

BUSINESS LEGISLATIONS

समर्पण

ॐ

शिरडी के साईं बाबा

के पावन, पवित्र चरणों में

जिनकी प्रेरणा एवं आर्शिवाद के बिना,

लेखक का यह

प्रयास असम्भव था

उन्ही को आभार सहित

सादर एवं सविनय

यह प्रस्तुति समर्पित है।

(डॉ. नीरज कुमार, सी–4/8, रिवर बैंक कालोनी, लखनऊ – 226018)

CONTENTS

PART "K" INDIAN CONTRACT ACT, 1872

PART "L" THE COMPANIES ACT, 1956

PART "M" RIGHT TO INFORMATION ACT, 2005

PREFACE TO THE SECOND REVISED EDITION

The reception to the first edition of this book within a very short span of about a-year-and-a-half has been a source of inspiration to me to undertake revision.

With the introduction of new Act in India, the Right to Information Act, 2005 has assumed a greater significance and has been incorporated as an important Act in various courses of Law and Management studies. These aspects have also been dealt in detail in the present volume. This chapters will not only be useful to students but will be of immense help to practising managers.

The basic aim of this book is to supply the students of management/business administration in various Universities and Institutes a realistic blend of survey of theory and practice in the field of Business Legislations comprehensively and adequately. Yet the thrust of the book with managerial problem-solving rather than mere descriptive of existing practices is one of its main feature. However, to make it more students' friendly, an exhaustive list of questions for discussions has been appended in the last.

A book, such as this one, incorporates the ideas of many people — authors, teachers and managers — most of them albeit unnamed. The author owes, as in previous edition, a deep sense of gratitude and offers his sincere thanks for the valuable suggestions and contributions that have been adopted wherever practicable in the present edition.

My great appreciation goes out to Himalaya Publishing House for their understanding, cooperation and expertise throughout this project.

While great care has been taken, errors do creep in. The author craves for indulgence of readers in deficiencies in analysis of errors, if any. Suggestions for further improvement of this volume are thankfully accepted from learned constructive critics.

C – 4/8, River Bank Colony,
LUCKNOW – 226 018.

Dr. NIRAJ KUMAR

PREFACE

Business Legislations is a subject that not only grows but also changes with the passage of time as per the requirements of the business of that country. It comprises laws of practical importance in the modern business world. Therefore, the study of Business Legislations, a compilation of various laws that affect the business and the business has to revolve around these laws, has been given a top priority for Commerce, Management and Law education by all universities and professional institutes. However, some authors have termed it as "Business Law or Laws" but I am of the firm view that since it is not a law in itself rather a compilation of various legislations that effect business the term "Business Legislations" is more appropriate.

There is abundant of literature available in the market of this subject. However, there still seems to be a need for a work which unfolds in an easily comprehensible manner the intricacies of the law and seeks to answer the tricky questions which might intrigue the mind of a curious reader. It is with this feeling that the present text has been written.

The object of this book "*Business Legislations*" is to set out the basic principles of various laws essential for business, simply and clearly. An attempt has been made to present the concepts as briefly and concisely as possible without sacrificing essential features. Leading cases have been provided for illustration. Section numbers of the relevant statutes have been given in order to facilitate reference. This book on Business Legislations covers the whole teeming ground in a manner differing from the usual textbook, by giving in one volume, a thorough, lucid and easily understandable explanation of the various principles of that branch of law which has to deal with business transactions and business community.

This book explains the fundamental principles of the subject and presents a comprehensive, coordinated, cohesive and accurate exposition of its statutory provisions in a lucid manner. Besides, the presentation is easy to gasp since each complicated provision has been explained with the help of illustrations and analogies.

The book is intended primarily as a textbook for graduate and postgraduate students preparing for the various University and Professional Examinations in Business Legislations, but it cannot fail to be useful to businessmen who have from time-to-time to deal with several branches of the subject. The aim is to explain the provisions of the different enactments, and in doing so, the book deals with the law, subject-by-subject, grouping together the sections of the respective acts so as to make them simple and logical to the student, convenient to the businessman and interesting to the casual reader who may care to use it as a reference. Even lawyers and practitioners will find the book of practical use inasmuch as it contains in a handy volume the whole range of Business Legislations, supported by citation of both English and Indian cases and references to the relevant sections of the various Acts. Where controversial points occur, the author has based the exposition on the general consensus of standard authoritative opinion of leading writers, and the considered judgements of the courts.

Practice questions have been given at the end of each chapter to enable the readers to evaluate their understanding of the subject.

The subject-matter has been organised in parts dealing with the laws relating to various aspects of business. The Chapters have been designed to explain topic-wise the statutory provisions, grouping together the relevant Sections. Both English and Indian decided cases have been cited at appropriate places with a view to securing the necessary authenticity and clarity of the subject.

I am grateful to my friend, philosopher and guide, Professor Emeritus Prof. Avtar Singh a leading authority in the field for his helpful suggestions and guidance. I also express my gratitude to the various authorities on the subject, both English and Indian, on whose works I have heavily drawn in preparation of this book.

Thanks are due to Sri S.P. Shukla, Nandit Srivastava, Rajan Misra and Rajesh Shukla all advocates of High Court of Judicature, Allahabad, Lucknow Bench for their valuable suggestions and providing their all possible support whenever required.

Thanks are also due to Sri Ashok Kumar Srivastava and many others for logistical support.

New Year, January 1, 2009

Dr. NIRAJ KUMAR

C – 4/8, River Bank Colony,
LUCKNOW – 226 018.
E-mail:
kumarniraj1000@rediffmail.com
nirajklko@yahoo.com, nirajklko@gmail.com

PART A

INTRODUCTION

CHAPTER

1

Business *vis-à-vis* Environment

In this chapter, we begin by answering the question, 'What is business'? and what is the relation between Business and Law. We then introduce the main topic — the legal environment of business and discuss the need for the business managers to understand the same.

What is Business?

Business may be understood as the organized efforts of enterprise to supply consumers with goods and services for a profit. Businesses vary in size, as measured by the number of employees or by sales volume. But, all businesses share the same purpose: to earn profits.

The purpose of business goes beyond earning profit. There are:

- It is an important institution in society.
- Be it for the supply of goods and services
- Creation of job opportunities
- Offer of better quality of life
- Contributing to the economic growth of the country.

Hence, it is understood that the role of business is crucial. Society cannot do without business. It needs no emphasis that business needs society as much.

BUSINESS TODAY

Modern business is dynamic. If there is any single word that can best describe today's business, it is change. This change makes the companies spend substantially on Research and Development (R & D) to survive in the market. Mass production and mass marketing are the norms followed by business enterprises. The number of companies with an annual turnover of Rs.100 crore each was only three in 1969-70.The figure has gone up by hundreds these days. Today's business is characterized by diversification, which may be:

Concentric Diversification — It refers to the process of adding new, but relates products or services.

Horizontal Diversification — Adding new, unrelated products or services for present customers is called Horizontal Diversification.

Conglomerate Diversification — It refers to adding new and unrelated products or services.

Going international is yet another trend followed by modern business houses.

Business houses are exposed to global competition, which argues well for consumers. Also occupying a major role is science in the global economic scenario.

Business is as old as civilisation itself. Also, it is the greatest thing in the world as no development could have taken place in the absence of business. Business provides to the society the things it needs in order to survive, enjoy life and improve its material and social well-being. Besides, it undertakes productive utilisation of wealth-producing resources of the society. It also leads to innovation and improvements in production process and thus enriches the life of people by enhancing the functional capacity of the available resources.

Industrial revolution and the development in the fields of communication, transportation, automation and the energy sources have influenced the life in a big way. Organisations engaged in business have grown in size; some of them beyond any expectations. The budgets of some of the multinational corporations today exceed the budgets of the States where they are operating.

Today, business enterprises dominate our lives. There was a time when business played very insignificant role in economic, social, political and technological affairs but now it plays a very significant one. It is not too much to say that the wealth of a country is, to a great extent, created and controlled by business. This gives business and executives thereof the "enormous power" to — affect the lives of different segments of society, such as customers, employees, shareholders, etc.

BUSINESS IN 21st CENTURY

Large organizations, with a large workforce will not exist. They will be 'Mini' organizations. Business during the 21st century will be knowledge-based, tomorrow's manager need not spend his time on file pushing and paper-shuffling. Information technology will take care of most of that work. Organizations will become flat. Linear relationship between the boss and manger and authority flowing downwards and obedience upward will disappear. Employees will have no definite jobs. Most of the jobs will last for two to five years. Remuneration will depend on one's contribution to organization.

BUSINESS GOALS

Profit — Making profit is the primary goal of any business enterprise.

Growth — Business should grow in all directions over a period of time.

Power — Business houses have vast resources at its command. These resources confer enormous economic and political power.

Employee satisfaction and development — Business is people. Caring for employee satisfaction and providing for their development has been one of the objectives of enlightened business enterprises.

Quality Products and Services — Persistent quality of products earns brand loyalty, a vital ingredient of success.

Market Leadership — To earn a niche for oneself in the market, innovation is the key factor.

Challenging — Business offers vast scope and poses formidable challenges.

Joy of creation — It is through business strategies new ideas and innovations are given a shape and are converted into useful products and services.

Service to society — Business is a part of society and has several obligations towards it.

What is the Environment of Business?

Environment refers to all external forces, which have a bearing on the functioning of business. Environment factors "are largely if not totally, external and beyond the control of individual industrial enterprises and their managements." The business environment poses threats to a firm or offers immense opportunities for potential market exploitation.

Systems approach considers business unit as an open system which has continuous interaction with its external environment for its survival and growth. Thus, a business unit exchanges information, materials and other resources with the environment. It gets inputs such as materials, capital, energy, human resources, and information from the environment. The inputs are transformed into goods and services which are supplied as outputs to the environment. Inputs of a system are the outputs of other systems and similarly its outputs are the inputs of other systems. Thus, all systems have interaction with a variety of other systems in the environment and also with the environmental suprasystem. That is why it is essential for business to understand their external environment and take steps to cope with the changing environment.

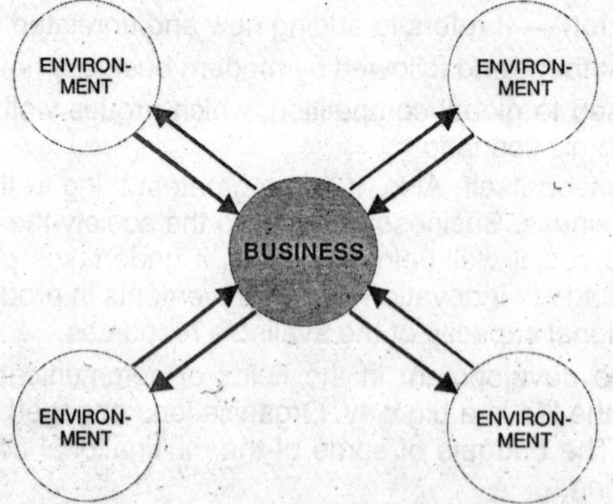

Fig. 1 Business and its Environment

Environment includes such factors as socio-economic, technological, supplier, competitor and the government. There are two more factors, which exercise considerable influence on business. They are physical or natural environment and global environment.

Technological Environment

Technology is understood as the systematic application of scientific or other organized knowledge to practical tasks. Technology changes fast and to keep pace with it, businessmen should be ever alert to adopt changed technology in their businesses.

Economic Environment

There is close relationship between business and its economic environment. Business obtains all its needed inputs from the economic environment and it absorbs the output of business units.

Political Environment

It refers to the influence exerted by the three political institutions, viz., legislature executive and the judiciary in shaping, directing, developing and controlling business activities. A stable and dynamic political environment is indispensable for business growth.

Natural Environment

Business, an economic pursuit of man, continues to be dictated by nature. To what extent business depends on nature and what is the relationship between the two constitutes an interesting study.

Global or International Environment

Thanks to liberalization, Indian companies are forces to view business issues from a global perspective. Business responses and managerial practices must be fine-tuned to survive in the global environment.

Social and Culture Environment

It refers to people's attitude to work and wealth; role of family, marriage, religion and education; ethical issues and social responsiveness of business.

Thus, business environment means the sum of all external forces and conditions that influence business and potentially affects its performance. These forces include economic factors, socio-cultural factors, politico-legal factors, suppliers of capital and materials, labour organisations, customers, regulating agencies, government, technology, etc.

Some of the environmental factors impose several constraints on the business enterprise, whereas some others act as facilitators. In fact, the same factor may impose some obligations and also bestow certain privileges on business. In any case, they have considerable impact and influence on the scope and direction of business activities. In fact, the performance of the business unit is to a great extent determined by these external forces.

Therefore, business environment is the totality of all such factors which influence the working and decision-making of a business organisation and encompasses the climate or set of conditions-economic, political, legal, social, institutional and technological — under which every business organisation has to operate. Business environment is a relative concept comprising monetary, fiscal, industrial, licensing, export-import, social and technological policies having great bearing on economic and business environment.

ENVIRONMENT – BUSINESS RELATIONS

Business is the product of the technological, political-legal, economic, social-cultural, global and natural factors amidst which it functions. Three features are common to this web of relationship between business and its environment.

- There is symbolic relationship between business and its environment and among the environmental factors. In other words, business is influenced by its environment and in turn, to certain degree, it will influence the external forces. Similarly, political-legal environment influences economic environment and vice versa. The same relationship between other environment factors too.

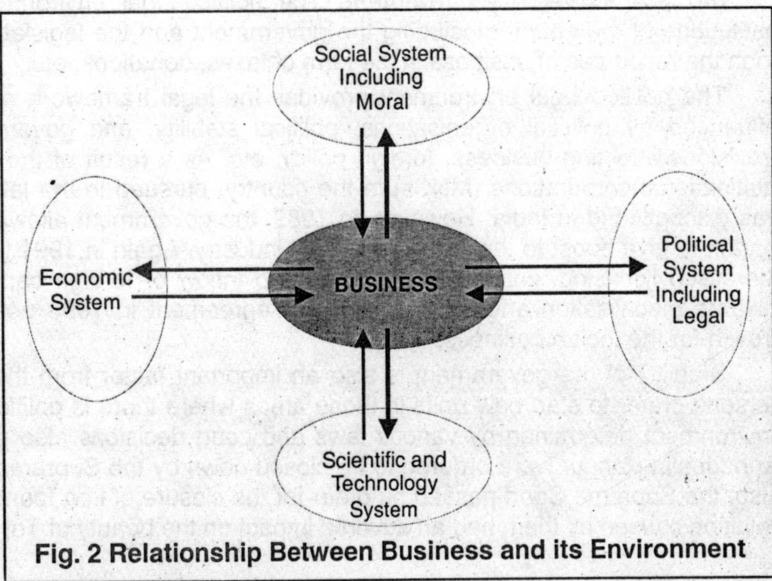

Fig. 2 Relationship Between Business and its Environment

- These environmental forces are dynamic. They keep on changing as years roll by, so does business.

The third feature is that a particular business firm, by itself, may not be in a position to change its environment. But along with other firms, business will be in a position to mould the environment in its favor.

While interacting with the environment, business has to take certain decisions, which are partly controlled by the external forces. Many a time, business has to identify itself completely with the environment and fit in with environmental framework. It is to be noted that while business is affected by its environment, it also affects its environment. Though it has very little control over its environment, nevertheless it does affect the different segments of the environment, some of them very significantly. These environmental factors constantly change, and therefore, business must adapt itself in order to survive and prosper.

Also, the relationship between business and its environment is one of mutual benefit and therefore, it has been shown as a two-way relationship in Fig. 2. This may be referred to as a 'symbiotic relationship' as business functions in such a way that it both takes from and gives nurture to the various segments of its environment. Only through such a relationship, a business can survive and prosper. Otherwise it will starve and wither away. Thus, business is influenced and shaped by its environment and also influences the segments which come into contact with it. In the latter sense, business has also been an instrument of change.

Segments Constituting Environment of Business

Business cannot function in isolation or in a vacuum. Its environment has, more or less, a direct bearing on its success or otherwise. Business is a part of the total environment in which we live, being influenced by it, while being a force in influencing it. As presented in Figure 1.2, social, political, scientific and technological and economic systems make up the external environment which has a tremendous impact on the development and growth of business. The environment of business comprises several segments which maybe classified as under:

(i) ***Social environment.*** Comprising customers and employees as well as social institutions which obtain benefit from business or provide benefit to it.

(ii) ***Economic environment.*** The economic environment encompasses the whole economy, the various economic institutions, including the competing business enterprise with which business has to deal. The economic environment is set by the type of national economic system including the nature of property rights, ownerships of means of production, production relations, role of planning, functions of price mechanism, etc. The government influences the economic environment of business through economic planning, monetary policies, fiscal policies and budgets, industrial regulations, Business Legislations, controls on prices and wages and commercial policies affecting export and import. For instance, if the government announces a cut in the excise duty on motor vehicles, the sales of business firms manufacturing motor vehicles will go up. Similarly, if the government exempts export units from income tax, such business units will get a boost.

The economic environment of business also includes all markets in which it buys and sells, raises funds, gets labour, etc. The business is invariably influenced by the conditions of various markets. For instance, if there is uncertainty in the capital market, it will not be advisable to go in for a public issue because of the risk of poor response.

(iii) ***Politico-legal environment.*** The politico-legal environment of business comprises political and legal institutions of the country including the government and the legislature which regulate business activity, and draws upon the resources of business in the form of taxes, donations, etc.

The politico-legal environment provides the legal framework within which business is to function. Business is influenced by political organisations, political stability, and government's intervention in business, constitutional provisions affecting business, foreign policy, etc. As a result of the government's policy of restricting the growth of multinational corporations (MNCs) in the country, pursued in the late seventies, the bottling and sale of Coca Cola was discontinued in India. However, in 1989, the government allowed another, MNC Pepsi Cola to enter the Indian market to give boost to the food processing industry. Again in 1991 the government revised its industrial policy which liberalised licensing, imports and exports and inflow of foreign capital and technology into the country. The trend towards globalisation and signing of GATT agreement in 1993 posed new challenges and created new vistas of growth for the Indian business.

Stability of the government is also an important factor from the point of view of growth of business. Business persons prefer to start new units in those areas where there is political stability and where rule of law prevails. Legal environment determined by various laws and court decisions also put pressure on business. For instance, several tanneries in Kanpur were ordered to be closed down by the Supreme Court, as they were polluting the Holy Ganges. Also, the Supreme Court passed on order for the closure of iron foundaries around the famous Taj Mahal because air pollution caused by them had an adverse impact on the beauty of Taj Mahal.

(iv) *Technological environment.* Technological environment of business comprises the know-how and production and management technology available to business at any point or during a particular period of time. The state of technology plays an important role in determining the type and quality of goods and services to be produced and the type of plant and equipment to be used. Nowadays, the pace of technological change is very fast. Technological environment influences business firms in terms of investment on technology consistent application of technology and the effects of technology on markets. Therefore, every business organisation has to be actively engaged in technological forecasting. Advancement in automation, information technology will create challenging situations for business firms in the not too distant future.

(v) *International environment* The forces in the international environment may have adverse or favourable impact on business. For example, the disintegration of USSR caused great miseries for Indian exporters in the early nineties. Not only their investment was blocked, further exports were also hindered. This compelled the Indian businesspersons to explore new export markets. Because of liberalisation of industrial licensing by developing nations and reduction of economic barriers between nations as a result of GATT agreement, 1993, several changes seem to be imminent in the near future. Multilateral trading among the nations will increase. The role of WTO, IMF, WB and other international institutions will change and new economic order will take place leading to globalisation of economies.

In modern times no state can afford to live in isolation. It has to cultivate relations with others states of the world out of sheer necessity. Just as no individual can live outside the society similarly no state can live outside the international community. Therefore, international relationship is as much a product of necessity as social existence itself. With the industrial revolution the world shrank and the distances were reduced.

As a result the regional and local problems began to assume world character. With this regional relations were transformed into international relations. The term international relations has been interpreted and defined in two senses — Narrow and Broad. In the narrow sense it is confined to the study of "***Official relations conducted by authorized leaders of the state.***"

By emphasizing official relations, the relations between businessmen, scientists, etc., of the various countries are excluded from the scope of international relations. In the broader sense international relations include ***"all intercourse among states and all movements of people, goods and ideas across national frontiers."***

TYPES OF RELATIONS

Usually, two types of relations exist between states – **cooperative and oppositional.**

- **Cooperative relations** — They are usually non-political and involve no power.
- **Oppositional relations** — The oppositional relations imply conflict among groups and demand use of power.

International relations include study of both. At initial stages, international relations studied only diplomatic history as conditioned by the happening of the past, but soon even to study of international law was included in its scope.

With establishment of the League of Nations, the study of international institutions was also included in its fold. Thus after World War I it came to study the diplomatic history, international law and the league organization. After World War II, its field was further widened and study of military science and regional areas was also included in it. The psychological study through personality and background analysis also gained prominence. Thus, at present international relations have become very extensive.

INTERNATIONAL RELATIONS APPROACHES

Broadly, speaking there are two approaches for the study of international relations.

- **The classical approach** considers the substance more important.
- **Scientific approach** attaches more importance to method and technique.

TYPES OF CLASSICAL APPROACH

The prominent amongst the classical approach are:

- ### Historical approach

Under it, diplomacy and interrelations of a particular period are studied. This approach is not possible in modern world, though it had the advantage of giving the students a deep understanding of the problems in their correct prescriptive.

- ### International organization approach

It studies the behavior of various states in the international organization to determine the attitude of a particular power. This theory does not take into account the activities of a state outside the international organization.

- **International law approach**

It considers the international law as the key to the interpretation of international relations. This approach however ignored the internal politics as a factor in determining the attitude of a power in the international sphere.

TYPES OF SCIENTIFIC APPROACH

The prominent scientific or modern approaches are:

- **Behavior approach** is based on psychology and tries to analyze international relations as strife between various national characters.
- Karl Detsch developed **Quantitative theory** and developed certain measurable indices of community development.
- **Decision-making approach** of Richar C. Synder emphasized the need of probing the minds of the decision makers. While probing their minds both internal and external settings were to be taken into account.
- **The systems theory** developed by Kapalan holds that a theory of international politics normally cannot predict individual actions because the interaction problem is very complex.
- **Equilibrium theory** of International relations and institutions was developed by Liska. He holds that the states seek to secure the best attainable position of equilibrium, and this is desirable.
- **Power approach or realist theory** It tries to understand international relations in term of state interests and holds that the statesmen are guided by interests rather than ideology, or motives.

The entry of MNCs into a country is not only associated with the inflow of technical know-how and capital, but it may also pose threat to the home industries. The units having collaboration with the multinationals may stand to gain, but others may have to face competition in the domestic market.

The dynamics of the business environment fostered by the drastic political changes in the erstwhile communist and socialist countries and the economic liberalization across the world has enormously expanded the opportunities for the multinational corporations, also known by such names as ***international corporation, transnational corporation, global corporation (or firm, company or enterprise) etc.***

The rapidity with which the MNC's are growing is indicated by the fact that while according to the World Investment Report 1997, there were about 45000 MNC's with some 280000 affiliates. According to the World Investment Report 2001, there were over 63,000 of them with about 822,000 affiliates. Only less than 12% of these affiliates were in the developed countries. China was host to about 3.64 lakh of the affiliates (i.e., more than 44% of the total) compared to more than 1400 in India. The MNC's account for a significant share of the world's industrial investment, production, employment and trade.

"A corporation that controls production facilities in more than one country, such facilities having been acquired through the process of foreign direct investment.

Firms that participate in international business, however large they may be, solely by exporting or by licensing technology are not multinational enterprises."

The various benchmarks sometimes used to define "multi nationality" are that the company must:

- Produce (rather than just distribute) abroad as well as in the headquarters Country
- Operate in a certain minimum number of nations (six for example)
- Derive some minimum percentage of its income from foreign operations (e.g., 25%)
- Have a certain minimum ratio of foreign to total number of employees, or of foreign total value of assets
- Possess a management team with geocentric orientations
- Directly control foreign investments (as opposed simply to holding shares in foreign companies).

MERITS OF MNC

The important arguments in favor of the MNCs are mentioned below:

- MNCs help increase the Investment level and thereby the income and employment in host country.
- The transnational corporation has become vehicles for the transfer technology, especially to the developing countries.
- They also kindle a managerial revolution in the host countries through professional management and the employment of highly sophisticated management techniques.
- The MNCs enable the host countries to increase their exports and decrease their import requirements.
- They work to equalize the cost of factors of production around the world.
- MNCs provide an efficient means of integrating national economies.

- The enormous resources of the multinational enterprises enable them to have very efficient research and development systems. Thus, they make a commendable contribution to inventions and innovations.
- MNCs also stimulate domestic enterprise because to support their own operations, the MNCs may encourage and assist domestic suppliers.
- MNCs help increase competition and break monopolies.

DEMERITS OF MNC

The various cases against MNCs are:

- The MNCs technology is designed for worldwide profit maximization, not the development needs of poor countries.
- Through their power and flexibility, MNCs can evade or undermine national economic autonomy and control, and their activities may be inimical to the national interests.
- MNCs may destroy competition and acquire monopoly powers.
- The tremendous power of the global corporations poses the risk that they may threaten the sovereignty of the nations in which they do business.
- MNCs retard growth of employment in the home country.
- The transnational corporations cause fast depletion of some of the non-renewable natural resources in the host country. They have also been accused of the environmental problems.
- The transfer pricing enables MNCs to avoid taxes by manipulating prices on intra company transactions.
- The MNCs undermine local culture and traditions; change the consumption habits for their benefits against the long-term interests of the local community.

PRESPECTIVE

Future holds out an enormous scope for the growth of MNCs. The changes in the economic environment in a large number of countries indicate this. A United Nation's report described several developments that points to a rapidly changing context for economic growth, along with a growing role transnational corporations in that process. These include:

- Increasing emphasis on the market forces and a growing role for the private sector in nearly all developing countries.
- Rapidly changing technologies that are transforming the nature of organization and location of international production.
- The globalization of firms and industries.
- The rise of services to constitute the largest single sector in the world economy and
- Regional economic integration, which involve both the world' largest economies as well as selected developing countries.

MULTINATIONALS IN INDIA

The inflow of foreign funds through MNCs in India is showing an upward trend in recent years. 1991 onwards, the Government of India has taken several steps to attract foreign investments and entry of the MNCs, such as:

- Abolition of industrial licensing
- Removal of restriction on investment under the MRTP Act
- Liberalization of policy and procedure for transfer of technology, import off capital goods, etc
- Existing companies are allowed to raise foreign equity upto 51%
- Provisions of the FERA have been relaxed. As a result, companies with more than 40% foreign equity can operate like any other Indian company.
- Foreign companies are permitted to use their trade in domestic markets.

During the nineties, there has been an increasing trend of foreign investments in India. The government approved 666 foreign collaborations in 1990. This number has become more than double to 1520 by 1992. At present, the USA is the largest investor in India, followed by Switzerland, Japan and UK. Foreign investment has largely been concentrated in sector such as fuel and oil refineries, power chemicals and electrical equipments and electronics.

THE RISE OF INDIAN MULTINATIONALS

After liberalization of Indian market in 1991 and in its due course, India INC. is flying high not only over the

Indian sky but globally. Though it took almost a decade when many Indian forms have slowly and surly embarked on the global path and lead to the emergence of the Indian Multinational Companies. With each passing day, Indian businesses are acquiring companies abroad, becoming worldwide popular suppliers and are recruiting staff across national boundaries.

While an Asian Paints is painting the world red, Tata is rolling out indicas from Birmingham and Sundaram Fasteners nails home the fat that the Indian company is an entity to be reckoned with.

- **TATA Motors** sells its passenger car – Indica in the UK through a marketing alliance with Rover and has acquired a Daewoo Commercial Vehicles unit giving it access to markets in Korea and China.
- **INFOSYS** has 25,634 employees including 600 from 33 nationalities other than Indian. It has 30 marketing offices across the world and 26 global software development centers in the US, Canada, Australia, the UK and Japan.
- **Ranbaxy** is the ninth largest generics company in the world. An impressive 76% of its revenues come from overseas.
- **Dr.Reddy's Laboratories** became the first Asia Pacific pharmaceutical company outside Japan to list on the New York Stock Exchange in 2001.
- **Asian paints are** among the 10 largest decorative paints makers in the world and has manufacturing facilities across 24 countries.
- Small auto components company **Bharat Forge** is now the world's second largest forging maker. It became the world's second largest forgings manufacturer after acquiring Carl Dan Peddinghaus a German forgings company last year. Its workforce includes Japanese, German, American and Chinese people. It has 31 customers across the world and only 31 percent of its turnover comes from India.
- About 80% of revenues for **Tata Consultancy Services** come from outside India. It raised in Asia's second —biggest tech IPO this year and India's largest IPO ever.
- **Sundaram Fasteners** is not merely a nuts and bolts company. It believes in thinking out of the box. Probably that is why it decided to acquire a plant in China. The plant in Jiaxin city in the Haiyan economic zone has ensures one fact; that its customers who were earlier buying Sundaram products in Europe and the US, did not have to go far from home to access the product.

Relationship between Business and its Environment from another View

The environment in which business is placed can also be described from another angle. There are various interest groups which contribute to the continuity and prosperity of business. These groups include consumers, employees, owners, creditors, suppliers, distributors and dealers, competitors, the Governments, etc. The survival and growth of business will depend upon its relations with all these interest groups. These interest groups (also known as "Publics") can be external. Fig. 3 shows business in relation to the different interest groups that constitute its environment.

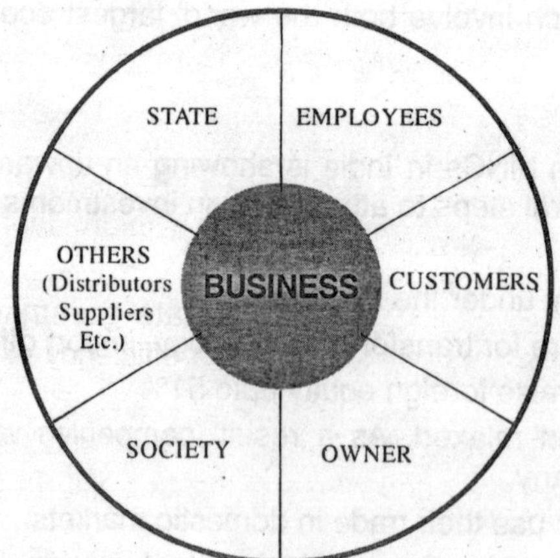

Fig. 3 Business and its Publics

CORPORATE GOVERNANCE

Corporate failures and widespread dissatisfaction with the way many corporate functions have led to the realization, globally, of the need to put in place a proper system for corporate governance.

Corporate governance is concerned with holding the balance between economic and social goals and between individual and communal goals. The governance framework is there to encourage the efficient use of resources and equally to require accountability for the stewardship of those resources.

The aim is to align as nearly as possible the interest of individuals, corporations, and society. The incentive to corporations and to those who own and manage them to adopt internationally accepted governance standards is that these standards will help them to achieve their corporate aims and to attract investment.

The incentive for their adoption by states is that these standards will strengthen the economy and discourage fraud and mismanagement.

RELEVANCE

At least three reasons have triggered off concern in corporate governance in our country.

- Since 1991, the country has moved into liberalized economy and one of the victims of the market-based economy is transparent fair business practice. Several instances of mismanagement have been alleged, with some well-known and senior executive being hauled up for non-performance and/or non-compliance with legal requirements.
- Both domestic as well as foreign investors are becoming more demanding in their approach towards the companies in which they have invested their funds. They seek information and want to influence decisions.
- Interests of non-promoter shareholder and those of small investors are increasingly being undermined. Several MNCs have sought to set up 100 per cent subsidiaries and transfer their businesses to them .In many cases, there was no thought of consultation with non-promoter shareholders.

In this context, some norms of behavior to ensure responsive behavior are of great help. Hence, corporate governance.

FOCUS

Corporate governance is concerned with the values, vision and visibility. It is about the value orientation of the organization, ethical norms for its performance, the direction of development and social accomplishment of the organization and the visibility of its performance and practices.

Corporate management is concerned with the efficiency of the resources use, value addition and wealth creation within the broad parameters of the corporate philosophy established by corporate governance.

IMPORTANCE

- Studies of firms in India and abroad have shown that markets and investors take notice of well-managed companies, respond positively to them, and reward such companies, with higher valuations. In other words they have a system of good corporate governance.
- Strong corporate governance is indispensable to resilient and vibrant capital markets and is an important instrument of investor protection.
- Corporate governance prevents insider trading.
- Under corporate governance, corporates are expected to disseminate the material price sensitive information in a timely and proper manner and also ensures that till such information is made public, insiders abstain from transacting in the securities of the company.
- The principle should be 'disclose or desist'. Good corporate governance, besides protecting the interests of shareholders and all other stakeholders, contributes to the efficiency of a business enterprise, to the creation of wealth and to the country's economy.
- Good corporate governance is considered vital from medium and longterm perspectives to enable firms to compete internationally in sustained way and make them, not only to improve standard of living materially but also to enhance social cohesion.

PRE-REQUISITES

A system of good corporate governance requires the following:

- A proper system consisting of clearly defined and adequate structure of roles, authority and responsibility.
- Vision, principles and norms, which indicate development path, normative considerations, and guidelines and norms for performance.
- A proper system for guiding, monitoring, reporting and control.

SOCIAL RESPONSIBILTY

Social responsibility is the obligation of decision-makers to take actions, which protect and improve the welfare of society as a whole along with their own interests. Every decision the businessman takes and every action he contemplates have social implications.

Be it deciding on diversification, expansion, opening of a new branch, and closure of an existing branch or replacement of men by machines, the society is affected in one way or the other. Whether the issue is significant or not, the businessman should keep his social obligation in mind before contemplating any action.

ARGUMENTS FOR SOCIAL RESPONSIBILITY

- Business has to respond to the needs and expectations of society.
- Improvement of the social environment benefits both society and business.
- Social responsibility discourages additional governmental regulation and intervention.
- Business has a great deal of power, which should be accompanied by an equal amount of responsibility.
- Internal activities of the enterprise have an impact on the external environment.
- The concept of social responsibility protects interests of stockholders.
- Social responsibility creates a favorable public image.
- Business has the resources to solve some of society's problems.
- It is better to prevent social problems through business involvement than to cure them.

ARGUMENTS AGAINST SOCIAL RESPONBILITY

- Social responsibilities could reduce economic efficiency.
- Social responsibility would create excessive costs for business.
- Weakened international balance of payments
- Business has enough power, and social involvement would further increase its power and influence.
- Business people lack the social skills necessary to deal with the problems of society.
- Business is not really accountable to society.

SOCIAL STAKEHOLDERS

Managers, who are concerned about corporate social responsibility, need to identify various interest groups which may affect the functioning of a business organization and may be affected by its functioning. Business enterprises are primarily responsible to six major groups:

- Shareholders
- Employees
- Customers
- Creditors, suppliers and others
- Society and
- Government.

These groups are called interest groups or social stakeholders. They can be affected for better or worse by the business activities of corporations.

SOCIAL RESPONSIVENESS

Social responsiveness (SR) is "the ability of a corporation to relate it operations and policies to the social environment in ways that are mutually beneficial to the company and to society."

In other words, it refers to the development of organizational decision processes whereby managers anticipate, respond to, and manage areas of social responsibility. The need to measure the social responsiveness of an organization led to the concept of social audit.

The social responsiveness of an organization can be measured on the basis of the following criteria:

- Contributions to charitable and civic projects
- Assisting voluntary social organizations in fund-raising
- Employee involvement in civic activities
- Proper reuse of material
- Equal employment opportunity
- Promotion of minorities
- Direct corporate social responsiveness investment

- Fair treatment of employees
- Fair pay and safe working conditions
- Safe and quality products to consumers
- Pollution avoidance and control

BUSINESS EHTICS

The two issues — an organization's social responsibility and responsiveness- ultimately depend on the ethical standards of mangers. The term ethics commonly refers to the rules or principles that define right and wrong conduct. Ethics is defined as the "discipline dealing with what is good and bad and with moral duty and obligation." Business ethics is concerned with truth and justice and has a variety of aspects such as expectations of society, fair competition, advertising, public relations, social responsibilities, consumer autonomy, and corporate behavior in the home country as well as abroad.

TYPES OF BUSINESS ETHICS

Moral management

Moral management strives to follow ethical principles and precepts, moral mangers strive for success, but never violate the parameters of ethical standards. They seek to succeed only within the ideas of fairness, and justice. Moral managers follow the law not only in letter but also in spirit. The moral management approach is likely to be in the best interests of the organization, long run.

Amoral management

This approach is neither immoral nor moral. It ignores ethical considerations.

Amoral management is broadly categorized into two types — intentional and unintentional.

- Intentional amoral managers exclude ethical issues because they think that general ethical standards are not appropriate to business.
- Unintentional amoral managers do not include ethical concerns because they are inattentive or insensitive to the moral implications.

Immoral management

Immoral management is synonymous with "unethical" practices in business. This kind of management not only ignores concerns, it is actively opposed to ethical behavior.

NEED FOR BUSINESS ETHICS

- Ethics corresponds to basic human needs. It is human trait that man desires to be ethical, not only in his private life but also in his business.

These basic ethical need compel the organizations to be ethically oriented.

- Values create credibility with public. A company perceived by the public to be ethically and socially responsive will be honored and respected.

The management has credibility with its employees precisely because it has credibility with the public.

- An ethical attitude helps the management make better decisions, because ethics will force a management to take various aspects — economic, social, and ethical in making decisions.
- Value driven companies are sure to be successful in the long run, though in the short run, they may lose money.
- Ethics is important because the government, law and lawyers cannot do everything to protect society.

ETHICAL GUIDELINES

- **Obeying the law:** Obedience to the law, preferably both the letter and spirit of the law.
- **Tell the Truth:** To build and maintain long-term, trusting and win-win relationships with relevant stockholders.
- **Uphold human dignity:** Giving due importance to the element of human dignity and treating people with respect.
- **Adhere to the golden rule:** "Do unto others as you would have others do unto you."
- **Premium Non-Nocere:** (Above all, do no harm)
- **Allow Room for participation:** Soliciting the participation of stakeholders rather than paternalism. It emphasizes the significance of learning about the needs of stakeholders.
- **Always Act When You Have Responsibility:** Managers have the responsibility of taking action whenever they have the capacity or adequate resources to do so.

TOOLS FOR ETHICAL MANAGEMENT

- **Top management commitment:** Managers can prove their commitment and dedication for work and by acting as role models through their own behaviors.
- **Codes of Ethics:** A formal document that states an organization's primary values and the ethical rules it expects employees to follow. The code is helpful in maintaining ethical behavior among employees.
- **Ethics committees:** Appointment of an ethics committee, consisting of internal and external directors is essential for institutionalizing ethical behavior.
- **Ethics Audits:** Systematic assessment of conformance to organizational ethical policies, understanding of those policies, and identification of serious deviations requiring remedial action.
- **Ethics training:** Ethical training enables managers to integrate employee behavior in ethical arena with major organizational goals.
- **Ethics Hotline:** A special telephone line that enables employees to bypass the normal chain of command in reporting their experiences, expectations and problem. The line is usually handled by an executive appointed to help resolve the issues that are reported.

LEGAL ENVIRONMENT OF BUSINESS

The law is almost a universal human need. No society can exist without a legal order. We need institutions and a framework of rules and regulations to provide firmness to our mutual relations. Without law, there would be complete anarchy in society. That is why we regard rule of law as the essence of civilized society. It provides certainty to our relationships. It emphasises that laws ought to be general in character so that there is no arbitrariness in their exercise. It also emphasises complete equality before law and equal conformity to law by officials and individuals.

But let us emphasise it once again that not all laws are conducive to human good or work to protect our rights or help those who are least advantaged by the system. There are, however, some laws which tend to destroy our freedom or human rights.

Law and business are closely related disciplines. They complement each other. Law is a major factor in business decision-making. Almost every aspect of business is regulated by law. Even the installation of a business unit itself may involve observance of some legal provision or the other. For instance, in the case of a company, the various provisions of the Companies Act, 1956 and other allied laws are to be complied with for incorporation and commencement of business. The contracts entered into by business with others may be held to be void or may be against public policy. Certain business practices may amount to monopolistic, restrictive or unfair trade practices. Products supplied may be defective. There may be deficiency in the service provided by business. The agreement between a manufacturer and his dealers may defeat the provisions of some law or the other.

Sometimes the law may require business to provide certain facilities to its employees, even when the contract does not provide therefore. For instance, the provisions of labour welfare laws impose a legal obligation on employers to provide certain benefits to their workers.

The Monopolies Enquiry Commission recommended the enactment of law to control concentration of economic power in the hands of business. This led to the adoption of Monopolies and Restrictive Trade Practices Act, 1969. Further, the labour union movement arose out of conflicts between workers and industry. This led to the enactment of a plethora of laws for the welfare of the workers. Furthermore, the consumer movement grew from consumer complaints about the defective goods and deficiency in services.

Law seeks to control concentration of economic power. It is assumed that business which has economic power will abuse it to the detriment of its "Publics" as it is rightly said that 'power corrupts and absolute power corrupts absolutely.' Therefore, the law will also be seen throughout this text as a means of limiting concentration and abuse of economic power of business. Let us have a look at the danger of such concentration.

Sometime ago, the Central Government gave complete freedom to Banks to fix interest rates, which was obviously aimed at triggering off competition in the Indian economy. But all nationalised banks in India tried to keep the prime lending rate artificially high by resorting to cartelisation which is violative of the MRTP Act, 1969. The banks arrived at the particular interest rate at the behest of the Indian Banks Association (IBA) and not by taking into consideration the cost of raising funds.

Thus, the legal environment of business is one of the major factors in regulating its conduct though some of the laws may act as facilitators for some segment of the business at some time or the other. Almost every aspect of business is controlled by law. Sometimes even the nature of the business organisation itself imposes legal fetters right from the time of its formation. The buying and selling, production, marketing and other functions of the business enterprise are to be conducted within a certain framework of legal environment. The decision making process of business, right from its very inception, will be guided by law. Certain conduct is illegal, and business which commits acts or omissions declared to be illegal is subject to sanctions. There may be fines or imprisonment if the conduct is declared a crime. The sanctions may include liability for damage if the conduct amounts to a breach of contract. In addition, the law and legal sanctions may be used to prevent certain conduct or to require that certain acts be done or to make business to comply to some requirement. Thus, business people must take decisions within the framework of law otherwise sanctions will be imposed. In this way, law is the foundation for the regulation of all business conduct and decisions. In this text, some of the more important laws controlling business decisions and conduct are explained.

Further, the courts interpret the legal provisions in the light of developments in social, economic and political changes in the country. They resort to what is known as 'judicial activism'. The real life situations pertaining to different legal aspects of business get reflected in judgements. Therefore, the present text has made use of case law profusely.

Further, law provides a mechanism by which disputes between different parties are settled. Thus, there may be a dispute between a business enterprise, on the one hand, and employee, customer, government, dealer, creditor, debtor, etc., on the other. If a shopkeeper sells a defective product to a consumer, then the latter has a number of remedies under different legal provisions, by which his rights will be vindicated.

These legal rights are vested in those who are 'injured', or 'aggrieved' or have suffered 'injustice' at the hands of others. Thus, selling a defective product to a customer 'injures' him; an injustice has been done to him. Therefore, this 'injury' or 'injustice' gives rise to the creation of certain rights in favour of the customer against the shopkeeper. Similarly, if the shopkeeper sells goods on credit to the consumer and the latter fails to make the payment after the term of credit has expired, then the shopkeeper has certain rights against the buyer. These rights are created by custom, statutes, judicial decisions, etc. In fact, there are a number of sources from which these rights arise.

Further, no one can have a right against himself. He can have a right against someone else. No one owes a duty to oneself. One owes a duty to another. Therefore, a right of one person involves imposition of duty on another person.

Moreover, there are no absolute rights; there is always some limitation or the other on the right of a person. For instance, a particular individual has a right to work and earn a living; but he is duty bound not to leak business secrets of his employer. This duty of the employee is nothing but a right of his employer, and it puts a limit on the right of the employee.

In this way, law recognises and adjusts claim of individual rights within a society. At times, important rights of different interests' conflict and the law help in balancing them. For instance, there may be a conflict between the right of a business enterprise granted to it by one law, and the right of its employees granted to them by another law. Also this conflict is increased due to the fact that no rights are absolute. There are always some fetters placed on the rights.

Another factor which must be kept in mind while studying legal environment is that the development of laws is closely associated with historical and social movements. For example, an understanding of such regulatory areas as unfair trade practices, foreign exchange and labour relations is enhanced by an appreciation of the historical movements that led to their creation.

Also, the law seeks to control concentration of power, on the premise that "power corrupts and absolute power corrupts absolutely." In the present text, our concern is with Business Legislations, many of which exist for controlling business power.

There are, however, no readily available answers to legal matters. Business managers cannot be absolutely assured of knowing all the legal ramifications of their decisions. Further, the existing laws are amended from time to time, and new laws are enacted. Many a time, ordinances are promulgated under the provisions of the Constitution of India. Now, for a business student, Business Legislations is at most a minor component of his curriculum. Also, general text books on Business Legislations are of little assistance in dealing with a practical situation by a manager. He has to deal very frequently with some legal document or the other. Sometimes, he may himself be required to draft such a document. At other times, he may be called to scrutinise drafts of legal documents prepared by others. Occasionally, it may be expected of him to interpret a particular part of a document. Further, he may be required to provide certain inputs for the drafting of a document. Frequently, the fate of huge sums of money may depend on the correct analysis and appreciation of one single word or group of words occurring in a particular document.

PERSPECTIVE 1

The Rs 2,800 Crore Enron-sponsored Dabhol Power Project in Maharashtra

The Enron Development Corporation of USA, which is one of the largest integrated natural gas companies in the world, started construction in Maharashtra, in April 1995, on the 695, MW gas fired plant. But the new government of Maharashtra-the Shiv Sena — BJP combine ordered a review of the project. The BJP had opposed the deal on various counts when it was being struck between Enron and then the government of Maharashtra headed by Congress party. Some of the counts on which the project was criticised were: (i) the social and environmental aspects of the project, (ii) the alleged bribes paid by Enron, (iii) the high cost of the project, (iv) the lack of transparency and (v) the absence of competitive bidding. The Congress leaders alleged that cancelling the project was a politically-motivated decision. Also, it is pertinent to refer to the ruling by the Bombay High Court in 1994, when it threw out a petition filed against the project by one of the leaders of BJP. In a strongly worded verdict the court had said, "The proposal was deliberated at length for two and a half years, draft agreements were prepared from time to time, and it was ultimately the eighth or ninth draft which was finalised. Nothing was done secretly. There was total transparency at every stage of negotiation. There is nothing to show that anybody was being favoured for any specific reason."

Also the Government of India had taken a series of decisions concerning inviting private sector participation in the power sector and announcing a list of incentives. Firstly, the first few private sector projects were to be given the status of pioneer projects what later came to be known as "fast track" ones, and were to be given every facility by the government. Secondly, for the first few projects, the government would not go in for public tendering. Naturally, Enron cannot be blamed for government policies.

PERSPECTIVE 2

Kentucky Fried Chicken (KFC)

The Kentucky Fried Chicken — the world's largest chicken-based fast food chain and part of the $28 million Pepsico group — decided to open about 100 outlets^in India, the first one being in Bangalore. The Bangalore City Corporation charged the outlet with serving chicken with levels of mono sodium glutamate (MSG) — a flavouring agent — far higher than those permitted under the Prevention of Food Adulteration Act, 1954. MSG goes under many names: 'Ajinomoto' and 'Chinese powder'. This flavouring agent stimulates the taste buds and makes them extra sensitive. Thus, the food is perceived to be tasty without actually making it tasty.

A local unit of a political party threatened to demolish outlet of KFC, claiming that it was a cultural invasion that focus unhealthy eating habits on the unsuspecting Indians. Is it a fault of KFC? Once the government allows the entry of KFC, knowing fully well the type of business being carried on by KFC, how can you criticise it on the ground of cultural invasion?

In Delhi also, the decision to permit Pepsi Food Ltd. to open a KFC outlet was criticised. This was in sequel to the action of the Bangalore City Corporation. It was alleged that the chicken sold led to several health problems.

The Indian Food and Drug Administration has put down a limit of 1 per cent for all food additives, and anything above that amounts to adulteration. It is alleged that the samples picked up from KFC contained 2 per cent of MSG. Also, it is insisted that packaged food containing MSG should declare the fact on the pack, along with the warning — "not suitable for infants under 12 months".

PRACTICE QUESTIONS

1. What is the significance of business in a modern society? Explain with reference to opening up of the Indian economy.
2. Enumerate the different segments constituting environment of business. Do these include international environment also?
3. Identify the different interest groups that constitute environment of business.
4. Who are the stakeholders of a business firm?
5. "Law and business are closely related disciplines". Comment.
6. "The study of law is not limited to learning legal rules; understanding the legal environment of business is very necessary". Explain.
7. "The study of law requires a broad understanding of the people, and basic trends that influence the relationship between law and business". Discuss.
8. "The development of legal rules and institutions is closely associated with historical and social movements". Discuss.
9. "Power corrupts and absolute power corrupts absolutely". Discuss the statement with reference to at least two laws concerning business.
10. "The concentration of power in private business is more dangerous to individual freedom than the concentration of power in government". Explain.
11. "The legal constraints tend to control or limit the discretion of the business on the grounds that absolute rights cannot be conferred in the modern society". Explain.
12. "The law seeks to control concentration of power - political or economic". Explain.
13. "The law recognises and adjusts claims of individual rights within a society". Discuss.
14. Are there any circumstances under which a society could exist without law?
15. Identify a recent change in the law which will have a significant impact on business organisations in general. The change in the law may be in the form of an Act of Parliament, delegated legislation or judicial decision.
16. Investigate the nature of the change and consider the implications of the change for the organisation itself and other interest groups likely to be affected, e.g., consumers, employees, investors.

CHAPTER

2

Nature & Scope of Business Legislations

NOMENCLATURE OF LAW

The nomenclature of Law denotes, rather indicates, the nature of provisions contained in it. For example, the Indian Penal Code obviously contains provisions which enumerate the whole nature of criminal offences. Similarly, the Indian Contract Act, as its name suggests lays down all the provisions relating to contracts namely valid and invalid contracts, consideration of a contract, vitiating factors of a contract, enforceability of a contract, remedies available in the case of breach of a contract. In the same way, the Sales of Goods Act incorporates the provisions of sale and purchase, negotiation of sales, compensation in case of goods sold are bad or sub-standard. The Transfer of Property Act deals in all cases of transfer of property; namely, by sale, gift, will, testament, mortgage, its kinds and so on. The Prevention of Corruption Act, deals in how corruption cases would be dealt. The Consumers Protection Act, provides for protection of consumer interests, the remedies and relief available. The Weights and Measures Act, determines all cases regulating measures, weighing scales, under-weighment and the like.

It is well-known that the law of the land, is divided into various categories, like Criminal Law, Civil Rights, Mercantile Law in each of which respectively, crimes committed by anyone would be punished with imprisonment, death and fine; violation of civil rights would be remedied by specific enforcement of right, money compensation in cases of deprivation of civil rights and innumerable kinds of relief, while Mercantile Law deals in provisions regulating trade, commerce, business and industry, the provisions for which are embodied in myriad laws framed by Parliament, the Central law-making body. The State Legislatures too in various states in the Indian Union have law-making powers on various subjects that are listed in the Constitution as state subjects in its Schedules.

APPROACH TO STUDY OF LAW

The usual approach while writing on any subject, or for making an in-depth study, is to define the basics or fundamentals. Definitions, however, explain the basic concept of the provisions of any particular law. Various enactment or Acts define the basic concept in each of these enactments. But, when we embark on the study of an entire group of laws that are classed under the category of Mercantile Law, the approach has to be different. Going through technical terms used in each enactment or their study would fail to give the student a comprehensive idea as to what is Mercantile Law or what is the *sine qua non* of grouping so many enactments under the broad category of Mercantile Law. In the same way, the question arises as to how innumerable enactments are classed under the category of Criminal Law. Similarly, why several enactments get grouped together under Civil Law.

It is, therefore, clear that while definitions might explain the technical terms and phrases used in a particular enactment and they may be fairly understood for invoking these provisions in seeking relief in Courts of Law, yet it is necessary to understand as to why of the innumerable enactments, some get classified as criminal enactments, others as civil laws and yet another group falls under the category of :

Mercantile Law. It can be said that definitions of technical terms simply explain the terms used in an enactment, but fail to reveal the spirit and thought that have formulated these concepts which we encounter as terms and phrases in various enactments. We will have to delve, though briefly, into the genesis or historical past that have shaped these concepts into technical terms and phrases embodied and defined in various enactments. Any definition of a technical term or phrase without comprehending its genesis would make the study of Mercantile Law or Business Legislations or Business Legislations futile. The various enactments that are grouped under Mercantile Law, like Laws of Contract, Sale of Goods, Transfer of Property, Laws relating to business and commerce, could be understood from their provisions, but Mercantile Law must be studied in the context of its genesis and historical past, in order to understand the thoughts and concepts incorporated in the terms and phrases used in these enactments.

We must, therefore, first deal briefly, if not at length, the genesis and historical past of Mercantile Law, its sources, evolution, sanctions, concepts and its transformation through various stages and the manner in which it came to be settled in the form as we know it today.

FOUNDATION OF LAW

We will have to peep into the past if we want to discover the roots of the law in general or of any particular law. The British Parliament is called the Mother of Parliaments. This means that democratic principles evolved by the British Parliament over the centuries, is the basis of democratic principles practised by democracies the world over. During this process of the British Parliament, the Law in general also shaped and developed which came to be known as the English Common Law. It was much later in this march forward that the English Common Law expanded both in content and concept and got divided into broad categories of Criminal Law, Civil Law and Mercantile Law. This development of English Common Law is both interesting and educative. It is interesting because it provides a picture of how a single nucleus-concept got enlarged into a mature and fully grown legal principle. It is educative because this journey would reveal how the nucleus concept grew, not as an organic body but voluntarily by taking into account new issues, fresh concepts, ever increasing demand for justice by the people, incorporating new situations and for meeting new requirements.

Law in general or, for that matter, the law administered by democracies the world over, have profusely drawn from the English Legal System, that is, the English Common Law. Most of the laws adopted and enforced in the democracies all over the world are founded on the principles contained in Laws of England. The English Legal System, which embraces the legal system of America and of most of the legal systems of the British Commonwealth countries have an immutable link with the evolutionary past of the English Common Law.

Members of the British Parliament in the early ages because of their religious convictions and inspired by their dynamic perceptions finally laid down the principle that the King was under God and the Law.

The clear-cut divisions of modern law as we know today into contracts, crimes and torts (civil wrongs), for which the remedy was damages in terms of money, did not exist in ancient law.

Juristic Rigmarole and ritualism of legal procedure and its intricacies in fact obscured substantive legal rights of wronged persons. Substantive legal rights were neither recognised nor contained in ancient laws.

Sir Henry Maine, and eminent jurist dwelling on the nature of early *English Law* has apathy said so *great is the ascendancy of the Law of actions in the infancy of the Courts of justice that substantive Law has atfirst the look of being gradually secreted in the intricacies of procedure.* As is amply clear, early English Law, which diversified into various branches of Law much later, is, the before a history of the *forms of action.*

FORMS OF ACTION

The question arises as to what were these *forms of action?* They were known as writs. In early English Law, a wrong could be redressed or relief was available if the wrong fell within the four comers of a writ. A writ was an order of the King, issued by the Lord Chancellor or his office calling upon the defendants to appear before the Court and show cause that he did not come within the ambit of the plaintiffs claim under the writ issued. The writ was available from the *ojJiciana brevium* or the *writs hop or ojJice.* If the *writ* purchased was a wrong one or, one which did not cover the wrong suffered by the plaintiff, then he could not get the relief. The early English Law was wedded to the concept or bound down to the principle *"wherever there was a remedy available, there was a wrong."* It was a *writ-system* for dispensing justice to the person wronged.

The Lord Chancellor had in his possession a specific number of *writs* or *forms of action,* which were the authorised orders of the King. If a wrong committed against anyone, that is, the victim, approached the Lord Chancellor for relief and justice, the person *"wronged"* that is the victim could get the desired relief if the wrong was covered by any specific writ, available with the Lord Chancellor. It was known as the *'Pigeon-Hole' Theory.* In actual practice it meant that specified number of writs were available with the Lord Chancellor; that is, one *writ or forms of action* in each 'Pigeon-Hole' for each recognised wrong. New wrongs went without remedy and a relief because no writ was available for the new wrong complained about by the plaintiff. This rule, as enunciated in Latin was *"Ubi remedium ibijus*", that is, where there was no writ there was no right for the plaintiff to have his wrong redressed.

This created a piquant situation. While more and more people suffered injuries yet they went without relief or remedy because no writ or form of action was available to give relief. The English Common Law was awfully rigid, conservative and unbending.

At this stage, the English Common Law was merely a law of civil wrongs for which the remedy was damages. The Law of Contract, or the law which bound down two persons under an agreement to make one to perform his obligations under the deed, and for the other to accept services, goods or benefits under it did not exist. The Law of Contract or Mercantile Law evolved much later. The English Common Law in its initial stages was, therefore, the law of civil wrongs or which was known as the *Law of Torts.*

LAW OF TORTS

The word 'tort' is a French term which in English is the same as 'wrong' and in Latin the word 'delict' means the same thing. After the Norman invasion of England, concepts of the Norman Law gradually permeated into English Law because the administration of justice was in the hands of the conquerors. The Norman jurists introduced the word 'tort' into the English Common Law. The term 'tort' is a contribution of Latin in which the word *'tortum'* means to *twist* and therefore, covers all kinds of conduct which was *twisted, abnormal, unnatural, unusual or tortuous* that is, *involved not straight forward.*

For the sake of interest proper understanding and appreciation as to how *Law Merchant or Mercantile Law* evolved and emerged from the development process of the English Common Law, we should try to study the evolution process. The evolution process was gradual. Hence, it would be appropriate to study this phase and observe and understand at which stage the English Common Law got diversified into various distinct branches, like Civil Law, Criminal Law and Law Merchant.

The initial stage in the development of the English Common Law is simply the law of civil wrongs, that is, Torts. Various jurists have tried to define the word tort. Tort denoted the general position of remedies being provided for wrongs committed by one person against another. The wrongs committed under the classification of wrongs as torts was a general duty, namely, no one was expected to commit a wrong against or cause an injury to anyone, say A, B, C or D. Later, when the law further developed, and the general duty of say X became specific against A, B, C or D then it acquired the semblance of a man to man obligation and took the shape of a contract. But, to understand the *Law of Contract or Law Merchant or Mercantile Law,* it would be proper to first understand the nature of a tort.

TORT DEFINED (OR TORT DEFINITIONS)

Several eminent jurists of those times have tried to define a tort. *Salmond* says *"Tort is a civil wrong for which the remedy is a common law action for unliquidated damages, and which is not exclusively the breach of a trust or other merely equitable damages".* Another jurist of the times, *Winfield* says *"Tortious liability arises from a breach of duty primarily fixed by Law. This duty is towards persons generally and its breach of duty primarily fixed by Law. This duty is towards persons generally and its breach is redressible by an action for unliquidated damages."*

Another eminent jurist of those times, *Underhill,* has given the most graphic and expressive definition of tort. *Underhill* says *"Tort is a wrong independent of contract and resulting (in):*

(i) In the infringement of some absolute right to which another is entitled, or

(ii) In the infringement of some qualified right of another causing actual damage, or

(iii) In the infringement of some public right causing some special and substantial damage to an individual beyond that which is suffered by the public generally."

Despite the above definitions, it can be said that it is difficult to define the term tort due to the following, amongst other, reasons:

(i) The Law of Torts is dynamic, it continues to grow; it is neither static nor stagnant.

(ii) The Law of Torts is not limited in its scope as it is not based on Statute Law but on case Law.

(iii) Because the legacy of the forms of action persisted. Due to the lingering tradition or the conservative adherence to the writ system of dispensation of justice inspite of newer writs being introduced it was commonly observed those days: *"The forms of action we have buried, but they rule us from their graves.*

(iv) Because by this time courts had been accorded equitable jurisdiction, newer wrongs could be remedied. The juristic dictum or the narrow rule of *'Ubi remedium ibi jus'* that is, where there was no writ (form of action) there was no right, or wherever there was a remedy there was a wrong had got enlarged into a more liberal view embodied in the juristic dictum or the liberal rule. *Ubi jus ibi remedium'* which meant that for every wrong a new writ or form of action could be availed that is wherever there is a legal right there is a legal remedy.

Finally, therefore, we can say that *a tort is a civil wrong independent of contract for which the appropriate remedy is an action of damages.* A civil wrong for which an action for damages will not lie is not a tort.

In the backdrop of these facts, and the historical account so far, it was not easy to define as to what was the Law of Torts? This piquant situation has been aptly summed by the eminent jurist Winfield:

The moment we *attempt to define the nature and scope of the Law of Torts, we are at once in a thicket of difficulties".*

TORT- NOT STATUTE LAW

These difficulties arise because the Law of torts has not been created by any Statute, but emerged and grew up effortlessly from the righteous decisions of courts of law and, as such, is the working product of the Common Law of England. The Law of Torts, despite progressive and liberal decisions of the Court of Law *"could not free itself from legal formalism."* Only that person could redress wrongs done to him, who could fit his claim into the recognised forms of action. In this context, it was a true comment: *"the forms of action* we *have buried but they rule us from their graves."* It is worthwhile remembering that the law at this stage was not in the neat divisions of the law into 'Torts'. 'Contract' and 'Criminal Law', as we know today, did not exist in the past. The entire law and its administration was confined to the supremacy and predominance of the law of *'forms of actions'*, that is, a wrong could be redressed only if a remedy existed or was available.

Thus, the Law of Torts was dynamic in olden times like the general law today, which took into account expectations of the people wronged; it grew and developed continually. Moreover, the Law of Torts was not codified then and, therefore, to confine it within the four comers of any kind of definition or to analyse its precise nature became all the more difficult.

The early English Law is, therefore, the history of the *forms of action.* It was much later that judges began to inquire, "Has the defendant infringed any legal right vested in the plaintiff? Has he broken any duty which he owed to the plaintiff?" Examined under the prevalent practice, the plaintiff's case succeeded only if it could be fitted into the four comers of any of the recognised forms of action. The usual question used to be "Has the plaintiff any form of action against the defendant and, if so, what form?"

SCOPE OF TORT ENLARGED

The *Law of Tort* to begin with was the *writ of trespass.* In order to remedy more and more wrongs, *the Writ of Trespass on the Case* was invented. Trespass, generally understood to be unauthorised entry into another persons land, in the past also included injury to land, goods or persons. The *Writ of Trespass* provided remedy to injuries which were the direct and the immediate consequence of the wrongful act. The *Writ of Trespass on the Case* had to be invented for providing remedy to injuries which were remote and indirect. The *Statute of Consimili Casu* was passed in 1325 AD in the reign of Edward I. This authorised the Chancery to issue the *Writ of Trespass on the Case* for providing remedies to new injuries. This enabled the law to march ahead swiftly and help acquire a wider scope and potential which the Law of Torts possesses today. The scope and potential and the liberal nature which the Law of Torts possesses today has been rightly summed up by the Latin adage *"Ubijus ibi remedium "*, that is, wherever there is a legal right, there is a legal remedy. This was a categorical statement of the advanced stage of law that there is no right without a remedy. Thus, it has been rightly said that the *Writ of Trespass* from which emerged the *Writ of Trespass on the Case* allowing a remedy for every infringed right, is the *"fertile mother of actions."*

BREACH OF CONTRACT

The Law of Torts, as we have seen above, was a civil wrong for which the remedy was damages under a *writ or form of action.* It was the earliest concept of what a contract was, that is, an agreement between two persons *inter-se* and the remedy that was provided for its breach, with the passage of time led to the establishment of a distinct branch of law, known as *Law Merchant or Mercantile Law.* The *Law Merchant or Mercantile Law,* following further development upto the modem times, brought under its umbrella, myriad Laws known today like the Law of Contract, Sales of Goods Act and the Transfer of Property Act.

The moot question, therefore, is how did the Law of Contract take shape. The earliest known remedies for a breach of contract were also available under *forms of action* or *writs* known as the *Writ of Debt, Writ of Covenant* and the *Writ of Detinue.* These early remedies were considered inadequate to cover all actions, deemed to be contractual. A new remedy, therefore, was introduced in the 14th century which was known as the *Action of Assumpsit* or the *Writ of Assumpsit.* The *Action of Assumpsit* was, in fact another form of the *Writ of Trespass on the Case* and this remedy ushered in a new era of progress in the field of the *Law of Contracts.*

The basic idea in the *Action of Assumpsit* was that if A undertook to perform some act for Band in case A misperformed, then B having suffered damage, was, therefore, entitled to recover damages from A. It is clear that only *acts of misfeasance* could be covered under the *Action of Assumpsit.* But, under the *Law of Contract,* apart from *acts of misfeasance,* newer wrongs cropped up like *acts of non-feasance,* that is, acts of non-performance of the obligations under the *Law of Contract.* The earlier situation was when in a contractual relationship between A and B, the case was of *misperformance,* but cases of *non-performance* went without remedy. A new *form of action* for covering cases of *non-feasance* or *non-performance* had to be devised. It was a new form of action known as *indebitatus assumpsit.*

Finally, the *forms of action* were abolished by the Common Law Procedure Act, 1872 and the Judicature Act of 1873. Rules based on these two enactments framed in 1875 required that every pleading should include in brief material facts on which the party claimed relief or which were vital to prove the pleading.

Earlier, procedure predominated the substance of the pleading. Following the above enactments and the rules framed thereunder the position got reversed making substance predominant over procedure. In this context, it is worth quoting a case: *In re United Australia Vs. Barclays Ltd. (1941 A. C.J.)* in which **Lord Atkin** Commenting on the zealous adherence to form (procedure) than substance, disapprovingly observed, *"When these ghosts of the past stand in the path of justice clanking their mediaeval chains the proper course for the judge is to pass through them undeterred."*

TORTS IN INDIA

In the process of historical development of the English Common Law in which the Law of Torts emerged in England and the manner in which it was made liberal, it would be interesting to know how and to what extent the law of torts or the law of civil wrongs was administered by courts of law during the British rule. The English Law of Torts was made applicable to Indian conditions as modified by *Acts of Indian Legislature.*

In the *'Post-Independence'* era there has been brisk legislative activity. Attempts were even made to codify the complex Hindu Law. Earlier, that is in the pre-independence era a bill or draft-law known as the The Indian Civil Wrongs Bill, was drafted by Sir Frederick Pollock at the instance of the Government of India, but it failed to become an Act of Legislature.

The Law of torts as prevailing in England was not imported and applied as a whole, but some of its parts were brought under certain enactments passed by the Indian Legislature from time to time in the form of the following Acts:

(1) The Fatal Accidents Act, 1855.

(2) The Carriers Act, 1865

(3) The Specific Relief Act, 1877.

(4) The Easements Act, 1882.

(5) The Workmens Compensation Act, 1923.

The English Law of Torts as we have seem is basically case law, because it evolved from the expanded jurisdiction of the *Writ System* or when it had been made more liberal by introducing new writs or *forms of Action* with a view to providing remedies for new wrongs. In order to understand the *Law of Torts* as applicable to India, we shall have to rely much upon the case-law based Law of Torts of England.

It is in the fitness of things to fully understand the Law of Torts because an action under it results in payment of damages to the plaintiff by the defendant. In the Law of Contracts too, which is an action by the plaintiff against the defendant the remedy is also payment of damages. The difference between the Law of Torts and the Law of Contracts is rather fine. In the former, the defendant could be anyone who has caused harm to the plaintiff, while in the latter, that is, the Law of Contracts, the defendant is specifically the only one who is bound by the agreement either to share profits, perform a duty, or render the service specified in the contract. The Law of Contracts is a subsequent manifestation of the English Common Law than the Law of Torts which emerged earlier. From the Law of Contract several other obligations and duties devolved in trade, business and commerce; the entire gamut of which came to be classed as *Law Merchant* or *Mercantile Law.* Let us therefore, study the characteristics of an action under the Law or Torts distinguished from other wrongs.

TORT AND OTHER WRONGS

A Tort has five characteristics:

(1) Tort is a civil wrong

A tort is a civil wrong. It is neither a crime, nor a breach of contract or a breach of trust and other civil wrongs. A breach of contract and a breach of trust are civil wrongs indeed, yet they are not torts.

(2) Torts is a right fixed by law

The right infringed in the commission of a tort must be right fixed by law. In an action under the Law of Contract, the right infringed is a right by consent of the parties to the contract or bound by the agreement under the contract.

(3) The right infringed must be right 'in rem'

Rights can be classified under two heads; one is a right *in rem,* while the other, is a right in *personam.* A right *in rem* is indeed vested in a specific person (either as a member of the community or personally), but is available against the world at large and becomes actionable against the person in the world at large, the moment he infringes that right. By way of example, every person possesses a right not to be defamed, but becomes actionable the moment by specific person indulges in an action of defamation. Let us take another example. Every person has the right to the beneficial enjoyment of his property against the world at large, but an act either damaging the property or an action of obstruction to the enjoyment, it becomes an actionable right under the *Law of Tort.*

A *right 'in personam'* is a right available against some specific or determinate person or body, in which the community at large has no concern Examples can better illustrate the point: A and Bare bound by a contact for the sale of a house, in which A agrees to sell his house to B for a specific sum of money under the contract. In case, A refuses to sell the house to B or B refuses to purchase the house an action would lie for breach of contract or for non-performance of the contract. The nature of duty in a *right in rem,* and in a *right in personam* are entirely different. In the case of a *right in rem* the duty is imposed by law and it is owed to the world at large. In the case of a *right in personam,* the duty is imposed fixed or undertaken by the will and consent of the parties to an agreement or contract, and is owed to a definite or specific person or persons.

(4) Tort is a Common Law action

The action available in tort should be a *Common Law* action. Common law actions of which actions in tort, are a variety are available only in England. *In India, however, there is no such thing as Common Law actions, but torts are recognised by various enactments in India and are also actionable: the plaintiff being entitled to damages for breach of duty under torts.*

(5) Nature of remedy

The remedy in an action under tort is by way of *'unliquidated'* damages, that is, damages which are not specified by any law, but determined by judicial discretion of courts of law. The remedy in an action under a contract, is by way of *'liquidated'* that is damages specified under the contract or determined under the agreement between the parties to the contract.

TORT AND BREACH OF CONTRACT

SIMILARITIES:

We have, by now fairly understood, the differences between an action under tort and an action under contract. But both the kinds of action have some similarities too.

(1) Both the commission of a tort or a breach of contract are civil wrongs. Both involve infringement of private rights. The society is not concerned with the violation of private rights. In either case, the aggrieved party has the right to claim damages.
(2) The injured or wronged person in both cases, namely, in the commission of a tort on in the breach of a contract, seeks the remedy. The action in both is by the person injured or wronged. The world at large or the society is not concerned the plaintiff is the person who has suffered or has sustained the harm.
(3) The remedy in both is in the form of compensation or damages. It may be recalled in torts they are unliquidated damages; in contract, they are liquidated damages.

DIFFERENCES:

(1) Nature of Right involved

A tort is a violation of a right *'in rem'* while a breach of contract is a violation of a right *'in personam'*. The action in tort being for violation of a right *in rem,* that is, against the whole world, materialises as soon as anyone in the society or in the world at large violates that right, on the other hand, an action in contract being a right available *in personam* that is against a definite person or persons, bound by the contract, materialises when that person or persons violate the contract.

(2) Nature of duty Involved

The duty imposed under tort is imposed by law and it is towards the society in general. Under contract, the duty is one imposed by the will and consent of the parties to the contract, while the duty is towards a specific or definite person or persons bound by the contract.

(3) Privity: Relationship between the wrongdoer and the person wronged

There is a *privity* between parties to a contract. It means that in a contract there is a legal relationship between the parties to the contract or bound by agreement: while there is no such *'privity relationship'* in the case of a tort. In order to understand the difference between torts and contract, let take the definitions framed for both by eminent jurists.

Professor Winfield has defined tortious liability in these terms: Tortious liability arises form the breach of duty primarily fixed by law, such duty is towards persons generally and its breach is redressible by an action of *unliquidated damages.*

Salmond, the well-known jurist has described the characteristics of contract in these terms:

"A contract arises only out of the exercise of the autonomous legislative authority entrusted by the law of private persons to declare and define the nature of their mutual rights and obligations."

(4) Consent of parties

In a contract, the duty arises from the consent of parties, while in a tort the duty arises independently without or irrespective of the consent of the parties.

(5) Remedy for breach of contract and for breach of a duty under Tort

Under a breach of contract, the damages claimed and awarded are *liquidated damages* that is a *pre-determined* and *a fixed sum of money.*

Under a breach of duty under the law of Tort, the damages claimed and awarded are *unliquidated damages,* which is not *predetermined or fixed sum of money,* but is a sum of money which the court in its discretion, may award.

It may be further clarified that in a breach of contract, the liquidated damages are claimed and awarded, because the sum of money payable is a part of the contract and if the sum of money is not specified in the contract, it is capable of being determined, or calculated according to damage clause and the terms and conditions incorporated in the contract.

In the case of torts, the breach of a duty is imposed by law of torts, the damages in terms of money have to be assessed and evaluated by the court which, in its discretion, it deems fit and appropriate for the purpose of providing relief to the plaintiff or person injured, who seeks the remedy. The court while awarding damages takes into consideration the nature of damage encountered.

Two points may be noted with respect to the damages awarded in the case of breach of a contact and in the case of breach of duty imposed by law under tort.

(i) Exemplary Damages

In a breach of contract, exemplary damages are not awarded, because the damages are in accordance to the damage clause incorporated in the contract. Exemplary damages may, however, be awarded in the case of a breach of contract to marry, because in such a case the girl, especially loses face and reputation in society.

In an action under tort, the court may, in its discretion, favour award of exemplary damages both for purposes of providing adequate compensation as a deterrent against repetitive breach of duty under torts by others.

(ii) Remoteness of Damages

The rule regarding the remoteness of damages to torts is different to that applicable in contract. A person in tort action may be held liable to pay damages arising out of special circumstances of which the person guilty of committing the tort had no knowledge.

The position in the case of breach of contract is entirely different. A person committing a breach of contract is not liable to pay damages arising out of special circumstances, if these special circumstances are not incorporated in the contract or agreement, or had no knowledge about them at the time of execution of the contract or while entering into the agreement.

6) Motive-Relevance:

In tort, the motive of the person guilty of the tort or committing the tort, is material and relevant; while in the case of a breach of contract the motive of the person committing a breach of a contract is not material; it is totally immaterial or irrelevant.

Views of Jurists

It would be interesting to go through the views expressed by eminent of jurists from time to time about how they appraised the English Law.

In 1498, it was commonly said: *"The Law of England is the most reasonable thing in the world."* Every ardent student of law on a deep study will find that the reason element in the law is vital because as we study the development of English Law we would discover that it is based on case law, whose decisions have been based on reason.

In the beginning of the seventeenth century, one of the most eminent of English Lawyer said:

"The reason of the law is the life of the law, for though a man can tell the law, yet if he know not the reason thereof, he shall soon forget his superficial knowledge, but when he find the right reason of the law and so bring it to his natural reason that he comprehends it as his own, this will not only serve him for the understanding of that particular case but of many others."

Later, in 1173, Lord Mansfield, Chief Justice, sounded a similar view: *"Very happily the more law is looked into, the more it appears founded in equity, reason and good sense."* In the development process, English law has taken into account different aspects at various stages. In the early period, some ideas of personal preferences, convictions and conscience got absorbed in the English Common Law. This led to the inclusion of features and ideas of different origins in the law. Despite this, the English Common Law maintained its dependence on reason. Social, political and economic changes later imparted to the old law a new face tackling new problems. But, founded on old soil, however, it retained its ancient fervour. English law for nearly a thousand years, adhered to an orderly path, linking the past and present, although, at times, it was a slow and staggered progress. It can be safely said that the English law was the outcome of the legal profession of England and of the people who themselves conceived and shaped their own laws, drawing marginally, if at all, from foreign systems or of systems of other countries English law, therefore, being insular, can be interpreted and best understood in context of its environments. Because English law is a law made by the people during different periods of times, we must study it with respect to the ages which shaped it. Following the Norman conquest, the law was laid by fierce and barbarous men seeking peace and good governance in the countries that followed. Later, the law broke its barriers drawn by the rigid and *unbending forms of action* or *writs* which held the law active for centuries. It was during this stage that the law imbibed the elements of equity, reason and good conscience.

In this backdrop, Sir Edward Coke, a great Lawyer spoke about English Law as the 'perfection of reason'. The rules of English law are undoubtedly, ideal; its concepts and procedure for its implementation evoke envy of laws of other countries. Although, statutory law has often altered the English law, yet its foundation remains firm because English law has primarily evolved out of judge-made rules.

Eminent jurist, Dicey, propounded the theory of the *Rule of Law,* which was subjected to criticism frequently, but despite this, the English Common Law ultimately came to occupy a place in the modern British constitution. While the English Common Law retained its liberal approach, yet this fell a victim in Western Europe under the autocratic Roman rule. Respect for law both by the rulers and ruled is a basic tenet of the English Common Law. The trial of Charles I, prior to his execution after a Court verdict goes to prove that the *rule of law* was at the roof of the English Common Law. Some views, however, hold that the trial was a sham or a mockery, not justifiable by law; but it did prove that the *rule of law* was vital to the English to the English Common Law even in its early stages.

The spirit behind the principle of the *'Rule of Law'* travelled to the laws of other countries as well. While the British were withholding the rights cherished and imbibed in the English Common Law for which the British Parliament fought for nearly a century for its American colonies, the American Constitution armed its Supreme Court with the powers to declare invalid acts of the American President or of the Congress. This delivers a message for the law in all ages, including the present one. It leads us to the rule that people should enjoy unfettered their liberties or fundamental rights, it was also considered necessary that courts of law should by headed by fearless and independent judges who could take courage to administer justice irrespective of the position, influence or status of those arraigned before them. It is, therefore, not possible to study law torn apart from the social economic and political factors woven in the history of development of the English Common Law.

Despite the significance of Common Law, there is yet no court known as the Court of the Common Law. There are only three divisions of the High Court of Justice of England. The three divisions of justice are the Queens Bench Division, the Chancery Division and the Probate, Divorce and Admiralty Division. It is the Queens Bench Division primarily which administers justice in cases arising from violation of the English Common Law, the Chancery Division deals with equity while the Probate, Divorce and Admiralty Divisions and adjudicate on that branch of Law which has its roots in the Roman and Canon Law. Even till this day, the three divisions of the High Court of Justice still exist. This proves two things; one is the strength of tradition, the other the vital role plays by judicial institutions in the development of the British legal system. It would, therefore, be appropriate to study the judicial institutions in order to understand the nature of the law which they gave us. In this study, we are bound to come across the contributions made by eminent lawyers practising law in these institutions. The judges of the Common Law Courts also helped shape the Common Law through their verdicts and decisions in matters that came up for hearing before them. Besides them, the judges in the Chancery Division made significant contributions to the growth and development of Common Law. Thus, the English Common Law was not the contribution of individuals, but drawn from many sources. In the medieval legal system, procedure was dominant in the dispensation of justice rather than the rules of liability or guilt of substantive offence. Because of this, an eminent jurist, Maine observed: *"Early substantive Law has the look of being secreted in the interstices of procedure".* The modem concept of law as against the medieval concepts however, is that procedure is an appendix of substantive Law.

The judges presiding over courts of law bound by procedural complexities had perforce to give decisions which had peculiar character. Changing circumstances and demands of society forced the judges to give decisions meeting the aspirations of the people and fulfilling their expectations despite the fact that the judges had no law-making powers. The demands of social, economic and political institutions were met by judges while deciding cases and they took recourse to judicial reasoning which may be termed as legal logic and by evolving and adopting means which may be called legal fiction. Legal fiction gradually faded giving place to legal understanding and interpretation of the law, while judicial reasoning still remains the basis of understanding English law.

LEGAL DEVELOPMENT — ANGLO-SAXON ERA

Having studied the general developmental trends of the English Common Law, it would be interesting to follow the development of law phase-wise according to historical eras. This study would help us to examine the development in each era.

The modem view is that the culture of the Anglo-Saxon era was either like the early Biblical pre-classical civilisation or like the culture of West Africa of the nineteenth century.

The Anglo-Saxon law was based primarily on custom. The law remained unwritten. Custom emanated from the lives of the people. This can be discerned and appreciated if we study the social pattern of this era.

After the Norman Conquest, the British people were brought under a somewhat archaic law.

It developed its own legal systems and judicial tribunals, but legal profession of any kind did not develop during this period.

ANGLO-SAXON LAW

Law is the mirror of its times; its development is inspired and helped by the social attitude and its progress depends upon the aspirations of the people seeking justice. The Anglo-Saxon era lasted for hundreds of years. Christianity also took root during this period. Its liberal attitude cannot be construed to have altered the Anglo-Saxon law much. The Anglo-Saxon era was marked by a wild way of life. Crime of all kinds was rampant. The Chrisiian influence could not tone down the trend. The repeated Danish invasions kept stability at bay.

The law during this period comprised mostly customary rules, modified sometimes by the *Dooms* of the Anglo-Saxon or Danish Kings. Customary rules were mostly ancient customs administered locally in shires or the hundreds of the various kingdoms. The objective of customary rules was primarily to prevent bloodshed by recognising some elementary rights of property and personal freedom and sometimes money compensation for injuries suffered instead of allowing the practice of blood feud marked by the rule: *an eye/or an eye* and *a tooth/or a tooth,* that is inflicting identical injury on the wrongdoer. The rules or law remained mostly unwritten in its traditional form.

SOURCES OF LAW

The Church and the State were not divided by clear cut dividing lines. The cleric or the priest, therefore, acted both the lawyer and the historian. The bulk of the customary rules and traditional practices could, at best, be gleaned from the documents or ecclesiastical records maintained in monasteries and churches.

Diplomata

The *'Diplomata'* were charters issued by landowners to persons who were required to hold the land as vassals (servants). These *diplomata* were at times forged documents framed inside monastries for providing a claim to customary rights. Besides these, a few Anglo-Saxon "Wills" giving authority over land and goods were also available, but they could not provide any understanding of the law in vogue.

Dooms

The *'Dooms'* were issued by later Kings starting from the Laws of Aethelbert and ending with the Dooms of Cnut, that is, from circa 600 to circa 1029. The Dooms of Alfred (circa 890) and of Cnut were rather important.

The *Dooms* though detailed were yet for the most part, unsystematic and piecemeal in nature, The *Dooms* provided fines and punishment tariffs for some offences, which proves their existence.

Some matters and problems were backed by the authority of the King and his Witan (Council of Wise Men), which functioned as a Court for noblemen. The rights of the Church constituted Alfreds Laws which helped develop the law of the times. These laws took care of officials and revenue matters regulating more of methods of proof and administration of justice. The Kings during the Anglo-Saxon era were more concerned about the enforcement of customary law rather than introducing amendments in it. The real effort was aimed at replacing of primitive law giving to individuals the right to self-help, namely allowing individuals the right to retribution summed by the saying; *An eye for an eye; a tooth for a tooth,* no new law was framed during this period. The punishments and the compensation for violent injury, later constituted the basis of criminal law and law of tort or of civil injury.

The law, during this period, was primarily concerned with simple matters like redress for violent injury sustained by the victim and sale of goods and chattels. Peoples life was intimately associated with ownership of land, but as time passed, it tended to become complex.

Anglo-Saxon Law

Even after the Norman conquest in 1066, "It was for centuries common to hark back to the good old law of the day when Edward the King was alive and dead." This conservatism was natural, applicable to all ages and peculiar to the primitive communities of the times, to resist change. But, however, the old law was gradually becoming redundant owing to the development after the Conquest. In order to comprehend the modem law, it is essential to study the law of the time and its historical development. It has to be conceded that before William I landed on the shores of England, there was some semblance of a government for centuries prior to the event. The administration of this government was founded on peoples tradition and the transformation in the laws that followed the Norman Conquest must have taken a long period of time.

Anglo-Saxon Law After the Norman Conquest

Much is not known about the position of the Anglo-Saxon Law. Its character can be judged from the observation of historical records and views of jurists Pollock and Maitland: "The Norman Conquest is a catastrophe which determined the whole future of English Law. We can make but the vaguest guesses as to the kind of law that would have prevailed in the England of the thirteenth century or the nineteenth had Harold repelled the invader."

The Norman Kings did not attempt to replace the custom-based English Law by Norman Law.

The Norman Kings granted charters by which they decreed that the people would continue to live under the law of Edward's era. While no attempts were made to change the law or substituted it with laws of the Norman Kings, yet efforts were made to restate the prevailing law.

The Normans were more civilised that the Saxons. William I and his successors to the throne could not much tamper with the laws laid down by Edward the Confessor, and also because he had strengthened his kingship by electing the Witan (Council of Wise Men). The Norman classed themselves different to the Anglo-Saxons and did not bother much about the law which the latter had laid down.

Immediate Effects of the Norman Conquest

Old customs of the Saxons were left untouched by the Norman conquerors. Land, constituting the country's wealth, came into the hands of the Normans and as such it came within the ambit of their law. This was the immediate effect of the Norman Conquest as land came to be governed by the Laws of Continental Feudalism. Land disputes came to the King's Court and were decided according to Norman Law. Norman land law virtually continued to apply to land till as late as the seventeenth century. Local customs also persisted in some measure until the customary tenure *'gavelkind'* was finally abolished by the Law of Property Act, 1922. New *'Pleas of the Crown'* replaced the old Criminal Law, which thus became exclusively reserved for the King's Courts. Land records could not be made throughout the first century after the Norman Conquest. Thus, the law of contract and tort were largely left to the local courts and were decided by local custom.

Changes in the Government

The most important change after the Norman Conquest was the establishment of a strong central government. All departments of administration, namely, legislative, executive and judicial, came within its control. Administration of justice in some of the most important branches became centralised under the wise rule of the Norman and Angevin Kings. Royal justice being strong and the law being administered by one set of Courts, established an uniform pattern of justice. As all disputes became centralised to the Kings Courts the legal system of England gradually got consolidated into Common Law. The Common Law became so strong and formidable that even after the Renaissance attempts by scholars and jurists to replace it with the more scientific and classical Roman Law were strongly resisted. Toughness entails weaknesses as well. Rigidity which was the backbone of toughness of law in the administration of centralised justice, ushered in equity jurisdiction and approach supplementing the Common Law. The unification of justice by one set of courts helped England acquire a strong centralised government unlike Continental countries which administered justice according to their different local customs.

Impact of the Norman Conquest

The impact of the Norman Conquest which entailed a change of hands in the governance of England can be studied best if we examine the social and economic conditions prevailing at that time.

England during this period was largely rural in composition; the urban population being negligible. Rural towns, therefore, were both independent and isolated from each other. They had their separate forms of administration of justice dependent upon individuals and local customs as handed over to them by their elders. In such a society, it was obvious that the village which formed part of the manor was opposed to change.

The whole of England was composed like its villages and the people sustained themselves on the produce of the land. The country despite being composed of dissimilar and unlinked to each other in the administration of justice, had only one thing in common. This was the Church, which was universal.

This being so, the conflict which existed between the Pope and the Emperor was unavoidable. The Church had vast estates of land, individual churchmen were not bound down to particular localities. The clergy was literate. Moreover, the church claimed its own sphere of influence and also its independence from secular rule. The conflict between the Pope and the Emperor became predominant and resulted in the murder of St. Thomas of Canterbury at the instigation of Henry II. The Emperor claimed jurisdiction over the clergy. Till the Reformation, two central authorities existed in England.

Main Effects of the Conquest

There were several effects of the Norman Conquest. According to jurists, *Pollock and Maitland,* some of the immediate effects of the conquest were:

(i) Introduction of official Latin and the official and popular hybrid dialect better known as Anglo-Norman or Norman-French;

(ii) Establishment of separate ecclesiastical courts;

(iii) Landholding coupled with seigniorial justice was adopted as a general principle.

Outcome of these Effects

(i) The introduction of official languages of the Continent carried along with them legal terms as well. Sharpness was also imparted to the prevalent legal language.

(ii) Bishops prior to the conquest sat along with ealdormen in the Courts of the Shire and the Hundred. The rights of the Holy Church was given attention by Dooms of the Anglo Saxon Kings. Later a conflict arose between the Holy Roman Emperor and the Pope regarding supremacy in the administration of justice. William the Conqueror, in order to win the favour of the Church fulfilled his promise and created separate Church courts. This led not merely to the establishment of two systems of courts but also two systems of administration of justice.

Ecclesiastical Courts administered Canon Law, peculiar in form and drew largely from the system practised in imperial Rome. Canon lawyers studied the Roman Civil Law, exercised jurisdiction over clerics and persons in minor matters associated with the Roman Church and later in certain matters over all persons. Judges of ecclesiastical courts like the royal judge of Common Law were mostly laymen. The Church Courts however, did inspire the Common Law lawyers to fill in the gap in the administration of justice, especially in the field of Contract Law. The concept of benefit of clergy in Criminal Law came into being due to the conflict between the secular royal courts and the ecclesiastical courts. It may be recalled that the law relating to marriage and divorce and probate of wills till the middle of the last century were under the jurisdiction of the Church courts, which later came within the ambit of the Royal secular courts.

(iii) William I insisted that all land was held from him. All landholders were expected to do *fealty* to him by the *Oath of Sarum,* irrespective of the fact whether they held land from him or as tenant *in capite* or from a *mesne* lord.

SEIGNORIAL JUSTICE

Feudalism was virtually administration of justice based on land tenure. It was also used as an effective instrument in the maintenance of law and order. The primitive concept prevailing during this time was that the lord could hold a court for all his tenants. There was little or no legislation.

The manorial courts got firmly in saddle. They also became a source of profit to the lord because of the dues paid by his tenant for whom he held the manorial courts. A severe conflict erupted between the seignorial courts and the common law courts. These feudal courts acquired important concurrent jurisdiction with the Kings Courts or Common Law Courts in several important matters like title to land. *Hundred Courts* on which private ownership had managed to survive for some time, while the non-feudal courts gradually vanished.

Development of Statute Law

The British Parliament came into existence much later. Parliament, therefore, could not be a source of Statute Law. Some statutes which were not Acts of Parliament were mistaken for statutes.

The separation between Parliament and Councilor the House of Lords and the House of Commons as they are known today began during the reign of Edward I. Distinction between ordinances and statutes took shape along with the division of the institutions of Parliament and Council. Statutes constituted the new law made by Parliament. But, it was difficult to draw a dividing line between statutes and the common law. The Council managed the administration and made ordinances for enforcing the existing law by means of regulations. These ordinances did not introduce any new law.

Petitions made to the King in Parliament and their disposal or decision considered best gave rise to statutes which were recorded on the statute roll. The House of Commons complained against the disposal method of petitions. These complaints surfaced during reign of Henry IV This led to framing of complaints in the manner in which relief was sought. These documents came to acquire the nomenclature of bill. The King in such a presentation had to either accept or reject it in the manner proposed by Parliament. Modern Statute Law took its form and shape during the fourteenth and fifteenth centuries. Parliament as a result of this practice acquired its legislative role subject to the consent of the House of Lords and the House of Commons, sitting separately. Several statutes were passed in this manner during this period.

Modern Law — Development

Some kind of confusion gripped the legal system of England during this period. Merchants, because of the different nature of their problems managed to have separate courts for their disputes.

It appeared that several legal systems were in vogue. Common Law Courts which had come into being were found competing with the older Courts of the *Shire* and the *Manor*. The Courts of the Church had gradually extended their jurisdiction over matters associated with the common man and over other lay matters. These courts were more keen on enforcing rules of morality. The Court of the Chancery came into being out of the weakness of Law. The law was unable to enforce its decisions. It was also not able to give relief which made people to prefer petitions to the King and his Council for seeking remedies. Each of these sets of courts adopted their separate legal principles, even while dealing with similar kinds of cases. This competition between different sets of courts helped develop the Common Law.

Social and economic factors also helped develop the law. Society had a feudal structure when Edward I ascended the throne. This system was on the wane when Henry VII came to the throne after much bloodshed. The system virtually vanished during the reign of the Tudor Kings. The feudal system received the worst jolt following the Black Death disaster of 1348. People had to forsake their land holdings, forsake their agricultural mainstay and had to undertake alternative careers for livelihood. The existing law, naturally had to change to take into account the changed social and economic pattern. This subjected the law to both change and growth.

The French wars and the Wars of the Roses which followed the Black Death broke society and its archaic composition. The chaos unleashed violence and disorder, which was mirrored in the legal institutions of the time. Preservation of family property became the prime concern of the people. This led to the establishment of the Law of Trusts. The Star Chamber was a product of the prevailing situation.

Development of Common Law

The judges, in fact, developed the law from the reign of Edward I till 1485. Two main factors somewhat staggered the growth and development of Common Law:

(i) The conservative character of the *forms of action,* and

(ii) Normal administration of justice was to some extent done by unruly barons; eruption of rebellions and civil war also hampered the growth of Common Law.

These retarding factors helped develop some angularities in the law. These were:

(i) Devices were invented by the judges in order to adapt the Common Law to the needs of the people;

(ii) Evolution of a new kind of jurisdiction to supplement the Common Law both in its substantive content and its procedural gaps; and

(iii) Intervention by the royal executive authority for maintenance of order and for dispensation of justice through the Council and Star Chamber.

LAND LAW

Holding of land being vital to society during the Middle Ages, Common Law was chiefly based on the law of the land. *Littleton, Tenures* was a classic written during this period. The contents were mostly general principles applicable to substantive rules. Another classic written during this period, namely, *coke on littleton* reveals that more maturity in the Common Law was yet to come. Somehow, notions of land property continued to be vital in the resolution of all disputes. The medieval origin of Common Law persisted for a long time in the resolution of disputes. Land tenure imposed certain obligations on landholders, like a knight was enjoined to serve his lord for 40 days in England or wherever there might be a war, or the right to refuse his consent to marriage which was unprofitable to him. Because of this legacy, lawyers too adopted logic peculiar to and emanating from the system.

THE LAW OF CONTRACT

Agreement between individuals was not accepted by early law as giving rise to any legal obligations. It was much later that the Chancery Courts and Ecclesiastical Courts took notice of such legal obligations. Judges began accepting such agreement as contract. They invoked the *Writ of Trespass* to provide remedy and relief in such cases. The Law of Contract, therefore, developed gradually, to acquire its modem concept. In fact, the Law of Contract, had no medieval origin.

LAW OF TORT

Tort, however, which related to liability arising independent of an agreement, was recognised by the early law. The Kings Courts took cognizance of wrongs involving violence or injury, when a person owing duty towards the community at large, committed a wrong and the victim required relief or remedy.

The Law of Torts during the medieval era was confined to specific ideas and concepts and had not enlarged its scope and ambit under which the modem Law of Torts took into it domain a variety of circumstances, causes and disputes. The earliest forms of actions in tort were simple cases resulting in physical damage to the victim. No regard or consideration was paid to the intention or objective of the wrongdoer.

Two factors were relevant during the early history of torts. Firstly, morality and the law remained awfully mixed up unlike their distinction accepted in modern times. The rule was that any law was right or wrong depending upon what the Law of God ordined. Secondly, any action causing damage was considered irrespective of the motive or intention of the wrongdoer. The *Writ of Deceit* was invented to check abuse of legal proceedings. Since the rule of Henry VI, the wrongs arising out of private transactions were brought within the ambit of the *Writ of Trespass*. Later, it was enlarged to include cases where relief or remedy was to be provided for failure to fulfill contractual obligations. Such cases where fraud was committed, like a vendor selling cattle not owned by him, was considered fit for giving relief or remedy.

The Law or Tort remained conservative and ineffective until 1846 like a huge branch falling and injuring someone stood forfeited as a deodand to the Crown. This shows that the position of the Law of torts was consideration of the actual damage and the physical cause for it, irrespective of the motive or intention behind it.

THE LAW OF EQUITY

During the medieval period, securing justice was dependant upon the availability of writ, which in turn, were limited in number. The Common Law jurisdiction, therefore, was limited in scope. But, people continued to seek justice where no writ existed. The itinerant justices which comprised the General Eyre tried to tackle such cases, but non existence of a Common Law writ prevented them from accommodating such requests. The general Eyre, in fact, became obsolete and inoperative in the reign of Edward III. Appeals and petitions for justice were naturally made to the king himself, as the fountain of Justice, for providing a remedy or relief, which was not available otherwise. The king, on his part, dispensed justice through his Council. This led to the establishment of two new Courts.

THE STAR CHAMBER

The star chamber remained identical to the Kings Council. It is often referred to as a Court of criminal equity. The Star Chamber proved to be a strong Court because it was linked directly to the executive authority or the king. It dispenses stronger justice than what was available in the Common Law Courts. The Star Chamber contributed to the English Legal System which can be called the Law related to criminal misdemeanour. The Star Chamber for centuries acted as a forum for safeguarding Law and order. It contributed to the growth of the English Legal System.

THE CHANCERY

A large number of petitions seeking justice in matters which could not be disposed off by the Common Law Courts came before the King in the hope of securing justice. These petitions were initially dealt with by the Kings Council. The Kings Council, considering them to be routine matters entrusted them to the Chancellor. The chancellor, in order to do justice to such cases, with the passage of time established his own Court of the Chancery. This Court gave relief in cases where the Common Law Courts, bound by the conservatism of the writ system could not do justice. Moreover, the relief given by the Chancery was also different to that given by the Common Law Courts. This practice ushered in the era of a more complete and effective English Legal System. The Chancery, at times, entertained cases which came within the purview of the Common Law Courts. In this process and due to the role played by the Court of Chancery, a sigular principle of the English Legal System got evolved. The *Court of the Chancery* came to be known as a *"Court of Conscience"*, meaning thereby that justice which was beyond the reach of the petitioner because of the rigidity of the law, namely, the *writ system,* confining relief to available *forms of action* through the Common Law Courts, could be secured from the *Chancery*. The vital principle was that the petitioner could secure justice normally denied, through the Chancery. The Chancery, in turn, was committed to the principle, that the petitioners conscience should not be smitten by remorse, that he failed to secure justice. During the Medieval Ages, the Chancellor chose to administer justice according to conscience because he felt that the law must have a moral base or that real law was derived from moral rules.

LAW MERCHANT

Business and commercial transactions during the Middle Ages were conducted by traders and merchants, travelling from one place to another or from one country to the other, namely, all over Europe and England. The traders and merchants had, during the early period, established their own special courts *affairs* and *markets,* which they visited. The traders and merchants began to petition the King by the time Edward I had come to the throne. They petitioned the King expecting that the King and his Council would do justice and settle their disputes. The Common Law system was unsuitable for them because they hailed from distant lands and foreign countries. Moreover, the Common Law was inapplicable, because the disputes of the traders and merchants related mainly to injuries to land, individuals in their trade dealings with each other and new kind of disputes Further, the Common Law had no provisions for redressing wrongs arising out of mercantile transactions. In fact, the trade and business transactions being of an international nature, the Law Merchant was derived more from Roman Law. The Law Merchant could not draw much inspiration from the insular nature of the Common Law of England.

During the reign of Edward I, a new Royal Court emerged which functioned under stewardship of the Admiral. This came to be known as the *Court of Admiralty* which entertained petitions from traders and merchants both in maritime and commercial or mercantile matters. By the year 1485, the Court of Admiralty had grown and developed considerably, had acquired a vast jurisdiction over mercantile disputes, and had laid the solid foundations of Law Merchant or Mercantile Law, which is familiar in this form in modern times. The Admiral, presiding over the Court of Admiralty, dispensing justice in mercantile disputes, drew strength from the patronage of the King of England, yet because of the international nature of mercantile disputes, was not a judge of Common Law. The judge of the Court of Admiralty was a civilian trained in Roman Law. This international nature of the Mercantile Law administered by the Court of Admiralty, is preserved in the Mercantile Law as we know it today.

INFLUENCE OF THE CHURCH ON COMMON LAW

The English Common Law peculiar to England is the basis of the English Legal System. But a controversy and conflict raged for a long time with the Church claiming supremacy over the Common Law jurisdiction. The Church was a very big land owner and its bishops, abbots and priors were powerful feudal lords, keen on augmenting their revenues. The Church frequently interfered in matters concerning the lay or ordinary people. The Church assumed the role of the custodian of morals of people and society. New disputes like the breach of contract and slander of a neighbour made their appearance during the medieval era. The Common Law Courts took notice of such disputes and tried to dispense justice in such cases. But, from the moral standpoint, the Church continued to dispense justice in matters of marriage, divorce and settlement of property with heirs and successors in the event of death of a person.

The laws related to marriage, divorce and property settlement on death remained within the domain of the Ecclesiastical Courts administered by the Church virtually till the end of the nineteenth century. It is natural that Ecclesiastical Courts enforcing justice according to rules of morality under the stewardship of the Church was bound to leave its lasting impact and influence on the English Legal System.

It can, therefore, be said that the English Legal System began to take form and shape in the two hundred years since the commencement of the reign of Edward I. While courts of different origins continued to dispense justice according to their thought, ideals, concept and background, yet the English Common Law had begun to formulate its structure during this period despite the conflict and jurisdictional claims of these courts. With the foundations of the English Common Law thus laid, the social, economic and political changes in the following centuries the English Common Law grew and developed into the shape and form in its various branches as we know today.

THE RENAISSANCE AND CIVIL WARS

This period was marked by a rivalry between the King and Parliament. It was a scene of judicial rivalry. The English Common Law had grown and had acquired a stable state. The law based on equity too had secured firm roots. It was also a period of major economic and social progress and development, and also of changes. The ancient feudal system was disintegrating while the merchant class was fast growing up. The Renaissance ushered in an intellectual revolution, which was followed by a natural phase of the Reformation which saw many changes.

Chancellors administering justice and guided by the moral rules were replaced by lawyers.

The dual sovereignty of the Church and the State was displaced by the sovereignty of the Central Government. As a finale, the sovereignty and authority of the Central Government was replaced by the sovereignty of Parliament. Further, equity jurisdiction no longer continued as an offshoot of natural justice because natural justice became a system of law.

The origin of modem law of contract and tort can be ascribed to the sixteenth and seventeenth centuries. New interpretations of old remedies and of old concepts of law stressing more on the sanctity of individual rights found acceptance in the English Common Law. Many rules of modem law also originated during this period.

COMMERCIAL LAW

Commerce, trade and mercantile activities had increased tremendously during the sixteenth and seventeenth centuries. Law Merchant had acquired a special position in the English legal system. But, the merchant for the most part, were a different class of people, dissimilar to the common law litigants, as the rules and law applicable to the latter did not apply to the former. The merchant guilds declined to seek justice in their disputes from the Common Law Courts. The rules applicable to the mercantile disputes were replaced by statutory rules and regulations. Mercantile transactions, however, continued to be governed by rules of custom or customary rules. Trading being international in character including its association with the continent, rules regulating its activities and for settlement of disputes were largely those drawn by lawyers from Roman Law. Many rules were opposed to the rules of the English

Common Law. For example, liability for a debt could be transferred by a negotiable instrument, which was not possible under the English Common Law. To meet the situation, the Court of Admiralty came into existence,. Merchants brought their disputes between merchants were brought before the Court of Admiralty. Its jurisdiction was expanded and strengthened by commissions issued by Henry VIII. Thus custom of merchants became the law administered by the Court of Admiralty. This administration of justice was supplemented wherever necessary by rules of Roman Law. The judges and the lawyers associated with this dispensation of justice were civilians. By the middle of sixteenth century the judges of the English Common Law Courts began to make efforts for restricting the jurisdiction of the Court of Admiralty. The Common Law judges succeeded to a great degree in restricting the jurisdiction to cases arising on the high seas. Despite this, Law Merchant had got firmly established in the hands of civilian judges. The Common Law Courts continued their efforts and devised a fiction by which they acquired jurisdiction over mercantile causes of action even though it had arisen in foreign territory. The remedy, however could be given only by using a fiction *'the action on the case'* which was based on custom of the merchants. This significance given to the custom of merchants laid the foundations for the development of Mercantile Law in the following centuries.

IRON AGE

The Iron Age marked the end of the political struggle in which Parliament was trying to wrest authority from the King. It also ushered in the struggle in which the common people were trying to wrest power of the Parliament from the gentry. It also marked the era of legislative intervention in the arena of rights and liabilities. The judges were left free to shape the law because Parliament was in the hands of a ruling class.

England expanded its horizons; conquests helped it to acquire colonial settlements which finally helped it to develop its mercantile marine. Napoleon disapproved England's transformation from an agricultural nation to a nation of shopkeepers. This business activity helped develop the concept of joint stock company. The East India Company was one such creation. Another class of traders who were not directly engaged in trade or business managed to participate through the operation of the joint stock company. Such companies managed to collect capital for trade and business from members of the community, who could be termed as *lesser traders,* and who without participating directly in trade or business managed to earn profits on the capital invested. This attracted the attention of the Legislature. In its bid to regulate this trading activity, the Legislature passed a Consolidation Act in 1908, followed by another in 1929 and another in 1948.

In the Middle Ages, Flemish weavers because of religious unrest, fled the continent in the seventeenth century and established home in England. Industrial activities increased. Underground mineral resources hitherto neglected, received attention. Mining of coal and iron began during the Iron Age. Markets having developed sufficiently, there was a steady growth of industrialisation. The Machine Age was round the corner and mass production was on the anvil. Men moved out from agriculture to towns and urban areas. A complex commercial organisation had developed which had its own complex problems like that of the master and servant and of one trader with another.

FOUNDATIONS OF COMMERCIAL LAW

The foundations of modem Commercial Law was laid in the eighteenth century. The dominance of Land Law related to agricultural activity was on the decline. A marked transformation was witnessed. The emphasis gradually changed from ownership of land to ownership of chattels and new forms of property came into existence like stocks and shares in Joint Stock Companies. The phenomenon was *"The old order changeth giving place to the new".* The changes were both social and economic. By the end of the century the new order had got firmly rooted and was also recognised. Parliament however, was still in the hands of the landed class. Traders businessmen and shopkeepers who had spread all over England, naturally wanted speedy justice sanctity of trade, and business agreements. This was possible if the administration of justice was cured of its technicalities and rigidity.

Two new developments took place in this transitional phase. Political thought and philosophy were getting crystalised, while religious predominance was on the decline. The Church Courts receded into the background. Canon Law or the Law administered by these Church Courts got confined to small nature of disputes.

Quite a few attempts were made by jurists to write treatises on the position of law. *Fortesque,* the Lancastrian Chief Justice and *Sir Thoman Smith* during Elizabeth's reign in their works, writing on the English constitution gave details about the theories of government. Fortesque stood for a limited monarchy, while Smith pleaded for the power of the King in Parliament. Yet another two thinkers, Hobbes and Locke came up with their theories separately. Hobbes in his work Leviathan in 1651 propounded the philosophy of the omnipotence of the State. He said the life of man without the government of State was "solitary, poor, nasty, brutish and short". *Locke* had stated earlier that Sovereign power should be subject to some kind of limitations. It was to some degree propounding the theory of separation of powers between the legislature, the executive and the judiciary. The theories of *Rousseau* stressing upon the rights of man and the *social contract theory* did not make much impact in England. Reforms in the law were delayed following alarm caused by the French Revolution. The two hundred years long constitutional power struggle prior of 1700 had shaken the belief of the judges that law was either right justice or was written in the hearts of the judges. As a result, the law-making authority of the King in Parliament acquired weightage. These conflicting political theories were counter-productive, as nothing positive emerged about the position of law. Conservatism, therefore, gained an upper hand on the development of the law during this era.

DEVELOPMENT OF LAW

Two major developments took during this era. Principles of equity became clear, while Common Law adopted Commercial Law.

EQUITY

Equity became part of the legal system. Equity had become a system of *case law* and this, in turn, was based on the *law of precedent.* The traditional concept of natural justice became obsolete.

Equity was applied for giving decisions wherever Common Law was silent or failed to give any clear direction. The judges were left with the residuary jurisdiction of *"judicial discretion."*

COMMERCIAL LAW

The second development was following the failure of Admiralty jurisdiction which made Mercantile Law come within the ambit of Common Law. There were some peculiar characteristics of mercantile activity. Ships operated under special documents known as charters; frequent communication between master and servant was impossible because of long and hazardous voyages of these chartered ships. Negotiable instruments which came into being for settling debts and bills of exchange foreign to the Common Law procedure of settling debts, helped devise a system under which purchasers of equity *"as holders of debt in due course"* were dealt with by Common Law. Goldsmiths became bankers and evolved their own law for dealing with complicated matters of credit and finance. Insurance contracts and guarantee contracts became the mode for carrying out trading and business. The basis, as some say erroneously, of the contract under Mercantile Law was the contract under Common Law. In fact, Mercantile Law was derived largely from the custom practised by merchants and not from the Law of Contract of England. Judicial conservatism stalled and development of Mercantile Law or Commercial Law.

REFORM AND LEGISLATION

We are not concerned here with the details of the various enactments that were approved by Parliament. Most of these enactments were designed to reform the involved rules of procedure. A host of enactments made their appearance from 1830 onwards. Finally, the Judicature Act 1873 put a final seal on the reforms carried out by the earlier enactments. The Judicature Act made sweeping changes. Under this Act, the old Common Law Courts, the Chancery Court and the Court ·of Appeal were merged and brought under the Supreme Court of Judicature. The High Court of Admiralty, the Probate Court and the Court for Matrimonial Causes also came under the Supreme Court of Judicature and got merged into it. Provision was also made for striking a balance between the rules of law and equity. The rules framed by the Supreme Court of Judicature laid the foundations of the modem law of practice and pleading. The rules thus framed enabled litigants to initiate action on an uniform pattern in simple terms shorn of the complex verbiage required under the ear1ierforms *of action.* The complaints made in this simple manner enabled the Supreme Court of Judicature to apply the law and give relief. These reforms finally bid good bye to the old rule of *'ubi remedium ibi jus* " that is , wherever there was a remedy there alone was any right admissible or fit for relief. The new order under the principles of *'ubi jus ibi remedium'* that is wherever there was a right, a remedy or relief had to be given or provided, became firmly rooted. Thus, the English Legal system had become liberal, travelling from the 'Pigeon-Hole' theory, of recognising certain rights fit for relief to the liberal and modem view that wherever a person's right had been infringed or an inquiry was caused the law must investigate, examine and provide relief and remedy.

SUBSTANTIVE LAW — REFORMS

Legislative activity increased during this period. Parliament became active; framed new laws defining new principles and obligations. New sections of the community, under the right to franchise granted to them, continued to clamour for enforcement of their rights. This phenomenon made the Parliament active.

The right to franchise coupled with the social, political and economic changes in English society motivated the framing of new laws. The business and trading community, as stated earlier, which had organised itself earlier into *'guilds'* began to press for their needs, despite the decline of these institutions. The business and trading community had organised itself afresh and more strongly now than in the form of guilds in the Middle Ages. In the new context, this organised community was more vocal and pressing. The law, therefore, grew and developed. Common Law was based on individualism or the injury caused to individuals was considered fit for relief. This catalysed the growth of statute law, which made Parliament enact fresh laws or statutes for providing relief for new kinds of injuries and breach of relationships or obligations.

The new trend of collectivism was on stage and was reflected by the law-making activity of Parliament. The doctrine of *laissez faire* had made its appearance. The Common Law recognised the need for protecting the legitimate trade interest and also the need for safeguarding the interests of other groups of traders against injury.

Commercial interests were on the ascendence during the nineteenth century, which made Parliament active. Social and industrial legislation marked Parliament's law-making activity during the twentieth country. Social legislation modified to a great degree the rights of owners of land. This was due to two reasons. Ones was the increased urbanisation of England, which saw people flock to cities from villages, while the other was the growing public conscience under which the well-off community also owed a duty towards the less privileged ones in society.

Social legislation indirectly made inroads into the domain of private law. Legislation made its appearance regulating employer-worker relations in factories; making it obligatory upon employers to insure its factory workers against injury suffered during work or by restricting a land owner from developing his land, subject to the needs of town or country planning rules.

This spate of social legislation, however, did not effectively regulate the master-servant relationship, which continued to fall within the ambit of the Common Law contract rules. Even the development of his land by its owner was subject to rules and law relating to creating a public nuisance, continued to be within the Common Law.

Legislation during this period did build up new concepts, principles and obligations. Such new concepts were contained in Bankruptcy Law and Company Law which were enacted during this period. New legal institutions also grew up to administer these new laws. The new social legislation or even the new laws enacted by Parliament did not alter the fundamental rights of citizens or of the people. These enactments also created new areas of responsibilities and liabilities. Examples of such legislation are many. To quote a few, the Factories Act imposed upon factory owners the responsibility of not installing machinery which might be dangerous to the personal safety of workers; or the Wages Councils Act under which factory owners were bound to include in the contract of employment of workers that the latter shall be paid a specified minimum wage; or the Housing Act, under which the local authority was empowered to clear a slum for construction purposes for general public good.

Industrial revolution witnessed in the nineteenth and early twentieth centuries catalysed the framing of new laws by the British Parliament. The Parliament became the supreme law-making body, whose composition in turn became more democratic dependent not on ownership of land, but on the basis of the majority elected under the new right of the vote or the right to franchise, while the 'King in Parliament' became the political sovereign, instead of a monarch on the principle of Kingship by descendence. The position of Parliament developed and grew into a legislative forum making laws recognising new rights, creating new obligations and liabilities and, the laws thus framed and dedicated to the principles of doing *"the greatest good to the greatest number."* The legislative activities of Parliament were not new in any way; it was only increased legislative activity accommodating the hopes and aspirations of the people, recognising the rights and duties of not merely individuals but of the community as a whole and taking into account new concepts needing regulation following the industrial revolution.

This era also saw a spate of social legislation which regulated and curbed the laws of private rights.

New laws were enacted by Parliament for meeting new and pressing demands of the people.

One such law was the Workmen's Compensation Act. This imposed upon employers additional liability than what was accepted in the contract for employment. The Land Transfer Acts and the Land Registration Act 1925, introduced the concept of registration of titles to land. The Housing Act enabled tenants to acquire concessions from landlords, that it restricted the rights of the latter. The Trade Disputes Act regulated trade disputes. The concepts of health and insurance guarantees were also introduced in terms of employment. Even minimum wages were made obligatory established by law. A Hire-Purchase Act framed in 1938 also introduced the concept for the first time.

Growth and development of commerce, business and trade created situations for framing another type of laws. Issues related to title to land and similar other matters were complex and required the legal acumen of lawyers. Business, trade and commercial matters required simpler laws. As a result, some aspects of Mercantile Law were codified during this era. The Bills of Exchange Act,1882, the Partnership Act, 1890, the Sale of Goods Act, 1893 and the Marine Insurance Act, 1906 were the enactments which codified some of the activities of trade and business and laid the foundations for codifying Mercantile Law.

CODIFICATION OF COMMON LAW

Codification was undertaken in several fields during this era. This was done in the field of crime contract, Tort, Equity and Mercantile matters.

MERCANTILE LAW

Rapid growth of Statue law was witnessed in the field in Mercantile Law during the nineteenth and early twentieth centuries. Commercial activities because of modem is at ion and advancement of life following introduction of the steam engine to atomic energy and airways necessitated framing of new rules which led to the enactment of new law. The new Acts or Statutes either made new law or propounded new concepts and principles or codified the existing rules and laws. Following the codification, customary law of the merchants was relegated to the background. These concepts, like chartering of ships, drawing up negotiable instruments for recognising debts of one merchant against another for or for transferring debts, or framing of insurance deeds, were not part of the English Common Law. But the fact remains that it was Mercantile Law which founded and developed the English Law of Contracts. Transactions under Mercantile Law did indeed exhibit the elements of the modern Law of Contracts. For example, a deed of insurance in operation was a deed of contract of mutual trust and good faith,. Failure to disclose and state the substance of the deed of insurance could make the insurance policy infructuous or even render invalid the sale of any goods or chattel. This implied that the person securing a deed of insurance of a policy of insurance must have an *"insurable interest "*, failing which the policy, in the nature of contract between two parties to the policy, would be rendered invalid. There were many customary rules of the merchants which got embodied in Statutes or enactments of Parliament.

The Reformation, social consciousness, moral responsibilities, colonisation, growth of trade union bodies, modernisation and various other factors were responsible for the growth and development of Mercantile Law and Industrial Law. The new laws so framed armed women with rights to purchase, dispose off or hold property. The right of the vote was granted to women by another law. Limiting the rights of landlords over their tenants was imposed by another law. No landlord was permitted to allow growth of slums on his property by an enactment as late as 1954. Similarly, under the New Towns Act, 1957, land, including that in villages, could be acquired for development for new townships. Under the Town and Council Planning Act, 1947, the owner of land could not change *"land use"* of his property, except with the permission of the government.

Modernisation and growth of merchant and industrial activity, a spate of new laws made their appearance. These law regulated and imposed restrictions on activities in trade and industry. By a specific law, goods transport vehicle owners were enjoined to pay their workers in money and not in kind. The activities inside factories were also subjected to conditions and restrictions. The Workmen's Compensation Act enforced the liability on factory owners to pay compensation to certain categories of workers injured in the *"course of their duties"* according to norms prescribed by the law. Further, factory owners engaged in certain production activities were enjoined to pay minimum wages to their workers as notified from time to time by the government. The spate of new laws, in fact, were framed to meet the need of a fast growing economy marked by a spate of trade and industrial activity.

GENERAL CONCEPT OF LAW

We have traced the history of how law evolved and manifested itself in various forms. We have also seen how custom of communities used to regulate relations, duties and obligations between members of these communities. When small communities grew and became larger and these customs became acceptable by the larger group, it became a sort of law.

The communities were primarily associated with land holdings. Cultivation used to be the mainstay for sustenance of members of the community. Sharing of agricultural produce was easy to begin with. But, when the size of land holdings increased and along with it the agricultural produce, it required additional hands for cultivation of the land. The natural question that cropped up was naturally the compensation to the additional hands employed by the owner or the landlord or land owner to the farm hand or farm labour. To begin with, it was sharing of the produce. Later, as society grew and developed the need for choosing a leader was felt and someone presumably the strongest developed the need for choosing a leader of this larger group, as time went by, became more powerful, raised a class dedicated to him, which was used by the leader for enforcement of custom or customary rules.

The leader of the bigger community acquired more powers and came to enjoy the attributes of kingship, whose word and orders became the law, although the law so enforced, was a body of customary rules. With the passage of time, the Feudal Lord, who had become some sort of a King or first amongst equals, in addition to enforcing customary rules and law, also made new rules which acquired the sanctity of law.

When the Feudal Lord, after becoming or acquiring the attributes of Kingship, increased his sway, became a bigger and powerful Feudal Lord he increased his law enforcing power; refusal to abide by the customary rules of their violation, became punishable by the feudal overlord. And, when the feudal overlord or King did not have any rival or competing king, he became a supreme power who could enforce his writ and directions of punish those at will, who disobeyed him.

The above discussion is not without reason. It helps us to understand the position of a King, Monarch or Sovereign the law which he was able to enforce, punish those who violated it; and he knew no superior who could superimpose his will over him.

It leads us to the inevitable position, which would greatly help us to understand or comprehend some vital aspects that govern modem society. These elements are custom or customary law, which later, was replaced by Statute Law, the position of the sovereign authority which enforces the law, visits those who refuse to obey it or violate it and does not have to consult or take orders from any competing sovereign authority.

Before we embark on examining various definitions of law it would be worthwhile to consider what eminent jurists have said on the questions of what is law; or what is the position of customary rules when Statue Law is available; why is violation of the law visited with punishment of fine, or why is there is a need for enforcing law at all.

Among the various jurists, let us first take up what Austin says about sovereignty and the supreme authority, namely, the sovereign which enforces law. According to the Austinian theory of Sovereignty, four elements must exist:

(1) Territory

(2) People or subjects

(3) Sovereign, who rules over the territory and subjects and has powers to enforce the law and punish those who violate it.

(4) Non existence of a super authority

Examining these elements, we may say that only that person would be a sovereign, who has a territory over which has writ reigns supreme; the territory must have people or subjects over whom the sovereign rules or governs and the sovereign enforces law or his orders which the subjects must obey; their defiance being subject to either punishment or fine or both, and lastly the sovereign must have no equal who can dictate terms to him or who has power to set aside the orders of the said sovereign.

One point may be noted here. The sovereign ofthe earlier times or feudal times, is today replaced by a government or sovereign authority, which is an elected body as in a democracy. Even an autocracy, dictatorship or a presidential form of government as in America, is a sovereign authority; has a territory to govern, has a law to enforce, has powers of punishing those who disobey the law or his orders with punishment of fine.

With the various forms of government available in modem times various states have appeared as Sovereign States. It would be interesting to find that the United Nations Organisation (UNO) or the world body, representing the comity of nations, is not a sovereign body. Comity means harmonious friendliness or courtesy. In this context of meaning of the word 'comity', the comity of nations means friendly recognition shown by one nation towards the laws, customs, rules, conventions, principles, practices, etc. of other nations.

It is because of this, International Law administered by the world body, that is, the UNO has been termed as the *'vanishing point of jurisprudence*'. A debate has gone on for a long time whether International Law is law at all? The main attribute of the law of any State is that the State which is a sovereign authority, has the powers to enforce the law on its subjects living in the territory which the State governs. The world body, namely, the UNO may have framed its own laws, that is International Law, but where does it possess the territory which the UNO governs or where are its subjects over which it can enforce its law, the International Law?

This paradox by itself explains that the UNO is not a sovereign authority The UNO is the world body, created by the consent of its member nations. Consent by nations only imposes the moral obligations on member-states to respect the decisions of or abide by the resolutions approved or passed by the UNO.

International Law not being enforceable as law as such, is often referred to by jurists that *"International Law is the vanishing point of jurisprudence."* In the strict terms of the connotation of law, International Law falls miserably short of the attributes of real law.

We can further digress interestingly into the arena of "police intervention" by the UNO in the affairs of sovereign states, as was witnessed in the North-South Korea conflict or in the recent Iran-Iraq war, in each of which the UN police force engaged itself directly in armed conflict. Examined strictly from the point of view of sovereignty of Nations or States, this kind or armed intervention by the UN "police force" or given the nomenclature of a "peace-keeping force" amounts to interfering with the sovereignty of nations.

We have taken up the foregoing discussion merely to explain the concept of law, which includes Mercantile Law. We have various kinds of law, namely, Civil Law, Criminal Law, Constitutional Law, Mercantile Law, Contract Law, Company Law, Business Legislations, Land Reforms Law, Revenue Law, Sales of Goods Law, Property Law, Patents Law, Official Secrets Law, National Security Law and so on.

The State, which is the sovereign authority, frames laws, makes newer laws, all with the objective of regulating the activities of its subjects over which it rules. The laws as we have seen are there to regulate individual to individual relations, individual to community relations, social relations, maintenance of internal peace and security, and for safeguarding the interests of the nations.

Law, therefore, may be defined in many ways. According to one view, *"Law includes all rules and principles which regulate our relations with other individuals and with the state."*

Similarly, the State, or the sovereign authority, regulates the conduct of its subjects or the people, whom it governs by a body of rules which is termed as law. Another view, therefore, would be "Law are rules of conduct approved by the State and enforced on the people which the State governs."

Holland, an eminent jurist, has defined Law thus: *"Law constitutes rules of external human action enforced by the sovereign political authority, namely, the State."*

Salmond, yet another notable jurist, in his treatise on Jurisprudence has defined law thus: *"Law is the body of principles recognised and applied by the State in the administration of justice."*

Woodrow Wilson, another jurist has defined law in a different way: *"Law is that portion of the established habit and thought of mankind which has gained distinct and formal recognition in the shape of uniform rules backed by the authority and power of the government."*

There are a host of definitions of law. Jurists have viewed law in different contexts. It would suffice here to say after analysing the above definitions, that firstly, law comprises a body of rules and regulations framed by the State, which is sovereign authority, for regulating the conduct of individuals, society at large, safeguarding the interests of the State with regard to internal peace and harmony and national integrity of the Nation. The law so framed by the State, is secondly, for the people governed to observe and abide by it both in letter and spirit; violation of which ends in punishment and fine or both. Thirdly, the State or the sovereign authority also reserves for itself the power to enforce the law, that is it is also armed with an enforcement machinery, namely, the administration both civil and police administration. The writ of the state runs over its entire territorial jurisdiction and covers all people, namely, each and every individual who are the citizens of that state. People aggrieved by the enforcement of the law, have been provided with the right of appeal. The appeal, however lies with the forums of judicial administration or the judicial set-up also provided by the State. But the state, or the sovereign authority making the law and enforcing it over its entire territory and on the entire populace, comprising its citizens, *"knows no equal or superior or sovereign authority"* which can superimpose its will or its dictates over the Sovereign State.

India is an Union of States. It is a "Sovereign Socialist Secular Democratic Republic", having a Parliamentary System of Government. The Republic is governed in terms of the Constitution, which was adopted by the Constituent Assembly on 26th November, 1949, and which came into force on 26th January, 1950.

No book on any branch of law would be complete without having a deep look on the kind of governance which India acquired through the Constitution. The nature of the Government may be gleaned from the Preamble of the Constitution. The Preamble is virtually *"A Guide to Governance of the People"*. It must be remembered by every student of law, by every citizen, by those who administer the country namely, the Legislature, the Executive and the Judiciary, the three main wings of the Government, also created by the Constitution.

The Constitution comprises not merely the enforceable aspect of law, but also the guidelines for governance. The Constitution has a host of provisions, some of which may be mentioned here as they relate to the interests of the students of law in general, not without exception, even for students of Mercantile Law. **The Constitution of India** lays down the rights and duties of those who govern and also for those who are governed by the State. It is a logical rule that if a person has rights, he must have duties too towards other individuals and the society at large. Even the Government has to abide by the norms of governance contained in the Constitution. The Preamble is being given to enable the students to understand these norms of governance and the rights, duties and limitations to which the people that is, citizens of India have been subjected to. The Preamble is as follows:

"WE, THE PEOPLE OF INDIA, having solemnly resolved to constitute India into a *SOVEREIGN SOCIALIST SECULAR DEMOCRATIC REPUBLIC * and to secure to all its citizens;

JUSTICE, social, economic and political;

LIBERTY of thought, expression, belief, faith and worship;

EQUALITY of status and of opportunity; and to promote to among them all

FRATERNITY assuring the dignity of the individual and *the unity and integrity of the Nation* ;

IN OUR CONSTITUENT ASSEMBLY this the twenty sixth day of November, **1949, do HEREBY ADOPT, ENACT AND GIVE TO OURSELVES THIS CONSTITUTION."**

It may be noted that the words within the first set of asteriks were introduced in the Constitution by the Constitution (Forty-second Amendment) Act, 1976 as also the words within the second set of asteriks by the same amendment. Both of these set of phrases became operative with effect from January 3, 1977.

The Constitution provides for a scheme of things that govern the entire Republic; namely, the Legislature, the Executive, the Judiciary, the States, the Republic itself and its people, that is citizens.

The Constitution has 22 Chapters, 10 Schedules, the 10th one having been repealed.

It may be interesting to note that the Constitution in its Chapter III or Part III, gives to citizens Fundamental Rights defined in Articles 14 to 35, but *'these rights are not absolute.'* To illustrate, Article 19 provides: 19(1) All citizens shall have the right — (a) to freedom of speech and expression; (b) to assemble peaceably and without arms; (c) to forms associations or unions; (d) to move freely throughout the territory of India; (e) to reside and settle in any part of India; and (f) to practise any profession, or to carry on any occupation, trade or business.

The student may note here that these fundamental rights given by the constitution were subjected to certain restrictions by the Constitution (Sixteenth amendment) Act, 1963, which inserted Article 19 (2) as follows:

"19(2) Nothing in sub-clause (a) of clause (1) shall affect the operation of any existing law, or prevent the State from making any law, in so far as such law imposes reasonable restrictions on the right conferred by the said sub-clause in the interests of *'the sovereignty and integrity o/India'* the security of the State, friendly relations with foreign States, public order, decency or morality, or in relation to contempt of court, defamation or incitement to an offence."

The student by examining the insertion of the above provision must have noted that these fundamental rights are not absolute; restrictions can be imposed by the State in the interests of one of the eight objectives mentioned in the amendment.

This discussion would help the student appreciate that laws that are made for meeting the aspirations of the people and for ensuring good governance.

When we mention about good governance, the moot question arises: Has the Constitution made any provisions for good governance? This question is natural because the earlier provisions from Article 14 to 35 deal with fundamental rights of citizens subject, however, to some restrictions as incorporated by Article 19(2).

Chapter IV or Part IV of the Constitution in Articles 39 to 43 lays down all the norms which the state or the Republic of India shall have to observe and abide by in the governance of the country. There is a vital difference between Fundamental Rights and the Directive Principles of State Policy. Fundamental rights are justiciable rights or such rights which can be enforced by courts of law. The Directive Principles of State Policy are not justiciable, that is, cannot be enforced through courts of Law. Article 37 provides: The provision in this part shall not be enforceable by any court, but the principles therein laid down are nevertheless fundamental in the governance of the country and it shall be the duty of the state of apply these principles in making laws."

Article 38 makes the position more clear. Articles 38 (1) says: "The State strive to promote the welfare of the people by securing and protecting as effectively as it may a social order in whichjustice, social, economic and political, shall form all the institutions of national life."

Article 38 (2) states: "The State shall, in particular, strive to minimise the inequalities in income, and endeavour to eliminate inequalities in status, facilities and opportunities, not only amongst individuals but also amongst groups of people residing in different areas or engaged in different vocations."

IGNORANCE OF LAW — NO EXCUSE

We have seen so far that law is intended to regulate the conduct of the people or citizens of the State which makes the law. The State also makes law for itself, namely the Directive Principles of State Policy under Articles 39 to 43 of the Constitution, while Articles 37 specifically states that these principles shall be "fundamental in the governance of the country" and "it shall be the duty of the State to apply these principles in making laws."

Besides the Constitutional provisions, there are myriad laws that have been enacted by Parliament, regulating human activity in all walks of life. The natural question is can a person rather a layman, have knowledge of all the laws, or be aware of the provisions in these enactments. The unlettered or the illiterate, that is, the common man may remain ignorant of these laws and their provisions. He may violate some provision or defy a positive directive of another law. Will such a person be excused or his acts be condoned?

In such a situation the rule stated in Latin; "*Ignorantia jusris non excusat*" would be involved.

It means, *Ignorance of law is no excuse.* Every person who is a citizen of the State is supposed to know the law and be aware of what the law permits and what it prohibits. It may be noted that almost all the enactments have provisions indicating what is right and what is wrong. In other words, a law punishes both acts of commission and acts of omission. The law, in fact, imposes a duty on those for whom they have been framed. Violation of the duty so imposed or failure to discharge the said duty would in either case become punishable. Because the law prescribes a rightful conduct and disapproves a wrongful conduct, none can plead or take shelter under the defence that he was ignorant of the law or not aware of it.

ACT OF COMMISSION & OMISSION

Every kind of law especially criminal law, imposes liability both for acts of commission and omission. For example, a husband is supposed to support his wife; if he fails to do so, he is liable to pay a maintenance to his wife, if he has abandoned her. Similarly, a husband is duty-bound to protect his wife against harm, a father is duty bound to undertake responsibilities for supporting his children.

It can therefore, be concluded, that law punishes both acts of commission and acts of omission.

Some more examples can be cited even in Civil Law. A person executes a deed to sell his property and some money (Consideration) has also been paid to the prospective seller by the buyer. If the seller refuses to sell his property on the expiry of the agreed upon period of time the purchaser can either claim damages for refusal to sell, or move a civil court for specific performance that is, he can be forced to sell the property as per the agreement to sell.

Similarly, an indemnity bond is an agreement by the person who executes it to compensate the person in favour of whom it has been executed. Take the case of a *'hundi'* which is a *'promise to pay'*. a kind of negotiable instrument, which places the person who issues it to honour it and pay the amount due under it, failure to do so will make the executor of the negotiable instrument or *'hundi'* liable not only for payment of the amount due under it but also for damages.

KINDS OF LAW

Every law that is an enactment has certain aims and objectives. Just below the title ofthe law or enactment or Act, is invariably given the *'statement of objects and reasons.'* This indicates the purposes for which the law has been made. For example, the Industrial Disputes Act, 1947, states as its objectives: "An Act to make provisions for the investigation and settlement of industrial disputes and for certain other purposes."

Take the case of the Industrial Disputes (Banking and Insurance Companies) Act, 1949. The aims and objectives of this enactment state: "An Act to provide for the adjudication of industrial disputes concerning certain and insurance companies."

Each set of law has specific aims and objects. It depends upon what kind of action is sought to be regulated by the enactment.

CLASSIFICATION OF LAW

Law which comprises rules for regulating affairs which are sought to be brought under it can be classified in a number of ways.

Classification may be attempted under two categories: (1) Law prescribing duties, liabilities and powers or (2) Law containing criminal rules and law containing civil rules.

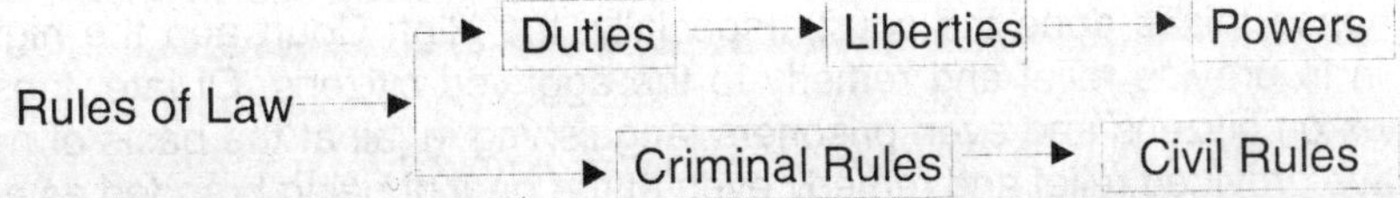

SUBJECT-WISE CLASSIFICATION

Laws enacted by the Legislature [(State Assemblies) or (Parliament)] may also be classified according to the subject they relate to. Such classification for example can be crimes, civil liabilities property dealings, contract, negotiable instruments, industrial disputes, workers' compensation, protection of tenants, minimum wages to factory workers, road offences, transport violations, matrimonial matters, inheritance in property, consumer protection, service matters, revenue matters, etc. A subject-wise list of the laws if drawn up, would virtually form a big book.

CLASSIFICATION — LEGAL REMEDIES

Yet another kind of classification of law can be made according to the legal remedies which the laws provide. The earlier classification according to duties, liberties and powers under one category and criminal rules and civil rules under the second category, may be one way of looking as the kinds of law available. The subject-wise classification poses difficulties because the subjects run into hundreds, may thousands, or even more.

The more effective and rather the most effective way of classifying the laws available would be remedy-wise. This classification would be more realistic because every law provides some kind of relief or remedy to the person aggrieved. Take the case of criminal law: it provides for varying periods of imprisonment, death sentence and even fine for different categories of acts which the law treats as crime. In the field of civil law, provisions exist for giving relief to the aggrieved person say when his right to beneficial user of his property or damage to it by another say that his rights to inheritance are jeopardized and so on.

Even, the earlier classification of legal rules into duties, liberties and powers, can be better understood when examined in the context of remedies or relief associated with them.

Duties imposed on persons when flouted ends in punishment or payment of compensation in fines. For example, failure by a person to perform his duty as a factory worker or as a government employee may respectively end in cut in wages or withholding of annual salary, increment or denial of promotion for say a year or two. Similarly, a husband's failure to support the wife makes the husband liable for paying maintenance to the abandoned wife.

Take the case of legal rules as liberties. A person has been given the liberty of beneficially enjoying his property. If the person in doing so puts up a construction which prevents or deprives his neighbour of light and air, the neighbour can sue the person for denying him the *right of easement.* The neighbour can even obtain an injunction or stay order from the civil court to stop the construction and, finally, if the construction has been completed, the disposal of the civil suit will force the person to pull down his construction. Take another example, if a person under debt refuses to repay it to the creditor and the debtor obtains a declaration of bankruptcy from the civil court, the court can order attachment of the debtor's immovable property and even order its public auction for satisfaction or repayment of the debt.

Let us examine the third category of law which invests powers to authorities. A local body, namely, a municipal board or municipal corporation having powers to acquire property, may do so, but not without offering compensation to the person whose property has been acquired under the law. Similarly, the municipal authority has the powers to pull down dangerous or dilapidated buildings on the ground that it is a hazard to public safety, but the municipal authority cannot do it straightaway. It must give a notice to the owner of the dangerous building specifying a period of time, say a month or fifteen days, to pull down the structure himself, failing which the municipal authority would do it itself and also recover the cost incurred in pulling down the structure.

Reverting to the premise of classifying the laws according to the remedy and relief they provide, it would produce a rather practical and more rational classification. After all, laws are made not to confound the people on whom they are applied; the objective of each law is to inform and educate the people and make them understand the limits within which they are immune to action under the law. Once they transgress these limits the law will come into operation and punish those who violate it or disobey it.

Moreover, laws are not enacted merely to punish the wrongdoers. Laws lay down the dividing line between rightful and wrongful conduct as well. Law is without passion and *'justice is blind'*; it does not discriminate between rich and the poor, the influential and the lowly or the mighty and the weak. Because of this trait, relief and remedy is also available to those aggrieved by arbitrary and spiteful police's administrative actions. If, *"Ignorance of law is no excuse"* for the people governed, it is equally true, *"Misuse, abuse or arbitrary use of the law is no excuse for those who govern or rule".* Once this is done the court, especially, the High Court and the highest court of the land, the Supreme Court step in to provide relief and remedy to the aggrived citizens. Of late, these apex courts have taken cognizance of atrocities on citizens and even prisoners languishing in jail at the basis of newspapers reports or even private petition and have provided relief and remedy even at the peril of being branded as an *"overactive judiciary".*

The remedy-wise classification could be as follows:

(1) Remedies for violation of the personal rights
(2) Remedies for violation of property rights
(3) Contractual remedies
(4) Matrimonial remedies
(5) Constitutional remedies
(6) Civil remedies
(7) Criminal remedies
(8) Consumer remedies
(9) Remedies under the Law of Torts

The above classification may need a little clarification personal rights include may things like the beneficial employment of property, rights to privacy, right to fresh air and light, right to personal security against injury or danger of life so on. Remedies for violation of personal rights would attract both civil action and for injuries to the person, criminal action.

In the same way, violation of property rights, would entail mostly civil action. Matrimonial causes would invoke the jurisdiction of Civil Courts or Matrimonial Courts wherever they exist.

Contractual remedies come within the ambit the whole gamut of Mercantile Law. Some of the liabilities arise out of unwritten contracts, like the duty of the trader to pay to government sales tax on goods sold, income tax on his personal income so earned, excise duty on the goods offered for sale, giving compensation to factory workers injured in the course or employment or work, paying overtime for work taken beyond the prescribed hours of works, giving of leave, sick leave, privilege leave to workers, weekly offs and holidays on gazetted holidays. In all such cases and many more like these there is no written contract between the person duty-bound to observe these laws and the persons or the government entitled to these benefits.

The other categories of liabilities under Mercantile Law arise from written agreements or contracts. A person bound under a contract, must discharge his obligations towards the other party to the contract. An Indemnity Bond enjoins the person executing it to compensate or indemnify the person in whose favour the bond has been executed for the losses incurred as envisaged under the bond. Chartering of road carriers, ships on the high seas, goods aircraft or rail wagons, the person hiring them is liable to pay the charges of transport. A negotiable instrument or a *'hundi'* has to be honoured at once when it is presented to the person for whom it meant. A person responding to a tender for undertaking supplies of goods or for executing a construction work, on acceptance of the offer or the tender, is duty-bound to complete the supplies or execute the construction work within the time specified in the tender failing which he, namely, the tenderer, is liable to pay damages as envisaged in the damage-clause of the tender.

Constitutional remedies form a distinctive class of remedies as provided by the Constitution under the head, Right to Constitutional Remedies. Articles 32 to 35. Article 32(1) state: The right to move the Supreme Court by appropriate proceedings for the enforcement of the rights conferred by this part is guaranteed [part being part II detailing Fundamental Rights — Articles 14 to 35]. Article 32 (2) provides: The Supreme Court shall have the power to issue directions or orders or writs, including writs in the nature of *habeas corpus, mandamus, prohibition, quo warranto and certiorari,* whichever may be appropriate, for the enforcement of any of the rights conferred by this part (Part being Fundamental Rights).

Civil Remedies include a vast range of relief under its provisions, stay orders, injunctions, decrees, declaration of rights and titles etc. are given under the Civil Procedure Code. Criminal Remedies are provided under the Indian Penal Code for injuries like theft, robbery, dacoity, homicide, culpable homicide, murder, assault, criminal assault, wrongful confinement, trespass, breach of trust, fraud, deceit, maintenance for criminal neglect of wife, defamation, libel etc. The remedy under the Indian Penal Code includes, imprisonment, including life imprisonment, death sentence, fine and imprisonment or both, damages, maintenance etc.

Consumer remedies is yet another class of relief which has come into the fore with the advancement of society. The consumer is no longer a 'sitting duck' who can be fleeced of his hard earned money without having relief or remedy for poor quality goods or products sold to him. In the earlier era when consumer consciousness had not developed, the warranty and guarantee clauses attached to equipment, machinery or electronic gadgets were not honoured by producers and manufacturers. Today, the purchaser, buyer and the consumer can knock at the doors of Consumer Courts and get relief by way of damages, compensation or even replacement of the equipment, machinery or electronic gadgets. The latest incident is a case in point. Mustard oil packs were taken back by manufacturers and money paid back to consumers when several brands were found to be adulterated with *'argemone'* oil declared by chemists, analysts and health authorities, to be responsible for causing dropsy.

Remedy under the Law of Torts are available, but there is no Statute which codifies the law. Take the example of some one throwing floor-sweepings or rubbish from first, second or third floors on a person down below on the road, it is an actionable cases under the Law or Torts. The person who is hit by the downpour of rubbish can sue the person throwing it and be awarded damages, of course, by a Civil Court.

Let us examine in some detail the nature of legal rules that comprise duties, liberties and powers.

DUTIES

Under the head of laws that impose duties on the people, fall under a special kind of laws. As already stated, a husband is duty bound to support the wife, a person who is a party to a contract, must perform his duty; if he refuses, the court may order specific performance of the contract. Similarly, a witness in the witness-box under oath is bound to speak the truth about facts which he is supposed to know; if he tells a lie or speaks untruth, he is liable for perjury and punishable under law. Even a false statement, say in an affidavit duly sworn in and submitted in a court by a person, make him liable for punishment as a contempt of the court.

Further, there are some rules or law which are prohibitory in nature. Their violation may not be a crime, but it is still actionable. If a person or trader does not deposit sales tax which he realises on goods sold by him, he can be proceeded against and fined. The fine can be realised by attachment of his property and its sale for recovering the amount due as arrears of land revenue. Breaking of traffic rules, or smoking at places where it is "prohibited" is punishable with fine. Similarly, the police cannot enter any private houses for search without a search-warrant issued by a magistrate.

LIBERTIES

Liberties have been given to the people in the shape of freedoms under the Constitution.

The Constitution guarantees to all citizens a number of fundamental rights which are in the nature of liberties. Article 19 gives these guarantees of freedoms.

Article 19 (1) All citizens shall have the right:

(a) to freedom of speech and expression;
(b) to assemble peaceably and without arms;
(c) to form associations or unions;
(d) to move freely throughout the territory of India;
(e) to reside and settle in any part of the territory of India; and
(e) to practise any profession, or to carry on any occupation, trade or business.

Notes: Clause (f) was deleted by the Constitution (Forty-Fourth Amendment) Act, 1978 with effect from June 20, 1979. These are popularly known as the "six freedoms" guaranteed by the Constitution. Being fundamental rights or freedoms or liberty, they are justiciable and enforceable through courts of law.

Some of the other liberties or freedoms in the nature of fundamental rights are Article 14: "equality of opportunity and equal protection of the Laws"; Article 15: "State shall not discriminate against any citizen on grounds only of religion, race, caste, sex, place of birth or any of them" with regard to access to shops, public restaurants, hotels and places of public entertainment or in the use of wells, tanks, bathing ghats, roads and places of public resort maintained wholly or partly out of State funds or dedicated to the use of the general public; Article 16: "there shall be equality of opportunity for all citizens in matters related to employment or appointment to any office under the State"; Article 20: "no person shall be convicted of any offence, except for violation of a law in force; no person accused of any offence shall be prosecuted and punished for the same offence more than once; no person accused of any offence shall be compelled to be a witness against himself and no person shall be deprived of his or personal liberty except according to procedure established by Law", Article 22: "no arrested person shall be detained in custody without being informed, as soon as may be, of the grounds of such arrest and nor shall be denied the right to consult, and to be defended by, a legal practitioner of his choice", "every person who is arrested and detained in custody shall be produced before the nearest Magistrate within a period of twenty-four hours of such arrest." Further on, the Constitution provides to citizens "Rights Against Exploitation" (Articles 23 & 24); "Right to Freedom of Religion" (Articles 25, 26, 27 & 28) "Cultural and Educational Rights" (Articles 29, 30) and 31, which was repealed by the Constitution (Forty-fourth Amendment Act, 1978 ") and "Right to Constitutional Remedies" (Article 32 to 35).

POWERS

Legal rules or laws giving powers are more relevant in trade and business. This kind of relationship is created by certain laws, like a seller is invested with the powers to sell his goods to anyone who wants to buy them. The buyer has the power to purchase a particular item from any seller. Once, a particular buyer proposes to buy a particular product and a particular seller agrees to sell and the transaction is completed, the sale under the offer made by the buyer and accepted by the seller completes the contract of the sale. The buyer has to pay the demanded price, while the seller has to supply the item of proper quality, and is bound to indemnify in damages or replace the item, if it is found wanting in quality defective or sub-standard, under the warranty clause.

We need not discuss the criminal and civil laws as most of us are aware about them. Moreover, reference has been made to them in the classification of law according to the kind of legal remedies available or the kind of relief provided.

Having dealt with the history of law in general and of Law Merchant or the basis of Mercantile Law of modern times, let us proceed to examine as to what comprises Business Legislations.

NATURE OF BUSINESS LEGISLATIONS

In an organised society, governed by the State, all human activity and transactions, are regulated by the state through laws made by it. Law is needed because without defining the rights, powers, limitations, liabilities, duties and responsibilities, activities are likely to go haywire, cause harm, injury, loss or damage. The law, therefore, provides, how such situations could be averted.

Business Legislations, like any other kind of Law regulates activities of business, trade, industry and commerce. The nature of Business Legislations can be understood if we examine the following two definitions:

(1) "Business Legislations is that portion of the legal system which guarantees any orderly conduct of business affairs and the settlements of legitimate disputes in a just manner.

(2) "Business Legislations establishes a set of rules and prescribed conduct that enables us to avoid misunderstandings and injury in our business relationships."

SCOPE OF BUSINESS LEGISLATIONS

We have already discussed the origin of Law Merchant, how it got evolved from Common Law of England. It would be worthwhile to examine how Business Legislations or Mercantile Law took root in India. This discussion would be useful before we deal with the scope of Business Legislations. It may, however be mentioned here that the scope of Business Legislations is very vast. Business Legislations encompass a large variety of matters like licences, large business units, monopolies, issues of securities, agency, property, contracts and agreements, foreign exchange, negotiable instruments, firms and partnerships, sales, insurance, companies, corporate bodies, warranties, guarantees, bailment, labour, factory workers, minimum wages, workmen's compensation, suretyship, consumer interest, indemnities, bankruptcy, taxation, unfair trade practice, institutional finance, shares, equities, procurement of raw material power, iron, steel-import-export rules, customs clearance, wharfage, storage, import of capital goods, marketing-laws, taxation-sales tax and income-tax and minimum wages-pollution control and a myriad other matters. Legislation at State level and by the Centre controls and regulates these matters through laws enacted by these legislative bodies from time to time.

BUSINESS LEGISLATIONS - INDIAN ORIGIN

The origin of Business Legislations in India is also essential for study. Law Merchant or Mercantile Law of England, as the mother of Business Legislations all over the world as part International activities as well has already been discussed. The Indian origin of Business Legislations is rather interesting.

The earliest form of Business Legislations is that contained in the Dharma Shastras. The names of Manu, Vishnu, Yajna-Valkya and Narada, is associated with it. It is they who dwelt at length on what is right or what is wrong. Their views might have been in the nature of moral rules, or exhortations, but, nevertheless they did lay down the basics. Under Hindu Law, views of Manu as laid down in the Dharma Shastras, is authoritative. Manu, in Hindu Law is considered the progenitor of the human race, the first King and the first lawmaker and lawgiver. Following development over the centuries and the growth of progressive views, persons, political leaders, and modem progressives, have discredited the laws of Manu. They say the Laws of Manu are conservative, orthodox, rigid, biased and obsolete in the context of modem times. It is no surprise because even the once famed Greek philosophers have found bitter critics. As an example Karl Marx and his political and economic theories have been discredited following the recent disintegration of the USSR into nine independent states.

Whatever may be the *pros* and *cons* of the laws and thoughts given by Manu or their criticism in the modem context, the Dharma Shastra deals extensively with civil rights, duties, responsibilities, morals, Wrongs, criminal law and the connected procedures which can be used for proving these concepts right or \Wrong.

The next in order is the Artha Shastra ofKautilya which dates back to 300 BC. Kautilya's Artha Shastra, covers rights, duties, Wrongs and responsibilities which devolve on the King. This masterpiece on law deals with myriad matters including economics diplomacy, treatment of official messengers from other Kings, strategies, the propriety of retaining certain matters in the King's control, namely, the Public Sector concept of modem democracies, and a host of other matters. It also dwells at length on the propriety of trade and business, the duties and responsibilities of those who engaged in it in private capacity and obligations of the 'public sector' or industries, trade and commerce in the King's control.

The Artha Shastra, as already stated also lays the foundations of the sanctity of contracts, the obligations to act according to it and fulfill what is agreed upon in contracts. It deals with all kinds of contracts, including sale, purchase, marriage, diplomatic commitments, treaties between Kings,. State to State agreements, and a host of other matters.

These principles propounded in the Artha Shastra are not mere gems of thought of a philosopher, but are solidly backed by reasoning. Logic, propriety and precision. The contract, according to Kautilya, would be valid if made openly between parties competent to enter into the agreement. It would be invalid Kautilya has stated, if the contract was made by parties not competent to enter into an agreement, or if made against the interests of the King, or against public policy and morals or was against the King's administration. Kautilya even conceived what modem Contract Law codifies, that a contract would stand vitiated or be invalid *ab initio* if the agreement was based on fraud and misrepresentation. Regarding competence of the parties entitled to enter into a contract, Kautilya clearly laid down that the parties should be of sound mind, capable of understanding the nature of the contract, where their consent to the contract or agreement should not be under duress but should be free and voluntary and that the contract should contain some transfer of interest or be for some consideration. The student must be aware that the Indian Contract Act contains all these elements of a valid contract, namely, the parties to the contract should be of sound mind, should not be minors, should act freely of their own will without duress and that the consideration of the contract which had been made while any of the above factors existed could be rescinded by either party to the contract and the person guilty of hiding the vitiating factors was liable to pay compensation or damages to the other party. Kautilya, in addition to specifying the relief of compensation or damages to the aggrieved party, also suggested that a penalty be imposed on the wrongdoer.

The Artha Shastra also provides for a number of other concepts which are in prevalence in modem Business Legislations like the concepts of debts, pledges, master-servant relationship, treatment of farm and industrial labour, duties towards those in employment of the King, those working in cooperatives. The Artha Shastra is virtually a complete treatise on statecraft, detailing at length even what is right or wrong for the King, or what are the duties and responsibilities of those who rule over people. The King in the Artha Shastra, is the modern democracy and government of modem times.

The treatise deals extensively with the subject of taxes, what kinds can be imposed and which taxes would be considered immoral. Details have also been given how tax should be collected, how should it be stored in the King's treasury and how should it be spent righteously.

The Artha Shastra outlines in detail the manner in which the King should spend the money from the treasury, which has been collected from the people through taxes. Expenditure which is right or wrong has also been given in the treatise. The expenditure by the King has to be for the people's welfare. The treatise, therefore, has given at length what expenditure should be considered for public good. Thus, what is public welfare, the modem concept, has been discussed at length in the Artha Shastra.

The student of Business Legislations or Mercantile Law would be well advised to go through a concise account of Kautilya's Artha Shastra. He should do so not merely to glean the concepts propounded in the treatise, but also for grasping the fundamentals and the reasons behind the adherence to these concepts. It would be a worthwhile study.

EAST INDIA COMPANY AND LAW

The history of the Indian legal system and laws begins with the advent of the East India Company. It was a major landmark. The British crown issued a Charter in 1600 to the East India Company for carrying on its legitimate trading activities in India. The Charter conferred on the East India Company a corporate character and gave juristic powers to the Company. The Charter empowered the Company to frame Laws for ensuring proper governance in its jurisdiction. The Company was also empowered to inflict punishment in the form of fines and penalties as may be necessary for enforcing the laws made by it.

Later in the year 1858, the British Crown assumed sovereignty over India appropriating it from the East India Company. The Government of India Act 1858, was enacted by the British Parliament, under which the British Government through the British Crown assumed direct rule over India. The Secretary of State for India assisted by a Council of 15 members exercised the powers of the Crown for purposes of administration under this Act. This Council of 15 members comprised members who were exclusively Englishmen. Some of these members were nominees of the Crown, while the other were representatives of the Directors of the East India Company. The Secretary of State for India was directly responsible to the British Parliament. The Secretary governed India through the Governor-General in Council which was an executive council. High officials of the Government were inducted into an executive council. The Government of India Act 1858 was a law which imposed the principle of imperial will and control in the governance of India, without allowing any kind of local participation in the administration of the country.

The Indian High Court Act, 1861, was a significant enactment in the development in Indian Legal History. It laid the foundations of setting up the system of judicial administration on a sound footing. The Indian High Courts Act abolished the dual system of administration of justice, one, by the Courts of the company and the other by the Courts under the Crown.

The next important enactment was the Government of India Act, 1919. This enactment provided for increased participation of Indians in every branch of administration of India in the governance of the country. The Act also aimed at the gradual development of self-governing institutions with the objective of progressive realisation of responsible government in British India as an integral part of the British Empire.

The next significant event was the enactment of the Government of India Act, 1935. This enactment introduced significant changes in the administration of British India. The earlier enactments known as Government of India Acts were different as they continued to propagate unitary nature of the Indian administration. The Government of India, 1935, transformed the unitary nature of India's administration into a Federation of provinces and the Indian Princely States as its units: The Federation, however, never came into existence, as the Princely India States given the option to join the Federation, decided not to do so. Although the Federation conceived under the 1935 Act never became a reality, the principle of provincial autonomy envisaged under the Act, came into effect from April, 1937. The Act provided for separation of legislative powers between the Provincial and Central Legislatures according to the scheme and limits defined by the Act. The Provinces were no longer delegates of the Central Government, but were autonomous units of administration. A governor appointed by the Crown exercised the executive authority of the Provinces on behalf of the Crown and not as a subordinate of the Governor-General. The Governor was required to act on the advice of ministers who were responsible to the State Legislature.

The Government of India Act, 1935, also provided for the establishment of Federal Court.

The Federal Court was a Constitution Court, the first of its kind in India. It was empowered with the primary function of interpreting the Government of India Act, 1935. Till the year 1949, that is, even two years after India gained freedom and became independent, the Federal Court continued to function. Its decisions were subject to the appellate authority of the Privy Council in England. The Federal Court was replaced by the Supreme Court of India, the highest court of the country, after India adopted its Constitution on 26th November, 1949.

The Indian Independence Bill, seeking to grant Independence to India, was introduced in the British Parliament on July 4, 1947 and on receipt of Royal Assent on July 18, 1947, became the Indian Independence Act. This Act provided that from August 15, 1947, in place of "India" as defined in the Government of India Act, 1935, two independent dominions of India and Pakistan, would come into being. The Act also provided that both the dominions of India and Pakistan will have their separate Constituent Assembly which would have the power to repeal any Act of British Parliament, including the India Independence Act, 1947,. India's Constituent Assembly adopted the Constitution on the 26th day of November, 1949, which became effective from January 26, 1950. It is because of this that India's Republic Day is observed every year on 26th January.

As we span the time from Kautilya's Artha Shastra of 300 BC, laws were made from time to time for regulating trade, business and industrial activities. New laws were framed, while old enactments considered obsolete and redundant from time to time, were repealed.

BUSINESS LEGISLATIONS — SOURCES

The sources of Business Legislations can be roughly classified as follows:

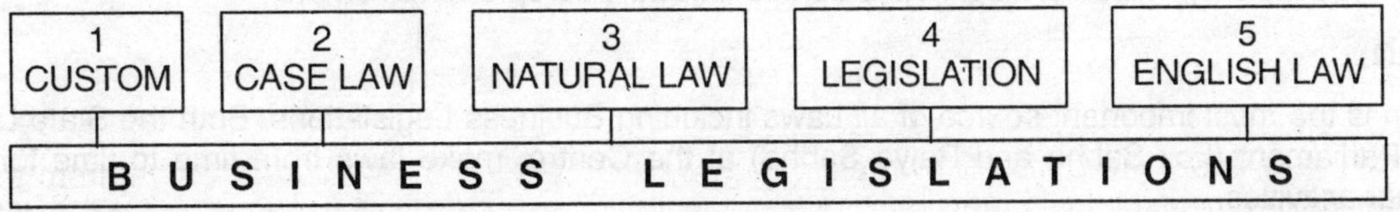

In general, we can say, the oldest law is Natural Law. This is the law given to humans by Nature around us. Next, when people constituted small social groups, the leader, amongst them, made the observance of custom the basis of the group welfare. When these social groups became stronger, a leader of the group decided disputes and the leader giving these decisions, began functioning as a court of law, both for the social group and for the leader on king who head the large group. Next came legislation. This is how the English Law grew and developed and gave us our modem civil and judicial administration. Let us take up each head of classification in some detail.

NATURAL LAW

Nature functions in its own orderly fashion. This gave to the people the idea that a social group must have rules of conduct. The law of the jungle is *"the survival of the fittest n"*. The might of the stronger vanquishes the weaker animals. People grouped in societies felt because being endowed with the human brain, the weak must be protected. This necessitated the adoption of rules of moral conduct under which the weak must be protected against the might of the strong.

When case law became available and legislative activity had gained momentum and newer laws were being enacted, the concept of natural justice also grew. That no person should be punished twice for the same offence was a concept which was incorporated in all kinds of criminal laws that were being enacted.

Yet another concept got weightage in the process of natural justice as more and more cases came up for decision before courts of law. The concept which became part of natural justice was that no person should be declared guilty until the charges against that person were proved. This concept of natural justice became crystalised into an addict that *"It is better that nine guilty persons may* go *unpunished rather than one innocent person be punished as guilty."*

Yet another principle of natural justice now finds place in the administration of just ice in the form of a well defined principle: *"Justice should not merely be done, but appear to have been done."*

The above discussion indicates that natural justice is the basic concept of what is termed as Natural Law. The case of the *National Textile Unions Vs. Ramakrishna* decided by the Supreme Court in 1983 proved how natural justice plays a vital role in the process of judicial decisions. The basic issue in the case was whether workers of a company had the right or a locus standi for being heard, whereas the Companies Act in its extensive provisions of 650 sections did not give the workers any such right of intervention or for being granted a hearing. The Supreme Court, despite the Companies Act being silent on the issue, in its epoch making judgement granted the workers this right of being heard, as the closure of the Company was vital to their interests and livelihood.

CUSTOM

Custom is an important source of all laws, including Business Legislations. Custom formed the basis of decision of disputes in societies even before they began getting organised and got active in evolving their law-making bodies. Custom secures the sanctity of law when courts of law invoke custom or customary rules and practice in deciding cases, including those in the field of Business Legislations.

Even enactments, particularly, in the field of Business Legislations, have specifically incorporated custom as part of the law. The Indian Contract Act provides that nothing herein contained, "shall affect any usage or custom of trade." The Negotiable Instruments Act similarly, provides that nothing herein contained "shall affect any local usage relating to instruments in an oriental language." This provision recognises the position of a 'hundi', invariably drafted in regional or state languages, as a valid negotiable instrument for payment of money to its holder immediately on presentation.

CASE LAW

Case Law is the most important source of law in general, Business Legislations, being no exception.

Case law is vital in the administration of justice because wherever the law is silent, the principles invoked in earlier decisions having similar facts were used in disposing off such cases. This is known as the Law of Precedents, which in practice means that judgments of earlier decided cases are used to settle cases in which clear law is not available. The judicial committee of the Privy Council in the *Moribibi Vs. Dharmodas Ghose* in the year 1903 gave a judgment that a contract with a minor is void. The Indian Contract Act, 1872, also provides that a contract is invalid on several grounds, like insanity, minority, illegal consideration, fraud, misrepresentation etc.

LEGISLATION

Legislation is the most important source of all Laws including Business Legislations. Both the State Legislatures in States and Parliament (Lok Sabha and Rajya Sabha) at the Centre, make laws from time to time for regulating human and other activities.

Business Legislations cover a wide range of subjects. Such laws include. The Indian Contract Act, The Negotiable Instruments Act, The Transfer of Property Act, and a wide rage of laws which cover subjects like import, export, customs excise, gifts, cess, wharfage, guarantee, indemnity, factories, wages, minimum wages, working hours of labour or factory workers, labour welfare, workmen's compensation, employees state insurance, company matters etc.

ENGLISH LAW

We have seen in the earlier discussion how the English Common Law evolved from custom, changed, grew and developed following the Norman Conquest, how Roman Law was invoked, the creation of merchant guilds later replaced by the Admiralty Court and the growth Law Merchant, the precursor of Mercantile Law, as we know it today.

It would not be wrong to say that the Indian Mercantile Law is largely derived from English Law and English enactments. The Sales of Goods Act which we follow has been taken directly from the English Sales of Goods Act, Similarly, the Indian Companies Act and the Indian Contract Act have also been drafted on the pattern of similar British enactments. Due to this background, instances are not wanting when Indian courts while deciding ticklish cases under these enactments, often has their decisions on English cases, because of the similarity of provisions of these laws.

DHARMA

'Dharma' is the oldest origin of Indian laws. 'Dharma' in this context, is not religion, but rules of morality, or rules that determine what is right and what is wrong. 'Dharma' is the main source oflaw of the ancient era of India. Those rules of 'Dharma' may no longer be applicable, but most of our modem enactments incorporate these concepts. A jurist, *AH Bashan,* has observed, "Though we know very little about the legal system of the Rigvedic period, it is clear that the idea of a divine cosmic order already existed."

Contract, customs and royal ordinances, constituted the basis of 'Dharma', and these concepts were also incorporated in ancient India textbooks on law. The earlier religious books may not have dwelt at length on these aspects, but they gained importance with the passage of time. Supplementary sources of law were also added into the ancient India Law. It was an universally accepted the concept that the rules of governance contained in 'Dharma' were superior to other sources of law. The Artha-Shastra, however, stressed that the royal ordinance would override other sources of law. This was the approach of the Mauryas who laid much stress on the royal edicts and directives.

In ancient times, protection of 'Dharma' was considered to be the duty of the King. The concept therefore, was King as the protector of' Dharma' was considered as 'Dharma' incarnate. Onwards from Ashoka's dynasty, the King was personified as 'Dharmaraj'. 'Dharmaraj' is another name or a synonym of 'Yamaraj', the God of Death. The analogy, therefore, was that both Yamaraj and Dharmaraj were duty bound to enforce the 'Dharma'; or, the sacred laws and did so, by punishing the evil doers or those who disobeyed 'Dharma' and protected the righteous, that is, those who obeyed the Laws.

'Dharma' continues to be the guilding principle in the interpretation of modem laws and is the basis of justice today. For example, in a case: *Ram Sarup Vs. Bansi mandir,* the decision declared a bond *null and void* under which the debtor who took a loan of Rs. 100 was and bound under it, was required to pay an exorbitant rate of interest and render manual labour to the creditor, the Bansi Mandir. The rules contained in 'Dharma' were invoked to declare the bond *null and void.*

BUSINESS

The term bushiness may be understood as the organised efforts of enterprises to supply consumers with goods and services and to earn profit in the process. Business is broad term and includes such varied activities as production, promotion, wholesaling, relating, distribution, transportation, warehousing, financing insurance, consultancy and the like. The two definitions on business given echo the same meaning.

1. Business is a "complex field of commerce and industry in which goods and services are created and distributed .... in the hope of profit within a framework of laws and regulations."
2. Business "comprises all profit seeking activities and enterprises that provide goods and services necessary to an economic system standard of living. Profits are a primary mechanism for motivating these activities."

Business is as important as it is vast in its scope. It is a unique institution which converts ideas into saleable products. From the time we get up early in the morning till we go to bed in the night, the products we consume and the services we use are all supplied to us by business. Business offers innumerable opportunities for us to earn money so that we can buy and enjoy the products. We depend so much on business that except for six or seven hours we sleep every day, the remaining hours we spend for or on bushiness. It is really shuddering to imagine what would happen to us without business. Indeed there is no life without business.

LAW IN NUTSHELL

Law refers to the principles and regulations established by a Government and applicable to people, whether in the form of legislation or of custom and policies recognised and enforced by judicial decision.

A few definitions of law are worth quoting in this context. According to Blackstone *"Law in its most general and comprehensive sense signifies a rule of action and is applied indiscriminately to all kinds of actions whether animate or inanimate, rational or irrational. "*

Salmond's definition of law may be recalled: *"Law is a body or principles recognised and applied by the State in the administration of Justice."*

Woodrow Wilson as stated earliar defines Law as *"That portion of the established habit and thought of mankind which has gained distinct and formal recognition in the shape of uniform of rules backed by the authority and power of the Government."*

Definitions of law frequently emphasise the coercive power of the State which stands behind the rules. And is true of many rules that failure to comply with them may lead to the use of coercion by officials. Thus, if a man refuses to perform his obligations under a contract, he is sued in a court for breach of contract, loses the suit and is ordered to pay damages. But many rules of law merely grant permission to do creative things, and if a citizen does not do what he is permitted to do, he is not subject to any coercion. Moreover, the government often induces people to do what it wants them to do by the lure of benefits. An entrepreneur, for example, is assured of certain concessions if he were to set-up his plant in a backward area. If he ignores the offer, he is not penalised, he simply does not get the concession.

BUSINESS LEGISLATIONS — OBJECTIVES

Business Legislations, as already stated, have been enacted with well-defined objectives, not merely for regulating business activities, but also for upholding certain laudable goals or objectives.

It would be worthwhile for the students to go through these objectives with a clear mind. A rule for normal or orderly conduct of business, also entails moral responsibilities. Let us try to examine what can be the sound objectives for business activity, which are either embodied in Business Legislations or incorporated in business practice. The following may be considered relevant.

(1) FAIR TRADE PRACTICE

All bushiness, trade and industrial activity are bound not merely by law, but also by rules of propriety, to conduct their activities in a 'fair manner'. For example, a company known as 'X' company has no right to run down or defame a rival company, 'Y' Company or damage its reputation doing similar business, for the sake of promoting its business or for promoting the sale of its product. Similarly, if a Company, known as 'Z' Company, producing a similar product for purposes of promoting its product, imposes sanctions on dealers against selling the same product of other companies, namely, 'X' Company and 'Y' Company, it would fall in the category of *"UNFAIR TRADE PRACTICE"* and is liable to be set aside by a Court of Law.

(2) RIGHTS OF BUSINESS TRADE AND COMMERCE

Business Legislations while observing *"fair trade practice"* obligatory on business, trade and commerce, also gives this sector certain rights as well.

This sector, like citizens, also has certain rights. These rights are enforceable through courts of law against individuals and the government. Business, trade, industry and commerce sector can invoke the jurisdiction of the High Court or the Supreme Court for enforcing this sector's right against its debtors or, violators of patent, copyright, trade mark, brand rights etc. This sector can also proceed against individuals or groups which indulge in removing genuine contents from sealed packages and refilling them spurious specimens or adulterating the contents with a view to harming the reputation of the product. The degree of success which this sector can achieve through courts of law depends upon the extent to which it can prove its claim.

(3) RIGHT TO FAIR COMPETITION

The business, trade, industry and commerce sector, under Business Legislations has the right to fair competition. Any unit in this sector expects fair competition under Business Legislations. This fair competition against other units in this sector amounts to the enforcement by the Business Legislations uniformly and fairly on all units like in the grant of permits, licences, tax or duty exemption procurement of raw materials, imports and exports, supply of water, power and other units. Fair competition also includes the right to raise equity through marketing of shares institutional finance from banks and other funding bodies without discrimination *vis a vis* similar other units. It might be recalled that Article 19(1)(e) gives to every citizen "the right to practise any profession, or to carry on any occupation, trade or business". In this context, every unit of business, trade, industry and commerce has the right to compete with others or the right of being considered for the grant of licences, permits, tax or duty exemption, imports and exports. It is immaterial whether a unit gets these advantages or not, it is vital that while issuing licences and permits, or granting import export licences, all units which have applied have been considered. In other words, every unit has the right to be dealt with uniformly with others in the application of Business Legislations.

MORAL DUTIES UNDER BUSINESS LEGISLATIONS

Business Legislations and other laws regulating business, trade, industry and commerce, have both positive and negative provisions. The negative provisions do not place these units under any kind of handicap, but impose moral duties on them to be fair and upright in many ways. These negative provisions can be classed as moral duties as follows:

(i) DUTY TOWARDS CONSUMERS

Every business trade industrial or commercial unit making and marketing any consumer product is duty bound to maintain quality, sell requisite quantity both by weight and volume as notified on the package. We have seen how producers of various brands of mustard oil had to withdraw their packages when the contents were found to be adulterated with *'argemone'* which caused widespread outbreak of dropsy. Similarly, the contents of packages should neither be underweight, nor less than the volume notified on the package.

(ii) DUTY TO SHUN PUFFERY

Producers and manufacturers have a moral duty to shun *'puffery'*. *'Puffery'* is the practice adopted by producers and manufacturers to claim efficacy of a product more than its worth. For example, a pain-relieving ointment may be stated to give relief for a particular kind of pain, but to say that it is magical or it can perform a miracle would amount to *'puffery '*. Similarly, a nutritive drink marketed by a producer can claim to provide the extent of nutrition to the degree notified on the package: it could also claim or advertise that the drink, though nutritive does not produce' cholesterol' (a substance which on getting deposited on artery walls constricting its passage, ultimately producing high blood pressure and heart attack), but it can not claim falsely that it helps to reduce cholesterol. A false claim or a claim which is untrue is puffery. *'Puffery'* has to be avoided by producers and manufacturers not merely as amoral duty, because a false claim about a product can lead to an action in the Law of Torts in a Civil Court which can award damages in terms of money compensation to the purchaser who pays the higher price for the product which fails to deliver the publicised result.

(iii) DUTY NOT TO CREATE ARTIFICIAL PRIORITIES OR A SCARE

Producers and manufacturers of products, consumer, goods electronic gadgets have a moral duty towards consumers and purchasers not to create artificial priorities or false preferences or produce a scare to promote sales of their products. For example, a producer or manufacturer cannot advertise that his product is the best amongst other brands in the market; he can, however, say that his product is of high quality. He also cannot say that other brands are dangerous, or a risk to personal safety. He also cannot say that his product is available for a specified period causing a rush for purchases, while it continues to sell indefinitely thereafter.

(iv) DUTY TO PROVIDE AFTER SALE SERVICE

This is in the nature of a social duty. Manufacturers of long-utility items like mopeds, motorcycles, scooters, cars, vans, trucks, buses, musical systems, television sets, washing machines and the like, are duty-bound to provide after-sale service for repairing breakdowns, provide spares for worn out parts, etc. This duty arises from the obligation under which the purchasers place the manufacturers under it because the latter after pocketing high prices for the item purchased are duty bound to ensure that the item functions to the full satisfaction of the purchaser.

(v) DUTY TO HONOUR WARRANTY AND GUARANTEE

Warranty is an undertaking by the producer or manufacturer of a consumer item like a motor-vehicle, or electronic gadget or any other utility gadget, to replace the item if it has any kind of manufacturing defect. Guarantee is an undertaking by the producer or manufacturer to ensure trouble-free and satisfactory performance of the item sold. Producers and manufacturers who refuse to replace the item with manufacturing defect now have to face action in consumer forums. The consumer forum has been created lately and the Consumer Act is a new law that protects consumer interest. Similarly, failure to back the guarantee attached to an item bought is also actionable. For example, a waterproof wrist watch which fails to prevent moisture from entering its mechanism, thereby putting it out of order, puts the manufacturer under a legal duty to replace the wrist watch. Warranty is a solemn undertaking for a specific period say six months during which the producer or manufacturer is duty-bound to replace a defective piece. Guarantee, on the other hand, binds the manufacturer to replace an item which fails to function or perform as claimed for a specific period say one or two years.

(vi) DUTY TO ABIDE BY PROVISIONS OF BUSINESS LEGISLATIONS

A number of Business Legislations have been enacted from time to time for regulating production and manufacturing processes, for enforcing orderly conduct of trade, industry and commerce. For example, a law exists which forbids exploitation of child labour, another which prohibits discrimination in wages on grounds of sex, caste or religion, law also exists which prohibits misuse of economic power against any section of society, also prevents reckless exploitation of economic resources which may be a permanent loss to posterity and also abolishes systematic disruption of ecology. Law also exists for providing compensation to workers suffering personal harm in the course of employment, like loss of a limb, eyes etc.; the compensation rates being prescribed by the law. Law also exists prohibiting employers from taking more than the prescribed hours or work; in the alternative binding them to make payment of double the normal hourly wage for the number of hours of work taken during overtime. Employers are also enjoined by law to ensure labour welfare facilities, employees state insurance benefits, housing facilities etc. for workers employed by them.

BUSINESS LEGISLATIONS — PROBLEMS:

Laws have been enacted to regulate human conduct. Laws which are designed to regulate business, trade, industrial and commercial activities also intend to safeguard public interest. However, perfect may be the law that is enacted, some lacunae are bound to come up during its enforcement and operation. Some of the problems that arise despite the prohibition and penal clauses in Business Legislations can be briefly summed up as follows:

(1) SELF-CREATED PROBLEMS

Business, trade, industrial and commercial units are apt to create problems for themselves due to non-observance of mandatory provisions of the law that apply to their functioning. For example, Article 39 of the Constitution under Part IV, that is, the Directive Principles of State Policy, categorically outlines the principles which ought to be observed both by the Government individuals and units in the commercial sector. It states: "The State shall, in particular, direct its policy towards securing:

(a) that the citizens, men and women equally have the right to an adequate means of livelihood;

(b) that the ownership and control of the material resources of the community are so distributed as best to subserve the common good;

(c) that the operation of the economic system does not result in the concentration of wealth and means of production to the common detriment;

(d) that there is equal pay for equal work for both men and women;

(e) that the health and strength of workers, men and women, and the tender age of children are not abused and that the citizens are not forced by economic necessity to enter avocations unsuited to their age or strength;

(f) that children are given opportunities and facilities to develop in a healthy manner and in conditions of freedom and dignity and that childhood and youth are protected against exploitation and against moral and material abandoment.

Note: Clause (f) above was added by the Constitution (Forty-second Amendment) Act, 1976 and was enforced with effect from January 3,1977.

Similarly, Section 67 of the Factories Act, 1948, prohibits employment of children below the age of 14 years.

Examining Article 39 and Section 67 of the Factories Act, it can be seen the childhood and youth are protected against exploitation under the Constitution and that employment of children below the age of 14 years is prohibited.

It is clear, therefore, business, trade industrial and commercial units may create a problem for themselves by exploiting child labour or by employing children below the age of 14 years. This act of omission is punishable under the law. Even the International Labour Organisation (ILO) in its 14th Convention has decreed that child labour should not be exploited. The Human Rights Commission also bans child labour. The private sector, however, continues to exploit child labour by employing children below the age of fourteen in hotels, restaurants, blacksmithy units, brick-making and construction establishments.

Similarly, provisions of Article 39(d) of the Constitution may be violated by business, trade, industrial and commercial sectors by paying women workers less than the wages paid to male workers. This problem can also be created by units in this sector by themselves.

Likewise, violation of the provisions of Article 39(e) of the Constitution can also produce a self-created problem. It clearly states that the health and strength of workers, men and women, and the tender age of children are not abused and that the citizens are not forced by economic necessity to enter avocations unsuited to their age or strength. Take the case of the bangle industry of Firozabad, where the workers have to brave the intense heat of high temperature of furnaces in front of which they have to work for long hours. Similarly, the lock industry of Aligarh, the carpet industry of Bhadoi (Mirzapur), the utensil industry of Moradabad, or even the modem plastic industry, where men, women and children, unmindful of their health and strength, are being employed by such units.

Again, the Factories Act, 1948, prescribes the minimum standards of cleanliness, lighting, ventilation, safety and other facilities, which are being grossly violated. This is another class of self-created problem.

Another kind of self-created problem arises by defying prohibitions prescribed by the Drugs Control Act. The combination of Tetracycline, an essential drug, with Vitamin C is banned for sale in India. A leading drug manufacturing company, in order to avoid prosecution is selling a product, "Oxyteracycline" (same as Tetracycline) in combination with Vitamin C.

(2) LAW ENFORCEMENT PROBLEMS

Business, trade, industrial and commercial units face yet another kind of problem which arises from lax and arbitrary enforcement of law or, misapplication of the law.

The Drugs Control Act is a Central enactment, while its enforcement is the responsibility of the State Governments. The State Governments, on their part, either do not set up a proper enforcement machinery or such machinery is inadequate for enforcing the law. Moreover, the Constitution devolves the control of business activity on State Governments. The State Governments have not set up proper machinery for enforcement of the Drugs Control Act, with the result often the intervention or use of civil and police administration in this area results inconnivance over the violations of the law.

Yet another law enacted some years ago decreed that certain vitamin preparations be stored in temperatures below 25 degrees centigrade. Several drug manufacturing companies violate this provision and also chemists and druggists who sell this preparation, with the result the efficacy of the vitamin preparation is lost to the detriment of interests of the users. Even transportation of this preparation by rail or road is being done in ordinarily higher temperatures than 25 degrees centigrade.

(3) PROBLEMS ARISING FROM HAZARDOUS OPERATIONS

Business, trade, industrial and commercial units are often found not to adopt safety measures in hazardous production or manufacturing operations, thereby landing themselves in situations to face such unanticipated problems.

Workers engaged in hazardous operations are supposed to be provided with safety measures and safety-wear while engaged in work. Workers, say employed in acid producing plants should be provided with acid-resistant rubber gloves and gumboots to avoid acid bums on their hands and feet. This is more often noticed in commercial units in their violation than observance.

Similarly, workers engaged in the production of strong alkalis and other fume-producing chemicals should be provided with special kind goggles for protecting their eyes, which is not done properly by many units.

Industrial units producing items or goods which during production produce a lot of harmful dust must be provided with protective gear to prevent inhalation of the dust, which inhaled may cause tuberculosis or other pulmonary diseases.

Some factories or industrial undertakings may be producing dust that may cause cancer or skin diseases. In such hazardous operations, employers are required by law to provide protective working gear to workers for safeguarding their health or tending to shorten their life span.

Some of the health hazards faced by workers in such units must be checked by the State Government for which it should create a proper machinery. This aspect is often neglected by State Governments and workers in such units continue to languish in life-taking or life-shortening environment inside factories and industrial units.

(4) PROBLEMS ARISING FROM OPERATIONS ENDANGERING PUBLIC HEALTH

Business, trade, industrial or commercial units may be running such units effluents from which may endanger public health. There are several units in this sector which let loose air pollutants or water pollutants or solid pollutants.

Most of the industrial units producing different kinds of items also produce 'wastes' that has to be disposed off. The 'waste' products may be in the nature of harmful gases, harmful liquid 'wastes' or solid 'wastes' that they continue to dump into air, rivers and surroundings causing untold miseries or health hazards to public health.

Both the Centre and the States have set up Pollution Control Boards, which are enjoined by law to prevent air, water and environmental pollution. These Pollution Control Boards are either under-staffed, or lack the proper enforcement machinery. The net outcome is that air, water and environmental pollution continues unabately putting public health at a premium.

Various laws exist for checking pollution, but industrial units continue to violate their provisions. Industrial units are required to have chimneys of certain height and specifications in order to discharge the flue gases high up in the atmosphere. There is hardly any check for observance of the law in this regard.

Of late, there has bean a growing consciousness for checking pollution of air, water and environment. The State as well as the Central governments have launched prosecution against errant industrial units in courts of law.

The Anti-Pollution Laws have made it mandatory for all industrial units to set up effluent treatment plants so that no kind of harmful effluents are discharged into air, water or environment.

Air-borne pollutants finding their way into people's breath may cause grave disease, while liquid pollutants discharged into rivers finds its way into drinking water inside homes which get their drinking water supply from city waterworks.

Solid pollutants dumped by industrial units outside factory boundaries also contain harmful ingredients or substances. During rains, these substances get absorbed into the soil causing loss of fertility of soil or destroy existing vegetation and greenery.

A case in point may be recalled. Some years ago, the Pollution Control Board moved the High Court and obtained an injunction against the tanneries of Kanpur which were dumping their liquid waste, full of acidic and alkaline constituents and also leather dust and shavings, all harmful to public health, into the Ganga. Drinking water after treatment of Ganga water with chlorine and alum, was being pumped into households. The water treatment by the waterworks was unable to destroy the harmful acidic and alkaline contents and also the leather dust, which found its way into drinking water. As many as 27 tanneries were closed. Even the Supreme Court before which the tannery owners had filed appeals refused to order re-opening of the tanneries unless they installed effluent treatment plants within their factory premises.

(5) PROBLEMS ARISING FROM PROFIT MOTIVE

Business trade industrial and commercial units and even producers of consumer goods may, due to their profit motive add ingredients harmful to health for making the product more attractive or apparently efficacious for fetching a higher price. For example, whole or un ground 'masalas' may be coloured with non-edible colour. Powdered 'masalas' may be similarly adulterated with baser substances harmful to health. Soaps or detergents, claiming magical cleansing powers, may have strong alkalis which may cause skin erosion. These are punishable offences but they continue unchecked due to inadequate enforcement machinery of the State Government or because it is hand in glove with the packagers or producers of such items. Branded mustard oil producers marketing it adulterated with 'argemone' oil, causing outbreak of dropsy, had to withdraw their packages from the market is a recent case in point. Some packagers were arrested and are now facing prosecution.

(6) PROBLEMS ARISING FROM NON-OBSERVANCE OF THE LAW

Business, trade, industrial and commercial units, employing a large work force, may face problems leading to prosecution if they blatantly refuse to enforce labour laws to provide labour welfare facilities and do not implements factory laws, workmen's' compensation law, etc.

Under the provisions of Labour Laws, an employer cannot take more than the prescribed hours of work; shall have to pay overtime at double the hourly wage, for extra work taken. There is a vast area of businessmen, trade, industrial and commercial activity which is covered by both Central and State enactments.

Different laws exist for different kinds of activities. Public utility services have their own set of laws which regulate their operations. The Industrial Dispute Act, 1947, enlists as many as 17 public utility industries. They are transport (excluding railways) for carriage of passengers or goods by land or water: banking, cement, coal, cotton textiles, foodstuffs, iron and steel, defence establishments service in hospitals and dispensaries, fire brigade services, India Government Mints, India Security Press, copper mining, lead mining, zinc mining, iron ore mining and service in any oil field.

The Labour Court can try offences under several Central enactments. Some of these enactments (16 in number) have been mentioned in the Industrial Disputes Act, 1947. They are the Trade Unions Act, 1926, The Payment of Wages Act, 1936, The Factories Act 1948 The Minimum Wages Act, 1948 The Employees' State Insurance Act, 1948 The Employees' Provident Fund and Miscellaneous Provisions Act, 1952; The Working Journalists and other Newspaper Employees (Conditions of Service) and Miscellaneous Provisions Act, 1955, The Motor Transport Act, 1961, The Maternity Benefits Act, 1961, The Payment of Bonus Act, 1965, The Beedi and Cigar Workers (Conditions of Employment) Act, 1966, The Contract Labour (Regulation and Abolition) Act, 1970, The Payment of Gratuity Act,

1972, the Sales Promotion Employee (Conditions of Service) Act, 1976; The Equal Remuneration Act, 1976 and the Inter-State Migrant Workmen (Regulation of Employment and Conditions of Service) Act, 1979.

Similarly, the Industrial Tribunal gives decisions on a wide variety of matters concerning the workers, their service conditions and allied matters, which are also regulated by Laws. Violation of these provisions attracts the operation of these laws and the Industrial Tribunal adjudicates on them. These matters are wages, including the period and mode of payment; compensatory and other allowance; hours of work and rest intervals; leave with wages and holidays; bonus, profit-sharing, provident fund and gratuity; shift-working otherwise than in accordance with standing orders; classification of grades; rules of discipline; rationalisation; retrenchment of workmen and closure of establishment; and any other matter that may be prescribed.

(7) PROBLEMS ARISING FROM FAILURE TO DISCHARGE DUTY IMPOSED BY LAW

There is a wide spectrum of laws under which business, trade, industrial and commercial units have to abide by there provisions and perform the mandatory duties imposed on them. These duties if left unfulfilled would subject these units to prosecution both with imprisonment of their proprietors or managers and also make them liable to pay fines.

Some of these duties include payment of sales tax dues now trade tax in U.P., file income returns and pay income tax, excise duty, production tax and other government dues. Units in this sector often postpone payment of government dues either with a view to earn more on the dues withheld or file false returns, but in its wake create problems for themselves. Sometimes, they also move courts of law and obtain stay orders on the basis of misrepresentation or on wrong facts. The temporary reprieve obtained from the court works havoc in the long run when the dues so withheld accumulate into heavy unpaid amounts finally forcing many an unit to close down, throwing hundreds and thousands of workers and employees out of job.

(8) PROBLEMS CREATED THROUGH FRIVOLOUS LITIGATION

It is often seen that business, trade, industrial or commercial units initiate frivolous litigation and obtain stay orders injunctions etc. This method is employed by units in this sector with a view to create and *alibi* or excuse to withhold legally sanctioned benefits to workers and employees or with a view to gaining public sympathy. The proprietors and heads of such units also through such orders on untenable grounds try to apportion responsibility and blame on courts of law for stalling that which they could have extended to their employees and workers. Take the case where such units on the basis of unreal balance sheets show losses instead of profit and try to stall payment of bonus to workers. As a result of such fake litigation raked up such units, the government very early after enacting the Bonus Act, amended it that a minimum of 8.33 per cent of the wages or salaries of workers and employees shall be payable to them, irrespective of losses shown in balance sheets.

The state of frivolous or fake litigation has made some jurists define various laws in a disparaging manner as follows:

German Law: Everything is forbidden except what is permitted.

French Law: Everything is permitted except what is forbidden.

Soviet Law: Everything is forbidden including what is permitted.

Italian Law: Everything is permitted specially what is forbidden.

Indian Law is somewhat more explicit. Indian enactments have a scheme in which the main section states the Law, while its proviso elaborates the exceptions to the rule in specific circumstances. The main sections of Indian enactment, therefore, prohibit some acts which may be classed as crime of a particular nature, but its proviso outlines the circumstances in which the crime defined in the main section would be treated as a lesser crime. Similarly, in enactments where the main section permits as legal some acts, the provision states the circumstances in which the permission given for some acts in the main section would no longer be permitted or, in other words, becomes forbidden.

A summary of some objectives of Business Legislations and the lacunae therein have been tabulated below for convenience of study for the students.

Objectives	Lacunae
(1) Defines the law and sanctions.	(1) Uncovered gaps or lacunae between law and practice or application of the Law.
(2) Defines enforceable rights.	(2) Laws enacted by the Centre, enforced by the State, produces piquant situations.
(3) Laws designed for industrial growth.	(3) Administrative delays or red-tape delay or hamper industrial growth.
(4) Laws designed to promote or achieve social justice.	(4) Taxes, levies, cess and other dues undo the social justice objective and failure to pay by units themselves produces similar results.
(5) Laws designed to fix priorities.	(5) Priorities often overlooked or withheld by commercial units themselves or stalled through courts on flimsy grounds.

IDEAL LAW AND EFFECTIVE BUSINESS LEGISLATIONS

There is no such thing as ideal law because law is regulatory in nature; prescribes *do's and don'ts.*

But for any law to be effective it must possess certain characteristics because the main objective of all laws is to help and not to obstruct or cause hardship for whom it is meant. Law is supposed to aid people not to harm them. Similar norms would apply to every kind of law, including Business Legislations. We may consider the following ideals norms which should exist to enable the people to greet the law and call it good law. Consider the following:

1. LAW SHOULD BE SIMPLE

Law should be simple, easily comprehensible, so that the people for whom it is meant may be able to understand it without the aid of a lawyer. It is a principle of jurisprudence that *'ignorance of law is no excuse'* which in Latin is stated thus: *'Ignorantia juris non excusat* '. If the Law is simple, the people would abide by its provisions. Benjamin Nathan Cardonzo says 'Law as a guide to conduct is reduced to the level of more futility, if it is unknown and unknowable'.

2. LAW SHOULD ATTRACT AND PROMOTE VOLUNTARY OBEDIENCE

Law which is simple and clear is bound to promote and attract voluntary obedience. Moreover, a law which has clear and honestly declared objectives like social justice, industrial growth, civic rights, peace and tranquillity is bound to evoke spontaneous response and obedience. A law which deals with people as criminals, industrial units as exploiters etc. is bound to arouse opposition and evasion. That law is best which needs a minimum enforcement machinery. Moreover, the reliefs and remedies which the law provides through courts should be available through easy procedures and not cumbersome methods. Examples can be observance of traffic rules, buying tickets for travel whose violations should be punished lightly. Ruthless or arbitrary punishments to violations of ordinary laws is likely to generate opposition and make people manufacture *alibis* to escape punishment.

3. LAW SHOULD BE JUST AND REASONABLE

Laws ban certain acts, providing punishments for violations. It is a wrong notion that people obey the laws out of fear. If the laws are just and reasonable, people are bound to obey them for their own convenience, and convince others to obey the law. This can be noticed in certain laws under which first offenders are punished leniently or juvenile offenders are put on probation for acquiring good conduct and are not punished.

4. LAW SHOULD NOT BE RIGID, BUT FLEXIBLE

Law should not be rigid; its violations being severely punished. Law which is flexible is welcomed by people. Flexibility of law does not mean that offences in penal laws should be loosely defined or its violations be assessed for a lesser crime. Flexibility in the laws has been incorporated in provisos of various section of a law. For example, a person acting in self defence inflicts an injury on another trying to kill or murder him, or even kill him, it would be not be treated as murder, but culpable homicide not amounting to murder. It will not merit a death sentence or life imprisonment, but seven years of imprisonment.

5. LAWS SHOULD BE CONSTITUTIONALITY VALID

All laws enacted by the State or Central legislature are expected to be within the provisions of the Constitution. No law would be considered just if it is *ultra vires* of the provisions of the Constitution for it is liable to be struck down by the Supreme Court, the highest Court of India. A relevant case is that because income of an individual cannot be taxed twice, led to the profession tax assessed on income was struck down by the Supreme Court as unconstitutional some two decades ago. Similarly, Article 20(2) of the Constitution guarantees it as a Fundamental Right that *'No person shall be prosecuted and punished/or the same offence twice.'*

Summing up the foregoing discussion on what is ideal Law or what can be called Effective Business Legislations, we can illustrate it in the following chart for ready reference. They can be termed as the objectives of Business Legislations.

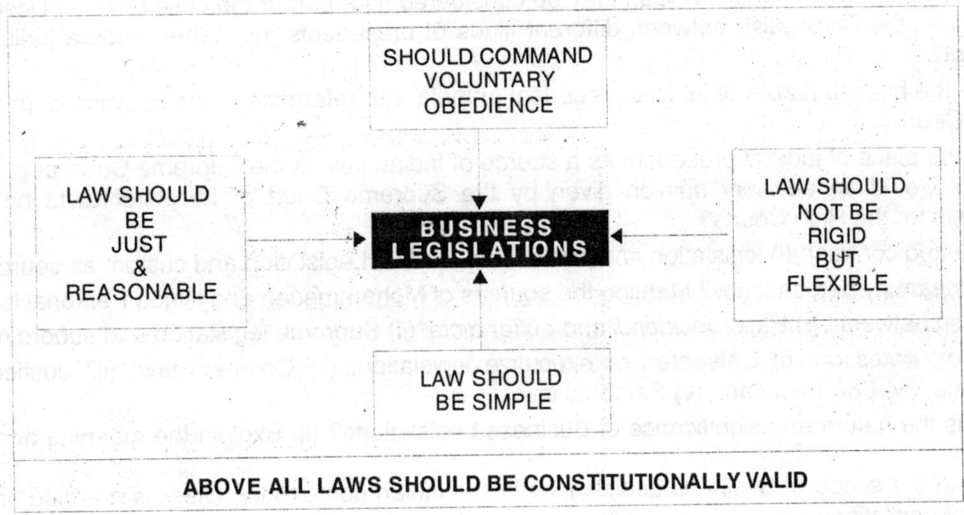

PRACTICE QUESTIONS

1. Why is law difficult to define? Give some examples of law in the widest sense of the term. How would you define law?
2. Enumerate some of the more important points you will keep in mind while defining law. Explain the meaning and nature of law.
3. Why should a definition of law emphasise enforcement? What are the two basic ideas involved in any law?
3. How would you distinguish law from morality? "Every law can be traced to some moral rule or the other." Do you agree?
4. "Law and morals by no means coincide, although they are closely related." Discuss the relationship between law and morality. If the personal morality of a person conflicts with the law, should he obey the law?
5. Do you agree with the statement: "Ignorance of law is no excuse". "*Ignorantia juris non-excusat.*" Explain.
6. You must have come across some law or the other which has either been amended or enacted recently. Describe its objectives, legal provisions and impact on business and society.
7. You must have come across some judgement or the other by some court recently. Describe its impact on business in general, or on a particular business or profession.
8. Investigate the new enactment, the change in the existing laws, or the judicial decisions from the viewpoint of different interest groups likely to be affected, such as consumers, employees and investors.
9. Subjects such as prohibition on running a lottery, smoking, employing child labour in carpet industry, industry pollution may be taken up for class room discussion. Their legal and moral aspects may be discussed.
10. Distinguish between: (i) Public law and private law; (ii) Criminal law and civil law; (iii) Substantive law and procedural law; (iv) Public international law and private international law; (v) Statutory law and. customary law.
11. Which is more important — Procedural law or Substantive law?
12. "A same action may result both in a civil case and a criminal case." Comment.
13. What are the sources of Indian Law? Discuss any one important source of law and justify why it is important.
14. Evaluate custom as a source of law. Mention the different kinds of custom, and distinguish between custom and usage.

15. What are the requisites of a valid custom? Does every custom become law?
16. "Custom is not law but only a source of law. It acquires the force of law. It becomes law only after it satisfies certain essential pre-requisites and is either embodied in a statute or recognised by a court." Comment and elucidate.
17. "Legislation is even today not the only source of law." Explain and illustrate.
18. Find out such examples as would show how Indian customs and the Constitution of India have proved to be important sources of law.
19. (i) What is meant by *obiter dicta*? Can they be considered as a part of the case law? (ii) Describe the importance of case law. (iii) Distinguish between different kinds of precedents. (iv) When does a judicial decision become precedent?
20. Examine the binding nature of judicial precedent in India with reference to the decision of (i) Supreme Court, and (ii) High Court.
21. Discuss the place of judicial precedent as a source of Indian law. Is the Supreme Court of India bound by its own decision? Could an advisory opinion given by the Supreme Court or its obiter dicta be considered judicial precedents for the High Courts?
22. Compare and contrast: (i) legislation and precedents, and fii) Legislation and custom as sources of law?
23. What is meant by personal law? Mention the sources of Mohammedan and Hindu Personal law, respectively?
24. Distinguish between: (i) Ratio *decidendi* and *obiter dicta*; (ii) Supreme legislation and subordinate legislation.
25. Write short notes on: (i) Delegated or executive legislation; (ii) Common law; (iii) Justice, equity and good conscience; (iv) Law merchant; (v) Personal law.
26. (i) What is the nature and significance of Business Legislations? (ii) Explain the meaning and scope of Business Legislations.
    (iii) Explain the scope of Business Legislations in the Indian context. (iv) Discuss the different sources of Indian Business Legislations.
27. Distinguish between natural person and artificial person.
28. "The true subject matter of law is persons." Elucidate.
29. What is incorporation? What are the advantages resulting therefrom?
30. Are the following persons?: (i) A child in the womb; (ii) A corpse of a person; (iii) a minor; (iv) A still born child; (v) A testator; (vi) An animal; (vii) A partnership firm; (viii) A Hindu idol; (ix) A company registered under the Companies Act, 1956; (x) A society registered under the Societies Registration Act; (xi) A co-operative society registered under the Co-operative Societies Act; (xii) A corporation established by a Special Act of Parliament.
    Answers: (i) Yes, (ii) No, (iii) Yes, (iv) No, (v) Yes, (vi) No, (vii) No, (viii) Yes, (ix) Yes, (x) Yes, (xi) Yes, (xii) Yes.
31. What do you understand by legal rights of persons? Illustrate.
32. Mention some of the important legal rights of persons.
33. Enumerate at least five characteristics of rights.
34. "The right has a source — either in contract, or in custom, or in natural law." Explain.
35. Distinguish between right *in personam* and *in rem*.
36. Distinguish between personal and proprietary right.
37. Explain the concept of property as understood in law.
38. Distinguish between: (i) Movable and immovable property; (ii) Personal and real property; (iii) Corporeal and incorporeal property.
39. "The concept of ownership is a bundle of rights *in rem* having certain characteristics namely of unspecified duration and use, and generally being inheritable and transferable." Comment.
40. "Possession, right or wrong, is protected by law." Explain Essentials of Law Discuss the different essentials which must be present in law in order to make it more effective.

REFERENCES

1. Blackstone: Commentaries Laws of England
2. Herbert Broom & Edward A Hadley: Commentaries on Laws of England (4 Vo1s)
3. Edward Jenks: History of English Laws
4. William Blackstone: Commentaries on the Laws of England
5. WS Holdsworth: A History of English Laws (12 Vo1s)
6. Thedore FT P1ucknett: A Concise History of the Common Law
7. GW Homes: Common Law
8. Roscoe Pound: Readings on the History and System of the Common Law
9. Sir Frederick Pollock & Frederik William Maitland: The History of English Law
10. AKRKirafy: Potter's Historical Introduction to English Law and its Institutions
11. GC Cheshire & Sir John Miles: Stephen's Commentaries on the Laws of England (4 Vo1s)
12. Kenneth Smith & Denis J Keenan: English Law
13. GR Rudd: The English Legal System
14. CHS Fifoot: History & Sources of the Common Law of Tort & Contract
15. GRY Radcliffe & Geoffrey Cross: The English Legal System
16. AT Carter: A History of the English Courts
17. WJV Windeyer: Lectures on Legal History
18. CHS Fifoot: English Law and its Background

PART B

BANKING REGULATION ACT, 1949

CHAPTER

3

Law of Banking

Introduction

'History is bunk', said Henry Ford, U.S. Business magnate. Although he may have been correct in some respects, there is no doubt that to understand clearly the present functions of banks it is useful to know something of their past. In this chapter, we propose to deal with the origin of banks followed by the main functions of commercial banks with special reference to the economic and monetary implications of modern banking operations and the present concept of social responsibility of banks.

1. Origin and Development of Banks

Early European History

According to some writers, the word 'bank' is derived from the Italian word 'banco' which means a bench. It was upon the bench in the marketplace that the early bankers, viz., the mediaeval European money — lenders and money changers, used to display their coins and transact business. The word has been in use from the middle ages in connection with the business of banking as money-changing was considered at that time as the most important function of a bank.

European banking has a long history dating back from the days of Greece and Rome, and was carried on by the Jews who are reported to have introduced Bills of Exchange in Europe as the most convenient method of transmitting money from one country to another. The Babylonians are known to have used their temples as banks as early as 200 B.C. Banking in ancient times was largely confined to money changing and money lending as conducted in mediaeval times. In mediaeval Europe, the bankers of Lombardy, a province in North Italy, were famous and due to wars at that time many important Lombardy families migrated to more settled countries such as Belgium, France and England. In London, they settled at the place now famous as Lombard Street.

The Bancc di Rialto was the first public bank started in Venice in the year 1584. Later on, banks were started at other places such as the Bank of Sweden (now known as State Bank of Sweden) in 1556, foreign exchange business and finance the trade of their countries with foreign countries. Subsequently, they took to deposit banking.

Indian History

The system of indigenous banking, as is well-known, dates back to very ancient times in India. All throughout the period of Indian History, money-lenders who were called either bankers or seths or shroffs are recorded to have existed and carried on the business of money-lending and banking on a large scale. Authoritative records of taking and giving of credit are to be found as early as between 2000 and 1400 B.C. during the vedic period. The question deposit and pledges has also been dealt with by the renowned Law giver Manu in his work at about the end of third century. The banking operations of ancient Indian resembled to those of modern private banking.

During the Moghul period, the indigenous bankers were most prominent in connection with the financing of trade and the use of instruments of trade. The house of "Jagat Seth" came to occupy the position of the most eminent bankers of their time during the reign of Aurangzeb and rendered much assistance to the British in the early days of their advent in India. From the early Vedic period right through the Moghul period as well as that of East India Company's rule until the middle of the nineteenth century, one finds evidence that indigenous bankers were the hub of the Indian financial system providing credit not only to the trade but also to the government of the day.

The advent of the British had an adverse impact on the business of the indigenous bankers not only because the monopoly position enjoyed by them for centuries was disturbed but also because there was a qualitative depreciation. The European bankers began to enjoy State patronage and the indigenous banker was gradually elbowed out. He concerned himself with providing credit to the agriculturists and the artisans, and with financing of internal trade.

It would be pertinent to note the primary distinction between the money-lender and the indigenous banker, as drawn by the Study Group on Indigenous Bankers appointed by the Banking Commission (1972). While the money-lender lends his own funds, the indigenous banker acts as a financial intermediary by accepting deposits or availing himself of bank credit. In other words, the indigenous banking system is regarded as a true financial intermediary in the sense that its ability to purvey funds is largely dependent on the outside resources it is able to mobilise. Another distinguishing feature between them is that the transactions of the money-lenders are conducted in cash while those of the indigenous bankers are based on the dealings in short-term credit instruments for financing the production and distribution of goods and services.

Money-Lenders

For a long time in the agricultural sector, money-lending process was controlled by the authoritative, profit-making and exploitative money-lenders. The interest charged by the private lenders had been unusually high and quite often they took undue advantage of illiterate, ignorant and superstitious farmers. Despite these evils, they continued to attract farmers due to their simple lending procedures and timely loans given on personal security. These had a profound effect on demand for money which had been quite large. It was, therefore, said that Indian farmers used to be born in debt live in debt and die in debt. Subsequently, owing to the legal restrictions imposed on the operations of money-lenders, the institutional agencies in the organised sector have been called upon to assume a more active role in the distribution of agricultural credit, particularly after nationalisation of 14 major commercial banks in 1969.

Indigenous Bankers

The indigenous bankers include Multanis, Gujarati Shroffs, and Marwaris in Western, Central and Northern India; Sindhi Multanis, Nattukotai Chetiars and Kallidaikurichy Brahmins in South India. As stated before, these indigenous bankers perform several functions like drawing and discounting hundis of two kinds, darshani (sight or demand) hundi and muttdati (usance) hundi, lending money, transmitting money from place to place, giving letters of credit to merchants and/or receiving deposits. They combine banking and trading activities and also at times act as commission agents. Indigenous bankers perform a useful role inasmuch as they make credit available to those sectors which are productive but which are not generally catered to by commercial banks either on grounds of cost or risk involved. Their methods of operation are expeditious and flexible.

Among the indigenous bankers, the Multani bankers are closest to the organised money market. Commercial banks provide accommodation to the indigenous bankers by discounting hundis endorsed in favour of the latter. The Multani hundi business is entirely unsecured, being based on the personal assessment by the Multani of the creditworthiness of the borrower. Since the hundi is a 90 days' instrument and the sanctity of the due date is observed, it provides a profitable short-term liquid form of investment to the banks.

So long as commercial banking was concentrated in metropolitan areas and important commercial centres, a very large proportion of credit requirements of rural and semi-urban areas continued to be met by the indigenous bankers and the money-lenders. With progressive extension of commercial banking geographically and to the priority sectors and the growth of cooperatives following the adoption of the integrated scheme or rural credit, the area of indigenous agencies has contracted further. At the same time, the changes in the strength and competition of demand for funds have led to new type of profitable lending. Thus, these agencies continue to play an important part in the unorganised financial system.

The Banking Commission (1972), recognising the valuable contribution of the indigenous bankers to the neglected sectors, has stressed the need for continued existence of such agencies which can offer personalised service. The Commission has also laid down certain requirements which the indigenous bankers should fulfill in order to be entitled to the discounting facilities with the commercial banks.

Development of Modern Banking

Historically, the genesis of banking on modern lines in India can be traced only to the beginning of the East India Company's trade relations with this country. The expanding trade interests of the English merchants compelled many English agency houses, which were essentially trading agencies, to add banking business to their activities. However, most of them came to grief owing to their participation in speculative ventures. The banking business of agency houses, which survived and continued to carry on trade and banking together, was progressively taken over by the Presidency banks. The three Presidency banks, viz., the Bank of Bengal (1806), the Bank of Bombay (1840) and the Bank of Madras (1854), were established under the Charter of the East India Company. These banks acted as bankers to the East India Company at Calcutta, Bombay and Madras and performed central banking functions for their respective areas. The three Presidency banks were amalgamated in 1921 to form the Imperial Bank of India which was nationalised in 1955 and renamed the "State Bank of India". Prior to the inauguration of the Reserve Bank of India in 1935, the Imperial Bank of India performed certain central banking functions, in particular, acting as banker to the Government, though primarily it remained as a commercial bank.

The Joint Stock Companies Act of 1850 was the first legislative enactment in the country to mould the corporate sector into an organic system. The principle of limited liability, however, was for the first time recognised in the Act of 1857 and extended subsequently to banking companies by the Act of 1860. This was the signal for new banking ventures in India. By 1894, there were 14 joint stock banks with limited liability in India, most of them run by Europeans. Initially, the joint stock banking in India developed on the lines of banking in the U.K. At the close of last century, the swedeshi movement gave fillip to the establishment of many joint stock banks owned and run by Indian capital and management. Of these, the Punjab National Bank Ltd. was founded in 1895; the Bank of India Ltd. in 1906; the Bank of Baroda Ltd. in 1908 and the Central Bank of India Ltd. in 1911. These four banks are of the "Big Five" in India today and the fifth, the United Commercial Bank Ltd., was founded in 1943.

State Bank of India and its Associate Banks

Commercial banking in India was concentrated in the port towns at Bombay, Calcutta and Madras and a few other important centres. Even as late as 1951, the bias in favour of larger population centres continued inasmuch as 63 per cent of the bank offices were in towns having a population of over 25,000 and only 37 per cent at centres with a population of 25,000 and less. Also commercial banks were mainly undertaking wholesale banking, apart from commodity financing in mandi towns. Banks considered small loan accounts as a costly proposition. The savings of the common man were channeled mainly into unproductive areas and his credit needs were met by the unorganised money market where the interest rates were exorbitant.

The lopsided nature of banking development, the absence of institutional avenues for savings, particularly in rural areas, and the urgency to take care of their credit needs required immediate remedying. July 1, 1955, is an important landmark in the history of Indian banking. On this day, in pursuance of the recommendation of the All India Rural Credit Survey Committee, 1954, the Government of India nationalised the Imperial Bank of India and the State Bank of India was formed under the State Bank of India Act, 1955. With a view to maintaining the commercial character of the State Bank of India, 92 per cent of the share capital is held by the Reserve Bank of India and the rest is allowed to be in the private hands.

The object of nationalisation, as stated in the preamble of the State Bank of India Act, 1955, are "the extension of banking facilities on a large scale, more particularly in the rural and semi-urban areas, and for diverse other public purposes." Having been designed to develop into an engine for surveying rural credit, the State Bank of India Act required the bank to establish not less than 400 additional branches within a period of five years, particularly at the district level and sub-divisional centres. The State Bank of India fulfilled this requirement a little ahead of the schedule.

Under the State Bank of India (Subsidiary Banks) Act, 1959, eight major state-owned/state-associated banks operating in the erstwhile princely states were taken over by the State Bank of India as its subsidiaries. Later, two of the subsidiaries were amalgamated, reducing the number to seven. Thus, an integrated framework was set up for extending banking and credit facilities into rural and semi-urban areas.

The subsidiaries, now referred to as Associate Banks, thus taken over are:

(1) The State Bank of Bikaner and Jaipur.
(2) The State Bank of Hyderabad.
(3) The State Bank of Indore.
(4) The State Bank of Mysore.
(5) The State Bank of Patiala.
(6) The State Bank of Saurashtra.
(7) The State Bank of Travancore.

Of these, three banks (State Bank or Hyderabad, State Bank of Patiala and State Bank of Saurashtra) are wholly owned by the State Bank of India. In the remaining four banks, the State Bank of India holds largely the share capital with minority share holdings by the public. The Chairman of the State Bank of India is the ex-officio chairman of the Board of Directors of subsidiaries. These banks had their own branch expansion programmes.

The State Bank of India, thus, spearheaded the development of commercial banking in the backward and underdeveloped areas of the country and made the first systematic and planned effort to spread banking in the rural areas. The State Bank of India also undertook the promotion and financing of small industries and supported rural credit operations through assistance to land mortgage banks and other cooperative institutions.

It may be stated that the provisions of the Banking Regulation Act, 1949, are also applicable to the State Bank of India and its subsidiaries to the extent there is no corresponding provision in the Act which have brought them into existence.

Joint Stock Banks

During the last about 100 years the banking industry suffered a number of setbacks in the form of bank failures, particularly during the period 1913-17 and 1931-38. Some of the serious defects which caused a large number of bank failures were: the admixture of banking and trading, inadequate capital resources, unsound investment policies, indiscriminate lending, uneconomic branch banking, dishonesty of the directors and managers, and lack of trained and experienced personnel. Efforts were made to rectify the undesirable features in the banking system from time to time through legislative measures. However, it was not before 1949 that for the first time a comprehensive piece of legislation (the Banking Companies Act, now called the Banking Regulation Act) was enacted to consolidate and amend the law relating to banking.

The Act which came into force on March 16, 1949, is a unique piece of legislation in the history of banking in India. It contains a comprehensive legislative framework covering all important aspects of commercial banking such as organisation, management, audit, liquidation etc. In fact, the Act laid the foundation for the growth of a healthy commercial banking system in the country. As and when experience showed that the provisions were inadequate, fresh provisions were added to the Act or the existing provisions were amended for the orderly growth of the banking system.

Amalgamation and Consolidation

Since 1949 an era of consolidation for the Indian banks set in and the total number of branches declined from 4,359 in 1949 to 3,959 in 1955. A few amalgamations also took place. Bharat Bank was absorbed by Punjab National Bank and four banks in Bengal formed the United Bank of India. This was considered as a healthy feature creating a sound base for future expansion.

The process of weeding out substandard non-viable banks through amalgamation or absorption of weaklings with stronger banking units was accelerated after the failure of Laxmi Bank and the Palai Central Bank in 1960. A number of small local banks which had developed at small towns were absorbed into larger banks with the result that there had been substantial decline in the number of commercial banks and a very remarkable increase in the number of their branches. The number of banks declined from 566 at the end of 1951 to 74 at the end of December 1973 and the number of bank offices increased from 4,151 to 16,503 during the same period, though an important aspect of growth in bank offices is the extension of banking facilities to the rural or less developed areas.

Social Control of Banks — Evolution of the Concept

In terms of such indices as the number of branches or the magnitude of bank deposits or bank credit, commercial banks grew considerably in stability and strength during the post-independence years. However, there had been persistent complaints, particularly in the 1960s, that the priority sectors such as agriculture, small-scale industries and exports had not been receiving their due share of bank credit and the bulk of bank advances was diverted to large and medium scale industries and big and established houses. This was so because commercial banks in the private sector did not change their policies to adapt themselves to the emerging need of the economy. This state of affairs was attributed to the pattern of ownership and control of commercial banks by large industrial and business interests. It was also felt that the banking system was not properly equipped to assist the attainment of the basic economic and social objectives namely, rapid economic growth, diffusion of economic power and channeling of credit in accordance with the priorities of the Five Year Plans.

Owing to these adverse features there was strong demand in political circles for total nationalisation of banking. The term "Social Control" over banking was adopted for the first time by the then ruling Congress Party in its 1967 election manifesto which stated that "It is necessary to bring most of the banking institutions under social control in order to serve the cause of economic growth and fulfill our social purposes more effectively and to make credit available to producers in all fields where it is needed." The Government thought that the purpose of nationalisation could be well served by social control without the special difficulties arising from Government ownership and management. The scheme of social control of banks was, thus, enforced through the Banking Laws (Amendment) Act, 1968. The Act sought to streamline the managerial and operational aspects of commercial banks with a view to diffusing economic power and checking the misuse of bank credit by vested interests. The important provisions of the Act are given below:

(i) Reconstitution of the Board of Directors

It was made obligatory for every banking company to reconstitute its Board of Directors so that not less than 51 per cent of the total number of directors consisted of persons having special knowledge or practical experience in banking, agriculture, small-scale industry, rural economy, etc., of use to a banking company. It was, thus, aimed to give a professional bent to bank management. The director of a bank shall not have a substantial interest and/or be employed in any large or medium sized industrial and business undertaking. Further, the Reserve Bank was given wide powers regarding the appointment of a director or an observer on the Board of a banking company.

(ii) Chairman

Each Indian Bank will have a whole-time chairman who should be a professional banker having special knowledge and practical experience of the working of a commercial bank or financial, economic or business administration. He will be the chief executive officer of the bank and will not be substantially interested in any other company or firm or otherwise actively connected with it. The appointment, removal or termination of services of the Chairman and the terms of appointment will require the approval of the Reserve Bank.

(iii) Foreign Banks

Each foreign bank operating in India will have to set up an Advisory Committee on the lines of the reconstituted Board of Directors of Indian banks. Further, foreign banks were required to get the accounts of their Indian business audited only by auditors registered in India.

(iv) Restriction on Loans to Directors

The Act prohibits the grant of any new loans, secured or unsecured, to directors or companies or firms in which they are interested. The existing loans were to be recovered on the expiry of the period specified in the relative contracts or where no period was specified within a period of three years.

(v) Government Powers to Take Over Banks

The Act contains a provision for nationalisation of any particular bank even without resorting to legislation. It gives powers to the Union Government to take over the business of any banking company if it has persistently failed to comply with the directions given by the Reserve Bank. Further, individual banks may be nationalised if it is in the interests of the depositors or in the interests of banking policy or for the better provision of credit in general or to particular sectors.

The Banking Laws (Amendment) Act, 1968, came into force on February 1, 1969. It must be said to the credit of commercial banks that they acted up to the idea of social control much earlier than it was passed into legislation. In several cases, the General Managers were appointed as Chairman and changes were voluntarily effected in the composition of their Boards on the lines indicated above. The banks also embarked upon various schemes to provide finance to agriculture and small-scale industry in compliance with the targets fixed by the National Credit Council.

The National Credit Council (NCC) was set up in February 1968 by the Government of India with the Finance Minister as Chairman and the Governor of the RBI as Deputy Chairman. Its main functions were periodically:

(a) to assess the demand for bank credit from various sectors of the economy;

(b) to determine priorities for grant of loans and advances, in particular to priority sectors of agriculture, small-scale industry and exports or for investment; and

(c) to coordinate the lending the investment policies as between commercial and cooperative banks and specialised agencies to ensure optimum and efficient use of overall resources.

Bank advances to the two sectors of agriculture and small-scale industry went up by Rs. 33.17 crores and Rs. 41.31 crores between June 1968 and April 1969. These trends showed that the scheme of Social Control was working satisfactorily. In fact, it was social control and the guidelines of the erstwhile NCC which brought about the first stirrings towards a major meaningful redeployment of bank credit in favour of priority sectors.

Nationalisation of Banks — Rationale

As indicated before, the Social Control policy was being followed since the beginning of 1968. However, there was sudden shift in the view of the Government and 14 major Indian private commercial banks with deposits of Rs. 50 crores or more were nationalised on July 19, 1969, by a Presidential Ordinance. The Ordinance became law by the Banking Companies (Acquisition and Transfer of Undertakings) Act, 1970, which received the assent of the President on March 31, 1970. The nationalisation was a momentous step in the history of Indian banking.

The primary objective of nationalisation were set forth as follows:

(1) To extend banking facilities in unbanked and underbanked centres, especially in rural areas.

(2) To ensure an increased flow of assistance to the hitherto neglected sectors.

(3) To foster the growth of new and progressive entrepreneurs.

(4) To give a professional bent to the banks' management with a view to removing control by a few.

The 14 nationalised banks, after dropping the prefix "The" and suffix "Limited" from their names, are:

1. Allahabad Bank
2. Bank of Baroda
3. Bank of India
4. Bank of Maharashtra
5. Canara Bank
6. Central Bank of India
7. Dena Bank
8. Indian Bank
9. Indian Overseas Bank
10. Punjab National Bank
11. Syndicate Bank
12. United Commercial Bank (since named as 'UCO Bank')
13. Union Bank of India
14. United Bank of India

At the time of nationalisation, the 14 nationalised banks together with the State Bank of India and its seven subsidiaries which already operated under public ownership accounted for four fifths (81 per cent) of the total number of branches and six sevenths (84 per cent and 83 per cent respectively) of deposits and credits of all scheduled banks in the country. Thus, the July 19 decision of the Government brought about a complete revolution in Indian banking as almost the whole of the banking business came under Government ownership.

Compelling Reasons for Nationalisation

The various compelling reasons which weighed with the Government in taking the momentous decision of bank nationalisation may be summarised as under:

(1) Concentration of Wealth and Economic Power

The foremost reason for nationalisation of banks was the charge that through their lending policies and practices the Indian commercial banks, which were under the control and management of big industrialists and business magnates, were responsible for the concentration of wealth and economic power in a few hands. Bank deposits were mobilised from many but credit needs of only a few were catered to. Bank loans were security-oriented rather than purpose-oriented and the consideration of security in terms of tangible assets had the effect of making big business as better credit risk. The extension of security-oriented credit, thus, helped the growth of economic power and intensification of disparities of income and wealth in the country, which is against the Directive Principles of the Indian Constitution. In order to bring about necessary changes in lending policies and procedures of banks, public ownership and control of large banks was considered an essential prerequisite.

(2) Resources Utilised by Directors

The financial stake of the shareholders of the banks was almost negligible, the ratio of paid-up capital and reserves to deposits having declined by more than 75 per cent from 9.7 per cent in 1951 to 2.2 per cent in 1969. The bank managements were, thus, operating almost exclusively with other people's money. It was stated that a large part of deposit resources of banks was utilised by the directors of the banks to promote their personal interests or was used in the business and industrial concerns in which the directors were personally interested and not for general economic development. In order to eliminate such malpractices, it was considered necessary to dissociate the big industrialists and businessmen from the top managements of banks.

(3) Branch Expansion

The urban bias of commercial banks was reflected in their geographical distribution. As the opening of the branches in the countryside is not a profitable proposition, private commercial banks were not enthusiastic about opening more and more branches in small towns and large villages. As a result, they failed not only in credit extension to deserving sectors but also in effective mobilisation of deposits. Besides, they drained the savings of some states and diverted them to others. Public ownership of banks was considered necessary in order to launch a massive programme of branch expansion in unbanked and underbanked areas as well as to prevent lopsided regional development.

(4) Neglect of Agriculture, Small-Scale Industry and Other Small Borrowers

In spite of the fact that agriculture is the basic industry of the country, private commercial banks had largely remained indifferent to the credit needs of farmers for agricultural operations. A large majority of the weaker sections of society, such as small entrepreneurs, retail traders, artisans, etc., were practically denied credit, however socially useful and economically viable the productive activity they were engaged in. Further, larger share of credit went to large industrial and business units and consequently small-scale industrial units and small borrowers were discriminated against. Due to these credit gaps and imbalances, it was considered necessary to bring about radical changes in the credit policies and practices of banks with a view to correcting and, if possible, eliminating the maldistribution of bank credit which was heavily weighed in favour of the large industrial and trade sectors.

(5) Five Year Plans and Commercial Banks

It was pointed out that private control of commercial banks was an obstacle to the achievement of the objectives of the Five Year Plans as they failed to contribute to the financial resources for the vital sectors of the economy. Banking institutions are the most important levers for achieving the social objectives of Plans and hence they ought to be under public ownership.

Non-Nationalised Sector

Small banks with deposits of less than Rs. 50 crores were not nationalised as their operations were limited to certain specific regions and they already catered mainly to the small borrowers. Such banks are part of the community in which they function and small businessmen and small industrialists have some say in their operations.

All the foreign banks — branches of banking companies incorporated outside India — were also excluded from the purview of nationalisation. In this context, the then Prime Minister, late Mrs. Indira Gandhi, in her statement in Parliament on July 22, 1969, said. "They (foreign banks) provide, by and large, business of a specialised nature such as facilitating foreign trade and tourism. The operations of banks of one country in another, subject to the laws of the land, is mainly for such purposes and is part of international facility. It has been the Government's general policy to confine the opening of new branches of foreign banks to major port towns where their specialised services are needed."

Foreign banks operating in India accounted for about 10 per cent of total deposits of all scheduled commercial banks. The activities of foreign banks were already being regulated under the Banking Regulation Act. With the nationalisation of major banks further restrictive orders were issued to the foreign banks in regard to credit-deposit ratio, branch expansion and deployment of foreign funds. The desirability of stepping up the pace of Indianisation of the personnel of their branches was also impressed on them.

The nationalisation provision does not apply to such of the branches of the nationalised banks as are situated outside India and where, under the law in force in the country concerned, it is not permissible for a bank, owned or controlled by the Government to carry on business there.

Nationalisation vs. Social Control

The question is often raised why nationalisation of banks was considered necessary on the heels of the scheme of Social Control which was working satisfactorily and why Social Control could not have been tried for a longer period. The answer was provided by the Government in pointing out certain weaknesses of the scheme of Social Control, as given below:

The major weakness of Social Control was, as stated by the Prime Minister in Parliament, that "in many banks people who had been controlling their policies in the past continued to exercise their influence over them in one way or another, sometimes by the continued presence of the chairman or vice-chairman of the boards." Thus, there was no basic change in the control of the banks' operations under the scheme of Social Control. The basic objective of Social Control was to develop a framework of credit planning without touching the ownership of banks. It was, however, felt that the ownership and credit policy could not be divorced to check misuse of credit.

Secondly, some of the banking companies were not obeying the instructions and directions given to them by the Government or the Reserve Bank wholeheartedly and with enthusiasm but were just carrying them out in word and ignoring them in spirit. It was, therefore, considered necessary to amend the structure of the 14 major private banks to bring it in line with the national economic strategy.

Finally, the Reserve Bank had limited powers to reconstitute the banks' board of management to bring their operations in line with national priorities. The Reserve bank could remove a director, for example, only in specified circumstances and under prescribed procedures. There was also a limitation on the number of additional directors it could appoint. The majority decision of the board of directors could not thus be bypassed by the Reserve Bank. It could issue directives in exceptional or unusual cases, but this power could not obviously be invoked in the daily operations of the banks.

Denationalisation

The constitutional validity of the Banking Companies (Acquisition and Transfer of Undertakings) Act,1969, was challenged and the Act was struck down by the Supreme Court by a majority of 10:1 on February 10, 1970 on two grounds. First, there was hostile discrimination against the nationalised banks in that it prohibited them from carrying on banking business, whereas other banks, foreign and Indian, were permitted to do so. It had also restricted these banks from carrying on business other than banking as defined in Section 5(b) of the Banking Regulation Act, 1949. Secondly, the methods by which compensation was to be determined could not be considered relevant and appropriate for such determination.

Renationalisation

A new validating Ordinance was issued by the President on February 14, 1970, to renationalise the 14 commercial banks with retrospective effect from July 19, 1969. It also protected all the actions taken by the nationalised banks between July 19, 1969, and February 14, 1970. The Ordinance made amendments to those aspects of the former Act against which the Supreme Court took objection and struck down the entire measure. It provided for bankwise compensation which added up to Rs. 87.40 crores against Rs. 75 crores provided under the earlier Act. Under the Ordinance, the companies whose banks were nationalised can start banking business again. But the new banks will have to have different names as they would be required to get licence from the Reserve Bank. The Bill to replace the Ordinance for regularising the renationalisation of 14 major commercial banks was passed by Parliament and became law on March 31, 1970, when the President accorded his assent to it.

Second Round of Nationalisation

By a Presidential Ordinance promulgated on April 15, 1980, the Union Government nationalised six banks in the private sector, whose demand and time liabilities in India as on March 14, 1980, amounted to not less than Rs. 200 crores. The six new nationalised banks, after dropping the prefix "The" and suffix "Limited" from their previous names are:

1. Andhra Bank,
2. Corporation Bank,
3. New Bank of India,
4. Oriental Bank of Commerce,
5. Punjab and Sind Bank, and
6. Vijaya Bank.

The preamble to the Ordinance for the acquisition and transfer of these six banking undertakings (since replaced by an Act of Parliament) states that these banks have been taken over, "having regard to their size, resources, coverage and organisation in order further to control the economy, to meet progressively and serve better the needs of the development of the economy and to promote welfare of the people in conformity with the policy of the State". Thus, the Government further extended the area of public control over the country's banking system. This was done in the light of emphasis that was being placed on the implementation of the 20-Point Economic Programme and raising of the share of advances to the priority sectors from 33.1/3 per cent to 40 per cent over the period of five years of the Sixth Plan, 1980-85.

With the nationalisation of the above six banks, the number of public sector banks has increased to 28 (comprising State Bank of India and its seven subsidiaries and 20 nationalised banks), exclusive of regional rural banks. All the 28 public sector banks accounted for 88.1 per cent of offices, 90.9 per cent of deposits and 90.5 per cent of advances of scheduled commercial banks in December 1980 as against 79.8 per cent of offices, 83.3 per cent of deposits and 83.8 per cent of advances before nationalisation of 14 major banks in July 1969. The share of the remaining private sector banks truncated to 9.1 per cent in deposits and 9.5 per cent in advances. Within this category of private sector, foreign banks accounted for 3.6 per cent in deposits and 4.0 per cent in advances.

As on March 14, 1980, the total deposits of six nationalised banks exceeded Rs. 2,356 crores and accounted for a little over 7 per cent of the aggregate deposits of the commercial banking system which amounted to Rs. 31,338 crores. According to the official sources, the Government would be able to ensure better that a higher percentage of bank deposits is utilised to fulfill the socio economic objective through control over the credit policy. Like other nationalised banks, the six banks will be guided by the directions in regard to matters of policy which the Central Government may make after consultation with the Reserve Bank of India, and are expected to reinforce Government policies.

2. MAIN FUNCTIONS OF COMMERCIAL BANKS

In the world of banking and finance nothing stands still. The biggest change of all is the scope of business of banking. Banking in the traditional form is concerned with the acceptance of deposit of money from the customers, the lending of the surplus of deposited money to suitable customers who wish to borrow, and transmission of funds. These are still the primary functions of banking, albeit on a much larger map, on a much larger scale and in a much more technologically advanced way that could be contemplated years ago. Banks have slowly expanded and diversified their functions embracing many aspects of economic activity.

Commercial banks in India, like their counterparts all the world over, have been trying to diversify their business activity during the past two decades and performing for their customers — and in some instances also for the public at large — host of service functions. But the two functions of (i) the acceptance of deposits and the repayment of these funds on demand or at a stipulated time in future, and (ii) provision of credit to different sectors of the economy, are the core functions of banking activity and form the mainstay of banking business in India. With deposits providing the major source of lendable or investible funds and with roughly 75 per cent or more of total revenues derived from advances, it can be readily appreciated why these functions constitute the basic functions of commercial banks.

Definition of Banking

The statutory definition of 'banking' in India was at first a part of the definition of 'banking company' (introduced in 1936 in the Indian Companies Act, 1913) and later given separately in the Banking Companies Act, 1949 (now known as the Banking Regulation Act, 1949). The Banking Regulation Act, 1949, specially defines 'banking' and 'banking company' in unambiguous terms. Section 5(b) of the Act defines banking as follows:

"Banking means the accepting, for the purpose of lending or investment, of deposits of money from the public, repayable on demand or otherwise, and withdrawable by cheque, draft, order or otherwise."

This definition which considers traditional functions makes it clear that the essential or minimum characteristics of 'banking' are four:

(1) accepting deposits of money from the public;
(2) for the purpose of lending or investment;
(3) repayable on demand or otherwise; and
(4) withdrawable by cheque, draft, order or otherwise.

Thus, the definition of banking makes it clear that the acceptance of deposits is the *sine qua non* for constituting banking business. It should be noted that the definition of banking is in terms of the nature of the business and does not vary due to differences in legal status of the persons who carry on such business, such as statutory corporations, joint stock companies, firms or individuals.

Section 5 (c) defines a 'banking company' as any company which transacts the business of banking in India. However, the acceptance of deposits by companies for the purpose of financing their own business is not regarded as 'banking' within the meaning of the Act. An explanation to this effect has been added to clause (c) of Section 5 to make it clear that any company which is engaged in the manufacture of goods or carries on any trade and which accepts deposits of money from the public merely for the purpose of financing its business shall not be regarded as a banking company.

One of the distinguishing features of commercial banking is the payment of cheques drawn by customers on current accounts. This concept is reflected by the subsequently enacted Section 49A of the Banking Regulation Act. According to this Section, no person other than a banking company or an approved banking institution can accept from the public deposits of money withdrawable by cheques.

According to Section 5(d) of the Banking Regulation Act, a 'company' means any company as defined in Section 8 of the Companies Act, 1956, and includes a foreign company within the meaning of Section 591 of that Act. Hence, a foreign company incorporated outside India and having a place of business within India will be a banking company if it performs functions (1) to (4) mentioned above.

It is obvious that an institution, in order to qualify as a bank, must satisfy two requirements: (1) It must be a company as defined in the Companies Act; and (2) It must undertake business of banking as defined in the Banking Regulation Act. A banking company may use any of the words 'bank', 'banker' or 'banking' as part of its name and all other companies are prohibited from using any of these words, as provided in Section 7(1) of the Banking Regulation Act, 1949. Thus, there is no room for any doubt about the meaning of words 'bank', 'banker' or 'banking' for the purpose of the Banking Regulation Act, 1949.

Acceptance of Deposits "from the Public"

Banking as defined in the Banking Regulation Act, 1949, is linked with the acceptance of deposits "from the public". The words "from the public" have been interpreted to exclude acceptance of deposits by a body, such as a Nidhi, from its members. Nidhis are companies incorporated under the Companies Act which accept deposits from their members and carry on lending activities. Further, if deposits from members are excluded from the scope of the definition of 'banking', cooperative credit institutions taking deposits only from their members go out of banking regulation. To plug this loop-hole in the definition, the Banking Commission has recommended that the expression "from the public" should be clarified as covering also the acceptance of deposits by a body from its members or shareholders (see the Banking Commission Report, 1972, Government of India, p. 476).

Private Bankers

The Banking Regulation Act applies only to companies and not to individuals or firms carrying on banking business. However, Sub-Section 2 of Section 7 of the Act prohibits firms, individuals and groups of individuals from using any of the words 'bank', 'banking' or 'banking company' as part of their name, but does not prohibit them from using the word 'banker'. This is why many of such individuals or firms call themselves as "private bankers" and accept

(a) current deposits withdrawable on demand through withdrawable forms (not by means of cheques because of prohibition imposed by Section 49A of the Act);
(b) collect cheques for credit of accounts; and
(c) lend by way of overdrafts or key loans.

They are not, however, required by any law to maintain and preserve accounts and records like a bank and it is open to them to change the constitution at any time.

Such private bankers may be able to make a legally valid claim to the status of a banker under the existing definition of a banker in the Negotiable Instruments Act, 1881. Section 3 of this Act merely describes a banker as "any person acting as a banker". This is the widest possible definition which may include even the firms and individuals, who can legally use the word 'banker' as part of their trade name. As banker, they may claim statutory protection under Section 128 of the Negotiable Instruments Act regarding payment of crossed cheques and under Section 85 and 10 of the Act regarding payment in due course of cheques. There is, therefore, the need to revise the definition of 'banker' in the Negotiable Instruments Act, 1881, so that it conforms to the definition of banking business under the Banking Regulation Act, 1949.

Permissible Business

Clause (a) of Sub-Section (1) of Section 6 of the Banking Regulation Act sets out the normal kinds of business which is essential for carrying on the business of banking or more or less incidental to such business. These functions which form the bulk of the bank activities and are called the main functions include the following:

(a) the borrowing, raising or taking up of money, the lending or advancing of money either with or without security;

the drawing, making, accepting, discounting, buying, selling, collecting and dealing in bills of exchange, hundis, promissory notes, coupons, drafts, bills of lading, railway receipts, warrants, debentures, certificates, scrips and other instruments, and securities whether transferable or negotiable or not;

the granting and issuing of letters of credit, traveller's cheques and circular notes;

the buying, selling and dealing in bullion and specie;

the buying and selling of foreign exchange including foreign bank notes;

the acquiring, holding, issuing on commission, underwriting and dealing in stock, funds, shares, debentures, debenture stock, bonds, obligations, securities and investments of all kinds;

the purchasing and selling of bonds, scrips or other forms of securities on behalf of constituents or others, the negotiating of loans and advances;
the receiving of all kinds of bonds or valuables, on deposit or for safe custody or otherwise;
the providing of safe deposit vaults;
the collecting and transmitting of money and securities.
the other important ancillary services as set out in clauses (b) to (o) of Sub-Section (1) of Section 6 are:

(b) acting as agents for any government or local authority or any person or persons;
the carrying on of agency business of any description including the clearing and forwarding of goods, giving of receipts and discharged and otherwise acting as an attorney on behalf of customers, but excluding the business of a managing agent or secretary and treasurer of a company;

(c) contracting for public and private loans and negotiating and issuing the same;

(d) the effecting, insuring, guaranteeing, underwriting, participating in managing and carrying out of any issue public or private, of State, municipal or other loans or of shares, stock, debentures or debenture stock of any company, corporation or association and lending of money for the purpose of any such issue;

(e) carrying on and transacting every kind of guarantee and indemnity business;

(f) managing, selling and realising any property which may come into the possession of the company in satisfaction or part satisfaction of any of its claims;

(g) acquiring and holding and generally dealing with any property or any right, title or interest in any such property which may form the security or part of the security for any loans or advances or which may be connected with any such security;

(h) undertaking and executing trusts;

(i) undertaking the administration of estates as executor, trustee or otherwise;

(j) establishing and supporting or aiding in the establishment and support of association, institutions, funds, trusts and conveniences calculated to benefit employees or ex-employees of the company or the dependents or connections of such persons; granting pensions and allowances and making payments towards insurance; subscribing to or guaranteeing moneys for charitable or benevolent objects or for any exhibition or for any public, general or useful object;

(k) the acquisition, construction, maintenance and alteration of any building or works necessary or convenient for the purpose of the company;

(l) selling, improving, managing, developing, exchanging, leasing, mortgaging, disposing of or turning into account or otherwise dealing with all or any part of the property and rights of the company;

(m) acquiring and undertaking the whole or any part of the business of any person or company, when such business is of a nature enumerated or described in this sub-section;

(n) doing all such other things as are incidental or conducive to the promotion or advancement of the business of the company;

(o) any other form of business which the Central Government may, by notification in the Central Gazette, specify as a form of business in which it is lawful for a banking company to engage.

Commercial banks in India perform for their customers many of the above functions but the range of services may vary depending upon the size and type of the bank. The Act specifically provides that banking companies shall not engage in any form of business other than those mentioned above [Section 6(1)]. Such restriction of activities of commercial banks is necessary for discouraging them from indulging in non-banking activities like trading.

Business Prohibited for a Banking Company

Section 8 of the Banking Regulation Act lays down that no banking company shall directly or indirectly engage in any trade or buying or selling of goods otherwise than in connection with the bills of exchange received for collection or negotiation. If in satisfaction of its claims in the course of banking business, any bank acquires immovable property in which it is not lawful for it to transact business, it should dispose of such assets within seven years (Section 9). The Reserve bank may extend the period by another five years if it is satisfied that such extension would be in the interest of the depositors of the banking company. The banking company shall have to dispose of such property within the prescribed period.

Section 19 of the Banking Regulation Act restricts the formation of subsidiary companies by a banking company may form a subsidiary company only for the purposes mentioned below:

(i) For undertaking and executing of trusts;

(ii) For undertaking the administration of estates as executor, trustee or otherwise; or

(iii) For providing safe deposit vault.

A subsidiary company may also be formed for such other purposes as are incidental to the business of banking, with the previous permission in writing of the Reserve Bank of India.

Subject to the above a banking company shall not hold shares in any company, whether as pledgee, mortgagee or absolute owner, of any amount exceeding 30 per cent of the paid-up share capital of that company or 30 per cent of its own paid-up capital and reserves, whichever is less.

A banking company cannot hold shares in any company, in the management of which its managing director or manager is interested.

Permission to Banks to Undertake Leasing Business

Since under Section 8 of the Banking Regulation Act, 1949, banks have been debarred from buying or selling or bartering of all movable properties except in connection with the realisation of the security held by them for lending or other purposes, banks were not able to enter into leasing activity. Nor were they allowed to form subsidiaries to undertake leasing under Section 19 (1) of the same Act. But the Banking Law (Amendment) Act, 1983, has widened the scope of Section 19 (1) by permitting banks to form subsidiaries for the purpose of carrying on any kind of approved business (including leasing) mentioned in Section 6 of the same Act and also for "undertaking of such other business which the Reserve Bank may, with the prior approval of the Central Government, consider to be conducive to the spread of banking in India or to be otherwise useful or necessary in public interest". Decks have been cleared through these amendments for the entry of commercial banks into the leasing business.

The RBI has allowed banks with its prior approval to either set up subsidiaries to transact equipment leasing business with not less than 51 per cent of share holding or investment in shares of other equipment leasing companies within the limit specified in Section 19 (2) of the Banking Regulation Act, i.e., upto 30 per cent of the subscribed capital of the concerned leasing company. The Reserve Bank has further stipulated that the investment of a bank in the shares of other leasing companies together with the investment in its own subsidiaries should not exceed 10 per cent of the paid-up capital and reserves of the bank, The RBI has wisely advised the banks not to engage themselves directly in the leasing business.

Permission to Banks to Conduct Business of Mutual Funds

Through amendment in the Banking Regulation Act, 1949, it has become lawful for a banking company to establish and conduct the business of mutual funds. The mutual funds would mean the business acquisition, holding management, trading or disposal of securities, participation certificates or any other instrument, income or growth participation business and unit trust schemes. The funds will be open to participation by the public through the subscription of shares or units or otherwise.

The State Bank of India has become the first commercial bank in the country to launch a mutual fund named as the SBI Mutual Fund, which began its operations on July 2, 1986. The fund is in the form of a trust with the SBI as settler, and is managed by the SBI's wholly owned subsidiary, SBI Capital Markets Ltd., as the Fund's trustee.

The first mutual fund scheme known as Magnum Regular Income Scheme, 1987, launched by the SBI Mutual Fund, opened for public subscription on November 30, 1987. The Scheme has offered $5^1/_2$ years 20 lakhs Magnums of Rs. 500 each at par, thus mobilising Rs. 100 crores.

The subsidiary of Canara Bank — Canbank Financial Services — started business on June 1, 1987, and has also launched a mutual fund scheme, 'Canstock Fund and Canshare Fund.'

On April 12, 1988, Punjab National Bank has launched a wholly owned subsidiary christened "PNB Capital Services Ltd." for undertaking merchant banking, equipment leasing and other allied activities, and thereby offers a 'financial package' to the industrial clients.

These companies have the potential of developing into specialised institutions dealing with all specialised financial activities. Some other banks are reported to be waiting to float mutual funds, perhaps each with its own pattern of assured income and liquidity.

Permission to Banks to Establish Subsidiaries to Provide Housing Finance

Though commercial banks, except the State Bank of India, were not prohibited from extending housing credit, they have not entered the housing finance field to any significant extent. After nationalisation in 1969, some banks introduced savings schemes linked with housing loans, but they were more of deposit schemes rather than the schemes for housing finance. A recent major development in the area of commercial banks' entry to housing finance is the establishment of subsidiaries by selected banks. So far three banks have been permitted by the Government to establish subsidiaries.

The SBI's Housing Promotion Finance Corporation Private Ltd. has an authorised capital of Rs. 25 crores and an initial paid-up capital of Rs. 5 crores. It has the equity participation of SBI Capital Markets, HDFC, and other institutions like LIC and GIC. It is to operate in Eastern and North-Eastern India.

Canara Bank's Can Fin Homes Ltd., which was established with an initial investment of Rs. 30 crores, has an equity participation from Canara Bank, Canara Bank Financial Services, HDFC and other financial institutions such as UTI. It is to cover the Union Territory of Delhi and South India.

Punjab National Bank's PNB Housing Services Ltd., with an authorised capital of Rs. 10 crores, will confine its operations in Northern India. While the SBI's housing subsidiary plans to take up development of housing estates and commercial complexes like shopping centres, market yards and hospitals, PNB's housing subsidiary has plans to finance partly or wholly setting up of new or satellite towns.

With the emergence of housing subsidiaries together with an apex institution, i.e., National Housing Bank (NHB) at the national level, the housing finance scenario will take a new turn in the years ahead.

Diversification of Banking Business

The Indian banking has undergone phenomenal transformation since the nationalisation of 14 major commercial banks in July, 1969. There has been unprecedented growth of business and the hallmark of this growth process has been functional diversification in new and complex areas. The experiments made by the Indian banking system in the area of social and development banking in the past 20 years is unique and has emerged as a model, eliciting keen interest the world over.

Qualitatively the period of rapid growth has also witnessed remarkable shifts in focus of banks' operations from traditional to non-traditional areas. Over the years, Indian banks have been experimenting, innovating, improvising and coming out with new types of services to cater to the emerging needs of their customers. Each bank has entered into merchant banking activity in a big way. Leading banks have started mutual funds, housing finance, sale of public sector bonds, etc. A few larger banks have also set up separate subsidiaries to effectively manage these new areas. Some banks are now entering into areas of equipment leasing. Further, in view of the growing equity culture in the economy, banks may have to become active in distributing stocks, debentures and bonds even to their own depositors.

In view of shortage of housing, especially in towns and metropolitan centres, banks will have to take interest in financing this activity through subsidiaries or otherwise. With the setting up of the National Housing Bank as an apex institution for housing finance, commercial banks can hope to enlarge their credit to this sector. It might be necessary for National Housing Bank to provide refinance to the commercial banks as is being done by the IDBI in respect of industrial finance and by NABARD in respect of finance to agriculture.

Several banks have expanded their overseas operations and have undertaken financing the import-export business of their clients in a professional manner, many times competing with some large international banks. The international banking scene has undergone drastic changes with the introduction of computer and telecommunication technology, which have led to geographical and functional integration of international financial markets in recent years. International banks have diversified their business into capital market operations since new profit opportunities have been noticed in this field. Responding to these changes in the international and domestic environment, commercial banks in India have also been trying to diversify their activities in such areas as consumer credit, credit cards, traveller's cheques, venture capital and factoring, apart from merchant banking, leasing and mutual fund. It is, however felt that we should not aim at something which is not in our competence and that overseas bank offices should be used more as centres for information for exports.

To conclude, while going in for diversification banks should ensure that the relevant activity is broad based so as to make it available to the community at large and not limited to only a privileged few. Moreover, such activities should have socio-economic relevance as per the national development priorities. Since most of the development schemes implemented hitherto have urban orientation, banks will have to consider whether any special schemes should be evolved for the people in rural areas and smaller towns.

A commercial banker must be a catalyst of change in a rapidly progressing society. He must study underlying social changes and the changing technologies relating to the demand for banking services. This will enable him to equip himself to tackle the challenging tasks ahead.

3. ECONOMIC AND MONETARY IMPLICATIONS OF MODERN BANKING OPERATIONS

Financial Intermediation

The financial institutions are now often referred to as "financial intermediaries" which provide a channel through which funds flow between lenders and borrowers. In this sense commercial banks are 'financial intermediaries' for they also borrow from those who are not immediately spending all their current receipts and they lend to those who have intentions of immediate spending on goods beyond the range of their current receipts. Banks lend for many purposes to a wide range of customers and accept funds from a great many sources. Clearly, by taking money from some people and lending it to others, banks play a vital part in a country's economy and in the well-being of the people. It is difficult to imagine a modern economy working without banks. Within the economy, individuals, companies and institutions all rely on efficient banking system.

When we consider the role of banks as financial intermediaries we are obviously concerned with the credit services provided by them to promote economic growth. Commercial banks can influence the economic trends through changes in their lending policies. Banks as financial intermediaries also help in other ways such as risk transformation, maturity transformation and reorganisation of funds.

The Economy and the Banks

Bank credit is a catalyst for bringing about economic development. Without adequate finance, there can be no growth or even the maintenance of a stable output. Bank investments determine not only the pattern but also the pace of a country's development as per the State priorities.

With the initiation of planned economic development in India and the ever growing demand for credit for financing an expanding economy, a high degree of emphasis has been placed on deposit mobilisation by banks as one of the main ways in which resources needed for the development of the economy can be enlarged. The growth of deposits depends upon savings. If institutional facilities to mobilise savings are increased, deposits may increase. Banks with their network of branches throughout the length and breadth of the country together with their wide experience of financial management have played an important role in the mobilisation of savings of the people. Of the three stages of capital formation — creation of savings, mobilisation of savings and acquisition of capital assets — banks can make a definite contribution both in the creation and mobilisation of savings and acquisition of capital assets — banks can make a definite contribution both in the creation and mobilisation of savings. Willingness to save may be influenced by banks to a great extent by extending numerous facilities to the existing customers and offering advice to the prospective customers by appealing to their propensity to save and invest.

Banks as Sources of Loans

The function of banks as sources of loans involves community's interest in the distribution, between different uses, of the resources that can be devoted to adding to the real capital of the nation. When a bank makes an advance, by allowing the customer to overdraw his account, the bank, in effect, exchanges its promise to pay immediately against the customer's promise to pay off the advance later on. The economic importance of this exchange of obligations — the essence of bank lending — is in the creation of readily available purchasing power at the disposal of the borrowers who do the spending that constitutes the total demand for goods and services. Thus, the activities of banks will influence the pressure of total demand.

The extent to which the community's productive resources are employed, and to some extent the prices (wages, etc.) at which they are employed, and the general level of prices of products, are all to a greater or less extent influenced by the pressure of total demand being exerted at any time. Hence the banks' activities, because they have effect on the monetary situation, have much bearing on the broad functioning of the economy, in the sense of the degree to which its productive resources are employed and the behaviour of the price levels. In fact, the 'monetary' influence on the country's economic activity is exercised by a wide range of financial intermediaries though the influence of banks on the level of total demand is over-whelmingly important.

Since the liabilities of the banks are 'money' with which payments are actually made, a failure of the growth of bank liabilities (deposits) to match a growth in the volume of transactions can set up a chain reaction that may eventually check the growth of total demand. Some economists lay heavy stress on this power of the banks, a power resting on their control of deposits, whereby the banks can influence the behaviour of total demand.

Risk Transformation

Those who put their surplus funds in a bank face less risk than in lending direct to a party perhaps not well-known to them. As a bank receives a large number of deposits from many sources and lends to a large number of borrowers, risks are spread widely. Banks specialise in risk assessment, ensuring that where appropriate an advance is properly secured and making sure it is repaid at the proper time, at the maturity date.

Maturity Transformation

Maturity transformation is of value both to borrowers and lenders. Generally speaking, lenders dislike tying up their money for long periods and they are interested in liquidity, the ability to have their money speedily without loss. Borrowers, on the other hand, normally seek funds for a period longer than is usually available from individual lenders. As banks are dealing with large number of depositors and borrowers and have both experience and expertise, they are able to reconcile the differing requirements of borrowers and lenders.

Reorganisation of Funds

Financial intermediaries receive and tend both small and large sums of money. A bank may use a large deposit to make a number of smaller advances — a disaggregation of funds — or funds may be aggregated, a number of deposits being used to make an advance. The process of borrowing and lending is assisted and encouraged by the standardisation of arrangements brought about by banks. A good example is the current or chequeing accounts of banks. The way they operate and the terms on which they are made available to bank customers are well known to the general public and they may be regarded as standard bank products.

Bank Deposits as Money

People use the banks not only as source of loans but also for the purpose of making payments. Banks are institutions whose debts — usually referred to as 'bank deposits' — are commonly accepted in final settlement of other people's debts. Demand deposits of a bank can be drawn upon by cheques without notice, without previous permission and without any loss or penalty. The transfer of bank deposits by cheque, credit transfer or standing order, etc., is one of the most important methods of debt settlement. The cheque itself is merely the instrument by which the bank is given instructions and cannot be described as money because it lacks general acceptability. But the bank deposit that can be transferred does serve as money, 'money' being the word we apply to anything ordinarily used in settlement of debts.

The general acceptability of bank deposits as a means of payment depends on complete confidence in the ability of the bank to exchange its own promise (the deposits) for other means of payment (directly or indirectly cash) on demand. To retain its customers, a bank must so conduct its business as to maintain liquidity. In practical banking, liquidity means capacity to produce cash on demand in exchange for deposits.

Bank deposits are not legal tender. Legal tender status is, as the words imply conferred by the law of the country, its substantial meaning is that a creditor to whom legal tender has been offered suffers certain restrictions if he refuses to accept the payment and thereafter seeks by legal process to enforce payment. So long as there is general confidence in the ability of a bank to convert its deposits into legal tender money, its deposits will be just as acceptable in settlement of debts as legal tender. Indeed, the great convenience and security of bank deposits may make them more acceptable for a wide range of transactions. Whether an instrument is a legal tender or not is, thus, of no importance from economic point of view, and it is the actual practice of people in the ordinary business of life that effectively determines what is and what is not money in the economic sense.

Bank as Administrators of Payment Mechanism

In developing countries like India where banking habits are not well developed, the system of payments by cheques is rather restricted and people demand for cash high. a factor which is generally responsible for this state of affairs in developing countries is the lack of facilities on an adequate scale as regards clearing arrangements and remittances which discourage people from taking to banks as payment mechanism at all levels of transaction. Needless to say that an efficient system of bank clearing and remittances is a must for sound banking in these countries.

Banks have developed the clearing system for exchange and settlement of cheques drawn on each other by making transfer entries in their accounts with the central bank. Much of the labour and inconvenience is done away with that is experienced in the individual system of clearance and settlement when the central bank enters into the picture. In India, this function is performed by the Reserve Bank of India and at places where the RBI is not established, the State Bank of India or any other public sector bank acts as agent of the RBI for this purpose.

The process of effecting settlement between the banks on the books of the central bank is not only comparatively simple but is also of utmost importance to the banking community. It is of considerable significance in economising the use of money in banking operations, more particularly when the central bank has branches or agents in different parts of the country and uses its branches and agents for local settlements. The clearing system is also a means of testing at any time the degree of liquidity which the community is maintaining — a matter which is essential for the central bank to know from day to day.

Though the number of clearing houses functioning in the country has progressively increased, there is still a large number of banked places which do not have clearing house facilities. It is obvious that with the growth of banking habit and banking facilities as well as the economic development of the country, cheque clearance will increase in the coming years. There is, thus, a need for a wider network of clearing houses throughout the country as also for simplification of clearing house procedures to avoid undue delay in the collection of local cheques by banks. The MICR (Magnetic Ink Character Recognition) cheque system introduced recently in the four metropolitan cities, viz., Bombay, Calcutta, Delhi and Madras, is a wise step in this direction and in promoting manifold growth of banking operations. It is reported that the clearing system is being revamped by the RBI through the use of electronic transfer of funds (Source Hindustan Times dated 21.11.1988).

Several banks have introduced teller system and mechanised accounting system at their selected branches to encourage use of cheques in the payment system. However, the process of bringing about such changes in the payment system covering a large country like India will have to be necessarily gradual and rather slow.

As regards collection of cheques and bills, the most frequent complaint against banks relates to the delay in collecting them and prompt return thereof in case of non-payment. In order to avoid inconvenience to customers, and as a measure of self-discipline, the Reserve Bank of India directed the banks in 1986 to extend the facility of automatic credit for outstation cheques of Rs. 2,500 or less and to credit interest at saving bank rate in case collection of outstation cheques is delayed beyond 14 days for cheques drawn on branches of the same bank and beyond 21 days for cheques drawn on the branches of other banks. Later on, the Reserve Bank of India gave revised instructions to the banks that they should give immediate credit for both local and outstation cheques up to Rs. 2,500. The RBI has now reiterated its aforesaid instructions as a large number of bank customers are not getting this facility despite specific instructions from the RBI (Hindustan Times, dated December 19, 1988).

The instruments for transfer of funds through banks are mainly drafts, mail transfers, telegraphic transfers and traveller's cheques of which drafts are by far the most important. At times, delays are caused in mail transfers due to negligence in preparing correctly and despatching promptly the relative transfer documents, while delays in respect of telegraphic transfers are caused by incorrect computation of check signals or mutilation of messages in course of transmission. The remedy in these cases lies in toning up the general administration and assigning priorities for different types of work.

The Process of Money Creation

As the demand deposits of banks are regarded as money, commercial banks 'create' money and are able to increase the money supply by creating new deposits on purchasing securities or lending to customers. Generally speaking, the commercial banking system as a whole can create deposits many times the initial cash reserve under which a bank keeps a certain portion of the deposits in reserves as cash and the remaining is lent out. The banks are able to add to the money supply (or create credit) and erect a pyramid of credit on a given cash base.

An Illustration

A simplified example will illustrate the process by which multiple credit expansion by commercial banks takes place. Let there be banks B1 and B2. It is assumed that these banks are under statutory obligation to maintain cash reserve of 10 per cent. Suppose an individual (X) deposits Rs. 100 in his bank B2. Given a cash reserve ratio of 10 per cent, the bank B1 has now an excess cash of Rs. 90 which it lends to another person (Y) to earn profit. It Y decides to pay Rs. 90 to any person (Z) who is a client of B2, then the bank deposit of B2 will rise by Rs. 90 when B2 receives Rs. 90 in cash. Given the 10 per cent cash deposit ratio, the bank now has Rs. 81 which it is in a position to lend to creditworthy borrowers. If these loans are lent to the clients of B1, then the deposit of B1 will rise by Rs. 81. After the cash transfer of Rs. 81 to B1, this bank will now be holding Rs. 72.90 (i.e., 90 per cent of Rs. 81) as excess cash which could be lent again and the whole process will be repeated. The total deposit creation will be given by the initial deposit of cash, i.e., Rs. 100 x 10 = Rs. 1,000.

In practice, this process of deposit and money creation is continuous, since every day banks are lending money to their customers. Also every day, the opposite is happening and some deposits are being destroyed.

Limitation of the Power to Create Credit

The power of the banks to create is not, however, unlimited and a number of factors limit the banks' money creating activities. It should be noted that an individual commercial bank can expand its loans and deposits only by the amount of excess cash reserve which is only a portion of the addition caused in its statutory reserves. The larger the excess cash reserves, the greater shall be the power of the banking system to create deposits through loans and advances. For the banking system as a whole, all the banks taken together expand credit by a multiple of addition to their reserves. Closely associated with this is the amount of capital of banks, for clearly a bank cannot increase its lending and size of its other assets if it has an inadequate capital base. To do so might be unsafe and would undermine people's confidence in the bank.

In practice, the power of banks to create credit is circumscribed by certain other well-known limits. Clearly, a bank can only increase its lending if there are people willing to borrow from the bank at the rates of interest and on the conditions the bank is prepared to offer. Prospective borrowers must have acceptable reasons for requiring finance and must meet the lending criteria established by the bank. Very often, banks are constrained in their lending activities by action of the central bank forming part of the monetary policy of the country.

4. PRESENT CONCEPT OF SOCIAL RESPONSIBILITY OF BANKS

The major objective of bank nationalisation in 1969 was to make banks more responsive to the needs of national development in pursuance of plan objectives of amelioration of poverty and modernisation of agriculture and small industries, and to the aspiration of the common man. Visualising the role of banks as a potent force in bringing about a socio-economic transformation in the country, the then Prime Minister, Mrs. Indira Gandhi, observed, "An institution such as the banking system that touches and should touch the lives of millions has necessarily to be inspired by a larger social purpose and has to subserve the national priorities and objectives." In consonance with this policy, the banking industry embarked upon the new phase of social banking, requiring reorientation of credit policy.

The term 'social banking' refers to the policy induced bank assistance to the designated priority sectors of the economy and weaker sections of the community. The major thrust on social functions of commercial banks has been to achieve more productive use of bank credit through: (i) a large credit flow to sectors of social and economic priorities; and (ii) special assistance within the priority sectors to the weaker sections of society at concessional rates of interest. Banking has, thus, emerged as an effective instrument and catalytic agent of socio-economic change through its integration with the process of economic planning.

The hitherto neglected sectors of the economy were brought within the ambit of commercial banking and declared as priority sectors for bank lending. The concept of "priority sector" is mainly intended to ensure that the assistance from the banking system flows in an increasing measure to those sectors of the economy which though contributing significant proportion of national product, have not received adequate support of institutional finance in the past.

The priority sector covers agriculture, small-scale and cottage industries, road and water transport operators, retail trade and small business and consumption loans. The 'weaker' sections of society within the priority sector consist of:

(i) Small and marginal farmers, tenant farmers, sharecropper and agricultural labourers in the agricultural sector;
(ii) Artisans, village and cottage industries with credit limit up to Rs. 25,000;
(iii) Scheduled Castes and Scheduled Tribes; and
(iv) Beneficiaries of poverty alleviation programmes, viz., Integrated Rural Development Programme and Differential Rates of Interest Scheme.

The prime requisite for diversifying the credit deployment for banks in a big country like ours with a vast population, was to have the dispersal of bank officer over a wide geographical area, especially in the rural hinterland where banks had hardly made their presence felt. There was also the imperative need for rectifying the inter regional disparities in the spread of banking facilities in the country. Banking services have been extended to a wider area and new branches have been opened in rural areas and unbanked centres, especially to enlarge the flow of commercial bank credit to agriculture, small industry and small borrowers

The philosophy and techniques in the sphere of bank lending have also changed to suit the needs of the priority sectors and weaker sections. Credit assistance is being provided to them on concessional interest rates without insisting on the usual security norms. Purpose and project are today the guiding factors in providing bank credit, and not capital and collateral as it used to be. Emphasis on bank lending is on disbursing credit based on the appraisal of the genuine productive requirements of the borrowers and the relevance of the project in the context of socio-economic growth. Repayment capacity of the borrower is judged on the basis of incremental income generated with the help of bank finance.

The banks are being urged to improve their skills for appraisal of schemes. Monitoring of post-disbursal of loans, recovery, etc. Banks have initiated measures to generate a proper climate within the organisation for social responsiveness and participation to bring about social orientation on the part of bank employees in operating situations. The investment of banks in priority sector lending has grown considerably since the early seventies and banks have embarked on the voyage of rural development in a big way.

Programmes of Social Lending

Because of the importance of agriculture in Indian economy, economic development of the country is synonymous with agricultural development and economic uplift of the underprivileged and weaker sections of society. In order to direct a larger flow of institutional credit for agricultural and rural development and to the weaker sections, a multi-agency approach has been adopted wherein the cooperatives and commercial and regional rural banks simultaneously service the agricultural and rural credit system. In recent years, the Government and the Reserve Bank have sponsored various schemes and taken a number of steps to help commercial banks to expand their activities to ensure increased flow of credit to agricultural and rural development in general and to the weaker sections in particular. The implication of such a policy is clearly to eradicate poverty particularly in rural areas and pull up the vast masses of the people, who are below the poverty line, above the level of subsistence by providing them gainful employment through a host of economic activities.

(1) Social Lending Targets and Sub-Targets

In order to channelise bank finance increasingly to priority sectors and weaker sections, the public sector banks are expected to achieve stipulated targets and sub targets connected with it which have been undergoing changes in response to the emerging needs of the economy. The existing stipulations prescribed by the Reserve Bank of India and the Government of India and achievements of the banks in meeting them are given below:

(a) Priority Sectors:

The advances to priority sectors should reach a level of at least 40 per cent of total credit by March, 1985 Banks are also expected to ensure that on an incremental basis 40 per cent of the total credit was extended to the priority sectors (This target has since been achieved by several banks individually and by the banking system as a whole. The share of priority sector advances in the net credit of public sector banks stood at 44.0 per cent at the end of March, 1987).

(b) 20-Point Programme:

Within the overall target fixed for priority sector advances, a significant proportion should be allocated to the beneficiaries of the 20-Point Programme. (More than 34 per cent of total priority sector advances of public sector banks were provided to the beneficiaries of this programme at the end of March, 1987).

(c) Direct Agricultural Advances:

Direct advances to agriculture should reach a level of at least 15 per cent of total credit by March, 1985, 16 per cent by March, 1987 and 17 per cent by March, 1989. (Public sector banks' direct agricultural advances formed 16.2 per cent of their total advances at the end of March, 1987).

(d) Weaker Sections:

The advances to the designated "Weaker Sections" in the priority sector should reach a level of at least 25 per cent of total priority sector advances or 10 per cent of total advances. (The advances granted by public sector banks to the weaker section constituted 11 per cent of their total advances at the end of March, 1987).

(e) Credit-Deposit Ratio in Rural and Semi-Urban Branches:

The credit-deposit ratio of the banks at their rural and semi-urban branches separately should not be less than 60 per cent to emphasis local deployment of deposits and to allay apprehensions that rural branches might become the conduit for the flow of resources from the rural to the urban areas. The banks have been asked to ensure that wide disparity in the ratios between different States/regions is avoided in order to minimise regional imbalances in credit deployment. (While this ratio was exceeded in the case of rural offices, the ratio at the end of June, 1985, being 65.6 per cent, the performance of semi-urban branches with a ratio of 52.8 per cent fell considerably short of the target).

(f) **Differential Rate of Interest (DRI) Advances:**

The banks should attain the ratio of DRI advances to total advances (at the end of previous year) of at least 1 per cent on an ongoing basis. The other stipulations for credit under this scheme are:

(i) 66.7 per cent of DRI advances should be routed through rural and semi-urban branches;

(ii) The share of Scheduled Castes and Scheduled Tribes in the total DRI advances should be at least 40 per cent; and

(iii) The share of women beneficiaries should not be less than 30 per cent.

(The target of 1 per cent was over fulfilled and the ratio stood at 1.15 per cent at the end of June, 1985).

(g) **Advances under IRDP:**

The banks should lend at least 30 per cent of their IRDP advances to Scheduled Castes and Scheduled Tribes.

The trend in credit portfolio of banks so far indicates that the banks are making concerted efforts to meet the prescribed targets. The target in respect of small-scale industries (i.e., 12.5 per cent of total advances) has already been surpassed.

(2) Differential Rate of Interest (DRI) Scheme

This scheme is in operation since 1972 as a part of priority sector lending and is specifically oriented to the weaker sections. Loans being given by the banks under the scheme are meant to cater to the requirements of the 'weakest' among the weak so as to extricate them from the morass of abject poverty. Those with annual family income not exceeding Rs. 2,000 per annum in rural areas and Rs. 3,000 per annum in urban or semi-urban areas are eligible for loans for starting any income generating viable project. (With effect from September 1986, these limits have been raised to Rs. 6,400 and Rs. 7,200 respectively). The maximum quantum of loan has been laid down under the scheme. Each commercial bank has been required to lend 1 per cent of net bank credit under the scheme at a highly concessional rate of interest of 4 per cent per annum on an ongoing basis. To facilitate the flow of funds to Scheduled Tribes banks are advised to use the medium of cooperatives, including LAMPS, organised specially for the benefit of the tribal population. The major problem faced by banks in administering this scheme relates to proper identification of beneficiaries from among a vast number of eligible borrowers so that the weakest among the borrowers benefit from the scheme.

(3) Integrated Rural Development Programme

This is a major programme of poverty alleviation in the rural areas. The programme was formulated by merging some of the existing schemes like SFDA, MFAL, etc., to make it more effective and was started during the Sixth Five Year Plan. The programme aimed at helping poor families living below poverty line, why institutional credit and government subsidy to enable them to acquire productive assets which would generate additional income for the family and leave which would be above the poverty line. The poverty line which was fixed at an annual family income of Rs. 3,500 has been raised to Rs. 6,400. However, for identification of the family, a lower cut-off point has been fixed at an annual income level of Rs. 4,800.

In July 1986, the RBI has increased the exemption limit for the requirement of collateral security or margin for loan from the existing limit of Rs. 5,000 to Rs. 10,000 in respect of IRDP beneficiaries. Upto this amount, the IRDP beneficiaries will not have to provide any collateral security and margin. Normally, subsidy would be equal to 25 per cent of the outlay and it would increase to 50 per cent for Scheduled Tribe beneficiaries and the ceiling on subsidy amount per family would be Rs. 3,000 for small farmers, marginal farmers, agricultural labourers, etc., Rs. 4,000 in Drought Prone Area Programme areas, and Rs. 5,000 for Scheduled Tribes. The secondary and tertiary sectors of the economy — industry, service and business — have been accorded the highest priority for the benefit of the rural poor who do not have any land for subsistence. The commercial banks, regional rural banks and cooperative banks are participating in the scheme.

During the Sixth Plan period, 15 million poor rural family were sought to be helped under the programme with an institutional credit of Rs. 3,000 crores. The identification of eligible borrower was to be done by a specially constituted District Rural Development Agency. The actual achievements in terms of families assists, and disbursement of credit and subsidy were a little more than the relative targets.

The strategy for IRDP during the Seventh Plan period was to consolidate the gains made during the Sixth Plan and help the beneficiaries who have not been able to cross the poverty line, by giving them a second dose of assistance. The old and new beneficiaries to be assisted would be around 20 million. The outlay has been fixed at Rs. 18,890 million of subsidy and about Rs. 40,000 million of institutional credit.

(4) Scheme for Self-Employment for Educated Unemployed Youth (SEEUY)

The Government of India in consultation with the Reserve Bank launched in September, 1983 a scheme for educated (matriculates and above) unemployed youth (age group 18-35 years) to undertake self-emplcyment ventures in industry, services and business in areas with a population of less than 10 lakhs. The idea was to give a major thrust in extending credit to unemployed youth to assist them in setting up any gainful activity. The criteria for identifying the borrowers under the scheme has been amended from time to time and the scheme has also been extended to 1990. Thus, it has now been made coterminus with the Seventh Five Year Plan.

In July 1986, the loan limit of Rs. 25,000 has been raised to Rs. 35,000 at a concessional rate of 10 per cent in backward areas and 12 per cent in other areas, and subsidy to the extent of 25 per cent is given by the Government of India. No margin money is required. The selection of the beneficiaries was to be done by a task force of the District Industries Centre. The family income of the proposed borrower shall not exceed Rs. 10,000 per annum. The ceiling limits for loan assistance to SSI units, Services enterprises and business shall be Rs. 35,000, Rs. 25,000 and Rs. 15,000 respectively, Loan is to be repaid in 3 to 7 years depending upon the income generating capacity of the activity.

(5) Self-Employment for Urban Poor (SEUP)

This scheme, launched by the Central Government on September 1, 1986, envisages providing self-employment to the urban poor living in metropolitan/urban cities and towns with a population exceeding 10,000 as per 1981 census. The objective of the programme is to enable eligible families living below subsistence level to undertake self-employment ventures with the help of subsidy and bank credit.

Urban the scheme, an urban wage earner, with an income of upto Rs. 600 per month and who is holding a ration card and has not obtained a bank loan before, would be eligible for a loan upto Rs. 5,000 without any margin and third party guarantee. The assets created by the loan like a rickshaw or equipment or even the trading stock would be the only security. Some 33 different types of employment like rickshaw pulling, shoe repair and carpentry have been identified for the scheme. The repayment would be in 33 equal monthly instalments after a grace period of 3 months.

The scheme is to be implemented by the selected branches of the public sector banks and they will select the beneficiaries at the rate of one for every 500 eligible persons in the locality per year. There would be a committee of bankers at each centre to supervise the operation and monitor the progress. The scheme would be applicable to all towns and cities not covered by the IRDP. The Central Government would provide capital subsidy of 25 per cent to the banks.

(6) The Revised 20-Point Programme

The restructured Programme presented to Parliament on August 20, 1986, lays special stress on removal of poverty, creation of employment opportunities, reduction of income disparities, raising productivity, ensuring equality for women and providing new opportunities for the youth. It renews the Government commitment to wage war on poverty as its first priority, remove economic disparities and ensure social justice. The emphasis continues clearly on rural development and poverty alleviation. Like the two earlier programmes of 1975 and 1982, banks are expected to contribute their might to the successful implementation of those items of the Programme which relate to them. Already banks have a number of schemes under priority sector for financing agriculture and allied activities, small business, retail trade, transport, etc., which can be extended to 20-point programme beneficiaries.

(7) The Deposit Insurance and Credit Guarantee Corporation Limited (DICGC)

As part of the credit policy to promote extension of small loans to borrowers of small means in the priority and other neglected sectors, the Reserve Bank of India promoted under the Companies Act, 1956, a new public limited company known as Credit Guarantee Corporation of India (CGCI) on January 14, 1971. In pursuance of its objective, the CGCI provided guarantee cover in respect of lending by commercial banks to the designated priority sectors and weaker sections of society. Earlier in July, 1960, the Government of India introduced, in consultation with the Reserve Bank of India, the Credit Guarantee Scheme to provide a measure of protection to commercial banks and certain other financial institutions against possible losses in respect of advances granted by them to small-scale industries. This scheme was administered by the Reserve Bank of India, designated as 'Credit Guarantee Organisation" (CGO), acting on behalf of the Government of India. The CGCI and CGO formed the much needed innovative institutional support for encouraging the banking system to provide credit assistance to the weaker sections and went a long way in creating salubrious atmosphere for increasing lending to priority sectors.

Subsequently in July 1978, the CGCI and CGO were merged with the Deposit Insurance Corporation of India established in 1962 for providing insurance cover on bank deposits, and converted into Deposit Insurance and Credit Guarantee Corporation Ltd. (DICGC). The DICGC is a subsidiary of the Reserve Bank of India and provides guarantee cover in respect of credit facilities extended by banks to certain specified categories of borrowers and also insures deposits (upto a given amount kept with eligible institutions).

The poor recovery of advances to priority sectors in some parts of the country has put substantial pressure on the DICGC and the claims by the banks over the years have been mounting. At the same time, since priority sector lending has become a way of life with the banking system, the advisability of continuing the guarantee support was in doubt. The RBI, therefore, set up a committee to go into the working of the DICGC and advise on its continuation. The report of the committee is under the consideration of the RBI and revised guidelines have been issued.

Concluding Remarks

To sum up, the functions and responsibilities of banks have undergone a sea-change in the post-nationalisation period with the commercial character of banking steadily yielding place to social and developmental orientation of banks. This is reflected in the shift from class banking to mass banking, from profit motive to welfare motive, from security orientation to purpose orientation in bank lending and from elitist urban bias to massive rural banking. Banks have emerged as active agents of socio-economic change and are being involved in a big way in development of the nation and in the process of achieving the social objective of reaching the fruits of progress to the smallest of small man in society. Their performance in dis-charging their social obligation and banking responsibilities has been creditable though it has touched the fringe of the problem of the weaker sections. What is required is an analysis of how far the loans given to the weaker sections contributed to generating a steady sustained income for them.

It has been increasingly realised that credit is only one of the inputs and the non-credit inputs, e.g., supply of seeds, fertilisers, market support to agriculture, are equally important. It is also being increasingly appreciated that it is basically the responsibility of non-credit institutions to create conditions conducive to the flow of credit to rural development, especially the weaker sections. Various agencies have been set up to look after these aspects in a coordinated manner. District Rural Development Agencies (for identifying the beneficiaries under IRDP) and District Industries Centres (for assisting small-scale industries) have been set up by the Government. The Reserve Bank of India has been taking necessary measures to ensure the greater flow of institutional credit for rural sector and improve the credit delivery system for the greater benefit of the weaker sections. The banking system and Government agencies are being adequately geared to play their part to meet the challenge with alacrity to take the country forward and transform it from a developing to a developed country.

CHAPTER

4

Banker and Customer

DEFINITION OF A CUSTOMER

According to Dr. D.L. Wast, "a customer is one who has an account with a banker or for whom a banker habitually undertakes to act as such." According to Lord Davey, "a customer is a person who has some sort of account, either deposit or current or some similar relation with the banker. "

According to Sir John Paget, "To constitute a customer there must be some recognisable course or habit or dealing in the nature of regular banking business." This means the customer should have dealing with the bank for fairly good period. An isolated transaction or even a series of transactions, not associated with banking is not sufficient. This is what is called as 'duration theory'.

The duration theory has, however, been discarded. According to Bailhache, J.[1] the relationship of banker and customer began as soon as the first cheque was handed over to the banker for collection and not when it was paid. In the case of *Commissioner of Taxation v. English, Scottish and Australian Bank Ltd.* 1920[2], their lordship pointed out that a person whose money has been accepted by a bank on the understanding that it undertakes to honour cheques up to the amount to his credit is, whether his connection with the bank is of short or long standing, a customer of the bank as per the statute.

Thus, if a person has a bank account and the banker undertakes to provide him the facilities as a banker, he is a customer. It is not necessary that the account must have been operated for quite some time. But what is important is that his dealings with the banker must be relating to the business of banking; because a banker performs a number of agency functions and renders services to general public, e.g., a person encashing a cheque received by him, will not become a customer. Similarly a person depositing valuable in the lockers, or depositing money to the credit of some individual or institution does not become a customer on account of these activities. These dealings are of casual nature. Thus the essentials of constituting a person as a customer of a bank are:

(i) He has an account with the bank whether savings, current or fixed deposit; and

(ii) His dealings with the bank must be of a nature of banking business.

A customer need not be a natural person. A firm, a society, a company can be a customer.

RELATIONSHIP BETWEEN BANKER AND CUSTOMER

(I) Primary Relationship

Relationship as Debtor and Creditor:

As soon as the customer hands over his money to the banker for safe custody he enters into a contractual relationship with the bank. The customer becomes its creditor and the banker his debtor. Both agree to abide by the rules and regulations, prevalent at the time. However, the relationship is reversed when the customer overdraws on his account. The moment he overdraws he becomes the debtor and the banker his creditor. When the banker advances loan on some security or allows the overdraft on security the banker becomes the secured creditor. But this privilege is never enjoyed by the customer who in all circumstances remains an ordinary creditor, that is to say, an unsecured creditor since he, in no circumstances, can secure any security from the bank on his deposits. In case of his deposits only a contractual guarantee is there that his money will remain in bank's safe custody and on demand it will be paid back.

The customer, after January, 1962, has become an insured creditor upto a certain limit of deposits. The Deposit Insurance Scheme covers the depositors' risk with the bank upto Rs. 30,000.

Lord Cottenham in *Foley v. Hill*, 1848 observed, "Money, when paid into a bank, ceases altogether to be the money of the principal; it is then the money of the banker who is bound to return an equivalent by paying a similar sum to that deposited with him when he is asked for it. The money paid into the banker's coffer is known to the principal to be placed there for the purpose of being under the control of the banker; it is then the banker's money; he is known to deal with it as his own; he makes what profit he can, which profit he retains to himself, paying back only the principal, according to the custom of bankers in some places ... That being established to be the relative situations of banker and customer, the banker is not an agent or factor, but he is a debtor."

But this is not the relationship of ordinary debtor and creditor. This special relationship requires the following conditions or special terms to be fulfilled.

(i) Demand by Customer is necessary

The general principle is that a request by the creditor is not necessary for the repayment of the debt. In case of a bank deposit, the depositor (creditor) is required to demand his deposit back then only the banker would refund the deposit.

The banker is under no obligation to return the deposit to the depositor, without demand. Lord Justice Atkins observed in *Joachimson v. Swiss Bank Corporation* (1971) case that "the relationship between banker and customer is that of a debtor and creditor but one of the implied contracts is that money lent to the banker is not payable except on demand". Demand of deposit by the customer is, therefore, a necessary but implied (not explicit) clause in this contractual relationship.

If he returns the deposited money on his own accord by closing the account, this may lead to dishonour of cheques issued by the customer and thereby damage letter's reputation. Hence, a deposit by a customer with a bank is different from an ordinary debt.

(ii) Proper Time and Place

The depositor should demand back his money at a proper time and place. Proper time means the specified working hours of the bank. By proper place we mean the branch of the bank where the account is opened. In *Jyothi Prasad Singh Deo Bhadur v. Chola Nagpur Banking Association*, it was observed that a bank is bound to pay the cheques of a customer at that branch only, at which he keeps his account. Though branches are agencies of one principal, they may be regarded as distinct for special purposes, for example that of entitling a banker to refuse payment of a customer's cheque except at the branch where he keeps his account. If a cheque drawn on one branch of a bank is cashed by its another branch, the latter does it, not as the banker of the drawer but on the credit of the person presenting the cheque, and can hold him liable in case the bank is put to any loss.

(iii) Demand must be made in proper manner

Sec. 5(b) of the Banking Regulation Act states that deposits can be withdrawn by cheques, drafts, orders or otherwise. The identity of the depositor must be disclosed and authenticated to the satisfaction of the banker. Demand should be made as per the common usage and it cannot be made verbally or through a telephonic message.

(II) Subsidiary Relationship

(1) Banker as Trustee:

Bank is a trustee not for the money deposited but for securities and valuables deposited for safe custody. A trustee is a person who keeps other's property for the latter's benefit and does not put them into his own use. Profits accruing from those properties belong to the beneficiary and not to the trustee. It is on these grounds a banker is not the trustee of the money deposited with him because he has a right to use it and pocket the profit made out of its use. He is not liable to return the identical notes deposited. It is for securities, valuables etc. that the banker acts as trustee. However, the line of demarcation is thin, e.g., for cheques sent for collection from another bank, the banker acts as a trustee till these are realised and credited to the customer's account. Thereafter he will become the debtor. If the bank purchases some securities from the money in the account of the customer, after the purchase of securities he becomes a trustee for the money which is now in the form of securities.

According to the Supreme Court[3], when a person delivers money to a bank, it is generally presumed that the relationship of debtor and creditor has arisen. But the presumption can be rebutted. In the following cases such presumption is rebutted and the banker is supposed to act as trustee:

(i) When a customer pays money to the banker with the special instruction to retain the same till further instructions or to pay over the same to another person who has no account with the bank; and the bank accepts the instructions or

(ii) A customer may order the bank to use the deposited money as per his (customer's) directions and the profit so earned will be credited to his (customer's) account.

(2) Banker as Agent:

When a banker buys or sells securities on behalf of his customer, he performs an agency function. Similarly when he collects cheques, bills, interest, dividends etc. or when he pays insurance premium out of customer's account as per customer's mandate, he acts as his agent.

OBLIGATIONS OF A BANKER

Though primarily the banker is a debtor but the special nature of relationship imposes certain obligations on banker. They are as follows:

1. OBLIGATION TO HONOUR THE CHEQUES OF HIS CUSTOMER

According to Mr. Jones, "The banker's primary contract is to repay money received for his customer's account usually by honouring his cheques." According to Section 31 of the Negotiable Instruments Act, 1881, the drawee bank, if having sufficient money in the customer's account, must honour the cheques when duly required to do so. If it does not pay on those cheques it will be liable to compensate the customer for any loss or damage caused by such default. Usually the rule of damage is 'higher the amount of cheque, lower the damages, lower the amount of cheque, higher are the damages.' The following are the essential conditions of this obligation:

(i) Sufficient funds:

It means funds in the credit of the customer's account are at least equal to the amount of cheque and the funds should be applicable to the payment of such cheque, e.g., where a cheque is drawn on a current account which is not having sufficient funds but the customer is having a saving account also the banker is entitled to dishonour the cheque because the funds of savings bank are not applicable to the cheques drawn on current account.

(ii) The Banker must be duly required to pay:

This means that the cheque must be in order i.e. complete in respect to the date, amount, payee's name, duly signed by the customer. It should have been presented within the time limit, i.e., within six months of the date specified on the cheque. It should not be post-dated. It should be in proper form.

Consequence of Dishonour

Dishonour of a cheque hurts a customer socially. He loses his goodwill though he may not suffer any monetary loss directly. It affects his future trading relations with the trading community. Therefore, in such cases the law grants damages by way of penalty which is contrary to the normal rule of damages (i.e. compensation for the monetary loss suffered). In this case the usual rule of damages is 'lower the amount of cheque higher are the damages.'

Exceptions:

There are certain exceptions to this obligation, i.e., in certain cases Bank has the right to dishonour or he may dishonour the customer's cheques and in others he has the obligation to dishonour and must dishonour the customer's cheques.

2. OBLIGATION TO MAINTAIN SECRECY OF ACCOUNTS OF HIS CUSTOMER

Another important obligation of the banker is to keep the secrecy of his customer's account. In the case of *Tournier v. National Provincial Bank*, Lord Justice Atkin observed that "one of the implied terms of the contract is that the bankers enter into a qualified obligation with their customer to abstain from disclosing information as to his affairs without his consent".[4]

In this case, Tournier was the customer with an overdraft of £9 8s 9d. He had promised to clear off this overdraft in installments of £1 a week. He ceased to pay after three installments. He was in the meantime on a 3-month employment contract in a company. The banker contacted the customer's employer to enquire his private address. During the conversation, banker disclosed Tournier's account and as a result Tournier's service agreement was not renewed. Held, banker was wrong in disclosing the particulars of the customer's account.

This obligation is so important that even after the nationalisation of banks in India, this clause has been retained in the Banking Companies (Acquisition and Transfer of Undertakings) Act, 1970. According to Sir John Paget, duty of secrecy continues even after the customer's death whether the account is in credit or overdrawn.

Exceptions:

In the following circumstances, this obligation is not adhered to.

(A) Legal Compulsions

The banker has to be governed by the law of the land. He may be required by other laws of the country to reveal the contents of his customer's account. Some of such laws are as follows:

(i) Income Tax Act, 1961

Under Section 133 of the Act, the banker may be asked to reveal the information.

(ii) Companies Act, 1956

Under Sections 240 and 251, the banker has to reveal the information to an inspector appointed under Section 235 and/or Section 237.

(iii) Reserve Bank of India Act, 1934

Reserve Bank has a right to obtain information regarding those who have secured loans and advances.

(iv) Banking Regulation Act, 1949

Under Section 26, banker has to submit a report regarding those accounts which are live in the banker's books but have not been operated for the last 10 years.

(v) Gift Tax Act, 1958

Under Section 36, banker may be required to reveal information about a customer's account.

(vi) Criminal Procedure Code, 1973

Section 94(3) empowers the police authorities to inspect a customer's account in banker's books.

(vii) Foreign Exchange Regulation Act, 1973

Those bankers who deal in foreign exchange, their books and other documents may be inspected by the Foreign Exchange Control Deptt. (Section 43).

(B) Others

(i) Practice and usage in banking business:

It is a practice among bankers to elicit information about their own customers, their guarantors, acceptors of bill of exchange, etc. from other bankers.

There is also a usual practice among the businessmen to elicit information about the credit worthiness of their debtors from the bankers. True, the information so received are kept secret by the businessman but the secrecy clause here does not remain binding on the banker in the larger interest of the business community as a whole.

While reporting on the credit worthiness of a party the banker ensures that:

(a) he gives only general statement and not factual one;

(b) he neither exaggerates the financial position in his general statement nor underestimates the same;

(c) he gives the report as an unbiased party and warns that he is reporting on the credit-worthiness of the party according to his own judgement and he will not be responsible for any loss etc. if the party proves otherwise;

(d) he is bound to rely upon the accounts maintained by his customer. He is not supposed to take notice of the opinion which others are having about his customer; and

(e) in no circumstance he has to resort to fraudulent misrepresentation.

(ii) Where customer consents:

A customer may give his willingness to such disclosures, e.g., a customer may ask the banker to disclose the balance of his account to his legal advisor. The willingness may be implied also.

(iii) Where interest of the bank so requires:

E.g. when the banker sues the customer for the recovery of an overdraft, it may disclose the customer's state of account before the court.

(iv) Public Interest:

If the activities of the customer are against the Public Interest, the banker can disclose the details of his account, e.g., there is a smuggler customer. His activities are prejudicial to the national interest.

For unjustified disclosures the banker is liable not only to compensate the customer for the loss suffered by him due to such disclosure but is liable to third party also for the loss suffered by him (third party) because of relying on the disclosed information.

3. OBLIGATION UNDER GARNISHEE ORDER

A Garnishee Order is an order of the court, issued under Order 21 Rule 46 of the Civil Procedure Code, 1908, attaching the funds of a debtor in the hands of his banker. When a debtor fails to pay his debt, his creditor may apply for such an order. After receiving this order banker comes under an obligation not to make any payment form the account concerned and will have to disclose the amount in the account and pay it to the Judgement creditor, the person against whom it is issued is called the judgement debtor and the banker who is asked to comply with it is called Garnishee. Garnishee Order is issued in two parts.

Order Nisi and Order Absolute

First the order of the court directs the banker to stop payment from the account of the judgement debtor and asks the banker to explain as to whom these funds should not be paid to judgement creditor. This order is called Order Nisi. After receiving this order the banker can neither pay any amount to the customer nor honour any of the cheques issued by the customer. He should immediately inform the customer about such an order.

Banker sends his explanation to the 'Order Nisi'. Thereafter if the court does not find any reasonable cause for stopping further proceedings, it may issue the 'Order Absolute' which attaches the entire balance in the account of the customer to the judgement creditor and the banker becomes liable to pay the garnishee funds to the judgement creditor. The effect of this payment is to discharge banker's liability to the customer.

A garnishee order may attach either the whole of the amount in the bank, (whether the debt owed to the judgement creditor is smaller than the amount) or a specified amount only. In the former case, the Bank can dishonour all subsequent cheques. But a cheque already marked as good for payment has to be paid. The order shall not apply to this cheque. But if the banker wants it can pay a part of the amount not exceeding the difference between the total amount in the account and the amount payable to judgement creditor together with the cost of legal proceedings. In the latter case, amount attached by the order is transferred to a Suspense Account (the account is allowed to be operated).

Garnishee Order applies even to the fixed deposit because it is a present debt, though, payable at a future date.

Non-applicability of the Garnishee Order

Garnishee Order is not applicable to the following cases:

(1) To the account of judgement debtor if it is overdrawn.

(2) To cheques, bills etc. deposited with the banker for collection, because banker is not a debtor of the customer for these transactions, he is acting as an agent of a trustee.

(3) To a new account opened by the customer after the garnishee order.

(4) To instructions received from the customer, before the receipt of garnishee order, for payment etc. to some party. Issue of cheques does not amount to such instructions.

(5) To those funds which the customer is holding in trust and the banker has knowledge of it.

(6) To a joint account of the customer.

(7) To the deposits of the customer in a foreign branch of the banker.

4. OBLIGATION OF REPAYMENT OF DEPOSITS (FREE OF LIMITATION)

Limitation Act, 1963 lays down that if a creditor does not claim back debt within a period of 3 years from the date of the payment of the debt to his debtor, he forfeits his right of recovering the debt back. It becomes time barred. But this rule does not apply to a deposit with a banker. The customer can demand back his deposit even after the expiry of three years and the bank is legally bound to honour the withdrawal order. In case of bank deposit, debt does not become due unless demand is made.

RIGHTS OF BANKER

We have already discussed the liabilities of the banker. But without rights, liabilities do not carry weight. In the following paragraphs we shall discuss the rights of the banker. They are as follows:

(1) Right of General Lien
(2) Right of Set-off
(3) Right of Appropriation
(4) Right of charging interest, commission, incidental expenses, charges etc.

(1) Right of General Lien

Lien is the right to retain property belonging to another until debt due from the latter is paid. While the charge like pledge, mortgage or hypothecation arises out of an agreement, right of lien is created by law.

Lien is generally of two types - (i) Particular lien and (ii) General lien. Particular lien can be enforced only for the recovery of labour charges and expenses incurred by the creditor on the goods which are retained under lien. While in general lien the creditor can retain the goods for the recovery of a general balance of account i.e. he can retain the property till all the due are cleared.

While a finder of goods, a Bailee, a Pawnee, an Agent (Indian Contract Act) and an unpaid seller (Indian Sale of Goods Act) have only particular lien, a banker enjoys a general lien. (Section 171 of the Indian Contract Act). Thus, a banker can retain securities etc. belonging to a customer till the customer clears the general balance due by him unless there is an implied contract inconsistent with right of lien.

In the case of *Brando v. Barnett* it was said that 'a banker's lien is more than a general lien; it is an implied pledge'. This means that the banker, in the event of default by the customer may proceed to sell the goods and securities retained. But a reasonable notice of this sale should be given. It continues on those securities also which were pledged for a particular loan and were not taken back by the customer after the repayment of that loan.

Exceptions:

Right of general lien does not apply to the following:

1. **Goods lodged for safe custody:** Because in respect of these articles the banker acts as bailee and a bailee does not have a general lien.
2. **Articles given for specific purpose:** Cheques, bills etc. for collection deposited with the specific instructions that the amount is to be utilised for specific purpose.
3. Money deposited for specific purpose.
4. **Trust Account:** General lien is not applicable to an account opened by the customer as a trustee.
5. Securities left negligently.
6. Securities deposited before the loan is sanctioned.

(2) Right of Set-off

When a customer has more than one account with the banker and one or more of the accounts are overdrawn, the banker has a right to adjust the debit balance in such account/accounts with the other account/accounts. This right is called the right of set-off, e.g., A, a customer has overdrawn his current account by Rs. 5,000 while he has Rs. 8,000 in his savings account. The banker can adjust the debit balance of Rs. 5,000 against the credit balance of Rs. 8,000. The following points should be considered in relation to this set off:

(1) The accounts must belong to the same customer under same rights e.g. if the other account is a trust account, right of set off is not applicable.
(2) The debt must have become due and must be of a certain sum of money. This right cannot be exercised against future debts or contingent debts, e.g., A has guaranteed a loan taken by B. B has not yet refused to pay the loan. The banker cannot set off this loan against A's accounts.
(3) There should not be a contract inconsistent with the right of set off.
(4) All branches of a bank are treated as one and the right of set off can be exercised by one branch over the account in the other branch.
(5) Right of set off can be exercised before the garnishee order becomes applicable, i.e., banker may first exercise the right of set off and the balance may be adjusted against the garnishee order.

(3) Right of Appropriation

(i) Several Accounts:

A banker may open more than one account in the name of his customer and may lend him money in different accounts at different times and on different terms. In such a case, if the customer pays a sum of money, the question arises to which debt this payment should be appropriated. This is called the problem of appropriation. Right of appropriation is governed by the Indian Contract Act (Section 59 to 61 — For details refer to Chapter on 'Performance of Contracts').

(ii) Single Account:

In case a customer has a single account and he deposits and withdraws money out of it, the order in which debit entry will be set off against the credit entry was laid down in the following case.

Clayton's Case[5]

There was a partnership firm carrying on business as bankers. Mr. Clayton has a current account with this firm. This account has a credit balance of £1713 at the time when Devaynes, one of the partners of the firm died, and the surviving partners carried on the business of banking under the same name in spite of the objections by Devaynes' executors against the use of Devaynes' name. After a year the firm became bankrupt and the creditors of the firm filed their claims against the estate of Devaynes, the deceased partner.

Clayton had continued to deal with the firm, making deposits and receiving payments. As a result, his credit balance was reduced from £1713 at the time of Devaynes' death to £453 at the time of bankruptcy. His withdrawals during this period had been more than £1713 but his deposits exceeded the withdrawals. Clayton claimed £453 from the estate of the deceased on the grounds that

(i) the withdrawals from the account after the death of the partner were paid out of the deposits made during the same period and, therefore,

(ii) the credit balance standing at the time of the partner's death was recoverable from the assets of the deceased partner.

His contention was not accepted by the Court in the following words: "This is the case of a banking account where all the sums paid in formed one blended fund, the parts of which have no longer any distinct existence. Presumably, it is the sum first paid in, that is first drawn out. It is the first item on the debit side of the account that is discharged or reduced by the first item on the credit side".

In case of running overdrafts or cash-credit accounts against securities, if 'the Rule in Clayton's Case' is allowed to operate, payments in would have the effect of discharging the secured debt, whereas payments out would constitute unsecured advances.

The 'Rule in Clayton's Case' is applicable only when the account is still running. If the account is broken, and a new distinct account is opened, the rule does not apply to the old account. To avoid the application of the rule, the banker closes the account and seeks customer's written consent to the opening of a new account.

The effect of the rule can be seen from the following example: X, the guarantor dies at the time when the principal debtor Y (i.e., the person whose account he has guaranteed) owes the banker Rs. 5,000. If the account is continued unbroken after the guarantor's death, all payments in will go to reduce the balance of Rs. 5,000 and all payments out will constitute a new debt unsecured by the guarantee. Thus, if Y pays into the unbroken account Rs. 5,000 after the death of X and draws out Rs. 2,000, the effect of the rule will be that the debt covered by the guarantee will be wiped out and will owe the banker Rs. 2,000 and this debt of Rs. 2,000 will be unsecured.

Where the customer is a trustee and his account consists partly of trust money and partly of his own, the customer, when drawing out money for his own use, is deemed to have drawn out his own money first and trust money later on.

But if the trust money paid into his own account belongs to different beneficiaries, then the first money paid in will be the first trust money drawn out e.g., 'X' has a credit balance of Rs. 5,000. He then pays in Rs. 1,000 belonging to another person 'P', then Rs. 2,000 belonging to 'Q' and further Rs. 2,500 belonging to 'R'. He then draws out and misappropriates Rs. 9,000. Of the remaining Rs. 1,500, P and Q would get nothing but R is entitled to the whole of the balance.

(4) Right to charge Interest, Commission etc.

Banker has the implied right to charge interest on the advances made by the banker to the customers. This right includes the right to debit this interest to the account of the customer. Interest due from a customer is also a debt and therefore interest is charged on unpaid interest also called compound rate of charging interest.

Banker is also entitled to charge commission for services rendered either as agent or trustee for collection of cheque, bills etc. The usual practice is to debit the customer's account but the banker must inform the customer about it.

CHAPTER

5

Accounts and Account Holders

TYPES OF ACCOUNTS

One of the primary functions of the banker is to solicit deposits from the customers. Customers deposit money for their own convenience. This convenience differs from one customer to another. Therefore, facilities expected by the customers are of a varied nature. The banks have, therefore, introduced different types of accounts which can be broadly classified into: Demand Deposits and Time Deposits.

(A) DEMAND DEPOSITS

Demand deposits are those deposits which do not require any prior notice for their withdrawal. They can be withdrawn on demand. Hence, they are called Demand deposits. Demand deposits include current accounts and savings accounts.

(1) Current Account

A current account is a running account, i.e., it can be operated upon any number of times during a working day. Banker is liable to honour all demands of the customer to the extent of the credit balance in his current account. Because of this obligation, this account is included in the current liability of the bank and the banker is liable to keep sufficient funds ready all the time to meet this liability.

Current accounts are suitable for big businessmen, joint stock companies, institutions, public authorities, industrialists etc. who enter into numerous transactions on every working day. They get the advantage of keeping their working capital safe and at the same time receiving and making payments with ease and efficiency, without directly involving themselves. For the Current Account holders, the banker provides the facilities of:

(1) collecting properly endorsed cheques, bills etc. which were drawn in favour of third parties.

(2) overdraft, through prior arrangements, for the same are usually made.

(3) granting loans and advances without cash transaction lending process is completed and credit creation is facilitated.

Reserve Bank of India prohibits the payment of interest on current account deposits, except with its prior approval. Banks do not make 'charge' for keeping a current account provided a minimum balance is maintained. This minimum balance compensates the bank for the work involved. Rules of minimum balance may differ from bank to bank.

(2) Savings Account

The object of this account is to mobilise the savings of the people belonging to lower and middle classes. This helps them meet their future needs and also earn an income from their savings. Since these accounts are designed to promote the habit of thrift among people banks usually impose restrictions on the number of withdrawals. In one year, not more than 150 withdrawals are allowed these days. A bank may allow additional withdrawals at its discretion. Withdrawals of less than one rupee or a sum which is not a multiple of one rupee is not permitted except when account is closed. The minimum amount for a cheque is Rs. 5. not less than 5 rupees can be deposited at a time. If cheque facility is granted, a minimum balance of 250 rupees is required to be maintained. If above limits are violated, banks impose a service charge of Rs. 10 per annum on these accounts as per a practice, recently introduced.

The facility of collection of cheques on behalf of the savings accounts holders is usually granted to those customers who have opened their accounts through a proper introduction. Banks do not accept cheques or other instruments payable to a third party and endorsed in favour of the account holder for the purpose of deposit in the savings account.

As per the direction of Reserve Bank the interest is allowed on savings deposit which at present is 6% p.a. Interest is calculated on monthly basis on the minimum balance from the 10th day of the month to the last day of the month. It is calculated on every complete sum of Rs. 10. It may be credited to the customer's account either quarterly or on longer rests.

Opening a Current or Savings Account

Opening an account makes the person a customer of the bank, thereby creating a special relationship between them which imposes several obligations on the banker. Therefore, banker should take adequate precautions regarding the identity of the customer. Following procedure is generally followed:

(i) Prescribed application form

Person who wants to open an account has to fill in a prescribed form which requires information about his name, occupation, full address, specimen signatures, introductory reference. Person opening the account has to sign a declaration that he has read the rules and will follow them and that any amendment to these rules shall also be acceptable to him.

(ii) Introductory Reference

Banker reserves the right not to open the account in the name of the person whose identity has not been established or who is considered as undesirable person, e.g., an anti-social element. Banker wants to be assured of his customer's character, honesty, social standing and goodwill. This information the banker gets from the person who introduces the customer to the banker. The introducer should sign the reference column of the application form only when he knows the applicant. Banker accepts an introducer if the banker knows that person and reposes his faith and confidence in him. Such a person can be an old customer or acquaintance or an employee of the bank or a respectable person of the locality. According to the advice of the Reserve Bank for employees of the government departments, police and armed forces their identity cards or pay books etc. should be considered sufficient for establishing their identity. The person introducing the applicant should be a respectable person commanding goodwill.

Advantage:

Introductory reference provides statutory protection to the banker. According to Section 131 of the Negotiable Instruments Act if the banker collects cheques or bills on behalf of a customer who has no title or his title is defective, the banker will not be liable if it has acted in good faith and without negligence. Obtaining introductory reference proves this good faith etc. Further, it is easy to trace such a person and recover the amount. Moreover, if by oversight an overdraft is granted to the customer the banker does not run the risk of loss if the customer is properly introduced.

If the customer opens only savings account and wants to make only cash transaction, the banker may not ask for introductory reference. To such a customer, no cheque book is issued and no cheques are deposited in his account for collection.

(iii) Specimen signatures

It is the duty of the banker to honour the cheques issued by the customer. If signatures on these cheques are forged the banker is liable. To ensure against the default of honouring forged cheques, banker keeps the specimen signatures of the customer and compares the signatures on the cheque or withdrawal forms with the specimen signature. These signatures are obtained both on the application form and on a card meant for this purpose.

(iv) Depositing money

After the above formalities are fulfilled the customer deposits some cash with the bank by filling the pay-in-slip and the banker opens his account and tells him his account number. Generally, the minimum amount required to be deposited is Rs. 10 for a Savings Account and Rs. 100 for a Current Account. After opening the account, the banker gives the customer (i) A Pay-in-slip Book, (ii) A Cheque Book and (iii) A Pass Book so that the customer can operate his account with ease.

Operating a Current or Savings Account

(i) Pay-in-Slip Book

This book contains a number of Pay-in-slips. Pay-in-slip is a prescribed form, to be filled up at the time when customer wants to deposit cash or cheque in this account with the banker. Information required to be filled up in the Pay-in-slip is the name of the account, account number, amount to be deposited with detailed denomination of currency notes and coins (for cash deposits), cheque number and name of the paying banker. These information are to be filled up both on the main slip as well as on the perforated counterfoil. Banker after having accepted the deposit signs the counterfoil and returns it to the depositor which serves as an acknowledgement of the receipt of the deposit.

(ii) The Cheque Book

This book contains a number of blank cheques. A cheque is a prescribed form of order to be given to the bank to pay a certain sum of money to or to the order of a certain person or to the bearer of the cheque. According to Negotiable Instrument Act, a cheque is a bill of exchange drawn on a specified banker. All cheques are serially numbered. Before issuing a cheque the customer should write the date and sign it, besides writing the name of the person to whom money is payable and the amount. Amount is written both in figure and in words so that no confusion persists about it. In case there is difference between the two, the banker may refuse to pay.

Withdrawal form

In case of Savings Account, cheque book is issued to those customers only who maintain a minimum balance as required by the rules of the banks. No cheque book is issued to customers who open savings accounts without reference to their credit. Other customers have to use the withdrawal form for withdrawing money from their accounts. It is also a prescribed form of requesting the banker to refund a stated sum of his (customer) deposit. This form is available as loose leaf, in bank's office only. Banks usually insist for the presentation of Pass Book along with the withdrawal form. It cannot, usually, be issued in favour of a third person. Hence, it cannot be used as a mode of settling the claim of a creditor. Personal presence during the working hours becomes necessary for withdrawing the money.

(iii) Pass Book

A Pass Book is a small handy book, issued by the banker to the customer's account, in the prescribed form for customer's use. It is called a 'Pass Book' because it passes from the hands of the customer to that of the banker and *vice versa*. Customer deposits the pass book with the banker periodically and the banker makes entries in it as they appear in the customer's account in banking ledger. Thus, 'Pass Book' is a true and certified copy of the customer's account as it appears in the bank's ledger. It helps the customer with a ready record of his bank transaction and helps the businessman in preparing bank reconciliation statement.

Legal Position of Entries in the Pass Book

Since there may be clerical errors in recording transactions in the pass book, the question arises whether a Pass Book is a conclusive evidence of the entries made therein.

Effects of Entries Favouring the Banker

There are divergent opinions on this subject. According to Sir John Paget'a pass book should be considered as a conclusive and unquestionable record of transactions between the customer and the banker and after full opportunity of examination on the part of the customer, all entries at least to his debit, ought to be subsequently final and not to be subsequently reopened, at any rate to the detriment of the banker'. It presumes that the customer is under obligation to verify the entries in the pass book and bring to the notice banker errors, if any.

In several legal judgements this viewpoint has been refuted. Mr. Justice Bray said "How absurd it would be to hold, that the taking out of the pass book and its return constituted a settled account." It is now well established that the customer is not bound to examine the pass book and therefore pass book is not a conclusive evidence of the debit entries therein.

Not with standing the above viewpoint, if the customer acts in a manner that his negligence towards the entries made in the pass book is proved and as a result of this negligence banker is adversely affected customer may not be allowed to dispute the accuracy of his account. It is, however, not clear as to what acts or omissions on the part of customer constitutes negligence. In *Essa Ismail v. Indian Bank Ltd.* in 1963, the Kerala High Court held that if the customer signs the confirmation slip about the accuracy of his account as contained in the pass book he will be bound by the debits made therein.

Effects of entries favouable to customer

If a bank makes wrong credit entries in the account of the customer, without knowing the fact, and intimates to its customer these credit entries and the customer acting upon the intimation of these credit entries, in good faith, alters his position to his prejudice, the bank is estopped from denying the credit entries. Customer cannot be asked to refund this money.

But two conditions are important in this regard. Firstly, that he should act in good faith, i.e., he should have no knowledge that these entries are false. Secondly, there should be no negligence on his part in detecting these false entries. If the customer regularly maintains his accounts' books and regularly receives the pass book or statement in lieu thereof, he will be deemed to be negligent in not detecting these errors. He will be deemed to have constructive notice of those entries and will not get the benefit of those entries.

(B) TIME DEPOSITS

Such deposits can be withdrawn only after the expiry of fixed period of time. Under this category are included Fixed deposits accounts, Recurring deposits accounts and Deposits payable at a specified notice.

(I) Fixed Deposit Accounts

Those persons who have money to invest for a longer period but do not want to take much risk, prefer to deposit their savings with commercial banks for a fixed period[1]. Since in fixed deposits money is payable only on th expiry of fixed period of time only, these deposits are termed at time liabilities of the bank. The rate of interest on fixed deposit is higher than that of Savings Account because the banker need not provide cash reserves for them. Rates of interest and other terms and conditions of fixed deposit are governed by the Reserve Bank of India (Sec. 21, and 35 A of the Banking Regulation Act, 1949). Fixed deposits are now classified into 8 categories on the basis of the period of their maturity, the minimum period being 15 days. Higher the period of deposit, higher is the rate of interest. This induces the investor to invest a larger part of their savings.

Interest is payable at the stipulated rate, only at the maturity of the deposit. However, banks also make arrangements to pay interest quarterly or half yearly also. Legally no interest is payable on overdue fixed deposits, i.e., after the expiry of the fixed period. Banks at their discretion do allow interest thereafter if the fixed deposit is renewed.

Opening the Account

If a person wants to open a fixed deposit account he should fill in the prescribed application form mentioning the amount of deposit and the time of deposit. He also gives his specimen signatures and deposits the money. He is issued a fixed deposit receipt acknowledging the receipt of the money. Date of interest is also mentioned on it. This receipt is not transferable and hence is not a negotiable instrument. But the debt covered by it can be assigned (Sir John Paget). Similar view was held in the case of *R.D. Sethna v. Hemmingway (Bombay).*

If the receipt is lost banker issues a duplicate one on request, after asking him to inform in writing about the loss and filling in a duly stamped letter of indemnity and making a note in the concerned ledger.

Payment before due date

Banks do permit encashment of fixed deposits even before the due date of maturity. But in accordance with the directives of Reserve Bank the rate of interest allowed on such deposits should be at least 1% less than the rate applicable to the deposits of the period for which this deposit was actually held by the bank.

Loans against FDR

The banker may grant a loan to the depositor against a FDR. Reserve Bank requires that interest on such loan shall be at least 2% higher than the interest payable by the banker on such deposit. Loans are generally granted upto 90% of the total fixed deposit. If the fixed deposit is made on joint account, the payment of the deposit on maturity will be received by the joint depositors.

(2) Recurring Deposit Account or Cumulative Deposit Account

This account has been designed to inculcate the habit of savings among people on a regular basis. The depositor has to deposit a certain sum, usually a multiple of Rs. 5 or Rs. 10 in his account every month. This may be done for a selected period of time say 2 years, 3 years etc., ranging from 1 year to 10 years. These accounts carry higher rate of interest than the savings accounts. It is almost equal to that of fixed deposit account. This account can be opened jointly or severally. A guardian can open such an account in the name of a minor. These accounts are transferable from one breach to another without any charge.

Besides the above important accounts banks also permit one or more of the following accounts and schemes to motivate people to save. These are Cash certificates, Recurring deposit schemes, Daily savings schemes, Minor's savings scheme, Monthly interest income schemes, Annuity or retirement schemes, Farmer's deposit schemes, Housing deposit scheme, Premium prize deposit certificates, Student deposit account, Cumulative-cum-sickness benefit deposit account, Non-resident (external) Account, Foreign currency (Non-Resident) Accounts, Annuity deposits, Super-savings package, State bank education plan, Re-investment plan, Credit cards, Gift cheques, Insurance linked savings bank account etc.

Insurance of Bank Deposits

After failure of the Palai Central Bank in 1960, a necessity was felt of protecting the interest of depositors against the failure of the banks. Consequently deposit insurance was introduced from 1 January, 1962 and for the purpose Deposit Insurance Corporation was established by an Act of Parliament on 15 July, 1978. This corporation was re-named as Deposit Insurance and Credit Guarantee Corporation.

Against a premium of 4 paise per annum for every 100 rupees, paid by the banks, it provides the insurance cover, to all deposits with the insured banks, in respect of unpaid balances due to a depositor up to Rs. 30,000 (Originally the limit was Rs. 1500. It was increased to Rs. 5000, then to Rs. 10,000, then to Rs. 20,000). Among the insured banks are all commercial banks scheduled or unscheduled, regional rural banks and cooperative banks. The corporation reimburses the depositor if the latter does not receive back fully his balance due to him on account of the failure of the bank or its amalgamation with another bank.

TYPES OF CUSTOMERS

Certain types of accounts require special care in their opening and operation. Hence, special rules are framed for them. These customers are as follows:

(1) Minor

A person who has not completed 18 years of age is called a minor as per Sec. 3 of the Indian Majority Act. According to this section, if a guardian of his person or property is appointed by the court before a person completes 18th year of his age, he shall attain majority at the age of 21 years. According to Sec. 11 of the Indian Contract Act, a minor is not competent to contract and the money lent to him cannot be recovered even if he falsely misrepresented his age.

No law bars the banker from dealing with a minor. The banker incurs no risk if it permits a minor to open and operate an account so long as it has a credit balance. But following special precautions are necessary:

(i) If an overdraft is allowed by mistake, it would not be recoverable. Therefore, minor's account should be opened in the name of his guardian, such account should be closed after the minor attains majority. Alternatively, the account can be opened in the name of the minor but operated by his guardians. Many banks permit a minor who has attained 12 years of age to operate his account by himself. Legally, there is no bar on the bank to allow a minor to operate his account.

(ii) Pledge of securities by a minor is invalid.

(iii) Advances granted to a minor, even on the guarantee of a third party, will not be recoverable because where the contract between the creditor and the principal debtor is void, guarantee is not enforceable. In practice, therefore the banker should include an indemnity clause making the surety liable as principal debtor.

(iv) According to Sec. 26 of the Indian Negotiable Instruments Act, 1881, a minor can draw, endorse and transfer any negotiable instrument but he himself is not bound by his actions though he can bind third parties by his actions.

(v) According to Sec. 182 of the Indian Contract Act, he can act as an agent of an other person his principal shall be bound by his dealings, to the banker. Thus, minor is not an ordinary customer.

(2) Lunatic

A person of unsound mind is called a lunatic. He is incapable of understanding a contract and of forming a rational judgement as to its effect upon his interest. Banker should not open as account with such a person and if the account is already in operation and the customer becomes insane, banker should stop all payments from his accounts and suspend all transactions till he receives an order from the court.

(3) Married Women

A married woman should not be considered as an agent of her husband for the purpose of granting loans. Banker should carefully evaluate her personal possessions for the purpose. If the loan granted to her is not repaid, the husband cannot be held liable except where:

(i) the loan was taken with his consent and authority.

(ii) the debt is taken for buying the necessities of life, because the husband did not provide the same.

(4) Pardanasheen Woman

There is always a doubt about her identity. Problem of impersonation may arise because she observes purdah. Because of her observing complete seclusion there is a presumption in law that she has been induced by undue influence to enter into a contract. Banker should, therefore, avoid such a woman to become a customer. If an account has to be opened in her name then her signatures should be attested by a responsible person, known to the bank, both at the time of opening the account as well as permitting withdrawals.

(5) Illiterate Persons

For this purpose, an illiterate person is one who cannot sign his name. In place of specimen signatures, his thumb impression serve the purpose. For identification, bank can take a copy of his recent photography duly attested by a first class magistrate.

(6) Insolvents

A banker should not open an account in the name of an undischarged insolvent. Where a customer becomes insolvent after opening an account, banker should not allow him to operate the account as all his properties vest in the official receiver.

(7) Joint Accounts

Joint accounts are those accounts which are opened in the joint names of two or more persons. Account opening form should contain the specimen signatures of all of them. Clear instructions must be obtained from all of them as to how the account will be operated. The name or names of the persons authorised to operate the account, withdraw the money, sign the cheque, must be clearly obtained. In no circumstances such authorised person can transfer his authority to another person unless all the joint holders of the account give their consent. In the absence of these instructions, banker should honour only those cheques which carry the signatures of all the joint holders. It should also be ascertained whether the person authorised to operate the account is empowered to overdraw the account. The operation of the joint account is suspended if any of the joint holders asks the banker, in writing, to do so. In case an overdraft is to be granted, the banker should obtain joint and several promissory notes executed by them.

According To Sect. 45 of the Indian Contract Act, the banker is liable to all of them jointly and if any one of them dies then to the living account holders and representative of the deceased jointly unless otherwise agreed. There is a practice of the account holders giving an instruction that the balance of the account shall be payable to 'either or survivor' which permits the banker to repay the money to the survivor alone.

(8) Joint Hindu Family (Hindu Undivided Family)

Joint Hindu family consists of all persons lineally descended from a common ancestor and includes their wives. It carries on ancestral business with ancestral properties. The properties and the business are managed by the head of the family called Karta (manager). If the family is governed by 'Mitakshara school' every male member of the family acquires an interest in the joint property by birth. He is called a co-parcener. According to Hindu Succession Act, 1956 on the death of a co-parcener his sons, wife, daughters and some other female relatives become joint successors to his property. According to 'Dayabhag school' during the life time of the father his sons have no right to the property of the father.

Therefore, while dealing with a Joint Hindu family a banker is faced with the problem of ascertaining the rights of various members of the family. Though Karta has the right to take a loan, execute necessary documents and pledge the family property, it will be binding on other members if it is necessary for the business (not speculative) or in the benefit of the family. To save itself from any possible dispute, the banker should ensure that the loan documents are executed by all adult male members of the family. This is important from another point of view, i.e., the co-parcener's liability, for a loan, is limited to the extent of his interest in the joint property unless he has jointly contracted for the loan or ratified the contract made by the Karta. But Karta's liability is always unlimited. It must be remembered that the death of co-parcener does not end the firm.

(9) Partnership Firm

According to the Indian Partnership Act, partnership is "the relation between persons who have agreed to share the profits of a business, carried on by all or any of them acting for all." From the banker's point of view, there are two important points in this definition firstly it should ascertain the terms of the agreement. Though the agreement can be oral also but if it is in writing, a copy of the agreement called 'partnership deed' must be obtained by the bank and the provisions of the deed must be carefully studied with regard to (i) names, addresses and occupation of partners; (ii) nature of business; (iii) management structure; (iv) rights and duties of the partners; (v) financial powers and liabilities; and (vi) the provision as to change in the rights and duties.

The second important aspect of the definition is that a partner may 'act for all', i.e., he can bind the other partners by his acts. This authority of the partner is called implied authority. The necessary conditions of the implied authority are—

(i) the act must be done in the name of the firm, expressing or implying an intention to bind the firm;
(ii) it must relate to the business of the firm;
(iii) it must be done in the usual way.

But partners among themselves may agree to put certain limitations on this implied authority. Banker should ascertain what those limitations are. Banker should be aware about the exceptions to this implied authority provided in the Partnership Act (Refer to Law of Partnership).

The precautions that a banker should take are:

(i) That the number of partners do not exceed the statutory limit laid down by Sec. 11 of the Companies Act, 1956.
(ii) Firm's account should not be opened in the name of individual partner/partners. It should always be opened in firm's name.
(iii) As far as possible consent of all the partners, for the opening of the firm's account, should be obtained. Specimen signatures of all the partners should be taken for record though right to operate the account may be with a few of them.
(iv) A partner who enjoys the authority to operate the firm's account cannot delegate the same to any other partner without the consent of all the partners.
(v) For the purpose of granting a loan, the banker may take into account the assets or properties of individual partners (because partners have unlimited liability) as well as their personal liabilities, because personal assets are to be applied, first to the payment of personal liabilities and then to the liabilities of the firm.
(vi) On the death of a partner, if the firm is not dissolved on account of an agreement to that effect, the banker should close the account of the firm to determine deceased partner's liability (in view of the Clayton's rule) and a new account should be opened to enable the firm to carry on business. Same procedure should be followed on the retirement of a partner, insolvency of a partner as well as on admission of a partner if the account shows a debit balance at the time of such retirement, insolvency and admission.

(10) Joint Stock Companies

It is an artificial person, having limited liability with perpetual succession and a common seal. Unlike a partnership firm, it is considered a separate legal person. Liability of the members is limited to the nominal value of the shares they hold. The following points deserve attention while dealing with a company:

(i) Banker should examine the certificate of incorporation to ensure that the company has acquired a separate legal entity. If the company is a 'Public Limited Co.' then the certificate to commence business should also be seen. However, company is required to deposit all receipts of money on account of issue of shares in a separate bank account, before the certificate of commencement of business is obtained.
(ii) Memorandum of Association of the company should be examined. The object clause of the memorandum determines the contractual capacity of the company. All acts of the company beyond the object clause are *ultravires* the company and not enforceable against the company.
(iii) Articles of Association should also be studied to ascertain the rights, duties, powers and liabilities of the directors, rules as to the conduct of the meeting and other details as to the conduct of the day-to-day business. Specific attention should be paid to the procedure and authority to draw and endorse cheques, bills, notes etc. on behalf of the company, and the procedure and authority for borrowings and mortgaging company's assets. Limit on borrowings should be clearly ascertained. It should be kept in mind that the Companies Act has also laid down limit on the powers of the directors to borrow.
(iv) It should seek a copy of the resolution of the Board of Directors wherein it has been appointed as a banker to the company and the name of the person/persons who are authorised to operate the accounts are stated. Resolution should also authorise the advances to be obtained if any, their limit, security and rate of interest etc.
(v) Sec. 125 of the Companies Act, 1956, requires certain charges, created by a company to be registered with the Registrar of Companies within 30 days of its creation. Banker should ensure that it has been complied with.
(vi) Before granting loan on the basis of charges, the banker should enquire about the charges already created. Sometimes, these charges do not permit a second charge to be created over them ranking above or at par with them 'Register of charges' maintained in the office of the registrar of companies should be inspected.
(vii) In case the director authorised to operate company's account, has a personal account also with the same banker and endorses a cheque, drawn in favour of the company to be credited to his personal account. The banker should ascertain whether there are genuine reasons for the same.

(II) Trustee

According to Sec. 3 of the Indian Trust Act, 1882, a trust is an obligation annexed to the ownership of property and arising out of a confidence reposed in or accepted by the owner or declared and accepted by him for the benefit of another or of another and 'the owner.' The person who reposes the confidence is called the settler or the author of the trust and person in whom confidence is reposed is called the 'trustee'. The document, through which trust is created, is called the 'trust deed'. Trustee may open a bank account in his name to operate the trust funds. Besides, he may have a personal account also with the same banker. Banker must ensure that the trust funds are not transferred to the personal account of the trustee.

'Trust deed' should be examined to ascertain the powers and duties of the trustees. In case of more than one trustee, clear instructions must be sought as to who will operate the account. Powers of borrowings and creating charge should be examined. In case, a trustee dies the powers will be vested in other trustees as per the provisions of the trust. If all of them die, new trustees have to be appointed by the court. Insolvency of a trustee does not affect the trust property and the creditors cannot recover their claims from trust property.

Bankers should take all precautions to save the interest of the beneficiary and should not allow the misuse of the funds of the trust if it has knowledge of it.

(12) Club, Societies, Charitable Institutions

Under this head fall the other institutions like religious institutions, libraries, schools, college etc. These institutions may be registered or unregistered. Registration may be done under the Societies Registration Act, 1860 or Companies Act, 1956 or Cooperative Societies Act. An unregistered society cannot be sued in a Court of Law. A Banker should:

(i) Examine the provisions of the relevant Act;

(ii) Examine the constitution of the society and the bye-laws framed thereunder. A copy of the same should be obtained to know the powers and functions of the persons managing its affairs;

(iii) Obtain a copy of the resolution of their Managing Committee wherein opening an account with the banker has been authorised and names of the persons to operate the account are mentioned. Other directions about the account may also be laid down.

(iv) Before granting any loan to such institutions, the relevant Act, its constitution and bye-laws should be studied to know whether it has power to borrow and whether there are limitations on this power.

In case of death of the person operating the account of the society, the banker should stop the operation of the account till another person is nominated by the society to operate the account. If person operating the society's account has a personal account with the banker, care should be exercised to ensure that society's funds are not transferred to his personal account.

(13) Local Authorities

In case of local authorities like municipal corporations etc. the relevant statutes should be studied. These statutes provide the name of the banker and the officer who can operate the account, e.g., in the case of Bombay Municipality, the Commissioner or Deputy Commissioner, jointly with one member of the standing committee and the chief accountant should sign the cheques. In case statutes do not provide the name of the banker, a resolution should be passed by such body to that effect. Banker must obtain a copy of the resolution. Power to borrow are laid down in the statutes and should be studied before granting loans.

EMPLOYMENT OF FUNDS

Banks are middlemen between those who have funds and those who do not have. They can better he described as financial intermediaries. They accept deposits from the public and lend or invest the same for a profit. But they cannot invest the entire funds in high income earning assets because of the obligation they owe to the depositors — the obligation to return their funds when they demand the same (in case of demand liabilities). Therefore, a part of the funds have to be kept in cash so as to meet this obligation. More the funds are kept in cash, lesser is the profitability. More the funds are invested in high income bearing portfolios, lesser is the liquidity of funds. This conflict between liquidity and profitability guides the policy of employment of funds by a banker. A good management is a better resolution of this conflict. Let us first discuss all the sources from which a bank obtains funds.

SOURCES OF FUNDS

The sources of a bank's funds can, like any other business enterprise, be divided into two categories, viz., owned funds and borrowed funds.

(A) OWNED FUNDS

Owned funds consist of the following:

1. Paid-up capital

They are the funds raised from its members or shareholders.

2. Reserve funds

Reserve fund is the profit earned by the banker in the past and not distributed among its members or shareholders on account of legal requirements, i.e., the legal minimum of retained earnings.

3. Undistributed profits

Over and above, the legal minimum a banker may set aside additional profits for meeting future contingencies. These profits become available in subsequent years for employment.

(B) Borrowed Fund

Borrowed funds consist of the following:

1. Public Deposits

Public deposits are deposits with the banker in the form of 'Fixed Deposits Accounts', 'Savings Deposits Accounts', 'Current Accounts', Recurring Deposits Account' etc. This source is the most important source of bank's funds and determines the lending policy of the banker. Around 90% of the total funds of a bank come through this source.

2. Borrowings from other Institutions

In case of need, usually of a short term nature, bank can borrow from:

(i) Reserve Bank of India
(ii) Other Banks
(iii) Life Insurance Corporation of India
(iv) Unit Trust of India
(v) Industrial Development Bank of India

3. Others

Banks can raise money through bonds and debentures, bills of exchange and other negotiable instruments cash certificates etc.

4. Credit creation

Over and above the initial public deposits banks create credit, e.g., bank grants a loan of Rs. 100 to A.A does not withdraw cash but retains it in a separate Loan Account with the bank and withdraws it according to it needs. The bank has raised his deposit by Rs. 100 without receiving any cash. Credit creation is an important function of banks.

EMPLOYMENT OF FUNDS

Let us, now, discuss how these funds are employed to earn a handsome return without jeopardising liquidity. Liquidity is the "ability of the banker to satisfy demand for cash in exchange of deposits." Since around 90% of the funds come from public deposits this requirement is most essential. A bank which fails to meet this requirement becomes bankrupt. Banking history is full of many such cases. Thus, liquidity is the most important requirement for the employment of a banker's funds. But liquid assets do not usually yield a good return and Bank has to pay interest on deposits. In the absence of profits, the very purpose of carrying on the business of banking will be defeated. Safety of funds has to be ensured. Hence, it is necessary to strike a balance between liquidity and profitability which involves a choice between safety and risk while deciding to employ the funds. The assets in which the funds of a banker are employed are:

(1) LIQUID ASSETS

As explained above, to save itself from insolvency, a banker must be able to return the funds of a depositor whenever he demands. For this reason, a part of funds is kept in the form of cash or near cash. This is usually referred to as 'Liquid Assets'. It consists of Non-earning and Earning Liquid Assets.

(A) Non-earning Liquid Assets

(1) Cash Balance

Immediate demand of the depositor is met with the cash in the 'cash chest' of the banker. The quantum of cash in the chest is determined by the following factors:

(i) Habit of the customers

Banker must study the habit of its customers as to the frequency of withdrawals and accordingly determine the amount to be kept in the 'chest'.

(ii) Nature of Accounts

Fixed deposit accounts do not require much cash to be kept but for current accounts a good portion is to be kept in cash. Saving Accounts fall between the two as regards the need for keeping cash in the chest.

(iii) Banker's clearing house

Dealing through a clearing house lesser funds are required in cash because bank has to provide only the difference between the cheques 'draw on it' and the cheques 'drawn in its favour'. In general, more the use of cheques lesser is the requirement of cash in chest. If both the Drawers and the Payee have their account in the same branch, no cash is required at all. Even if it involves another bank through the clearing house the need of cash is reduced.

(iv) Nature of Advances and facility of Refinance

Reserve Bank of India provides assistance to the banker in case of need. But this is of bills. If these assets from the portfolio of the bank, then accommodation of the Reserve Bank can be sought and the need of maintaining large cash balance is obviated.

(2) Statutory Balance with Reserve Bank of India Cash Reserve (CRR)

Under Sec. 42 (1) of the Reserve Bank of India Act, 1934, every scheduled bank is required to maintain with the Reserve Bank of India a cash reserve of 3% of its aggregate demand and time liabilities. i.e., average daily balance from Friday to next Saturday. This is a statutory requirement and is also termed as Statutory Cash Reserve Ratio. This ratio can be increased upto 15 % and higher. In the previous years, over and above 15%, an additional reserve of 10% of the incremental deposits after a particular date, was also required. This additional 10% has been withdrawn w.e.f. 3.4.92.

(3) Balance with other banks

Scheduled banks maintain balances with other banks in India and abroad in current account. These balances are as liquid as balances held by themselves. They may be withdrawn as and when necessary. These balances constitute the first line of defence of a bank since its solvency depends upon them.

(B) Earning Liquid Assets

(1) Money at Call and Short Notice

Depending upon the need of clearing, bank may be left with surplus funds, on a particular day and may face deficiency on another. While one bank may have surplus on a day, another may face shortage the same day. Inter-bank call money market provides a channel utilising surplus of one bank by another, of course at a rate of interest. Such loans are repayable at call or at short notice.

(2) Investment in Securities

Bank may keep a part of its funds in securities transacted at the Stock Exchange or otherwise. The securities are:

(i) Government securities

(ii) Semi-Government Securities (Trust Securities)

(iii) Shares and Debentures of Joint Stock Companies

Govt. Securities are the loans and bonds raised by Central or State Governments called Public Debt. Semi-Government securities include Fort trust, Improvement trust and Municipal bond, and Debentures. They are considered very safe. The former two are 'approved securities' because they are approved by the Reserve Bank of India for investment under statutory obligation. There are also referred to as gilt edged securities because it is safest investment, Investment in corporate securities is insignificant.

(3) Treasury Bills

Reserve Bank of India issues treasury bills on behalf of the central government. These bills are for a short period usually for 91 days. They are available on top throughout the week. Banks prefer to invest their surplus funds in them because besides earning interest, there is the facility of rediscounting with Reserve Bank.

(4) Excess Reserves with Reserve Bank

Over and above the statutory minimum of 3% (or more) a bank may keep a higher amount with Reserve Bank. This fetches an interest of 10.5% per annum.

Statutory limit of Liquid Assets (SLR)

According to Sec. 24 of the Banking Regulation Act, 1949 both scheduled and non-scheduled banks must maintain in India, (in addition to the minimum cash balance with the Reserve Bank of India) cash, gold or unencumbered approved securities, at the close of business on any day, of an amount not less than 25% of their demand and time liabilities. Called Statutory Liquidity Ratio (SLR), this can be increased upto 40%. At present, it stands at 38.5% on deposits as on 3.4.92 and 30% of incremental deposits after 3.4.92. Since cash and gold do not yield any income, a major part of this investment is made in approved securities.

(II) PROFITABLE ASSETS (LOANS AND ADVANCES)

Granting of loans and advances is one of the most important functions of a bank. Essentially, banking business is lending. Deposits are accepted from the public for the purposes of lending or investing so as to earn a profit. Loans and advances, therefore, constitute the most important asset of the bank because a major portion of its funds are invested in this asset. Therefore, this part of the chapter is to be discussed in greater detail. This will be discussed under the following sub-heads:

(A) General Principles governing Loans and Advances

(B) Form of Loans and Advances

(C) Modes of securing Loans and Advances

(D) Principles governing Evaluation of Security

(E) Types of Securities

(A) General Principles Governing Loans and Advances

While lending its funds, the Banker has to reconcile the following requirements:

(1) Safety

Banker, basically, invests others' funds. It cannot, therefore, afford to lose them. Loans must be granted after careful consideration of the chances of its being repaid, along with the interest, as per the terms and conditions. For the purpose, borrower's capacity and willingness to pay must be inquired into. He should be a man of integrity, good character and reputation. Proper references should be obtained about him. Over and above this, the bank should try to secure loan by creating appropriate charges.

(2) Liquidity

Money should be advanced on terms that repayment should be quick because bank is under legal obligation to repay on demand to the depositors. For this requirement, short-term loans are advisable. Liquidity sometimes depends upon the type of securities received. These assets should be easily marketable and their prices should not be subject to wide fluctuations. Land, building, plants etc. are not easily marketable.

(3) Profitability

Since the objective of the business of a banker is to make profit, profit has to be the guiding principle of loans and advances. Their profit is the difference between the interest they earn on their assets and the interest they pay to their depositors. A bank has to ensure a regular income by charging interest. As regards the interest, it should strike a balance between minimum risk and maximum profit. A customer with a high reputation may be charged a lower interest. This need to choose a optimum combination of minimum risk and maximum profit has been beautifully summarised in the following words 'caution bears fruits. Timidity may mean health but adventure combined with caution may give vigour, enthusiasm and this leads to a profitable future'.

(4) Purpose of Loan

Purpose of the loan determines both its liquidity and profitability. Loan will be taken by a customer for productive or unproductive purposes. Productive loan is both profitable and liquid. Loans taken for hoarding and speculative activities do not fulfill these requirements, besides being opposed to social objective. After nationalisation of major banks, purpose of the loan has become an important factor in obtaining assistance from bank. If the purpose is in consonance with national policy, it becomes an approved purpose.

(5) Diversification of Risks

Business history is full of depressions and recessions not only of different trades and industries but also of different national economies as well as at the international level. Natural calamities or political disturbances may affect a part of the country. The banker can guard itself, at least against the recessionary conditions in one or more trade by following the maxim 'do not keep all your eggs in one basket'. This means that loans should be dispersed over different industries and trade and if possible in different regions and among different customers. It should not be concentrated in a few big customers either. This diversifies the risk involved in lending. If a few big customers meet misfortune or recession affects a few industries adversely or a region becomes politically instable, banker's overall position does not suffer.

(B) Form of Loans and Advances

Advances granted by commercial banks in India usually fall in the following categories:

(1) Cash Credit

Cash credit is the main method of lending by banks in India and accounts for about 70% of the total bank credit. Under this arrangement, a customer is allowed to borrow upto a limit called cash credit limit already laid down against the security of the assets. Cash credit limit is generally determined by the banker usually on annual basis. Customer has to open a separate cash credit account. The customer may draw the cash credit whenever he likes either all at a time or in parts. Interest is charged only on the amount actually drawn. No interest is charged on the unused balance. In order to fulfill commitments the bank keeps ready cash. Current account relating to cash credit is a regular, active running account. Customer may deposit in this account or withdraw from it as he likes. There is not specific date of its repayment. However, banker has no control on the use of funds, since the limit once set, can be used by the customer for purposes other than those for which the facility was granted.

By depositing surplus cash in the cash credit account, the borrower is able to reduce the interest charges on this advance. Every withdrawal from this account is an advance which does not require repetitive documentation.

(2) Overdraft

When a customer having a current account with the bank is permitted to draw more than the amount standing to the credit of his account, he is deemed to have obtained an advance called 'overdraft'. This may be granted purely on personal security, though bank may insist on some collateral security. A limit is usually agreed in advance to which customer's cheques will be honoured over and above his credit balance. But interest is charged on the actual amount overdrawn.

Cash Credit and Overdrafts compared

(i) In both the cases, limits are set in advance. In cash credit, it is generally done on annual basis.

(ii) In both the cases, interest is charged on actual amount used.

(iii) Overdrafts are generally granted against personal security of the customer or a promissory note though bank may insist on the customer or a promissory note though bank may insist on security of tangible assets also. But cash credit is generally granted against the security of stock.

(iv) In case of cash credit facility, a separate cash credit account is to be opened while overdraft relates to the existing current account of the customer and no separate account is required.

(v) While overdraft is a temporary arrangement but cash credit is permanent.

(vi) In order to fulfill its commitment regarding cash credits, the bank has to keep ready cash to honour the cheques etc. But overdrafts, generally do not impose such restraints.

(3) Loans

Under this system, assistance is provided by the bank for a definite purpose and for a specific period. While money is withdrawn by the customer at one time, its repayment is in instalments spread over the period of loan. If customer wants additional fund, he is to apply and negotiate for the same separately. Each of them is a separate contract, requiring separate documentation. Banker has the right to refuse or reject or approve such request. Interest accrues on the entire amount. Assets purchased with the loan are generally hypothecated with the bank.

Loan account is temporary because it is closed when loan is repaid. But cash credit account continues. Amount deposited in loan account cannot be withdrawn again but from cash credit account customer may withdraw as per his choice. In loan account, instalments are deposited regularly for pre-agreed amount but in cash credit irregular and uneven amounts can be deposited.

Types of Loans

Loans are granted by commercial banks for short-term, medium term as well as long-term. Short term loans are granted to meet working capital requirements, medium-term loans are granted for purchase of durable items like buses, tractors, professional equipment etc. Long-term loans are granted to industrial undertakings for extension, alterations, modernisation or for the purpose of acquisition of fixed assets. Usually, a loan granted for a period of less than 15 months is called short-term loan. If the period of loan varies between 15 months to 5 years, it is referred to as Medium-term loan. If the period is more than 5 years, it is called a long-term loan. When a loan is granted both for the purpose of meeting working capital requirement and fixed capital requirement, it is called a 'composite loan'. The term 'consumption loan' refers to advances granted for meeting expenses for education, medical, marriage, religious ceremony etc. When a financial institution is unable to shoulder the risk of big loan to an industrial undertaking, it may request the commercial banks to join in this risk. A loan granted by one or more commercial banks or a financial institution and one or more than one banks together, is called a Participative loan'. 'Personal Loans' are sanctioned to help the people of fixed income group to raise their living standard, e.g., for the construction and repair of a house, etc.

(4) Discounting of Bills

Regarding bill of exchange the banker provides the service of collecting it from the drawer on behalf of its customer (the drawer or payee). In the capacity of a collecting banker, it just acts as an agent of the customer and does not lend its funds, i.e., no credit is given to the customer till the realisation of the bill. When the bank purchases or discounts a bill it is said to have granted a loan to the person who has written the bill. In the Balance Sheet, these bills are shown as part of loans and advances. When a bank discounts a bill the customer who is the holder, endorses the same in the name of the banker so as to constitute the banker as the transferee. This is done for a settled price or at a current rate of discount. Banker gives the credit to the customer for the entire amount without waiting for realisation and becomes a holder for full value. He is not a trustee or agent. He can pledge it, endorse it. Discounting of demand bills is known as purchase of bills because they are payable immediately. Discounting of usance bills is called discounting of bills.

Discounting must be distinguished from pledging of a bill. When a customer takes a loan on the security of a bill of exchange, he is said to have pledged it. Banker acquires an interest in th bill only to the extent of the amount advanced. He does not become the holder, the bill remains the property of pledgor. Discounting of bills is very popular and profitable business of the banker.

Advantages

(i) Safety of Bank's funds

The amount advanced is secured because on the failure of the drawee to honour the bill the banker has the right to debit the entire amount of the customer's account. Still the banker must ensure that both the parties to the bill are of standing and good reputation.

(ii) Self-Liquidating

Chances of realising a bill are higher because it generally originates from an actual commercial transaction (except accommodation bill). Debtor is, therefore in a position to pay after disposing of the goods.

(iii) Re-finance facility

Reserve Bank of India helps the banker, in case of need by rediscounting these bills. Thus, banker can obtain financial assistance, by granting loans in this form. This obviates the need of keeping large cash reserves. It is discussed in detail in the following paragraph.

(iv) Stability in value

The value of a bill as security does not fluctuate while the value of tangible assets, given as security against loans does fluctuate. Bill is a legally enforceable instrument and the parties can be summarily sued.

(v) Profitability

In case of other loans, interest is payable either quarterly or half yearly, but in case of bills the banker deducts the interest (called discount) at the time of advancing the credit. As a result, the actual earning is higher than the rate of discount, e.g., If a bill of Rs. 1000 payable after 3 months is discounted @ 8% per annum the banker pays only Rs. 980 (Rs. 1000-20). Thus, he earns Rs. 20 on an advance of Rs. 980 for 3 months, the actual yield comes to 8.16% p.a.

Precautions

Bills of only those customers should be discounted who enjoy regular credit limits. The credit-worthiness of the drawee should be ascertained. Only genuine trade bills should be discounted because they are self-liquidating. Accommodation bills should be avoided. Customer should be a drawer of the bill and not an endorsee as far as possible.

Re-finance Facility

Refinance facility by the Reserve Bank of India, on the basis of discounted bills of exchange is provided under the following two heads:

(a) By rediscounting the bills under Sec. 17(2) (s).

(b) By granting loans on the security of isuance promissory notes of their customers under Sec. 17 (4) (c).

On the basis of above two provisions Reserve Bank introduced the following two schemes:

(a) Bills Re-discounting Scheme

This scheme was introduced with effect from 1 November, 1970 under Sec. 17 (2) (a). Under this scheme, all licensed scheduled commercial banks are eligible to offer their bills of exchange for re-discounting. For the purpose a limit is to be fixed annually and the banker has to apply for the same on the basis of estimated requirements. The bills which are eligible for the purpose are:

(i) Genuine trade bills, in which a licensed scheduled bank is the drawee, or has accepted it jointly with the purchaser of the goods or has signed it in support of an unscheduled bank. The bill should not have a maturity of more than 90 days. Bills of 120 days maturity are also eligible if at the time of rediscounting, their maturity is not more than 90 days. Nature of transaction should be mentioned on the bill. Reserve Bank may indicate from time to time the commodities, bills drawn on whose purchase will not be discounted.

(ii) Bills drawn on and accepted by buyer under an irrevocable letter of credit and certified by the banker of the buyer who has opened the letter of credit.

(iii) Bills drawn on and accepted by buyer and endorsed by the seller in favour of his bank with certain conditions etc.

Banks availing this facility must retire and take delivery of the bills at least three working days before the respective dates of their maturities. For the re-discounting, the value of each bill should not be less than Rs. 1000 and the value of all such bills should not be less than Rs. 5000.

In the early years, scheme made much progress till 1977-78. Thereafter, it declined sharply. In view of the general policy of restrictive credit, Reserve Bank has been using it on a discretionary basis and amount sanctioned is negligible.

(b) Bill Market Scheme

Introduced under Sec. 17(4)(c) in January, 1952, under this scheme scheduled banks can avail demand loans from Reserve Bank against promissory notes of their customers. They must be iSaunce promissory notes maturing within 90 days. These bills are lodged with Reserve Bank as security for advances and are not rediscounted. The borrowing banks can withdraw any of these bills and can replace them with others.

Borrowing bank has to get the limit fixed, for the purpose, in respect of each of its customer whose bills it will be lodging with the Reserve Bank. It has to submit various details about the party to the Reserve Bank. Reserve Bank may approve or reject a party or approve a lower limit. The borrowing bank can reduce its liability to Reserve Bank under this scheme by depositing its surplus funds even for a short period.

(C) MODES OF SECURING LOANS AND ADVANCES

The banker has to ensure the safety of funds lent to a customer. This is done by creating a charge on tangible assets of the borrower besides relying on the character, capacity and capital of the borrower. This is called credit-worthiness. In fact unsecured loans (called clean advance) are also granted to persons of sound financial position possessing tangible assets. But their assets are not charged. Bank relies primarily on the personal guarantee or sometimes on the guarantee of a third party. In secured advances, assets are charged to the loan. Assets may be charged in any of the following manners.

(1) Lien

The banker enjoys a general lien on all securities of the customer in terms of Sec. 171 of the Indian Contract Act. This has already been explained under 'rights of the banker'. Another aspect of lien is the declaration given by the customer that certain specific of his assets are free from encumbrances and that he will not dispose them or created a charge over them without the permission of the banker. Though banker cannot realise its dues from those assets but that ensures some 'realisable assets' with the customer for the purpose of pursuing the realisation of loan.

(2) Pledge

According to Sec. 172 of the Indian Contract Act, pledge is the 'bailment of goods as security for payment of a debt or performance of a promise'. The person delivering the goods is called the pledgor or pawner and the person to whom the goods are delivered is called the 'pledgee' or 'pawnee'. The ownership of the goods remains with the pledgor but the pledgee acquires a special property and lien. So long as his loan is not repaid no other creditor can take away the goods or its price. In the case of *Bank of Bihar (now State Bank of India) v. State of Bihar and others*, sugar pledged with the Bank of Bihar was seized by the government of Bihar. It was held that the government was liable to reimburse the bank for such amount that the bank would have realised, in the ordinary course, by the sale of sugar.

Delivery of goods is essential to constitute pledge. Delivery need not be physical. It may be constructive or symbolic, e.g., where bank puts his own lock on the godown of the customer storing pledged goods, it is constructive delivery. Same is true of handing over of documents of title like Bill of Lading, Railway Receipt after proper endorsement. But goods left with the banker for safe custody or for a special purpose, is not pledge.

(3) Hypothecation

Hypothecation is another method of creating a charge over the movable goods. Under this mode of creating charge, neither ownership nor actual possession of the goods is transferred to the banker. Only an equitable charge is created in favour of the banker. Goods remain with the borrower, who is bound under the agreement, to give the possession to the banker, whenever required. On such demand, hypothecation gets converted into pledge and the banker acquires the rights of a pledgee. The possession with the borrower is deemed to be on behalf of the banker and not in his own right as the owner of goods. Hence, they are deemed to be in the constructive possession of the banker.

Hypothecation is done where pledge is not convenient or practicable e.g. raw material, work-in-progress etc. Borrower needs the use of the goods for the continuance of the business. He is, therefore, allowed to use the stock, sell it and replenish it. The charge over such assets is called a floating charge because the value of the security varies from time to time. Banker should, therefore, obtain periodical statements from the customer about the figure of such assets. In case the borrower is a joint stock company, this charge should be registered with the registrar of companies. This facility should be granted to those parties whose honesty and integrity are not in doubt. Banker should ensure that the hypothecated stocks are fully insured against fire or other risks. Periodical inspection of the assets should be carried out to verify the correctness of the statements submitted by the borrower. A name plate of the bank stating that the stocks are hypothecated to it, must be displayed at all conspicuous places in the premises where such assets are kept so that no second charge is created. If the similar facility is enjoyed by the borrower from different banks their respective assets (specially stock) should be segregated with separate stock books.

(4) Mortgage

Mortgage has been defined by Sec. 58 of the Transfer of Property Act, 1882 as "the transfer of an interest in specific immovable property for the purposes of securing the payment of money advanced or to be advanced by way of loan, an existing or future debt, or the performance of an engagement, which may give rise to a pecuniary liability." The transferor is called the mortgagor and the transferee is called the mortgagee. The document by which the transfer is effected is called the 'mortgage deed'. Main characteristics of a mortgage are:

1. Specific Immovable Property

Only specific immovable property is accepted as a mortgage. By specific immovable property, we mean the property which is of specific value, identify, size, measurement, situation etc. These particulars must be enclosed with mortgage deed.

2. Transfer of Interest

Unlike sale where complete ownership is transferred, in mortgage only some of the rights of ownership are transferred, in mortgage only some of the rights of ownership are transferred. Mortgagor retains the right of redeeming the property.

3. Possession

The actual possession of property is not transferred to the mortgagee in all cases.

4. Right of Sale

The mortgagee has the right to sell the property if the mortgagor fails to pay the debt.

5. Re-conveying the interest in Property

On payment of loan the interest in the property is re-conveyed to the mortgagor. If the property is transferred in discharge of a debt it is not a mortgage.

Legal Mortgage Vs. Equitable Mortgage

From the point of view of transfer of rights in the property, mortgage is divided into two categories viz. legal mortgage and equitable mortgage. In the legal mortgage legal title to the property is transferred to the mortgagee through a mortgage deed and getting it registered by paying registration charges and stamp duty. In case of equitable mortgage only documents of title are deposited with the mortgagee. The mortgagor, however, undertakes to execute a legal mortgage in case he fails to pay the debt. Equitable mortgages do not involve expenses of registration, stamp duty etc. This undertaking is called Memorandum of Deposit. In legal mortgage though legal title to the mortgaged property is transferred to the mortgagee, mortgagor has the right to redeem the property upon repayment of the loan.

In equitable mortgage, the mortgagee can apply to the court for conversion of equitable mortgage into legal mortgage on the non-payment of loan. This mortgage is preferred by customers because their credit does not suffer. Due to absence of registration, outsiders do not know about the mortgage transaction. Equitable mortgage, however, involves certain risks. They are:

(a) In a legal mortgage effected prior to an equitable mortgage to the banker, legal mortgagee will rank before the banker. But he will lose this right where he was a party to the creation of this equitable mortgage to the banker.

(b) A legal mortgage created after an equitable mortgage will also have priority over the latter.

(c) As between two or more equitable mortgages created on the same property, the one who is in possession of the documents of title shall have priority over others. Banker, therefore, should be very careful in giving the documents of title back to the mortgagor even for a short period.

(d) If the mortgagor makes a binding agreement to sell property before effecting an equitable mortgage of the same, banker's equitable charge shall be postponed to the purchaser's equitable charge.

Banker should, therefore, be very careful about it. He should examine the title deeds properly. In suspicious circumstances, he should make proper enquiries. It should be used in relation to those customers whose integrity is not in question. However, in spite of these risks the advantages of equitable mortgage outweigh the risks involved.

Forms of Mortgage

Section 58 of the Transfer of Property Act, 1882 recognises the following six forms of mortgage:

(a) Simple Mortgage

There is no transfer of possession of mortgaged property but there is an agreement, express or implied that the mortgagee can sell the mortgaged property if the loan is not repaid. But this right is to be exercised only through the intervention of the court.

(b) English Mortgage

Under this form of the mortgage, the mortgagor transfers the mortgaged property absolutely to the mortgagee subject to his right of redemption. On default of the mortgagor in repayment, the mortgagee has a right to sell the property without seeking the permission of the Court in special circumstances. The mortgagee is entitled to immediate possession and to retain possession until the payment is received.

(c) Mortgage by Deposit of title deeds

Where the mortgagor delivers only documents of title it is known as mortgage by deposit of title deeds. This is called equitable mortgage. But according to Transfer of Property Act, mortgage by deposit of title deeds is restricted to the towns of Calcutta, Madras and Bombay and in any other towns which the state government may, by notification in the official gazette, specify.

(d) Mortgage by conditional sale

In this case, the mortgagor almost sells the property to the mortgagee on the condition that—

(i) on default of payment of loan, the sale shall become absolute

(ii) on payment of loan, the sale shall become void and the buyer shall transfer the property to seller.

(e) Unfructuary Mortgage

In this case, over and above transferring or agreeing to transfer the possession of the mortgaged property, mortgagor further authorises the mortgagee to received rents and profits accruing from the property and to appropriate the same in lieu of interest or mortgage debt. Since the mortgagor does not bind himself personally to repay the mortgage debt, no suit of repayment of mortgage debt can be filed. The mortgagee cannot file a suit for sale or foreclosure of property. He can only retain possession and recover income accruing therefrom.

(f) Anomalous Mortgage

A mortgage that does not fall in any of the above categories is called an anomalous mortgage.

Rights of Mortgagee

According to Transfer of Property Act, mortgagee enjoys the following rights:

(a) Right of Foreclosure

This right consists in seeking court's permission debarring the mortgagor of his right to redeem his property. This permission can be obtained in 'conditional sale' and 'anomalous mortgage' on default of payment by mortgagor.

(b) Right of sale

The mortgagee has a right to obtain court's permission to sell the property on the non-payment of mortgage money. However in case of 'English Mortgage' or where such right is expressly conferred on the mortgagee by the mortgage deed, permission of the court is not required for sale.

(c) Right to sue for Mortgage Money

The mortgagee has a right to sue the mortgagor for the recovery of mortgage debt under simple mortgage as well as in cases where the agreement expressly so provides.

(d) Right to possess, accession to mortgaged property

If any accession takes place to the mortgaged property, the mortgagee can hold the same as security.

(e) Right to recover money spent on mortgaged property

There should not be a contract to the contrary.

Difference between Pledge and Mortgage

1. Pledge relates to movable property while mortgage relates to immovable property.
2. In pledge, possession of the goods passes to the pledgee (whether actual or constructive). But in mortgage transfer of possession is not always necessary, Mortgage can take place by depositing documents of title only.
3. Under pledge, written deed is not necessary. Therefore, the necessity of its registration also does not arise. But mortgage is always by a written deed and except in case of equitable mortgage it is to be compulsorily registered if the value is more than Rs. 100.
4. The pledgee has the power to dispose of the pledged goods and realise his debt. Such powers are not available to a mortgagee unless he obtains permission of the court that effect.

Difference between Pledge and Hypothecation

Though in both cases, it is movable property which is accepted as security but the two differ in respect of the following:

1. In pledge possession of goods, actual or constructive, is transferred to the pledgee but in hypothecation no such transfer of possession takes place.
2. In case of pledge, goods, subject to charge, remain in the possession of pledgee but in case of hypothecation goods remain with the hypothecator till, as per the terms of the hypothecation, they are acquired by the banker.

3. The pledgor can neither use the goods nor sell them. But hypothecator not only uses the goods but can sell them if the terms of the agreement so permit or where prior permission of the banker has been obtained.
4. Pledgor can sell the goods and realise his debt on the default of the pledgor to pay. But hypothecator has no such right unless the agreement so provides.

(D) PRINCIPLES GOVERNING EVALUATION OF SECURITIES

While granting loans and advances against the securities offered by the borrower, the banker must adhere to the following principles:

(1) Realisability

The securities must be readily realizable, i.e., they should be capable of being encashed easily. If the borrower fails to pay the debt and the banker does not find a buyer for the security or the buyer is not to be found easily, the banker will stand to lose.

(2) Encumbrance

As far as possible, the banker must accept the securities which are free from any prior charge. Where it is already encumbered, the value of the security should be adequate enough to cover all the advances granted by the bank till the loan is repaid.

(3) Margin

The term margin refers to the difference between the market price of the security and the amount of advance granted, e.g., If Bank advances a sum of Rs. 5000 and obtains pledge of shares of the market value of Rs. 8000, Rs. 3000 is the margin. Margin is required both to cover the risk of the price of the security going down as well as to recover the interest on loan. For the purpose, the banker considers the likely fluctuations in prices of the securities, financial, position of the issuing company, financial position of the borrowing company etc. If the security consists of commodities subject to credit control of the Reserve Bank of India, the latter prescribes the rules of margin.

(4) Valuation

Care must be taken to ensure that securities are valued properly. Adequate obsolescence and depreciation are provided. Stocks and shares which are dealt on a Stock Exchange or commodities for which organised markets are there may be evaluated easily. But, securities for which no such ready sources are available, must be referred to experts.

(5) Stability in Value

The value of the security should not be subject to wide fluctuations otherwise all calculations about margin etc. would go wrong.

(6) Documentation

Appropriate documents should be executed to ensure the stipulated rights of the banker over the securities so as to avoid possible misunderstandings or disputes in future.

(7) Cost of Supervision

Bank should, generally, prefer securities that do not require much supervision, e.g., where banker accepts as security goods of the borrower kept in the latter's godown, he will have to supervise it regularly. No such supervision is required in case of government securities, stocks and shares etc.

(8) Yield

Where security yields some incomes like dividends on shares. The banker can obtain borrower's permission to appropriate the same to the loan. Such securities should be preferred to others.

(9) Durability

Perishable goods like vegetables, meat etc. or goods, requiring special care in storage like gur, chillies, woollen clothes, or those grains or oilseeds which last for one or two seasons only should generally be avoided as security.

(10) Transferability

The security should be of such nature that in case of need it can be sold easily. In this regard, immovable securities do pose some problem. An elaborate legal procedure is required to transfer the title.

(E) TYPES OF SECURITIES

Advances may be granted by a bank against the following securities:

(1) Against goods
(2) Against documents of title to the goods
(3) Against Stock Exchange securities
(4) Against Life Insurance Policies
(5) Against Fixed Deposit Receipts
(6) Against Land and Buildings

(1) Advances against Goods

Goods are preferred over personal guarantees because in the latter case if both the principal debtor and surety become insolvent banker has to incur the loss. Moreover, it may involve costly legal proceedings. But where goods are pledged, banker has something tangible in his possession to fall back upon. Goods which are necessities of life are free from wide fluctuations in normal times. They can be sold easily in comparison to immovable property. Their value can be easily ascertained from market. They can be kept under banker's lock and key.

But goods face the risk of deterioration. Fruits and vegetables decay very soon while commodities like wheat if stored for more than six months face the danger of spoilage by insects. If goods are not necessities of life, their prices are likely to fluctuate heavily. Verification of goods and their quality is a difficult task and the customer may commit fraud on bank. Large storage spaces have to be hired for storing them and vigilance is required so that godown keeper may not join hands with the borrower and replace the goods. Due the their bulk and weight, transportation becomes a difficult task. Since goods are susceptible to loss by theft and fire, they should be insured. In case goods require licences, the banker should inspect the licences. The most important precaution is that the customer should be trustworthy.

(2) Advances against Documents of title to goods

The term document of title has been defined to include a bill of lading, dock warrant, warehouse keeper's certificate, wharfinger's certificate, railway receipt, warrant or order tor delivery of goods or any other document used in the ordinary course of business as evidence of the possession or control of goods or authorising or purporting to authorise either by endorsement or by delivery, the possession of the documents to transfer or receive the goods thereby represented. Since documents represent goods, advance against documents is, ultimately advance against goods. Let us discuss advances against various document.

Bill of Lading

When the goods are delivered on board, the ship, the shipowner or his agent issues an acknowledgement to that effect together with an undertaking to deliver them in the same condition to the consignee or his agent provided freight and other charges are duly paid. It can be transferred by endorsement and delivery and the transferee of the bill of lading can sue in his own name. But the transferor. Therefore, it is not negotiable instrument.

Advances should be given only against 'Shipped Bill of Lading' and not against 'Reserved for shipment' or 'Through Bill of Lading' because in the former case goods have been delivered on board the ship while in other two cases delivery on board may be delayed and goods may deteriorate. Goods should be insured against the perils of the sea.

Railway Receipt

Like a bill of lading, a railway receipt also confers title to the transferee on being endorsed and delivered. The title of the transferee will not be better than that of the transferor, though the unpaid seller cannot stop the goods in transit. Banker should check the particulars of the railway receipt with that of the invoice as regards the description, weight and destination of goods. Date of the receipt is also important because in case of an old receipt goods might have arrived at the destination, incurring demurrage.

Warehousekeeper's Certificate or Receipt

It is an acknowledgement of the receipt of specified goods in the warehouse and held at the disposal of the person named therein. Usually, such an acknowledgement is non-transferable. Banker should, therefore, obtain such a certificate in his own name. Goods should be insured against theft and fire.

Dock Warrants

It is a certificate issued by a dock company acknowledging the receipt of goods held at the disposal of the person named therein. It is also transferable by endorsement and delivery but does not convey a better title to the transferee. Trustworthy customers should be given advances against it.

Delivery Orders

The owner of the goods for the purpose of transferring possession, either on account of a sale or otherwise, may give written order to the warehousekeeper where his goods are stored to deliver the goods of specified description or weight to the person named therein. This order is also transferable by endorsement and delivery. Precautions similar to that of warehousekeeper's certificate should be observed in this regard too.

(3) Advances against Stock Exchange Securities

Securities which are dealt on a Stock Exchange are called 'Stock Exchange Securities'. They are:

Government Securities

Securities issued by central as well as state governments from time to time against the loans raised by them are called government securities. They are very safe because there is hardly any risk of loss. Moreover, they are easily saleable in the market. On these accounts they are referred to as gilt edged securities. Their valuation can be easily done and their prices do not fluctuate widely. These securities may consist of 'inscribed stock,' 'bearer bonds' or 'promissory notes'. 'Promissory notes' are more common and are negotiable instruments, i.e., their 'holders — in due course' get a better title than that of the transferor. Keeping a margin of 10 to 15% for the possible fluctuation of prices and interest, the banker should require an authorisation from the borrower to sell the securities in case of default in payment of loan.

Semi-Government Securities

Bonds and debentures issues by bodies like Port Trust, Improvement Trusts, Municipal Corporations etc. are called Semi-government securities. They are also quite safe and liquid and the bankers grant loans against them quite often.

Corporate Securities

Corporate securities refer to shares and debentures of Joint Stock Companies. As regards shares, they have the advantages of tangible security, easy realisability, easily valuable, easily transferable etc. But the shares or every company do not enjoy all these advantages. This depends upon the age and reputation of the company and its directors, its financial position including reserves and prospects of the company in general. Therefore, every bank prepares a list of such companies in advance, whose shares can be accepted as securities. Shares should not be partly paid, otherwise the banker may be called upon to pay the calls. Care is to be exercised against the forged share certificates. Share price should not be subject to wide fluctuations. Banker should send a letter to the company so that a duplicate certificate may not be issued.

As regards debentures it should be found out whether they are secured or unsecured. Unsecured debentures do not usually find favour with banks, unless the company enjoys a high reputation. Terms of issue, type of charge enjoyed by debentureholders, regularity of payment of interest should be enquired into. Above all, their marketability should be specifically ascertained.

(4) Advances against Life Insurance Policies

These days it is the commoniy acceptable security because longer they are held, the higher is their surrender value. Advances linked with the surrender value and not with the amount of the policy, are most safe. It can be assigned to the bank that entitles the banker to receive payment on maturity or death of the borrower. It has the drawback that on account of non-disclosure of material facts by the insured, the insurance company may be absolved of its liability and the banker loses the value of the security. Banker also runs the risk of non-payment of premium by the insured. Age of the insured should have been admitted by the Life Insurance Company. Endowment policies should be preferred to whole life policies because they have a definite maturity.

(5) Advances against Fixed Deposit Receipt

Advance should be granted only the person in whose name the deposit receipt is issued. If the deposit receipt is issued by another banker, then no advance should be granted as the issuing banker may have paramount lien on it. If the deposit receipt is in the name of two or more persons, all of them should sign the letter of authority and discharge on revenue stamp. Their signatures must be tallied with the specimen signatures. Bank should make a note in the fixed deposit register and ledger. One branch of the same bank granting loan on fixed deposit receipt issued by another branch should obtain confirmation that no loan has already been granted against it. Interest on loans against FDR is now governed by the Reserve Bank of India. Banks are required to charge at least 1% above the interest payable on such deposits.

(6) Advances against Land and Buildings

Though they are tangible assets but they suffer from the defect that the title of the owner may not be easily ascertainable. In case of agricultural land, records are not properly maintained. Rules of succession are complicated. Therefore, person claiming the ownership may not be the absolute owner. There are restrictions on transfer of agricultural land. Its sale is not easy because of complicated legal formalities. Buyers may not be easily available. Its value cannot be easily ascertained. Administering such properties is a difficult task, i.e., carrying out repairs, collecting rents and keeping accounts is a time consuming process.

However, in advancing loans against this security, Banker should prefer a legal mortgage. Experts should be engaged to ascertain its true value. Cost so incurred should be charged to the borrower. Property should be insured against fire, riot etc. Banker should ensure that mortgagor is regularly paying the lease or ground rend and other taxes. An adequate margin ranging between 33% to 50% is normally kept. Above all, the title of the mortgagor should be thoroughly investigated.

LETTER OF CREDIT

Apart from accepting deposits and advancing loans, banker also provides several useful services. Among these services, letter of credit is the most useful since it solves numerous problems of the business world particularly relating to foreign trade. It is a document issued by a bank, addressed to another bank, authorising the latter to grant a specified amount to a third party named therein, undertaking to pay the money paid under the letter of credit. This promise of the issuing banker is honoured on a global basis. Letters of credit are of two types:

(1) Letters of commercial credit

(2) Travellers' letter of credit

COMMERCIAL LETTER OF CREDIT

This is most useful in solving the problems of foreign trade. In foreign trade, goods are despatched and documents of title are sent together with a bill of exchange which the buyer has to accept. Where the exporter of goods does not know the importer intimately, he faces the risk of exporting the goods but the importer not accepting the bill or not paying the bill. If the banker of the importer undertakes to accept such bill, the exporter is relieved of the problem. It is because banks enjoy world-wide reputation for honouring such commitments. In the letter of credit, details regarding goods, the date by which they must be despatched etc. are mentioned. It is the duty of the exporter to honour all such conditions, otherwise the banker issuing the letter of credit will not be bound by his promise.

The importer of goods at whose behalf such letter of credit is given, is called the applicant or opener. The banker who issues such letter is called the issuing bank or opening bank. The exporter in whose favour such letter is given is called the beneficiary. The issuing bank sends such letter through another banker, its agent in the country of the exporter. Such agent is called advising bank. The exporter, after having received the bill, discounts the same with his banker, called 'negotiating banker' because exporter negotiates for payment with such banker. Sometimes, the issuing bank may impose a restriction that the bill is to be negotiated with a special banker. Such letter of credit is called a 'restricted letter of credit'. All others are called 'open letter of credit'.

Advantages

1. Certainty of Payment

The exporter is certain that the bill will be accepted and paid because of the banker undertaking its acceptance and payment. Therefore, goods can be exported to far and wide without bothering much about the importers.

2. Immediate Payment

The exporter can negotiate this bill with his banker and can obtain the payment immediately. Negotaiting banker will easily agree to this because of the involvement of the opening banker.

3. Risk of exchange restriction avoided

Opening Banker's commitment would be made only after confirming that the exchange regulations of the country permit the transfer of money. This risk is therefore avoided.

4. Obtaining loan

The exporter may need money for arranging for goods to be exported. If there is a letter of credit from the importer's bank, exporter may be able to obtain advance from his banker.

5. Importing at the credit of the banker

It would have been difficult for the importer to satisfy the exporter, particularly when importing goods from varied and new sources.

6. Importer's interests are protected

The importer is assured that bill will be accepted only when conditions in the letter of credit have been complied with.

Types

(1) Documentary and Clean Letter

The letter of credit may require that the bill will be accepted only when documents of the title to the goods, i.e., Bill of lading, insurance policy, invoice, certificate of origin etc. are attached with the bill. Such a letter is called documentary letter of credit and the one that does not require these documents, is called a clean letter.

(2) Revocable and Irrevocable Letter

If the opening banker reserves the right to cancel or change the credit at any time even without prior intimation to the beneficiaries, such letter of credit is called revocable letter. But if a bill is drawn without having the knowledge of such revocation, the issuing banker is bound by it. Where no such rights are reserved by the issuing banker, it is called an irrevocable letter. Revocable letter does not constitute dependable guarantee and is not generally accepted by exporter.

(3) Fixed and Revolving Letter

If the issuing banker fixes the amount beyond which bills should not be drawn otherwise it would not be liable for acceptance or payment it is called a fixed letter of credit. In case of revolving letter of credit issuing, banker specifies the total amount upto which bills drawn remain outstanding at a time upto a specified time. Thus, on the payment of a bill, the beneficiary can draw another bill under the same letter of credit.

(4) Confirmed and Unconfirmed Letter

At the request of the issuing bank, the advising bank may confirm the credit by appending its signatures on it. By this advising bank also assumes the same liability as that of an issuing bank. This is called confirmed letter of credit. This assures the payment doubly. Letter not having such confirmation is called an unconfirmed letter of credit.

(5) With or Without Recourse Credit

If the letter contains the words 'With course to the drawer', the banker, as the holder of the bill can recover the amount of the bill from the drawer also if the drawee fails to pay the same. In letter containing words 'without course', the drawer is not liable after it is negotiated by him.

(6) Transferable and Non-Transferable

Usually, the right to draw the bill is with the beneficiary only. Such a letter is called 'non-transferable'. Under 'transferable letter', the beneficiary can transfer the right to draw the bill to somebody else. This happens when he is an intermediary in the transaction. But it can be transferred only once.

(7) Back to Back Letter of Credit

If on the security of a letter of credit a bank issues a letter of credit to the beneficiary of the former, it is called a back to back letter of credit.

(8) Restricted Letter of Credit

Sometimes, a issuing bank imposes a restriction that the bill is to be negotiated with a special banker such letter of credit is called a 'restricted letter of credit'. All others are called 'open letters of credit'.

Liability of the Issuing Banker

A letter of credit is an implied contract of payment between the exporter (seller) and the issuing banker which is separate from, though incidental to, the contract of purchase between the purchaser (importer) and the seller (exporter). Though this original contract may provide for the right of the buyer to reject the goods under certain circumstances, but that does not give him a right to an injunction restraining the seller from dealing with the letter of credit. However, if the seller commits a fraud in complying with the terms of the letter of credit, issuing banker's liability will cease.

Right of the Issuing Banker

The issuing banker has the right to claim payment on the letter of credit from the buyer of goods. Any objection to the non-compliance of condition should be raised by the buyer within a reasonable time.

TRAVELLER'S LETTER OF CREDIT

Persons travelling within the country or abroad may not like to take the risk of carrying cash with them. They may carry letter of credit from the banker and utilise them at different stations and destinations. These may be of the following types:

1. Circular Letter of Credit

In these letters, the issuing bank orders its other branches or a representative bank to pay a specified amount to the beneficiary. On the back of it, paying bankers fill in the particulars of payment made. To facilitate payment by the paying banker, a letter of identification is issued wherein the signatures of beneficiary are attested. Paying bank realises the money from issuing banker.

2. Circular notes

These letters are written on paper where a specific amount say Rs. 100, 500 or 1000 is printed. They are issued in favour of the beneficiary with the serial number printed on it. Beneficiary need not fill the amount on it.

3. Circular cheques

They are printed in different colours and are generally issued by foreign branches of a bank to a beneficiary intending to visit the country of the issuing bank. After selling these cheques, the foreign branches send a report to their head office. The beneficiary may receive the payment from any branch of the same bank or agency or head office, a list of which is given to the beneficiary. Colour indicates the maximum amount.

4. Traveller's cheques

These cheques are also of specified denominations printed thereon. But unlike a circular note, no letter of identification is given. Buyer of the cheque has to sign on the cheque before the issuing bank and again before the paying bank and the two signatures must tally. Traveller's cheques may be issued by any branch but circular cheques are issued only by foreign branches of a bank.

BANK SECURITIES SCAM

A recent development of great public concern relates to the detection of serious irregularities in securities transactions of certain banks and other financial institutions. Though this has not adversely affected the reforms, yet it has tended to sideline the otherwise far reaching reform measures and structural changes that are being implemented or are under way to make the financial system much more competitive, efficient and transparent. This sordid episode has come to be known as "Bank Securities Scam" (or securities scam or bank scam) that has rocked the Government as well as the country. The multi-crore bank securities scam was exploded in April, 1992 because of the brokers' strike in Bombay, causing severe damage to the image of the banking institutions. Annexure I gives the glossary of a few important terms commonly used in securities transactions.

Banks have been undertaking transactions in securities: (i) on their own investment account, (ii) on account of PMS Client's Account in their fiduciary capacity, and (iii) on behalf of their other constituents including brokers purely as an agency function. In the normal course, banks' transaction in securities on their own investment account are expected to be in Government and other trustee securities account which are intended to comply with SLR requirements, except a very small fraction consisting of PSU bonds, shares and debentures which would have devolved on them on account of their underwriting commitments. Banks' portfolio in respect of PMS Clients' Account is expected to generally consist of high coupon bearing capital market instruments like PSU bonds, corporate debentures and shares. These PMS Accounts are mostly of public sector undertakings or other corporate entities. The transaction in securities on behalf of their other clients like brokers undertaken as an agency function would be both in Trustee securities and other corporate bonds, debentures and shares because the broker-client may be dealing in both trustee securities as well as in corporate bonds, debentures and shares.

The commercial banks are required by law to keep certain percentage of their funds invested in Government securities to meet the requirements of Statutory Liquidity Ratio (SLR) prescribed by the Reserve Bank of India from time to time. The commercial banks, therefore, buy and sell Government securities from time to time as a part of a funds management exercise in the banks. They buy and sell Government securities through the brokers and transactions in Government securities are required to be reported to the Public Debt Office (PDO) of the Reserve

Bank of India (RBI) which maintains the record of inter-bank transacitons of investment in Government securities by commercial banks through the Subsidiary General Ledger (SGL) Accounts. It came to the notice of the Reserve Bank of India that some banks were undertaking large scale transactions in Government securities through brokers and in the process they were violating the guidelines issued by the Reserve Bank of India in July, 1991, as stated below. The matter was under investigation by the Reserve Bank of India for quite some time.

1. THE RESERVE BANK OF INDIA GUIDELINES

The Reserve Bank circular of July, 1991 (DBOD No. FSC. 46/C469 - 91 92 dated 26th July, 1991) much talked of now, gives the types of irregularities and transactions in which certain banks were engaged and which they should not have undertaken. Such transactions included:

(i) Ready-forward (buy-back) deals at rates having no relevance to the market rates, *inter alia*, with a view to window dressing their balance sheet/compliance of SLR requirements.

(ii) Double ready forward deals with a view to covering the oversold position in a specific security.

(iii) Sale transaction by issue of Bank Receipts (BRs)/SGL forms without actually holding the securities/without having sufficient balance in their SGL accounts.

(iv) Issuing BRs/SGL forms on behalf of their broker-clients without safeguarding banks' interest.

In the said circular, the RBI had also advised the banks to frame and implement a suitable investment policy to ensure that operations in securities are conducted in accordance with sound and acceptable business practices and, while evolving the investment policy with the approval of their respective boards, to keep in view the following guidelines:

(i) Under no circumstances, the banks should have oversold position in any security (that is to say, no sale transactions should be put through without actually holding the security in its investment account).

(ii) All the transactions put through by the banks either on outright basis or on ready forward basis and whether through the mechanism of SGL Account or BR should be reflected on the same day in their investment accounts and accordingly for SLR purposes, wherever applicable.

(iii) Transactions between banks should not be put through the broker's accounts.

(iv) For issue of BRs, the banks should adopt the format prescribed by the Indian Banks' Association (IBA) and strictly follow the guidelines prescribed by them in this regard and banks should issued BRs covering their constituents including brokers.

(v) Banks should be circumspect while acting as agents of their broker clients for carrying out transactions in securities on behalf of brokers.

(vi) Any instance of return of SGL from the PDO of the RBI for want of sufficient balance in the account should be immediately brought to the notice of the RBI with details of the transaction.

Times of India Report

However, on 23rd April 1992, The Times of India carried a report indicating that there was a shortfall in Government securities held by the State Bank of India to the extent of about Rs. 700 crores. It was noticed that the transactions were put through the issue of Bank Receipts (BRs) by selling banks in respect of transactions in securities. Some of the BRs were found to be disproportionate to the funds of the banks issuing them. In some cases, the BRs issued by banks were not delivered to the other banks and they were kept with the brokers who raised money against such BRs and diverted the funds for operations in the stock market which fueled a wave of high flying boom in the stock market. This boom in the stock market was attributed to the liberalisation of economic policies of the Government of India, expectation of a large flow of the foreign funds from abroad for investment in India and the use of funds received from abroad.

2. JANAKIRAMAN COMMITTEE'S REPORT

On the basis of information received that some banks were undertaking large-scale transactions in Government securities through the medium of brokers in the course of which they were violating the Reserve Bank's guidelines issued to them in July 1991, the Reserve Bank of India constituted a committee under the Chairmanship of Shri R. Janakiraman, Deputy Governor, Reserve Bank of India on 30th April 1992 to investigate into the possible irregularities in funds management by commercial banks and financial institutions and, in particular, in relation to the dealing in Government securities, public sector bonds, UTI units and similar other instruments. The Committee submitted six reports dated May 31, July 5 and August 23, all of the year 1992 and March 6, 1993 which were released to the press immediately, and has rung the curtain down on its labour after submission of two further reports — fifth and sixth ones

— simultaneously. Soon after submission of each report, stern follow-up action has been initiated expeditiously by the Reserve Bank and the Government of India.

A statistical analysis of the transactions in securities in banks brings out the extent to which the system had degenerated, as shown below:

Firstly, of the astronomical figure of transactions of the face value of Rs. 1,285,549 crore (two times the country's GDP and five times the size of bank deposits), during the period of a year and half from January 1991 to June 1992, only Rs. 69,192 crore (or 5.4 per cent) was for outright or such other similar sales and purchases, the others were ready-forward or double ready-forward or other transactions.

Secondly, of the total amount, Government securities constituted Rs. 6,07,627 crore (47.3 per cent). While PSU bonds Rs. 4,94,415 crore (38.5 per cent). With 35,352 transactions in PSU bonds, the amount of Rs. 10,681 crore held by banks has been roughly turned over 46 times in the short period of a year and a half.

Thirdly, the large indulgences have not been entirely due to PMS clients. Own-account transactions aggregated Rs. 8,65,449 crore (67.3 per cent) while transactions relating to PMS clients worked out to Rs. 3,40,303 crore (26.5 per cent) with another Rs. 79.979 crore (6.2 per cent) attributed to transactions on behalf of others including brokers.

Fourthly, brokerwise analysis of the transactions reveals that bulk of what are shown as direct transactions pertain to transactions with routing banks where the counter parties were in fact brokers. The transactions essentially involved brokers. Assuming that transactions for Rs. 1,000,000 crore out of Rs. 1,285,549 crore were undertaken through brokers and if brokers earned a net profit of 0.5 per cent out of total amount of these transactions, an amount of Rs. 5,000 crore would have been generated as profit for the broker community during less than 14 months between April 1, 1991 and May 23, 1992. The Committee has identified as many as 24 brokers who have shared the booty. There top brokers, namely, Harshad Mehta, Hiten Dalal and Bhupan Champak Lal Devidas have accounted for 31.3 per cent of the transactions booked through brokers.

Apart from Central Bureau of Investigation (CBI), other agencies such as Enforcement Directorate and the Income Tax Department have also initiated investigation in the business activities of certain bankers, financial institutions, public sector undertakings and brokers. Very unfortunately, even the central bank of the country got involved in the controversy. No doubt, 34 out of 180 banks and the financial institutions have been involved but the guilt is concentrated in a few banks and institutions. The Joint Parliamentary Committee (JPC) draft report has clearly brought out the nexus between the leading brokers who were on the select list and top management executives in banks like State Bank of India, Syndicate Bank, UCO Bank, Andhra Bank, Vijaya Bank and Bank of Madura Ltd. apart from Bank of Karad Ltd. and Metropolitan Co-operative Bank, now both under liquidation. Further, four foreign banks, namely, Citi-bank, Standard Chartered Bank, Bank of America and ANZ Grindlays Bank had their role in the securities scam. Others involved in securities scam were senior officials of certain institutions and organisations which included National Housing Bank, SBI Caps, Canfina and Canbank Mutual Fund, Andhra Bank Financial Services Ltd. (ABFSL); Oil India Development Board among PSUs. and Fairgrowth Financial Services Ltd. (FFSL) among the private sector financial institutions. The JPC draft report has also exposed the linkage between leading brokers with particular banks, to show as to which particular broker was on the most favourable terms with which bank like Harshad Mehta with State Bank of India and Dalal Group with foreign banks.

Root Causes of the Scam

The clearing mechanism in Bombay market was "rudimentary and inefficient." Government securities were cleared through Public Debt Office (PDO) of the Reserve Bank of India by entries in Subsidiary General Ledger (SGL). The evidence of sale and purchase between banks was through SGL notes which were delivered to the Public Debit Office and recorded to the debit of selling bank's account and the credit of purchasing bank's account.

Owing to the inefficiency of Public Debt Office (PDO), there were often lengthy delays in recording transactions, Inadequate registration and delivery systems for public sector unit bonds made it difficult for banks to settle themselves quickly and efficiently. Often the bonds were simply unavailable.

To overcome these problems, a bank receipt mechanism had been devised. A bank receipt is simply a receipt for money received and a promise to deliver the relevant security at a later date. Although bank receipts are not transferable, they became the widely used media by which banks transferred securities between themselves via brokers.

The role of brokers was key to understanding what happened. Brokers not only acted as intermediaries between principals in arranging deals but also acted as clearing agents in the sense that they would take cash from a purchaser, deliver to the seller and accept securities for delivery in return. With the inefficiencies in both the PDO and the Bank Receipt Section and the dual capacity of brokers as agents and principals, there was ample opportunity to take advantage of the systematic weaknesses to obtain double financing against securities or to deploy cash in the booming stock market.

Widespread market dealings had grown up for ready forwards in public sector unit bonds. Ready forwards involve the sale of a security by one bank to another and its repurchases for a fixed price at a given future date. The Reserve Bank of India guidelines prohibited ready forwards in public sector unit bonds. Nevertheless the practice continued but the ready forwards were not recorded in banks' accounts. Consequently, the market in ready forwards in public sector bonds was essentially an oral one with the brokers playing a pivotal role. Again, the market was wide open for abuse.

Degraded market practice at a time of an unprecedent boom in stock market activity coincided to create a situation which devalued ethical standards and fostered a climate of opportunism. All the elements needed for a scam were there.

There was collusion between bank officials and brokers. This fraudulent activity made banks more, vulnerable than others to loss arising from widespread abuse of the market, malpractice and dishonesty. If the basic norms had been observed, on broker would have had unbridled freedom to indulge in "hera-pheri" of billions of rupees.

As the Janakiraman Committee has emphasised, the irregularities have arisen cut of attempts to circumvent RBI guidelines. The banks and institutions involved in the securities scam pushed ahead with their irregular activities in two forms, namely, the portfolio management scheme (PMS) with assured rates of return and for duration for less than one year contrary to RBI guidelines, and the financing of brokers through illegal ready forward and double forward deals through money market operations and discounting of fictitious bills. Such activities became so blatant and widespread that they almost emerged as market practices and several banks and other financial institutions joined the fray but a few continued to dominate the scene.

Banker-Broker Nexus

The Janakiraman Committee has identified seven types of irregularities committed by banks in the operation of PMS system:

(i) indicating assured rates of return;

(ii) providing of funds under the PMS scheme to brokers under ready forward transactions;

(iii) failure to ensure that PMS funds were in fact invested in areas in which clients were legally permitted to invest.

(iv) attempts to siphon off the excess earnings of PMS funds through artificial rates shown in the books so that actual earnings remained close to the indicated rates;

(v) the crediting of lower yield rates on PMS accounts than those credited to the banks' own accounts whenever composite sales were made;

(vi) failure to provide full details of PMS accounts to banks' clients and finally;

(vii) fictitious transactions of loaning customers unit holding to the bank concerned and siphoning off the income in PMS accounts to the credit of banks.

Interestingly, in all these irregularities the Citibank has been singled out for mention by the Janakiraman Committee. The total amount of funds so generated on PMS accounts on Units by Citibank was Rs. 411.21 crore (Source: Economic and Political Weekly, 5 June, 1993).

The banks and financial institutions involved in PMS irregularities were four foreign banks (Stand chart, Citibank, ANZ Grindlays and Bank of America), Canfina, Andhra Bank Financial Services, Syndicate Bank and Vijaya Bank. The beneficiaries were all brokers. The PMS funds as also large amount of their own funds were lent by banks to brokers in the form of ready forward transactions. As ready forward transactions could only be entered into with banks and only in respect of Government Securities, transactions were recorded as though made with certain counter-party banks, but their actual beneficiaries were brokers. To accomplish, certain banks acted as 'routing' banks for brokers. The 'routing' bank, in turn, purchased and sold securities without indicating that they were acting on behalf of broker. When securities did not exist, they even created fictitious BRs. Many fictitious entries were made debiting the cost of purchases to the brokers' accounts. As many as nine major banks functioned as 'routing' banks in favour of brokers. Brokers liberally used banks as counter-parties, sometimes even without their knowledge. Many purchasing banks were unaware of the fact that they were dealing with brokers and not with counter-party banks. When delivery was not effected of the securities for which payment has been made the liability was denied by banks whose names were shown as counter-party banks.

A significant part of the problem has arisen on this account and related to certain transactions which have resulted in problem exposure and the links between the banks and the borrowers in this regard. The Janakiraman Committee has now updated and worked out the gross problem exposure of banks at Rs. 4,024,45 crore — a significant increase from the first report's estimate of Rs. 3,078.63 crore — comprising (a) total value of investment made by banks for which they do not hold any securities, SGL form or valid BRs (Rs. 2,262,57 crore); (b) total exposure against BRs/SGL transfers issued by Bank of Karad Ltd. and Metropolitan Cooperative Bank Ltd. (both now under liquidation) for which there appears to be no security backing (Rs. 1,473,47 crore); and (c) other items (Rs. 288,41 crores). The gross problem exposure does not include the depreciation or losses suffered by banks as ready-forward transactions could not be reversed and the banks were left holding securities which had depreciated in value. Only a small amount of Rs. 600 crore or so is in sight as having been recovered by banks.

The most revealing aspect of Janakiraman Committee's report relates to the close nexus between brokers and certain banks which enables the brokers to have unlimited access to the funds. There are also examples of nexus among banks whereby one bank was used as a source of funds and another as disburser of funds.

The key element in the perpetration of the irregularities was the BRs which were used to generate transactions that had no security backing. BRs were used almost as negotiable instruments and transferred from one bank to another and also third party BRs were accepted by banks. As the Janakiraman Committee argues," the indiscriminate use of BRs without security backing created a kind of paper money which circulated from bank to bank like a stage army of soldiers and provided an opportunity to brokers to avail of funds of increasingly large amount." All these irregularities were possible because of the complete breakdown of the system of internal control in a number of banks.

Committee's Findings and Remedial Action

The findings of the Janakiraman Committee have indicated serious irregularities and deficiencies in the functioning of banks and financial institutions involved. These included: absence of necessary internal control in various functions; raising money without the backing of genuine securities; diversion of call money to the currents accounts of chosen brokers; and massive collusion between the concerned officials and brokers involved in dealings in Government securities, public sector bonds, units, etc. The Committee has listed the devices adopted for diversion of funds from the banking system to individual accounts of certain brokers which prima facie constitute evidence of fraudulent misrepresentation. Funds management operations have been conducted in gross violation and with utter disregard of the instructions and guidelines issued by the RBI from time to time. The breakdown of essential discipline regarding the issue and recording of Banker's receipts (BRs), the receipt and delivery of securities and the receipt and payment for settlement of transactions have been detailed in the report. The Committee has also come across instances wherein brokers have been financed by banks through the discounting of bills not supported by genuine transactions.

The Janakiraman Committee has made recommendations for taking a series of steps so that remedial action is taken to introduce proper control system, strengthen monitoring and remove lacunae in the existing system and procedures so as to prevent recurrence of similar lapses in future. The Reserve Bank and the Government have taken a number of steps with a view to unearthing the entire ramifications of the episode, to recover the banking dues, to punish the guilty, and to set in motion enduring measures of preventive nature. The avowed objective of the Reserve Bank and the Government is to restore confidence, both in India and abroad, in the country's financial system and to ensure that it becomes stronger and much more efficient by undertaking appropriate follow-up measures.

The measures include examination of the entire securities transaction of banks and financial institutions for the last one year; placing Bank of Karad Ltd., under suspension; placing Bank of Madura Ltd., under a Reserve Bank observe; proceeding against Metropolitan Cooperative Bank Ltd. (Reserve Bank accorded its sanction for winding up of this bank on June 19,1992); the delisting of three brokers from the Reserve Bank's list of approved brokers' entrusting the entire investigation to the Central Bureau of Investigation (CBI); attaching the properties of all those involved; establishment of a Special Court to exclusively attend to cases relating to securities transaction of banks and financial institutions; appointment of reputed firms of Chartered Accountants to conduct special audit of treasury operations of major players in the market under the provision of Section 30 (IB) of the Banking Regulation Act, 1949. issuance of special guidelines including the prohibition of inter-bank ready-forward deals in dated securities and approved/trustee securities except Treasury Bills of all maturities; and prohibition of double ready-forward deals in Government securities including Treasury Bills.

The other important aspects of the guidelines are:

(i) The existing prohibition of buy-back deals between banks in other securities such as PSU bonds and units will continue.

(ii) Banks should ensure that Subsidiary General Ledger (SGL) transfer forms covering their sale transactions in Government/approved securities are issued only if they have sufficient balance in their respective SGL accounts in the Public Debt Office of the Reserve Bank of India. In the event of bouncing of SGL transfer forms, banks will render themselves liable to penal action.

(iii) BRs should not be issued under any circumstances in respect of transaction in Government securities for which SGL facility is available. BRs may be issued in the case of other securities for ready transactions only under exceptional circumstances; and

(iv) BRs should not be issued covering transactions relating to either portfolio management scheme clients or other constituents including brokers.

Detailed profiles of large-scale frauds, misdemeanor and irregularities involving commercial banks and other financial institutions the world over reveal that each one of them is *sui generis* with unique and distinct characteristics. Fraudulent practices are committed with great ingenuity by individuals by always by subverting the rules of the game with connivance and collusion. It is because of such connivance and collusion that all frauds continue for a long period before they are detected; the detection is often accidental as such frauds do not get revealed in the case of normal reporting to the regulatory authorities. The occurrence of frauds is neutral to the type of institutional set-up or the nature of supervisory regulations. Frauds have occurred in most competitive conditions and also in fairly controlled systems. They have occurred in tight regulatory environment as much as they have occurred in liberal environment. One single feature which is common to almost all frauds is that the funds so generated have generally been deployed in stock markets.

Critical Analysis of the Report

While the Janakiraman Committee has unearthed the various dimensions of the irregularities with commendable insight and thoroughness, it is on a weak wicket at least on two counts, namely, first, in its perception of the environment which facilitated the perpetration of these irregularities and second, in its analysis of the reasons shy the irregularities could not be detected earlier. In explaining the environment, the Committee has advanced argument similar to what the protagonists of liberalisation have been putting forth, namely, that the rigid regulatory environment created arbitrage opportunities for banks whereby funds could be borrowed cheap and relent dear. The Committee's argument run on these lines:

First, with the withdrawal of budgetary support, the PSUs had to raise funds massively in the market. With the short-term money market closed to them, they needed an investment avenue yielding more than the coupon rate on their bonds. Therefore, the PSUs raised huge funds from the banks and relent them through the portfolio management scheme (PMS).

Secondly, the stock market was booming and the 'bulls' needed to finance their overbought position, never mind the high badla rates.

Thirdly, bankers who faces rigid controls on interest rates and cash reserves and liquidity requirements and who accepted high cost funds from PSUs, saw that the only avenue which yielded with enough returns was financing of stock brokers in a booming stock market.

Essentially, the predatory instincts of a few foreign banks and some Indian banks overtook the system. In the first place, PSUs did not require the funds for investment and yet they were allowed to borrow massive funds through PSU bonds. It was a system of frauds perpetrated with the connivance of banks, brokers and PSUs. It clearly brought out a scenario in which the "umpires" who were supposed to check the "foul play", too ironically became the "players" in the game of fraud with public money. Secondly, it is a moot point if the share prices would have boomed but for the availability of these scam-generated funds for the brokers. Thirdly, nowhere in the banking world could yield rates in the short-term money market ensure regular returns higher than yield rates on long-term bond. Fourthly, the irregularities were not restricted to PSU funds, fictitious and artificial funds were generated out of thin air through BRs and SLGs just to finance the brokers illegally. If the supervisory system remains weak, frauds will occur in any environment, controlled or liberal.

In fact, banks have incurred losses on a massive scale, inclusive of about Rs. 800 crore through depreciation in the value of PSU bonds. This suggests that there was hardly any trace of professional ingenuity, competence and calculation on the part of banking personnel who indulged in arbitrage arbitration; it was a crude method of financing brokers which enticed the bankers with the prospects of book margins and profits.

As for the reasons why the irregular, could not be detected earlier, the Janakiraman Committee appears to be soft on all the three major parties, that is, the bank management, the supervisory authority (i.e., the RBI) and the banks internal auditors who should have detected the irregularities. There is no doubt that failures everywhere have been at the top for want of professional commitment and competence. In the banking industry, over the years, the quality of personnel in the higher echelons has been deteriorating. Likewise, in the case of Reserve Bank, the Janakiraman Committee argues that in emphasising the quality of banks' assets, provision for doubtful debts, etc., the bank did not perhaps give sufficient importance to banks' treasury functions. It also points out that the RBI had nonetheless detected some of the irregularities earlier. This may be true and may redound to the credit of lower-level functionaries in the RBI. Even so, irregularities on such a massive scale for so long a period since the mid-80s could not have occurred, had firm steps been taken by the concerned authorities to nip the evil in the bud.

3. JOINT PARLIAMENTARY COMMITTEE

After the bank securities scam was exposed, the Government constituted, on August 9, 1992, a Joint Parliamentary Committee (JPC) comprising 30 members from both the Houses of Parliament under the Chairmanship of Shri Ram Niwas Mirdha, M.P. to probe into the entire gamut of issues concerning the serious irregularities in the securities transaction of the banks and the financial institutions. The members of Parliament belonging to the ruling Congress Party and the opposition parties are members of the JPC as well as the drafting Committee with the Chairman, Shri Mirdha being a Congress Party M.P.

As the terms of reference of JPC cover substantially the same ground as envisaged by the terms of the Janakiraman Committee and its investigation would involve duplication of work, the Janakiraman Committee proposed to confine its future work to an examination of the findings of the scrutiny already undertaken by the Reserve Bank inspecting officers under its directions and to report thereon.

The JPC is finalising the report, after extensive sittings, after recording all the evidence, after enough time had been given to all interested parties to come forward and disclose evidence and depose before the JPC. The final report is expected to be submitted shortly. The JPC may keep apart the probe into the controversial Rs. one crore pay-off allegedly made by Harshad Mehta (touched later) and submit its report to Parliament on Rs. 5,000 crore bank securities scam which was its basic mandate. The controversy about the alleged payoff is getting deeper with new points or charges coming to light necessitating for the JPC to look into the fresh issues is completed (See Annexure 11 for JPC Final Report).

4. PAYOFF CHARGE

On 16 June, 1993, Stock broker, Harshad Mehta, a key figure in the unprecedented financial scandal, made the sensational allegations at a Press Conference at Bombay that he had paid Rs. one crore directly to the Prime Minister P.V. Narasimha Rao "for his political patronage and guidance" in two installments on two consecutive days. He said that at 10.45 A.M. on November 4, 1991 he handed over a suitcase containing Rs. 67 lakhs personally to the Prime Minister P.V. Narasimha Rao at his 7 Race Course residence and that the remaining amount was paid on the following day.

On the same day, Prime Minister P.V. Narasimha Rao categorically denied the allegation that he had received Rs. 1 crore from stock broker Harshad Mehta and said, I am shocked and surprised that a malicious and unfounded story has been made up. I have not got any money from Mr. Mehta I deny the allegations made. People can well understand the motive behind the allegations." (Source: Hindustan Times dated 17 June, 1993).

People are to judge who of the two is right. As regards burden of proof, Section 101 of the Indian Evidence Act provides: "Burden of Proof: Whosoever desires any court to give judgement as to any legal right or liability dependent on the existence of fact which he asserts, must prove those facts exits. When a person is bound to prove the existence of any fact, it is said that the burden of proof lies on that person." In the light of this provision, since Harshad Mehta has made the allegation, burden of proving them beyond all reasonable doubt lies on him. However, Mr. Mehta has failed, by all counts, to provide any evidence to prove his allegations beyond any doubt.

The Joint Parliamentary Committee (JPC) who is also seized of this case, sent questionnaires to nine persons who recently figured in the deposition given by the stock broker, Harshad Mehta and also summoned certain documents from the Prime Minister's office and residence relating to the records of telephone calls, visitor's registers etc., of November, 1991. The questionnaires were returnable by June 20, 1993 (Source: Hindustan Times Dated 14.7.1993).

While the CBI had in its latest status report to the JPC stated that it did not find any substantive material to take up the investigation into the allegation, the JPC has yet to decide if it should also drop the matter or pursue it by calling the Prime Minister for evidence. There is nothing, of course, to prevent the high power forum from pursuing its enquiry in the manner it deems most proper and productive. To examine all aspects of the sordid affair and also to keep sights clearly and firmly at the substantive issues at stake, the one-crore poser should elicit a response that does not put off the answer to the 5,000-crore question.

Concluding Observations

Soon after presentation of the 1993-94 Union Budget, the capital market was booming with Bombay Stock Exchange index going upto 4500 and above in April 1992. The boom in the stock market was attributed to several factors including the introduction of economic reforms leading to policies of liberalisation in the filed of trade, industry and commerce. However, this boom proved to be short lived with the outbreak of security scam exposing several irregularities in security transactions between banks and brokers and as a result of these revelations the confidence of investing public in the stock market declined and the share prices started collapsing with the Bombay Stock Exchange index declining to around 2500 in May, 1992.

The Janakiraman Committee scrutinised the way in which the banks took active part in the brokers' systematic loot of public money. Paper instruments called BRs (Bank Receipts) which are as good as banker cheques, bounced. SGLs (Subsidiary General-Ledgers) accounts were grossly misused. The Portfolio Management Scheme (PMS) which was introduced to help investors to use their funds prudently, became "deposits" for the banks and a perennial source of fund for unscrupulous brokers and their obliging friends in the banks and the Government.

The JPC draft report has now shed some light on the murky doings of bankers and brokers. Brokers made money using other's money. Many bankers know what was happening but did little to check what was going on. Some of the bankers who failed the banks and the depositors have been thrown out of their jobs. The Government has also taken action against others found responsible for negligence and complicity.

In its final report, the JPC has an opportunity to go beyond the "systemic failure" which has been conclusively identified. The "system", after all, is not a totally inanimate object — it is run by human beings. And, clearly, some of them are responsible for the way in which the "system" was manipulated, and the crime committed against the nation. Apart from identifying the culprits and exposing the guilty, it is necessary that JPC suggest adequate safeguards and corrective measures for the overhauling of the entire system so that such a colossal tragedy does not occur again.

The securities scam has revealed several weaknesses in the working of commercial banks, particularly in their procedures evolved for control mechanism. The commercial banks will, therefore, have to think in terms of strengthening their control mechanism for evolving appropriate procedures. The Government had announced in 1993-94 budget the setting up of a separate Board for Financial Supervision to strengthen the RBI's supervisory role over the banks. But this has yet to be set up.

The annual report of the Reserve Bank of India for 1992-93 (July-June) refers to the securities scam and stresses the need for a strong and alert system of surveillance. The mechanism of internal control and audit and the system of supervisions had failed to detect financial operations of a collusive and fraudulent character. The RBI is of the view that there should be a quick fraud detection mechanism, accompanied by a machinery for its proper enforcement. Necessary measures in this regard will be adopted shortly.

ANNEXURE 1

GLOSSARY OF TERMS COMMONLY USED IN SECURITIES TRANSACTIONS

Bank Receipt (BR)

Bank Receipt is a receipt issued by a selling banker in favour of a purchasing banker in token of having received the payment towards sale of security. Bank Receipt acknowledges that the selling bank holds the security on behalf of the purchasing bank. Bank Receipts are to be issued in the prescribed format, as prescribed by Indian Banks Association (IBA), on security paper and are required to be serially numbered and dated according to IBA rules. Bank receipts must be exchanged for actual scrips within a period of 90 days. BR is non-transferable. Normally, no BR should be issued where SGL facility is available. BR can be accepted from any one of the following institutions:

(i) All member banks of IBA.

(ii) Financial institutions like IDBI, IFCI, ICICI, NABARD, UTI, LIC, GIC.

(iii) Public Sector Undertakings (PSUs).

(iv) Any other institutions specified by the IBA/RBI.

SGL (Subsidiary General Ledger) Account

Subsidiary General Ledger (SGL) Account is maintained by the Public Debt Office (PDO) of the Reserve Bank of India (RBI) by the banks loanwise through which the transactions pertaining to Central/State Governments securities can be put through. It is similar to current accounts maintained by banks. The transfer is effected by the Reserve Bank of India from one banker's account to another banker's account by posting the credit/debit SGL transfer form. This form does not require any stamp duty. The officers of the bank who are authorised to sign the SGL transfer forms are required to get their Power of Attorney registered with the RBI. After verification of the signature of the concerned officials of the seller bank/purchasing bank, the transaction will be put through by the PDO, RBI, subject to availability of credit in the particular security account.

Ready Forward Contract

Transactions entered into towards sale/purchase of securities by one bank with another bank with the arrangement for purchase/sale thereof on a specified date with the predetermined price. It is permitted from one bank/financial institution to another bank/financial institution. The facility is applicable in respect of approved securities.

Double Ready Forward

These are Ready Forward Transactions undertaken to cover another Ready Forward Transaction with, an intention to acquire a particular security against another security. For example, acquisition of 11.50% GOI Loan 2010 against sale of 11.50% Loan 2008. This consists of two Ready Forward Transactions.

JOINT PARLIAMENTARY COMMITTEE FINAL REPORT

The final report of the Joint Parliamentary Committee on the multi-crore Bank Securities Scam was presented to both Houses of Parliament on 21 December 1993. The JPC comprising 30 members from both the Houses of Parliament and belonging to both the ruling party and the opposition parties, was specially appointed through a resolution passed in the Lok Sabha in August 1992. It was the Lok Sabha which set out its terms of reference and the basic task for the JPC by authorising it go into the irregularities, to fix individual and institutional responsibility for the fraud and to make recommendations regarding policy and regulations so that the scam did not occur again. The bulky report in two volumes is a "consensus" document of the 30-member committee and is a product of 16 months of JPC labour. At the end of its long journey, when the JPC could produce a unanimous report, it was definitely a positive achievement.

The report came to the broad conclusion that the scam was "basically a deliberate and criminal misuse" of public funds with the aim of "illegally" siphoning the funds of the banks and public sector undertaking to "select brokers." The report gives three figures about the size of the scam Janakiraman Committee's figures of Rs. 4,024 crore, CBI's figure of Rs. 8,383 crore and of office of the Custodian, Rs. 3,650 crore. The aggregate value of transactions runs into some twelve lakh crore of rupees of which the foreign banks were involved in Rs. 6,82,427 crore between April 1991 and May 1992. The report blames the commercial banks, the stock market, the financial institutions, public sector undertakings, the Reserve Bank of India and "even the Ministry of Finance, (and) other economic ministries in varying degrees." The JPC is very harsh on the foreign banks, principally the Citibank, ANZ Grindlays, Standard Chartered and Bank of America. The JPC is equally harsh on the Indian banks, in particular the State Bank of India, and has made severe criticism of public sector undertakings. The report also goes for the brokers and states that "the close nexus between certain PSUs, banks and brokers enabled them to have unauthorised access to funds leading to diversion of huge public funds from the banking sector to the brokers."

The JPC then goes to criticise the RBI and the Ministry of Finance. On the RBI, the JPC observes that "it was the top management of the RBI which was wholly responsible for the RBI's contribution to the scam." "Shri S. Venkitaramanan as the Governor of the Bank during the crucial period must be held no less responsible." According to the JPC, the "acts of omission and commission" by the former governor, S. Venkitaramanan, included "a display of unusual interest" in a bank account of the chief scamster, Harshad Mehta, besides helping foreign banks evade rules and regulations and hamstrunging official efforts to discipline banks and discourage permissive portfolio management scheme. The Report also blames two deputy Governors and Chief Officer of the Department of Banking Operations and Development of the RBI, for their role in the scam.

The JPC in its report indicted in varying degrees Finance Minister, Dr. Manmohan Singh, present Health Minister, Mr. B. Shankaranand and Minister of State, Mr. Rameshwar Thakur for their lapses. The JPC holds that the FM has "constructive responsibility" for the scam. To affirm the general principle of constitutional responsibility of a minister of Parliament is one thing but to apportion blame to a minister on a particular case irrespective of the specific circumstances is quite another and is hardly justified. Dr. Singh's constructive responsibility for his ministry, as stressed by the JPC, is certainly undeniable, but this is not by any means comparable to the plain culpability of some others. The sharp and spicy comments in the report about the Finance Minister's 'slumber' (though changed later) is a caution against complacency rather than a charge of complicity.

Mr. Shankaranand has come for adverse comments for his role as Chairman of Oil Industries Development Board (OIDB) under the Ministry of Petroleum when he was the Minister for petroleum. The Report concluded that OIDB under Mr. Shankaranand had shown favour to Canfina and Syndicate Bank in making investment of huge surplus funds under PMS. Minister of State, Mr. Rameshwar Thakur has been censured by the JPC for delaying action against Big Bull, Harshad Mehta, in a particular case for over a month. Both Mr. Shankaranand and Mr. Rameshwar Thakur have refuted the charges made against them in the JPC report.

Harshad Mehta's Allegations

The JPC did not probe into the allegations of the political pay-off by Bombay broker, Mr. Harshad Mehta, to Prime Minister P.V. Narasimha Rao, in November 1991. The report, however, reproduced the evidence tendered by CBI Director and others that the Bombay broker had failed to make out a *prima facie* case on charges of corruption and the CBI did not take up the enquiry. The Committee did not draw any conclusion.

But there is a note appended to the JPC Report, given by 13 members belonging to the opposition parties in the Committee, which demanded an enquiry to be set up under the Commission of Inquiry Act. They did not want the matter to be dropped. On the other hand, the Congress members in their note appended to the report maintained that there was no substantive material to merit an enquiry. These and other notes given by the individual members have been made a part of the report though they have not been treated as notes of dissent.

Fallout of the Report

In the aftermath of the IPC Report, two events of significance took place:

(i) Resignation by Finance Minister, Dr. Manmohan Singh, and

(ii) debate in both Houses of Parliament on JPC Report on 29th and 30th December 1993.

Resignation

The Role of the Finance Minister, Dr. Manmohan Singh, came for adverse comments in the final report at several places, though it is a case of his constructive responsibility and accountability to Parliament. The JPC observed that "despite the Minister of Finance being aware of what was happening in the stock market he did not address himself seriously to check the unhealthy trend." The JPC in a severe indictment of the Finance Ministry held that it failed to respond purposely when the scam came to the surface and failed to manage adequately when it broke out. What was worse was the Finance Ministry did not punish the guilty in time.

In keeping with the healthy democratic traditions following the JPC's indictment of the Finance Ministry and to uphold principles and values in public life, Dr. Manmohan Singh submitted his formal resignation letter to Prime

Minister P.V. Narsimha Rao on 23rd December 1993. Dr. Singh took the reins of the Finance Ministry on June 21, 1991 after the Congress Party headed by Narasimha Rao formed the Government. Dr. Singh, a well-known Economist and dynamic Finance Minister, was responsible for various economic reforms and had pulled the nation's economy out of a deep crises and put it back on the rails. He is known as a person of impeccable personal integrity and character and the JPC Report did not cast any aspersions on his integrity. It was, however, felt that if Dr. Singh's resignation is accepted it was sure to give a bad signal to the international financial institutions about the course of future economic reforms in India. Both the industry sources and the foreign institutional sources expressed their concern at this sudden development and they hoped that the Prime Minister would still be persuaded to retain Dr. Singh in the cabinet.

The week-long suspense over the resignation of Finance Minister, Dr. Manmohan Singh ended on 31st December 1993 with the Prime Minister officially rejecting Dr. Singh's resignation letter. In his rejection letter, the Prime Minister is reported to have pointed out that he is not in a position to accept "the resignation of his valued colleague" in view of the ongoing economic reforms. In resigning the Finance Minister has shown moral courage and in not accepting the resignation the Prime Minister has acted in national interest.

Parliamentary Debate

According to newspaper reports, the Congress Party, during the two-day debate on the JPC report in Parliament on December 29 and 30, 1993, attacked or disowned its findings, in both the Houses of the Parliament. Several opposition members, both in the Lok Sabha and Rajya Sabha wanted to know if this kind of denigration of the JPC and its work was the Government's thinking on the role and authority of the Joint Parliamentary Committee.

Finance Minister, Dr. Manmohan Singh, however, paid compliments to the JPC in the Lok Sabha for its labour and the work done by it and said that the Government accepted the report, though he had some reservations about certain aspects of the conclusions. A major outcome of the debate in Parliament on the JPC report was the Prime Minister's assurance that corrective action will be taken wherever it is called for. It may be added that not only action should be taken against the culprits in the biggest financial scandal in the country's history but fool proof measures should be worked out to ensure that public money is not siphoned off on such a colossal scale in future.

Prevention

The central issue before the JPC was not only to find out who the guilty were but also to deal with "systemic failures". In fact, the principal issue which concerns the average citizen is why did the scam occur and how to prevent such scams in future.

Unfortunately, on these central issues the JPC is content to make only passing references. For instance, Para 16.31 of the report states "that 10 top executives of the 20 nationalised banks have during the past few years been found involved in serious irregularity is a telling commentary on the process of selection and appointments by the Government." The JPC, however, did not go into this issue which is at the heart of management of the banking system in India, that is, why are people with dubious records appointed top executives of the banks.

PRACTICE QUESTIONS

1. Define 'banking' under the Banking Regulation Act, 1949.
2. Define a customer. What are the obligations of a banker towards his customer?
3. When must a banker refuse payment of a cheque?
4. What are the accepted norms the banks should follow to minimise the risk involved in lending?
5. Distinguish between 'development banking' and 'commercial banking'.
6. What are the advantages of branch banking?
7. Explain the factors determining liquidity of banks.
8. 'Money today is highly the creation of Banking system" – Comment.
9. Mention the principles that should guide a commercial bank in investing in Funds.
10. What are the reasons for nationalisation of banks in India?
11. Explain the reasons for underdeveloped Indian money market.
12. Define crossing and explain different types of crossing
13. What are the essential features of a banker-customer relationship?
14. How and when a banker may disclose information regarding the customer's account?
15. Discuss the legal position of a banker regarding fixed deposits.

16. Bring out clearly the functions of a pass book.
17. Explain the importance of liquidity and profitability in commercial banking.
18. Explain the essential functions of Reserve Bank.
19. Explain the recent trends in Indian Money Market.
20. The relation between banker and customer is primarily that of Debtor and Creditor. How does this differ from similar relationship arising out of ordinary commercial debts? Discuss.
21. "Is a banker legally bound to honour his customer's cheques?" Discuss.
22. Explain the legal position of wrong entries in the pass book.
23. What precautions a banker should take while opening the current of Joint Stock Companies?
24. Distinguish between secured and unsecured advances of the bank. What precaution should a banker take while making unsecured advances?
25. Define 'Endorsement'. Explain the essentials of valid endorsement.
26. Write a note on 'banking ombudsman scheme'.
27. "Skill of successful banking lies in arranging maturity pattern of liabilities and assets sub-serving the principle of liquidity." Comment.
28. "The combination of 'account payee' crossing and 'not negotiable' crossing gives fullest protection to a cheque." Comment.
29. "A banker's right to set-off is nothing but the right to combine the accounts." Comment.
30. A bank disbursed a loan to one of its customers after obtaining from him a demand promissory note. Later on, it is noticed that the promissory note was not stamped. Bank wants your advice on the following available options:
    — to affix necessary stamp duty on the promissory note which has already been executed; or
    — to obtain a fresh promissory note duly stamped and executed from the customer.
31. A letter of credit is valid upto 10th April, 2005 for shipment and 25th April, 2005 for negotiation. Amendment is received extending the date of shipment upto 10th May, 2005. What will be the validity period of the letter of credit?
32. Prakash is the managing director of a limited company. In his capacity as the managing director, he is authorised to sign alone for operating the company's bank account which is maintained with Kripa Bank Ltd. in Chennai. Prakash's personal account is also with the same bank, where he has maintained an average credit balance of Rs. 15,000.

    Prakash draws a cheque on the company's account in favour of himself for Rs. 1.85 lakh and deposits it with the Kripa Bank Ltd. for credit to his personal account. The cheque is duly collected by the Kripa Bank Ltd. and the proceeds credited to his account. Subsequently, the company goes into liquidation and the liquidator files a suit against the Kripa Bank Ltd. for recovery of the money on the ground that there had been fraudulent conversion. What is the position of the Kripa Bank Ltd.? Give reasons for your answer.
33. The Blessed Bank Ltd. had advanced a loan for purchasing a truck and deed of hypothecation was executed by the owners in favour of the bank under that agreement, the truck was pledged with the bank for due repayment of the loan advanced by the bank. The truck remained in the possession of the owners and was plied by the driver engaged by the owners. The truck collided with a passenger bus due to which some passengers of the bus were injured. The injured persons preferred separate claim applications. It was claimed that the bank along with owners of the truck should be held liable vicariously. Decide whether the hypothecating bank can be held liable for payment of compensation to the victims of the accident caused by the owners' employee. What is the status of the hypothecating bank — only as a debtor or as a creditor?
34. Raju has a current account with a bank. His clerk forged his signature to a cheque for Rs. 15,000 and encashed it at the bank. Raju, having come to know of this irregularity, claims the amount from the bank. Meanwhiie, the banker claims that it has paid the cheque in due course. Can the banker escape from its liability? Give reasons.
35. "Financial sector reforms have changed the face of public sector banks in India." Do you agree? Explain what should be the mission for banking sector in India.
36. What precautions a bank should take before opening a letter of credit (L/C) limit for the use of importers?
37. What is a Commercial Bank? How is financial management done in commercial banks? Also discuss major banking laws and regulations.
38. Discuss the growth and trends of development banking in industrial financing in India.

References

1. Ladbroke & Co. v. Todd.
2. Times Law Report, March 1920.
3. New Bank of India v. Perey Lal (1962).
4. Tournier v. National Provincial Bank.
5. Devaynes v. Noble (1816) 1 Men 572 (Clayton's case).
6. Paget, Sir John, Law of Banking, Butterworth & Co., 1966.
7. Sayers, R.S., Modern Banking, Oxford University Press, London, 1960.
8. Charler, Lord, Law of Banking, Banking Regulation Act, 1949
9. Hart, Law of Banking.
10. Times of India Report, 1972
11. RBI Bulletin, of 1973 and others.

PART C

NEGOTIABLE INSTRUMENTS ACT, 1881

PART C

NEGOTIABLE INSTRUMENTS ACT, 1881

CHAPTER

6

Negotiable Instruments

Backdrop

In the field of monetary dealings and commercial transactions, some papers of specific conditions are used which are called "negotiable instruments". The 'negotiable' word denotes transferable from one person to another in return for consideration and 'instrument' denotes a written paper which provides a right in favour of some person. Thus, a 'negotiable instrument' is a piece of written paper which entitles a person to a sum of money and which is transferable from one person to another by mere delivery or by endorsement and delivery. The person in favour of whom it is so transferred becomes entitled to transfer it again.

Negotiable Instrument, however, is an exception to the maxim of law *nemo dat quod non habet* (no person can transfer a better title than he himself has).

Willis in his book "The Law of Negotiable Securities" defined as "a negotiable instrument is one, the property in which is acquired by any one who takes it bonafide and for value notwithstanding any defect of title in the person from whom he took it."

Negotiable Instruments Act 1881 deals with the law relating to negotiable instruments. This Act came into force on Ist day of March, 1882. Act is applicable to whole of the India.

Definition of Negotiable Instrument

The definition of term Negotiable Instrument as such is not given in the Negotiable Instruments Act. According to section 13 of the Act, 1881, "a negotiable instrument means a 'promissory note', 'bill of exchange' or a 'Cheque' payable either to order or to bearer." The sphere of Act, however, does not exclude any other instruments which satisfies the conditions of negotiability and can be added to the list of negotiable instruments.

It is clear from the section 13 of the Act that instrument payable to order are negotiable also, but an order instrument can only be negotiated by endorsement and genuiness must be in endorsement.

Characteristics of a negotiable instrument

Followings are the special characteristics of a negotiable instrument.

(a) Freely Transferable

The instrument should be freely transferable from one person to another by:

(i) delivery in case the instrument is payable to bearer, or

(ii) by endorsement and delivery in case the instrument is payable to order.

(b) Holder's title free from all defects

A person who takes an instrument for value known as a holder in the due course. A holder in due course acquires a good title notwithstanding any defect in a previous holder of title. He must have taken the instrument in food faith and without notice of any defect in the instrument or in the title of the person negotiating it to him.

(c) Recovery

The holder in due course can sue upon a negotiable instrument in his own name for the recovery of the amount.

(d) A negotiable instrument can be transferred any number of times, till its maturity.

Applicable presumptions to negotiable instruments

Section 118 and 119 provides following presumptions in favour of all negotiable instruments, unless the contrary is proved.

1. Consideration

Every negotiable instrument is presumed to have been made or drawn for consideration. Consideration in a promissory note is different from that which was alleged in the plaint. The note was still presumed to have been issued for valid consideration.[1]

When once the court finds that the defendant has executed the promissory note, then the burden is on the defendant to proved that there is no consideration. The initial burden rests on the plaintiff who has to prove that the promissory note is executed by the defendant. If there is an admission by the defendant, there is no burden on the plaintiff to prove the execution of the 'promissory note' where execution is admitted or proved, a presumption is raised in favour of consideration having been passed and the burden to prove lack of consideration is then with the defendant.[2]

2. Date

Every negotiable instrument bearing a date is presumed to have been made or drawn on such date.

3. Time of acceptance

When a bill of exchange has been accepted, it is presumed that it was accepted within a reasonable time of its date and before its maturity.

4. Transfer time

It is presumed that every transfer of a negotiable instrument has been made before its maturity.

5. Order of Endorsement

The endorsements on a negotiable instrument are presumed to have been made in the order in which they appear thereon.

6. Stamp

When an instrument has been lost, it is presumed that it was duly signed and stamped.

7. Holder in due course (Sec. 118)

It is presumed that the holder of a negotiable instrument is a holder in due course. The burden to show that holder of a negotiable instrument is not a holder in due course lies upon the opposite party. But when it is shown by the lawful owner or custodian of the instrument that it was obtained from him by means of an offence or fraud or for unlawful consideration then the presumption is rebutted and burden of proving is shifted to the holder.[3]

8. Proof of Protest (Sec. 119)

In a suit upon an instrument which has been dishonoured, the court, on proof of the protest, presumes the fact of dishonour until such fact is disapproved.

Reserve Bank of India Act, 1934

The provisions of sections 31 and 32 of the Reserve Bank of India Act, 1934 are not by the Negotiable Instruments Act. Section 31 prevents private persons from infringing the government's monopoly in issue of paper currency in India. The provisions of section 31 and 32 are given below.

According to section 31, no person (other than Reserve Bank or the Central Government) can draw, accept, make or issue any bill of exchange or promissory note payable to bearer on demand.

Section 31 further lays down that no person (other than the Reserve Bank or the Central Government) can make or issue any promissory not, payable to the bearer of the instrument.

Section 32 provides that if a person issues bills or notes payable to bearer on demand or a note payable to bearer he shall be punishable with fine.

Kind of Negotiable Instruments

Negotiable Instruments may be of following kind.

(1) Instruments negotiable by statute or
(2) Instruments negotiable by custom or usage.

1. Instruments negotiable by Statute

Section 13 of Negotiable Instruments Act 1881, provides only three kinds of Negotiable Instruments. These instruments are:

(i) Promissory notes

(ii) Bill of Exchange and

(iii) Cheques

2. Instruments negotiable by Custom of Usage

The character of negotiability to certain other instruments is given by the usage or custom of trade. Infact every document which authorises a person to a sum of money and which is transferable by delivery also, is entitled to be called 'negotiable instrument'. In Smith Leading cases, 535 (12th edn 1915)[4] it is observed:

"Where an instrument is by the custom of trade transferable in this country, like cash, by delivery and is capable of being sued upon by the person holding it pro tempore (for the time being) there it is entitled to the name negotiable instrument, and the property in it passes to a bona-fide transferee for value." In England, the following instruments have been held to be negotiable by custom, viz., exchequer, bills, bank notes, share warrants, circular notes, bearer debentures, dividend warrants, share certificates with blank transfer deeds, etc. The practice of English courts in according the character of negotiability to other instruments is usually followed by the courts in India. Thus, in India, Government promissory notes, banker's drafts and pay orders, hundis, delivery orders and railway receipts for goods have been held to be negotiable by usage or custom.

The section clearly provides that instruments payable to order are also negotiable. But an order only can be negotiated by endorsement and the endorsement must be genuine.

Promissory Note (Sec. 4)

Section 4 of the Negotiable Instruments Act defines a promissory note as an instrument in writing (not being a bank note or a currency note) containing an unconditional undertaking signed by the maker, to pay a certain sum of money to, or to the order of, a certain person or to the bearer of the instrument.

The person who makes the promissory note and promises to pay is called the maker.

Illustrations

The following are the illustrations of promissory notes :

(a) "I promise to Pay 'B' or order Rs. 500."

(b) "I acknowledge myself to be indebted to 'B' in Rs. 1000, to be paid on demand for value received".

But, the following are not Promissory Notes.

(a) "Mr I.O.U. (I owe you) Rs. 1000."

(b) "I promise to pay B Rs. 500 and all other sums which shall be due to him."

(c) "I promise to pay B Rs. 500, first deducting there out any money which he may owe me."

(d) "I promise to pay B Rs. 500 seven days after my marriage with C."

(e) "I promise to pay B Rs. 500 on D's death, provided D leaves me enough to pay that sum."

(f) "I promise to pay B Rs. 500 and to deliver to him my black horse on Ist January next."

A promissory note is a promise in writing by a person to pay a sum of money to a specified person or to his order.

Specimen of a Promissory Note

Rs 1,000 — Kanpur
October 24, 1996

Six months after date, I promise to pay Anil Kumar or order the sum of one thousand rupees for value received.

To,
Mr. Anil Kumar
B-74 Indira Nagar
Lucknow

Stamp
Sd/-

Although this is the normal form, but no particular form of words is required for a promissory note.

Essential elements of a Promissory Note

From the definition of a promissory note as defined in section 4 of the Act, the following essential elements are required for an instrument to become a valid promissory note.

1. In Writing

All negotiable instruments must be in writing, only verbal engagement to pay a sum of money is not enough. The writing may be in ink or even in pencil.

2. Promise to pay

The instrument must contain a promise to pay. A mere acknowledgement of indebtedness is not sufficient. There should be an express promise to pay the money. A mere receipt for money does not constitute a promissory note. But if the receipt is coupled with a promise to pay, it should be a promissory note.

In Akbar Khan Vs. Attar Singh 4-A, a document was made in following words:

This receipt is hereby executed by B ...... for Rs. 43,000 .... received from A. The amount to be payable after two years. Interest at the rate of Rs. 5-4-0 per cent to be charged.

Where the note read as "Received from Mr and Mrs T. Claydon the sum of £10,000 as a loan to be paid in full by July 1, 1983 with interest rate of 20% per annum."[5]

The document was held to be not a promissory note.

"We have received a sum of Rs 9,000 from Shri R.R. Sharma. This amount will be repaid on emand. We have received this amount in cash." Held, this is a promissory note.[6]

3. Unconditional

The promise to pay the money should not be conditional. It must be definite and unconditional. Thus an instrument payable on performance or non-performance of a particular act or on the happenings or non happening of a event is not a promissory note.

Examples

(i) A promises to pay B Rs. 10,000 when he delivers the goods, is not promissory note.

(ii) A promises to pay B Rs. 500 by installments with a condition that no payment shall be made after his death, is not a promissory note.

(iii) A promises to pay B Rs. 5000 seven days after his marriage with C, is also not a promissory note.

(iv) I promise to pay B a sum of Rs. 500 when C will give me Rs. 1000, is again not a promissory note.

But where the promise to pay with a condition which is so certain, necessary and is bound to happen (like death) the instrument will be a valid promissory note. Thus, where A promises to pay a sum of Rs. 5000 on the death of C, the promise is a valid promise for it is certain that C shall die.

5. Certain Sum of Money

The sum payable on a promissory note must be certain and specific and must not be capable of contingent additions or subtractions. Where rate of interest is specified, the sum shall be deemed to be certain. But where expression market rate of interest is used it cannot be said that amount is certain and specific because market rate may vary with source of borrowing, purpose of borrowing, financial standing of the borrower and so on.

The following instruments are not promissory notes as the sum of money is not certain.

(i) A promise to pay B Rs. 5000 with the fine according to the rules.

(ii) A promises to pay B Rs. 1000 with all other sums due to him.

(iii) A promises to pay B Rs. 10,000 with interest, but the rate of interest is not stated in the instrument.

However, a promissory note containing an undertaking to pay the amount 2% above the 'bank rate' shall be a valid note.

6. Promise to pay money only

The promissory note should contain a promise to pay money and money only. A promises to pay something other than money or something in addition to money, is not a promissory note. Thus

"I promise to pay B Rs. 300 and also deliver him one quintal of Rice."
"A promise to pay B Rs. 1000 and deliver 5 books."
"I promise to deliver to B 10 bags of sugar."

These are not promissory notes as promise to pay is not money only.

7. Maker's Signature

The promissory note must be signed by maker, otherwise it is incomplete and ineffective. If it is not signed by the maker, it shall not be a valid promissory note. 'Signature' means the writing of a person's in order to authenticate the contract contained in the instrument.

Signature by authorised attorney (agent) of a trading firm shall be valid.[7]

8. Certain parties

The instrument must point out with certainty as to who is the maker and who the payee is. Both the maker and the payee must be indicated with certainty on the fact of the instrument. A promissory note cannot be made payable to the maker (promisor) himself. Such a note is a nullity. But, if it is endorsed by the maker to some other person, or endorsed in blank, it becomes a valid promissory note.[8]

A promissory note may be made payable to the holder of an office without naming him. However, a note made "Payable to the Secretary for the time being of the Indian Society or Order" was held bad, JERVIS CJ said ".......... we must hold that to make a promissory note there must be a payee ascertained by name or designation."[9]

An instrument which does not use the words "bearer or order" after the name of payee is valid.[10]

A promissory note cannot be made payable to bearer on demand. Section 31 of the Reserve Bank of India prohibits issue of such promissory notes except by the Reserve Bank of India itself or the Central Government.

9. Stamping

A promissory note must be duly stamped under the Indian Stamp Act. Stamps of the requisite amount must have been affixed on the instrument and such stamp must be duly signed by maker's signatures or initials or otherwise.

10. Payable on demand or after a definite period

A promissory note payable 'on demand' means payable immediately or at anytime till it becomes time-barred. It becomes time-barred on completion of 3 years from the date it bears.

Lack of any requirements mentioned in section 4 of Negotiable Instrument Act will not make a document a 'promissory note' (Bapanna Krishnayya V. Chaparala Baburab).[11]

Bill of Exchange

Section 5 of the Negotiable Instruments Act defines a Bill of Exchange as an instrument in writing containing an unconditional order, signed by the maker, directing a certain person to pay a certain sum of money only to, or to the order of a certain person or to the bearer of the instrument.

The common form of a Bill of Exchange is as below:

Rs. 1000

Bombay
October 27, 1998

Six months after date pay to Ram or order the sum of Rupees
One thousand only for value received.

To,

Jai Ram
LUCKNOW

Stamp
Mohan

Although this is the common form of Bill of Exchange but no specified form is prescribed.

The above Bill of Exchange indicates that Jai Ram of Bombay buys goods on credit from Mohan of Bombay for Rs. 1000 to be paid 6 months after date. Mohan buys goods from Ram of Bombay for Rs. 1000 on same terms. Now Mohan may order JaiRam to pay the sum of Rs. 1000. This order of Mohan will be a Bill of Exchange.

Parties to a Bill of Exchange

There are three parties to a Bill of Exchange, these are (a) drawer (b) the drawee (c) the payee.

(a) 'Drawer'

The drawer of a Bill of Exchange is a person who gives the order to pay or who makes the bill.

(b) 'Drawee'

The drawee of a Bill of Exchange is the person who is directed to pay.

'Drawee in case of need' When in the bill or in any endorsement thereon the name of any person is given in addition to the drawee to be restored to in case of need, such person is called a "drawee in case of need". Thus, a person whose name is mentioned as an alternative drawee is called a "drawee in case of need". Originally, the bill must be presented to the drawee and only when he refuses or fails to accept then it may be presented to the drawee in case of need.

When the drawee accepts the bill, he is called the "acceptor". When a bill of exchange is refused by the original drawee to accept and any person accepts supra protest for honour of the drawee or any one of the endorsers, such person is called an "acceptor for honour".

(c) Payee

The person to whom the payment is to be made is called the payee. Where the payee named in a bill is a fictitious or non-existing person, the bill is treated as payable to bearer (Clutton Attenborough)[12].

The drawer or the payee who is in possession of the bill is called the holder. The holder must present the bill to the drawee for his acceptance. If it is not accepted, is does not become invalid, it only becomes dishonoured buy non-acceptance. The usual mode of acceptance is that the drawee will sign his acceptance on the free. Section 7 requires that the drawee should sign his assent and return it to the holder or give notice to him that he has done it and then he becomes the acceptor. An unqualified signature without any express words of acceptance is a sufficient signification of assent. The acceptor will be estopped from denying his signature[13].

Section 33 provides that a bill can be accepted by the drawee or by all or some of several drawees or by a person mentioned in the bill as drawee in case of need or by a person who accepts it for the honour of the drawee. No other person can bind himself by acceptance.

Section 34 declares where there are several drawees of a bill who are not partners, each can accept for himself and not for other, unless so authorised.

Essential Elements of Bill of Exchange

A bill of exchange must basically comply with requirements of section 5. A bill of exchange in fact is the order of a creaditor upon his debtor requiring him to pay money to specified person. The followings are the essential elements of bill of exchange.

1. It must be in writing.
2. It must contain an order to pay and not a promise or request. Example —

   "Please pay Rs. 500 to Shyam on demand and oblige."

   There is a request and not order to pay therefore it do not constitute a bill of exchange.

   The order to pay may be in the form of a request but it should be imperative. But if the language of the draft does not show any "order to pay", the draft will not be a bill of exchange.

   In Little V Sluckford[14] the defendant issued a paper addressed to the plaintiff in the following words:

   "Mr. Little, please to let the bearer have seven pounds, and to place them to my account, and you will oblige. Yours humble servant R Slackford."

   This is not a bill of exchange as it contains a request and not an order.
3. The order to pay must be unconditional. The word "unconditional" has the same meanings as has already been discussed in promissory note.
4. A bill of exchange requires three parties, i.e., 'drawer' — who makes the bill of exchange, 'drawee' — The person to whom the bill of exchange is addressed and 'Payee' — The person to whom the payment is to be made.

   The detail explanation has already been given in 'parties to the bill of exchange'.

5. The parties must be certain

All three parties must be indicated with reasonable certainty. Sometimes, the drawer and the payee are the same persons where a bill is drawn "pay to me or my order" in such a case, there are only two parties but without this minimum of two there cannot be a bill of exchange.

6. Money only

The order must be to pay money and money only. The amount ordered to be paid must be certain.

7. The sum payable must be certain or capable of being made certain.
8. It must be signed by the drawer.
9. It must be duly stamped as per the Indian Stamp Act.

Cheque

Section 6 of the Negotiable Instrument Act defines a "Cheque" is a bill of exchange drawn on a specified banker and not expressed to be payable otherwise, than on demand.

Thus, a cheque is a bill of exchange with two additional features, viz.,

(i) it is always draw on a specified banker

(ii) it is always payable on demand and not otherwise.

All cheques are bills of exchange but all bills of exchange are not cheques. A cheque being a bill of exchange must possess all the essentials of a bill and should also meet the requirements of section 6. It must be signed by the drawer. It must contain an unconditional order of a specified person or the bearer of the cheque. In Bevins Vs. London and South Western Bank Ltd,[15] a company issued a cheque on its bankers. A receipt was appended to the cheque and it ordered the banker to make the payment "provided the receipt from at foot hereof is only signed, stamped and dated". The cheque was held to be invalid because its payment was made conditional upon signature of the receipt. But it does not require acceptance as it is intended for immediate payment.

As section 6 says that a bill of exchange to become a cheque has two special feature. First a cheque must be drawn on a specified banker. In R. Pillai V S. Auuar[16] answer to question who is banker is given. Where a district board deposited its funds in Government Treasury and used withdraw money by issuing order inform of cheques. The question was whether a unconditional order having been issued in writing was a cheque or not. Ayyar J. held that "Treasury is not a bank" and therefore the order was not a cheque under section 6, but a bill of exchange under section 5. The reason is that every person who receives the money of another and pays it according to his orders cannot be regarded as a banker, unless he establishes that business of profit. Ayyar J. Cited Hart's definition who says in his law of Banking, "A banker is one who in the ordinary course of his business honours cheques drawn upon him by persons from and for whom he receives money on current accounts."

Second, the cheque must be payable on demand. Parke B in Ram Charun Mullick Vs. Luchmee Chand Radakissen[17] said that a cheque "is a peculiar sort of instrument, in many respects resembling a bill of exchange, but in some entirely different. A cheque does not require acceptance, in the ordinary course it is never accepted, it is not intended for circulation, it is given for immediate payment, it is not entitled to days of grace....... ."

Lord Wright approved and cited above passage in Bank of Baroda Vs. Punjab National Bank.[17-A]

Specimen of Cheque

No. Date......19....

ALLAHABAD BANK
Aishbagh Branch Lucknow.

Pay .... or bearer.
the sum of Rs. ....

Rs................. Sd/-

Special features of Cheque

1. Written instrument

All cheques must be in writing. The writing may be in pencil or in ink.

2. On a Specified Banker only

A cheque can only be drawn on a specified banker.

3. Certain sum of Money

The sum payable on a cheque must be certain and specifies. The orders asking the banker to deliver securities or certain things cannot be regarded as cheque.

4. Payee to be certain

A valid cheque must be payable to a certain person. The term person includes legal person also. The cheque, thus can be drawn in favour of a body corporate, local authorities, clubs institutions etc.

5. Cheque should be unconditional

A cheque must contain an unconditional order. The word order or its equivalent word is not necessary to be used to make the document a cheque.

6. Cheque Amount

The cheque must have a clear amount. The amount should be written both in words as well as figures to avoid mistakes.

7. Payable on demand

A valid cheque must be payable on demand. When the drawer does not specify the time for its payment, the cheque is payable on demand.

8. Dating of cheque

A cheque without a date is considered incomplete and is returned unpaid by the bank. A post-dated cannot be honoured.

In England, cheque can remain in circulation for a period of 12 months while in India it is only six months.

Distinction between Promissory note and a bill of exchange

Promissory Note	Bill of Exchange
There are only two parties one is maker the and other is payee.	There are three parties — the drawer drawee and the payee — although any two of those capacities may be filled by one and the same person.
There is a unconditional promise by the maker to pay the payee.	It contains an unconditional order to the drawee to pay according to the drawer's directions.
Prior acceptance is not required.	It must be accepted by the drawee or his agent before presented for payment.
There is primary and absolute liability of the maker.	The liability of the drawer is secondary and conditional upon non-payment by the drawee.
If it dishonoured, does not require any notice to be given.	Notice of dishonour must be given by the holder and immediate endorsers to hold them liable thereon.
A promissory note cannot be made payable to the maker himself.	The drawer and the payee may be one and same person.
The maker of the note in immediate relation with the payee.	The maker or drawer does not stand in immediate relation with the acceptor or drawee.

Distinction between Cheque and Bill of Exchange

Cheque	Bill of Exchange
A cheque is always drawn on a banker.	A bill may be drawn on any person, including a banker.
A cheque requires no acceptance.	A bill must be accepted before the drawee can be called upon to make payment upon it.
A cheque is not entitled to any days of grace.	A bill is entitled to three days of grace.
A cheque is always payable on demand.	A bill may be payable demand or after specified time.
Notice of dishonour is not necessary. The parties thereon remain liable, even if no notice of dishonour is given.	Notice of dishonour is necessary hold the parties liable thereon. A party is given who does not receive a can escape its liability thereon.
A cheque is not required to be noted or dishonour.	A bill may be noted or protested for dishonour.
A cheque can be crossed.	Crossing of bill is not possible.
The payment of cheque may be countermanded by the drawer.	Payment of bill cannot be countermanded.

CHAPTER

7

Holder and Holder in Due Course

Holder

Holder means either the bearer or endorsee of an instrument. The expression holder is defined under section 8 of the Negotiable Instruments Act. According to Section 8, a holder of a negotiable instrument is "a person entitled in his own name to the possession thereof and to receive or recover the amount due thereon from the partied thereto."

Where the note, bill or cheque is lost or destroyed, its holder is the person so entitled of the time of such loss or destruction.

The phrase "entitled in his own name" used in above definition is significant, due to the institution of 'benama'. In *Suraj Bali Vs. Ram Chandra*[18] the actual holder of a promissory note had disappeared but was civilly alive. His son sued for the amount on maturity but court on the ground that he was not entitled "in his own name" to the possession of the instrument dismissed his action.

Where a person obtains possession of an instrument by theft or under a forged endorsement, is not a holder as he is not entitled to recover the amount of the instrument. But where in the absence of a holder, a person who is heir of the deceased holder by giving a valid discharge to the maker or acceptor of the instrument may acquire the status of a holder and can sue on the instrument to recover the amount due thereon.

Holder in due Course

A person who takes an instrument "in good faith and for value" becomes the true owner of the instrument and is known as a "holder in due course."

Section 9 is as follows:

'Holder in due course' means any person who for consideration become the possessor of a promissory note, bill of exchange or cheque if payable to bearer, or the payee or endorsee thereof, if payable to order, before the amount mentioned in it became payable and without having sufficient cause to believe that any defect existed in the title of the person from whom he derived his title.

Essential elements of Holder in due course

Following four elements must be fulfilled to make a person holder in due course:

1. For Consideration

A negotiable instrument contains a contract and therefore must be supported by consideration. Where a person receives a negotiable instrument without consideration, he will not be holder in due course and he cannot enforce it.

2. Holder must have obtained instrument before maturity

In order to be a holder in due course the holder must have obtained the instrument before its maturity. In Down v. Halling[19] held that "if a bill or note or cheque be taken after it is due", the person taking it takes at his peril. He "can have no better title to it than the party from he takes it, and therefore, cannot recover upon it if it turns out that it has been previously lost or stolen."

3. The instrument must be complete and regular

The other essential element is that the instrument should be complete and regular on the face of it. An instrument may be defective in several ways. It may be incomplete without any drawer's name. In *Hogarth v. Latham and Co.*,[20] the held that the plaintiff who took two bills of exchange without any drawer's name, could not recover upon the bills.

An instrument may also be incomplete because it is not properly dated and stamped.

4. Holder must have taken the instrument in good faith and without of any defect either in the instrument or in the title of the person negotiating it to him. There are two methods of ascertaining a person's good faith, one in subjective and the other is objective. In subjective test, the court has to see the holder's own mind and the only question is "did he take the instrument honestly?" On the other hand, in objective test, the court has to go beyond the holder's mind and see whether he expressed as much care in taking the security as a reasonably careful person ought to have done.

Privileges of a Holder in Due Course

A holder in due course gets title to a negotiable instrument. A holder in due course is given certain additional privileges under the Negotiable Instrument Act, which are not available to a holder. These are as follows:

(1) Inchoate Stamped Instrument

Section 20 of Negotiable Instruments Act provides that a person, who has signed and delivered to another a stamped but otherwise inchoate (incomplete) instrument, is stopped from assertaining, as against a holder in due course, that the instrument has not been filled in accordance with the authority given by him, the stamp being sufficient to cover the amount.

(2) Liability of Prior Parties

As per section 34, every prior party to a negotiable instrument, i.e., the maker or drawer, the acceptor and all the immediate endorsers continue to remain liable to a holder in due course until the instrument is duly satisfied.

(3) Fictitious Payee (Section 42)

Where a bill of exchange is drawn by a fictitious person and a payable to his order, the acceptor cannot be relieved from his liability to the holder in due course. The holder in due course shall, however, have to prove that the instrument was endorsed by the same hand as drawer's signature.

"Fictitious payee" means a person who is not in existence or, being in existence, is never intended by the drawer to have the payment. Where the drawer intends the payee to have the payment, then he is not a fictitious payee and the validity of the cheque will affect with forgery of his signature.

(4) Conditional Delivery (Section 46)

Where an negotiable instrument is negotiated to a holder in due course, the other parties to the instrument cannot escape liability on the ground that the delivery of the instrument was conditional or for a special purpose only.

(5) Instrument Cleaned of all defects

Section 53 provides that once a negotiable instrument passes through the hands of a holder in due course, it gets cleansed of its defects provided the holder was himself not a party to the fraud.

(6) Presumption

According to section 118, every holder is presumed to be a holder in due course. The burden of providing his title does not lie on him. Once it is shown there the bill is tainted with fraud the burden is shifted to the holder to prove that he is a holder in due course.[21]

Parties to a Negotiable Instrument

Every person who is competent to make a contract can become party to a negotiable instrument. According to section 11 of the Indian Contract Act 1872, every person is competent to contract who is of the age of majority according to the law to which he is subject, and is of sound mind and is not disqualified from contracting by any law to which he is subject. Thus, incapacity to contract may arise from; (i) minority (ii) mental incompetent and (iii) status. Thus a person competent to contract can become party to a negotiable instrument. Such a person may, however, draw, endorse, deliver and negotiate a bill or a note so as to bind all parties except himself (Section 26).

Minor

A minor is not competent to contract and, therefore, he cannot bind himself by becoming a party to a negotiable instrument. But he may draw, indorse, deliver and negotiate a negotiable instrument so as to bind all parties except himself. A instrument does not become void because a minor is a party. It remains binding upon all other parties. Under instrument, minor's right are not affected.

For eg: If he is the payee or endorsee or holder, can be enforced by him or on his behalf.[22]

Unsound mind person

Like minors, bills and notes drawn or made by lunatics, idiots and drunken persons are void against them but the other parties remain liable.

Corporation

A corporation or a company, being an artificial creation of law, their capacity to insure liability on a negotiable instrument depends upon the only those powers which its memorandum or Articles confer upon it. If memorandum or Articles expressly or implied by authorises a corporation or a company to do so, it may become a party to a negotiable instrument in any capacity, otherwise its contract shall be *ultra vires*.

Agents (Section 27)

A person who has the capacity to contract may accept or make or otherwise become party to an instrument either himself or through duly authorised agent. But a general authority to transact business and to receive and discharge debts does not confer upon an agent the power of accepting or endorsing bills of exchange so as to bind his principal. An authority to draw bills of exchange does not of itself impart an authority to endorse.

In one of following two ways, an agent signs a negotiable instrument for his principal—

(1) Agent may sign the principal's name, for it is immaterial what hand actually signs the principal's name, if in fact there exists an authority to put it them.

(2) He may sign by procuration (agency, the instrument giving power to do this) stating on the face of the instrument that he signs as agent.

An agent can bind his principal by acting on his behalf in the manner in which he is duly authorised to become a party to a negotiable instrument. The agent has to make it clear that he is acting in representative capacity by using the words 'for and on behalf of' or '*per pro*'. The form of signature must show that he intends to act as "agent" or that does not intend to incur personal liability. (Section 28).

An agent is personally liable if he:

(1) puts signature to an instrument without indicating thereon that he signs as agent.

(2) executes an instrument without, or in express of his authority.

Legal representative (Section 30)

A legal representative of a deceased person who signs his name to a promissory note, bill of exchange or cheque is personally liable thereon unless he limits liability to the extent of the assets of the deceased received by him as a legal representative.

Joint Hindu Family

Karta of a Hindu Undivided Family has an implied authority on behalf of the family to borrow money on a note or bill where he carries on family business. Such bill or note binds all the members of the joint family including the minor members to the extent of their shares. Minors are not, however, personally liable.

CHAPTER

8

Negotiation and Liability

One of the important characteristics of a negotiable instrument is that it should be freely transferable from one person to another. There are only two ways by which the transfer of negotiable instrument may take place, these are:

(1) by way of negotiation or

(2) by way of assignment.

1. By Way of Negotiation

Section 14 of the Negotiable Instruments Act "negotiation". According to which, when a promissory note, bill of exchange or cheque is transferred by one person to another, so as to constitute the transferee a holder is called "negotiation", and the instrument is said to be negotiated.

An instrument payable to bearer can be by simple delivery. The person to whom the instrument is delivered becomes the holder. However, a person steals or finds a bearer instrument is not the holder because instrument is not delivered to him. So if 'x' gives a instrument to 'y' for keeping it safely, the instrument is not negotiated to 'y' as delivery of the instrument to 'y' does not make him its holder but a mere bailee.

2. By way of assignment

When the holder of promissory note or bill of exchange or cheque transfers it to another person so as to confer a right on the transferee to receive the payment of the instrument, transfer by way of assignment takes place.

Thus, there is a transfer of the right to receive the payment of a debt in both negotiation and assignment but the basic difference is that the rights of instrument transferee are superior in negotiation to those of an assignee.

The transfer of negotiable instrument by way of assignment is not dealt by The Negotiable Instrument Act.

Distinction between negotiation and assignment

The points of difference are stated as below —

1. In case of negotiation, a holder in due course (transferee) gets a better title than its transferor. While in assignment, the title of the transferee (assignee) is subject to the defects and equities in the title of the transferor.
2. In negotiation, consideration is always presumed. In case of assignment, the transferee must prove consideration. He has to prove that he has given consideration for assignment.
3. 'Negotiation' can be effected by mere 'delivery' if the instrument is a bearer one and by endorsement and delivery in case it is an order instrument. An assignment can only be made in writing signed by the transferor.
4. An assignment does not bind the debtor unless a notice of the assignment has been given to him and he has assented to it. In negotiation, notice of transfer to the debtor by the transferee is not necessary.

Negotiation by Delivery

Section 47 provides that an instrument payable to bearer is negotiable by delivery thereof. Thus, an instrument payable to bearer is negotiated by simple delivery of the instrument. The person to whom the instrument is delivered becomes the holder. Delivery is an important formality. No possessor is constituted as the holder of the instrument without delivery of instrument.

Delivery may be actual or constructive. Actual delivery means change of actual possession of instrument.

Example:

A, the holder of a negotiable instrument payable to bearer, delivers it to B's agent to keep it for B. The instrument has been negotiated.

Constructive delivery takes place when the instrument is delivered to the transferee's agent, clerk or servant on his behalf.

Example:

A is the holder of a negotiable instrument payable to bearer. The instrument is in the hands of A's banker who is also at the time the banker of B also. A directs the banker to transfer the instrument to B's credit in his banker's account. The banker does so, and accordingly new possesses the instrument as B's agent. The instrument has been negotiated and B has become the holder of it.

Exception to section 47

A promissory note, bill of exchange or cheque delivered on condition that it is not to take effect except in a certain event is not negotiable (except in the hands of a holder for value without notice of the condition) unless such event happens.

Payable to Bearer

An instrument is payable to bearer where (i) it is made so payable; (ii) it is originally made payable to order but the only or the last endorsement is in blank. A cheque which is originally drawn payable to bearer remains bearer even through it is subsequently endorsed in full. The rule is once a bearer cheque always a bearer cheque of (iii) the payee is a fictitious person.

Negotiation by Endorsement and Delivery

An instrument payable to order is negotiated by endorsement and delivery.

The term endorsement in its literal sense means writing on an instrument. In its technical sense it means the writing of a person's name (otherwise than as maker) on the face or back of a negotiable instrument or on a slip of paper called 'allonge' annexed thereto for the purpose of negotiation. The person who so signs the instrument is called the endorser and to whom the instrument is endorsed is called the 'endorsee'. Thus endorsement requires two formalities. First, the holder should endorse it and then deliver it to his endorsee. Where endorser posted instrument to deliver endorsee, it is deemed to have been delivered to the endorsee as soon as it is posted. Bombay High Court in a case where endorser sent a bank draft by post to endorse issued instruction to the bank not to pay the draft, held that delivery of bank draft became effective from the date of posting and draft can not be cancelled by the endoser[23].

Who may Endorse?

The rightful person to make the first endorsement of an instrument is the payee. Subsequent endorsement may be made by anyone who has become the holder of the instrument. Section 15 provides that the maker of a note and the drawer of a bill cannot endorse. But if any of them has become the holder in his own right, he, may endorse the instrument. Section 51, however, provides that every sole maker, drawer, payee or endorse or all of several joint maker, drawers, payee or endorsees may indorse and negotiate the instrument.

Essentials of Valid Endorsement

Following essentials are required for a valid endorsement in order to operate as a negotiation.

1. Endorsement must be on the instrument itself. But when no space is left on the back of the instrument it must be on a slip of paper annexed to the instrument, called 'allonge'.
2. Endorsement must be genuine and not forged. Where a person takes an instrument through a forged Endorsement, he and the parties that acquire the instrument after him, get no good title[24]. The maker, acceptor or endorser can cancel or revoke his signature before delivery of instrument but not after delivery.[25]
3. Where a bill or note payable to order, the name of endorsee or payee is wrongly spelt, he should sign the instrument in the same manner as given in the instrument. He may write the correct spelling within brackets.
4. It must be completed by the delivery of the instrument. The delivery of the instrument to the endorsee with the intention of passing the property in it is important.
5. The endorsement must be of the entire instrument. A partial endorsement does not operate as a negotiation of instrument.

Kinds of Endorsements

According to Negotiable Instrument Act, an instrument may be of following kinds:

1. Endorsement in Blank

Where endorser signs only his name on the back of the instrument without specifying the endorsee for the purpose of negotiating it, the endorsement is said to be in blank. (Section 16). Endorsement in blank converts an order instrument into bearer instrument (Section 54). Endorsement in blank may be negotiated by simple delivery and bearer is entitled to its payment.

Example: A cheque is payable to Ram or order and Ram signs on the back of the cheque. This is an endorsement in blank by Ram and the cheque is payable by mere delivery.

2. Endorsement in Full

Where endoser along with his signature specifies the name of endorsee whom or to whose order, he wants the instrument to be paid. Such endorsement is called endorsement in full (Section 16).

Example: Ram wants to make a cheque in endorsement in full to B. He would write thus "Pay B or order". Signature Ram.

This is a common form of endorsement in full but there is no prescribed form.

An instrument with endorsement in full can only be paid to the endorsee and further can only be negotiated by his endorsement.

An endorsement in blank may be converted into endorsement in full merely by adding the name of a person before the endorser's signature.

3. Restrictive Endorsement

The restrictive endorsement prohibits or restricts the further negotiation of instrument. It merely entitles the holder of the instrument for a specific purpose.

The endorser may express words in the endorsement restricts or take away the right of further negotiation or may constitute the endorsee an agent to endorse the instrument, or to receive its contents for the endorse or for some other specified person (Section 50).

The following illustrations are given in section 50 of the Act:

B signs the following endorsement on different negotiable instrument payable to bearer:

(a) "Pay the contents to C only."
(b) "Pay C for my use."
(c) "Pay C or order of the account of B."
(d) "The within must be credited to C."

These endorsements exclude the right of further negotiation by C.

(e) "Pay C."
(f) "Pay C value in account with the Oriental Bank."
(g) "Pay the contents to C, being part of the consideration in a certain deed of assignment executed by C to the endorser and others."

These endorsements do not exclude the right of further negotiation by C.

4. Conditional Endorsement

A conditional endorsement limits or negates the liability of the endorser. Conditional endorsement makes the transfer of the property in a negotiable instrument from the endorser to the endorsee dependent upon the fulfillment of stated conditions. Thus, according to section 52, where an endorser makes his liability on the instrument conditional on the happening of a particular event, it is called conditional endorsement. Though such event may never happen.

For example, where the endorsement states

(i) "Pay B or order on his birthday"
(ii) "Pay B or order on the arrival of Delhi"

In above cases, B can claim payment on the instrument only if stated conditions will be fulfilled.

A conditional endorsement is different from a restrictive endorsement. A restrictive endorsement imposes restriction on the negotiability of the instrument while a conditional endorsement limits the liability of the endorser.

5. Endorsement 'Sans Recourse'

Where the endorser of a negotiable instrument may be express words in the endorsement exclude his own liability thereon (section 52). Such endorsement is called 'Endorsement Sans Recourse'. The endorser may impose a stipulation in his endorsement for restricting his liability. He can do so by adding the words 'Sans Recourse' (without recourse) to the endorsement.

For examples endorser may write his endorsement such as

(i) "Pay A or order sans recourse."
(ii) "Pay Y or order without recourse to me."
(iii) "Pay D or order at his own risk."

These words exclude the liability of the endorser and endorser will not be liable on the instrument if it is dishonoured.

6. Partial Endorsement

Endorser can not indorse an instrument to endorsee for a part of its amount only.

Examples:

(i) An instrument for Rs. 200/-, it cannot be endorsed for Rs. 100/- only.
(ii) A is the holder of a bill for Rs. 100/- he cannot endorse to B for Rs. 50/- only.
(iii) A, the holder of a bill for Rs. 400/-, endorsers it 'Pay Rs. 200/- to B or order and Rs. 200/- to C or order. A cannot endorse instrument in such a way and B and C cannot sue or endorse.

But partial endorsement can only be possible where due amount has already been party paid, a note to that effect may be made on the instrument and it may then be negotiated for the balance (Section 56).

7. Facultative Endorsement

The Endorsement is termed as facultative endorsement where such words are added to an endorsement whereby the endorser waives his right to receive notice of dishonour.

Liability of Parties

Liability of parties to negotiable instruments is dealt with section 30 to 32 and 35 to 42 of the Negotiable Instruments Act, which are discussed as below.

Liability of drawer (Section 30)

The drawer of a bill of exchange is liable before its acceptance by the drawee. But as soon as it is accepted by the acceptor, he becomes the primarily liable and then the liability of the drawer becomes secondary to that of the acceptor.

Liability of drawer of a Cheque (Sec 30)

The drawer if a cheque is liable to compensate the holder if the cheque is dishonoured by the banker provided that due notice of dishonour has been received by the drawer.

Thus, it is clear from the above facts that the liability of drawer of a cheque is primary and not the secondary while in case of bill of exchange the liability of drawer before the acceptance by the drawee is primary and it becomes the secondary after its acceptance.

Liability of drawee of Justified Cheque (Sec 31)

The person who keeps an account with a banker is called a 'Customer' and the drawee of a cheque is always a banker. The banker and his customer has a contractual relationship. It is the contractual obligation of the banker to honour his customer's cheque as long as he has sufficient balance of his credit applicable to the payment, the drawee, i.e., the banker, must compensate the drawer for any loss or damage caused by such default.

However, obligation of paying banker to honour his customer's cheque is subject to the following conditions.

(1) The paying banker is under an obligation to honour only those cheques which are drawn against the account maintained at that branch of the bank where the cheques are presented.

(2) The paying banker is bound to pay only such cheques as are presented to him for payment within reasonable time.

(3) Cheques presented after banking hours have no legal effect and therefore banker cannot be held liable for refusing payment on such cheques.

(4) Funds must be sufficient and available.

(5) Cheques which are not drawn in the proper form are refused by the paying banker. Section 5 and 6 of the Negotiable instrument Act provide that the banker should examine the contents of the cheque to ensure that it is perfectly a valid instrument containing an unconditional order to pay a certain sum of money.

Liability for unjustified Dishonour

"The relation between banker and the customer is that of debtor and creditor with a super added obligation on the part of the banker to honour the customer's cheques when the account is in credit."[26] An unjustified dishonour of cheque is not merely a breach of contract, but also a tort as it damages the customer's reputation."[27]

Where a banker has agreed to provide credit or overdraft facility to a customer and forgetting that agreement refuses the customer's cheque, the banker is liable in damages.[28]

The banker has to be careful in the choice of words that he uses in returning the customer's cheques. The words "not sufficient" have been held to be defamatory. The banker's remark must be consistent with the truth and should be expressed in least defamatory words.[29]

When Banker Justified in refusing payment of cheque

In following circumstances the banker is justified to dishonour a cheque without incurring any liability thereon:

(1) Where the Cheque is post-dated

Refusal to pay a post-dated cheque before the ostensible date does not amount a banker liable for wrongful dishonour.

(2) Where the cheque is out dated

Where the cheque is presented after a period of six months from the date of its issue. The cheque is then known as a stale cheque.

(3) Where a cheque is not duly presented

A cheque presented after business hours shall be deemed not to have been duly presented.

(4) When the funds of the customer are in sufficient

The banker is justified in refusing the payment of a cheque when the funds in the customer's account is not sufficient to meet.

(5) Where the Customer Countermands the Payment

Where the customer requests the banker by a notice not to pay a particular cheque is known as "countermand". A Countermand to be effective must reach the banker before he has paid the cheque in the ordinary course. The notice regarding 'stop payment' should be honoured only if it is signed by the customer and must give correct particulars (number, date, the name of the payee and cheque amount) of the cheque[30].

In case of joint account or partnership accounts any of the joint account holders or any of the partners can request the banker to stop the payment. But in such cases any request to remove the stop payment must be signed by all the required signatories. A telephone or telegraph message is not sufficient because in that case the banker has to ascertain the authenticity of the message. In Curtis Vs. London City and Midland Bank (1908)[31] due to Clerk's negligence the telegram was not brought to the banker's notice until after payment, the banker to the banker's notice until matter payment, the banker was held not liable. It a banker a proper stop notice has been received, he cannot debit the account of his customer, but he can recover the money from the party who has received the payment as money paid under a mistake of fact.[32]

(6) Where the Customer has died

The payment of cheques presented after death of customer must not be made. But, where the payment is made without knowing the fact of the customer's death, bank cannot be held liable.

(7) Where the Customer has become insolvent

Any cheques presented after the adjudication of a customer as insolvent or of presentation of an insolvency petition against him must be refused payment.

(8) When the Customer has become a person

A person of unsound mind is not competent to contract. A cheque being a contract, therefore, a banker should refuse payment on cheques drawn and received after the receipt of notice of the customer's insanity.

(9) Where a Garnishea order has been issued

Where a Court order (Garnishea) attaching the customer's balance has been received by banker the payment of cheques after the receipt of such an order must be refused. If Garnishea order is absolute, the whole balance stands attached even if it is in excess of what is due to the judgement creditor.[33] But if Garnishea order is for a particular amount, leaving that specified amount, cheques for remaining amount should be honoured.

(10) Where the cheque is of doubtful Validity

The Validity of a cheque may be in doubt where it is not drawn in the proper form. Such cheques are refused by the paying banker. The mandate in such cheques is not clear. The doubtful Validity of such cheques may be due to without date or the amount in words and figures are different or its endorsements are not proper or regular or there is some other confusion about the cheque.

(11) When the cheque is mutilated.

(12) Where the customer's signature does not agree.

(13) Where the customer has countermanded payment.

Criminal Liability of drawer in case of dishonour of cheques for in sufficiency of funds in the account

A new chapter XVII in Negotiable instruments Act 1881 is added by the Banking, Public Financial and Negotiable Instruments laws (Amendment) Act 1988. The chapter comprises section 138 to 142. The main provisions of these sections are as given below:

Section 138 Dishonour of cheque for funds insufficiency in drawer account

The criminal liability arises when a cheque is dishonoured on account of insufficiency of funds standing to the credit of the drawer's account or the amount of the cheque exceeds the amount of credit facility allowed to the customer.

He shall be punished with imprisonment extending upto one year or with fine extending upto twice the amount of the cheque or with both. It is necessary that the cheque should have been presented by the payee or holder in due course within a period of six months from the date on which it is drawn or in special cases it may be reduced to a shorter period by a notice on the face of the cheque.

Holder, after receiving information from the bank that the cheque has been dishonoured, should make a demand to the drawer for payment within fifteen days. If drawer fails to make the payment with in fifteen days of such notice period, the offence becomes complete and the cause of action starts against drawer from the 16th day onwards.

Post-dated cheques — A Controversy

The Kerala High Court in *Manoj Kumar Seth v. Fernandez* (1992)[34] observed that in the case of the post-dated cheque, the same can be presented only on or after the date of the cheque. Thus, if a post-dated cheque is presented within 6 months from the date it bears, the presentation shall be deemed to be in order and hence cause of action shall lie under section 138.

In *Babu Xavier vs. Lalchand Munoth* (1992)[35] Madras High Court observed otherwise.

In *Gulshan Rai vs. Anil Kumar* (1993)[36], the Punjab and Haryana High Court endorsing Babu Xavier's case observed that the post dating of the cheque does not make it invalid, but when such a cheque is post dated in a manner that the date of presentation is beyond the period of six months of the date on which it is drawn, it can be presumed that the payee had the knowledge that in the event of its dishonour for want of funds, the criminal liability created under section 138 will not be attached.

Controversy Resolved

The Supreme Court in *Anil Kumar vs. Gulshan Rai* (1993) resolved the controversy by reversing the aforesaid decisions of Punjab and Haryana High Court and the Madras High Court. Supreme Court observed that in case of a post dated cheque, upto the date shown on the cheque, it remains a mere bill of exchange and becomes a cheque only from the date written on it. A cheque is an instrument payable on demand. A post dated cheque which is not payable on demand till the particular date is not a cheque in the eyes of law till the date it becomes payable on demand.

The period of 6 months is, therefore, to be reckoned from the date of the cheque.

Thus, the decision of the Kerala High Court in *Manoj Kumar Seth v. Fernandez* stands endorsed.

The question whether section 138 is attracted when the cheque is returned with the memorandum "Account closed" was considered in the case of *S. Prasanna vs. R. Vijaya Lakshmi* (1993).[37] The Madras High Court observed as follows:

Section 138 is attracted when a cheque is returned by the bank unpaid in two circumstances, viz., (i) the amount of money standing to the credit of that account is insufficient to honour the cheque or (ii) it exceeds the amount arranged to be paid from that account.

It does not include a situation where the cheque is returned because the account is closed.

Presumption in favour of holder (Sec. 139)

It may be noted that the holder of a cheque shall be presumed to have received the cheque for discharge, in whole or in part, of any debt or other liability.

Defence which may not be allowed in any prosecution under section 138 (Sec. 140)

It shall not be a defence in a prosecution for an offence under section 138 that the drawer had no reason to believe that when he issued the cheque that the cheque may be dishonoured for the reasons mentioned in section 138.

Offences by Companies (Sec. 141)

When the drawer of a dishonoured cheque is a company, the company will, of course, be liable to be proceeded against, but liability will also be incurred by every person who at the time was in charge of and responsible to the company for the conduct of its business. Further, a director, manager, secretary or other officer of the company shall be deemed to be guilty of that offence and shall be liable to be prosecuted against and punished accordingly in case the offence has been committed with has consent or connivance, or its attributable to any neglect on his part in this regard. But under this section a person will not be liable in case —

(i) Where such person proves that the offence was committed without his knowledge or
(ii) Where he had exercised all due diligence to prevent the commission of such offence.

Cognizance of Offences (Section 142)

(i) No Court shall take cognizance of any offence punishable under section 138 except upon a complaint in writing made by the holder of cheque.
(ii) Such complaint should be made within one month of the cause of action arising under section 138.
(iii) Further, no court inferior to that of a metropolitan magistrate or a judicial magistrate of the first class shall try any offence punishable under section 138.

Rasing of Amount

Where with reasonable precautions the customer has drawn his cheque but some dishonest person has altered and raised the amount of cheque by using some technique, so that the banker, not knowing the forgery, has paid the increased amount. In such circumstances, the banker bear the loss. He cannot recover the excess amount from the customer.

But where the customer has left unusual spaces which facilitate interpolation of words and figures and that becomes the cause of forgery, the loss falls on the customer. Lord Finlay, LC described it as "sound in principal, said:

"As the customer and the banker are under a contractual relation in this matter, it is obvious that in drawing a cheque, the customer is bound to take usual and reasonable precautions to prevent forgery ——. If the cheque is drawn in such a way as to facilitate or almost invite an increase in the amount by forgery if the cheque should get into the hands of a dishonest person, forgery is not to remote, but a very natural consequence of neglect of this description."

Forgery of Signature

No protection is granted to paying banker for making payment of cheques bearing forged signature of the customer. Payment of a cheque bearing forged signature of a customer is deemed to be a payment constitutes breach of the implied contract between banker and the customer. The banker is not absolved of this liability even where the signature are so cleverly forged that it is difficult to detect with reasonable care Forgery is nullity. A forged cheque is a nullity. In *Prabhu Dayal v. Jwala Bank*,[38] the decision of Allahabad High Court is an illustration.

One of the bank rules provided that "the customer should keep cheque books under look, and key, otherwise the bank is not liable for any loss in this connection. "The customer, however, left his cheque books in an unlooked box. A leaf was stolen, the customer's signature forged and the cheque was presented and duly paid by the bank.

The banker was held for the loss. The customer was no doubt negligent, but his negligence was not the proximate cause of the loss.

However, the banker can debit his customers account where the loss is caused directly by the conduct or negligence of the customer. Where the customer has asserted that signature on the cheque is genuine, the banker cannot be held liable for paying such a cheque, if latter the signature is proved to be forged one.

In joint account case, all signatures must be genuine. If any signature is a forged one, payment should not be made thereon, otherwise the banker shall be liable.

Estoppel against Forgery

The banker can recover the total amount from the forger as money paid a mistake. It is the duty of the customer to inform the banker as soon as he learns of the forgery of his signature. The banker may take action against the forger. If the customer withheld this information and in result of which the banker loses his remedy against the forger, the customer will be estopped from relying upon the forgery of his signature. In *Greenwood v. Martins Bank*, the decision given by House of Lords[39] is a illustration of this principle.

The plaintiff's wife repeatedly forged her husband's signature to cheque and drew out money and invested it for her own use. The husband became aware of the forgeries but being persuaded by his wife to say nothing about them, he kept silent for eight months. When he finally decided to disclose the forgeries to the bank, the wife shot herself dead. The plaintiff claimed that the banker should not be allowed to debit his account.

But Lord Tomlin rejected above contention and said:

The Plaintiff owned a duty to the bank to disclose the forgeries when he became aware of them and so enable the defendants to take steps towards recovering the money wrongfully paid on the forged cheques, that through his failure to fulfill his duty they were prevented from bringing an action against the wife for the tort of forgery, and therefore, the plaintiff was estopped from asserting that signature to the cheques were forgeries.

There is no estoppel where the information, even when given promptly, would have been too late to help the banker. There is no estoppel also where at the time of disclosure the banker's rights against the forger. Similarly there is no estoppel where the information, even when given promptly, would have been too late to help the banker.

Forgery in Endorsement

The consequences of forgery in endorsement are, however not so fatal because a special protection in section 85(1) is given, which says that "where a cheque payable to order purports to be endorsed by or on behalf of the payee, the drawee (the paying banker) is discharged by payment in due course." It means that the banker is protected if he pays the amount in accordance with the apparent tenor of the instrument in good faith and without negligence and to a person under circumstances not affording a reasonable ground for believing that he is not entitled to receive the payment. The banker can debit his customer's account with the amount so paid even though —

(i) The endorsement by the payee might turn out to be a forgery or

(ii) The endorsement might have been placed on the cheque by the payee's agent with out his authority.

Example

A cheque is drawn 'payment to B or order'. It is stolen and B's endorsement is forged. The banker pays the amount in due course. The banker is discharged from liability (*Charles v. Blackwell*).[40]

The banker can debit his customer with the amount so paid. Section 85 grants this protection to the banker because he is not expected to know the signatures of all the persons, excepting his customers. A banker can hardly be called upon to acquaint himself with the handwriting of several persons who may a cheque. The banker may have no means to find out whether a particular endorsement is genuine or forged. A banker can only assure is that the cheque should appear to be properly indorsed and that the payment is made in good faith and without negligence. But the banker will not be protected if there is an apparent irregularity in endorsement.[41]

Liability of Transferor by Delivery

A bearer instrument can be transferred by simple delivery. A person who so transfers, it is known as "transferor by delivery". The Negotiable Instruments provides nothing about the position and liability of such a transferor. Transferor by delivery incurs no liability because his name does no appear on the instrument in any capacity.

Liability of Endorser (Section 35)

The endorser of a negotiable instrument before maturity is liable to all subsequent holders in case of dishonour of the instrument provided —

(i) There is no contract to the contract,

(ii) The endorser had not limited or qualified his liability by using appropriate words, and

(iii) Due notice of dishonour has been given to, or received by, such endorser.

Every endorser after the dishonour of the instrument is liable as upon an instrument payable on demand. The endorser can exclude his liability by express words in the endorsement or can make it conditional.

Liability Under Accommodation Bills (Section 43 - 45)

Instrument Without Consideration (Section - 43)

An accommodation instrument means an instrument that had been accepted, made, drawn, indorsed or Transferred without consideration or for consideration which fails, creates no obligation of payment between the parties to the transaction.

But, if any such party has transferred the instrument with or without endorsement to a holder for consideration, such holder, and every subsequent holder deriving title from him, may recover the mount due on such instrument from the transferor for consideration or any prior party thereto. But the ultimate liability should be of the party for whose accommodation the instrument was made or indorsed. He should pay it and relieve the party who helped him in his difficulty. When he pays it, he himself cannot recover from any party.

Where an instrument has been given to a person for a consideration which he fails to perform in full, he cannot recover beyond the value of the consideration given by him.

Partial Failure of Consideration (Sec 44)

Where, instead of total absence or failure of consideration, the consideration fails only partially, the claim of the holder standing in immediate relation with the maker shall be proportionality reduced.

The drawer of a bill; of exchange stands in immediate relation with the acceptor. The maker of a promissory note, bill of exchange or cheque stands in immediate relation with the payee and the endorser with his endorsee. Other signers may by agreement stand in immediate relation with a holder.

Holder's Right to Duplicate (Sec 45-A)

Where before maturity of bill holder lost it, he may request the drawer to provide a duplicate copy of it. The holder will have to give security against the consequences if the original bill is found. If the drawer refuses to oblige he can be compelled to do so.

CHAPTER

9

Presentment of a Negotiable Instrument

Presentment means showing an instrument to the drawee, acceptor or maker for acceptance sight or payment. There are three kinds of presentment.

(1) Presentment of bills of exchange for acceptance.

(2) Presentment of promissory notes for sight.

(3) Presentment of negotiable instrument for payment.

1. Presentment for Acceptance

Only bills of exchange require presentment for acceptance. It is not all but certain kinds of bills must be presented for acceptance. Bills which are payable on demand or on a fixed date need not be presented for acceptance. But the following bills must be presented for acceptance otherwise the parties to the bill will not be liable thereon:

A — A bill payable after sight. Such a bill has to be presented for acceptance to fix maturity of the bill.

B — A bill which contains an express stipulation that it should be presented for acceptance before it is presented for payment.

In case where presentation for acceptance is not necessary but optional, it is always desirable to get a bill accepted as soon as possible in order to obtain as soon as possible in order to obtain; (i) the additional security of the acceptor's name on the bill, or (ii) an immediate right of resource against the drawer and the other parties in case the bill is dishonoured by non-acceptance.

Presentation for acceptance must be made at a reasonable hour on a business day and before the bill is overdue (Sec. 61).

Essentials of a Valid Acceptance

(1) The word accepted must be written on the face of the bill and drawee must signs below it.

(2) It must be signed by the drawee personally or through a duly authorised agent. Because without acceptance the drawee is not liable.

(3) Accepted bill must be delivered to the holder acceptance has not effect until bill is not delivered to the holder.

(4) Where the bill is drawn in a set, the acceptance should be put on the part only (Section 7 para 3). If the drawee signs his acceptance on more that one part, he may become liable on all the parts.

Mode of acceptance

An acceptance may be general or qualified.

General acceptance

When the drawee does not attach any condition or qualification while accepting, the bill, it is called general acceptance. If the acceptance is not absolute, the holder may treat the bill the bill as dishonoured by non-acceptance.

Qualified acceptance

When an acceptance is given subject to some condition or qualification, it is called qualified acceptance. The holder may in such a case refuse to take a qualified acceptance, and treat the bill as dishonoured by non acceptance. But if he takes a qualified acceptance, he does so at his own risk and discharges all the parties prior to himself, unless he obtains their consent to such acceptance. An cceptance is qualified when it is —

(1) Conditional as, for example, "Accepted payable when in funds" or Accepted payable when a cargo consigned to me is sold.

(2) Partial, i.e., of a part only of the amount of the bill as, for example, when a bill is drawn for Rs. 1,000 and is 'Accepted for Rs. 200 only.'

(3) Qualified as to time, i.e., to pay at a time other than that given in the bill as, for example, a bill drawn payable three months after date, but 'Accepted payable six months after date.'

(4) Qualified as to place, i.e., to pay only at a specified place and not else where or to pay at a place different from the place mentioned in the bill. An acceptance to pay at a particular place is a general acceptance, but if it expressly stated that the bill is to be paid there only and not elsewhere, it is a qualified acceptance.

(5) Acceptance by some of the drawees, but not all, as, for example a bill drawn on A, B and C (Who are not partners) but accepted by A only.

Presentment to whom for acceptance

Presentment for acceptance may be made to —

(i) the drawee or his duly authorised agent, or

(ii) all or some of several drawees or

(iii) all the drawees, where there are several drawees, unless they are partners and one has express or implied authority to accept on behalf of all.

(iv) the legal representative, if the drawee has died or

(v) official receiver or assignee, when the drawee has been declared insolvent (Sec 75).

Place of Presentment for Acceptance (Sec. 61)

The bill should be presented at the place which is specified for presentment. If no places for presentment is specified the bill should be presented at the drawee's place of business or residence, where the bill is presented at the residence, it must be at the reasonable hour.

The holder must allow the drawee forty eight hours (exclusive of public holidays) to consider whether he will accept the bill or not. If the holder allows more time, the other parties will be discharged from their liability to him. The proper approach for the holder is to treat the bill as dishonoured if it is not returned to him after acceptance within forty-eight hours (Section 63 and 83).

Time for Presentment for Acceptance

Where a time for presentment is specified, it must be presented within that time and before its maturity. Where no time is specified and the presentment is obligatory, it must be made within reasonable time. Reasonable time is a question of fact that depends upon the means of communication available and the usages of a particular trade.

The presentment must also be made on a business day and within business day.

Non-presentment effect

Where a bill is obligatory and the holder of a bill fails to present it for acceptance, the drawer and all the indorsers are discharged from liability to him. He is not entitled to a decree, nor can be base his claim on the original consideration.

Excuse from presentment for acceptance

Presentment for acceptance is excused under following circumstances.

(1) Where the drawee cannot, after reasonable search be found (Sec 61).

(2) Where the drawee is dead or insolvent, But in such a case, the bill may be presented for acceptance to the legal representative of the decreased or the official assignee of the insolvent (Sec 75).

(3) Where the drawee is a fictitious person or incapable of contracting, i.e., minor or of unsound mind. (Sec 91)

(4) Where, although presentment is irregular, the acceptance is refused on some other ground.

2. Presentment For Sight

In case of a promissory note, the acceptance is not required because maker of it is primarily liable. A note payable at a certain period after sight must be presented to the maker for sight in order to fix its maturity. The presentment is excused and instrument may be treated as dishonoured when the maker cannot be found after reasonable search. In default of such presentment, no party thereto is liable thereon to the person making such default (Sec 62).

3. Presentment for Payment (Sec. 64)

A negotiable instrument must be presented for payment to the maker, acceptor or drawee, there of, as the case may be, by the holder or his agent. In case of the default, the parties to the instrument other than the maker, acceptor or drawee are not liable to such holder.

In case of a promissory note, presentment for payment is not required where it is payable on demand and is not payable at a specific place.

Time for presentment

Where an instrument is payable after a fixed period of time, it should be presented for payment on its maturity (Sec 66). The presentment for payment must be made during usual hours of business, and in case of a cheque, within banking hours (Sec 65). However, where the presentment is made at an unreasonable hour but the payment is refused on some other ground, the instrument is deemed to be duly presented for payment.

If a promissory note is payable in installments, it should be presented for payment on the third day after the date fixed for each installment. Non payment of a single installment has the same effect as dishonour of the instrument at its maturity (Sec 67).

A negotiable instrument payable on demand must be presented for payment within a reasonable time after receipt by the holder (Sec 74).

Place of Presentment

Where a negotiable instrument is made payable at a specified place and not elsewhere, it must be presented for payment at that place in order to make any party liable thereon otherwise no party would be liable to the holder (Section 68 and 69). Where, no place is specified, it must be presented for payment at the place of business, if any or at the usual residence of the make, drawee or acceptor, as the case may be (Section 70). If the acceptor or maker has no known place of business or fixed residence and no place is specified in the instrument, the presentment may be made to him wherever found (Sec 71).

When Presentment of Payment not necessary (Sec. 76)

No presentment for payments necessary is where —

(1) The maker, drawee or acceptor internationally prevents the presentments of the instrument.

(2) The instrument is payable at the place of the business of the maker, acceptor or drawee of the note, bill or cheque, and such place on the due date during the usual business hours is closed. In such a case the presumption is that the person liable to pay wants to avoid payment.

(3) The instrument is payable at a specified place, and neither the maker, acceptor or drawee, nor any other person authorised to pay it is present, during the usual business hours.

(4) There is a promise to pay not with standing non-presentment.

(5) The instrument is not payable at a specified place, and the payer cannot after due search be found.

(6) The presentment for payment is expressly or implied by waived by the party entitled to presentment.

(7) The drawer could not suffer damage for want of presentment.

(8) The drawee is a fictions person or incompetent to contract.

(9) The drawer and drawee are the same person.

(10) The presentment has become impossible.

(11) The bill is dishonoured by non acceptance.

Maturity of Instrument (Sec. 21-25)

The provisions of presentment for payment are mostly related with the maturity of instrument. Payment can be only possible when it is due. Payment is only possible at the maturity of the instrument. The provisions of maturity of instrument are given in section 21 to 25 of the Act.

According to section 22, "the maturity of promissory note or bill of exchange is the date at which it falls due". Section 21 provides, a note or bill of exchange payable "at night or on presentment" is payable on demand. It is due for payment as soon as it is issued. It is mature for payment on its very issue when a note is payable "after sight", it should first be sighted to the maker. Then if it is payable "on demand after sight", its payment can be at once demanded but if it is payable after a specified period after sight, it is mature on the expiry of that period.

Days of Grace (Section 22)

Section 22 declares "Every promissory note or bill exchange which is not expressed to be payable on demand, at sight or on presentment is at maturity on the third day after the day on which it is expressed to be payable".

It means that where an instrument is payable after a fixed period of time, the party who has to pay is entitled to three days of grace after its maturity. Instrument which are payable on demand, after sight or on presentment are not entitled to any days of grace. The days of grace are calculated after the date of maturity. Maturity is calculated in accordance with the following principles.

(a) Instrument payable so many months after date or sight (Section 23)

When an instrument is payable some months after its date, its maturity will be on the day of the month which corresponds with the date of the instrument. If the month in which the period would terminate has no corresponding day, the period shall be held to terminate on the last day of such month. for example, if the instrument is dated October 31 and is payable after 4 months, its maturity will be on February 28 or 29, whichever may be the last day of February month.

(b) Instrument payable after some days (Section 24)

Where an instrument is payable after a specified number of days, the day of presentment shall be excluded. If it is payable on the happening of an event or after sight, the day of sight or of the happening of the event shall be excluded.

Where the day of maturity is public holiday, the instrument shall be at maturity on the next proceeding business day (Sec. 25).

CHAPTER

10

Dishonour of Negotiable Instrument

A bill of exchange may be dishonoured either by non acceptance or by non payment.

1. Dishonour by non-acceptance

Section 91 of the Negotiable instruments Act enumerates the circumstances when a bill will be considered as dishonoured by non-acceptance. These are:

(i) When the drawee does not accept it within 48 hours from the time of presentment by non-acceptance,

(ii) When presentment for acceptance is excused and it remains unaccepted,

(iii) When the drawee is a person incompetent to contract,

(iv) When the drawee could not be found after a reasonable search,

(v) Where the acceptance is qualified,

(vi) Where one or more of the several drawee refuse to accept the bill.

2. Dishonoured by non-payment

A negotiable instrument is said to be dishonoured by non-payment when the maker, acceptor or drawee, as the case may be, makes default in payment upon being duly required to pay the same (section 92).

A negotiable instrument is also dishonoured by non payment is excused and the instrument remains unpaid after maturity (section 76).

Notice of Dishonour

In both the cases is a negotiable instrument dishonoured by non-acceptance or non payment, the holder must give notice of dishonour to drawer and all other parties whom he seeks to make liable. It is however, not necessary to give such a notice to the maker of the promissory note, or the drawee or acceptor of the dishonoured bill of exchange or cheque (section 93). Each party receiving notice of dishonour must in order to render any prior party liable to himself give notice of dishonour to such party within a reasonable time after he has received it (section 95). The notice may be oral or in writing though for safety it is advisable to give a written notice. A notice may be sent by post. It may be in any form. But it should inform the recipient, expressly or by reasonable instrument has been dishonoured and in what way dishonoured, and that he will be held liable on it. If the notice is duly directed and sent by post, and miscarried, such miscarriage does not render the notice invalid. A notice should be directed to the party's place of business, or where he has no such place, to his residence.

Effect of Dishonour

The effect of dishonour of a negotiable instrument whether by non-acceptance or non payment is to render the drawer and all the endorsers liable to the holder. However, their liability can be invoked only if the holder gives then notice such dishonour.

The drawer is liable only if the instrument is dishonoured by non-payment.

When notice of dishonour not necessary?

Section 93 of the Negotiable Instruments Act requires that when a negotiable instrument is dishonoured by non-acceptance or non payment, the holder must give notice of dishonour to the drawer and all other parties whom he seeks to make liable.

However, section 98 of the said Act enumerates the following circumstances in which notice of dishonour is not necessary:

(i) When it is dispensed with by the party entitled there to.
(ii) In order to charge the drawer when he has countermanded payment, notice of dishonour is unnecessary because the instrument is dishonoured by the express mandate of the drawer himself.
(iii) When the party charged could not suffer damage for want of notice.
(iv) When the party entitled to notice cannot after reasonable search be found.
(v) Where the party liable to give notice is unable without any fault of its own to give it, e.g. death or serious illness of the holder or his agent or any other accident.
(vi) Where the promissory note is not negotiable.
(vii) In case the drawer himself is the acceptor, no notice is necessary to charge the drawer.
(viii) When the party entitled to notice, knowing the facts promises unconditionally to pay the amount due on the instrument.

Noting and Protesting

Noting (Sec. 99)

Noting is a convenient method of authenticating the fact of dishonour. Where an instrument is dishonoured, the holder can, after giving due notice of dishonour, sue any or all prior parties liable thereon. But before he does that, he may get the fact of dishonour authenticated by "Noting" by a Notary Public. In such a case the Notary makes a formal demand upon the maker or drawee or acceptor, for acceptance or payment, as the case may be. On refusal by the maker or drawee or acceptor, he records the noting on the instrument. Noting means the recording of the fact of dishonour by a Notary Public upon the instrument, or upon a paper attached there to or partly upon each, within a reasonable time after dishonour. Noting must contain specific date of dishonour and the reason for such dishonour. If the instrument has not been expressly dishonoured the noting should state why the holder treats it as dishonoured. It must contain the Notary charges.

Noting is not compulsory in the case of an inland bill or note, but foreign bills must be protested. If so required by the law of the place where drawn.

Protesting

When a promissory note or bill of exchange is dishonoured by non-acceptance or non payment, the holder may, within a reasonable time cause such dishonour to be noted and certified by a Notary Public. Such certificate is called a 'protest'.

A valid protest must contain the following particulars (Section 101):
(i) The instrument itself or a literal transcript of instrument.
(ii) The name of the person for whom and against whom the instrument is protested.
(iii) The place and time of dishonour.
(iv) The fact and reason of dishonour.
(v) Signature of the notary public.
(vi) In case of acceptance for dishonour or payment for dishonour, the name of the person by whom or the person for whom, and the manner in which, such acceptance or payment was offered and effected.

Protest for better Security [Sec. 100(2)]

Sometimes, a bill is protested for better security. When before the maturity of a bill, the acceptor of a bill has become insolvent, or has suspended payment or his credit has been publicly impeached, the holder may through a notary public, demand better security from the acceptor. If the acceptor refuses it the fact may also be noted and certified by the notary. Such certificate is called a protest for better security. The demand for better security should be made within reasonable time.

Notice of Protest (Sec. 102)

When a promissory note or bill of exchange is required by law to be protested, notice of such protest must be given instead of notice of dishonour, in the same manner and subject to the same conditions as notice of dishonour. But the notice of protest may be given by the notary public who makes the protest.

Protest for non-payment after dishonour by non-acceptance (Sec. 103)

A bill which has been dishonoured by non-acceptance may be protested for non-payment if it is payable at some place other than the residence of the drawee.

Protest of foreign bills (Sec. 104)

Foreign bills of exchange must be protested for dishonour when such protest is required by the law of the place where they are drawn.

Advantages of Protest

(1) It is a certified evidence of dishonour to the drawer and endorsers.

(2) In a suit of dishonoured instrument, the court shall, on proof of the protest, presume the fact of dishonour unless such facts are disproved.

Distinction between Noting and Protesting

(1) Noting is the preliminary step to "protesting".

(2) Noting is made by the notary public by way of memorandum while a protest is authentic formal certificate on basis of noting.

(3) All dishonoured bills should be noted through notary public if definite instructions are not given regarding protest.

(4) At places where there is a notary public is not appointed under Notaries Act, 1952 the dishonoured bills cannot be noted and, therefore, these should be protested.

Compensation (Section 117)

Section 117 lays down rules for determining the amount of compensation to the holder or endorsee when a negotiable instrument is dishonoured. These rules are as below:

(1) The holder is entitled to recover the amount due upon the instrument, with interest on the principal sum and expenses incurred in presenting, noting and protesting the instrument [Sec. 117 (a)].

(2) Where a person resides in a country different from that in which the instrument is payable, holder is entitled to receive the compensation at the current rate of exchange between the two countries on the date of dishonour [Sec. 117(b)].

Compensation to Endorser

(1) If an endorser has paid the amount due on the instrument is entitled to the amount so paid with 18% interest per annum [interest rate from 6% to 18% increased by the Banking, Public Financial institutions and Negotiable Instruments laws (Amendment) Act 1988] from the date of payment until tender or realisation, with all expenses caused by the dishonour and payment. But he can recover the amount only if at the time of payment he was liable on the instrument [Sec. 177(c)].

(2) When the person charged and the endorser are residents of different countries the current rate of exchange between the two countries shall apply [Sec. 177(d)].

Re-draft

The party entitled to compensation may draw a bill upon the party liable to compensate him, for the amount due to him together with all expenses incurred by him. Such a bill is called a 're-draft'. Such bill must be accompanied by the instrument dishonoured, and the protest, if any. If such bill 're-draft' is dishonoured, the party dishonouring the same is liable to make compensation in the same manner as in the case of original bill [Sec. 117 (e)].

Compensation against banker

There is no provision in this Act for determining the compensation payable by a banker who wrongfully dishonours his customer's cheques, therefore, the rule as it prevails in England seems to be applicable in India.

In English law, such compensation will include damages to credit and reputation of the drawer, and the court would normally award exemplary or vindictive damages.

CHAPTER

11

Discharge of a Negotiable Instrument

The term 'discharge' in relation to a negotiable instrument is used in two senses, viz., (1) discharge of the instrument, and (2) discharge of one or more parties from liability on the instrument.

Discharge of the Instrument

An instrument is said to be discharged when all rights of action under it are completely extinguished and when it ceases to be negotiable. A negotiable instrument is discharged when the party ultimately liable on the instrument is discharged from liability. After a negotiable instrument is discharged, the rights against all the parties there to come to an end, and no party, even a holder in due course, can claim the amount of the instrument from any party there to. The discharge of one or more of the parties to a bill or note does not discharge the instrument.

The different modes of discharge of an instrument are given as below:

(1) When the party Primarily liable on the instrument (i.e., the maker of the note, acceptor of the bill or drawee bank) makes the payment in due course to the holder at or after maturity (Sec. 78). A payment by a party who is secondarily liable does not discharge the instrument because in that case the payer holds it to enforce it against prior endorsers and the principal debtor.

(2) When the maker of a note or the acceptor of a bill becomes its holder at or after its maturity in his own right, the instrument is discharged (Sec. 90).

(3) When the party primarily liable becomes insolvent, the instrument is discharged and the holder cannot make any other prior party liable thereon. Notice that in the case of insolvency, the acceptor or maker is unable to pay and it is only on refusal to pay that the instrument is deemed to be dishonoured and prior parties can be made liable thereon. Similarly, an instrument stands discharged when the primary party liable is discharged by material alteration in the instrument (Sec. 87), or by lapse of time making the debt time barred under the limitation Act.

(4) Where an instrument is intentionally cancelled by the holder or his agent and the cancellation is apparent thereon, the instrument is discharged and ceases to be negotiable (Sec. 82).

Discharge of one or more parties

A party is said to be discharged from his liability when his liability on the instrument comes to an end. When only some of the parties to a negotiable instrument are discharged, the instrument continues to be negotiable and the undischarged parties remain liable on it. A party or parties to a negotiable instrument is/are discharged from liability in any one of the following ways:

1. By Cancellation [Sec. 82 (a)]

When the holder of a negotiable instrument or his agent cancels the name of the party on the instrument to discharge him, and the cancellation is apparent thereon, such party and all subsequent parties who have a right of recourse against the party whose name is canceled are discharged from liability to the holder. The subsequent parties are in the position of sureties to the prior party whose name is canceled and discharge of the principal debtor automatically discharges the sureties. Thus the first endorser is a surety to prior parties and a principal to subsequent.

It is important to note that where the cancellation is done under a mistake or without the authority of the holder it would be inoperative and will not discharge any party.

2. By release [Sec. 82 (b)]

Where the holder of a negotiable instrument releases any party to the instrument by any method other than cancellation of names (i.e., by a separate agreement of waiver, release, or remission), the party so released and all parties subsequent to him, who have a right of action against the party so released, are discharged from liability.

3. By payment [Sec. 83 (c) and (Sec. 78)]

When the party primarily liable on the instrument makes the payment in due course to the holder at or after maturity, both the instrument and the parties to the instrument stand discharged.

Payment is an effective discharge only if it is "payment in due course". According to section 10 of Act 'payment in due course' means in accordance with the apparent tenor of the instrument in good faith and without negligence to any person in possession thereof under circumstances which do not afford a reasonable ground for believing that he is not entitled to receive payment of the amount there in mentioned.

Thus, the first requirement of an effective payment is that payment should be made on the maturity of the instrument. A payment before maturity is no discharge unless the instrument is cancelled or the fact of payment is conspicuously recorded on it.

Secondly, section 78 says that payment should be made to the holder otherwise it shall not be a good discharge to the party liable to pay.

4. By allowing drawee more than 48 hours (Sec. 83)

If the holder of a bill of exchange allows the drawee more than 48 hours (exclusive of public holidays), to consider whether he will accept the same, all previous parties who do not consent to such allowance are thereby discharged from liability to such holder.

5. By Delay in presenting cheque (Sec. 84)

The holder is under a duty to present cheque for payment within reasonable time of its issue. If he fails to present and in the mean while the bank fails causing damage to the drawer, the drawer is discharged as against the holder to the extent of the actual damage suffered by him.

6. By Qualified Acceptance (Sec. 86)

The holder of a bill who presents it for acceptance should insists that the bill be accepted without any conditions or qualifications. If the holder of a bill acquiesces in a qualified acceptance, all the previous parties whose consent is not obtained to such acceptance are discharged from liability. They will be liable if on a notice being given to them they give their assent to such acceptance.

7. Material alteration

Sometimes negotiable instruments are altered between drawing and presentation period without authority from the drawer. Some alterations are material and some are immaterial. An alteration is material if it alters materially or substantially the operation of the instrument and there by the rights are liabilities of the parties.

Section 87 of the Negotiable instruments Act says, "Any material alteration of a negotiable instrument renders the same as void as against any one who is a party there to at the time of making such alteration and does not consent there to, unless it was made in order to carry out the common intention of the original parties." An alteration is material in following conditions:

(A) Intentional Alteration

The alteration must be intentional. It must be such to which the other parties can assent. In *Hong Kong and Shanghai Banking Corporation v. Lo Lee Shi*[42] it is observed "The alteration contemplated is one to which all parties might assent. It is not reasonable to assume parties assenting to a part of the document being effected by the operation of a mouse, by the hot end of a cigarette or by any of the other means by which accidental disfigurement can be effected. It cannot reasonably apply to the ravages of a rat, white-ant or any other animal pest."

(B) Material Alteration

Secondly, alteration should be in the material part of the instrument. An alteration is material if it alters the business effect of the instrument if it has some business effect. In *Coonkaran Sethiya v. Ivan E. John*[43], it is stated by Supreme Court that:

"A material alteration is one which varies the rights, liabilities or legal position of the parties as ascertained by the deed in its original state, or otherwise varies the legal effect of the instrument as originally expressed, or which may otherwise prejudice the party bound by the deed as originally executed."

Examples of material alteration are:
Alteration regarding

(i) date,
(ii) the place of payment,
(iii) the time of payment,
(iv) the sum payable,
(v) the number of parties,
(vi) the relationship between parties,
(vii) legal character of the instrument,
(viii) opening a crossed cheque,
(ix) converting an order cheque into a bearer cheque.

These alterations vitiate the instrument. The following alterations do not vitiate or avoid the negotiable instrument:

(1) An alteration, though in a material part, made before the instrument is issued.
(2) An alteration made for the purpose of correcting a mistake.
(3) An alteration which is not material.
(4) An alteration made with the consent of the parties.
(5) An alteration made to carry out the common intention of the original parties, e.g. insertion of the words 'or order' where the drawer of a bill forgets to use these words.

The Act itself permits three kinds of alteration which do not vitiate the instrument.

(1) The person who issued a blank instrument is authorised to complete (Sec. 20).
(2) Conversion of a blank endorsement into an endorsement in full (Sec. 49).
(3) Crossing of a uncrossed cheque or conversion of general into special crossing or making not negotiable (Sec. 125).

Further the banker to whom a cheque has been crossed specially may cross it especially to another banker or his agent. The principle also does not apply to the following cases:

Firstly, Section 88 says "An acceptor or endorser of a negotiable instrument is bound by his acceptance or endorsement not with standing any previous alteration of the instrument."

Secondly an alteration is made to carry out the common intention of the original parties does not render the instrument void (Sec. 87).

(c) Apparent Alteration (Sec. 89)

Section 89, however, grants protection to the paying banker where the alteration is apparently not noticeable and the payment is made in due course as per section 10. Section 89 provides that where an instrument has been materially altered but does not appear to have been so altered, the party paying it will be discharged by payment in due course. But in such a case the acceptor is liable only for the original tenor of the instrument and not for its altered tenor. It was held by the House of Lords in *Schalfiled v. The Earl of Condesborough*[44], that the acceptor was liable only for what he accepted to pay. The acceptor of a bill of exchange is not under a duty to take precautions against fraudulent alteration in the bill after acceptance.

Where an alteration is apparent, i.e., observable on reasonable examination, the party taking it gets no rights.

Effect of material alteration

The effect of material alteration of a negotiable instrument is only to discharge those who become parties there to prior to the alteration. But if an alteration is made in order to carry out the common intention of the original parties, it does not render the instrument void.

Section 87 expressly provides that any material alteration, if made by an endorser, the endorser will be discharged from his liability to him even in respect of the consideration. So, when a cheque is altered, it ceases to be a cheque altogether and a banker who makes payment cannot debit the customer's account. Thus, if the alteration is not under the full signature of the drawer, the cheque should be returned with the remarks "Alteration requires full signature of the drawer."

8. By Negotiation Back (Sec. 90)

The acceptor of bill of exchange becomes its holder when that instrument comes back to the acceptor by process of negotiation, which is known as 'negotiation back'. If this process of negotiation happens at or after maturity, all liability on the instrument comes to an end.

Section 90 of Act provides: "If a bill of exchange which has been negotiated is, at or after maturity, held by the acceptor in his own right, all rights of action there on are extinguished."

CHAPTER

12

Crossed Cheques

There are following two types of cheques.

(1) Open cheques and

(2) Crossed cheques.

Open cheques

They are payable in cash across the bank counter. There is a great risk in open cheque while it is in circulation. Where the holder of such cheque loses it its finder may get payment from concerned bank unless its payment has already been stopped. The custom of crossing of cheque was introduced to prevent the risks of open cheque.

Crossed cheques

Crossing of cheques had its origin in London Clearing House. It is a peculiar method of modifying the instrument to the banker for payment of the cheque. A crossed cheque is one which bears across its face two parallel transverse lines. The lines are usually drawn on the left hand top corner of the cheque. But they may be drawn any where. Crossing affects the mode of payment of the cheque. Such cheque is not payable to holder or payee at the counter of the bank. The payment of such a chequo can bo obtained only through a banker. Thus, crossing Is a dlrection to the drawee banker to pay the amount of money on a crossed cheque generally to a banker or a particular banker so that the party who obtains the payment of the cheque can be easily traced, because he has to operate through a banker. The crossing affords security and protection to the owner of the cheque, as the cheque is payable only through a banker.

Kinds of crossing

There are basically two kinds of crossing, namely:

(1) General crossing and

(2) Special crossing

A new type of crossing known as 'restrictive crossing' has been adopted by banking and commercial usage.

1. General Crossing (Sec. 123)

A cheque is said to be crossed generally where it bears no words between two parallel transverse lines or when there are some words but not the name of a bank. Section 123 provides "where a cheque bears across its face an addition of the words 'and company' or any abbreviation thereof, between two parallel transverse lines or of two parallel transverse lines simply, 'either with or without the words' not negotiable, that additional shall be deemed crossing and the cheque shall be deemed to be crossed generally."

The containing of words between the lines of crossing makes no difference.

And Company	& Co.	Not negotiable	N/N & Co.	
(1)	(2)	(3)	(4)	(5)

Specimen of General Crossing

2. Special Crossing (Sec. 124)

Where the lines of crossing bear the name of a banker with or without any additional words, the cheque is said to be crossed specially and to be crossed to that banker. Transverse lines are not necessary in case of special crossing.

Section 124 in this regard, provides : "Where a cheque bears across its face, an addition of the name of a bank, either with or without the words 'not negotiable', that addition shall be deemed a crossing, and the cheque shall be deemed to be crossed to that banker." "Drawing two parallel lines is not necessary in case of a specially crossed cheque."

(1)	(2)	(3)	(4)
Allahabad Bank	Allahabad Bank	Not negotiable Allahabad Bank	A/c payee only Allahabad Bank

Specimen of Special Crossing

The payment of a specially crossed cheque can be obtained only through the particular banker whose name appears across the face of the cheque or between transverse lines, if any. Where a cheque is crossed specially the banker on whom it is drawn shall pay it only to the banker on whom it is crossed or his agent for collection (Sec.126).

Account payee only

Sometimes the lines of crossing contain the word "account payee only", which is the version of general crossing. Such crossing is a mere direction to the collecting bank that the amount collecting on the cheque is to be credited to the account of the payee. It should however be noted that "A/c payee only" cheques are negotiable.[45]

The addition of "A/c payee only" to a crossing has no legal sanctity and the paying banker may ignore such a direction without beiing liable for any damages.

"Not Negotiable" Crossing (Section 130)

When the lines of crossing carry the words "not negotiable" the crossing is said to be 'not negotiable crossing'. Section 130 states the effect of the words "not negotiable". These words "not negotiable effect upon thenegotiable character of the cheque. The effect is that the title of the transferee of such a cheque cannot be better than that of its transferor. The addition of the words "not negotiable does not restrict the further transferability of the cheque, it only takes away the main feature of negotiability, which is, that of holder with a defective title can give a good title to a subsequent holder in due course. Anyone who takes a cheque marked 'not negotiable' takes it as his own risk.

The object of crossing a cheque 'not negotiable' is to afford protection to the drawer or holder of the cheque against miscarriage or dishonesty in the course of transit by making it difficult to get the cheque so crossed cashed, until it reaches its destination. In *Wilson and Meoson v. Pickering*[46], a blank cheque marked "not negotiable" was fraudulently completed by an agent and transferred to a person to whom the agent was indebted, it was held that the transferee was affected by the fraud.

Who may cross a cheque (Sec. 125)

A cheque may be crossed by any of the following:

1. By Drawer

The drawer of a cheque may cross the cheque generally or specially.

2. By Holder

Where a uncrossed cheque is issued, the holder may cross it generally or specially. If the cheque is crossed generally, the holder may cross it specially. Where it is crossed generally or specially, the holder may add the words "not negotiable".

3. By Banker

Where a cheque is crossed specially, the banker to whom it is crossed may again cross it specially in favour of another banker. The latter banker in such a case acts as the agent of the former for collection.

Payment of crossed cheques (Sec. 126)

The banker who makes the payment of a crossed cheque is called the 'paying banker'. Thus, 'paying banker' is a banker upon whom a cheque is drawn. The paying banker is under a duty to pay a crossed cheque only to another banker and to pay a cheque crossed specially only to the banker to whom it is crossed. On such payment, the paying banker is discharged from his liability to the same extent as if the payment has been made to the true owner. This will be so even if the content of the cheque do not reach the true owner (Sec. 128) .

Where, the payment is not made in above stated manner, the paying banker becomes liable to the actual owner for any loss sustained by him owing to the irregular payment (Sec. 129).

In *Madras Provincial Co-operative Bank Ltd., Madras v. South Indian Match Factory Ltd.*[47], the banker who paid a crossed cheque over the counter to the company's liquidator, was held liable to the company, the liquidator having misappropriated the amount.

Section 89 provides another protection of the paying banker. Where a cheque does not at the time of presentment appear to be crossed or where the crossing is obliterated, the banker, paying the cheque in good faith and without negligence, will be discharged from the liability on the cheque.

Section 127 stated that, where a cheque is crossed specially to more than one banker, except when necessary for collection, the banker on whom it is drawn should refuse payment.

The Collecting Banker

The bank which receives the payment of a crossed cheque on behalf of its customer is known as the collecting banker. The collecting banker may be described as a link between the payee of a cheque and its drawee (Paying banker). Though not obligatory, this service of collection of cheques on behalf of the customers has become an accepted part of banker's functions due to the great use of crossed cheques which are not payable otherwise than through a banker.

Protection of the Collecting Banker (Sec. 131)

There are a great risks for collecting bank in receiving payment of crossed cheques. The cheque is collected by collecting bank on behalf of the customer who may turn out to be not entitled to the cheque. The banker may thus become liable to the true owner of the cheque for conversion in having helped a person to receive money to which he was not entitled; Section 131 extends protection to the collecting banker. This section protects bankers who, in good faith and without negligence, collect crossed cheques for a customer who had no title to them. This section states "A banker who has in good faith and without negligence received payment for a customer of a cheque crossed generally or specially to himself shall not, in case the title to the cheque proves defective, incur any liability to the true owner of the true owner of the cheque by reason only having received such payment.

Thus, the requirements of this statutory protection to a collecting banker are as follows:

1. For a customer

The protection can be claimed only for those cheques which the banker collects as an agent for his customers. A banker who allows the facility of collection to a stranger does so at his own risk. The term 'customer' is not defined in any of the statutes. A 'customer' means a person who keeps an account with the bank. Thus, a customer is a person who has some sort of account with a banker. The duration of the relationship is immaterial. A account may be a current account or a deposit account.

In *Landbroke v. Todd* (1914)[47], it was observed; "The relation of banker and customer begins as soon as the first cheque is paid in and accepted for collection and not merely when it is paid". But mere casual acts of service do not create the relationship of banker and customer (*Commissioner of Taxation v. English, Scottish Australian Bank Ltd.* (1920)[48] and merely because a banker performs a causal service for a person does not make that person a customer. A person who goes to the bank to remit his life insurance premium to the Life Insurance Corporation, or to buy a draft or cash a cheque issued to him by someone else, is not a customer. A person who is customer must have some sort of account with the banker. The relationship between a banker and his customer is essentially contractual. A banker before accepting a person as a customer, as a general rule must take reasonable care to satisfy himself that the person is of good reputation. 'Reasonable Care' depends upon facts and circumstances of each case.

2. Collecting Banker as an agent

A collecting banker acts as an agent of customer if receives payment of the crossed cheque and credits to the customer's account with amount of the cheque after it is actually realised. When collecting banker acts as an agent has no better title than of his customer.

Section 131 enunciates the rule that where a banker collects payment on a crossed cheque for his customer is protected, if the customer's title to the cheque turns out to be defective and he would not be liable to the true owner for conversion. Following conditions are essential for the protection —

(1) That the collecting banker acts in good faith and without negligence.
(2) That the collecting banker receives payment of the crossed cheque for a customer.
(3) That the collecting banker acts as an agent for collection for the customer.
(4) That the protection applies to crossed cheques and that the cheque must have been crossed before it gets into the hands of the collecting banker.

Explanation to Section 131 extends a further protection to the collecting banker, where the collecting banker credits his customer's account with the amount of the crossed cheque before receiving payment thereof, the banker is protected in that case also.

3. For Crossed cheques only

The protection of section 131 is available to the collecting banker only with regard to crossed cheques. This protection is not available to banker in case of open cheques. If the cheques are uncrossed, the banker is not protected, if the customer's title is defective and he cannot secure the protection by subsequently himself crossing the cheque.

Section 131-A provides that protection extends to any crossed draft to the same extent as if it were a cheque.

4. Good faith and without negligence

Lastly, the collecting banker must have received payment in good faith and without negligence. There should be nothing in the circumstances of the cheque to create a suspicion about the customer's title. If there is any cause of suspicion, due inquiries should be made, failing which the banker may be held guilty of negligence. The facts of *A.L. Underwood Ltd. v. Bank of Liverpool and Martins and Barclays Bank*[49] are most illustrative of the circumstances which demand inquiry. In this case Underwood who was the sole director and principal shareholder of the plaintiff company. A large number of cheques payable to the order of company were endorsed by him to himself and paid into his personal account with the defendant bank for collection. When the company went into liquidation, the liquidator commenced action against the bank for conversion of its cheques.

The bank was held liable for guilty of negligence. The banker should have inquired how and for what reason the director was diverting the Company's cheques into his personal account.

The extent of inquiry depends upon the circumstances of each case. An inquiry is necessary in all cases where an agent or servant is dealing with the cheques of his master in an unusual manner. Thus, in *Lloyds v. Savory and Co.* (1933)[50] two dishonest clerks of a stock brokers firm (Savory and Co.) stole the cheques which were issued by the firm to customers. Both clerks paid the cheques in the head office of the Lloyds Bank for collection and transmission of the proceeds in one case into the clerk's personal account in a branch of the bank and in the other case into the account of the clerk's wife.

The bank was held guilty of negligence and liable to refund the money. They should have inquired in one case the name of the clerk's employer's and in the other case the name of the customer's husband.

Inquiry may also be made in obtaining the proper introduction of customer at the time of opening account. In *Landbroke v. Todd* (1914)[51], an account was opened without seeking proper introduction, the banker was held responsible for having acted negligently.

Where a party unknown to the banker opened an account after giving the name of a stranger as reference. The banker was held negligent for taking no steps to check the reference (Guardians of *S. John's Hampstead v. Barclay's Ltd.* (1923).[52]

Similarly, in *Vysya Bank Ltd v. Indian Bank AIR* (1988) 256 Mad[53], an introduction by an authorised signatory of another account holder was not considered as proper introduction and hence the banker was held negligent.

Inquiry is necessary only when the circumstances demand or justify it. The banker is not bound to regard every new customer as a potential criminal. A long and detailed scrutiny of every available piece of evidence is not required.

CHAPTER

13

Rules of Evidence, Estoppel and International Law

Act provides special rules of evidence, estoppel and international law for negotiable instruments.

Presumptions (Sec. 118-119)

Section 118 and 119 lays down a number of presumptions and apply to all negotiable instruments, unless otherwise is provided. These presumptions are as follows.

1. As to Consideration

Every negotiable instrument is presumed to have been made, drawn, accepted, endorsed negotiated or transferred for consideration. This would help a holder to get a decree from a court without any difficulty. The consideration mentioned in a promissory note differed from that which was alleged in the plaint. This did not destroy the presumption of consideration. The note was still presumed to have been issued for valid consideration.[53]

2. As to Date

Every negotiable instrument is presumed to have been made or drawn on the date appears on it.

3. As to Acceptance

When a bill of exchange has been accepted, it is presumed that it was accepted within a reasonable time after the date mentioned therein and before the date of its maturity.

4. As to Transfer

Every transfer of a negotiable instrument is presumed to have been made before its maturity.

5. As to order of Endorsements

The endorsements appearing on a negotiable instrument are presumed to have been made in the order in which they appear thereon.

6. As to Stamp

When an instrument has been lost, it is presumed that it was duly stamped.

7. As to holder in due course

The holder of negotiable instrument is presumed to be a holder in due course. The burden lies on the opposite party to show that he is not a holder in due course. When this is shown the presumption is rebutted and the burden of proving that he is a holder in due course is then shifted to the holder.[54]

8. Proof of protest (Sec. 119)

If a suit is filed upon an instrument which has been dishonoured, the court, on proof of the protest, presumes that the fact of dishonour, unless such fact is disaproved.

The above presumptions can be rebutted by evidence. These presumptions would not arise where an instrument has been obtained by any offence, fraud, or unlawful consideration.

Estoppels

The Negotiable Instruments Act lays down the following rules of estoppel.

(i) Against Denial of Validity of Instrument (Section 120)

The maker of a promissory note, the drawer of a bill or cheque and the acceptor of a bill for the honour of the drawer are not permitted, as against a holder in due course, to deny the validity of the instrument as originally made or drawn.

(ii) Against Denial of Payee to Endorse (Section 121)

The maker of a promissory note and the acceptor of a bill of exchange payable to order are not permitted, as against a holder in due course, to say that the payee is not in capacity at the time to endorse the instrument.

(iii) Against Endorser (Section 122)

The endorser of a negotiable instrument is not permitted, as against a subsequent endorser, to deny the signature or capacity of any prior party to the instrument.

Bills in Sets (Section 132)

A Bill of exchange is sometimes drawn in parts, especially when it has to be sent from one country to another (foreign bills), this is known as drawing a bill 'in a set'. Each part of the bill is known as a 'via' and with the acceptance and payment of any part, the other parts become inoperative.

All the parts together make a set, but the whole set constitutes only one bill. The entire bill is extinguished when payment is made on one of the parts. The drawer must sign each part of the bill and deliver all parts. But the stamp is affixed on one part only and only one part of the whole set needs to be accepted.

If, however, any person endorses different parts of a bill in favour of different persons, he and the subsequent endorsers of each are liable on such part as if it were a separate bill (exception to section 132).

International Law (Sections 134-137)

The rules of International Law relating to foreign negotiable instruments are as follows:

1. Liability on Foreign Instruments (Section 134)

The liability of the maker or drawer of a foreign promissory note, bill of exchange or cheque is regulated in essential respects by any law of the place where the instrument has been made.

"Foreign instrument" has not been defined. Definition of "Inland instrument is given in section 11. Section 11 says that a Promissory note, bill of exchange or cheque drawn or made in India are payable in or drawn upon any person resident in India is an inland instrument. According to section 12, a foreign bill is negotiable instrument which is not an inland instrument, as defined in section 11. Thus, a foreign bill of exchange is—

(a) drawn in India upon a person resident outside India and made payable outside India, or

(b) drawn outside India and payable in India.

The respective liability of the acceptor and endorser is determined by the law place where the instrument is payable.

Law in respect of dishonour (Section 135)

Where a promissory note, bill of exchange or cheque is made in a different Country from the one where it is made payable shall determine what constitutes dishonour and what notice of dishonour is sufficient.

Example — A bill of exchange drawn and endorsed in India, but accepted payable in France, is dishonoured. The endorsee causes it to be protested for such dishonour and gives notice thereof in accordance with the law of France. The notice is sufficient.

3. Foreign instruments made in accordance with Indian law (Section 136)

If an instrument is made, drawn accepted or endorsed out of India but in accordance with Indian law, the fact that the instrument is invalid according to the law of the country where it is made, does not invalidate any subsequent acceptance or endorsement of the instrument made within India.

Presumption as to foreign law (Section 137)

The law of the foreign country regarding promissory notes, bills of exchange and cheques is presumed to be the same as that of India, unless it is proved to be different.

CHAPTER

14

Acceptance and Payment for Honour

The acceptance of a bill is the indication by the drawee of his assent to the order of the drawer. Section 7 of the Negotiable Instruments Act says that an acceptance is the signature of the drawee of a bill who has signed his assent upon the bill and delivered it or given notice of such signing to the holder to some person on his behalf. An acceptor is the drawee who has signed his assent upon the bill and delivered it to the holder or has given notice of his so doing to the holder. Writing the word "accepted" is immaterial to the establishment of the drawee's responsibility. But an oral acceptance or writing of the words accepted without the drawee's signature is not an acceptance. An acceptance to be valid must be (a) in writing, (b) signed by the drawee or his agent, (c) on bill of exchange, and (d) completed by delivery to the holder or by notice of acceptance to him or some person on his behalf.

Kinds of Acceptance

An acceptance of a bill may be general or qualified.

General Acceptance

An acceptance without any conditions or qualification is called general acceptance.

Qualified Acceptance

Where certain condition or qualification is imposed for acceptance which varying the effect of the bill as drawn is called qualified acceptance. The acceptance by law must be general and therefore the holder is at liberty to refuse to take a qualified acceptance. When he refuses to take bill with certain qualification, the bill shall be dishonoured by non-acceptance. But, if he accepts the qualified acceptance, even then it binds only him and the acceptor and not the other parties who do not consent thereto.

The explanation to Section 86 of the Negotiable Instrument Act lays down the following qualified acceptance.

(a) where it is conditional declaring the payment to be dependent upon the happening of event therein stated.
(b) where it undertakes the payment of part only of the sum ordered to be paid.
(c) where it undertakes the payment at a time other than that at which under the order it would be legally due.
(d) where place of payment is not specified on the order, it undertakes the payment at a specified place, and not otherwise or elsewhere, or where, a place of payment being specified in the order, it undertakes the payment at some other place and not otherwise or elsewhere.

Who may Accept?

The following persons may accept a bill of exchange.

(1) The drawee of the bill.
(2) Where there are more than one drawees, by all or some of them. Only those who accept become liable on the instruments.
(3) A drawee in case of need.
(4) An agent of any of the person mentioned above.
(5) An acceptor for honour.
(6) An agent of the acceptor for honour.
(7) In case no drawee is mentioned in the bill and a person accepts it, he becomes an acceptor by estoppel.

Acceptance for honour (Section 108)

When a bill of exchange has been noted or protested for non-acceptance or for better security, any person who is not already liable on the bill may with the consent of the holder, accept the bill for honour of any party.

The acceptance should be by writing on the bill, signed by the acceptor for honour. He should also declare in the same writing that he is accepting it for the honour of the drawer or of a particular endorser whom he names, or generally for honour (Section 109) where the acceptor does not state for whose honour it is made, it shall be deemed to be made for the honour of the drawer. (Section 110)

Payment for Honour (Section 113)

The general rule of law is that no person by voluntarily paying the debt of another can make himself his creditor. But, in case of negotiable instruments section 113 makes an exception saying that "when a bill of exchange has been noted or protested for non-payment, any person may pay the same for the honour of any party liable to pay the same, provided that the person so paying or his agent in that behalf has previously declared before a notary public the party for whose honour he says, and that such declaration should have been recorded by the notary public.

Right to Payer for honour (Section 114)

The person who pays for honour has the same rights as the holder has against all the parties. In particular, as against the party for whose honour he pays, he has the right to recover all sums he has paid, and also interest on them and the expenses properly incurred in making such payment.

Drawee in case of need (Section 115)

Where a drawee in case of need is named in the bill itself or in any endorsement on it, the bill is not dishonoured till it has been dishonoured by such drawee.

A drawee in case of need can accept the bill or pay it without any previous protest (Section 116) .

PRACTICE QUESTIONS

1. Explain the term 'Instrument'.
2. What do you understand by 'negotiable instruments'?
3. Explain the meaning of 'negotiability'.
4. Name the instruments which are recognised as negotiable instruments by the Negotiable Instruments Act, 1881.
5. Give the different forms in which an instrument must be payable so as to constitute a negotiable instrument.
6. Write explanatory notes on the following: (i) Ambiguous instruments, (ii) inchoate instruments, (iii) Lost or stolen instruments.
7. State briefly the presumptions as to negotiable instruments under the Negotiable Instrument Act.
8. "The capacity of a party to draw, accept, make or endorse a negotiable instrument is co-extensive with his capacity to enter into a contract."
9. (i) What are the essential requirements of a valid promissory note? (ii) Give some examples of instruments which: (a) are promissory notes, (b) are not promissory notes. (iii) Enumerate the different parties to a promissory note.
10. What is a bill of exchange? State its essential characteristics. How does a promissory note differ from a bill of exchange?
11. Distinguish between (i) inland and foreign bills; (ii) time and demand bills; (iii) clean and documentary bills; and (iv) general acceptance and qualified acceptance.
12. When is a bill deemed to have been dishonoured by non-acceptance?
13. (i) Define a Cheque (ii) What are the various requisites of a cheque? Comment.
14. Distinguish between a cheque and a bill of exchange.
15. 'A cheque is a bill of exchange drawn on a banker'. Comment.
16. What do you understand by - (i) a stale cheque, (ii) an overdue cheque, (iii) bank iraft or demand draft.
17. Define the term 'holder', 'holder for value' and 'holder in due course'. Enumerate B privileges of a 'holder in due course'.
18. Explain the term 'negotiation'. Distinguish it from assignment.
19. Distinguish between a (i) 'bearer' and an 'order' instrument, (ii) conditional endorsement and restrictive endorsement.
20. Write a short note on essentials of a valid endorsement of a negotiable instrument.
21. Write a note on 'once a bearer always a bearer'.
22. Write short notes on (i) presentment for acceptance and payment, (ii) maturity of an instrument.
23. What is meant by (i) dishonour for non-acceptance, (ii) dishonour for non payment?
24. Explain the provisions relating to 'Noting' and 'Protesting' of a bill which has re=n dishonoured by the acceptor.
25. Write a note on crossed cheques.
26. Explain clearly the meaning of 'general' and 'special' crossing and "crossing after the issue of a cheque".
27. Cheques crossed 'not negotiable' are nevertheless transferable. Explain.
28. Explain the effect of (i) Notnegotiable crossing (ii) "Account payee only" crossing.

29. When is payment on a negotiable instrument said to be payment in due courses?
30. Has a holder of a cheque any remedy against the banker for wrong dishonour of the cheque?
31. "Issuing of a cheque that bounces is an offence." Comment.

References

1. Beni Madhab Nath v. Juyendra Nath AIR 1979 Gau. 46
2. Marimutha Kounder v. Radhakrishan and others AIR 1991 Ker. 39.
3. Banque Belge v. Hambrouck (1921) 1 K B 321 (CA).
4. Smith Leading case 535 (12th edn.) 1915.

4A. Akbar Khan v. Attar Singh RIL (1936) 17 Lah 557 (PC)

5. Claydon v. Bradley, The Times, Dec 15, 1986, 1987 J.B.L. 137.
6. Surjit Singh v. Ram Ratan, AIR (1975) Gan 15.
7. Meenakshi v. Chettiar AIR (1957) Mad 8.
8. Gay v. Landol (1848) L.T. CP 286.
9. Cowie v. Stirling (1856) 119 E.R. 889.
10. Pulluree Vajrama v. More Agaish AIR 1979 A.P. 2.
11. Bapanna Krishnayya v. Chaparala Baburao AIR (1977) A.P. 42.
12. Clutton v. Attenborough (1897) A.C. 90.
13. Union Bank of India v. Swastic Motors, AIR 1983 Delhi 240.
14. Little v. Slackford (1828) (M and W 171).
15. Bevins v. London and South Western Bank Ltd. (1900) 1 K. B. 270.
16. R. Pillai v. S. Ayyar (1930) 43 Mad 816.
17. Ram Chandra Mullick v. Luchmee Chandra Radakissen (1854) 9 Moore P.C. 46: 14 ER 215.

17A. Bank of Baroda v. Punjab National Bank, (1944) A.C. 177 at 184.

18. Suraj Bali v. Ram Chandra 1950 ALJ 610.
19. Down v. Halling (1825) K.B. 107 E.R. 1082.
20. Hogarth v. Lathan and Co. (1878) 3 Q.B.D. 643.
21. Banku Behari Sikdar v. Secretary of State of India (1908) 36 Cal. 239.
22. Ram Prasad v. Srinivasa 27 Bom. L.R. 1122.
23. Tukaram Bapuji v. Belgaum Bank AIR 1976 Bom. 185.
24. Arnold v. Cheque Bank (1876) 1 CPD 578 at P 584.
25. Bank of Van Diemen's Land v. Bank of Victoria (1871) L.R. 3 CP 526.
26. LORD FINLAY LC in London Joint Stock Bank Ltd. v. Macmillan and Arthur, (1918) AC 777.
27. Marzetti v. Williams (1830) 109 E.R. 842, 1B and Ad 415.
28. Fleming v. Bank of New Zealand (1900) AC 577.
29. Davidson v. Barclays Bank (1940) 1 All E.R. 316.
30. Westminister Bank v. Hilton (1927) 136 LT 315.
31. Curtis v. London city and Midland Bank (1908) 1 K.B. 273 (C.A.)
32. Barclays Bank Ltd v. W.J. Sins (1980) Q.B. 677.
33. Rogers v. Whiteley (1892) A.C. 118 (HC)
34. Manoj Kumar Seth v. Fernandez (1992) 73 Comp Cas. Kerala High Court.
35. Babu Xavier v. Lalchand Munoth (1992) 74 Comp Cas. Madras High Court.
36. Gulshan Rai v. Anil Kumar (1993) Comp Cas. 685 Punjab and Haryana High Court.
37. S. Prasanna v.R. Vijayalakshmi (1993) 76 Comp Cas 522. Madras High Court.
38. Prabhu Dayal v. Jwala Bank ILR 1938 All 634.
39. Green wood v. Martins Bank (1933) AC 51.
40. Charles v. Blackwell (1872) 2 CPD 115.
41. Slingsby v. District Bank (1932) 1 KB 544, C.A.
42. Hong Kong and Shanghai Banking Corporation v. Lo Lee Shi (1928) A.C. 181 (P.C.)
43. Loonkaran Sethiya v. Ivan E. John (1977) 1 Sec at 394.
44. Scholfiled v. The Earl of Londesborough (1896) A.C. 514.
45. British Bank of Middle East v. Almal Bros. 66 CWN 285.
46. Willson and Meeson v. Pickering (1946) 1 All ER 394.
47. Landbroke v. Todd (1914) 111 L.T. 43.
48. Commissioner of Taxation v. English, Scottish Australian Bank Ltd. (1920) A.C. 683.
49. A.L. Underwood Ltd. v. Bank of Liverpool and Martins and Barclays Bank (1924) 1 K.B. 775.
50. Lloyds Bank v. Savory and Co. (1933) A.C. 201.
51. Landbroke v. Todd (1914) 111 L.T. 43.
52. Guardians of S.John's Hampstead v. Barclay's Ltd. (1923).
53. Beni Modhab Nath v. Jayendra Nath AIR 1979 Gau 46.
54. Banque Belge v. Hambrouck (1921) 1 K.B. 321 (R.A.).

PART D

INDIAN PARTNERSHIP ACT, 1932

CHAPTER

15

The Law of Partnership

Introduction

Previously the law relating to partnership was contained in chapter XI of India Contract Act 1872 but, in 1932 Chapter XI of Contract Act was repealed and re-enacted by Indian Partnership Act (IX) of 1932.

Definition and Nature of Partnership: Definition (Section 4)

The term "partnership" is defined in section 4 of The Partnership Act as "the relationship between persons who have agreed to share profits of business carried on by all or any of them acting for all."

Essentials of Partnership

It is evident from the above definition of "partnership" that following are essentials of a "partnership".

(i) Partnership is an association of two or more persons.
(ii) Partnership is the result of an agreement.
(iii) Partnership is organised to carry on a business.
(iv) Business must be carried on by all or any of them acting for all.
(v) The agreement must be to share profits of the business.

(i) Association of two or more persons

A single person can not form a partnership because it is not possible to become a partner with himself. There must be minimum two persons to consented a partnership.

(ii) Result of an agreement

The partnership can be created by contract only. It is not a product of status as in the case of a joint family business. Partnership can arise only by an agreement between the parties concerned.

A formal or written agreement is not essential for partnership. An agreement to create a partnership may as well arise from the conduct of the parties concerned. It is need by the court in *Abdul v. Century Wood Industries*. "If two or more persons put together certain amounts of money in certain shares for the purpose of purchasing properties and selling them for profit for common benefit, it has to be said that such a transaction amounts to a partnership concern. An agreement of partnership need not be express. It can arise out of mutual understanding shown by a consistent course of conduct."

(iii) To Carry on a Business

A partnership exist in business and business alone. Section 2 Clause (b) says that the term 'business' "include every trade, occupation and profession". Unless the persons join for the purpose of carrying on a business is that of a joint operation for two sake of gain. Thus, partnership does not exist between members of a charitable society or religious association or a building scheme. A club is also not a partnership (*Caldicott v. Griiffiths*)[2]

The business may be temporary or permanent but the business must be in existence for partnership. The agreement of business at a future time does not result in Present Partnership (*R.R. Sharma v. Reuben*)[3]

(iv) Business must be carried on by all or any of them acting for all, i.e., "Mutual Agency"

Every partner assumes a dual role that of principal and of an agent. Partnership is based on the idea of mutual agency. Each partner is an agent of other partners who are his principals and each partner is again a principal, who is bound by the acts of the other partners. It is not necessary that every partner must actively participate in the conduct of the business.

In *Cox v. Hiickman*,[4] Lord Cranworth said, "The liability of one partner for the acts of his co-partner is in truth the liability of a principal for the acts of his agent. Where two or more persons are engaged as partners in any ordinary trade, each of them has an implied authority from the other to bind all by contracts entered into according to the usual course of business in that trade. Every partner in trade is, for the ordinary purposes of the trade, the agent of his co-partners, all are, therefore, liable for the ordinary trade contract of the other. The public have a right to assume that every partner has authority from his co-partners to bind the whole firm in contracts made according to the ordinary, wages of trade."

(v) Sharing of profits of the business

Sharing of profits is an essential condition of partnership. Sharing of profits also involves sharing of losses, but in partnership sharing of loses is not essential. Thus, a person may become a partner under a distinct understanding that he will share the profits only and will not share the losses. In *Cox v.Hickman*[5], the House of Lords in a historic decision held that no man is a partner unless he has the right to share the profits of the business. But every man who received profits is not necessary a partner. Thus sharing of profits is only a prima facie evidence of the existence of a partnership. The conclusive test of existence of partnership is that of mutual agency. The provision for sharing of loss is not essential (*Walker West Developments v. F.J.Emmett*).[6]

'Partners', 'Firm' and 'Firm Name' (Section 4)

Persons who constitute partnership with one another are individually called partners and collectiively called "a firm" and the name through which their business is carried on is called the "firm name".

In law, a "firm" has no legal existence except from their partners. A firm is nothing more than a compendious name of the partners farming it. A firm is not a body corporate. The rights and obligations of the individuals composing the firm.

Partner can choose any name as their firm's name but name should not be such which mislead the people with a reputed firm already in existence. Section 58(3) says that a firm shall not contain any of the following words 'Crown', 'King', 'Queen', 'Emperor', 'Empress', 'Imperial', 'Royal', or words expressing or implying the sanction approval or patronage of government except with the written consent of the state government.

Mode of determining existence of partnership

Section 6 of Act lays down that "in determining whether a group of persons is or is not a firm or whether a person is or is not a partner in a firm regard shall be had to the real relation between the parties, as shown by all relevant facts taken together."

Thus, when there is name the use of the "partner" does not make a partnership. But, if all the relevant facts taken together show that all the essentials of partnership are present, the group of persons will be called partnership, otherwise not.

It is observed in *Badly v. Consolidated Bank*[7] that "it is quite plain now, ever since *Cox v. Hickman*, that what we have to get at in the real agreement between the parties. It is no longer right to infer either partnership or agency form the mere fact that one person shares the profits or another."

The true test of partnership is agency, and not sharing of profits.

Non Parnership Interests

Section 6 of Act gives the list of persons who share the profits of a business but who do not by that reason alone become partners. They can be described as Wolders of non partnership interests, such persons are

1. Lender of Money Receiving Profits

A person who has lent money to a person or firm engaged in business and has agreed to take in addition to, or in place of his interest, a portion of the profits of the business, he does not by, that reason become a partner in the business, in *Mollwo March and Co. v. The Court of Warde*[8], their Loreships said:

If appears to be now established that although a right to participate in the profits of trade is a strong test of partnership and that there may be cases where, from such participation alone, it may, as a presumption, not of law, but of fact, be inferred, yet whether that relation does or does not exist depends on the real intention and the conduct of the parties.

2. Joint Owners Sharing Gross Returns

Joint ownership is not a business. The joint owners of property who share the profits or gross returns arising out of the property do not become partners.

In *Govind Nair v. Maga*[9], A and B jointly purchased a tea shop and incurred additional expenses for purchasing pottery and utensils for the job. Each of them contributed a half of the total expense. The shop was then leased out on rent which was shared equally by them.

The High held, "Nothing more is done by the parties than utilising the common property and obtain a return for such use by leasing the property for rent." Their investment made them only co-owners and not partners. They never carried on any business.

3. Widow or Child of Deceased Partner

On the death of a partner, the other surviving partners sometimes agree to give a share in the profits to the widow or the child of the deceased partner. Such a widow or child does not of itself become a partner in the firm (*Income Tax Commissioner v. Kesharmal Keshade*[10]).

4. Seller of Goodwill

The persons who sells his business with the goodwill in sometimes given a share in the profits of the business he has sold, but such a person does not of itself become a partner in the business.

5. Servant or Agent receiving Profits

Generally, servant or agent of business is permitted a portion of profits of that business. This portion of profit may be in addition to or in place of regular remuneration but that never make him a partner in the business. The decision in *Munshi Abdul Latif v. Gopeshwar Chattoraj*[11] affords a good illustration. In this case a contractor of loading and unloading of railway wagons appointed a servant to manage it. The term of employment was to receive 75% of the profits and was to bear all losses. It was held that servant was not his partner he was only the agent of contractor. In another case I.T. *Commissioner v. Kesharmal Keshardeo,*[12] a person joined in a firm of chartered Accountants E as a salaried partner only and property, profits and goodwill remaining that of E. It was held that, salaried partner became a partner but he was not entitled as an order of dissolution because he had no interest in assets.

Maximum Number of Partners

According to section 11 of the companies Act 1956 a partnership for carrying on banking business the maximum number of partner should be 10 and for all other business the maximum number of partners are not more than twenty. If this number of partners is exceeded, the partnership must be registered as a company under the companies Act.

Difference between Partnership and certain Similar organisations

1. Partnership and Co-ownership

If there are assets in a firm that assets are the joint property of the partners, to this extent partners are co-owners also. Co-ownership means joint ownership. But co-ownership and partnership is not the same thing. The points of difference between partnership and the co-ownership are as follows.

(i) A partnership can arise only by agreement. A Co-ownership may arise by status.

(ii) Co-ownership may exist without any business but business is necessary for the existence of a partnership.

(iii) Each partner is the agent of other partners while co-owners are not the agent of the other co-owners.

(iv) A co-owner may transfer his share without consent of the other co-owners. But a partner can not transfer his interest without the consent of all other partners.

(v) A partner can sue his co-partners for dissolution and accounts while a co-owners can sue for partition of the joint estate.

2. Partnership and Company

There are following distinctions between a company and a partnership.

(i) A company has a legal status distinct from its members. A partnership firm has no legal existence apart from its partners. It is a collection of partners.

(ii) A member of a company is not an agent of other members. Partnership is based on the principle of mutual agency. Partners are mutual agents.

(iii) The liability of members of company is limited but liability of a partner is unlimited. The own personal assets of partners are liable for the debts of the firm.

(iv) The shares of a company are freely transferable, while a partner can not transfer his interest without the consent of all other partners.

(v) If the agreement is not contrary, death, retirement or insolvency of a partner results in the dissolution of the firm. But death or retirement or insolvency of a member can not affect the existence of the company. A company enjoys a perpetual succession.

3. Partnership and Joint Hindu Family

There are some common features in partnership and a Joint Hindu family carrying on business. But section 5 expressly excludes a Joint Hindu family carrying on business from the operation of the Act. This section provides that the relation of partnership arises from agreement and not from status, and in particular the members of a Hindu undivided family carrying on a business as such are not partners in such business. However, the Act does not prohibit the members of Hindu undivided family to enter into partnership amongst themselves. The main points of difference between partnership and a Joint Hindu Family carrying on business are as follows:

(i) A Partnership is created only by an agreement between the parties, but a Joint Hindu Family cannot be created by an agreement. It is the result of status.

(ii) In Joint Hindu Family, a person becomes a member by mere fact of birth and he is entitled to get an equal share in assets and profits, where as a new partner is admitted into partnership only with the consent of all the partners.

(iii) Partners are mutual agents but members of a family are not mutual agents. The Karta is only representative of the family.

(iv) A female member is not a member of a Joint Hindu Family business, though she can become a partner of partnership business.

(v) If the agreement is not contrary the death of a partner dissolves the firm but there is no affect in Joint Hindu Family business with the death of its member.

(vi) Every partner is liable to an unlimited extent. Partner's liability is personal and joint both. The liability of Co-Parceners is limited to the extent of his share of assets and profits. He is not personally for business obligations of the family.

Partnership at will (Section 7)

A partnership is a partnership at will when (i) no provision is made by contract between the partners for the limited period of time of their partnership or (ii) when no provision is made for the termination of their partnership.

Such type of partnership can be dissolved by any of the partners at any time notifying his willingness to do so.

Particular Partnership (Section 8)

A partnership which is formed for a particular adventure or a particular undertaking is called particular partnership. Particular partnership is usually dissolved when such particular adventure or undertaking is completed.

Relations of Partners to one another

Relations of partners to one another are regulate by two fundamental principles the first principle provides freedom to partner for settlement of their mutual rights and duties by contract between them. This is contained in section 11 of the Act,

Section 11, Determination of rights and duties of Partners by contract between the partners.

(1) Subject to the provision of this Act, the mutual rights and duties of the partners of a firm may be determined by contract between the partners, and such contract may be expressed or may be implied by a course of dealing.

Such contract may be varied by consent of all the partners, and such consent may be expressed or may be implied by a course of dealing.

The second principle is that relations of partners to one another are based on the absolute good faith trust and confidence among the partners is a necessary condition of their relations. Section 9 of Act says that "Partners are bound to carry on the business of the firm to the greatest common advantage, to be just and faithful to each other,........

Duties of Partners

1. General Duties of Partners (section 9) partners are bound

(a) to carry on the business of the firm to the greatest common advantage,

(b) to be just and faithful to each other,

(c) and to render true accounts and full information of all things affecting the firm to any partner or his legal representative.

Thus it is duty of partners to secure maximum profit for the firm with absolute good faith.

2. Duty to Indemnity for loss caused by fraud (section 10)

Every partner shall indemnfiy the firm for any loss caused to it by his fraud in the conduct of the business of the firm.

It should be the main object of the partners to deal honestly with the customers of the firm. If a fraud is committed by a partner upon a customer of the firm and the firm with all partners has been held liable, the firm may recover indemnity from partner who is guilty of the fraud.

3. Agreement to restraint of trade [section 11(2)]

If restrained by an agreement with other partners, a partner has a duty not to carry on any business other than that of the firm while he is a partner.

4. To indemnify the firm for his willful neglect [section (13f)]

It is the duty of partner of firm that he shall indemnify the firm for any loss caused to it by his willful neglect in the conduct of the business of the firm.

If a firm is suffered a loss due to willful negligence of a partner, he is bound to indemnify the firm for the same. His liability is limited to his degree of negligence only.

5. Attend diligently to his duties [section 12(b)]

Every partner is bound to attend diligently to his duties in the conduct of the business.

6. Duties without any remuneration [sec. 13(a)]

It is the duty of partners to attend diligently to his duties in the conduct of the firm's business without any remuneration.

7. Firm's property proper use [sec. 16(a)]

Every partner of the firm is under a duty to use the property of the firm only for the purposes of business of the firm. If he uses the firm's property for any private purpose, he must account for the advantages and profit gained from such use and pay it to the firm.

8. Duty not to Compete [Section 16(b)]

It is the duty of partners not to carry on any business similar to or in competition with the business of the firm and if a partner does any such business, he shall account for any pay to the firm all profits made by him in that business.

Rights of Partner

Mutual rights of partners depend upon the provision of agreement. But subject to their agreement the Act provides following rights to all partners.

1. Right to take in Business [sec. 12(a)]

"Every partner has a right to take part in the conduct of the business." Right to take part in business of firm must be applied to increase the interest of firm and not to destroy it.

2. Majority Rights [sec. 12(c)]

Every partner has a right to express his opinion on any matter but in case of any difference arising as to ordinary matters related to the business he is bound by majority decision. But a nature of business can only be changed with the consent of all the partners.

3. Access to Books [sec. 12(b)]

"Every partner has a right to have access to and to inspect and copy any of the books of the firm."

But right of partners to inspect papers does not include the right to carry them without the consent of the other partners to any other place than the registered office of the company[13].

4. Right to Indemnify [sec. 13(e)]

Section 13 (e) gives partner's right to recover indemnity from the firm. This section says.

"The firm shall indemnify a partner in respect of payments made and liabilities incurred by him —

(i) in the ordinary and proper conduct of the business and
(ii) in doing such act, in an emergency, for the purpose of protecting the firm loss as would be done by a person of ordinary prudence, in his own case, under similar circumstances."

Thus, there is two kinds of indemnity, first is to recover any expenses incurred by partner in the ordinary and proper conduct of business from the firm. The second indemnity is only recoverable when a partner has done an act of expenditure to protect the loss of the firm threatened by a emergency. But the act of partner should be as a reasonable man would have acted in his own case under similar circumstance.

5. Right to Profits [sec. 13(b) and (c)]

If there is no otherwise agreement every partners is entitled to share equally in the profits earned by the firm. In the same way partners are bound to contribute equally in the losses sustained by firm.

6. Right to Interest [sec. 13(c) and (d)]

When a partner has advanced some money beyond the amount of capital that he agreed to subscribe for promoting the business of firm, he is entitled to claim interest at the rate of 6 per cent per annum.

Section 13(c) says "Where a partner is entitled to interest on the capital subscribed by him, such interest shall be payable only out of profits."

Thus partners are not entitled to any interest on the capital subscribed by him.

7. Rights to Remuneration [sec. 13(a)]

Section 13(a) Provides:

"A partner is not entitled to receive remuneration for taking part in the conduct of business;"

But agreement of partnership may provide remuneration to working partners.

Rights and Duties of Partners after the expiry of the term of Partnership

Generally, it is found that firm which is created for a fixed term or for particular business remains continue even after the expiry of such term or completion of such business without adopting new agreement. Section 17 of Act enacted to meet such cases. This section lays down following three changes in which mutual rights and duties are not affected unless otherwise agreed.

(a) Change in Constitution of the firm

Where a change occurs in the constitution of the firm, the mutual rights and duties of the partners remain the same as they were immediately before the change.

(b) After Expiry of Term

Where a firm is constituted for a fixed term but continues to carry on business after the expiry of that term, the mutual rights and duties will remain the same, but only in so far as they are consistent with a partnership at will.

(c) Where additional undertakings are carried out

The mutual rights and duties will remain the same where a firm carries out other adventures or undertaking which was previously constituted for one or more adventures. Such firm has the status of firm "at will" and will survive as are consistent with a firm.

The Property of the Firm

Section 14 of the Act lays down that subject to contract between the partners the property of the firm means all property and right and interest in property which (a) originally brought into stock of the firm or (b) acquired by purchase or (c) otherwise, by or for the firm or (d) for the purposes and in the course of the business or the firm including the goodwill of the business also.

A property of the firm can only be used for the business of the firm and any partner is not entitled to use any part of the property in his personal use. But a property of a partner will not be the property of the firm only by its use in the business of the firm. Such property of the partner will become the property of the partnership only if there is express or implied agreement[14].

Goodwill

Goodwill is also a part of firm's property and has exchangeable value. But the definition of goodwill is given in the Act.

It may be described as the advantage which is acquired by a business beyond the mere value of the capital, stock, fund or property employed therein as a result of the general public patronage and encouragement that it receives from constant or habitual customers. Goodwill means the whole advantage, whatever it may be, of the reputation and connection of the firm, which may have been built up by years of honest work organised by lavish expenditure of money. It is treated as part of the assets of the firm. It represents the business reputation. The goodwill is the very sap and life of a business, without which the business will yield little and no fruit. When the goodwill of a firm is sold out to a new come, he stems into the shoes of the original owner.

In *Stewart v. Gladstone*, Jessel, M.R. observed that the goodwill is not an available asset in the sense that you can draw upon it or that you turn it into money or pay it out to the parties.

Relation of Partners to Third Parties

Section 25 of the Act lays down the rule that every partner is liable with all of his co-partners jointly and severally for all acts of the firm done while he is a partner. The rule is as follows.

25 — Liability of a partner for acts of the firm — Every partner is liable, jointly with all the other partners and severally, for all acts of the firm done while he is a partner. The important condition of while partner's liability is that the act of the firm shall have been done which he is a partner. An act done prior to or after a partner ceases to be the partner will not bind him.

Section makes it clear that partners of a firm are jointly and severally liable for all acts of the firm. Thus, a partner can be sued individually and jointly also with other partners for every act of the firm. There is a small difference in English law. Section 9 of the English partnership Act 1890 makes partners jointly liable for contractual liabilities and make them jointly and severally liable for liabilities in respect of the wrongs of the firm.

The Doctrine of Implied Authority

The partners are liable for the acts of the firm. The acts of the firm are performed by the partners. Section 18 and 19 of the Act tells the acts of the partners which are considered as acts of the firms section 18 declares every partner to be an agent of the firm for the purposes of the business of the firm.

Section 18. Partner to be agent of the firm - Subject to the provisions of this Act, a partner is the agent of the firm for the purposes of the business of the firm.

A partner is both principal and agent. But he is an agent only for the business purposes of the firm. Thus the act of a partner done by him as an agent in the usual course of business is an act of the firm.

Lord Wensley in a leading case *Cox v. Hickman* (1860)[16] held "A man who allows another to carry trade whether in his own name or not, to buy and sell, and to pay over all the profits to him, is undoubtedly the principal, and the person so employed is the agent, and the principal is liable for the agent's contract in the course of his employment so if two or more agree that they should carry on a trade, and share the profits of it, each is a principal and each is an agent for the other, and each is bound by the other's contract in carrying on the trade, as much as a single principal would be by the act of an agent , who was to give the whole of the profits to his employer".

So the act of partner performed by him in capacity of an agent of the firm is called the implied authority of a partner.

The Extent of Implied Authority

Section 19(1) says:

Subject to the provisions of section 22 the act of a partner which is done to carry on, in the usual way, business of the kind carried on by the firm, binds the firm.

Thus the nature and the usual way of carrying on a business is directly related with extent of authority. Since the requirements of one business may be wholly different from those of another business, the nature of the business and the practices, customs and usages of businessmen engaged in that kind of business, must be known before it can be said by what acts a partner can bind the firm.

If the partnership be of a general commercial nature, he may pledge or sell the partnership property, he may buy goods on account of partnership, he may borrow money, contract debts, and pay debts, he may make, draw or accept or otherwise deal with negotiable instruments on account of the firm. A partner of a trading or non trading firm may buy or hire on credit the kind of goods that are used in the firm's business[17]. Thus where a partner hired an elephant for the purpose of trapping wild elephants which was the business of the firm and the hired elephant died in the course of the operations, the firm was held liable. A partner may take a lease of premises on behalf of the firm or mortgage the assets of the firm should that be necessary for purposes of business[18]. Where the nature of a firm's business did not warrant entering into a surety ship, the firm was held not liable for the act of a partner in giving a guarantee on behalf of the firm[19].

Where the act of a partner is within the scope of his implied authority but it has been done by him, to the knowledge of the third party, not for the firm, but for his own purposes, the firm is not liable. Thus payment by a partner of a personal debt from the funds of the firm does not bind the firm and the firm can recover back the money[20].

The Reason implied authority

The authority which partners of a firm have is not in nature of an indifferent or separate authority but is implied in the very "nature of partnership." It is the result of the relation of agent and principal conferred by law upon every partner in relation to third persons.

Restrictions on Implied Authority (Ss. 19 & 20)

There are two kinds of restrictions on the implied authority of partners. Such restrictions are namely, (1) statutory restrictions and (2) restrictions imposed by partnership deed.

(1) Statutory Restrictions [Section 19(2)]

The section lays down that in the absence of any usage or custom of trade to the contrary, provides statutory restrictions. The implied authority of a partner prohibits him from doing the following acts:

(a) to submit a dispute relating to the business of the firm to arbitration,

(b) to open a banking account on behalf of the firm in his own name,

(c) to compromise or relinquish any claim or portion of claim by the firm,

(d) to withdraw a suit or proceeding filed on behalf of the firm,

(e) to acquire immovable property on behalf of the firm,

(f) to transfer immovable property on behalf of the firm,

(g) to enter into partnership on behalf of the firm.

(2) Restrictions imposed by partnership deed

The second kind of restrictions are those restrictions which may be imposed by the partnership deed or any agreement between the partners. Section 20 says that —

The partners in a firm may by contract between the partners, extend or restrict the implied authority of any partner.

What will be the effect of such restrictions upon those persons who are dealing with the firm section 20 provides that — not with standing any such restriction, any act done by a partner on behalf of the firm which falls within his implied authority binds the firm, unless the person with whom he is dealing knows of the restriction or does not know or believe that partner to be a partner.

Thus the implied authority of a partner can by contract between the partners, be extended or restricted. Inspite of the restriction, the firm will be liable to third person, provided the act done by the partner on behalf of the firm falls within his implied authority unless it is proved that

(i) The third party contracting with the partner had knowledge of the restriction, or
(ii) he did not know or believe the partner who did the act to be a partner.

A good illustration on this point is the case of *Motilal v. Unnao Commercial Bank.*[21] In this case, one partner of trading firm borrowed money by accepting a bill of exchange despite restrictions on borrowing contained in the partnership deed. The plaintiff did not know nothing of the restriction. The trading firm was held liable.

The difference between statutory restrictions and the restrictions imposed by partnership deed is that the former are effective against all the word whether a particular person contracting with the firm has knowledge of them or not, while the latter are not effective against a party who has no knowledge on them.

Partner's authority in an emergency (Section 21)

Section 21 says:

A partner has authority, in an emergency; to do all such acts for the purpose of protecting the firm from loss as would be done by a person of ordinary prudence, in his own case, acting under similar circumstances, and such acts bind the firm.

A partner of firm is entitled to perform all such acts in an emergency which are required for the purpose of protecting the firm from loss provided he has acted as a reasonable man would have acted in his own case under similar circumstances and such acts bind the firm.

Essential Ingredients

According to provisions of section 21, the following ingredients are essential in order to bind the firm with the acts of a partner in an emergency.

(i) An emergency should be there.
(ii) The acts done by a partner to protect the firm from loss in an emergency.
(iii) The act done by partner must be reasonable in the circumstances.

The test of reasonableness is that the partner must have taken such steps as would been done by a man of ordinary prudence in his own case under similar circumstances.

Mode of Exercising Authority (Section 22)

The manner in which a partner is to act on behalf of the firm is given in section 22, which says —

In order to bind a firm, an act or instrument done or executed by a partner or other person on behalf of the firm shall be done or executed in the firm name, or in any other manner expressing or implying an intention to bind the firm.

Thus it is the duty of partner acting for the firm to bring in notice of other party that he acts for the firm and it is in the knowledge of the other party that he is the partner of the firm. If partner acts in his individual name and not for the firm he will become liable to personally and the firm may not be liable. In *Ghisulal v. Haji Md*[22], firm was held not liable where a pronote was signed by a partner describing himself as proprietor of the firm.

Admission by a Partner (Section 23)

Section 23 provides —

An admission or representation made by a partner concerning the affairs of firm is evidence against the firm, if it is made in the ordinary course of business.

Within the scope of partnership business the partners are agents of each other. All admissions (statements of acknowledgment of fact) and representations made by a partner in the ordinary course of the business of the firm are binding on all other partners. But an admission or representation made by a partner will not bind the firm if his implied authority on the point is restricted and the other party has the knowledge of that restriction. The restrictions must be as listed in section 19(2) of Act.

The admissions and representations will affect the firm when tendered by third partners, but they may not have the same weight in matters of disputes among the partners *inter se*.

An admission or representation made by a partner may be a piece of evidence against the firm even though made in fraud of his Co-partners, but this rule will not be applied if there is collusion with the other party.

Effect of Notice to a Partner (Section 24)

Section 24 says —

Notice to a partner who habitually acts in the business of the firm of any matter relating to the affairs of the firm operates as notice to the firm, except in the case of fraud on the firm committed by or with the consent of that partner.

Notice to a partner is equivalent to notice to all other partner of the firm. Section 24 laid down following requirements of notice to a partner of firm.

(1) The notice must be 'actual' and not constructive notice.

According to Lindley [22]

"The equilable doctrine of constructive notice that a person is deemed to know that which be might have discovered on inquiry is not to be imported into commercial transactions."

(2) The notice must be given to a partner who habitually takes part in the management of the business of the firm, that is, to an active partner and not a sleeping or dormant partner. A person who is admitted as a partner into a firm will not ordinarily be affected with notice of matters relating to the affairs of the firm that may have happened before he was admitted as a partner[23]. A partner who goes out of the firm or otherwise ceases to be a partner of the firm will not ordinarily be affected with notice of matters relating to subsequent matters[24].

(3) The partner receiving notice should not have with held it from the firm either by his own fraud or in conspiracy with the third party. In *Bignold v. Waterhouse*[25], the other partners were held not liable for the loss of such packages as notice of their value was deliberately from them by working partner.

Liability of the firm for wrongful acts of partner (Section 26)

Section 26 lays down the principle of firm's liability for wrongful acts of partner in ordinary course of business. This section says —

Where, by the wrongful act or omission of a partner acting in the ordinary course of the business of a firm, or with the authority of his partners, loss or injury is caused to any third party, or any penalty is incurred, the firm is liable there for to the same extend as the partner.

A firm is liable to the same extent as the partner himself for any loss or injury caused by him to a third party by his wrongful act or omission done in the ordinary course of the business of the firm or with the authority of his partners.

The liability of the firm for wrongful act of a partner is based on the same principle on which the liability of a master is based for the tortious act of his servant. This section provides for the liability of wrongful acts of a partner in general.

There are following two requirements for the liability of the firm for wrongful acts of the partner.

(1) The wrongful act must be done in the ordinary course of the business of the firm,

or

(2) The wrongful act must be done witn the authority of his Co-partners.

Thus in Hamlyn v. John Houston and Co[26], one of the two partners bribed the clerk of the plaintiff and induced him to give secret information about plaintiff's customers and prices. Consequently, the plaintiff lost business to the tune of £750. The plaintiff and defendant were two grain merchant and # competitor of each other. The plaintiff sued the defendant firm.

It was held that both the partners were responsible in damages to plaintiff.

Another illustration is the case of *Rapp v. Latham,*[27] where plaintiff engaged a firm of two partners to buy and sell wine on commission basis. The plaintiff left money with the firm for the purpose. The active partner rendered false accounts of purchase and sale to the plaintiff and misappropriated the money. The firm was held liable. Court laid down that all partners are liable to a third party for wrongful act or omission of one of its partners committed in the ordinary course of the business, and on the same principle innocent partners have been held liable for the ordinary business of the firm.

In another case *Longmen v. Pale,*[28] a partner of one firm colluded with partner of another firm, in a matter within the regular course of dealings between the two firms. The partners of plaintiff firm sustained injury, the innocent partners of the defendant firm were held liable to the firm that sustained loss as a result of collusive acts of their partners.

In this connection, it is essential to mention that, where the wrongful act or misconduct of a partner not acting in the ordinary course of the business of the firm does not render the other partners of firm liable.

An illustration in this connection is a case *T.N. Waterworks Co. v. Jones.*[29]

J. and G. were two partners in a firm. G. was appointed as a secretary to the plaintiff company. Property was purchased by the company and transferred to in the name of G. for its own convenience. G. fraudulently mortgaged the property for his personal dept. The other partner was not held liable for this fraud. If he had misconducted himself as secretary and caused loss to the company, the firm would have been liable. But it was no part of a secretary's duties to accept a transfer of property in his name. The company had by its own conduct enabled the secretary to commit the fraud by placing him in a position which it was not in the scope of partnership business for him to accept.

Similarly a fraud committed by a partner while acting on the own separate account was held not imputable to the firm, although without being a partner of the firm, he might not have been able to commit fraud.[30]

Liability of firm for misappropriation of property and money received from third parties (Section 27)

Section 27 lays down two following rules relating to liability of firm for misappropriation of firm's property or money by a partner.

(1) Where a partner acting within his apparent authority receives money or property from a third party and misapplies it, or

(2) Where a firm in the course of its business receives money or property from a third party, and the same is misapplied by any of the partner while it is in the custody of the firm, the firm is liable to make good the loss.

Every partner is a general and accredited agent of the firm and every act done by him in the ordinary course of the partnership business is binding on the firm. The liability of the firm arises when the money or property is received by a partner within his "apparent authority" or by the firm "in the course of business." Thus, there two elements are in substance same thing because a firm itself does not receive any property and apparent authority of a partner to receive money depends upon the ordinary course of the firm's business. The only difference is that where the property is deemed to be received by a partner, the firm will be liable only when that particular partner misappropriates it, but when it is deemed to be received by the firm, it will be liable when any partner misappropriates it.

A well-known illustration is *Rhodes v. Moules*[31] case. In this case the plaintiff applied to R, a member of a firm of solicitors to raise a loan on the mortgage of his property. R obtained the loan, but falsely told the plaintiff that lender demanded some additional security. The plaintiff accordingly deposited with R. Share warrants payable to bearer. R. sold the warrants, misappropriated the proceeds and absconded.

His Co-partners were held liable for the plaintiff's loss. According to LINDLEY LJ "The only conclusion at which I can arrive is that the plaintiff's certificates came into R's hands when acting within the scope of his apparent authority."

In *Plumer v. Gregory,*[32] the plaintiff gave £1,300 for investment on a specified security to J. and W who were working as solicitors in partnership. After wards, the plaintiff gave another sum of £ 1,700 to W on his representation that it would be invested on some other security without knowledge of J. J died and both sums were misappropriated by W.

The estate of J. was held liable for the sum of £ 1,300 but not for £ 1,700 as it was no part of the firm's business to receive money for investment generally.

Where the money or property is received by a partner of the firm for purposes unconnected with the firm's business does not make the liability of the firm.

Thus in *Cleather v. Twisden*,[33] A partner of a firm of solicitors received from a friend certain bonds payable to bearer for safe custody in the strong room of the firm. The other partner misappropriated the bonds.

The firm was held not liable because no partner had authority to receive valuable paper for that purpose.

Liability for Holding out (Section 28)

The term holding out means to represent. Thus, sometimes a person who is not partner in fact, represents himself as a partner and incurs liability for his acts in certain conditions. Such type of liability is based on the principle of holding out.

The principle of this liability is well illustrated by EYRECJ in *Wough v. Carver*[33] in following words:

"Now a case may be stated in which it is the clear sense of the parties to the contract that they shall not be partner, that A is to contribute neither labour nor money, and, to go still further, not to receive any profits. But if he will lend his name as a partner he becomes as against all the rest of the world a partner, not on the ground of real transaction between them, but upon principles of general policy, to prevent frauds to which creditors would be liable, if they were to suppose that they lent their money upon the apparent credit to three or more persons, when, in fact, they lent it only to two of them, to whom without the others they could have lent nothing."

Substantially the rule is that a person who is not a partner in fact a and represents himself to be a partner in a firm, becomes liable as a partner in that firm to those have faith on him as a partner.

The doctrine of "holding out" is incorporated in section 28 of the Act:

Holding out — (1) Any one who by words spoken or written or by conduct represents himself or knowingly permits, himself to be represented, to be a partner in a firm, is liable as a partner in that firm, to any one who has on the faith of any such representation given credit to the firm, whether the person representing himself or represented to be a partner does or does not know that the representation has reached the person so giving credit.

(2) Where after a partner's death the business is continued in the old firm name, the continued use of that name or of the deceased partner's name as a part there of shall not of itself make his legal representative or his estate liable for any act of the firm done after his death.

The principle underlying the doctrine of "holding out" has application in case of —

(a) a former partner who retires from the firm without giving a proper public notice, and
(b) a partner abandoning without public notice a firm which is continued by the remaining partners.

The requirements of this liability are as follows:

(1) Representation

The person sought to be charged with liability for "holding out" must have represented himself to be a partner in the firm. Representation may be made either by words, written or spoken or by conduct. An express representation takes place when a person allows his name to be used in the affairs of the firm, for example, in the name, title or signboard of the firm.

In Kirkwood v. *Cheetham and Smith*,[34] a dealer of butter appointed Smith as servant and start business under the name of Smith and Co. and the goods were supplied to the firm. The defendants were jointly held liable, Smith holding himself out as partner and Cheetham as the real principal.

Similarly, in *Bevan v. The National Bank Ltd.*,[35] the business was carried on under the name M.W. and Co. in which M.W. was the manager.

M.W. was held liable to those who gave credit to the firm on the faith of that representation that he was a partner.

Holding out may also arise where a person "knowingly permits" himself to be represented as a partner.

Thus in *Martyn v. Gray*,[36] defendant introduced a person to plaintiff as his partner, when in fact he was not so and silently stood by, he was held liable by holding out.

2. Knowledge of Representation

The person who is seeking to make another person liable by holding out or estoppel must show that he had knowledge of representation and acted on it. It must be proved as Per Lord WENSLYDALE in *Dickinson v. Valpy*[37] laid down:

------"That the defendant had held himself out to be a partner not 'to the world' — for that is a loose expressions —but to the plaintiff himself, or under such circumstances or publicity as satisfy a jury that the plaintiff knew of it and believed him to be a partner. He would (then) be liable to the plaintiff in all transactions in which he engaged and gave credit to the defendant (or the firm) upon the faith of his being such partner."

The liability of holding out is only incurred when plaintiff has acted on the faith of representation. This liability is not applicable for the tort, crime or other wrongful conduct of a partner because it has nothing to do with the fact of representation.

The principle underlying the doctrine of "holding out" has an important application in case of partner retires and a public notice of retirement is not given. The retired partner remains liable by holding out to those customers of the firm who have given credit without knowledge of the retirement. The customer can sue only one either the old firm or the new firm as constituted after retirement but not both.

But doctrine of holding out on retirement without giving public notice has no application in cases (i) Deceased partner (ii) Insolvent partner and (iii) Dormant partner.

(i) Deceased Partner

The doctrine of holding out has no application to the cases of a deceased partner. The estate of a deceased partner is not liable for any act of the firm done after his death because death is a notice by itself and needs no separate notice.

(ii) Insolvent Partner

Liability of a partner terminates as soon as he declared insolvent and his partnership in a firm ceases from the date of insolvency.

(iii) Dormant Partner

A partner is dormant or sleeping partner who has never taken part in the conduct of business of firm and not known to the customers of the firm. His liability for the acts of the firm is the same as that of any acting partner. But when he retires, public notice is not needed to terminate his liability.

Transferee of Partner's Interest (Section 29)

Rights of transferee of a partner's interest —

(1) A transfer by a partner of his interest in the firm, either absolute or by mortgage, or by the creation by him of a charge on such interest, does not entitle the transferee, during the continuance of the firm, to interfere in the conduct of the business, or to require accounts or to inspect the books of the firm, but entitles the transferee only to receive the share of profits of the transferring partner, and the transferee shall accept the account of profits agreed to by the partners.

(2) If the firm is dissolved or if the transferring partner ceases to be a partner, the transferee is entitled as against the remaining partners to receive the share of the assets of the firm to which the transferring partner is entitled, and, for the purpose of ascertaining that share, to an account as from the date of the dissolution.

Being trust and confidence are essential parts of a partnership, a new partner shall only be introduced with the consent of all the existing partners, on the same grounds no partner can transfer his own interest in the firm to transferee in order to make him partner in his place unless all the Co-partners agree to accept that person as a partner. This principle is recognised by section 29 of the Act. The section says that the transferee of a partner's interest does not have the right, during the continuance of the firm:

(i) to interfere in the conduct of the business of the firm,
(ii) to require accounts, or
(iii) to inspect books of the firm.

This will be so whether the transfer is by way of absolute sale, or by way of mortgage or by the creation of a charge on the partner's interest. In no case the transferee acquires the status or rights of a partner. If any partner objects to the transfer he can apply for dissolution of the firm.

The transferee has two rights:

(i) First right is that the transferee has the right to receive the share of profits of the transferring partner to which he (transferring partner) is entitled. Transferee is not entitled to inspect the accounts.

(ii) Second right is that transferee is entitled to receive the transferring partner's share in the assets of the firm on the dissolution of the firm or when the transferring partner ceases to be a partner. He is entitled to an account as from the date of the dissolution for the purpose of ascertaining that share.

Minor as Partner (Section 30)

Section 30 Minors admitted to the benefits of Partnership —

(i) A person who is a minor according to the law to which he is subject may not be a partner in a firm, but, with the consent of all the partners for time being, be admitted to the benefits of partnership.

(ii) Such minor has a right to such share of the property and of the profits of firm as may be agreed upon, and he may have access to and inspect and copy any of the accounts of the firm.

(iii) Such minor's share is liable for any acts of the firm but the minor's is not personally liable for any such act.

(iv) Such minor may not sue the partners for an account or payment of his share of the property or profits of the firm, save when severing his connection with the firm, and in such case the amount of his share shall be determined by a valuation made as far as possible in accordance with the rules contained in section 48:

Provided that all the partners acting together or any partner entitled to dissolve the firm upon notice to other partners may elect in such suit to dissolve the firm, and there upon the court shall proceed with the suit as one for dissolution and for settling accounts between the partners, and the amounts of the share of the minor shall be determined along with the shares of the partners.

(v) At any time within six months of his attaining majority, or of his obtaining knowledge that he had been admitted to the benefits of partnership, which ever date is later, such person may give public notice that he elected to become or that he has elected not to become a partner in the firm, and such notice shall determine his position as regards the firm:

Provided that, if he fails to give such notice, he shall become a partner in the firm on the expiry of the said six months.

(vi) Where any person has been admitted as a minor to the benefits of partnership in a firm, the burden of proving the fact that such person had no knowledge of such admission until a particular date after the expiry of six months of his attaining majority shall lie on the persons asserting that fact.

(vii) Where such person becomes a partner —

(a) his rights and liabilities as a minor continue up to the date on which be becomes a partner, but he also becomes personally liable to third parties for all acts of the firm done since he was admitted to the benefits of partnership, and

(b) his share in the property and profits of the firm shall be the share to which he was entitled as a minor.

(viii) Where such person elects not to become partner —

(a) his rights and liabilities shall continue to be those of a minor under this section up to the date on which he gives public notice,

(b) his share shall not be liable for any acts of the firm done after the date of the notice, and

(c) he shall be entitled to sue the partners for his share of the property and profits in accordance with sub section (4).

Nothing in sub-sections (7) and (8) shall affect provisions of section 28.

Section 11 of Indian Contract Act says that a contract of minor is absolutely void.[38] Partnership is created by contract, not by status. It would be correct to say that partnership is the result of a contract and a minor is not competent to contract, therefore, he cannot become a partner in a firm. There cannot be a partnership consisting of all minors or of one adult and all other minors.[39] But section 30(1) gives a relief to minor. This section lays down that a minor be admitted to the benefits of partnership with the consent of all the existing partners.

It has been held that in order, to prove whether a minor has been admitted to the benefits of the partnership, it must be proved that there was a consent of all partners and there was an agreement as contemplated under section 30(2).[40]

Rights and duties of minors

When a minor is admitted to the benefits of an existing firm, he has following rights and liabilities.

(1) The minor has the right to receive his agreed share of the property and of the profits of the firm.

(2) He may have access to and inspect and copy any of the accounts of the firm.

(3) He is not personally liable for any act of the firm during his minority. He is entitled to only what would fall to his share after paying off the liabilities of the firm.[41]

(4) On attaining majority it is depend upon him to decide that he shall remain in the firm or leave it within the period of six months. He should give a public notice of his choice within this period. But, if he fails to give any notice, he automatically becomes a partner on the expiry of six months.

If he becomes a partner on attaining majority his rights and liabilities as a minor continue up to the date on which he becomes a partner but he also becomes personally liable for all the acts of the firm done since he was admitted to the benefits of the firm. His share in the property and profits remains the same as was before so far not altered by agreement.

If he does not elect to become a partner—

(a) His rights and liabilities shall continue to be those of a minor up to the date of public notice,

(b) His share shall not be liable for any of the acts of the firm done after the date of notice.

(c) He shall be also entitled to sue the partners for his share of the property and profits as given in section.48

Incoming and Outgoing Partners

Incoming Partner

Introduction of a Partner (Section 31)

Section 31(1) Subject to contract between the partners and to the provisions of section 30, no person shall be introduced as partner into a firm without the consent of all the existing partners.

(2) Subject to the provisions of section 30, a person who is introduced as a partner into a firm does not thereby become liable for any act of the firm done before he became a partner.

Introduction of a Partner

The relationship of partner is based on the mutual trust and confidence, therefore, a new partner can be introduced in the firm with the consent of all the partners. Such consent is essential for the harmonious working of the firm. Thus, a person who is admitted as a partner into an already existing firm with the consent of all the existing partners is called as "incoming partner."

The rule mentioned above is, however, subject to contract between the partners of firm. The partners may agree between themselves that on the death of a partner his executors shall become partners. If such an agreement exists and a valid nomination is made. The nominee will be entitled to all rights of a partner. But nominee is not bound to become a partner. It is a matter of his opinion but if he comes to accept, the nomination he must, in that case, fulfil such conditions in his behalf as may be contained in the original agreement such as executing a proper deed or otherwise.[42]

The article of a partnership between two person contained a clause that one would have the right to bring his son into the partnership on attaining age 21 year. The other partner refused to accept the son. But it was held that he could not do so, the partnership articles being a contract.[43]

Liability of an Incoming Partner [Section 31(2)]

The general rule, as section 31(2) says That "a person who is introduced as a partner into a firm does not thereby become liable for any act of a firm done before he became a partner." Thus the liability of the new partner is only for those acts of the firm which are done subsequent to his becoming partner. He is not liable for acts done prior to his admission. But a new partner may agree with his Co-partner to become himself liable for liabilities and obligations incurred by the firm before the date of his admission. Such agreement does not give the right to any creditor to sue the new partner for debts prior to his admission.

A new partner can only be made liable to the creditors for debts incurred prior to date of becoming a partner, when (1) he by an agreement assumes the liability for the past debts and (2) where the creditors knowing that new partner has taken over all the assets and liabilities incurred before his admission.

On the fulfilments of above conditions the new partner becomes liable to those of the creditors who expressly or impliedly accept the new agreement. An implied rejection of new partner occurs when creditor, having knowledge of admission of new partner, continues to deal with old partner alone. The important illustration on this point is case of *British Home Insurance Corporation v. Peterson*[44].

Where, the plaintiff corporation appointed B their solicitor and instructed him to act for them in mortgage transaction. While the business was pending, B took the defendant P into partnership and gave the plaintiffs notice in writing. The plaintiffs paid no attention to the notice, continued to correspond with B in his own name and finally sent the money to advance on the mortgage by cheque made payable to his order and accepted his receipt in his own name. B paid the money into his own account and misappropriated it. The plaintiffs sued the new partner.

It was held that the plaintiffs had by their conduct declined to accept the liability of the new partner. They had elected to deal with the old partner alone and could not after wards hold the new partner liable.

Outgoing Partner

A partner who leaves a firm in which the rest of the partners continue to carry on business is called outgoing or retired partner.

A partner may retire from the firm in one of the following ways:

1. By Consent (Section 31)

A partner may retire with the consent of all his partners.

2. By Agreement (Section 32)

A partner may retire in accordance with an express agreement by the partners. In case of such an agreement, a partner has a right to retire whether his Co-partners agree or not at the time of retirement.

In *Vishnu Chandra v. Chandrika Pd,*[45] it is held by the supreme court that an agreement which permitted a partner to retire by giving one month's notice is valid.

3. By Notice (Section 32)

Where the partnership is at will, a partner may retire by giving notice in writing to all the other partners of his intention to retire. The retirement becomes effective from the date mentioned in the notice or, if no date is mentioned, from the date of service.

Liabilities of Retired Partner

Liabilities of retired partner may be of two kinds:

(a) Liability for Acts done before Retirement.

(b) Liability for Acts done after Retirement.

(a) Liability for Acts done before Retirement [Section 32(2)]

The general rule is that a retired partner remains liable for all acts of the firm done before his retirement. But his Co-partners may, however through an agreement release him from such debts. But two things are required to obtain such release.

(i) The copartners must have agreed with the retired partner to release him from the existing debts and liabilities.

(ii) Secondly, the creditors should be informed of the retirement and the reconstitution of firm.

It is to be noted that a partner who has committed a tort or an infringement of a trade mark remains liable to the injured party even though he had retired before the suit was filed.[46]

(b) Liability for Acts done after Retirement [Section 32(3)]

A retiring partner continues to remain liable to third parties for all acts of the firm untill public notice is given of his retirement. Such notice may be given either by the retiring partner or by any member of the reconstituted firm. So long such public notice is not given the retiring partner is to be liable as a partner to the third parties for any act done by him or by any of the other partners which would have been an act of the firm done before the retirement. A retiring partner will not be liable to any third party who does not know that he is a partner in the firm with which the third party deals.

The procedure of giving public notice is prescribed in section 72 of this Act. In the case of a registered firm, (1) a copy of the notice is to be sent to the Registrar of firms, and (2) a copy must be published in the local official Gazette and in at least one Vernacular newspaper circulating in the district where the firm has its place or principal place of business. In the case of unregistered firms, only (2) is necessary.

Expulsion of Partner (Section 33)

(1) A partner may not be expelled from a firm by any majority of the partners, save in the exercise in good faith of powers conferred by contract between the partners.

(2) The provisions of sub section (2), (3) and (4) of section 32 shall apply to an expelled partner as if he were a retired partner.

Section 33(1) embodies a general rule, that a partner cannot be expelled from a firm by any majority of partners. But a partner may be expelled if the terms of partnership agreement confer the power of expulsion. The power of expulsion must be exercised in absolute good faith in the interest of the firm. In *B Lisset v. Daniel,*[47] majority of the partners expelled a partner because he had opposed the appointment of one of the partner's son as manager, the court held the expulsion to be unwarranted and an abuse of power.

Expulsion may be justified where a partner commits a breach of duties as a partner[48]. In *Ganesh Chandra v. Gopal Chandra,*[49] the Calcutta High Court justified the expulsion of a partner who paralysed the business of the firm by giving notice to the firm's bankers not to pay the firm's cheques and offered no explanation for his conduct after given a full opportunity to him.

The power of expulsion can be exercised by a majority and not by a single partner.

Rights of an expelled Partner

An expelled partner is entitled to get the entire amount contributed by him towards capital. He is also entitled to share the partnership profits upto the date of his expulsion.

Liabilities of an expelled Partner

A partner who is expelled is in the same position as that of a retire partner [sec. 33(2)] .

Where the expulsion is not proper, it is of no effect. Sub-section 2 of section 33 puts an expelled partner on the same tooting as a retired partner as regards his liabilities for existing and future debts of the firm.

Insolvency of a Partner (Section 34)

When a partner in a firm is adjudicated an insolvent he ceases to be a partner from the date of his insolvency, whether the firm is dissolved or not

Effects Resulting from Insolvency

(1) In the absence of a contract to the contrary, the firm is dissolved from the date of the order of adjudication.

(2) The estate of the insolvent is not liable for any act of the firm subsequent to the date of the order of adjudication. Adjudication of insolvency is a notorious event and so no further notice is needed to that effect either to old or new customer of the firm.

(3) The firm cannot be held liable for any act of the insolvent partner from the date of the order of adjudication.

Liability of estate of deceased Partner (Section 35)

A partner ceases to be a partner on his death. In the absence of a contract to the contrary, the firm is dissolved by the death of a partner. Thus, if there is a contract between the partner that the firm will not be dissolved on the death of a partner the estate of a deceased partner is not liable for any act of the firm done after his death.

Section 28(2) says that where after a partner's death the business is continued in the old firm name, the continued use of that name or the deceased partner's name as a part there of shall not of itself make his legal representative or his estate. So, the doctrine of holding out does not apply to the case of a deceased partner.

Rights of outgoing Partner (Section 36, 37 and 38)

An outgoing partner is a partner in a firm who goes out from a firm either by retirement or expulsion or insolvency or by death. Followings are the rights of the retired partner.

1. Right to carry on competing business (Section 36)

An out going partner in a firm in the absence of a contract may carry on any business competing with that of the firm. He may set up his new business at a place next door to the firm or anywhere else. He may advertise his business in rivalry with the business of the firm.

But there are following restrictions to out going partner as imposed by Act to protect the interest of firm which he has left.

(i) He may establish his new business under any other name but he cannot use the name of the firm left by him.

(ii) He cannot represent himself as he is carrying on the business of the firm.

(iii) He may not solicit the customers of the firm who were dealing with the firm before he ceased to a partner. In *Trego v. Hunt*[50] the retiring partner was restrained from drawing a list of the firm's customers.

Agreement in restraint of trade

Section 36 (2) imposes certain restrictions on an out going partner in order to prevent unfair competition.

A partner may make an agreement with in partners that on ceasing to be partner he will not carry on any business similar to that of the firm within a specified period or within specified local limits.

Such agreement shall be valid if the restrictions imposed are reasonable which is ordinarily void under section 27 of the Indian contract Act 1872. Reasonableness is to be judged by the character and nature of the business and of its customers.[51]

2- Right to share subsequent profit (Section 37)

Where any member of a firm dies or otherwise ceases to be a partner as a result of retirement, expulsion, insolvency, or any other cause and the surviving or continuing partner conduct the business with the property of the firm without any final settlement of accounts as between them and the out going partner or his estate, at that time, in the absence of a contract to the contrary, the out going or deceased or his estate has the option to claim:

(a) Such a share of the subsequent profits as may be attributable to the use of his share of the property of the firm, or

(b) Interest on the amount of his share in the property of the firm at the rate of 6% per annum.

This right exists even when only a part of the retired partner's share of assets is used in business, although in that case comparatively less profit would be attributable to his share.[52]

Where the representative of a deceased partner opted for interest, it was held that the estate of the deceased partner was not thereby deprived of its normal right to benefit from an increasing value of the assets pending realisation.[53]

When by contract between the partner's an option is given to continuing partner's to purchase the retired partner's share in the firm. When this option is exercised the right to share subsequent profits is lost. But the right will revive if the purchasing partners do not in all material respects comply with the terms of the purchase.

But if the surviving or continuing partners have not pursued exactly option which has been given, it will fail and the partnership will remain an unliquidated partnership, to a due share of the profits of which the estate of the deceased or outgoing partner will continue to be entitled until liquidation actually takes place.

3. Revocation of Continuing Guarantee (Section 38)

In the absence of a contract to the contrary, a continuing guarantees given to a firm or to a third party in respect of the transactions of a firm is revoked as to future transaction from the date of any change in the constitution of the firm. The revocation of continuing guarantee commences from the date of any change in the constitution of firm. It applies to future transaction. The rule is undoubtedly intended to protect the surety's interest.

In *Neel Lomul Mookerjee v. Bipro Das Mookerjee*,[54] the conduct of a firm's cashier was guaranteed. Subsequently the constitution of the firm was altered and its name changed from 'N.C. Mookerjee' to "N. Mookerjee and son." The Calcutta High Court held that surety was not liable for the misconduct of the cashier after the change.

DISSOLUTION

The discontinuance of the jural relation between all the partners of the firm is called dissolution. Section 39 says:

Dissolution of a firm — The dissolution of partnership between all the partners of a firm is called the "dissolution of the firm."

Thus, the dissolution means complete break up of the relation of partnership between all the partners. When one or more of its members ceased to be partners in a firm while others remain, the firm is not said to be dissolved.

The dissolution is different from the retirement, death or insolvency of a partner, because in these events the business of firm is continued by one or more of the partners. The firm in such a case is called a reconstituted firm. Reconstitution of a firm involves a change in the relation of partners where as in case of dissolution there is complete discontinuance of relationship between all partners[55].

Modes of Dissolution

A firm may be dissolved in any one of the following ways:

(1) By Agreement (Section 40)
(2) By Consent (Section 40)
(3) Compulsory Dissolution (Section 41)
(4) Contingent Dissolution (Section 42)
(5) By Notice (Section 43)
(6) Dissolution by Court (Section 44)

1. By Agreement (Section 40)

A firm may be dissolved in accordance with a contract between the partners. The contract providing for dissolution may be contained in the partnership deed itself or in a separate agreement. Thus, if the agreement of partnership provides that a partner or partners will have the right to dissolve the firm in certain events, the dissolution in pursuance of the agreement will be binding on the other partners even though when any of these events occur they will be unwilling to accept it.

When, there is a partnership of two partners only and one partner retires by virtue of an agreement in between the two partners, it amounts to the dissolution of partnership.[56]

2. By Consent (Section 40)

A firm may at any time be dissolved with the consent of all the partners. The consent of all the partners may be express or it may be inferred from the conduct or other circumstances. Dissolution by consent applies to all cases whether the firm is for a fixed period or at will.

3. Compulsory Dissolution (Section 41)

A firm is compulsorily dissolved on the happening of the following contingencies.

(a) Insolvency of Partners

If all or all but one of the partners are adjudicated as insolvent. Because there must at least be two partners competent to carry on the business.

(b) Business of the firm becomes unlawful

When some event has happened which makes it unlawful for the business to be carried on in partnership.

If the firm is carrying on more than one business, the illegality of one or more does not cause the dissolution of the firm in respect of its lawful business.

4. Contingent Dissolution (Section 42)

Where, there is no contract to the contrary, a firm is dissolved on the happening of any of the following contingencies.

(a) If the firm is constituted for a fixed term, on the expiry of that term.
(b) If the firm is constituted to carry out one or more adventures or undertakings, when they are completed.

(c) By the death of a partner.

(d) By the adjudication of a partner as an insolvent.

5. By Notice (Section 43)

Section 7 says that partnership is deemed to be partnership at will when:

(i) No fixed period has been agreed upon for the duration of partnership and

(ii) There is no provision made as to the determination of partnership in any other way.

If one of the above two above conditions exist the partnership is called as partnership at will.

Where the partnership is at will, it may be dissolved by giving notice in writing to the other partners of his intention to dissolve the firm. The notice must (i) state the intention to dissolve the firm, and (ii) notice should be in writing, signed by the partner it and should be served upon all the partners. The firm is dissolved as from the date mention in the notice as the date of dissolution or if no date is mentioned then from the date of communication of the notice. Filing a suit for dissolution is not a notice as required by the section. The date of passing of the preliminary decree for dissolution in such cases will be the date of dissolution.[57]

6. Dissolution by Court (Section 44)

At the suit of a partner, the court may dissolve a firm on any of the following grounds:

(a) Partner unsound mind

When one of the partners has become a person of unsound mind, any partner including the insane, may apply for dissolution.

(b) Permanent incapability

When any partner, other than the partner suing becomes permanently incapable of performing his duties as a partner, any partner may apply for dissolution. The incapability in permanent nature may arise due to illness, mental or Physical. In *Whitwell v. Arthur*[58], a partner suffered from paralysis attack which on medical evidence was found as curable and not permanent, the dissolution was not granted.

(c) Misconduct affecting the business

When a partner, other than the partner suing, is guilty of conduct which is likely to affect prejudicially the business of the firm the court may order dissolution. The misconduct of a partner towards third parties should be connected in the course of business. Thus in a mercantile partnership if a partner was guilty of adultery, it was held that this was not a ground for dissolution of the firm.[59] But the act of a partner of a mercantile firm, in speculation in cotton was regarded a sufficient ground for dissolution of the firm.[60] Similarly, when a partner of a firm of solicitors was convicted of travelling on the railway without a ticket and with intent to defraud, dissolution was granted.[61]

(d) Wilful and Persistent breach of agreement

When a partner, other than the partner suing, wilfully and persistently commits breach of the partnership agreement relating management or otherwise so conduct himself in matters relating to the business that it is not reasonably practicable for the other partners to carry on business in partnership with him, the court may order dissolution. Conduct of a partner which is destructive of mutual confidence between the partners,[62] keeping erroneous accounts and not entering receipts,[63] refusal by a partner to attend on matters of business,[64] have been held sufficient to justify a dissolution.

(e) Transfer of Interest

If a partner, other than the partner suing transfers his whole interest in the firm to a third party or allows it to be sold in, the recovery of arrears of land revenue, or of any dues recoverable as arrears of land revenue, the court may dissolve the partnership. A partner can transfer the whole of his share to a Co-partner in the firm.

(f) When business cannot be carried on save at a loss

The court may also dissolve a partnership when it is satisfied that the business of the firm cannot be carried save at a loss. The fact that partnership is for a fixed term or for a particular adventure cannot fetter the discretion of the court.[65]

(g) Just and equitable

The court may dissolve a firm on any other ground which in opinion of the court just and equitable for dissolution. In *Baring v. Dixon*,[66] it was held that court would dissolve a firm where appears that the business cannot be carried on in accordance to true meaning of the articles of partnership.

This is a residuary power which gives the court wide discretion and jurisdiction to dissolve a firm on any reasonable ground other than those mentioned in clause (a) to (f) of section 44 of the Act.

Consequences of Dissolution

Public Notice and liability for acts done after dissolution (Section 45)

Despite the dissolution of the firm, the partners will continue to be liable to third parties for their acts if done before its dissolution until public notice is given that the firm is dissolved. Thus public notice is necessary to terminate the liability of the partners by holding out and of the firm by estoppel, for, without it, the firm and every partner would continue to be liable to third parties for any act done by them which would have been an act of the firm if done before its dissolution. Until public notice is not given the whole number of partners remains liable[67]. The notice may be given by the firm or any partner.

There are three instances in which the outgoing partner or his estate would not be liable to third parties for acts done after the date on which he ceases to be a partner, even if no notice of dissolution is given. They are as given below.

(i) Where a partner dies

(ii) Where a partner is adjudicated an insolvent.

(iii) Where dormant partner who has retired.

Right of partners to have business would up after dissolution (Section 46)

Section 46 says that every partner or his representative has a right against the other partners (i) to have the property of the firm applied in payment of the debts and liabilities of the firm, and (2) to have the surplus distributed amongst the partners or their representatives according to their respective rights on the dissolution.

The rights of a partner enunciated in this section is also called as partner's lien.

Authority of partners in winding up (Section 47)

After dissolution, a partner cannot bind the firm in any case, except.

(i) in so far as it may be necessary to wind up affairs the firm, and

(ii) to complete transaction begun but unfinished at the time of dissolution.

Where a partner of a dissolved firm accepted a bill of exchange to pay an existing debt,[68] or paid moneys into a bank to meet current bills[69] or sold goods to pay the debts of the firm,[70] the act in each case was held to be binding upon the representatives of the partner whose bankruptcy had caused the dissolution.

A partner who has been adjudged an insolvent cannot bind the firm in any case after the adjudication has been passed.

Liability to share personal profits (Section 50)

In the absence of a contract to the contrary, if a partner, after dissolution and before the affairs of the partnership are wound up, earns any profit from any transaction connected with the firm or from any use by him of the firm's property, name or business connections, he must share it with the other partners and the legal representatives of the deceased partners under the principle of section 16(a).

But where a partner or his representative has bought the goodwill of the firm, he will not be bound to share profits earned by use of the firm's name.

Where a partner terminated the partnership by notice, but before that obtained renewal of the petrol agency in his personal name and continued with it, the other partner was allowed to recover his share of the profits.[71]

Mode of settlement of Accounts (Section 48)

Section 48 lays down two fundamental principles relating to the mode of settlement of accounts, first, as to payment of losses, and second, as to application of assets.

Losses, including deficiencies of capital, shall be paid first out of profits, next out of capital, and lastly, if necessary, by the partners individually in the proportion in which they were entitled to share profits.

The assets of the firm, including sums contributed by partners to make up deficiency of capital, shall be applied in the following manner.

(i) In paying the debts of the firm to third parties.
(ii) In paying each partner rateably, for advances made by him to the firm as distinct from capital.
(iii) In paying to each partner rateably what is due to him on account of capital.
(iv) The residue in paying each partner in accordance with his share in the profit of the firm.

Some of these rules found application in Garner v. Murray[72]

Under the terms of a partnership, the partners contributed capital in unequal shares, but shared profits in equal shares. The firm was dissolved and the assets, after paying of outside creditors and paying back the advances of partner, were not sufficient to pay back the partner's capital. Two partners contributed their shares of the deficiency and the third one failed to do so.

It was held, in the first instance, that every partner was bound to contribute equally to make up the deficiency, and secondly, that if a partner failed to contribute his share of the deficiency, the other partners were not bound to make contribution in respect of that default.

Refund of Premium (Section 51 and 52)

Where some one is admitted into an established firm for a fixed term as a partner and paid a sum of money to the old partners as a premium for admission. It is a kind of compensation to the old partners for the goodwill they have created and of which the new partner will enjoy benefits. If after the premium is paid the firm is dissolved before the expiration of that term, he (new partner) shall be entitled to repayment of the premium or of such part there of as may be reasonable (regard being had to the terms and to the length of time during which he was a partner) unless,

(i) the dissolution is due to the death of a partner, or
(ii) to his own misconduct, or
(iii) the dissolution is in pursuance of an agreement containing no provision for the return of the premium or any part of it.

But, if he was induced to join the firm by the fraud of any partner, he may, on discovering the fraud, rescind the agreement and have refund not only of the premium but also of the capital paid. His rights in case of fraud are given in section 52 and are as follows:

(i) He has a right to retain, or exercise lien on, the partnership property, which is left after paying partnership debts, for any sum paid by him to purchase a share in the firm and for any capital contributed by him.
(ii) He is entitled to rank as a creditor of the firm in respect of any payment made by him towards the debts of the firm.
(iii) He has the right to recover indemnity from the partner guilty of the fraud or misrepresentation against all the debts of the firm.

Right to restrain from use of firm name or firm property (Section 53)

After a firm is dissolved, every partner or his representative may in the absence of a contract between the partners to the contrary restrain any other partner or his representative from carrying on a similar business in the firm name or from using any of the property of the firm for his own benefit, until the affairs of the firm have been completely wound up.

Provided that where any partner or his representative has brought the goodwill of the firm, nothing in this section shall affect his right to use the firm name.

Thus, section 53 imposes two following restriction on the use of firm's name or property by its partners or his representative until the affairs of the firm have been completely wound up. If there is no contrary contract between the parties.

(i) From carrying on a similar business in the firm name, or
(ii) From using any of the property of the firm for his own benefit.

Such restrain provides a good check over abuse of section 50 and prevent any prejudice to the value of the goodwill which is saleable under section 55.

The section however is subject to the proviso that where any partner or his representative has brought the goodwill of the firm, nothing in this section shall affect his right to use the firm name.

Agreements in Restraint of Trade (Section 54)

Partners may, upon or in anticipation of the dissolution of the firm, make an agreement that some or all of them will not carry on a business similar to that of the firm. The agreement shall be valid — (i) if it specifies the period or local limits of restraint, and (ii) the restriction imposed is reasonable.

This constitutes an necessary exceptions to the general rule contained in section 27 of the contract Act which renders agreements in restraint of trade void.

In *Dev Sharma v. Laxmi Narain*, two persons constituted a partnership for carrying on a business as selling agents of a mill. They agreed that on the termination of the agency the firm would be dissolved and neither partner would undertake the same selling agency. The agency was determined by the mill and the firm was consequently dissolved. One of the partners then obtained a renewal of the agency in his favour. The other partner sued to restrain him in terms of the agreement.

It was held that the agreement was in restraint of business and could not be enforced.

Payment of partnership debts (Section 49)

Where there are joint debts due from, the firm and also separate debts due from any partner, the property of the firm shall be applied in the first instance in payment of the debts of the firm, and if there is any surplus, then the share of each partner shall be applied in payment of his separate debts or paid to him. The separate property of any partner shall be applied first in the payment of his separate debts, and the surplus (if any) in the payment of the debts, of the firm.

This section deals with the order in which the joint debts and separate debts of partners are to be paid from their joint and separate property.

Section 14 says that goodwill is an asset of the firm. On the dissolution of a firm, its goodwill is included in the assets of the firm. This is, however, subject to a contract to the contrary between the partners. The goodwill of the firm is saleable separately or alongwith other property of the firm. If goodwill is not separated from the other assets of the firm it remains a part of those assets. Where a partnership between two partners was dissolved on terms that the assets would be taken over by one of them, no mention being made of goodwill, it was held that goodwill went to the partner relating the assets and he could restrain the other partner from canvassing the customers of the old firm.[74]

Where the goodwill of a firm is sold after dissolution, every partner has a right to carry on a similar business in completion with purchaser, but he cannot do so under the former name of the firm, nor can he represent himself as continuing or succeeding to the same business. He may advertise his business, but he must not solicit the customers who were dealing with the former firm. But he cannot do the following:

(i) He cannot use the name of the firm.
(ii) He cannot represent himself as carrying on the business of the firm.
(iii) He cannot solicit old customers of the firm who were dealing with the firm before its dissolution. But he may deal with old customers of the firm if they come to him of their own accord.[75]

Agreement in restraint of trade

Section 55(3) says that any partner may upon the sale of the goodwill of a firm make an agreement with the buyer that such partner will not carry on any business similar to that of the firm with in specified period or within specified local limits. And such restraint imposed must be reasonable both as to the limit or period specified in the agreement. The reasonableness of the restriction must be judged by the character or nature of the business and its customers. In *Krishnarao v. Shanker*,[76] the restriction was held reasonable where a partner of a firm sold the business to the other partner and agreed not to carry on a similar business of manufacturing and selling bakelite goods for three years within the city of Bombay.

Thus, this section is subject to a exception to section 27 of the Indian contract Act which lays down the rule that every agreement by which any person is restrained from exercising a lawful trade or business of any kind is to that extent void.

Registration of Firms

Section 57 of Partnership Act says that the state Government may appoint Registrars of firms for the purposes of this Act. Accordingly, an office of the Registrar of Firms exists in every state. Registrar is a public servant within the meaning of section 21 of the Indian penal code. Registration is obtained by filing an application with the Registrar of Firms. The application should be on the prescribed form and accompanied by the prescribed fee, stating following particulars.

(a) The name of firms
(b) The place or principal place of the firm.
(c) The names of any other places where the firm carries on business.
(d) The date when each partner joined the firm.
(e) The names in fill and permanent addresses of the partners.
(f) The duration of the firm.

The application form should be signed and verified by each partner or by their duly authorised agents. After the satisfaction of Registrar about the fulfillments of requirements for registration, the firm's name enters in the Register of Firms and issues a certificate of registration. Where the Registrar acts bonafide and follows the prescribed procedure, his satisfaction on the said points is not open to question in a court of law.[77] But the registration is optional and not compulsory and it may be done at any time.

In *Gandhi and Co. v. Krishna Glass (P) Ltd.*,[78] the Bombay High Court held that the suit of the firm was not maintainable where the name of a partner was not shown in the register of firms on the date of the filing of the suit.

Section 58(3) provides that the name of the firm shall not contain any of the following words, namely-

"Crown", "Emperor", "Empress", "Empire", Imperial", "King", "Queen", "Royal", or words expressing or implying the sanction, approval or patronage of Government except when the state Government signifies its consent to the use of such words as part of the firm name by order in writing.

Change of firm's Particulars

An alteration is made in the firm name or in the location of the principal place of business of a registered firm requires a new registration and all formalities of registration should be complied as given in section 58.

The Registrar should be informed in following cases by any partner or agent of the firm.

(i) When the business of registered firm is discontinued at one place or extended to a new place (section 61), or
(ii) When a partner changes his name permanent address (section 62), or
(iii) When a firm is dissolved (section 63(1)), or
(iv) When a partner retires or joins or a minor having been admitted, elects to become or not to become a partner [section 63 (2)].

Rules of evidence (Section 68)

Any statement, notice or intimation recorded or noted with the Registrar by any person is a conclusive proof against him of the fact stated. Entries relating to a firm in the Registrar of Firms may be proved by producing certified copies of the entries.

Penalty for furnishing false particulars (Section 70)

A person is liable to penalties if knowingly or without belief in its truth furnishes false or incomplete declaration in any document sent to Registrar.

Effects of Non-Registration (Section 69)

Registration of firms is optional and not compulsory. Act does not impose penalties to unregistered firms. But the rules regarding to the consequences of non registration of firm make registration necessary at one time or the other because section 69 disqualifies an unregistered firms and its partners to sue. For instance a firm which is not registered will not be allowed to enforce its claims against third parties in the courts.

Following two important requirements must be fulfiled before a suit can be instituted to enforce a contractual right by the firm or on behalf of the firm:

(1) that the firm is a registered one, and
(2) that the persons suing are or have been shown in the Register of Firms as partners.

The effects of non-registration are given as below:

1. Suits between Partners and Firm

A Partner of a registered firm whose name appears in registration can only sue the firm or his present or post Co-partners for the enforcement of any right arising from a contract or conferred by the partnership Act. In Ram Kumar v. Dominion of India,[79] it was held that where in the registration documents of a firm all the partners presently in the firm were not shown, suit was not allowed. When a suit is filed without registration, it is liable to be dismissed and cannot be rectified by subsequent registration.[80] In *Jagdish Chandra Gupta v. Kajaria Traders (India) Ltd.*[81] the partnership deed provided that in case of any dispute between the partners the matter will be referred to arbitration. One of the partner brought an action to enforce the arbitration clause of the deed. The other partner contended that the firm was not registered and therefore the suit was not maintainable.

The Supreme Court has settled the controversy by holding that the registration of a firm is a precondition for filing a suit.

2. Suits between Firm and Third Parties

Any third party can not be sued by an unregistered firm for the enforcement of any right arising from contract. A suit can only be brought by persons whose names appears as partners in the register of firms. A fresh suit will have to be field after registration provided that it is still within the period of limitation.

In a recent case of *M/s Shreeram Finance Corpn v. Yasin Khan,*[82] the Supreme Court laid down that where on account of the admission of some new partners and of some minors into the benefit of the firm, there was a discrepancy between the names on the register and the names included in the suit, the suit was not maintainable.

Exceptions

The provisions of section 69 admits following exceptions:

(1) An unregistered firm and its partners can bring an action for dissolution of a firm or for accounts of a dissolved firm.

(2) The Power of an official assignee, receiver or court to reliase the property of an insolvent is not affected by non registration of firm.

(3) Any suit or claim not exceeding Rs. 100 in value.

(4) Third parties are free to sue a firm whether registered or not. The Provisions of section 69, however do not affect the right of a third party to sue against the unregisterd firm or its unregistered partners.

(5) A firm whether registered or unregistered can sue for their statutory and non contractual rights. Thus a person who damages the property of the firm can be sued whether the firm is registered or not.

PRACTICE QUESTIONS

1. What is a partnership? Briefly state special features of a partnership on the basis of which its existence can be determined under the Indian Partnership Act?
2. (a) Explain the procedure for getting a partnership firm registered. When is such a registration treated as complete? (b) State the effects of non-registration of a firm, (c) What are the advantages of registration of a partnership firm?
3. Explain the following: (i) Partner by holding out, or by estoppel, (ii) Dormant or sleeping partner, (iii) Nominal partner, (iv) Sub-partner, (v) Working partner, (vi) Incoming partner, (vii) Outgoing partner, (viii) Limited partnership.
4. What are the provisions of the Indian Partnership Act with regard to the admission of a minor into the partnership? What will be his rights and liabilities during his minority and after he has attained the majority?
5. Enumerate the rights and duties of partners *inter se.*
6. What is meant by the implied authority of a partner to bind the firm? State the acts of a partner for which he does not have the implied authority to bind the firm.
7. Write a short note on 'liability of a firm for wrongful acts of a partner'.
8. Explain the conditions under which a partner may be expelled from the firm State the consequences of such an expulsion.
9. In what circumstances is partnership dissolved: (i) automatically, (ii) compulsorily by the court?

10. What is meant by disso'ution of a firm? Is it different from the dissolution of partnership?
11. Describe the mode of settling accounts of a firm after dissolution with special reference to a case where one of the partners has become insolvent and nothing is recoverable from his estate.

References

1. Abdul v. Century Wood industries AIR 1954 Mys33
2. Calelicott v. Griffiths (1853) 8 EX Re, 898.
3. R.R. Sarma v. Reuben AIR 1946 Oudh 68.
4. Cox v. Hickman (1860) 8 Hcl 288.
5. Cox v. Hickman (1860) 8 Hcl 268.
6. Walker West Developments v. F.J. Emmett (1978) 252 EG. 1171, C.A.
7. Badby v. Consolidated Bank (1888) 38 ChD 238.
8. Mollwo March and Co. v. The Court of Wards (1872) LR 2 CP 419.
9. Govind Nair v. Maga (1888) 38 Ch.D 238.
10. I.T. Commissioner v. Kesharmal Keshardeo AIR 1968 A and N. 68.
11. Munshi Abdul Latif v. Gopeshwar Chattoraj AIR 1933 Cal 204.
12. I.T. Commissioner v. Kesharmal Keshardeo, AIR 1968 A & N 68.
13. Floydd v. Cheney (1970) Ch 602.
14. Arjun Kanoji v. Santaram Manoji (1969) 1 SCC 555.
15. Slewart v. Gladstone (1879) Ch. D. 626
16. Cox v. Hickman (1860) 8 HLC 268.
17. Bond v. Gibson (1808) 1 Camp 185, 10 R.R. 665.
18. Jafferali Bhallo Lakha v. Standard Bank of S. Africa (1927) 107 Ic 453, AIR 1928 Pc 135.
19. Porbander Commercial Co-op Bank Ltd. v. Bhanji Lavji (1985) 26 (1) Guj. LR 49.
20. Kendall v. Wood, (1871) L.R. 6 Ex 243.
21. Motilal v. Unnao Commercial Bank (1930)32 Bom L.R. 1571.
22. Lindley on Partnership, 172 (12 the dn by Scamell 1962)
23. Williason v. Barker (1877) 9 Ch. D. 529.
24. Adams v. Bingley (1836) 1, M & W 192
25. Bignold v. Water house (1813) 1 M and S 255: 105 ER 95.
26. Hamlyn v. John Houston and Co. (1902) 87 L.T. 500: (1903) 1 KB 81.
27. Rapp v. Latham, 2 B & A 795: (1819) 21 R.R. 495.
28. Longmen v. Pale (1828) Don and L 1126
29. T.N. Waterworks Co. v. Jones (1903) 2ch 615
30. Munshi Bashiruddin v. Surja Kumar (1908) 12 Cal. W.N. 716.
31. Rhodes v. Moules (1895) 1 ch d. 236.
32. Plumer v. Gregory (1974) LR 18 Eq. 621.
33. Wough v. Carver 2 H. Blacks 235: 14 R.R. 845.
34. Kirkwood v. Cheetham and Smith (1862) 2F & F 798.
35. Bevan v. The National Bank Ltd. (1906) 2 TLR 65
36. Martyn v. Gray (1863) 14 CB (NS) 824.
37. Dickinson v. Valpy, 10 B and C 128, 140: 34 R.R. 348, 355.
38. Mohori Bibee v. Dharmodas Ghose(1903) 30 IA 114: 30 Cal 539.
39. Shivram v. Gaurishankar, AIR 1961 Bom 136.
40. Venkideswara Prabhu v. Surendra Nath Prabhu AIR (1985) Kar 265.
41. Sahai Bros v. Commissioner of Income Tax AIR (1958) Paf 177.
42. Wootney v. Trist (1876) 45 LJ ch. 412.
43. Byrne v. Reid (1902) 2 ch. 735.
44. British Home Insurance Corp. v. Peterson (1902) 2 ch. 404.
45. Vishnue Chandra v. Chandrika Pd. AIR (1983) SC. 523.
46. Thomas Bear and Sons v. Rulia Ram AIR (1934) Lah 625.
47. Elisset v. Daniel (1853) 10 Hare 493: 90 R.R. 454.
48. Green v. Howell (1910) 102 LT 347 (CA):(1910) 1 ch. 495.
49. Ganesh Chandra v. Gopal Chandra AIR (1976) Cal. 459.
50. Trego v. Hunt (1896) AC 7.
51. Krishnarao v. Shankar (1954) A Bom 532: 56 Bom LR 973.
52. Ramakrishna Ayyar v. Muthuswami Ayyar AIR (1929) Mad 456.
53. Barclays Bank Trust Co. Ltd. v. Bluff (1981) 3 All ER 232.
54. Neel Comul Mookerjee v. Bipro Das Mookerjee (1901) 28 Cal 597.
55. Wajid Ali v. CIT, AIR (1988) SC. 757.
56. Erach F.D. Mehta v. Minoo F.D. Mehtab AIR (1971) SC. 1653.
57. Banarsi Das v. Kanshi Ram AIR (1963) SC. 1165.

58. Whitwell v. Arthur (1865) 35 Beav 140.
59. Snow v. Milford (1868) 18 LT N2.
60. Pearce v. Foster 17 QBD 536.
61. Carmichael v. Evans (1940) 1 ch. 486.
62. Harrison v. Tennant (1856) 21 Beav 482.
63. Cheeseman v. Price, (1865) 35 Beav 142.
64. De Beenger v. Hamel, 7 Jar Byth, 2nd. edn, 25
65. Rahmatunnisa v. Price (1918) 42 Bom 380 P.C.
66. Baring v. Dixon (1786) 29 ER 1134.
67. K. Lakshmi narayanan v. Lakshmi Venkata (1988) 25 Reports (AP) 327.
68. Robinson, ExP, (1833) 3 Dea & ch. 376: 38 R.R. 39.
69. Woodbridge v. Swan (1833) 4 B & Ad 633.
70. Fraser v. Kershaw (1856) 2K & J 496.
71. Pathirana v. Pathirana (1967) 1 AC 233 on appeal to the Privy Council from ceylon.
72. Garner v. Murray (1904) 89 LT: (1904) 1 ch. 57.
73. Dev Sharma v. Laxmi Narain AIR (1956) Punj 49.
74. Jennings v. Jennings (1898) 1 ch. 378.
75. Leggot v. Barret (1880) 15 ch. D. 306, 313.
76. Krishnarao v. Shanker, (1954) 56 Bom LR 973.
77. Girdhari Lal v. S. Dinga Singh and Co. (1954) AIR M.P. 52.
78. Gandhi and Co. v. Krishna Glass (P) Ltd. AIR (1987) Bom 348.
79. Ram Kumar v. Dominion of India,AIR (1977) Cal 37.
80. Union of India v. Durga Dutt AIR (1961) Assam 2.
81. Jagdish Chandra Gupta v. Kajaria Traders (India) Ltd. AIR (1964) SC. 1882.
82. M/S Shreeram Finance Corporation v. Yasin Khan AIR (1989) SC. 1769.

PART E

SALE OF GOODS ACT 1930

CHAPTER

16

Sale of Goods

Backdrop

Sale of goods is one of the specific forms of contracts. The laws relating to such contracts is contained in the Sale of Goods Act 1930. Before the passing of the Sale of Goods Act, 1930, the law relating to the Sale of Goods was contained in the chapter VII of the Indian Contract Act 1872. The unrepealed provisions of the Indian Contract Act 1872, however, continue to apply in contract for the Sale of Goods. If the Provisions of the Contract Act are inconsistent with the express provisions of the Sale of Goods Act, 1930, then the latter shall apply (Sec.3). Further, the expressions used but not defined in the Sale of Goods Act, 1930 and in the Contract Act, 1872, have the meanings assigned to them in the Contract Act (Section 2 (15)). The Sale of Goods Act, 1872 deals with the 'Sale' but not with 'mortgage' or 'Pledge' which comes with in the purview of the transfer of Property Act and the Indian Contract Act, respectively. Secondly, the Act deals with 'goods', not with all movable property. For e.g., actionable claims are contained in the Transfer of Property Act.

The Sale of Goods Act, 1930, came into force on Ist July, 1930. It is substantially based on the English Sale of Goods Act, 1893. It extends to the whole of India, except Jammu and Kashmir.

Formation of the Contract of Sale

Definition and Essentials of Contract of Sale

Definition

Section 4 of the Sales of Goods Act defines 'Sales' as follows:

"A Contract of Sales of goods is a contract whereby the seller transfers or agrees to transfer the property in goods to the buyer for price".

Essentials of a Contract of Sale

The definition emphasises the following essential features of a Sale.

1. There must be at least two parties

A Sale has to be a bilateral agreement, since the property in goods has to pass from one person to another. The seller and buyer, therefore, must be two different persons because the seller cannot buy his own goods.

A Sale is said to be consensual because it is necessary that the parties should agree with their free consent. A forced purchase or procurement is an acquisition and not a sale.

2. The Consideration is money

The Consideration for sale of goods has necessarily to be money, called the price. Where the property in goods is transferred for any consideration other than money, it will not be regarded as a sale. If, for instance, goods are offered in consideration for goods, it will not amount to sale, since it is similar to 'barter', where, there is no consideration, it amounts to gift and not sale. Where goods are sold for a definite sum and the price is paid partly in terms of goods and partly in cash, is not considered as a sale. For example, when an old car is returned to the dealer in exchange of a new one against the difference is paid in cash, it will amount to a sale.

In Aldridge v. Johnson, fifty-two bullocks, valued at pond 6 a piece, were exchanged for 100 quarters of barely at pond 2 per quarters, the difference to be made up in cash, the contract was treated as one of sale.

3. Goods

The subject matter of the contract must necessarily be goods. Sale of immovable property is not covered under the sale of Goods Act. The expression "goods" is defined in section 2(7) of the Act.

"Good means every kind of movable property, other than actionable claims and money, and includes stock and shares, growing crops, grass and things attached to or forming part of the land which are agreed to be severed before sale or under the contract of sale."

Thus every kind of movable property except money or actionable claim is not a good. Goodwill, trade mark, copyright patents, water, gas electricity and ship, all are goods. A decree can also be sold as goods.

4. 'A contract of sale may be absolute or conditional.'

Sale and Agreement to Sell

The distinction between the two is important because legal repercussion of the two are vastly different. Section 4(3) states the basic difference between the two in following words.

"Where under a contract of sale, the property in the goods is transferred from the seller to the buyer, the contract is called a sale, but where the transfer of the property in the goods is to take place at a future time or subject to some condition there after to be fulfilled, the contract is called an agreement to sell."

Sale of goods is a contract where by the seller transfers or agrees to transfer the property in the goods to the buyer for a price. The effect of sale is, therefore, the transfer of property in the goods from the seller to the buyer. Where under 'agreement to sell' the transfer of property in goods is to take place at a future date or subject to some condition there after to be fulfilled. The following are the points of difference between them.

(1) A sale is an executed contract. An agreement to sell is an executory contract.
(2) In a sale the property in goods passes to buyer and seller can sue the buyer for the price of the goods. In an agreement to sell, in case of breach, the seller can only sue for damages.
(3) A sale creates a right in rem while an agreement to sell creates a right in personam.
(4) In a sale, a subsequent loss or destruction of the goods is the liability of the buyer, but the liability remains with the seller where the transaction only amounts to an agreement to sell.

When Agreement to sell becomes sale (Section 4(4))?

Section 4(4) says that an "an agreement to sell becomes a sale when the time elapse or the conditions are fulfilled subject to which the property in the goods is to be transferred."

Thus, when in an agreement to sell the passing of property is fixed at a future date, the agreement becomes sale on the due date and if certain conditions are imposed for passing of property, it becomes a sale prior to those conditions being fulfilled.

Agreement to Sell and Hire Purchase

A hire-purchase agreement is a contract where by the owner of the goods lets them on hire to another person called hirer on Payment of rent to be paid in installments and upon an agreement that when a certain number of such installments is paid, the ownership in goods will pass to the hirer. The hirer may return the goods at any time without any obligation to pay the balance installment.

Whether an agreement is a hire-purchase agreement or a contract of sale, the test would be whether or not any option has been given to the hirer to terminate the contract. If the answer is in the affirmative, it would be a hire purchase agreement and if the answer is in the negative it would be a contract of sale. The hirer must not, however, be compelled to exercise the option. But where a buyer has no right to terminate the agreement and is bound to pay the price, the agreement is a sale.

Main Points of distinction between sale and an agreement to sell are given below:

Sale

(1) Ownership is transferred from the seller to the buyer as soon as the contract is entered into.
(2) The position of the buyer is that of the owner.
(3) The buyer cannot terminate the contract and as such is bound to pay the price of the goods.
(4) If the payment is made by the buyer in installments, the amount payable by the buyer to the seller is reduced, for the payment made by the buyer is towards the price of the goods.

Hire purchase agreement

(1) Ownership is transferred from the seller to the hire-purchaser only when a certain agreed number of installments are paid.
(2) The position of the hire purchaser is that of the bailer.
(3) The hire purchaser has an option to terminate the contract at any stage, and cannot be forced to pay further installments.
(4) The installments paid by the hire purchaser are regarded as hire charges and not as payment towards the price of the goods till option to purchase the goods is exercised.

The hire purchase agreements are governed by Hire Purchase Act, 1972. Sale tax is not leviable on a hire purchase until it becomes a sale.[3]

Sale and Barter or Exchange

Where property in goods is transferred from the seller to the buyer for a price, it is called a sale and where goods are exchanged for goods, the transaction is called a barter and not a sale. Where money is exchanged for money, it is a transaction of exchange and not a sale. But if the consideration for transfer of property in goods consists partly in goods and partly in money, the contract is a sale.

Sale and Bailment

In a sale, the property in goods is transferred from the seller to the buyer. In a bailment, there is only transfer of possession from the bailer to the bailee. This may be for any one of the objects, namely safe custody, use of carriage from one place to another, etc. In a sale, the buyer can deal with the goods in any way he likes to. The bailer can deal with the goods according to the direction of the bailer.

Sale and contract for work and materials

The Sale of Goods Act applies to a contract of sale and not to a contract for work and materials. A contract of sale contemplates the delivery of goods, where as a contract for work and material involves exercise of skill and labour by one party in respect of materials supplied by another, the delivery of goods being only subsidiary or incidental.[4]

Examples

(a) A dentist agreed to supply a set of artificial teeth to a patient. The material was wholly found by the dentist, held the contract was for the sale of goods (*Lec v. Griffin*).[5]
(b) A contract involved the repair of a car and the supply of parts for that purpose, held it was a contract for work and materials (*Myers and Co. v. Brent cross service Co.*).[6]
(c) A contract with an artist who agreed to paint a picture, for an agreed sum, on the canvas and with the materials to be supplied by the other party, was held to be a contract for work and labour and not for sale of goods. (*Robinson v. Graves*).[7]
(d) 'F' contracted for the sale of a fur coat of special design and colour to a customer's requirements, held it was a sale of goods not with standing the degree of skilled work and labour involved in its production (*J. Marcel (Furriers), Ltd. v. Tapper (1953) 1 All ER15*).[8]
(e) A contract for fabrication, supply, erection and installation of two types of rolling shutters to be manufactured according to the specifications, drawings, designs and instructions and also to be erected and installed at the premises, have been held by the supreme court to be contracts of work and not of sale. (*Sentinel Rolling Shutters v. C.S.T.*).[9]

Subject- Matter of Contract of Sale (Section 6)

Goods form the subject-matter of a contract of sale only. According to section 2(7):

'Goods' means every kind of movable property other than actionable claims and money, and includes stock and shares, growing crops, grass, and things attached to or forming part of the land which are agreed to be severed before sale or under the contract of sale. Trade marks, copyrights, patent rights, goodwill, electricity, water, gas are all goods and may be the subject matter of a contract of sale.

Actionable claims and money are not goods. An actionable claim is something which can only be enforced by action in a court of law. A debt due from one person to another is an actionable claim, once cannot be bought or sold as goods. It can only be assigned. Money here means current money and not old rare coins.

The definition of the term 'goods' also suggests that it includes stocks and shares, growing crops, grass and things attached to or forming part of land which are agreed to be severed from land before sale. Growing crops and grass are included in the definition of the terms 'goods' because they are to be severed from land. Trees which are agreed to be severed before sale or under the contract of sale are goods (*Badri Prasad v. state of M.P.11*).

Classification of Goods

The goods which form the subject of a contract of sale may be either existing goods or future goods (section 6(1) or contingent goods (section 6(2)).

(1) Existing goods

These are the goods which are owned and possessed by the seller at the time of sale (Section 6). Instances of sale of goods possessed but not owned by the seller are sales by agents and pledges. Only existing goods can be the subject matter of a sale. The existing goods may be —

(i) Specific goods

These are the goods which are identified and agreed upon at the time of contract of sale is made [section 4(14)] as for example a specified watch, dog or horse, goods are, however, not specific merely because the source of supply is identified.

(ii) Ascertained goods

Though commonly used as similar in meaning to specific goods these are the goods which become ascertained subsequent to the formation of contract of sale. *In re* wait (1927) 1 ch 606,[12] Lord Atkin observed that ascertained probably means "identified in accordance with the agreement after the time a contract of sale in made."

(iii) Generic or unascertained goods

These goods are goods indicated by description and not specifically identified.

Example

A who wants to buy a television set goes to showroom where four sets of Janta model are displayed. He sees the performance of a particular set, which he agrees to buy. The set so agreed to be bought is a specific set. If after having bought one set be marks a particular set the set so marked becomes ascertained. Till this is done, all sets are unascertained.

(2) Future goods

These are the goods which a seller does not possess at the time of the contract. Such goods will be manufactured, or produced or acquired by the seller after making the contract of sale [section 2(6)]. A contract of present sale of future goods though expressed as actual sale, purports to operate as an agreement to sell the goods and not a sale [section 6(3)]. This is because the ownership of a thing cannot be transferred before that thing comes into existence.

The Railway Administration entered into a contract for sale of coal all that might accumulate during the period of contract, held the contract amounted to an agreement to sell.[13]

An agreement to sell future crops of a particular field implies an agreement to sell future goods.

(3) Contigent goods

These are the goods the acquisition of which by the seller depends upon a contingency which may or may not happen [section 6(2)].

Example-1

A agree to sell specific goods in a particular ship to B to be delivered on the arrival of ship. If the ship arrives but with no such goods on board, the seller is not liable, for the contact is to deliver the goods should they arrive.

Example-2

Where A agrees to sell to B a certain furniture only if C, its present owner, sell it to him. This furniture is classified as contingent goods.

Contingent and future goods

The procurement of contingent goods depends upon a contingency where as it is not so in case of future goods. On non acquisition of contingent goods, the parties are discharged where as on non acquisition or non production of future goods the parties are not discharged.

Effect of Destruction of goods

1. Goods perishing before making of contract (section 7)

A contract for the sale of specific goods is void if at the time of the contract, the goods have, without the knowledge of the seller, already perished or become so damaged as no longer to answer their description in the contract. Thus, this rule applies subject to the following conditions:

(1) The "specific goods" must be for the contract of sale.

(2) 'Specific goods' must have perished before the contract is made and without the knowledge of the seller.

Examples

(1) A sale of cargo of goods is void if unknown to the seller the goods have before the contract, become heated and sold at an intermediate part[14] or destroyed before loading by floods following an earthquake. [15]

(2) The principle is also applied where a part only of goods are lost in circumstances which makes the rest of the goods useless for the buyer. The important illustration is *Barrow Cane and Ballard v. Phillips.*[16]

The seller made a contract to buyers for the sale of a parcel of 700 bags of Chinese groundnuts. This was unknown to the seller that 10 bags had been stolen at the time of contract. The seller delivered the remaining 591 bags and, on the buyer's refusal to take them, brought an action for the price.

It was held that buyers could not be compelled to take less quantity of goods and they were not liable to take or pay for the remaining bags. The contract had accordingly become void by reason of the loss of the goods.

The principle will apply even where the goods have lost their commercial value. A leading illustration is *Asfar and Co. Ltd. v. Blundell.*[17]

A Cargo of dates was sold. The dates were contaminated with sewage so as to be unsaleable as dates, through they could be used for making spirits. It was held that the contract was void as the dates no longer answered their description in the contract.

2. Goods Perishing after the agreement to sell (Section 8)

An agreement to sell specific goods becomes void if subsequently the goods, without any fault on the part of the seller or buyer perished or become so damaged as no longer to answer their description in the agreement before the risk passes to the buyer.

A leading illustration is *Howell v. Coupland.*[18] The defendant agreed to sell to plaintiff 200 tons of regent potatoes. The defendant sowed sufficient land to grow more than 200 tons but a disease attacked the crop, and he was able to deliver only about eight tons. The agreement was held to have become void.

'Fault' means wrongful act or default [section 2(6)]. This rule is based on the ground of impossibility of performance.

Section 7 and 8 apply only to specific goods and not to unascertained goods.

Documents of title to goods [Section 2(4)]

A document of title to goods is one used in ordinary course of business as any document used as proof of the possession or control of goods, authorising, or purporting to authorise, either by endorsement or by delivery, the possessor of the document to transfer or receive goods there by represented.

It symbolises the goods and confers a right on the purchaser to receive the goods or to further transfer such right to another person. This may be done by mere delivery or by proper endorsement and delivery. Conditions to be fulfilled by a document of title to the goods:

(i) It must be used in the ordinary course of business.

(ii) The undertaking to deliver the goods to the possessor of the document must be entitled to receive the goods unconditionally.

Section 2(4) recognises the following as documents of title to goods:

(1) **Bill of lading:** It is a document which acknowledges receipt of goods on board of a vessel and is signed by the Captain of the ship or his duty authorised representative.

(2) **Dock warrant:** It is a document issued by a dock owner giving details of the goods and certifying that the goods are held to the order of the person named in it or endorses. It authorises the person holding it to receive possession of the goods.

(3) **Warehouse-keeper's or wharfinger's certificates:** It is a document issued by a warehouse keeper or a shatfinger stating that the goods are specified in the document are in his warehouse or in his warf.

(4) **Railway receipt:** It is a document issued by the railway acknowledging receipt of goods. It is to be presented by the holder or consignee at the destination to take delivery of the goods.

(5) **Delivery Order:** It is a document containing an order by the owner of the goods to the holder of the goods on his behalf asking him to deliver them to the person named in the document.

The Price (Section 9 and 10)

The price in a contract of sale means the money consideration for sale of goods. It forms an essential part of the contract. It must be expressed in money. It in the consideration for the transfer or agreement to transfer the property in goods from the seller to the buyer. If it is not fixed and is not capable of being fixed, the whole contract is *Void-initio*. As to how the price is to be fixed.

Ascertainment of Price

According to section 9 the price in a contract of sale may be (i) either fixed by the contract or (ii) may be agreed to be fixed in a manner provided by the contract, e.g., by a valuer, or (iii) it may be determined by the course of dealings between the parties. Thus in *Browne v. Byrine*,[19] a usage to deduct discount in determining the price was implied from the course of dealings (iv) In case, price is not capable of being fixed in any of the above ways, the buyer is bound to pay reasonable price. What is reasonable price will vary from case to case. However, where there is a market price, that may be a reasonable price.

Agreement to sell at Valuation (Section 10)

The parties may agree to sell and buy goods on the terms that price is to be fixed by the such valuation of a third party. If such third party cannot or does not make such valuation, the agreement becomes void. But if the goods or any part there of have been delivered to, and appropriated by the buyer, he shall pay a reasonable price thereof. If the third party is prevented from making the valuation by the fault of the seller or buyer, the party not in fault may maintain a suit for damages against the party in fault.

Earnest

Quite often in a contract of sale the buyer may give some tangible thing as a token of good faith as a guarantee or security for the due performance of the contract (*Howe v. Smith*[20]). This is known as earnest. If the contract is duly performed, the earnest is returned or if it is in the form of the money it is adjusted against the purchase price. If the contract is not or cannot be performed through the default of the buyer, the buyer forfeits the earnest unless otherwise agreed.

An 'earnest' must be distinguished from part payment, it is forfeited if through the buyer's default, the contract goes off. But if there has been a part payment, and the contract goes off through the buyer's default the buyer may recover the part payment, but he remains liable to the seller for such damages as the seller has sustained by reason of the breach.

Stipulations As To Time (Section 11)

Stipulation as to time in a contract of sale fall under the following two heads:

(1) Stipulations relating to time of payment.

(2) Stipulation not relating to time of payment e.g., delivery of goods, etc.

Stipulations relating to time of payment are not of the essence of a contract of sale unless a different intention appears from the contract, As regards other stipulations time may be of the essence of the contract but the essentially depends on the terms of the contract. In a contract of sale, stipulation other than those relating to the time of payment are regarded as of the essence of the contract. Thus, of a time is fixed for the delivery of goods, the delivery must be made at the fixed time, otherwise the other party is entitled to put an end to the contract.

Condition and Warranties

Before a contract of sale is entered into, a seller frequently makes representations or statement which influence the buyer to conclude the bargain. Such representations or statements differ in character and importance. Whether any statement or representation made by the seller with reference to the goods in a stipulation forming part of the contract or is a mere representation forming no part of the contract, depends on the constructions of the contract. If there are no such representations, the ordinary rule of law 'Cavet Emptor' i.e., "Let the buyer beware" — applies.

This means it is the buyer's duty to select goods of his requirement and it is no part of the seller's duty to point out the defects in the goods to buyer.

A stipulation in a contract of sale with reference to goods which are the subject there of may be a condition or a warranty (Section 12(1).

Condition

A Condition is a stipulation which is essential to the main purpose of the contract. It goes to the root of the contract. Its non-fullfilment upsets the very basis of the contract. Explaining the term condition section 12 (2) says

"A condition is a stipulation essential to the main purpose of the contract, the breach of which gives rise to a right to treat the contract as repudiated.

Thus, the effect of a breach of a condition is to give the aggrieved party a right to treat the contract as repudiated, i.e., if price has been paid, the buyer can claim the refund of price plus damages for breach.

Warranty

A warranty is a stipulation which is collateral to the main purpose of the contract. It is not of such vital importance as a condition. Defining a warranty, the section 12(3) says:

"A warranty is a stipulation collateral to the main purpose of the contract, the breach of which gives to a claim for damages but not to a right to reject the goods and treat the contract as repudiated".

It is defined in *Wallis v. Pratt* as an "obligation which though it must be performed, is not vital that a failure to perform it goes to the substance of the contract". If there is a breach of warranty, the aggrieved party can only claim damages and it has no right to treat the contract as repudiated.

Whether a stipulation in a contract of sale is a condition or a warranty depends in each case on the construction of the contract as a whole. The court is not to be guided by the terminology used by the parties to the contract. A stipulation may be a condition through called a warranty in the contract. (Section 12(4)). The court may access the relative importance of the stipulation in dispute in the light of all the circumstances including the intention of the parties. The concept of a condition is well illustrated by the case of *Baldry v. Marshall*.[22]

The plaintiff consulted the defendants, motor car dealers for a car "suitable for touring purposes". The defendants suggested that a "Bugatte" car would be appropriate and the plaintiff accordingly bought one. The car turned out to be unfit for touring purposes and the plaintiff sought to reject it. The defendants relied upon a term in the contract which guaranteed the car for twelve months against mechanical defects and excluded every other guarantee or warranty.

But is was held that the suitability of the car for touring purposes was not a guarantee or warranty, but a condition of the contract. Then term was so vital that its non-fulfilment defeated the very purpose for which the plaintiff bought the car. He was therefore, entitled to reject and have refund of the price.

An illustration of a warranty is Harrison v. Knowles and Foster[23]

The plaintiff bought two small ships from the defendants relying upon particulars furnished by the defendants that the dead weight capacity of each ship was 460 tons. The capacity was in fact only 360 tons.

The plaintiff sought to reject the ships. It was held that the representation of capacity was not a condition but a warranty, for which the plaintiff could have sued in damages had liability for warranties not been excluded.

Similarly in *Meyer v. Klvisto,*[24] there was sale of timber properly seasoned for shipment, the requirement as to seasoning was held to be a warranty and not a condition.

Distinction between a Condition and Warranty

1. Difference as to Value

A condition is a stipulation which is essential to the main purpose of the contract. A warranty is a stipulation which is collateral to the main purpose of the contract.

2. Difference as to breach

If there is a breach of a condition the aggrieved party can repudiate the contract of sale, but in case of breach of a warranty the aggrieved party can claim damage only.

3. Difference as to treatment

A breach of a condition may be treated as a breach of warranty. This would happen where the aggrieved party is contented with damages only. A breach of a warranty how ever cannot be treated as a breach of a condition.

When Condition to be treated as warranty (Sec 13)

In following circumstances, a breach of condition is to be treated as a breach of warranty.

1. Voluntary Waiver of Condition

Where a contract of sale is subject to any condition to be fulfilled by the seller, the buyer may (a) waive the condition or (b) elect to treat the breach of the condition as a breach of warranty (Section 13(1)). If the buyer once decides to waive the condition he cannot afterwards insist on its fulfillment.

2. Acceptance of goods by buyer

If the contract of sale is not severable and the buyer has accepted the goods or part there of, the breach of any condition to be fulfilled by the seller can only be treated as a breach of warranty, unless there is a term of the contract express or implied to the contrary (Section 13 (2)).

The provisions of section 13 do not affect the cases where the fulfilment of any condition or warranty is excused by law reason or impossibility or otherwise (Section 13 (3)).

Express and Implied Conditions and Warranties

In a contract of sale of goods, conditions and warranties may be express or implied. Express Conditions and Warranties are those which are expressly provided in the contract. Implied conditions and warranties are those which are not being expressly provided for. The law implies them in any particular contract on operation of its own rules.

Section 16(4) further provided that an express warranty or condition does not negative an implied warranty or condition unless the express warranty or condition inconsistent with the implied warranty or condition. Implied conditions and warranties are stated in sections 14 to 17.

Implied Conditions: The following are two implied conditions.

1. Condition as to title

Section 14(a) provides that in a contract of sale unless the circumstances of the contract are such as to show a different intention there is an implied condition on the part of the seller that—

(a) in the case if a sale he has a right to sell the goods and

(b) in the case of an agreement to sell, he will have a right to sell the goods at the time when the property is to pass.

In *Rowland v. Divall,*[25] R purchased a car from D who had no title to it. R used it for four months and after that, the true owner spotted the car and demanded it from R. Held R was bound to hand over the car to its true owner and that R could successfully Sue D. The seller without title for the recovery of the purchase price even though several months had passed.

If the goods delivered can only be sold by infringing a trade mark, the seller has broken the condition that he has a right to sell the goods. The expression "right to sell" is wider than "the right to property".

In *Niblett v. Confectioners materials Co. Ltd,*[26] plaintiff brought 3000 tins of condensed milk from the U.S.A. The tins were labelled in such a way as to infringe the Nestle trade mark. As a result they were detained by customs authorities. To get the Clearance Certificate from the Customs authorities, he had to remove the labels and sell the tins at a loss. Held the seller had broken the condition that he had a right to sell.

Where a seller having no title to the goods at the time of the sale, subsiquently acquires a title that title feeds the defecture titles of both the original buyer and the subsequent buyer (*Butterworth v. Kingsway Botors*[27]).

However, this condition may be neglected by an express term, as in sales by custom authorities or by courts.

2. Sale by description (Section 15)

Where there is a contract for the sale of goods by description there is an implied condition that the goods shall correspond with the description. The rule of law contained in section 15 is summarised in the following maxim:

"If you contract to sell peas, you cannot oblige a party to take beans. If the description of the articles tendered is different in any respect, it is not the article bargained for and the other party is not bound to take it". (*Bower v. Shand*).[28]

If the sale is by sample as well as description the goods must not only correspond with the sample but also with the description.

Example: (1) A ship was sold by description, viz., "Copper-fastened vessel" but actually it was only partly copper-fastened. Held, that the goods did not correspond to description and hence could be returned or else, if the buyer took the goods, he could claim damages for breach. This was so even though the ship was sold subject to all faults and defects (*Shepherd v. Kain*).[29]

(2) A car is sold as a "new singer car". The buyer finds it to be used one. The buyer may reject the car or retain the car and claim damages (*Andrews Ltd. v. Singer and Co. Ltd.*).[30]

Sale of goods by description may include the following situations.

(a) Where the buyer has not seen the goods and relies on their description given by the seller

The expression "sale by description", says CHANNEL J, "must apply to all cases" where the purchaser has not seen the goods, but is relying on the description alone. A leading illustration is *Varley v. Whipp.*[31]

The buyer bought a reaping machine which he had never seen and which the seller stated "to have been new the previous year and used to cut only 50 or 60 acres". On delivery, the buyer found the machine to be extremely old and returned it. Held, buyer could return the machine as it did not correspond with the description.

(b) Where the buyer has seen the goods but he relies not on what he has seen but what was stated to him and the deviation of the goods from the description is not apparent.

This happened in *Nicholson and Venn v. Smith Marriott,*[32] where in an auction sale of a set of napkins and table cloths these were described as "dating from the seventeenth century." The buyer bought the set after seeing it. Subsequently, he found the set to be an eighteenth century set. Held, he could reject the set. The discrepancy between the description and the quality could not have been discovered by the causal examination.

In *Beale v. Taylor,*[33] a car was advertised for sale as a "Herald Convertible white 1961 model." The buyer saw the car before buying it. After buyer the car, he discovered that while the rear part of the car was part of a 1961 model, the front half was part of an earlier model. Held, the buyer could return the car.

(c) Packing of goods may sometimes be a part of the description

In *Moore and Co. v. Landauer and Co.*[34] there was a contract for purchase of 3,000 tins of Australian fruits packed in cases containing 30 tins. The seller tendered a substantial portion in cases containing 24 tins. Held, the purchasers were entitled to reject the whole consignment as the goods were not packed according to the description given in the contract as the method in which the fruit was packed was an essential part of the description.

Sale by Description as well as by Sample (Section 15)

In a sale by description, there is an implied condition that the goods shall correspond with the description. Section 15 further provides that if the sale is by sample as well by description, the goods must not only correspond with the sample but also with description. If the goods supplied correspond only with the sample and not with the description or *vice-versa*, the buyer is entitled to reject the goods. The bulk of the goods must correspond with both.

Examples: In Nichol v. Godts[35]

"Foreign refined rape oil" was sold warranted to be equal to sample. The sample was actually not" foreign rape oil "but a mixture of "hemp oil". Held, the buyer could reject the oil though the bulk corresponded with the sample.

In *Wallis v. Pratt*[36] the agreement was for the sale of English saintoin seeds, exhibited by a sample. The bulk did corresponded to the sample but, the seeds supplied were giant saintoin and not the English sainfoin. Held, there was a breach of condition and the buyer was entitled to recover damages.

3. Condition as to quality or fitness (Section 16)

Normally in a contract of sale there is no implied condition as to quality or fitness of the goods for a particular purpose. The buyer must examine the goods thoroughly before he buys them in order to satisfy himself that the goods will be suitable for the purpose for which he is buying them. Thus, if the goods purchased turn out to be unsuitable for the purpose for which he bought them, the seller cannot be asked to compensate.

Exceptions

There are, however certain exceptions, to this general rule. It is only in these exceptional circumstances that there is an implied condition as to quality or fitness. Section 16 provides for following exceptions:

(i) Fitness for Buyer's purpose [Section 16 (1)]

Sub Section (1) requires the seller in certain circumstances to supply goods which shall be fit for the buyer's purpose. It runs thus:

(a) Where the buyer, expressly or by implication, makes known to the seller the particular purpose for which goods are required, so as to show that the buyer relies on the seller's skill or judgement and the goods are of a description which it is in the course of the seller's business to supply (Whether he is the manufacturer or producer or not), there is an implied condition that the goods shall be reasonably fit for such purpose.

For this kind of exception to operate, the following three conditions must be fulfilled, (a) the purpose must have been expressly or impliedly disclosed, (b) the buyer must have relied on the seller's skill or judgment, and (c) the seller's business must be to sell such goods.

Examples:

(i) A person who was a draper and had no special knowledge of hot water bottles, purchased a hot water bottle from a chemist. The bottle burst and injured his wife. Held, breach of condition as to fitness was committed and thus chemist was liable for refund of price plus damages (*Priest v. Last*)[37]

(ii) A sold a refrigerator to B. The refrigerator performed all other functions but failed to make ice. Held, it amounted to a breach of an implied condition (Evens v. Stella Benjamin)[38].

(iii) In case of food articles, there is an implied condition that the article is fit for human consumption. Thus in *Frost v. Aylesbury Dairy Co. Ltd.*,[39] A supplied F with milk. The milk contained typhoid germs. F's wife who consumed milk was infected and died. Held, there was a breach of condition as to fitness and A was liable to pay damages.

The above exception does not apply where the specific goods are sold under their patent or trade name.

Example:

A buyer ordered a Patent smoke consuming furnace by its patent name for his brewery. The furnace supplied was found to be unsuitable for the purpose. Held, the buyer had no cause of action against the seller (*Chanter v. Mopkins*).[40]

The mere mention of the name of product, or patent does not exclude the condition, for even then the buyer may rely on the seller's skill and judgement. In *Baldry v. Marshall*,[41] buyer told to motor car dealer, that he wanted a comfortable car suitable for touring purpose. Dealer recommended a "Bugatte" car, a trade name, and buyer there upon bought one. The car was uncomfortable and unsuitable for touring purpose. Held, buyer could reject the car and recover the price and the mere fact that he bought the car under its trade name, which was part of the description of the car did not necessarily exclude the condition of fitness.

(b) Where buyer purchases goods for particular use and goods is suffering from an abnormality and it is not made known to the seller at the time of sale, implied condition of fitness does not apply.

Thus in case Griffiths v. Peter Company Ltd.,[42] A woman purchased a tweed coat which caused her dermatitis due to her unusually sensitive skin. Held the seller was not liable being the cloth fit for any one with normal skin.

(c) Where the goods can be used for a number of purposes the buyer must till the seller the particular purpose for which he requires the goods. If he does not show particular purpose, can not hold the seller liable if the goods do not suit the particular purpose for which he buys the goods.

A woolen merchant who was also a tailor bought by a sample indigo cloth for the purpose of making liveries. This fact was not brought to the notice of the seller. Held the seller was not liable when on account of latent defect in the cloth the cloth was unfit for making liveries but was fit for other usual purposes. (Jones v. Padgett).[43]

2. Condition as to Merchantable quality

The other leading condition exception created by section 16 is that a dealer who sells goods by description is bound to deliver goods of merchantable quality. Sub section (2) says:

Where the goods are brought from a seller who deals in goods of that description (Whether he is a manufacturer or producer or not) there is an implied condition that the goods shall be of merchantable quality.

This means goods should be such as are commercially saleable under the description by which they are known in the market at their full value. If goods are of such a quality and in such a condition that reasonable person acting reasonably would accept them after having examined them thoroughly, they are of merchantable quality (*Bristal Tramways Co. v. Flat motors Ltd.*).[44] Thus a watch that will not keep time, a pen that will not write, and tobacco that will not smoke, cannot be regarded as merchantable under such names.

The expression "merchantable quality" has now received in England its statutory definition. Section 7(2) of the supply of goods (Implied Terms) Act 1973, provides that merchantable quality means that the goods shall be as fit for the purpose or purposes for which goods of that kind are commonly bought as it is reasonable to expect having regard to any description applied to them, the price (if relevant) and all other relevant circumstances.

In *Gardner v. Gray,*[45] it is said that the article "must be saleable in the market under the denomination mentioned." In other words, the quality of the article should be such that reasonable men would accept the article as performance of a promise.

Examples:

(i) In *Jones v. Just,*[46] there was a contract of sale of Manila hemp. The hemp that was supplied, though Manila hemp, was so damaged by sea water that no one in the market would accept it as Manila hemp. Held, the goods were not of merchantable quality.

(ii) Where a part of the goods are defective, the buyer may reject the whole lot even if he had accepted some deliveries before finding out the defect. Thus in *Jackson v. Rotax Motor and Cycle Co.,*[47] a manufacturer supplied 600 horns under a contract. The buyer accepted a few and rejected the rest as being dented, badly polished and otherwise of faulty manufacture. The seller's suit for the price was dismissed as they were not of merchantable quality. KENNEDY J. said:

"There was here a substantial failure on the part of the seller to deliver goods of a merchantable quality .... and the buyers were entitled to treat this as one contract and to reject the goods. They were entitled to treat this as one contract and to reject the goods. They were not bound to go picking and choosing. The seller cannot say "pick out the various portions which are good and pay for those."

(iii) In *Jackson v. Watson and Sons,*[48] there was a sale by a grocer of tinned salmon which was poisonous. It resulted in the death of the wife of the buyer. Held, the buyer could recover damages including a sum to compensate him for being compelled to hire some one to perform the services which were rendered by his wife.

(iv) In *Godley v. Porry,*[49] seller sold a plastic catapult to a boy of six year. The catapult broke while it was using due to defective material used in its manufacture, and the boy was blinded in one eye. Held, seller was liable as the catapult was not of merchantable quality.

The proviso to section 16 (2) says that

Where the buyer examines the goods prior to sale, there is no implied condition as to merchantability as regards defects which such examination ought to have revealed. Thus, an leading illustration of this proviso is in the case of *Thornett and Fehr vs. Beers and Sons.*[50]

A buyer contracted to buy a quantity of glue. The goods were contained in casks which were lying on the seller's godown. The seller took the buyer to the godown and offered to show him the glue. But, being pressed for time, the buyer did not ask that any of the casks should be opened. He contended himself with looking at the casks. The glue turned to be defective and not of merchantable quality.

The buyer contended that he had not actually examined the goods and, therefore, the proviso was not attracted. But the court held that the requirement of the proviso is satisfied when the seller gives the buyer full opportunity or not should make no difference.

The proviso applies only to patent defects, which means a defect which is obvious to the eye an is apparently noticeable. In sale of motor car the defects of the engine are latent as to them the proviso will not apply.[51]

3. Conditions implied by Trade usage (Section 16(3))

Section 16(3) provides statutory force to conditions implied by the usage of a particular trade. It says:

"An implied warranty or condition as to quality or fitness for a particular purpose may be annexed by the usage of trade."

In some case, the purpose for which the goods are required may be ascertained from the acts and conduct of the parties to the sale, or from the nature of description of the article purchased for instance, if a perambulator or a bottle of milk is purchased, the purpose for which it is purchased is implied in the thing itself. In such a case the buyer need not tell seller the purpose for which he buys the goods.

In *Priest v. Last*[52] Priest purchased hot water bottle from Last, a retail chemist. He was supplied one which burst after a few days use and injured priests wife. Held, retail chemist was liable for breach of implied condition because priest had sufficiently made known the use for which he required the bottle.

A bought a set of false teeth from a dentist. The set did not fit into A's mouth. Held, he could reject the set as the purpose for which anybody would by it was implicity known to the seller, i.e., the dentist (Dr. *Baretto v. TR Price*).[53]

An unreasonable custom will not, however, affect the parties contract. "If the custom went to the length of saying that there should be no remedy for any variation in the quality contracted for, it would course be unreasonable, for it would absolutely alter the nature of contract."[54] The custom should not be inconsistent with the express terms of the contract.[55]

4. Express Terms (Section 16(4))

Parties are free to include any express conditions and or warranties in their contract. But an express warranty or condition does not negative a warranty or condition implied by the Act unless the express terms are inconsistent with the implied conditions.

Thus, for example, where sleepers supplied to a railway company were required to be approved by its experts, it was held that did not exclude the implied condition of merchantableness[56].

Sale by sample (Section 17))

Section 17(1) defines sale by sample. It says that "a contract of a sale is a contract for sale by sample where there is a term in the contract, express or implied, to that effect". Thus, it cannot be assumed that in all cases, where sample is shown, the sale is a sale by sample. In cases where there is no term to the effect, it is assumed that the sample is not shown as a warranty, but only to enable the buyer to form a reasonable judgment of the commodity.

In a sale by sample, the law implies three following conditions.

(i) That the bulk shall correspond with the sample in quality.

(ii) That the buyer shall have a reasonable opportunity of comparing the bulk with the sample.

(iii) That the goods shall be free from any defect rendering them unmerchantable which would not be apparent on reasonable examination of the sample.

The first condition implies that the bulk of the goods delivered must be same with the sample in quality.

In *Gardiner Gray*[57] twelve bags of waste silk were sold to the plaintiff after his agent had inspected a sample. The buyer wanted to reject on the ground that the bulk did not correspond with the sample. Lord ELLEBROROUGH said:

"This was not a sale by sample. The sample was not produce as a warranty that the bulk corresponded with it, but to enable the purchaser to form a reasonable judgment about the commodity."

In *Leonard v. Fowler,*[58] there was a sale of a large quantity of beans contained in a number of packages. The seller exhibited an average sample which he obtained by taking a small quantity from each package and mixing them together. It was held that no single package could be rejected for failing to match the sample in quality, the test was whether the bulk as a whole achieved that standard.

The second implied condition is that the buyer shall have a reasonable opportunity of comparing the bulk of the goods with the sample.

The third condition requires the goods must be free from any defect, which renders them unmerchantable and which is not apparent on reasonable examination. It means that this implied condition applies only to latent defects, i.e., defects which are not discoverable on a reasonable examination of the sample. The seller is not responsible for the defects which are patent, i.e., visible or discoverable by examination of the goods. In such a case there is no breach of implied condition as to merchantability. A leading illustration is the case *Drummond and Sons v. Van Ingen.*[59] There was sale by sample of mixed worsted coatings to be in quality and weight equal to the samples. It was found that the goods owing to latent defect would not stand ordinary wear when made up into coats. The same defect was there in the sample but could not be detected on a reasonable examination of the sample.

The House of Lords held that the defect was a latent one and, therefore, the goods were unreasonable. Lord MACNAGHTEN explained the meanings and effect of a sample in the following words:

"Correspondence of the goods with the sample does not relieve the seller from his obligation to supply goods fit for the purpose for which they were intended. After all the office of a sample is to present to the eye the real meanings and intention of the parties with regard to the subject matter of the contract which owing to the imperfection of language it may be difficult or impossible to express in words. The sample speaks for itself."

Miscellaneous or Innominate Terms

Through the Act has classified mostly all the terms of a contract into the categories of warranties and conditions, even so there may be terms in a contract which will answer neither category.

In *Cahavenv v. Bremer Handelsge Sellschat*[60] case, there was a contract for shipping "in good condition" some tons of citrus pellets. A part of the cargo was damaged by over-heating and the buyer rejected the consignment on the ground that it had not been shipped "in good condition". Lord DENNING MR said:

In my opinion, therefore, the term shipped "in good condition" was not a condition strictly so called, nor was it a warranty strictly so called, nor was it a warranty strictly so called. It was one of those intermediate stipulations which gives no right to reject unless the breach goes to the roof of the contract.

The breach being not of that category, the buyer was advised to be content with damages.

IMPLIED WARRANTIES

In a contract of sale of goods, the following warranties are implied by law.

1. Warranty of quiet possession (section 14 (b)

In a contract of sale of goods unless there is a contrary intention, there is an implied warranty that the buyer shall have and enjoy quiet possession of the goods. If the buyer is in any way disturbed in the enjoyment of the goods by the seller or any other person, the buyer is entitled to sue the seller for damages. Thus in *Rowland v. Divall,*[61] juice the plaintiff purchased a motor car from the defendants. The car turned out to be stolen property and the plaintiff had to restore it to the true owner.

The plaintiff was held entitled to recover the whole of the price paid by him despite the fact that he had used the car for some months.

2. Warranty of Freedom From Encumbrances {Section 14(c)}

In addition to the above warranty, the buyer is entitled to a further warranty that the goods are not subject to any charge or right in favour of a third party. If his possession is in any way disturbed by reason of the existence of any charge or encumbrance on the goods in favour of any third party, he shall have a right to claim damages for breach of this warranty. Thus this warranty will not be applicable where the buyer has been informed of the encumbrances or has notice of the same. It was held in Collinge v. Heywood,[62] that the claim under this warranty shall be available only when the buyer discharges the amount of encumbrance.

Doctrine of Caveat Emptor

Caveat Emptor is a fundamental principle of the law of sale of goods. It means "Caution Buyer" i.e., "Let the buyer beware". In other words, in sale of goods the seller is under no duty to point out defects of his own goods. The buyer must inspect the goods to find out its usefulness and defects. If the goods turnout to be defective or do not suit his purpose, or if he depends upon his own skill and judgement and makes a bad selection, he cannot blame anybody excepting himself.

The doctrine of Caveat Emptor is enunciated in the opening words of section 16 which runs thus; "Subject to the provisions of this Act and of any other law for the time being in force, there is no implied warranty or condition as to the quality of fitness for any particular purpose of goods supplied under a contract of sale ...."

One illustration of the application of this principle in *Ward v. Hopps*[63]. Some pigs were sold by auction without any warranty in respect of any fault, error or description. These pigs, beings infected, caused typhoid to other healthy pigs of the buyer. The House of Lords held that the seller was not bound to disclose that the pigs were unhealthy. The rule of law being 'Caveat Emptor': Lord O' HOGAN said:

Although a vendor is bound to employ no artifice or disguise for the purpose of concealing defects in the article sold, since that would amount to a positive fraud on the vendee, yet under the general doctrine of caveat emptor, he is nor ordinarily bound to disclose every defect of which he may be cognizant, although his silence may operate virtually to deceive the vendee.

Exceptions: The doctrine of Caveat Emptor has certain important exceptions. The case law on these has already been discussed. Section 16 provides the following exceptions which are however briefly referred to.

1. Fitness for buyer's purpose {Sec 16 (1)}

Where the buyer expressly or by implication, makes known to the seller the particular purpose for which he requires the goods and relies on the seller's skill or judgement and the goods are of a description which it is in the course of the seller's business to supply, the seller must supply the goods which shall be fit for the buyer's purpose.

2. Sale under a patent or trade name {Proviso to sec 16(1)}

In the case of contract for the sale of a specified articles under its patent or other trade name, there is no implied condition that the goods shall be reasonably fit for any particular purpose.

3. Merchantable Quality {Section 16(2)}

Where goods are bought by description from a seller who deals in goods of that description (where he is the manufacturer or producer or not) there is an implied condition that the goods shall be of merchantable quality. But if the buyer has examined the goods there is no implied condition as regards defects which such examination ought to have revealed.

4. Usage of trade {Section 16(3)}

An implied warranty or condition as to quality or fitness for a particular purpose may be annexed by the usage of trade.

5. Consent by fraud

Where the consent of the buyer in a contract of sale, is obtained by the seller by fraud or where the seller knowingly conceals a defect which could not be discovered on a reasonable examination (i.e., where there is a latent defect in the goods), the doctrine of Caveat Emptor does not apply.

Exclusion of Implied Terms (section 62)

Section 62 enables the parties to a sale to exclude liability for implied terms. Section 62 says:

Where any right, duty or liability would arise under a contract of sale by implication of law, it may be negatived or varried by express agreement or by the course of dealing between the parties, or by usage, if the usage is such as to bind both parties to the contract.

The section recognises three modes by which liability for implied terms may be negatived —

(1) by express contract,
(2) by course of dealing, and
(3) by usage.

1. By Express Contract

Courts have strictly construed seller liability for breach of implied terms unless the liability is excluded by very appropriate terms. If liability is not excluded by very appropriate terms the seller is held responsible. Thus a case *Baldry v. Marshall*[64], where in a sale of car "fit for touring purposes", the seller excluded liability for all guarantees and warranties, the court held him liable as the unfitness of the car supplied for touring purpose was not a breach of a guarantee or a warranty but of a condition.

2. Course of Dealing

The implied terms of a contract of sale can also be negatived by a course of dealing between the parties. There should be a clear proof of the existence of a course of dealing. "........[A] course of dealing may arise with equal force from a written or oral Bargain, or from the repeated occurrence of similar methods as between the parties. In each case the question is as to the implication to be drawn from the pait as applied to a new transaction."[65]

But a single transaction is not sufficient to establish a course of dealing. Thus the fact that on one occasion a party paid against delivery Telegrams was held not sufficient to exclude the implied incidents of a c.i.f. contract by which the buyer has to pay only against shipping documents[66].

3. Trade Usage

Implied terms may be excluded by trade usage. Thus, on a sale of meat by a butcher which was seized and condemned as unfit for human consumption, the seller was allowed to give evidence of the fact that by the usage of the market no warranty of fitness for food was implied[67]. The buyer was however, allowed to recover damages in respect of the fine and costs and for his loss of trade.

Passing of Property (Sections 18 to 26)

Passing of Property

Passing of property means passing of ownership. 'Property in goods' implies ownership of goods. 'Property in goods' is not the same thing as possession of goods'. The possession of goods refers to the custody of goods. Property in the goods is said to pass to the buyer when he acquires proprietary rights over them. Through normally a person who is in possession shall also be its owner but it need not be necessarily so. There may be situations where a person is the owner of certain goods but is not possession of the same or *vice-versa.*

When does the property in the goods pass from the seller to the buyer is one of the most important question in a contract of sale of goods. It is important to find out the exact point of time of passing of ownership from the seller to the buyer.

Property passes when intended to pass (Section 19)

Property passes when intended to pass —

(1) Where there is a contract for the sale of specific or ascertained goods the property at such time as the parties to the contract intend it to be transferred.
(2) For the purpose of ascertaining the intention of the parties regard shall be had to the terms of the contract, the conduct of the parties and the circumstances of the case.
(3) Unless a different intention appears, the rules contained in section 20 to 24 are rules for ascertaining the intention of the parties as to the time at which the property in the goods is to pass to the buyer.

The heading of section 19 is "Property passes when intended to pass." Thus passing of property, though one of the natural result of a sale, is not the inevitable result. In *McEntire v. Crossley Ltd*[68] case Lord WATSON said:

It does not in the least follow that, because there is an agreement of sale and purchase, the property in the thing which is the subject-matter of the contract has passed to the purchaser. That is a question which entirely depends upon the intention of the parties. The law permits them to settle the point for themselves by an expression of their intention upon the point.

Thus the intention of the parties reigns supreme in this area. An illustration is the case of *Sacks v. Tilley.*[69]

Certain diamonds were sent to the buyers by post by a foreign firm. A bill for the price was sent along with them and it was condition of the contract that property would pass on the bill being accepted. The invoice was marked "settled by acceptance". The bill was never accepted.

In such cases, property passes when the documents are forwarded, but that rule was held to have been ousted by the express declaration of the parties intention, that acceptance was necessary for the property to pass.

It is obviously necessary that such intention must be embodied in the contract itself, for when once the rules apply, a subsequent attempt to modify them will be of no avail.

Rules Regarding Transfer of Property

Where the intention of the parties is not apparent from their contract, their intention will be ascertained in accordance with the rules laid down in section 18 and 20 to 24. These sections deal with three kinds of situations.

(1) Sale of specific or ascertained goods,
(2) Sale of goods on approval, and
(3) Sale of unascertained goods.

Sale of specific or Ascertained Goods (Section 20 to 22)

In reference to sale of specific or ascertained goods the property in them in transferred to the buyer as soon as the contract is made. Section 20 laid down the basic conditions of such sales. Section 20 says:

Where there is an unconditional contract for the sale of specific goods in a deliverable state, the property in goods passes to the buyer when the contract is made, and it is immaterial whether the time of payment of the price or the time of delivery of the goods or both is postponed.

Thus basic conditions of such sales are (i) the sale must be that of specific goods (ii) the goods must be in a deliverable state and (iii) the contract must be unconditional.

Specific Goods

'Specific goods' means goods identified and agreed upon at the time a contract of sale made. (Sector 2 (14)). It means the identity of the goods has already been established at the time of the sale and their individuality must be there. In *Shanker Das v. Bhanna Ram*[70] case, file buses were sold, the price to be paid by instalments and the ownerships and route permits to be transferred within a week after the last instalments. It was held that this was a sale of specific goods and the property passed when the contract was made.

1. Deliverable State

The goods should be in a deliverable state. Section 2(3) states "Goods are said to be in a deliverable state when they are in such state that the buyer would under the contract be bound to take delivery of them."

Thus in the case of specific goods, in a deliverable state, property in them passes at the time when the contract (unconditional) is made. The fact that the time of payment or the delivery of goods, or both, is postponed does not affect the passing of the property.

In the case of specific goods to which something has to be done by the seller to put them in a deliverable state, property passes only when such this is done, and the buyer has notice there of (Section 21). Thus if the seller has to paint the car to make it acceptable to the buyer, it is not in a deliverable state until it is so painted. This becomes apparent from the case of *Underwood Ltd. v. Burgh Caste Bricl and Cement Syndicate.*[71]

Where, a Conden Sing engine fixed at a particular place agreed to be sold F.O.R. (Free on Rail) for a fixed and the engine was damaged while being taken to the Railway.

Held, the property had not passed to the buyer, as the seller was required, under the contract, to place it on rail before it could be said to be in a deliverable state.

Further in *Rugg v. Minett*,[72] there was a sale of the whole of turpentine oil lying in a cistern. The oil had to be filled by the seller in casks which was partly done in the buyer's presence, but before he could remove the casks the whole oil was consumed by fire. The buyer had to bear the loss for the casks which had been filled up because everything had been done by the seller which lay upon them to perform in order to put the goods in deliverable state.

Where the goods are already in that state, the mere fact that the seller has to perform some collateral act, does not prevent the property from vesting in the buyer.

Where there is a contract for the sale of specific goods in a deliverable state but the seller is bound to weigh, measure, test or do some other things with reference to them, for ascertaining the price, the property does not pass till such act or thing is done and the buyer has notice of it (Section 22).

A leading illustration is on this point is *Zaguny v. Furnell,*[73] where a stock of bark was sold at an agreed price per ton. The bark was to be weighed by the agents of the seller as also of the buyer for ascertainment of the price. A part of the bark was weighed and carried away by the buyer's agent and servant, but the remaining was swept away by the flood. It is held that the loss of the remainder should be borne by the seller, since the property in the remainder had not passed because the required weight was not done.

However, it should be noted that the section applies only where, by contract, the seller has to do something mentioned therin. Thus, if the weighing etc has to be done by the buyer for his own satisfaction, the section does not apply (*Turley v Bates*[74]).

2. Sale of Goods on Approval

Where goods are delivered to the buyer 'on approval' or 'on sale or return' or similar terms, the property passes to buyer. Section 24 lays down the rules in such cases:

(a) When he signifies his approval or acceptance to the seller or does any other act adopting the transaction,

(b) If he does not signify his approval or acceptance to the seller but retains the goods without giving notice of rejection, then, if a time has been fixed for the return of the goods, on the expiration of such time, and, if no time has been fixed for the return of the goods, on the expiration ofsuch time, and if no time has fixed, on the expiration of a reasonable time.

Thus, the rule is that the property passes either by acceptance or by failure to return within reasonable time.

(1) By Acceptance [Sec 24(1)]

The property passes when the buyer signifies his acceptance or approval or otherwise adopts the transaction. The acceptance may be express or implied from conduct. An implied adoption takes place when the buyer deprives himself of the power to return the goods. The leading illustration is the case of *KirKhan v. Allenborough.*[75]

Some jewellery were delivered by a manufacturing jeweller to one Winter "on sale or return". Winter pledged the jewellery with the defendant, Allenborough, a Pawn-broker. Winter failed to pay the price. The plaintiff then commenced an action against the pawn-broker to recover the goods. But it was held that the plaintiff should have sued Winter for the price and not the defendant, who had acquired a good title because Winter, by pledging the goods, had adopted the transaction and the property then passed to him.

Lord ESHER MR, explaining the meaning and consequences of sale on approval, said:

The contract by which goods are delivered 'on sale or return' means this: the purchaser may return the goods within a reasonable time, and the option to return belongs solely to the purchaser, the other party cannot even ask for the return of the goods and his only right is to sue for the price if the goods are not returned.

His lordship then quoted the section and continued.

Acceptance means acceptance of that part of the contract which makes him the purchaser absolutely ...... That will be some act which signifies that he intends to be the absolute purchaser. If he does some act which would be right only if he were the absolute purchaser that signifies an acceptance or adoption within the statuto........... (H)e pawned the goods. He had not then the power of returning the goods, unless he repaid the amount advanced by the pawnee. That is inconsistent within free power of returning the goods.

In *Genor v Winkel,*[76] this principle has been followed.

In this case, the plaintiff delivered diamond to the defendant on 'sale or return'. The defendant delivered them to a third party to a fourth on the same terms. The last party lost them, meanwhile the plaintiff remained unpaid.

It was held that by depriving himself or the power to return the goods, the defendant had adopted the transaction and consequently was liable for the plaintiff's loss.

(II) By Failure to Return [Section 24(2)]

The second circumstances in which the property passes to the buyer is when the latter fails to return the goods within reasonable time or if a time has been fixed on the expiration of that time. Till the expiry of such time the goods remain the property of the seller. A leading illustration is case of *Elphiek v. Barness.*[77]

A horse was delivered to the defendant on terms that he should try it for eight days and then return it if he did not like it. The horse died on the third day without the fault of the defendant.

The seller could not recover the price from the defendant, the horse, being still his property when it perished.

On failure to return within the specified time, the property passes to the buyer and the seller may then sue for the price. Where no time is fixed, the goods should be returned within reasonable time. What is reasonable time is a question of fact in each case. *Poole v. Smith's car sales (Balham) Ltd*[78] is an authority in point.

In August, the plaintiff delivered a second hand Vauhall car to Smith's car sales on "sale or return". No time was, however, fixed for its return. It was not returned till October. Then the plaintiff wrote to them that if it was not returned by November 10, it would be deemed to have been sold to them. Even so it was not returned till November end and that too in a very bad condition, the car having been damaged by the defendants employees.

ORMEROD LJ rejected the defendant's contention that reasonable time for the return of the car had not expired. Drawing upon the knowledge which came to him in the ordinary course of life and through sittings in the courts, he found that there was a market for second-hand cars in holidays which end with September and not to have returned the car before that was its retention beyond reasonable time.

Difference between "Sale or return" and "Sale for cash only or return"

In "Sale for cash only or return", the property does not pass to the buyer until paid for. In such a case, if the buyer creates a pledge, it will be invalid and the seller will have a right to recover the goods from the pledge.

3. Sale of Unascertained Goods(Sec 18 and 23)

There are two sections — 18 and 23 relating to the provisions of passing of property on sale of unascertained goods.

Sec 18, Goods must be ascertained — where there is a contract for the sale of unascertained goods, no property in the goods is transferred to the buyer unless and untill the goods are ascertained.

Example:

A agree to sell B 400 quintals of Rice out of a larger quantity lying in X's store. The agreed price is to be paid on the day appointed under. The contract, unless and until the required quantity of 200 quintals is separated from the larger quantity and the goods have thus been ascertained, property cannot pass from the seller to the buyer.

Sec. 23 Sale of unascertained goods and appropriation.

(1) Where there is a contract for the sale of unascertained or future goods by description and goods of that description and in a deliverable state are unconditionally appropriated to the contract, either by the seller with the assent of the buyer or by the buyer with the assent of the seller, the property in the goods there upon passes to the buyer, such assent may be express or implied, and may be given either before or after the appropriation is made.

On analysis of the above provisions of section 23, it will be noted that, in such a case, for pass, the following conditions must be fulfilled:

(A) Goods of the contract description must be produced or obtained.

(B) They must be in a deliverable state, i.e., "the goods are in such state that the buyer would under the contract be bound to take delivery of them."

(C) They must be unconditionally appropriated to the contract. Thus, where the sellers did not separate the goods contracted for from the general stock with them or put them in any receptacle sent by the buyers, if was held that an inspection of the general stock by the buyer and approval of the quality of goods, fixation of price and agreement regarding payment of freight and tax charges between the parties, was not sufficient to pass the properly to buyer.

Thus, ascertainment of the goods is the first condition and their appropriation to the contract, the second, and there upon the property passes to the buyer.

"Ascertainment" is the process by which the identity of the goods to be delivered under the contract is established. But "a mere setting apart or selection by the seller of the goods which he expects to use in performance of the contract is not enough."[78] They must also be appropriated to the contract. The distinction between ascertainment and "appropriation" is that ascertainment can be a unilateral act, that is, the seller alone may set apart the goods. But "appropriation" involves "the element of common intention." "To constitute an appropriation of the goods to the contract, the parties must have had, or be reasonably supposed to have had, an intention to attach the contract irrevocably to those goods, so that those goods and no others are the subject of the sale and become the property of the buyer." One of the conditions adopted by the Coffee Board of India for auction sale of coffee is that the property would not pass to the bidder until full price was paid and the coffee sold was weighed and set apart for delivery to him. This act of setting apart is known as "ascertainment" and it would amount to appropriation if it has the assent of the buyer.[79] Selection of the goods with the exclusive intention of using them in performance of the contract and with the mutual consent of the parties is what constitutes "appropriation."

The unconditional appropriation may be made.

A. By the Buyer with the seller's Assent

Normally goods shall be appropriated by the seller. But, where goods are in possession of the buyer who is a warehouse-man for the seller in respect of 500 bags of sugar and agrees to buy 100 bags of them, the buyer, i.e., warehouse-man may, with the seller's assent select 100 out of 500 bags, and when he has done so, the goods (100 bags) become appropriated and the ownership in them passes to the buyer.

B. By the seller with the Buyer's assent

Where the seller appropriates the goods to the contract, the property shall pass to the buyer only when he (the buyer) has assented to the appropriation. The assent may, however, be given before or after appropriation.

For example, if the 500 bags of sugar were lying with the seller and he selected 100 bags out of the lot with the buyer's assent, the ownership of those 100 bags would pass to the buyer's as soon as this is done.

Notice that whether the appropriation is made by the seller or buyer, the assent of the other party must be sought. Thus, where the contract was for the sale of machines made by the seller, who packed the machines and before sending them asked the buyer to name the conveyance by which they should be sent. There was no reply from the buyer. It was held that there was no valid appropriation as the buyer had not assented (*Atkinson v. Bell*).[80]

Appropriation by the seller may be done

(i) by putting the quantity contracted for in suitable receptacles, for example, by putting the goods into boxes, or gunny bags, or putting the oil into bottles or other suitable receptacles, with the assent of the buyer.

(ii) by delivery to the carrier or other bailee for transmission to the buyer, without reserving the right of disposal. Thus, if goods are tendered by the seller to the buyer with a stipulation that delivery is only against payment in cash, no property shall pass till cash payment is made.

Whether or not the seller has retained the right or disposal over the goods even after delivering them to a common carrier, is a question of fact depending on all the surrounding circumstances. But when the railway receipt (R/R) or Bill of lading (B/L) is taken in the name of the buyer or his agent, it is presumed (though it can be rebutted) that the seller did not retain the right of disposal, and if it is made out in the seller or his agent's name, presumption is that the right of disposal is reserved by him.

Where the seller of goods draws on the buyer for the price and transmits the bill of exchange and bill of lading to the buyer together, to secure acceptance or payment of the bill of exchange, the buyer is bound to return the bill of lading if he does not honour the bill of exchange, and if he wrongfully retains the bill of lading the property in the goods does not pass to him [section 25(3)].

Transfer of Risk (sec. 26)

The provisions relating to transfer of risk are given in section 26.

Risk prima facie passes with property — Unless otherwise agreed, the goods remains at the seller's risk untill the property therein is transferred to the buyer, but when the property therein is transferred to the buyer, the goods are at the buyer's risk whether delivery has been made or not.

Thus 'risk' and 'property' go together, both are not inseparable. Sterns ltd. v. Vickers Ltd. [81] is illustrative to this.

There was a sale of 1,20,000 gallons of white spirit out of 2,00,000 gallons in a tank belonging to a third party. A delivery warrant was given to the buyer and it accepted by the owner of the tank. But the buyer did not take delivery of the spirit for some months for his own convenience. The spirit deteriorated. The loss fell upon the buyer, both because the property had passed by attornment, and even if it had not, because the buyer delayed taking delivery.

(1) Sometimes risk may be in one party and 'property' in another. In second paragraph section 26 says.

Provided that, where delivery has been delayed through the fault of either buyer or seller, the goods are at the risk of the party in fault as regards any loss which might not have occurred but for such fault.

A clear illustration is *Demby Hamilton and Co. Ltd. v. Barden (Endeavour wines) Ltd.*[82]

The defendant contracted to buy of the plaintiffs 30 tons of apple juice. Delivery was to the made in weekly truck loads. The plaintiffs crushed all the apples they had for the season and put the juice in casks to enable them to perform the contract. Deliveries would have been completed by February, 1946, but for the buyer's request that they should be held up. They took some deliveries subsequently and then stopped altogether. The juice was still waiting for their orders up to November when it deteriorated.

It was held that in the circumstances the loss fell upon the buyer.

(ii) 'Risk' and 'Property' may be separated by a trade custom. An illustration in this point is *Bevington v. Dale.*[83]

Certain furs were delivered to a buyer on approval. By a custom of the fur trade the goods were at the risk of the person ordering them on approval. They were stolen before the time of approval expired. The loss fell upon the buyer although the property had not yet passed to him.

(iii) "Risk" and "Property" may be separated by the agreement of the parties. Section 40 also provides that where the seller agrees to deliver the goods at his own at a distant place from where they are, the buyer has, unless otherwise agreed, to task any risk of deterioration incident to the transit.

(iv) Risk and property may be separated by a term of the contract.

Consolidated Coffee Ltd. v. Coffee Board[83]

In this case, one of the terms adopted by the coffee board for auction of coffee was that the property in coffee knocked down to a bidder would not pass until the payment of full price and, in the meantime, the goods would remains with the seller but at the risk and responsibility of the buyer. The clause was regarded as a valid and effective.

Transfer of Title

The general rule is that owner of goods can only transfer a good title. No one can give a better title than he has himself. This rule is expressed by the maxim "*Nemo dat quod non habet,*" which means "that no one can give what he himself has not". Section 27 of the Indian sale of Goods Act in this regard says:

Sale by person not the owner-subject to the provisions of this Act and of any other law for the time being in force, where goods are sold by a person who is not the owner thereof and who does not sell them under the authority or with the consent of the owner, the buyer acquires no better title to the goods than the seller had.

Examples

'A' finds a ring of 'B' and sells it to a third person who purchases it for value and in good faith. The true owner 'B' can recover from that person, for 'A' having no title could pass non the better (*Faruquaharson v. King*).[84]

Exceptions to the rule

There are several exceptions upon the above rule. These exceptions are mentioned in sections 27 to 30 and are as follows:

Estoppel (sec. 27)

The purchaser may get a good title if:

The owner of the goods is by his conduct precluded form denying the seller's authority to sell.

Thus where a person sold his father's goods in his presence and no objection was made by him against this sale then he was not subsequently permitted to deny his son's authority to sell and the sale was binding on him. Estoppel arises from a representation that the seller has the authority to sell. Representation may arise from words or declarations or it may arise from an act or omission. An omission to perform one's duty may create an estoppel. But the duty must be a legal obligation."

2. Sale by Mercantile Agent (sec. 27, Proviso)

A buyer of goods acquires good title from a mercantile agent, who is in possession of either the goods or documents of title to the goods with the consent of the owner and sells the goods in the ordinary course of business as a mercantile agent, if the buyer buys the goods in goods faith and for value.

The expression, "mercantile agent" is defined in section 2(9) as follows:

"Mercantile agent" means a mercantile agent having in the customary course of business as such agent authority either to sell goods, or to consign goods for the purpose of sale, or to by goods, or to raise money on the security of goods.

The definition was explained in *Lowther v. Harris.*[85]

The plaintiff engaged one prior, a shopkeeper, to act for him in the disposal of some tapestry. Prior obtained possession of the goods by fraud and sold them to a bonafide purchaser. Prior misappropriated the sale proceeds.

It was held that the purchaser acquired a good title.

The mercantile agent should be in possession of the goods as mercantile agent. If the goods are entrusted to him in any other capacity, he cannot convey a good title. This was so held in staffs *Motor Guarantee Ltd. v. British Wagon Ltd.*[86]

A dealer in second-hand cars sold his lorry to a company and then immediately took it back from the company under a hire purchase agreement. He then resold the lorry to another company, which claimed that it had good title to the lorry having bought it from a mercantile agent in good faith.

The court refused to sustain this claim. The lorry had been handed back to the dealer not as an agent but as a hirer and, therefore, as its bailee.

The goods should be in the possession of the mercantile agent "with the consent of the owner." A mercantile agent obtained possession of a car against a bogus cheque. Immediately on learning that the cheque was not met the principal instructed the agent to return the car but he, instead sold if off to a bona-fide buyer for value. The sale was held to be valid. He had obtained possession with consent though the consent itself was caused by fraud.

The mercantile agent sell the goods "when acting in the ordinary course of business of a mercantile agent." Thus where a broker, who was entrusted with certain diamonds for sale, pledged them through a friend, the transaction was held to be invalid. It was not the ordinary course of business of a mercantile agent to ask a friend to pledge goods entrusted to him, but to pledge them himself.

The buyer must act in good faith and should not have notice that the seller has no authority to sell. This was explained in *Oppenbeimer v. Fraze & Wyatt.*[87]

A firm purchased certain goods from a mercantile agent, who within knowledge of one of the partners, though not of the others, had obtained possession of the goods by larceny by a trick, it was held that the requirement of good faith was not satisfied and, therefore, the firm did not acquire a good title.

3. Sale by a joint owner (sec. 28)

Where one of several joint owner of goods has the sale possession thereof, with the consent of the others, any purchaser from such person, for value without notice at the time, of the seller's want of authority to sell, acquires a good title there to against the other joint-owners.

In case of sale by co-owner, good title can pass to the purchaser only if the co-owner was in possession with the consent of the other co-owners.

4. Sale by a person in possession under a voidable contract (sec. 29)

When a person has obtained possession of goods under a voidable contract on the grounds of fraud, misrepresentation, coercion, or under influence and makes a sale of them, the buyer gets a good title provided the contract has not been avoided at the time of the sale and the buyer acts in good faith and without notice of the seller's defect in the title.

An illustration in the case of Phillips v. Brooks.[88]

A fraudulent person posed himself to be a respectable person and obtained from a shopkeeper a valuable ring by giving a worthless cheque. Before the fraud could be discovered the rogue had pledged the ring with a bona fide pledgee. It was held that pledgee obtained a good title. The contract was voidable by person of the fraud and before it was rescinded the goods had gone to the hands of a third person.

5. Seller in Possession after sale [sec. 30(1)]

Section 30(1) says: where a seller having sold goods, continues in possession thereof or of documents of title to the goods, the delivery or transfer by such person or by a mercantile agent acting for such person, of the same, by way of sale, pledge or other disposition, will pass a good title to the transferee, if such latter person has acted in good faith and without previous sale. For the section to apply two following conditions must be satisfied.

(i) The seller must be in possession of the goods as seller and not in any other capacity. Thus, where the buyer asks the seller to keep the goods as his bailee, In staffs *Motor Gaurantee Ltd. v. British wagon Co. Ltd.*,[89] the owner of a lorry sold it to the defendants and took it back on hire purchase. He then resold it to the plaintiffs. The latter would not get a good title because the seller was not in possession "as seller" but as a bailee under a hire purchase agreement. The section will not apply.

(ii) The purchaser must be a bonafide purchaser and for value.

6. Sale by buyer in possession of goods [sec. 30(2)]

Where a person having bought or agreed to buy obtain, with the consent of the seller, possession of the goods or of the documents of title to the goods, the delivery or transfer by such person or by a mercantile agent acting for such person, of the goods or documents by way of sale, pledge or other disposition thereof will be valid and effective, if the person receiving the same acted bonafide and without notice of the seller's lien, if any.

The sale may have been made by actually transferring the goods or by transfer of documents of title. The second buyer should act in good faith and without notice of the seller's rights.

In *Marten v. Whale*,[90] the plaintiff agreed to buy a plot of land from one T in return for a car subject to the condition that his approved the title of land. Before anything was done in this connection, the plaintiff gave the possession of his car to T, who sold it to the defendant, the latter acting in good faith. It was held that the car in the possession of a person who had agreed to buy it and, therefore, the defendant acquired good title.

Possession obtained under a hire purchase agreement does not make the possession a buyer in possession so that a sale by him will not convey a good title to the buyer.

Performance of the Contract

Section 31 says that it is the duty of the seller to deliver the goods and of the buyer to accept and pay for them, in accordance with the terms of the contract of sale. Delivery of the goods and payment of the price are concurrent conditions. Seller cannot demand payment of price in advance unless there is a stipulation to that effect.

Delivery

Delivery is defined in the Act as 'a voluntary transfer of possession from one person to another' [sec. 2(2)]

The mode of delivery is stated in section 33 in following terms:

Delivery: Delivery of goods may be made by doing anything which the parties agree shall be treated or which has the effect of putting the goods in the possession of the buyer or of any person authorised to hold them on his behalf.

Therefore, it is clear that in addition to transfer of Physical possession, any other act which the parties agree to treat as equivalent there to has the effect of delivery.

Delivery of the goods may be:

(1) Physical or Actual Delivery — In this, the Physical possession of the goods is handed over by the seller to buyer.
(2) Symbolic delivery — Delivery is made by delivering some symbol that carries with the real possession or control over the goods, e.g. delivery of the key of a warehouse.
(3) Constructive Delivery or Attornment

In this kind of delivery, there is neither change of Physical possession of goods, nor delivery of a symbol, but there is only an acknowledgement by the person in possession that he holds there on behalf of another. Such type of delivery may be effected in three ways:

(A) Where the buyer, who is already in possession of goods as bailee of the seller, holds them as his own, after the sale,

(B) Where the seller, who is in possession of goods, holds them as bailee of the buyer after the sale, and

(C) Where a third person, like a carrier or a warehouse man, who holds the goods as bailee for the seller agrees and acknowledges to hold them for the buyer.

Part Delivery (sec. 34)

Effect of Part delivery — A delivery of part of goods, in progress of the delivery of the whole, has the same effect, for the purpose of passing the property in such goods, as a delivery of the whole, but a delivery of part of the goods, with an intention of serving it from the whole, does not operate as a delivery of the reminder.

The effect of the provision is that the delivery of a part of the goods amounts to a delivery of the whole for the purpose of passing the property provided that a part of the goods are delivered in progress of the delivery of the whole.

Thus, where a wharfinger was ordered to deliver the goods to the buyer and the buyer weighed and took away a part of them, that was held to be a delivery of the whole.[91] Where a part of the goods is delivered with the intention of serving it from the whole, that does amount to a delivery of the whole of the goods. Thus, where, on sale of a stack of hay, the buyer was permitted to cut and remove a part of the stack, that did not amount to delivery of the whole, as the permission related only to a part of the goods.[92]

Rules Regarding Delivery (sec. 36)

Rules as to delivery: whether it is for the buyer to take possession of the goods or for the seller to send them to the buyer is a question depending in each on the contract, express or implied, between the parties. Apart from any such contract, goods sold are to be delivered at the place at which they are at the time of the sale, and goods agreed to be sold are to be delivered at the place at which they are at the time of the agreement to sell, or if not then in existence, at the place at which they are manufactured or produced.

The section lays down the following rules regarding delivery.

1. Place of Delivery

Whether it is for the buyer to take possession of the goods or for the seller to send them is a question that depends on the intention of the parties as express in their contract. In the absence of any contract to the contrary, goods sold are to be delivered at the place at which they are at the time of sale. In the case of an agreement to sell, the goods are to be delivered at the place where they are at the time of the agreement, or if the goods are not then in existence, at the place where they are manufactured or produced.

2. Time of Delivery

Where under the contract of sale the seller is bound to send the goods to the buyer, but no time for sending them is fixed, the seller is bound to send them within a reasonable time. If the seller fails to do so he will be guilty of breach even of the delivery is subsequently prevented by the intervention of war or some government order.

3. Delivery by Attornment

Where the goods are in the possession of a third person, there is no delivery unless and until such third person acknowledges to the buyer that he holds the goods on his behalf. Once the third person does this, that amounts to delivery the buyer, and, therefore, the third person cannot afterwards refuse to deliver on the ground that the goods have to be paid for or that the buyer has become insolvent.

This rule is however, subject to the transfer of documents of title, because where, for example a bill of lading is transferred, the transferee is deemed to have got possession of the goods even when they are in the hands of a carrier who has not acknowledged to the buyer.

4. Time for Tender of Delivery

Goods sold must be demanded by the buyer at a reasonable hour and in the same way the seller should them at a reasonable hour. What is a reasonable hour is a question of fact.

5. Expenses of Delivery

Unless otherwise agreed, the expenses of and incidental of putting the goods into a deliverable state shall be borne by the seller.

Delivery of wrong Quantity (sec. 37)

Delivery of wrong quantity: where the seller delivers to the buyer a quantity of goods less than he contracted to sell, the buyer may reject them, but if the buyer accepts the goods so delivered he shall pay for them at the contract rate.

This section lays down the following rules as to the effects of delivery of wrong quantity.

1. Short Delivery

Where the seller delivers to the buyer a quantity of goods less then he contracted to sell, the buyer may reject them.

A buyer can reject on the ground of short delivery only if the misdelivery goes to the root for the contract.

2. Excess Delivery

Where a larger quantity is delivered, the buyer may accept the goods included in the contract and reject the rest or he may reject the whole. If the buyer accepts the whole of the goods so delivered, he shall pay for them at the contract rate.

3. Delivery of Mixed Goods

Where the goods of the contract description are mixed up with other goods, the buyer may accept the goods which are in accordance with the contract and reject the rest or may reject the whole. Thus, in Micolson v. Bredford Union,[93] coal that was supplied was partly according to contract and partly not. Held the buyer was entitled to reject the whole.

The last sub-section of section 37 declares that the above rules as to delivery of wrong quantity are subject to any usage of trade, special agreement or course of dealing between the parties.

Instalment Deliveries (sec. 38)

Section 38 (1) provides: "unless otherwise agreed, the buyer of goods is not bound to accept delivery thereof by instalment". The contract to make instalment deliveries may be either express or implied.

In a contract of sale of 25 tons of pepper "October - November shipment", the seller shipped 20 tons in November and 5 tons in December. Held, buyer could refuse the whole (*Reuter v. Sala*).[94]

Where the contract for the sale of goods provides for installment deliveries which have to be separately paid, for and either buyer or seller commits a breach of contract, section 38(2) provides the answer. It says that:

It is a question in each case, depending on the terms of the contract and the circumstances of the case, whether the breach of contract is a repudiation of the whole contract, or whether it is a severable breach giving rise to a claim for compensation, but not to a right to treat the whole contract as repudiated.

The section thus leaves the whole matter to be determined on the merits of each case.

Generally, failure to deliver or pay for one installment, does not amount to repudiation or breach of the whole contract. But where the breach is such as to lead to a reasonable inference that similar breaches will be committed with reference to the subsequent installments also, the other party is entitled to treat the whole contract as repudiated.

Example

X sold to Y 1,500 tons of meat and bone meat of a specified quality to be shipped, 125 tons monthly in equal weekly installments. After about half the meat had been delivered and paid for Y discovered that it was not of the contract quality and, therefore, refused to take further deliveries. Held, he could do so as he was not bound to take the risk of having put upon him further deliveries of goods which did not conform to the contract (*Robert A. Munso and Co. v. Meyer*).[95]

Delivery to carrier or Wharfinger (sec. 39)

Section 39(1) Provides:

Delivery to Carrier or Wharfinger — Where, in pursuance of a contract of sale, the seller is authorised or required to send the goods to the buyer, delivery of the goods to a carrier, whether named by the buyer or not, for the purpose of transmission to the buyer, or delivery of the goods to a Wharfinger for safe custody, is prima facie deemed to be delivery of the goods to the buyer.

A seller took the goods to a wharf, where he was told that they would be conveyed to the foreign buyer by the ship "commerce". The seller informed the buyer of this. But unknown to the seller the ship was fully laden and the goods were sent by another ship. Even so it was held that the goods had been delivered to the buyer, and he must pay the price, although the goods were lost on the way.[96]

Where, however, it is agreed that the goods are to be delivered at a particular place, for example, at the buyer's mill, delivery to a carrier does not amount to delivery to the buyer.[97]

Seller's Duty [sec. 39(2)]

The seller has to make with the carrier such contract as may be reasonable having regard to the nature of goods and the other circumstances of the case. The purpose of this duty is to secure for the buyer such contract of carriage as will enable the buyer to sue the carrier in case the goods are lost. If the seller fails to make such contract the buyer may refuse to treat the delivery to the carrier as delivery to himself or may hold the seller liable in damages.

In *Clarke v. Hutchins,*[98] the carrier to whom the goods were delivered in this case notoriously required a notice that the goods were over the value of £ 5, otherwise he was not liable for any loss. The seller gave no such notice. It was held that he had failed in his duty of making a reasonable contract, and, therefore, was liable for the loss.

These principles can be excluded by a contract to the contrary.

Sea Transit [sec. 39(3)]

Where the goods have to be sent by sea transit where insurance is usual, the sellers should give to the buyer such notice as will enable him to insure the goods.

Contracts involving Sea Routes

Contracts which usually involve sea routes and known as "international sale" are of three kinds. They are namely —

1. F.O.B. Contracts

F.O.B. means "free on board." In other words, the seller has to place the goods on board a ship at his own expense. He has only to bear the expenses of loading the goods. There after the goods are at the buyer's risk and he is responsible for freight, insurance and subsequent expenses.

2. C.I.F. Contracts

C.I.F. means the price is to include cost, insurance and freight. The duties of the seller under a C.I.F contract have been thus stated by lord ATKINSON in *Johnson v. Taylor Bros and Co. Ltd.*[99]

"The seller in the absence of any provisions to the contrary is bound by his contract to do things:

(i) to make out an invoice of the goods sold.

(ii) to ship at the port of shipment goods of the description contained in the contract.

(iii) to procure a contract of afreightment under which the goods will be delivered at the destination contemplated by the contract.

(iv) to arrange for an insurance upon the terms current in the trade which will be available for the benefit of the buyer.

(v) with all reasonable dispatch to send forward and tender to the buyer these shipping documents, namely, the invoice, the bill of lading and the policy of insurance, delivery of which to the buyer is symbolical of delivery of the goods purchased, placing the same as the buyer's risk and entitling the seller to payment of their price...... If no place be named in the C.I.F contract for the tender of the shipping documents they must *prima facie* be tendered at the residence or place of business of the buyer."

If the seller fails to deliver the shipping documents with in a reasonable time, that is a breach of contract. The shipping documents must include the policy of insurance and not merely the certificate of insurance.

The buyer has to pay and receive the documents without waiting for the arrival of the goods.

3. Ex Ship Contracts

Under an "*ex ship*" contract the seller has to deliver the goods to the buyer at the port of destination. Lord SUMNER explained the incidence of an "*ex ship*" contract in *Yangtsze Ins. Association v. Luckmanjee* 100 in following words:

In the case of a sale '*ex ship*', the seller has to cause delivery to be made to the buyer from a ship which has arrived at the port of delivery and has reached a place therein which is usual for the delivery of goods of the kind in question. The seller has, therefore, to pay the freight or otherwise release the ship owner's lien and to furnish the buyer with an effectual direction to the ship to deliver. Till this is done the buyer is not bound to pay for the goods. Till this is done he may have insurable interest in profits, but none that can correctly be described as an interest 'upon goods', nor any interest which the seller, as seller, is bound to insure for him. If the seller insures he does so for his own purposes and of his own motion.

In this case, there was a contract for "*ex ship*" sale of Indian first class teak squares. The first installments of logs was shipped on board at Colombo. It was discharged at the port of destination, and was lost in a gale. The seller had insured the timber and the buyer sought to enforce the policy. It was held that he could not do so. At the time of insurance, the timber was the property of the seller and not of the buyer, because in an "*ex ship*" contract the property passes on delivery at the port of destination. The buyer had no insurable interest when the goods were shipped.

Whether a particular contract is an '*ex ship*' contract or a c.i.f. contract does not depend upon the terminology used by the parties but upon the essence of the transaction. "The true effect of all its terms must be taken into account, though, of course, the description c.i.f. must not be neglected." This opinion was expressed and applied by the House of Lords in Comptoir Achat *et de vente du* Boerenbond Belge *S.A v. Luis de Ridder Limitada.*[101]

Deterioration During Transit (sec. 40)

Section 40 provides:

Risk where goods are delivered at distant place — where the seller of goods agrees to deliver them at his own risk at a place other than that where they are when sold, the buyer shall, nevertheless, unless otherwise agreed, take any risk of deterioration in the goods necessarily incident to the course of transit.

In *Bull v. Robinson*[102] case ALDERSON held, "A manufacturer who contracts to deliver a manufactured article at a distant place, must indeed stand the risk of any extraordinary or unusual deterioration, but the vendor is bound to accept the article if only deteriorated to the extent that it is necessarily subject to in its course of transit from one place to another."

Acceptance (sec. 42)

A buyer cannot reject the goods after he had accepted them. Section 42 says that the buyer is deemed to have accepted the goods in the following circumstances.

(1) When he intimates to the seller that he has accepted them.

(2) When the goods have been delivered to him and he does any act in relation to them which is inconsistent with the ownership of the seller.

(3) When, after the lapse of a reasonable time, he retains the goods without intimating to the seller that he has rejected them.

In Hardy *Co. v. Hillerns and Fowler,*[103] a quantity of wheat arrived on c.i.f terms. The buyers without making proper inspection, resold various parcels to sub-buyers. Three days later the buyers found that the wheat was not of contract quality and therefore sought to reject it.

It was held that they had lost the right of rejection. Thus, any dealing by the buyer with the goods in a manner inconsistent with the seller's ownership amounts to acceptance and deprives the buyer of his right to reject.

But dealings with documents of title does not amount to acceptance.

Right to Examination (sec. 41)

Section 41(1) Provides:

Buyer's right to examining the goods — where goods are delivered to the buyer which he was not previously examined, he is not deemed to have accepted them unless and until he has had a reasonable opportunity of examining them for the purpose of ascertaining whether they are in conformity with the contract.

Thus, by accepting the documents of title the buyer is not deemed to have accepted the goods. He still has the right of examining the goods on their arrival.

In *Isherwood v. Whatmore,*[104] the seller refused to allow the buyer to open the cases which contained the goods. Held no sufficient opportunity had been given to the buyer to inspect the goods and hence there was no valid offer of delivery by the seller. Buyer was not bound to accept them.

Section 41(2) further provides:

Unless otherwise agreed, when the seller tenders delivery of goods to the buyer, he is bound, on request, to afford the buyer a reasonable opportunity of examining the goods for the propose of ascertaining whether they are in conformity with the contract.

In the absence of an agreement to the contrary, the proper place of inspection is the place of delivery.

Carrying the goods from the place of delivery to some place amounts to acceptance. A mere pledging of shipping documents received under a c.i.f contract does not amount to acceptance, and, therefore, the buyer will have the right to reject if the goods turn out to be defective.

Duty after Rejection (sec. 43)

43 Buyer not bound to return rejected goods

Unless otherwise agreed, where goods are delivered to the buyer and he refuses to accept them, having the right so to do, he is not bound to return them to the seller, but it is sufficient if he intimates to the seller that he refuses to accept them.

Thus, if the buyer wants to reject he must intimate to the seller his intention to reject. But he is not bound to return the goods to the seller. The principle applies when the rejection is rightful and there is no agreement to the contrary.

Liability of the Buyer (sec. 44)

When the seller is ready and willing to deliver the goods and request the buyer to take delivery and the buyer does not within a reasonable time after such request take delivery of the goods, he is liable to the seller for any loss occasioned by his neglect or refusal to take delivery, and also for a reasonable charge for the care and custody of the goods. This rule does not affect the seller's right to treat the buyer's refusal or neglect as a repudiation of the contract.

Unpaid Seller and His Rights

A seller who has only received a part of the price is an unpaid seller. Section 45(1) provides the definition of unpaid seller.

45(1) The seller of goods is deemed to be an "unpaid seller" if:

(a) the whole of the price has not been paid or tendered,

(b) When a bill of exchange or other negotiable instrument has been received as conditional payment, and the condition on which it was received has not been fulfilled by reason of the dishonour of the instrument or otherwise.

The term "seller" includes any person who is in the position of a seller, eg an agent of the seller.

Rights of unpaid Seller

Rights of an unpaid seller may broadly be classified under two heads namely.

(1) Rights against goods

(2) Rights against the buyer personally.

1. Rights against goods

Section 46 seeks to protect the interest of an unpaid seller by conferring upon him the following rights against the goods.

(i) a lien on the goods for price while he is in possession of them,

(ii) in case of the insolvency of the buyer a right of stoppage of the goods in transit after he has parted with the possession of them,

(iii) a right of resale as limited by the Act.

(1) Lien on the goods (sec. 47 - 49)

The words 'lien' means to retain possession of goods until certain charges due in respect of them are paid. Section 47 provides that an unpaid seller who is in possession of goods, is entitled to retain them in his possession until payment or tender of the price in the following cases.

(a) Where the goods have been sold without any stipulation as to credits,

(b) Where the goods have been sold on credit, but the term of credit has expired,

(c) Where the buyer becomes insolvent.

The right of lien is linked with possession and not with title. The unpaid seller may exercise his lien not withstanding that he is in possession of the goods as agent or bailee for the buyer. Where the goods are sold on credit, the right of lien is suspended during the term of credit. But on the expiry of that term, if the goods are still in the possession of the seller, his lien revives.

Lien can be exercised only for non-payment of the price, and not for any other charges due against the buyer. For instance, the seller cannot claim lien for godown charges for storing the goods in exercise of his lien for the price.

In *Somes v. British Empire Shipping Co.*[105] the house of lords held that where the price has been tendered, the seller cannot claim to retain the goods further for the expenses incurred by him on storage during the period that he was holding the goods in the exercise of his lien.

Part delivery (sec. 48)

Section 48 further provides that the right of lien of an unpaid seller is available even after part delivery of the goods has been made, unless such part delivery is made under such circumstances as to show an agreement to waive the lien.

Termination of Lien (Section 49)

Section 49 says that an unpaid seller loses his lien in the following cases:

(a) when he delivers the goods to a carrier or other bailee for the purpose of transmission to the buyer, without reserving a right of disposal of the goods, e.g., takes R/R or Transport Receipt in the name of buyer or his agent,

(b) when the buyer or his agent lawfully obtains possession of the goods,

(c) by waiving the right of lien.

It should, however, be noted that an unpaid seller does not lose his lien by reason only that he has obtained a decree for the price of the goods [sec. 49(2)]

Lien of an unpaid seller is a possessory lien it means once the possession is lost, lien is lost. In *Bhameha v. Wadilal,*[106] on sale of certain shares the relevant share certificates and transfer forms duly signed were handed over by the seller to the buyer against payment of price by cheque. On the buyer becoming subsequently insolvent, it was held that the seller had no lien on the share certificate or transfer forms, for his lien ceased when he parted with their possession.

(ii) Right of stoppage-in-Transit

Section 50 Provides:

Subject to the provisions of this Act, when the buyer of goods becomes insolvent, the unpaid seller, who has parted with the possession of the goods, has the right of stopping them in transit, that is to say, he may resume possession of the goods as long as they are in the course of transit, and may retain them until Payment or tender of the price.

Section 50 confers this right upon the unpaid seller. Requirements of this right are that the

(a) seller should be unpaid,

(b) buyer should have become insolvent

(c) property should have passed to the buyer.

It means this right is earned only when the right of lien is lost.

(d) the goods should be in the course of transit.

Distinction between Lien and stoppage in transit

Following are the points of difference —

(1) Unpaid seller's lien is available only when the goods are in the possession of the unpaid seller.

Right to stoppage in transit is available when unpaid seller has parted with the possession of the goods.

(2) The seller's lien attaches when the buyer is in default whether he solvent or insolvent.

The right of stoppage in transit only arises when the buyer is insolvent.

(3) When lien ends the right of stoppage in transit commences.

Duration of Transit (sec. 51)

Since, the right of stoppage in transit can be exercised only during transit, the question of duration of transit is of great importance. Goods are deemed to be in course of transit from the time when they are delivered to a carrier or other bailee for the purpose of transmission to the buyer, until the buyer or his agent in that behalf takes delivery of them from such carrier or other bailee.

Section 51 tries to solve the difficulty by laying down basic propositions which govern the commencement and end of transit.

(1) Delivery to the buyer [sec. 51(1)]

Transit ends when the goods are delivered to the buyer or his agent.

(2) Interception by the Buyer [sec. 51(2)]

The transit ends when the buyer or his agent takes delivery of the goods from the carrier before their arrival at appointed destination.

(3) Acknowledgement to the Buyer [sec. 51(3)]

The transit ends if after the arrival of the goods at the appointed destination, the carrier or the other bailee acknowledges to the buyer or his agent that he holds the goods on behalf of the buyer or the buyer's agent. It is immaterial that a further destination of the goods was indicated by the contract.

(4) Rejected by the Buyer [sec. 51(4)]

If the goods are rejected by the buyer and the carrier or other bailee continues in possession of them, the transit is not at an end. This will be so even if the seller himself has refused to take back the goods.

(5) Delivery to ship chartered by the Buyer [sec. 51(5)]

When the goods are delivered to a ship it becomes a question of fact depending on the circumstances of the particular case whether they are in the possession of the master as carrier, or as an agent of the buyer. If the ship is chartered by the buyer or is one belonging to the buyer, the transit comes to an end as soon as the goods are loaded on the ship, unless the seller had reserved the right of disposal of the goods.

(6) Wrongful refusal to Deliver [sec. 51(6)]

Where the carrier wrongfully refuses to deliver the goods to the buyer or his agent, the transit is at an end. It is obvious that the goods should have arrived at their destination, because otherwise the carrier has the right to refuse to deliver them.

(7) Part Delivery [sec. 51(7)]

Where the goods have been delivered in part, the seller may stop the remainder of the goods, unless the part delivery shows an agreement to give up the possession of the whole.

How Right of stoppage-in-transit effect (sec. 52)?

The unpaid seller may exercise his right of stoppage in transit:

(a) either by taking actual possession of the goods, or

(b) by giving notice of his claim to the carrier or other bailee in whose possession the goods are.

The notice of stoppage may be given either to the person in actual possession of the goods or to his principal. In the latter case the notice, to be effectual, must be given at such time and in such circumstances, that the principal by the exercise of reasonable diligence, may communicate it to his servant or agent in time to prevent a delivery to the buyer.

On receipt of the notice from the seller, the carrier or other bailee in possession must re deliver the goods to, or according to the directions of the seller. The expenses of such — re delivery shall be borne by the seller.

Effect of sub-sale or Pledge by Buyer (sec. 53)

The rule is that the unpaid seller's right of lien or stoppage in transit, is not affected by any sale or other disposition of the goods which the buyer may have made, unless the seller has assented thereto.

In *Knights v. Wiffen*[107] A sold to B 80 maunds of grain out of a granary. B then out of 80 maunds sold 60 maunds to C.C after receiving from B the delivery order presented it to A. A told C that the grain would be delivered in due course, B then became insolvent. A's right against the 60 maunds is lost since A recognised the title of C — the sub buyer.

Exceptions

Following are the exceptions to the above rule.

1. Where a document of title to the goods has been issued, or lawfully transferred to any person as buyer or owner of the goods, and that person transfer the document to a purchaser in good faith and for valuable consideration, the unpaid seller's right of lien or stoppage in transit is destroyed [Dreyfus Co's case].[108]
2. Where the document of title to the goods issued, or lawfully transferred to the buyer has been transferred by him, to a bonafide purchaser for consideration, by way of pledge, the right of lien or stoppage in transit can only be exercised subject to the right of the pawnee.

Right of Re-Sale (sec. 54)

Sale not generally rescinded by lien or stoppage-in-transit

Subject to the provisions of this section, a contract of sale is not rescinded by the mere exercise by an unpaid seller of his right of lien or stoppage in transit.

Thus, the unpaid seller, who has retained possession of the goods in exercise of his right of lien or who has resumed possession from the carrier upon insolvency of the buyer, can re sell the goods:

(1) If the goods are of a perishable nature, without any notice to the defaulting buyer.

(2) In other cases, the seller should give a notice to the defaulting buyer of his intention to resell. If the buyer does not the price within reasonable time after receiving the notice, the seller may resell the goods. He can recover from the defaulting buyer any loss occasioned by his breach of contract. He can also keep any profit which may occur on the resale. But if the unpaid seller sells the goods without serving upon the buyer a reasonable notice, the seller can not recover damages for the breach and he has also to hand over any profit to the buyer made on the resale.

Right of re-sale is also available where by the contract, seller has expressly reserved a right of re-sale in case the buyer makes a default. In such a case no notice of sale is necessary. The contract is automatically rescinded when the seller resells the goods. He does not resell as an unpaid seller, but as an original owner of the goods. What is a reasonable time will be determined by the fact of the case.

Measure of Damages

The measure of damages in case of re-sale is the difference in the contract price and resale price plus the expenses of re-sale.

Seller's Remedies against Buyer

Following remedies may be enjoyed by the seller personally.

1. Suit for Price (sec. 55)

If buyer does not pay the price in terms of contract when the property in the goods has passed to him, the seller may sue him for the price of the goods.

Where under a contract of sale the price is payable on a day fixed irrespective of delivery or of passing of property and the buyer wrongfully neglects or refuses to pay the price, the seller may sue the buyer for the price.

2. Suit for Damages (sec. 56)

Where the buyer wrongfully neglects or refuses to accept and pay for the goods, the seller may sue him for damages for non acceptance. Section 73 and 74 of contract Act laid down the principles of assessment of damages.

Buyer's Remedies against seller

Following are the remedies of buyer against seller.

1. Damages for Non-Delivery (sec. 57)

Where the seller wrongfully neglects or refuses to deliver the goods to the buyer, the buyer may sue the seller for damages for non-delivery.

2. Remedy for Breach of warranty (sec. 59)

Where there is breach of warranty or where the buyer elects or is compelled to treat the breach of condition as breach of warranty, the buyer cannot reject the goods. He setup the breach of warranty in extinction or diminution of the price payable by him and if the loss suffered by him is more than the price, he may sue the seller for damages. If he has already paid the price, his only remedy is an action for damages.

3. Specific Performance (sec. 58)

Where the contract is for the sale of specific or ascertained goods and the seller refuses to deliver them the court may require him to deliver the goods in terms of the contract instead of permitting him to retain them on Payment of damages.

There are certain conditions to this remedy.

(1) The contract must be for the seller of specific or ascertained goods.

(2) The power of the court to order specific performance under section 58 is "subject to the provisions of chapter II of the specific Relief Act 1877" (Now S. Relief Act of 1963). Chapter II of the specific Relief Act empowers the court, in its discretion, to order specific performance whenever damages would not be an adequate remedy.

Anticipatory Breach (sec. 60)

According to section 60 if a party to a contract of sale repudiates the contract before delivery date, the other party has the choice between two courses. He may immediately accept the breach and bring an action for damages or he may wait till the date of delivery. In the first alternative the contract is thereby rescinded and damages will be assessed according to the prices prevailing at that time. In second alternative, the contract remain open at the risk and benefit of both parties. Not only the party repudiating may subsequently choose to perform but also damages will be assessed according to the prices on the day stipulated for delivery.

Recovery of Interest (sec. 61)

Section 61 lays down following provisions about recovery of interest.

Interest by way of damages and special damages

(1) Nothing in this Act shall affect the right of the seller or the buyer to recover interest or special damages in any case where by law interest or special damages may be recoverable, or to recover the money paid where the consideration for the payment of it has failed.

(2) In the absence of a contract to the contrary, the court may award interest at such rate as it thinks fit on the amount of the price —

 (a) to the seller in a suit by him for the amount of the price — from the date on which the price was payable.

(b) to the buyer in a suit by him for the refund of the price in a case of a breach of the contract on the part of the seller — from the date on which the payment was made.

PRACTICE QUESTIONS

1. State the essentials of a contract of sale under the Saie of Goods Act, 1930.
2. Distinguish between (i) Sale and hire purchaser agreement, (ii) Sale and 'contract for work and labour', (iii) sale and agreement to sell.
3. What is meant by goods?
4. What is meant by (i) ascertained and unascertained goods, (ii) specific and generic goods, (iii) existing and future goods?
5. What do you understand by a 'document of title to goods'? Give at least two examples of documents which are recognised by the Sale of Goods Act as being documents of title to goods.
6. What are the rules as given in the Sale of Goods Act, 1930, regarding fixation of price?
7. What do you understand by earnest money?
8. Distinguish between condition and warranty. State the circumstances under which a condition can be waived and treated as a warranty.
9. Distinguish between 'express warranty' and 'implied warranty'.
10. State the implied conditions in a contract of sale.
11. Explain the rule of *caveat emptor* and exceptions thereto. What is the modern approach to this rule?
12. State briefly the rules regarding the transfer of ownership from the seller to the buyer.
13. What is the practical importance of knowing the exact moment when the property in goods passes from the seller to the buyer? State and illustrate the rules which determine such moment, or 'Risk *prime facie* passes with property'. Elucidate.
14. When may a seller give a better title to the buyer than he himself has in the goods sold? or 'No one can give what he himself has not'. Elucidate.
15. Explain the rules relating to delivery of goods.
16. What is (i) an R.O.B. contract, (ii) a C.I.F. contract?
17. Define an unpaid seller. What are the different rights of an unpaid seller?
18. Distinguish between the right of lien and stoppage in transit.
19. State the circumstances when the right of stoppage in transit ends.
20. When can a seller resell the goods?
21. What remedies are available to a seller for breach of contract of sale?
22. Discuss the buyer's remedies against seller where there is a breach of contract *Sale by*

References

1. Aldridge v. Johnson (1857) 7 E & B 885: 26 LJQB 296
2. Badische Anilin and Soda Fabric v. Hickson (1906) AC 419
3. K.L. Johar and Co. v. Deputy Commercial Tax officer AIR. 1965 SC 1082
4. State of Gujrat v. Variety Body Builders AIR 1976 SC 2109
5. Lee v. Griffin (1861) 30 LJQB 252
6. Myers and Co. v. Brent cross service Co. (1934) IKB 46
7. Robinson v. Graves (1935) IKB 579
8. J. Marcel (Furriers) Ltd. v. Tapper, (1953) 1 All ER 15
9. Sentional Rolling shutters v. C.S.T (1978) 4 sec 260
10. Rash Behari v. Emperor 1936 41 CWN 225: AIR 1936 cal 753, commr of sales Tax v. M.P. Electricity Board AIR 1970 SC 732
11. Badri Prasad v. State of M.P. AIR (1970) SC 706
12. In re wait (1927) 1 CR 606
13. Union of India v. Tara chand AIR (1976) M.P. 101
14. Couturier v. Hastie (1856) SHLC 673: 101 RR 329
15. Smith v. Myers (1871) 1 QB 139 Exch.
16. Barrow Lane and Ballard v. Phillips (1929) 1 KB 574
17. Astar and Co. Ltd. v. Blundell (1861) 1 QB 123
18. Howell v. Coupland (1876) 1 QBD 258
19. Browne v. Byrine (1854) 118 ER 1304
20. Howe v. Smith (1884) 27 CHD 89
21. Wallis v. prott (1910) 2 KB 1012

22. Baldry v. Marshall (1925) 1 KB 260
23. Harrison v. Knowles and Foster (1917) 2 KB 606
24. Meyer v. Kivisto (1930) 40 TLR 162
25. Rowland v. divall (1923) 2 KB 500
26. Niblett v. Confectioners Materials Co. Ltd. 1921 3 KB 387
27. Butterworth v. Kingsway botors (1954) 1 WLR 1286
28. Bower v. Shand (1877) APP cas 455
29. Shepherd v. Kain (1821) 5 B and Ald 240
30. Andrews Ltd. v. Singer and Co. Ltd.(1934) 1 KB 17
32. Nicholson and Venn v. Smith Marriott (1947) 177 LT 189
33. Beale v. Talor (1967) 3 All ER 253
34. Moore and Co. v. Landauer and Co. (1921) 2 KB 519, CA
35. Nichol v. Godts (1854) 10 Ex 191
36. Wallis v. Pratt (1911) A.c 399
37. Priest v. last (1903) 2 KB 148
38. Evens v. Benjamin AIR 1950 cal 470
39. Frost v. Aylesbury Dairy Co. Ltd. (1905) 1 KB, 608
40. Chanter v. Hopkins (1938) M and W 399
41. Baldary v. Marshall (1925) 1 KB 260
42. Griffths v. Peter Conway Ltd. (1939) 1 All ER 685
43. Jones v. Padgett (1890) 24 QBD 650
44. Bristol Tramways Co. v. Flat Motors Ltd. (1910) 2 KB 831
45. Gardner v. Grey (1814) 4 comp 144
46. Jones v. Just (1867) LR 3 QB 192
47. Jackson v. Rotax Motor and cycle Co. (1910) 2 KB 937
48. Jackson v. Watson and sons (1909) 5 KB 193 CA
49. Godley v. Perry (1960) 1 All ER 36
50. Thornett and Fehr v. Beers and sons (1919) 1 KB 486
51. G. Mekenzie and Co. v. Nagendra Nath (1945) 50 CWN 213
52. Priest v. Last (1903) 2 KB 148
53. Dr. Barctto v. TR Price, AIR (1939) Nag. 19
54. In re walkers, Winser and Hamon and Shaw Co. Ltd. (1904) 2 KB 152 at 158
55. Rusttonsi Rowji v. The Bombay united wearing and spinning Co. ILR (1916) 41 Bom 518
56. Bombay - Burma Trading corpn v. Aga Mohomed(1911) 38 IA 169
57. Gardiner v. Gray (1815) 4 camp 144
58. Leonard v. Fowler (1871) 4 NY 289
59. Drummond & Sons v. Van Ingen (1887) 12 APP cas 184
60. Cehavenv v. Bremer Handelsge Sellschaft (1975) 3 All ER 739, (1976) QB 44
61. Rowland v. Divall (1923) 2 KB 500
62. Collinge v. Heywood (1839) 9 A and E 633
63. Ward v. Hobbs (1878) 4 aPp cas 13
64. Baldry v Marshall (1925) 1 KB 260
65. M. Cardie J in Poeahontas Fuel Co. v. Ambatulos (1922) 27 Com cas 148, 152-3
66. Steel Bros and Co. v. Dayal Khatao and Co. ILR (1923) 47 Bom 924
67. Cointal v. Mytham and son (1913) 2 Kb 220
68. Me Entire v. Crossley Bros Ltd. (1895) AC 457
69. Sacks v. Tilley (1915) 32 TLR 148
70. Shanker Das v. Bhanna Ram AIR 1926 Lah 606
71. Underwood v. Burgh Castle Syndicate (1922) 1 Kb 343
72. Rugg v. Minett (1809) 11 East 210
73. Zaguny v. Furnell (1809) 2 camp 240
74. Turley v. Bates (1863) H & C 200
75. Kirkhan v. Allenborough (1897) 1 QB 201, CA
76. Genn v. Winkel (1911) 28 TLR 483
77. Elphick v. Barnes (1880) 5 CPD 321
78. Per PEARSON J in carlos Federspiel & Co. SA v. Charles Twigg & Co. Ltd. (1957) 1 lioyd's Rep 240 at 255
79. Consolidated Coffee Ltd. v. Coffee Board (1980) 3 sec 358
80. Atkinson v. Bell (1828) 108 ER 1046
81. Sterns Ltd. v. Vickers Ltd. (1923) 1 KB 78, CA
82. Demby Hamilton & Co. Ltd. v. Barden (1949) 1 All ER 435
83. Consolidated Coffee Ltd. v. Coffee Board (1980) 3 sec 358
84. Faruquaharson v. King (1902) AC 325
85. Lowther v. Harris (1927) 2 KB 393

86. Staffs Motor Gauarantee Ltd. v. British Wagon Ltd. (1934) 2 KB 305
87. Oppenheimer v. Fraze and Wyatt (1907) 2 KB 50 CA
88. Phillips v. Brooks (1919) 2 KB 243
89. Staffs Motor Gaurantee Ltd. v. British Wagon Co. Ltd. (1934) 2 KB 305
90. Marten v. Whale (1917) 2 KB 480
91. Mammond v. Anderson (1803) 1 B and P.N.R 69
92. Bunnery v. Poyntz (1833) 4 B and Ad 568
93. Nicolson v. Bredford union (1866) LR 1 QB 620
94. Reuter v. Sala (1879) 4 C.P.D 239
95. Robert A Munso and Co. v. Meyer (1930) 2 KB 312
96. Cooke v. Ludlow, (1806) 2 B and PNR 119
97. Sadasook Kothari v. Chaitram Rambilash (1925) 29 cal WN 808- AIR 1926 cal 218
98. Clarke v. Hufchins (1811) 14 East 475
99. Johnson v. Taylor Bros and Co. Ltd. (1920) AC 144
100. Yangftsze Ins. Association v. huckmanjee (1918) AC 585 at 589 Pc
101. Computer d' Achat et de Vente du Boerendond Belge S.A v. Luis de Ridder Limitada (1949) 1 All ER 269
102. Bull v. Robinson (1854) 10 Ex 342 at 346
103. Hardy and Co. v. Hillerns and Fowler (1923) 2 KB 490 CA
104 Isherwood v. Whatmore (1843) 11 Mand W 347
105. Somes v. British Empire Shipping Co. (1860) 8 HLC 338
106. Bhameha v. Wadilal, 28 Bom LR 777 P.C.
107. Knights v. Wiffen (1870) LR 5 QB 660
108. Dreyfus Co's case (1943) KB 40

PART F

THE CARRIERS ACT, 1865

CHAPTER

17

Law of Carriage

Common Carrier

The Carriers Act, 1865, was passed at a time when the profession of carrying goods or passengers was growing and the carriers had an open opportunity to contract out of liability even for negligence or misconduct with the result that the consigners were left wholly at their mercy. Now, the Carriers Act does not permit exclusion of liability in such cases.

The liability stated under the act and its provisions are attracted only when a carrier comes within the description of "common carrier" as given in Section 2 of the Act. This Section is the "interpretation clause" and the first concept defined is that of common carrier. The definition is in these words:

'Common Carrier' denotes a person, other than the Government, engaged in the business of transporting for hire property from place to place, by land or inland navigation, for all persons indiscriminately.

The definition is based upon the English common law. "The common law in England developed from quite early times to make the profession of common carriers a kind of public service, or as stated by Lord Holt in an early case "a public trust"[1]. It is where such a public trust has been undertaken as distinct from a private contract that a carrier ceases to be a private carrier and becomes a public carrier or as English law calls him "a common carrier". Explaining the distinction between a mere carrier and a common carrier, AIDERSON B said in *Ingate v. Christie*.[2]

Everybody who undertakes to carry for anyone who asks him, is a common carrier. The criterion is, whether he carries for a particular person only, or whether he carries for every one. If a man holds himself out to do it for everyone who asks him, he is a common carrier; but if he does not do it for everyone, but carries for you and me only, that is a matter of special contract.[3]

The definition given by Story in his book on BAILMENT is more or less to the same effect:

"A common carrier is one who undertakes for hire or reward to transport the goods of such as choose to employ him from place to place."[4]

If he reserves to himself the right to reject goods of any kind or from any person, he is not a common carrier. An illustration in point is *Belfast Ropework Co. v. Bushell*.[5]

The defendant described his business as that of an automobile engineer and haulage contractor. He owned two lorries intended for sale. With these and others which he hired when necessary he carried sugar from Liverpool to Manchester. At Manchester, he invited offers of goods of all kinds except machinery for carriage to Liverpool and other places. These offers he accepted or rejected according as the rate, route and class of goods were or were not satisfactory. He accepted the plaintiff's hemp for carriage to Liverpool. In the course of the transit the hemp was damaged by fire without negligence of the defendant.

It was held that inasmuch as he reserved to himself the right of rejecting or accepting offers of goods for carriage he was not a common carrier and, therefore, was not absolutely liable for the loss of the goods.

The concept was considered by the Supreme Court in *River Steam Navigation Co. Ltd. v. Shyam Sunder Tea Co.*[6]

The defendant company was providing steamer service in the river Brahmputra between Dibrugarh and Calcutta, and was engaged mostly for carriage of tea chests. In this respect, the company admitted that it was a common carrier. In order, however, to facilitate the transportation of tea from the interiors to the main Ghats on the river, the company provided boats on request to the tea gardeners on the tributaries of the river and nothing was charged for this service. The plaintiff delivered certain tea chests on board the company's boat on a tributary point for transportation to the main Ghat and onward to Calcutta. The boat sank owing to negligence. The company was accordingly sued and it contended that it was not a common carrier on feeder lines and should, therefore, not he held liable.

But the Court held that the company had become a common carrier even on the feeder routes. One of the agents of the company told the Court that they always tried to give facility to the interior tea gardens and to all customers wherever they required any help. It, therefore, became obvious that they accepted goods wherever they were available indiscriminately from all customers and brought them to the main routes. This was a sufficient public profession of their being regarded as common carriers for that purpose. It was immaterial that there were no fixed rates for feeder services. The Court cited Blackburn J in *G.W. Ry. Co. v. Sutton*[7] as saying that "there was nothing in the common law to hinder a carrier from carrying for favoured individuals at an unreasonably low rate, or even gratis. All that the law required was that he should not charge any more than was reasonable."[8]

It also makes no difference that he carries only for a part of the route or only certain kinds of goods.

A person may profess to carry a particular description of goods only, for instance, cattle or dry goods, in which case he could not be compelled to carry any other kind of goods, in which case he could not be compelled to carry place to another, as from Manchester to London and then he would not be bound to carry to or from the intermediate places.[9]

Similarly, it has been observed that "at common law no person is bound to carry as a common carrier any goods of a kind which he does not profess to carry."[10]

A common carrier may limit his liability by a special contract and he does not thereby cease to be a common carrier, though, of course, the contract would be valid only if it does not offend the provisions of the Act. He remains a common carrier and liable as such even where he has forwarded the goods to another carrier outside his own system.[12]

Thus, the legal requirement is the public profession to carry goods for persons indiscriminately and not as a casual operation or some individuals. It is on this basis that a licence is issued under the Motor Vehicles Act for the profession of public carrier.[13]

Once a person qualifies as a common carrier within the meaning of this definition, he becomes bound to accept the type of goods which he professes to carry on his routes. Any refusal by him is an offence for which a civil as well as a criminal action lies. As explained by Lord Holt in an early case.[14]

Wherever a subject takes upon himself a public trust for the benefit of the rest of his fellow subjects, he is *co ipso* bound to serve the subject in all the things that are within the reach and comprehension of such an office, under pain of an action against him. If on the road a shoe fall off my horse, and I come to a Smith to have one put on, and the Smith refused to do it, an action will be against him, because he has made profession of a trade which is for the public good. If an inkeeper refuse to entertain a guest when his house is not full, an action will lie against him; and so against a carrier, if his horses be not loaded, and he refuse to take a packet proper to be sent by a carrier.

This statement has been cited with approval by Patel J of the Bombay High Court in *Husainbhai v. Motilal*,[15] but the learned judge added:

Though for improper refusal he is liable to indictment, there does not appear to be a single case of conviction.[16] In this country, there can be no prosecution for a refusal, since it is not made an offence. Obligation to carry may, however, be enforced in different ways such as for example, a suit for damages for refusal.

He can, however, justly refuse to carry if there is no room in his vehicle, or the goods are not of the type which he professes to carry; or the destination is not on his routes or if the goods are unlawful, dangerous or improperly packed.

LIABILITY OF CARRIER

Certain preliminary points made out by the Carriers Act about the liability of a carrier may be noted first.

Liability for goods mentioned in the Schedule [Section3]

The Carriers Act mentions in its schedule certain types of property. The schedule is reproduced below. Section 3 deals with liability for such property. Because the properties mentioned are of special value, for example, gold and silver, the Section requires the value or description to be given and provides that the carrier would not be liable beyond one hundred rupees unless the value was declared or description given.

SCHEDULE

Gold and Silver coin.

Gold and Silver in a manufactured or unmanufactured state.

Precious stones and pearls.

Jewellery.

Time-pieces of any description.

Trinkets.

Bills and hundis.

Currency-notes of the Central Government or notes of any Banks, or securities for payment of money, English or foreign.

Stamps and stamped paper.

Maps, prints and works of art.

Writings.

Title-deeds.

Gold or Silver plate or plated articles.

Glass.

Chino.

Silk in a manufactured or unmanufactured state, and whether, wrought up or not wrought up with other materials.

Shawls and lace.

Cloths and tissues embroidered with the precious metals or of which such metals form part.

Articles of ivory, ebony or sandalwood.

Art pottery and all articles made of marble.

Furs.

Government securities.

Opium.

Coral.

Musk, Itr, Sandalwood oil, and other essential oils used in the preparation of itr or other perfumes.

Musical and scientific instruments.

Feathers.

Narcotic preparations of hemp.

Crude India-rubber.

Jade, Jade-stone and amber.

Gooroochand or Gooroochandan.

Cinematograph films and apparatus.

Zahir Mohra Khatai.

Platinum.

Iridium.

Palladium.

Radium and its preparations.

Tantalum.

Osmium.

Ruthenium.

Rhodium.

Agarwood.

The Section is as follows:

Carriers not to be liable for loss of certain goods above one hundred rupees in value unless delivered as such. — No common carrier shall be liable for the loss of or damage to property delivered to him to be carried exceeding in value one hundred rupees and of the description contained in the schedule to this Act, unless the person delivering such property to be carried, or some person duly authorized in that behalf, shall have expressly declared to such carrier or his agent the value and description thereof.

In a case before the Calcutta High Court,[17] the consignor declared the goods as stationery. The consignment contained other goods besides stationery and included silk handkerchiefs of the value in excess of Rs. 100 and other gold and silver articles which fell within the schedule. Each class of such articles was of the value of less than Rs. 100. Two boxes of such goods were lost. The ruling of the Court appears from the judgement of Mitter J.[18]

The next point taken is that the consignor is guilty of fraud as it did not give the declaration in respect of the scheduled articles ..... and that therefore the consignor is not entitled to get the price of the non-scheduled articles also as the Court should refuse all relief where the transaction is vitiated by the fraud of the party seeking relief. there is no foundation for this contention under the English Law, when a package containing both scheduled and non-scheduled articles is lost, the value of the non-scheduled articles may be recovered though the value of the scheduled articles exceeding the statutory limit cannot be recovered.[19] This is also the law in India in case of carriers who are governed by the Carriers Act.

In this case, certain classes of articles were less than Rs. 100 in value, but the aggregated value of all such classes exceeded Rs. 100 whether in such cases the claim should be allowed or not was not considered by the Court as this point was not raised at the appropriate stage.

In another case before the Calcutta High Court.[20], six packages of matka silk thread were made over to the carrier as undeclared luggage. The steamer had gone only about two and a half miles that it caught fire and the goods were lost. The company resisted the claim on the ground that the nature and value of the goods, being scheduled articles, were concealed from the company, and also higher charges were not paid on them.

The Court held that Section 3 is subject to the declaration in Section 9 which holds the carrier liable where the loss is due to his negligence. The loss in this case being due to the carrier's negligence he was held liable.

Had the matka silk thread been lost otherwise than through the negligence of the company, they would not have been liable for the loss, as the value and description of the property had not been declared as provided by Section 3 and as there was no payment of a special rate as provided by Section 4. But as the property was lost owing to the negligence of the company, we are of opinion that they are liable for the loss, although the value and description of the property were not declared and a higher charge was not paid for them and that in such a case Section 3 and 4 of Act III of 1865 do not afford any protection to the carrier.[21]

The Court also rejected the contention that because the goods were booked as luggage and not as general merchandise there should be no liability for the loss of general merchandise. Section 8 speaks of liability for "property delivered" which words would include "luggage as well as goods."[22]

Extra Charges [Section 4]

Section 4 is supplementary of the provision in Section 3. It enables the carrier to charge extra for the risk in respect of the scheduled articles. Such extra charges must be exhibited at the place of booking in English as well as the language of the place.

The Section runs as follows:

For carrying such property payment may be required at rates fixed by carrier. Every such carrier may require payment for the risk undertaken in carrying property exceeding in value one hundred rupees and of the description aforesaid at such rate of charge as he may fix:

Section 3 and 4 would not be attracted where the goods in question do not come within the schedule. In a case before the Andhra Pradesh High Court, [23] the question was whether "Leno" was within the schedule. The only clause to which it came near states: "clothes and tissues embroidered with the precious metals or of which such metals form part." The Court held that "Leno" which according to the Concise Oxford Dictionary means "kind of cotton gauge for caps, veils, curtains etc." could not "by any stretch of imagination be brought within the ambit of this item." If the goods have been declared by the consignor, he has done his duty and the failure of the carrier to charge extra on the basis of the declaration will not make any difference as to the carrier's liability.[24]

Recovery of Charges [Section 5]

If the value and nature of the goods have been declared as required by Section 3 and the carrier has levied special charges, the consignor will be entitled to recover in case of loss of such goods, not merely the value of the goods, but also the charges paid by him in respect of the special risk. Section 5 provides for this right in the following words:

The person entitled to recover in respect of property lost or damaged may also recover money paid for its carriage. In case of the loss or damage to property exceeding in value one hundred rupees and of the description aforesaid, delivered to such carrier to be carried, when the value and description thereof shall have been declared and payment shall have been required in manner provided for by this Act, the person entitled to recover in respect of such loss or damage shall also be entitled to recover any money actually paid to such carrier in consideration of such risk as aforesaid.

Recovery under this Section is allowed to the person on whose behalf the goods were booked and not to the agent or the forwarding carrier unless he booked on his own account.[25]

Liability for Non-Scheduled Goods [Section 6]

The Section runs as follows:

In respect of what property liability of carrier not limited or affected by public notice. The liability of any common carrier for the loss or damage to any property delivered to him to be carried, not being of the description contained in the schedule to this Act, shall not he deemed to be limited or affected by any public notice;

Limitation of Liability

Thus, liability for the loss of goods not falling within the schedule cannot be limited by public notice but can be limited by special contract made with each consignor. The clauses of the contract by which the liability is limited must be brought to the notice of the other party. In a case before the Madras High Court,[26] the party's agent signed the consignment note which carried conditions overleaf limiting liability for loss to Rs. 500 only. The goods having been lost, the consignor claimed that neither he nor his agent had knowledge of the clause. Ramachandra Iyer J. reminded him as follows:

It is comparatively rare to find any common carrier to convey goods under such liability, (absolute liability) as it is invariably the practice with common carriers to enter into a contract, defining and limiting their liability. That practice is so universal that in the normal course of things one would expect any consignor of goods to look into such conditions which are found in consignment notes. To say that in every case the carrier should prove that he drew the attention of the consignor to the clause ... is extending the rule beyond its limits.[27]

Limiting clause are strictly construed and against the party who inserted them. One protection is contained in the Section itself which requires that the contract containing such clauses should be signed by the owner of the property or by his duly authorised agent. Oral stipulations will not be sufficient. Thus where, in a case before the Rajasthan High Court [28] the carrier pointed out to one of those attending loading of cotton on a gas plant truck that it was exceptionally risky and he agreed to take it, the carrier was nevertheless held liable when the gas plant materialised the risk by putting the truck with its load of cotton on fire.

Liability as Common Carrier [Section 7, 8 and 9]

The provisions relating to the liability of the common carrier for the loss of or damage to the goods entrusted to him for carriage are to be found in Section 7, 8 and 9. The main provision is in Section 8. Section 7 extends the liability stated under Section 8 to the operators of railroads or tram roads under the Court saying that "a carrier is in the nature of an insurer; where the goods were damaged by rats, notwithstanding that he had kept cats on board, that being the only protection available against rats at the time, where the goods were stolen by a forcible robbery while the ship was lying in the river Thames, the Court saying: "a common carrier must make good a loss though even robbed," where the goods were taken away from the ship by means of a trick.[29]

The position of the carrier in India is the same except as modified by the Carriers Act, "since the great case of *Irrawaddy Flotilla Co. Ltd. v. Bugwan Das,*[30] it is well settled that the duties and obligations of a common carrier are governed by the English common law as modified by the provisions of the Indian Carriers Act."[31] In the above cited Privy Council case:

Certain bales of cotton were delivered to a carrier for carriage to Rangoon by a ship. A fire broke out suddenly, and was not due to any negligence on the part of the servants; all precautions were taken on the night of the fire; when the fire was once detected, everything possible was done to stop it, but its progress was so exceedingly rapid that nothing could be saved. That is how the goods were destroyed.

The carrier pleaded that he had accepted the goods on the terms and conditions that he would be bound to take only such care of the goods as is defined in Section 151 of the Contract Act, namely the bailee's duty of reasonable care and he, having taken that degree of care, should not be held liable. Thus the question was whether the liability of the common carrier in India was to be governed by the Carriers Act or by Section 151 of the Contract Act. The question had already excited controversy between the High Courts in India, for the Bombay High Court had taken the view in *Kaverji Tulsidas v Great Indian Peninsular Ry. Co.*[32] that Section 151 being applicable to "all cases of bailment" and a delivery of goods for carriage being also a bailment, the Section would apply to carriers, and the Calcutta High Court in *Moothoora Kant Shaw v. Indian General Steam Navigation Co.*[33] had held that this was not so and Section 8 of the Carriers Act must govern the question of the carrier's liability. After considering these cases, Lord Macnaghten, who delivered the opinion of the Board, concluded:

These considerations lead their Lordships to the conclusion that the Act of 1872 [the Contract Act] was not intended to deal with the law relating to common carriers, and notwithstanding the generality of some expressions in the chapter on bailments, they think that the common carriers are not within the Act. They are therefore compeiled to decide in favour of the view of the High Court of Calcutta, and against that of the High Court of Bombay.[34]

The reason why their Lordships so held was that the Carriers Act was in force at the time when the Contract Act was passed and there is nothing in it to show that it intended to repeal the Carriers Act.

Thus the position of the common carrier in India is that he is liable for the loss or damage of the goods just like an insurer except where the loss falls within any of the admitted exceptions. His liability is absolute except as modified by the Carriers Act. And what is the modification? The modification is that he is permitted by making a special contract with each consignor and not by a general public notice, to limit his absolute liability in any way he likes except that he cannot exclude his liability for negligence or criminal act. Ordinarily he is absolutely liable; he may limit his liability by a special contract, but he will always be liable for his own or his servant's negligence or criminal act. For example, in *G.M. Roadways Co. v. P.G. Industries*,[35] copper wires were handed over to a transport company at Calcutta to be conveyed to Tatanagar. The contract provided that the goods were received wholly at the risk of the owner. A part of the consignment was stolen enroute probably with the connivance of the drivers. This being a criminal act on the part of the carrier's servants, the carrier was held liable notwithstanding that he had agreed to carry the goods only at the owners risk.[36] Similarly, the Madras High Court held the carrier liable when certain bales of cotton being carried by him by his lorry were lost in an accidental fire.[37] Rajasthan High Court faced a similar problem in Vidya Ratan v. Kota Transport Co. [38] A truck-load of cotton was booked with a transporter over a long distance route. The truck was operated by gas plant. The carrier told the consignor that it was risky to carry cotton by a gas plant truck, but even so he said that he would run the risk. The risk materialised. The gas plant set the cotton on fire and only a nominal part of it could be salvaged and delivered. For the rest, the carrier was held liable. Kan Singh J. cited from Halsbury's Laws of England statements under the heading "construction of special contracts."[39]

The liability of a common carrier for loss, injury or delay in respect to the goods carried may be varied by contract. If the contract is such as to obliterate or destroy his character of a common carrier, he must be regarded for the purpose of that particular contract as a private carrier, but if the contract does not so obliterate or destroy that character, and merely limits his liability in some respects, in all other respects he remains under a common carrier's liability.

No such written special contact having been proved in this case, the leaned judge quite naturally came to the conclusion that the carrier was a common carrier and, therefore, responsible for the loss.

To the same effect is the decision of the Calcutta High Court in *River Steam Navigation Co. Ltd. v Jumunadas Ram Kumar.*[41] The consignment note in this case excluded the liability of the carrier for negligence of their servants. Referring to this Mitter J. observed.[42]

Even in England it has been held that where a carrier made a contract with their customers that they would not be liable for any loss however occasioned such a contract was bad and unreasonable and could not be enforced in any part of it.[43] The portion of the contract which exonerates the Steam Navigation companies from the negligence of their servants or agents is bad both as being unreasonable and as being in contravention of Section 8.

Holding the carrier liable for his failure to deliver goods at the destination, Takru J. of the Allahabad High Court observed:[44]

The opening words of this Section [Section 8] make it perfectly clear that its provisions override those of Section 6. In other words, that whatever kinds of liability the carrier may be able to limit by special contract.. He cannot limit his liability for the criminal act or negligence of himself or any of his agents or servants. This prohibition is a statutory prohibition, with the result that if a special contract contains a stipulation in derogation of it, it would be void to that extent as offending Section 8.[45]

EXCEPTIONS

That being the general principle of liability, exceptions have been admitted. Just as the principle of absolute liability is a tradition, the exceptions are also a part, of the same tradition. These exceptions do not have the statutory force in India because they are not stated in any Section of the Carriers Act. But they have become a part of our law by virtue of the frequent declarations by the Courts, including the Supreme Court,[46] that English common law applies to common carriers in India with all its exceptions except as modified by the Carriers Act. The exceptions are as follows:

1. Act of God

A carrier is not liable for any loss or destruction of the goods where such loss or destruction is due to an "act of God" without the intervention of human forces. The exception was elaborately considered in *Nugent v Smith*:[47]

A loss is a loss by the act of God if it is occasioned by the elementary forces of nature unconnected with the agency of man or other cause; and a common carrier is entitled to immunity in respect of loss so occasioned if he can show that it could not have been prevented by any amount of foresight, pains and care reasonably to be expected of him.

In the above case, the defendant, a common carrier by sea from London to Aberdeen, received from the plaintiff a mare to be carried to Aberdeen on hire. In the course of the voyage the ship encountered rough weather and the mare received such injuries that she died. The jury found that the injuries were caused partly by reason of fright and consequent struggling.

It was held that the defendant was not liable for the death of the mare. "The carrier does not insure against the irresistible act of nature, nor against defects in the thing carried itself; if he can show that either the act of nature or the defect of the thing itself, or both taken together, formed the sole, direct and irresistible cause of the loss, he is discharged. In order to show that the cause of the loss was irresistible it is not necessary to prove that it was absolutely impossible for the carrier to prevent it, but it is sufficient to prove that by no reasonable precaution under the circumstances it could have been prevented."

Similarly, where the goods were thrown over board from a barge in a storm to lighten the barge[48] and where the goods were lost by tempest, [49] the carrier was held not liable. Thus, "however stringent the law is as to liability of a carrier, it does not put upon him the obligation to insure goods at all hazards against such superior forces as the agencies of nature — a force against which his skill and care cannot possibly provide."[50]

The Kerala High Court faced a problem of this kind in *R.R.N. Ramalinga v. Narayana*.[51]

The plaintiff booked 18 bags of green gram with the defendant for transportation from Kaniyakumari to Quilon in one of his lorries. The lorry was waylaid by a jatha while it was just only $1\frac{1}{2}$ miles from Quilon and the unruly mob which formed the jatha robbed the goods. The jatha was being taken out as a part of the food agitation. The agitators needed food and they jumped upon the lorry which carried it. The carrier stood as a silent spectator to see the irresistible happening.

The defendant being common carrier by road, he could be protected from liability only if the exception relating to act of God applied. Holding the carrier liable, Poti J. refused to agree that "all inevitable accidents must be taken as acts of God." [52] He said: "some of the well known instances of acts of God are the storms, the tides and the volcanic eruptions.... Accidents may happen by reason of the play of natural forces or by intervention of human agency or by both.... But it is only those acts which can be traced to natural forces and which have nothing to do with the intervention of human agency that could be said to be acts of God."[53] The learned judge concluded: The criminal activities of unruly mob which robbed the goods cannot certainly be an act of God so as to absolve the defendant from the rule of absolute liability as a common carrier. Hence, the defendant will be answerable for the loss of the goods.[54]

The case is a pictorial monument in its facts, though not in its result, to Mahatama Gandhi's observation that to a hungry man God appears in the form of food.

Where damage was done to a cargo by water escaping through the pipe of a steam boiler, in consequence of the pipe having been cracked by frost, it was held that this was not an act of God, but negligence in the captain in filling his boiler before the time for heating it, although it was the practice to fill overnight when the vessel started in the morning.[55] Where the goods were put in a boat which was towed by a steam vessel to a pier to take in passengers and had to be twice stopped for another vessel to leave the pier and in the second stoppage the tide overturned it, it was held that the damage was not caused by the act of God and the carrier was liable. "The act of God means something overwhelming, and not merely an accidental circumstance."[56]

2. National Enemies

The second defence available to a carrier is the act of the hostile foreign enemies. A carrier is not liable for loss or damage caused by alien enemies, whether they be person belonging to an enemy country or the enemy state itself. This kind of risk usually materialises during times of war. If, for example, a ship or a lorry on its way is torpedoed or bombarded the carrier will not be liable for the consequences. But if the war intervenes on account of something wrong on the part of the carrier himself, he will not be allowed this defence. For example, in *James Morrison and co. Ltd. v. Shaw, Savill and Alibion Co. Ltd.*, [57] a ship touched a port which was not on its customary route so that the deviation increased the voyage by about fifty miles and when it was just only seven miles away from its destination it was torpedoed by a German submarine and sank with her cargo. The carrier was not permitted to plead the defence of king's enemies. Swinfen Eady LJ said: "The question is whether the defendants are protected from liability as carriers by the fact that the loss occurred through the King's enemies. If they, as carriers, were duly performing their contract of carriage, they would not be liable for loss occasioned by the king's enemies. But they were breaking their contract. They are quite unable to show that the loss must have occurred in any event, and whether they had deviated or not."

3. Inherent Defects

A common carrier is not liable for an injury to goods caused by an inherent defect or vice in the goods themselves. Thus where a bullock was consigned with a railway company and it escaped by its own exertions and not due to any negligence and was killed, the railway company was held not liable.[58] Similarly, in *Lister v. Lancashire and Yorkshire Ry. Co.* [59]

A railway company contracted with the plaintiffs to carry for him an engine from his yard to a neighbouring town on their railways. The engine was on wheels and fitted with shafts to allow of its being drawn by horses. While the defendants were drawing the engine with their horses to the railway station one of the shafts, owing to its being rotten, broke; the horses took fright and upset the engine, which was damaged. The defective condition of the shaft was not known to either party, and could not have been discovered by any ordinary examination.

It was held that as the engine was not in fact fit to be carried in the way in which it was intended to be carried, and the damage resulted in consequence of that unfitness, the defendants were excused.

For the same reason, a carrier was held not liable when he was carrying wine in pipes and one of them burst owing to the wine being already on the ferment; this being an inherent development in the goods themselves.[60]

If the goods suffer loss of weight during transit, it can be due to their wasting nature as much as due to the carrier's negligence. But in either case burden lies upon the carrier to explain it.[61]

4. Improper or Bad Packing

If the goods are lost or damaged on account of improper, insufficient or defective packing, the carrier is not liable. Where goods are delivered to a common carriage insufficiently packed and are damaged in the course of the transit, the carrier's knowledge of their condition at the time of their receipt will not preclude him from setting up as a defence that the damage was due to the insufficient packing. This was pointed out in *Gould v. South Eastern and Catham Ry. Co.*[62]

A glass show case was consigned with a railway company. The case was not packed in a manner that the brittle nature of the goods demanded, and though the company knew this, it was not held liable when the case was damaged solely on account of its insufficient packing.

Similarly, where unpacked furniture was sent, the railways were held not liable for damage due to that condition.[63]

5. Justified Delay

A common carrier of goods is not, in the absence of a special contract, bound to carry within any given time, but only within a time which is reasonable, looking at all the circumstances of the case, and he is not responsible for the consequences of delay arising from causes beyond his control. For example, *in Sims and Co. v. Midland Ry. Co.*[64]

Perishable goods were consigned, no time for delivery being fixed. During the transit, a general strike of railway workers, including the defendants workers, broke out and the defendants were unable to forward the goods to their destination. The goods becoming deteriorated, the defendants sold them. The carrier was held not liable. The delay was caused by factors beyond their control and the delay caused the deterioration.

In another case,[65] delay was caused by an obstruction caused by the conduct of another company which carried power lines over the railway line, the railway company was held not liable.

6. Misconduct or Default of Consignor

It is the duty of the consignor to disclose to the carrier the true nature, quality and value of the goods so that he may take precautions accordingly. Any loss or damage due to the consignor's failure in this respect will not render the carrier liable. It is not the duty of the consignor in every case to disclose the contents of his goods, particularly where the goods are not dangerous or are not within the Schedule.

If a box with money be delivered to a carrier, he is bound to answer for it, if he be robbed, though it was not told him what was in it. It is immaterial that the sender told the carrier of somethings in the box and not all, for he need not tell the carrier all the particulars in the box.[66]

But where the goods are of dangerous nature that fact ought to be disclosed. For example, where carboys of corrosive fluid were consigned without disclosure and they leaked causing damage to other goods, the sender was held liable.[67]

Burden of Proof [Section 9]

Plaintiffs, in suits for loss, damage, or non-delivery, not required to prove negligence or criminal act. In any suit brought against a common carrier for the loss, damage or non-delivery of goods entrusted to him for carriage, it shall not be necessary for the plaintiff to prove that such loss, damage or non-delivery was owing to the negligence or criminal act of the carrier, his servants, or agents.

When the goods are not delivered at the destination, there is a presumption that they must have been lost due to the negligence or some other fault of the carrier. The consignor has to prove nothing except this that the goods have not been delivered at the destination. The burden lies upon the carrier to prove that there was no negligence or fault on his or his servants' part. The loss of goods is an evidence of negligence which the carrier will have to disprove.[68] The presumption is not displaced merely by showing that there was a storm. Thus in *Niranjanlal v B.S. Navigation Co.*[69] the carrier proved a newspaper report of the storm during the night that the goods were lost and he also proved that the godown in which the goods were stored at the time of loss was sufficiently safe, yet this was held to be not sufficient to displace the presumption of negligence. No witness was produced to depose from his personal knowledge how the storm affected the building and in what manner the goods were damaged. Mehrotra CJ said: "The defendants will not be liable to pay damages only if they succeed in proving that the damage was the direct and exclusive result of the storm."[70]

To the same effect is the decision of the Calcutta High Court in *C. Doogur v. River Steam Navigation Co.*[71] The goods were lost by fire while they were on board the defendant's flat for carriage to Calcutta. The defendant gave evidence showing the state of things before the fire occurred, the circumstances leading to the discovery of the fire (but not the cause or origin of it), and the measures taken to extinguish the fire. It was held that the occurrence of a fire disclosed in the case, without any explanation as to the origin of its was, of itself, evidence of negligence and the defendant had not discharged the onus cast upon them by law, of showing that there was no negligence.[72]

The Madras High Court also held a carrier liable for the loss of bales of cotton by fire while he was carrying the goods by his lorry, and it was not sufficient for his to show that there was no negligence on his part.[73] But where the parties have placed before the Court all the evidence on which they rely, it is for the Court to say upon that evidence whether or not the loss was caused by negligence, Pointing this out in *Central Coacher Tea Co. v. River Steam Navigation Co.*[74] were chests of tea where damaged in river navigation, Petheram CJ said that the evidence showed that while negotiating a bend, the flotilla came opposite the shoal, the captain stopped and then reversed the engine and that in consequence of this action the flotilla drifted with the current down and across the stream until it struck the left bank and that nothing appears to have been done which was inconsistent with due care and caution and the presumption of negligence was rebutted.

Notice of Loss [Section 10]

Notice of loss or injury to be given within six months — No suit shall be instituted against a common carrier for the loss of, or injury to, goods entrusted to him for carriage, unless notice in writing of the loss or injury has been given to him before the institution of the suit and within six months of the time when the loss or injury first came to the knowledge of the plaintiff.

Notice of loss should be given to the carrier before the action is brought and the notice should be given within six months from the date on which the plaintiff first learned of the loss.[75] Notice has to be given even where the carrier knows of the loss,[76] but if the carrier does not raise any objection on that ground that is a waiver.[77] A notice given to the local agent is sufficient.[78]

PRACTICE QUESTIONS

1. Mention the enactments in which the law relating to carriage of goods contained.
2. Define the term 'contract of carriage'.
3. What are the different types of carriers.
4. Define 'Common Carrier'.
5. Explain the following terms:
   (i) Private carrier and (ii) Gratuitous carrier.
6. Differentiate between common carrier and private carrier.
7. Who are common carriers? What are their liabilities?
8. "The rule at common law is that a common carrier is an insurer of goods: entrusted to him and is, therefore, liable for any loss or damage, whether caused due to his negligence or not." Comment. State the exceptions to the rule.
9. Discuss the rights and duties of a common carrier.
10. Discuss the liabilities of a common carrier.
11. Write an explanatory note on 'strict liability' of common carriers.
12. Describe the situations when the principle of strict liability of common carrier is not applicable.
13. How does the liability of a railway administration in India different from that of other carriers?
14. What are the conditions implied in a contract for the carriage of goods by sea? If any of the conditions is broken, what is the legal consequence?
15. What is a charter party? Mention the usual terms included in a charter party.
16. "A bill of lading is negotiable only in a popular sense and not in a technical sense." Comment.
17. Distinguish between a bill of lading and a charter party.
18. What warranties are implied in a charter party.
19. Mention the different documents of carriage by air.
20. What is an airway bill? Who prepares it? Can the correctness of its contents be called in question?
21. Is an airway bill a document of title?
22. Mention the minimum liability of a carrier by air under the Indian Carriage by Air Act? Can it be varied by a special contract?
23. Is a carrier by air liable to compensate for loss caused by negligent pilotage?
24. If carriage of goods by air is to be performed by various successive carriers, against whom will the action for compensation lie?
25. How far is a carrier by air liable for death or bodily injury to a passenger and for loss of, or damage to goods?

References

1. Lane v. Cotton (1701) 1 com 100; Empire Digest vol. 8 p.14,17.
2. (1854) 3 Car & Kir 61; N.P.
3. River Steam Navigation Co. Ltd. v. Shyam Sunda Tea Co. 1962 2 SCR 802 at p.807.
4. R.R.N. Ramlinga v. Narayna, AIR 1971 Ker 197 at p.199.
5. (1918) 1 K B 210; 87 LJ KB 740.

6. India General Navigation and Ry. Co. Ltd. v. Dekhari Tea Co., (1923) SI JA 28.
7. (1869) LR 4HL 226 at p.237.
8. Professor Otto Kahn Freund in "The Law of Carriage By Inland Transport, 190 (3rd Ed.).
9. Johnson v. Midland Rail co. (1849) and Ex. 367 at p.373.
10. Dickinson v. Great Northern Rail Co. (1886) 18 QBD 176 at p.183, CA.
11. Ali Mohammad v. G.P.P. Ry. Co. AIR 195 Nag at p.7.
12. Tugun Ram v dominian of India, AIR 1966 Nag. 260 ;
    Madura Co. Ltd. v P.C. Xavier, AIR (1931) Mad 115 ;
    Indira General Navigation and Rly. Co. v Dekhari Tea Co., ILR 51 Cal. 304 ;
    IA 28; AIR 1924 P.C. 40.
13. Husainbhai v Motilal, AIR (1963) Bom 208 LR 152.
14. Lane v Cotton (1701) 1 Com 100.
15. Johnson v Midland Ry. Co. (1849) 18 LJ Ex. 366.
16. Halsbury's Laws of England 137 (Vol. 4-3rd Ed.).
17. River Steam Nagivation Co. Ltd. v. Jamunadas Ram Kumar, AIR (1932) Cal. 344.
18. *Ibid.*
19. Flowers v S.E, Ry. Co., (1867) 16 LT 329.
20. Indian General Navigation & Rly. Co. v. Gopal Chandra Guin (1914) 41 ILR Cal 80.
21. Narang Rai Agarwalla v River Steam Navigation Co. Ltd. (1907) ILR 34 Cal 419.
22. Cahill v London and N.E. Ry. Co. (1862) 13 CBN 5818., Great Northern Ry. Co. v Shephand (1852) 8 L x 30; Hossein v Bengal and N.W. Ry. Co., (1909) ILR 36 cal 819.
23. Alopati Suryanaraynan v Puvvada Pullayya, (1968) 1 Andh LT 317.
24. (1892) 19 Cal 538.
25. D.P. Narasa Reddy v Ellisetti, AIR 1964 AP 71.
26. Indian Airlines Corpn. V. Jothaji, AIR 1959 Mad 285.
27. The count relied on Luddit, Guiger Coole Airways, (1947) AC 233.
28. Vidya Ratan v Kota Transport Co. Ltd.
29. Forward v Pittard, 1785 1 Term Rep. 27; Lavoroni v Drury, (1852) 8 E x ch 166;
    Barclay v Cuculla and Gana, (1784) 3 Dough KB 389 ;
    Gibbon v Paynton, (1769) 4 Burr 2298; Mors v Slaw (1672)2 Keb 866.
30. 18 IA PC 121.
31. Sukul Bros. v Kavrana AIR (1958) Cal p.732.
32. ILR 3 Bom 109.
33. ILR 10 cal 166.
34. Ibid.
35. AIR 1971 Cal 494.
36. *Ibid.*
37. P.K. Kalasami v K. Ponnusami, AIR 1962 Mad 44.
38. AIR 1965 Raj 200.
39. 3rd Ed. Vol. 4 para 407.
40. *Ibid.*
41. AIR 1932 cal 344.
42. *Ibid.*
43. Ashendon v London And Brighton South Coast Ry. Co. (1880) 5 Ex. D. 190.
44. Tugum Ram v Dominion of India AIR 1966 All at p.204.
45. Madura Co. Ltd. v P.C. Xavier, AIR 1931 Mad 115.
46. River Steam Navigation Co. v. Shyam Sunder Tea Co. 1962 2 SCR 802.
47. (1876) 1 CPD 423. 34 LT 827 CA.
48. Mouse's case (1608) 12 Co. Rep. 68. 77 ER 1341.
49. Amies v Stevans, (1718) 1 Stra 127; 93 ER 428.
50. Cohen v Gandit, (1863) 3 R & F 455, N.P.
51. AIR 1971 Ker 197.
52. *Ibid.*
53. Nugent v Smith (1876) 1 CPD; Chidambakrishna v South Indian Rly. Co. 21 Trav .
54. *Ibid.*
55. Stordet v Hall (1828) 4 Bing 607; 130 ER 902.
56. Oakley v Portsmouth and Ryds steam Packet Co., (1856) 11 Exch 618, 156 ER 977.
57. (1916) 2 KB 783; 115 LJ 508 CA.
58. Blower v Great Western Ry. (1872) LR 7C P 655
59. (10903) K.B. 878; LU KB 385.
60. Farrar v Adams (1711) Bull NP 69.
61. Hawkes v Smith (1842) Car and M 74 N.P.
62. (1920) 2 KB 186; 123 LT 256.

63. Barbo v South Eastern Ry. Co. (1876) 34 LT 67.
64. (1913) 1 KB 103. 82 LJ KB 67; 107 LT 700.
65. Taylor v Great Northern Ry. Co. 1866 LR 1 CP 385.
66. Kenrig v Eggleton (1648) 82 ER 932.
67. Great Northern Ry. Co. v. L.E.P. Transport (1922) 2 KB 94.
68. Irrawaddy Flotilla v Bugwandas, 18 ILR Cal 620.
69. AIR 1967 A and N 74.
70. River Steam Navigation Co. v. Shyam Sunder Tea Co. AIR 1955 ASS 65.
71. ILR (1897) 24 Cal 787.
72. Tugun Ram v Dominion of India, AIR 1966 All 260 at p.265.
73. Kalaswami v Ponnuswami, AIR 1962 Mad 44.
74. See (1897) 24 Cal 788.
75. River Steam Navigation Co. v. State of Assam AIR 1962 ASS 110.
76. Br. b Foreign Marine Ins. Co. v. India etc. Rly. Co. AIR (1918) Cal 896.
77. U Be Tin v U Tun On. AIR 1938 Rang 437.
78. General Navigation & Ry. Co. Ltd. v. Girdhari Lal, AIR 1927 Cal 394.

PART G

INSOLVENCY LAWS (AMENDMENT) ACT, 1978

CHAPTER

18

Law of Insolvency

Objects of Insolvency Laws

In an old case, Lord ELLENBOROUGH stated: The principle of bankruptcy laws is to prevent persons craftily obtaining into their hands great substance of other men's goods, and at their own wills and pleasures consuming the substance obtained by credit of other men, and it is always to be remembered that it is the protection of persons who have so given credit which is the professed object of bankruptcy laws.

In another case, JAMES L J stated: The bankruptcy law is a special law having for its object the distribution of an insolvent's assets equitably amongst his creditors and persons to whom he is under liability, and, upon this *cessio bonorum*, to release him under certain conditions from future liability in respect of his debts and obligations.

Insolvency laws are designed to serve two basic purposes: Firstly, they enable a person to get rid of the burden of debts which his assets are no longer in a position to pay so that when freed from his burden, he may have a fresh start in life. Secondly, whatever has remained of his assets, they should be taken charge of by a third person and distributed equally among those who have claims against the insolvent.

Acts of Insolvency [S. 9 PTIA & S. 6 PIA]

The first step necessary to initiate insolvency proceedings against an individual is to prove that he has committed an "act of insolvency." A rough idea of this expression is that he has done an act which shows that in all probability he shall not be able to pay his debts. This requirement is designed as a natural check upon frivolous insolvency proceedings. Following acts are regarded as "acts of insolvency."

1. If, in India or elsewhere, he makes a transfer of all or substantially all his property to a third person for the benefit of his creditors generally.

The transfer should be for the benefit of the creditors generally, and not merely for a creditor or two or for a class of them. Where a sale deed was executed directing the transferee to pay a particular creditor out of the money left in his hand, this was held to be no act of insolvency. An out and out sale to a creditor on consideration is also not an act of insolvency, even if the consideration is left in the hands of the transferee for the benefit of the other creditors. Section 6 (a) is attracted when the transfer looks like an endeavour on the part of the debtor to put his property into a course of distribution among his creditors. But when a debtor, having transferred his properties to a near relation for a consideration which he distributed among his creditors, totally ignoring the petitioning creditor that was held to be a fraudulent transfer and, therefore, an act of insolvency within the meaning of S.6. A creditor to whom the transfer is made or who has assented to the transfer cannot rely on the transfer as an act of insolvency, unless he revokes his consent.

2. If, in India or elsewhere, he makes a transfer of his property or of any part there of with intent to defeat or delay his creditors.

Where a debtor transferred a part of his property to a creditor in order to satisfy a decretal debt, this was not viewed as a transfer to defeat his creditors. It is not necessary that the debtor should divest himself of all the rights in the property. Where a debtor leased out his business machinery on a monthly rent with a condition that he would not demand possession as long as the lessee used them in business, this was held to be a sufficient transfer so as to be viewed as an act of insolvency within the meaning of clause (b). In a case before the Bombay High Court, a person who was already indebted in respect of a past debt transferred to the creditor all the goodwill and interest in his business with all its stock in trade etc. The court agreed that a sale or mortgage by the debtor of the whole or substantially the whole of his property in consideration of a past debt, that is a debt already incurred, is an act of insolvency, whatever the motives of the parties may have been, but a transfer of only a part of his property for a past debt does not amount to an act of insolvency. Since it was not proved in this case by the petitioning creditor whether the deed of sale comprised all the debtor's available property, it could not be taken as an act of insolvency. Where the property conveyed exceeded the value of the debtor's liability by two-thirds and there was a trust for the surplus for the benefit of the debtor, it was held to be an act of insolvency. Where there was an assignment by way of mortgage by a trader of a portion of his effects as security for an existing debt, it was held that the assignment was not per se an act of insolvency in the absence of fraud, though the effect of putting the instrument in force would be to stop the trader's business. Where a debtor sold his property and soon after it made payments to some creditors, it was held that both transactions must be taken together in judging his intention and that these transactions must inevitably defeat or delay those creditors who did not receive any share in the sale price and, therefore, was an act of insolvency.

3. If, in India or elsewhere, he makes any transfer of his property or of any part there of, which would, under this or any other enactment for the time being in force, be void as fraudulent preference if he were adjudged an insolvent.

The expression "fraudulent preference" is considered subsequently in connection with Section 54 which authorises the avoidance of transactions amounting to fraudulent preference.

4. If with intent to defeat or delay his creditors

(i) he departs or remains out of the territories to which the Act extends;

(ii) he departs from his dwelling house or usual place of business or otherwise absents himself;

(iii) he secludes himself so as to deprive his creditors of the means of communicating with him.

If a debtor leaves the country with intent to defeat or delay his creditors, only then it will be an act of insolvency. If the departure is not accompanied with such intent, it is no act of insolvency. It is not, however, necessary that a particular creditor should actually be delayed. If the necessary consequence of a trader's departure is that his creditors must be delayed, he thereby commits an act of insolvency. A man is to be considered as foreseeing and meaning to bring about the necessary consequences of his own acts. Where a person went beyond sea, on account of having killed his wife and his creditors were thereby in fact prevented from recovering their debts, it was held to be an act of insolvency, the court, however, adding that it would have been otherwise if creditors were not prevented from recovering their debts. The same would be the effect of departure to avoid an arrest. In another case, a debtor left England with a woman, who, the debtor being a married man, refused to live with him as mistress unless he took her abroad. It was held that the effect of going abroad was to delay his creditors and, therefore, it was an act of insolvency, irrespective of his object in so doing.

In the case of a domiciled person, the fact of his departure to avoid a debtor's summons would be a strong presumption that he intended to defeat or delay his creditors, this presumption will not apply to a foreigner returning to his own country. Where a debtor absents himself for three years and thereby delays his creditors, the intent to delay will be presumed, although he may be pursuing his regular course of business. A debtor's own letters to a creditor written from different countries, were held to be admissible in evidence as proof of his intent in staying abroad to defeat his creditors. If a trader goes abroad, leaving a general power of attorney with his clerk to transact all his business for him, but provides no means of paying his debts as they fall due, he commits an act of insolvency. This will be so even if he keeps writing home of his intention of returning.

5. If any of his property has been sold in execution of the decree of any court for the payment of any money.

Section 9 of the Presidency Towns Insolvency Act makes this difference that in addition to sale of property in execution of a decree, an attachment of the debtor's property for twenty-one days is also regarded as an act of insolvency.

Decree for the payment of any money has been taken to mean a decree against the debtor personally so as to be realisable out of his property generally. A decree for the enforcement of a mortgage by selling the property mortgaged has been held to be not an act of insolvency. The Madras High Court laid down on the facts of a case before it that:

There is a distinction between a decree based upon a purely personal claim and a decree based upon a mortgage or charge antecedent to the suit. What is contemplated by the expression "in execution of the decree for the payment of money" is a decree capable of execution by the arrest of person or against the general estate of the person against whom the decree is passed. Where a particular property is hypothecated for a debt either by way of mortgage or charge the relief can only be against that particular property and not against the general estate. It is not capable of being enforced against the debtor or his general estate until the property mortgaged or charged is exhausted.

In a case before the Supreme Court, a person was declared insolvent because his property was sold in execution of a decree. He contended that he had wiped out the act of insolvency within one month of the sale by depositing the entire decretal amount and consequently the sale was set aside; his insolvency order should also be set aside. The court, however, refused to oblige him, as this would have been against the spirit of bankruptcy laws. Explaining this HIDAYATULLAH, J. said:

The object of the law of insolvency is to seize the property of an insolvent before he can squander it and to distribute it amongst his creditors. It is, however, not every debtor, who has borrowed beyond his assets or even one whose property is attached in execution of his debts, who can be subjected to such control. The jurisdiction of the court commences when certain acts take place which are known as acts of insolvency and which give a right to his creditors to apply to the courts for his adjudication as an insolvent. Some are voluntary acts of the insolvent and some others are involuntary. The involuntary acts are of a kind by which a creditor is able to compel a debtor to disclose his insolvent condition even if the insolvent is careful enough not to commit a voluntary act of insolvency. One such act is that the insolvent has been imprisoned in execution of a decree of any court for payment of money. In this case, the property of the appellant was sold in execution of a money decree and therefore, there is no doubt that he was guilty of an act of insolvency.

The court found on evidence that not only he had committed an act of insolvency, but he was also not able to pay his debts. Hence, his insolvency could not be condoned:

An act of insolvency once committed cannot be explained or purged by subsequent events. The insolvent cannot claim to wipe it off by paying some of his creditors. This is because the same act of insolvency is available to all his creditors. By satisfying one of the creditors the act of insolvency is not erased unless all creditors are satisfied because till all creditors are paid the debtor must prove his ability to meet his liabilities.

6. If he petitions to be adjudged an insolvent.

The debtor's petition for getting himself adjudicated an insolvent is in itself an act of insolvency giving the court the jurisdiction to adjudge, and the debtor has the right to be adjudged, an insolvent. Even if the debtor's petition fails, the act of insolvency remains and can be made use of by any of his creditors for proceeding against him provided that he does so within three months. If the petition is competent and the conditions prescribed by the Act have been fulfilled, the order has to follow as a matter of course.

7. If he gives notice to any of his creditors that he has suspended, or that he is about to suspend, payment of his debts.

The notice need not be in writing. It is enough if notice is given to any one of the creditors. No particular form is prescribed. There is nothing said in the Act about the debtor's intention. The question is what effect would the communication have on the minds of the persons to whom it is addressed. All that is required is that a communication proceeding from the debtor, made seriously, should give to the creditors or any of the creditors, to understand from the state of circumstances as disclosed that the debtor has suspended or is about to suspend payments. A debtor wrote to one of his creditors: "Be it known to you that your dunning me over and over for money is entirely useless. I am now so much indebted that I cannot pay off my debts. You do what you like". This was held to be a sufficient evidence of an act of insolvency. Similarly, where the debtor said: "I cannot pay your debts, you can do what you like." These words were held to be sufficient to indicate the intention of the debtor to suspend payment. Facts must show that the debtor is not merely refusing to pay a particular creditor, but has declined to pay any creditor and intends to give the same treatment to his creditors as a body. Where the debtor said that a large number of debts had become payable, his property was being sold in execution and he could not pay more than half on his debts and the creditors replied that they would be satisfied if they are paid to the extent of three-fourth, this was held to be no act of insolvency.

Where a debtor in a communication to his creditors expressed his inability to pay them and invited them to a meeting where he said he would present a statement of his affairs for their consideration and decision, it was held to be a sufficient indication of the intention to suspend payments.

8. If he is imprisoned in execution of the decree of any court for the payment of money.

Act of Insolvency by Agent

An explanation to Section 9 of the Presidency Towns Insolvency Act, which deals with the acts of insolvency provides that for the purposes of the section the act of an agent may be the act of the principal, even though the agent has no specific authority to commit the act. The last words, namely, "even though the agent has no specific authority to commit the act" are not there in the explanation to Section 6 of the Provincial Act. Apparently, the omission of these words should make no difference. All that the explanation in either case means to say is that the act of an agent may be regarded as an act of insolvency of the principal whether or not the agent was given any authority to commit the act. If the act was otherwise authorised, this explanation need not be taken in aid.

It is sufficient if the authority follows from his general position as an agent. Where all that was alleged was that certain creditors went to the Bombay office and were told by the agent there that his master had stopped payment, that would not be a notice of suspension by the debtor, since, in the ordinary course, an agent does not have an authority within the general scope of his agency to commit an act of insolvency on behalf of his master.

Who can be Adjudged Insolvent?

A person can be adjudged insolvent if he has committed an act of insolvency and is subject to the jurisdiction of the court.

Non-Residents or Foreigners [S.11 PTIA and]

A person who has not committed an act of insolvency in India cannot be adjudged an insolvent in India. An act of insolvency committed abroad will not do, even if the person committing it has resided in India or has carried on business or incurred trade debts. An act of insolvency committed in India will be sufficient even though the person concerned has left India before the petition. It is further necessary under Section 11 of the Presidency Towns Insolvency Act that the debtor, within a year before the petition, has ordinarily resided, or had a dwelling house or has carried on business either in person or through an agent within the jurisdiction of the court. In a Bombay case the debtor carried on business in Bombay which he closed six years before carried on business in Bombay which he closed six years before the petition. He left Bombay and settled elsewhere but without paying the outstanding debts. The question was whether it would be said of him that he was carrying on business within year before the petition. The court cited English cases including the decision of the House of Lords in *Theophile v. Solicitor General* where it was held that a debtor who had carried on business in England continued carrying on business in England until all the trade debts were paid. Their Lordships said that "there is a series of cases which in unbroken sequence have decided that trading does not cease when the shutters are put up but continues until the sums due are collected and all debts paid. Accordingly it was held that his business debts being still outstanding six years after the closure of his business, he was still in trade for the purposes of insolvency laws.

Minors

A minor, being absolutely incapable of contracting, he cannot be debtor and, therefore, cannot be adjudged insolvent. Even where, on attaining majority, he ratifies debts incurred by him during minority, the ratification being inoperative, he cannot he made insolvent in respect of such debts. If a minor is admitted to the benefits of a firm his share of profits and property may be applies in the insolvency of the firm, but he cannot personally be declared an insolvent. Section 99(2) of the P.T.I.A. provides that where a minor is a partner. His insolvency cannot be sought even for non-payment of articles of necessity supplied to him. Even in respect of necessaries there is no debt personally against him.

Married woman

In India, a married woman can be declared an insolvent in respect of her separate property whatever be her religion.

Persons of Unsound Mind

In India the position of a person of unsound mind is more or less the same as that of a minor. He is not capable of contracting and, therefore, cannot be a debtor; nor is he capable of committing an act of insolvency which involves a specific intent. He may, however, be adjudged insolvent for debts incurred by him during periods of sanity or lucid intervals.

Partners and Partnership Firms *[S.99 P.T.I.A. and 79(2)(c) of Prov I.A.]*

The cases in which a firm can be declared an insolvent were explained by the Supreme Court in *Mukand Lal (Firm) v. Purushottam Singh.* The court said that according to English law the act of bankruptcy must be a personal act and, therefore, a firm as such cannot commit an act of bankruptcy and no adjudication can be made against a firm in the firm's name. But under Section 99 of the Presidency Towns Insolvency Act an adjudication order may be made against the firm in the firm's name and such an order operates as if it were an order made against each of the persons who at the date of the order was a partner in the firm. There is, however, no provision corresponding to this section in the Provincial Act. But Section 79 (2) (c) provides for rules to be made by the High Court as to the procedure to be followed when the debtor is a firm. The section, therefore, assumes that an adjudication order can be made under the Provincial Act also against a firm in the firm's name, if the proper conditions are satisfied.

In order to support an adjudication against a firm there must be a proof that each of the partners has committed some act of insolvency. If, however, a joint act of insolvency is relied upon it must be shown to be the act of all the partners. An order of adjudication can also be made against a firm if there was an act of insolvency by an agent of the firm which was such as must necessarily be imputed to the firm. Whether an act of insolvency of one or more partners can be regarded as an act of all the partners is a question of fact. For instance, *in Re* Mohammed Hasham & Co., one of the partners in a firm consisting of two partners departed from the usual place of business with intent to delay and defeat the creditors of the firm, it was held that the firm could not be adjudged insolvent unless the other partner had also departed with like intent. Similarly, where one of the partners closed the business of the firm which amounted to an act of insolvency, it was held that it could not be regarded an act of the firm without some evidence to show that the other expressly or impliedly authorised the same. In the case before the Supreme Court, all that was proved was that one of the partners had transferred his personal property to his son, which was an act of insolvency. It was quite obviously held that no order of adjudication could be passed against the firm on that ground.

Joint Debtors

Just as partners can be joined in a single petition against them for insolvency, so also joint-debtors liable upon a joint debt, who have each committed either a joint or a separate act of insolvency can be joined. The Rangoon High Court thus allowed a joint petition against a Buddhist husband and wife who had committed a joint act of insolvency. The contrary Calcutta view has been described as not good law.

Joint Hindu Family

Section 99 of the Presidency Towns Insolvency Act applies expressly only to partnership firm and not to a joint Hindu family firm. But by analogy the same principle has been extended by the courts to the case of a family also. A joint family firm is a peculiar kind of partnership and there is nothing to show that the provisions of Section 99 are limited to any particular kind of partnership. Where the property of a family remained attached for more than twenty-one days and insolvency proceedings were instituted, an order was passed adjudicating the firm with two of the partners insolvent; two other members of the firm who were minors were not so adjudicated. The liability of the member who takes no part in the management of the firm is limited, like that of a minor, to his interest in the joint family property. Thus, sleeping and minor members cannot be adjudged insolvent.

The Petition [S.10]

Procedure under the Presidency Towns Insolvency Act

Section 10 provides that if a debtor commits an act of insolvency, an insolvency petition may be presented either by a creditor or by the debtor himself. The court may make an order adjudging him an insolvent. This order is called an order of adjudication. The presentation of a petition by the debtor himself is itself an act of insolvency and that gives jurisdiction to the court to adjudge him an insolvent.

Restriction on Jurisdiction [S.11]

The court will have jurisdiction to pass an order of adjudication only where:

(1) the debtor is, at the time of the petition, imprisoned for non-payment of a decree in a prison in which debtors are ordinarily committed by the court in the exercise of its ordinary original jurisdiction; or

(2) the debtor, within a year before the petition, has ordinarily resided or had a dwelling house, or has agent within the limits of the ordinary original civil jurisdiction of the court; or

(3) the debtor personally works for gain within those limits; or

(4) in the case of a firm of debtors, the firm has carried on business within a year before the date of the petition within those limits.

Creditor's Petition [S.12]

A creditor can present a petition only in the following cases:

(1) The debt owed by the debtor should amount to at least five hundred rupees. This should be so either in reference to a single creditor or where more than two creditors join, the amount owing to them should total up to at least five hundred rupees,

(2) The debt should be a liquidated one either payable immediately or at some certain future time, and

(3) The act of insolvency on which the petition is grounded has occurred within three months before the petition. If the court is closed on the day on which such three months expire, the petition may be presented on the day that the court reopens.

If the petitioning creditor is a secured creditor, he should state that he is willing to relinquish the security for the benefit of the creditors in the event of the debtor being declared insolvent, or that he will give an account of the value of the security. If the value is less than the amount due, he may be treated for the balance as an unsecured creditor.

Where the alleged act of insolvency is the attachment of property for twenty-one days, the period of three months is to be reckoned from the expiry of 21 days. The fact that the attachment continues for more than one day does not make it a continuing act of insolvency. Nor is there a repetition of the act of insolvency at the expiration of every twenty-one days there after. Once 21 days have expired, the act of insolvency is complete. A petition, therefore, must be presented within three months of the completion of the first 21 days though the attachment may continue for more 21 days.

The debt of Rs. 500 or more should exist not only at the time when the petition was presented, but also at the time of the hearing of the petition and at the moment of time immediately prior to the making of an order of insolvency.

The debt must be liquidated one. A debt does not cease to be a liquidated sum, because it can be arrived at only after making some simple calculation; but if it is not readily ascertainable without enquiry, then it is an unliquidated claim. It is only when the account is of a simple nature that it can form the basis of insolvency proceedings. If there are entries in the accounts which are open to serious disputes, and the amount is subject to counter claims and an enquiry is necessary to ascertain which items and which counter claims are true, then it is not a claim for a liquidated sum.

Proceedings on Creditor's Petition [S.13]

The creditor should verify the contents of his petition by an affidavit or some one else who has knowledge of the facts should certify it on his behalf.

At the hearing, the court requires the proof of the following:

(1) The debt of the petitioning creditor;

(2) The act of insolvency, or if more than one acts are alleged, proof of at least one of them.

The court may then either adjourn the hearing or order service on the debtor. In the following cases, the court is bound to dismiss the petition:

(1) If the court is not satisfied with the proof of the above two facts.

(2) If the debtor appears and satisfies the court that he is able to pay his debts, or that he has not committed an act of insolvency or that for some other sufficient cause no order ought to be made.

The court may pass an insolvency order if the requisite facts are proved or if the petition was adjourned and inspite of having been served upon the debtor, he did not appear. But the court may refuse the order if it is of opinion that the petition should have been presented in some other court.

Where the debtor appears and says that he is not indebted to the petitioner or that he is not indebted to the requisite extent, the court may order him to pay to the petitioner any debt which may be established against the debtor in due course of law and may stay the proceedings for such time as may be required for the trial of the question relating to the debt. Where such stay has caused delay and another creditor has demanded insolvency, the court may pass an insolvency order and dismiss the petition on which the stay order was based.

A creditor cannot withdraw his petition without leave of the court.

Sub-section (4) gives a chance to the debtor to convince the court that he is in a position to pay his debts, and then no order will be passed against him. the court will be so convinced if the debtor shows that he has present means of paying his debts. It has been held that although a debtor may have assets which, if liquidated, would provide sufficient money to discharge his debts, yet if he has no liquid assets wherewith to pay his debts at present, he is not able to pay his debts within the meaning of Section 13(4).43 In a Calcutta case the assets of a joint family were locked up in family disputes and pending suits, but were otherwise sufficient, nor any of the members had denied payment or proposed compromise, the court dismissed the petition because no act of insolvency had committed. This is necessary to prevent creditors from converting insolvency proceeding into economic and swifter way of realizing debts. Where a debtor is possessed of assets substantially exceeding his liabilities, his temporary absence from his normal and convenient place will not justify an insolvency order.

The words "other sufficient cause" are not to be taken *'ejusdem generis'* to mean that any other cause similar to those mentioned before. These words give a discretion to the court which can be exercised on any justifying cause, for example, if the petitioner's conduct is unworthy or abuse of the right, the court may order dismissal of his petition. Where a creditor persisted with his proceeding inspite of the fact that the court ordered his payment out of the funds deposited by the debtor that was held to be a sufficient cause for the dismissal of his petition. But adjudication cannot be refused on the ground that the debtor has deposited the whole of the amount due to the petitioning creditor. If other creditors are not provided for there is a chance of the proceedings being repeated.

Debtor's Petition [S.14]

Section 14 states the conditions on which a debtor can apply:

(1) The debt must amount to rupees five hundred or more; or

(2) He has been arrested and imprisoned in execution of a decree of any court for the payment of money; or

(3) An order of attachment in execution of such a decree has been made and is subsisting against his property.

It is sufficient if the debtor proves any one of the above conditions. If he presents a petition when none of the above conditions is satisfied, that will be an abuse of the process of the court. Where his adjudication has been once annulled, and he files another petition, that will be an abuse and the court can reject it.

Section 15 provides that the debtor shall allege in his petition that he is unable to pay his debts and if the debtor proves that he is entitled to present a petition, the court may make an order of adjudication. In such a case, the court will refuse adjudication only if the debtor is abusing the insolvency proceedings. A person who has already been declared an insolvent and is not yet discharged, can be proceeded against for another order of insolvency if he has contracted fresh debts after the commencement of his insolvency.

A debtor cannot withdraw his petition without the leave of the court. When the debtor's petition is admitted, he shall produce all books of account and file such list of creditors and debtors and afford such assistance to the court as the court may prescribe. It he fails to do so the court may dismiss his petition.

Procedure under the Provincial Act

Contents of Petition [S.13]

A debtor's petition should contain the following particulars:

(1) A statement that he is unable to pay his debts;

(2) the place where he ordinarily resides or carries on business or personally works for gain, or, if he has been arrested or imprisoned, the place where he is in custody.

(3) the court by whose order he has been arrested or imprisoned, or his property attached and the particulars of the decree;

(4) the amount and particulars of all pecuniary claims against him, names and residence of his creditors as are known to him or can be ascertained with reasonable diligence;

(5) the amount and particulars of all his property, its valuation, the place where it can be found and a declaration of his willingness to place all his property at the disposal of the court which is otherwise available for insolvency;

(6) a statement whether he had filed any petition on a previous occasion and, if he had, whether it was dismissed or an adjudication order was passed and whether the same has been annulled or not.

A creditor's petition should specify the particulars stated in point (2) above and shall also state (1) the act of insolvency and the date of commission (2) the amount of his or their claim against the debtor.

Withdrawal [S.14]

A petition cannot be withdrawn either by the creditor or by the debtor except with the leave of the court.

Consolidation of Petition [S.15]

Where more than one petitions have been presented against the debtor or separate petitions have been presented against joint debtors, the court may consolidate them on such terms as it thinks fit.

Power to change carriage of Proceedings [S.16]

Where it appears to the court that the petitioner is not proceeding with due diligence on his petition, the court may substitute any other creditor to whom the debtor may be indebted in the like amount.

Death of Debtor [S.17]

If the debtor dies, the proceedings may be continued, as the court may order so far as may be necessary for the realisation and distribution of the property of the debtor.

Procedure on Admission [S.19]

The court may make an order fixing a date for the hearing of the petition. Notice shall be given to all the creditors and where the debtor is not the petitioner, notice shall be given to him also.

Interim Receiver [S.20]

In the case of creditor's petition, the court may, and in the case of debtor's petition, shall, appoint an interim receiver of the property of the debtor, directing him to take immediate possession of the property.

Interim Proceedings against Debtor [S.21]

The court can also make any of the following orders:

(1) require the debtor to give reasonable security for his appearance and, in default to detain him in civil prison;

(2) his attachable property to be attached and sold in execution of a decree;

(3) issue a warrant for his arrest and detention in civil prison and that he shall be released on reasonable terms as to security.

Such detention or attachment order shall not be made unless the court is satisfied that the debtor has absconded or is likely to abscond to delay and defeat his creditors or has failed to disclose or has concealed his property. This may sometime require investigation and an order made without the requisite investigation may be declared to be illegal. Accordingly the Calcutta High Court declared the attachment of a shop to be illegal. Another man was claiming ownership of the shop and the order was passed without looking into the truth of his claim. The court cited with approval the following statement from a judgement of the Allahabad High Court.

Where certain property was attached before the petitioner was declared an insolvent and a receiver appointed, it was held that the court was bound to hear and adjudicate upon any claim which might be preferred by persons alleging themselves to be in fact the owners of such property. Proceedings under this section are analogous to attachment before judgement under the Civil Procedure Code.

Duties of Debtors [S.22]

The following duties are imposed upon the debtors by Section 22 of the Provincial Act. These duties arise when an order is made admitting the petition:

(1) To produce all books of account.

(2) To prepare an inventory of his property and lists of his creditors and debtors as and when required.

(3) To submit himself to such examination in respect of his property or creditors, and attend at such times before the court or receiver, execute such instruments and generally do such acts as may be required by the court or receiver.

The Calcutta High Court examined the scope of this section in *Akshaychand Bagwani v. Emperor* and laid down that the first duty arises only at the first stage of the proceeding when the petition is admitted and is not applicable to the case of an order made on a creditor's petition. The rest of the duties, however, apply to both classes of cases, namely, orders made on the creditor's as well as on the debtor's petitions and to all stages of the proceedings that follow the order admitting the petition, leaving it to the court or receiver to make the requisition at the appropriate stage, and not only upto the order of adjudication.

Release of Debtor [S.23]

The court is given the power to release the debtor if he is already under arrest in the execution of a money decree against him. The order may be subject to such terms as to security as may be reasonable and necessary. The court also has the power to order rearrest. For either kind of order under this section, the court has to record its reasons in writing. The protection under this section can be given only against actual arrest in the execution of money decree and not against any other kind of arrest.

Procedure at Hearing [S.24]

On the day of hearing, the court has to require proof of the following matters:

(1) That the creditor or the debtor is entitled to present the petition. If the debtor is the petitioner the court will only require a *prima facie* proof of his contentions.

(2) That the debtor, if he did not appear on a petition presented by a creditor, has been served with notice of the order admitting the petition.

(3) That the debtor has committed the alleged act of insolvency.

(4) The court has the power to examine the debtor as to his conduct in reference to his property and the creditors shall also have the right to question him.

(5) If sufficient cause is shown the court can grant extension of time to any creditor or debtor for proving any fact necessary to the petition.

(6) The judge shall make a memorandum of the evidence which shall form part of the record of the case.

Dismissal of Petition [S.25]

In the case of a creditor's petition, if the court is not satisfied of his right to petition, or of service of notice upon the debtor, or of the alleged act of insolvency, or is satisfied that the debtor is able to pay his debts or that for some other sufficient cause no order should be made, the court shall dismiss the petition.

In the case of a debtor's petition the court shall dismiss it, if it is not satisfied of his right to present.

Award of Compensation [S.26]

Where a creditor's petition is dismissed and the court finds that the petition was frivolous or vexatious, the court can, on the application of the debtor, order the petitioner to pay to the debtor any amount, not exceeding Rs. 1,000, as reasonable compensation for his expenses and injury to his reputation. The amount can be realised from the creditor as if it were a fine imposed upon him by the court. The award shall have the effect of preventing any other suit for compensation in respect of the same petition.

Order of Adjudication [S.27]

If the court does not dismiss the petition, it shall make an order of adjudication and shall specify in the order the period within which the debtor should apply for his discharge, though, of course, the court shall have the power to extend such time and publish notice of the extension in such manner as may be necessary.

If the petitioning creditor has brought his case within the framework of the Act, he is entitled to an adjudication order and the court has no choice but to pass such order.

Effects of Order of Adjudication [S.17, PTI and S.28, PIA]

Section 17 of the Presidency Act gives the effect of the order of insolvency. It says that on the passing of an order of insolvency, the property of the insolvent, wherever situate, shall be vested in the official assignee. The property then becomes divisible among his creditors.

The second outstanding effect of the order is that after the property has been vested in the official assignee, no creditor, during the of insolvency proceedings, can have any remedy against the property of the insolvent, or can commence any suit or proceedings except with the leave of the court and that also on such terms as the court may impose. This, however, does not affect the rights of any secured creditor to deal with the property covered by his security.

The Provincial Insolvency Act states in Section 20 the effects of the order in the following points:

(1) The insolvent should help the court to the utmost of his power in the realisation of his property and the distribution of the proceeds among his creditors.

(2) The whole of the property of the insolvent shall vest in the court, or in a receiver and be divisible among his creditors. No claims or proceedings against the insolvent can be commenced except with the leave of the court.

(3) The property of the insolvent shall include all goods in his possession, order or disposition, at the time of the presentation of the petition, provided that they are with him in his trade or profession and, if they belong to someone else, then it will be necessary that they are in his possession with the consent of the true owner and under such circumstances that the insolvent is the reputed owner of those goods.

(4) If the insolvent acquires any property or any property devolves upon him during the tendency of the proceedings, that will also vest in the receiver and shall be available for distribution.

(5) The property of insolvent shall not include any property (not being books of account) which is exempted by the Code of Civil Procedure from attachment and execution sale.

(6) The power of a secured creditor to deal with his security is not to be affected by the order.

(7) The order relates back to, and takes effect from, the date of the presentation of the petition.

Thus the vesting of property for distribution among creditors and what that property includes are the two main effects of these provisions.

Vesting of Property

A petition for insolvency begins as a proceeding between a creditor and his debtor, but upon the issue of the order the proceeding is transformed in its character. The State then intervenes as a guardian of the creditors and of commercial morality. In a popular case which goes by the name *In re A Debtor,* where the insolvent's request that publicity should not be given to the proceedings was turned down by the court, COLLINS L. J. made pertinent remarks about the object of these provisions. His Lordship said that in the absence of proper publicity, the insolvent might as well go on trading and trapping other creditors.

"Why should those persons to whom is entrusted by law the guardianship, not only of the interests of the particular creditors and of the particular debtor, but of public morality and the interests that every member of the public has in the observance of commercial morality, stand by and allow the debtor to go on trading? Now then what is the scheme of the Act. It is quite obvious that the cardinal point is that all these proceedings, from the beginning to the end, shall be kept under the eye of the Government — under the eyes of the public authority. There is another and a larger interest to be safeguarded than the interest of the particular creditors, that is the interest of public.

An insolvency order thus operates in favour and for the benefit of all the creditors. It puts all the creditors on equality and prevents preference of one over the other. Where with the consent of all his creditors, an insolvent sought rescission of the order against him, ESHER M.R. replied:

Although the consent of all the creditors has been obtained, the court will still consider whether what they have agreed to is for the benefit of the creditors as a whole, and also whether it is conducive or detrimental to commercial morality and to the interests of the public at large and also whether what is proposed will not place his future creditors, who must come into existence immediately, in a position of imminent danger.

In another case, his Lordship laid down that when a receiving order has been made the court will not, even though the proceedings under it have been stayed, rescind the order merely upon the consent of the petitioning creditor. The court has a discretion in the matter, and will not rescind the order without a full investigation of all the circumstances, including the conduct of the debtor.

Vesting under the Presidency Towns Insolvency [S.17]

Section 17 operates to vest the insolvent's property in the official assignee. Where two orders of adjudication have been passed against the same insolvent, the one which is passed earlier will operate to vest the property in the official assignee and the subsequent order will remain infructuous even though the petition on the basis of which it was passed was of an earlier date. The order no doubt relates back to the date of petition but not for the purpose of divesting property which has already been vested in the official assignee.

Property which is acquired subsequently to the adjudication but before discharge also vests in the assignee, but not automatically. The official assignee has to intervene and demand the property and then it will indefeasibly vest in him. Where the plaintiff insolvent had filed a suit against a bank for damages for unjustified dishonour of his cheques and impleaded the official assignee as a second defendant, the assignee's plea that the decree, if any, should be passed in his favour, was held to be a sufficient intervention for the purpose of vesting the property in him.

The property of the debtor which has already been attached, but not yet sold, shall also vest in the assignee. In a Madras case, there was a pending suit for recovery of money under a hypothecation deed and an attachment of the debtor's immovable property was effected, but before the final decree was passed, the debtor became insolvent and the official assignee sought cancellation of the attachment, it was held that the result of an adjudication is that any attachment of his property would become cancelled and the property would be vested in the official assignee and this will be so even if the attachment was made with the consent of the debtor. A consent attachment does not give better rights than what an ordinary attaching creditor would have. The list of property would be prepared as from the date on which the first act of insolvency was committed.

Under Section 17 and 51 of the Presidency Towns Insolvency Act (III of 1909) the insolvency commences on the date of the commission of an act of insolvency. At that date the property of an insolvent vests in the official assignee who has distributed it among creditors who prove their debts. If a creditor's debt is not barred at the date of the act of insolvency on which a debtor is adjudicated an insolvent, even though it may be barred at the date of the order of adjudication, such a debt can be proved in the insolvency.

An amount standing to the credit of an insolvent in the hands of the Regional Provident Fund Commissioner and which has not been paid to the insolvent, does not vest in the official assignee. This is so by virtue of the provisions of the Employee's Provident Funds Act, which override those of the Insolvency Acts. But on payment to the insolvent this immunity ceases.

All properties, in India, movable or immovable, are vested in the assignee automatically including any interest in any property. Similarly, movable property outside India is also vested in the assignee automatically. Vesting of foreign immovable property would require final transfer in accordance with the law of that country.

Vesting under Provincial Insolvency Act [S.28]

The property is vested in the court and then in the receiver when a receiver is appointed. Vesting is not postponed to the appointment of a receiver. The principles stated above are also applicable under this Act.

One of the most important effects of vesting is that the insolvent cannot deal with his property. No buyer from the insolvent can get a good title. The power of disposal after adjudication is vested in the receiver or assignee.

Bar and Stay of Suits and Other Legal Proceedings

S.17 Presidency Act and Ss. 28 (2) & (6) and 29 Provincial Act

One of the most important effects of adjudication is upon the proceedings by or against the insolvent, under both the Acts.

The creditors of the insolvent, during the period of insolvency, and in respect of debts provable in insolvency, cannot file any suit or proceeding or make any claim against him or his property, except with the leave of the court and on such terms as the court may impose. The provision prevents filing of new claims, and does not say anything about pending suits. Section 18 of the Presidency Act contains a provision about pending suits also. It says that the insolvency court can stay any suit or other proceeding pending against the insolvent before any court or judge which is subject to the superintendence of the court. The court in which any such proceeding is pending is also given the power to stay it or allow it to continue on such terms as the court may impose. This provision is not there in the Provincial Act. Instead Section 29 provides that the court in which any proceeding is pending may either stay it or allow it to continue on such terms as the court may impose.

Section 18A of the Presidency Act further provides that if any court which is subject to the superintendence of the insolvency court has passed an order of adjudication against the same person, the court can annul it. If any act was done by such court or receiver in the mean time, that will remain valid, but for further action the property will be vested in the Official Assignee.

Appointment of Special Manager [S.19 PTIA]

If the court is of opinion that the nature of the debtor's estate or business or the interest of his creditors require the appointment of a special manager to assist the official assignee, the court may make an appointment accordingly. The time for which he will function is to be determined by the court. His powers will be those as may be entrusted to him by the official assignee or as the court may direct.

Notice or Advertisement of Adjudication [S.20 Presidency and S.30]

Notice of every order of adjudication has to be published in the Official Gazette. The notice should specify the name, address and description, of the insolvent, the date of adjudication, the court by which the order has been made and the date of the presentation of the petition.

Subsequent proceedings

Protection Order [S. 25 Presidency and S.31 Provincial]

If the insolvent applies for protection, the court may make an order for his protection against arrest or detention. The court may give a blanket protection against all debts or against some of them only. The commencement of protection and its duration are in the discretion of the court. The order is also revocable at the discretion of the court. Any revocation of such order or annulment of adjudication shall not affect the rights of the creditors.

Creditors are entitled to appear and oppose the grant of a protection order.

These are the main provisions of Section 31 of the Provincial Act. Section 25 of the Presidency Act contains more or less the same provisions, with only minor differences. The court can grant protection after the insolvent has submitted his schedule. But the court may grant protection without the schedule if the court thinks it necessary to do so in the interest of the creditors. Another difference under the Presidency Act is that where a creditor appears to oppose the grant of protection, the insolvent shall be prima facie entitled to protection if he produces a certificate from the official assignee that he has been conforming to the provisions of the Act.

Arrest after Adjudication [S.32 Provincial]

If any creditor or the receiver brings it to the notice of the court that the insolvent has absconded or departed from the jurisdiction of the court in order to avoid his obligation, the court may issue a warrant for his arrest. On his appearance before the court, he may be released on such security as may be reasonable or necessary. It he fails to furnish the security, the court may direct his detention in a civil prison which may extend to three months.

Schedule of Creditors [S.33 Provincial, S.24 Presidency]

After the order of adjudication it becomes the right as well duty of persons who claim themselves to be the creditors of the insolvent to tender proof of their claims together with evidence of the amount due and its particulars. The court shall then determine the list of persons who have proved themselves to be the creditors of the insolvent stating also the amount due. This list is called the schedule of creditors. If the court finds that the value of an alleged debt is not capable of being fairly estimated, the court may make an order to that effect and then that debt will not be included in the schedule. A copy of the schedule has to be posted in the court house.

It a creditor happens to be omitted from the list, he can also, before the insolvent is discharged, tender proof that his debt is provable. The court will give notice to the receiver and other creditors to hear their objections, if any, the court may either order the debt to be included or reject the application.

Section 24 of the Presidency Act contains the following provisions in reference to the insolvent's schedule.

(1) The debtor has to prepare and submit to the court a schedule verified by affidavit relating to his affairs.

(2) The schedule has to be submitted within the following times —
   (a) if the order is make on the petition of the debtor, within thirty days from the date of the order;
   (b) if the order is made on the petition of a creditor, within thirty days of the date of the service of the order.

(3) If the insolvent fails to do so without any reasonable excuse, the court can make an order for his committal to the civil prison. The official assignee can get the list prepared at the expense of the insolvent's estate to make good his default.

Debts Provable [S.34 Provincial]

Debts provable include all debts and liabilities, whether present or future, certain or contingent. It is necessary that the debtor should be subject to such debts at the time of adjudication or he may become subject to them before his discharge provided that the obligation for which they become due was incurred before the date of adjudication.

Debts provable do not include claims which are not capable of being fairly estimated and also demands in the nature of unliquidated damages. But demands in the nature of unliquidated damages arising by reason of contract or breach of trust are provable.

The main points stated by the section can be put in terms of the following propositions:

(1) Present and future debts, certain and contingent debts are provable if they existed at the time of adjudication or if they arose subsequently but before discharge, it is necessary that the obligation in respect of which they arose was incurred before adjudication.

(2) Debts which are not capable of being fairly estimated are not provable.

(3) Claims sounding only in unliquidated damages are not provable except in respect of a contract or breach of trust.

It has been held in some English cases that the decree of a Divorce court ordering a man to pay alimony for the rest of his and his wife's life is not a debt provable in insolvency. A claim of alimony is not capable of proper estimation because the man an compromise with his wife at any time and also because the court can alter the amount at a subsequent stage. It has been held by the Madras High Court that a claim for maintenance is different from a claim for alimony and is provable in insolvency.

An adjudication order was passed in 1933 against a debtor. His wife had obtained in 1932 a decree against him for her mahar (dower) and maintenance. In 1934 she applied for the execution of this decree.

The court held that a part of the debt having been incurred before adjudication and being for a certain amount was provable in insolvency. She could not, therefore, seek execution without the leave of the Insolvency court. The court said:

There is a clear distinction between orders for alimony and decree for maintenance. Orders granting alimony were always subject to modification and change. A maintenance decree ordinarily remains immutable and although the debtor may take separate proceedings to have it modified, it can never be modified retrospectively as the order for alimony in England can.

Where an insolvent's debt has been discharged by a joint debtor, the claim for contribution from the insolvent is provable; it is not a claim for damages.

The Madras High Court held in a case that damages for use and occupation are of the nature of unliquidated damages and would, therefore, come within the provisions of Section 34 (1) of the Act which prohibits the proving of such debts in insolvency. Claim for damages for occupation after the adjudication order is also not provable being not in respect of obligations incurred before adjudication. A personal liability created by the debtor by mortgaging his property is provable and if not proved in insolvency, it would he discharged by the discharge of the debtor. In a case before the Nagpur High Court.

A person was declared insolvent for his business debts. His brother had joined the business before the insolvency by contributing a sum of money, for which a promissory note was given to him when he left the business. He sought to prove his claim in the insolvency.

He was permitted to do so. On his retirement, the firm became dissolved and he became a creditor for his claim. The court stated the following principle of English law.

The rule in English law is that a partner in a firm against which a commission of bankruptcy issues shall not prove in competition with the creditors of the firm who are in fact his own creditors, and shall not take part of the fund to the prejudice of those who are not only creditors of the partnership, but of himself; but it is essential for its application that there should be some creditors proving under the bankruptcy for a debt or debts in respect of which the present or former partner whose proof is excluded, and the bankrupt were jointly liable.

A promissory note issued after presentation of the petition but before adjudication is not provable.

The corresponding provisions in the Presidency Act are in Section 46.

Annulment of Adjudication [S35 Provincial, S 21 Presidency]

Annulment of adjudication means that subsequent to an order of adjudication the court finds some reason which shows that the debtor should not have been declared an insolvent or that the insolvency order should be lifted, the court cancels the order of adjudication. Under the Provincial Act, the court can pass such an order in the following cases:

(1) Where, in the opinion of the court, the debtor ought not to have been declared an insolvent.

(2) Where it is proved to the satisfaction of the court that the debts of the insolvent have been paid in full.

(3) Where the adjudication was made on the petition of the debtor himself, the court may annul it if it is proved on an application by the receiver or any creditor that the conditions of Section 10 (2) were not satisfied and, therefore, the debtor was not entitled to an order of adjudication.

An order of annulment can be passed on the application of the debtor or any other interested person. The Presidency Act does not mention the word "debtor" and, therefore, entitles "any interested person" to apply for annulment.

The second sub-section of Section 21 of the Presidency Act further explains as to what is meant by payment of a debt in full. It says that a debt disputed by a debtor shall be considered as paid in full, if the debtor enters a bond in such sum and with such securities as the court approves that he will pay the amount. The Act also provides that a debt payable to a creditor who cannot be found or cannot be identified shall be considered to be paid in full if the payment is made into the court.

Another ground on which adjudication can be annulled is when the court has approved a scheme of compromise or arrangement in accordance with the provisions of the Act.

An adjudication can also be annulled where the debtor does not apply for his discharge within the time allowed to him or does not appear on the day fixed for hearing for an order of discharge.

Concurrent Proceedings [S. 36 Provincial and 22 Presidency]

If it is proved to the court which has passed an order of adjudication that proceedings against the same debtor were pending in another court and the property of the debtor can be more conveniently handled by that other court, the court may either annul the order or stay all proceedings on it. This provision is alike in both the Acts.

The provision enables the court to cancel or stay its own proceedings and not those of any other court.

Proceedings on Annulment [S. 37 Provincial and S. 23 Presidency]

An order of annulment has to be notified in the Official Gazette and also in such manner as the court may prescribe.

Annulment will have no effect upon sales or dispositions of property or payments made by the court or the receiver before the date of annulment. Such transactions will remain valid. For the future, the property of the debtor will be vested in the person whom the court may appoint for the purpose. If the court makes no such appointment, it shall revert to the debtor to the extent of his rights and interests in it and subject to such conditions as the court may by order impose.

The Presidency Act makes this further provision that if the debtor was in prison at the time of adjudication and he was released because of the adjudication, then upon the annulment of the order of his adjudication, the debtor will be recommitted to his former custody. The jailor to whom he is so recommitted shall be bound to receive him. The proceedings which were then in force against the debtor shall again take force as if no release order had ever been made.

"The object of the section is to preserve accomplished acts. In this particular case, no property had vested in anybody. All that happened was that property had been directed to be sold because it was thought that a sale was necessary for the payment of the insolvent's debts. But it afterwards turned out that it was wholly unnecessary. The learned judge should have reviewed the order by cancelling it: The fact that a sale might have caused the parties to cease quarrelling does not seem to be relevant."

In a Calcutta case, the court passed an order like this: "Annulled. The assets to remain in the hands of the Official Assignee subject to the further order of the court." The court held that the effect of the order was that the assets of the debtor were reverted to him.

"The section provides for terms and conditions to be applied only to the debtor on reversion — otherwise no conditions are necessary. The effect of the order was that the property of the debtor reverted to him, but on condition that the assets already in the hands of the Official Assignee were to remain in his hands subject to the further order of the court. The property which was neither in the hands of the Official Assignee, nor vested in him, was not affected by the order."

It has been held by the Bombay High Court that when a dividend has been declared in favour of a creditor, it ceases to be the property of the debtor. It per chance it could not be paid to the creditor it will not revert to the debtor but shall be vested in the State.

Where an order of annulment reserves a fund for the benefit of the creditors, it will not be available to the debtor and will have to be dealt with as if it were subject to the insolvency. The official assignee becomes a trustee for the amount. But the surplus, if any, left in his hands which is not claimed by any creditor can be ordered by the court to be paid back to the debtor.

Meeting of Creditors [S. 26 Presidency]

There are two further provisions in the Presidency Act about proceedings consequent on an order of adjudication. One of them provides for meetings of creditors. The court which passes an order of adjudication can at any time order a meeting of the creditors to be called. The order can be passed on an application by any creditor or by the official assignee. The purpose of the meeting is to consider the circumstances of the insolvency, the insolvent's schedule and his explanations of his schedule. The meeting can also consider generally the mode of dealing with the property of the insolvent.

The rules stated in the First Schedule are to be observed in summoning and for the proceedings of a meeting.

Public Examination of the Insolvent [S. 27 Presidency]

The court which has passed an order of adjudication is required to hold a public sitting on any day to be fixed by the court. The notice of such sitting should be given to the creditors in the prescribed manner. The purpose of the sitting is to subject the insolvent to a public examination. The insolvent is bound to attend. He can be examined as to his conduct, dealings and property.

The date of examination should be after the expiry of the time for filing of the insolvent's schedule, but should be fixed as soon as convenient.

Any creditor who has tendered a proof may, himself or through a legal practitioner acting on his behalf, ask any questions concerning the insolvent's affairs and the causes of his failure. The official assignee has also to take part in the examination. Subject to any directions that the court may give, the official assignee may be represented by a legal practitioner. The court can ask expedient questions to the insolvent.

The insolvent has to take oath and answer all such questions as the court may put or allow to be put. The court may make such notes of his answers as it thinks proper. The notes should be read by or to the insolvent and signed by him. They constitute evidence against the insolvent and have to be available to the creditors at all reasonable times for inspection.

When the court is satisfied that the affairs of the insolvent have been sufficiently investigated, the court may close the examination. But this will not preclude the court from summoning him for further examination if necessary.

The court may exempt the insolvent from public examination if he is a lunatic or is suffering from such mental or physical affliction or disability as make him unfit for such examination or if the insolvent is a woman who according to the customs or manners of the community ought not to be compelled to appear in public. The court can in such cases either dispense with the examination altogether or direct the time, manner and place at which the insolvent should be examined. The court should not, however, lightly dispense with it. The Calcutta High Court pointed out in a case.

...... although there may be power under the Act to dispense with the public examination of a debtor, in a case in which a composition is being proposed, it is a very strong thing to dispense with the public examination. In the present case the scheme is extremely informal, hazy and unsatisfactory, and, apart from that, there has been no investigation into the matter; and until there has been an investigation no creditor can know whether it is in his interest to accept the scheme of composition.

Composition and Schemes of Arrangement [S. 38 Prov. and S. 28 Pres.]

The debtor who has been adjudged an insolvent has a right to submit to the court a proposal for a composition in satisfaction of his debts, or a proposal for a scheme of arrangement of his affairs. If he does so, the court should fix a date for the consideration of the proposal and issue a notice to all the creditors. If the proposal is approved by a majority in number and who are creditors to the tune of 3/4 in value and who are present either personally or through a pleader, the proposal shall be deemed to be duly accepted by the creditors. The debtor can make any amendments in his proposal at the meeting if the court is of opinion that the amendment is calculated to benefit the general body of creditors. The court should consider the report of the receiver, if any, and the objections of the creditors, and then, if it appears that the terms of the proposal are not reasonable or are not calculated to benefit the general body of creditors, the court should refuse to affirm the scheme. If any fact is proved which would entitle the court to refuse, suspend or attach conditions to the debtor's discharge, the court may refuse to approve the proposal unless reasonable security is given that at least six annas in a rupee would be paid to all such unsecured creditors whose claims are provable against the debtor's estate. Further, no scheme should be approved unless it provides for prior payment of all such debts as are directed to be paid in preference to other debts in the administration of the property of the insolvent.

Apart from these considerations, the court has been given a discretionary power to refuse approval on any grounds as may be reasonable in the circumstances.

Stated in other words, the conditions for the approval of a scheme are as follows:

(1) The scheme should be approved by the requisite majority of creditors.

(2) Its terms should be reasonable and calculated to benefit the general body of creditors.

(3) Where the debtor would not be entitled to a clean discharge, he should assure six anna payment in a rupee to his unsecured creditors.

(4) Priority of payments as directed by the Act should be assured.

The Presidency Act makes a few further provisions. A creditor can express his assent or dissent by means of a letter which should reach the official assignee a day before the meeting. Such assent or dissent will have the effect as if the creditor was personally present.

Section 29 of the Presidency Act deals with approval of the proposal. It incorporates the conditions stated above and makes two additional provisions. The proposal is not to be heard until after the conclusion of the public examination of the insolvent, except where the administration is of a summary nature or special leave of the court has been obtained. A creditor can speak against the scheme and the court shall hear him not with standing that at a meeting of the creditors he voted for the acceptance of the proposal. Before approving the scheme the court is required to hear the report of the official assignee, the objections of the creditors and also to take into account the conduct of the insolvent.

In a case before the Calcutta High Court, the insolvent had connived at the presenting of a false claim at a meeting of the creditors summoned for the purpose of approving a scheme of composition. The court laid down the following principles:

In rejecting or accepting proof of debts for the purpose of Section 28, the official assignee does only discharge his functions as the chairman of the meeting. He is not a court within the meaning of the Criminal Procedure Code.

A debtor after adjudication cannot settle with his creditors out of court. Such settlement is possible only by a scheme of composition under the Act.[76]

Under the Presidency Act a scheme of composition or arrangement can be submitted only after adjudication, whereas under the Provincial Act a proposal of this kind can be submitted either before or after adjudication.

It is really the approval of the court which makes the scheme binding. If the court approves the proposal the terms must be embodied in an order of the court and the adjudication must be annulled.

The jurisdiction of the insolvency court does not terminate even on the approval of a composition or scheme. Though the adjudication is annulled, the composition is made with the approval of the insolvency court and the court retains jurisdiction to give effect to it. The effect of the approval of a scheme is to substitute the scheme for the bankruptcy. The scheme remains under the control of the court. The payment of any instalment due under a composition may be enforced by an application to the court.

Insolvency proceeding is admittedly a proceeding in a court within the meaning of Section 195, Cr. P.C., it follows that the offence of lodging having been committed in relation to a proceeding in a court and without any complaint in writing by that court the Magistrate was debarred from taking congnizance of the same.

There can be no doubt that in an insolvency proceeding the function of the official assignee is chiefly and primarily administrative. At the same time it cannot be denied that the official assingee is given judicial powers also in certain respects along with his administrative powers. He, for example, is given judicial powers in the matter of proof of debts.

A scheme which has been approved by the court cannot be subsequently amended by any party whatsoever, including the official assignee, except with the approval of the court. In a case before the Patna High Court,[78] a scheme as approved by the court provided for simple interest in favour of a bank until full payment and also that certain persons will transfer on trust to the official assignee certain properties from the income of which the assignee will pay the bank. The trust deed provided for compound interest. The court held that even supposing that the trust deed was a supplementary part of the scheme and so was the provision for compound interest, the compound interest was not recoverable. Compound interest can be recovered only when the regular instalments are not paid in time. The provision for compound interest being a part of the scheme, it could not be enforced through any other court than the insolvency court.

The court also emphasised that an agreement of composition with creditors requires the strictest good faith. An agreement which attempts to give preference to one creditor as against the others and behind their back cannot be enforced. A scheme of composition is not *nudum pactum*,[79] but an agreement which is supported by good consideration, the consideration being the common sacrifice by the creditors who join the scheme. The very nature of this consideration makes it necessary that no creditor should be allowed to score off a secret advantage for himself or to commit any act which may amount to a breach of faith with the other creditors. The courts have consistently refused to enforce transactions which have been entered into in disregard to "commercial morality" even though the other creditors may not have been prejudiced in any way. This is so because one question always is that whether the judgment of the creditors has been influenced by the supposition that all are to suffer in the same proportion.

Order on Approval [S. 39 Prov. and S. 30 Pres.]

If the court approves the proposal its terms should be embodied in an order of the court. The adjudication should be annulled. Section 37 which deals with annulment will apply. All the creditors shall become bound by the scheme in reference to debts which are provable in insolvency.

Sub-section (2) of Section 30 of the Presidency Act further provides that the provisions of the composition or the scheme may be enforced by the court on an application by any interested person. Any disobedience of an order of the court made on any such application shall be deemed a contempt of the court. The scheme will operate as a discharge of the insolvent in respect of debts which were provable but which were not brought before the court.

Readjudication as Insolvent [S. 40 Prov. and S. 31 Pres.]

The court has been given the power to declare that the debtor is an insolvent again. This power can be exercised in the following cases:

(1) If a default is made in payment of any installment due under the scheme or compromise.

(2) If it appears to the court that the composition or scheme cannot proceed without injustice or undue delay.

(3) If the approval of the court was obtained by fraud.

Upon readjudication as insolvent, the composition or scheme becomes annulled, but without prejudice to the validity of any transfer or payment duly made or of anything duly done under or in pursuance of the scheme. Any debts otherwise provable and contracted by the debtor before readjudication shall become provable in the insolvency.

The property will vest back in the official assignee.

When a debtor is "adjudicated", or "re-adjudicated" or "freshly adjudicated" under Section 31, such adjudication is not independent of the original insolvency, although, no doubt, between the date when the scheme was approved and the date when the debtor is re-adjudged an insolvent, he is a free man. His legal position is analogous to that of an insolvent who has obtained his discharge but whose discharge ultimately is cancelled. During that period he is a person *sui juris;* but, after the acceptance and approval of the scheme the jurisdiction of the court continues, and the scheme, when accepted and approved operates only as a conditional discharge, and subject to Section 31 (2) upon annulment and re-adjudication the *status quo ante* is restored. It follows, therefore, that where a scheme has been approved and is subsequently annulled, and the debtor dies after approval but before annulment, Section 93 (Pres.) applies; and, notwithstanding the death of the debtor any person interested (in this case the widow of a creditor) has a locus stand to apply that the debtor be readijuged an insolvent for the purpose of the further administration in insolvency of the deceased debtor's estate.

In considering whether the debtor should be readjudged, the court should have regard to the position of the creditors, and if the court is of opinion that the creditors will not be benefited by an order annulling the scheme and readjudicating the debtor, in ordinary circumstances the court will not make an order of adjudication.

Another additional provision in the Presidency Act is Section 32. This section provides that a scheme, even though approved by the court, shall not bind any creditor as regards a debt or liability from which an insolvent would not be discharged by an order of discharge from insolvency unless the creditor has assented to the proposition or the scheme.

Control over Person or Property of Insolvent:

Duties of Insolvent as to Realisation and Discovery of Property [S. 33 Pres.]

The section lays down the duties of the insolvent as to discovery and realisation of his property.

The first duty is to attend any meeting of his creditors which the official assignee may call and to submit to be examined by the meeting and to give such information as the meeting may require.

The second duty is to submit such information relating to the following matters as the official assignee or special manager may require or may be ordered or prescribed by the court:

(1) an inventory of his property, list of his creditors and debtors, and of the debts due to and from them respectively;
(2) submit to be examined by the creditors in respect of his property or his creditors;
(3) wait at such times and places on the official assignee or special manager;
(4) execute such powers of attorney, transfers and instruments;
(5) generally do all such acts and things in relation to his property and distribution of the proceeds among his creditors as may be necessary.

The third duty is that the insolvent shall aid, to the utmost of his power, in the realisation of his property and the distribution of the proceeds among his creditors.

If the insolvent wilfully fails to perform these duties or to deliver to the official assignee any property which is divisible amongst his creditors, it will be a contempt of the court, apart from any other punishment to which it may subject the insolvent.

In the Provincial Act, the provisions parallel to these are to be found in Sections 22, 28 and 69.

Arrest of Insolvent [S. 34 Pres.]

The court of its own motion, or at the instance of the official assignee or any creditor, order arrest of the insolvent, or, if he is already under arrest, to be detained, for such time as the court may order. The court can exercise this power in the following circumstances:

(1) If the court has reason to believe that he has absconded or is about to abscond with a view of avoiding examination in respect of his afairs, or of otherwise avoiding, delaying or embarrassing proceedings in insolvency against him.
(2) If it appears to the court that he is about to remove his property with a view of preventing or delaying the official assignee from taking possession of the property.

For the purposes of Section 36 the court shall have the same power to issue commissions and letters of request for the examination on commission as it has for the examination of witnesses under the Civil Procedure Code.

Discharge of Insolvent [S. 41 Prov and S. 38 Pres.]

It is the duty of a debtor to apply to the court for a discharge. He can make an applicaiton at any time, but, if the court has fixed a period for this purpose, he must apply before the time expires. The court will fix a date for hearing the application and give such notice as may be necessary so as to enable the persons concerned to raise their objections, if any. After hearing the creditor's objection and after considering the receiver's report, if any, the court may—

(1) either refuse or grant an absolute order of discharge;
(2) suspend the operation of the order for a specified time;
(3) grant an order of discharge subject to any conditions with respect to his subsequent earnings or after acquired property.

The purpose of discharging the insolvent from insolvency is that he ought not to remain for ever a slave of the official assignee:

"The overriding intention of the legislature jn all Bankruptcy Acts is that the debtor on giving up the whole of his property shall be a free man again, able to earn his livelihood, and having the ordinary inducement to industry. Sometimes it is not right that the bankrupt should be free immediately; he must pass through a period of probation; and theoretically there may be cases in which he ought not to be free at all, but prima facie he is to give up every thing he has, and on doing that he is to be made a free man."

The Rangoon High Court followed this principle and refused an order of discharge to an insolvent who was a dangerous man; who succeeded in putting all his assets beyond his creditor's reach; who destroyed documents in order to make it more difficult for the official assignee to recover his property; who still occupied an expensive house and moved about in a motor car registered in another name.

In the exercise of its discretion the court has to consider whether having regard to the welfare of the community on the or has concealed, or is about to conceal or destroy any of his property or any books, documents or writings which might be of use to his creditors in the course of his insolvency.

(3) If he removes any property in his possession above the value of fifty rupees without the leave of the official assignee.

A provision parallel to this in the Provincial Act is to be found in Section 32.

Redirection of Letters [S. 35 Pres.]

The court can order that letters, registered or ordinary, parcels and money orders addressed to the debtor shall be redirected or delivered by the postal authorities to the official assignee. The order can be issued for such time as the court may fix but should not exceed three months.

Discovery of Insolvent's Property [S. 36 Pres.]

The court can summon the insolvent or any other person suspected or known to have in his possession any property of the insolvent, or suspected to be indebted to the insolvent, or any person who can give information about the insolvent, his dealings or property and the court may require such person to produce any documents in his possession relating to the insolvent, his dealings or property.

The person so summoned should appear on being tendered a reasonable sum for the purpose and produce the things required unless he makes known to the court some legal impediment. If he fails to do so the court can have him apprehended and brought up for examination. The court can then examine him as to any matter relating to the insolvent, his dealings and property. He has a right to be represented by a legal practitioner. If his examination reveals that he is indebted to the insolvent the court may order him to pay up to the official assignee and also order that such payment shall operate as a full or partial discharge of his liability. If he owns that he has with him a property of the insolvent, the court can order delivery of the same to the official assignee.

Provisions paralled to these are to be found in Section 59A of the Provincial Act. One hand and the right of a subject normally to live his life as a free man, an order of discharge should be granted or not.

Discharge operates from the date of the order, though the order has not been formally drawn up or signed. The Calculta High Court held in a case of this kind that once the debtor has been ordered to be discharged he cannot be considered to be an undischarged insolvent, though the registrar has not done his duty in implementing the order and the property coming to the insolvent after such order cannot be regarded as an after-acquired property.

Where the operation of an order has been suspended for a certain period, the order becomes automatically effective on the expiry of that period and no further order is necessary. In a case before the Bombay High Court, the operation of an order of discharge was suspended for one year. Three years later the insolvent acquired a business and the official assignee, knowing that no final order has been made, sought to recover the business for the benefit of the unpaid creditors.

It was held that the official assignee could not do so. The court pointed out that the practice of the Bombay High Court requiring an insolvent whose discharge has been suspended to appear and obtain the final and absolute discharge after the expiry of the period of suspension is contrary to law.

Cases in which absolute discharge should be refused [S. 42 Prov and S. 39 Pres.]

On proof of any of the following facts, the court should refuse an absolute order of discharge:

(1) The insolvent's assets are not equal to eight annas (fifty paise) in the rupee on the amount of his unsecured liabilities. The court can, however, ignore this fact if it is not due to circumstances for which he cannot justly he held responsible.

(2) The insolvent has not maintained such books of account as are usual and proper in his business and as sufficiently disclose his business transactions and financial position within three years preceding to his insolvency.

(3) The insolvent continued to trade after knowing himself to be insolvent.

(4) The insolvent has contracted a debt which is provable against him without any responsible or provable ground of expectation that he would be able to pay it. The burden lies upon him to show that he felt he would be in a position to pay.

(5) The insolvent has failed to account satisfactorily for any loss of assets or for any deficiency of assets to meet his liabilities.

(6) The insolvent contributed to his insolvency by rash and hazardous speculations or by unjustifiable extravagance in living, or by gambling or by culpable neglect of his business affairs.

(7) The insolvent, being unable to pay his debts within three months prior to the petition, gave an undue preference to any of his creditors.

(8) Prior to the present proceeding, the insolvent had already once before become an insolvent or and made a composition or arrangement with his creditors.

(9) The insolvent has concealed or removed his property wholly or partly or has been guilty of any other fraud or fraudulent breach of trust.

For the purposes of these provisions, the report of the receiver shall count as evidence and the court can presume the correctness of the statements in the report. The section also provides that the power of suspending discharge or attaching conditions to it can be exercised concurrently. This means that the court can make the order conditional as well as suspend its operation.

Section 39 of the Presidency Act puts these in the sub-section (2), and also adds the following additional grounds for refusing an order of discharge:

(1) The insolvent has put any of his creditors, who had sued, to an unnecessary expense by forth a frivolous or vexatious defence.

(2) The insolvent, within three months before the petition, incurred unjustifiable expenses by bringing a frivolous or vexatious suit.

Another difference that the Presidency Act makes is that in reference to the first ground, it provides for four anna payment instead of eight annas [55 p. instead of 50 p.] .

Sub-section (1) of Section 39 of the Presidency Act is worded differently. It says that the court shall refuse discharge in all cases where the insolvent has committed an offence under the Insolvency Act or under Section 421 to 424 of the Indian Penal Code.

One proof of any of the above stated facts the alternatives available to the court are—

(1) to refuse the discharge;

(2) to suspend the discharge for a specified period;

(3) to suspend the discharge until a dividend of four annas (25 p.) in the rupee has been made to the creditors;

(4) to require the insolvent to agree to a consent decree which will be passed in favour of the assignee for payment out of the subsequently acquired property or income any provable debts which have not been paid at the time that the insolvent has asked for his discharge. The decree shall be capable of being executed only with the leave of the court which leave will be granted only on proof of the fact that the insolvent has obtained an income or acquired a property which is available for payment of his debts.

When an order of discharge has been suspended waiting for four anna payment in the rupee, then as soon as such payment has been made or a sum sufficient for such payment has come into the hands of the official assignee, the suspension automatically terminates and the discharge becomes effective.

Following the decision of the English Court of Appeal *in Re* Hawkins, the Rangoon High Court has held that:

"as soon as the official assignee has in hand a sum sufficient to declare the required dividend of four annas in the rupee, plus, of course, the expenses of the proceedings and his commission, the discharge of the insolvent is complete and if any further sums should come into the official assignee's hands they are the property of the insolvent and must be refunded to him".

In the above-mentioned English case the facts were that an insolvent's discharge was suspended until he paid to the trustee a sum sufficient to pay his creditors a dividend of five shillings in the pound. Before any such sum was received by the trustee, a considerable legacy was left to the insolvent and the question before the Court of Appeal was whether the legacy vested in the trustee. Lord ESHER M R and LOPES L J held that the whole of the legacy vested in the trustee because it was a property acquired before the discharge became absolute, although their Lordships agreed that the discharge became complete as soon as the trustee received the legacy. FRY L J on the other hand felt that the trustee should receive only that part of the legacy as was sufficient to assure five shillings payment in the pound and the rest should belong to the insolvent. It is, however, manifest that if the legacy had been received in two parts and the second after the first was proved sufficient to assure the requisite payment, the second part would have gone to the insolvent. The court added:

"This is not to say that in such cases it is never possible for the creditors to receive a dividend of more than four annas. It may be that owing to an unexpected windfall, or owing to some creditors waiving their claims, it may be possible for the official assignee to pay more dividend out of the moneys received prior to the discharge becoming absolute."

Annulment on Failure to apply for Discharge [S. 43 Prov and S. 41 Pres.]

If the insolvent does not appear on the day fixed for hearing his application for discharge or if he does not apply for an order of adjudication is annulled. Section 37 then applies and, therefore, subject to payments which have already been made, the property will revert back to the insolvent.

Another effect of the annulment is that if the debtor was released from a prison by virtue of the insolvency law, he will go back to the prison and be again subject to the same process to which he would have been but for the release.

The Presidency Act makes the following additional provisions:

Renewal of Application for Discharge [S. 42 Pres.]

Where the court refuses the discharge of an insolvent, the court may subsequently permit him to renew his application and on such terms etc. as the court may impose.

Where a conditional order of discharge has been made and after the expiration of two years the insolvent satisfies the court that there is no reasonable probability of his being able to comply with the condition, the court may modify the terms of the order subject to such terms and conditions as it may think fit to impose.

Duty of Discharged Insolvent [S. 43 Pres.]

It is the duty of the insolvent, notwithstanding his discharge, to help the official assignee in the realisation and distribution of his property as is already vested in the assignee. If fails to cooperate, it will amount to contempt of court and, in addition, the court can also revoke his discharge.

Fraudulent Settlements [S. 44 Pres.]

Certain kind of settlements in consideration of marriage have been declared by the section to be open to revision by the court. The section affects the following two kinds of settlements:

(1) settlements before and in consideration of marriage made at a time when the settlor is not able, without the aid of the property comprised in the settlement, to pay all his debts;
(2) any covenant or contract in consideration of marriage to settle property in future on the settlor's wife or children, which is not that of his wife and in which he has not at the date of marriage any estate or interest.

Such transactions will become void if the settlor is adjuged insolvent or compounds or arranges with his creditors and it appears to the court that the transaction was made to defeat or delay creditors, or was unjustifiable having regard to the state of the settlor's affairs. The court may on this ground either refuse an order of discharge or suspend it or grant an order subject to conditions or refuse to approve a compromise or arrangement.

Effect of order of Discharge [S. 44 Prov, S. 45 Pres.]

An order of discharge does not release the insolvent from the following debts:

(1) any debt due to the Crown;
(2) any debt or liability incurred by means of any fraud, or fraudulent breach of trust to which he was a party;
(3) any debt or liability in respect of which he has obtained forbearance by any fraud to which he was a party;
(4) any liability under an order for maintenance made under Section 488 of the Code of Criminal Procedure, 1898 [Section 125 of the New Code].

But, subject to these surviving liabilities, an order of discharge releases the debtor from all debts which are provable against him under the insolvency law.

The order of discharge does not release any person who, at the date of the petition, was a partner or co-trustee with the insolvent, or was jointly bound or had made any joint contract with him or any person who was surety for him.

Section 45 (3) of the Presidency Act makes this additional provision that an order of discharge shall be conclusive evidence of the insolvency and of the validity of the proceedings.

The debt due to a secured creditor is not a debt provable in insolvency. The order of adjudication and the subsequent order of discharge does not affect the rights of the secured creditor which flow from the mortgage contract. There is no difference in this respect between the Provincial and the Presidency Towns Insolvency Acts. Where a mortgagor has been adjudicated an insolvent with reference to certain debts which were provable in insolvency, the order of adjudication and the order of discharge do not and cannot affect the legal rights of the creditor against the debtor in respect of debts which were not provable in insolvency.

It has been held by the Calcutta High Court that where a person has been declared insolvent by two different courts and one of them, without having the proceedings in the other stayed, passes an order of discharge, the order is ineffective. Explaining the reasons, the court cited the following passage from a judgment of SIR JOHN WALLIS`C J of the Madras High Court.

In British India we have not only four insolvency jurisdictions under the Presidency Towns Insolvency Act, but also the very numerous jurisdictions under the Provincial Insolvency Act, so that cases like the present may not infrequently arise. In all such cases, it should be recognised that vesting depends on priority of adjudication, and that steps should at once be taken to annul the prior adjudication when it is convenient that the estate should be administered by another jurisdiction. Great confusion might ensue if competing assignees or receivers were to have concurrent authority to realise the insolvent's estate independently of one another, instead of the insolvency being in one jurisdiction only at a time and other jurisdictions being required to act in aid of it, if necessary.

ADMINISTRATION OF PROPERTY

Methods of Proof of Debts

Future Debts [S. 45 Prov]

A future debt means a debt which is payable at a future date and, therefore, its payment is not presently due. The section enables the claimant of a future debt also to prove his claim along with those claims which are presently due. He may also receive dividends along with the others. The only thing is that while making payment to him interest at the rate of six per cent should be deducted from the date of dividend to the date on which the payment would have been due.

Debts Provable [S. 45 Prov]

Following points are laid down by this section in respect of provable debts:

(1) Demands in the nature of unliquidated damages are not provable. Thus tort action are excluded, such as, for example, a claim for damages for negligent handling of a motor car. But claims arising out of a breach of contract or breach of trust are provable even if the claim is in the nature of unliqauidated damages.

(2) A person who comes to know of the presentation of a petition against the debtor is not allowed to prove any claim incurred by the debtor subsequent to such notice.

(3) Subject to the above exceptions, all debts incurred by the insolvent before his adjudication are provable. The Act says that all debts and liabilities, present or future, certain or contingent, to which the debtor is subject at the date of insolvency or to which he may become subject before his discharge, shall be provable in insolvency.

(4) Where the debt is of contingent nature or by reason certain value, the official assignee should make a just estimate of such a claim. If he feels that the value cannot be fairly estimated, he should issue a certificate to that effect, and thereupon the claim shall be deemed to be not provable in insolvency.

(5) The explanation appended to these provisions says that the term "Liability" includes any compensation for work or labour done; any obligation or possibility of an obligation to pay money for the breach of any express or implied covenant, contract, agreement or undertaking, even if the breach has not occurred, or is not likely or capable of occurring before the discharge of the insolvent. any express or implied engagement, agreement or undertaking to pay money or money's worth, whether the amount is fixed or unliquidated, or whether it is payable presently or in future, certain or dependent on contingencies, capable of being ascertained by fixed rules or as a matter of opinion.

The corresponding provisions in the Provincial Act are in Sections 33 and 34, which have been noted before.

The scope of the phrase that only such debts are provable to which the debtor is or may be "subject" has been explained in a decision of the Madras High Court. The court said that a debt will be provable even if the liability is not of a personal nature. "Though a personal liability is a necessary fou1ndation for an order of adjudication, it is not a necessary condition for a debt provable in insolvency. It is enough if there is a 'proprietary liability' to use the language of Lord Bown, i.e., a liability in respect of property."

"What is, therefore, required is, there must be a debt or liability to which the debtor was subject on the date of the receiving order or order of adjudication. 'Subject' means 'liable', i.e., liable personally or in respect of property. Therefore if the debtor is liable to pay a debt or satisfy a liability from and out of the property in his hands it would be a provable debt in insolvency."

Accordingly, it has been held that the damages awarded to a petitioner in a Divorce Court against a correspondent though they will not support a bankruptcy petition against the correspondent, are nevertheless a debt provable in insolvency. Following these principles the court held that if on the date of the order of adjudication, the insolvents were under a liability to pay a debt from and out of the joint family property in their hands or from and out of the separate property inherited by them from their father, such a liability would be a debt provable in insolvency. In this case the creditor had received a part payment under a compromise out of the assets of the insolvent in Ceylon, and for the balance he was allowed to prove for payment out of the assets in India.

A debt arising out of an indemnity bond which was executed to receive delivery of goods is a debt provable in insolvency. A promissory note executed after the presentation of a petition but before discharge is a post-insolvency debt and is, therefore, not provable. The Act does not prevent the insolvent from creating new liabilities. It only prevent such debts from being proved in insolvency. They can, however, be enforced against the insolvent independently of the insolvency proceedings.

Mutual Dealings and Set-off [S. 46 Prov, S. 47 Pres.]

Where a creditor also owes something to the insolvent, the question can arise whether such cross debts can be mutually set off. The above sections provide the answer. It says that where there have been mutual dealings between an insolvent and a creditor who has presented a claim, an account shall be taken of what is due from the one party to the other, and the same shall be mutually set off and only the balance will be paid by one side to the other.

The Presidency Act adds this proviso that a creditor who at the time of giving the credit had notice of the presentation of the insolvency petition shall not be allowed to claim a set-off against the property of the insolvent.

"The surety's liability under a guarantee may be made the subject of a set-off or counter-claim by the creditor in an action brought against him by the surety; and conversely, the surety, when sued on the guarantee, may raise a set-off or counter-claim against the creditor."

In India, in the absence of a contract to the contrary, a joint promise creates a joint and several obligation. If A sues B and C who are jointly and severally liable, B can set off a debt due to him separately from A. On the other hand, if A and B sue C for the recovery of a debt due from C to A and B, C cannot set off a debt due to him from A alone. Under Section 45, Contract Act, the claim of A and B is joint and to allow C to plead set off in such a case will be to enable C to obtain payment from B who is in no way indebted to C.

Similarly, if a bank is liable under a fixed deposit receipt payable to either A or B or survivor, in a suit for recovery of the deposit by B, the bank cannot set off a separate debt due from A to the Bank, unless the deposit though standing in the name of A and B is really and truly the property of A.

The right of set off given by the insolvency law is wider than that given by the general law. The Insolvency Acts generally enlarge the scope of the subject-matter of the plea of set off.

The Presidency Act does not state on what date the right of set off is to be ascertained. Section 46, however, shows that all debts and liabilities to which the debtor is subject when he is adjuged an insolvent may be proved. The dividing line, therefore, in the case of a proof of debt is the date of adjudication, and the same dividing line is to be taken for the purpose of as-certainment of the date of set off. The line which is drawn for defining what debts are provable must also be the line for defining what cross claims are to be set off. "If the line were to be drawn at different times for the two purposes of proof and set off the result might be unjust."

In the case of a guarantee the right of set off will depend upon the form of the guarantee and the nature of the equities arising in the case. If the guarantee is in the form of a joint and several promise, in a suit to enforce such promise, the surety can set off a separate debt due to him. If the guarantee is in the form of a collateral obligation, there is no doubt that the surety's liability under a guarantee be set off against a debt due to the surety.

The fact that the debt is not payable at the date of insolvency is wholly immaterial. A debt payable in future may be set off.

If as security for the debt of A,B charges in favour of C, the creditor of A, a debt due to B from C without incurring any personal obligation for the repayment of the debt of A, no doubt B is a surety for some purposes. It has, however, been held that on the bankruptcy of C, A cannot set off the debt due to B from C against the debt due to C from A.

In the case before the Calcutta High Court,

On the date of the order for winding up of a bank, one Badrinarayan was a guarantor for the whole of the debt due to the Bank from Annapurna and was liable personally to the Bank for the repayment of the debt. at the same time the bank was on that date indebted to Badrinarayan. The court held that there was no doubt that there were mutual dealings between Badrinarayan and the Bank and the debt due to him from the Bank must be set off against his liability as guarantor for the debt of Annapurna.

In another case before the same High Court,

The question was whether in a suit by X against A to recover a separate debt due from A to X, A can set off a debt repayable under a contract with A and B to either or survivor?

The court said:

There is no doubt that if the debt is a debt jointly due to A and B, A cannot set off such debt. The debt due to A and B is not legally recoverable by A alone from X and cannot, therefore, be set off under Order 8, Rule 6, C.P.C. In this respect in the absence of special circumstances equity follows the law. The set off is also not permissible under Section 47, Presidency Towns Insolvency Act read with Section 229, Indian Companies Act 1913, because there is no matual credit between A and X in respect of such debt.

The court cited the following statement by LINDLEY L J:

"*Prima facie* a separate debt cannot be set off against joint debt either at law, in equity or under the mutual credit clauses of the Bankruptcy Act. There is no authority for the bankers having a general lien in such a case as the present."

The court also cited with approval a decision of the Lahore High Court. In that case,

A bank had issued a fixed deposit receipt in favour of A and his wife B payable to either or survivor. In a suit by B against the bank to recover the deposit, the bank claimed to retain the the moneys and asserted a lien thereon on the ground that A was severally indebted to the bank. This defence was negatived and it was held that the bank could not appropriate the amount of the fixed deposit against the debt severally due from A either in law or in equity.

In still another Calcutta case, the court stated the following principles.

Long before the making of statutory provisions on the subject it was the practice in bankruptcy, where there was debtor and creditors account between the bankrupt and another person, to take the amount between them and to adjust the balance, provided that the debts were connected with each other. The statutory provisions on the subject extended the same rule to cases where the debts were unconnected with each other. These provisions are based on manifest justice; otherwise the receiver in insolvency would be able to recover the full amount due to the insolvent leaving the other person to take a pro rata dividend only. *In re* Daintry, Ex p. M Mant, it was argued that the trustee in bankruptcy could recover 20 shillings in the pound from Mant and say that Mant must be content with a dividend on the debt due to them from the bankrupt, but LINDLEY M R repelled the contention as unarguable. The term 'mutual dealings' has been given by the decisions a very extended meaning. It includes not only the case where a person owes a debt to the insolvent but also where there is a claim for rent.

Secured Creditors [S. 47 Prov]

Where a secured creditor realises his security, he may prove for the balance due to him, after deducting the amount so realised. Where, however, he relinquishes his security for the general benefit of the creditors, he may prove for his whole debt. Where he does not either realise or relinquish his security, then, before proving his claim, he shall have to furnish the particulars of his security and the value at which he assesses it. He can then claim only the balance amount after deducting the value so assessed. The court can also redeem the property to the creditor on payment of the assessed value. If the creditor, after making such valuation, also realises the security, the net amount realised shall be substituted for the amount of valuation and it shall then be considered as an amended valuation. If the creditor does not comply with these provisions, he shall be excluded from all share in any dividends.

Interest [S. 48 Prov]

Where on a particular debt interest is due, but the rate is not reserved or agreed, interest at the rate of six per cent can be claimed. If the debt is due on a written instrument, such interest can be claimed from the date of the instrument. If there is no writing about the debt, interest can be claimed from the date on which a demand is served that interest will be claimed.

Where the instrument itself specifies the rate of interest or any other consideration in place of interest or consideration shall not exceed six per cent for the purpose of payment of dividends. This, however, does not prejudice the right of the creditor to recover more interest, if more is due, after all the debts proved have been paid in full.

Mode of Proof [S. 49 Prov]

A debt can be proved by delivering or sending by registered letter to the court an affidavit claiming and verifying the debt. The affidavit should refer to or contain a statement of account showing the particulars of the debt and should specify the vouchers, if any, by which the same can be substantiated. The court can call the production of the vouchers.

Disallowance and Reduction of Entries in Schedule [S. 50 Prov.]

If the receiver finds that a debt has been improperly entered in the schedule, he can apply to the court. The court will give notice to the creditor and, after making necessary enquiries, may either expunge such entry or reduce the amount of the debt.

Where no receiver has been appointed, or if the receiver refuses to interfere in the matter of an improper entry, any creditor can apply to the court and in the case of a composition or scheme, any debtor can apply. In either case, the court will make necessary inquiry and may either expunge the entry or reduce the debt.

The corresponding provisions in the Presidency Act relating to secured creditors, interest, and proof of debts are given in the second schedule.

Antecedent Transactions

Restriction of Rights of Creditors under Execution [S. 51 Prov. S. 53 Pres.]

Sometimes it so happens that a creditor has obtained a decree and an execution order against the property of his debtor and then insolvency intervenes. If the property has already been sold in the execution of the decree before the date of admission of the petition, then it has already gone beyond the reach of the insolvency laws. But if the petition is admitted before the actual execution, then no one can have the benefit of the execution against the receiver. It would, therefore, be better to stay the execution.

The provision does not affect the rights of a secured creditor in respect of the property against which the decree is executed.

A person who purchases the property in good faith in an execution sale shall acquire a good title against the receiver.

The criterion for determining "good faith" must be taken in reference to the general scheme of the Insolvency Acts.

"The fundamental aim of bankruptcy law is to combine and regulate two great objects, namely, the distribution of the debtor's properties in the most expeditious, equal and economical manner, and, secondly, to secure the debtor's release from his creditors, if certain conditions prescribed by the statute have been fulfilled. The scheme of the insolvency enactment will require that the best price possible for the debtor's property should be obtained, so that the creditors might get as much as possible for their dues".

This statement occurs in a Madras case in which certain properties of a debtor were being sold in the execution of some decrees against him and he had requested the court to stay the sale disclosing that a petition for his insolvency had been filed. Thus the purchaser had come to know of the tendency of the proceeding. The question was whether he was a purchaser in good faith. The court stated that the effect of an insolvency order was that neither the insolvent can give title to any person with respect to his property after the date of the act of insolvency, nor his rights could validly be sold in proceedings in invitum. An exception has, however, been ingrafted on this rule. That is Section 53 which protects bona fide purchasers and Section 57 purchasers without notice. Section 57 invalidates a transaction if there was notice of the insolvency petition, whereas, under Section 53 what has to be proved is that the purchaser made the purchase in good faith. Under Section 53 the decree-holder will not get the benefit of the execution, but the purchaser will get good title to the property sold. This being an exception to the general rule of relation back, the burden of proving good faith will be on the person seeking advantage of the exception.

There are two conflicting principles, (1) the safeguarding of the rights of a third party purchaser in execution sale, and (2) the safeguarding of the rights of the general body of creditors. Section 53 (3) attempts to reconcile these two conflicting principles. Where the purchaser is unaware of the proceedings and the sale is also fair, there would really be nothing to the prejudice of the general body of creditors, inasmuch as the assets realised will be available for them.

Where, however, the purchase is made with the knowledge of the insolvency proceedings, the burden of proving good faith on the part of the purchaser will be greater than in a case where he has no such knowledge. In such cases unless the purchaser is satisfied that the petition is frivolous he must be deemed to have had knowledge that the rights of the general body of creditors might intervene.

In a Madras case, the court expressed the view that mere knowledge of the proceedings would not be sufficient to negative good faith.

In that case an interim receiver had been appointed prior to the date of the sale. The interim receiver applied to the executing court to stay the sale, but the court allowed the sale to proceed. The act of the court was held to be improper. Nevertheless, it was held that the purchaser, although aware of the tendency of the insolvency proceedings, must be regarded as one acting in good faith, because he made the purchase on the faith of the court's order.

However, divergent views have been expressed by different High Courts It seems that the court should lay emphasis upon the fairness of the sale. The assignee has in any case to sell and he cannot hope to realise more than a fair price. Thus, if the purchaser has given a fair price, knowledge of proceedings should not matter. Such knowledge can co-exist with good faith.

Section 52 of the Provincial Act supplements the provisions of Section 51. It provides that where before actual sale, notice is given to the executing court that an insolvency petition is pending, the court shall direct the property to be delivered to the receiver if it is in possession of the court. However, the costs of the suit in which the decree was passed and of execution, shall constitute the first charge on the property so delivered. The receiver can sell the property or any adequate part of it in order to satisfy such costs.

Avoidance of Voluntary Transfer [S. 53 Prov, S. 55 Pres.]

Generally, a transfer of the property of the insolvent made two years before the presentation of the petition is voidable at the option of the receiver and can be annulled by the court. The section, however, does not apply to transfers made in consideration of marriage or those made in good faith and for valuable consideration. In other words, a transaction can be avoided: (1) if it was made within two years before the petition and (2) was not made in consideration of marriage or in good faith for a valuable consideration.

Where a man owning one-half interest in a property, the other half being with his wife, released his interest in favour of his wife at a time when he was very heavily involved in debts, it was held that the device of release was adopted to screen his half share from being proceeded against by his creditors and, being a fraud on the creditors, could not be said to have been made in good faith. The court pointed out that the word "transfer" is wide enough to cover all sorts of devices that may be practised or suffered by an insolvent to deprive the creditors of the benefit of his property and that, as such, the remission of debt without consideration amounts to a transfer within the meaning of the Act and the transaction is liable to be impugned. The court gave the following illustration.[114]

Suppose that the only property a person has is a large sum of money due to him from a relation of his and, in order to defeat his creditors, he remits the debt, is there any principle on which the case can be distinguished from one where makes a gift of the debt to a third person. We think not. No authority has been cited for such a distinction being drawn, and it would open a wide door to fraud if the remission of a debt is placed on a different footing from a transfer.

The Privy Council laid down in Pope v. Official Assignee, Rangoo:

Where a receiver appointed under the Presidency Towns Insolvency Act, 1909, seeks to set aside under Section 55 of the Act a transfer for consideration made by the insolvent within two years of the insolvency, it is for him to prove that the transferee is not a purchaser in good faith. If the transaction was a real and not a fictitious one, it is not brought within the section unless the receiver proves that the transferee knew that the transferor was insolvent when the transfer was made, even where the transfer was of the whole of the available assets and the consideration was a payment in reduction of a bank overdraft which the transferee had guaranteed.

The facts were that in carrying on her business, one Mrs. Young financed it by means of an overdraft permitted to her on a guarantee by a third person, who deposited the title deeds of his house with the bank as a security and also gave a joint promissory note with the lady. The bank pressed the guarantor for payment. He obtained a deed of sale of her properties from Mrs. Young and paid off the bank. Mrs. Young became bankrupt and the receiver sought to avoid the sale deed. But their Lordships held that it had not been proved that the transaction was not made in good faith or that the guarantor had knowledge that Mrs. Young was bankrupt at the time.

Avoidance of Preference in Certain Cases or Fraudulent Preference [S. 54 Prov, S. 56 Pres.]

It is not desirable that a person, who is not able to pay his debts as and when they become due, should use up his assets in paying some of his creditors and leaving the others totally unpaid. That would be a fraud upon the other creditors. No person who is going to face an impending solvency should have the right to select the creditors whom he is going to pay. The law of insolvency tries to prevent such preference under the principle of fraudulent preference.

The principle is that if a person is not able to pay his debts from his sources as they become due and he is declared an insolvent, then any transfer of property, or every payment made, or every obligation incurred or any judicial proceeding taken or suffered by him within three months before the presentation of a petition against him, shall be deemed to be fraudulent preference and shall be void. It shall be annulled by the court.

The conditions necessary for this doctrine to apply are:

(1) there must have been some transfer of property, or making of payment, or an obligation incurred or a proceeding taken or suffered;

(2) the person concerned must be at the time unable to pay his debts;

(3) any of these things was down with a view to giving preference to a creditor over the others, and

(4) within three months of the transaction the person concerned has been adjudicated insolvent.

The doctrine will not upset any such transaction in favour of a person who in good faith and for valuable consideration has acquired a title through or under a creditor of the insolvent.

It is necessary that the transaction should have been entered into by the debtor as a free agent, and not under compulsion of any kind. The intention of the debtor to prefer is the most material factor. Thus where payments were made by a debtor into his banking account to wipe out his overdraft at a time when the debtor was not able to pay his other creditors and insolvency followed within three months the payments were held to constitute a fraudulent preference. But where a person issued a bill to his wife to secure her bona fide advances to him and had subsequently to replace the bill because of a technical flaw, that was held to be not a fraudulent preference. Similarly, payments made under compulsion of legal proceedings by a creditor or under pressure by a creditor; to repay trust money which had earlier been misapplied by the debtor; to protect himself from criminal proceedings; to revive a time-barred debt; enable himself to carry on the business in the ordinary course, have been held to be not a fraudulent preference.

The intention of the debtor is material but not that of the creditor. The person who alleges that the transaction is a fraudulent preference will have to prove fraudulent intention on the part of the debtor.

When a creditor to whom some property has been transferred by way of fraudulent preference, has himself transferred it further to a bona fide buyer, the right of such buyer is protected. When the person who receives the payment is in fact preferred, he cannot retain it only on the ground that he had no knowledge of the debtor's insolvency or of his intention to prefer.

Where the dominant motive of the debtor is to benefit himself and the preference, if any is only incident to that, the debtor will not be regarded as guilty of making fraudulent preference. Thus where a debtor, on pressure being exerted by a creditor, gave him a security for an outstanding debt, but only on receiving a further advance which he needed to pay other creditors, it was held that he had no intention to prefer.

Any such transaction can be challenged by the Official Receiver. It can also be challenged by a creditor who has proved his claim, but only with the leave of the court, which will be granted when it is proved that the creditor requested the receiver but the latter refused to make such petition.

Protection of bonafide Transactions [S. 55 Prov]

Certain transactions are not allowed to be affected by the fact of insolvency and that is why they are called protected transactions. It is necessary that such transactions should have taken place before the order of adjudication and the person favoured had no knowledge of the tendency of the insolvency proceedings. Such transactions are:

(1) any payment by the insolvent to any of his creditors;

(2) any payment or delivery to the insolvent;

(3) any transfer by the insolvent for valuable consideration; and

(4) any contract or dealing by or with the insolvent for valuable consideration.

This principle is in essence an exception to the doctrine of relation back. One effect of "relation back" is that because the order of adjudication becomes effective from the date of the petition, therefore, all transactions after the date of the petition become void. This doctrine in some cases resulted in real hardship. Experience demanded that transactions made with a person in good faith who had no knowledge of the pending proceedings should be protected and this is what the section seeks to do.

Realisation of Property [S. 56 Prov and S. 58 Pres.]

The court can appoint a receiver at the time of the order of adjudication or at any time afterwards. One of his functions is to receive the property of the insolvent and that is why the section says that upon his appointment the property of the insolvent shall stand vested in him. The court can prescribe any condition for the appointment of a receiver, but the following two points the court has to fix in any case:

(1) The court shall require the receiver to give such security as it thinks fit so that he may duly account for his receipts etc.

(2) The court shall fix the amount that the receiver shall receive as his remuneration out of the assets of the insolvent.

After the appointment of a receiver the court can order the removal of any person from the possession of the property of the insolvent, but not a person whom the insolvent has no present right to remove. In order to enable the court to exercise real control over the receipts and disbursements by the receiver, the section provides that if the receiver fails to submit his accounts at periods and the form in which the court prescribes, or fails to pay the balance due from him as the court directs or causes loss to the property by his wilful default or gross negligence, the court may direct his property to be attached and sold. The proceeds can then be applied to make good any loss or any balance due from the receiver. These provisions are applicable to interim receivers also.

Power to appoint Official Receivers [S. 57 Prov]

The State Government can keep a panel of persons to be called Official Receivers from whom receivers can be appointed according to needs. Where no receiver is appointed, the court can exercise all the rights of and exercise all the powers of a receiver.

Duties and Power of Receiver [S. 59 Prov. and S. 68 Pres.]

The receiver's duty is, with all convenient speed, to realise the property of the debtor and to distribute dividends amongst claimants who are entitled to them. For this purpose he can exercise the power,

(a) to sell all or any property of the insolvent,

(b) to give receipts for any money received by him.

He can also exercise the following powers with the leave of the court:

(a) to carry on the business of the insolvent in so far as it may be necessary for the beneficial winding up of his affairs;

(b) to institute, defend or continue any suit or other legal proceedings relating to the property of the insolvent;

(c) to employ a pleader or other agent to take any proceedings or do any business as the court may sanction;

(d) to accept anything as a consideration for any sale of the insolvent's property which operate as a security for future payment;

(e) to mortgage or pledge any property of the insolvent for the purpose of raising money for the payment of his debts;

(g) if a particular property is not easily saleable, the receiver may distribute the property among claimants according to the estimated value of the property.

Power to require Information [S. 59 A Prov]

The State Governments have the power to authorise the courts or any officer of the court to summon before it any person who has with him any property of the insolvent or who can give any information about the dealings or property of the insolvent. If he fails to appear even after reasonable expenses have been tendered to him, he can be apprehended by warrant and brought before the court. He may be examined by the court as to the property of the insolvent and his dealings. He can engage a legal practitioner to represent him.

Sale of Agricultural Property [S. 60 Prov]

Agricultural land cannot be sold by the receiver himself. The receiver has to show to the court the gap between receipts and payments after realisation of the other properties and the court may ask the local Collector to raise money on the land according to further needs.

Realisation of Property under the Presidency Act [S. 58]

The official assignee has to take, as soon as possible, possession of the deeds, books and documents of the insolvent and all other parts of his property which are capable of manual delivery. For this purpose, his status is that of a person appointed as receiver under the Civil Procedure Code.

Where the property consists of stocks, shares in ships, charges or other property which is transferable in the books of any company etc., the official assignee will have the same power to effect the transfer as the insolvent.

Seizure of Property [S. 59]

The court can order the seizure of the property of the insolvent and for this purpose breaking open of any house or building or receptacle. If the court is satisfied that the property is lying concealed at a particular place, the court can order the search of that place.

Appropriation of Salary [S. 60]

Salary can be attached for payment of the debts of the insolvent to the extent to which it is otherwise attachable in the execution of a decree.

Where an official assignee succeeds to the office of a former assignee the property shall pass from one assignee to the other and shall vest in the official assignee for the time being during his continuance in the office without any transfer whatever.

Distribution of Property

Priority of Debts [S. 61 Prov]

Following debts are payable in priority to all other debts:

(a) all debts due to the Government or to any local authority;

(b) all salaries or wages, not exceeding Rs. 20 in all, of any clerk, servant or labourer in respect of services rendered to the insolvent during four months before the presentation of the petition.

These debts are payable in full. But if the property is not sufficient they shall abate in equal proportions. The assignee may also reserve amounts for necessary expenses.

In the case of partners, the partnership property shall be applicable in the first instance to the payment of partnership debts, and the separate property of each partner is applicable in the first instance to the payment of his personal debts. Where there is a surplus of the separate property of the partners, it shall be dealt with as part of the partnership property; and where there is a surplus of the partnership property, it shall be dealt with as part of the respective separate property, it shall be dealt with as part of the respective separate property, it shall be dealt with as part of the respective separate property in proportion to the rights and interests of each partner in the partnership property.

All other debts are payable rateably without any preference. The surplus, if any, can be utilised in paying interest at the rate of six per cent to the creditors from the date on which the debtor has been adjudged an insolvent.

Calculation of Dividends [S. 62 Prov]

In calculating dividends the receiver has to keep in his hands sufficient assets to meet the following claims:

(1) Debts due to persons who are residing in such distant places that in the ordinary course of communications they have not had the time to tender their proofs.

(2) Debts provable under the Act in respect of which the subject of claims has not yet been determined.

(3) Disputed proofs or claims.

(4) The expenses necessary for the administration of the estate.

Subject to this, the rest of the money can be distributed as dividends.

Creditor who could not prove before Declaration [S. 63 Prov]

A creditor, who fails to prove his debt before the declaration of a dividend, is not entitled to disturb the dividends already paid, but he shall be entitled to his share before any further dividend is paid.

Final Dividend [S. 64 Prov]

When the receiver has realised the whole of his property or as much as can be realised without needlessly delaying the work, he should declare a final dividend. Before so doing, he should give notice to those whose claims have been notified but not proved. If they do not prove their claims within the time specified in the notice, then the receiver can pay the final dividend ignoring their claims. The property of the insolvent is to be distributed among the creditors entered in the schedule without regard to the claims of any other persons.

No suit for Dividend [S. 65 Prov]

No suit can be brought against the receiver for a dividend. But where the receiver refuses to pay any dividend to a claimant on the schedule, he can apply to the court, which may order the dividend to be paid, and also order the receiver to pay interest from his pocket for the period of the delay and the costs of the application.

Management by and allowance to Insolvent [S. 66 Prov]

There court can appoint the insolvent himself to superintend the management of the property of the insolvent or of any part of it or to carry on his trade for the benefit of the creditors and also in any other way to aid in administering the property in such manner and on such terms as the court may direct.

The court can, from time to time, make reasonable allowance to the insolvent out of his property for the support of himself and his family or in consideration of his services if he is engaged in winding up his estate. The court can at any time withdraw such allowance or vary it.

Right to the Surplus [S. 67 Prov]

When all the creditors on the schedule have been paid in full and the expenses of winding up have been met, the surplus if any, is to be handed over to the insolvent.

Committee of Inspection [S. 67 A Prov and S. 88 Pres.]

The court can authorise the creditors, who have proved their debts, to appoint a committee of inspection. The committee will superintend the functions of the receiver in respect of the administration of the insolvent's property. Only a creditor who has proved his debt can be appointed a member or a person holding his power of attorney. The court can prescribe the extent of control that the committee shall exercise over the activities of the receiver.

Appeal to court against Receiver [S. 68 Prov, S. 86 Pres.]

If the insolvent or any of the creditors or any person is aggrieved by any act or decision of the receiver, he may apply to the court. The court will have the power to confirm, reverse or modify the act or decision of the receiver or make any other suitable order in its place.

PENALTIES

Punishment for offences [S. 69 Prov, S. 103 Pres.]

Following acts on the part of the insolvent are punishable whether they are done by him before or after the order of adjudication:

(1) When he wilfully fails to perform the duties imposed upon him by Section 22 or to deliver possession of property which is divisible among his creditors.

(2) When fraudulently with intent to conceal the state of his affairs or to defeat the objects of the Act, he has destroyed or prevented the production of his documents, or has kept false books, or has made false entries or withheld entries in his books.

(3) When fraudulently with intent to diminish the sum to be divided among his creditors or to give undue preference to any of them, he has discharged or concealed any debt due to or from him, or has charged or mortgaged any part of his property.

The punishment is imprisonment which may extend to one year. Under the Presidency Act, the term can extend to two years.

Where necessary the court can refer any of the above offences for further investigation to a Magistrate. The above proceeding can be taken even if the insolvent has been discharged or a scheme of compromise or arrangement has been approved or accepted.

Where an undischarged insolvent takes credit beyond fifty rupees, that too is punishable with a fine, or imprisonment upto six months or both.

Disqualifications of Insolvent [S. 73 Prov, S. 103 A Pres.]

A person who has been adjudged insolvent, shall be disqualified as follows:

(1) being appointed or acting as a Magistrate;

(2) being elected to any office of any local authority, where the appointment to such office is by election or holding or exercising any such office to which no salary is attached;

(3) being elected or setting or voting as member of any local authority.

These disqualifications shall stand removed or cease when the order of adjudication is annulled or the insolvent obtains from the court an order of discharge, whether absolute or conditional, with a certificate that his insolvency was caused by misfortune without any misconduct on his part.

The court has the discretion to grant such certificate or refuse it, but the order of refusal shall be subject to appeal.

SUMMARY ADMINISTRATION

Small Insolvencies [S. 74 Prov, S. 106 Pres.]

Where the court is satisfied that the property of the debtor is not likely to exceed Rs. 500, the court can order summary administration of the property of the insolvent. Such order brings about the following alterations in the ordinary procedure:

(1) Unless the court orders otherwise, notice of insolvency shall not be published in the Official Gazette;

(2) On the admission of a petition by a debtor, the property of the debtor shall vest in the court as a receiver;

(3) At the hearing of the petition the court shall inquire into the debts and assets of the insolvent and it shall not be necessary to prepare a schedule of creditors;

(4) The property of the debtor shall be realised with all reasonable dispatch and then, as soon as possible, it shall be distributed among the creditor by way of a single dividend;

(5) The debtor should apply for his discharge within six months from the date of adjudication;

(6) The court may make any suitable order for minimising expenses.

Under the Presidency Act such order can be made when the property of the debtor is not likely to exceed three thousand rupees. The Act also contains some other provisions.

(1) No appeal shall lie from any order of the court, except by leave of the court;

(2) No examination of the insolvent shall be held except on the application of the creditor or official assignee.

OFFICIAL ASSIGNEE

Appointment and Removal [S. 77 Pres.]

The High Court of Madras has been given the power to maintain a panel of persons who shall be appointed official assignees or deputy official assignees. For the States of Bengal and Bombay, this power is to be exercised by the State Government in consultation with the Chief Justice of the Calcutta or Bombay High Court.

Duties as regards the Insolvent's Conduct [S. 79 Pres.]

The duties of an official assignee shall have relation to the conduct of the insolvent and to report to the court in connection with his application for discharge, stating whether there is reason to believe that he has committed any offence which would justify the court in refusing, suspending or qualifying an order for his discharge.

(1) To make such other report concerning the conduct of the insolvent as the court may prescribe.

(2) To take such part and to take such assistance in the prosecution of the fraudulent insolvent as the court may prescribe.

He is also under duty to furnish to a creditor, on demand, the list of creditors [S. 80 pres.]

Misfeasance [S. 82]

The court has the power to call upon the official assignee to account for any misfeasance, neglect or omission which may appear in his accounts or otherwise. If such misconduct has caused any loss to the estate, the court may require him to make good such loss.

Control over Discretionary Power [S. 85 Pres.]

In the administration of the property of the insolvent and its distribution amongst creditors, the official assignee shall be bound to have regard to the resolutions that may be passed by the creditors at a meeting. He can summon such meetings from time to time to ascertain the creditors' wishes. But it shall be his duty to call a meeting when it is so required by the court or by ¼ in value of the creditors.

The official assignee can apply to the court for directions in reference to any matter. subject to these controls, the official assignee has to use his own discretion in the management of the estate and its distribution among the creditors.

If the insolvent, or a creditor or any other person is aggrieved by any act or decision of the official assignee, he may appeal to the court. The court can confirm, reverse or modify the decision complained of.

Control of the Court [S. 87 Pres.]

If the court is apprised that the official assignee is not performing his functions faithfully, the court may, after enquiry, take such action as may be necessary. The court can examine him for this purpose and can also order inspection of his books and vouchers.

Doctrine of Reputed Ownership

The property of the insolvent which is available for the purpose of distribution among his creditors also includes any property which is within his "reputed ownership" at the commencement of his being insolvent. A property is said to be within his reputed ownership if the property has been lying with him under such circumstances that reputedly he is the owner of the property. For this principle to apply it is necessary that the property in question should have come into his possession or trade with the consent of the owner and under circumstances which create the impression that to all appearance and purposes he was the owner of the property. The owner should have given over the property to the insolvent for use in his business and not generally. Where the owner of a car had given over the car to the insolvent on hire but did not know that he was using it in his business, it was held that the car was not within the principle of reputed ownership. Possession and open use in business may give rise to the inferénce of ownership. For example, a building contractor would look like to be the owner of the building material which is going to be applied, but not of the loose material on the site. Where there is a known custom that merchants may be using goods for their business which belong to others, the inference of repudiated ownership may not arise in such cases.-

PRACTICE QUESTIONS

1. What is an 'act of insolvency'? Normal Describe what constitutes 'act of insolvency'.
2. Under what circumstances may a person be adjudicated an insolvent?
3. At whose instance may *a* person be adjudicated an insolvent?
4. Who can be adjudged an insolvent?
5. Who cannot be adjudged an insolvent?
6. What is an 'order of adjudication'? What are its effects?
7. "The object of an adjudication is to free the debtor from the claims of credit which are to be satisfied out of the insolvent's estates, which the court *am* possession of and distributes among his creditors." Discuss.
8. Define insolvent's property. What property of the insolvent (i) is divisible (ii) is not divisible among his creditors?
9. What debts are provable in insolvency?
10. What debts are not provable in insolvency?
11. State the duties of an insolvent as to discovery and realisation of proper:
12. Write explanatory notes on:
    (i) Disclaimer of onerous property; (ii) Doctrine of relation back'; (iii) Doctrine of 'reputed ownership', (iv) Fraudulent preference
13. What is the mode of distribution of property of the insolvent?
14. Discuss the effect of insolvency on antecedent transactions.
15. When may insolvency court annul an order of adjudication. State the effect of the annulment order.
16. What is meant by discharge of an insolvent?
17. What is an order of discharge? What are its effects?

18. State the powers of an insolvency court in deciding an insolvent's application for his discharge.
19. What matters must the court consider in deciding the application for discharge?
20. State the cases in which the court must (i) absolutely refuse the discharge; refuse to grant an absolute discharge.
21. What are the disabilities of an undischarged insolvent.
22. "In matters arising out of insolvency the official assignee or the official receiver a higher title than the insolvent." Discuss.
23. "The effect of the doctrine of reputed ownership is to take one man's property and pay another man's debts". Discuss the statement, explaining the range and scope of the doctrine.
24. "A debtor may not by stipulation with a creditor, provide for a different distribution of his effects, in the event of his insolvency from that which the law provides". Elucidate.
25. Write explanatory notes on the following:
    (i) Public examination of the insolvent.
    (ii) Protection order and its effect.
    (iii) Protection transactions.
    (iv) Preferential debts.

References

1. Sulton v. Wedey (1806) 7 East 442; ER 171.
2. Re Levy (1881) Ch. 746, CA.
3. Subbu Chetti v. Arunachalam Chettiar AIR 1930, Mad 382; Re Philips 19002 Q.B. 329.
4. Pydimari Venkateshwarlu v. Jalamma, AIR 1969 AP 318.
5. Ramalhal Anni v Kanniapa Mudaliar AIR 1928 Mad 480.
6. Re Sunderland (1911) 2 KB 658.
7. *In re* Bholanath Chatterjee, AIR 1968 Cal 521.
8. MS Kumar & Co. v. Official Assignee of Bombay AIR 1956 Bom 38.
9. Adamali Mahomedali Nulvala *In re* AIR 1932 Bom 580.
10. Smith v. Cannan (1853) 2 El & Bl 35; 22 LJ Q.B. 291.
11. Young v. Wand (1852) Ex 221; 22 LJE x 27.
12. Jethanand Murijmal v Ghanshamdas AIR 1935 sind 53.
13. Re woodier, 1739 Bull NP 39.
14. Raikes v. Pareau 1786 Cook's Bankrupt Laws (7th ed. p.80).
15. Re Cripson (1873) 8 ch App 374.
16. Wood, 1841 2 Mont D & De Gui.
17. Hawson v. Maig, (1824) 2 Bing 99; 130 ER 242.
18. Re Bryant (1837) 3 Mont & A 722.
19. Lakshmayya v. Subha Rao, AIR 1937 Mad 433.
20. Laldhari Singh v. Count of Words (1911) 14 CIJ 639.
21. Yenumula Mallu Dora v Peruri Seetharatnam, 1966 2 SCR 209.
22. Jamal Din v. Vishambar Dayal, AIR 1929 Lah. 72; 109 IC.
23. *In re* Gopaldas Aurora, AIR 1926 Col. 640.
24. Piare Lal v. Sallamutullah Khan, AIR 1937 All 435.
25. Chanabalu Siva Reddy v O.R. Ballry, AIR 1937 Mad 13.
26. Lakhi Pd. v. Ugrah Misra AIR pat 461.
27. Kaurhal Kishore v Ram Dev AIR 1955 Purj 193.
28. Crook v Morley (1891) A C 319.
29. Alagappa Chelliar v. Nagindas AIR 1926 Bom 383.
30. Ex Parte Girdhari Lal Shanker Dave, AIR 1971 Bom 362.
31. (1950) AC 186.
32. Goverdhan Das v. Parry & Co. ILR 48 Mad 795.
33. Shivgonda Ramji Patil v. Chandrakant AIR 1965.
34. AIR 1968 SC 1182.
35. Exp. Blaim (1870) Ch D 522.
36. 2 Bom LR 861; AIR 1923 Bom 107.
37. Gopal Naidu v. Mohan Lal ILR 49 Mad 189.
38. Maung Kyi oh v. Arunachallam AIR 1925 Rang 36; Kalichanada Saha v. Hari Mohan Basak (1919) 24 Cal. WN 461; 58 IC 551.
39. Gokuldal Goverdhandas v. Parry & Co., AIR 1925 Mad 1249; 91 IC 127.
40. Annupma Devi v. Gurdas Chatterji ILR 57 Cal. 10274.
41. Ahmad Mohomed v. Prafulla Nath AIR 1939 Cal 35.
42. Ratnasami Naidu v. Subba Reddiar, AIR 1943 Mad 766.
43. Pratapmal Rameshwar v Chunilal Jouhari 1833 Cal. 417; 144 IC 142.

44. Kanhya lal Bhargava v. Banwari Cal. AIR 1936 Cal. 269.
45. J. MC Iver v. Allagappa, AIR 1936 Mad 27.
46. Harsukdas Balkissendas, Exp. AIR 1924 Cal. 964.
47. Bhawanidas v. Jethsing, AIR 1938 sind 82.
48. Chattarpal Singh Dagar v Kharag Singh Luchmiram (1916) 44 Cal. 535.
49. Patil Paban Daw v. Hari Sadhan ILR 1938 Cal. 245; Hasmat bibi v Bhagwan Das (1913) ILR 36 All 65, 67.
50. (1934) 61 ILR Cal. 537; AIR 1934 Cal. 409.
51. (1901) 84 LT 666.
52. In re Hester, 22 QBD 632 at p.639.
53. *In re* Flatan (1893) 2 QB 219.
54. Official Assignee v. Haradagiri, AIR 1963 SC 754, 757 - 758.
55. Mohamed Hussain Saheb v. The Chartered Bank (1964) 1 Mad 1012.
56. R. Manick Chettiar v. The Official Assignee 1944 1 Mod LJ 116.
57. Byramji Bomanji Talati v. Official Assignee of Bombay 1935 ILR 60 Bom 444.
58. Pearly Achew v Oficial Assignee, AIR 1966 Bom 121, 67 Bom LR 651.
59. Linton v Linton (1885) 15 Q.B.D. 239; 54 LJ Q.B. 529.
60. Mamihabeebi v. Minndeen, AIR 1939 Mad 183.
61. Mohammad Ali Metab bhai In re AIR 1930 Bom 144.
62. Chengalraya v. O.R., AIR 1947 Mad 338.
63. Venkata Hanumantha Rao v. Ram Krishnaiya AIR 1945 Mad 239.
64. Syed Faizuddin v N.v. International Co. 1937 Wag 410.
65. *In re* Douglas 1930 Ch 97; 142 LT 379.
66. Nagin Lal Maganlal JaiChand, in re AIR 1925 Bom 543.
67. Thangavelu v Chock lingam AIR 1944 Mad 129.
68. *In re* Mirza Md. Masru Ali Khan AIR 1942 Cal 150.
69. Sidick Haji v. Official Asignee AIR 1935 Bom 310.
70. Pareshram v. Official Assignee of Calcutta AIR 1933 Cal 387.
71. Motilal viswas v. Empror, AIR 1929 Cal 80.
72. Narayan Singh v. Attar Singh AIR 1933 Cal p.130.
73. S. 28 (4) Presidency.
74. Kedar Nath v. Amulya Ratan AIR 1942 Cal 79; Cr. L.J. 402.
75. Beardsell & Co. v. Nilgiri Abdul Gani Saheb, AIR 1914 Mad 474.
76. *In re* Shivlal Rathi, AIR 1917 Bombay L.R. 349.
77. *In re* Krishna Kishore Adhikasi AIR 1928 Cal 21.
78. Banares Bank Ltd. v. George Machnald Falkmer, AIR 1942 Pat 493.
79. Coldrey v Bartrum 1880 19 ChD 394, SILJ Ch 265.
80. Mallew v Moldgon (1861) 117 ER 1045; Knight v. Hunt 1829 E R 1127.
81. Ganpat Rai v. Kanti Ram AIR All 293.
82. Exp. Bacan, (1881) 17 ChD 447; *In re* Krishna Kishore Adhicary AIR 1928 Cal 21.
83. Per Warchan William L.J. *in Re* Gaskell (1909) 2 KB 478: 78 L.J. K.B. 656.
84. Mansa v. M.E.A. Majid, AIR 1931 Rang 275.
85. Official Assignee of Calcutta v. Frederick Lionel Harcount, AIR 1932 Cal 162.
86. (1892) 1 QBD 890.
87. Section 40 of the Presidency Act.
88. Niaz Ahmed v. Phul Kunwar AIR 1932 All 336.
89. Rustamjee Dorabjee v. K.D. Bros, AIR 1927 Cal 163.
90. Official Assignee of Madras v. Official Assignee of Rungoon (1918) 42 Mad 121; 35 MLJ 533; 49 IC 210; LW
91. Chokkalingam v Official Assignee AIR 1940 Mad 837.
92. *Ibid.*
93. *In re* O Gormon (1899) 2 QBD 62; LJ QB 650.
94. Halsbury's Laws of England, Vol. 16 Arl 89 p.36.
95. Illustration (f) and g to 0.8, Rule C.P.C., of it 94 vol. 29 Art 696; Flitcher v. Dyke (1787) 2 TR 32.
96. Section 43 Indian contract Act, 1872; Re Pioneer Bank, AIR 1951 Cal 519
97. Simla Banking Co. v. Bhagwan Kuar 1928 Lah 316; Panikar v. Travamcore National and Quilon Bank Ltd. AIR 1942 Mad 351.
98. Sovereign Life Ass. Co. v. Dodd 1892 IQB 573 at p.578.
99. Re Daintrey, (1900) 1 QB 546 p.555.
100. New Bank of India v. Banwarilal 1949 Comp cas 236; Jeffery v. official Assignee of Rangoon, 6 Rang 46.
101. Ex. p. Prescote (1753) 1 Atk 230; Smith v wood (1929) 1 Ch 14; *In re* Travancore National and Quilon Bank Ltd., AIR 1941 Mad 622.
102. *In re* The Pioneer Bank AIR 1951 Cal 519.
103. Nath Bank Ltd. v. Sisir Kumar Sarkar AIR 1954 Cal. 303.
104. Bow year v Pawson (1881) 6 Q.B.D. 540; Storey: Equity Jurisprudence Art. 439.
105. Wolstenholme v. Sheffield Union Banking Co. (1886) 54 LT 746 p.748.

106. Krishna Chandra v Patna Dhana - bhandar Co. AIR (1935), Cal 225.
108. 1900 1 QB 546.
109. Mersey. Steel & Iron Co. Ltd. v. Naylor, Benzone & Co. 1884 9 APP Cas 434; 58 LJ 637.
110. Raghava Reddy v. Official Assignee AIR (1964) Mad 549 p.552.
111. Muttan Chettiar v. Venkitaswami Naicker AIR 1936 Mad 819.
112. *Ibid.*
113. Dina Nath Saligram Marandee v Maroti Totaram, AIR 1959; Bom 105. Guruiah v Rangiah, 1942 Mad 614.
114. Official Assignee v. T.D. Tehrani, AIR 1972 Mad 187; Official Assginee v. Kamiah Naidu, ILR 58 Mad 702; Lakhmiammal Sinivasa Iyenger, AIR 1916 Mad 481.
115. 60 IA 362; AIR 1934 P.C. 3; Rang 105.
116. *In re* Kushler Ltd., 1943 Ch 248; In re Fweedle (1892) 2 QB 216.
117. Sharp v Jackson 1899 AC 419.
118. *In re* Goldsmid (1886) 18 QBD 295.
119. *In re* Lane (1889) 2 QBD 74.
120. *In re* Cohen (1924) 2 Ch 515.
121. Racburn & v. Zoolikofer & Co. AIR 308.
122. S. 54A Provincial Insolvancy Act, 1920.
123. S. 58 Provincial Insolvency Act, 1920.

PART H

LAW OF AGENCY

CHAPTER

19

Law of Agency

Introduction

(1) Agency is the relationship which exists between two persons, one of whom expressly or impliedly consents that the other should represent him or act on his behalf, and who similarly consents to represent the former or so to act. The one who is to be represented or on whose behalf the act is to be done is called the principal. The one who is to represent or act is called agent. Any person other than the principal and the agent may referred to as a third party.

(2) In respect of the acts which the principal expressly or impliedly consent that he shall do, the agent is said to have authority to act; and this authority constitutes a power to affect the principal's legal relations with third parties.

(3) Where the agent's authority results from a manifestation of consent that he should represent or act for the principal to the agent himself, the authority is called actual authority, express or implied. Where the agent's authority result from such a manifestation made by the principal to a third party, the authority is called apparent authority[1].

The Law of Agency in India is codified as part of Indian Contract Act 1872. It is enshrined in Section 182 to 238 of the Indian Contract Act, and therefore all references in this work is directed towards interpretation of sections relating to Agency of aforesaid Act.

The Indian Contract Act is based on English Common Law and particularly on English law of Contract.

In English Law, Contract of agency is "the employment of one person by another in order to bring the latter into legal relations with a third person". It is based on Latin maxim *'Qui Per Allum Facit Perseipsum Facere Videtur',* i.e. He who does an act through another is deemed in law to do it himself. This is may be shortened as *'Qui Facit per alium facit perse'* i.e. He who act by another act by himself."

There is a statutory recognition of agency in the Partnership Act (1932), Transfer of Property Act India, Companies Act (1956), Negotiable Instrument Act (1881) etc.

The concept of Agency is fundamental to the whole branch of law, since it provides the paradigm situation for the application of typical rules to govern so many vivid relations in Today's life, of an individual, a corporation (private or public), or either a public sector undertaking or being multinationals in India to snatch direct or indirect agency so as to unsurp and grab, age old valuables of India.

2. Essential of Agency

An Agreement: The basic notion behind law of agency can be explained in these terms. The mature law recognises that a person need not always do things that change his legal relations himself, he may utilise the services of another to change them, or to do something during the course of which they may be changed. Thus where one person, the principal, requests another, the agent to act on his behalf, and the other agrees or does so, the law recognises that the agent can affect the principal's legal position by certain acts which, though performed by the agent, are not necessarily to be created as the agents own acts, but are to be treated in certain respects as if they were acts of the principal. This results is not confined to cases where the agent has specific instructions for it, if this were so, the notion would be of very limited application. and agent may be requested generally to act according to his own discretion within certain limits. The justification for the whole concept of agency is doubtless the idea of unilateral manifestation of willingness to be bound: there is no conceptual contract between principal and agent.

The same concept is extended to cases where the law regards two persons as having agreed that one shall act for other, regardless of whether their intentions did actually coincide in this respect to cases where one person has the power to act on another, behalf as if there had been agreement and finally to cases where law treats a third party as entitled to regard one person as having been authorised to act as agent for another, even though nothing has occurred from which the law would draw that conclusion if the matter were in issue between the supposed principal and supposed agent only.[2]

The model situation, in which the parties infact agreed in this work called agency by express agreement.

The first extension is called agency by implied agreement. The second is dealt with under the heading of ratification; the third, which occurs principally in cases of necessity, is called agency by operation of law. The fourth is treated under the title of agency by estoppel and apparent authority.

It will be seen from this that the basic case is that in which the agent and principal agree that one should act for the other. This is the model and it is from their similarity in various respect to this situation that others derive their legal force.

Thus the term agency is here assigned to this basic relationship, which involves the consent of both parties. The other cases may fairly be regarded as derivatives. Ratification cases can, but only with difficulty.

Be assimilated into model situation, agency of necessity occurs where ex-hypothesis no agreement can be found so that it is reasonably described as arising solely by operation of law; and agency by estoppel and apparent authority cases only affect third parties in the first instance, so to do not give rise to the full range of results flowing from the model situation.[3]

In conclusion, it can be said that it is the law that imposes certain consequences on the facts in all cases. Therefore, all types of agencies arise by operation of law and the insistence on the element of consent of parties as the ground base of agency is old and out dated. However, it can also be said that cases of genuine express agreement are now become exception rather than rule and that the objective interpretation imposed by law is so clearly predominant that it, and not subjective consent should be regarded as the connecting link between cases of agency.

The approach of English Courts reflected in the words of **Lord Cranworth**: No one can become the agent of another except by the will of that other person. More than a century later Lord Pearson said: "The relationship of principal and agent can only be established by the consent of the principal and agent. Thus, the notions of will and consent may be objectively determined while they clearly remain fundamental.[4]

3. Concept of Authority and Power:

The description of results which the law puts on a true agency conditionality is to say that agent has a power to affect the principal's legal relation however, it is more commonly said that the agent has authority. ON analyis, this authority amount to no more than a power of special sort. a power by doing an act to affect the principal's legal relations as if he had done the act himself. Yet is may be said that authority and power are different This is so in the sense that where such a power is voluntarily — conferred by one person on the another (the model agency case), the person on whom it is conferred is said to be authorised by the other or to have his authority. But the power may exist in a person on whom it cannot be said to have been voluntarily conferred. In common law, such cases seem exceptional and it is said that there is only authority by operation of law or apparent or legal authority. Yet, the power is same there is no temptation to talk of apparent power or real power.[5]

It seems that authority like possession carries the image of a model can justify a legal result. The concept of powers neutral and simply states the result regardless of the reason for it.[6]

4. Real and apparent authority

The placing of real and apparent authority together can be misunderstood but for actual authority arises where there is agency by agreement. Whereas apparent authority can be said to be no authority at all, in that there is no agreement between principal and agent even if a third party is entitled to assume that there has been. But these two types of authority commonly spoken of together, and have certain common consequences; it seems not correct therefore, to reflect this usage at the outset.

It can also be said that in both cases the authority stems from principles objectively determined consent the difference being that in one case the consent is manifested to the agent and in the other to the third party.

5. Vivid use of agency rationale

The ruling norm is that the acts of an agent are in certain circumstances to be deemed as having the same legal effect as if they had been done by the principal. Reasoning along these lines may be found in the spheres of contract, property, tort, quasi contract, evidence, administration, law, taxation, labour law and else where. But this approach has value in imposing some unity on the law applicable to situations where one party represents or acts for another. It should not be taken too literally. It is erroneous to assume that a single set of principles, valid for the whole law, relating to the representation of one person by another can be evolved under the title of agency.

The main application of such rationale in the law of contact, where it is obviously desirable for rules to exist under which a person may make a contract for another, and such reasoning was necessary to render the principal liable in assumpsit's.[7]

6. Other forms of representation

It should be acknowledged that the law of the agency traditionally embraces also various forms of representation where a person is appointed to act on behalf of another but often cannot bind his principal by contract, dispose of his property, or indeed directly affect his legal position at all except in minor ways. Such a person is not strictly an agent; yet having fiduciary duty like agent.

Such as solicitors, estate agent and commission merchant, public agents private agents, foreign agents, general agents, special agents, co-Agents, sub-Agents etc.

7. Certain concepts relevant to the contract of agency

(1) A disclosed principal, is principal, whether identified or unidentified, whose existence as principal is known at the time of the transaction to the person dealing with agent.

(2) An undisclosed principal, is a principal whose existence as principal is not known at the time of transaction to the person dealing with the agent.

(3) An independent contractor is one who undertakes to produce a given result, but so that in the actual execution of the work he is not under the order or control of a person for whom he does it, and may use his own discretion in things not specified before hand.

(4) A servant is person employed by another to do work for him on terms that he, the servant, is to be subject to control and directions of his employer in respect of the manner in which his work is to be done.

(5) A general agent is an agent who has authority to act for his principal in all matters concerning a particular trade or business, of a particular nature; or to do some act in the ordinary course of his trade, profession or business as an agent, on behalf of his principal.

(6) A special agent is an agent who has only authority to do some particular act, or to represent his principal in some particular transaction, such act or transaction not being in ordinary course of his trade, profession or business as an agent.

(7) A Factor is an agent whose ordinary course of business is to sell or dispose of goods, of which he is entrusted with the possession or control by his principal.

(8) A Broker is an agent whose ordinary course of business is to negotiate and make contracts for sale and purchase of goods and other property, of which he is not entrusted with possession or control.

(9) A del credere agent is an agent who, in consideration of extra remuneration, called a del credere commission, guarantees to his principal that third persons with whom he enters into contracts on behalf of the principal shall duly pay any sums becoming due under those contracts On basis of these parameters, we shall unfold the kind of agents.[8]

8. Kinds of Agents:

1. Factor and Brokers:

A Factor is an agent entrusted with possession and control of the goods to be sold by him for his principal. And in this respect he differs from a broker — the latter not having such possession or control, but being a mere negotiator empowered to effect contract of sale or purchase for others unless otherwise agreed between him and him principal. A factor has a general lien over goods belonging to the principal and entrusted to him, in the course of his agency in respect of any claim that he may have against his principal provided that it arises out of agency. A factor is entitled to contract in his own name and to receive payment but a broker has normally no authority to do either, nor to cancel a contract which he has affected for his principal.[9]

2. Del Credere Agents

An agent for the sale of goods some time acts under a del credere commission, that is a higher reward than is usually given he becomes responsible for the solvency of the buyer; or in other words he guarantees, in every case of sale, the payment of price of goods sold when ascertained and due. He does not become responsible to the buyer for the due performance of seller's contract and principal may not litigate with a del credere agent dispute arising out of contract made by him.

A del credere agency may be implied, or inferred from a course of contracts, but an agreement between stock broker by which one party agreed in consideration of receiving half commission on business introduced by him to bear half of any loss ascertained by the other in connection with such business was held to constitute not a del credere agency but a contract of indemnity. A del credere does not need to be in writing because being merely incidental to another transaction, it is not a promise to answer for the debt, default or miscarriage of another within the meaning of section 4 of the statute of fraud of England or elsewhere. [10]

3. Auctioneers:

An auctioneer is an agent to sell at an open sale, but not to give warrantees as to the property auctioned unless he has been expressly authorised to do so and he is a trustee for the vendor both as to what is sold and as to the purchase money.

Although he is primarily and agent for the vendor, he is also the agent of a purchaser to sign a contemporary memorandum sufficient to satisfy the requirement of law.

In an English case: Chancy v. Maclow[11] the highest bidder at an auction of real property refused to sign the contract but did not repudiate it. The auctioneer. Later signed and was authorised to do so as his authority has not been withdrawn.

The authority of auctioneer to sign arises directly when the contract is concluded and at any rate on part of vendor is irrevocable. The authority does not extend to auctioneer's clerk unless the purchaser assent to the clerk's signing for him.

The Shipmaster: The master of a ship has wide power as an agent for the owners to do all things necessary for the due and proper prosecution of the voyage; by way of contracting for usual employment of the ship, for repairs and necessaries and his authority is some what enlarged in cases of emergency. He may also be entitle in some circumstances to act an agent for the cargo owners. But his authority is less extensive as regards the enlarged powers in emergency, when he can communicate with the ship and cargo, owners, as now-a-days he normally can.

The Indian Contract Act, sections 186 and 187 deals with creation of agency, express and implied. It is said an implied agency includes an agency by estoppel; agency by holding out, and an agency of necessity.

The relationship of principal and agent need not be expressly constituted, it can be brought about by implication of law in a particular situation or from the necessity of the case.

In all cases, whether an instrument is contract of agency or sale has to be determined from substance of the case.

9. Agent and servant:

The supreme Court of India discussed distinction between an agent and a servant in *Lakshminaraynan Ram Gopal & Sons v. Hyderabad Government*,[12] speaking through Mr. Justice Bhagwati J. held.

(1) An agent has the authority to act on behalf of his principal and to create contractual relations between the principal and a third party. This kind of power not generally enjoyed by a servant.

(2) A principal has right to direct what the agent has to do, but a master has not only that right, but also the right to say how it is to be done. A servant acts under the direct control and supervision of his master and is bound to conform to all reasonable orders given to him in the course of his work. But an agent, though bound to exercise his authority in accordance with all lawful instructions and is not subject in its exercise control or supervision of the principal.

(3) The made of remuneration generally different a servant is paid by way of salary or wages but an agent receives commission on basis of work done.

(4) A master is liable for wrongful act of his servant if it is committed in the course of servant's employment A principal is liable for agents wrong done within the scope of authority.

(5) A servant usually serves only one master, but an agent may work for several principal at the same time.

Though an agent is as such not a servants, a servant is generally for some purposes his master's implied agent, the extent of agency depending upon the duties or position of the servant. It is true that a director of the company is not a servant, but an agent in as much as the company cannot act in its own person but has only to act through director who qua the company have the relationship of an agent to its principal.

A managing director has a dual capacity. He is a director as well an employee. It is therefore evident that in the capacity of managing director he may be regarded as having not only as persona of a director but also the persona of an employee, and as an agent depending upon the nature of his work and the terms of him employment. Where he is so employed the relationship between him an managing director and the company may be similar to a reason who is employed as a servant or as agent, for the term employed is facile enough to corner any of these relationships.

11. Agency by Estoppel

This type of agency arises where by his conduct plead B to believe that C is his agent.

In such a case, if his conduct discloses a certain set of circumstances as existing, he cannot later repudiate the truth of such statements which led the other to believe the said circumstances.

In an English case Lord Halsbury said:

"Estoppel arises when you are preluded from denying the truth of any thing which you have represented as a fact, although it is not a fact" [13]

In analysis if A tells B in the hearing of C that he (A) is C's agent. C does not contradict this. B bonafide believing the statement of A (since C does not repudiate it) enters into a transaction. In suit between C and B, C can not deny that A was his agent, though in fact a Was never his agent.

Likewise in a case of agency by estoppel it is immaterial to consider if the ostensible agent acted in fraud of principal , having no authority at all of if he merely exceeded his authority.

In Moorgate Mercantile Co Ltd. v Twitchings, [14] the plaintiffs a finance company, by a hire purchase agreement let a car on hire purchase to M, who paid some advance, the rest being payable in 24 instalments. The practice was that all hire purchase transaction were registered with Hire Purchase information Ltd. (HPI) to whom all enquiries had to be addressed. The HPI represented the defendants, the vendor from M, that the car was not registered with them, thereby implying that plaintiff had no interest in the car. M paid only four instalments. M offered the car for sale to the defendant, a motor car dealer who was an affiliated member of HPI. M told the defendants that the car was not subject to any hire purchase and stated that he was the owner.

As a result of the answer given by the HPI that the car was not registered with them, the defendant bought the car from M. Soon after that the car was resold to a private person. M paid four instalments of hire to the plaintiff to keep then quite but he did not pay any further instalments. Sometime later, the plaintiff discovered that the car had been sold. They sued the defendant for conversion. It was held that the plaintiff's claim failed since they were stopped from ascertaining their title to the car against the defendant for the following reasons:

(1) Since the plaintiff had entrusted HPI, an organisation set up for very purpose of supplying information about hire purchase transactions, the plaintiffs were responsible for the answer given by HPI to the defendant that the car was not subject to any hire purchase agreement. Accordingly, it would be inapplicable to allow the plaintiffs to depart from what they led the defendant to believe.

(2) HPI had become its members' agent to answer on their behalf enquiries from dealers. Agents representations in the course of agency constituted estoppel against the principal.

(3) The plaintiffs were under a duty to assure registration of the transaction with HPI because they knew that dealers would reply on information supplied by HPI.

12. Some Special Kinds of Agents:

1. Solicitors:

A solicitor has implied authority to accept service for his client. But unless so authorised he cannot institute an action for him except where this can be inferred from the terms of the retainer. A solicitor's act bind the client, when done in the ordinary course of practice. He can effect a compromise in a suit. If solicitor acts within the terms of his authority and the other party has no notice of any limitation on it, the client is bound by he act of solicitor. If the client acted under a misappropriation he should withdrawn his consent before a consent order is passed by court.

2. Home Agent and Land Agents:

Where a vendor seeks an agent to negotiate with a purchaser, the agent has authority to describe the property and make statements as to its value so as to bind his principal. He can receive a deposit but he cannot conclude a contract of lease or sale without express authority. He can sign the sale for his principal . But cannot with special conditions. It is his duty to inform the principal of the best offer before any sale is signed by the principal.[15]

3. Dealers and Finance companies:

Regulation authorises the dealer to act as agent for the finance company, to provide finance for hire purchase, credit sale, conditional sale and to receive notice of cancellation, revocation of offer and rescission. He can be its agent for other matters also.[16]

4. Sheriff:

A Sheriff is an agent of court executing its warrants. He is not an agent of the creditor who obtained judgement.[17]

5. Common Agent:

There can be an a gent for more than one principal e.g. a society is the agent of all its members likewise Trade Union Office bearers are deemed Agent of its members.

Thus, the concept of agency is a complex concept of contractual relations and having no precisely definable limits. Because its an ever growing field and various superior courts continue their drive to unfold various new facets of the concept of agency. But one thing is core of concept of agency under which an agent ought to represent his principal and principal ought to discharge his obligations towards the third parties created for him by his agent. Under express, implied authority and authority of necessity.

2. Appointment and authority of agents. Indian Contract Act 1872 Ss 182-189.

"Agent" and "principal" defined an "Agent" is a person employed to do any act for another or to represent another in dealings with third person. The person for whom such act is done or who is so represented is called the principal".

According Section 182 an agent is one;

(i) who is employed by another

(ii) to do any act for another

(iii) to represent another is dealing with third persons.

In short an agent is the connecting link between the principal and third persons and serves as a conduit pipe or middle man. This middle man has the power to create legal relationship between the principal and third parties. He has competency to make the principal responsible to the third person. He is different from a servant who mechanically carries out the master's order and has no power to represent his master or create legally binding relationship with third parties affecting his master.

In certain circumstances, an agent may act as a trustee. If his principal entrust him with money to utilise the same in a particular manner, if he uses in some other manner his liability is that of a trustee. If he mingles that amount with his own and deals with them as he pleases, he is not a trustee but a debtor to his principal. A secretary of a fund is an agent and not a trustee. To constitute a trust, there must be a distinct fund or property which the trustee is bound to preserve intact and account for. In a contract of agency, there is no such fund, agent can spend the principal's monies subject to accountability. The beneficiary under a contract has only a personal claim against promisor a beneficiary under a trust has the beneficial interest in trust property.[18]

The definition of agent in section 182 is indeed wider than that in English law. It may embrace even a servant pure and simple, even a casual employee, a man who is engaged by me in the street to black my boots, but it cannot for a moment be contented that they are therefore all to be placed in the same category.[19]

In a Rangoon case posited that the term agent may include a person employed to sell unredeemed articles from a pawnshop on behalf of the employer. In a Calcutta case it was pointed out that the definition does not limit the employment of an agent to one by the principal only. It includes any employment by any authority authorised by law to make the employment.[20]

The concept of agency explained by Ramaswami of Madras High Court in *Krishna v. Ganapati*[21].

"In legal phraseology, every person who acts for another is not an agent. A domestic servant renders his master personal service; a person may till another's field or tend his flocks or works in his ship or factory or mine or may be employed upon his roads or ways; one may act for another in aiding in the performance of his legal or contracted obligation to third person .... In none of these capacities, he is agent and he is not acting for another in dealing with third persons. It is only when he acts as a representative of other in business negotiations, that is to say that, in the creations, modifications or termination of contractual obligations between that other and third persons, that he is agent.................. Representative character and derivative authority may briefly be said to be the distinguishing feature of an agent."

The Apex Court in *Lakshminrain Ram Gopal v. Hyderabad Government*.[22]

Speaking through Bhagwati J. adopted following distinction stated in Powell's Law of Agency and Halsbury's law of England

(i) An agent has the authority to act on behalf of his principal and to create contractual relations between the principal and a third party. This kind of power is generally not enjoyed by the servant.

(ii) A principal has the right to direct what the agent has to do, but a master has not only that right, but also the right to say. A servant act under the direct control and supervision of his master and is bound to conform to all reasonable orders given to him in the course of his work. But an agent, though bound to exercise his authority in accordance with all lawful instructions ....is not subject to the exercise to the direct control or supervision of the principal.

(ii) The mode of remuneration is generally different. A servant is paid salary or wages, an agent receives commission on the basis of work done.

(iii) A master is liable for wrongful act of his servant is the course of employment. A principal is liable for the wrong done within the scope of authority.

(v) A servant usually serves only one master, but an agent may work for several principals at the same time.

2. Co-Agents and Co-Principals

(i) In case of joint authority to co-agents, it would be necessary for them to act jointly and only then their principal would be bound. In cases where in given authority is joint and several any one of them would be competent to act for principal.[23]

(ii) An agent who represent more than one principal in one and same transaction, he should account for to all of them jointly, for an account given to one many not absolve him from his liability to another.[24]

3. Nature and Essentials of Agency:

In the Halsbury's Law of England it is said: The term agency and agent have in popular use a for number of different meanings, but in Law the word agency is used to connote the relation which exists where one person has authority or capacity to create legal relations between a person occupying the position of principal and third parties. The relation of agency arises, whenever one person, called the agent has authority to act on behalf of another called principal and consents to act. Whether that relation exists in any situation depends not in the precise terminclogy employed by parties to describe their relationship. If an agreement in substance contemplates the alleged agent acting on his own behalf and not on behalf of the principal, then although he may be described in the agreement as an agent, the relation of agency will not have arisen.

Conversely, the relation of agency may arise despite a provision in the agreement that it shall not. Servant or an independent contractor, though not necessarily the employer's agent, may often have authority to act as such when relations with authority are involved. Nevertheless an agent as such is not a servant.[25]

In Phimpton v Binkimshaw,[26] it was stated that a person appointed to carry on a business under the power of attorney of a person incapable of managing his affairs or under a deed of arrangement for the benefit of creditors is an agent. An agent is bound by the terms of his authority. If he is authorised to buy or sell property for the principal but seeks to sell his own property to his principal or to buy the property of the latter for himself, he clearly violates the first condition of his employment and changes the intrinsic nature of contract between them.

As to the competency of the principal it is settled law that during the period of hostilities (hostilities) with the country of which he is subject, that is an alien enemy, is wholly incompetent to contract or to act as principal but he may appoint an agent to enter into contract on his behalf. However, principal who is minor is not liable for any tort committed by his agent unless committed with his direct consent.[27]

4. Creation of agency

The creation of agency may be takes place by:

(i) a written document.

(ii) operation of law

(iii) subsequent ratification

(iv) inference from the circumstances and conduct of parties.

According to Chitty, the creation of agency thus:

"This relationship of principal and agent is created by an express or implied agreement, which may but need not be contractual, by the ratification of the agents's by the principal and by the operation of law in the cases of agency of necessity and in certain other situations. Furthermore, the principal may be bound under the doctrine of apparent authority or agency by estoppel.[28]

Therefore, where a person by words or conduct represents to third party that another has authority to act on his behalf, he may be bound by acts of such person, as if he had in fact authorised him. This doctrine called the doctrine of apparent or ostensible authority implied authority and applicable to cases:

(i) Where a person allows another who is not his agent at all to appear as his agent.

(ii) Where a principal allows his agent to appear to have more authority than he actually has

(iii) Where a principal makes reservations in his agent's authority that limits the authority which such agent would normally have, but fails to inform third party of this,

(iv) Where a principal allows it to appear that an agent has authority when such authority has infact been terminated. The doctrine of estoppel said to have an application. The doctrine of estoppel however as normal rules being leniently applied, particularly as regards reliance on the representation.

It is obviously clean that the definition given in section 182 is not exhaustive it covers also implied agency (section 186) , of course the definition in Section 182 is of wider import than in English Law where agency is possible only at the will of the other. In India, the definition did not require that the employment should be by the person by whom the agent is employed to act or whom he is employed to represent. [29]

The Judicial committee of P.C. had also elaborated the extended meaning of the term agency thus:

"In many trades — particularly in motor car trade — the so called agent is merely a favoured and a favouring buyer, one who under an overriding contract, undertakes to do his best to find a market for the manufacturer's stock, who is given some special advantage, such as a special advantage, such as a special discount or preference in complying with his orders, but who in each particular contract act as a buyer from manufacturer, and sells as whatever price he can get, unless he is forbidden to sell too cheap".[30]

An agent is under the supervision and control of the principal and is liable to account to latter.

Where a document is ambiguous, parole, evidence can be admitted to show who the real principal is under contract. But where the contract is in writing, the said document cannot be used so as to contradict the written contract what is essential is the incidents of the contract as disclosed by the evidence justifying the finding as to the agency Mere writing of letters or offering advice cannot establish an agency. Agency can be proved by direct evidence of conferral of authority, or though a cause of conduct justifying an inference of such authorisation A formal agreement is not absolutely necessary to create an agency. [31]

According to Lord Denning L J in *Shephard v. Cartwright*,[32] an infant can not appoint an agent to act for him neither by means of a power of attorney nor by any other means. If he purport to appoint an agent, not only is the appointment itself void, but everything done by the agent on behalf of the infant is also void and incapable of ratification.

His Lordship further said:

An infant has not sufficient discretion to choose an agent to act for him. He is all two likely to choose a wrong man; and so the law declares him to be incapable of choosing an agent at all.

But in situations where a minor is capable of binding himself by contract he may appoint an agent.

According Bow Stead:

An infant or a lunatic is a bound by a contract made by his agent with his authority, where the circumstances are such that he would have been bound if he had himself made the contract.

However, there is nothing in the Act which prohibits guardian of a minor to inter into a contact.

5. Examples of Agency:

1. Where a firm was appointed sole banian of a company to sell its manufactured goods, to be responsible to the company for the movies due by the buyers, to guarantee the performance of the guarantee of the buyers through them, it was held the firm was a del credere agent of the company.[33]
2. When goods are despatched through post office by the V.P.P. system, it is the post office that is an agent of the seller for recovery of the price; so if it fails to recover the price but delivers the goods, it is liable in damages to the seller A post office is an agent of the payee.[34]
3. A person can appoint one branch of a bank as agent for him but in such a case all other branches of the bank cannot thereby become his agent.[35]
4. Where the defendant Bank was appointed agent of the plaintiff for merely handling over documents. Thus, through the conduit pipe of the defendant bank privity of contract was established between the plaintiff and the second defendant who thus became a substitute agent for purposes of arranging reshipment.[36]
5. Where A was employed to invest money on B's behalf an represent him in dealings with debtors, and A did exhibit such conduct and entered into transaction on behalf of B the relation ship was clearly one of principal and Agent.[37]
6. A military contractor was required to deposit a certain sum a security in a certain recognised Bank. He did so in the name of the military authorities and forwarded the receipt. The bank went into liquidation. It was held an agency can be inferred from the transactions and acting of the parties. Consequently the authorities was liable for the return of the amount. Once the fact of agency is established the question of negligence cannot arise.[38]
7. There was no contract of agency in writing. But the evidence disclosed that the plaintiff purchased and resold the goods on behalf of the defendant. was held that there was a contract of agency.[39]
8. A pays treasury Bill to Bank B for collection. Bank B passes on the bill to Bank C for collection. The treasury paid the amount of Bill of Bank B. It was held A is the principal, Bank B the agent and Bank C is the sub-agent.[40]
9. Where a shareholder appoints a 'proxy' to attend on his behalf the company meeting the proxy is the agent of the shareholder. The world 'Proxy' connotes 'some agent properly appointed.[41]
10. There can be a purchasing agent (e.g. Paddy) for the Government of India. In the instant case the agent had a further responsibility for milling Paddy in Bihar, with a view to supply to nominees of the Government of India but that was held to be in his capacity as independent contractor; merely because the milling was to be done at the mills specified by the Government cannot be interpreted to make him as the agent for the Government in that field also.[42]
11. A commission agent may agree to be the agent of his principal to procure certain goods. The transfer of goods by him to his customer principal is then as his agent. It is not a sale within the meaning of the Sale of Goods Act.[43] But it may be that the term 'Commission agent' may be in a document and yet the relationship may be one of vendor and vendee. In such a case the person is not exactly an agent of the other party. The question is if the agent acts in the transaction on his own behalf or of his principal.[44]
12. "A broker is an agent employed to make a bargain for another and receive a commission on the transaction which is usually called brokerage. He has usually neither the custody nor the possession of the goods. It is the broker's duty to establish privity of contract between the principal and the third party-The broker cannot sell in his own name nor can be sued on the contract."[45] In *Fowler v. Hollins,*[46] it was said:............he is an agent employed to make bargains and contracts between other persons in matters of trade, commerce and navigation .... he is throughout merely the negotiator between the parties. And therefore by the civil law brokers were not treated as ordinarily incurring any personal liability by their intervention unless there was some fraud on their part."
13. A Railway company is an agent of the consignor of perishable goods to carry and not to sell. But as agents of necessity they can sell the goods provided it was impossible to get instructions from the owner. They have further to show that the sale was in the circumstances the only reasonable business cause to be taken. [47]
14. The Post Office is an agent of the addressee when money is sent by insured cover, provided the addressee has expressly or impliedly asked the sender to send or remit the amount by post. [48]
15. A, the plaintiff, agreed to supply mutton to military authorities. A deposited necessary security in Bank B who issued a deposit receipt in the name of Divisional Disbursing Officer, Lahore. A sent the receipt to the proper Military Authorities. The deposit was renewed in the same officer's name at his instance. Later the plaintiff submitted no demand certificate to the military who however due to negligence did not return the deposit receipt

in time. Meantime the Bank B went into liquidation. A sued the Secretary of State to recover the amount. It was held that Bank B was an agent of the defendant and so the defendant was liable to A.[49]

16. A clerk in charge to Savings Account in a Bank in an agent of the Bank. He is in the know if a constituent overdraws. He is liable to the Bank for any negligence on his part in that regard unless the Bank permits overdrawal up to a limit.[50]
17. A is employed by B to invest monies on his behalf and to represent him in his dealing with debtors. A is an agent of B.[51]
18. Where a Deshmuk, entitled to certain fees out of the revenue collected in Poona, got this done by Ajahat Gumashtas, hereditarily appointed by the old Peshwa's Government. These gumashtas did not pay amount collected to the plaintiff, the Deshmuk. It was held the defendants were plaintiff's agent though their appointment and removal was not in his hands[52].
19. Where A arranges transport of goods with one transporting agency which utilises other agencies' services also, the latter are the agents of the contracting agency.[53]
20. In *Goenka Cotton Spinning and Weaving Mills v. Duncan Stratton & Co.* [54] A, a firm ordered machinery from Firm B, some from B's stock with fixed prices and others to be imported by B. The price of the later was fluctuating. B was to get certain commission and was to act as A's agent for shipping and clearing. Later A sold the machinery to C and asked B to place all sums advanced to the credit of C, C also confirmed this by his letter to B. Some time later in B's firm, one D because the sole proprietor in place of E, the old one. C sued B. It was held that B was C's agent as to the imported machinery whose price was fluctuating and was a principal so far as the other machinery (stable price) was concerned. The changes in B's firms would not affect the position as B was a legal entity as a firm. Further as A had transferred all his rights to C, B was the agent of C also consequently.
21. Two brothers owning estate, can act as agent other, so that the estate can be managed by one in the absence of the other.[55]
22. A Director or Managing Director of a company is its agent for carrying on its business and not a mere servant of the company.[56]
23. Under the Indian trade in Calcutta, each indent is an offer by the person placing the order which is accepted by the person who imports the goods by sending the corresponding placement report. The importer is the agent of the dealer who places the order. The fact that the goods are to be bought by the seller at a stated place C.I.F. and no commission is payable by the dealer, cannot convert the transaction into a sale.[57]
24. The plaintiff purchased grain for the defendant and stored it. He charged the defendant with the purchase price and storage rent. He later sold the grain as per defendant's instructions and this resulted in a loss. Plaintiff sued the defendant for the amount due to him. It was held that there was a contract of agency as between the parties, carrying with the right of indemnity to the agent who merely carried out his principal's instruction.[58]
25. A, a creditor agreed to pay off the debts of B to his other creditors on B executing a sale deed for a particular amount. It was agreed that if creditors demanded more, B should pay the excess to A. Actually A managed to get clearance from the creditor by paying less. B claimed the balance. It was held that A was not entitled to retain the remission as he acted as the agent of B in the settlement with the creditors.[59]
26. Where A was appointed by a company as its cloth dalals for the whole of India, to sell the cloth, A was clearly an agent of the company who cannot dictate to A the manner or method of doing the work of the sole selling agency. For A was not a servant of the company but an agent.[60]
27. The Companies Act does not define 'sole selling agent' but it means an individual, or a firm or a company given exclusive right to sell goods of another person in a particular area. Courts have to determine if there was in reality such an agency. The mere inclusion of a term that business will be as between principal and principals does not carry on far. In the instant case the court construed the agreement as a whole as creating a sole selling agency coming within the purview of Section 294 of the Companies Act (1956).[61]
28. Where Income-tax assesses non-resident Company carries on business in former native State and Sells goods to buyers in British India and instructs his Bank in the Native state to collect hundies etc. the Bank is a collecting agent of the assesses. Buyer posts a cheque to the assesses seller, the Post Office is agent of the latter. When draft is sent by buyer through post with no such request from sells, the post office is agent of the buyer. The later is not taxable when received in a native State.[62]
29. The relationship of a Bank and a constituent is that of a principal and agent and that of a creditor and debtor. So where A, petitioner, gave the respondent Bank B certain treasury bills for collection, B passed them on to C, the Federal Bank of India for collection. The Treasury paid the amounts to C before C went into liquidation. B claimed

from the official liquidator of C the said amounts. B and the official liquidator entered into an arrangement by which B was to be paid in full quite fifty per cent of the amount. A applied under Section 45B of the Banking Companies Act claiming the entire amount from C. It was held A was entitled to priority to the extent of the entire amount as A and B were principal and agent. C was only B's sub-agent. There was no privity to contract between A and C.[63]

30. Where shares in a Bank were hypothecated by A to B and the deed authorised B to draw the dividends from the Bank and appropriate same for interest due on the debt. B stood in the position of an agent to A *vis-a-vis* Bank dividends. The agency is one as contemplated under Section 202. A cannot extinguish the right of the creditor B to receive the dividends in contravention of Section 242.[64]
31. Where a Post Office delivers a V.P.P. parcel to the addressee but fails to recover the amount from him, the Post Office is liable to make good the amount to the sender by way of damages. For the Post Office is but the agent of the sender as laid down by the Supreme Court in AIR 1959 SC 1934 approving the principle enunciated in LRR 28 Mad 213.[65]
32. There was sale of goods in British India by assessee trading in Native State. The buyers in British India used to send sale proceeds through negotiable instruments by post on the assessee's. The negotiable instruments when posted are to be received by the assessee in British India and therefore taxable.[66]
33. Where a dealer is appointed wholesaler under Madras Food Grains (Procurement) Order, 1947, etc. it was held the dealer is the agent of the Government who is bound under law to indemnify him. For when an act is done by one person at the request of another and such act turned out to be injurious to the rights of the third party, the person doing it was entitled to an indemnity from him who requested that it should be done.[67]
34. A Kaccha Adatiya acts as agent with personal liability on himself so far as third party is concerned. A pakka Adatiya is himself generally responsible to his constituent and he may act as principal. The crucial test is if the pakka Adaitiya has any personal interest of his own when he entered into the transaction in suit or whether that interest was limited to his commission agency charges and pocket expanses coupled with the right to be indemnified by the principal in the event of any loss. So when the defendant Pakka Adatiyas transacted business on plaintiffs behalf with third parties and further had not allocated any of the suit dealings to themselves, it was held that they were mere commission agents just as in the case of Katcha Adatiya; so they would be liable to pay the amount in their hands on account of the principal as per Sections 217 and 218.[68]
35. Under Section 44 of the Post Office Act, 1898, the remitter has full control over the amount in the money order till it is paid to the payee. In such an event, the post office is the agent of the remitter. If the payee specifically directs or instructs the remitter to send money by means of a money order, then the Post Office is the agent of the payee.[69]
36. In *Parashar Singh v. Hindustan Manganese Mines Ltd.*,[70] A contracted with B company for service which was being managed by C company under Managing agency agreements. D was director of B company and also managing director of company. D terminated A's service. It was held D will not be liable either in tort for procuring breach of contract with managed company, or for breach of contract by terminating the service of A. For D was in the position of an agent of the managed company.
37. In *Harichand Madan Gopal v. State of Punjab*,[71] an agency contract was for working as clearing agents of foodgrains for the whole of the undivided Punjab. It was a continuing contract and so under clause 2(d) of the Punjab Partiion (Contracts) Order 1947, it was held that the obligation of the agent continued even after partition though the contract between the appellants (agents) and the undivided Punjab was not a completed contract. The services were rendered for undivided Punjab and so the contract could not be deemed to be in force after the partition.
38. Where a colliery supplied coal to a company in pursuance of order of Coal Commissioner and the wagons were arranged by the Deputy Coal Commissioner and freight charges were payable by the company, it was held that the colliery was an agent for the company for the purposes of entering into a contract of consignment.[72]

When a person is not deemed an Agent

1. A cement stockist operating under the W.B. Cement Control Act (1948) was held to be not a constituted agent of Government.[73]
2. Where a person merely signs letters purporting to emanate from the Military Secretary and he signs over the words "for the Military Secretary" he cannot be deemed as an agent of an Ex-Ruler. He was merely performing the ministerial act of signing for the Military Secretary. He is in no sense the agent of the Ex-Ruler who had directed the Military Secretary to place the orders.[74]

3. Where a broker does not act as merely a middleman helping the parties to negotiate the deal, but undertakes to buy or sell goods for his employer, his role is merely that of his employer's representative. So, he cannot without the permission of his principal act simultaneously as the agent of both parties.[75]
4. Mere Undertaking to pay rent to the Zamindar cannot make him a *cestui que* trust nor is the tenure-holder an agent for him.[76]
5. An executor or administrator is not an agent of the legatees since they have not appointed him. So he cannot bind the legatee by entering into contracts. Ordinarily, the executor's contract is personal. If it is entered into for the benefit of the estate, he can by special clause exempt himself from personal liability.
6. Where an Official Receiver acknowledges the insolvent's liability, he is not an agent of the insolvent as there is no authority conferred on him to do so. But differing from this opinion it was posited in a Madras case that under Section 28(2) of the Provincial Insolvency Act at the properties of the insolvent vest in the Official Receiver, and that he is really the person against whom 'such property or right' as to acknowledgement is within the meaning of Section 19 new Section 18 of the Limitation Act. Consequently an acknowledgment by him can furnish a starting point of limitation.[77]
7. A commission agent sells goods in his won right and he is responsible to the principal only for the sale proceeds. The sale is not by him as agent of the principal.[78]
8. An unregistered Association or club is not a legal person. So the secretary or steward of a club cannot be the agent of party who is not a legal person. He has power to act and bind the club only within the authority given to him under the bye-laws of the club.[79]
9. Export licence holders are not agents. The Government regulatory order merely says that exports have to be made only through licensed exporters. This does not make the transaction one of agency since the principal does not sell to his agent. By the very act of purchase the exporter becomes the principal. The exporter does not become the agent of the seller at any time.[80]
10. In *Balthzar and Sons v. E. M. Abowath*[81] the Privy Council considered a case where A offered to buy sugar from B, who was not a producer. B contracted with C for purchase and delivery of sugar in six instalments. A was to pay commission to B. C failed to deliver after a few instalments. A sued B for damages for nondelivery after a few instalments. A sued B for damages for nondelivery. B pleaded he was nearly an agent. It was held that B was not the agent of A or C. A and B acted as principals between with them selves. Mere mention of Commission was not in consistent with this position and make a middle man an agent.
11. A took a building contract from a Railway Company. A gave a sub-work to B in the regard on a percentage basis. A got money from Railway. B used A for rendition of accounts. It was head the suit was incompetent as A and B were not in the relationship of principal and agent.[82]
12. Where no vesting order had yet been passed, the Official Receiver sold the insolvent's property and the insolvent's son sued him. The official receiver later obtained the vesting order with retrospective effect. It was held at the time of sale, the Receiver was not the agent of the Court and as such the court cannot ratify and an unauthorised sale by him.[83]
13. An Official Liquidator of a bank is not the bank's agent. He is an officer of the Crown acting within the terms of his appointment.[84]
14. A Secretary to a joint stock company is not its agent. He has authority to give effect to the decisions of Directors. However, recent changes in company law and practice made him agent also in cases issuance of prospectus by a joint stock company.[85]
15. A contracts to purchase from B on behalf of C. A undertake to B a definite sum of money in case of default on the specified date. A defaults. It was held A is not the agent of C in this regard. He is personally liable to B. A person working on his won account and not liable to any other for profit or loss is not an agent.[86]
16. A subsequent mortgagee who pays a prior encumbrance cannot be deemed to be an agent of mortgagor.[87]
17. A mortgagee may request the mortgagor to appoint a manager of the estate of the mortgaged property so as to inspire confidence in the mortgagee as to the safeguarding of the property for his dues. Such an agent is in law only the agent of the mortgagor and not of the mortgagee. So the mortgagee is in no way liable for the negligence of the manager.[88]
18. A person who merely advises is not an agent. An agent must represent or act for the principal on the latter's authorisation. He must aid the principal in bringing him in contractual relation with the named third person.[89]
19. An insurance Agent collecting premiums from the insured does not act as the agent of the Insurance Company.[90]

20. An Agent is never a servant, though the concept of a servant may in a sense involve an element of agency.[91]
21. A license under Section 3, Import (Control) Order, 1995, when he issues a letter of authority to a person to import the goods virtually effects a sale, liable to sales tax. The holder of letter of authority importing the goods and selling to licensee cannot be called an agent of the licensee.[92]
22. The word 'Agent' in paragraph (6) of the Indo-Pakistan Travel Scheme has been held not to mean a hired agent or a commissioned business agent.[93]
23. There is no agency when sales are made to export license holders in India and not to overseas buyers direct due to the obligation of the seller to follow the procedure as under the Cotton Textile (Export Control) Order. No. agency arises in this transaction since a principal does not sell to his agent. Even if this was the only way by which an export can be effected that would not render the role of the exporter as the agent of the seller. For by the very act of purchase, the exporter became a principal and bought as such.[94]
24. A person voluntarily working for a candidate for election cannot be deemed to be his agent. The Representation of People Act, 1951, defines 'agent' to include a person specifically engaged by the candidate or his election agent to work for him, as also a person who works for him and whose services have been accepted by the candidate., The political party ad its prominent members who set up his candidature and worked for him may be aptly called the 'agent'. But an intermeddler is not an agent, as there can be no basis for even implied acceptance by the candidate of the intermeddler's work. [95]
25. An Official Receiver is not an agent at all of the insolvent. He is the custodian of the assets of the insolvent with duties to discharge under the insolvency law. An insolvent cannot take the role of a principal and give directions to the Official Receiver.[96]
26. A director of a company is not necessarily the agent of the company or its shareholders. If he acts as agent he must specifically say so. So where in his written statement a director did not raise such a plea, he is deemed to have acted only in his personal capacity. So a suit against him alone in not barred by Sections 230 and 235 of the Contract Act. [97]
27. A undertook to pay the price of coal to be supplied by B to C. It was held A was not a mere del credere agent in the eye of law. A was liable to B for damages for breach of contract. The terms of the contract override the provisions in the Colliery Control Order, 1945. The liability of A was for the full price of the goods supplied. [98]
28. Where Government appoints defendants as agent for purchase of paddy and allows defendant to have full responsibility as to millowner, he cannot be deemed to be an agent of the Government for milling. That the defendant is but a contractor. [99]
29. Where mill owners are appointed as licensees to buy and sell paddy at rates fixed by Government, they are not exactly agents of Government. They are bound by the terms of the license. To the extent of procurement they may be agents. When the licensee stipulates fixation of price by Government the Government is acting like the master directing the servant mill-owner to sell only at a particular rate If the servant sold in excess of the rate, he is bound to make good the excess price to the principal. He cannot pocket it for himself., When the order of the Government under Sections 3(2), 4 and 14 of the Essential Supplies (Temporary) Powers Act, 1946, is for such a refund, the mill-owner cannot repudiate the validity of such an order having earned his commission under that very order. He cannot both approbate and reprobate. [100]
30. Under the U.P. Improvement. Trust Act, 1819 a scheme was entered into under which Government land was placed at the disposal of the Trust on certain terms and conditions. In Sinha J's words: "placing the property at the disposal of the Trust does not signify that the Government had divested itself of its title to the property and transferred the same to the Trust. Clause 12 of the agreement (Ex. D5) to the effect that 'Government may at any time on giving six months' notice terminate the agreement' clearly indicates that the Government had created agency not on a permanent basis but as a convenient mode of having its schemes of improvement implemented by a single agency with wide powers of management and expenditure of funds place at its disposal, either by way of income from the property or by way of advance from Government funds .... on a consideration of those rules (of the Trust) we are satisfied that they are more consistent with the Trust being a statutory agent of the Government which has to maintain separate accounts in respect of Nazul Property. [101]
31. Agency is not spelt out by mere name as 'sole selling agent'. It is determined by conduct of parties and the purport of their dealings. Thus facts may demonstrably show that a sole selling agent is not in fact an agent but a buyer with the sole right to sell the goods of a manufacturer. [102]
32. A stockist of cement under W.B. Cement Control Act (1948) is not an agent of the Government merely because the buyer was told by the Government to deposit the price with the stockist, cannot impute agency with the stockist, The Act merely bring stockists under control and supervision of Government. [103]

33. Under the Hyerabad General Sales Tax Act, 1950, any person engaged in the business of buying, selling or supplying goods in Hyderabed State either on commission, remuneration or other basis is a dealer. An agent in the State, of a non-resident dealer is deemed also to be a dealer under Section 18 of the Act. For an agent to be regarded as a dealer authority to buy on behalf of the principal is not necessary.[104]
34. A broker in his capacity as negotiator acts for both the buyer and seller of the goods. He is not incompetent to act as the agent of the other party because he is employed by his first principal to find someone with whom he may contract. But where the broker undertakes to buy or sell goods for his employer he acts merely as hid employer's representative. So he may not without his principal's permission act simultaneously as the agent of both the parties. [105]
35. A sub-lessee of a mining lease in not agent of the lessee. So if there is an injunction against the lessee and the sub-lessee is not a party to the suit the lessee cannot be held responsible for disobedience of injunction by the sub-lessee.[106]
36. A broker is a mere negotiator and for that purpose alone he may function as an agent. He is not concerned with the result of the contract. He cannot be sued for breach of contract by a party to the contract. A borker merely established contract between the parties to the contract and does not accept any liability for the fulfiment of the contract. [107]
37. Where a contractor contracts with the Government for supply of materials and execution of work, and the risk is borne by the contractor till delivery of materials at work site, and insurance is in the joint names of the contractor and Government, is was held severable from rent of the contract which was for sale of the materials, The sale was held liable to tax. The use of words like 'agent' and 'commission' in the agreement do not denote agency.[108]
38. A company contracted with a purchaser to sell goods which it did not, have. It subsequently entered in to a contract with a firm dealing in such goods. Such a transaction could be only in aid and benefit of the purchaser. But the contract between the purchaser and the company and that with the company and the firm are quite independent, distinct and different in terms, price and time. Further, all the payments for goods are made only by the purchaser through the company, the purchaser not having any direct contract or correspondence with the firm. It was held that the contractors are not one composite contract. The company is clearly to an agent but was only a middleman. The test for agency is as to who is to pay the price. The distinction between an agent and a middleman is whether the contract is independent and enforceable as such. [109]

Promoter of a Company, if an agent

39. As to the exact legal status of promoters, the statutory provisions " both in England and in this country are silent in most part except for a couple of sections in the Specific Relief. Act, both old and new ones. It appears that a promoter is neither an agent nor a trustee of the Company under incorporation, but certain fiduciary duties have been imposed on him both under the English Companies Act, 1948 and the Indian Companions Act, 1956. He is not an agent because there is no principal and he is not a trustee because there is a non-existing cestri qui trust. It is on this ground that the doctrine of ratification by the Company was regarded as inapplicable to the actual promoter *vis-a-vis* the company under incorporation. However, company may its promoters acts.
40. Independent buyers, even when working as commission agents, were regarded to be not agents. [110]
41. Where certain important persons representing two communities(Hindus and Muslims) signed a settlement of peace under section 107, Cr. P.C. the rest of the members of the two communities were allowed to plead that the settlement was not binding on them. If it had been a compromise in a suit the representatives would have been regarded as their agents.[111]

41A Where the mortgagor gave right to the mortgagee to sell the mortgaged property without intervention of court, the mortgagee could not be said to be an agent of the mortgagor in selling the property. The mortgagee exercises his rights under a superior claim which is not under the mortgagor but against him. [112]

Liability of Corporate Body as Principal — Where the responsible officers of a corporate body commit fraud by knowingly representing certain false facts, the corporate body will be liable. [113]

Principal and Agent

DUTIES OF AGENT

Mutual rights and duties of principal and agent may be wholly provided for in their contract. But the following duties of general nature are imposed by law upon every agent.

1. Duty to execute mandate or Command

The first and the foremost duty of every agent is to carry out the mandate of his principal. He should perform the work which he has been appointed to do. Any failure in this respect would make the agent absolutely liable for the principal's loss. Thus, it has been held in a number of cases that:

The rule of equity is, that if an order is sent by a principal to a factor to make an insurance, and he charges his principal, as if it was made, if he never make an insurance, he never in fact made that insurance, he is considered the insurer himself.

In such cases the agent becomes liable to the principal for the amount which would have been recovered if the goods had been insured. An example is *Pannalal Jankids v. Mohanlal.*[114]

A commission agent purchased goods for his principal and stored them in a godown pending their despatch. The agent was under instruction to insure them . He actually charged to premium for insurance, but failed to insure the goods, The goods were lost in an explosion in the Bombay harbour.

The agent was held liable to compensate the principal for his loss minus the amount received under the Bombay Explosion (Compensation) Ordnance, 1944, under which the Government paid compensation up to fifty per cent in respect of the uninsured merchandise lost in the explosion.[115]

2- Duty to follow instructions or customs [S.211]

211. Agent's duty in conducting principal's business — An agent is bound to conduct the business of his principle according to the direction given by the principal, or in the absence of any such directions, according to the custom which prevails in doing business of the same kind at the place where the agent conducts such business. When the agent acts otherwise, if any loss be sustained, he must make it good to his principal, and if any profit accrues, he must account for it.

Illustrations

(a) A, an agent engaged in carrying on for B a business, in which it is the custom to invest from time to time, at interest, the moneys which may be in hand, omits to make such investment. A must make good to B the interest usually obtained by such investments.

(b) B, a broker, in whose business it is not the custom to sell on credit, sells goods of A on credit to C, whose credit at the time was very high, C, before payment becomes insolvent, B must make good the loss to A.

The section provides that an agent is bound to conduct the business of principal according to the directions given by the principal. In the absence of direction, the agent has to follow the custom which prevails in business of the same kind and at the place where the agent conducts such business. When the agent acts otherwise, if any loss be sustained, he must make it good it his principal, and if any profit accrues, he must account for it in *Lilley v. Doubleday.*[116] An agent was instructed to warehouse his principal's goods at a particular place. He placed a part of them at a different warehouse which was equally safe, But ht goods were destroyed without negligence.

The agent was held liable for the loss. Any disobedience of, or departure form the instructions makes the agent absolutely liable for the loss.

Where the principal gave instructions of ambiguous nature which were capable of the two meanings, he was not permitted to argue as against the agent that he should have read the instructions in the other sense than what he actually did.

In the absence of instructions, business customs must be followed, Where, for example, the customs of a particular trade require that goods should not be sold on credit or in return for a negotiable instrument, the agent should not do so. If he does so, he would be liable to the principal for any loss resulting from the transaction.[117]

3. Duty of reasonable care and skill [S.212]

212. Skill and diligence required from agent — An agent is bound to conduct the business of the agency with as much skill as is generally possessed by persons engaged in similar business, unless the principal has notice for his want of skill. The agent is always bound to act with reasonable diligence ad to use such skill as he possesses; and to make compensation to his principal in respect of the direct consequences of his own neglect. Want of skill of misconduct, but not in respect of loss or damage which are indirectly or remotely caused by such neglect, want of skill, or misconduct.

Illustrations

(a) A, a merchant in Calcutta, has an agent, B, in London, to whom a sum of money is paid on A's account, with orders to remit, B retains the money for a considerable time, A , in consequent of not receiving the money, becomes insolved. B is liable for the money and interest from the day on which it ought to have been paid, according tot he usual rate, and for any further direct loss — as e.g., by variation of rate of change — but not further.

(b) A, an agent for the sale of goods, having authority to sell on credit sells to B on credit without making the proper and usual enquiries as to the solvency of B.B, at the time of such sale in insolvent. A must make compensation to this principal in respect of any loss thereby sustained.

(c) A, an insurance broker employed by B to effect an insurance on a ship, omits to see that the usual clauses are inserted in the policy, the ship is afterwards lost. In consequence of the omission of the clauses nothing can be recovered from the underwriters, A is bound to make god the loss to B.

(d) A, a merchant in England, directs B, his agent at Bombay, who accepts the agency to send him 100 bales of cotton by a certain ship, B. Having it in his power to send to cotton, omits to do so. The ship arrives safely in England, Soon after her arrival the price of cotton rises. B is bound to make good to A the profit which he might have made by the 100 bales of cotton at the time the ship arrived, but not any profit he might have made by the subsequent rise.

Section 212 lays down the standard of care and skill required of an agent.[118]

Every agent is bound to carry on the business of agency with reasonable skill and care. For example, a bank was instructed by the plaintiff to collect a certain amount on his behalf and to remit it to him. There was no specific instruction as to the manner of remittance. The bank sent the amount by draft placed in a letter sent by ordinary post. The bank was held negligent in sending the draft like that.

The standard of care and skill which an agent has to bestow depends upon the nature of his profession. An agent, having authority to sell on credit, must take care to ascertain the solvency of his buyer. An insurance broker must see that usual clauses for the protection of the principal are inserted in the policy. An estate agent should know the land laws and also must take care to ascertain the solvency of the tenant. If an agent is retained for assisting his principal for lending money on a mortgage, he must make reasonable inquiry about the value of the property. A stock broker should know the regulations of the stock exchange.

If the principal suffers any loss owing to the agent's want of care or skill, the agent must compensate the principal for such loss. Section 212 limits the agent's liability to "direct consequences". It provides that the agent must "make compensation to his principal in respect of the direct consequences of his neglect, want of skill or misconduct but not in respect of loss or damage which are indirectly or remotely caused by such neglect, want of skill or misconduct". If for example, an agent fails to send to principal's money in time, he may be liable for the money and the loss of interest. But not if the principal becomes insolvent by that reason. The meaning of the expression "direct consequences" has been explained by the Supreme Court in *Pannalal Jankidas v. Mohanlal.*[119]

An agent, having been instructed to insure certain goods, failed to do so, The goods were lost in an explosion at the docks, Even if the agent had taken out a fire insurance policy in the usual form it would not have covered a loss of this kind, as fire due to explosion would have been an excepted peril, But the Bombay Government passed on Ordinance under which it undertook to pay half loss in cases of uninsured goods. Thus the principal got only half of what he would have got if the goods had been insured.

The agent contended that as the passing of the Ordinance could not have been anticipated, the loss was too remote, But, it was held by a majority, that the loss was the direct result of the agent's negligence. The court, following English decisions, felt that the intervention of the Government Ordinance did not break the chain of causation. KANIA CJ said "Once misconduct is admitted or proved that fact that the Ordinance did not exist and could not have been in the contemplation of the parties is irrelevant for deciding the question of liability."

Where the agent informed his principal that purchases have been effected on his behalf and subsequently confirmed it by reporting that the goods would be despatched as soon as transport strike was over whereas, in fact, he had done nothing in the matter, it was held by the Supreme Court that such a neglect and misconduct of the agent misinforming the principal was squarely within the wide terms of Section 212. "He must bear the brunt to pay damages," the court said.[120]

In cases of difficulty the agent's duty is to use all reasonable diligence in communicating with his principal and in seeking to obtain his instructions, if the principal can be communicated with by reasonable care, before taking any steps in facing the difficulty or emergency. Where an estate agent received an offer and communicated it to the principal, but failed to communicate a higher offer which received some five days later, this was regarded as a breach of the duty to show proper skill and care.[121]

Where a booking agent did not prepare airway bill with proper skill and diligence in as much as the relevant boxes relating to the items as to cash on delivery and collection of charges by the carrier were left blank by him he being in breach of duty he was not allowed to recover his expenses in arranging consignment of the goods.[122]

Duty to maintain confidence — Aim to this is the duty to maintain the business secrets of the principal. A bank is under similar duty of Secrecy so far as the customer's dealings with him are concerned and would be liable in damages if any loss is caused to the customer by leakage of secret information. Certain currency notes were deposited with a bank for demonetisation. The bank informed the Income tax Authorities and the customer there by lost the utilisation of the money. Eve the customer's action against the bank failed. The bank was under a higher national duty which superseded the duty to the customer.

An agent is also under a duty to maintain confidence, secrecy and non-disclosure of any sensitive information about the affairs of principal. A banker may be liable if the state of his customer's account is leaked, except where the disclosure is under compulsion of law, e.g. duty to obey an order under the Bankers Books Evidence Act, or under a higher duty owed to state or public institutions which supersedes a lower duty or under any statement in a formal claim or with the customers permission.[123]

4. Duty to avoid conflict of interest [S. 215]

215. Right of principal when agent deals on his own account, in business of agency without principal's consent.—If an agent deals on his own account in the business of the agency, without first obtaining the Consent of his principal and acquainting him with all material circumstances which have come to his own knowledge or the subject, the principal may repudiate the transaction, if the case shows, either that any material fact has been dishonestly concealed from him by the directs or that the dealings of the agent of the have been disadvantageous to him.

Illustration

(a) A directs B to sell A's estate B buys the estate for himself in the name of C.A. on discovering the, B has bought the estate for himself, may repudiate the sale, if he can show that B has dishonestly concealed any main fact, or that the sale has been disadvantageous to him.

(b) A directs B to sell A's estate. B on looking over the estate before selling it, finds a mine on the estate which is unknown to. B informs A he wishes to buy the estate for himself, but conceals the discovery of the mine A allows to buy in ignorance of the existence of the mine or adopt the sale at his option.

An agent occupies fiduciary position and, therefore it is his duty not to do anything which would bring his personal interest and his duty to the principal in conflict with each other. This conflict invariably arises when the agent is personally interested in the principals transaction, for example, where he buys himself the property he is appointed to sell or delivers his own goods when he is instructed to buy on behalf of the principal. Thus, where a stock broker was instructed by his principal to buy the share of a particular company, and the agent, instead of buying them in the open market, sold him shares which he himself owned, the court allowed the principal to set aside the sale. A well-known illustration is the case of *De Busche v. Alt.*[124]

The plaintiff consigned a shop to a company in China for sale "at 90,000 payable in cash". With the consent of the plaintiff, the company appointed the defendant, a Japanese agent, to sell the ship. The defendant attempted to sell the ship, but having failed to find a customer bought the ship himself and without disclosing this, remitted the above sum through the company to the plaintiff. Soon thereafter a war broke out and ships were again in great demand. A Japanese prince bought it from the defendant at 1,60,000. The plaintiff sued the defendant to recover the profit made on resale.

He was held bound to account for the profit. There would have been nothing wrong if the agent had bought the ship after disclosing the fact to his principal. The agent might have been honest in this particular case. But if his contention was accepted. Many an agent would make secret profits by feigning inability to sell.

This principle is incorporated in Section 215, which provides that if an agent deals on his won account in the business of agency, without first obtaining the consent of his principal and acquainting him with full facts, the principal may repudiate the transaction if he can show that —

(a) a material fact has been dishonestly concealed from him, or
(b) the dealing of the agent has been disadvantageous to him.

The first illustration to the section says that if the agent has secretly bought the principal's property for himself, the principal may repudiate the transaction if he can show that the agent has concealed any material fact or that the sale has been disadvantageous to him. Where, for example, the agent discovers a mine on the principal's estate and without disclosing this fact buys the estate for himself, the principal may repudiate the transaction. The mere fact of the agent buying the principal's property brings his interest in conflict with his duty to the principal and it has been pointed out that the conflict is in itself a sufficient disadvantage to the principal.

5. Duty not to make secret profit [S. 216]

216. Principal's right to benefit gained by agent dealing on his won account in business of agency.— If an agent, without the knowledge of his principal, deals in the business of the agency on his own account instead of on account of his principle, the principal is entitled to claim from the agent any benefit which may have resulted to him from the transaction.

Illustration

A directs B, his agent, to buy a certain house for him, B tells A it cannot be bought, and buys the house for himself, A may, on discovering that B has bought the house compel him to sell it to A at the price he gave for it.

Another aspect of this principle is the duty of the agent not to make any secret profit in the business of agency. His relationship with the principal is of fiduciary nature and this require absolute good faith in the conduct of agency. What is meant by secret profit? It means any advantage obtained by the agent over and above his agreed remuneration and which he would not have been able to make but for his position as agent. Acceptance of bribe is a profit of this kind, even "if the employers are not actually injured, and the bribe fails to have the intended effect."[125] A military officer who took bribe and allowed goods to pass under the authority of his uniform was held liable to account for the same to the Crown.[126] Similarly, where an auctioneer received from the buyer commission in addition to what his principal paid him, he was held bound to hand over the commission to the principal.[127] Where an agent sells his own stock to the principal without disclosing the fact, he is bound to account for any profit he made in the transaction. It is immaterial that the agent charged only the prevailing market price.[128] A principal agreed to buy horses from a dealer provided that his veterinary surgeon would pass them as sound. The seller bribed the surgeon and obtained his certificate. The horses turned out to be unsound. The principal was held justified in rejecting them and countermanding the cheque which he had issued for the price.[129]

Knowledge which is acquired by an agent in the course of business of agency and which he converts into his advantage does not require accountability if the agent neither uses the principal's property in the process nor diverts his business opportunities. [130]

As a part of the agent's duty to be honest to his principal it is necessary that the agent should not disclose any confidential information received by him from his principal, If he does so, the principal may terminate the contract and hold the agent liable in damages for his loss, if any. One of the aspects of this duty is that the principal can restrain his agent, even after the expiry of the term of agency, from making use of the information which he acquired during the course of the agency. Where an agent was induced by the third party by paying bribes to contract with him, the court upheld the principal's right to avoid such a contract as against the third party. In addition the principal can sue the third party for damages for any loss suffered by him on account of the bribery and it will be immaterial that the principal had already recovered the bribe money from the agent.[131]

6. Duty to remit sums [S. 218]

218. Agent's duty to pay sums received for principal — Subject to such deductions, the agent is bound to pay to his principal all sums received on his account.

The agent is bound to pay to his principal all sums received on his account. The agent is however, entitled to deduct his lawful charges, but subject only to this right, the principal's money must be remitted to him even if it has been received in pursuance to a void or illegal contract. Proper performance of this duty requires that the agent should keep proper accounts of his principal's money or property and render then to him on demand.

7. Duty to maintain accounts [S. 213]

213. Agent's accounts — An agent is bound to render proper accounts to his principal on demand.

Accounts are necessary for the proper performance of the agent's other duties, for example, the duty to remit sums to the principal.[132]

There is no provision in the Act enabling an agent to institute a suit for accounts against the principal. The Supreme Court in *Narandas v. Papammal* [133] laid down that the provisions of the Contract Act are not exhaustive in this regard and that the right of an agent to sue the principal for accounts is an equitable right arising under special circumstances One of those special circumstances is where all the accounts are in the possession of the principal. In a case before the Madras High Court,[134] an agent was running a mill which was taken over by the owners. The agent claimed that he lost his account in the process of take over and, therefore, claimed accounts from the principal. The court did not provide him any relief because he was not able to give any proof of the loss of this accounts Where an agent was appointed to secure orders for supply of goods, his commission to be payable when the principal received payment for supplies, it was held that quite naturally an account would have to be maintained by the principal and the agent had the right to demand an account.[135]

8. Duty not to delegate [S. 190]

'Delegatus non protest delegare' is a well-known maxim of the law of agency. The principal chooses a particular agent because he has trust and confidence in his integrity and competence. Ordinarily, therefore, the agent cannot further delegate the work which has been delegated to him by his principal. But there are exceptions. In the following cases the agent may delegate the work to another.

(1) *Nature of work* — Sometimes, the very nature of work makes it necessary for the gent to appoint a sub-agent. For example, an agent appointed to sell an estate may retain the services of an auctioneer and the one authorised to file a suit may engage a lawyer. A baker instructed to make payment to a particular person at a particular palce may appoint a banker who has an office at that place.[136] A baker authorised to let out a house and collect rents may entrust the work to an estate agent.[137]

(2) *Trade custom* — Secondly, a sub-agent may be appointed and the work delegated to him if there is ordinary custom of trade to that effect. Thus, architects generally appoint surveyors.[138]

(3) *Ministerial action* — An agent cannot, of course, delegate acts which he has expressly or impliedly undertaken to perform personally; e.g., acts requiring personal or professional skill. But the agent may delegate acts which are purely ministerial in nature, e.g., authority to sign.[139]

(4) *Principal's consent* — The principal may expressly allow his agent to appoint a sub-agent. His consent may also be implied from the conduct of the parties. The principal may ratify his agent's unauthorised delegation.

Effects of Delegation

A person who is appointed by the agent and to whom the principal's work is delegated is known as "sub-agent". Section 191 defined "sub-agent" as "a person appointed by and acting under the control of the original agent in the business of the agency". The significance of the words 'acting under the control of the original agent" appears from a judgement of the Supreme Court.[140] The plaintiff had sent an article by V.P.P. (value payable post) to Pakistan. The Pakistani authorities received the dispatch, delivered it to the addressee and received the value from him. Commencement of hostilities at this stage resulted in suspension of the postal services agreement between the two countries. The amount was not received by the Government of India. Even so the plaintiff sued the Government contending that the failure of the Government was a failure of sub-agent for which the original agent is liable. The Supreme Court did not consider it possible for anybody to say that by virtue of the postal treaty a foreign Government had become the sub-agent of the Union of India. The Court said that when two sovereign powers enter into an agreement, neither of them can be described as an agent of the other. had the Pakistan Government been really a sub-agent. Payment to them would have been as good as payment to the Union of India but that is not the case here. Under the arrangement entered into between the two sovereign powers, Union of India and Pakistan, neither could beside to be employed by or acting under the control of the other.

Now, when a sub-agent is appointed, what relationship is constituted between the principal and the sub-agent and the agent? The answer depends upon whether the sub-agent has been properly or improperly appointed.

1. Improper delegation [S. 193]

193. Agent's responsibility for sub-agent appointed without authority — Where an agent, without having authority to do so has appointed a person to act as a sub-agent, the agent stands towards such person in the relation of a principal to an agent, and is responsible for his acts both to the principal and to third persons; the principal is not represented by or responsible for the acts of the persons so employed, nor is that person responsible to the principal.

Delegation is improper when it is not authorised that is, when it is not within any of the recognised exceptions. The effect is that the principal is not bound by the appointment. He is not represented by that person, nor bound by his acts. That person is also not responsible to the principal. But the agent will be responsible to the principal for any acts of that person. The agent stands is the position of principal towards the person and is as such responsible for his acts to third parties[141].

2. Proper delegation [S.192]

192. Representation of principal by sub-agent properly appointed — Where a sub-agent is properly appointed, the principal is, so far as regards third persons, represented by the sub agent and is bound by and responsible for his acts as if he were an agent originally appointed by the principal.

Agent's responsibility for sub-agent — The agent is responsible to the principal for the acts for the sub-agent.

Sub-agent's responsibility — The sub-agent is responsible for his acts to the agent, but not to the principal, except in case of fraud or wilful wrong.

In *Calico Printers' Association v. Barclay's Bank*[142] WRIGHT J explains the effect of proper delegation:

Even where the sub-agent is properly employed, there is no privity between him and the principal ; the latter is entitled to hold the agent liable for breach of the mandate, which he has accepted, and cannot, in general claim against the sub-agent for negligence or breach of duty.

The following effects of the appointment are stated in Section 192

(1) Principal represented by sub-agent — In the first place, so far as regards third persons, the principal is represented by the sub-agent, He is bound by and responsible for his acts as if he were an agent originally appointed by the principal.[143]

(2) Agent's responsibility for sub-agent — Secondly, the agent is responsible to the principal for the acts of the sub-agent. If, for example, the sub-agent has misappropriated the principal's property or its sale proceeds, the agent is responsible for the same. There is no privity of contract between the principal and the sub-agent and therefore, he cannot sue the sub-agent, except for fraud or wilful wrong. Even where fraud or wilful wrong is established, the principal has the choice to sue either the agent or the sub-agent. But the agent may exempt himself from such liability.[144]

(3) Sub-agent's liability to principal — The sub-agent is not directly liable to the principal, except for fraud and wilful wrong, A well-known illustration is Calico Printers' Association v. Barclays Bank:[145]

A sub agent failed to insure the principal's goods, which were destroyed by fire. But the principal could not recover against the sub-agent.

Similarly, in Summan Singh v. National City bank of New York,[146] the plaintiff in a foreign country appointed the NC Bank to deliver a sum of money to one Pritam Singh of Jullundar, whose address was given. The Bank instructed its Bombay branch appointed to Punjab National Bank which delivered the money to a wrong person.

The plaintiffs action against either bank failed. The Punjab National Bank was however not liable to the principal except whether he is guilty of fraud or wilful wrong. The wrong delivery was due only to negligence the NC Bank had exempted itself from the consequences of wrong delivery sub-agent is, however, bound by all the duties of an ordinary agent.

A sub-agent is, however, bound by all the duties of an ordinary agent.

Substituted agent [Ss. 194 and 195]

194. Relation between principal and person duly appointed by agent to act in business agency — Where an agent. Holding an express or implied authority to name another person to act for the principal in the business of the agency, has named another person according such person is not a sub-agent but an agent of the principal for such part of the business the agency as is entrusted to him.

Illustrations

(a) A directs B, his solicitor, to sell his estate by auctions, and to employ an auctioneer for purpose, B names, C an auctioneer, to conduct the sale, C is not sub-agent, but is A's agent for the conduct of the sale.

(b) A authorises B, a merchant in Calcutta to recover the moneys due to A from C & Co. instructs D, a solicitor, to take legal proceedings against C & Co, for the recovery of the money D is not a sub-agent, but is solicitor for A.

195 Agent's duty in meaning such person — In selecting such agent for his principal agent is bound to exercise the same amount of discretion as a man of ordinary prodder could exercise in his own case; and if he does this, he is not responsible to the principal acts or negligence of the agent so selected.

Illustrations

(a) A instructs B, a merchant, to buy a ship for him, B employs a ship survivor or of reputation to choose a ship for A. The survivor or makes the choice negligently and the ship to out to be unseaworthy and is lost. B is not but the survivor or is, responsible to A.

(b) A consigns goods to B, a merchant, for sale, B, in due course, employs an auctioneer of good credit to sell the goods of A, and allows the auctioneer to receive the proceeds of the sale. The auctioneer afterwards becomes insolvent without having accounted for the proceeds. B is responsible to A for the proceeds.

A sub-agent has to be distinguished from a substituted agent. Sections 194 and 195 contain special provisions about substituted agents. According to Section when an agent has an express or implied authority of his principal to name a person to act for him and the agent has accordingly named a person, such person is not sub-agent, but he becomes an agent for the principal in respect of the business which is entrusted to him. The two illustrations to the section further explain the position of a substituted agent. A solicitor is appointed to sell an estate by auction and employ an auctioneer for the purpose. The auctioneer thus appointed is not sub agent but an agent of the employer himself for the purpose of the sale. Similar by when an agent is authorised to recover debts and he appoints a solicitor for purpose, the latter is not a sub-agent, but a full-fledged agent for the purpose.[147]

One of the effects of appointing a substitute is that a direct privity of contract is established between the principal and the "substitute". The agent is not concerned about the work of the substitute. His only duty is to make the selection of the substitute with reasonable care. Section 195 says that "in selecting such agent for his principal, an agent is bound to exercise the same amount of discretion as a man of ordinary prudence would exercise in his own case; and, if he does this he is not responsible to the principal for the acts or negligence of the agent so selected". The two illustrations appended to the section explain the point. A merchant is instructed to buy a ship for his principal. The merchant employs a ship surveyor of good reputation to choose a ship for the principal. The surveyor makes the choice negligently, the ship turns out to be unseaworthy, and is lost. The surveyor, but not the agent, is liable to the principal. In the second illustration, goods are consigned to a merchant for sale, The merchant employs an auctioneer of good credit to sell the goods and allows him to receive the proceeds. The auctioneer becomes bankrupt without having accounted for the proceeds to the principal. The agent is not liable.

Principal's remedies

The rights of the principal on agent committing breach of duty were briefly stated by Lord SUMNER in *Christogorides v. Terry.*[148]

Principal have three rights as against agents who fail in their duty — they can recover damages for want of skill and care, and for disregard of the terms of the mandate; they can obtain an account and payment of secret and illicit profits, which have come to the hands of their agents; and they can resist an agent's claim for commission and for indemnity against liability incurred as mandatory by showing that the agent has acted as a principal himself and not merely as an agent. Each remedy is distinct and is directed to a specific irregularity.

Another remedy against a defaulting agent is that he can be dismissed instantly and summarily, where the managing director of a company had taken bribes from a third party for favouring him by engaging his ships, the company was held justified in dismissing him without notice.[149]

RIGHTS OF AGENT

(1) Right to remuneration [S. 219]

219. When agent's remuneration becomes due — In the absence of any special contract, payment for the performance of any act is not due to the agent until the completion of such act; but an agent may detain moneys received by him on account of goods sold, although the whole of he goods consigned to him for sale may not have been sold, or although the sale may not be actually complete.

Every agent is clearly entitled to his agreed remuneration, or if there is no agreement, to a reasonable remuneration. The difficult question is as to when remuneration becomes due. Section 219 says that "in the absence of any special contract, payment for the performance of any act is not due until the completion of such act....."

The provision raises two questions. When is the act complete and secondly, is the act a result of the agent's services? Both questions depend "first and last on particular terms of the particular contract"[150]. Thus, where an agent was appointed to secure orders for advertisements in a newspaper, the commission in respects to commission on orders actually obtained by him although the advertisements which the orders related were not published until after the termination of employment. As against it, where an agent was engaged to negotiate for the purchase of house at a commission of 2 per cent on the purchase price, he was held not entitle to any commission till the completion of the purchase of the house.[151] Much depend upon the nature of the service that the agent undertakes to provide. Thus, in a case before the Allahabad High Court, an agent was appointed to introduce a purchase willing to purchase the defendant's property. He did introduce one and even sale was settied and earnest money paid but it could not be completed through the purchaser's inability to find money. The agent was nevertheless held entitled to agreed commission.[152]

Secondly, the transaction that results must be due to the agent's services. The bargain must be the direct result of his service. In *Green v. Bartlett*[153]. an agent was appointed to sell a house. He held an auction but failed to find a purchaser. One of the persons attending the auction obtained from him the address of the principal and purchased the house from him without intervention of the agent. Even so the transaction was held to be a result of the agent's effort entitling him to his commission. The principle of this case has been followed by the Bombay High Court.[154] The defendants appointed the plaintiff, a broker, to obtain a loan on the mortgage of premises. He introduced the manager of bank who would have made an advance if the security offered had not proved to be insufficient. Ultimately, the bank did make an advance, but through another broker, The plaintiff was held entitled to commission.

Where the agent's services are only remotely connected with the transaction his remuneration is not earned. *Tribe v. Taylor*[155] is an apt illustration.

The defendant requested the plaintiffs to introduce a purchaser of his premises or a source of capital, The plaintiff introduced one Wood who advanced a sum of money by way of loan. The agreed commission was paid to the plaintiffs. Subsequently, Wood entered into partnership with the defendant and advanced a further sum. The plaintiff's action to claim commission on the second advance failed.

"The question which arose was....'Whether the subsequent advance was the result of any act of the plaintiffs'. If .... the plaintiffs had introduced any new person, which had advanced the money, I should have thought the defendant would have been bound to pay the commission claimed. If they had induced Wood to become a partner and to introduce further capital, I should have thought they would have been entitled to commission on that................. Was the subsequent partnership the result of the introduction or of an independent negotiation? *Cause proximo* is not the question; the plaintiffs must show that the act of theirs was the cause causans. It is true that the (second) advance might not, and probady would not have been made by Woods but for the regional introduction by the plaintiff. But that is not enough.

The principal is, of course, under duty not to prevent the agent from earning his commission. But this does not prevent the principal form selling the property himself or from refusing to sell at all. A well-known case is *Luxzor (Eastborne) Ltd. v. Cooper.*[156]

An agent was promised his commission if he brought about the sale of the defendant's cinemas. The agent introduced a customer but the company refused to sell. The agent brought an action for his commission.

The House of Lords held against him. "There was no implied term that the principal would not dispose of the property himself, or through other channels or other whose act so as to prevent the agent from earning his commission.[157] Viscount Simon LC said.[158] The agent necessarily incurs certian risks, e.g., the risk that his nominee cannot find the purchase price and will not consent to terms reasonably proposed to be inserted in the contract of sale.... The agent also takes the risk of his principal to be inserted in the contract of sale .... The agent also takes the risk of his principal to being willing to conclude the bargain with the agent's nominee. The last risk is ordinarily a slight one for the owner's reason for approaching the agent is that he wants to sell.

Effect of misconduct [S. 220]

220. Agent not entitled to remuneration for business misconduct — An agent who is guilty of misconduct in the business of the agency in not entitled to any remuneration in respect of that part of the business which he has misconducted.

Illustrations

(a) A employs B to recover 1,00,000 rupees from C, and lay it out on good security. B recovers the 1,00,000 rupees and lays out 90,000 rupees on good security, but lays out 10,000 rupees on security which he ought to have known to be bad, whereby A loses 2,000 rupees, B is entitled to remunerations for recovering the 1,00,000 rupees and for investing the 90,000 rupees, He is not entitled to any remuneration for investing the 10,000 rupees and he must make good the 2,000 rupees to B.

(b) A employs B to recover 1,000 rupees from C. Through, B's misconduct the money is not recovered, B is entitled to no remuneration for his services, and must make good the loss.

An agent is not entitled to any commission in respect of that part of the business which he has misconducted. Section 220 accordingly provides that an agent who is guilty of misconduct in the business of agency, is not entiltled to any remuneration in respect of that part of the business which he has misconducted[159]. The effect of misconduct is two-fold. Firstly, the agent forfeits his right to commission. This is irrespective of any loss suffered by the principal. "The principal underlying the rule is that a principal is entitled to have an honest agent and it is only the honest agent who is entitled to any commission." The commission if forfeited only is respect of that part of the agency business which has been misconduct.[160]

Secondly, the principal is entitled to recover compensation for any loss caused by the misconduct. The illustrations to the section make it clear that payment of damages caused by the misconduct is in addition to the for forfeiture of commission or remuneration.

(2) Right of retainer [S. 217]

217. Agent's right of retainer out of sums received on principal's account — An agent may retain, out of any sums received on account of the principal in the business of the agent. All moneys due to himself in respect of advances made or expenses retain only such expanses properly incurred by him in conducting such business, and also such remuneration as may be payable to him for acting as agent.

The agent has the right to retain his principal's money until his claims, if any, in respect of this remuneration or advances made or expenses incurred in conducting the business of agency are paid. The right can be exercised on any sums received on account of the principal in the business of the agency. He can retain only such money as is in his possession. He is not entitled to an equitable lien , that is, the right to have his claims satisfied in preference to other creditiors out of the principal money not in his possession. But a solicitor or vakil is entitled to an equitable lien on the proceeds of an auction conducted by him till his costs are paid. His fee is a first charge on the proceeds even if they are not in his possession. He is also entitled for this purpose, to have the proceeds pass through his hands.[161]

(3) Right of lien [S. 221]

221. Agent's lien on principal's property — In the absence of any contract to the contrary an agent is entitled to retain goods, papers and other property, where the movable, or immovable, of the principal received by him, until the amount due to himself for commission, disbursements and services in respect of the same has been paid or accounted for to him.

In addition to the above right of retainer, the "agent has the right of retain goods, papers and of the property, whether movable or immovable, of the principal received by him, until the amount due to himself for commission, disbursements and services in respect of the same has been paid or accounted for to him".[162] The conditions of this right are:

(1) The agent should be lawfully entitled to receive from the principal a sum of money by way of commission earned or disbursements made or services rendered in the proper execution of the business of agency.

(2) The property over which the line is to be exercised should belong to the principal and it should have been received by the agent in his capacity and during the course of his ordinary duties as agent. The property is considered to be sufficiently in the possession of the agent where he has been dealing with it. Thus, where an auctioneer was engaged to sell furniture at the owner's house, he was held to be sufficiently in possession to exercise lien for his commission.[163] The property held by an agent for a special purpose cannot be subjected to lien. The existence of a special purpose smartly excludes the right. Similarly, where possession is obtained without the principal's authority or by fraud or misrepresentation. there is no lien. Briefly, the agent's possession must be lawful.

(3) The agent has only a particular lien. A particular lien attaches only to the specific subject-matter in respect of which the charges are due. No other property can be retained. For example, in Bombay Saw Mills Co., *Re.*[164]

The secretaries and treasurers of a company claimed lien over the company's property for their advances.[165]

SCOTT J rejected the claim 'because the sums advanced and expended were not, as required (by Section 221) 'disbursements and services in respect of the property on which the lien was claimed, but were loans made on behalf of the company generally and for the purpose of the whole concern."

An agent who falls in the category of bailees listed in Section 171 will have a general lien, that is to say, that he can retain any property belonging to his principal. The list includes bankers, factors, wharfingers, policy-brokers and solicitors.[166]

Effect of lien — The effect of lien as between the principal and the agent has been thus stated by *A H Khan in Goplads v. Thakurdas.*[167]

The agent's lien does not give unrestricted authority to the agent to deal with the property in any manner the agent may like. The right is limited in nature; it enables the agent to retain the property till his dues are paid, both this confers no authority on the agent to sell or otherwise dispose of the property without the consent of the owner.

Where, however, in terms of his agreement, with the principal, the agent has become a pledgee of the goods, he may sell them after giving a notice to the principal of his intention to sell.[168]

As against third parties the lien is effective only to the extent of the principal's rights on the property. If the principal has limited rights, the lien will be equally limited. If the property is already subject to some rights or equities in favour of third persons the lien will also be subject to them. But where the property on which the lien is exercised is a negotiable instrument, the agent will become a holder for value to the extent of his lien and will acquire a title free of prior equities if he acts in good faith and without notice of them.[169] It the principal creates any charge on the property subsequently to the attachment of the lien, that will be subject the lien.

Loss of lien — The agent's lien is lost in the following circumstances:

(1) Lien being a possessory right, is to lost as soon as possession is lost, Possession is lost when the agent delivers the goods to the principal himself or to some carrier for the purpose of transmission to the principal. In the latter case the agent cannot revive his lien by stopping the goods in transit. But where the property has been delivered for a special purpose, like safe custody, which is consistent with lien, the line is not lost. As long as the agent remains in possession, his lien is effective, and in not affected by the fact that the company to which the goods belonged has been ordered to be wound up,[170] or that the principal has become insolvent. The agent's possession is not terminated where property has been obtained from him by unlawful means or by fraud or misrepresentation.

(2) The lien is lost hen the agent waives his right. The waiver may arise on of an agreement, express or implied, or may be inferred from conduct inconsistent with the right.

(3) The agent's lien is subject to a contract to the contrary and, therefore, does ot exist where the agent has by his agreement with the principal excluded it.[171]

(4) The right to indemnity [Ss. 222 and 223]

The right to indemnity is entained in the statutory provision contained in Section 222 of the Indian Contract Act.

222. Agent to be indemnified against consequences of lawful acts — The employer of an agent is bound to indemnify him against the consequences of all lawful acts done by such agent in exercise of the authority conferred upon him.

Illustrations

(a) B, at Singapore, under instructions from A of Calcutta, contracts with C to deliver certain goods to him. A does not send the good. B sues B for breach of contract B informs A of the suit, and A authorizes him to defend the suit, B defends the suit and is compelled to pay damages and costs, and incurs expenses. A is liable to B for such damages, costs and expenses.

(b) B, a broker an Calcutta, by the orders of A, a merchant, there, contracts with C for the purchase of 10 cases of oil for A, Afterwards A refuses to receive the oil, and C sues B,B informs A, who repudiates the contract altogether. B defends, but unsuccessfully, and has to pay damages and costs and incurs expense /A is liable to B for such damages, costs and expenses.

223. Agent to be indemnified against consequences of acts done in good faith — Where one person employs another to do an act, and the agent does the act in good faith, the employer is liable to indemnify the agent against the consequences of that act, thought it is causes an injury to the rights of third persons.

Illustrations

(a) A, a decree-holder and entitled to execution of B's goods, requires the officer of the Court to seize certain goods representing them to be the goods of B. The officer seizes the goods, and is sued by C, the true owner of the goods. A is liable to indemnify the officer for the sum which he is compelled to pay to C, in consequence of obeying A's direction.

(b) B, at the request of A, sells goods in the possession of A, but which A had no right to dispose of B, does not know this, and hands over the proceeds of the sale to A. Afterwards C, the true owner of the goods, sue B, and recovers the value of the goods and costs. A is liable to indemnify B for what he has been complelled to pay to C and for B's own expenses.

The right to indemnity extends to all losses and expenses incurred by the agent in the conduct of the business. Where, for example, a stockbroker, on the instructions of a solicitor, contracted to sell certain shares and had to incur liability to the purchase by reason of the owner's refusal to complete the sale, the stockbroker was held entitled to recover indemnity from the principal.[172]

The agent must have been damnified in the lawful conduct of the business of agency. A wagering agreement is not unlawful. It is only void. Accordingly, the Supreme Court in *Kishanlal v. Banwarilal.*[173] allowed an agent to recover indemnity for losses incurred by him in wagering transactions entered into on instructions of his principal.

Where the act done by the agent instructions from his principal is apparently lawful, but it turns out to be unlawful or injurious to a third person, the agent is entitled to indemnity against the consequences of the act.

One of the illustrations appended to Section 223 seems to be based upon the facts of *Adamson v. Jarvis.*[174] An auctioneer sold certain cattle on instructions from the defendant and was held liable to the true owner for conversion. He recovered indemnity from the principal because the act in question was apparently lawful.

Where an agent, on the instructions of his principal reserved a shipping space but the principal did not send the goods and, consequently, the agent had to pay the shipowner damages for dead freight, the agent was allowed indemnity for his loss from the principal.[175]

Where, however, the act in question is apparently unlawful or criminal, such as beating a person or publication of a libel, the principal will not be liable upon an express or implied promise to indemnify the agent against the consequences of such act. For example, and agent appoint to import adulterated mustard oil, suffered loss and punishment, but he could not recover indemnity.[176] Where, however, the plaintiff on instruction from the defendant, paid a sum of money to the casts panchayat to have the defendant's caste disqualifications removed, he was allowed to recover the money from the defendant.[177]

224. Non-liability of employer of agent to do a criminal act — Where one person employ another to do an act which is criminal, the employer is not liable to the agent, either upon an express or an implied promise, to indemnify him against the consequences of that act.

Illustration

A employs B to beat C, and agrees to indemnify him against all consequences of the act, thereupon beats C, and has to pay damages to C for so doing. A in not liable to indemnify B those damages.

Where the act in question is apparently tortuous, the agent, who has been held liable for it, may recover contribution from the principal (not indemnity) under the Law Reform (Married Women and Tortfeasors) Act, 1955.

(5) Right of compensation [S. 225]

225. Compensation to agent for injury caused by principal's neglect — The principal make compensation to his agent in respect of injury caused to such agent by the principal neglect or want of skill.

Illustration

A employs B as a bricklayer in building a house, and puts up to seaffolding himself. The scaffolding is unskilfully put up, and B is in consequence hurt. A must make compensation to B.

Thus, every principal owes to his agent the duty of care not to expose him to unreasonable risks. The illustration appended to the section makes the point clear.[178]

Principal And Third Parties

AGENT'S AUTHORITY

The acts of the agent within the scope of his authority bind the principal. Section 226 of the Contract Act gives statutory effect to the principal by declaring that:

226. Enforcement and consequences of agent's contracts — Contracts entered into through an agent, and obligations arising from acts done by an agent, may be enforced in the same manner, and will have the same legal consequences, as if the contracts had been entered into and the acts done by the principal in person.

The declaration is followed by two illustrations:

(a) A buys goods from B, knowing that the is an agent for their sale, but not knowing who is the principal. B's principal is the person entitled to claim from A the price of the goods, and A cannot, in a suit by the principal, set-off against that claim a debt due to himself from B.

(b) A, being B's agent, with authority to receive money on his behalf, receives from C a sum of money due to B, C is discharged of his obligation to pay the sum in question to B.

It is necessary for this effect to follow that the agent must have done that act within the scope of his authority. The authority of an agent and more particular its scope are subjects of some controversy. The uncertainty is largely due to the fact that the authority of an agent does not depend upon one source. It emanated from the principal, but its dimensions depend upon legal inferences, which in turn, depend upon the purpose of the agency. The surrounding circumstances and a desire to protect bona fide commercial transaction. For, agency came into being to promote and not to hinder commerce.

The authority of an agent means his capacity to bind to the principal, It refers to "the sum total of the acts it has been agreed between principal and agent that the agent should do on behalf of the principal."[179] When the agent does any of such acts, it is said he has acted within his authority.

Actual authority [Ss. 186-187]

186. Agent's authority may be expressed or implied — The authority of an agent may be express or implied.

187. Definitions of express and implied authority — An authority is said to be express when it is given by words spoken or written. An authority is said to be implied when it is to be inferred from the circumstances of the case; and things spoken or written, or in the ordinary course of dealing. May be accounted circumstances of the case.

Illustration

A owns a shop in Serampore, living himself in Calacutta, and visiting the shop occasionally. The shop is managed by B, and he is in the habit of ordering goods from C in the name of A for the purposes of the shop, and of paying for them out of A's funds with A's knowledge. B has an implied authority from A to order goods from C in the name of A for the purposes of the shop.

Actual authority of an agent is the authority conferred on him by the principal. It is of two kinds, namely, express or implied.

(1) Express authority [S.186] — Where the authority is conferred by words spoken or written, it is called express authority. A power of attorney, for example which is a kind of deed and authorise the agent to do certain acts, is an illustration of express authority. But however precisely the authority of an agent may be drawn disputes as to its scope are likely to arise. The scope of express authority is works out by construction of the words used in the document. For example, where a principal, while going abroad, authorised his agent and partner to carry on the business and his wife to accept bills on his behalf for his personal business, he was held not bound when his wife accepted bills for the business which the agent was conducting and which was different from his personal business. The decision has been criticised particularly, because the agent and the third party had acted in good faith to meet the principal's genuine business needs. Accordingly, in a subsequent case of agency by power of attorney where the agent obtained a loan outside his authority by signing a cheque on behalf of his principal to pay the principal's workmen, the principal was held bound. Where the appointment was for "fixing" a steamer the intention being to let it out, the principal was held liable when the agent instead hired a steamer.[181]

Where the third party has knowledge of the limitation on the agent's authority or could have discovered it by reasonable examination of the documents of authority he would be bound by it. Thus, where an agent was given very wide power or with drawing the principal's money "without restriction", the principal was held no bound when the agent gave a cheque to a car dealer to purchase a car for himself. And paid a few cheques into his banking account to wipe out his overdraft.[181] In either case, it was the duty of the third party to make a reasonable inquiry whether the agent had the authority to use the principal's money for his personal purposes.

An agent cannot borrow on behalf of his principal unless he has clear authority to do so. The power to draw or endorse bills or notes does not include the power to borrow. The power to sell will not authorise the agent to borrow money or to pledge goods.[182] Where the agent has the power to borrow, the fact that he borrowed beyond the authorised limit, does not prevent the third party from holding the principal liable, because the third party has no means of ascertaining that fact. Similarly, the fact that an agent has acted for improper motive does not take the case beyond the scope of his authority. Thus, in *Humber v. Burnard.*[183]

An agent was appointed to underwrite policies, He underwrote a policy which in fact amounted to a guarantee of a company's debts. He knew the precarious condition of the company, but being interested in it, wanted to help it. The principal was held liable because the third party could not have known with what motive the agent was underwriting a particular policy.

(2) Implied authority [S. 187] — "An authority is said to be implied when it is to be inferred from the circumstances of the case, and things spoken or written or in the ordinary course of dealing, may be accounted circumstances of the case." This definition of implied authority in Section 187 is illustrated thus:

A owns a shop in Serampur, living himself in Calcutta and visiting the shop occasionally. The shop is managed by B, and he is in the habit of ordering goods from C in the name of A for the purpose of the shop, and paying for them out of A's funds with A's knowledge, B has an implied authority from A to order goods from C in the name of A for the purposes of the shop.

Implied authority is an instance of real or actual authority for it is conferred upon the agent by the conduct of the principal as interpreted in the circumstances of the case.

The distinction between express and implied authority is not fundamental but depends merely on whether the authority is delimited by words or by conduct. If P tells A that he is to act as manager this is really a compendious way to stating that he is to do all the acts as manager should ordinarily do. Those acts might well be termed as express authority. However, it is often said that if an agent is placed in a certain position he has implied authority to do all the acts a person in that position ordinarily does.[184]

An illustration of implied authority is to be found in *Ryan v. Pilkington.*[186] An estate agent was appointed to find a purchaser for certain property. He accepted a deposit from a prospective customer and misappropriated it. The principal was held liable, because an estate agent has an implied authority to take a deposit. He cannot however receive payment or give any warranty unless actually authorised.[187]

Thus, the extent of an agent's authority, whether express or implied, depends upon —

(1) The nature of the act or business he is appointed to do;

(2) things which are incidental to the business or are usually done in carrying it out;

(3) the usual customs and usages of the trade.

Scope of authority

This is the essence of Section 188 which defines the extent of the agent's authority in the following words:

188. Extent of agent's authority — An agent, having an authority to do an act, has authority to do every lawful thing which is necessary in order to do such act.

An agent having an authority to carry on a business has authority to do every lawful thing necessary for the purpose, or usually done in the course, of conducting such business.

(a) A is employed by B, residing in London, to recover at Bombay a debt due to B, A may adopt any legal process necessary for purpose of recovering the debt, and may give a valid discharge for the same.

(b) A constitutes B, his agent to carry on his business of a ship-builder. B may purchase timber and other materials, and hire workmen, for the purpose of carrying on the business.

A well-know illustration is the case of *Dingle v. Hare*.[187]

An agent was authorised to sell artificial manure. He had no authority to give any warranty about the goods. Yet he warranted to the buyer that the manure contained 30 per cent phosphate of lime.

The warranty turned out to be false and the principal was sued for its branch. He was held liable, because it was usual in the artificial manure trade to give a warranty of this kind. BYLES J said.

When the jury found that is was usual to sell these artificial manures with a warranty, the nice distinction as to the extent of the agent's authority became quite immaterial. An agent to sell has general authority to do all that is usual and necessary in the course of such employment.

Thus, every agent has the implied authority to act according to the customs and usages of a particular marker or trade. The principal is bound by such usages even if he is unaware of them or even if they conflict with his instructions. Thus a bill-broker in London was entrusted with certain bills for discounting, and he pledged them the principal was held bound as it was usual for bill-brokers in London to raise money by depositing their customers' bills en bloc.[189] But the custom or usage must not be unlawful or unreasonable. Where a custom or usage is unlawful for example which converts the agent into a pricipal, is unreasonable. *Robinson v. Mollet*[190] is an illustration in point.

R authorised broker M to purchase for him 50 tons of tallow. M supplied his own tallow as there was a custom in his trade to buy large quantities of tallow in his own name and then to allocate it to his principals.

The House of Lords held the custom to be unreasonable. It made M a wholesaler more than agent. It also created a conflict between his duty to the principal and his personal interest.

Similarly, a custom which gives the agent liberty to adjust his personal account by way of set-off or otherwise for the claims of the principal is unreasonable, Thus, where an agent was authorised to collect from the underwriters a sum of money due under policy of insurance, he was not allowed to set off his personal debts to the underwriters against that money although a custom to that effect was alleged.[191] The Principal would, however, have been bound by this custom if he were aware of it.

The principle of *Dingle v. Hare*[192] applies to all cases where the agent acts as a seller. For example, an agent appointed to sell a horse may warrant it as good if the principal is a horse dealer, or if the sale of being held at a market-place, but not if it is a private sale. Similarly, an agent to sell a property has authority to state the condition and value of the property to a proposed purchaser and an agent to discount a bill may warrant it as a good bill, but he cannot endorsee it.[193]

It seems almost as a natural corollary of the authority to sell goods that the agent would have the authority to receive payment also, But this is not essentially so. An agent was appointed to sell certain coats. The purchaser of the coats paid the agent but the latter did not pay the pricipal. The principal successfully sued the purchaser for the price.[194] The court relied upon an earlier authority where it was said.[195] That an agent authorised to sell has as a necessary legal consequence authority to receive payment is a proposition utterly untenable and contrary to authority.

The court, however agreed that the purchaser could show that the agent was expressly, impliedly or ostensibly authorised to receive payment or that the circumstances were such that payment to the agent was in essence payment of the principal. But nothing of the sort was shown.

Authority of special agents

Factor — A factor is a mercantile agent who is put in possession of the goods of his principal for sale He has the authority to sell the goods in his won name, to warrant they if it is usual to do so to fix the selling price and to receive payment.

Broker — A broker is a mercantile agent appointed to sell the goods of his principal, but he is not given possession thereof, He may sell the goods in his own name, and may receive payment. But if he discloses the name of the principal, he cannot receive payment. He may act according to the usual course of business except he here a usage is unreasonable or unlawful. He may sell on reasonable credit.

Estate or house agent — A house or estate agent is in a different position from a broker at the stock exchange owing to the peculiarities of the property with which he has to deal and which does not pass by a short instrument as stocks and shares do, but has to be transferred after investigation of title as to which various stipulations might be of particular concern to the owner, may have to be inserted in a concluded contract relating to such property. The parties, therefore, do not ordinarily contemplate than the agent should have the authority to complete the transaction in such cases. That is why is it has been held both in England and here, that authority given to a broker to negotiate a sale and find a purchaser, without furnishing him with all the terms means 'to find a man willing to become a purchaser and not to find him and make him a purchaser.' This passage occurs in the judgement of the Supreme Court in *Abduall a Ahmed v. Animendra Kissen Mitter.*[197]

The facts of the case were that an state broker was appointed with an authority for one month to negotiate the sale of property on certain terms as to price and with which his commission was also linked. Before the expiry of the month he found a customer ready and willing to purchase and communicated the fact to the principal. The principal terminated the authority of the agent and directly enter into a contract with a nominee of the person found by the agent. The agent claimed his commission.

It was held that the agent having negotiated the sale and secured a buyer who made a firm offer acquired the right to commission on the basis of the proffered price subject to the condition that the buyer should complete the transaction, and as this condition was fulfilled, the agent's right to commission became absolute and could not be affected by the circumstances that the principal for some reason of his own sold the property at a lower price.

Auctioneer — An auctioneer is an agent appointed to sell goods at a public auction. He therefore, does not have the authority to sell by private contract. He cannot sell on credit, or accept any payment other than cash, or warrant the goods.

Ostensible or apparent authority [S. 237]

The apparent authority of an agent is thus explained by DENNING LJ: [197]

Ostensible or apparent authority is the authority of an agent as it appears to others. It often coincides with actual authority. Thus, when the board (of directors) appoint one of their members to be a managing director they invest him not only with implied authority, but also with ostensible authority to do all such things as fall within he usual scope of that office. Other propel people who see him acting as managing director are entitled to assume that he has the usual authority of a managing director. But sometimes ostensible authority exceeds actual authority. For instance, when the board appoint the managing director, they may expressly limit his authority by saying he is not to order goods worth more than £500 without sanction of the board. In that case his actual authority is subject to the limitation, but his ostensible authority includes all the usual authority of a managing director The company is bound by his ostensible authority in his dealings with those who do not know of the limitation. Thus, if he orders goods worth £1,000 the company is bound to the party who does not know of the (£500) limitation.

Thus, "when it is said that an agent's act was within the scope of his apparent authority all that is meant is that the act appeared to be authorised."[198]

A leading authority is *Wattean v. Fenwick*: [199]

The defendants had forbidden the manager of their hotel from buying cigars on credit. The plaintiff gave cigars to the manager on credit, which were used in business. The manager's name appeared over the board and the plaintiff trusted him and had never heard of the defendants. Being unable to recover the price from the manager, the plaintiff sued the defendants.

The court found that "cigars were .... such as would naturally be supplied to and dealt in such an establishment." WILLIS J, therefore, held that "once it is established that the defendant was the real principal, the ordinary doctrine as to principal and agent applied, that the principal is liable for all the acts of the agent which are within the authority usually confided to an agent of that character, notwithstanding limitations, as between the principal and the agent. Put upon that authority." In another similar case, the manager of a public house was authorised to buy spirits only from A, but he bought them from another person telling him that he was a manager. The principal was held not liable, because the fact of agency was disclosed and it was well-known that such managers had authority to buy only from authorised sources.[200] But in above case the fact of agency had not been disclosed, the principal would have ben liable in the manner of a dormant partner.

Similarly, in a case before the Kerala High Court,[201] it was held that a person having responsibility to carry on the business of the store of a co-operative society must be deemed to have authority to purchase goods on credit notwithstanding that the society had advanced him enough money for the purpose. A decision of the Allahabad High Court furnishes another illustration.[202]

In pursuance of an agreement the plaintiff despatched a wagon load of potatoes to the defendant. The latter refused to take delivery., The plaintiff then sent his agent to the agent a less sum of money in full payment, which the agent accepted. The plaintiff received the money but brought an action for the balance.

It was held that the defendant could presume that the agent who was sent to sell at the available price had the ostensible authority to settle with the defendant at a less price.

In the above-cited Kerala case the court adopted from Smith and Watt's MERCANTILE LAW,[203] the following statement on the distinction between "implied" and "ostensible" authority:

Implied authority is real authority, the exercise of which is binding not only as between the principal and the third party, but also between principal and agent. It differs only from an express authority in that it is conferred by no express words, but is to be gathered form surrounding circumstances. The term "ostensible authority", on the other hand. Denotes no authority at all. It is a phrase conveniently used to describe the position which arises when one person has clothed another, or allowed him to assume, an appearance of authority to act on his behalf, without actually giving him any authority either express or implied, by which appearance of authority third party is misled into believing that a real authority exists.

The statement portrays the truth in Lord ELLENBOROUGH'S observation that "apparent authority is the all authority."[204] Whether there is appearance of authority in a particular case depends upon the facts of the case. An appearance of authority in a particular case depends upon the facts of the case case. An appearance of authority may, for example arise from the course of business. A well-known authority is *Humber v. Burnard.*[205] Where an agent was authorised to underwrite insurance policies. The principal was held liable when he underwrote a guarantee policy because under writing of guarantee policies was within the ordinary course of business of a Lloyd's underwriter. An appearance of authority may arise from the position occupied by the agent. Where the secretary of a company, having no actual authority to do so, hired on behalf of the company expensive self-drive cars and used them for his own purposes, the company was held liable. His position as secretary warranted the authority for certain types of administrative or ministerial acts. Hiring a car was one such act.[206]

An appearance of authority may arise from the course of dealing adopted in a particular case. Thus, where a principal once authorised his servant to purchase iron on credit and paid for it, he was liable when on a subsequent occasion he sent the servant with ready cash, but the servant again incurred credit.[207] But if the original act had been unauthorised, the principal would not have been liable for the second, even if he had paid for the first. "Thus in *Barret v. Irvine*[208], it was laid down that a mother who has once paid for a horse for her infant son does not thereby raise an inference of a general authorisation to him to pledge her credit for his future equine purchases.[209]

A representation of authority has to emanate from some conduct of the principal. There must be some conduct on his part which enables the agent to occupy a position of apparent authority. For example, a principal used to order goods from the plaintiff. He has a servant whom he never authorise or ever sent out for buying goods. The servant was dismissed and after that on two occasions he bought goods from the plaintiff in the principal's name. Each time the principal paid the account in ignorance. He was held entitled to recover back the money, for he had done nothing to enable his servant to acquire an appearance of authority.[210] The Privy Council has recently held that an apparent authority cannot be inferred from the fact that the act itself was of class which the principal had previously authorised the agent to do. An agent was instructed not to carry, on evaluations for a group of companies because of the group's failure to pay for the past services. The agent later became director of one of the companies and, without the employer's knowledge, performed a number of evaluations for them. The evaluations had been negligently done and the person who suffered loss by relying on them, sued the employer. It was held that no authority to perform these evaluations could be inferred form the fact that the employer had authorised the employee to perform certain others.[211] On the other hand, in the American case of *Kannelles v. Locke,*[212] the principal was held liable for the act of complete imposter. The plaintiff arrived at night at a small hotel. She was greeted by a man in the corridor. He booked a room for her and took charge off her valuable articles and issued a receipt in the principal's name. He disappeared with the articles. The hotel-keeper was held liable because the imposter could not have occupied that position of apparent authority without the hotel-keeper's negligence. In *Panorama Developments (Guidord) Ltd. v. Fideis Furnishing Fabrics Ltd.*[213] the facts were:

The plaintiff ran a car on hire service. The defendant company's company secretary hired cars from the plaintiff ostensibly for the company's business, telling him that the cars were wanted to carry the important customers of the company. he wrote on the company's paper ordering the cars signing himself, "company secretary". Only fact he used the cars for his own purposes and not for those of the company.

It was held that the secretary had ostensible authority to enter into contracts for hiring cars for which the company must pay.

An apparent authority once created continues to exist unless it is terminated by a notice to the third party. It cannot be terminated or restricted privately. Thus, a principal who had terminated the authority his agent who had occasionally bought wool for him was nevertheless held liable for the agent's further purchases as the supplier had no notice of the termination.[214] Similarly, where a man lived with his mistress, as husband and wife and used to pay for the mistress's purchases, he was held liable for the purchases made after he had left her, because the supplier did not know of that fact.[215]

Statutory provision about apparent authority — The doctrine of ostensible authority is given statutory shape in Section 237 of the contract Act. The section is as follows:

237.Liability of principal inducing belief that agent's unauthorised acts were authorized — When an agent has, without authority, done acts or incurred obligations to third persons on behalf of his principal, the principal is bound by such acts obligations to third persons on behalf of his principal, the principal is bound by such acts or obligations if he has by his words or conduct induced such third persons to believe that such acts ad obligations were within the scope of the agent's authority.

Illustrations

(a) A consigns goods to B for sale, and gives him instructions not to sell under a fixed price. C, being ignorant of B's instructions, enters into a contract with B to buy the goods at a price lower than the reservations price. A is bound by the contract.

(b) A entrusts B with negotiable instructions endorsed in blank B sells them to C in violation of private orders from A. The sale is good.

The provision has been used in quite a few cases to fix the principal with liability for unauthorised acts of his agent. The prominent among them seems to be a decision of the Nagpur High Court, where a banking firm was held liable for the misappropriation of the funds of a customer by a person who, to the knowledge of the firm was accepting deposits from customers. The court said: Their Lordships of the Judicial Committee of the Privy Council ruled in *Ram Pertab v. Marshall*[216] that the right of a third party against the principal on the contract of his agent though made in excess of the agent actual authority was nevertheless to be enforced when the evidence showed that the contracting party had been led into an honest belief in the existence of the authority to the extent apparent to him."[218]

Actual or constructiveness of lack of authority — Where, however, a person contracting with the agent has actual or constructive notice of any restriction on the agent's ostensible authority, he is bound by the restriction. Thus, where an agent authorised by a power of attorney to operate a business, but not the borrow money produced the power of attorney to a lender whom he asked for a loan, but the lend did not read it and advanced a loan, he could not recover it from the principal he had constructive notice that the agent had no power to borrow.[218]

Where a broker was permitted to receive payment for his principal's goods, B drawing upon the seller a bill of exchange and securing his acceptance to it. Payment made in the that manner become binding upon the principal. But where the broker was authorised to receive payment only in respect of one previous contract he was held to be not sufficient to create an apparent authority to receive such payments in the future also.[219] Once an ostensible authority is created, the principal becomes bound by his agent's acts within the scope of such authority. He cannot rely upon any private restrictions on the agent's authority.[220]

Just and reasonable solution — The ultimate question is whether the circum stances under which a servant has made a fraudulent misrepresentation which had caused loss to an innocent party contracting with him are such as to make it just for the employer to bear the loss. Such circumstances exist where the employer by words or conduct has induced the injured party to believe that the servant was acting in the lawful course of the employer's business. They do not exist where such belief although it is present, has been brought about through misguided reliance on the servant, when what he is purporting to do is not authorised to do what he is purporting to in his position is usually authorised to do and when the employer has done nothing to represent before it, the House of Lords held that where an agent was authorised dispose of a ship, a charter-party granted by him did not bind the principal. The sale of a ship backed by a three-year charter-party is a transaction of wholly different character from a straightforward sale.[221]

Agent's authority in emergency [S. 198]

189. Agent's authority in an emergency — An agent has authority, in an emergency, to do all such acts for the purpose fo protecting his principal from loss as would be done by person of ordinary prudence, in his own case, under similar circumstances.

Illustrations

(a) An agent for sale may have goods repaired if it necessary.

(b) A consigns provisions to B at Calcutta, with directions to send them immediately to C, at Cuttack, B may sell the provisions at Calcutta, if they will not bear journey to Cuttack without spoiling.

Where agent exceeds authority [Ss. 227-228]

227. Principal how for bound, when agent exceeds authority — When an agent does most then he is authorised to do, and when the part of what he does, which is within his authority can be separated from the part which is behind his authority, so much only of what he does as is within his authority is bending as between him and his principal.

A, being owner of a ship and cargo, authorises B to procure and insurance for 4,000 rupees on the ship, B procures a policy for 4,000 rupees on the ship, and another for the like sum on the cargo, A is bound to pay the premium for the policy on the ship, but not the premium for the policy on the cargo.

228.Principal not bound when excess of agent's authority is not separable — When an agent soen more than he is authorised to do, and what he does beyond the scope of his authority cannot be separated from what is within it, the principal is not bound to recognise the transaction.

Illustration

A authorises B to buy 500 sheep for him. B buys 500 sheep and 200 lambs for one sum of 6,000 rupees, A may repudiate the whole transaction.

Where an agent exceeds his authority, actual or apparent, the principal is not bound by the excess work, but where is separable from the authorised work the principal is bound to that extent. For example, an agent is authorised to insure a shop, He insures the ship as well as the goods under separate policies. The principal is bond only by the policy on the ship. If he had taken only on policy in excess of instructions, the principal would not have been bound.[222] Where the agent was authorised to sell half a right over a property and he contracted to sell all the rights, the principal became bound only to the extent of half the rights authorised by him, they being separable from the rest.[223]

Where the authorised work is not separable from the rest, the principal may repudiate the whole of the transaction.[224] For example, an agent is authorised to buy 500 sheeps, He buys 500 sheeps and 200 lambs for one sum of 6,000 rupees. The principal may repudiate the whole transaction. Where an agent was authorised to draw bills up to Rs 200 each, the principal was held not liable when the agent drew upto Rs. 100[225] Similarly, where an agent was instructed to contract of the purchase of cotton to be delivered at the end January, purchase of cotton to be delivered at the end of January, the principal was held not liable when the agent contracted for delivery in the middle of that month.[226]

Effect of notice to agent

229. Consequences of notice given to agent — Any notice given to or information obtained by the agent, provided to be given or obtained in the course of the business transacted by him for the principal, shall, as between the principal and third parties, have the same legal consequences as if it had been given to or obtained by the principal.

Illustrations

(a) A is employed by B to buy from C certain goods, of which C is the apparent owner, and buys them accordingly, In the course of the treaty for the sale, A learns that the goods really belonged to D, but B is ignorant of that fact. B is not entitled to set-off a debt owing to him from C against the price of the goods.

(b) A is employed by B to buy form C goods of which C is the apparent owner., A was, before he was so employed, a servant of C, and then learnt that the goods really belonged to D, but B is ignorant of that fact, In spite of the knowledge of his agent, B may set-off against the price of the goods a debt owing to him from C.

The effect of the provision is the notice given to or information obtained by an agent in the course of the business transacted by him on behalf of his principal, shall as between the principal and third parties, have the same legal consequences as if it had been given to or obtained by the principal. Acting on the principle the section the Calcutta High Court held that where the secretary of a society was de facto as well as decure incharge of the affairs of the society, a notice given him of the fact that a partner of a firm with which the society had dealings retired, operated as a notice to the society.[227]

Knowledge of broker — Where a broker is acting as a agent of the assured or the insurer, depends upon the facts of each case. It has been held that when broker has the power to bind the insurer, popularly known as "binder", he will be an agent of the insurer and his knowledge will be deemed to be the knowledge of the insurer. Thus, where a member of the border's firm knew of the criminal past of the assured, the insurer was not permitted to deny liability on the ground the past had not been disclosed.[228]

In such circumstances an assurance given by the broker would bind the insurer. In one such case, the broker orally assured that the new car purchased by the assured would be substituted for the old. The insurer was held liable thought he was not in a position to give such substitution.[229]

Liability for agent's wrongful acts [S. 238]

Section 238 of the Contract Act lays down the principle by which the liability of the principal for the wrongful acts of the agent is to be determined. The section provides:

238. Effect, on agreement, of misrepresentations or fraud by agent — Misrepresentation made, or frauds committed, by agents acting in the course of their business for their principal have the same effect on agreements made by such agents as if such misrepresentations frauds had been made or committed by the principals; but misrepresentations made and frauds committed by agents, in matters which do not fall within their authority, do not affect their principals.

Illustrations

(a) A, being B's agent for the sale of goods, induces C to buy them by a misrepresentation, which he was not authorised by B to make. The contract is voidable, as between B an C, at the option of B.

(b) A, the captain of B's ship, sign bills of lading without having received on board the goods mentioned therein. The bills of lading are void as between B and the pretended consignor.

To fix the principal with vicarious liability for the wrongs of his agent, is necessary that the wrong must have been committed in the course of the principal business. Although the particular act may not be authorised but, if it is done in the course of carrying on the authorised business, the principal is liable.[230]

A master is liable for the wrongs of his servant committed in the course of the servant's employment, whereas a principal is label for wrongs done by the agent in the course of business. The expression "course of business" has been generally taken to mean to same thing as "course of employment". Accordingly, the principles governing the master and servant relationship have been applied to that of principal and agent and also to partners. To quote Professor Street: "There has never been a time when cases on master and servant were not cited as authority in the law of principal and agent."[231]

Secondly, although Section 238 speaks of "misrepresentations' and "frauds" in reference to "agreements made by agents" the principle is applicable to all cases whether an agreement is involved or not.

Misrepresentations and frauds — An agent appointed to sell his principal's goods or property has often to make statements concerning the nature and quality of the property and in his enthusiasm to find a customer make exaggerated statement. The law does not like to hold the principal liable for the agent's extravagant statements unless it finds some fault with the principal himself, If for example the principal has authorised a false statement to be made, or knows that it is being made by the agent or keeps the real facts from the agent, obviously the principal is liable. The liability of the principal is enforced, at the option of the third party, by avoiding the contract if it is still executory or by holding the principal; liable in damages. Such liability came to the principal in the following three cases:

Fuller v. Wilson:[232] An estate agent stated to the purchaser that the house under sale was free from rates and taxes. The principal was aware, but the agent was not, that the house was subject to taxes and taxes were levied soon after the plaintiff purchased the house. The principal would have been held liable if the plaintiff had relied on the representation. DENMAN CJ said: "............ if the purchaser was actually deceived in his bargain, the law will relieve him form it. We think the principal and his agent are for this purpose completely identified, and that the question is, now what was passing in the mind of either, but whe than the purchaser was in fact received by them or either of them."

London County Freehold and Leasehold Properties Ltd. v. Barkerly Property and Investment Co. Ltd.[233] Negotiations were afoot for the sale of a block of flats by the defendant company to the plaintiff company. The solicitors of the plaintiff company, while going through the draft agreement. Put a marginal note enquiring whether all the tenants were paying their rents regularly. The solicitors of the defendant company consulted the property manager of the company and then informed the plaintiffs, also by way of marginal note to the draft the tenants were paying rents regularly with immaterial exceptions. The statement turned out to be false. The defendant company was held liable in fraud because one of its agents (property manager) who knew the real facts had made a false statement, and the company has necessarily to act thought its agents.

Briess v. Wooley: [234] Selector director of a company started negotiations for a contract without any authority and made fraudulent misrepresentations. Subsequently, he was authorised to complete the contract, but did nothing to correct the misrepresentations. The company was held liable.

In the following cases the principals were held not liable:

Cornfoot v Fowke: [235] The plaintiff had employed an agent to let a house. The defendant was in contact with the agent for a house. The defendant. Asked the agent: "if there was any objection to the house", to which he answered that there was not; the defendant entered into and signed the agreement, but afterwards discovered that the adjoining house was a brothel, and on that ground declined to fulfil the agreement. He claimed the right to avoid the agreement as there was fraudulent concealment of a material fact. But he was held bound by the agreement. There was no guilt in the principal because he held bound by the agreement. There was no guilt in the principal because he neither knew nor had authorised the statement to be made. There was no guilt in the agent because he did not know that there was a brothel.

This decision has been criticised.[236] It should be the duty of the principal to apprise the agent of the whole situation, otherwise he creates the risk of innocent misrepresentation being made by the agent. Moreover, recession is allowed even for innocent misrepresentation and there was no reason on why this should not have been attributed to the principal. If the principal had himself said "there was no objection to the house" he would have been guilty of fraud, and when he gives an ostensible position to his agent to make this statement, the elementary principle that "he who acts through another is deemed to act himself" should have been followed. Despite the criticism the decision has been followed in Armstrong v. Strain.[237]

On Mr Strain, a retired practitioner, "owned a bungalow in an area notoriously prone to produce settlements because of the heavy clay 'sub-soil. The bungalow had suffered severely from this scourge and had already been underpinned three times."[239] He was naturally noxious to dispose it of and entrusted it to his partners. His partners arranged it with another firm, which found Armstrongs as buyers. The bungalow was described to be "in a very nice condition" and one of the partners of the latter firm valued it at £2,000 for mortgage purposes. The agents knew of the last underpinning but not of the two earlier ones. Within two months of the transaction the bungalow collapsed finally. But Armstrong's action to hold the principal liable in damages for the fraud failed. The court fund no conscious falsehood and, therefore, acquitted the principal, " and the unfortunate Armstrongs were left with the ruins of a bungalow".

The decision has been described by L C B Gower as one that is socially undesirable and logically unsatisfying.[239] The learned writer has stated the position of English law in the following words: "The law is that a principal is not liable for fraud in respect of his agent's act unless — (a) he intends or knowingly permits the agent to make a false statement, or (b) his agent acting within the actual or apparent scope of his authority makes a statement with knowledge of its falsity or recklessly not caring whether it be true or false."

Agent's torts — "One who chooses to do business through an agent may in certain situations be liable for a tort committed by the agent. The doctrine of respondent superior (let the superior answer) will be applied to make the principal liable where the gent commits a tort while engaged in the business for the principal, or, as it is commonly said, when the tort is committed by the agent while acting in the course of and within the scope of his agency".[240] An agent kicked a boy form a moving street car. The principal was held liable for assault and battery.[241] An agent, employed to collect evidence for his principal in a pending law suit, offered to bribe a witness. It was held that the act was within the course of the employment of the gent and that the principal was bound by it.[242]

It is not necessary that the act should have been done by the agent for the principal's benefit. The House of Lords in their decisions in *Lloyd v. Grace Smith and Co.*[243] clearly ruled that the only condition of the principal's liability is that the act in question must be within the course of the agency business. The facts of the case were as follows:

Grace Smith and Co were a firm of solicitors of some repute and respectability. MRs. Lloyd, a widow, being dissatisfied with the income of her two cottages, consulted the firm's clerk, who was incharge of the conveyancing business, as to how to improve the income. He advised her to dispose of the cottages. He converted these papers into a sale deed to himself and subsequently disposed of the property and misappropriated the proceeds. It was held "that the firm was responsible for the fraud committed by their representative in the course of his employment."

PERSONAL LIABILITY OF AGENT [S. 230]

230. Agent cannot personally enforce, nor be bound by, contracts on behalf of principal — In the absence of any contract to that effect, an agent cannot personally enforce contracts entered into by him on behalf of his principal, nor is he personally bound by them.

Presumption of contract to contrary — Such a contract shall be presumed to exist in the following cases —

(1) Where the contract is made by an agent of the sale or purchase of goods far a merchant resident abroad;

(2) where the agent does not disclose the name of his principal ;

(3) where they principal, though disclosed, cannot be sued.

It has already been seen that the chief function of an agent is to establish contractual relationship between his principal and third parties, the agent then drops out. He can neither sue nor be sued on contracts made by him on his principal's behalf. Section 230 accordingly provides that in the absence of any contract to that effect, an agent cannot personally enforce contracts entered into by him on behalf of his principal nor is he personally bound by them.

This is known as the principle of the agent's immunity from personal liability. This rule applies even where the agent has contracted beyond his authority and the principal would not be liable. Even then the agent cannot be sued on the contract if he professed to act for the principal thought he will be liable to the third party for the deception played by him.[244]

Where a charter-party agreement was signed by agents adding to their signature the words 'as agents" and though their principal was not named, they were held to be not liable in respect of the agreement. Their signature "as agents" clearly indicated that they were acting only in that capacity.[245] In another case, goods were contracted to be sold on behalf of named principals by their agents who signed clearly and expressly as agents. Their principals refused to deliver the goods. The third party sued the agents for non-delivery, but the action failed.[246] This rule applies even where the agent has contracted beyond his authority and the principal would not be liable. Even then the agent cannot be sued on the contract if he professed to act for the principal though he will then be liable to compensate the third party for his loss.

But here are certain circumstance in which the agent incurs personal liability. Section 230, which incorporates the principle of agent's immunity from personal liability, says that there may be a contract to the contrary., In other words, the agent may contract to undertake personal liability. The section further goes on to provide that such contract is presumed in the following cases:

(1) Foreign principal [S.230(1)]

When an agent contracts for "a merchant resident aboard" their is the presumption that the agent undertakes personal liability. The original presumption of English law was that the agent alone was liable and he had nor right or pledge the credit of a foreign principal. The presumption still stand, but is has declined in importance. The perception was needed at a time when it was difficult to sue foreign principles and for the convenience of merchants a usage came into existence that the agent of a foreign principle incurs personal liability. But now on account of changed conditions of international trade, merchants trust each other and agents do not like to incur personal liability. The presumption being still a part of the law, an agent can only overthrow it by contracting in a manner showing an intention not to incur personal liability. Thus, where a contract was signed "by the authority of our principals ..... as agents", it was held that this was sufficient manifestation of the intention to exclude liability.[247]

The presumption has statutory force in India. An agent can only overthrow it by contracting in a manner showing an intention not to incur personal liability. Thus, where a contract was signed "by the authority of our principal...... as agents" or "Greenwich Marine Incorporated as agents for Trader Export, SA", is was held that theis was sufficient manifestation of the intention to exclude personal liability.[249] A company registered in England, and having a place of business in India, has been held to be a foreign principal for the purposes of this presumption and the Indian agent acting for it was held personally liable.[249]

(2) Principal unnamed [S.230(2)]

The presumption of agent's personal liability arises when he "does not disclose the name of his principal". Where an agent contracts for an undisclosed principal, he definitely is personally liable, being a party to the contract. But when he contracts for an unnamed principal, there is only a presumption of his personal liability. The presumption may arise even where the agent discloses his representative character, but not the name of his principal. Accordingly, the honorary secretary of a school was held personally liable for the rent of a house hired by him in his own name though for purposes of the school. But where an agent disclosed his characters the secretary of a club, personal liability could not be imposed on him.[250] The same result would follow where the representative character is already known of the third party.[251] But in every such case the form of contract will be the deciding factor. In an English case, a broker signed a contract in his own name, but had added: "Messrs. Southwell, to my principal etc." It as held that he was not personally liable.[252] Thee is nothing whatever in the contract to show that the defendant intended to act otherwise than as broker. Where an order was placed over telephone by a broker to another broker for the supply of bunkers, the ordering broker was held to be not personally liable. The general practice in placing orders by telephone was not to disclose the name of the principal and, moreover, the supplier already knew that the order was sent by a broker. Where, on the other hand, the usual mode of operation over telex of a forwarding agent was to remark, without disclosing the name of the principal, "We can do this for you," he ws held personally liable, though in that case he indicated the name of the liner to whom he was forwarding the goods.[253]

The presumption of personal liability in this case also is rebutable. One of the circumstances which excludes the presumption is sale of specific goods by an auctioneer for an unnamed principal. In one case,[254] an auctioneer auctioned a car for an unnamed principal. In another case,[255] an auctioneer auctioned a car of an unnamed principal. It subsequently came to light that the car, being already subject to a hire-purchase agreement, could not be transferred. The buyer sued the auctioneer for breach of warranty. The action failed because the auctioneer had not given any warranty about his principal's right to sell. The court pointed out that if it were a sale of unascertained goods the presumption would have prevailed.

(3) Non-existent or incompetent principal [S. 230(3)]

An agent is presumed to incur persònal liability where he contracts on behalf of a principal who, "thought disclosed cannot be sued." An agent who contract for a minor, the minor being not liable, the agent become personally liable. This result may not however, follow where the other party already knows that the principal is a minor. Similarly, where promoters buy goods on behalf of a projected company they become personally liable to pay for them. The company, being not in existence at the time of the contract, cannot be sued. The Calcutta High Court did not permit an agent of the Russian Government to be sued personally because it was neither averred nor proved that the Government of Russia could not be sued in India or elsewhere. The mere fact that such a suit required permission of the Government of India could not be taken to mean that no suit was possible.[256]

Election by third party [S. 232]

232. Performance of contract with agent, supposed to be principal.—Where one man makes a contract with another, neither knowing nor having reasonable ground to suspect that the other is an agent, the principal ,if he requires the performance of the contract, can only obtain such performance subject to the rights ad obligations subsisting between the agent and the other party to the contract.

Illustration

A, who owes 500 rupees to B, sells 1,000 rupees worth of rice to B, A is acting as agent for C in the transaction, but B has no knowledge nor reasonable ground of suspicion that such is the case. C cannot compel B to take the rice without allowing him to set-off A's debt.

In all the above situations "where the agent is personally liable, a person dealing with him may hold either him or his principal, or both of them, liable."

This seems to be a departure from the English law, where the third party has to elect between the liability of the principal or agent and the election once made is final and binding on him. If, for example, he has obtained judgment against the agent, he cannot afterwards sue the principal even if the judgement against the agent has remained unsatisfied. But this rule has been criticised. "Clearly it is contrary to justice that It should not be able to sue P is his judgment against A is unsatisfied. The rule works particularly harshly where It does not even know of P's existence until after he has obtained judgement against A.[257]

It is perhaps for this reason that the Indian Legislature marked a departure form the English rule and allowed the third party to sue the agent and the principal jointly. COUTTS-TROTTER CJ of the madras High Court doubted whether this was the intent of the Legislature and opined that the English rule should be followed. But a subsequent Division Bench of the same High Court disagreed with him. LEACH CJ said: "There is no ambiguity in the language used in the section and I am unable to see anything unreasonable in he rule, which it embodied had been obtained against the agent in an earliest is another matter but we are not called upon to consider that question here." Earlier, the Bombay High Court had also held that the section plainly intends to create joint liability. But is seems that even under this section some kind of election is likely to be involved. The third party has to choose between the liability of the agent, or the principal or both and the choice once made shall bind him.[258]

(4) Pretended agent [S. 235]

235. Liability of pretended agent — A person neutrally representing himself to be the authorised agent of another, and thereby inducing a third person to deal with in as such agent, is liable, if his alleged employer does not ratify his acts, to make compensation to the other in respect of any loss or damage which he has incurred by so dealing.

Thus, where a person pretends to act as the agent of another, he any be saved by the principal by ratifying his act. But if no ratification is forthcoming the pretended agent becomes personally liable to the third party for any loss that he may have suffered by relying upon the representation of authority. The false representation must be the cause of the contract. If the truth is already known to the other party, no liability arises. The false representation must be the cause of the contract. A person who acknowledged the liability of a firm pretending acknowledgement. Since the action in such cases is under the tort of deceit tort principles as of damages would apply rather that those applicable to breach of contract.[259]

Where the pretension is as to a matter of law, the agent would not be liable. For example, the borrowing power of a company is a matter of interpretation of its constitutional documents and governing statutes. A misrepresentation as to this will not create liability.[260] But whether borrowing powers have been exhausted, is a question of fact. Liability would follow if this fact is misrepresented.[261]

The agent himself cannot sue on a contract which he has made pretending to be an agent. This disability is clinched upon against by Section 236.

236. Person falsely contracting as agent not entailed to performance — A person with whom a contract has been entered into in the character of agent is not entitled to require the performance of it if he was in reality acting not as agent, but on his own account.

When a person has, in fact, no principal, yet persuades the other to contract with him as an agent of another, he is estopped from saying that the he had no principal, and since the contract was with his principal and not with him he has no locus to sue under that right. This will be so whether he feigns a named or unnamed principal. Where a shipping agent and did not do so, he held personally liable to the principal for the tort of conversion and for breach of contract under Section 73 of the Contract Act.[262]

(5) Breach of warranty of authority

Closely allied to the liability of a pretended agent is the liability of an agent for breach of warranty of authority. Where a person is in fact an agent, but exceeds his authority or represents to have a kind of authority which he in fact does not have, he commits breach of warranty of authority ad is personally liable to the third party for any loss caused to him by reason of acting on the false representation. This is the principal of *Collen v. Wright*.[263]

W was land agent for one G.W. agreed to grant to the plaintiff a lease fo G's farm for 12 $^1/_2$ years. He honestly believed that he had the authority to do so. But W refused to execute the lease and he proved that he had given no such authority to the agent. W, having died in the meantime. The plaintiff used his executors for the loss he had suffered in entering upon the farm, and they were held liable.

WILLES J said: "The fact that the professed agent honestly thinks that he has authority that affects the moral character of his act; but his moral innocence, so far as the person whom he has induced to contract is concerned, in no way aids such person, or alleviates the inconvenience and damage which he sustains. The obligation arising in such a case is well expressed by saying that a person, professing to contract as agent for another, impliedly, if not expressly, undertakes to or promises the person who enters into such contract upon the faith of the professed agent being duly authorised, that the authority which he professes to have does in point of fact exist."

Similarly, in *Young v. Toynbee*[264] an agent was held liable for prosecuting action even after his principal, though unknown to him, had become insane, for the insanity had determined the agent's authority at once. A bank as induced by an agent to transfer some stock (shares) standing in the name of his principals, the agent producing a transfer form signed apparently by the principals,. Signature turned out to be forged. The bank had to restore the stock to the principals. For the loss thus caused, the bank was allowed to hold the agent liable for the fraud committed through falsely warranting authority.[265] An agent was held liable to a person to whom he chartered his principal's ship without authority of the principal who repudiated the transaction.[266]

An agent gives warranty of his authority; he does not give a guarantee that the contract is within authority, the principal would not commit breach.

RIGHTS AND LIABILITIES OF UNDISCLOSED PRINCIPAL

The rights and liabilities of a principal under contracts made by his agent depend upon whether-(a) the principal's existence and name were disclosed by the agent; (b) the principal's existence was disclosed but not his name and; (c) neither existence nor name of the principal were disclosed.

Where principal disclosed

Where the existence of the principal is disclosed, Section 226 applies, according to which the agent's acts and contracts "will have the same legal consequence as if the contracts had been entered into and the acts done by the principal in person". The principal may sue the third party upon the contract and vice versa. For example, where the agent is authorised to receive payment, a payment to him discharges the third party from his liability to the principal. The agent can neither sue nor be sued upon a contract made by him on behalf of his principal. "The contract is the contract of the principal, not that of the agent, and prima facie at common law the only person who can sue is the principal and the only person who can be sued is the principal." [267]

Unnamed principal

Even where the agent does not disclose the name of his principal but discloses his representative character, the contract will be the contract of the principal, unless there is something in its form or signature to show that he intended to be personally liable. Where an agent signed the contract as a broker, "to my principals", but did not disclose who the principals were he was not personally liable. "There is nothing whatever on the contract to show that the defendant intended to act otherwise than as a broker.[268]

Undisclosed principal

The doctrine of undisclosed principal comes into play when the agent neither discloses the existence of his principal nor his representative character. In such circumstances, the question arises what are the mutual right and liabilities of the principal, the agent and the third party. There is nothing unusual in this doctrine insofar as the relations between the agent and the third party are concerned. Since the agent has contracted in his own name, he is bound by the contract. He may be sued on it and he has the right to sue the third party and the principal in not liable is such cases. But the principal too has the right to intervene and assert his position as an undisclosed party to the contract.[269] The right of the principal is protected by the Contract Act itself. Section 231 declares;

231. Rights of parties to a contract made by agent not disclosed — If an agent makes a contract with a person who neither knows, nor has reason to suspect that he is an agent, his principal may require the performance of the contract; but the other contracting party has, as against the principal, the same rights as he would have had as against the agent if the agent had been principal.

It the principal discloses himself before the contract is completed, the other contracting party may refuse to fulfil the contract , if he can show that, if he had known who was the principal in the contract or if he had known that the agent was not a principal, he would not have entered into the contract.

The right of the principal has been described as "anomalous" because it does not fit in any of the established principals of the law of contract.

The rule which permits an undisclosed principal to sue and be sued on a contract to which he is not a party, though well-established, is itself an anomaly.

Yet the doctrine has business convenience to recommend itself. But for this doctrine, the property or money of one person would have gone to enrich the estate of another person. If, for example, an agent sells his principal's property in his own name and receives the price, the principal is obviously entitled to trace his money and recover it, even if the agent has gone bankrupt. An action of this kind was allowed as early as *Gurratt v. Cullum*[270].

The right of the undisclosed principal to intervene and use the third party is, however, subject to the following qualifications:

Firstly, the other contracting party would have against the principal "the same rights which he would have had against the agent if the agent had been principal." S 232 which says that "the principal, if he requires the performance of the contract, can only obtain such performance subject to the rights and obligations subsisting between the agent and the other party to the contract. The main concern of these sections is to ensure that the third party is not put to any disadvantage by the intervention of the principal.

S 232. Performance of contract with agent supposed to be principal — Where one man makes a contract with another, neither knowing nor having reasonable ground to suspect that the other is an agent the principal, if he requires the performance of the contract, can only obtain such performance subject to the rights and obligation subsisting between the agent and the either party to the contract.

Illustration

A, who owes 500 rupees to B sells 1,000 rupees worth of rice to B.A. is acting as agent for C in the transaction, but B has no knowledge nor reasonable grounds of suspicion that such is the case. C cannot compel B to take the rice without allowing him to set off A's debt.

If, for example, the agent owes some money to the third party, which the latter could have set off against the price of the goods sold to him, he would have the same right if the principal sues him for the price. *Montague v. Forwood*[271] is an illustration in point.

The plaintiffs, who were acting for the owners of a cargo, employed B & Co. as their agents to collect from underwriters contributions is respect of general average loss. B & Co. not being brokers, employed the defendants, who were brokers at Lloyd's, to collect the money, and they did so. At the time when the defendants received the money there was a debt due to them from B & Co. The defendants did not know and there was nothing to lead them to suppose that B & Co. were not acting as principals in the matter and the defendants believed that B & Co were acting as principal.

It was held that the defendants were entitled to stand in the position in which they would have stood if B & Co. had really been principal's; and that consequently, the defendants were entitled to set off against the demand of the plaintiffs for the money which they had collected the debt due to them from B & Co.

The illustration appended to Section 232 is more or less to the same effect.

A, who owes 500 rupees to B, sells 1,000 rupees worth of rice to B, A is acting as agent for C in the transaction, but B has no knowledge nor reasonable ground of suspicion that such is the case. C cannot compel B to take the price without allowing him to set off A's debt.

But where the third party does not believe the agent to be a principal or there are suspicious circumstances, he may not be able to claim a set off. Thus, for example, in *Cook v. Eshelby*.[273]

L & Co. sold cotton to C, in their own names, but really on behalf of an undisclosed principal. C knew that L & R Co. were in the habit of dealing both for principal and on their own account and had no belief on the subject whether they made this contract on their won account or for a principal.

It was held that C could not, in an action brought by the principal for the price of cotton, set off a debt due from L & Co.

Secondly, if the principal discloses himself before the contract is completed the third party may repudiate the contract if he can show that if he had known who the principal was or that the agent was not the principal, he would not have contracted. The right of the third party to repudiate the contract arises only when, the identity of the undisclosed principal would have been so material to him that if he had known the true facts, he would not have contracted. Thus, in *Said v. Butt*.[273]

A theatre ticket was purchased by person through an undisclosed agent knowing fully well that a ticket would not have been issued to him on personal grounds. It was held that the theatre-owner had the right to repudiate the contract and exclude him form admission.

It means that an undisclosed principal cannot intervene when he knows that the other party would not have dealt with him. This principle will apply only when "some personal consideration (forms) a material ingredient". In *Dyster v. Ryndall*,[274] a piece of land was purchased by somebody for an undisclosed principal. The owner would not have sold the land to him, yet he was allowed to intervene and enforce the contract.

Lastly, an undisclosed principal cannot intervene if some express or implied term of the contract excludes him from the contract. The world like "owner"[275] "proprietor,[276] show an intention to make a personal contract and consequently preclude the undisclosed principal from intervening. But where, in a contract of letting out, the agent described himself as the "landlord", evidence was allowed to show that he was only an agent, Similarly, "the description in a charter party of one of the contracting parties as 'charterer' does not, of itself, designate him as the only person to fill that position", and the undisclosed principal was allowed to sue for the breach of the charter-party.[277]

Third party's right against undisclosed principal — Just as the undisclosed principal has the right to sue the third party, the latter has the right to sue the principal. Difficult questions in this connection have arisen where the principal has already paid the agent, trusting that he has paid or will pay the third party, but the agent has defaulted or has gone bankrupt before payment. This happened in *Davison v. Donaldson*.[278]

The managing owner and the master of a ship purchased goods on credit from the plaintiff for the purposes of the ship. The undisclosed partner settled his account with the husband believing that the latter had paid the plaintiff. But he had not done so and had gone bankrupt. The plaintiff sued the principal. The court said: "When a person is supplied with goods it is his duty to see that the seller is paid....... Partners ought not to settle with their co-partners without satisfying themselves that the payments have been actually made."

RATIFICATION OF AGENTS ACTS

The doctrine of ratification comes into play when a person has done an act on behalf of another without his knowledge or consent. The doctrine gives the person on whose behalf the act is done an option either to adopt the act by ratification on to disown it. Ratification is thus a kind of affirmation of unauthorised acts. It is thus explained in Section 196.

196. Right of person at to acts done for him without his authority: Effect of ratification — Where acts are done by one person on behalf of another, but without his knowledge or authority, he may elect to ratify or to disown such acts. If he ratifies them, the same effect we follow as if they had been performed by his authority.

Where, for example, a person insures the goods of another without his authority the owner may ratify the policy and then the policy will be as valid as if the agent had been authorised to insure the goods.[279]

Ratification may be express or implied. Section 197 provides;

197. Ratification may be expressed or implied — Ratification may be expressed or may be implied in the conduct of the person on whose behalf the acts are done.

The Section carries the following illustrations:

(a) A, without authority, buys goods for B. Afterwards B sells them to C on his own account B's conduct implies a ratification of the purchase made for him by A.

(b) A, without B's authority, lends B's money to C. Afterwards B accepts interest on the money from C. B's conduct implies a ratification of the loan.

Where the manager of an insurance company effected an assurance which he had no authority to do, but the company accepted the money which was receive under the policy, that was held to be a sufficient ratifications.[280]

Conditions of ratification

A valid ratification has to fulfil certain conditions. Some of them are as follows.

1. On behalf of another

In the first, it is necessary that the act in question must have been done on behalf of the person who wants to ratify it. The agent must profess to act as an agent on behalf of an identifiable principal. "It is not necessary that he should be named, but there must be such a description of him as shall amount to a reasonable designation of the person intended to be bound by the contract." If the agent act in his own name and "makes no allusion to agency"[270] his act cannot be ratified by any other person even if the agent in his secret mind intended to act for another. This is the principle of the famous case of *Keighley, Maxsted & Co. v. Durant*.[281]

K M & Co., authorised their agent to buy Karachi wheat at specified rates on their joint account. Wheat was not obtainable at those rates. He bought wheat from Durant at a higher rate. He did so in the hope and confidence that his act would be adopted by the principals, but he never mentioned the principals and contracted in his own name. The principals approved the purchase, but, when the price of wheat fell, refused to take delivery. Durant sued the agent and the principals for breach of contract.

But the principals were held not liable. The agent, having contracted in his own name, his act was not open to anybody's ratification and, therefore, the purported ratification was ineffective. LORD MACNAGHTEN said: "...Obligations are not to be created by or founded upon undisclosed intentions."

Similarly, Lord James Said:

To establish that a man's thoughts unexpressed and unrecorded can form the basis of a contract so as to bind other persons and make them liable on a contract they never made with persons they never heard of, seems a somewhat difficult task.

The words "on behalf of another" as used in Section 196 expressly recognise this rule.[282]

A construction company took out a policy of insurance in which the assured was described as "the company, all its subsidiary, associated and related companies, all contractors and sub-contractors and/or suppliers". An employee of one of the sub-contractors who was engaged to work at a particular site suffered an accident and obtained judgment against the sub-contractor and the latter claimed the amount from the insurer. Supposing that no formal notification of ratification was necessary and that the filing of a claim under the policy amounted to ratification, the questions still remained whether the policy was taken out on behalf of the sub-contractor to enable him to ratify and whether the ratification was within reasonable time. On the first question, the judgement was that the contract should be made on behalf of a person who is presently assertible. Since the sub-contractor did not then exist, he was possibly only a future beneficiary and, therefore, not entitled to ratify. The court, however, did not accept the argument that the contract was not ratifiable after the occurrence of the loss.[283]

The section, however, does not insist upon the name of the principal being disclosed. Marine insurance policies are often effected on behalf of anybody interested and are, therefore, open to anybody's ratification. Where the act is purported to be done on behalf of another, that other may ratify even if the agent used his name to commit a fraud upon the third party.[284]

2. Competence of principal

Since ratification relates back to the date when the contract was originally made by the agent, it is necessary that the principal who purports to ratify must be in existence at the time of the contract and should also be competent. It is this principle which prevents a person from ratify a contract made in its name before its incorporation. But this is subject to the provisions of the Specific Relief Act, 1963, Section 15 of which provides that if a pre-incorporation contract is for an object which is within the objects for which the company incorporated, the company may ratify it and, if does ratify it becomes binding an the other party can also enforce it against the company.

3. What acts can be ratified? [S.200]

Only lawful acts are open to ratification. An act which is void from the very beginning cannot be ratified. The Privy Council observed in a case that ratification "must be in relation to a transaction which may be valid in itself and not illegal" Where money was entrusted to a person for investment and he put it to his own use, it was held by the Privy Council that the doctrine of ratification could not be used to validate this breach of fiduciary obligation. Subject to this any act may be ratified "whether it is founded on a tort or on a contract". A forgery of signatures being a crime, cannot be ratified. A minor's agreement being void cannot be ratified by him on attaining majority.[285]

Similarly, acts which would become injurious to others by ratification cannot be ratified. This principle is incorporated in Section 200 which says that an act cannot be ratified which by ratification "would have the effect of subjecting a third person to damages." The following illustrations are given in the section.

(a) A, not being authorised thereto by B, demands, on behalf of B, the delivery of a chattel the property of B, from C, who is in possession of it. This demand cannot be ratified by B, so as to make C liable for damages for his refusal to deliver.

(b) A holds a lease from B, terminable on three months' notice. C, an unauthorised person gives notice of termination to A. The notice cannot be ratified by B, so as to be binding on A.[286]

Acts done on behalf of Government — Such acts are ratifiable in the same way in which private acts can be. In one of the cases it was observed: "If their had been any doubt about the original intention of the Government, it has clearly ratified and adopted the acts of its agents which according to the principle in *Burot v. Denman*[277] is equivalent to previous authority." Thus, acts of public servants if excess of their authority may be ratified by the Government.

Where public officers exceed their authority, the State will be liable only to the extent it has expressly or impliedly ratified or approved the acts of such officers. Collector *Musulipatam v. Patam Cavaly Vencata Narrianpah*,[288] where the court said:

The acts of a Government officer bind the Government only when he is acting in the discharge of certain duty within the limits of the authority or if he exceeds that authority, when the government, in fact or in law, directly or by implication ratifies the excess.

4. Knowledge of facts (S. 198)

Section 198 declares: "No valid ratification can be made by a person whose knowledge of the facts is materially defective." "To constitute a binding adoption of acts as a prior unauthorised these conditions must exist: (1) the acts must have been done for and in the name of the supposed principal, and (2) there must be full knowledge of what those acts were, or such an unqualified adoption that the inference may properly be drawn that the principal intended to take upon himself the responsibility for such acts, whatever they were."

5. Whose transaction (S. 199)

"A person ratifying any unauthorised act done on his behalf, ratifies the whole of the transaction of which such act forms a part."[289] A person cannot ratify a part of the transaction which is beneficial to him and repudiate the rest. So, a ratification of a part of a transaction operates of the whole of the transaction.

6. Within reasonable time

A ratification to be effective must come within reasonable time. If a time is fixed for performance of the contract, ratification must come before that time otherwise it will be too late. For example, a tender for supply of eggs was approved by a board, but not formally. The time for commencement of performance was September. Before this date the tender was withdrawn. The board ratified its approval of the tender on October 6. It was held that this was too late as it was done after the date fixed for performance. Similarly, a policy of fire insurance was allowed to be ratified after the occurrence of the loss, because the owner himself could to have insured at that time. The only exception is marine insurance, where a policy can be ratified even after the owner has come to know of the loss. In a case before the Court of Appeal of New South Wales, exception of marine insurance, a period before occurrence of loss. The court said that "a ratification-after-loss rule promotes loss distribution which is the rationale of insurance and is best calculated to serve the needs of the commercial and the side community".[290]

Effects of ratification

Ratification has the following effects:

(1) It establishes the relationship of principal and agent insofar as the act ratified is concerned between the person ratifying and the person doing the act.

(2) Ratification establishes the relationship of contract between the principal and the third party.

7. Doctrine of relation back

Ratification relates back to the date on which the agent first contracted. Section 196 declares that if an unauthorised act is ratified by the person on whose behalf it was done, "the same effects will follows as if they had been performed by his authority". Thus, there is a contract between the principal and the third party not from the date of ratification, but from the date when the agent first contracted. One of the effects of relation back is demonstrated by *Bolton v. Lambert*.[291]

The defendant made an offer to the managing director of a company, who having no authority to do so, accepted it. That gave the company an option to ratify the contract. But the company ratified only after the defendant had withdrawn his offer. The company sued the defendant for specific performance.

The company was held entitled to it. The company's ratification related back to the date on which the managing director first accepted the offer. Thus, there was a contract between the company and the defendant from that date. The defendant's revocation of his offer was ineffective.

The decision has been criticised on the ground that it leaves the third party in a worse position that he would have been if he had contracted with the principal, for then he would have revoked his offer until the principal had accepted it. But if he contracts through an unauthorised agent, he neither has a contract (until ratified) nor can withdraw from it. The AMERICAN RESTATEMENT suggests a different rule:

To constitute a ratification, the affirmance of a transaction must occur before the other party has manifested his withdrawal from it either to the purported principal or to the agent, and before the offer or agreement has otherwise terminated or been discharged.[292]

The decision has also been justified. The defendant had contracted to sell the property for a certain price and was given the same terms. The ratification had not caused him any prejudice. But the general trend of opinion is against the decision. That is why, it is not to be extended and was not followed in Watson v Davies.[293]

The defendant offered to sell his property to a charitable institution. The offer was accepted by a few members of the board "subject to approval by full members of the board." The day on which the board was to meet, the defendant withdrew his offer. The board ratified it and brought an action for specific performance.

The ratification was held to be too late, and the revocation effective. Maugham J said: "An acceptance by an agent....subject in express terms to ratification by his principal is legally a nullity until ratified, and is no more binding on the other party than an unaccepted offer which can, of course, be withdrawn before acceptance."

Determination of Agency

201. Termination of agency — An agency is terminated by the principal revoking his authority; or by the agent renouncing the business of the agency; or by the business of the agency being completed; or by either the principal or agent dying or becoming of unsound mind; or by the principal being adjudicated an insolvent under the provisions of any Act for the time being in force for the relief of insolvent debtors.

The relationship of principal and agent may end in any of the ways mentioned in Section 201. The section provides for the following modes of termination:

(1) Revocation.

(2) Renunciation by agents.

(3) Completion of business

(4) Principal or agent's death.

(5) Principal or agent becoming person of unsound mind.

(6) Expiry of time.

1. By revocation (s. 203)

The principal may revoke his agent's authority and that puts as end to the agency. Section 203 clearly declares;

203. When principal may revoke agent's authority — The principal may, save as is otherwise provided by the last preceding section, revoke the authority given to his agent at any time before the authority has been exercised so as to bind the principal.

Section 207 further provides that revocation may be express or implied from the conduct of the principal. An illustration appended to the section says:

A empowers B to let A's house. Afterwards A lets it himself. This is an implied revocation of B's authority.

Thus, where the owner of a colliery appointed a sole selling agent for his coal for seven years, it was held that the owner could sell the colliery even before the expiry of this period and thus terminate the agency. He was not bound to keep his colliery. Lord Penance, pointed out that no principal can be compelled to keep the business open whether it is profitable to him or not and only for the benefit of the agent and the commission that he may receive.[294]

An agent provided a charter-party to the owner of a ship to run for a period of 18 months, the agent receiving commission on hire paid and earned. The owner sold the ship to the charterers within four months. The charter-party ended and so did the agency. The agent could not recover any damages, for the principal was not bound to keep the ship for the period of charter-party.[295] Where an agent was appointed by a shirt manufacturer as a canvasser and traveller for five-year period to sell such goods as may be forwarded to him and the principal's factory was burned down by a chance fire while there were still three years for the agency to go; the principal never resumed business and ended the agency, he was held liable in damages as the agency seemed to have been created for a definite term.[296]

An agency was deemed to have ended automatically by operation of law when a war broke out between the two countries to which the principal and agent respectively belonged. This is so because "agency as a contract is determined by any event which terminates a contract."[297]

Revocation is subject to the following conditions:

1. Revocation operates prospectively (s.204)

Even where the agent has partly exercised his authority, the principal may revoke it for the future. But it is irrevocable "as regards such acts and obligations as arise from acts already done in the agency". Where, for example an agent has been appointed to buy something for the principal and he has purchased it by involving his personal liability, his authority cannot be revoked.[298] The following illustration are appended to Section 204.

(a) A authorises B to buy 1,000 bales of cotton on account of A, and to pay for it out of A's money remaining in B's hands. B buys 1,000 bales of cotton in his own name, so as to make himself personally liable for the price. A cannot revoke B's authority so far as regards payment for the cotton.

(b) A authorises B to buy 1,000 bales of cotton on account of A, and to pay for it out of A's money remaining in B's hands. B buys 1,000 bales of cotton in A's name, and so as not to render himself personally liable for the price. A can revoke B's authority to pay for the cotton.

Where the agent carries on business even after his authority has been revoked by the principal, the latter cannot have any claim to remuneration for a period after the revocation. He can, however, claim compensation for wrongful dismissal. He may even restrain his principal from appointing any other person in his place if there was a restrictive covenant to that effect.[299]

2. Notice precedent to revocation(S. 206)

Where an agency has been created for a fixed period, a reasonable notice would be necessary to terminate it. The length of notice will depend, among other things, upon the length for which the agency has continued. Thus, the Privy Council has held that " the notice of 3 1/2 months given by the respondents was inadequate to determine an agency which had lasted for nearly 50 years, under which a very large business had been built up, and great expense incurred by the agents".[300] Their Lordships would have accepted without question that two years was reasonable notice. In a Madras case reasonable notice for premature determination was not given. The agent was earning Rs 4000 per month. The court allowed Rs 12,000 as compensation in lieu of reasonable notice which should at least have been for three months.[301]

3. Liability to compensate (Ss. 205-206)

205. Compensation for revocation by principal, or renunciation by agent — Where there is an express or implied contract that the agency should be continued for any period of time the principal must make compensation to the agent, or the agent to the principal, as the case may be, for any previous revocation or renunciation of the agency without sufficient cause.

206. Notice of revocation or renunciation — Reasonable notice must be given of such revocation or renunciation; otherwise the damage thereby resulting to the principal or the agent as the case may be, must be made good to the one by the other.

If the agency is determined without reasonable notice, "the damages thereby resulting to the agent must be made good" by the principal. Where an agency has been created for a fixed period, compensation would have to be paid for its premature for a period of five years. The function of the agent was to sell "any shirts or other goods manufactured or sold" by the principal. After two years, the principal's action against him for breach of contract succeeded. The decision went by the fact that the agency was not merely for things manufactured by the principal but also for things sold by him.[302]

The liability to pay compensation does not arise where the agency is not for a fixed period. The Madras High Court did not allow any compensation to the agent for the unilateral termination of an agency which, though created without any stipulation for its duration, has lasted from 1952 to 1964. [303] Thus, no compensation is payable in the following case:

(1) Where the agency has not been created for any definite period.

(2) Where, though created for a specified length of time, reasonable notice for its termination has been given or the termination is otherwise based upon a sufficient cause.

1. Agency coupled with interest [S. 202]

In certain circumstances, however, an agency becomes irrevocable. This happens when the agent is personally interested in the subject-matter of agency. Section 202 provides:

S. 202. Termination of agency, where agent has an interest in subject-matter — Where the agent has himself an interest in the property which forms the subject-matter of the agency cannot in the absence of an express contract, be terminated to the prejudice of such interest.

Illustrations

(a) A gives authority to B to sell A's land, ad to pay himself out of the proceeds, the debts due to him from A. A cannot revoke this authority nor can it be terminated by his insanity or death.

(b) A consigns 1000 bales of cotton to B, who has made advances to him on such cotton and desires B to sell the cotton, and to repay himself, out of the price, the amount of his own advances A cannot revoke this authority, nor is it terminated by his insanity or death.

In the well-known case of Smart v. Sanders[304] WILDE C J stated the rule thus: "Where an agreement is entered into on a sufficient consideration, whereby an authority is given for the purpose of securing some benefit to the donee of the authority, such an authority is irrevocable, This is what is usually meant by an authority coupled with an interest, and which is commonly said to be irrevocable," The simplest case of such agency occurs when the principal owes something to the agent and authorises him to sell the principal's goods and pay himself out of the sale proceeds. But an authority to pay the debts which the principal owes to some third person does not make the agency irrevocable. In a case before the Madras High Court, a person was entitled to be maintained out of the income of a property. The authority was held to be not revocable. In another case before the High Court, in consideration of advances made the plaintiff, all the properties of a division were given over to him on lease for 18 years with authority to receive rents. That was held to be an authority coupled with interest and, therefore, irrevocably Thus the essence of the matter is that "[T]he agent has, as it were, bought his authority in order to endure the payment of a debt due from the principal" Where the promoter of a company was given an authority by an underwriter that 1,000 shares may be allotted to him if they are not taken up by the public, he was not subsequently permitted to withdraw that authority. It was given for consideration. [305]

An agency of this kind is to even terminated by the principal's death. A principal owed a sum of money to his agent and gave him an accepted bill of exchange with an authority to fill the drawer's name. The principal died before the agent could complete the bill. His authority to fill in the drawee's name was held to be not terminated. [306] But the matter is not free from controversy. For, in *Watson v. King*[307] Lord ELLENBOROUGH said: "How can a valid act be done in the name of a dead man?" Commenting upon the decision Powell says: The decision overlooks the fact that an authority coupled with an interest is really a transfer of property." [308] An authority coupled with interest is also not determined by the principal's insolvency.[309]

But the doctrine of agency coupled with interest is not without qualification. In the first place, the interest of the agent must exist at the time of the creation of the agency. "[T]his doctrine apples only to cases where the authority is given for the purpose of being a security or....as a part of the security; not to cases where the authority is given independently and the interest of the donee of the authority arises afterwards, and incidentally only."[310] This statement of the law occurs in *Smart v. Sanders*. In this case, goods were consigned to a factor for sale and he subsequent made advances to his principal on the credit of the goods. It was held that subsequent advance could not convert the agency into one coupled with inter that the authority to sell shall be no longer revocable, but such an effect will not arise independently of agreement."

Secondly "the test to be applied for finding out whether a power of attorney given to an agent is irrevocable or not is to see whether the primary object in giving the power was for the purpose of protecting or securing any interest of the agent. It the primary object was to recover on behalf of the principal the fruits of his decree and, in doing so, the agent's rights were also incidentally protected, then his power is revocable" Similarly, the prospect of earning a commission is not on interest for this purpose. Against a "mere arrangement that the plaintiff's salary should be paid out of the rents could not be regarded as giving to the agent interest in the property, the subject-matter of the agency, within the meaning Section 202" [310]

2. By renunciation by agent [S. 206]

An agent may renounce the business of agency in the same manner in which the principal has the right of renunciation. In the first place, if the agency is for fixed period, the gent would have to compensate the principal for any pervious renunciation without sufficient cause. Secondly, a reasonable notice of renunciation is necessary. Length of notice is to be determined by the same principals which apply to revocation by the principal. If the agent renounces without proper notices, he shall have to make good any damage thereby resulting to the principal.

3. Completion of business [S. 201]

An agency is automatically and by operation of law determined when its business is completed. Thus, for example, the authority of an agent appointed to see goods ceases to be exercisable when the sale is complete. He cannot afterwards alter the terms of the sale. But the Allahabad and Calcutta High Courts have held that agency is not terminated on the completion of the sale but continues until payment of the sale proceeds to the principal. [311]

4. Death or insanity [S. 201]

An agency is determined automatically on the death or insanity of the principal or the agent. [312].

5. Principal's insolvency [S. 201]

An agency ends on the principal being adjudicated insolvent.

6. On expiry of time

Where an agent has been appointed for a fixed term, the expiration of the terms puts an end to the agency, whether the purpose of the agency has been accomplished or not.

Effects of termination [S. 208]

208. When termination of agent's authority takes effect as to agent and as to third persons — The termination of the authority of an agent does not, so far as regards the agent, take effect before it becomes known to him, or so far as regards third persons, before it becomes known to them.

Illustrations

(a) A directs B to sell for him, and agrees to give, B five per cent commission on the price fetched by the goods. A afterwards, by letter, revokes B's authority. B, after the letter is sent, but before he receives it, sells the goods for 100 rupees. The sale is binding on A, and B is entitled to five rupees as his commission.

(b) A, at Madras, by letter, directs B to sell for him some cotton lying in a warehouse in Bombay, and afterwards, by letter, revokes his authority to sell, and directs B to send the cotton to Madras B after the second letter enters into a contract with C who knows of the first letter, but no of the second, for the sale to him of the cotton. C pays B the money, with which B absconds. C's payment is good as against A.

(c) A directs B, his agent, to pay certain money to C, A dies and D takes out probate to his will, B after A's death, but before hearing of it, pays the money to C, The payment is goods as against D, the executor.

As between the principal and the agent, the authority of the agent ends when he comes to know of the termination. Where, for example, the authority of an agent appointed to sell goods is revoked, but he sells the goods before receiving the letter of revocation, the sale is good.

But as regards third persons the agency does not terminate until they come to know of the fact of termination. Where, for example, an agent sells the principal's goods even after receiving notice revoking his authority, the sale is binding on the principal and the buyer gets a good title provided he did not know of the fact of termination.

Even when the agency is terminated by the death of the principal, the termination is effective only when it comes to the knowledge of the agent.

Section 210 provides that the termination of an agent' authority amounts to termination of all sub-agents appointed by him. Section 209 charges the agent with duty to protect his principal's interest where the principal has died or has become a person of unsound mind.

Agent's duty on termination [S. 209]

209 Agent's duty on termination of agency by principal's death or insanity — When an agency is terminated by the principal dying or becoming of unsound mind, the agent is bound to take, on behalf of the representatives of his late principal, all reasonable steps for the protection and preservation of the interests entrusted to him.

PRACTICE QUESTIONS

1. The defendant employed the plaintiff to find a tenant for his premises. While the plaintiff was telephoning to a prospective tenant X, a third person, overheard the conversation ascertained the locality from X, went to the premises where there was a "To let" board with address of the defendant and engaged the premises. The plaintiff claims his remuneration. Is the claim tenable?
2. A enters into a contract with B for buying B's motor-car as agent of C and without C's authority, B repudiated the contract before C comes to know of it. C subsequently ratified that contract and sues to enforce it. How would you decide?
3. A power of Attorney was given by A to B, his agent to present a document for registration. The Registrar was aware of the death of A and registered the document. Examine the position.
4. "The law which superadds the liability of the agent does not detract from the liability of the principal." Examine this statement, pointing out the circumstances in which the agent is personally liable, for contracts enter in to by him on behalf of the principal.
5. To what extent is the principal liable for an act done by the agent in excess of his authority? When is the agent personally liable?
6 A holds a lease from B, terminable on three months' notice. C, without B's authority, gives notice of termination to A. B ratifies the notice and files a suit for ejectment. Is B entitled to get a decree?
7. An agent, who was appointed by a power of Attorney borrowed money on a representation that the power gave him full authority to borrow. The agent produced the power, which did not authorise the borrowing but the lender, without reading it, relief on the agent's representation. Is the principal bound by the loan?
8. "The effect of a contract made by an agent varies according to the circumstances under which the agent contracted." Discuss.
9. At a sale by auction without reserve the auctioneer is instructed not to sell for less than a certain price. The auctioneer accepts the highest bond side bid which, however, is lower than that price. Is the auctioneer liable to the principal for his action?
10. A, not being authorised thereto by B, demands on behalf of B the delivery of a chattel, the property of B, from C, who is in possession of it. C refuses to deliver, Can B ratify the demand and render C liable of damages for non-delivery?
11. B, a broker at Calcutta, by the order of A, a merchant of Singapore, contracts with C for the purchase of 10 cakes of oil for A. Afterwards A refuses to receive the oil and C sues. B. B informs A, who repudiates the contract altogether. B defends but is unsuccessful and has to pay damages and costs and incurs expenses. Examine the liability of A to B for such damages. Costs and expenses.
12. X consigns goods to Y, merchant, for sale. Y, in due course, employs an auctioneer of goods credit to sell the goods of X and allows the auctioneer to receive the proceeds of the sale. The auctioneer becomes insolvent without having accounted for the proceeds. S seeks to hold Y responsible for the proceeds. Can he do so?
13. A directs B his agent, to pay a certain sum to C. A dies and D takes our probate late to his Will. After A's death but before hearing of it, B pays the money to C. Is the payment good against D?
14. P's name was forged by A to a joint and several promissory note for 20 purporting to be made by P and A in favour of X. In order to save A, P later signed the following memorandum: 'I hold myself responsible for a bill, dated November 7th for 20, bearing my signature and that of A. Examine the liability of P.
15. P Instructed A solicitor, to defend an action on his behalf, but become in insane after the action was beginning. Incongruence of P's insanity; in ignorance of P's insanity A entered an appearance; delivered a defence and took other steps in connection with the litigation. When the plaintiff learned of P's condition he got the proceedings struck out and then no sued out and then sued to recover his costs from A. Is A liable?
16. 'Ratification is tantamount to prior authority.' Explain pointing out the limitations to the principal.

17. Explain the exact scope of the principal's liability for the acts of his agent when the agent has acted: (i) with ostensible authority; (ii) in the course of his business
18. A entered into a contract with B for the sale of a pair of horses to him subject to the condition that X, B's agent, should certify that the horses were sound. A secretly offered X a certain sum (if the sale would be completed) by way of bribe. X, having accepted the offer of A, certified that the horses were sound. On coming to know of X's duplicity B refused to affirm the contract. Is A entitled to enforce the contract against B? Decide, giving reasons.
19. The defendant employed a firm of estate agents to sell his bungalow for him. One S. A member of the firm represented to the plaintiffs that 'any building society would lend Rs. 12,000 on it.' That is it was a property of considerable value. In fact, this was quite untrue as the bungalow has been underpinned several times in order to prevent it from falling down. The defendant knew that the bungalow was in poor condition, and he had not authorised S to make the representative, nor had he employed him with that end in view. S has no knowledge of the underpinning. The plaintiffs brought an action against the defendant for damages for the loss suffered though his fraud. Will they succeed? If yes, on what ground?
20. Define and distinguish 'sub-agent' and 'substituted agent.' Discuss the position of the agent, sub-agent principal where a sub-agent is (i) properly appointed and (ii) not properly appointed
21. A instructs B, a merchant, to buy a ship for him. B employs C, a ship survey on or of goods reputation, to choose a ship for A. C makes the choice negligently and the ship turns out to be unseaworthy and is lost. Who is liable to A for the loss of the ship?
22. Am at the request of a party. B purchased and sent certain goods to C, C appropriated the goods for himself and wrote to A that he would pay him the price in a few days. B was declared insolvent. A sued C of the price of the goods. Is C liable to pay A?
23. 'The essential characteristic of an agent is that he is invested wit ha legal power to alter his principal's legal relations with third parties: the principal is under a correlative liability to have his legal relations alterd.' Discuss.
24. I owned some cottages and consulted G. & Co., solicitors. She was seen by S, their managing clerk, who had authority to transact conveyancing business on behalf of his employers. S fraudulently induced L to sign deeds, which infact transferred the cottages to S With the help of the documents, S sold the cottages and absconded with the proceeds. L sued G. & Co., for the recovery of the price of the property. Will she succeed?
25. A enters into a contract with B to sell him 100 bales of cotton and afterwards discovers that B was acting as agent for C. Who is liable to A for the price of the cotton?
26. 'An apparent and ostensible agency is as effective as an agency deliberately created. Apearance and reality are one.' Comment?
27. H, the owner of a restaurant, sold the restaurant to F, who continued H as manager. W, who knew nothing of this transaction or of F, sold cigars to H for use of the restaurant. H had been expressly for bidden by F to purchase cigars on credit. Being unable to obtain payment from H, W sued F. If W entitled to recover form F.
28. 'The relation of principal and factor is a special form of agency as well as a special from of bailment. 'Amplify'.
29. Sanders, who was a corn factor, was entrusted by Smart with a certain quantity of wheat to sell on his behalf. Sanders subsequently advanced the sum of 3,00 to Smart, which Smart failed to repay. Smart gave orders that the wheat was not to be sold. Notwithstanding this Sanders sold it to secure his advance, In the action against him Sanders pleaded that the agency was irrevocable. Decide.
30. Delegates non protest delegate (a delegate cannot further delegate). Discuss the implications of this maxim in relation to Agency and state the exception to the rule.
31. Z instructs his lawyer in another town to engage an estate agent to sell his house in that town. Accordingly, the lawyer selects B, the leading a goods price. But B delays to remit the purchase amount to Z and meanwhile becomes insolvent. Z hold has lawyer responsible for the loss. How would you decide? State your reasons.
32. Z, a wholesale cloth dealer, appoints Y as his agent for the sale of cloth on the basis of 5 per cent commission on the sales done by him. Y had an agreement with his principal Z that he could retain part of the sale amount of goods to adjust the commission due to him. Z terminates the agency of Y. Y refuses to hand over the cloth in his possession to Z and claims that he is vested with authority coupled with interest and that the agency could not be terminated. How would you decide?
33. 'A principal has the power to revoke the authority of the agent, but he does not have the right to do so. Explain and illustrate the truth of this statement.
34. A, who had contracted to construct a building, borrowed money from B. As security for the loan, A gave B a power-of-attorney, authorizing him to collect and receive all money due under the contract. Late A revoked the

power-of-attorney and demanded money due under the contract, B also demanded the money. Who should get it, and why?

35. 'No one can become the agent of another person except with the will of that other person." Examine the truth of this statement.
36. A was running a way-side hotel. At 1 a.m., B applied and was received as a guest in the hotel and paid Rs. 10 for a room to which he was taken by a man who appeared to be in charge. B handed over Rs. 5,000 in bank notes to the man for safe-keeping by the hotel proprietor. The man gave B a receipt for the money signed by him for and on behalf of A. In the morning, B presented the receipt to A and demanded back his money, when learnt that the man was not in the employ of A and had no authority to receive the money. The man having disappeared, is B entitled to reverser the money form A?
37. The conductor of a bus, who had temporarily taken over the wheel from the bus driver, injured A, a passerby, by his negligent driving. A claims damages from the bus company, Will he succeed? Give reasons.
38. Explain how agency may arise: (i) by implication: (ii) by estoppel and (iii) by necessity.
39. D, a carrier, discovers that a consignment of tomatoes owned by E has deteriorated badly before the destination has been reached. He therefore sells the consignment for what he can get: this is about a third of the market price for good tomatoes. E has now sued D for damages D claims he was an agent of necessity. Advise him.
40. In what circumstances may a person ratify a contract made on his behalf but without his authority?
41. 'An apparent or ostensible agency is as effective as an agency, deliberately created.' Explain this proposition.
42. A asks B to sell his cycle in the market. A directs B not to sell it below Rs. 100 and in any case not to sell it to C. Disregarding both the directions, B sells the cycle to C for Rs. 80 only. What are the rights of A against B and C?
43. A enters into a contract with B to sell him 100 bales of cotton. A afterwards discovers that B was acting as an agent for C. What are the rights of A against B and C?
44. "He who does anything by another does it himself." Explain
45. A holds a lease from B terminable with three months' notice. C on behalf of B, but without his authority, gives notice of the termination of the said lease of A. B ratifies the notice and seeks to eject A. Will he succeed?
46. A appointed B as agent for sale of coal for a period of seven years. After some time, A had to close his colliery and so he could not supply and could to B. Can B sue A for compensation for premature termination of agency? Discuss.
47. "Agency in law connotes an authority or capacity in one person to create legal relations between a person, occupying the position of principal and third parties."

    Critically examine the concept of "agency". Explain the duties of an agent to Principal. Also point out the difference between a 'contract of sale' and a 'contract of agency for sale'.
48. Certain millers were appointed licences by the Government to buy wheat at a fixed price and to sell the same to particular persons at a price fixed by the Government. The said millers received commission for their labour. Did the Relationship of principal and agent exist between the Government and the said millers? Explain with reason.
49. "In order to constitute agency, it is not necessary to have a formal agreement. The test of agency is whether the person is purporting to enter into the transaction on behalf of the Principal or not."
50. Bhikam was appointed as an agent for the Government of India to procure paddy in Sri Lanka. He was to have full responsibility for getting it milled at one of the mills in Tamil Nadu specified in the letter of appointment of agency and was to deliver an equivalent amount of rice to such Governments as was directed by the Government of India.

    Was Bhikam agent both for procuring paddy as well as for getting it milled?
51. P represents to Q that he (P) is acting as agent for R. Relying on that representation Q delivers goods to P as buyer. Is there a valid contract between P and Q? Does any property pass he (P) make a valid sale or a valid pledge *vis-a-vis* those goods?

References

1. Bowslead: On Agency (14th Ed.) 1976 p.1. London, Sweet and Maxwell
2. See v. G. Ram Chandran: Law of Agency; 1985 Ed.Easteren Book Company, Lucknow
3. See Simpson "The analysis of legal concepts" (1964) 80 L.Q.R. 35
4. Bow Stead: *Op. cit* p.3
5. Bowstead *op. cit* p.4
6. Bowslead *Op. cit* p.4.
7. Bow slead p.5, Ltd Powell pp. 148-149. how of Ageney, London, Ser Isac, pitman and sons Ltd seeond Edition 1961.
8. Powell *op cit* pp 148-149

9. vG. Ram Chandran *op. cit* p2
10. *op. cit* p.3
11. Chancy v Maclow (1829) Ch. D. 691
12. Lakshmi Narayan Ram Gopal & Sons v. Hyderabad Government AIR 1954 SC 364.: Ram Chandran *op. cit.* p.6
13. Lord Halsbury: Mac Fisheries v. Harisison 1924 LJKB 811.
14. Moorgate Mercantile Co. Ltd. v. Twitchings, (1975) 3 All ER 314
15. Keppel v. Wheeler (1927) 1 K.B. S 77; Burchell v. Goweir & Blackhouse Collieries Ltd. 1910 A.C. 614, 625.
16. Finacnings v. Stimsion (1962) WLR 1184.
17. Bare Lays Co Ltd. v. Roberts (1954) WLR 1212
18. Repidaman v. Surinder Kumar, AIR (1959) ISI, ER.
19. Kalyan Ji Kumar Ji v. Trika Sheo Lal, AIR (1938) Nag. 254.
20. Sukumari Gupta v. Dhivendra Nath Roy, AIR 1941 Col 643
21. Krishna v. Ganpati AIR 1955 Mad 648.
22. Lakshmi Narain Ram Gopal v. Hyderbad Government AIR 1954 SC 364.
23. Brown v. Andrew 1849 LJ Q.B. 153.
24. Raghubar Dyal v. Piare Lal AIR 1933 1 ALL 93
25. VG. Ram Chandran *op cit* p-21.
26. Phinpton v. Binkinshow, 1908, 2 K.B. 572 CA
27 Burnard v. Haggis (1803) 14 c BN 45.
28. Chitty: Vol I.p. 22 1977 Ed.:Vol II p.6 1977 Ed.
29. Sukumari Guptaa v. Dhirendra Nath Roy, AIR 1951 Col 643.
30. H. Pruthemene & Cov Hamel & Hardy Ltd. AIR 1925 Col 161.
31. VG. Ram Chandran op. cit p.24
32. Shephard v. Cartwright 1953 Ch. 728
33. Srivilas v. Tinnevelly Municipal Council, 106 IC 334.
34. Union of India v. Firm Ram Gopal, AIR 1960, All. 672 at 682.
35. Jai Prasad v. Chartered Bank of India etc. AIR 1927 Lah. 562
36. Ghambhir Mullv Indian Bank Ltd. AIR 1963 Cal. 163 at 169-70.
37. Khubchand v. Chitter Mall AIR 1931 All. 372.
38. Hari Singh v. Secretary of State AIR 1932 Lah 34 at 35.
39. (Firm) Devi Sahai Ramjidas v Tirath Ram, AIR 1923 Lah 473 at 474.
40. R.L. Rhakna v. Simla Banking and Industrial Company Ltd. AIR 1959 Punj 100.
41. Visvanathan v. Tiffin's Barytas Asbestos and Paints Ltd. MLJ 346 at 356.
42. Government of India v. Janunadkar, AIR 1960 Pat. 19 at 25.
43. Panna Lal v Commissioner of Sale Tax, AIR 1956 All 710.
44. Ganesh Export and Import Co. v Mahadeilal Nathmal, AIR 1956 Cal 188.
45. K. Rama Krishna Rao v. Province of Madras AIR 1952. Mad 718 at 772. 718-to 772.
46. Fowter v. Hollins 1872 LRQB 616 at 623.
47. Union of India v. Satyananda, AIR 1963 Ori 17 at p. 18
48. Union of India v. Lallan Prasad Singh, AIR 1963 Pat 216 at p.217.
49. Hari Singh v Secretary of State, AIR 1932 Lah 34.
50. Benares Bank Ltd. v. Ram Prasad AIR 1930 All 573.
51. Khubchand v. Chittar Mal AIR 1931 Al 372.
52. Maloji Rao Narsingha Rao v. Keshav Moreshwar, AIR 1939 Bom 126.
53. Madura Coy. u. vP.C. Xavier AIR 1931 Mad. 115.
54. Goenka Lotton Spinning and Weaving Mills v. Duncun Stration & Co. AIR 1938 Lah 277.
55. Asghar Ali Khan v. Khurshed Ali Khan (PC) (1902) 24 All 27, 37.
56. Gulab Singh v. Punjab Zamindara Bank Ltd., AIR 1942 Lah 47.
57. Holmes Wilson & Co. Ltd. v. Bata Kristo De, AIR 1927 Cal 668.
58. Devi Sahai Ram ji Das v. Tirath Ram, AIR 1923 Lah 473.
59. Godde Venkatrayudu v. Anumlu, AIR 1937 Mad 810.
60. Sarabhai & Co. v New Swadeshi Mills, 8 Guj LR 345.
61. Shalagram Jhaj Jharia v. Natronal Co. Ltd. (1965) 69 CWN 369
62. Hira Mills Ltd. v. Commissioner of incometex (1965) 57 ILR 103 Bo; AIR (1959) SC 1070.
63. R.L. Khanna v. Simla Banking and Industries Co, AIR 1959 Punj 100.
64. Maria Kutty v. Chaladean Syrian Syrian Bank Ltd. Trichur, AIR (157) Tr.
65. Union of India v. Ram Gopal Hukum Chand AIR (1960) All772.
66. Dharangada Trading Co (P) Ltd. v. Commissioner of Income Tax Bombay ILR 1965 Guj 215.
67. Ganapati Alluraiah v. State of A.P. , AIR (1963) AP 394.; of bid relied on AIR 1946 AP 472 and 1924 AC 177.
68. Harpool Chand Ganeshi Lal v. Kishori Lal Jagannath Prasad, ILR (1961) 11 Raj
69. Harbhagwan Ram Lal v. Punjab & Pepsi Finances Ltd. AIR Punjab and Hariyana, p. 340.
70. Parashar Singh v Hindustan Maganese Mines Ltd. 1968 MPLJ 846.
71. Harichand Madan Gopal v. State of Punjab, AIR 1973 SC 381.

72. Kuchwar Lime and Stone Co. v. Dehri Rohlas Light Ry (1969) SCR 359; AIR 1969 SC 193.
73. S.N. Barick v State of W.B., AIR 1963 Cal 79 at 82.
74. Mohanlal v. H.H. Sawai Man Singhji, AIR 1962 SC 73 at p. 76.
75. Messrs S. Laxmi Ginning & Oil Mills v Amrit B. Co. Ltd., AIR 1962 Punj 56 at pp. 58, 59.
76. K.G. Mukherji v. Raj Kiran Chandra, 42CWN 1212.
77. Currimbai v. Ahmed Ali, AIR 1939 Bom 91.
78. Satyanarayana v State of Madras, 1955 Andh W.R. 83.
79. Craff v Evans, (1932) 1 KB 6 (C.A.)
80. State of Mysore v. Mysore Spinning and Mfg. Co. AIR 1958 SC 1002-1005.
81. (1921) 63 IC 521 (PC)
82. Muhammad Shafi v. Fazal Din, AIR 1930 Lah 1062.
83. P. Basava v. G. Narasimhalu, AIR 1927 Mad 1 (FB)
84. Dentish Asiatische Bank v. Hiralal Burdhan & Sons, AIR 1919 Cal 1078.
85. Khulna Loan Co. Ltd. v. Jahir Goldar 24 IC 209
86. Kuchwar Limestone Co. v. Secretary of State AIR 1936 Pat 372 , 376
87. Totaram v. Ram Lal, 54, All 897
88. Motilal Dass v. The Eastern, Mortgage Agency Co. Ltd. AIR 1921 PC 118
89. Mahesh Chandra Bose v. Radhakrishna Bhattacharya, (108) 12 CWN 28.
90. New India Rubber Works (P) Ltd. v. Oriental Fire and General Insurance Co. (1969) 1 Lah LJ 153; refers to AIR 1962 Cal 625.
91. Kotharda Raman K. R. v. Commissioner of Income tax, AIR Mad 143 ; relies on AIR 1964 SC 364.
92. Rajeshwari Mills Ltd. v. State of Madras, AIR 1964 Mad 162.
93. Mediator Co. Ltd. v. The State of W.B.
94. State of Mysore, Mysore Spinning and Mfg. Co. Ltd. AIR 1958 SC 1002.
95. Nani Gopal Swami v. Abdul Hamid Chowdhury, AIR 1959 Ass 200.
96. Ramgopal Naicker v. Muthu Krishna Iyer, AIR 19578 Mad 1. Dissents from 58 Bom 505.
97. Raja Ram Jaiswal v. Ganesh Parshad, AIR 1959 All 29.
98. F.&v Merchant & Co. v. Pura Golaknath Coal Coy., AIR 1960 Pat 364, relies on (1955) 1 All ER 180. Distinguishes (1914) 3 KB 1272.
99. Govt. of India v. Jumnadhar Rungta , AIR 1960 Pat 19.
100. State of Madras (now Andhra Pradesh) by Collector W. Godavari v. Sri Jayalakshmi Rice Mill, AIR 1959 Andh Pra 352.
101. F & v Merchuant Union v Imporvement Trust Delhi, AIR 1957 SC 344 at 351-352.
102. Shalagram Jhajharia v. National Coy, Ltd., 69 CWN 369; See also AIR 1963 Pat 407.
103. S.N. Barick v. State of W.B., AIR 1963 Cal 79.
104. Srinivas Gopikissen Badruka v. State of Andhra Pradesh, (1962) 13 STC 303 (SC).
105. Lakshmi Ginning and Oil Mills v. Amrit Banaspati Co. Ltd. AIR 1962 Punj 56.
106. Mineral Development Ltd. v. State of Bihar, AIR (196c)[2] Pat 443 relies on AIR 1938 PC 295.
107. Alapati Ramamurthi G. Krishnamoorthy & Co. v. J. Ramanujam, AIR 1961 Andh Pra 408.
108. Srilal Agarwalla v. State of Orissa, ILR 1961 Cut 709; relies on AIR 1959 SC 887.
109. Modi Vanaspathi Mfg. Co. v. K.J. Mills, AIR 1969 Cal 497; follows AIR 1967 SC 151.
110. Weaver Mulls v. Balki's Ammal; AIR 1969 Mad 462 at p. 469 per Veerasami, J.
    3rd Edition, Vol. 6, para 194.Varsha Eng. P. Ltd. Vijay Traders Baroda, AIR 1983 Guj 66.
111. Shaikh Pir Bux v. Kalandi Poti Poo, (1968) 2 SCR 563: AIR 1970 Sc 1988.
112. Navandas Karsondas v S.A.K., (1977) 3 SCC 247, 255 (1977) 2 SCR 341' AIR 1977 SC 774.
113. R.C. Fhakkar v. Gujrat Housing Board, AIR 1973 Guj 34.
114. AIR 1951 SC 144: 1950 SCR 979: (1951) 21 Comp Cas: 53 Bom LR 472.
115. See also illustration (d) to Section 212.
116. Section 212. See illustrations appended to the u/section.
117. Ireland v. Livingston, (1872) 27 LT 79.
118. See Trojan & Co. v. Nagappa Chettiar, 1953 SCR 786: hAIR 1953 SC 235.
119. Heys v Tindall (1861) 1 B & S 296. Baxter v. Gapp & Co Ltd. (1939) 2 KB 27. AIR 1951 SC 144:1950 SCR 979: (1951) 21 Comp Cas 53 Bom LR 472.
120. Jayabharathi Corpn v. SUPNSNR Nandar, (1993), Sup I SCC 401: AIR 1992 SC 596.
121. Section 214; Keppel v. Wheeler (1927) 136 LT 203.
122. Sinclair Freight and Chartering Consultants P. Ltd. v. Fiel Traders, AIR 1987 Cal 201. For another case of failure of agent to follow instructions see Fersikringselshapet Vasta v Butcher (1986) 2 All ER 488 QBD.
123. Shankerlal v. State Bank of India, AIR 1987 C 129
124. Armstrong v. Jackson, (1916-17) All ER Rep 1117: (1917) 2 KB 822 (1878) 8 Ch D 828.
125. Harrington v. Victoria Graving Dock Co (1878) 3 QBD 549. Also Industries and General Management Co v Lewis (1949) 2 All ER 573.
126. Reading v. The King, (1951) AC 507.
127. Andrews v. Ramsay & Co. (1903) 2 KB 635. The Priniple of these cases is incorporated in Section 216 The following illustration is appended. A directs B, his agent, to buy a certain house for him. B tells A it cannot be bought and buys the house for himself. A may, on discovering that B has bought the house, compel him to sell it to A at the price he gave for it.

128. Bentley v. Craven, (1853) 18 Beav 75: 104 RR 373; Damodar Das v . Sheoramdas, (1970) 29 All 730
129. Shipway v. Broadwood, (1899) LT 11: (1899) 1 QB 369.
130. Novdisk Insulin Laboratorium v. CL Bencard, (1953) CH 430, Aas v Benham, (1967) 2 Ch 244 (CA) For accountability of a pretended agent see Phipps v. Boardman, (1967) 2 AC 46. For the position of an agent drawing commissio from both sides see Fullwood v Hurley, (1928) 1 KB 498.
131. LS Harris Trustees v. Power Packing Services (1970) 2 Lloyd's Rep 65. The agent can also be restrained by means of an injunction from disclosing confidence. Anton Piller KG v. Mfg. Processes Ltd. (1976) Ch 55, Burden of proving breach of duty is on the principal , Gokal Chand Jagannath v. Nand Ramm Das Atma Ramm, (1939) AC 106.
132. As a part of the obligation to render accounts the agent has to produce voucher in support of expenditure incurred by him. See S Paul & Co v. State of Tripura AIR Cal 378.
133. AIR 1967 SC 333.
134. State of Tamil Nadu v. Alagir Subramanian, AIR 1988 Mad 248.
135. There is no right to demand accounts where the claimant is not an agent but an independent contractor Dalmia Cement (Bharat) Ltd. v. TV Omen, 1987 Reports 8 Ker 588; Saroj Kapur v Nitin Castings Ltd. AIR 1987 Delhi 149.
136. Summan Singh v. National City Bank of New York, AIR 1952 Punj 172:ILR 1952 Punj 189.
137. Mohinder v. Mohan, AIT 1936 All 188' Union of India v. Amar Singh (1960) 2 SCR 75: AIR 1960 SC 233 ILR (1960) Punj 536.
138. Moon v. Wime Union, (1837) 43 RR 802.
139. Mason v. Joseph (1804) I Smith KB 406.
140. Union of India v Mohd. Nazim (1980) 1 SCC 284.
141. A person who was appointed as a sole agent was held to have no authority to delegate. John Mc Cann & CovPour[1974] 1 WLR 1673.
142. (1931) 145:T 51.
143. Raghunath Prasad v. Sewa Ram, AIR 1980 All 15.
144. Nesukhdas v. Birdichand (1917) 19 Bom LR 948. Summan Singh v. National City Bank of New Yorki, AIR 1952 Punj 1952 Punj 172: ILR 1952 1952 Punj 189.
145. (1931) 145 LT 51
146. AIR 1952 Punj 172: ILR 1952 Punj 189.147.
147. Supreme Court in Qamar Shaffi Tyabji v. Commr, Excess Profits Tax 19 3 SCR 546: AIR 1960 SC 1269, where a person named as an agent for the companby with the approval of the board of directors was held to be a substituted agent; Aggarwal Chamber of Commerce Ltd. Ganpat Rai Hira Lal (1958) SCR 938: AIR 1958 SC 269, privity of contract established.
148. (1924) All ER Rep 815.
149. Boston Deep Sea Fishing Co v. Ansell, (1888) 59 LT 345.
150. Seller v. London County Newspapers (1951) 1 All ER 554.
151. Ayyanath Chetty v. Subramania Iyer (1923) 45 Mad LJ 409 . The court relised upon the following statement of Lord ESHER in Peacock v Freeman, 4 TLR 541: "Land Could only be said to have been sold whe the conveyance was complete, not when there was a mere contract to sell."
152. Sheikh Farid Baksh v. Hargulal Singh, AIR 1937 All 46. See also Saraswati Devi v Moti Lal, AIR 1982 Raj 108 1982 Raj LR 251, where the commission was payable to an estate agent as and when he introduced a ready and willing customer, but the principal refused to sign the agreement, commission to the agent allowed. The court followed Abdulla Ahmed Animendra Kissen Mitter, 1950 SCR 30: AIR 1950 SC 15: 1950 SCJ 153 and Jaques v Lloyd D George (1968) 1 WLR 625; Alpha Trading Co v Dunn-Shaw Patten Ltd (1981) 2 WLR 169 (CA)
153. (1863) 14 CB (NS) 681: 8LT 503: 11 WR 834: 32 LJCP 261.
154. Vasanji Mooli v. Karsondas Tejpal, AIR 1928 Bom 270.
155. (1876) CPD 505.
156. See Alpha Trading Co v. Dunn-Shaw Patten Ltd. (1981) 2 WLR 169 (CA) where the agent introduced a customer ready and willing to buy, but the principal refused to complete the sale, the agent was allowed his commission: Saraswati Devi v Moti Lal, AIR 1982 Raj 108: 1982 Raj LR 251, the agent introduced a ready and willing customer who offered a cheque in part payment, the principal refused to sign; the agent was allowed to recover his commission. (1941) AC 108.
157. Chorely and Tucker, Cases on Mercantile Lw 118 (1962, 4th edn.)
158. For the purposes of his remuneration he has the right to demand accounts from the principal though there is no statutory provision on it, Narandas v. Papammal AIR 1967 SC 333, 335.
159. Sirdhar Vesanta Rao v. Gopal Raw, AIR 1940 Mad 299 at 301, quoting Lord Alverstion CJ in (1903) 2 KB 635 at 638.
160. Purushottam v Amruth Ghee Co, AIR 1961 AP 143.
161. Bombay Saw Mills Co. Re, ILR (1888) 13 Bom 314, where the claim of secretaries and treasure of a company, who had advanced money to the company, to be paid first out of the company's money was rejected, because they were not in possession of the money. This right does not confer any ownership on the agent. The money remains that of the principal. Turner Morrison & Co. Ltd. v. CIT, 1953 SCR 520 AIR 1953 SC 140;
162. Lord Ellenborough in Houghton v Mathew, (8 B & P 494 (A) described 'lien' to be the right in one man to retain that which is in his possession belonging to another untill certain demands of the person who is in possession are satisfied" . Cited by A H Khan J in Gopaldas v. Thakurdas, AIR 1957 MB 20 at 22.
163. Williams v Millidgton, (1788) 1 HB BI 81: 2 RR 724.
164. ILR (1888) 13 Bom 314
165. Who were a sort of managing agents, now banned.

166. Near East Relief v. King Chasseur & Co Ltd. (1930) 36 Ll LR 91, where an ordinary agent was not allowed to claim general lien.
167. AIR 1957 MBJ 20 at 22.
168. Gopaldas v. Thakurdas, AIR 1957 MB 20 at 22.
169. London and Joint Stock Bank v. Simmons (1892) AC 201.
170. Chidambaram Chettiar v. Tinnevelly Sugar Mills Co (1908) 31 Mad 123.
171. Ram Prasad v. State of MP (1969) 3 SC 24, 27, (1970) 2 SCR 677: AIR 1970 SC 1818, the right is excluded where the property is accepted for a special purpose.
172. Hichens v. Jackson, (1943) AC 266 HL.
173. AIR 1954 SC 500.
174. The Supreme Court had held in A Thangal Kunju Musaliar v. M Venkatachalam Potti, (1955): AIR 1956 SC 246, that there can be no agency for the commission of a crime. The wrongdoer would be personally liable.
175. Anglos Oveseas Transport Ltd. v. Titan Industrial Corpn, (1959) 2 Lloyd's Rep 152.
176. Ram Kumar v. Laksmi Narayan AIR Cal 157.
177. Hazarimal v. Khemchand, AIR 1962 Raj 86.
178. Federal Ins Ca v. Nakano Singapore P Ltd. (1992) 1 Current LJ 539 CA Singapore, liability for weak scaffolding.
179. Hazarimal v. Khemchand, AIR 1962 Raj 86.
180. Federal Ins Co v Nakano Singapore P Ltd. (1992) 1 Current LJ 539 CA Singapore, Liability for weak scaffolding.
181. Polestar Electronic (P) Ltd. v Addl Commr (1978) I SCC 636 sales made through branch agents regarded as sales of the principal.
182. JL Montrose, Actual and Apparent Authority, (1938) 16 Can BR 757 at 761. See further, Municipal Corpn, Delhi v. Jagdish Lal (1969) 3 SCC 389: (1970) 1 SCR 579: AIR 1970 SC 7.
183. A power of attorney can be executed by several persons in favour of one agent. See Syed Abdul Khader v Rami Reddy, (1979) 2 SCC 601: AIR 1979 SC 553 , where the Supreme Court explains the principles relating to interpretation of powers of attorney; Attwood v. Munnigs, (1827) 7 B & C 278. Reid v Rigby, (1827) 7 B & C 278. Weigall v Runciman (1916) 85 LJ KB 187.
184. Reckitt v Barnet, Preembroke & Slater (1929) AC 176; Midland Bank Ltd. v Reckitt, (1933) AC 1
185. Jacobs v Morris (1902) 1 Ch 816 ; Timblo Irmaos Ltd. v. Jorge Anibal Matos Sequeira (1977) 3 SCC 474.
186. (1904) 2 KB 10 (CA).
187. JL Montrose, Actual and Apparent Authoirty8 (1938) 16 Can BR 757 at 764.
188. (1959) 1 WLR 403: 1 All ER 689 (CA)
189. Foujdar Kameshwar Dutt Singh v Ghanshyamdas, 1987 Supp SCC 689, where the elder brother sold property and was held to be impliedly authorised by long acquiescence with open knowledge.
190. (1859) 7 CB (NS) 145 LJ (CP) 143: ILT 38.
191. Scott & Harton v Godfrey, (1901) 2 KB 726.
192. Foster v. Pearson (1835) 1 CM & R 489: 4 LJ Ex 120.
193. (1874) LR 7 HL 802: 44 LJ CP 362: 33 LT 544.
194. Sweeting v Pearee, (1859) 7 CB (NS) 449.
195. (1859) 7 CB (NS) 145: 29 LJ (CP) 143: ILT 38.
196. Howards v. Sheward, (1866) 2 CP 148 ; Brooks v Hassal, (1883) 48 LT 569; Brady v. Todd, (1861) 9b CB (NS) 592: 127 RR 797; Mullens v Miller (1882) 22 Ch D 194; Fenn v Harrison (1791) 3 TR 757.
197. Butwick v. Grant (1924) All ER Rep 274.
198. Drakeford v. Piercy (1866) 7 B & S 216.
199. 1950 SCR 30: AIR 1950 SC 15:" 1950 SCJ 153.
200. Hely-Hutchinson v. Brayhead Ltd.[1967] 3 All ER 98: (1968)I Comp LJ 263 at 267.
201. J.L. Montrose, Actual and Apparent Authority, (1938) 16 Can BR 757 at 765.
202. [1893] 1 QB 346.
203. Daun v Simmins, (1879) 41 LT 783.
204. Valapad Coop Stores Ltd v Srinevasa Iyer, AIR 1964 Ker 176.
205. Ishaq v Madan Lal, AIR 1965 All 34.
206. Cited by MATHEW J at 177 (8th edn. 1924.
207. Pickering v Busk, (1812) KB 15: 13 RR 364: 15 East 38.
208. [1904] 2 KB 10.
209. Panorama Developments (Guildford) Ltd v Fidelis Furnishing Fabrics Ltd. [1917] 1 WLR 440: [1971] 3 All ER 16, CA.
210. Hazard v Tredwell, (1722) 1 Stra 506.
211. (1907) 2 Ir R 462.
212. Borrowed from Hanbury, THE PRINCIPLES OF AGENCY, p 28 (1952 edn.).
213. Bailey & Whites Ltd. v House, (1915) 31 TLR 583.
214. Keooragang Investments v Richardson and Wrench, [1981] 3 WLR 439 PC.
215. (1919) 12 Ohio App 210.
216. [1971] 2 QB 711: [1971] 1 WLR 440: [1971] 3 All ER 16, CA
217. Dodsley v Varley, (1848) 12 QB 460.
218. Ryan v Sams, (1848) 12 QB 460.

219. Raj Bahadur Benilal Abir Chand v Kabulchand, ILR (1945) Nag 204.
220. ILR (1898) 26 Cal 701.
221. Jacobs v. Morris, [1902] 1 Ch 816.
222. Kamal Singh Deegar v Corporated Engineers Ltd, AIR 1963 Cal 454.
223. Sarshar Ali v. Roberts Cotton Assn. (1963) 1 SC 244 (Pak); Ram Pratab v. Marshall, ILR (1898 26 C 701; Moosa Bhoy v. Kristiah, AIR 1952 Hyd 79.
224. Armagas Ltd v. Mundagas SA. The Queen Frost, [1986] 2 All ER 585 HL.
225. Bains v. Ewing, (1866) 1 Ex. 320.
226. Ahammed v. Mammad Kunhi, AIR 1987 Ker 228.
227. Section 228.
228. Prembhai v. Brown, (1873) 10 BH C 319.
229. Avalpa Nayak v. Narsi Keshawji, (1871) 8 BHCAC 19.
230. Jani Nautam Lal Venishanker v. Vivekanand Coop Housing Society, AIR 1986 Guj. 162
231. Woolcott. V. Excess Insurance Co. Ltd. (1978) 1 Lloyd's Rep 163.
232. Stockton v. Mason; (1978) 1 Lloyd's Rep. 633.
233. There can be nc agency for wrongful acts. A thangal Kunju Musaliar v M Venkatachalam Potti, (1955) 2 SCR 1196: AIR 1956 SC 246.
234. Street, U/L Vol. 2, p. 454.
235. (1842) 3 CB 58.
236. [1936] 2 All ER 1039.
237. [1954] AC 333: (1954) 2 WLR 832: [1954] 1 All ER 909 HL.
238. (1840) 6 M & W 358: 55 RR 655.
239. For a critical analysis of this and contrary decisions see Patrick Devlin, Fraudulent Misrepresentation Division of Responsibility between Principal and Agent, (1937) 53 LQR 344.
240. [1952] 1 All ER 139 CA.
241. L C B Gower, Agency and Fraud, (1952) 15 Mod LR 232.
242. Ibid at 234.
243. Atlantic Die Casting v. Whiting Tubular Products Inc. 337 Mich 414: 60 NW 2d 174, reported in Stimpson and Lazar, Recent Cases and Materials And Business Legislations p. 131 (1955 Ed.).
244. Schultz v. La Goses City Railway Co. (1907) 133 wis 420.
245. Chicago City Railway Co. v Mc. Mohan (1882) 103 ILJ 485.
246. (1912) AC 716.
247. Under Section 235 as a protended agent. See Lewis v. Nicholson, (1852) 18 QB 502: 88 RR 683.
248. Universal Steam NavigationCo. Ltd v James McKelvie, (1903) 129 LT 595.
249. Gadd v. Houghton & Co. (1876) 35 LT 222.
250. Miller, Gib & Co. v. Smith & Tyre Ltd. [1917] 2 KB 141.
251. Tudor Marine Ltd. v. Trader Export, SA, [1976] 2 Lloyd's Rep 135; Miller, Gib & Co. v Smith & Tyre.
252. Tutika Basavraju v. Pary & Co. (1903) 27 Mad 315, See also Radhakrishna Srivadutta Tai v Tayballi Dawoodbhai, 1962 Supp (1) SCR 81, 101, 103: AIR 1962 SC 538; JS Holt & Moseley (London) Ltd v Sir Charles Cunningham Partners, (1950) 83 Llyod's Rep 141, where the contract did not show any contemplation of personal liability. Gopal Chandra Ghose v Orissa State Financial Corpn. AIR 1994 Ori 143, loaning agreement made by the Corporation as an agent of the State, the Corporation allowed to sue by itself without bringing in the State Government into the matter.
253. Bhojabhai v. Hayen Samuel, (1898) 22 Bom 754.
254. North-Western Provincess Club v. Sadullah, 91898) 20 All 497; Mackinon v. Lang. (1881) 5 Bom 584.
255. Southwell v. Bowditch, (1876) 1 CPD 374.
256. N & J Vlaspulas v. Ney Shipping Ltd. (1977) 1 Lloyd's Rep 478; (1977) 2 Lloyd's Rep 57.
257. Benton v Cambell Parker & Co. Ltd [1925] All ER Rep 187.
258. Shet Manibhai v. Bai Rupaliba, (1899) 24 Bom 166; Kalner v. Baxter, (1866) 2 CP 174; Union of India v. Chinoy Chablani & Co. AIR 1976 Cal 467.
259. Kendall v. Hamilton, (1879) 4 App Cas 50 ; Powell, THE LAW OF AGENCY p. 270 (2nd edn., 1961)
260. Kuttikrishan v. Appa Rao, (1926) 49 Mad 902: AIR 1926 U/C ad1213; Shamsuddin v Shaw Wallace & Co. (1939) Mad 282: AIR 1939 mad 520; Shivlal Motilal v Birdi Chand (1917) 19 Bom LR 370; The opinion is expressed in Pollock & Mulla, THE INDIAN CONTRACT AND SPECIFIC RELIEF ACTS, p. 71 (8th edn, 1957), ed by Setalved & Goodesson.
261. Addison v. Gandasequi, (1812)4 Taunt 574; Scarf v. Jardine, (1882) 7 App Cas 345; Clarkson Booker Ltd v. Andjel, [1964] 2 QB 775 (CA).
262. Shet Manibhai v Bai Rupaliba, (1899) 24 Bom 166, a mother representing herself to be the agent of his minor son, was held not liable as the other party already knew the principal's minority; Bheck Chand v. Prabhuji, AIR 1963 Raj 84: (1963) 13 Raj 84; Vairavan Chettar v. Avicha Chettar, (1915) 38 Mad 275.
263. Saffron Walden, Building Society v Rayner, [1880] 14 Ch D 406.
264. Oliver v. Bank of England, [1901] 1 Ch 652, 660; Rashdall v Ford, (1886) LR 2 EQ 750; Cherry v Colonial Bank of Austrasia, (1869) LR 3 P/c 24; Weeks v Property, (1873) LR 8 CP 427.

265. Sewdutt Roy Muskara v. Napapiet, (1907) 54 Cal 628; Nand Lal Roy v Gurupada Haldar, (1924) 51 Cal 588: 81 IC 721: Shree Shree Gopal Sridhar v. Shasibhushan, (1932) 60 Cal 111: AIR 1933 Cal 109 ; Nepal Food Corpn. v. U P T Import and Export Ltd., AIR 1988 Cal 283.
266. Ganpat Prasad v Sarju, (1911) 9 All LJ 8. (1857) 8 E & B 647: 27 LJ QB 215: 30 LT 209.
267. [1901] 1 Ch 344.
268. Starkey v. Governor of Bank of England (1903) 88 LT 244.
269. Weigoll v. Runciman (1916) 85 LJ KB 187.
270. Montgomeric v. United Kingdom Steamship Assn. [1891] 1 QB 370 at 371, per WRIGHT J.
271. Southwell v Bowditch, (1876) 1 CPD 374.
272. J Thomas & Co v. Bengal Jute Baling Co. AIR 1979 Cal 20.Evidence is admissible to show that the agent contracted on behalf of an undisclosed principal. See Feod. Drughom Ltd v. Rederriskt, [1918-19] All ER Rep 152.
273. (1710) Bull NP 42: Willes 400, 405- 406.
274. [1893] 2 QB 350 (CA).
275. (1887) 12 App Cas 271.
276. [1920] 3 KB 497.
277. [1926] Ch 932.
278. Humble v. Hunter, (1848) 12 QB 310 at 317.
279. Formby Bros v. Formby, (1910) 102 LT 116.
280. Fred Drughorn Ltd. v. Rderiaktieb Olaget Transatlamic [1919] AC 203.
281. (1882) 9 QBD 623.
282. Williams v. North China Insurance Co. (1876) ICPD 757
283. Hukum Chand Insurance Co. v. Bank of Baroda AIR 1977 Kant 204
284. Chishire and Fefoot; The Law of contract p. 405 (6th Ed.1964)
285. (1901) AC 240
286. Raja Rai Bhagwat Dayal v. Debi Dayal Sahu (1908) 35 IA at 58, Raghavachari v. Pakkiri Mohd. (1976) 30 Mad LJ 497 , 501
287. Trident General Insurance Co. Ltd. v Mc Nice Brothers Pty Ltd. Mar 31, 1987, 1987 LBL 378
288. Boston Fruit Co. v. Britirish and Foregin marine Insurance co. 1906 AC 336; Tiedamann & Leadermann Fieres , Re (1899) 2 Q B 66
289. Law Banque Jacques Curtior v. La Bangued d' Epargne. (1987) 13 App Cas 111; Maumgappa Chetti Official Assignee of Madras (1937),64IA 343 AIR 1937 PC 296 ; Brook v. Hook (1871) Exch 89
290. Cassin Ahmed v. Eusuf Hazi Azam (1916) 23 Cal LJ 453
291. (1848) 2 Ex. 167
292. (1861) 8 Moore IA 529, 554 PC
293. S. 199
294. Metrophlitan Asylum Board v. Mathews (1910) 2 KB 401; Williams v. North China Insurance Co. Ltd. v. Mc. Niece Brothers Pty Ltd. Mar 31, 1987: 1987 JBL 378
295. (1889) 41 Ch D 295
296. Section 88
297. (1931) 1 Ch 455
298. Rhodes v. Forwood (1876) 1 App Cas 256
299. L French & Co. Ltd., Leeston Shipping Co. Ltd. 1922 All ER Rep 314
300. Turner v. Goldsmith (1891) 1 QB S 44:(1891) AllER Rep 384
301. Stevenson & Sons Ltd. v. Akt. Fur Cartonnagen Industries (1917) IQ 842 Treitel, Law of contract 570 (5th Ed. 1979)
302. Kishni Devi v. State of Raj, AIR 1992 Raj 24
303. Hirihar Prasad Singh v. Kesho Prasad Singh AIR 19 Pat 68; Ibid; Decrowall International SAv Practicioners in Marketing Ltd., (1971) 2 All ER 216 (CA)
304. Sohrabji v. Oriented Government Security Assurance Co AIR 1946 PC 9
305. JK Sayani v. Brighat Brothers AIR 1980 Mad 162
306. Turner v. Goldsmith (1891) 1 QBS 44
307. Bright Brothers v. J.K. Sayani AIR 1976 Mad 55
308. (1848) 75 RR 849: (1948) SCB 895
309. Pestanji v. Matett 1870 BHCAC 10 ;Clerk v. Laurie, 1857 2H & N 197 Paliyankoton Kuruvan Param Bath & Chathu Kutti Nair v. Kundon Appa AIR 1932 Mad 70; Powell , the law of Agency 392 (2nd Ed. 1961) Hanan's Empress Gold Mining Co. Ltd. Re; Charmichael ex p. (1886) 75 LT 45
310. Palani v. Krishnaswami 1946 ILR 121.
302. Babu Ram v. Ram Dayal 189012 All 541.
303. Nasib Kaur v. Chandan Singh (1991) 99 Punj LR 216.

PART I

CONSUMER PROTECTION ACT, 1986

CHAPTER

20

Consumer Protection & Guidance

Importance of the consumer to the business has yet to be realised fully. Business makes profit only when goods are consumed or services utilised. This presupposes consumer existence. Business is entirely dependent on the consumer not only for its very survival but also for its growth.

Consumer movement

The problem of consumers have been felt and recognised with the growth of industrialisation and urbanisation and along with the rapid growth of industrialisation, new market techniques were developed which influenced the economic and social culture. The common law maxim "Caveat Emptor, ('let the buyer beware') which placed once on the buyer to protect his won interest, protected the seller against any action for damages sustained due to defects in goods. However, with the growth of laisse fair competition, it was accepted that the interest of buyer served best by free competition between sellers. With further increase in the volume of production and distribution, the problem of consumers became prominent and consumer groups started asserting their claims. Consequently, both an national and international level the consumer protection movement started.

Consumer seeks protection, advice and information when his rights are adversely affected. The shift from buyer beware to seller beware has increased the role of Government in promoting the consumer's right to safety, the right to be informed, the right to choose, the right to be heard, the right to redress and right to represent. These consumer rights constitute Consumer Bill of Rights. In 1962, President John F. Kennedy, in his consumer message, summed up these rights of consumers and paved the way for organised consumerism in the U.S.A. and all over the world.

Consumer Protection in India

In general, consumers are scattered over the country. They are highly disorganised. Individually, they have very weak bargaining power. They are not professional or shrewd buyers. Besides, in India, they have an additional handicap, namely, majority of consumers are ignorant and usually lack information to make intelligent purchases. In many cases, they are incompetent to protect their interests, particularly when they deal with fully organised, united and well-informed professional sellers. Above all, apathy, indifference and inertia of the public are the perpetual enemies and they are simply appealing. These are serious obstacles to the sound and sustained development of consumerism and consumer protection in India.

In India where the majority of consumer is illiterate and ill-informed, and has limited purchasing power and are not in a position to meet the basic necessities of life. A large number of non-essential, traders by means of unfair practices and deceptive methods, Competition in the market is often reduced to competition in advertising, as companies spend more and more money on exaggerated, misleading and deceptive advertising claims, rather than improving and functional features, making the distribution system more efficient or reducing the price.

In economics, it is said that the act of production is not complete until the commodity is in the hands of the ultimate consumer. All production is, in fact, for consumption directly or indirectly. It is true that consumption should be the sole end and purpose of all production. In a free market economy, it is said that consumer is the king. He communicates his decision or wish through price, every rupee representing a ballot paper and the prime regulator of our economic life. He rules the economy through pricing. He brings about the so-called optimum allocation of scarce economic resources through the all powerful mechanism of pricing governed by the impersonal and, therefore, impartial general relations of demand and supply.

In reality, consumer is not a king. At the most, he is a prince without a privy purse and is often indistinguishable from a serf or a pauper. He is the main sufferer of inflation, sometimes controlled or otherwise naked. He pays more and earns much less in the real terms. He is the one to suffer most from acute shortages (man-made or god-made) of essential commodities. He is the one who is often cheated and fleeced — even given shoddy and adulterated goods. Short weights and measures, deceptive packaging, misleading advertising, hoarding, profiteering and countless frauds committed by trade on the poor and innocent consumers clearly indicate gross exploitation of the consumer by industry, trade and by organised labour. By and large, during the last 25 years, the consumer in India has been a victim of Central Government's various policies. It resorted to enhancing from time to time excise duties and commodity taxes which heavily leaned on the consumer. Indirect taxes hit the consumers most particularly when they can be easily transferred to consumers in the form of price rise. In the seller's market, the producer can do so without any danger of reduction in demand. Heavy investment in capital goods industry and the neglect of consumer goods industry led to an era of scarcity, rising prices and misery for the consumer. Extraordinary finance for financing huge projects under planned economy was secured through deficit financing. Of all the taxes perhaps, inflation is the most ruthless and its impact on the low-income consumers is probably the highest. Above all, extraordinary growth of population in India further complicates the problem of distribution.

During inflation, we have a persistent rise in prices. When there is a labour dispute, wages and bonuses are increased and immediately employers and managements conveniently raise prices due to higher cost of production. If the price is controlled, they demand Government's sanction for a price hike or rise. In any event, the price spiral (rise) is in full swing and inflation is accentuated. The victim of inflation once again is the consumer.

The foregoing state of affairs incidentally happens to be the profile of Indian economic situation for the last thirty years and strongly emphasises the immediate need for consumer protection, consumer guidance and consumer education in India.

Unless there is a general awakening in the consumer-public, consumer movement and consumer guidance or protection cannot have firm and strong foundation. Consumer education assumes considerable importance in evolving a favourable climate for exercising the sovereign right to grumble, right to protest, right to demand justice and fair trade right to grumble, right to protest, right to demand justice and fair trade practices. Businessmen usually take full advantage of general apathy, indifference and helplessness on the part of the consumer and adopt anti-consumer policies to earn larger profits.

We have monuments to the unknown soldier, statues for martyrs, tablets for freedom fighters. But so far, in no country there is a single memorial for the conveniently forgotten man and the victim of our society — the poor and helpless consumer.

What is Consumer Protection?

Consumer protection is essential is essential for a healthy economy.

We need physical protection of the consumer, for instance, protection against products that are unsafe or endanger the health and welfare of consumer.

We need protection of the consumer against deceptive and unfair trade practices. Consumer must have adequate rights and means of redress against business malpractices and frauds.

Ecological and environmental effects of chemical, fertiliser or refinery complexes will have to be seriously considered because they pollute water, air and food and endanger human life. Consumer wants due protection against all types of pollution, he wants a healthy environment free from pollution.

We must have adequate protection of consumer public against the abuse of monopoly position and/or restrictive trade practices. Protection delayed is protection denied.

Greater and free competition in the market is of definite advantage to the consumer. Competition can reduce prices, enhance quality and stimulate innovation in product-mix and marketing-mix. Innovation means progress and progress means life, a prosperous life. Competition is the dispenser of justice to the consumer and producer alike.

Why Consumer Protection?

The `why' of consumer protection is evident at least in India.

Consumer has no voice in the product which is manufactured for his consumption. Hence, consumer naturally demands the existence of fair trade practices which would ensure physical safety when he consumes the product. Similarly, fair trade practices will enable him to get the real value for his money.

It is very difficult to effectively organize consumers in country as vast as India. The backwardness of people is a further obstacle to consumer organization.

A majority of the population is illiterate and ignorant.

Poverty, lack of education, lack of information, traditional outlook of indias to suffer in silence (considering poverty and misery as a god-given things-all these negative sides of our life have enabled unscrupulous businessmen to exploit consumers in India. To prevent this ruthless exploitation, we need a forceful well-organised consumerism or consumer movement coupled with Government support and patronage in the form of special legislation. Of course, legislation can protect consumers only when consumers themselves assert their rights and exert pressure on the producers, dealers and the Government. Then only the prevailing malpractice like profiteering, blackmarketing, hoarding, adulteration, short measures and weights, misleading advertisement, faulty packaging, mail-order frauds etc., can be cured or reduced to the minimum.

The march of science and technology has increased the difficulties of the consumer along with his opportunities of selection from a very wide variety of goods (many of them highly sophisticated and complicated). Increasing technical complexity of consumer goods, especially those containing machinery clearly points out that consumers (who are not professional buyers) cannot know the ins and outs of such goods. Rational choice between and among such goods would require the skills of amateur electrician, mechanic dietician, mathematician, etc. Marketing is now becoming increasingly impersonal (professional).

The consumer choice is influenced by mass advertising and other promotional devices, utilising highly developed art of persuasion. Commercial sources are the core of the existing information system. But consumers find that most advertising and promotion today are deceptive or misleading. Hence, consumer cannot know whether drug preparations meet the minimum standards of safety, quality and efficacy. He usually does not know whether one professed food has more nutritional value than another. He may not know whether the performance of a product will in fact meet his needs or whether the large economy size, or the best buy is really a bargain.

Consumers wish to meet producers as equals. They want value for money, reasonable quality, prices related to the cost of production, transport, etc. Too many producers are bringing out products that people do not really need any cannot afford. But aggressive advertising and salesmanship make people want the things. In many cases, people spend the money they otherwise need for food, clothing and shelter on gadgets that are not really needed. The advertising industry in the U.S.A. spent $ 150 per person per year (in 1978) to push up goods on consumers. The consumer wants protection against deceptive and misleading advertisements and sales promotion devices.

Therefore, in the present intricate and complicated market, he is just an amateur. In short, consumers do need protection and guidance under the present circumstances.

After evaluating the scope, need and significance of consumer protection, let us now deal with the alternative ways and means of securing reasonable consumer guidance and protection.

There are three agencies for ensuring consumer protection:

Self-help, i.e., consumer organisation itself.

Business, by self-regulation and by giving a fair deal to the retailers.

Government, by having special Acts and implementing those laws strictly. Mere legislation is not enough. More important is their enforcement not only in letter but also in spirit. The legislation ensures competition, provision of information to buyers, and regulation of unfair trade practices.

How To Provide Consumer Protection?

The consumer interest in the market place is the focus or the heart of enlightened marketing mix. The business and consumerism both aim at the protection of consumer interest-business through self- regulation and consumerism through self-help. Consumerism invokes Government assistance when business misbehaves and fails to fulfill special responsibilities.

In exchange relationship normally, we have only two parties: (1) Seller and (2) Buyer. However, in the modern market, the seller is organised and has professional skill, whereas the buyer is usually unorganised and amateur. Hence, we need consumer legislation and consumerism.

Consumer Legislation Consumer Projection in Marketing Place Business Consumerism (Self-Regulation) (Self-help)

If business morality is high and if moral values are at a premium, there is no reason why self-regulation by traders and their associations should fail to give meaningful guarantee or money back to consumers. In reality, the problem of consumer protection is bilateral. (1) Organised consumer movement inducing consumers to take intelligent interest in consumer democracy, and (2) Self- regulation and self-discipline by producers and traders. Government intervention takes place only to protect the weaker party in the market (consumer) and to prevent exploitation by the stronger party (businessmen).

It should be noted the consumer legislation is a rough substitute for self-regulation of business. It appears as a last resort, when consumerism is recognised as a shame on marketing. Consumer legislation offer insurance against business malpractice and ensures distributive justice to amateur consumers.

Consumer Ombudsman (Lokayukta)

What is the Consumer Ombudsman?

The Consumer Ombudsman (a Consumer Protection Agency) is the Commissioner for Consumers — a chief officer of Central Consumer Council appointed by the Government. He is in charge of enforcing and administering the consumer protection Acts. He can speed up legal processes in dealing with trade practices.

The aim of Fair Trade Practices Act is to protect consumers against misleading advertising, deceptive packaging, misbranding, mislabeling, false warranties and other undesirable commercial marketing, i.e., all activities undertaken in order to increase the sale of goods and services by greedy sellers.

The cleaning up of advertising, sales promotion and other marketing practices, which can be achieved with the aid of the consumer legislation, may in turn help to make it easier for consumers to make their decisions when buying goods and services.

The Consumer Ombudsman (at the Central and State levels) checks that advertising contains no misleading information about products, prices, quality, etc. The supervision of the Ombudsman covers all kinds of commercial marketing carried out by all business enterprises. He scrutinises advertisements in newspapers and periodicals and on packages, as well as direct mail advertising, outdoor advertisement, film radio and T.V. advertisements, etc.

Consumer Ombudsman protects consumers from undesirable conditions which may appear in the printed sales agreement forms which are used when capital goods such as household appliances, television sets, books, etc., are sold. For instance, these contracts may have small prints improperly favouring the seller at the cost of the buyer — a clause reserving the right of the seller alone to decide whether the goods sold are defective or there may be a price increase clause, giving unilateral right to the seller to raise the agreed price.

He tries to get the matter put right voluntarily, by discussing in with the seller or his representative, e.g., advertising agency.

If correction by a voluntary agreement is impossible, the case is referred to a special court dealing with unfair trade practices. The court's decision is final.

In matters of minor importance, the Consumer Ombudsman can himself issue 'cease and disist' order prohibiting a misleading marketing action.

Consumer Ombudsman is accessible to all consumers or their associations. In Sweden, we have Consumer Ombudsman since 1971 under the Marketing Practices Act and under the Act Prohibiting improper contract terms.

A consumer Ombudsman or a consumer protection authority (Lokayukta) can survey the whole field of consumer protection in consultation with consumer associations and take necessary steps for speeding up legal processes in dealing with trade malpractice. There is a compelling need for a through survey of the real as opposed to the theoretical protection offered to the consumer by present legislation. A Consumer Ombudsman may be the answer to our consumer problems in India. He can act as a statutory agency empowered to enforce genuine claims on behalf of Indian consumer.

The Act: An Historical Step

In India, until the advent of independence, there were hardly and laws which were directed to the protection of consumer interests. The Sale of Goods Act, the Drugs and Cosmetics Act did not directly deal with the subject of consumer interest. Under Constitution of India, fundamental right have been declared and procedure for the their enforcement has been laid down. Many civic and criminal statutes define and deal with the right of the citizens and courts and tribunal have been set up for remedying the wrongful acts done to them. However, in context of the growing needs of the citizens many problems relating to their routine necessities, do not find effective measure for verifying wrongful acts and for compensation due to consequent loss to them. For example, the supplier of adulterated or spurious articles of food can be prosecuted and punished but the victim or consumer will not get any compensation or awards for the damage or loss done to him.

Likewise, under Civil Procedure Code, a person may file suit for recovering the damages but due to complexities of the procedure delay in disposal and expensive litigation, such procedure was not considered desirable, particularly for the enforcement of the rights of the protection of the rights of the consumers who are the victim of the delay and negligence on the part of the supplier of goods or services and sustained personal loss while consuming goods or utilizing services.

After the report of Sachhan Committee, the Consumer Protection Bill, 1986 was introduced in the Parliament and received assent of the President on December 24,1986.

The Act became effective from January 7, 1987. It provided better protection of the interests of consumer and for establishment of consumer council and other authority for the speedy settlement of the consumer disputes and matters connected therewith.

Objects of Consumer Protection Act, 1986:

In the statement of objects and reasons, it is said that the Act seeks to provide speedy and simple redressal to consumer dispute, a quasi judicial machinery is sought to be set up at the District, State and Central levels. The quasi-judicial body will observe the principles of natural justice and have been empowered to give relief of a specific nature and to award, wherever appropriate, compensation to consumer, penalty for non compliance of orders given by the quasi-judicial body have also been provided.

The Act seeks to protect the consumers in the following respects. Section 6 of the Act spells out these object as follows:

1. The right to be protected against the marketing of goods and services which are hazardous to life and property.
2. The right to be informed about the quality, quantity, potency, purity, standard and price of goods to protect the consumer against unfair trade practices.
3. The right to be assured whenever possible, with regard to access to a variety of goods at the competitive prices.
4. The right to be heard and to be assured that consumer's interest will receive due consideration at the appropriate forums.
5. The rights to redressal against unfair trade practices of unscrupulous exploitation of consumers and,
6. The right to be consumer education.

(A) Protection against hazardous goods:

The act says that the consumer has a right to be protected against the marketing of those goods which are hazardous to life and property, e.g., gas cylinder, if not sealed and delivered properly, may cause injury to life.

There are many laws intended to safeguard these interests, e.g., Food Adulteration Act 1954, Besides there is provision for I.S.I. and Agmark in order to secure these interests.

But the problem is of honest and efficient enforcement of standards laid down in these laws.

Consumer Protection Act, 1986 provides protection to consumes from such goods if any how they have got place in the market and have caused and injury to consumer or his property.

Donoghue v. Steveson quotes where a bottle of drink sprang the remains of a dead shell to the fright of the consumer at a restaurant, who had already taken a part of the contents, aggravating her illness and the manufacturer was held liable to the distant user.[1]

(B) Right to information:

The consumer has the right to be informed about the quality, quantity, potency, purity standard and prices of goods.

In *Indian Photographic File Co. v. H.D. Shourie case*,[2] it was held that the importer of film was not able to print the price of the film on the film, because the nature of trade was such that it did not permit him to do so. He was directed to make it a condition with his retailers to attach price tag to each film before they delivered the same.

This has been done in order to save consumer from unfair trade practices and to save them from false and misleading description about the quality and nature of the product.

(C) Right of access to variety:

Consumer has right to choose from a variety at competitive prices. For this objective, all the dealers are supplied with the variety of goods so that they can offer variety of goods to consumer and to resist monopoly of a dealer or manufacturer. It is the duty of the central council, constituted under this Act, to ensure that consumer enjoys variety of goods at competitive prices and they are not being cheated by a dealer.

(D) Right to be heard:

The right to be heard pertain to the post-purchase. It has two aspects, one is that the supplier of goods or services should attend to the complaint and the other is that the consumer should have a legal remedy in the event of non-redress by the supplier.

To be heard, appropriate forum has been constituted under this Act, so that consumers receive due consideration at the hands of the appropriate redressal forums.

(E) Unscrupulous Exploitation:

The consumer has been given right to seek redressal against unfair trade practices or unscrupulous exploitation.

Angela Fonese v. Corol Lawn[3] states, Plaintiff booked the lawn for marriage and this booking was done on a non-refundable deposit. It was held to be unfair trade practice and deposited money was ordered to be refunded with interests when plaintiff, due to preponement of marriage date, was not allowed to usé the lawns though lawn was free on that date.

(F) Consumer Education:

It has been found that despite of various remedies, people do not exercise their legal remedies and thus do not get any benefits of such Acts. Thus, it was felt consumers should be informed about the remedies available under this Act, so that they can exercise this legal right. The Consumer Protection Act, 1986 assigns to the central council set-up under the Act, the task of organizing consumer education.

Once people are rendered conscious of their rights they may feel energised to struggle against exploitation by manufacturers and traders.

Consumer Rights:

***Helvetica Right to Protection of Health and Safety*:** There are unsafe products, unstated dangers in product performance and inadequate services after sale. Right to safety means protection against the marketing of goods that are unsafe to health and life.

Products should not cause any physical danger to consumers or put them in difficulty due to sudden failure. Consumers must have assurance regarding quality, reliability and performance. There are so many common household items now available to consumers containing potentially harmful substances. Food additives, food colouring and pesticides further add new potential dangers.

In the case of food and drugs, we need safety to consumers. In many sophisticated products, e.g., toys, appliances, flammable fabrics, etc, we need considerable safety. Fortunately, the recent trend in legislation for consumer safety shows a continuous shift in emphasis for consumer buyer responsibility to seller-trader responsibilities for damages and losses arising out of unsafe and dangerous products. Food and Drug Acts now hold the seller responsible for product safety. With the advance of science and technology, consumer products have become highly complex and intricate. In many instances, responsibility for safety of finished products is directly place on producers and distributors. Legislation to achieve consumer protection against unsafe products is only the first step. Equally important is vigorous and sincere imaginative enforcement of law by adequately — staffed agencies.

By misleading advertisement, consumers are led to expect higher performance levels than the product can deliver. For instance, Zippers jam, food products are adulterated, wash and wear clothes need ironing, appliances do not perform as advertised, cosmetics fail to fulfill even the minimum expectation, etc. Not only is the product quality poor but also after sales service is deplorable. In all these respects, consumers have a right of reasonable protection

Helvetica Right to be Informed: Consumers demand positive obligation of full disclosure to be placed on the manufacturer and dealer. We must have adequate, accurate and up-to-date information on the quality, performance and other vital characteristics of products.

Full information will enable consumers to exercise intelligently their decision to buy before they part with their money in exchange of good. The consumer must protected against fraud. The establishment of standard weights and measures, truth in labeling and packaging, performance testing in drugs, grade labelling, tel-tags (informative labels), standardization and so on will help consumers to get reliable information. Consumer must have all facts needed make informed choices. We have frequently inadequate and misleading information, deceptive advertising, deceptive packing, misleading warranties, scanty information on product contents, and operating instruction, or care of the products, collusive pricing, deceptive credit terms, etc. The trader takes undue advantage of consumer ignorance and he is deceived as to quality, quantity, price, weight, size and any other factor involved in buying. Once the right to information is legally recognised, many of the aforesaid malpractices will be reduced to the minimum.

The seller should ensure that his advertisement mean what they say and the say what they really mean. Unfortunately, such sincere seller are rare in the market. Advertising causes us to buy goods we do not want at prices we cannot pay, and on terms we cannot meet. Want of objective information is a great obstacle in consumer satisfaction and many a time, they have a bad bargain. A house-wife buys what is should to her. It is packaged. She buys it on good faith. Unscrupulous sellers may exploit such a situation.

Helvetica Right to Choose: It should be the keystone of dealer's policy. The widest possible selection of quality brand names at fair price should be offered to the customers.

Right to choose implies that monopoly is disliked by consumers. They want to buy a product of their will. They want to exercise their option to choose a particular brand or to decide about the quantity. If the market has ample quantity and variety of products at competitive prices, buyers have an opportunity of wise selection. Collusion among sellers, price fixing understanding among leading competitors, cartel movement, etc cannot give wider choice to consumers. Competition assure consumers the right to choose.

Competition and consumer legislation provide ample protection for the consumers. More efficient information system will enable consumers to make a satisfactory choice. Competition provides wider choice of good and services. Consumer legislation and Government regulations provide official system to make a wise selection or best bargain.

Helvetica Right to Heard: Consumer has a right to dissatisfaction and get his complaint heard and weighed. This even greater importance. Even if consumer have the rights to safety, to be informed and to chose, but do not enjoy the right to be heard, would be no real control on the other three rights. If this rights. If this right to be heard is denied to consumers, there would be no body to listen to their complaints and the very purpose of granting them other rights would be simply defeated. The right to be heard implies the existence of a legal framework and Government intervention to safeguard consumer interest. Many business firms are utterly indifferent to consumer grievances and protests.

Helvetica Right to Redress: Today, a new right is being recognised. It is the right to redressal or to settlement of just and deserving clams or grievances of consumer. This consumer right was not part of the original consumer's bill of rights. It is a good addition. This is the right to expect every product to perform as advertised when it is used as directed. If the performance and quality is short of expectation, a consumer has a right of redress. The product must be repaired, replaced or taken back by the seller. Warranties such as money back guarantee, if dissatisfied must be meaningful. Then only consumers will have confidence in the seller.

In fact, the right to be heard further implies the existence of a mechanism through which other rights can be asserted: in particular, by ensuring the right of redressal (to set right or rectify) of legitimate consumer grievances. The consumer adviser of ombudsman *Helvetica (Lokayukta)* and the Government authorities often receive complaints and attempt to resolve them. If we have a standing grievance machinery for listening to the complaints of consumers and for the settlement of their grievances, consumer relation with the business will be very cordial and harmonious. Such a bridge of understanding or communication is necessary for assuring protection. A business firm should have a consumer affairs department to receive customer complaints and problems and to resolve them amicable. The new department should be directly attached to the top management.

Helvetica Right to a Physical Environment that will Enhance the Quality of Life: This right has been recently to the consumer bill of rights thereby considerably the scope and significance of modern consumerism. Indeed, consumerism is now defined broadly as an organised expression for an improved quality of life. The environmental problems do affect the life of consumers. Air pollution, water pollution, food pollution and noise pollution are the legacies of reckless industrialization. The social costs of the aforesaid forms of pollution are at the cost of social benefits. Please note that each form of pollution destroys the social benefits already existing. Industry is directly responsible for many forms of pollution. Investment decisions of industry, e.g., chemical and fertilizer complex, refineries, etc., must ensure quality of community life by preventing or reducing the evil effects of air, water and food pollution.

Consumer, Guidance or Education

Consumer education has been defined as conscious preparation of the individual in the skills, concepts and understandings that are required for everyday living to achieve, within the framework of his/her own values and culture, the maximum satisfaction and utilization of his/her resources.

Consumer education is necessary when we have in the marketplace varied and numerous consumer goods and services demanding adequate information regarding safety and performance or correct use of the products. Consumer awareness and education will be necessary to bring about balanced control among buyers and sellers.

Consumer education will also enable buyers to protect themselves against exploitation by unscrupulous sellers indulging in unfair trade practices. In the modern complicated retail markets, we must make consumer aware of business malparctices and sales gimmicks. Consumer should be enabled to discern deceptive advertising, deceptive packaging and misleading labels. Consumer must be aware of the tactics of high pressure salesmanship and high powered advertising.

Consumer welcomes education and guidance so that he/she cannot be fooled and cannot be made to pay more than what he/she to pay by law. Consumer education gives confidence to the buyer that he cannot be cheated in the market by fraudulent sellers.

Scope of Consumer Education

Consumer education should cover efforts to give opportunities in acquiring an understanding of market economy, knowledge of consumer and agencies serving consumer interest.

It should also cover a general familiarity with legal rights and responsibilities of consumers, and those of manufacturers and dealers. A buyer should know the implication involved in a purchase contract specially in durable goods.

Consumer should have adequate information on standards of quality, knowledge of technical and commercial terms used in the market of goods and services.

He should have a general awareness of fraudulent and misleading advertisements, deceptive packaging and labelling, misbranding and adulteration, and such other common dishonest practices prevalent in business. Such awareness prevents consumer victimisation to a great extent.

Consumer education and awareness will be necessary for self-insurance against sharp selling practices and usual unfair trade practices. To accomplish all these skills effectively, consumer education must focus on everyday living situations of a given group of consumers.

Consumers in India need more knowledge about nutrition and food use (cooking recipes and substitute food) and their corresponding food value. They should know the ways and means to reduce waste, to find out low cost housing materials, low cost clothing, etc. They should be educated in safety on roads and streets, and they should have overall ability to assess and judge critically the comparative values of goods in the current market in order to get maximum satisfaction in all their daily wants.

How to Become a Better Buyer?

Buymanship: We have ample literature on advertisement, salesmanship; marketing, etc. filled with numerous ways and means for successful selling. Hence, we have professional sellers in the market. However, we have comparatively limited literature on buymanship particularly for consumers. Books on purchasing invariably concentrate on industrial purchasing or merchandise useful for industrial buyers and merchants

Better buymanship substitutes rational on intelligent action for emotional consumer action in the market. An alert and informed consumer is his own best friend and needs no consumer advocates or world savers to protect him. He needs no protection from big, bad business, which is incidentally the producer of largest verities and best quality of goods and services in the world. Better buymanship is insurance against high pressure salesmanship advertising and high powered sales promotion. Remember, however, that the consumer-buyer is an amateur while the seller, by and large, is a professional. Better buymanship is the counterpart of modern salesmanship and to that extent it will certainly ensure more equal and balanced contest in the market.

Ingredients of Better Buymanship

Be prepared with adequate and up-to-date information. Professional purchasing agent is always an informed buyer. One can collect relevant information from consumer magazines, e.g., 'Keemat', from informative labels and advertisements and from other buying guides.

Watch for lures and traps, such as bad and switch advertising, deceptive levels, etc. Bait advertising is used to lure innocent consumers into a store. The low-priced advertised item may not be shown on the sales counters and the salesman may urge you to see more expensive item and persuade you to buy it. Buymanship helps you to guard against such deceptive and fraudulent sales methods.

Avoid Impulse buying: Average consumer buys on impulse at least on 50 per cent occasions. The sellers exploit the buyer's tendency to purchase impulsively. You should be aware of impulse purchase traps.

Watch for Sales: During certain seasons, buying is profitable. Seasonal purchases can give you 20 per cent savings. In addition to seasonal sales, we have annual sales, special sales, one-day sales, reduction sales, and so on.

Shopping around before actual buying can save easily 20 per cent of your income. It is desirable to have price comparison study of a product in several stores. Consumers who shop around, comparing quantity, quality and price get definite reduction in their purchase bills. One can save easily fifty rupees per month on all monthly purchases (worth Rs. 300/-), through shopping around. A careful shopper does this with interest.

It is not true that you get what you pay for. There is no close correlation between price and quality. Seller wants us to believe that higher price means higher quality. Out of 100 items surveyed in one marked survey, only 25 had significant price quality correlation, 20 items actually had negative correlation, i.e., lower priced was associated with higher quality. The remaining 55 items had very low correlation. Hence, shopping around is justifiable particularly in buying costly articles.

Bargain for lower prices and other concessions or services. This is possible even under the so-called one price system. In retail trade, retailer would not allow himself to be undersold. He is prepared to meet competitor's prices. Careful buyer must compel him to give price reductions directly or indirectly (for example free home delivery or free installation).

When we have normal supplies, careful buyer can buy in bulk and secure special price concession in bulk purchase.

Read carefully labels, warranties and the freshness date or the expiry date particularly in foods and medicines.

Check the quantity; do not be fooled by the size of the package. Label points out net weight, measure or count. Find out whether the package is full or semi-empty.

Always adopt cash and carry system. Credit costs money. Cash purchases are economical and free from future worries. As far as possible daily necessaries should be bought on cash at competitive prices.

Check prices and totals on the bills. When unit pricing becomes universal, price checking will be easier. There may be clerical errors in calculations and totals.

Keep records and receipts of purchases. This will help you to protest and get quick redress against your complainants.

In case you decide to exercises your to protest and get redress, e.g., the article bought is defective, follow the procedure given below:

Give the seller opportunity to redress.

If he is not prepared to give justice to you, approach the Consumer Organization for further action.

You may write to the manufacturer direct and send a copy of your protest to the concerned Government authority.

You may also approach Fair Price Trade Practices Association and lodge your complaint formally.

Consumer Protection Act, 1986: 2002 Amendments — Laurels and Loopholes

Section 2 (d) of the Consumer Protection Act, 1986, defines 'consumer' as any person who —

(i) buys any goods for a consideration which has been paid or promised or partly paid and partly promised, or under any system of deferred payment and includes any user of such goods other than the person who buys such goods for consideration paid or promised or partly paid or partly promised, or under any system of deferred payment when such use is made with the approval of such person, but does not include a person who obtains such goods for resale or for any commercial purpose; or

(ii) hires or avails of any services for a consideration which has been paid or promised or partly paid and partly promised, or under any system of deferred payment and includes any beneficiary of such services other than the person who hires or avails of the services for consideration paid or promised, or partly paid and partly promised, or under any system of deferred payments, when such services are availed of with the approval of the first-mentioned person.

Legal terminology apart, every human being at some point or other, has donned the role of a consumer in his/her lifespan. When we buy an electric appliance for the home, get the monthly ration or buy a brand new car — we become consumers. When we pay some fees to a doctor for the medical services provided by him/her, when we pay the telephone bill or when we post a registered letter — we become consumers of the doctor, telephone department and the postal services respectively.

Thus, it would not be an exaggeration to point out that the Consumer Protection Act, 1986, is one of the most important legislations that governs the life of every human being in his transactions with the society for availing goods and services provided by others. It not only comes into daily use but prevents the exploitation of common man, the consumer, at the hands of the affluent and moneyed business man or service provider. Hence any change or amendment whatsoever, in the Act directly affects the common people thereby needing a close scrutiny of the amendments thereto.

This analysis seeks to take a look at some of the most profound amendments to the Consumer Protection Act, 1986 brought about by the Consumer Protection (Amendment) Act, 2002, the subsequent repercussions of those respective amendments, the shortcomings which have still not been rectified despite the amendment and also the benefits that are resultant of certain amendments.

Some major loopholes of the Act still left unplugged by the 2002 Amendments are discussed here:

(1) One of the biggest achievements of the Consumer Protection (Amendment) Act, 2002, was the conferment of First Class Magistrate's powers to the Consumer Forums or Commissions

The main problem regarding the above empowerment and the relevant provision is the fact that the Gazette notification for the conferment of First Class Magistrate's powers to the Consumer Forums or Commissions is still not issued. Thus it is practically impossible for the Forums or Commissions to exercise this power conferred by the Act.

(2) Another lacuna present in the amended Act is the relatively softer approach adopted by the Act towards the judgment debtor in its certain provisions. The amendment of 2002 has not done anything concrete to fill this lacuna. For instance, S. 24 of the Consumer Protection Act, 1986, which reads as follows:

S.24: Finality of order:-

Every order of a District Forum, State Commission or the National Commission shall, if no appeal has been preferred against such order under the provisions of this Act, be final.

Thus this provision implies that non-preferment of appeal renders the order final. Conversely, preferring an appeal means that order is not final. Hence, once an appeal is preferred by the judgement debtor, he gets a stay against the execution and thus there cannot be any execution.

The judgement debtors have certainly misused this provision of the Act. It is a general pattern that judgement debtors just buy time before the Forum or Commission stating that appeal has been preferred. Even if the appeal is not admitted and may take quite some time for the purpose, even if the required bank guarantee is yet not given and the stay is still not granted, the consumer cannot get the execution of the original order done. Thus justice still eludes the hapless consumer while the seller (judgement debtor) more often than not manages to get adjournment. The Act is silent regarding a 'stay order'. Even the Amendment Act of 2002 disappoints in this regard. This Section urgently calls for amendment substituting the words "appeal preferred" with the words stay granted.

(3) Another important confusion is created by the amended S.25 of the Act that reads as under:

S.25: Enforcement of orders by the Forum, the State Commission or the National Commission: — (1) Where an interim order made under this Act, is not complied with the District Forum or the State Commission or the National Commission, as the case may be, may order the property of the person, not complying with such order to be attached.(2) No attachment made under sub-section (1) shall remain in force for more than three months at the end of which, if the non-compliance continues, the property attached may be sold and out of the proceeds thereof, the District Forum, or the State Commission or the National Commission may award such damages as it thinks fit to the complainant and shall pay the balance, if any, to the party entitled thereto.(3) Where any amount is due from any person under an order made by a District Forum, State Commission or the National Commission, as the case may be, the person entitled to the amount may make an application to the District Forum, the State Commission or the National Commission, as the case may be, and such District Forum or the State Commission or the National Commission may issue a certificate for the said amount to the Collector of the district (by whatever name called) and the Collector shall proceed to recover the amount in the same manner as arrears of land revenue.

If we carefully give a perusal to the above provisions of the above section, we find that by virtue of S.25 (1) the provision of attachment is against the interim order and not the final order. But looking at the pattern of judgements, it can be clearly discerned that generally attachments are aimed at awarding compensation to the aggrieved party, mostly the consumers. Compensations are usually awarded as part of the final order and the interim order almost never awards compensation. Interim orders aim at compelling or restraining any agency for the commission or omission of some act but these interim orders are seldom used by the Forums or Commissions to attach or seal the property of any business person, manufacturer, banks, medical establishments, etc. for the simple reason that the Forums/Commissions are not aware if there will be any compensation order against them at the conclusion of the proceedings before Consumer Protection Agencies. Since no recovery proceeding is provided under the Act, there cannot be any assessment of the dues and thus no interim attachment order. Thus, a more practically feasible approach would be to replace the word interim order with all orders.

(4) Also S. 25 (3) provides for issuance of a certificate to the Collector for recovery of the amount due from any concerned person. The consumers have to contact the Collector for recovery of their dues because there is no further provision as to what is the role of Consumer Forums/Commissions after that. After a long wait for the order from the Forum, the hapless consumers still have to undergo the rigor of going to the collector for the realization of the dues. There is no clarity regarding who is responsible for the follow up with the revenue department and the stipulated time limit thereto. Thus the concerned provision of S. 25 (3) should provide for the revenue department to send the arrears to the Forum itself for reimbursement to the consumer.

Thus, an amendment is required to take care of the afore-mentioned problem. However, while critiquing certain provisions of the Act, at the same time it is necessary to point out certain other provisions which are the product of the 2002 Amendments and have plugged many loopholes by their progressive wording. These provisions brought about by the amendment have gone a long way in doing away the perennial problems of delay.

(1) Amendment to Section 11 enhances the jurisdiction of the District Forum to entertain complaints where the value of the goods or services and the compensation claimed does not exceed rupees twenty lakhs. This will be more convenient for the complainants and also reduce the number of complaints filed with the State Commission and National Commission.

(2) Section 12 is substituted to provide that every complaint filed with the District Forum shall be accompanied with such amount of fee as may be prescribed. It also provides that the admissibility of the complaint shall ordinarily be decided within twenty-one days from the date on which the complaint is received and that once admitted a complaint shall not be transferred to any other Court or Tribunal. This will help to quicken disposal of complaints.

(3) The amendments to section 13 require the District Forum to refer a copy of the admitted complaint within twenty-one days from the date of its admission to the opposite party to give his version within the prescribed time. It also provides the much needed provision for ex parte order as well as dismissal of complaint on non-appearance of complainant.

It includes a new sub-section (3A) to provide that complaint shall be heard as expeditiously as possible and endeavour made to decide the complaints within the prescribed period. Adjournments would ordinarily not be granted, and if granted for reasons to be recorded in writing by the forum, an order as to the costs occasioned by the adjournment would also be made by the forum. It is also provided that in the event of a complaint being disposed of after the period so specified, the District Forum shall record in writing, the reasons for the same at the time of disposing of the said complaint.

It further includes a new sub-section (3B) to enable the District Forum to pass interim orders where required. It also includes a new sub-section (7) for the substitution of parties in accordance with the provisions of Order XXII of the First Schedule to the Code of Civil Procedure, 1908 in the event of death of the complainant or opposite party.

These amendments will facilitate quicker disposal of cases, enable complaints to get immediate relief where required to the hapless consumers. The procedural delays will be done away with.

1) New section 19A provides that endeavour shall be made to dispose of appeals filed before the State Commission or the National Commission within ninety days from the date of admission.

The Consumer Protection Act, 1986 was further amended and the changes became effective March 15, 2003. Let us look at a few amendments and their relevance.

The Act will no longer be available for commercial purpose

What does this mean? An answer must be preceded by looking at how the old Act was used to expand the scope of the Consumer Protection Act of 1986. The old Act allowed small businesspersons — for example, a tailor — to seek redress for free repair or replacement of the tools/machinery used in their business. But lawyers have the ability to expand the scope of any law, and with the District Fora and the State Commission lax in their approach, large companies began to benefit by this law. A main advantage was that they did not have to pay the heavy stamp fee to the courts. Thus, for example, a large textile mill, which bought a few gensets, approached the consumer forum seeking replacement of a defective one.

Soon the consumer fora and the State Commissions were loaded with litigations which could have been handled by civil and criminal courts. The latest amendment shuts the door for any commercial activity. Not even a tailor can approach the consumer forum for redress.

While this is welcome, the amendment could have been such that the spirit of the primary act was retained. For instance, the amendment could have allowed only individual, who are defined as consumers, and those who practice a trade or run single-person enterprises to seek redress under the CPA.

Pecuniary jurisdiction of the redress tiers raised

A new amendment allows the District Consumer Fora to entertain complaints up to Rs 20 lakh. But how many articles bought by individuals cost so much? Why, then, raise the pecuniary jurisdiction? Consumer fora and the State Commission award little compensation for loss of income, mental agony and anguish, etc. Compensation rarely exceeds a few lakh rupees. Continuing this to allow original complaints at the National Commission of pecuniary jurisdiction beyond Rs. 1 crore, to my mind, is simply ridiculous.

District forum or the State Commission can pass interim order.

This is a good amendment. With the application of other provisions in the Consumer Protection Act, and including the clauses taken out from the MRTP Act on unfair trade practices, this amendment becomes very useful. The use of this provision will be available in many other instances also. For instance, an insurance company receives an accident claim, say, for Rs. 50,000. The insurance company wants to settle for Rs 10,000. But the consumer is not satisfied and therefore petitions the District Forum. The District Forum can order an interim payment, if convinced with the consumer's case, and ask the insurance company to pay a minimum sum.

This provision will also help say if large-scale adulteration is detected. While the District Forum or the State Commission can take up this matter on a petition, they can immediately on receipt of the petition order the alleged defaulter to stop selling the product. This amendment can be very useful in restraining unscrupulous traders, manufacturers and service providers from taking advantage of consumers.

State Commission to have multiple benches

This is an important amendment, especially as thousands of cases remain pending for years. With little support from the Department of Consumer Affairs, and the Consumer Welfare Fund, it is possible to set aside some money to create multiple benches for all State Commissions.

District Fora empowered to give punitive awards

Again, this is an important amendment, as the District Fora can now be a little more generous in awarding damages. The District Fora should be able to award punitive damages when a registered appointment letter is not delivered on time frame and a person fails to secure a job. Of course, the consumer must be able to prove that an appointment order fixing a date of joining duty was not received on time and, therefore, an opportunity was lost for a career.

Similarly, the loss of a limb or disability due to negligence leading to loss of income for a period must also be considered for punitive damages. As also in certain cases of insurance claims. While the amendment offers considerable scope, the problem may lie in proving a petitioner's point of view.

Review of orders by National Commission

It is possible that the petitioner/consumer does not agree with an order of the National Commission. Instead of going on appeal to the Supreme Court, it is now possible for ask for a review of the order.

Power for the district forum to attach property

A survey of how effective were the orders of the District Fora and the State Commissions revaled thatin many a case though the consumer got a favourable order, the final outcome was zero as the order could not be enforced. A new amendment to the act allows the Consumer Fora and State Commission to ask the District Collector to recover the amount due to the consumer by attachment and sale of property. This is an important and useful amendment.

While all these changes are useful, for the Consumer Protection Act to be consumer friendly, further amendments are necessary. But the most important thing to remember is that the consumer protection law was intended to be quick, simple, effective and inexpensive. One hopes that the Consumer Protection Act will be implemented with its original spirit and zeal.

When the Consumer Protection Act was initially enacted in 1986, goods purchased for commercial purpose (excluding those purchase for earning one's livelihood) were excluded from the purview of the Act. Yet, surprisingly services availed or hired for commercial purposes were amenable to the jurisdiction of the consumer courts. To remove this anomaly, the CP Act was amended in the year 2003, so that services for commercial purposes (except those availed of for earning one's livelihood) stood excluded from the purview of the CP Act. This amendment was made with the objective of excluded commercial disputes, as the CP Act was basically for the common man.

Now, the National Consumer Disputes Redressal Commission has interpreted the meaning of "commercial purpose" in such a manner that business houses can also file complaints under the CP Act. This authoritative judgement was recently passed on December 3, 2004 by a bench of the National Commission comprising of Justice MB Shah and Rajyalakshmi Rao in a bunch of appeals requiring the interpretation of the term "commercial purpose."

The issue before the National Commission was whether insurance policies taken by commercial units could be held to be hiring of services for commercial purpose and thereby excluded from the purview of the Consumer Protection Act, 1986 (as amended in 2003). The issue came up in a bunch of appeals against the orders passed by the Gujarat State Commission which had held that commercial units which had availed of insurance services were not maintainable as services for commercial purpose were excluded from the purview of the CP Act.

After considering the definitions of the words "consumer," "service," and "commercial purpose," the National Commission observed that an insured who takes an insurance policy cannot trade or carry on any commercial activity with regard to the insurance policy taken by him.

Hence, hiring of services of insurance companies by taking insurance policies by persons / parties carrying on commercial activities cannot be held to be a commercial purpose. This is because the policy is taken for reimbursement or for indemnity for the loss which may be suffered due to various perils. There is no question of trading or carrying on commerce in insurance policies by the insured, even though the insurance coverage is taken for commercial activity carried out by the insured.

While arriving at this conclusion, the National Commission referred to Halsbury's Laws of England, Volume 25, 4th Edition, and observed that insurance is a contract of indemnity and, therefore, the insured can recover the actual amount of loss and no more. Hence, an insurance policy is for protection of the interest of the insured in respect of articles or goods, and not for making any profit or trading for carrying on commercial purpose.

The National Commission also referred to various judgements of the Supreme Court and held that services in respect of any connected commercial activity would continue to remain within the purview of the Act. What is excluded would only be those goods purchases or services availed or hired where profit is the main aim.

Thus, the test to determine "commercial purpose" would determine whether the goods are purchased for resale or for any commercial purpose or the services are availed for any commercial purpose, i.e., for generating profit.

The National Commission gave illustrations to explain how to interpret its judgement. For example, if a manufacturer cannot file a complaint under the CP Act in respect of any defect in raw material, as this would be for commercial purpose.

As against this, if the same manufacturer purchases a refrigerator, a television or an air-conditioner for his use at his residence or even in his office, it cannot be held to be for commercial purpose, and for this purpose he is entitled to approach the consumer forum under the Act. Similarly, when a hospital which hires the services of a medical practitioner, it would be a commercial purpose; but if a person avails of such services for his ailment it would be held to be not a commercial purpose.

In short, "commercial purpose" would mean goods purchased or services hired should be used in any activity directly intended to generate profit. Profit is the main aim of commercial purpose. But, in a case where goods purchased or services hired in an activity which is not directly intended to generate profit, it would not be commercial purpose.

This landmark judgement will help business houses to avail of the benefits of a welfare legislation like the CP Act, but it might prove to be detrimental to the interest of the common man whose cases will get delayed because of the increase caused in the work load of the Consumer Fora which will once again have to entertain disputes filed by business houses and industries.

These are just some of the useful amendments and the afore-mentioned list is definitely not exhaustive. In fact all the amendments made to the Consumer Protection Act by the 2002 Amendments aim at furthering the efficiency of the Act and doing away with procedural delays which render the consumers disillusioned and dissatisfied. These Amendments have been fruitful in providing 'protection' to the consumers in the real sense of the term and served the purpose of the Act. It is hoped that further amendments would aim at even more efficiency and render the position of the consumers much stronger in this era of globalization and privatization where the sudden unchecked advent of Multi National Companies has to be balanced with the protection of the rights of the consumers by the legislature and the judiciary.

PRACTICE QUESTIONS

1. Discuss the main features of the Consumer Protection Act, 1986.
2. What are the objects which the Consumer Protection Act, 1986 seeks to achieve?
3. In which way the Consumer Protection Act can help the consumers in the of their grievances.
4. Define the following terms as per the Consumer Protection Act 1986: (a) Consumer; (b) Consumer dispute; (c) Defect;
   (d) Deficiency, (e) Manufacturer; (f) Restrictive trade practice; (g) Unfair trade practice; (h) Service; (i) Trader.
5. Can the following be regarded as consumers? (a) A patient of a government hospital., (b) A person who registers himself for a telephone connection; (c) A person sending a telegram.
6. Will the following constitute deficiency in service? (a) Delay of 1 year in settlement of a life insurance claim, (b) Delay of 6 months in settlement of a fire insurance claim, (c) The failure of BSNL to send bill by registered post in spite of a request by the subscriber in that regard against payment of the registration charges.
7. Examine the rights of a consumer enshrined under the Consumer Protection Act 1986.
8. Who can file a complaint under the Consumer Protection Act?
9. What sort of complaint may be lodged under the Act?
10. Where and how can a complaint be made? State the jurisdiction of the various redressal agencies in this regard.
11. What are the major amendments made from time to time in the Consumer Protection Act, 1986.
12. How have the amendments made the Consumer Protection Act more meaningful and powerful?

PART J

INFORMATION TECHNOLOGY ACT, 2000

CHAPTER

21

Information Technology

Backdrop

Modern Communication systems and advanced technology have become a part and parcel of businessmen's life. An awakening is beginning in the way people transact business. Not only business class, but even common man has started using computers to create, store, transmit information in an electric form instead of the traditional custom of using paper documents. Such Information stored in computers i.e. electronic forms has many advantages like being cheaper, easier, retrieval and speedy.

The term 'information technology' (IT) is generally applied to broad area of activities and technologies associated with the use of computers and communication. We can explain information technology as an application of computers to create, store, process and use of information particularly in the field of commerce. Basically, information technology enables the corporate management to have access to timely, accurate and relevant data, with the use of computers, communication, telephone, Internet, etc., which helps in informed decision-making, minimises the response time and enables better coordination in the organisation resulting in reduced costs or increased profits.

The Model Law provides for equal legal treatment of users of electronic communication and paper based communication. Pursuant to a recent declaration by member countries, the World Trade Organisation is likely to form a work programme to handle its work in this area including the possible creation of multilateral trade deals through the medium of electronic commerce.

It was proposed to provide for legal recognition of electronic records and digital signatures. It was also proposed to provide for a regulatory regime to supervise the Certifying Authorities issuing digital signature certificates to prevent the possible misuse arising out of transactions and other criminal liabilities for contravention of the provisions of the proposed legislation.

With a view to facilitate Electronic Governance, it was also proposed to provide for the use and acceptance of electronic records and digital signatures in the government offices and its agencies.

It was also proposed to make consequential amendments in the Indian Penal Code and the Indian Evidence Act, 1872 to provide for necessary changes in the various provisions which deal with offences relating to documents and paper based transactions. It is also proposed to amend the Reserve Bank of India Act, 1934 to facilitate electronic fund transfers between the financial institutions and banks and the Banker's Book Evidence Act, 1891 to give legal sanctity for books of account maintained in the electronic form by the banks.

Prologue

Connectivity via the Internet has greatly abridged geographical distances and made communication even more rapid. While activities in this limitless new universe are increasing incessantly, laws must be formulated to monitor these activities. Some countries have been rather vigilant and formed some laws governing the net. In order to keep pace with the changing generation, the Indian Parliament passed the much-awaited Information Technology (IT) Act, 2000. As they say, "It's better late than never."

Many laws such as Indian Contract Act 1872, and Negotiable Instruments Act, 1881 govern paper based records and documents which are signed and witnessed by, individuals, with the evolution of electronic communication system, Paper based system of communication and collection of information on Paper in files becoming obsolete, The computers heap in creating, transmitting, storing and retrieving information in electronic form rather than in traditional paper form. The business transactions through electronic form, now popularly known as, electronic commerce or e-commerce.

History

From Charles Babbage's first computer far back in the 1800s to the military network of 40 computers in the US connected by links and lines in 1969 called the Advanced Research Projects Agency Network (ARPANET) to the internet as we know it today, a world wide web that links the globe through 50 million nodes, a network of 233.3 million computers and a user group of 163 million individuals/entities, technology and therefore life has progressed into a world which seeks to obliterate barriers of economy, polity, society and administration.

When you gaped at one's description of his life on the net from business through entertainment to shopping for fresh vegetables, one will agree with this. But today the net has indeed overtaken conventional living. Business on the net is easy and with the variety of services offered it is of little wonder that people are increasingly turning to the net for everyday living. The future lies there — in a network of computers spanning the globe.

It becomes imperative then that government services are also delivered online. This could prove to be a blessing for the net entails transparency and accessibility of information: the lifeblood of any democracy. Corruption and red tapism, the greatest evils of modern governments can be thwarted fairly successfully. And for ordinary users — if they can buy vegetables and pay their bank dues on the net shouldn't they also be able to pay their electricity bills and apply for is licences online?

If e-governance and e-commerce are to be viable options, electronic records and digital signatures must gain legal validity. If the courts of law refuse to enforce a contract or validate a licence, entered into or obtained on the net, the growth potential of the internet will be severely retarded.

And yet the internet is not all goodness and opportunity. The World Wide Web is the playground of a new sort of criminal — one who revels in the anonymity offered by a network of millions of computers and whose apprehension legal systems across the world are battling with rather unsuccessfully. The internet challenges every single convention and belief that traditional legal systems are based upon. Benjamin Wittes is said to have remarked:

Suppose you wanted to witness the birth and development of a legal system. You would need a large complex system that lies outside of all other legal authorities. Moreover, you would need that system somehow to accelerate the seemingly millennial progress of legal development, so you would witness more than a moment of progress. The hypothetical system might seem like a social scientist's fantasy, but it actually exists. It's called the Internet.

It is to enable online governance and to grant legal recognition to electronic records and digital signatures that the Information Technology Act was passed. The act attempts to regulate life on the net and counteract known dangers to security and privacy of information. In doing so, it has set up a regulatory mechanism that is distinguished by the stranglehold the central government has been granted on all matters pertaining. The act has been the subject of severe criticism for the extent of executive discretion, immunity for executive actions, disproportionate penalties and the introduction of a system so tedious and complex that it is bound to hamper the progress of life on the net for Indians. Worse still is the extensive power granted to the state to impinge on the privacy of netizens.

Every invention needs to be protected and regulated uniformally, electronic commerce has now been accepted as an alternative to paper based system of communication. While activities in electronic commerce are increasing, laws must be formulated to monitor those activities. Regulations with global uniformity have to keep pace with electronic progress.

The United Nations Commission on International Trade Law adopted a model law on electronic commerce in 1896. General Assembly of the United Nations by Resolution dated 30-01-1997 has adopted the model Law on electronic commerce and recommended to all member errantries for favorable consideration. The Government of India, being a signatory to the model law, considered necessary to give effect to the said resolution to promote efficient delivery of Government services by means of reliable electronic records. The Department of Electronics in July 1998 drafted the bill. The Central Cabinet approved the bill on May 13, 2000 and both the houses of Parliament finally passed it by May 17, 2000, The Presidential Assent was finally received in the month of June 2000.

The Indian Parliament enacted the Information Technology Act, 2000. This Act is based on the Resolution A/RES/51/162 adopted by the General Assembly of the United Nations on 30th January 1997 regarding the Model Law on Electronic Commerce earlier adopted by the United Nations Commission on International Trade Law (UNCITRAL) in its twenty-ninth session. This resolution recommends that all States give favourable consideration to the Model Law on Electronic Commerce when they enact or revise their laws, in view of the need for uniformity of the law applicable to alternatives to paper-based methods of communication and storage of information.

It was a foresight on the part of the Government of India to initiate the entire process of enacting India's first ever information technology legislation in the year 1997 itself and it was done because of three reasons:

1. To facilitate the development of a secure regulatory environment for electronic commerce by providing a legal infrastructure governing electronic contracting, security and integrity of electronic transactions
2. To enable the use of digital signatures in authentication of electronic records
3. To showcase India's growing IT prowess and the role of Government in safeguarding and promoting IT sector and attracting FDI in the said sector.

Enumerated below are the main principles of the Information Technology Act, 2000:

- Defining data, computer database, information, electronic form, originator and addressee
- Creating civil liability if any person accesses or secures access to computer, computer system or network
- Creating criminal liability if any person accesses or secures access to computer, computer system or network
- Declaring any computer, computer system or computer network as a protected system
- Imposing penalty for breach of confidentiality and privacy
- Setting up a hierarchy of regulatory authorities, namely adjudicating officers, the Cyber Regulations Appellate Tribunal etc.

The Indian Information Technology Act, 2000 is one of the most important pieces of legislation in the recent past. This statute reaffirms India's commitment towards building a knowledge-based society and keeping pace with the rest of the world by providing a legal framework within which such a society can flourish.

The Act not only addresses issues related to electronic commerce by providing a framework for the establishment of a Public Key Infrastructure in the country, but it also addresses the issues of cyber crime and admissibility of digital evidence through the various provisions incorporated within the Act in itself and by way of amendments in other statutes.

However, the ever changing and dynamic information technology sector has already, within three years of the commencement of the Act, made it imperative to review the Act as there seems to be an ever increasing view by the industry, academicians, professionals and the general public that the Act needs to be re-analyzed in its entirety. This need for analysis arises so that the weaknesses that were already present in the Act and have later crept into it, creating ambiguities, can be eliminated.

Object of the Information Technology Act, 2000

The "Statement of Objects and Reasons" appended to the "Information Technology Bill, 2000," explains the rationale behind the IT Act, 2000. Excerpts from the said statement are given below:

"New communication systems and digital technology have made dramatic changes in the way we live. A revolution is occurring in the way people transact business. Businesses and consumers are increasingly using computers to create, transmit and store information in the electronic form instead of traditional paper documents. Information stored in electronic form has many advantages. It is cheaper, easier to store, retrieve and speedier to communicate. Although people are aware of these advantages, they are reluctant to conduct business or conclude any transaction in the electronic form due to lack of appropriate legal framework. The two principal hurdles which stand in the way of facilitating electronic commerce and electronic governance are the requirements as to writing and signature for legal recognition. At present, many legal provisions assume the existence of paper based records and documents and records which should bear signatures. The law of evidence is traditionally based upon paper based records and oral testimony. Since electronic commerce eliminates the need for paper based transactions, hence to facilitate e-commerce, the need for legal changes have become an urgent necessity. International trade through the medium of e-commerce is growing rapidly in the past few years and many countries have switched over from traditional paper based commerce to e-commerce."

"There is a need for bringing in suitable amendments in the existing laws in our country to facilitate e-commerce. It is, therefore, proposed i provide for legal recognition of electronic records and digital signature. This will enable the conclusion of contracts and the creation of rights on obligations through the electronic medium."

"With a view to facilitate Electronic Governance, it is proposed provide for the use and acceptance of electronic records and digital s natures in the Government offices and its agencies."

What is a Cyber Crime?

"Cyber" refers to imaginary space, which is created when the electronic devices communicate, like network of computers. Cyber crime refers to anything done in the cyber space with a criminal intent. These could be either the criminal activities in the conventional sense or could be activities, newly evolved with the growth of the new medium. Cyber crime includes acts such as hacking, uploading obscene content on the Internet, sending obscene e-mails and hacking into a person's e-banking account to withdraw money.

Is There any Law for Cyber Crimes?

Cyber crime can involve criminal activities that are traditional in nature, such as theft, fraud, forgery, defamation and mischief, all of which are subject to the Indian Penal Code. The abuse of computers has also given birth to a gamut of new age crimes that are addressed by the Information Technology Act, 2000. The act does not define 'cyber crime'. However, any activities which basically offend human sensibilities would come within its ambit. Child Pornography on the Internet constitutes one serious cyber crime.

The Information Technology Act 2000 deals with the following subjects:

(i) Secure electronic transactions to facilitate e-commerce,

(ii) Attribution of electronic messages,

(iii) Legal status to electronic signature and electronic records by providing for the appointment of a Controller of Certifying Authority,

(iv) Offences regarding electronic records

(v) Privacy and confidentiality of information,

(vi) Filing of electronic records with and maintenance by government,

(vii) Regulatory infrastructure by providing for a Controller of certifying authorities,

(viii) Exclusion of liability of network service providers (ISPS) for context on the internet where he has exercised all due diligence to prevent the offence.

Preamble

The Preamble of the Act states that it aims at providing legal restriction for transactions carried out by means of electronic data interchange and other means of electronic communication, commonly referred to as "electronic communication", which involve the use of alternations to paper based methods of communication and storage of information and aims of facilitating electronic filing of documents with the government agencies.

The General Assembly, of the United Nations had adopted the Model Law on Electronic Commission on International Trade Law (UNCITRAL) in its General Assembly Resolution. The Indian Act is in keeping with this resolution that recommended that member rations of the United Nations enact and modify their Laws according the Model Law.

Thus with the enactment of this Act, Internet Transactions will now be recognised, on-line entreats will be enforceable and e-mail will be legally acknowledged. It will tremendously augment domestic as well as international trade and commerce.

Scope of the Act

The main objectives of the Act as reflected in the preamble of the Act are: -

(i) To grant legal recognition for transitions carried out by means of electronic data interchange and other means of electronic communication commonly referred to as based methods of communication,

(ii) To give legal recognition to digital signature for authentication of any information or matter which required authentication under any law,

(iii) To facilitate electronic filing of documents with government departments,

(iv) To facilitate electronic storage of data.

(v) To facilitate and give legal sanction to electronic fund transfers between books and financial institutions,

(vi) To give legal recognition for keeping books of account by bankers in electronic form,

(vii) To amend the Indian Penal Act 1810, the Indian Evidence Act 1872, The Banker's Book Evidence Act, 1891 and the Reserve Bank of India Act 1934.

(viii) To provide for matters corrected Therewith or incidental there to.

The Act is arranged in 13 Chapters comprising of 93 Sections along with Four Schedules.

The Act simultaneously amended the following Acts —

The Indian Penal Code Act, 1860;

The Indian Evidence Act, 1872;

The Reserve Bank of India Act, 1934;

The Banker's Book Evidence Act, 1891.

Application

The Act extends to whole of India. The provisions of the Act shall apply also to any offence or contravention committed out side India by any person irrespective of the nationality provided that the act or conduct constituting the offence or contravention involves a computer, computer system, or computer net work located in India.

The Act, however, shall not apply to:

(i) A negotiable instrument (other than a Cheque) as defined in section 13 the Negotiable Instrument Act, 1881.

(ii) A power-of-attorney as defined in section 1A of the Power of Attorney Act, 1881.

(iii) A trust as defined in section 3 of the Indian Trusts Act, 1882.

(iv) A will as defined in clause (h) of section 2 of the Indian Succession Act 1925, including any, other testamentary disposition by whatever name called.

(v) Any contract for the sale or conveyance of immovable property or any interest in sale property.

(vi) Any such class of documents or transactions as may be notified by the Central Government in the Official Gazette.

DEFINITIONS

"Access" means gaining entry into, instructing or communicating with the logical, arithmetical or computer system or computer network.

"Addressee" means a person who is intended by the originator to receive electronic record but does not include any intermediary.

"Adjudicating officer" means adjudicating officer appointed under section 46(1).

"Affixing digital signature" means adoption of any methodology or procedure by a person for the purpose of authenticating an electronic record by means of digital signature.

"Appropriate government" means as respects any matter –

Enumerated in list II of the seventh schedule to the Constitutlon.

Relating to any state law enacted under list III of the seventh schedule to the Constitution.

The state government and in any other case, the Central Government.

Asymmetries crypto system" means a system of a secure key pair consisting of a private key pair for creating a digital signature and a public key to verity the digital signature.

"Certifying Authority" means a person who has been granted a license to issue a digital signature certified under section 24.

"Certification practice statement" means a statement issued by a certifying authority to specify the practices that the Certifying Authority employs in issuing Digital Signature Certificates.

"Computer" means any electronic magnetic, optical or other high speed data processing device which performs logical, arithmetic, and memory functions by manipulation of electronic, magnetic optical impulses, and includes all input, output, processing, storage, computer software, or communication facilities which are connected or related to the computer in a computer system or computer network.

"Computer network" means interconnection of one or more computer through—

(i) The use of satellite, microwave, terrestrial line or other communication media, and

(ii) Terminals or a complex consisting of two or more interconnected computers whether or not the interconnection is continuously maintained.

"Computer resource" means computer, computer system, computer network, data, computer database or software.

"Computer system" means a devices or collection of devices including input and output support devices and excluding calculators which are not programmable and capable of being used in conjunction with external files, which conation computer programmers, electronic instructions, input data and output data that performs logic, communication control and other functions.

"Controller" means the Controller of Certifying Authorities appointed under section 17 (1).

"Cyber Appellate Tribunal" means the Cyber Regulations Appellate Tribunal established under section 48.

"Data" means a representation of information, knowledge, fests, concepts or instructions which are being prepared or have been prepared in a formalised manner, and in intended to be processed, is a computer system or computer network, and may be in any form including computer printouts, magnetic or optical storage media, punched cards, punched tapes or stored internally in the memory of the computer.

"Digital Signature" means authentication of any electronic record by a subscriber by means of an electronic record by a subscriber by means of an electronic method or procedure in accordance with the provision in section 3.

"Digital Signature Certificate" means a digital signature certificate issued under section 35(1).

"Electronic form" with reference to information means any information generated, sent, received or stored in media, magnetic, optical computer memory or similar device.

"Electronic record" means data, record or data generated image or sound stored, received or sent in an electronic form.

"Sanction" in relation to a computer, includes logic, control, arithmetical process, deletion, storage and retrieval and communication or telecommunication form or within a computer.

"Information" includes data, fist, images, sound, codes computer programmers, software and databases.

"Intermediary" with respects to any particular electronic message means any person who on behalf of another person receives stores or transmits that message or provides any service with respect to that massage.

"Key Pair" in an asymmetric crypto system, means a private key and its mathematically related public key, which are so related that the public key can verify a digital signature created by the private key.

"Law" includes any Act of Parliament or of a State Legislature Ordinances promulgated by President or a Governor, as the case may be. Regulations made by the President under Article 240, Bills enacted as president's Act under sob clause (a) of clause (1) of article357 of the Constitution and includes rules, regulations, by laws and order's issued or made hereunder.

"License" means a license granted to a certifying authority under section 24.

"Originator" means a person who sends generates, store or transmits any electronic message or courses any electronic message to be sent, generated, stored or transmitted to any other person but does not include an intermediary.

"Prescribed" means prescribed by rules made under this Act.

"Private Key" means the key of key pair used to create a digital signature. Public key means the key of a key pair used to verify, digital signature and listed in the digital signature certificate.

"Security Procedure" means the security procedure prescribed under section 16 by the central government.

"Security System" means computer hardware, Software and procedure that –(a) are reasonably secure from instruction and misuse, (b) provide a reasonable level of reliability and correct operation, (c) are reasonably suited to performing. The intended functions, and (d) adhere to generally accepted security procedures.

"Subscriber" means a person in whose name the Digital Signature Certificate is issued.

"Verify" in relation to digital signature, electronic record or public key, with its grammatical variations and cognate expression means to determine whether —

(a) The initial electronic record was affixed with the digital signature by the use of private key corresponding to the public key of the subscriber,

(b) The initial electrified record is retained intact or has been altered since such electronic record was so affixed with the digital signature.

DIGITAL SIGNATURE

A Digital Signature functions for electronic documents like a handwritten signature does for printed documents. The signature is an unforgeable piece of data that asserts that a named person wrote or otherwise agreed to the document to which the signature is attached. In the Information Technology Act, 2000 for the words "digital signature" occurring in the Chapter, section, sub-section and clause referred to in the words "electronic signature" have been substituted by the Information Technology (Amendment) Act, 2006, vide Bill No. 96 of 2006.

A Digital Signature actually provides a greater degree of security than a handwritten signature. The recipient of a digitally signed message can verify both that the message originated from the person whose signature is attached and that the message has not been altered either intentionally or accidentally since it was signed. Furthermore, secure Digital Signatures cannot be repudiated; the signer of a document cannot later disown it by claiming the signature was forged.

The General Clauses Act does not define signature anywhere but explains 'sign' with its grammatical variations and cognate expressions, with reference to person, to mean affixing of his handwritten signature or any mark on any document. It is argued that if a person can introduce such information to any document so as to authenticate authorship, it will be construed as a signature whether written or printed and so digital signatures are also covered.

Section 3 provides that digital signature means an authentication of any electronic record by a subscriber by means of on electronic method or procedure in accordance with the other provisions of the Act. The Act has adopted the Public Key Infrastructure (PKI) for securing electronic transactions. As per Section 2(1)(p) of the Act, a digital signature means an authentication of any electronic record by a subscriber by means of an electronic method or procedure in accordance with the other provisions of the Act. Thus, a subscriber can authenticate an electronic record by affixing his digital signature. A private key is used to create a digital signature whereas a public key is used to verify the digital signature and electronic record. They both are unique for each subscriber and together form a functioning key pair.

In other words, Digital Signatures enable "authentication" of digital messages, assuring the recipient of a digital message of both the identity of the sender and the integrity of the message.

Digital Signature means authentication of any electronic record by a subscriber by means of an electronic method or procedure **[Sec.2(p)]**.

Any subscriber may authenticate an electronic record by affixing his Digital Signature **[Sec.3(l)]**.

A person in whose name the Digital Signature Certificate is issued on application to Certifying Authority is a subscriber **[Sec.2(zf)]**.

Affixing Digital Signature means adoption of any methodology or procedure by a person for the purpose of authenticating an electronic record by means of Digital Signature **[Sec.2(d)]**.

The authentication of the electronic record shall be effected by the use of asymmetric crypto system and hash function which envelop and transform the initial electronic record into another electronic record **[Sec.3(2)]**.

Asymmetric crypto system: It means a system of a secure key pair consisting of a private key for creating a Digital Signature and a public key to verify the Digital Signature **[Sec.2(f)]**.

Cryptography: In Greek, it means secret writing. It is the science of codification, which converts a normal text into junk characters (known as cipher text). The process of coding is called encryption and the process of decoding is called decryption. Encryption and decryption is done through software. These softwares are called Public Key and Private Key. Private Key is kept secret and the Public Key is made public.

'Cryptography' involves the process of encryption and decryption. Encryption is the process of transforming plain text into unintelligible form and decryption is the process of converting the unintelligible data back into the original plain text. Encryption can be used for two purposes: (1) Maintaining the confidentiality of the message; and (2) Affixing a digital signature.

In the former case, the text itself is converted using an algorithm into cipher text so as to ensure that those who are not intended to read the message do not read it. The process used is called symmetric cryptography, or secret key cryptography. In this process the same key or algorithm that is used to encrypt also has to be used to decrypt. Owing to the disadvantages of symmetric cryptography, the asymmetric crypto system came into place.

The system envisages the use of two keys — a public key and a private key. The explanation to sub-section (2) to section 3 reads "For the purpose of this sub-section, 'hash function' means an algorithm mapping or translation of one sequence of bit into another, generally smaller set known as 'hash result' such that an electronic record yields the same hash result every time the algorithm is executed with the same electronic record as its input making it computationally infeasible —

(a) to derive or reconstitute the original record from the hash result produced by the algorithm;

(b) that two electronic records can produce the same result using the algorithm."

Hash function: This means an algorithm mapping or translation of one sequence of bits into another, generally smaller, set known as "hash result" such that an electronic record yields the same hash result every time the algorithm is executed with the same electronic record as its input, making it computationally infeasible —

(a) to derive or reconstruct the original electronic record from the hash result produced by the algorithm;

(b) that two electronic records can produce the same hash result using the algorithm **[Expln. to Sec.3(2)]**.

Therefore, it means that the authentication of the electronic record shall be effected by the use of asymmetric crypto system and hash function which envelop and transform the initial electronic record into another electronic record. Asymmetric crypto system means a system of a secure key pair consisting of a private key for creating a digital signature and a public key to verity the digital signature. Hash function means an algorithm mapping or translation of one sequence of bits into another, generally smaller, set known as "hash result' such that an electronic record yields the same hash result every time the algorithm is executed with the same electronic record as its inputs, making it computationally infeasible —

(a) to derive or reconstruct the original electronic record from the hash reset produced by the algorithm.

(b) that two electronic records can produce the same hash result using the algorithm.

Electronic record means data, record, or data generated, image or sound stored, received or sent in an electronic form or micro film or computer generated micro fiche [Sec.2(s)].

Any person by the use of a public key of the subscriber can verify the electronic record. The private key and the public key are unique to the subscriber and constitute a functioning key pair **[Secs.3 (3) & (4)]**.

Public key: It means the key of a key pair used to verify a Digital Signature and listed in the Digital Signature Certificate **[Sec.2(zc)]**.

Private key means the key of a key pair used to create a Digital Signature **[Sec.2(zb)].**

Key pair: This in an asymmetric crypto system means a private key and its mathematically related public key, which are so related that the public key can verify a Digital Signature created by the private key **|Sec.2(w)].**

Communication of compromise of private key: Where the private key corresponding to the public key listed in the Digital Signature Certificate has been compromised, the subscriber shall communicate the same without any delay to the Certifying Authority. An application for revocation of the key pair shall be made in Form online on the web site of the concerned Certifying Authority to enable revocation and publication in the Certificate Revocation List. I The subscriber shall encrypt this transaction by using the public key of the Certifying Authority. The f transaction shall be further authenticated with the private key of the subscriber even though it may have | already been compromised **[Reg. 6]**.

In short, it can be said that the process of digital signature involves the converting electronic record into secret code first, and then translating the codes into a small number by applying a formula. Each licensed Subscriber uses unique secret code and formula, which is known to him only. This is done through private key. Based on private key techniques, public key is designed.

Manner in which information be authenticated by means of Digital Signature:

A Digital Signature shall —

(a) be created and verified by cryptography that concerns itself with transforming electronic record into seemingly unintelligible forms and back again;

(b) use what is known as "Public Key Cryptography", which employs an algorithm using two different but mathematical related "keys" — one for creating a Digital Signature or transforming data into a seemingly unintelligible form, and another key. for verifying a Digital Signature or returning the electronic record to original form. The process termed as hash function shall be used in both creating and verifying a Digital Signature.

Computer equipment and software utilising two such keys are often termed as "asymmetric cryptography" **[Rule 3]**.

Creation of Digital Signature:

To sign an electronic record or any other item of information, the signer shall first apply the hash function in the signer's software. The hash function shall compute a hash result of standard length which is unique (for all practical purposes) to the electronic record. The signer's software shall transform the hash result into a Digital Signature using signer's private key. The resulting Digital Signature shall be unique to both electronic record and private key used to create it. The Digital Signature shall be attached to its electronic record and stored or transmitted with its electronic record **[Rule 4]**.

Verification of Digital Signature:

In relation to Digital Signature, electronic record or public key, expression "verify" shall mean to determine whether —

(a) the initial electronic record was affixed with the Digital Signature by the use of private key corresponding to the public key of the subscriber;

(b) the initial electronic record is retained intact or has been altered since such electronic record was so affixed with the Digital Signature **[Sec. 2(zg)]**.

The verification of a Digital Signature shall be accomplished by computing a new 'hash result' of the; original electronic record by means of the hash function used to create a Digital Signature and by using the public key and the new hash result, the verifier shall check:

(i) if the Digital Signature was created using the corresponding private key; and

(ii) if the newly computed hash result matches the original result which was transformed into Digital Signature during the signing process.

The verification software will confirm the Digital Signature as verified if:

(a) the signer's private key was used to digitally sign the electronic record, which is known to be the case if the signer's public key was used to verify the signature because the signer's public key will verify only a Digital Signature created with the signer's private key; and

(b) the electronic record was unaltered, which is known to be the case if the hash result computed by the verifier is identical to the hash result extracted from the Digital Signature during the verification process **[Rule 5].**

Use of Digital Signature for authentication

Suppose Piyush wants to send a signed message to Prashant. He creates a message digest by using a hash function on the message. The message digest serves as a "digital fingerprint" of the message; if any part of the message is modified, the hash function returns a different result. Piyush then encrypts the message digest with her private key. This encrypted message digest is the digital signature for the message.

Piyush sends both the message and the digital signature to Prashant. When Prashant receives them, he decrypts the signature using Piyush's public key, thus revealing the message digest. To verify the message, he then hashes the message with the same hash function Piyush used and compares the result to the message digest he received from Piyush. If they are exactly equal, Prashant can be confident that the message did indeed come from Piyush and has not changed since she signed it. If the message digests are not equal, the message either originated elsewhere or was altered after it was signed.

Note that using a digital signature does not encrypt the message itself. If Piyush wants to ensure the privacy of the message, she must also encrypt it using Prashant's public key. Then only Prashant can read the message by decrypting it with his private key.

It is not feasible for anyone to either find a message that hashes to a given value or to find two messages that hash to the same value. If either were feasible, an intruder could attach a false message onto Piyush's signature.

Specific hash functions have been designed to have the property that finding a match is not feasible, and are therefore considered suitable for use in cryptography.

One or more Digital IDs can accompany a digital signature. If a Digital ID is present, the recipient (or a third party) can check the authenticity of the public key.

DIGITAL SIGNATURE CERTIFICATE

Digital Signature Certificate is issued by the Certifying Authority to a subscriber **[Sec.2(q)]**. Certifying Authority is a person who has been granted a licence to issue a Digital Signature Certificate **[Sec.2(g)]**. Any person may make an application to the Certifying Authority for the issue of a Digital Signature Certificate in such form as may be prescribed by the Central Government. Every such application shall be accompanied by such fee not exceeding Rs.25,000 as may be prescribed by the Central Government, to be paid to the Certifying Authority **[Sec.35(I)(2)]**.

Every such application shall be accompanied by a Certification Practice Statement or where there is no such statement, a statement containing such particulars as may be specified by regulations **[Sec.35(3)]**.

Certification Practice Statement:

Certification Practice Statement is a statement issued by a Certifying Authority to specify the practices that the Certifying Authority employs in issuing Digital Signature Certificate **[Sec.2(h)]**. The Certification Practice Statement of the Certifying Authority shall comply with, and be governed by, the laws of the country **[Rule 19]**.

On receipt of an application, the Certifying Authority may, after consideration of the Certification Practice Statement or other statement and after making such enquiries as it may deem fit, grant the Digital Signature Certificate **[Sec.35(4)]**.

Compliances for issue of Digital Signature Certificate:

The Certifying Authority before granting the Digital Signature Certificate should be satisfied that —

(a) the applicant holds the private key corresponding to the public key to be listed in the Digital Signature Certificate;

(b) the applicant holds a private key, which is capable of creating a Digital Signature; (c) the public key to be listed in the certificate can be used to verify a Digital Signature affixed by the private key held by the applicant **[Proviso to Sec.35(4)]**.

Besides the above compliances, the Certifying Authority shall, for issuing the Digital Signature. Certificate, also comply with the following, namely:

(a) The Digital Signature Certificate shall be issued only after a Digital Signature Certificate. Application in the form, with the particulars given in the Model Form given in Schedule-IV, provided by the Certifying Authority has been submitted by the subscriber to the Certifying Authority and the same has been approved by it.

(b) No interim Digital Signature Certificate shall be issued.

(c) The Digital Signature Certificate shall be generated by the Certifying Authority upon receipt of an authorised and validated request for:

(i) new Digital Signature Certificates; (ii) Digital Signature Certificate's renewal.

(d) The Digital Signature Certificate must contain or incorporate by reference, such information, as is sufficient to locate or identify one or more repositories in which revocation or suspension of the Digital Signature Certificate will be listed, if the Digital Signature Certificate is suspended or revoked.

(e) The subscriber identity verification method employed for issuance of Digital Signature Certificate shall be specified in the Certification Practice Statement and shall be subject to the approval of the Controller during the application for a licence:

(i) where the Digital Signature Certificate is issued to a person (referred to in this clause as a New Digital Signature Certificate) on the basis of another valid Digital Signature Certificate held by the said person (referred in this clause as an Originating Digital Signature Certificate) and subsequently the originating Digital Signature Certificate has been suspended or revoked, the Certifying Authority that issued the new Digital Signature Certificate shall conduct investigations to determine whether it is necessary to suspend or revoke the new Digital Signature Certificate;

(ii) the Certifying Authority shall provide a reasonable opportunity for the subscriber to verify the contents of the Digital Signature Certificate before it is accepted;

(iii) if the subscriber accepts the issued Digital Signature Certificate, the Certifying Authority shall publish a signed copy of the Digital Signature Certificate in a repository;

(iv) where the Digital Signature Certificate has been issued by the licensed Certifying Authority and accepted by the subscriber, and the Certifying Authority comes to know pf any fact, or otherwise, that affects the validity or reliability of such Digital Signature Certificate, it shall notify the same to the subscriber immediately;

(v) all Digital Signature Certificates shall be issued with a designated expiry date **[Rule 24]**.

Before the issue of the Digital Signature Certificate, the Certifying Authority shall also — (i) confirm that the user's name does not appear in its list of compromised users;

(ii) comply with the procedure as defined in his Certification Practice Statement including verification of identification and/or employment;

(iii) comply with all privacy requirements;

(iv) obtain a consent of the person requesting the Digital Signature Certificate, that the details of such Digital Signature Certificate can be published on a directory service **[Rule 26]**.

The Certifying Authority, for reasons to be recorded in writing, may reject the application. No application shall be rejected unless the applicant has been given a reasonable opportunity of showing cause against the proposed rejection **[Second Proviso to Sec.35(4)]**.

Legal status of documents signed with Digital Signatures

It may be noted that digital signature is unlike a conventional signature. It is nothing but transformation of an electronic record into another electronic record with the help of private key. If digital signatures are to replace handwritten signatures they must have the same legal status as handwritten signatures, i.e., documents signed with digital signatures must be legally binding. NIST has stated that its proposed Digital Signature Standard should be capable of "proving to a third party that data was actually signed by the generator of the signature." Furthermore, U.S. federal government purchase orders will be signed by any such standard; this implies that the government will support the legal authority of digital signatures in the courts. Some preliminary legal research has also resulted in the opinion that digital signatures would meet the requirements of legally binding signatures for most purposes, including commercial use as defined in the Uniform Commercial Code (UCC). A GAO (Government Accounting Office) decision requested by NIST also opines that digital signatures will meet the legal standards of handwritten signatures.

However, since the validity of documents with digital signatures has never been challenged in court, their legal status is not yet well-defined. Through such challenges, the courts will issue rulings that collectively define which digital signature methods, key sizes, and security precautions are acceptable for a digital signature to be legally binding.

Digital signatures have the potential to possess greater legal authority than handwritten signatures. If a ten page contract is signed by hand on the tenth page, one cannot be sure that the first nine pages have not been altered.

However, if the contract was signed with digital signatures, a third party can verify that not one byte of the contract has been altered.

Currently, if two people want to digitally sign a series of contracts, they might first sign a paper contract in which they agree to be bound in the future

by any contracts digitally signed by them with a given signature method and minimum key size.

Several efforts are underway to legislate the legality and use of digital signatures. Utah has implemented laws qualifying digital signatures. Similar legislation is under way in California and New York, with other states following.

Fees for issue of Digital Signature Certificate:

The Certifying Authority shall charge such fee for the issue of Digital Signature Certificate as may be prescribed by the Central Government.

Fee may be payable in respect of access to Certifying Authority's X.500 directory for certificate downloading. Where fees are payable, Certifying Authority shall provide an up-to-date fee schedule to all its subscribers and users which may be done by publishing the fee schedule on a nominated web site.

Fees may be payable in respect of access to Certifying Authority's X.500 directory service for certificate revocation or status information. Where fees are payable, Certifying Authority shall provide an up-to-date fee schedule to all its subscribers and users which may be done by publishing the fee schedule on a nominated web site.

No fee is to be levied for access to Certification Practice Statement via internet. A fee may be charged by the Certifying Authority for providing printed copies of its Certification Practice Statement **[Rule 31]**.

Representations upon issuance of Digital Signature Certificate:

A Certifying Authority while issuing a Digital Signature Certificate shall certify that —

(a) it has complied with the provisions of this Act and the rules and regulations made thereunder;

(b) it has published the Digital Signature Certificate or otherwise made it available to such person relying on it and the subscriber has accepted it;

(c) the subscriber holds the private key corresponding to the public key, listed in the Digital Signature Certificate;

(d) the subscriber's public key and private key constitute a functioning key pair;

(e) the information contained in the Digital Signature Certificate is accurate; and

(f) it has no knowledge of any material fact, which, if it had been included in the Digital Signature Certificate, would adversely affect the reliability of the representations made in clàuses (a) to (d) above **[Sec.36]**.

Digital Signature Certificate Standards:

All Digital Signature certificates issued by Certifying Authorities shall conform to ITU X.509 Version 3 Standard [Rule 7]. The Information Technology (IT) architecture for Certifying Authorities may support open standards and accepted de-facto standards, the most important standards that may be considered for different activities associated with the Certifying Authorities functions, are as under **[Rule 6]**.

The Product	The Standard
Public Key Infrastructure	PKIX
Digital Signature Certificates and	X509 version 3 certificates as specified in ITU
Digital Signature, revocation list	RFC 1422
Directory (DAP and LDAP)	X500 for publication of certificates and Certification Revocation Lists (CRLs)
Database Management Operations	Use of generic SQL
Public Key Algorithm	DSA and RSA
Digital Hash Function	MD5and$HA-l
RSA Public Key Technology	PKCS # 1 RSA Encryption Standard (512, 1024,2048 bit) PKCS # 5 Password Based Encryption Standard PKQS # 7 Cryptographic Message Syntax Standard PKCS # 8 Private Key Information Syntax Standard PKCS # 9 Selected Attribute Types PKCS # 10 RSA Certification Request PKCS # 12 Portable format for storing/ transporting a user's private keys and certificates.
Distinguished name	X520
Digital Encryption and Digital Signature	PKCS # 7
Digital Signature Request Format	PKCS # 10

Contents of Digital Signature Certificate:

Digital Signature Certificate shall *inter alia* also, besides above standards, contain the following data, namely —

(a) Serial Number (assigning of serial number to the Digital Signature Certificate by Certifying Authority to distinguish it from other certificate);

(b) Signature Algorithm Identifier (which identifies the algorithm used by Certifying Authority to sign the Digital Signature Certificate);

(c) Issuer Name (name of the Certifying Authority who issued the Digital Signature Certificate);

(d) Validity period of the Digital Signature Certificate;

(e) Name of the subscriber (whose public key the Certificate identifies); and

(f) Public Key information of the subscriber **[Rule 7]**.

Generation of Digital Signature Certificate:

The generation of the Digital Signature Certificate shall involve —

(a) receipt of an approved and verified Digital Signature Certificate request;

(b) creating a new Digital Signature Certificate;

(c) binding the key pair associated with the Digital Signature Certificate to a Digital Signature Certificate owner;

(d) issuing the Digital Signature Certificate and the associated public key for operational use;

(e) a distinguished name associated with the Digital Signature Certificate owner; and

(f) a recognized and relevant policy as defined in Certification Practice Statement **[Rule 25]**.

Certificate Lifetime:

A Digital Signature Certificate shall be issued with a designated expiry date. In the event of suspension of Digital Signature Certificate, on withdrawal of suspension, the Digital Signature Certificate shall return to the operational use. Digital Signature Certificate shall expire automatically upon reaching the designated expiry date at which time —

(i) the Digital Signature Certificate shall be archived, on expiry, shall not be re-used;

(ii) the period for which a Digital Signature Certificate has been issued shall not be extended. A new Digital Signature Certificate may be, however, issued after the expiry of such period **[Rule 26]**.

Normally, a key expires after some period of time, such as one year, and a document signed with an expired key should not be accepted. However, there are many cases where it is necessary for signed documents to be regarded as legally valid for much longer than two years; long-term leases and contracts are examples. By registering the contract with a digital time-stamping service at the time it is signed, the signature can be validated even after the key expires.

If all parties to the contract keep a copy of the time-stamp, each can prove that the contract was signed with valid keys. In fact, the time-stamp can prove the validity of a contract even if one signer's key gets compromised at some point after the contract was signed. Any digitally signed document can be time-stamped, assuring that the validity of the signature can be verified after the key expires.

Archival of Digital Signature Certificate:

A Certifying Authority shall archive —

(a) application for issue of Digital Signature Certificate;

(b) registration and verification documents of generated Digital Signature Certificate;

(c) Digital Signature Certificate;

(d) notices of suspension;

(e) information of suspended Digital Signature Certificates;

(f) information of revoked Digital Signature Certificates;

(g) expired Digital Signature Certificates, for a minimum period of seven years or for a period in accordance with legal requirement **[Rule 28]**.

Compromise of Digital Signature Certificate:

Digital Signature Certificates in operational use that become compromised shall be revoked in accordance with the procedure defined in the Certification Practice Statement of Certifying Authority.

Digital Signature Certificates shall —

(a) be deemed to be compromised where the integrity of —

(i) the private key associated with the Digital Signature Certificate is in doubt;

(ii) the Digital Signature Certificate owner is in doubt, as to the use, or attempted use of his key pairs, or otherwise, for malicious or unlawful, purposes;

(b) remain in the compromised state for only such time as it takes to arrange for revocation **[Rule 29]**.

Suspension of Digital Signature Certificate:

The Certifying Authority may suspend the Digital Signature Certificate on receipt of a request from the subscriber listed in the Digital Signature Certificate or from any person duly authorised to act on behalf of the subscriber. The Certifying Authority may also suspend the Digital Signature Certificate if it is of the opinion that the Digital Signature Certificate should be suspended in public interest.

A Digital Signature Certificate shall not be suspended for a period exceeding 15 days unless the subscriber has been given an opportunity of being heard in the matter. On suspension of a Digital Signature Certificate, the Certifying Authority shall communicate the same to the subscriber **[Sec.37]**.

Revocation of Digital Signature Certificate:

The Certifying Authority may revoke a Digital Signature Certificate issued by it —

(a) where the subscriber or any other person authorised by him makes a request to that effect; or

(b) upon the death of the subscriber; or

(c) upon the dissolution of the firm or winding up of the company where the subscriber is a firm or a company.

A Certifying Authority may also revoke a Digital Signature Certificate, if it is of the opinion that —

(a) a material fact represented in the Digital Signature Certificate is false or has been concealed;

(b) a requirement for issuance of the Digital Signature Certificate was not satisfied;

(c) the Certifying Authority's private key or security system was comprised in a manner materially affecting the Digital Signature Certificate's reliability;.

(d) the subscriber has been declared insolvent or dead or where a subscriber is a firm or a company, which has been dissolved, wound-up or otherwise ceased to exist.

Digital Signature Certificate shall be revoked. and become invalid for any trusted use, where —

(a) there is a compromise of the Digital Signature Certificate owner's private key;

(b) there is a misuse of the Digital Signature Certificate;

(c) there is misrepresentation or errors in the Digital Signature Certificate;

(d) the Digital Signature Certificate is no longer required **[Rule 30(1)]**.

The revoked Digital Signature Certificate shall be added to the Certificate Revocation List (CRL) **[Rule 30]**.

A Digital Signature Certificate shall not be revoked unless the subscriber has been given an opportunity of being heard in the matter. On revocation of a Digital Signature Certificate, the Certifying Authority shall communicate the same to the subscriber **[Sec.38]**.

Publication of notice of suspension or revocation:

Where a Digital Signature Certificate is suspended or revoked, the Certifying Authority shall publish a notice of such suspension or revocation, as the case may be, in the repository or repositories specified in the Digital Signature Certificate for publication of such notice **[Sec.39]**.

Digital Signatures help detect altered documents and transmission errors:

A digital signature is superior to a handwritten signature in that it attests to the contents of a message as well as to the identity of the signer. As long as a secure hash function is used, there is no way to take someone's signature from one document and attach it to another, or to alter the signed message in any way. The slightest change in a signed document will cause the digital signature verification process to fail. Thus, authentication allows people to check the integrity of signed documents. Of course, if a signature verification fails, it may be unclear if there was an attempted forgery or simply a transmission error.

DUTIES OF SUBSCRIBERS

Subscriber means a person in whose name, the Digital Signature Certificate is issued **[Sec.2(zf)]**.

The method used to verify and authenticate the identity of a subscriber is known as "Subscriber Identity Verification Method" **[Rule 2(k)]**.

1. *Generating key pair:* Where the public key of any Digital Signature Certificate corresponds to the private key listed in the Digital Signature Certificate of that subscriber, then the subscriber shall generate the key pair by applying the security procedure **[Sec.40]**.

Secure Digital Signature: If, by application of a security procedure agreed to by the parties concerned, it can be verified that a Digital Signature, at the time it was affixed, was —

(a) unique to the subscriber affixing it;

(b) capable of identifying such subscriber;

(c) created in a manner or using a means under the exclusive control of the subscriber and is linked to the electronic record to which it relates in such a manner that if the electronic record was altered, the Digital Signature would be invalidated, then such Digital Signature shall be deemed to be a secured Digital Signature **[Sec.15]**.

2. *On acceptance of Digital Signature Certificate:* The Digital Signature Certificate must have been accepted by the subscriber. A subscriber shall be deemed to have accepted a Digital Signature Certificate, if he publishes or authorises the publication of a Digital Signature Certificate to one or more persons, in a repository, or otherwise demonstrates his approval of the Digital Signature Certificate in any manner **[Sec.41(I)]**.

By accepting a Digital Signature Certificate, the subscriber certifies to all who reasonably rely on the information contained in the Digital Signature Certificate that —

(a) the subscriber holds the private key corresponding to the public key listed in the Digital Signature Certificate and is entitled to hold the same;

(b) all representations made by the subscriber to the Certifying Authority and all material relevant to the information contained in the Digital Signature Certificate are true;

(c) all information in the Digital Signature Certificate that is within the knowledge of the subscriber is true **[Sec.41(2)]**.

3. ***Control of private key:*** Every subscriber shall exercise reasonable care to retain control of the private key corresponding to the public key listed in his Digital Signature Certificate and shall take all steps to prevent its disclosure to a person not authorised to affix the Digital Signature of the subscriber. If the private key corresponding to the public key listed in the Digital Signature Certificate has been compromised, then, the subscriber shall communicate the same without any delay to the Certifying Authority in such manner as may be specified by the Regulations. The subscriber shall be liable till he has informed the Certifying Authority that the private key has been compromised. **[Sec.42].**

4. ***To extend facilities to decrypt information:*** If the controller is satisfied that it is necessary or expedient in the interest of the sovereignty or integrity of India to safeguard the security of the State, friendly relations with foreign States or public order or for preventing incitement to the commission of any cognizable offence, for reasons to be recorded in writing, by order, direct any agency of the Government to intercept any information transmitted through any computer resource. The subscriber or any person incharge of the computer resource shall, when called upon by any agency which has been directed as aforesaid, extend all facilities and technical assistance to decrypt the information. The subscriber or any person who fails to assist the agency shall be punished with an imprisonment for a term which may extend to seven years **[Sec. 69].**

5. **If the PIN does not appear to work:** use the "copy" and "paste" commands from the Edit menu to copy your PIN from the E-mail you received and paste it into the field on the page you use to get your Digital ID. If copying and pasting does not work with your software, and you must type the PIN, make sure: the PIN includes 16 or 32 characters, the characters include only the numerals 0 (zero) 9 and the letters A through F; there are no spaces before, after, or within the PIN.

6. **When you try to download your Digital ID you get the message "private key not found":** In such a situation, when you retrieve your Digital ID, we automatically check to make sure that the private key created in your hard drive during enrollment matches the public key in your Digital ID. In order for these to match, you must be using the same web browser, in the same directory, on the same computer as you were when you requested the Digital ID.

ELECTRONIC GOVERANCE

Information Technology is changing the way the society functions.

Internet is the biggest revolution in human history. The impact of ITcan be felt in all economic and social activities in every conceivable manner. The convergence of all forms of communications on the digital playfield is opening up immense new possibilities of achieving speed, versatility and space-time independence.

Governments are no exception to this phenomenon. In the post liberalization era, governments across the country have been engaged in improving internal efficiencies, responsiveness, coordination and integration between various government departments and external agencies, citizens and businesses. The global trends also point out to the emergence of e-Government revolution after the Internet and ecommerce revolutions.

We often hear a number of words coined to describe this newly founded love between the Governments and the computers — "Good Governance", "SMART Government" and "e-Government". It is pertinent to state clearly what they mean.

'Good Governance' connotes the widest meaning of the three phrases. It encompasses the entire process of public administration, the processes underlying the formulation of public policies, the HRD efforts required for re-skilling the government machinery, prioritization, efficient management of public resources and above all re-designing the various instruments used to realize the concept of a welfare state. 'SMART Government' is an acronym for Simple, Moral, Accountable, Responsive and Transparent Government. It is the image of an ideal government through the eyes of its constituents.

e-Government is a subset of the concepts of Good Governance and SMART Government. It is the very specific task of using the tools offered by Information Technology in various aspects of the process of governance with the objective of achieving efficiency, transparency, accountability and user-friendliness in all the transactions that the citizens and businesses conduct with the Government – that is, providing digital interface in the G2C and G2B interactions.

In the last decade of twentieth century, we heard a hue and cry about E-Commerce.

Experts estimated that in future E-Commerce transactions would overtake conventional transactions throughout the world. A vast employment opportunity of E-Commerce-personnel was also expected. In commensurate with the actions of other countries, Govt. of India enacted Information Technology Act, 2000 to facilitate E-Commerce transactions, inter alia other objectives.

In a broad sense, Electronic Commerce (E-Commerce) includes not only Internet commerce but also transactions through other electronic medium. In other words it can be described as —

(1) transaction between a company and its customers, i.e., buying and selling of goods, services and information (including after-sale service and support);

(2) exchange of structured business information between two or more companies, e.g., Electronic Data Interchange (EDI); and

(3) internal commerce involving work flow re-engineering, product and service customization, Supply Chain Management (SCM) etc; by using electronic devices.

Electronic devices used for E-Commerce are – (i) Bar Code Machines, (ii) Vending Machines, (iii) Telephone & Telegraphs, (iv) Fax, (v) Television, (vi) Stand alone Computers, (vii) Computer Network, (viii) Internet, WWW & E-mail.

When Internet is used as the medium of transaction, it is called *Internet Commerce (I Commerce)*. At present, the words E-Commerce and I-Commerce have become synonymous. It is because the concept of E-Commerce became popular only during the Internet era, although it was in practice for decades. In future, with the convergence of communication technologies, E-Commerce can be accomplished through any of the networks that make up the Information Superhighway (I-way).

Types of E-Commerce

One way of classifying E-Commerce is based on parties involved in the transaction. Major types are mentioned below:

- Business to Customers (B2C)
- Business to Business (B2B)
- Government to Business (G2B)
- Government to Citizens (G2C)
- Academic Institutions to Students (AI2S)

The name of a type indicates the parties involved in that type of E-ommerce transactions. It may be noted that this list is not exhaustive.

Legal Recognition of Electronic Records

Section 4 of the Act states that when under any particular law, in any information in to be provided in writing or typewritten or printed form, then notwithstanding that law, the same information can be provided in electronic form which can also be accessed for any future reference. This non-obstanate provision will make it possible to enter into legally binding contract on-line.

Therefore, the Act provides for legal recognitions of electronic records and digital signatures in Government and its agencies. Electronic Governance is recognition by Government to accept communication, storage of information, acceptance of digital signatures in electronic forms and retention of electronic records and giving it a legal sanctity.

Legal Recognition of Digital Signature

Section 5 provides that when any information or other matter needs to be authenticated by the signature of a person, the same can be authenticated by means of digital signature affixed in a manner prescribed by the Central Government.

Under Section 10, the Central Government has powers to make rules prescribing the type of digital signature, the manner in which it shall be affixed, the procedure to identify the person affixing the signature, the maintenance of integrity, security and confidentiality of electronic records or payments and rules regarding any other appropriate matters.

Furthermore, these digital signatures are to be authenticated by Certifying Authorities (CAs) appointed under the Act. These authorities would *inter alia*, have the license to issue Digital Signature Certificates (DSCs). The applicant must have a private key that can create a digital signature. This private key and the public key listed on the DSC must form the functioning key pair.

Once the subscriber has accepted the DSC, he shall generate the key pair by applying the security procedure. Every subscriber is under an obligation to exercise reasonable care and caution to retain control of the private key corresponding to the public key listed in his DSC. The subscriber must take all precautions not to disclose the private key to any third party. If however, the private key is compromised, he must communicate the same to the Certifying Authority (CA) without any delay.

Network Related Terminologies

1. Computer Network — Connection between two or more computers through cable line or through satellite. It is a hardware link managed by software.

Following types of computer networks are found:

LAN (Local Area Network) — Normally within an organization.

MAN (Metropolitan Area Network) — Normally within a Metro.

WAN (Wide Area Network) — Normally within a State/Country.

Internet (International Network) — WANs located in different parts of the world are connected to form a worldwide network of computers. It is a networking of the networks. Internet connections may be — (a) Dial up line, (b) ISDN line, (c) Leased line etc.

2. Web Server — It is the software, with the help of which websites are published. Examples of **HTTP** (Hyper Text Transfer Protocol) based Web Servers are — Apache, Quid Quo Pro, Quid Pro Quo, Front Page, Website Professional etc. Servers based on other protocols are FTP, Gopher, NNTP, Database etc.

3. Web Browser — The software that fetches and displays websites. Example — NCSA Mosaic (being the first, developed in 1993), Internet Explorer,

Netscape Navigator etc. It is also called **Client.**

4. Server Computers — These computers host web servers and are located at the place of Internet Service Providers.

5. Client Computers — The computers located in offices, at homes etc. through which we access to web sites.

6. Hypertext — It is that type of text (used in web), which facilitates hyper linking of web documents containing text, graphics, animation, audio, video, images or programs. It is also called hypermedia.

7. Web Pages — Hypertext documents in the Internet are called web pages.

Each page is a hypertext file. A set of web pages of a particular organisation is called Web Site. The first page is called Home Page. It is also called **Web or Domain.**

8. WWW (World Wide Web) — It was the first website developed at CERN, Switzerland, in 1989. Presently websites as a whole are called WWW. WWW is also the name of an Internet search tool.

9. Portal — Websites, which have the facility of search engines, e-mail and other value added services, are called portals.

10. Search Engine — Some websites facilitates searching of web addresses relating to a particular subject. If we type the subject matter in the designated text box, the search engine will give a complete list of web addresses, which contain the subject matter.

11. Cyber (Cybernetics) — Cybernetics is the science of communication and control in biological system. Computer systems also have a built-in mechanism of communication and control. However, the word 'cyber' has become synonymous with the word Internet.

12. Protocol & Protocol Suite — A protocol consists of software and it is the communication language spoken by the computers in the network. A *protocol suite* is a set of protocols. At present, two protocol suites are in use — (i) TCP/IP (ii) ISO/OSI (International Standard Organization/ Open System Interconnection).

13. TCP/IP (Transmission Control Protocol/Internet Protocol) — Developed in mid-seventies. The purpose of TCP/IP was to connect different network (i.e., copper wire, radio, microwave) and still enable the host computers to talk to each other coherently.

14. URL (Universal Resource Locator) — Another name of website address. It helps to locate web resources. It is also called **Domain Name.**

15. ISP (Internet Service Provider) — The agency that provides service related to Internet. Example — VSNL, BSNL, Satyam etc.

16. Gateway — It is the main gate through which Internet links with other countries are maintained. Example — VSNL in India.

17. Modem (Modulator Demodulator) — Computers are digital but telephone lines are analog. For data communication through Internet, conversion from analog to digital and *vice-versa* is required. A modem serves this purpose.

However, where the telephone line is digital, use of modem is not required.

18. Firewall — A firewall a security system for network. It consists of hardware, software or both that isolates a private network from a public network. It allows insiders full access to the public network but allows only selective access from the public network.

19. M-commerce — E-commerce with the help of mobile phone/laptop etc. is called M-commerce.

20. VAN (Value Added Network) — It is a network that works as a storehouse/ mailbox. It is used in EDI and cell phone network. A data deposited in a VAN can be retrieved according to the convenience of the receiver.

ELECTRONIC RECORDS

Where any law provides that information or any other matter shall be in writing or in the typewritten or printed form, then, notwithstanding anything contained in such law, such requirement shall be deemed to have been satisfied if such information or matter is —

(a) rendered or made available in an electronic, form; and

(b) accessible so as to be usable for a subsequent reference **[Sec.4]**.

Electronic form: It means any information generated, sent, received or stored in media, magnetic, optical, computer memory, micro film, computer generated micro fiche or similar device **[Sec.2(r)]**.

Access means gaining entry into, instructing or communicating with the logical, arithmetical, or memory function resources of a computer, computer system or computer network **[Sec.2(a)]**.

Computer: It means any electronic, magnetic, optical or other high speed data processing device or system which performs logical, arithmetic, and memory functions by manipulations of electronic, magnetic or optical impulses and includes all input, output, processing, storage, computer software, or communication facilities which are connected or related to the computer in a computer system or computer network **[Sec.2(i)]**.

Computer network: This means the interconnections of one or more computers through — (i) the use of satellite, microwave, terrestrial line or other communication media; and (ii) terminals or a complex consisting of two or more interconnected computers whether or not the interconnection is continuously maintained **[Sec.2(j)]**.

Computer resource: It means computer, computer system, computer network, data, computer database or software **[Sec.2(k)]**.

Computer system: It means a device or collection of devices, including input and output support devices and excluding calculators which are not programmable and capable of being used in conjunction with external files which contain computer programmes, electronic instructions input data and output data, that performs logic, arithmetic, data storage and retrieval, communication control and other functions **[Sec.2(l)]**.

Data: It means a representation of information, knowledge, facts, concepts or instructions which are being prepared or have been prepared in a formalised manner and is intended to be processed, is being processed or has been processed in a computer system or computer network and may be in any form (including computer printouts, magnetic or optical storage media punched cards, punched tapes) or stored internally in the memory of the computer **[Sec.2(o)]**.

Function: In relation to a computer function, includes logic, control, arithmetical process, deletion, storage and retrieval and communication or telecommunication from or within a computer **[Sec.2(t)]**.

Information: Information includes data, text, images, sounds, voice, codes, computer programmes, software and databases or micro film or computer generated micro fiche **[Sec.2(u)]**.

Information asset: This means all information resources utilised in the course of any organisation's business and includes all information, applications (software developed or purchased), and technology (hardware, system software and networks) **[Rule 2(f)]**.

Use of electronic record and digital signatures in Government and its agencies

Section 6 states where any law provides for the following –

(a) The filings of any form, application or any other document with any office, authority, body or agency owned or controlled by the appropriate Government in a particular manner,

(b) The issue or grant of any license, permit, sanction or approval by whatever name called in or a particular manner,

(c) The receipt or payment of money in a particular, then, such requirement shall be deemed to have been satisfied if such filing, issue, grant, receipt or payment, as the case may be, is effected by means of such electronic form as may be prescribed by the appropriate Government.

Accordingly the appropriate Government may, by rules prescribe —

(a) the manner and format in which such electronic records shall be filed, created or issued,

(b) the manner or method of payment of any fee or charges for filing, creation or issue any electron record.

Electronic form means any information generated, sent, received or stored in media, magnetic, optical, computer memory, micro film, computer generated micro fiche or similar device **[Sec.2(r)]**.

Retention of electronic records (Section 7)

Where any law provides that documents, records or information shall be retained for any specific period, then, that requirement shall be deemed to have been satisfied if such documents, records or information are retained in the electronic form, if

(a) The information contained therein remains accessible so as to be usable for a subsequent reference,

(b) The electronic record in retained in the format in which it was originally generated, sent or received or in a format which can be demonstrated to represent accurately the information originally generated, sent or received,

(c) The details which will facilitate the identification of the origin, destination, date and time of the dispatch or receipt of such electronic record are available in the electronic record. This clause shall not apply to any information which is automatically generated solely for the purpose of enabling an electronic record to be dispatched or received.

The above provisions shall not apply to any law that expressly provides for the retention of documents, records or information in the form of electronic records **[Sec. 7]**.

Publication in Electronic Gazette (Section 8)

Electronic Gazette means official Gazette published in the electronic form **[Sec.2(ra)]**. Where any law provides that any rule, regulation, order, bye, law, notification or any other matter shall be published in the official Gazelle, then, such requirement shall be deemed to have been satisfied if such rule, regulation, order, bye-law, notification or any other mailer is published in the Official Gazette. However, where any rule, regulation, order, bye-law, ratification or any other mailer is published in the Official Gazette, the date of publication shall be deemed to be the date of the Gazette which was first published in any form **[Sec.8]**.

Protected System

The appropriate Government may, by notification in the Official Gazette declare that any computer, computer system or computer network to be a protected system. The appropriate Government may, by order in writing, authorise the persons who are authorised to access protected systems notified. Any person who secures access or attempts to secure access to a protected system in contravention of this provision shall be punished with imprisonment of either description for a term which may extend to 10 years and shall also be liable to fine **[Sec.7]**.

Appropriate Government, in respect of any matter, enumerated in List-II of the Seventh Schedule to the Constitution and relating to any State law enacted under List-III of the Seventh Schedule to the Constitution means the State Government. In any other case, the appropriate Government means the Central Government **[Sec.2(e)]**.

No right conferred to insist that document should be accepted in electronic form.

The above provisions shall not confer a right on any person to insist that any ministry or department of a Central Government or the State Government or any authority or body established by or under any law or controlled or funded by the Central or State Government should accept, issue, create, retain and preserve any document in the form of electronic records or effect any monetary transaction in the electronic form **[Sec. 9]**.

Power to make rules by Central Government in respect of Digital Signature (Section 10)

The Central Government may, for the purposes of this Act, by rules prescribe —

(a) The type of digital signature,

(b) The manner and format in which the digital signature shall be affixed,

(c) The manner and procedure which facilitates certification of the person affixing the digital signature.

(d) Control processes and procedures to ensure adequate integrity security and confidentiality of electronic records or payments and

(e) any other matter which in necessary to give legal effect to digital signatures.

Manner in which information be authenticated by means of Digital Signature:

Where any law provides that information or any other matter shall be authenticated by affixing the signature or any document should be signed or bear the signature of any person, then, notwithstanding anything contained in such law, such requirement shall be deemed to have been satisfied, if such information or matter is authenticated by means of digital signature affixed in such manner as may be prescribed by the Central Government **[Sec.5]**.

A Digital Signature shall —

(a) be created and verified by cryptography that concerns itself with transforming electronic record into seemingly unintelligible forms and back again;

(b) use what is known as "Public Key Cryptography", which employs an algorithm using two different but mathematical related "keys" — one for creating a Digital Signature or transforming data into a seemingly unintelligible form, and another key for verifying a Digital Signature or returning the electronic record to original form. The process termed as hash function shall be used in both creating and verifying a Digital Signature.

Computer equipment and software utilising two such keys are often termed as "asymmetric cryptography" **[Rule 3]**.

Attribution, Acknowledgement and Dispatch of Electronic Records (Section 11 to 13)

Attribution

Section 11 states that an electronic record shall be attributed to the originator as of it was sent by him or by a person system programmed to operate on behalf of the originator.

Electronic record means data, record or data generated, image or sound stored, received or sent in n electronic form or micro film or computer generated micro fiche **[Sec.2(s)]**.

An electronic record shall be attributed to the originator —

(a) if it was sent by the originator himself;

(b) by a person who had the authority to act on behalf of the originator in respect of that electronic record; or

(c) by an information system programmed by or on behalf of the originator to operate automatically **[Sec.II]**.

Qriginator means a person who sends, generates, stores or transmits any electronic message or a uses any electronic message to be sent, generated, stored or transmitted to any other person but does not include an intermediary [Sec. 2(z)].

Intermediary with respect to any particular electronic message means any person who on behalf of another person receives, stores or transmits that message or provides any service with respect to that message **[Sec.2(v)]**.

Mode of acknowledgement of receipt

As per section 12, the addressee may acknowledge the receipt of the electronic record either in particular manner or form as desired by the originator and in the absence of such regiment, by communication of the acknowledgement to the addresses or by any conduct that would sufficiently constitute acknowledgement **[Sec. 12(1)]**.

Addressee means a person who is intended by the originator to receive the electronic record but does not include any intermediary **[Sec.2(b)]**.

Normally if the originator has stated that the electronic record will be binding only on receipt of the acknowledgement, then unless acknowledgement in received, the record in not binding and unless acknowledgement has been so received, i.e., electronic record shall be deemed to have been never sent by the originator **[Sec.12(2)]**.

However, of the acknowledgement is not received within stipulated time period or in the absence of the time period, within a reasonable time, the originator may notify the addressee to send the acknowledgement, failing which the electronic record will be treated as never been sent **[Sec. 12(3)]**.

Time and place of dispatch and receipt of electronic record (Section 13)

(1) Subject to the agreement between the originator and the addressee, the dispatch of an electronic record occurs when it enters a computer resource outside the control of the originator.

(2) Subject to an agreement between the originator and the addressee, the time of receipt of an electronic record shall be determined as follows:

(a) If the addressee has designated a computer resource for the purpose of receiving electronic records —

(I) receipt occurs at the time when the electronic record enters the designated computer resource, or

(II) If the electronic record in sent to a computer resource of the addressee that in not the designated computer resource receipt occurs at the time when the electronic record in received by the addressee.

(b) If the addressee has not designated a computer resource along with specified timings, if any, receipt recurs when the electronic record enters the computer resource of the addressee.

An electronic record in deemed to be dispatched at the place where the originator has his place of business, and in deemed to be received at the place where addressee has his place of business.

If the addressee or originator has more than one place of business, an electronic record in deemed to be dispatched at the place where the originator has his place of business, and in deemed to be received at the place where addressee has his place of business.

If the addressee or originator has more than one place of business, the principal place of business shall be the place of business. If the originator or the addressee does not have a place of business, his usual place of residence shall be deemed to be the place of business, the "usual place of residence" in relation to a body corporate, means the place where it is registered.

Utility of electronic records and digital signatures in Government Audits Agencies:

According to the provisions of the Act, any forms or applications that have to be filed with the appropriated Government office or authorities can be filed or any licence, permit or sanction can be issued by the Government in an electronic form. Similarly, the receipt or payment of money can also take place electronically.

Moreover, any documents or records that need to be retained for a specific period may be retained in an electronic form provided the document or record is easily accessible in the same format as it was generated, sent or received or in another format that accurately represents the same information that was originally generated, sent or received. The details of the origin, destination, date and time of the dispatch or receipt of the record must also be available in the electronic record.

Furthermore, when any law, rule, regulation or byelaw has to be published in the Official Gazette of the Government, the same can be published in electronic form. If the same are published in printed and electronic form, the date of such publication will be the date on which it is first published.

However, the above mentioned provisions do not give a right to anybody to compel any Ministry or Department of the Government to use electronic means to accept, issue, create, retain and preserve any document or execute any monetary transaction. Nevertheless, if these electronic methods are utilised, the Government will definitely save a lot of money on paper.

SECURE ELECTRONIC RECORDS

Section 14 states that where any security procedure has been applied to an electronic record at a specified point of time, then such record shall be deemed to be a secure electronic record from such point of time to the point of verification.

SECURE DIGITAL SIGNATURE (Sections 15)

If by application of a security procedure agreed to by the parties concerted it can be verified that a digital signature, at the time it was affixed, was —

(a) unique to the subscriber affixing it,

(b) capable of identifying such subscriber,

(c) created in a manner or using a means under the exclusive control of the subscriber and is linked to the electronic record to which it related in such a manner that of the electronic record was altered the digital signature would be invalidated, then such digital signature shall be deemed to be secure digital signature.

SECURITY PROCEDURE (Sections 16)

The Central Government shall prescribe the security procedure having regard to the commercial circumstances prevailing at the time when the procedure was used, including:

(a) The nature of the transaction,

(b) The level of sophistication of the parties with reference to their technological capacity,

(c) The volume of similar transactions engaged in by other parties,

(d) The availability of alternatives offered to by other parties,

(e) The procedures in general use for similar types of transactions or communications.

CONTROLLER AND CERTIFYING AUTHOITIES

Appointment of Controller and other officers (Section 17)

The Central Government may, by notification in the Official Gazette, appoint a Controller of Certifying Authorities for the purposes of this Act. The Controller shall discharge his functions under this Act subject to the general control and direction of Central Government, there shall be a seal of the office of the Controller. Central Government may also by ratification appoint such number of Deputy Controllers and assistant Controllers as it deems fit. The Deputy Controllers and Assistant Controllers shall perform the functions assigned to them by the Controller under the general superintendence and control of the Controller.

The qualification, experience and term and conditions of the service of Controller, Deputy Controllers and Assistant Controllers shall be such as may be prescribed by the Central Government.

The Head Office and Branch Office of the Controller shall be at such places as the Central Government may specify, and these may be established at such places as the Central Government may specify, and these may be established at such places as the Central Government may think fit.

Functions of Controller (Section 18)

The Controller may perform all or any of the following functions namely:

(a) Exercising supervision over the activates of the certifying authorities.

(b) Certifying public keys of the certifying authorities.

(c) Laying down the standards to be maintained by the certifying authorities.

(d) Specifying the qualifications and experience which employees of the certifying authorities should possess.

(e) Specifying the conditions subject to which the certifying authorities shall conduct their business.

(f) Specifying the contents of written printed or visual material and advertisements that may be distributed or used in respect of a Digital Signature Certificate and the public key.

(g) Specifying the form and content of a Digital Signature Certificate and the key.

(h) Specifying the form and manner in which accounts shall be maintained by the certifying authorities.

(i) Specifying the terms and conditions subject to which auditors may be appointed and to which auditors may be appointed and the remuneration to be paid to them.

(j) Facilitating the establishment of any electronic system by a certifying authority either solely or jointly with other certifying authorities and regulation of such systems.

(k) Specifying the manner in which the certifying authorities shall conduct their dealings with the subscribers.

(l) Resolving any conflict of interests between the certifying authorities and the subscribers.

(m) Laying down the duties of the certifying authorities.

(n) Maintaining a data-base containing disclosure record of every Certifying Authority containing such particulars as may be specified by regulations.

Power's of Controller

(1) Recognition of Foreign Certifying Authorities (Section 19)

The Controller may with the previous approval of the Central Government and by notification in the Official Gazette recognize any foreign certifying authority as a certifying authority for the purpose of this Act. Thereupon the Digital Signature Certificate issued shall be valid for the purposes of this Act. However, the Controller may, if he is satisfied that any foreign certifying authority has contravened any of the conditions as restrictions subject to which it was granted recognition, he may, for reasons to be recorded in writing by notification in the Official Gazette, revoke such recognition.

(2) Controller to act as Repository (Section 20)

The Controller shall be the repository of all Digital Signature Certificates issued under this act.

The Controller shall:

(a) Make use of hardware, software and procedures that are secure from intrusion and misuse.

(b) Observe such other standards as may be prescribed by the central Government to ensure that the secrecy and security of the digital signatures are assured. The Controller shall maintain a computerized database of all public keys in such manner that such database and public key are available to any member of the public.

(3) To delegate (Section 27)

The Controller, any, in writing, authorize the Deputy Controller, Assistant Controller or any officer to exercise any of the powers of the Controller.

(4) To investigate contraventions (Section 28)

The Controller or any officer authorized by him in this behalf shall take up for investigation any contravention of the provisions of this Act, rule or regulations made thereunder. The Controller or any office authorized by him in this behalf shall exercise the like powers which are conferred on Income-Tax authorities under Chapter XIII of the Income-Tax Act., 1961 and shall exercise such powers, subject to such limitations laid down under that Act.

(5) Access to Computers and data (Section 29)

The Controller or any person authorized by him shall, if he has reasonable cause that any contravention of the provisions of this Act, rules or regulations made thereunder has been committed, have access to any computer system any apparatus, data or any other material connected with such system, for the purpose of searching or causing a search to be made for obtaining any, Information or data contained in or available to such computer system. The Controller or any person authorized by him may, by order, direct any person incharge of, or otherwise concerned with the operation of the computer system, data apparatus or material, to provide him with such reasonable technical and other assistance as he may consider necessary.

(6) To give directions (Section 68)

The Controller may by order, direct a certifying authority or any employee of such authority to take such measures or erase carrying on such activities as specified in the order if those are necessary to ensure compliance with the provisions of this act, rules or any regulations made there under.

(7) To direct any agency to intercept any information (Section 69)

If the Controller is satisfied, for reasons to be recorded in writing, that it is necessary or expedient in the interest if the sovereignty or integrity if India, the security, if the state, friendly relations with foreign states or public order or for preventing incitement to the commission of any cognizable offence, by order, direct any agency of the government to intercept any information transmitted through any computer resource. The subscriber or any person incharge if the computer resource shall, when called upon any agency, extent all facilities and technical assistance to decrypt the information.

CERTIFYING AUTHORITY

Licensing of certifying authorities:

According to Sec 2(g) of the Act, a certifying authority is a person who has been granted a license to issue digital signature certificates.

Who may apply? (Section 21)

Any person may make an application to the Controller, for a license to issue digital signature certificates.

The applicant shall however, fulfill such requirements with respect to qualifications, expertise, manpower, financial recourses and other infrastructure facilities, which are necessary to issue digital signature certificates as may be prescribed according to Sec. 21(1)(2) of the Act as enumerated herein after.

The following persons may apply for grant if a license to issue digital signature certificates:

1. an individual, being a citizen if India and heaving a capital if five crores of rupees or more in his business and profession.

2. a company having—

(1) paid up capital if not less than five crores of rupees; and

(2) net worth of not less than fifty crores of rupees.

No company, in which the equity share capital held in aggregate by the Non-Resident Indians, Foreign Institutional Investors or Foreign Companies exceeds forty-nine per cent of its capital, shall be eligible for grant of license.

In a case where the company has been registered under the Companies Act 1956 during the preceding financial year or in the financial year during which it applies for grant of licence under the Act and whose main object is to act as certifying authority, the net worth shall be the aggregate net worth of its majority shareholders, beings the Hindu Undivided Family, firm or company holding at least 51% of paid equity capital. The majority shareholders shall not include non-resident Indians, foreign nationals, foreign institutional investor and foreign company.

The majority shareholders of company whose net work has been determined on the basic and such majority shareholders, shall not, without prior approval of the Controller, sell or transfer its equity share hold in such company unless such a company acquires or has its own net work of not less than fifty crores of rupees.

3. a firm having—

(1) Capital subscribed by all partners of not less than five crores of rupees, and

(2) net worth of not less than fifty crores of rupees.

No firm, in which the capital held in aggregate by any non-resident Indian and foreign national exceeds forty-nine per cent of its capital, shall be eligible for grant of licence.

In case where the firm has been registered under the Indian Partnership Act, 1932 during the proceeding financial year or in the financial year during which it applies for grant of license under the Act and whose main object in to act as Certifying Authority, the net worth shall be the aggregate net worth of all of its partners. The partners shall not include Non-Resident Indian and foreign national.

The partners of a firm, whose net worth has been determined on the basis of such partners, shall not, without the approval of the Controller, sell or transfer its capital held in such firm unless such firm has acquired or has its own net worth of not less than fifty crores of rupees.

4. Central Government or a State Government or any of the Ministries or Departments, Agencies or Authorities of such Governments.

Conditions to be complied with:

The applicant being an individual, or a Company or a firm shall submit a performance bond or furnish a banker's guarantee from a scheduled bank in favour of the Controller in such form and in such manner as may be approved by the Controller for an amount of not less than five crores of rupees. The performance bond or bankers guarantee shall remain valid for a period of six years from the date of its submission. The company and firm shall submit a performance bond or furnish a bankers guarantee for ten crores of rupees. This shall not apply to the company or firm after it has acquired or has its net worth of fifty crores of rupees.

The performance bond or bankers guarantee may be invoked –

(1) When the Controller has suspended the license,

(2) For Payment of an offer of compensation made by the Controller, or

(3) For Payment of liabilities and rectification costs attributed to the negligence of the Certifying Authority, its officer's or employees, or

(4) For Payment of the costs incurred in the discontinuation or transfer of operations of the licensed Certifying Authority, if the Certifying Authority's license or operation is discontinued, or

(5) Any other default made by the Certifying Authority in complying with the provisions of the Act or rules made there under.

Besides invocation of performance bond, penalty may be imposed or prosecution may be initiated for any offence under the Act.

How a application for license to be made? (Section 22)

Every application for issue of a licence for a Licensed Certifying Authority shall be made to the Controller in the form at Schedule-I to Information Technology (Certifying Authorities) Rules, 2000. Every application for issue of a licence shall be accompanied by—

(a) a Certification Practice Statement in the framework given in Annexure-I to Information Technology (Certifying Authorities) Regulations, 2001;

(b) a statement including the procedures with respect to identification of the applicant;

(c) a statement for the purpose and scope of anticipated Digital Signature Certificate technology, management, or operations to be outsourced;

(d) certified copies of the business registration documents of Certifying Authority that intends to be licensed;

(e) a description of any event, particularly current or past insolvency that could materially affect the applicant's ability to act as a Certifying Authority;

(f) an undertaking by the applicant that to its best knowledge and belief it can and will comply with the requirements of its Certification Practice Statement;

(g) an undertaking that the Certifying Authority' s operation would not commence until its operation and facilities associated with the functions of generation, issue and management of Digital Signature Certificate are audited by the auditors and approved by the Controller;

(h) an undertaking to submit a performance bond or banker's guarantee within one month of Controller indicating his approval for the grant of licence to operate as a Certifying Authority;

(i) any other information required by the Controller **[Sec.22 & Rule 10]**.

Application for grant of a licence shall be accompanied by a non refundable fee of Rs.25,000 payable by a bank draft or by a pay order in the name of the Controller **[Rule 12(1)]**.

Terms and conditions of licence to issue Digital Signature Certificate:

Every licence to issue Digital Signature Certificates shall be granted subject to the terms and conditions set out in Regulation 3 of Information Technology (Certifying Authorities) Regulations, 2001 **[Reg.3]**.

Issuance of Licence:

The Controller may, within four weeks from the date or receipt of the application after considering the documents accompanying the application and such other factors, as he may deem fit, grant or renew the licence or reject the application. No application shall be rejected unless the applicant has been given a reasonable opportunity of presenting the case.

In exceptional circumstances and for reasons to be recorded in writing, the period of four weeks may be extended to such period, not exceeding eight weeks in all as the Controller may deem fit.

If the application for licensed Certifying Authority is approved, the applicant shall —

(a) submit a performance bond or furnish a banker's guarantee within one month from the date of such approval to the Controller;

(b) execute an agreement with the Controller binding himself to comply with the terms and conditions of the licence and the provisions of the Act and the rules made thereunder **[Sec.24 and Rule 47]**.

Validity of Licence:

A licence granted shall be valid for a period of five years from the date of its issue. The licence shall not be transferable [**Rule 14**] or heritable. A licence shall be subject to such terms and conditions as may be specified by the Regulations **[Sec.21]**.

Every Certifying Authority shall display its licence at a conspicuous place of the premises in which it carries on its business **[Sec.32]**.

Commencement of operation by Licensed Certifying Authorities:

The licensed Certifying Authority shall commence its commercial operation of generation and issue of Digital Signature only after —

(a) it has confirmed to the Controller the adoption of Certification Practice Statement;

(b) it has generated its key pair, namely, private and corresponding public key, and submitted the public key to the Controller;

(c) the installed facilities and infrastructure associated with all functions of generation, issue and management of Digital Signature Certificate have been audited by the accredited auditor; and

(d) it has submitted the arrangement for cross certification with other licensed Certifying Authorities within India to the Controller **[Rule 21]**.

Renewal of License (Section 23)

An application for renewal of license shall be.

(a) in such form as may be prescribed by the Central Government,

(b) in the form of electronic record subject to such requirements as the Controller may deem fit **[Rule 16(3)]**;

(c) Accompanies by such fees not exceeding Rs.500 as may be prescribed by the Central, **[Rule 12(2)]**.

and

(d) Shall be made not less than 45 days before the date of expiry of the period of validity of the license **[Sec.23 & Rule 16]**.

However, an application for the renewal of the license made after the expiry of the license may be entertained on payment of such late fee, not exceeding Rs. 500, as may be prescribed.

Procedure for grant or rejection of license (Section 24)

The Controller may, on receipt of an application under section 21, after considering the documents accompanying the application and such other factors as he deems fit, grant the license or reject the application, however no application shall be rejected unless the applicant has been given a reasonable opportunity's of presenting his case.

The Controller may refuse to grant or renew a licence if —

(i) the applicant has not provided the Controller with such information relating to its business, and to any circumstance likely to affect its method of conducting business, as the Controller may require; or

(ii) the applicant is in the course of being wound up or liquidated; or

(iii) a receiver or manager has been appointed by the court in respect of the applicant; or

(iv) the applicant or any trusted person has been convicted, whether in India or out of India, of an offence the conviction for which involved a finding that the applicant or such trusted person acted fraudulently or dishonestly, or has been convicted of an offence under the Act or these rules; or

(v) the Controller has invoked performance bond or banker's guarantee; or

(vi) a Certifying Authority commits breach of, or fails to observe and comply with the procedures and practices as per the Certification Practice Statement; or

(vii) a Certifying Authority fails to conduct, or does not submit the returns of the audit;

(viii) the audit report recommends that the Certifying Authority is not worthy of continuing Certifying Authority's operation; or

(ix) a Certifying Authority fails to comply with the directions of the Controller **[Rule 18]**.

Revocation of license [Section 25(1)]

The Controller may, revoke the license, if he in satisfied, after making such inquiry as he may think fit, that a Certifying Authority has —

(a) made a statement in the application for issue or renewal of the license, which is incorrect or false in material particulars,

(b) fail to comply with the terms and conditions subject to which the license was granted,

(c) failed to maintain the procedures and standards specified,

(d) contravened any provision of this Act, rule, regulation, or order made thereunder.

No license shall be revoked unless the Certifying Authority has been given a reasonable opportunity of showing cause against the proposed revocation.

Suspension of license [Section 25(2)]

The Controller may, if he has reasonable causes to believe that there in any ground for revoking a license by order suspend such license pending the completion of any inquiry ordered by him.

No license shall be suspended for a period exceeding ten days unless the Certifying Authority has been given reasonable opportunity of showing cause against the proposed suspension.

No Certifying Authority whose license has been suspended shall issue any Digital Signature Certificate during such suspension.

The license granted to the persons shall stand suspended when the performance bond submitted or the banker's guarantee furnished by such persons is invoked **[Rule15]**.

Notice of suspension or revocation of license (Section 26)

Where the license of the Certifying Authority in suspended or revoked, the Controller shall publish notice of such suspension or revocation, as the case may be, in the data base maintained by him.

Where one or more repositories are specified, the Controller such publishes notices of such suspension or revocation, as case may be, in all such repositories.

The database containing the notice of such suspension or revocation, as the case may be, shall be made available through a website which shall be accessible round the clock. The Controller may, if he considers necessary, publicise the contents of data base in such electronic or other media, as he may consider appropriate.

Surrender of license (Section 33)

Every Certifying Authority whose license is suspended or revoked shall immediately after such suspension or revocation, surrender the license to the Controller.

Where any Certifying Authority fails to surrender a licence, the person in whose favour a licence is issued, shall be guilty of an offence and shall be punished with imprisonment which may extend upto six months or a fine which may extend upto Rs. 10,000 or with both.

Obligations and duties of Certifying Authority

1. Follow procedure (Section 30)

Every Certifying Authority shall —

(a) make use of hardware, software and procedures that are secure from intrusion and misuse,

(b) provide a reasonable level of reliability in its services which are reasonably suited to the performance of intended functions,

(c) adhere to security procedures to ensure that the secrecy and privacy of the digital signatures are assured, and

(d) observe such other standards of may be specified by regulations.

(e) the standards for every Certifying Authority to be carried out for different activities associated with its functions are set out in Regulation 4 of the Information Technology (Certifying Authorities) Regulations, 2001.

2. Compliances by Employees (Section 31)

Every Certifying Authority shall ensure that every person employed or otherwise engaged by it in the course of employment or engagement complies with the provisions of this Act, rules, regulations and orders made thereunder.

3. Display of license (Section 32)

Every Certifying Authority shall display its license of a conspicuous place of the premises in which it carries on its business.

4. Disclosure (Section 34)

Every Certifying Authority shall disclose in the manner specified by regulations the following —

(a) its Digital Signature Certificate which contains the public key corresponding to the private key used by that Certifying Authority to digitally sign another Digital Signature Certificate,

(b) any certification practice statement relevant thereto,

(c) notice of the revocation suspension of its Certifying Authority Certificate, if any, and

(d) any other fact that materially and adversely affects either the reliability of a Digital Signature Certificate, which that Authority has issued, or the Authority's ability to perform its services **[Sec. 34(1) & Reg. 5(1)]**.

This disclosure shall be made available to the Controller through filling online forms on the Website of the Controller on the date and time the said information is made public. The Certifying Authority shall digitally sign the information **[Reg. 5(2)]**.

Where in opinion of the Certifying Authority any event has occurred or any situation has arisen which may materially and adversely affect the integrity of its computer system; or the conditions subject to which a Digital Signature Certificate was granted, then, the Certifying Authority shall –

(a) Use reasonable efforts to notify any person who is likely to be affected by that occurrence, or

(b) Act in accordance with the procedure specified in its certification practice statement to deal with such event or situation **[Sec.34(2)]**.

5. Cross certification:

The licensed Certifying Authority shall have arrangement for cross certification with other licensed Certifying Authorities within India which shall be submitted to the Controller before the commencement of their operations.

Any dispute arising as a result of any such arrangement between the Certifying Authorities or between Certifying Authorities or Certifying Authority and the Subscriber, shall be referred to the Controller for arbitration or resolution.

The arrangement for Cross Certification by the licensed Certifying Authority with a Foreign Certifying Authority along with the application, shall be submitted to the Controller in such form and in such manner as may be provided in the regulations made by the Controller. The licensed Certifying Authority shall not commence cross certification operations unless it has obtained the written *ot* digital signature approval from the Controller **[Rule 13]**.

6. Security guidelines for Certifying Authorities:

The Certifying Authorities shall have the sole responsibility of integrity, confidentiality and protection of information and information assets employed in its operation, considering classification, declassification, labelling, storage, access and destruction of information assets according to their value, sensitivity and importance of operation.

Information Technology Security Guidelines and Security Guidelines for Certifying Authorities aimed at protecting the integrity, confidentiality and availability of service of Certifying Authority are given in Schedule-II and Schedule-III respectively to Information Technology (Certifying Authorities) Rules, 2000.

The Certifying Authority shall formulate its Information Technology and Security Policy for operation complying with these guidelines and submit it to the Controller before commencement of operation. Any change made by the Certifying Authority in the Information Technology and Security Policy shall be submitted within two weeks to the Controller **[Rule 20]**.

Issuance, Suspension and Revocation of Digital Signature Certificates (Section 35)

As per section 35, any interested person shall make an application to Certifying Authority for the issue of Digital Signature Certificate. The application shall be accompanied by filing fees not exceeding Rs. 25,000 and a certification practice statement or in the absence of such statement, any other statement containing such particulars as may be prescribed by the regulations. After scrutinizing the application, the Certifying Authority may either grant the Digital Signature Certificate or reject the application furnishing reasons in writing for the same.

While issuing the Digital Signature Certificate, the Certifying Authority must *inter alia* ensure that the applicant holds a private key which is capable of creating a digital signature and corresponds to the public key to be listed on Digital Signature Certificate. Both of them together should form a fine-tuning pair.

The Certifying Authority also has the power o suspend the Digital Signature Certificate in public interest on the request of the subscriber listed in the Digital Signature Certificate or any person authorized on behalf of the subscriber. However, the subscriber must be given an opportunity to be heard of the Digital Signature Certificate is to be suspended for a period exceeding fifteen days. The Digital Signature Certificate shall communicate the suspension to the subscriber **(Section 37)**.

There are two cases in which the Digital Signature Certificate can be revoked by a Certifying Authority. Firstly, as per section 38(1), it may be revoked either on the request or death of the subscriber or when the subscriber is a firm or company, on the dissolution of the firm or company, or on the winding up of the company. Secondly, according to section 38(2), the Certifying Authority may sue moto revoke it if some material fact in the Digital Signature Certificate is false or has been concealed by the subscriber or the requirements for issue of the Digital Signature Certificate are not fulfilled or the subscriber has been declared insolvent or dead.

On revocation of the certificate, the Certifying Authority shall communication the same to the subscriber. However, the certificate shall not be revoked unless the subscriber has been given an opportunity of being heard in the matter.

Notice of the suspension or revocation

As per Section 39, where a Digital Signature Certificate is suspended or revoked under section 37 and 38, the Certifying Authority shall publishes a notice of such suspension or revocation in the repository specified in the certification for publication of such notice. In cases one or more repositories are specified, the Certifying Authority shall publish notice of such suspension or revocation in all such repositories.

Confidential Information:

The following information shall be confidential* namely:

(a) Digital Signature Certificate application, whether approved or rejected;

(b) Digital Signature Certificate information collected from the subscriber or elsewhere as part of the registration and verification record but not included in the Digital Signature Certificate information;

(c) Subscriber agreement **[Rule 34]**.

Access to confidential information: Access to confidential information by Certifying Authority's operational staff shall be on a "need-to-know" arid "need-to-use" basis.

Paper based records, documentation and backup data containing all confidential information shall be kept in secure and locked container or filing system, separately from all other records.

The confidential information shall not be taken out of the country except in a case where a properly constitutional warrant or other legally enforceable document is produced to the Controller and he permits to do so **[Rule 35]**.

Audit

The Certifying Authority shall get its operation audited^annually by an auditor and such audit shall include *inter alia* —

(i) Security policy and planning;

(ii) physical security;

(iii) technology evaluation;

(iv) certifying Authority's services administration;

(v) relevant Certification Practice Statement;

(vi) compliance to relevant Certification Practice Statement;

(vii) contracts/agreements;

(viii) by the Controller;

(ix) policy requirements of Certifying Authorities Rules, 2000.

The Certifying Authority shall conduct —

(a) half yearly audit of the Security Policy* physical security and planning of its operation;

(b) a quarterly audit of its repository.

The Certifying Authority shall submit copy of each audit report to the Controller within four weeks of the completion of such audit. Where irregularities are found, the Certifying Authority shall take immediate appropriate action to remove such irregularities **[Rule 32]**.

Auditor's relationship with Certifying Authority: The auditor shall be independent of the Certifying Authority being audited and shall not be a software or hardware vendor which is, or has been providing services or supplying equipment to the said Certifying Authority.

The auditor and the Certifying Authority shall not have any current or planned financial, legal or other relationship, other than that of an auditor and the audited party **[Rule 33].**

Database of Certifying Authorities:

The Controller shall maintain a database of the disclosure record of every Certifying Authority, Cross Certifying Authority and Foreign Certifying Authority, Containing *inter alia* the following details:

(a) the name of the person/names of the Directors, nature of business, Income-tax Permanent Account Number, web address, if any, office and residential address* location of facilities associated with functions of generation of frigital Signature Certificate, voice and facsimile telephone numbers, electronic mail address, administrative contacts and authorized representatives;

(b) the public key, corresponding to the private key used by the Certifying Authority and recognized Foreign Certifying Authority to digitally sign Digital Signature Certificate;

(c) current and past versions of Certification Practice Statement of Certifying Authority;

(d) time stamps indicating the date and time of —

(i) grant of licence;

(ii) confirmation of adoption of Certification Practice Statement and its earlier version by Certifying Authority;

(iii) commencement of commercial operations of generation and issue of Digital Signature Certificate by the Certifying Authority;

(iv) revocation or suspension of licence of Certifying Authority;

(v) commencement of operation of Cross Certifying Authority;

(vi) issue of recognition of Foreign Certifying Authority;

(vii) revocation or suspension of recognition of Foreign Certifying Authority **[Rule 23].**

Duties of Subscribers.

Subscriber means a person in whose name; the Digital Signature Certificate is issued. The method used to verity and authenticate the identity of a subscriber is known as "Subscriber Identity Verification Method".

1. Generating key pair

Where the public key of any Digital Signature Certificate corresponds to the private key listed in the Digital Signature Certificate of that subscriber, and then the subscriber shall generate the key pair by applying the security procedure (Section 40).

2. Acceptance of Digital Signature Certificate

The Digital Signature Certificate must have been accepted by the subscriber. A subscriber shall be deemed to have accepted a Digital Signature Certificate, of his publishes or authorizes the publication of a Digital Signature Certificate to one or more persons, in a repository, or otherwise demonstrates his approval of the Digital Signature Certificate in any manner.

By accepting a Digital Signature Certificate, the subscriber certifies to all who reasonably rely on the information contained in the Digital Signature Certificate that —

(a) The subscriber holds the private key corresponding to the public key listed in the Digital Signature Certificate and in entitled to hold the same,

(b) All representations made by the subscribed to the Certifying Authority and all material relevant to the information contained in the Digital Signature Certificate are true,

(c) All information in the Digital signature Certificate that is within the Knowledge of the subscriber in free (Section -41).

3- Control of Private Key

Every subscriber shall exercise reasonable care to retain control of the private key corresponding to the public key listed in his Digital Signature Certificate and shall take all steps to prevent its disclosure to a person not authorized to affix the private key corresponding to the public key listed in the Digital Signature Certificate has been compromised, then the subscriber shall communicate the same without any delay to the Certifying Authority in said manner as may be specified by the Regulation. The subscriber shall be liable till he has informed the Certifying Authority that the Private Key has been compromised (Section 42).

CYBER CRIMES & PENALITIES

"Cyber" refers to imaginary space, which is created when the electronic devices communicate, like network of computers.

Cyber crime refers to anything done in the cyber space with a criminal intent. These could be either the criminal activities in the conventional sense or could be activities, newly evolved with the growth of the new medium. Cyber crime includes acts such as hacking, uploading obscene content on the Internet, sending obscene e-mails and hacking into a person's e-banking account to withdraw money.

Cyber crime can involve criminal activities that are traditional in nature, such as theft, fraud, forgery, defamation and mischief, all of which are subject to the Indian Penal Code. The abuse of computers has also given birth to a gamut of new age crimes that are addressed by the Information Technology Act, 2000. The act does not define 'cyber crime'. However, any activities which basically offend human sensibilities would come within its ambit. Child Pornography on the Internet constitutes one serious cyber crime.

The act recognizes three kinds of offences which are:

1. Tampering with computer source documents

Whoever knowingly or intentionally conceals, destroys or alters or intentionally or knowingly causes another to conceal, destroy or alter any computer source code used for a computer, computer programme, computer system or computer network, when the computer source code is required to be kept or maintained by law for the time being in force, shall be punishable with imprisonment upto three years, or with fine which may extend up to two lakh rupees, or with both.

Explanation — For the purposes of this section, "computer source code" means the listing of programmes, computer commands, design and layout and programme analysis of computer resource in any form.

2. Hacking with computer system

(1) Whoever with the intent to cause or knowing that he is likely to cause wrongful loss or damage to the public or any person destroys or deletes or alters any information residing in a computer resource or diminishes its value or utility or affects it injuriously by any means, commits hack:

(2) Whoever commits hacking shall be punished with imprisonment up to three years, or with fine which may extend upto two lakh rupees, or with both.

3.Publishing of information which is obscene in electronic form

Whoever publishes or transmits or causes to be published in the electronic form, any material which is lascivious or appeals to the prurient interest or if its effect is such as to tend to deprave and corrupt persons who are likely, having regard to all relevant circumstances, to read, see or hear the matter contained or embodied in it, shall be punished on first conviction with imprisonment of either description for a term which may extend to five years and with fine which may extend to one lakh rupees and in the event of a second or subsequent conviction with imprisonment of either description for a term which may extend to ten years and also with fine which may extend to two lakh rupees.

CYBER LAW & INFORMATION TECHNOLOGY

Success in any field of human activity leads to crime that needs mechanisms to control it. Legal provisions should provide assurance to users, empowerment to law enforcement agencies and deterrence to criminals. The law is as stringent as its enforcement. Crime is no longer limited to space, time or a group of people. Cyber space creates moral, civil and criminal wrongs. It has now given a new way to express criminal tendencies. Back in 1990, less than 100,000 people were able to log on to the Internet worldwide. Now around 500 million people are hooked up to surf the net around the globe.

Until recently, many information technology (IT) professionals lacked awareness of and interest in the cyber crime phenomenon. In many cases, law enforcement officers have lacked the tools needed to tackle the problem; old laws didn't quite fit the crimes being committed, new laws hadn't quite caught up to the reality of what was happening, and there were few court precedents to look to for guidance. Furthermore, debates over privacy issues hampered the ability of enforcement agents to gather the evidence needed to prosecute these new cases. Finally, there was a certain amount of antipathy — or at the least, distrust — between the two most important players in any effective fight against cyber crime:

Law enforcement agencies and computer professionals. Yet close cooperation between the two is crucial if we are to control the cyber crime problem and make the Internet a safe "place" for its users.

Law enforcement personnel understand the criminal mindset and know the basics of gathering evidence and bringing offenders to justice. IT personnel understand computers and networks, how they work, and how to track down information on them. Each has half of the key to defeating the cyber criminal.

IT professionals need good definitions of cybercrime in order to know when (and what) to report to police, but law enforcement agencies must have statutory definitions of specific crimes in order to charge a criminal with an offense. The first step in specifically defining individual cybercrimes is to sort all the acts that can be considered cybercrimes into organized categories.

United Nations' Definition of Cybercrime

Cybercrime spans not only state but national boundaries as well. Perhaps, we should look to international organizations to provide a standard definition of the crime. At the Tenth United Nations Congress on the Prevention of Crime and Treatment of Offenders, in a workshop devoted to the issues of crimes related to computer networks, cybercrime was broken into two categories and defined thus:

(a) Cybercrime in a narrow sense (computer crime): Any illegal behavior directed by means of electronic operations that targets the security of computer systems and the data processed by them.

(b) Cybercrime in a broader sense (computer-related crime): Any illegal behaviour committed by means of, or in relation to, a computer system or network, including such crimes as illegal possession [and] offering or distributing information by means of a computer system or network.

Of course, these definitions are complicated by the fact that an act may be illegal in one nation but not in another.

There are more concrete examples, including

(i) Unauthorized access

(ii) Damage to computer data or programs

(iii) Computer sabotage

(iv) Unauthorized interception of communications

(v) Computer espionage

These definitions, although not completely definitive, do give us a good starting point — one that has some international recognition and agreement — for determining just what we mean by the term cybercrime.

In Indian law, cyber crime has to be voluntary and willful, an act or omission that adversely affects a person or property. The IT Act provides the backbone for e-commerce and India's approach has been to look at e-governance and e-commerce primarily from the promotional aspects looking at the vast opportunities and the need to sensitize the population to the possibilities of the information age. There is the need to take in to consideration the security aspects.

In the present global situation where cyber control mechanisms are important we need to push cyber laws. Cyber Crimes are a new class of crimes to India rapidly expanding due to extensive use of internet. Getting the right lead and making the right interpretation are very important in solving a cyber crime. The 7 stage continuum of a criminal case starts from **perpetration** to **registration** to **reporting**, **investigation**, **prosecution**, **adjudication** and **execution**. The system can not be stronger than the weakest link in the chain. In India, there are 30 million policemen to train apart from 12,000 strong Judiciary Police in India are trying to become cyber crime savvy and hiring people who are trained in the area. Each police station in Delhi will have a computer soon which will be connected to the Head Quarter. The pace of the investigations however can be faster; judicial sensitivity and knowledge need to improve. Focus needs to be on educating the police and district judiciary. IT Institutions can also play a role in this area.

Technology nuances are important in a spam infested environment where privacy can be compromised and individuals can be subjected to become a victim unsuspectingly. We need to sensitize our investigators and judges to the nuances of the system. Most cyber criminals have a counter part in the real world. If loss of property or persons is caused the criminal is punishable under the IPC also. Since the law enforcement agencies find it is easier to handle it under the IPC, IT Act cases are not getting reported and when reported are not necessarily dealt with under the IT Act. A lengthy and intensive process of learning is required.

A whole series of initiatives of cyber forensics were undertaken and cyber law procedures resulted out of it. This is an area where learning takes place every day as we are all beginners in this area. We are looking for solutions faster than the problems can get invented. We need to move faster than the criminals.

The real issue is how to prevent cyber crime. For this, there is need to raise the probability of apprehension and conviction. India has a law on evidence that considers admissibility, authenticity, accuracy, and completeness to convince the judiciary. The challenge in cyber crime cases includes getting evidence that will stand scrutiny in a foreign court.

For this, India needs total international cooperation with specialised agencies of different countries. Police has to ensure that they have seized exactly what was there at the scene of crime, is the same that has been analysed and the report presented in court is based on this evidence. It has to maintain the chain of custody. The threat is not from the intelligence of criminals but from our ignorance and the will to fight it. The law is stricter now on producing evidence especially where electronic documents are concerned.

The computer is the target and the tool for the perpetration of crime. It is used for the communication of the criminal activity such as the injection of a virus/worm which can crash entire networks.

The Information Technology (IT) Act, 2000, specifies the acts which have been made punishable. Since the primary objective of this Act is to create an enabling environment for commercial use of I.T., certain omissions and commissions of criminals while using computers have not been included. With the legal recognition of Electronic Records and the amendments made in the several sections of the IPC vide the IT Act, 2000, several offences having bearing on cyber-arena are also registered under the appropriate sections of the IPC.

During the year 2003, 60 cases were registered under IT Act as compared to 70 cases during the previous year thereby reporting a decline of 14.3 per cent in 2003 over 2002. Of the total 60 cases registered under IT Act 2000, around 33 per cent (20 cases) relate to Obscene Publication/Transmission in electronic form, normally known as cases of cyber pornography. 17 persons were arrested for committing such offences during 2003.

There were 21 cases of Hacking of computer systems wherein 18 persons were arrested in 2003. Of the total (21) Hacking cases, the cases relating to Loss/Damage of computer resource/utility under Sec 66(1) of the IT Act were to the tune of 62 per cent (13 cases) and that related to Hacking under Section 66(2) of IT Act were 38 per cent (8cases).

During 2003, a total of 411 cases were registered under IPC Sections as compared to 738 such cases during 2002 thereby reporting a significant decline of 44 per cent in 2003 over 2002. Andhra Pradesh reported more than half of such cases (218 out of 411) (53 per cent).

Of the 411 cases registered under IPC, majority of the crimes fall under 3 categories, viz., Criminal Breach of Trust or Fraud (269), Forgery (89) and Counterfeiting (53).

Though, these offences fall under the traditional IPC crimes, the cases had the cyber tones wherein computer, Internet or its related aspects were present in the crime and hence they were categorised as Cyber Crimes under IPC.

During 2003, number of cases under Cyber Crimes relating to Counterfeiting of currency/Stamps stood at 53 wherein 118 persons were arrested during 2003. Of the 47,478 cases reported under Cheating, the Cyber Forgery (89) accounted for 0.2 per cent. Of the total Criminal Breach of Trust cases (13,432), the Cyber frauds (269) accounted for 2 per cent. Of the Counterfeiting offences (2,055), Cyber Counterfeiting (53) offences accounted for 2.6 per cent.

A total of 475 persons were arrested in the country for Cyber Crimes under IPC during 2003. Of these, 53.6 per cent offenders (255) were taken into custody for offences under Criminal Breach of Trust/Fraud (Cyber) and 21.4 per cent (102) for offences under 'Cyber Forgery'. The age-wise profile of the arrested persons showed that 45 percent were in the age-group of 30-45 years, 28.5 per cent of the offenders were in the age-group of 45-60 years and 11 offenders were aged 60 years and above. Gujarat reported 2 offenders who were below 18 years of age.

Fraud/Illegal gain (120) accounted for 60 per cent of the total Cyber Crime motives reported in the country. Greed/Money (15 cases) accounted for 7.5 per cent of the Cyber Crimes reported. Eve-teasing and Harassment (8 cases) accounted for around 4 per cent. Cyber Suspects include Neighbours/Friends/Relatives (91), Disgrunted employees (11), Business Competitors (9), Crackers Students/Professional learners (3). Cyber crime is not on the decline. The latest statistics show that cyber crime is actually on the rise. However, it is true that in India, cyber crime is not reported too much about. Consequently there is a false sense of complacency that cyber crime does not exist and that society is safe from cyber crime. This is not the correct picture. The fact is that people in our country do not report cyber crimes for many reasons. Many do not want to face harassment by the police. There is also the fear of bad publicity in the media, which could hurt their reputation and standing in society. Also, it becomes extremely difficult to convince the police to register any cyber crime, because of lack of orientation and awareness about cyber crimes and their registration and handling by the police.

A recent survey indicates that for every 500 cyber crime incidents that take place, only 50 are reported to the police and out of that only one is actually registered. These figures indicate how difficult it is to convince the police to register a cyber crime. The establishment of cyber crime cells in different parts of the country was expected to boost cyber crime reporting and prosecution. However, these cells haven't quite kept up with expectations.

Netizens should not be under the impression that cyber crime is vanishing and they must realize that with each passing day, cyberspace becomes a more dangerous place to be in, where criminals roam freely to execute their criminals intentions encouraged by the so called anonymity that internet provides.

The absolutely poor rate of cyber crime conviction in the country has also not helped the cause of regulating cyber crime. There has only been few cyber crime convictions in the whole country, which can be counted on fingers. We need to ensure that we have specialized procedures for prosecution of cyber crime cases so as to tackle them on a priority basis. This is necessary so as to win the faith of the people in the ability of the system to tackle cyber crime. We must ensure that our system provides for stringent punishment of cyber crimes and cyber criminals so that the same acts as a deterrent for others.

Threat Perceptions

UK has the largest number of infected computers in the world followed by the US and China. Financial attacks are 16 events per 1000, the highest among all kinds of attacks. The US is the leading source country for attacks but this has declined. China is second and Germany is third. It is hard to determine where the attack came from originally.

The number of viruses and worm variants rose sharply to 7,360 that is a 64% increase over the previous reporting period and a 332% increase over the previous year. There are 17,500 variants of Win.32 viruses. Threats to confidential information are on the rise with 54% of the top 50 reporting malicious code with the potential to expose such information. Phishing messages grew to 4.5 million from 1 million between July and December 2004.

Some Indian Case Studies

1. Pune Citibank Mphasis Call Center Fraud

US $ 3,50,000 from accounts of four US customers were dishonestly transferred to bogus accounts. This will give a lot of ammunition to those lobbying against outsourcing in US. Such cases happen all over the world but when it happens in India it is a serious matter and we can not ignore it. It is a case of sourcing engineering. Some employees gained the confidence of the customer and obtained their PIN numbers to commit fraud. They got these under the guise of helping the customers out of difficult situations. Highest security prevails in the call centers in India as they know that they will lose their business. There was not as much of breach of security but of sourcing engineering.

The call center employees are checked when they go in and out so they can not copy down numbers and therefore they could not have noted these down. They must have remembered these numbers, gone out immediately to a cyber café and accessed the Citibank accounts of the customers.

All accounts were opened in Pune and the customers complained that the money from their accounts was transferred to Pune accounts and that's how the criminals were traced. Police has been able to prove the honesty of the call center and has frozen the accounts where the money was transferred.

There is need for a strict background check of the call center executives. However, best of background checks can not eliminate the bad elements from coming in and breaching security. We must still ensure such checks when a person is hired. There is need for a national ID and a national database where a name can be referred to. In this case, preliminary investigations do not reveal that the criminals had any crime history. Customer education is very important so customers do not get taken for a ride. Most banks are guilt of not doing this.

2. Bazee.com case

CEO of Bazee.com was arrested in December 2004 because a CD with objectionable material was being sold on the website. The CD was also being sold in the markets in Delhi.

The Mumbai city police and the Delhi Police got into action. The CEO was later released on bail. This opened up the question as to what kind of distinction do we draw between Internet Service Provider and Content Provider. The burden rests on the accused that he was the Service Provider and not the Content Provider. It also raises a lot of issues regarding how the police should handle the cyber crime cases and a lot of education is required.

3. State of Tamil Nadu Vs. Suhas Katti

The Case of Suhas Katti is notable for the fact that the conviction was achieved successfully within a relatively quick time of 7 months from the filing of the FIR. Considering that similar cases have been pending in other states for a much longer time, the efficient handling of the case which happened to be the first case of the Chennai Cyber Crime Cell going to trial deserves a special mention.

The case related to posting of obscene, defamatory and annoying message about a divorcee woman in the *yahoo message group*. E-Mails were also forwarded to the victim for information by the accused through a false e-mail account opened by him in the name of the victim. The posting of the message resulted in annoying phone calls to the lady in the belief that she was soliciting.

Based on a complaint made by the victim in February 2004, the Police traced the accused to Mumbai and arrested him within the next few days. The accused was a known family friend of the victim and was reportedly interested in marrying her. She however married another person. This marriage later ended in divorce and the accused started contacting her once again. On her reluctance to marry him, the accused took up the harassment through the Internet.

On 24-3-2004 Charge Sheet was filed u/s 67 of IT Act 2000, 469 and 509 IPC before The Hon'ble Addl. CMM Egmore by citing 18 witnesses and 34 documents and material objects. The same was taken on file in C.C.NO.4680/2004. On the prosecution side 12 witnesses were examined and entire documents were marked as Exhibits.

The Defence argued that the offending mails would have been given either by ex-husband of the complainant or the complainant her self to implicate the accused as accused alleged to have turned down the request of the complainant to marry her.

Further, the Defence counsel argued that some of the documentary evidence was not sustainable under Section 65 B of the Indian Evidence Act. However, the court relied upon the expert witnesses and other evidence produced before it, including the witnesses of the Cyber Cafe owners and came to the conclusion that the crime was conclusively proved. Ld. Additional Chief Metropolitan Magistrate, Egmore, delivered the judgement on 5-11-04 as follows:

"The accused is found guilty of offences under section 469, 509 IPC and 67 of IT Act 2000 and the accused is convicted and is sentenced for the offence to undergo RI for 2 years under 469 IPC and to pay fine of Rs.500/-and for the offence u/s 509 IPC sentenced to undergo 1 year Simple imprisonment and to pay fine of Rs.500/- and for the offence u/s 67 of IT Act 2000 to undergo RI for 2 years and to pay fine of Rs.4000/- All sentences to run concurrently."

The accused paid fine amount and he was lodged at Central Prison, Chennai. This is considered as the first case convicted under section 67 of Information Technology Act 2000 in India.

4. The Bank NSP Case

The Bank NSP case is the one where a management trainee of the bank was engaged to be married. The couple exchanged many e-mails using the company computers. After sometime, the two broke up and the girl created fraudulent e-mail IDs such as "indianbarassociations" and sent e-mails to the boy's foreign clients. She used the banks computer to do this. The boy's company lost a large number of clients and took the bank to court. The bank was held liable for the e-mails sent using the bank's system.

5. SMC Pneumatics (India) Pvt. Ltd. Vs. Jogesh Kwatra

In India's first case of cyber defamation, a Court of Delhi assumed jurisdiction over a matter where a corporate's reputation was being defamed through emails and passed an important ex-parte injunction.

In this case, the defendant Jogesh Kwatra being an employ of the plaintiff company started sending derogatory, defamatory, obscene, vulgar, filthy and abusive emails to his employers as also to different subsidiaries of the said company all over the world with the aim to defame the company and its Managing Director Mr. R K Malhotra. The plaintiff filed a suit for permanent injunction restraining the defendant from doing his illegal acts of sending derogatory emails to the plaintiff.

On behalf of the plaintiffs, it was contended that the emails sent by the defendant were distinctly obscene, vulgar, abusive, intimidating, humiliating and defamatory in nature.

Counsel further argued that the aim of sending the said emails was to malign the high reputation of the plaintiffs all over India and the world. He further contended that the acts of the defendant in sending the emails had resulted in invasion of legal rights of the plaintiffs.

Further, the defendant is under a duty not to send the aforesaid emails. It is pertinent to note that after the plaintiff company discovered the said employ could be indulging in the matter of sending abusive emails, the plaintiff terminated the services of the defendant.

After hearing detailed arguments of Counsel for Plaintiff, Hon'ble Judge of the Delhi High Court passed an ex-parte ad interim injunction observing that a prima facie case had been made out by the plaintiff. Consequently, the Delhi High Court restrained the defendant from sending derogatory, defamatory, obscene, vulgar, humiliating and abusive emails either to the plaintiffs or to its sister subsidiaries all over the world including their Managing Directors and their Sales and Marketing departments. Further, Hon'ble Judge also restrained the defendant from publishing, transmitting or causing to be published any information in the actual world as also in cyberspace which is derogatory or defamatory or abusive of the plaintiffs.

This order of Delhi High Court assumes tremendous significance as this is for the first time that an Indian Court assumes jurisdiction in a matter concerning cyber defamation and grants an ex-parte injunction restraining the defendant from defaming the plaintiffs by sending derogatory, defamatory, abusive and obscene emails either to the plaintiffs or their subsidiaries.

6. PARLIAMENT ATTACK CASE

Bureau of Police Research and Development at Hyderabad had handled some of the top cyber cases, including analysing and retrieving information from the laptop recovered from terrorist, who attacked Parliament. The laptop which was seized from the two terrorists, who were gunned down when Parliament was under siege on December 13 2001, was sent to Computer Forensics Division of BPRD after computer experts at Delhi failed to trace much out of its contents.

The laptop contained several evidences that confirmed of the two terrorists' motives, namely the sticker of the Ministry of Home that they had made on the laptop and pasted on their ambassador car to gain entry into Parliament House and the the fake ID card that one of the two terrorists was carrying with a Government of India emblem and seal.

The emblems (of the three lions) were carefully scanned and the seal was also craftly made along with residential address of Jammu and Kashmir. But careful detection proved that it was all forged and made on the laptop.

7. Andhra Pradesh Tax Case

Dubious tactics of a prominent businessman from Andhra Pradesh was exposed after officials of the department got hold of computers used by the accused person.

The owner of a plastics firm was arrested and Rs. 22 crore cash was recovered from his house by sleuths of the Vigilance Department. They sought an explanation from him regarding the unaccounted cash within 10 days.

The accused person submitted 6,000 vouchers to prove the legitimacy of trade and thought his offence would go undetected but after careful scrutiny of vouchers and contents of his computers it revealed that all of them were made after the raids were conducted.

It later revealed that the accused was running five businesses under the guise of one company and used fake and computerised vouchers to show sales records and save tax.

8. SONY.SAMBANDH.COM CASE

India saw its first cyber crime conviction recently. It all began after a complaint was filed by Sony India Private Ltd., which runs a website called www.sony-sambandh.com, targeting Non Resident Indians. The website enables NRIs to send Sony products to their friends and relatives in India after they pay for it online.

The company undertakes to deliver the products to the concerned recipients. In May 2002, someone logged onto the website under the identity of Barbara Campa and ordered a Sony Colour Television set and a cordless head phone.

She gave her credit card number for payment and requested that the products be delivered to Arif Azim in Noida. The payment was duly cleared by the credit card agency and the transaction processed. After following the relevant procedures of due diligence and checking, the company delivered the items to Arif Azim.

At the time of delivery, the company took digital photographs showing the delivery being accepted by Arif Azim.

The transaction closed at that, but after one and a half months the credit card agency informed the company that this was an unauthorized transaction as the real owner had denied having made the purchase.

The company lodged a complaint for online cheating at the Central Bureau of Investigation which registered a case under Section 418, 419 and 420 of the Indian Penal Code.

The matter was investigated into and Arif Azim was arrested. Investigations revealed that Arif Azim, while working at a call centre in Noida gained access to the credit card number of an American national which he misused on the company's site.

The CBI recovered the colour television and the cordless head phone.

In this matter, the CBI had evidence to prove their case and so the accused admitted his guilt. The court convicted Arif Azim under Section 418, 419 and 420 of the Indian Penal Code — this being the first time that a cyber crime has been convicted.

The court, however, felt that as the accused was a young boy of 24 years and a first-time convict, a lenient view needed to be taken. The court therefore released the accused on probation for one year.

The judgement is of immense significance for the entire nation. Besides being the first conviction in a cyber crime matter, it has shown that the Indian Penal Code can be effectively applied to certain categories of cyber crimes which are not covered under the Information Technology Act 2000. Secondly, a judgment of this sort sends out a clear message to all that the law cannot be taken for a ride.

9. Nasscom vs. Ajay Sood & Others

In a landmark judgement in the case of National Association of Software and Service Companies vs. Ajay Sood & Others, delivered in March, '05, the Delhi High Court declared `phishing' on the internet to be an illegal act, entailing an injunction and recovery of damages.

Elaborating on the concept of 'phishing', in order to lay down a precedent in India, the court stated that it is a form of internet fraud where a person pretends to be a legitimate association, such as a bank or an insurance company in order to extract personal data from a customer such as access codes, passwords, etc. Personal data so collected by misrepresenting the identity of the legitimate party is commonly used for the collecting party's advantage. court also stated, by way of an example, that typical phishing scams involve persons who pretend to represent online banks and siphon cash from e-banking accounts after conning consumers into handing over confidential banking details.

The Delhi HC stated that even though there is no specific legislation in India to penalize phishing, it held phishing to be an illegal act by defining it under Indian law as "a misrepresentation made in the course of trade leading to confusion as to the source and origin of the e-mail causing immense harm not only to the consumer but even to the person whose name, identity or password is misused." The court held the act of phishing as passing off and tarnishing the plaintiff's image.

The plaintiff in this case was the National Association of Software and Service Companies (Nasscom), India's premier software association.

The defendants were operating a placement agency involved in head-hunting and recruitment. In order to obtain personal data, which they could use for purposes of head-hunting, the defendants composed and sent e-mails to third parties in the name of Nasscom.

The high court recognised the trademark rights of the plaintiff and passed an *ex-parte* adinterim injunction restraining the defendants from using the trade name or any other name deceptively similar to Nasscom. The court further restrained the defendants from holding themselves out as being associates or a part of Nasscom.

The court appointed a commission to conduct a search at the defendants' premises. Two hard disks of the computers from which the fraudulent e-mails were sent by the defendants to various parties were taken into custody by the local commissioner appointed by the court.

The offending e-mails were then downloaded from the hard disks and presented as evidence in court.

During the progress of the case, it became clear that the defendants in whose names the offending e-mails were sent were fictitious identities created by an employee on defendants' instructions, to avoid recognition and legal action. On discovery of this fraudulent act, the fictitious names were deleted from the array of parties as defendants in the case.

Subsequently, the defendants admitted their illegal acts and the parties settled the matter through the recording of a compromise in the suit proceedings. According to the terms of compromise, the defendants agreed to pay a sum of Rs. 1.6 million to the plaintiff as damages for violation of the plaintiff's trademark rights. The court also ordered the hard disks seized from the defendants' premises to be handed over to the plaintiff who would be the owner of the hard disks.

This case achieves clear milestones: It brings the act of "phishing" into the ambit of Indian laws even in the absence of specific legislation; It clears the misconception that there is no "damages culture" in India for violation of IP rights; This case reaffirms IP owners' faith in the Indian judicial system's ability and willingness to protect intangible property rights and send a strong message to IP owners that they can do business in India without sacrificing their IP rights.

10. Infinity e-Search BPO Case

The Gurgaon BPO fraud has created an embarrassing situation for Infinity e-Search, the company in which Mr. Karan Bahree was employed.

A British newspaper had reported that one of its undercover reporters had purchased personal information of 1,000 British customers from an Indian call-center employee.

However, the employee of Infinity eSearch, a New Delhi-based web designing company, who was reportedly involved in the case has denied any wrongdoing. The company has also said that it had nothing to do with the incident.

In the instant case the journalist used an intermediary, offered a job, requested for a presentation on a CD and later claimed that the CD contained some confidential data. The fact that the CD contained such data is itself not substantiated by the journalist.

In this sort of a situation we can only say that the journalist has used "Bribery" to induce a "Out of normal behaviour" of an employee. This is not observation of a fact but creating a factual incident by intervention. Investigation is still on in this matter.

PENALTIES AND ADJUDICATION (Section 43 to 47)

1. Penality for damage to Computer and Computer system

As per the Act, civil liability and stringent criminal penalties may be imposed on any person who causes damage to a computer or computer system. The offender would be liable to pay compensation not exceeding Rs. 1 Crore (10 million) for gaining unauthorised access to a computer or computer system, damaging it, introducing a virus in the system, denying access to an authorised person or assisting any person in any of the above activities.

If a person cause damage to a computer or computer system by any of the toll owing way without permission of the owner or any other person who is charge of computer, computer system, computer network shall be liable to damages; by way of compensation not exceeding Rs 10 lakhs.

(a) accesses or secures access to it,

(b) down loads, copies or extracts any data, computer database of information from it,

(c) introduces or causes to be introduced any computer contaminant or computer virus into it,

(d) damages or causes to be damaged any computer, etc., data, computer database or any other programs residing in such computer, etc.,

(e) disrupts or causes disruption of any computer, etc.

(f) denies or causes the denial of access to any person authorised to access any computer, ate,

(g) provides any assistance to my person to facilitate access to a computer, ate, in contravention of the provisions of this Act,

(h) charges of services availed of by a person to the account of another person by tampering with or manipulating any computer, etc.

2. Penalty for failure to furnish information, return, etc. (Section 44)

It any person who in required under this Act, etc. to —

(a) furnish any document, return or report to the Controller or the Certifying Authority fails to furnish the same, he shall be liable to a penalty not exceeding Rs. one lakh and fifty thousand for each such failure,

(b) file any return or furnish any intimation, books or other documents within the times specified there for in the regulations fails to file return or furnish the same within the time specified therefore in the regulations, he shall liable to a penalty not exceeding Rs.5,000 for every day during which such failure continues,

(c) maintain books of accounts or records fails to maintain the same, he shall be liable to a penalty not exceeding Rs 10,000 for every day during which the failure continues.

3. Residuary Penalty (Section 45)

The Act defines specific penalties for violation of its provisions or of any regulations made thereunder. However, if any person contravenes any rules or regulations framed under the Act for which no specific penalty is prescribed; he will be liable to pay compensation not receding Rs. 25,000.

Power to Adjudicate (Section 46)

The adjudicating court also has the powers to confiscate any computer, computer system, floppies, compact disks, tape drives or any accessories in relation to which any provisions of the Act are being violated. No penalty or confiscation made under this Act will affect the imposition of any other punishment under any other law in force.

If penalties that are imposed under the Act are not paid, they will be recovered as arrears of land revenue and the licence or Digital Signature Certificate shall be suspended till the penalty is paid.

Adjudicating Officer

The Central Government shall appoint an officer not below the rank of Director to the Government of India or equivalent officer of the State Government as an adjudicating officer to adjudicate upon any inquiry in connection with the contravention of the Act. Such officer must possess such experience in the field of Information Technology and legal or judicial experience as may be prescribed by the Central Government. Every adjudicating officer shall have the powers of civil court which are conferred on the Cyber Appellate Tribunal under section 58 and —

(a) all proceedings before it shall be deemed to be judicial proceedings under the Indian Penal Code,

(b) shall be deemed to be a civil court for the purposes of sections 345 and 346 of the code of criminal Procedure, 1973.

The Adjudicating officer must give the accused a reasonable opportunity to be heard and after being satisfied that he violated the law, penalize him according to the provisions of the Act.

CYBER REGULATION APPELLATE TRIBUNAL

Establishment

A Cyber Regulations Appellate Tribunal (CRAT) is to be set up for appeals from the order of any adjudicating officer. Every appeal must be filed within a period of forty-five days from the date on which the person aggrieved receives a copy of the order made by the adjudicating officer. The appeal must be the appropriate form and accompanied by the prescribed fee. An appeal may be allowed after the expiry of forty-five days if 'sufficient cause' is shown.

The Central Government shall, by notification one or more appellate tribunals to be known as Cyber Regulations Appellate Tribunal **[Sec. 48]**.

A Cyber Regulations Appellate Tribunal shall consist of one person only to the known as the Presiding Officer **[Sec. 49]**.

The qualifications of the Presiding Officer shall be a judge of a High Court or a member of the Indian Legal Service holding a post in Grade I of that service for at least three years **[Sect. 50]**.

The Presiding Officer shall hold officer for a term of five years or until he attains the age of 65 years, which ever is earlier **[Sec. 51]**.

The Tribunal shall ordinarily hold its sittings at New Delhi. However, if at any time, the Presiding Officer is satisfied that it is necessary to have sittings of the Tribunal at any other place, the Presiding Officer may direct to hold the sittings at any such appropriate place **[Rule 13]**. *[Rules referred in this Chapter areframed under Cyber Regulations Appellate Tribunal (Procedure) Rules, 2000 (CRAT Rules)]*.

The Presiding Officer may by notice in writing addressed to Central Government, May by order, removal of the Presiding Officer on the ground of proved misbehaviors or incapacity **[Sec. 54]**.

No order of the Central Government appointing any person as the Presiding Officer shall be called in question. No act or proceeding before the Tribunal shall be called in question on the ground merely of any defect in constitution of the Tribunal **[Sec. 55]**.

Appeal to Cyber Regulation Appellate Tribunal

Any person aggrieved by on order made by on adjudicating officer may prefer an appeal to the Cyber Appellate Tribunal from an order made by an adjudicating officer with the consent of the parties. Every appeal must be filed within a period of 45 days from the date of the receipt of the order by the aggrieved person.

The appeal filed before the Cyber Appellate Tribunal shall be dealt with by it as expeditiously as possible and endeavour shall be made by it to dispose of the appeal finally within six months from the data of receipt of the appeal **[Sec. 57]**.

A penalty imposed under this Act, if it is not paid, shall be recovered as an arrear of land revenue and the license or the Digital Signature Certificate shall be suspended till the penalty in paid **[Sec. 64]**.

Procedure for filing applications

Ah application to the Tribunal shall be presented to the Registrar in Form-1 annexed to the CRAT Rules in person or through a legal practitioner. The application shall be presented in six complete sets In a paper book form alongwith one empty full size envelope bearing full address of the respondent **[Rule 3]**, Every application shall be accompanied by a fee of Rs.2,000 **[Rule 6]**.

The Registrar shall endorse on every application the date on which it is presented. If on scrutiny, the application is found to be in order, it shall be duly registered and given a serial number. If the application is found to be defective and the defect is formal in nature, the Registrar may allow the party to rectify the same. If the defect is not formal in nature, the Registrar may allow the applicant such time to rectify the defect as he may deem fit. The Registrar shall decline to register the application if the applicant fails to rectify the defect. An appeal from this order shall lie to the Tribunal within 1.5 days and the decision of the Tribunal shall be, final **[Rule 4]**.

Every application shall set forth concisely under distinct heads, the grounds of such application which shall be numbered consecutively and typed in double space on one side of the paper. No separate application is required to seek an interim order or direction if the application contains a prayer to that effect. Separate application is required for seeking interim order or direction subsequently **[Rule 7]**.

Every application shall be accompanied by a paper book containing a certified copy of the order against which the application has been filed arid copies of the documents relied upon by the applicant. The documents annexed may be attested by an Advocate or a Gazetted Officer **[Rule 8]**.

An application shall be based upon a single cause of action. More reliefs may be sought provided they are consequential to one another **[Rule 9]**.

A copy of the application in the paper book shall be served on each of the respondents by the Registrar. The applicant shall pay alee for service or execution, of processes **[Rule 10]**.

The respondent shall file six complete sets containing the reply to the application alongwith the documents in a paper book form with the Registrar within one month from the date of service of the notice of the application on him. The respondent shall also serve a copy of the reply alongwith the copies of the documents to the applicant or his Advocate **[Rule 11]**.

Orders:

On receipt of an appeal, the Cyber Appellate Tribunal may, after giving the parties to the appeal, an opportunity of being heard, pass such orders thereon as it thinks fit, confirming, modifying or setting aside the order appealed against.

Every application shall be heard and decided by the Tribunal, as far as. possible, within six months of the date of its presentation **[Rule 14]**.

Ever order of the Tribunal shall be in writing and shall be signed and dated by the Presiding Officer **[Rule 18].**

Every order shall be communicated to the applicant and to the respondent **[Rule 20]** and to the concerned Controller or adjudicating officer. The Tribunal may make such orders or give such directions as may be necessary or expedient to give effect to its orders or to prevent abuse of its process or to secure the ends of justice **[Sec.57 and Rule 22]**.

Procedure and Power of the Tribunal (Section 58)

The Cyber Appellate Tribunal shall be guided by the principal of natural justice. Subjects to other provisions of the Act and the Rules, the Tribunal shall have power to regulate its own procedure including the place at which it shall have its sittings. The Tribunal shall have same power as are vested in a civil court under the Code of Civil Procedure 1908 in following matters —

(a) summoning and enforcing the attendance of any person and examining him on act,

(b) requiring the discovery and production of documents or other electronic records.

(c) receiving evidence and production of documents or other electronic records,

(d) issuing commissions for the examination of witnesses or documents,

(e) reviewing its decisions,

(f) dismissing an application for default or deciding it expert

(g) any other mater which may be prescribed.

The appellant may appear in person or authorise legal practitioners or any of its officers to present his case before the Tribunal **[Sec. 59]**.

The provisions of Limitation Act 1963 shall apply to on appeal made to the Tribunal **[Sec. 60]**.

No court shall have the jurisdiction to entertain any matter that can be decided by the adjudicating officer or Cyber Regulations Appellate Tribunal.

However, a provision has been made to appeal from the decision of the Cyber Regulations Appellate Tribunal to the High Court within sixty days of the data of communication of the order or decision of the Cyber Regulations Appellate Tribunal. The stipulated period may be extended if sufficient cause is shown. The appeal may be made on either any question of law or question of fact arising from the order **[Sec. 61]**.

Compounding of contraventions (Section 63)

Any contravention under two Act may, either before or after institution of adjudication proceedings, be compounded by the Controller or the adjudicating officer as the case may be. Such sum shall not exceed the maximum amount of penalty which may be imposed for the contravention so compounded.

The compounding benefit shall not be available to a person who commits the same or similar contravention within a period of three years from the date on which a previous contravention was compounded.

OFFENCES

1. Tampering with Computer Source Document (Section 65)

Whoever knowingly or intentionally conceals destroys or alters any computer source code wed for a computer or computer or computer programs, computer system or computer network, when the computer source code in required to be kept or maintained by law for the time being inforce shall be punishable with imprisonment upto three years, or with fine which may extend upto Rs. 2 lakh or with both.

2. Hacking with Computer System (Section 66)

Whoever knowingly or intentionally causes wrongful loss or damage to the public or destroys or deletes or alters any information reading in a computer resource or diminishes its value or utility or affects it injuriously by any means commits hacking shall be punished with imprisonment up to three years with fine which may extend to Rs. 2 lakh or with both.

3. Publishing of information which is obscene in electronic form (Section 67)

Any person publishes or transmits or causes to be published in electronic form shall be punished on first conviction with imprisonment of either description for a term which may extend to five years or with fine which may extent to five years or with fine which may extent to Rs. One lakh. In the event of subsequent conviction, the imprisonment may extend to 10 years and the fine may extend to Rs. 2 lakhs.

4. Power of Controller to give directions (Section 68)

The Controller may, by order, direct a Certifying Authority or any employee of such Authority to take such measures or cease carrying on such activities as specified in the order it those are necessary to ensure compliance with the provisions of this Act, Rules or any regulations made thereunder. Any person who fails to comply with any such order shall be liable on conviction to imprisonment for a term not exceeding three years or to fine not exceeding Rs. 2 lakh or both.

5. Directions of Controller to a subscriber to extend facilities to decrypt information (Section 69)

If the Controller is satisfied, for reasons to recorded in writing, that it is necessary or expedient in the interest of sovereignty or integrity of India, the security of the state, friendly relations with foreign states or public order for the preventing, incitement to the commission of any cognizable offence, by order direct any information transmitted through any computer resource. The subscriber or any person in charge of the computer resource shall extend all facilities and technical assistance to decrypt the information, if he fails to provide the necessary assistance, then he shall be punished with an imprisonment for a term which may extend to 7 years.

6. Protected system (Section 70)

The appropriate Government may declare that any computer, computer system or computer network to be a protected system. Any person who secures access or attempts to secures access to a protected system without authority from the appropriate government shall be punished with imprisonment upto 10 years and shall also liable to fine.

7. Penalty for misrepresentation (Section 71)

Any person for obtaining a license or Digital Signature Certificate makes misrepresentation to, or suppresses any material fact from the Controller or the Certifying Authority shall be punished with imprisonment upto two year or with fine which may extend to Rs. one lakh or with both.

8. Breach of confidentiality and privacy (Section 72)

Any person who has secured access to any electronic record, book, register, correspondence, information, document or other material discloses the same to any other person without the consent of the person concerned shall be punished with imprisonment upto two years or with fine which may extend to Rs. 1 lakh or with both.

9. Publication of Digital Signature Certificate for purpose (Section 74)

Any person knowingly creates, publishes or other wise makes available a Digital Signature Certificate for any fraudulent or unlawful purpose shall be published with imprisonment upto two years or with fine which may extend to Rs. one lakh or with both.

10. Offene or contravention committed outside India (Section 75)

The provisions of this act shall apply also to any officer by any person irrespective of his nationality. The act or conduct constituting the officer or contravention involves a computer, computer system or computer network located in India.

11. Confiscation (section 76)

Any computer, computer system, floppies, compact disks, tape drives or any other accessories relied thereto, in respect of which provision of this act, rules, order or regulations made thereunder has been contravened shall be liable to confiscation.

12. Penalties and confiscation not to interfere with other punishment (Section 77)

The penalty imposed or confiscation made under this act shall not prevent the inpositioning any other punishment to which the person affected thereby is liable under any other law for the time being inforce.

13. Power to investigate offences (Section 78)

A police officer not below the rank of deputy superintendent of police officer shall investigate any offence under this act.

Network Service Providers not liable in certain cases:

To quote Section 78, it states:

"For the removal of doubts, it is hereby declared that no person providing any service as a network service provider shall be liable under this Act, rules or regulations made thereunder for any third party information or data made available by him if he proves that the offence or contravention was committed without his knowledge or that he had exercised all due diligence to prevent the commission of such offence or contravention."

"Explanation — For the purposes of this section —

(a) 'network service provider' means an intermediary;

(b) 'third party information' means any information dealt with by a network service provider in his capacity as an intermediary."

Thus, a plain reading of the section indicates that if the network service provider is unable to prove its innocence or ignorance, it will be held liable for the crime.

Miscellaneous Provisions of the act

Important miscellaneous provisions are as below:

Section-80 says a police officer not below the rank of deputy superintendent of police has the power to enter any public place and arrest any person without a warrant if he believes that a cyber crime has been committed or in about to be committed.

Section 81 enumerates that this act shall have overriding effect notwithstanding any thing non-consistent contained in any other law for the time being inforce.

The Negotiable Instruments Act, 2002 has amended one section of the Information and Technology Act 2000 and inserted a new section '81 A' as follows:

81 A — application of the act to electronic cheque and truncated cheque.

For the purposes of this act, the expressions "electronic cheque" and truncated cheque shall have the same meaning as assigned in section 6 of the Negotiable Instruments Act 1881.

Section 82 declares that Controllers, Deputy Controller, Assistant Controllers shall be public servants within the meaning of section 21 of the Indian Penal Code. The presiding officer and other officers and employees of a cyber appellate tribunal, the Controller, The Deputy Controller and the Assistant Controllers shall be deemed to be public servants within the meaning of section 21 of the IPC.

It has been argued that it is not clear whether this is sufficient to bring it within the ambit of The Prevention of Corruption Act. What is far more worrying is section 84 which reads thus:

No suit, prosecution or other legal proceedings shall be against the Central government, the state government, the controller or any person acting on behalf of him, the presiding officer, adjudicating officers and the staff of the cyber-appellate tribunal for anything which is in good faith done or intended to be done in pursuance of this Act or any rule, regulation made thereunder.

Section 83 empowers the Central Government to give directions to any state government for execution of any of the provision of this act, or of any rule, regulation or order made thereunder.

Section 84 provides that no suit, prosecution, legal proceeding shall lie against the Central Government. The state government, The Controller, The Presiding Officer, Adjudicating Officer and the staff of Cyber Appellate Tribunal for anything done or intended to be done in good faith in pursuance of the Act, or rule regulations or orders made thereunder.

Section 85 makes a specific provision in the case of companies.

Section 86 empowered the Central Government to make provisions when any difficulty arises in giving effect to the provision of the act.

Section 87 provides power to central government to make rules under the act.

Section 88 provides for constitutions of the cyber regulation advisory committee.

Section 89 empowers the Controller to make regulations under the act.

Scetion 90 empowers the state government to make rules.

Section 91 to 94 provide for the amendment of the Indian Penal Code 1860, the Indian Evidence Act 1872, the Banker's Books Evidences Act 1891 and the Reserve Bank of India Act 1934.

DRAWBACKS OF THE ACT

BASIC SHORT COMINGS OF THE INFORMATION TECHNOLOGY ACT

After having discussed the important provisions of the act, attention should also be draw to some of its shortcomings.

1. Inapplicability

The first and foremost setback is that the provisions of the act does not apply to the following:

(1) A negotiable instrument as defined in section 13 of the Negotiable Instruments Act 1881,

(2) Power of attorney as defined in section 1A of the Powers-of-Attorney Act 1882,

(3) A trust as defined in section 3 of the Indian Trusts Act 1882,

(4) A will as defined in section (h) of section 2 of the Indian Succession Act, 1925, including any other testamentary disposition by whatever more called.

(5) Any contract for the sale or conveyance of immovable property or any interest in such property.

It is envisaged that the efficacy of the act may not be considerable owing to its restrictive applicability.

2. No Intellectual Property Rights Protection Guaranteed

The act deals with the commercial and criminal areas of law as affected information technology and, does not deal with certain other issues, such as intellectual property rights, particularly copyright on the internet. The act does not discuss the implications of any copyright violations over the net. It has no provisions to penalize copyright infringers for their activities over the net. Internet privacy is a major problem has not been tackled by this act.

3. Digital signatures

Act deals only with public key infrastructure (PKI) framework for authentication. it does not recognize any other authentication procedure though the ambit of 'legal record' is wide. This may cause problems for e-commerce transactions that may not necessarily use the public key infrastructure system for authentication and security purpose.

4. Qualifications and powers of adjudicating unclear

The Act is unclear as to the qualifications of an adjudicating officer and the manner in which he shall adjudicate.

The Act does not indicate the powers of the adjudicating officers when a person commits a cyber crime or violates any provisions of the law from out side India. The Act does not lay down any provisions where by extradition treaties can be formed with countries where the cyber criminal is located.

5. The Information Technology Act 2000 is silent as regards taxation of goods and services traded through e-commerce.
6. The Information Technology Act makes no provision for jurisdictional aspects of electronic controls, i.e., jurisdictional of courts and tax authorities.
7. No provision has been made for payment of stamp duty on electronic documents.

8. Misuse of Police Powers

The search arrest powers given to Police Officers are without any definite guidelines and may be ill used.

However, if the Act did give the Police Department Powers to enter people's houses without search warrants, it would amount to an invasion of the right to privacy and create pandemonium. Keeping this in mind, the legislature has tried to balance this provision so as to serve the ends of justice and at the same time, avoid any chaos.

On being, arrested, the accused person must, without any unnecessary delay, be taken or sent to the magistrate having jurisdiction or to the officer-in-charge of a police station. The provisions of the Code of Criminal Procedure, 1973 shall apply in relation to any entry, search or arrest made by the police officer.

9 Possible Violation of Fundamentals Rights

The provision that no order of the central government appointing any person as the Presiding Officer of a Cyber Regulations Appellate Tribunal (CRAT) shall be called in question in any manner and no act or procedure before CRAT shall be called in question in any manner merely because there is a defect in the constitution of the CRAT may be viola eye of the fundamental rights on the citizens under the constitution of India. This provision could be misused by the Central Government in an unfair and arbitrary manner. It is recommended that this provision be modified so that the interests of the public at large are safeguarded.

10. Qualifications and Powers of Adjudicating Officers Unclear:

The Act is unclear as to the qualifications of an adjudicating officer and the manner in which he shall adjudicate.

Moreover, though the statute is supposedly a 'long arm statute', it does not indicate the powers of the adjudicating officers when a person commits a cyber crime or violates any provisions of the law from outside India. Several practical difficulties may also arise in importing the cyber criminal to India. The Act does not lay down any provisions whereby extradition treaties can be formed with countries where the cyber criminal is located. Therefore, the extra-territorial scope of the Act may be difficult to achieve.

Furthermore, the powers to impose a penalty for a computer crime upto Rs. 1 crore offers a large discretion to adjudicating officers and may turn out to be harmful.

1 . ISP Liability — Responsibility for Content Regulation not attributable:

While Section 78 absolves a network service provider of its liability if it can prove its ignorance and due diligence, it fails to specify as to who would be held liable for such contravention in such an event. This provision will certainly cause problems when an offence regarding third party information or provision of data is committed.

Issue of Privacy

The line between the real world and the mechanical world is becoming more and more blurred every day. But it is not that humans are turning into automatons or becoming slaves to machines. No, we are simply growing towards each other. In the Blue Nowhere machines are taking our personalities and culture — our language, myths, metaphors, philosophy and spirit.

It becomes important, in this context, for any law-making body to think through on what the consequences of its actions will be. The issue of privacy is a serious one which the Act impacts on very unfavourably as the appendix reveals.

Privacy is the ability of an individual or group to seclude either themselves or information about themselves and thereby reveal themselves selectively. Privacy as a concept involves what privacy entails and how it is to be valued. Privacy as a right involves the extent to which privacy is (and should be legally protected). "The law does not determine what privacy is, but only what situations of privacy will be afforded legal protection." It is interesting to note that the common law does not know a general right of privacy and the Indian Parliament has so far been reluctant to enact one.

As of now there is no enactment on Privacy in India but the Constitution of India has embodied many Rights in Part III, which are called Fundamental Rights.

These are enumerated in Article 14-30 of the Constitution. But judicial activism has brought the Right to Privacy within the sphere of Fundamental Rights. Article 141 of the Constitution states "the law declared by the Supreme Court shall be binding on all courts within the territory of India."

Therefore, the decisions of The Supreme Court of India become the Law of the Land. The Supreme Court of India has come to the rescue of common citizen, time and again by construing "right to privacy" as a part of the Fundamental Right to "protection of life and personal liberty" under Article 21 of the Constitution, which states "no person shall be deprived of his life or personal liberty except according to procedures established by law". In the context of personal liberty, the Supreme Court has observed "those who feel called upon to deprive other persons of their personal liberty in the discharge of what they conceive to be their duty must strictly and scrupulously observe the forms and rules of the law."

The Supreme Court has reiterated the Right to Privacy in the following cases: Kharak Singh v. State of UP, Gobind v. State of M.P., Gobind v. State of M.P., People's Union for Civil Liberties (PUCL) v. Union of India, District Registrar and Collector v. Canara Bank and many others.

If one follows the judgements given by the Supreme Court, three themes emerge:

(1) That the individual's right to privacy exists and any unlawful invasion of privacy would make the 'offender' liable for the consequences in accordance with law.

(2) That there is constitutional recognition given to the right of privacy, which protects personal privacy against unlawful governmental invasion.

(3) That the person's "right to be let alone" is not an absolute right and may be lawfully restricted for the prevention of crime, disorder or protection of health or morals or protection of rights and freedom of others.

Privacy is closely connected to Data Protection. An individual's data like his name, address, telephone numbers, profession, family, choices, etc. are often available at various places like schools, colleges, banks, directories, surveys and on various websites. Passing on such information to interested parties can lead to intrusion in privacy like incessant marketing calls.

It is factually wrong to say that India does not have data protection legislation at all. The fact is that there exists data protection legislation in India and it has been dealt within the Information Technology Act, 2000 but not in an exclusive manner. Therefore, data protection is a Central subject and only the Central Government is competent to frame legislations on issues dealing with data protection.

13. Danger of Violation of Civil Rights

The Information Technology Act raises very real concerns. It demonstrates a legislature deeply sceptical of the internet, rooted in the conventions of the past, yet battling with the need for an information technology law in the present-day circumstances. This straddling of the known and the unknown has strange results. In its desperate need to bring in some security for activity on the net, it relies heavily on the executive, little realising that it can result in violation of civil rights particularly, in the light of India's infamous emergency. The absolute control it attempts to achieve over certifying authorities is worrying for the same reason. The act lacks balance.

Epilogue

The IT Act is a comprehensive piece of legislation which aims at policing some of the activities over the Internet. The fundamental approach of the Act is towards validating and legalising electronic and on-line transactions. Business transaction costs will be curtailed and transaction volumes will grow manifold. Computer and Cyber Crimes will hopefully be curbed and offenders will be strictly penalised. Policing these crimes is extremely necessary. At the same time, the police officers who occupy large powers under the IT Act must also be educated in computers and Internet. This would help them in executing their powers effectively and efficiently.

But in order to curb computer crimes, the police alone cannot make all the difference. Awareness regarding these cyberlaws must be created. Private and Non Governmental organisations must play an active role in communicating this message to the masses. Moreover, the judiciary will also have to play a proactive role in adjudicating cyber trials. A large part of the judiciary is probably unaware of cyberlaws and their implications. They must themselves study the laws carefully and effectively enforce them. Co-ordination amongst the organisations, police and judiciary will definitely create some impact and minimise the crime rate.

However, the working and implementation of this law will depend greatly on the rules and regulations that will be formed by the Government and other authorities constituted under the Act. The Act is only a skeletal figure, while it is the rules and regulations that will form the fleshy content.

The Information Technology Act 2000, is not the end but only a beginning to a plethora of legislation that still needs to be formed. It leaves various issues untouched, some and them relating to intellectual property rights, data protection and taxation. No concrete regulations have also been formulated for cross border issues. These issues are of immense importance and the Parliament must specially frame laws to govern them.

India is amongst few of the countries in the world which have any legal framework for e-commerce and e-governance. Indian industry projections indicate that business transactions over the net have crossed Rs. 2500 crore by 2002. The correct and honest implementation of this act would definitely be a boon to the Indian InfoTech sector. The Act has been passed at a time when the internet population in India is low and therefore it is hoped that implementing the law should not be very difficult.

Amendments to the Information Technology Act

The expert committee constituted for an in-depth review of issues relating to the Information Technology Act, 2000, and to consider suitable legislation for data protection (privacy) is understood to favour widening the ambit of computer offences as defined under the legislation, in the wake of rapid technological advancements.

"Computer has been narrowly defined in the Act and hence computer offences too have not been defined in a manner that would reflect technological advancements," sources said.

For instance, Phishing (the act of sending an e-mail to a user falsely claiming to be an established legitimate enterprise in an attempt to scam the user into surrendering private information that will be used for identity theft) was not widely known way back in 1999. "New laws cannot be enacted every two-three years and hence we are looking at making the type of offences more generic to take into account newer forms," the sources added.

The committee was set up after the controversy generated over the arrest of Baazee.com CEO in December 2004 in a case involving the sale of a sexually explicit clip on the auction site. The industry had subsequently called for an amendment in the IT Act.

Making the Baazee.com case as a reference point, the committee is re-looking at ways of balancing the rights of enforcement authorities with the rights of those who could be potentially accused. For instance, in the US, the practice is that an auction site is given an opportunity to take an offending product off its Web site once intimated. If the site fails to take off the offending item within a specified time, action can be taken against it. Therefore, the committee is understood to be looking at factors such as examination of due diligence.

With the IT Act 2000 in its present form covering only digital signatures, the expert committee is in favour of extending it to other forms of e-signatures, such as bio-metrics and fingerprint. "A big shift has been a suggestion to make it technology neutral," the sources added.

On the issue of data protection and data privacy, the committee is believed to be looking at issues such as how data should be collected by entities such as hospitals, telephone companies and banks, and how it should be used.

"It is not as if IT services clients are not satisfied about the data protection in India while offshoring work. The idea is to reassure Indian public that their information and data relating to credit card, mobile phone and even IPO issue application, is safe," the sources pointed out.

The committee, constituted was headed by Mr Brijesh Kumar, Secretary, Department of Information Technology, and includes Dr. A.K. Chakravarty, Scientist-G, DIT; Mr. Kiran Karnik, President of Nasscom; Mr. Ajay Chowdhry, Chairman, HCL Infosystems Ltd; Mr. Ajit Balakrishnan, CEO, Rediff; and Mr. R. Ramraj, CEO, Sify Ltd.

Now let us discusses the recent amendments to the IT Act 2000 that clarify its provisions and give it teeth. In the backdrop of e-fraud in banking and BPO, one can clearly lays out the shortcomings that existed in the IT Act and how these have been addressed in its latest avatar.

With the recent amendments being approved by the Cabinet, the Information Technology Act 2000 (The Act) is all set to silence critics with its new Avatar. The Act, much maligned for its supposed inadequacies, has undergone major surgery. Malignant parts have been removed and life-saving transplants have been made. Whether, the surgery has been able to able to expunge the inadequacies still remains to be seen.

Not surprisingly, popular belief links cyber law to punishments for hacking. The reasons are not hard to find. Hacking seems to conjure images of dark, shadowy alleyways, populated with Keanu Reeves's 'Neo'isque figures juggling with the world of bits and bytes that magically transform into six and nine digit figures in the hacker's bank account and dodge bullets,

Not many may know that the Act is more about the complex and highly versatile world of digital signatures than it is about the fascinating world of hacking. Personally, though, I believe cryptography (on which the concept of digital signatures is based) will give hacking a run for its money if measured by the yardsticks of romanticism and intrigue.

This brings us to the first failing of the Act, that of being technology specific. Critics said, "by specifying that only digital signatures can be used to authenticate electronic records, the Act shut its doors all other forms of electronic signatures, such as scanned thumbprints, signatures or PINs", which can also be used for authentication.

Digital signatures are an application of asymmetric key cryptography and their security is based upon the fact that it is computationally infeasible to compromise the application with the computing power currently at our disposal. What if due to some technological innovation, a path breaking invention or a remarkable discovery, we should be able to overcome this limitation. Digital signatures can no longer be used as authentication mechanisms and the whole legal superstructure built around the concept will collapse, necessitating an overhaul of the Act itself.

What about the money and the effort spent by organisations to comply with the requirements of the Act? Well, the answer is not too hard to guess. The first major amendment, then, introduces the concept of electronic signatures in place of digital signatures. This provides an alternative to a digital signature system which was the only option available earlier. But the amendment states that authentication may be done, "….in such other electronic form as the Central Government may prescribe from time to time."

As of right now, the Central Government has "prescribed" rules for the implementation of digital signatures only and not for anything else. So it is easy to say which form of signature organisations have to adopt to comply till such time the Central Government prescribes, "…such other electronic form….." (Which may be today, tomorrow, next week, next month, next year…..you get the idea!!)

Since its coming into force in the year 2000, I have received this query umpteen number of times from professionals and individuals from different walks of life, "does a law court recognize an agreement entered into through e-mails?" The answer is, yes.

An agreement, the terms of which have been transmitted through an e-mail or the contents of which are saved in a word file, i.e., in electronic form, is a valid agreement. A court of law will not refuse to admit an agreement solely because it is in electronic form. Just that, as in the case of an agreement made in any other form, it has be proved that such an agreement was indeed entered into between the parties concerned.

Earlier, this was not expressly stated in the Act and had to be inferred from a reading of the provisions. A new chapter titled, "Electronic Contracts", Chapter IIIA, now expressly states this, removing any ambiguities that may have existed in the minds of many.

The next piece of amendment will be of much interest to certifying authorities and to the subscribers who have obtained digital signature certificates from licensed certifying authorities. The provision which provided for the Controller to act as a repository has been omitted. Repositories are now to be maintained only by certifying authorities. The reasons provided are that maintaining a repository is the primary responsibility of a certifying authority, not the Controller and that it is an undue burden on the Controller.

For the uninitiated, a repository in a public key infrastructure serves as a storehouse of digital signature certificates. The idea is, if a person wants to verify the authenticity of a public key, he can retrieve the corresponding digital signature certificate from the repository and do so.

The very fact that the person has been able to retrieve a valid digital signature certificate from the Controller's repository provides the element of trust, so important for a digital signature system to exist. There is simple logic behind this. The Controller is a public servant and the highest ranking authority under the Act. He has been entrusted with the task of licensing certifying authorities. Thus, trust in him is highest.

If a subscriber can verify the antecedents of a certifying authority or of another subscriber from the Controller's repository, the trust that he would put into such verification would be much higher than from any other source. Considering the fact that public key infrastructure in India is still in its infancy, this would have given much needed reassurance to a subscriber about the genuineness of the system and would have helped popularise it.

Admitted, as the number of subscribers increase, it would not be easy for the Controller's office to manage the repository. But isn't that a small price to pay for so big an idea?

The next series of amendments to the Act is significant as it deals with privacy. Protection of privacy and personal data had never been addressed directly by any law in force in India. Protection was finally given by the Supreme Court in the form of a ruling which referred to privacy as a right flowing from the constitutionally guaranteed right to life. The picture regarding privacy and data protection laws will now be somewhat clear because of these amendments.

The first in the series of amendments involving privacy protection involves providing compensation of up to ten million rupees by an organisation,"...that owns or handles sensitive personal data or information in a computer resource that it owns or operates." If such an organisation has been negligent in implementing and maintaining "reasonable security practices" and procedures to protect "sensitive personal data", it shall be liable to pay compensation to any person affected by such negligence.

But for this to be workable the government has to move quickly and formulate rules on two aspects. First, it has to prescribe "reasonable security practices" to address cases where such practices are not defined in a contract. Secondly, it needs to define what constitutes "sensitive personal data." Till then, the law, though made in letter, will be inoperative in spirit.

The next amendment in the series of privacy related amendments deals with disclosure of information by intermediaries and service providers. Section 72 of the Act penalised those agencies which "in pursuance" of the powers conferred on them by the Act, (e.g., certifying authorities) having access to personal information disclosed it without authorisation. It had limited scope because it could only be applied to those cases where an agency disclosed personal information to which it was privy because of requirements under the Act.

The amendment to the section now does away with this limitation and penalises any intermediary who discloses subscriber information to which it is privy by reason of that subscriber availing of the services provided by the intermediary. A simple example would be all the providers who provide free services on the Internet. Almost all of them require the subscriber to fill in forms with personal information before he is allowed to avail of the services offered. The amendment penalises disclosure of such information without the consent of the concerned subscriber.

However, there is a catch. The provision states that if an intermediary discloses this information, "without the consent of such subscriber and with intent to cause injury to him...." the subscriber is entitled to a compensation of upto twenty five lakh rupees. It is interesting to note that no intermediary would ever disclose such information with the intent to cause injury to any subscriber. Rather the disclosure would most likely be caused by the intent to derive profit with the knowledge that injury might result from such disclosure. Without going into legal callisthenics, let me just say that the language in which the provision is couched will make it extremely difficult for a subscriber to get compensation from the errant intermediary.

The other amendment in this series addresses the scourge of mobile phone cameras. We have come across numerous incidents involving gross violation of privacy where a mobile phone camera has been surreptitiously used to take photographs or video clippings of private moments and private parts and then used to circulate these snaps or clips around using either the telecom network or the Internet. This can be extremely embarrassing and distressing to the victim.

The amended provision penalises intentional captures or broadcast of an image of a private area of an individual without his consent. It is also applicable to cases where an individual is unaware (and therefore unable to give consent) that he is being photographed or that a video clipping of his is being shot. The section provides for fine of upto twenty-five lakh rupees and imprisonment of upto one year for the offenders. For action to be taken under this section, the person aggrieved must file a written complaint before a magistrate. An F.I.R before the police is not enough. The section is comprehensive in its definitions and explanations and will definitely deter miscreants once a few cases are prosecuted.

The spate of events that may have prompted these provisions is well known. In mid 2005, a major scam involving the BPO company MSource in Pune was discovered where a team of Msource employees had siphoned off more than $425,000 using personal information of Citibank customers. Later that year, the well-known British tabloid Sun, in a sting operation, was able to obtain personal information of around 1,000 British citizens from the employee of another BPO outfit, Infinity E-search at the price of £5.5 per employee. More recently, in June 2006, another BPO fraud in Bangalore worth £233, 000 through HSBC came to light.

Earlier, MMS clips of a high school girl and a boy showing intimate acts were being circulated across the country. More clips followed, this time shot from hidden cameras placed in night clubs, bathrooms, swimming pools and hotel rooms. In most cases, the victims never had an inkling of the fact that their activities would be recorded and circulated around the country where perfectly normal private moments could become so outrageously public.

These incidents were a clarion call to the government to take action. Organisations handling personal data realised they had to have the best information security practices implemented in their organisations. These also highlighted the fact that organisations which compromised on sensitive personal data by sacrificing security practices for shoring up bottom lines could get away with it. Reason, there was simply no law in place which acted as a deterrent to prevent them from doing so.

The amendments will certainly help stem public outcry abroad against outsourcing to India, especially in services and will help bring back some confidence to the companies giving outsourcing contracts to Indian firms.

With the European Union's Directives on Data Protection being very stringent, major companies from the European Union have mostly stayed away from outsourcing to India where such outsourcing involved handling personal data, notably in the financial, legal and healthcare sectors. Although, a comprehensive legislation on privacy and data protection would have been more welcome, this is by no means a small achievement by our lawmakers.

Discussion now shifts to the more popular subject of cyber crimes. Obviously, then, the first section that we will discuss has to relate to hacking. In what is sure to raise the eyebrows of many, the proposed amendment to the provision which penalised hacking does not define hacking. Instead, the section has been renamed as a more stolid, "computer related offences", which in hindsight is perhaps right after all. Let me explain.

The earlier section defined hacking so widely that almost every conceivable computer crime fell within its purview. This, by itself, is perfectly acceptable till we consider the fact that you and I understand hacking as unauthorised access. Thus the commonly accepted definition and the legal definition were altogether different. This caused confusion even in the mind of the most diligent student to whom the difference had been explained time and again. To this, add the fact that purists in the field scoff at the idea of defining hacking as an illegal activity. Instead, they say, we mean cracking when we say hacking. Hackers, it seems are a benign lot, working only for the benefit of the wide wired world, which is now increasingly turning wireless!

Now, all this has been put to rest by simply not defining hacking at all! The provision has been divided into two parts. One part lays down a punishment of upto a year in jail or fine of up to rupees two lakh or both. Unauthorised access, unauthorised downloading of data and causing denial of access, if done for dishonest or fraudulent purposes fall under this category.

The other part penalises introduction of a virus, disruption of an electronic resource, credit card frauds and time thefts, aiding or assisting in illegal activity and damaging a computer resource. The penalty for the said offences is two years' imprisonment or rupees five lakh fine or both.

Another topic which has always attracted much debate is pornography. The provision penalising publishing and transmission of pornography has undergone substantial change. Intermediaries have been excluded from the scope. This will bring much needed relief to services based companies like Google and eBay, which will now not be liable for third party pornographic material being accessed through their sites.

More importantly, distinction has now been made between adult and child pornography and penalty has been reduced to two years imprisonment for adult pornography and three years imprisonment for child pornography. Only those people have been made liable who are "intentionally or knowingly" involved in transmission or publishing of pornographic material.

The inclusion of the phrase "intentionally and knowingly" means that innocently forwarded e-mails with adult content will now be outside the scope of this provision. The offence is punishable with two years' imprisonment (in cases of adult pornography) which automatically makes it non-cognisable and bailable. So, any person arrested by law enforcement agencies on charges of transmission or publishing will have to be released on bail.

There is more. Pictures, images and representations in electronic form which are proved to be justified as being for the public good on the ground of promotion of science, literature, art or learning are excluded form the purview of this provision. Material used for religious purposes is also excluded. This will please advocates of free speech and expression who have always argued that (adult) pornography be made legal.

Intermediaries will also be relieved by the fact that their liability extends only to those cases in which their active collusion is proved. The earlier section, which made them liable for not taking due diligence to prevent the transmission, has been removed. Considering the fiasco in the Baazee.com case which led to the arrest of the CEO simply because a posting relating to sale of a CD containing offensive material was found on Baazee.com, this is certainly a laudable step by the legislators. Cyber café owners will also heave a sigh of relief, as they are included within the definition of intermediaries.

The Act was had been criticised by all and sundry for giving arbitrary powers to the police. Under the Act, the police could enter any public and search and arrest without a warrant if they suspected commission of an offence under the Act. This made all offences under the Act cognisable. (Cognisable offences are those offences for which the police can arrest a suspected offender without a warrant.) This provision has now been removed, making life easier for the common man who feared arbitrary police action.

A small but significant change has also been made to the provision which specified offences relating to companies. Generally, when an offence committed by a company as a legal person, the person(s) managing the affairs of the company are made liable. The amended Act now provides that such a person will not be liable merely because he is in charge. Liability can only be pinned when it is proved that the person knowingly connived to commit the offence and failed to prevent the offence. Thus, it is not possible to prosecute directors or managers unless active connivance is proved by the complainant. Mere knowledge of the offence is not enough.

An overall feel of the amendments seems to have rectified most of the drawbacks in the original Act. Despite the Act being in force since 2000 and the increasing use of computers in every sphere, we haven't seen much court action involving the Act.

One find it hard to believe that this can be attributed to a lack of incidents. Is the Act so comprehensive that it forces litigants to settle maters amicably or is this due to a lack of awareness about cyber law or can this be attributed to enforcement woes attributable to rapidly changing technology and the mode of committing crimes?

PRACTICE QUESTIONS

1. Describe the objectives of the IT Act, 2000.
2. What do you understand by the term Information Technology? Explain the rationale behind the Information Technology Act, 2000.
3. Explain the terms "e-commerce" and "e-governance" with reference to Information Technology Act, 2000.
4. Enumerate the instruments, documents or transactions to which IT Act is not applicable.
5. Define the following terms: (i) Certifying Authority; (ii) Computer Resource; (iii) Digital Signature; (iv) Key Pair (v) Private Key; (vi) Public Key; (vii) Asymmetric Crypto System; (viii) Data.
6. What are the objectives of Cyber Laws? Explain. Who may authenticate an electronic record? How is it effected?
7. Write short notes on: (i) Legal recognition of electronic records, (ii) Legal recognition of digital signatures, (iii) Retentions of electronic records.
8. Describe the provisions as regards attribution, acknowledgement and despatch of electronic records.
9. Define the following terms as used in the Information Technology Act, 2000:

   (i) Digital signature; (ii) Asymmetric crypto system; (iii) Electronic record; (iv) Private key an Public key; (v) Computer network; (vi) Originator; (vii) Computer database; (viii) Computer virus.

10 Describe the provisions as regards secure electronic records and secure digital signatures.

11. Describe the provisions as regards appointment of the controller of Certifying Authorities.
12. Discuss the functions of the controller.
13. Who can grant a licence to issue Digital Signature Certificates? Give the requirements a person must complete for getting the licence.
14. Discuss the powers of "Controller of Certifying Authorities" under the Information Technology Act, 2000.
15. In which cases the licence to issue Digital Signature Certificates can be suspended or revoked?
16. Discuss the duties of "Certifying Authority" under the Information Technology Act, 2000.
17. Who is authorised to issue a Digital Signature Certificate? What type of representations is made by the Certifying Authority at the time of issue of a Digital Signature Certificate?
18. Explain the duties of the subscriber.
19. Enumerate the activities relating to computer, computer network etc., which are subject to sanction and penalised, if indulged without the permission of the owner or the person-in-charge.
20. What penalty is provided for damage to computer, computer system or computer network?
21. Enumerate the power of the Adjudicating officer.
22. How is "Cyber Appellate Tribunal" established? What are its powers under the Information Technology Act, 2000? Discuss.
23. Give provisions relating to establishment and composition and functions of the Cyber Appellate Tribunal.
24. Write explanatory notes on the following: (i) Tampering with computer source documents; (ii) Hacking with computer system; (iii) Protected system; (iv) Breach of confidentiality and privacy; (v) Offences by companies.

References

1. Kalakota, Ravi & Whinston, Andrew B. (2000), Frontiers of Electronic Commerce, Addison-Wesley, Delhi.
2. Treese, G. Winfield & Stewart, Lawrance C. (2000), Designing System for Internet
3. Commerce, Addison-Wesley, Delhi.
4. Jain, V. K. & Hemlata (2001), Enterprise Electronic and Mobile Commerce, Cyber-Tech Publications, New Delhi.
5. Rayudu, C. S. E. (2004), E-Commerce: E-Business, Himalaya Publishing House, Mumbai.Information Technology Act, 2000.
6. Asian School of Cyber Laws Search - Recommendations made to Government of India for amendments to the Information Technology Act, 2000
7. Deaver, Jeffrey; The Blue Nowhere; Pocket Star Books
8. "Digital and Electronic Signatures" http://members.aol.com/Winchel3/Links/Legal/Signatures/SignaturesLegalLinks.htm
9. Prannoy Roy hosted a talk show on BBC about the Y2K issue in which Sabeer Bhatia participated. Sabeer Bhatia is CEO Arzoo.com.
10. Dhar, Ravi Kumar "State Surveillance, Citizens' Civil Rights and Cyber Crime: Indian Information Technology Act-2000 in Retrospect"; http:/jcmc.huji.ac.il/vol2/Issue1/intro.html
11. A/RES/51/162 dt 30th January 1997.
12. Article 5: Legal Recognition of Data Messages Information shall not be denied legal effect, validity or enforceability solely on the grounds that it is a data message.
13. Ryder, Rodney D.; Guide To Cyber Laws (Information Technology Act, 2000, E-Commerce, Data protection and the Internet); Wadhwa.
14. Article 7 of the UNCITRAL Model Law
15. Kamath, Nandan; Law Relating to Computers, Internet and E-Commerce — A Guide to Cyberlaws; Universal Law Publishers.
16. Basu, Subhajit and Jones, Richard "Legal Issues Affecting E-Commerce: A Review of the Indian Information Technology Act, 2000"; http://www.bileta.ac.uk/02papers/basu.html
17. Sood, Vivek; Cyber law Simplified; Tata McGraw-Hill Publishing Co.
18. Vishwanathan, Suresh T; The Indian Cyber law; 2nd Edition; Bharat Publishing House, New Delhi, 2001; p 42.
19. Mittal, D P; Law of Information Technology (Cyber law), Taxmann,
20. Greenleaf, Graham "Privacy Implications of Digital Signatures"; http://www.anu.edu.au/people/Roger.Clarke/DV/DigSig.html
21. Lemos, Robert "Digital signatures a threat to privacy?"; http://zdnet.com.com/2100-11-519795.html?legacy=zdnn
22. Kaner, Cem "The Insecurity of the Digital Signature"; http://www.badsoftware.com/digsig.htm
23. Schneier, Bruce "Why Digital Signatures Are Not Signatures?"; http://www.counterpane.com/crypto-gram-0011.html
24. Berst, Jesse "Sign of Trouble: The Problem With E-Signatures";
    http://www.zdnet.com/anchordesk/stories/story/0,10738,2604099,00.html
25. D.P.Mittal, Law of Information Technology (Cyber Law) with Information
    Technology (Certifying Authorities) Rules, *2000,* Taxmann Allied Services Pvt. Ltd., New Delhi.
26. Taxmann, *Information Technology Act, 2000,* Taxmann Allied Services Pvt. Ltd., New Delhi.
27. Madan, Sushila, Students' Guide to Information Technology, Taxmann Allied Services Pvt. Ltd., New Delhi.
28. Sandeep Oberoi, "e-security and you", The IT Act explained, Tata McGraw-Hill.

PART K

INDIAN CONTRACT ACT, 1872

CHAPTER

22

Nature of Contracts

Object

The main object of the law of contract is to introduce definiteness in business transactions. The Law of Contracts differs from other branches of Law. It does not lay down so many rights and duties which the law will protect and enforce. It determines the circumstances in which promises made by the parties to a contract shall be legally binding on them. Its rules define the remedies that are available in the Court of Law against a person who fails to perform his contract, and the conditions under which the remedies are available. It affects all of us in one way or the other. It is, however, of particular importance to people engaged in trade, Commerce and industry.

The Indian Contract Act, 1872

The law relating to contracts is codified in the form of Indian Contract Act, 1872. The scope of the Indian Contract Act may be classified into two main groups, namely:

1. General principles of contracts (Sections 1 to 75) include rules and laws relating to communication, acceptance and revocation of proposals, voidable contracts, void agreements, contingent contracts, performance of contracts, certain relations resembling those created by law and consequences of breach of contract.

2. Specific kinds of contracts only (Sections 124 to 238) These are Contracts of Indemnity and Guarantee, Bailment and Pledge and Agency.

Law of Contract creates right-in-personam and not right-in-rem. "Right-in-personam" means a right against or in respect of a specific person. "Right-in-Rem" means a right against or in a respect of whole world.

Law of Contract is not the whole law of agreements nor the whole law of obligations.

There are several agreements which do not give rise to legal obligations. They are, therefore, not Contracts, similarly, there are certain obligations which do not necessarily spring from an agreement, e.g., (i) judgment of courts (ii) torts or civil wrongs (iii) quasi-contracts. These obligations are not contractual in nature. But even then they are enforceable.

Definition of Contract

Section 2(h) of the Indian Contract Act, 1872 defines a contract, as follows:

An agreement enforceable by law is a contract.

Thus, there must be (1) an agreement, and (2) the agreement should be enforceable by law.

Section 2(e) defines agreement as "every promise and every set of promises forming the consideration of each other."

Section 2(b) defines promise in these words: "when the person to whom the proposal is made signifies his assent thereto, the proposal is said to be accepted. A proposal, when accepted, becomes a promise."

It is obvious from the above definition of promise that an agreement is an accepted proposal. The two elements of an agreement are:

(i) offer or a proposal, and

(ii) An acceptance of that offer or proposal.

What agreements are Contracts?

All agreements are not contracts. Only those agreements which are enforceable at law are contracts. Thus every contract is an agreement, but every agreement is not a contract. Agreements which are not enforceable in a court of law are not contracts. Thus, a contract consists of two elements:

(i) an agreement; and

(ii) legal obligation i.e., enforceable at law.

However, there are several agreements which do not give rise to legal obligations. They are, therefore, not contracts. Similarly, there are certain obligations which do not necessarily spring from an agreement, e.g., (i) torts or civil wrongs (ii) quasi-contracts, (iii) judgements of courts (iv) relationship between trustee and beneficiary. These obligations are not contractual in nature, but are enforceable in a court of law.

Salmond has observed that the law of contract is "not the whole law of agreements, nor is it the whole law of obligations. It is the law of those agreements which creates obligations, and those obligations which have their sources in agreements."

Characteristics of an Agreement

1. Plurality of persons:

Agreement is an expression of common intention of two or more persons. It is impossible for one person to make an agreement with himself.

2. Consensus ad-idem:

The persons making an agreement must consent to some determination with a view to create a right in one party and corresponding duty on the other party. These determinations are known as promises. Promises are formed only when there is meeting of the minds of the parties who must agree to the same thing in the same sense.

Promise or Reciprocal Promises

When the person to whom the proposal is made signifies his assent thereto, the proposal is said to be accepted. Offer and acceptance together constitute an agreement. Agreement is, thus, a promise or a set of "reciprocal promises". "Promise which form the consideration or part of the consideration for each other are called reciprocal promises" {Section 2(f)}.

Kinds of Agreement

1. Valid Agreement

A valid agreement is one, which is enforceable by law.

2. Void Agreement

An agreement which is not enforceable by law is said to be void agreement {Section 2(g)}.

3. Voidable Agreement

A voidable agreement is one which is enforceable by law at the option of one or more of the parties thereto, but not at the option of other or others {Section 2(i)}.

4. Unenforceable Agreement

Such an agreement is valid in the eyes of law, but can not be enforced in the courts because of some technical defect in procedural matters of formation and enforcement.

5. Social Agreements

They are of social nature and do not enjoy the benefits of law. They are not enforceable and can not be called 'Contracts'.

6. Illegal Agreement

An agreement which is against the provision of law is called illegal agreement.

7. Agreements for future

An agreement to agree in future is a contradiction and is not a contract.

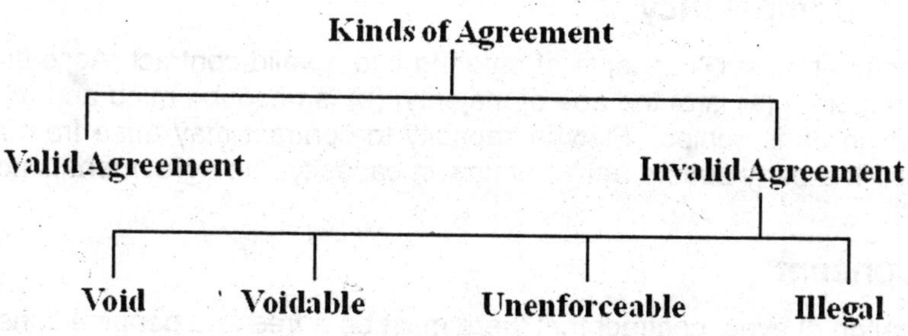

Figure No. 1

Essentials of a Valid Contract

According to section 10, all agreements are contracts if they are made by the free consent of parties competent to contract, for a lawful consideration and with a lawful object, and are not hereby expressly declared to be void.

Thus, the essential elements of a valid contract can be summed up as follows:

1. Agreement

As already mentioned, to constitute a contract there must be an agreement. An agreement is composed of two elements - offer and acceptance. The party making the offer is known as the offeror, the party to whom the offer is made is known as the offeree. Thus, there must be two persons or groups of persons to form a contract. There must also be privity of contract between the two parties. They both must be thinking of the same thing in the same sense. Thus, the offer and acceptance must be 'consensus ad-idem'.

2. Intention to create legal relationship

When two parties enter into an agreement, their intention must be to create legal relationship between them. If there is no such intention, there can be no contract between the parties. Agreements of a social or domestic nature do not contemplate legal relationship. As such they are not contracts. In *Balfour v. Balfore*[1] a husband agreed to pay $10 to his wife every month while he was abroad. On failure to pay, his wife sued him for the recovery of amount. It was held that it was a domestic agreement which did not intend to create legal relations.

However, even in the case of agreements of purely social or domestic nature, there may be intention of the parties to create legal obligations. In that case, the social agreement is intended to have legal consequences and, therefore, becomes a contract. In commercial and business agreements, the presumption is usually that the parties intended to create legal relations. But this presumption is rebuttable which means that it must be shown that the parties did not intended to be legally bound.

In *Rose and Frand Co. v. Crompton Bros*[2], there was an agreement between Rose company and Crompton company, where of the former were appointed selling agents in North America for the latter. One of the clauses included in the agreement was: "This agreement is not a formal or legal agreement and shall not be subject to legal jurisdiction in the law courts." It was held that there was no binding contract as there was no intention to create legal relationship.

In *Jones v. Vernon's Pools Ltd.*[3], there was an agreement containing a clause that it "shall not give rise to any legal relationships or be legally enforceable, but binding in honour only."

Held: The agreement did not give rise to legal relations and, therefore, was not a contract.

3. Lawful Consideration

The agreement to be enforceable by law must be supported by consideration on both sides. The term consideration means "something in return". The agreement is legally enforceable only when both parties give something and get something in return. A promise to do something, getting nothing in return, is usually not enforceable by law. Consideration need not necessarily be in cash or kind. It may be an act or abstinence (refraining from doing something) or promise to do or not to do something. The consideration may be past, present or future. But it must be real, definite, lawful, and of some value. The intention of the parties to create legal relationship can only be ascertained by the presence or absence of consideration.

4. Capacity of Parties — Competency

The parties to the agreement must be capable of entering into a valid contract. According to Section 11, every person is competent to contract if he (a) is of the age of majority, (b) is of sound mind and (c) is not disqualified from contracting by any law to which he is subject. Flaw in capacity to contract may arise from minority, lunacy, idiocy, drunkenness, etc, and status. If a party suffers from any flaw in capacity, the agreement is not enforceable except in some special cases.

5. Free and Genuine Consent

It is essential to the creation of every contract that there must be a free and genuine consent of the parties to the agreement. The consent of the parties is said to be free when they agree upon the same thing in the same sense. The parties are said to have identity of mind or agreed on the same thing in the same sense when all the terms of the consent are put in the form of an offer or proposal by one party and the other party says "yes" to it. There is absence of free consent if the agreement is induced by coercion, undue influence, fraud, misrepresentation, mistake etc. (Section 14)

6. Lawful Object

The object of the agreement must be lawful. It is lawful unless it is forbidden by law, or is of such a nature that, if permitted, it would defeat the provisions of any law, or is fraudulent, or involves or implies injury to the person or property of another, or is immoral or opposed to public policy (Section 23). If an agreement suffers from any legal flaw, it would not be enforceable by law.

7. Agreement not declared void

The agreement must not have been expressly declared void by any law enforce in the country (Section 24 to 30 and 56).

8. Certainty and Possibility of Performance

The agreement must be certain and not vague or indefinite (Section 29). If it is vague and it is not possible to ascertain its meaning, it cannot be enforced.

An agreement to do an act impossible in itself cannot be enforced. This is based on the maxim '*lex non logit ad impossibilia*' which means that law does not compel to do what is impossible.

9. Legal Formalities

An agreement may be oral or in writing. There is no difference between a contract in writing and a contract made by word of mouth. Where it is to be in writing, it must comply with the necessary legal formalities as to writing, stamping, registration and attestation. Further, an agreement is to be made in the presence of requisite witness. If the agreement does not comply with these legal formalities, it cannot be enforced by law. (Section 10)

An agreement with all the above elements is legal or valid agreement. But if any of the elements is missing, the contract is either voidable, void, illegal or unenforceable in the eyes of law.

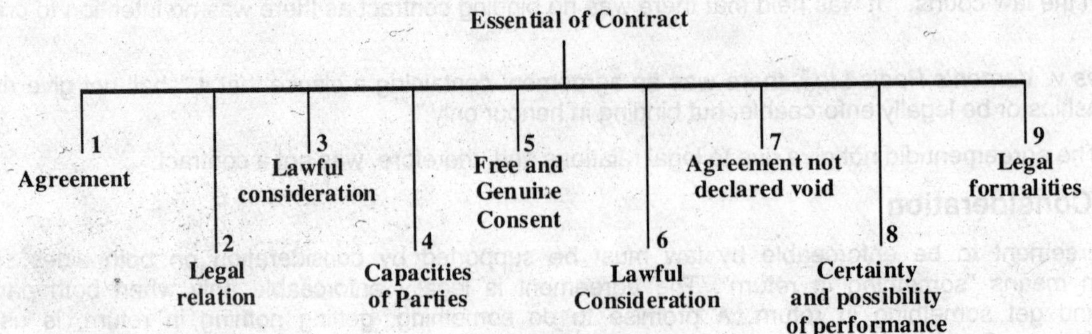

Figure No. 2

Classification of Contracts

Contracts may be classified in terms of their

(1) Validity or enforceability

(2) Mode of formation or

(3) Performance

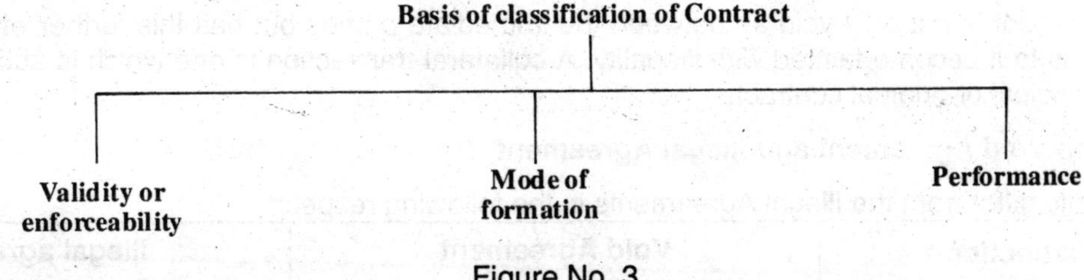

Figure No. 3

1. Classification according to Validity

Contracts may be classified according to their validity as

(i) Valid,

(ii) Voidable,

(iii) Void contracts or agreements,

(iv) Illegal or

(v) Unenforceable.

(i) Valid Contracts

A valid contract must have all the essential elements discussed above. If one or more of these elements is/are missing, the contract is either voidable, void, illegal or unenforceable.

(ii) Voidable Contracts

An agreement which is enforceable by law at the option of one or more of the parties thereto, but not at the option of the other or others, is a voidable contract [Section 2(1)]. This happens when the essential element of free consent in a contract is missing. When the consent of a party to a contract is not free i.e. it is caused by coercion, undue influence, misrepresentation or fraud, the contract is voidable at his option (Sections 19 and 19/A). The party whose consent is not free may either rescind the contract or elect to be bound by it. A voidable contract continues to be valid till it is avoided by the party entitled to do so.

Example: Mohan promises to sell his house plot to Ram for Rs. 60,000/- but his consent is taken by use of force. The contract is voidable and Ram may avoid the contract.

A Contract becomes voidable in the following two cases also —

(1) When a person promises to do something for another person for a consideration but the other person prevents him from performing his promise, the contract becomes voidable at his option (Sec. 53).

(2) When a party to a contract promises to perform an obligation within a specified time, any failure on his part to perform his obligation within the fixed time makes the contract voidable at the option of the promises. (Sec. 56).

(iii) Void Contract or Agreement

An agreement not enforceable by law is said to be void [Sec. 2(g)]. A void agreement does not create any legal rights or obligations. It is nullity and is destitute of legal effects altogether. It is *void ab initio*, i.e. from the very beginning as for example, an agreement with a minor or an agreement without consideration.

(iv) Void Contract

A contract which ceases to be enforceable by law becomes void when it ceases to be enforceable [Sec. 2(i)]. A contract, when originally entered into, may be valid and binding on the parties, e.g., a contract to import goods from a foreign country. It may subsequently become void, e.g. when a war breaks out between the importing country and the exporting country.

(iv) Illegal agreement

An illegal agreement is one the consideration of which is (1) forbidden by law, or (2) defeats the provisions of any law, or (3) is fraudulent, (4) involves or implies injury to the person or property of another, or (5) against public policy or criminal in nature or immoral.

An illegal agreement is not only void as between the immediate parties but has this further effect that even the collateral transactions to it become tainted with illegality. A collateral transaction is one which is subsidiary, incidental or auxiliary to the principal or original contract.

Distinction between Void Agreement and Illegal Agreement

Void agreements differ from the Illegal Agreements in the following respect:

Basis of distinction	Void Agreement	Illegal agreement
1. Void/illegal	All void agreements need not necessarily be illegal.	All illegal agreements are always void.
2. Effect on collateral agreements.	The collateral agreements do not become void.	The collateral agreements also become void.
3. Restoration of benefit received.	If a contract becomes void subsequently, the benefit received must be restored to the other party.	The money advanced or thing given can not be claimed back.

(v) Unenforceable Contract

An unenforceable contract is neither void nor voidable, but it cannot be enforced in a court of law because of some technical defect such as writing, registration or stamping or where the remedy has seen barred by lapse of time. The contract may be carried out by the parties concerned, but in the event of breach or repudiation of such a contract, the aggrieved party will not be entitled to the legal remedies.

2. Classification according to mode of formation

There are different modes of formation of contract-

(i) Express Contract

Where, the terms of a contract are expressed by words spoken or written at the time of the formation of the contract, the contract is said to be an express contract.

(ii) Implied Contract

Where, the terms of a contract are not expressly stated but which are inferred from the circumstances of the case and conduct of the parties.

(iii) Quasi Contract

It is an obligation imposed by law, regardless of agreement.

3. Classification according to Performance

To the extent to which the contracts have been performed may be classified as —

(i) Executed Contracts

It is a contract which is wholly performed by both the parties. Nothing remains to be done in terms of the contract.

(ii) Executory Contracts

It is a contract in which promises of both of parties have yet to be performed. An executory contract is one which is wholly unperformed, or in which there remains something further to be done.

The executory contract becomes an executed one when completely performed.

Another classification of contracts according to the performance is as follows:

Unilateral Contract: It is contract where only one party has yet to perform his obligation.

Bilateral Contract: It is a contract where both the parties have yet to perform their obligation.

Classification of Contracts in English Law

In English Law, contracts are classified into:

(1) formal contracts and

(2) simple contracts

(1) Formal Contracts

These include (a) contracts of record, and (b) contracts under seal. No consideration is necessary in the case of Formal Contracts, such contracts do not find any place under Indian Law as consideration is necessary under section 25.

A contract of Record is either (i) a judgement of a court or (ii) recognizance. An obligation imposed by the judgement of a court and entered upon its records is often called a Contract of Record.

Contracts of Record are not contracts in the real sense as the consensus-adidem is lacking. They are only obligations imposed by the court upon a party to do or refrain from doing something.

A contract under seal is one which derives its binding force from its form alone. It is in writing and is signed, sealed and delivered by the parties. It is also called a deed or a speciality contract. No consideration is, however, necessary in the case of contracts under seal.

Contracts of record and contracts under seal are known as formal contracts because their validity depends on the form in which they are made.

2. Simple Contracts

All Contracts which are not made under seal are simple contracts. They may be in writing or may be made by word of mouth. All simple contracts must be supported by consideration.

CHAPTER

23

Offer and Acceptance

A contract is made by the process of lawful offer by one party and the lawful acceptance of the offer by the other party to whom it is made.

Meaning of Offer

An offer is a proposal by one party to another to enter into a legally binding agreement with him. The term proposal is defined in section 2(a) of the Indian Contract Act, 1872, thus, "when one person signifies to another his willingness to do or to abstain from doing anything with a view to obtaining the assent of that other to such act or abstinence, he is said to make a proposal". The person making the offer is known as "offeror or proposer or promiser" and the person to whom the offer is made is called "offeree or promisee". For example, A says to B "will you purchase my scooter for Rs. 10,000/-?" A, in this case, is making an offer to B as he signifies to B his willingness to sell his scooter to B for Rs. 10,000/- with a view to obtaining B's assent to purchase the scooter.

Characteristics of Offer

The definition of offer involves the following important points:

(1) It must be an expression of willingness to do or to abstain from doing something.

(2) It must be made to another person.

(3) It must be made with a view to obtain the assent of other person to such act or abstinence.

(4) The expression of willingness must be made with a view to create legal obligations.

Types of Offer

There are following three types of offer:

1. Express and Implied Offer

An offer may also be made by express words, spoken or written. This is known as an express offer. The written offer can be made by letters, telegrams, telex messages, advertisements, etc. The oral offer can be made either in person or over telephone.

When, an offer is made otherwise than in words, the offer is called an implied offer. In so far as such proposal is made otherwise than in words, the promise is said to be implied.

Examples of Implied Offer

1. In a self service restaurant, there is an implied promise to pay for consuming eatables.

2. A transport company runs a bus on a particular route, there is an implied offer by the transport company to carry passengers for a specified fare.

2. Specific and General Offer

When an offer is made to a specific person, it is called a specific offer.

When offer is made to the world at large which could be accepted by anyone, e.g., reward to a person supplying information pertaining to something, it is called a 'General Offer' or 'Offer at large'.

3. Positive and Negative Offer

The offer may be positive or negative. Thus, an offer may be to do something or not to do something. An offer to do something is a positive offer and an offer not to do something is a negative offer.

Offer and Invitation to Offer

An offer must be distinguished from invitation to offer. 'Invitation to offer' are 'offers to negotiate'. On the other hand, offer is a final expression of willingness by the offeror to be bound by his promise, should the other choose to accept it.

Example

1. A prospectus issued by a college for admission to various courses is not an offer. It is only an invitation to offer. A prospective student by filling up an application form attached to the prospectus is making the offer.
2. A display of goods with a price on them in a shop window is construed an invitaiun to offer and not an offer to sell.

Legal rules and Essentials Regarding Offer

The Contract Act contains various rules regarding offer/ proposal. They can be summed up as follows:

1. Offer must intend to create legal relationship

An offer will not become a promise even after it has been accepted unless it was made with a view to create legal obligations. In *Blafour v. Balfour*[4], it was held that mere statement of intention in the course of conversion will not create binding promise. In this case husband agreed to pay some fixed money to his wife per month during his stay in abroad but he failed to pay promise amount to his wife.

2. Terms of offer must be definite

The offer must not be ambiguous, uncertain and vague. The terms must be definite, unambiguous and certain. If it is loose, vague and indefinite its acceptance cannot create any contractual relationship and it does not amount to a lawful offer. In Could v. Could[5], husband on leaving his wife promised to pay her £15 a week "so long as I can not manage it." It was held that although the husband and wife, who lived apart because of break-up of their marriage, could enter into a legally binding agreement, the vague or discretionary terms of the arrangement indicated an intention not to create legal relations.

3. Offer must be Communicated

An offer is effective only when it is communicated to the offeree. Unless an offer is communicated to the offeree by the offeror there can be no acceptance of it.

Fitch v. Snedker[6], S offered a reward to anyone who returned his lost dog. F brought the dog to S without having heard of the offer. Held, F was not entitled to the reward.

Lalman v. Gauri Dutt[7], G sent his servant L, to trace his missing nephew. He then announced a reward for information relating to his nephew. L traced the nephew in ignorance of this announcement. Subsequently, when he came to know of the reward, he claimed it. Held, he was not entitled to the reward on the ground that he did not know about the offer when he discovered the missing boy.

4. The Offer must express the final willingness of the offeror

The terms of the offer should be such that they contain final willingness of the offeror. Sometimes, a party does not express his final willingness. But proposes certain terms on which he is willing to negotiate. In such cases, he is not making an offer because he is not expressing his final willingness to enter into a contract.

5. An offer may be made to specific person or class of persons or to anyone in the world at large.

In Carlill v. Carbolic Smoke Ball Co[8], it was held that, when an offer is made to world at large any persons to whom the offer is made can accept it.

6. The offer may be expressed of implied.

7. The offer may be positive or negative.

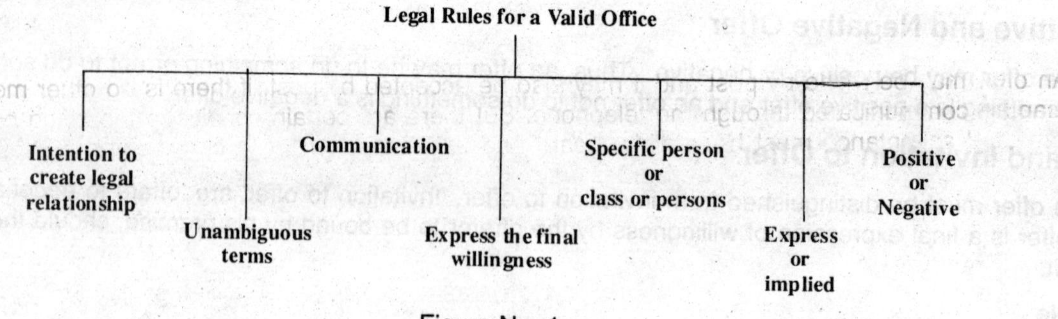

Figure No. 1

Tenders

A tender (in response to an invitation to offer) is an offer. However, a tender may be either —

(i) a definite offer to supply specified goods or services or

(ii) a standing offer to supply goods periodically or in accordance with the requirements of the offeree.

In the case of a definite tender, the suppliers submit their offers for the supply of specified goods and services. The offeree may accept any tender (generally the lowest). This will result in a contract.

Special Terms in a Contract

Where any special terms are to be included in a contract, these must be duly brought to the notice of the offeree at the time when the proposal is made. If it is not done, then there is no valid offer and if offer is accepted, and the contract is formed, the offeree is not bound by the special terms which were not brought to his notice. These special terms should be presented in such a manner that a reasonable man can become aware of them before he enters into a contract.

In *Olley v. Marlborough Court Ltd.*[9], a hotel put a notice in a bed room, exempting the proprietor from liability for loss of clients' goods. Held, the notice was not effective as it came to the knowledge of the client only when the contract to take a room had already been entered into.

If the conditions limiting or defining the rights of the acceptor are not brought to his notice, then they will not become part of the offer and he is not bound by them.

In *Henderson v. Stevenson*[10], a passenger was traveling with luggage from Dublin to white haven on a ticket, on the back of which there was a term which exempted the shipping company from liability for the loss of luggage. He never looked at the back of the ticket and there was nothing on the face of it to draw his attention to the terms on its back. He lost his luggage and sued for damages.

Held, he was entitled to damages as he was not bound by something which was not communicated to him.

Also, if the conditions are contained in a document which is delivered after the contract is complete, then the offeree is not bound by them. Such a document is considered a non-contractual document as it is not supposed to contain the conditions of the contract.

Cross Offers

When two parties make identical offers to each other, in ignorance of each other's offer, the offers are known as cross offers and neither of the two can be called an acceptance of the other and, therefore, there is no contract.

In *Tinn v. Hoffman and Co.*[10], H wrote to T offering to sell him 800 tons at 695 per ton. On the same day T wrote to H offering to buy tons at 695. Their letters crossed in the past. T contended that there was a good contract. Held, that there was no contract.

Mode of communication of offer

An offer should be communicated to other party by word of mouth, by writing, or by conduct. The process of making a proposal is completed by the act of communicating it. Section 3 lays down the modes of communication. A written offer may be contained in a letter or a telegram. A circular or advertisement or a notice may be written in such a language that it amounts to an offer.

Offer by post and telephone

An offer may be made by post and it may also be accepted by post, if there is no other mode of acceptance. Offer can be communicated through the telephone. But there are certain conditions regarding oral communication. The offer and acceptance must be audible, heard and understood. If these conditions are satisfied and the other essential elements of contract exist, the parties are bound through a telephone conversation.

A tramway car and a bus going along a street and picking up passengers are examples of offers by conduct.

Lapse and Revocation of Offer

An offer is made with a view to obtain assent thereto. As soon as an offer is accepted it becomes a contract. But before it is accepted it may lapse or may be revoked. Section 6 deals with various modes of revocation or lapse of an offer. In all these cases, an offer comes to an end.

1. By Notice of Revocation

An offer can be revoked at any time before acceptance, the offeror doing so by giving notice of revocation to offeree. A revocation of offer must be communicated to the offeree. It is necessary that the communication of revocation should be from the offeror or from his duly authorised agent.

2. Lapse of time

A proposal is revoked by the lapse of time prescribed in such proposal for its acceptance. If no time is prescribed that proposal is revoked by the lapse of a reasonable time {Section 6(2)}.

3. By Failure of the Acceptor to fulfill a condition precedent to acceptance

If there is a condition therein the proposal, before fulfilling of which, the acceptor cannot accept the proposal, the proposal will naturally be revoked if the acceptor fails to fulfill the condition precedent {Section 6(3)}.

4. By Failure to accept according to the mode prescribed

An offer is revoked, if the offeree fails to accept it according to the mode prescribed by the offeror. If no mode is prescribed, the offer must be accepted according to some reasonable or usual mode.

5. By Death or Insanity of the Offeror

Death or insanity of the offeror puts an end to the offer, provided the fact of the death or insanity comes to the knowledge of the offeree before acceptance. But if the offeree accepts the offer in ignorance of death of offeror, the acceptance is valid as against the heirs of offeror.

6. By Rejection

An offer lapses as soon as it is rejected by offeree. An offer is rejected, if the offeree

(i) communicates his rejection to the offeror or

(ii) makes a counter-offer or

(iii) accepts the offer subject to conditions.

7. By subsequent illegality or destruction of subject matter

An offer lapses if it becomes illegal after it is made but before it is accepted.

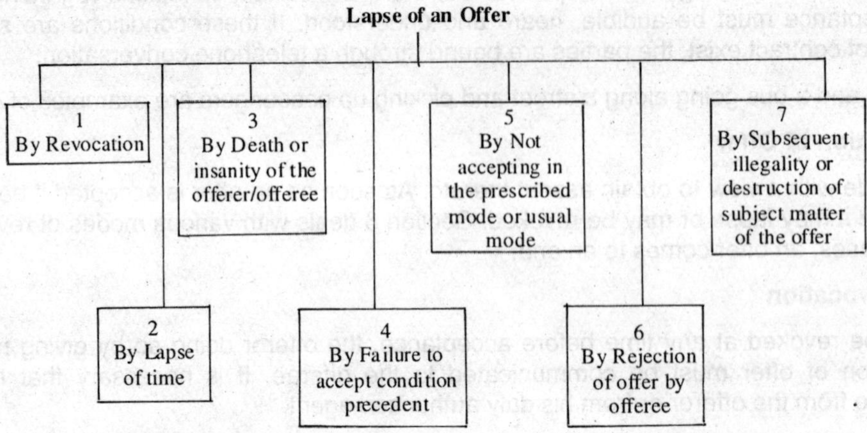

Figure No. - 2

Communication of Revocation of Offer

According to section 3, the revocation of a proposal or an acceptance is deemed to be made by any act or omission of the party by which he intends to communicate such revocation or which has the effect of communicating it. The communication of revocation is complete: (i) as against the person who makes it, when it is put into a course of transmission to the person who makes, when it is made, so as to be out of the power of the person who makes it, (ii) as against the person to whom it is made, when it comes to his knowledge.

Counter Offer

An offer terminates by counter offer by the offeree. When in place of accepting the terms of an offer as they are, the offeree accepts the same subject to certain condition or qualification, he is said to make a counter offer. The following have been held to be counter offers:

(i) Where an offer to purchase a house with a condition that possession shall be given on a particular day was accepted varying the date of possession.

(ii) An offer to buy a property was accepted upon a condition that the buyer signed an agreement which contained special terms as to payment of deposit, making out title completion date, the agreement having been returned unsigned by the buyer.

(iii) Where an acceptance of a proposal for insurance was accepted in all its terms subject to the condition that there shall be no assurance till the first premium was paid.

(iv) An offer to sell rice was accepted with an endorsement on the sold and bought note that yellow and wet grain will not be accepted.

CHAPTER

24

Acceptance

An acceptance is defined in section 2(b) of the Act as:

"When the person to whom the proposal is made signifies his assent thereto, the proposal is said to be accepted. A proposal, when accepted, becomes a promise."

The person making the proposal is called the "promiser" and the person to whom it is made is called the "promisee" [Section 2(c)]. Thus, acceptance is the manifestation by the offeree of his assent to the terms of the offer.

Essentials and Legal Rules of a Valid Acceptance

There are some legal rules which make the acceptance effective so as to give rise to a valid contract. These are as follows:

1. Acceptance must be absolute and unconditional (Section 7)

The acceptance must be absolute and unconditional and according to the exact terms of the offer. A proposal must be accepted in total and partial acceptance is no acceptance.

In *Neale v. Merrett*[11], M offered to sell land to N for £280. N replied purporting to accept and enclosed £80, promising to pay the balance of £200 by monthly installments of £50 each. Held, that N could not enforce acceptance because his acceptance was not an unqualified one.

However, a mere variation in the language which does not involve any difference in substance would not make the acceptance ineffective.[12]

Also if some conditions are implied as a part of the contract and the offeree accepts the offer subject to those conditions, the acceptance will be treated as valid.

2. Acceptance must be according to the mode prescribed or usual and reasonable mode (Section7)

Acceptance must be expressed in some usual and reasonable manner, unless the proposal prescribes the manner in which it is to be accepted. If the proposal prescribes a manner in which it is to be accepted, and the acceptance is not made in such manner, the proposer may, within a reasonable time after the acceptance is communicated to him, insist that his proposal shall be accepted in the prescribed manner, and not otherwise, but if he fails to do so, he is bound by the acceptance.

3. Acceptance must be given within a reasonable time

If any time limit is specified, the acceptance must be given within that time. If no time limit is specified, it must be given with in a reasonable time.

In *Ramsgate Victoria Hotel Co. v. Montefiore*[13], 'M' offered to take shares in 'R' Company on June 8. A letter of acceptance was received by him on November 23. He refuse to take the shares.

Held, M was entitled to refuse as his offer had lapsed as the reasonable period during which it could be accepted had elapsed.

4. Acceptance can not precede an offer

The acceptance must be in response to offer. There can be no acceptance without offer. There can, therefore, be no acceptance before the communication of the offer. For instance, no allotment of shares in a company can be made unless the allottee has applied for them before hand. (Section 41 of the Companies Act, 1956).

5. Acceptance must be made before the lapse or revocation of an offer

The acceptance must be made before the offer lapses or is terminated, revoked or withdrawn. If the offer lapses, then there is nothing to accept.

6. Acceptance must be by an ascertained person

Acceptance given by a person other than the offeree or by a person who is not authorised to give acceptance is ineffective in law. Likewise information received from an unauthorised person is ineffective.[14]

7. Acceptance must show to fulfill a promise

Acceptance, in order to be valid, must be made under circumstances which would show that the acceptor intends to fulfill the terms of the promise. If not such intention is present, the acceptance is not valid.

8. Acceptance may be express or implied

Acceptance must be communicated to the offeror by spoken or written words or conduct. When acceptance is made by words spoken or written, it is an express acceptance. If it is accepted by conduct it is an implied acceptance. The acceptor must have done something to signify his intention to accept. If the acceptor never communicates his acceptance to the proposer, there will be no binding agreement. It is essential that the proposer must know that his proposal has been accepted.

9. Acceptance of offer means acceptance of all terms attached to the offer

If the terms are to apparent in the fact and no reasonable caution is taken do draw the attention of the acceptor, then those terms will not be binding.

10. Acceptance cannot be implied from silence

The acceptance of an offer cannot be implied from the silence of the offeree or his failure to answer. Unless the offeree has by his previous conduct indicated that his silence means that he accepts.

Essentials and Legal Rules of a Valid Acceptance

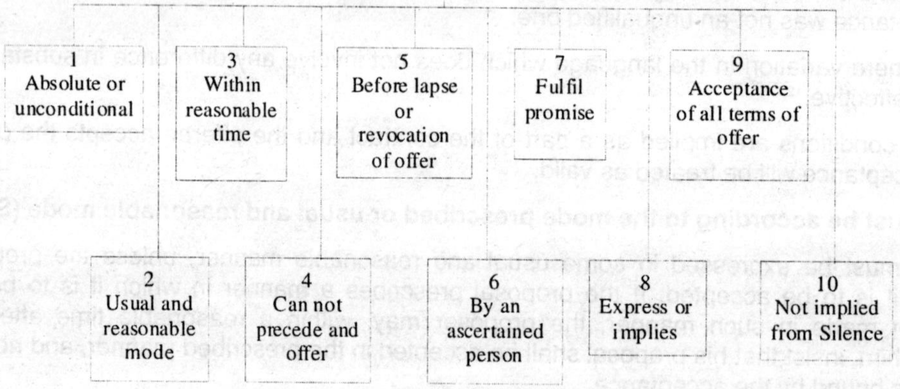

- 1 Absolute or unconditional
- 2 Usual and reasonable mode
- 3 Within reasonable time
- 4 Can not precede and offer
- 5 Before lapse or revocation of offer
- 6 By an ascertained person
- 7 Fulfil promise
- 8 Express or implies
- 9 Acceptance of all terms of offer
- 10 Not implied from Silence

Figure No. 1

Communication of Acceptance (Section 4)

According to Section 4, the communication of a proposal is complete when it comes to the knowledge of the person to whom it is made.

Example:

A proposes by letter, to sell a house to B at a certain price. The communication of the proposal is complete when B receives the letter.

The completion of communication of acceptance has two aspects:

(i) As against the proposer

The communication of acceptance is complete, as against the proposer, when it is put in a course of transmission to him so as to be out of the power of the acceptor.

(ii) As against the acceptor

The communication of acceptance is complete as against the acceptor when it comes to the knowledge of the proposer.

Example

Mohan proposes by letter to sell his car to Ram at a price of Rs. 95,000. Ram accepts Mohan's proposal by a letter sent by post. The communication of acceptance is complete — (a) as against Mohan when the letter is posted by Ram. and (b) as against Ram, when the letter is received by Mohan.

Thus, it will be seen that during the time the acceptance is on its way, the proposer is bound but not the acceptor. When the offeror and offeree are at two different places, the post office comes in. In such a case, the rules as referred to above apply.

As regards the communication of acceptance as against the proposer is concerned, once the letter of acceptance properly addressed and stamped is posted the acceptance is made and binds the offeror, as he is deemed to have received the acceptance at the moment when it is despatched so as to be out of power of the acceptor and it becomes a promise on which the acceptor can sue. Even if the letter of acceptance is lost in transit and is not delivered to the offeror, the contract is deemed to be concluded when the letter is posted.

Communication of Revocation [Section 4 Para 3]

Revocation means "taking back" "recalling" or "withdrawal". It may be a revocation of offer or acceptance. The communication of a revocation is complete:

(i) As against the person who makes it: when it is put into course of transmission to the person to whom it is made, so as to be out of the power of the person who makes it, and

(ii) As against the person to whom it is made: when it comes to his knowledge.

In *Byem and Co. v. Van Tienhoven*[15], T wrote a letter revoking his offer on 18th. The letter was received by B on 20th. Held, the revocation was of no effect until it reached B. A contract was made on 11th October when B accepted the offer. Lindley J. observed in this case. "A state of mind not notified cannot be regarded in dealing between man and man, and that an uncommunicated revocation is, for all practical purposes and in point of law, no revocation at all".

Loss of letter of acceptance in postal transit

Acceptance is complete as against the offeror as soon as the letter of acceptance is posted. The contract is complete even if the letter of acceptance goes astray or is lost through an accident in the post. But in order to bind the offeror, it is important that the letter of acceptance is correctly addressed, sufficiently stamped and posted. If it is not correctly addressed and sufficiently stamped, the communication of acceptance is not complete within the meaning of section 4 even if it is posted. Lord Cottenham L.C., in delivering the judgement in the House of Lords in *Dunlop v. Higgins* enunciated the principle in the following words: "If the letter of acceptance is posted in due time, the acceptor is not responsible for any casualities in the post office. If the party accepting the offer puts his letter into post on the correct day, has he not done everything he was bound to do? How can he be responsible for that over which he has no control?"

Contracts over telephone or telex or oral communication

Now-a-days most of the commercial transactions are carried on through telephone or telex. A contract by telephone or telex has the same effect as an oral agreement entered into between the parties when they are face to face. No contract can arise unless the offeree's acceptance is audible, heard and understood by the offerer.[16]

An example given in *Entores v. Miles Far East Corporation* (1955)[17] is enlightening in this connection:

"Now take a case where two people make a contract by telephone. Suppose, for instance, that I make an offer to a man by telephone, and, in the middle of his reply, the line goes 'dead' so that I do not hear his words of acceptance. There is no contract at that moment. The other man may not know the precise moment when the line failed. But he will know that the telephone conversation was abruptly broken off, because people usually say something to signify the end of the conversation. If he wishes to make a contract, he must, therefore, get through again so as to make sure that I heard".

The principle of the above case was endorsed by the Supreme Court in *Bhagwan Dass Kedia v. Girdharilal.*[18]

Revocation of Proposal (Section 5)

A proposal may be revoked at any time before the communication of acceptance is complete as against the acceptor, but not afterwards.

Example:

A proposes, by a letter sent by post, to sell his house to B. b accepts the proposal by a letter sent by post.

A may revoke his proposal at any time before or at the moment when B posts his letter of acceptance, but not afterwards.

Capacity of Contract (Section 10-12)

One of the essential conditions for the enforceability of an agreement is that the concerned parties must be competent to enter into an agreement. According to section 10, an agreement becomes a contract if it is entered into between the parties who are competent to contract. Thus, an agreement is valid and enforceable only if the parties to it are competent to enter into contract.

Meaning of Contractual Capacity

The 'capacity to contract' means the competence of the parties to enter into a valid contract. The term 'capacity of contract' is defined in section 11 of the Act. Section 11 provides that

"Every person is competent to contract who is of the age of majority according to the law to which he is subject, and who is of sound mind, and is not disqualified from contracting by any law to which he is subject".

Thus section 11, declares the following persons to be incompetent to contract:

(1) Minors,

(2) Persons of unsound mind, and

(3) Persons disqualified by any law to which they are subject.

1. MINORS

Meaning of Minor

According to section 3 of the Indian Majority Act, 1875, a minor is a person who has not completed eighteen years of age. However, a minor for whom a guardian has been appointed by court or when his property is managed by the Court of wards, he becomes a major only on his completing the age of 21 years.

Minor's Contracts

The Contract Act does not expressly specify whether minor's contracts are void or voidable. The position of minor's contract is summed up as follows:

1. A Contract with or by a minor is void and a minor, therefore, cannot, bind himself by a contract. A minor is not competent to contract. The Privy Council affirmed this view most emphatically in the leading case of *Mohiri Bibi v. Dharmodas Ghose*[19]

In this case, a minor mortgaged his house in favour of a money-lender to secure a loan of Rs. 20,000 out of which the mortgagee (the money-lender) paid the minor a sum of Rs. 8,000. Subsequently, the minor sued for setting aside the mortgage, stating that he was underage when he executed the mortgage.

The Privy Council decided that section 10 and 11 of the Indian Contract Act, make the minor's contract void. The mortgagee prayed for refund of Rs. 8000/- by the minor. The Privy Council further held that as a minor's contract is void, any money advanced to a minor cannot be recovered.

2. A Minor can be a promisee or a beneficiary

In capacity of minor to enter into a contract means incapacity to bind himself by a contract. There is nothing which debars him from becoming a beneficiary. Such contracts may be enforced at his option, but not at the option of the other party. The law does not regard him as incapable of accepting a benefit.

In *Raghavachariah v. Srinivas*[20], a mortgage was executed in favour of a minor. Held, he could get a decree for the enforcement of the mortgage.

In Abdul *Ghaffar v. Prem Piare Lal*[21], a minor, under a contract of sale delivered goods to the buyer. Held, he was entitled to maintain a suit for the recovery of price.

3. A Minor's agreement cannot be ratified by the minor on his attaining majority

An agreement made by a minor (during his period of minority) cannot be ratified by him on attaining majority because minor's agreement is void ab initio (i.e., void in the very beginning). Even, if a new agreement given by a minor relating to an earlier agreement (during minority) can not be enforced because the new agreement (during majority) is not supported by new consideration.

In *Indran Ramaswamy v. Anthiappa Chettiar*[22], M, a minor borrows Rs. 5,000/- from L and executes a Promissory note in favour of L, After attaining majority, he executes another Promissory note in settlement of the first note. The second promissory note is void for want of consideration.

In *Smith v. King* (1892) 2 Q.B.543[23], K, an infant, speculated on the stock exchange and became liable to the stock broker for £547. Subsequently to his attaining the age of majority he gave two bills for £50 each in satisfaction of the original debt. Held, K was not liable on the bills.

However, service rendered at the desire of the minor expressed during his minority and continued at the same request after his majority form a good consideration for a subsequent express promise by him in favour of the person who rendered the services (*Sindha v. Abraham*[24]).

4. No Estoppel against a Minor

A minor can always put forth the plea of minority and will not be estoppeled, i.e., prevented from doing so, even when he has entered into a contract falsely representing himself to be a major.

In *Leslie v. Shiell*[25], 'S', a minor, by fraudulently representing himself to be of full age, induced 'L' to lend him £400. He refused to repay it and 'L' sued him for the money. Held, the contract was void and 'S' was not liable to repay the amount.

Lawrence J. observed in this case: "whenever the infant is still in possession of any property in specie which he has obtained by his fraud, he will be made to restore it to its former owner. But I think it is incorrect to say that he can be made to repay money which he has spent, merely because he received it under contract induced by his fraud."

The court may, where a loan or some property is obtained by the minor by some fraudulent representation and the agreement is set aside, direct him, on equitable considerations, to restore the money or property to the other party, whereas the law gives protection to the minors, it does not give them liberty "to cheat men".

It is to be noted that if money could be traced then the court would have, on equitable grounds, asked the minor for restitution, as minor does not have a liberty to cheat. In the case of a fraudulent misrepresentation of his age by the minor, inducing the other party to enter into a contract the court may award compensation to that other party under section 30 and 33 of the Specific Relief Act 1963.

Example

A minor fraudulently mortgaged and sold certain properties. On the cancellation of the agreement at the instance of the minor, the lender and purchaser were awarded compensation. The lender and purchaser did not know about the fact that the seller was a minor. In fact, the minor fraudulently represented that he was of full age.

5. A minor can not be a partner in a partnership firm

A minor can not be a partner in a partnership firm. But he may be admitted to the benefits of an already existing partnership with the consent of the other partners. (Section 30, The Indian Partnership Act 1932).

6. Minor's parents will not be liable for the debts incurred by him even for necessaries of life. However, the parents are liable where the minor is acting as an agent of the parents or the guardian.

7. There can be no specific performance of the agreements entered into by him as they are *void ab initio.* A contract entered into on his behalf by his parent/guardian or the manager of his estate can be specifically enforced by or against the minor provided the contract is

(a) within the scope of the authority of the parent/guardian/manager, and

(b) for the benefit of the minor.

8. No liability in Contract or in Tort arising out of contract

The term 'tort' may be defined as any wrong for which a civil suit can be brought (except for breach of contract or breach of trust). We have already discussed that a minor's agreement is absolutely void. Moreover, he is not liable either for breach of contract or for damages on account of tort of deceit (fraud). If a minor enters into an agreement by misrepresenting his age, he cannot be sued either in contract or in tort for deceit. Because of the injured party is allowed to sue, it would be an indirect way of enforcing the void agreement. It may however, be noted that the minor is not liable for tort, only where the tort is directly connected with the contract.

9. Minor's liability for necessaries

A minor is liable to pay out of his property for necessaries of life supplied to him or to anyone whom he is legally bound to support. This obligation is cast on the minor not on the basis of any contract but on the basis of an obligation resembling a contract (Section 68). However, there is no personal liability on a minor for the necessaries of life supplied. It is only the property of the minor which is liable for meeting the liability arising out of such contracts.

The term necessaries is not defined in the Indian Contract Act, 1872. The English Sale of Goods Act defines necessaries as "goods suitable to the condition in life of the minor and to his actual requirements at the time of sale and delivery" (Section 2). Such goods need not necessarily belong to a class of useful goods, but they must be

(i) suitable to the position and financial status of the minor, and

(ii) necessaries both at the time of sale and at the time of delivery.

Necessary Include —

(a) Necessary Goods

Necessary goods are not restricted to articles which are required to maintain a bare existence, such as bread and clothes, but include articles which are reasonably necessary to the minor having regard to his station in life. A watch may well be considered to be necessaries, but not a vanity bag bought for the minor's finance.

In *Nash v. Inman*[26], 'I', a minor, was studying in B. Com. in college. He ordered 11 fancy coats for about £45 with 'N', the tailor. The tailor sued 'I' for the price. "I's" father proved that his son had already a number of coats and had clothes suitable to his condition in life when the clothes made by the tailor were delivered. Held, the coats were not necessaries and 'I' was not liable to pay for any of them.

In *Byrant v. Richardson*[27], Martin, B said that "a coat of superfine broadcloth may be a necessary for a son of a noble-man, although it is impossible not to say that the coarse material of a ploughman's coat would be sufficient to keep a nobleman's coat would be sufficient to keep a nobleman's body worm."

(b) Services rendered

Certain services rendered to a minor have been held to be necessaries. These include: Provision of education, medical and legal advice, provision of a house on rent to a minor for the purpose of living and continuing his studies.

As regards contracts which are not for the supply of necessaries but which are undoubtedly beneficial to the minor, the private estate of the minor is liable.

In *Roberts v. Gary*[28], 'G', a minor, entered into a contract with 'R', a noted billiards player, to pay him a certain sum of money to learn the game and play matches with him during his world tour. 'R' spent time and money in making arrangements for billiards matches. Held, 'G' was liable to pay as the agreement was one for necessaries as it was in effect "for teaching, instruction, and employment and was reasonable and for the benefit of the infant".

Loans for necessaries

A loan taken by a minor to obtain necessaries are also binds him and is recoverable by the lender as if he himself had supplied the necessaries [*Martin v. Gale*[29]].

But the minor is not personally liable. It is only his estate which is liable for such loans.

2. PERSON OF UNSOUND MIND

Meaning of Sound Mind

Section 12 lays down a test of soundness of mind. Section 12 says. "A person is said to be of unsound mind for the purpose of making a contract, if at the time when he makes it, he is capable of understanding it and of forming rational judgement as to its effects upon his interests."

Section 12 further states that (i) a person who is usually of unsound mind, but occasionally of sound mind may make a contract when he is of sound mind, and (ii) a person who is usually of sound mind but occasionally of unsound mind may not make a contract, when he is of unsound mind.

Illustrations

(a) A patient in a lunatic asylum, who is at intervals of sound mind, may contract during those intervals.

(b) A sane man who is delirious from fever or who is so drunk that he cannot understand the terms of the contract when he is of unsound mind.

Test of Soundness of Mind

The tests of soundness of mind are:

(i) the capacity to understand the contents of the business concerned and

(ii) the ability to form a rational judgement as to its effect on his interests.

If a person is incapable of both these elements, he suffers from unsoundness of mind. Whether a party to a contract is of sound mind or not is a question of fact to be decided by the court. There is a presumption in favour of sanity. If a person relies on unsoundness of mind, he must prove it sufficiently to satisfy the court.

The decision of Patna High Court in *Inder Singh v. Parmeshwardhari Singh*[30] is an illustration. In this case, a property of value about Rs. 25,000/- was agreed to be sold by a person for Rs. 7,000/- only. His mother proved that he was a congenital idiot, incapable of understanding the transaction and that he mostly wandered about. Holding the sale to be void, Sinha J stated that it is not necessary that a man must be suffering from lunacy to disable him from entering into a contract. "A person may to all appearances behave in a normal fashion, bit at the same time, he may be incapable of forming a judgement of his own, as to whether the act he is about to do is to his interest or not. In the present case (he) was incapable of exercising his own judgement."

Mental Incompetents

(A) Lunatics and Insane Persons

A Lunatic is one, whose mental power has been deranged. Insane persons are those persons who are sometimes sane and sometimes insane. Such persons may enter into contract during their lucid intervals i.e. period in which they are in senses. Such persons can always plead lunacy or insanity as a ground for avoiding a contract. It is for the plaintiff to prove that the contract was entered into during the lucid interval of the defendant. However, their property is liable for necessaries supplied to them.

(B) Idiots

An idiot is a person who is permanently of unsound mind. He does not have lucid intervals. He is incapable of entering into a contract and, therefore, a contract with an idiot is void. However, like a minor, his properties, if any, shall be liable for recoveries on account of necessaries of life supplied. Also he can be a beneficiary.

(C) Drunkards

A person under the influence of intoxication or drug stands on the same footing as a lunatic. He also suffers from temporary incapacity to contract. Contract by a drunken person is absolutely void and can not be ratified. But in order to make a contract by a drunkard void, the drunkenness should be effective and absolute, so that rational judgement cannot be formed by the contracting party. The drunken person should be incapable of understanding the contents of the contract and its legal consequences.

Under the English Law, contracts made by persons of unsound mind are voidable and not void.

The liability for necessaries of life supplied to persons of unsound mind is the same as for minors (Section 68).

3. Persons disqualified by any law to which they are subject

Besides minors and persons of unsound mind, there are some other persons who are incompetent to contract, partially or wholly, so that the contracts of such persons are void. Incompetency to contract may arise from political status, corporate status, legal status, etc.

Alien Enemy (Political Status)

An alien enemy is a person (including an Indian citizen) who is domiciled in a country which is at war with India. It is, therefore, the place of residence of an individual that decides whether he is an alien enemy or not. An alien enemy cannot enter into contracts with an Indian citizen nor can be file a suit in an Indian Court.

Foreign Sovereigns and Ambassadors

Foreign sovereigns and accredited representatives of a foreign state or Ambassadors enjoy some special privileges, they cannot be sued in our courts unless they choose to submit themselves to the jurisdiction of our courts. They can enter into contracts and enforce those contracts in our courts. But an Indian citizen has to obtain a prior sanction of the central government in order to sue them in our law courts. An ex-king can, however, be sued against in our courts without any such sanction (*Mighell v. Sultan of Johore*[31])

The Central Government grants permission to sue a foreign sovereign or ambassador etc.

(i) when he has instituted a suit in a Court against the person desiring to sue him, or

(ii) where he himself or through his agent carries on trade within the jurisdiction of the court, or

(iii) where he is in possession of immovable property in the jurisdiction of the court and is to be sued with reference to such property or

(iv) when he has expressly waived the privilege accorded to him.

Corporations (Corporate status)

A corporation is an artificial person created by law, having a legal existence apart from its members. It may come into existence by a special Act of the legislature or by registration under the Companies Act 1956. The contractual capacity of corporations (Corporate bodies) is restricted by the statutes governing them. They can not enter into contracts which are beyond their object and powers (i.e. *ultra vires*), nor can they make contracts which are associated with physical existence like contract of marry, because they are only artificial persons.

Married Woman (Marital status)

A married woman has full contractual capacity and can sue and be sued in her own name. She is not incompetent to contract. According to our constitution the right of a woman to be treated on a footing of equality with a man is a fundamental right guaranteed to her.

Bankrupt or Insolvent (Solvency status)

An undischarged insolvent cannot be appointed or acting as a magistrate, or elected to any office of local authority. He is also disqualified from being elected, sitting or voting as member of any local authority.

Felons and Convicts

Persons undergoing sentences of imprisonment cannot enter into contracts. He can, however, enter into, or sue on, a contract if he is lawfully at large under a licence called "ticket of leave". Their capacity to enter into a contract, and to sue is only suspended during the period of sentence and is regained after its expiry. The convict, however, does not suffer from the rigours of the Law of Limitation. Limitation is held is abeyance during the period of his sentence.

CHAPTER

25

Consideration

Consideration in one of the essential elements to support a contract. Subject to certain exceptions, an agreement made without consideration is *nudum pactum* (a nude contract) and is void.

Definition

Consideration has been variously defined. The simplest definition is given by **Blactstone:**

"Consideration is the recompense given by the party contracting to the other."[32]

Sir Frederick Pollock defines consideration as "Consideration is the price for which the promise of the other is bought, and the promise thus given for value is enforceable".[33]

Another simple definition is by **Patterson J.**

"Consideration means something which is of some value in the eye of law .... It may be some benefit to the plaintiff or some detriment to the defendant."[34]

In the English case of *Currie v. Misa*,[35] Consideration was defined by **Lush J.** as follows —

"A valuable consideration in the sense of the law may consist either in some right, interest, profit or benefit accruing to one party, or some forbearance, detriment, loss or responsibility given, suffered or undertaken by the other."

From the foregoing definitions it is clearly brought out that the term 'Consideration' is used in the sense of 'quid-pro-quo' which means 'something in return'. This 'something' may be some benefit, right, interest or profit or it may also be some forbearance, detriment, loss or responsibility upon the other party.

In India, the definition of consideration is contained in Section 2(d) of the Indian Contact Act 1872. This section defines "Consideration" as "when, at the desire of the promiser, the promisee or any other person has done or abstained, from doing or does or abstains from doing, or promises to do or to abstain from doing, some thing, such act or abstinence or promise is called a consideration for the promise."

Elements of Consideration

The definition of consideration in section 2(d) shows that the following are the essential parts of the consideration.

1. The consideration is an act, or abstinence

The definition of consideration in section 2(d) emphasises that an act or abstinence which is to be a consideration for the promise must be done or promised to be done in accordance with the desire of the promisor. For example, in Durga *Prasad v. Baldeo*[35], the plaintiff constructed a market at the instance of the collector of a district. The defendant, who was occupants of the shops in the said market promised to pay plaintiff a commission on articles sold through their shops. Held, there was no consideration because the money was not spent by the plaintiff at the request of the defendants, but voluntarily for a third person and thus the contract was void.

Notice that although the promisee must give consideration at the desire of the promiser, it is not necessary that the promiser himself should benefit by the consideration. The promise would be valid even if the benefit accrued to a third party.

For example, in *National Bank of upper India v. Bansidhar*[36], 'A' owed Rs. 20,000/- to 'B'. He (A) persuaded 'C' to sign a promissory note in favour of 'B'. 'C' promised 'B' that he would pay the amount. On the faith of promise by 'C', 'B' credited the amount to "A's" account. Held, the discharge of "A's account was consideration for C's promise.

2. Such act or abstinence may be done by the promisee or any person

The second feature of the definition of consideration in section 2(d) is that the act or abstinence which is to constitute a consideration may be done by the promisee or any other person. It means, therefore, that it is necessary that consideration must move at the desire of the promisor, it may be supplied either by the promisee or any other person. The case of *Chinnayya v. Ramayya*[37] is a good illustration on the point.

In this case, 'A' a lady, by a deed of gift transferred certain property to her daughter, with a direction that the daughter should pay an annuity to A's brother, as had been done by 'A'. On the same day, the daughter executed a writing in favour of the brother, agreeing to pay the annuity. Afterwards, she declined to fulfill her promise saying that no consideration had moved from her uncle ('A's brother).

The court, however, held that the words "the promise or any other person" in section 2(d) clearly show that the consideration need not necessarily move from the promisee, it may move from any other person. Hence, "A's" brother was entitled to maintain the suit.

Under the English law, consideration must move from the promisee. (*Tweddle v. Atkinson*[38]). Under the Indian law, consideration may move from the promisee or any other person, i.e., even a stranger.

3. Such act or abstinence is either already executed or is in the process of execution or may be still executory.

Legal Rules Regarding Consideration

1. Consideration is required both for formation and discharge of an agreement or contract.

According to section 25 of the Indian Contract Act 1872 "An agreement without consideration is void". Hence, the rule "No consideration, no contract, with few exceptions provided under section 25 and section 185 of the Act.

2. Consideration may be Past, Present or Future

The words used in section 2(d) are: "has done or abstained from doing or does or abstains from doing, or promises to do or to abstain from doing" indicate that consideration may be past, present or future.

(a) Past Consideration

When consideration by a party for a present promise was given in the past, i.e., before the date of the promise, it is called to be past consideration.

Example

'A' saves "B's" life. B promises to pay 'A' Rs. 1,000/- out of gratitude. The consideration for B's promise is a past consideration, something done before making of the promise.

In India, past consideration is a good consideration. In *Sindha v. Abraham*[39] (1895), a minor was given the benefit of certain services by the plaintiff, who rendered those services, not voluntarily but at the desire of minor and these services were continued even after majority at the request of minor who subsequently promised to pay an annuity to the plaintiff. It was held that the past consideration was a good consideration.

But, under English Law, past consideration is no consideration as, in the words of Anson, it is "a mere sentiment of gratitude or honour prompting a return for benefits received."

(b) Present or Executed Consideration

Consideration which moves simultaneously with the promise is called present consideration. 'Cash sales' is an excellent example of present consideration.

Example

A received Rs. 100 in return for which he promises to deliver certain goods to B. The money A receives is the present consideration for the promise he makes to deliver the goods.

(c) Future or Executory Consideration

When the consideration is to move at a future date, it is called future or executory consideration. It takes the form of the promise to be performed in the future.

A promises B to deliver him certain goods after 10 days. B promises to pay the price on delivery. Consideration in this case is future or executory.

3. The Consideration may be either Positive or Negative.

According to section 2(d) of the Indian Contract Act the consideration may be a promise to do something or to abstain from doing something. Thus, a consideration may be an act 'to do' or 'not to do' something i.e. it may be positive or negative.

The consideration may be forbearance to sue.

The term 'forbearance to sue' means that the plaintiff has a right of action against the defendant or any other person, and on a promise by the defendant, the (plaintiff) refrains from bringing the legal action. The forbearance to sue is regarded as a valid consideration.

4. The consideration must be done or promised to be done at the desire of the promiser.

The consideration may be furnished by the promisee or any other person (Details are given under heading 'Elements of Consideration').

5. Consideration must be lawful

According to section 10 — "All agreement are contracts if they are made ..... for a lawful consideration ..... ".

Section 24 further provides "if any part of a single consideration for one or more objects, or any part of any one of 'several considerations for a single object, is unlawful, the agreement is void." Thus, where part of the consideration is unlawful the whole agreement is void unless the part which is unlawful can be separated from the one which is legal.

6. Consideration need not be adequate

Consideration means "something in return". This "something in return" need not necessarily be equal in value to "something given". The law simply provides that a contract should be supported by consideration. So long as consideration exists. The courts are not concerned as to its adequacy. Provided it is of some value. "The adequacy of the consideration is for the parties to consider at the time of making the agreement, not for the court when it is sought to be enforced."[40] Consideration must, however, be something to which the law attaches value though it need not be equal in value to the promise made. The courts do not exist to repair bad bargains.

7. Consideration must be real and not Illusory

Although consideration need not be adequate, it must be real competent and of some value in the eyes of the law.

In *Collins v. Godfrey*[41], it was held that when a witness who has received summons to appear at a trial, a promise to pay him anything beyond his expenses is void for want of consideration, because the witness was bound to appear and give evidence.

But, a promise made to stranger to perform an existing contract, is enforceable because the promiser undertakes a new obligation upon himself which can be enforced by the stranger.

8. The Consideration must not be the performance of existing duties.

The term 'existing duties' includes legal obligations or Contractual obligations. A person may be bound to do something by law. The consideration must be something more than that what the promisee is already bound to do by law.

The performance of legal duty is not consideration for promise.

Exceptions to the general rule 'a contract made without consideration is void'

The general rule is that an agreement made without consideration is void (Section 25). "A bargain without consideration is a contradiction in terms and cannot exist"[42].

However, there are certain exceptional circumstances under which an agreement, even though without consideration, shall be enforceable. These exceptions are contained in sections 25 and 185 of the Indian Contract Act. These circumstances are:

Natural love and affection

An agreement made in writing and registered and is made on account of natural love and affection between parties standing in a near relation to each other [Section 25(1)].

An agreement without consideration is valid under section 25(1) only if the following requirements are complied with:

(i) The agreement is made in a written document.

(ii) The document is registered according to the law relating to registration in force at the time.

(iii) The agreement is made on account of natural love and affection

(iv) The parties to the agreement stand in a near relation to each other.

In simple words, a written and registered agreement based on natural love and affection between near relatives is enforceable even if it is without consideration [*Ram Dass v. Krishan Dev*[43]].

Venkataswamy v. Rangaswamy[44]

An elder brother on account of natural love and affection, promised to pay the debts of his younger brother. The agreement was put to writing and was registered. But elder brother did not repay the debt. The younger brothre repaid the debt out of his own and then sued the former for recovery of money. Held, the brother has the right to do because the agreement was valid under Section 25(1).

Rajlukhy v. Bhoothnath[45]

A Hindu husband, after referring to quarrels and disagreements between him and his wife executed a registered document in favour of his wife agreeing to pay her for maintenance, but no consideration moved from the wife. Held the agreement was void for want of consideration. "It was not made out of natural love and affection. Therefore, it was not a valid contract".

Compensation for voluntary services [Section 25(2)]

An agreement made without consideration is also valid and enforceable if it is a promise to compensate, wholly or in part, a person who has already voluntarily done something for the promiser, or something which the promiser was legally compellable to do. In order that a promise to pay for past voluntary services is binding, the following conditions must exist:

(i) The services should have been rendered voluntarily.

(ii) The services must have been rendered for the promiser and not anybody else. If the services are rendered not voluntarily but at the desire of the promiser, then it is covered under 'past consideration' and not under the exception.

(iii) The promiser must, be in existence at the time when the services were rendered.

(iv) The promiser must have intended to compensate the promisee.

(v) The promiser should be competent to contract at the time when the act was done.

(vi) It is to be noted that there is no need of having any written contract for this purpose.

3. Promise to pay a time barred debt [Section 25(3)]

A promise by a debtor to pay a time-barred debt is enforceable provided it is made in writing and is signed by the debtor or by his agent generally or specially authorised in that behalf. The promise may be to pay the whole or any part of the debt. The debt must be such "of which the creditor might have enforced payment but for the law for the limitation of suits".

A debt is barred by limitation if it remains unpaid or unclaimed for a period of three years. Such a debt becomes legally irrecoverable.

4. Completed Gift (Explaination 1 to section 25)

In the case of a gift actually made, not being an agreement to make a gift, no consideration is necessary although the donor and the donee may not be standing in near relation to each other, and even if they do, there may not be any natural love and affection between them.

5. Agency (Section 185)

Besides the exceptions mentioned in section 25 of the Act, there are also certain other types of agreements which are enforceable by law even without consideration.

Section 185 of the Act says that "No consideration is necessary to create an agency."

6. Remission (Section 63)

No consideration is necessary for an agreement to receive less than what is due known as remission.

7. Guarantee (Section 127)

A contract of guarantee is made without consideration.

Stranger to Consideration and Stranger to Contract

In is a general rule of law that only parties to a contract may sue and be sued on that contract. This rule is known as the doctrine of 'privity of contract'. Privity of contract means relationship subsisting between the parties who have entered into contractual obligations. It implies a mutuality of will and creates a legal bond or tie between the parties to a contract.

There are two propositions of the doctrine of privity of contract:

(i) A person who is not a party to a contract cannot sue upon it even though the contract is for his benefit and he provided consideration.

(ii) A contract cannot confer rights or impose obligation arising under it on any person other than the parties to it.

Thus, doctrine of 'Privity of Contract' means that a contract is a contract between the parties and no third person can sue upon it even if it is avowedly made for his benefit. This doctrine was affirmed by the House of Lords in *Dunlop Pneumatic Tyre Co. v. Selfridge and Co.*[46]

Defendant 'S' bought tyres from the plaintiff's Dunlop Rubber Co. and sold them to 'D', a sub-dealer, who agreed with 'S' not to sell below Dunlop's list price and to pay the Dunlop Co. £5 as damages on every tyre D undersold. D sold two tyres at less than the list price and there upon the Dunlop Co. sued him for the breach. Held, the Dunlop Co. could not maintain the suit as it was a stranger to the contract.

The above two propositions is not at all applicable in India. The second notable feature of the definition of consideration in section 2(d) is that the act which is to constitute a consideration may be done by "the promisee or any other person". It means, therefore, that, it is not necessary that consideration should be furnished by the promisee. A promise is enforceable if there is some consideration for it and it is quite immaterial whether it moves from the promisee or any other person.

It is necessary, in this context to distinguish between a stranger to a consideration and a stranger to a contract. If consideration is furnished not by the promisee but by a third person, the promisee becomes a stranger to the consideration, and as such he cannot enforce the promise. Similarly, a person who is not a party to a contract cannot claim any rights under the contract even though the contract may be for his benefit and such a person is known as 'stranger to the contract'.

It is now a settled law in India that stranger to a contract cannot sue on the contract because, there being no privity of contract between him and the contracting party. A contract can not confer rights or impose obligations on any person other than the parties.

Thus, in India stranger to the consideration may maintain a suit but a stranger to the contract can not maintain a suit.

Exceptions

In the course of time, the courts have introduced a number of exceptions to the rule that a stranger to a contract (rule of Privity of Contract) can not sue. Many of the exceptions are connected with the special branches of the law of contract, such as negotiable instruments, agency, bill of lending, railway receipts, transfer of property, etc. Certain well recognised exceptions are given below:

(i) A Trust or Charge

A person (beneficiary) in whose favour a trust or other interest in some specific immovable property has been created can enforce it even though he is not a party to the contract.

In *Khwaja Mohammad Khan v. Hussaini Begum*[47], 'H' sued her father-in-law 'K' to recover Rs. 15,000. Being the arrears of allowance called Kharchi-i-Pandan, the money payable to her by 'K' under an agreement made between K and "H's" father in consideration of "H's" marriage to "K's" son D. Both 'H' and 'D' were minors at the date of marriage.

It was held that the plaintiff, although no party to the agreement, was clearly entitled to proceed in equity to enforce her claim. "Here the agreement executed by the defendant specifically charges immovable property for the allowance which he binds himself to pay to the plaintiff, she is the only person beneficially entitled under it".

In *Rana Uma Nath Bakhs Singh v. Jang Bahadur*[48]

U was appointed by his father as his successor and was put in possession of his entire estate. In consideration thereof U agreed with his father to pay a certain sum of money and to give a village to J, the illegitimate son of his father, on his attaining majority.

It was held in the circumstances mentioned above a trust was created in favour of J for the specified amount and the village. Hence, he was entitled to maintain the suit.

2. Marriage settlement, Partition or other family arrangements

When an arrangement is made in connection with marriage, partition or other family arrangements and a provision is made for the benefit of a person, he may sue although he is not a party to the agreement.

In *Daropti v. Jaspal Rai*[49]

The defendant's wife left him because of his cruelty. He then executed an agreement with her father, promising to treat her properly, or, if he failed to do so, to pay her monthly maintenance and to provide her with a dwelling. Subsequently she was again ill-treated by the defendant and also driven out. Held, she was entitled to enforce the promise made by the defendant to her father.

Another interesting case in *Shuppu Ammal v. Subramantyam*,[50] two brothers, on a partition of joint properties, agreed to invest in equal shares a certain sum of money for maintenance of their mother. Held, she was entitled to require her sons to make the investment.

In Commissioner of Wealth Tax v. Vijayaba[51]

A mother agreed to pay to her younger son in the event of failure by the elder son to pay to the younger son the amount which fell short of the younger son's share in the assets left by their father. The agreement was made to purchase peace for the family. Held, it was a valid family arrangement creating liability of mother.

3. Acknowledgement or Estopple

Where by the terms of a contract a party is required to make a payment to a third person and he acknowledges it to that third person, a binding obligation is thereby incurred towards him. Acknowledgement may be expressed or implied.

In *Devaraja Urs v. Ram Krishniah*[52], the sale price was left in the hands of a buyer of a house for payment to a creditor, and the buyer made part payment, promising to remit the balance soon to the creditor, the creditor was allowed to recover the balance.

Covenants running with the land

In cases of transfer of immovable property, the purchaser of land with notice that the owner of the land is bound by certain conditions or covenants created by an agreement affecting the land shall be bound by their although he was not a party to the original agreement which contained the conditions or covenants.

In *Smith and Snipes Hall Farm Ltd v. River Douglas Catchment Board*[53], the defendants (the Board) agreed with certain land-owners adjoining a stream to improve the banks of the stream and to maintain them in good condition. The landlords on their part paid proportionate costs. Subsequently one of the landlords sold his land to the first plaintiff and he to the second plaintiff. There was negligence on the part of the Board in maintaining the banks, which burst and the land was flooded.

The court of appeal allowed the plaintiffs who were strangers to the agreement to sue the board for breach of the contract, for the whole arrangement was for the benefit of the landowners whoever they might be and not merely the parties of the agreement.

5. Assignment of a Contract

The assignee of rights and benefits under a contract not involving personal skill can enforce the contract subject to the equities between the original parties (*Krishan Lal Sadhu v. Promila Bala*[54]). Thus the holder in due course of a negotiable instrument can realise the amount on it even though there is no contract between him and the person liable to pay.

CHAPTER

26

Free Consent

Definition of Consent (Section 13)

Section 13 defines 'Consent' as follows:

"Two or more persons are said to consent when they agree upon the same thing in the same sense".

If parties do not consent, i.e., do not understand the same thing in the same sense, there can be no agreement, because consent is like the very roots of an agreement. If there is no consent the parties are not said to be ad idem, i.e., of the same mind.

In *Foster v. Mackinnon*[55], the defendant had purported to endorse a bill of exchange which he was told was a guarantee. The Court held that his signature, not being intended as an endorsement of a bill of exchange, there was no consent and consequently no agreement entered into by him, and therefore, he was not liable on the Bill.

Free Consent (Section 14)

To make a contract valid not only the presence of a consent of the other party is necessary but this consent should also be free.

Definition of Free Consent

Section 14 defines Free Consent as follows:

Consent is said to be free when it is not caused by:

(i) Coercion, as defined in Section 15 or

(ii) Undue influence as defined in Section 16 or

(iii) Fraud as defined in Section 17, or

(iv) Misrepresentation as defined in Section 18, or

(v) Mistake, subject to the provisions of Sections 20, 21 and 22.

Consent is said to be so caused when it would not have been given but for the existence of such coercion, undue influence, fraud, misrepresentation or mistake.

Consent thus gets vitiated by the presence of coercion or undue influence or misrepresentation. Accordingly, these are known as vitiating elements, and when any one of them is present in the consent given, then is said to be flow in consent. When consent to a contract is caused by coercion, undue influence, fraud, or misrepresentation, the agreement is a contract voidable at the option of the party whose consent was so caused.

For various flows in consent refer to the chart given below:

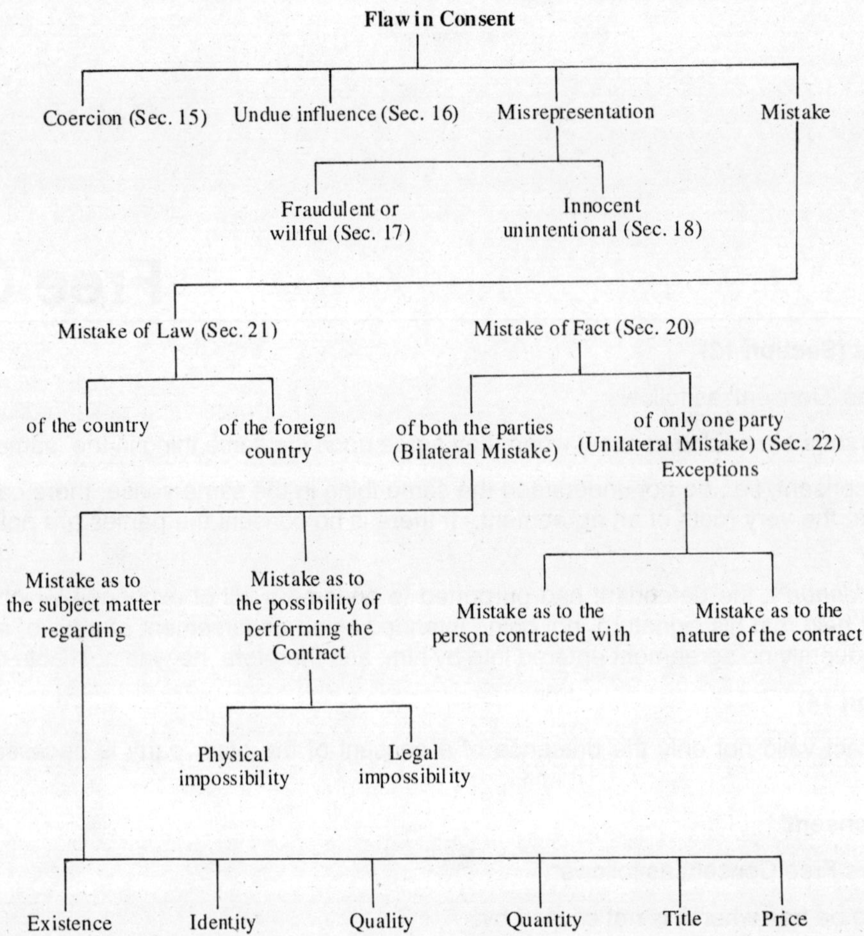

Coercion (Section 15, 19 and 72)

When a person is compelled into a contract by the use of force by the other party or under a threat, coercion is said to be employed. Coercion is defined by the section 15 of the Act as follows:

"Coercion is (i) the committing or threatening to commit any act forbidden by the Indian Penal Code, or (ii) the unlawful detaining or threatening to detain any property to the prejudice of any person whatever, (iii) with the intention of causing any person to enter into an agreement". It is immaterial whether the Indian Penal Code is or is not in force in the place where the coercion is employed.

The threat amounting to coercion need not necessarily proceed from any party to the contract. It may proceed even from a stranger to the contract. Likewise, it may be directed against any body —not necessarily the other contracting party. The intention of the person using coercion should, however, be to cause any person to enter into an agreement.

Consent is said to be caused by coercion when it is obtained by:

1. Committing or threatening to commit any act forbidden by the Indian Penal Code, 1860

Thus, in *Ranganayakamma v. Alwarsetti*[56], a Hindu widow of 13 years was forced to adopt a boy by her husband's relative who prevented the removal of dead body of her husband until she consented to the adoption. Held, the consent was not free but was induced by the coercion. Consequently, the adoption was set aside.

2. The unlawful detention of any property

Thus, in *Muthain Chettiar v. Karuppan Chette*,[57] an agent refused to hand over the account books of a business to the new agent unless the principal released him from all liabilities. The principal had to give a release deed as demanded. Held, the release deed was given under coercion and was voidable at the option of the principal.

An other case *Bansraj v. The Secretary of State*[58], the government gave a threat of attachment against the property of plaintiff for the recovery of the fine. The son of the plaintiff paid the fine. Held, the contract was induced by coercion.

(3) The threat to commit any act forbidden by Indian Penal Code

In *Amiraju v. Seshamma*[59], a release deed was obtained by a person from his wife and son under a threat of committing suicide. The transaction was set aside on the ground coercion, as suicide is forbidden by the Indian Penal Code.

Effect of coercion

When the consent to an agreement is caused by coercion, the agreement is a contract voidable of the option of the party whose consent was so caused (Section 19). In other words, aggrieved party can have the contract set aside or if he so desires to insist on its performance by the other party.

According to section 72, a person to whom money has been paid, or anything delivered by mistake or under coercion, must repay or return it.

Example

A railway company refuses to deliver certain goods to the consignee except upon payment of an illegal charge for carriage. The consignee pays sum charged in order to obtain the goods. He is entitled to recover so much of the charge as was illegally excessive.

Duress

In the English law, the near equivalent of the term 'Coercion' is "duress". Duress has been defined as causing, or threatening to cause bodily violence or imprisonment, with a view to obtain the consent of the other party to the contract. Duress differs from coercion on the following grounds:

(i) Coercion can be employed against any person, where as 'duress' can be employed only against the other party to contract or the members of his family.

(ii) Coercion may be employed by any person, and not necessarily by the promisee. 'Duress' can be employed only by the party to the contract or his agent.

(iii) Coercion is wider in its scope and includes unlawful detention of goods also. 'Duress' on the other hand does not include unlawful detention of goods. Only bodily violence or imprisonment is duress.

Undue Influence (Section 16 and 19-A)

Sometimes a party is compelled to enter into an agreement against his will as a result of unfair persuasion by the other party. This happen a special kind of relationship exists between the parties such that one party is in position to exercise influence over the other. Section 16(1) defines "undue influence" as follows:

"A contract is said to be induced by 'undue influence' where the relations subsisting between the parties are such that one of the parties is in position to dominate the will of the other and uses that position to obtain an unfair advantage over the other."

Example:

1. A, a man enfeebled by disease or age is induced by B's influence over him as his medical attendant to agree to pay B an unreasonable sum for his professional service, B employs undue influence.

   A person is deemed to be in a position to dominate the will of another:

   (a) where he holds a real or apparent authority over the other e.g., master and servant.

   (b) where he stands in fiduciary relation to the other, e.g., father and son,

   (c) where he makes a contract with a person whose mental capacity is temporarily or permanently effected by reason of age, illness or mental or bodily distress e.g., an old literate person.

Example:

(i) In *Mannu Singh v. Umadat Pandey*[60], a spiritual guru induced his devotee to gift to him the whole of his property in return of a promise of salvation of the devotee. Held, the consent of the devotee was given under undue influence.

(ii) *Ranee Annapurni v. Swaminath*[61], a poor Hindu widow was persuaded by a money lender to agree to pay 100% rate of interest on money lent by him to her. She needed the money to establish her right to maintenance. Held, it was a case of undue influence and the court reduced the rate of interest to 24%.

(iii) In *Inche Noriah v. Shaikh Allie Bin Omar*[62], an illiterate elderly woman made a deed of gift of practically the whole of her property to her nephew who managed her affairs. Held, the gift should be set aside on the ground of undue influence.

(iv) In *Sher Singh v. Pirthi Singh*[63], an illiterate villager aged about 90 years, physically infirm and mentally in distress, executed a deed of gift under the influence of his nearest relatives (who at one time formed a joint family) who looked after his daily needs and managed his cultivation. Held, the relatives were in position to dominate his will.

(v) *Niko Devi v. Kripa*[64], a minor female child who had lost her parents was living with her cousin brother who was in the position of loco parents (in the place of parents). A deed was executed by her in favour of latter. Held, there was undue influence.

Burden of Proof [Section 16(3)]

In an action to avoid a contract on the ground of undue influence, the plaintiff or the defendant, as the case may be, must satisfy the court:

(i) that the other party was in position to dominate his will, and

(ii) that he actually used that position for obtaining an unfair advantage for himself. Unfair advantage means gain, benefit or advantage obtained by unrighteous or undesirable means.

In *Saraswathi v. Lakshmi Kantam*[65], it was held that, mere proof of nearness of relationship is not sufficient for the court to assume that one relation was in position to dominate the will of the other.

In *Kanwarani Madna Wati v. Raghunath Singh*[66], an illiterate woman enfeebled by physical and mental distress, with none to advise her, executed a mortgage. Held, the burden is on the mortgagee to prove that the woman fully understood what she was doing.

Undue influence when presumed

The following relationships usually raise a presumption of undue influence, parent and child, guardian and ward, trustee and beneficiary, religious adviser and disciple, doctor and patient, solicitor and client, and fiance and fiancee.

There is, however, no presumption of undue influence in the case of landlord and tenant,[66] creditor and debtor, husband and wife.[67] In these cases, the party alleging undue influence must prove that undue influence must existed.

Effect of Undue Influence (Section 19-A)

An agreement caused by undue influence is a contract voidable at the option of the party whose consent was thus secured. While setting aside such a contract, the court may impose conditions as to the return of any benefit received under the contract by the party at those instance it is set aside. The aggrieved party may, if he desires, treat the agreement as binding and enforce it against the other party.

The following illustrations are appended to the section 19-A.

(a) A's son has forged B's name to a promissory note, B under threats of prosecuting A's son, obtains a bond from A for the amount of the forged note. If B sues on this bond, the court may set the bond aside.

(b) A, a money-lender, advances Rs. 100 to B, an agriculturist, and, by undue influence, induces B to execute a bond for Rs. 200 with interest at 6% per month. The court may set the bond aside ordering B to repay the Rs. 100 with such interest as may seem just.

Contracts with Pardanashin women

A contract with a pardanashin woman is presumed to have been induced by undue influence. She can avoid the contract unless the other party can show that it was her "intelligent and voluntary act". There is, however, no statutory or judicial definition of the term "Pardanashin woman." In *Shaik Ismail v. Amir Bibi*[68], Bombay High Court opinion is that a woman does not become pardanashim simply because "she lives in some degree of seclusion." The concept probably means a Pardanashin woman is one who observes complete seclusion because of the custom of the particular community to which she belongs.

In *Kalibaksh Singh v. Ram Gopal Singh*, the Privy Council pointed out that the proof must go so far as to show affirmatively and conclusively that the deed was not only executed by, but was explained to, and was really understood by, the grantor.

Any person who enters into a contract with a pardanashin woman has strictly to prove that no undue influence was used and that she had free and independent advice, understood the contents of the contract and exercised her free will. The law throws around her a special cloak of protection. The court, when called upon the deal with a deed executed by a paradanashin woman must satisfy upon evidence:

First, that the deed was executed actually by her with full understanding of what she was about to do.

Secondly, that she had full knowledge of the nature and effect of the transaction in which she is said to have entered, and

Thirdly, she had independent and disinterested advice in the matter.

Distinction between Coercion and Undue Influence

In both Coercion and Undue Influence, the consent of one of the parties is not free, his freedom of will is impaired and he is under the influence of another. However, the two differ in the following respects.

1. Relationship

In case of coercion relationship between the promiser and promisee is not necessary, while in case of undue influence some sort of relationship generally exists between the two parties.

2. Domination

Under Coercion, the consent of the affected party is obtained under the threat of an offense, i.e., committing or threatening to commit an act forbidden by the Indian Penal code or detaining or threatening to detain property of some other person unlawfully. But in undue influence, the consent of the aggrieved party is obtained by the exercise of domination by the other party securing unfair advantage.

3. Criminal Act

Coercion involves a Criminal Act and there is a criminal liability but in undue influence no criminal act is involved.

4. Character

Coercion is mainly of a physical character. It involves mostly use of physical or violent force. But on the other hand, uninfluenced is of moral character. It involves use of moral force or mental pressure. Hence, it is known as moral coercion.

5. Consent

In the case of coercion, consent is destroyed whereas in the case of undue influence, consent is induced by improper means.

6. Place

An act of coercion may be committed out side India but undue influence should be exercised in India in order that the law may take notice of it.

CHAPTER

27

Fraud [Section 17 and 18]

Fraud means deceit by making certain mis-statement deliberately. So, when a mis-representation is made by a party with full knowledge that it is not true or without belief in its truth or recklessly, not caring whether it is true or false, it is said to be fraudulent.

Definition

According to section 17 of the Indian Contract Act, 'fraud' means and includes any of the following acts committed by a party to a contract or with his connivance, or by his agent, with intent to deceive another party thereto or his agent, or to induce him to enter into the contract:

(i) the suggestion, as to a fact, of that which is not true, by one who does not believe it to be true,

(ii) the active concealment of a fact by one having knowledge or belief of the fact.

(iii) a promise made without any intent of performing it,

(iv) any other act fitted to deceive,

(v) any such act or omission as the law specially declares to be fraudulent.

To constitute fraud, the act complained of must be brought within any of the above five categories.

Essentials of Fraud

On analysis of the above definition, fraud seems to contain the following essentials elements.

(1) A suggestion as to a fact

There must be a representation or assertion and it must be false. Without a representation or assertion there can be no fraud except in cases (a) where silence may itself amount to fraud or (b) where there is an active concealment of a fact.

In *Ward v. Hobbs*[69], defendant sold certain pigs to plaintiff. The pigs were suffering from some fever and this was in the knowledge of defendant. The pigs were sold "with all faults". Defendant did not disclose the fever to plaintiff. Held, there was no fraud.

(2) The active concealment of a fact

If a person purposely and actively conceals a fact, which is his duty to disclose, it will be taken as a fraud, on his part.

In *Peak v. Gurney*[70], the prospectus of a company deliberately avoided reference to a particular document which would have disclosed certain liabilities. This was done to create an impression that the company was prosperous though in fact it was not. It was held that this amount to fraud and anyone who purchased shares on the faith of this prospectus could avoid the contract.

(3) The representation must relate to material facts

The representation or assertion alleged to be false must be of a fact. A mere expression of opinion, puffery does not constitute fraud.

In *Bisset v. Wilkinson*[71], the vendor of a piece of land told a prospective purchaser that, in his opinion, the land would carry 2,000 sheep. In fact the land could carry only a number less than this. Held, there was no misrepresentation as the statement was one of opinion which was honestly held.

(4) Fraud by a party or his agent to the contract

Fraud must be committed by a party to the contract or with his connivance or by his agent. It should not be committed by a stranger. That is when a person is induced by a stranger to subscribe towards shares of a company on false information, cannot set aside the contract on the basis of fraud.

(5) The representation must in fact deceive

If the person on whom the fraud was practised was not in reality deceived, then he is in just the same position as if no false representation had been made to him.

In *Horsefall v. Thomas*[72], 'T' bought a cannon from 'H'. The cannon was defective but 'H' had plugged it. 'T' did not examine the cannon, but when he used it, it burst. Held, there was no fraud because 'T' would have bought it even if no deceptive plug had been put. He was not in fact deceived by it.

(6) Suffered Damage

The plaintiff must suffer some damage by relying upon the presentation. The damage may consist of actual and temporal injury, i.e., some loss of money or money's worth, or some tangible deteriment capable of assessment.

Silence amounting to fraud

According to explanation to section 17:

"Mere silence as to facts likely to affect the willingness of a person to enter into a contract is not fraud, unless the circumstances of the case are such that, regard being had to them, it is the duty of the person keeping silence to speak, or unless his silence is, in itself equivalent to speech."

The following rules can be deduced from the above explanation to section 17.

(1) Mere silence is not fraud

Ordinarily, of course, mere silence as to facts likely to affect the willingness of person to enter into a contract is not fraud.

In a Supreme Court case *Shri Krishan v. Kurukshetra University*, a candidate, who had full knowledge of the fact that he was short of attendance, did not mention this fact in his examination form. This was held to be no fraud, it being the duty of the university to scrutinise forms and to call for verification or information in case of doubts. The university, having failed to do so, it was estopped from canceling the examination of the candidate[73].

(2) Silence is fraudulent

"If the circumstances of the case are such that, regard being had to them, it is the duty of the person, keeping silence to speak." The duty to speak or putting expression or hear say or flourishing description, does not amount to representation of fact.

Traders and manufactures are inclined to speak optimistically of their products, e.g. "X products are the best in the market." Such statement does not amount to fraud, unless a clear intention to deceive is proved.

(3) The representation or statement must be made with the knowledge that it is false or without believing in its truth or recklessly, not caring whether it is true or false.

(4) The representation must induce other party to act upon it. To establish fraud it is necessary to show that the complainant was induced to act on the basis of representation.

(5) Silence is fraudulent where the circumstances are such that "silence is in itself equivalent to speech". Example — A says to B, "if you do not deny it, I shall assume that the horse that you are selling me is sound." If B says nothing his silence is equivalent to speech.

Consequences of Fraud (Section 19)

The party defrauded has the following remedies:

1. He can avoid the performance of the contract.
2. He can insists that the contract shall be performed and that he shall be put in the position in which he would have been if the representation made had been true.

Example —

A fraudulently informs B that A's estate is free from encumbrance. B, therefore, buys the estate. The estate is subject to mortgage. B may either avoid the contract, or may insist on its being carried out and the mortgage deed redeemed.

3. He can sue for damages.

Exceptions, i.e., where the contract is not voidable. In the following cases the contract is not voidable:

(a) when the party whose consent was caused by misrepresentation or fraud had the means of discovering the truth with ordinary diligence (exception to Sec. 19)

(b) where a party, after becoming aware of the misrepresentation or fraud, takes a benefit under the contract or in some other way affirms it.

Fraudulent Silence and Good faith Contracts

Mere silence is not fraud: The general rule is that a person need not disclose to the other party the mental facts which he knows but he must refrain from active mis-statement. This means mere silence is not fraud. Thus, silence does not amount to a representation and cannot amount to fraud. In ordinary contract of sale, for example, the buyer must take care of himself. The seller is under no obligation to disclose material facts.

Exception to the general rule

It is fraud for one to conceal material facts which he is under an obligation to disclose when he is entering into a contract with another. This duty to disclose does not arise in cases of all contracts. It arises only in the following cases:

(i) Statutory obligation to disclose:

Certain statutory provisions require parties to a contract to make disclosure of material facts. Thus, section 55 of the Transfer of Property Act requires a seller of real estate property to disclose all defects as to his title and tells the buyer that his property is free from all encumbrances, the buyer may treat the contract as void even if he buys the property, in case the property, in case the property turns out to be mortgaged or subject to similar encumbrances.

(ii) Duty to disclose in contracts of Uberrima fides (Utmost Good Faith)

Where parties to a contract stand in such a relationship that utmost good faith is required of them, they must disclose all material facts, e.g., a contract between father and mother and son just come of age. Nondisclosure in such a case would be treated as fraudulent. The following are a few instances of contracts uberrima fides.

(a) Insurance Contracts

An insurer contracts on the basis that all material facts should be communicated to him. So non disclosure would vitiate the contracts.

In a proposal for fire insurance contract, non disclosure of the refusal of mother insurance company would entitle the insuring Company would entitle the insuring company to repudiate the contract.

(b) Contracts relating to Family Settlements

Full disclosures of all material facts are necessary when family disputes are settled by mutual agreement.

(c) Contracts for the allotment of shares in companies

A company inviting the public to subscribe to its share must disclose all information regarding itself in the prospectus with strict accuracy.

(d) Contracts of Partnership

Mutual trust and confidence is the basis of partnership. It requires utmost good faith between parties before and after the formation of partnership.

(e) Contract of Suretyship

Section 143 of the Contract Act lays down that any guarantee which the creditor has obtained by means of keeping silence as to material circumstances is invalid. A creditor must disclose all material circumstances to the surety.

(f) Contracts in which parties stand in a Fiduciary relation to each other

Parties standing in a fiduciary relation to each other are duty bound to disclose all facts to the other party which are likely to effect his willingness to enter into a contract, e.g., solicitor and client, father and son, doctor and patient. In all cases, silence and non-disclosure of fact will itself amount to fraud.

(g) Contracts to marry

Strictly speaking, Contracts of marriage are not Contracts of utmost good faith. However, in Haji Ahmad *Yarkhan v. Abdul Gani*[74], the Nagpur High Court observed that, "But contract to marry may also come under this category though the case law on the subject is meagre and conflicting". Never the less, since a marriage cannot be nullified on the ground of non-disclosure, when the contract is still in the executory stage, one party may set aside the contract and defend the suit for damages, if the other party failed to disclose the material facts, in accordance with the decision in the case cited above.

(iii) Silence is in itself, equivalent to speech

Silence will amount to fraud in all those cases where it shall be considered equivalent to speech.

CHAPTER

28

Mispresentation (Sections 18 and 19)

Like fraud, misrepresentation is incorrect or false statement but the falsity or inaccuracy is not due to any desire to deceive or defraud the other party, it is innocent. The party making it believes it to be true.

Definition

Section 18 of the Contract Act defines "misrepresentation". The section includes the following types of misrepresentation:

1. Unwarranted statements

When a person positively asserts that a fact is true when his information does not warrant it to be so, though he believes it to be true.

In a case *Oceanic Steam Navigation Co. v. Soonderdas Dharmasey,*[75] the defendants chartered a ship from the plaintiffs, who stated that the ship was certainly not more than 2,800 tonnage register. As a matter of fact the ship had never been in Bombay and was wholly unknown to the plaintiffs. She turned out to be of the registered tonnage of more than 3,000 tonnes.

It was held that the defendants were entitled to avoid the charter party. "There was the positive assertion by the plaintiffs about the ship — an assertion not warranted by any information the plaintiff had at the time, and which was not true."

Where the seller of car stated that the car had done only 20,000 miles, the representation being untrue, the buyer was allowed to recover compensation for the misrepresentation.[76]

A statement is said to be warranted by the information of the person making it when he receives the information from trustworthy sources. It should not be a mere hearsay.

In a case *Mohanlal v. Sri Gungaji Cotton Mills Co.,*[77] B told the plaintiff that one C would be director of a company. B had obtained this information not from C direct, but from another person, called L. The information proved untrue.

MACLEOD J said: "I am inclined to think that if B relied on second-hand information he derived from L, he was warranted in making the positive assertion that C would be a director."

Where a representation acquires the status of being a term of the contract, and in turns out to be untrue, the disadvantaged party may, not only avoid the contract but also sue for damages for breach.

In *Rickview Construction Co. v. Raspa,*[78] the seller stated in the course of negotiations for the sale of lamb, that the whole of the lot was fully serviced, whereas this was not so the buyer was allowed damages for the breach of the warranty.

2. Breach of Duty

When there is any breach of duty by a person which brings an advantage to the person committing it by misleading another to his prejudice.

In one case *Oriental Banking Corporation v. Johe Fleming*[79], the plaintiff, having no time to read the contents of a deed, signed it as he was given the impression by the defendant that it contained nothing but formal matters already settled between them. The deed, however, contained a release in favour of the defendants.

Accordingly, the plaintiff was allowed to set aside the deed, "The defendant", the court said, was under no obligation, legally or morally, tc communicate the contents of the deed. But the plaintiff placed confidence. It then became his duty to state fully without concealment, all that was essential to a knowledge of the contents of a documents."

3. Inducing mistake about subject matter

When a party causes, however innocently, the other party to the agreement to make a mistake as to the substance of the thing which is the subject of the agreement.

In a case, *Nursey Spinning and Weaving Co., Re*[80], the directors of a company, while acting within their authority, sold on the company's behalf a bill of exchange to the bank. The company denied liability on the bill.

But the bank was held entitled to recover the amount of the bill from the company as money received to the use of the bank. "The bill was different from what it was expressly represented to be by the agents of the company."

Requirements of Misrepresentation

A misrepresentation of relevant if it satisfies the following requirements:

(i) It must be a representation of a material fact, mere expression of opinion does not amount to misrepresentation even if it turns out to be wrong.

(ii) It must be made before the conclusion of the contract with a view to inducing the other party to enter into the contract.

(iii) It must be made with the intention that it should be acted upon by the person to whom it is addressed.

(iv) It must actually have been acted upon and must have induced the contract.

(v) It must be wrong but the person who made it honestly believed it to be true.

(vi) It must be made without any intention to deceive the other party.

(vii) It need not be made directly to the plaintiff. A wrong statement of facts made to a third person with intention of communicating it to the plaintiff, also amounts to misrepresentation.

In a case, *Babul v. R.A. Singh*[81], defendant told to his wife within the hearing of their daughter that the bridegroom proposed for her was a young man. The bridegroom, however, was over sixty years. The daughter gave her consent to marry him believing the statement by her father. Held, the consent was vitiated by misrepresentation and fraud.

Misrepresentation results not only from mis-statement of facts but also from suppression of material facts (*R. V. Kylsant*[82]).

Effect of Misrepresentation

In case of misrepresentation the contract becomes voidable and the aggrieved party can

(i) avoid the agreement, or

(ii) insist that the contract be performed and he shall be put in the position in which he would have been if the representation made had been true.

A person seeking to avoid a contract on the ground of misrepresentation must prove:

(a) that the representation related to a matter of fact,

(b) that it was made before or at the time when the contract was entered into,

(c) that it was untrue,

(d) that it was made to induce the other party to enter into the contract, and

(e) that it did, in fact, induce him to enter into the contract.

(iii) If the party to whom the innocent misrepresentation is made had the means of discovering the truth with ordinary diligence, the contract is not voidable (Sec. 19). "Ordinary diligence" means such diligence as a reasonably prudent man would consider necessary, having regard to the nature of the transaction.

Distinction between Fraud and Misrepresentation

(1) Intention

Both in fraud and misrepresentation there is a statement which is false but in case of fraud, the party making a false or untrue representation makes it with the intention to deceive the other party to enter into a contract. Misrepresentation on the other hand, is innocent, i.e., without any intention to deceive or to gain an advantage.

(2) Damages

The party aggrieved by fraud can sue the person guilty of the fraud for damages for any damage he may have suffered by reason of the fraud (the fraud having been successfully played on him). In the case of an innocent misrepresentation, the aggrieved party cannot sue for damages, but can only avoid the agreement.

(3) Rescission

The remedy of rescission of the contract is available when the contract is vitiated by fraud as well as when it is vitiated by innocent misrepresentation. However, in the case of fraud right can be exercised even after the contract has been performed. Where as it is an innocent misrepresentation the remedy of rescission can not be exercised after the contract has thus been executed.

(4) Whether truth can be discovered with ordinary diligence

In the case of misrepresentation, the aggrieved party cannot avoid the contract if it had the means of discovering the truth with ordinary diligence. But in fraud, as a rule, the contract is voidable even though the aggrieved party had the means of discovering the truth with ordinary diligence.

(5) Criminal act

Fraud, in certain cases can be criminal act and punishable under Indian Penal Code. But misrepresentation does not show any criminal intent on the part of the maker of the statement and it not criminally punishable.

(6) Silence

Silence can not constitute an act of misrepresentation but silence in certain of cases can be construed as fraud.

Mistake

Mistake may be defined as an erroneous belief about something. Mistake is of two kinds:

(1) mistake of fact and

(2) mistake of law.

(1) Mistake of fact

Mistake of fact may be

(i) a bilateral mistake or

(ii) a unilateral mistake.

(i) Bilateral mistake

Where both the parties to an agreement are under a mistake as to a matter of fact essential to the agreement, there is a bilateral mistake. In such a case, the agreement is void (Section 20). The following two conditions have to be fulfilled for the application of section 20.

(a) The mistake must be mutual, i.e. both the parties should misunderstand each other and should be at cross-purposes.

Example —

A agreed to purchase B's motor car which was lying in B's garage. Unknown to either party, the car and garage were completely destroyed by fire a day earlier. The agreement is void.

(b) The mistake must relate to a matter of fact essential to the agreement. As to what facts are essential in an agreement will depend upon the nature of the promise in each case.

In a case, *Galloway v. Galloway*[83] a man and a woman entered into a separation agreement under which the man agreed to pay a weekly allowance to the woman, mistakenly believing themselves lawfully married. Held, the agreement was void as there was mutual mistake on a point of fact which was material to the existence of the agreement.

But an erroneous opinion as to the value of a thing which forms the subject-matter of an agreement is not to be deemed a mistake as to a matter of fact (Explanation to Sec 20)

Following are the cases which fall under bilateral mistake:

(1) Mistake as to the subject matter.

Where both the parties to an agreement are working under a mistake relating to the subject-matter, i.e., they assume that a certain state of things exists which in fact does not exist, the agreement is void. Mistake as to the subject-matter covers the following cases:

(a) Mistake as to the existence of the subject matter.

If the both parties believe the subject-matter of the contract to be in existence, which in fact at the time of the contract is non-existent, the contract in void.

In *Couturier v. Hastie*[84], A agreed to sell a cargo of corn supposed at the time of the contract to be in transit from Salonica to the United Kingdom. Unknown to the parties, the corn had become fermented and had already been sold by the master of the ship a Tunis. Held, the agreement was void and the buyer was not liable for the price.

(b) Mistake as to the Identity and Quality of the subject-matter

Where both the parties are mistaken as to the identity of the property which is the subject-matter of the contract. A mistake as to the quality of an article is not material unless it is a mutual mistake, regarding some attribute of the article, without which the article is of an essentially different character from the article in the mind of the parties.

In a case, Raffles v. Wichelhaus[85]

Defendant agreed to buy from plaintiff a cargo of cotton "to arrive ex-pearless from Bombay" There were two ships of that name sailing in October and the other in December. Defendant meant the former ship but plaintiff meant the latter. Held, there was a mutual or a bilateral mistake and there was no contract.

In *Nicholson and Vann v. Smith Marriott*[86], table napkins were sold at an auction by a description "with the crest of Charles I and the authentic property of that monarch". In fact, the napkins were Georgian. Held, the agreement was void as there was a mistake as to the quality of the subject-matter.

(c) Mistake as to the quantity of the subject-matter:

There may be a mistake as to the quantity or extent of the subject matter, which will render the contract void.

In a case, *Cox v. Prentice*[87], a silver bar was sold under a mistake as to its weight. There was a difference in value between the weight of the bar as it was and as it was supposed to be. Held, the agreement was void.

(d) Mistake as to the title to the subject matter

If the seller is selling a thing which he is not entitled to sell and both the parties are acting under a mistake, the agreement is void.

In *Cooper v. Phibbs*[88], a person took a lease of a fishery which, unknown to either party, already belonged to him. Held, the lease was void.

(e) Mistake as to the Price of the subject matter.

There may sometimes be a genuine mistake as to the price of an article for sale in which case the contract will be void.

In a case *Webster v. Cecil*[89], defendant wrote to plaintiff offering to sell certain property for £1,250. He had earlier declined an offer from plaintiff to buy the same property for £2,000. Plaintiff knew that this offer of £1,250 was a mistake for £2,250, immediately accepted the offer. Held, plaintiff knew perfectly well that the offer was made by mistake and hence the contract could not be enforced.

(ii) Mistake as to the Possibility of performing the Contract

Consent is nullified if both the parties believe, at the time of entering into contract, that the contract is capable of being performed when in fact this is not the case. The contract in such cases, is void on the ground of impossibility of performance. Impossibility may be:

(a) Physical

Example, A contact for the hire of a room for witnessing the coronation proceeding of Edward VII was held to be void because, unknown to the parties, the procession had already been canceled (*Griffith v. Brymmer*[90]).

(b) Legal

A contract is void if it provides that something shall be done which cannot, as a matter of law, be done.

2. Unilateral Mistake

When in a contract only one of the parties is mistaken regarding the subject matter or in expressing or understanding the terms or the legal effect of the agreement, the mistake is unilateral mistake.

According to section 22, "A contract is not voidable merely because it was caused by one of the parties to it being under a mistake as to a matter of fact."

A unilateral mistake is not allowed as a defence in avoiding a contract unless the mistake is not allowed as a defence in avoiding a contract unless the mistake is brought about by the other party's fraud or misrepresentation.

Exceptions:

To the above rule, however, there are the following exceptions:

(i) Mistake as to the Identity of Persons contracted with:

This mistake is material only where the personality of the other party is of importance to the person making the error, and may arise out of either the negligence or the fraud of the other party.

If, for example, A intends to contract with B but finds be has contracted with C, there is no contract if the identity of B was a material element of the contract and C knows it. Likewise, if A makes an offer to B, C cannot give himself any rights in respect of the contract by accepting the offer. If he does so, the contract will be void. The following cases are important illustrations of the point-

(1) In *Lundy v. Lindsya and Co.*,[91] one Blenkarn, knowing that Blenkiron and Co., were the reputed customers of Lindsay and Co., ordered some goods from Lindsay and Co., by imitating the signature of Blenkiron. These goods were then sold to Lundy, an innocent purchaser. In a suit by Lindsay against Lundy for recover of goods, it was held that as Lindsay never intended to contract with Blenkarn, there was no contract between them and as such even an innocent purchaser of the goods from Blenkarn did not get a good title, and must return them or pay their price.

(2) Similarly, in *Lake v. Simmons*[92], a lady X induced Y to deliver possession of two pearl necklaces falsely representing that she was the wife of Baron Z and that she wanted them for showing them to her husband for his approval. held, Y intended to contract only with the wife of the Baron and not with X herself. Hence, the contract was void and X could not convey and title even a bonafide buyers.

(3) In another similar case, *Solwer v. Potter*[93], in May 1938, a lady by the name of Ann Robinson was convicted of permitting disorderly conduct in her cafe. In July of the same year she assumed another name, Ann Potter, and took a lease of Sowler's premises. Held, the lease was void ab initio because of Sowler's mistaken belief that Ann Potter was not Ann Robinson.

It should be noted that the principle holds good only when the identity of the contracting party is of importance.

In *Ingram v. Little*[94], A advertised his car for sale. B who falsely called himself Hutchinson agreed to buy the car, and when he offered to pay by cheque A said the deal was over. Then he gave an address which A checked in the telephone directory and found that it corresponded with the name B had given. A thereupon agreed to accept the cheque which was subsequently dishonoured. The car was subsequently sold to L who bought it in good faith. Held, there was no contract between A and B, as A intended to enter into contract only with Hutchinson and as B had no title to the car, he could pass none to L.

(ii) Mistakes as to the Nature of Contract

A contract is void when one of the parties to it does not intend to enter into it, but through the fault of another and without any fault of his own, makes a mistake as to the nature of the contract.

Thus, in *Foster v. Mackinnon*[95], an old illiterate man of poor sight, was made to sign a bill of exchange, by means of a false representation that it was a guarantee. Held, the contract was void.

It should be noted that the plea of mistake will be available only when it relates to the nature of the contract, and not to the terms of the contract (Bay v. Pollara and Morris[96]).

Effect of Unilateral Mistake

According to Sec. 22, "A contract is not voidable merely because it was caused by one of the parties to it being under a mistake as to a matter of fact."

Thus unilateral mistake does not generally affect the validity of a contract.

Mistake of Law

Mistake of law may be —

(1) mistake of law of the country, or

(2) mistake of law of a foreign country.

(1) Mistake of law of the country

In this regard, the rule is "*Ignorantia juris non excusat*", i.e., ignorance of law is no excuse. Following this principle, Section 21 declares that "A contract is not voidable because it was caused by a mistake as to any law enforce in India." A party cannot be allowed to get any relief on the ground that it had done a particular act in ignorance of law.

Thus, where 'A' and 'B' make a contract grounded on the erroneous belief that a particular debt barred by the Indian Law of Limitation, the contract is not avoidable.

A mistake of law is, therefore, no excuse, and the contract cannot be avoided (Solle v. Butcher[97]).

(2) Mistake of law of a foreign country

The above maxim that 'ignorance of law is no excuse' applies only to the law of the country and not to foreign law. The mistake of foreign law is to be treated as a mistake of fact. Section 21 reads, "A mistake as to a law not enforce in India has the same effect as a mistake of fact."

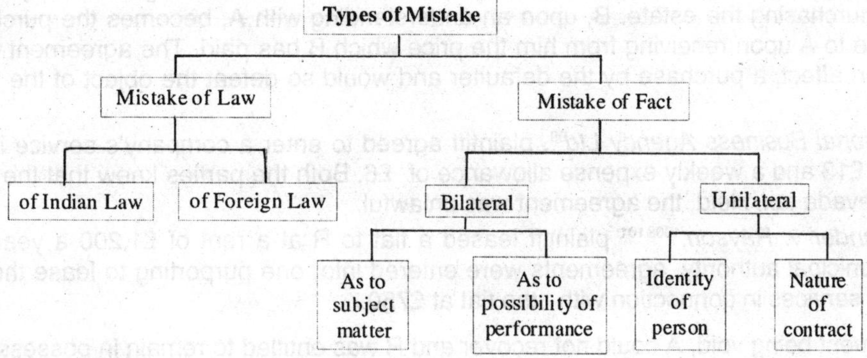

Figure No. 1

Remedies for Mistake

(i) If the consent is caused by mistake of both the parties, then agreement is void (Section 20)

(ii) Where the contract is void on account of mistake, any person who has received it or make compensation for it to the person from whom he received it. (Section 65)

Note: Whatever one party is playing fraud, but the other has been induced to enter into a contract under mistake, the case would be decided on the basis of mistake.

Legality of Object

An agreement will not be enforceable if its object or the consideration is unlawful. Section 23 of the Contract Act states that the object or consideration of an agreement is unlawful in the following cases —

(i) where it is forbidden by law, or

(ii) where it defeats the provisions of any law, or

(iii) where it is fraudulent, or

(iv) where it is injurious to another person or his property, or

(v) where it is immoral or

(vi) where it is opposed to public policy.

(i) Where it is forbidden by Law

If the object or the consideration of an agreement is the doing of an act forbidden by law, the agreement is void. An act is forbidden by law when it is punishable by the Criminal Law of the country or when it is prohibited by special legislation or regulations made by a competent authority under power derived from the Legislative.

Examples —

(a) A promises to drop a prosecution which he has instituted against B for robbery, and B promises to restore the value of the things taken. The agreement is void, as its object is unlawful [Illustration (h) to Section 23]

(b) In a case *Velu Payachi v. Siva Sooriam*[98], a partnership entered into for the purpose of doing business in arrack on a licence granted only to one of the partners, is void ab-initio whether the partnership was entered into before the licence was granted or afterwards as it involved a transfer of licence, which is forbidden and penalised by the Akbari Act and the rules thereunder.

(c) In *Srinivas v. Raja Ram Mohan*, a loan granted to the guardian of a minor to enable him to celebrate the minor's marriage in contravention of the Child Marriage Restraint Act is illegal and cannot be recovered.

(ii) Where it defeats the provisions of any law

Sometimes, the object or consideration of an agreement is not directly forbidden by the law. But it is of such a nature that, if permitted, it would defeat the provision of law. In such cases, the object or consideration is unlawful. The agreement with such an object or consideration is unlawful and void.

Examples

(a) A's estate is sold for arrears of revenue under the provisions of an Act of the legislature, by which the defaulter is prohibited from purchasing the estate. B, upon an understanding with A, becomes the purchaser and agrees to convey the estate to A upon receiving from him the price which B has paid. The agreement is void, as it renders the transaction, in effect, a purchase by the defaulter and would so defeat the object of the law [Illustration (i) to Section 23].

(b) In *Napier v. National Business Agency Ltd*[99], plaintiff agreed to enter a company's service in consideration of a weekly wage of £13 and a weekly expense allowance of £6. Both the parties knew that the expense, allowance was a device to evade tax. Held, the agreement was unlawful.

(c) In a case, *Alexander v. Rayson*,[100&101] plaintiff leased a flat to R at a rent of £1,200 a year. With the object of deceiving the municipal authority, agreements were entered into, one purporting to lease the flat at £450 a year and the other for services in connection with the flat at £750.

Held, the agreement being void, A could not recover and R was entitled to remain in possession of the flat for the remainder of the terms of the lease.

The following are held if permitted, it would defeat the provisions of any law:

(a) An insolvent debtor agreeing to pay in full to one creditor in preference to other creditor (void under Insolvency Law).

(b) A person agreeing to give annuity to the natural fatter of the person who is taken in adoption by him. (void under Hindu Law).

(c) A landlord agreement to pay consideration to a tenant to induce him to vacate possession of his premises (Illegal under Rent Restriction Control Act).

(d) An agreement by a debtor not to raise the plea of limitation (void under Limitation Act).

(iii) Where it is fraudulent

An agreement which is made for a fraudulent purpose is void. Thus, an agreement with a view to defraud other is void.

The word 'fraud' means (a) the quality of being deceitful (b) the criminal deception (c) the using of false representations to obtain an unjust advantage or to injure the rights or interests of another.

Examples —

(a) A, being an agent for a landed proprietor, agrees for money, without the knowledge of his principal, to obtain for B a lease of land belonging to his principal. The agreement between A and B is void as it implies a fraud by concealment by A, on his principal [Illustration (g) to Section 23].

(b) In a case *Scott v. Brown Doering Mc Nab*[102], the plaintiff entered into a contract with a broker that he should purchase the shares of a particular company at a premium so as to induce a public belief that the shares were worthy of being bought at a premium. Later, he discovered that the broker had sold his own shares to him and had bought no shares in the market at all. He applied to the court for rescission for the fraud committed on him.

No relief was allowed to him. The object of the agreement was to commit a fraud on the public. The sale object of the purchase was to cheat and mislead the public.

(c) In *Sujan Singh v. Mokham Chand*[103], an agreement between two bidders not to bid against each other with an understanding that the successful bidder would give half the property to the other has been held to be not against public policy.

(iv) where it is injurious to another person or his property

Any agreement between two person to injure the person or property of another is unlawful. If the object of an agreement is such that it involves or implies injury to the person or property of another, the agreement is unlawful. Thus, an agreement to pull down another's house is unlawful. The word 'injury' means criminal or wrongful harm. Loss which ensures to a trader as a result of competition by a rival trader is not injury within the meaning of this clause.

Examples —

(a) *W.H Smith and Sons v. C Clington,*[104] A requested B an editor of a Newspaper to publish a defamatory article (Libel) against C and promised to indemnity B against the consequences arising from the libel published. Held, that the agreement is void as it involves injury to C and the editor can recover the amount from A.

(b) *Ram Saroop v. Bansi Mandar,*[105] B borrowed Rs. 100 from L and executed a bond promising to work for L without pay for a period of two years. In case of default, B was to pay interest (at a very exorbitant rate) and the principal sum at once. Held, the contract was void as it involved injury to the person of B.

(c) *Gherulal Parekh v. Mahadeo,*[106] an agreement between some persons to purchase shares in a company with a view to induce other persons to believe, contrary to the fact, that there is a bonafide market for the shares is void.

(v) Where it is immoral

Sometimes, the object or consideration of an agreement is such that it is regarded as immoral. In such cases, the object or the consideration is unlawful. The agreement with such an object or consideration is unlawful, and void. The term 'Immoral' depends upon the standard of 'morality' prevailing at a particular place and time. But certain acts have been regarded as immoral since times immemorial, e.g., interference with marital relations.

Examples —

(a) In *Baivijli v. Nansa Nagar*[107], a married woman was given money to enable her to obtain divorce from her husband and then to marry the lender could not recover the money.

(b) A agrees to let her daughter to B for concubinage (state of living together as man and wife without being married). The agreement is unlawful being immoral.

(c) A, who is B's mukhtiar promises to exercise his influence as such with B in favour of C, and C promises to pay Rs. 1000 to A. The agreement is void, because it is immoral.

However, agreement for immediate separation between a husband and wife, both in England and in India, are enforceable. The principle underlying this is presentation of the peace and reputation of families. Similarly agreements in respect of post separation are also valid.

(vi) where it is opposed to public policy

An agreement is unlawful if the court regards it as opposed to public policy. The term "Public Policy" in its broadest sense means that sometimes the courts will, on considerations of public interest, refuse to enforce a contract. An agreement is said to be opposed to public policy when it is against public interest, i.e., when it is harmful to the public welfare. The following agreements have been held to be opposed to public policy:

(1) Trading with enemy,

(2) Agreements interfering with course of justice,

(3) Agreements in restraint of legal proceedings,

(4) Agreements for stifling prosecution,

(5) Agreements tending to an abuse of legal process,

(6) Agreements to oust the jurisdiction of courts,

(7) Agreements to vary periods of limitation,

(8) Agreements for the sale of Public Offices,

(9) Agreements to influence election to public offices,

(10) Agreements tending to create interest opposed to duty,

(11) Agreements tending to create monopolies,

(12) Agreements in restraint of parental rights,

(13) Agreements restricting personal liberty,

(14) Agreements in restraint of marriage,

(15) Marriage brokerage agreements,

(16) Agreements interfering with marital duties,

(17) Agreements in fraud of creditors,

(18) Agreements to defraud revenue authorities,

(19) Agreements in restraint of profession,

(20) Agreements in restraint of trade.

CHAPTER 29

Agreements Declared Void (Section 26-30)

The Indian Contract Act 1872 declares certain agreements to be void. A void agreement is one which is without legal effects. A void agreement does not create any legal rights and obligations. A void agreement is one which is not enforceable by law [Sec. 2(g)]. Such agreements are *void ab initio* (i.e. void from the very beginning) and without any legal effect. Following are the various types of void agreements. These are contained in Sections 11, 20 23 to 30 and 56 of the Indian Contract Act.

(1) Agreements by persons who are not competent to contract (Section 11)

(2) Agreements under a mutual mistake of fact mention to the agreement (Section 20)

(3) Agreement with unlawful consideration or object (Sec. 23)

(4) Agreements, the consideration or object of which is unlawful in parts (section 24)

(5) Agreements without consideration (Sec. 25)

(6) Agreements in restraints of marriage (Sec.26)

(7) Agreements in restraints of Trade (Sec. 27)

(8) Agreements in restraints of Legal proceeding (Sec. 28)

(9) Agreements the meaning of which is uncertain (Sec. 29)

(10) Wagering agreements (Section 30)

(11) Agreements to do impossible acts (Sec. 56)

Void agreements are explained as below:

Agreements Against Public Policy

The term 'Public Policy' is not capable of being defined with any degree of precision because 'Public policy', in its nature, is highly uncertain and fluctuating. It keeps on varying with the habits and fashions of the day, with the growth of commerce and usage of trade. In simple words, however, it may be said that an agreement which conflicts with morals of the time and contravenes any established interest of society, it is void as being against public policy. Thus, an agreement which tends to be injurious to the public or against the public good is void as being opposed to Public.

According to F. Pollock, "Agreements may offend against the public policy, or tend to the prejudice of the state in time of war (trading with the enemies etc.), by tending to the perversion or abuse of municipal justice, (stifling prosecution, champerty, maintenance) or in private life by attempting to impose inconvenient and unreasonable restrictions on the free choice of individuals in marriage or their liberty to exercise any lawful trading or calling."

In the words of Burrough J in a case *Richardson v. Mellish*,[108] "Public policy was a very unruly horse and when once you get astride it you never know where it will carry out."

In Janson v. *Driefontein Consolidated Mines Ltd*,[109] Lord Davey observed that "Public policy is always an unsafe and treacherous ground for legal decisions ...... and that categories of public policy are closed, and that no court can invent a new head of public policy." But this represents a very rigid and narrow view. According to this 'narrow view' school courts cannot create new heads of Public Policy.

According to the current school of thought, known as the "broad view" school, the principles governing public policy must be and are capable on proper occasion, of expansion or modification. Danckwerts, L.J. in Nagle v. Fielden[110] observed: "The law relating to Public Policy cannot remain immutable. It must change with the passage of time. The wind of change blows upon it".

The Indian also adopt the broad view. It has been held Ratanchand Hirachand v. Askar Nawaz Jung[111], that in a modern progressive society with fast changing social values and concepts, new heads of public policy need to be evolved whenever necessary. Law cannot afford to remain static. It has, of necessary, to keep pace with the progress of society and judges are under an obligation to evolve new techniques to meet the new conditions and concepts.

The following words of Subba Rao J (as he then was) in *Gherulal v Mahedeo Das*[112] enshrine the present position of the Doctrine of public policy in India.

"The principles have been crystallised under different heads and though it is permissible for courts to expound and apply them to different situations, it should only be invoked in clear and incontestable cases of harm to the public, though the heads are not closed and though theoretically it may be permissible to evolve a new head under exceptional circumstances of a changing world, it advisable in the interest of stability of society not to make any attempt to discover new heads in these days."

Some of the agreements which are, or which have been held to be opposed to public policy and are unlawful are as follows:

1. Agreements of trading with enemy

An agreement made with an alien enemy in time of war is illegal on the ground of public policy. This is based upon one of the two reasons: either that the further performance of the agreement could involve commercial intercourse with the enemy, or that the continued existence of agreement would confer upon the enemy an immediate or future benefit, contracts which are entered into before the outbreak of war are either suspended or dissolved according as the intention of the parties can or cannot be carried out by postponing performance till the end of hostilities.

2. Agreement to Commit a Crime

Where the consideration in an agreement is to commit a crime, the agreement is opposed to public policy. The court will not enforce such an agreement. Likewise an agreement to indemnity a person against consequences of his criminal act is opposed to public policy and hence unenforceable.

Examples

(a) A promises to indemnify B in consideration of his beating C. The agreement is opposed to public policy.

(b) In a case, *W.H. Smith and Sons v. Clinton*, A promises to indemnify a firm of printers and publishers of a paper against the consequences of any libel which it might publish in its paper. Held, A's promise could not be enforced in a law court where the firm was compelled to pay damages for a published libel.

3. Agreement which interfere with administration of justice

An agreement the object of which is to interfere with the administration of justice is unlawful, being opposed to public policy. It may take any of the following forms:

(a) Interference with the course of justice

An agreement the object of which is to interfere with the administration of justice is unlawful. Thus an agreement for using improper influence of any kind with the judges or officers of justice is unlawful. An agreement to delay the execution of a decree, and promise to give money to induce a person to give false evidence, have been held void. An agreement to perform "Puja" to secure success to the defendant in a litigation was held void.[114]

(b) Stifling prosecution

It is in public interest that if a person has committed a crime, he must be prosecuted and punished. Hence, an agreement not to prosecute an offender or to withdraw a pending prosecution is void if the offence is of public nature. Such agreements are called agreements to stifle prosecution. The law is "you cannot make a trade of felong. You cannot convert a crime into a source of profit."

Thus, where A promises to drop a prosecution which he has instituted against B for robbery and B promises to restore the stolen property, the agreement is unlawful.

But, where a compromise agreement is made before my complaint is filed, it would not amount to stifling prosecution, even if it is implemented after the filing of a complaint which is then withdrawn. This was pointed out by the Supreme Court in *Ouseph Poule v. Catholic Union Bank.*[115]

A bank found that the goods in a godown, which was pledged to it against a loan, were either fraudulently overvalued or withdrawn in collusion with bank officials. The borrowers agreed to make up for the deficiency by hypothecating more property. Some delay having taken place in the hypothecation, the bank filed a complaint which was withdrawn after the hypothecation was completed. The agreement was held to be valid.

Maintenance and Champerty

'Maintenance' is an agreement to assistance, financial or otherwise, to another to enable him to bring or defend legal proceedings when the person giving assistance has got no legal interest of his own in the subject-matter. For example, A offers to pay B Rs. 2,000/- if B will sue C. A's motive is to annoy C. This agreement between A and B is a maintenance agreement.

'Champerty' is a bargain whereby one party is to assist another in recovering property and in turn, is to share in the proceeds of the action. For example, A agrees to pay the expenses if B sues C, and B agrees to give A one-half of any proceeds received by B as a result of the said suit. This is a champertous agreement. Under the English Law, both these agreements are void. The Indian law, however, does not make them absolutely void. If the object of a contract is just to assist the other party in making a reasonable claim arising out of a contract and then to have a fair share in the profit, the contract is valid.

4. Agreements in restraint of marriage

According to section 26 of the Contract Act, "Every agreement in restraint of the marriage of any person, other than a minor, is void." This is because the law regards marriage and married status as the right of every individual.

Examples

(a) In, *Lowe v. Peers*[116], defendant promised to marry plaintiff only and none else and to pay him a sum of Rs. 2,000/- if he married someone else. Defendant married X. Held plaintiff could not recover the sum agreed as the agreement was in restraint of marriage.

(b) In *Maheswar Das v. Sakhi Dei*[117], the consideration under a sale deed was for marriage expenses of a minor girl aged 12 years. Held the sale was a void transaction, being opposed to public policy.

5. Marriage brokerage or brocage agreements

An agreement to procure the marriage of a person in consideration of a sum of money is called marriage brokerage contract. Such agreement are void being opposed to public policy. Accordingly, dowry is marriage brokerage and hence unlawful and void.

Examples

(a) In *Venkatakrishna v. Venkatachalam*[118], a sum of money was agreed to be paid to the father in consideration of his giving his daughter in marriage. Held, such a promise amounted to a marriage brokerage contract and was void.

(b) In *Vaidyanathan v. Ganagrazu*[119], a purohit was promised a certain sum of money in consideration of procuring a second wife for the defendant, it was held that the promise was opposed to public policy and thus void.

6. Agreements in restraint of Legal Proceedings

Section 28 which deals with these agreements renders void two kinds of agreements, viz..

(a) Agreements in restricting enforcement of rights —

An agreement which wholly or partially prohibits any party from enforcing his rights under or in respect of any contract is void to that extent.

(b) Agreements curtailing period of limitation —

Agreements which curtail the period of limitation prescribed by the law of limitation are void because their object is to defeat the provisions of law.

An agreement purporting to oust the jurisdiction of courts is contrary to public policy. But an agreement between two or more parties to refer to arbitration any disputes which have arisen or which may arise between them is perfectly valid.

7. Agreement in restraint of trade

An agreement which interferes with an individual's right to engage himself in any lawful trade, occupation or profession is called an "agreement in restraint of trade". It is in the interest of the community that every man should be at liberty to work for himself of the fruit of his labour, skill or talent by any contract that he enters into. He should also be at liberty to take up any trade or business and use his skill or talent by any contract that he enters into. He should also be at liberty to take up any trade or business and use his skill to the best of his capacity.

Where an agreement is challenged on the ground of its being in restraint of trade, the onus is upon the party supporting the contract to show that the restraint is reasonably necessary to protect his interests. Once this onus is discharged, the onus of showing that the restraint is nevertheless injurious to the public is upon the party attacking the contract. (*Niranjan Shanker v. Century Spinning and Mfg. Co. Ltd.*[120])

Examples

(a) In case *Shaikh Kalu v. Ram Saran Bhagat*[121], out of 30 makers of combs in the city of Patna, 29 agreed with defendant to supply him and to no one else all their output. Defendant was free to reject the goods if he found no market for them. Held, the agreement was void.

(b) In another case, *Madhav v. Raj Coomar*[122], A, who was carrying on business of brazier (Pan for holding burning coal), promised another person B, carrying on a similar trade in the same locality, to stop his business in consideration of B giving him a certain amount which he had advanced to his workers. B subsequent to A's closing the business, refused to pay. A filed a suit for the recovery of the amount. Held, the agreement was void.

In England, originally, all agreements in restraint of trade were void. But now, the rule is that though total restraint will be bad, reasonable restraint will be enforceable. In *Nordenfelt v. Maxim Nordenfelt* etc. Co.,[123] the House of Lords held that "the real test for determining the validity of agreements in restraint of trade was, whether the restraint imposed was reasonable, for good consideration, not prejudicial to the interests of the public, and not more onerous than necessary for the protection of the party imposing the restraint".

In India, the law on the subject is contained in section 27 of the Indian Contract Act 1872, which provides that "every agreement in restraint of trade is to that extent void." The reason for this being that not only a person is restricted in his choice but the society as a whole suffers is skills of individuals are permitted to go waste.

Thus, in India, all agreements in restraint of trade, whether general or partial, qualified or unqualified, are void. It is, therefore, not open to the courts in India to enter into any question of reasonableness or otherwise of the restraint (*Khemchand v. Dayaldas*[124]).

Exceptions

The following are the exceptions to the rule that "an agreement in restraint of trade is void".

1. Sale of Goodwill

An agreement between seller and buyer of goodwill, that the seller will not carry on similar business within specified local limits so long as the buyer or his representatives carry on the business is valid, provided in the opinion of the court, the limits are reasonable. Reasonableness of restrictionswill depend on many factors e.g. (i) the area in which the goodwill is effectively enjoyed, (ii) the price paid for it, (iii) the nature of the business, and (iv) the time of restrictions. (Section 27 exception 1).

2. Exceptions under Partnership Act

The Indian Partnership Act, 1932 also contains certain exceptions as follows:

(i) Existing Partner's Agreements

Section 11(2) of the Indian Partnership Act 1932 provides that an agreement between existing partners of a firm may provide that a partner shall not carry on any business other than that of the firm while he is a partner.

(ii) Agreement with outgoing partners

Section 36(2) of the Indian Partnership Act 1932 provides that an outgoing partner may agree with his partners not to carry on a business similar to that of the firm within a specified period or within specified local limits.

Notwithstanding anything contained in Section 27 of the Contract Act, as such agreement shall be valid if the restriction imposed are reasonable.

(iii) Agreement upon Dissolution

Partners may, upon or in anticipation of the dissolution of the firm, make an agreement that some or all of them will not carry on a business similar to that of the firm within a specified period or within specified local limits (Section 54 of the Indian Partnership Act 1932).

(iv) Sale of firm's Goodwill

Any partner may, upon the sale of the goodwill of a firm, make agreement that such partner will not carry on any business similar to that of the firm within specified period or within in specific local limits such agreement shall be valid if the restrictions imposed are reasonable (Section 55(3)of the Indian Partnership Act 1932).

3.Service Contract

Sometimes an employed by the terms of his service agreement is prevented from accepting—

(i) any other engagement during his employment

and/or

(ii) a similar engagement after the termination of his services.

A regards the first restraint, it is void and not is in restraint of trade these days it is a common practice to appoint management trainees. A lot of time, money and energy is spent in training the selected candidates in the management techniques. So, it will be a waste on the part of such organizations if these persons left for other organizations immediately after training. Therefore, a service bond is normally got signed whereby the trainee agrees to serve the organisation for a stipulated period. Such agreements, if reasonable, do not amount, to restraint of trade and hence are enforceable.

Examples

(a) Doctors are usually barred from private practice during term of their employment in hospitals.
(b) Where an employee undertaken to serve his employer for a period of 3 years but leaves the service after one year, he may be asked to abide by the agreement. (*Deshpande v. Arvind Mills*[125]).

As regards the second restraint, it is void if its object is merely to restrain competition by an employee in his employer's business. Therefore, a restraint on an employee not to engage in a similar business, or not to accept a similar engagement, after the termination of his services, is void.

In *Brahamputra Tea Company v. Searth*[126], it was held that an agreement restraining an employee from taking service or engaging in any similar business for a period of 5 years after the termination of his service was void.

If a restraint imposed on the employee is to operate after the expiry of the period of his service it shall *prima facie* be void. (*Krishria Murgai v. Superintendence Co. of India*[127])

Similarly, a restraint on an actor that he would not act in any theatre other than that of the employer during his tour of India was held to be void, being in restraint of trade (*Cohen v. Wilkie*[128])

If a restraint is intended to protect an employer against an employee making use of trade secrets learned by him in the course of his employment, the restrain is valid provided it is not for any other purpose also.

Examples—

(a) A was chiefly engaged in making glass bottles. B, his works manager, was instructed in certain confidential methods concerning correct mixture of gas and air in the furnaces. B agreed that during the five years after the termination of his service, he would not carry on in the United Kingdom, or be interested in, glass bottle manufacture. Held, A was entitled to protection and that the restraint was reasonable (*Forster and Sons Ltd. v. Suggett*[129])
(b) A servant copied the names and addresses of his employer's customers for use after he left his employment. Held, he could be restrained from using the list (*Robb v. Green*[130]).
(c) H employed A on a highly skilled work with access to the manufacturing data. In his spare time A worked for B on a similar work in competition with H. Held A was in breach of his duty and could be restrained from working for B. (*Hivae Ltd. v. Park Royal*[131])

However, an employer cannot prevent an employee earning his living by the exercise of his skill and the use of his knowledge.

Example — A, a tailor, employed as his assistant L under a contract by which L agreed on the termination of his employment not to carry on business as a tailor within 16 kms. of A's establishment. Held, the agreement was void (*Attwood v. Lamont*[132]).

4. Trade Combinations

A voluntary agreement among the members of the Trade Associations or Chambers of Commerce etc., to regulate their areas of operation or to fix prices of goods and commodities is not void under section 27. Nowadays, traders carry on their trade in an organised way. There are combinations of manufactures, grain merchants etc. Such combinations bring about standardised goods, fixed prices and eliminate cut throat competition. Thus, regulations as to the opening and closing of business in a market, licensing of traders, mode of dealings etc. are not invalid, even if there is incidental diminution of freedom of trade.

Example — An agreement between certain ice manufacturing companies not to sell ice below a stated price and to divide the profits in a certain proportion is not void under Section 27. Such agreements are neither in restraint of trade nor opposed to public policy (*S.B. Fraser and Co. v. Bombay Ice Mfg. Co.*[133]).

But a combination which tends to create monopoly and which is against public interest is void. Similarly, where the intention in such an agreement is to raise prices to an unreasonable extent, the agreement would be void under section 27. Same is the case when two firms enter into an agreement to avoid competition (*Jai Ram v. Kahna Ram*[134]).

5. Exclusive Agency

The principal may restrain his agent from dealing in goods of any other rival. For example, Reliance Textiles Co. Ltd. may grant a selling agency to Maharaja and Company on the condition that it will not deal in the goods of any other manufacturer.

6. Agreements in restraint of Parental rights

A father and in his absence the mother, is the legal guardian of his/her minor child. This right of guardianship cannot be bartered away by any agreement. If he enters into any such agreement, it shall be void on the ground of Public Policy.

Example

A father having two minor sons agreed to transfer their guardianship in favour of Mrs Annie Besant and also agreed not to revoke the transfer. Subsequently he filed a suit for recovery of the boys and a declaration that he was the rightful guardian, the court held that he had the right to revoke his authority and get back the children (*Giddu Narayanish v. Mrs. Annie Besant*[135]).

7. Agreements restricting personal liberty

Agreements which unduly restrict the personal freedom of the parties to it are void as being against Public Policy.

Example

A debtor agreed with his money-lender that he would not, without the lender's written consent, leave his job, or borrow money or dispose of his property or change his residence. Held, the agreement was void. (*Horwood v. Millar's Timber and Trading Co.*[136])

8. Agreements for the sale of Public Offices and Titles

Traffic by way of sale in Public Offices and appointments obviously tends to the prejudice of the public service by interfering with the selection of the best qualified persons. Such sales, are, therefore, unlawful and void.

Examples

(a) Where A promises to pay a sum to B in order to induce him to retire so as to provide room for A's appointment to the public office held by B, the agreement is void. (*Saminathag v. Muthusami*[137])

(b) The secretary of a college promised Col. Parkinson that if he made a large donation to the college, he would secure a knighthood for him. Held, the agreement was against public policy and thus void. (*Parkinson College of Ambulance Ltd.*[138])

Agreements the meaning of which is uncertain (Section 29)

Agreements, the meaning of which is not certain, or capable of being made certain, are void.

Illustrations

(a) A agrees to sell to B "a hundred tons of oil". There is nothing whatever to show what kind of oil was intended. The agreement is void for uncertainty.

(b) A agrees to sell to B one hundred tons of oil of specified description, known as an article of commerce. There is no uncertainty here to make the agreement void.

(c) A, who is a dealer in coconut oil only, agrees to sell to B "one hundred tons of oil". The nature of A's trade affords an indication of the meaning of the words, and A has entered into a contract for the sale of one hundred tons of coconut oil.

(d) A agrees to sell to B "all the grain in my granary at "Ram Nagar". There is no uncertainty to make the agreement void.

(e) A agrees to sell to B "one thousand mounds of rice at a price to be fixed by C". As the price is capable of being made certain, there is no uncertainty here to make the agreement void.

(f) A agrees to sell to B "my white horse for rupees five hundred or rupees one thousand." There is nothing to show which of the two prices was to be given. The agreement is void.

An interesting illustration is *Gathing v. Lynn*[139], a horse was bought for a certain price coupled with a promise to give £5 more if the horse proved lucky. The agreement was held to be void for uncertainty.

In *Pushpabala v. L.I.C. of India*,[140] A agreed to pay a certain sum when he was able to pay. Held, the agreement was void for uncertainty.

Wagering Agreements

According to section 30 of the Indian Contract Act 1872 "agreements by way of wager are void. The section does not define 'wager."

Definition

The section does not define 'wager' Sir William Anson defines 'wager' as a promise to give money or money's worth upon the determination or ascertainment of an uncertain event.

Lockburn C.J. defined it as "A contract by 'A' to pay money to 'B' on the happening of a given event in consideration of B's promise to pay money to 'A' on the event not happening". Thus, a wagering agreement is an agreement under which money or money's worth is payable, by one person to another on the happening or non-happening of a future, uncertain event.

The most illustrative definition of wager is that given by Hawkins J. in *Carlill v. Carbolic Smoke Ball Co.*[141].

"A wagering contract is one by which two persons, professing to hold opposite views touching the issue of a future uncertain event, mutually agree that, dependent on the determination of that event, on shall pay or hand over to him, a sum of money or other stake, neither of the contracting parties having any other interest in that contract than the sum or stake he will so win or lose, there being no other real consideration for the making of such contract by either of the parties. It is essential to a wagering contract that each party may under it either win or lose, whether he will win or lose being dependent on the issue of the event, and, therefore, remaining uncertain until that issue is known. If either of the parties may win but cannot lose, it is not a wagering contract."

Examples

(a) A and B bet as to whether it would rain on a particular day or not. A promising to pay Rs. 100 to B if it rained, and B promising an equal amount to A, if it did not. This agreement is wager.

(b) A and B agree to deal with the differences in prices of a particular commodity. Such an agreement is a wager.

Essentials of Wagering agreement

(1) Uncertain event

(2) Mutual Chances of gain or loss

(3) Neither party to have control over the event

(4) No other interest in the event and

(5) The promise must be to pay money or money's worth.

(1) Uncertain Event

The promise must be conditional on an event happening or not happening. A wager generally contemplates a future event, but it may also relate to a post event provided the parties are not aware of its result or the time of its happening.

(2) Mutual Chances of gain or loss

The second essential feature is that upon the determination of the contemplated even each party should stand to win or loss. If there are no such mutual chances of gain or loss, there is no wager. Thus, in Babasaheb v. Rajaram.[142]

Two wrestlers agreed to play a wrestling match on condition that the party failing to appear on the day fixed was to forfeit Rs. 500 to the opposite party, and the winner was to receive Rs. 1,125 out of the gate money. The defendant failed to appear in the ring and the plaintiff sued him for Rs. 500.

It was held that the agreement could not be looked upon as one of wagering in law. "It is of the essence of wager that each side should stand to win or lose according to the result of the uncertain event." In the present case neither side stood to lose according to the result of wrestling match, "The stakes did not come out of the pockets of the parties, but had to be paid from the gate money provided by the public." The prize would not have been recoverable if it was to be subscribed by the competitors themselves.

A chit fund does not come within the scope of 'wager'. It is no doubt true that some chance gain may come to some of the members, but none of them stands to lose his money for his periodical deposits are refunded to him at the end of the scheme (*Narayan Ayyangar v. K Vallachami Ambalam*[143]).

(3) Neither party to have control over the event

Neither party should have control over the happening or non-happening of the event one way or the other. If one of the parties has the event in his own hands, the transaction lacks an essential ingredient of a wager.

(4) No other interest in the event

Neither party should have any interest in the happening or non happening of the event other than the sum or stake he will win or lose. Thus, an agreement is not a wager if the party to whom money is promised on the occurrence of an event has an interest in its non-occurrence. That is why a contract of insurance is not a wagering agreement.

(5) Promise to pay money or money's worth

The wagering agreement must contain a promise to pay money or money's worth.

Lotteries

A lottery, which is a game of chance, is a wagering agreement. An agreement to buy a ticket for a lottery is also a wagering agreement. Section 29-A of the Indian Penal Code 1860 provides that anyone who keeps any office or place for the purpose of drawing any lottery (Other than a State Lottery of a lottery authorised by the State Government) shall be punished with imprisonment for a term which may extend to six months or with fine or with both. Where a wagering transaction amounts to a lottery, it is illegal as per section 29-A of the I.P.C. In Sir *Darabji Tata v. Edward F. Lance,*[144] where the Government of India had sanctioned a lottery, the court held that the permission granted by the government will not have the effect of overriding Sec.30 of the Indian Contract Act and making such a lottery legal. Its only effect was that the persons responsible for running the lottery **would not be punishable under the Indian Penal Code.**

However, in *H. Anraj v. Govt. of Tamil Nadu,*[145] the Supreme Court upheld lotteries with the prior permission of the Government as legal, thereby conferring upon the winner of a lottery, a right to receive the prize and the sale of lotteries subject to payment of sales-tax. Supreme Court held that a sale of lottery ticket confers on the purchaser thereof two rights (a) a right to participate in the draw and (b) a right to claim a prize contingent upon his being successful in the draw.

Insurance Contract

Contract of insurance are not wagering agreements even though the payment of money by the insurer may depend upon a future uncertain event. Contracts of insurance differ from the wagering agreements in the following respects:

(i) It is only person possessing an insurable interest that it is permitted to insure life or property, and not any person, as in the case of a wager.
(ii) In the case of fire and marine insurance, only the actual loss suffered by the party is paid by the company, and not the full amount for which the property is insured. Even in the case of life insurance, the amount payable is fixed only because of the difficulty in estimating the loss caused by the death of the assured in terms of money, but the underlying idea is only indemnification.
(iii) Contracts of insurance are regarded as beneficial to the public and are, therefore, encouraged. Wagering agreements, on the other hand, are considered to be against public policy.
(iv) A contract of insurance is based on scientific and actuarial calculation or risks. A wagering agreement is just a gamble.

Exceptions

The following transactions have been held not to be wagers:

1. Horse Race

The section does not render void a subscription or contribution, or an agreement to subscribe or contribute, toward any plate, prize or sum of money, of the value or amount of five hundred rupees or upwards to the winner or winners of any horse races (Exception to Sec. 30).

2. Crossword Competitions and cross-word puzzle

A crossword competition involving a good measure of skill for its successful solution. A crossword puzzle in which solution can be made by only one word is not a game of chance but it is game of skill. A crossword competition is not a wager since it involves skill. But in *Coleys v. Odham's press,*[146] it was held that a crossword puzzle in which prizes depend upon correspondence of the competitor's solution with a previously prepared solution kept with the editor of a newspaper is a lottery and therefore, a wagering transactions.

3. Sports Competitions

Competitions such as athletics, wrestling, indoor games of any type (Carom, Judo, Billiard, Table tennis, playing Cards etc.) Boxing, Football, cricket, Hockey, etc, are not games of chance. It is decided by skill or judgement. Therefore, competition is not a wager.

Thus, an agreement to enter into a wrestling contest in which the winner was to be rewarded by the entire sale proceeds of tickets, was held not to be wagering contract. (*Babalalteb v. Rajaram*[147])

4. Contract of Insurance

Contract of insurance is not a wagering one. In this contract, the insured has insurable interest in the property or life. The insurer promises to pay a certain sum of money on the death of insured provided the insured pays the premium regularly to the insurance company.

Effects of Wagering Transactions

A wagering agreement being void cannot be enforced in any Court of Law. Section 30 expressly declares that "no suit shall be brought for recovering anything alleged to be won on any wager, or entrusted to any person to abide the result of any game of other uncertain event on which any wager is made". Thus, the amount won on a wager cannot be recovered. In a case before the Calcutta High Court, *Badridas Kothari v. Meghraj Kothari*[148], a promissory note given on a wagering debt was held to be not enforceable.

Illegal Agreements

The term 'illegal agreement' may be defined as the agreement which is expressly or impliedly prohibited by law, e.g., by Indian Penal Code or by some special legislation etc. Thus, an agreement to commit a murder, or to publish a libel (a defamatory statement) is an illegal agreement. Moreover, the agreement, which are immoral or opposed to public policy, are also illegal. As a matter of fact, the illegal agreements are void and do not confer any rights and obligations on the parties concerned. As a result of this, they are not enforceable in a Court of Law.

Illustrations:

(i) A, B, and C entered into an agreement to carry on the business of smuggling and agreed, to divide the profits in equal shares. It is an illegal agreement as to smuggling is forbidden by law.
(ii) A agreed with B, a prostitute to give her certain ornaments on hire. A knew that B had to use those ornaments in the furtherance of her trade. B failed to pay the hire charges, and A filed a suit for the recovery of the same. It was held that the agreement was illegal and void. And thus, A could not recover anything from B.

Effect of Illegal Agreements

The effects of illegal agreements may be discussed under tow heads —

(i) Effects on Main Transaction and

(ii) Effects on Collateral Transaction

(i) Effects on Main Transaction

An illegal agreement is void ab initio (i.e., void from the very beginning) and without any legal effects. As a matter of fact, the illegal agreement is non-existent, and the law will not permit the parties to enforce any right under it. This is so because the law treats the illegal agreement as if it had not been made at all. Therefore, no remedy is available to either party. Thus, nothing can be recovered under the illegal agreement. And if something has been paid by any party, that party cannot get it back from the other party.

The general principle of law that no suit can be filed in respect of an illegal agreement, is based on the following two maxims:

(a) From an illegal cause, no action arises. Thus, the Courts refuse to help either party. Moreover, the law discourages people from entering into an illegal agreement which arise from an illegal cause.

(b) In case of equal guilt, the defendant is in a better position. Thus the party, who has paid some money against an illegal agreement, cannot get it back. In other words, the defendant can keep whatever has been received by him against the illegal agreement. This is because of the fact, that the Courts do not help either party.

(ii) Effects on Collateral Transactions

Collateral transaction is an incidental or parallel transaction. In other words, it is the transaction which is subsidiary to the main transaction, e.g., the loan taken for the purpose of carrying an illegal business such as smuggling. The collateral transaction, to an illegal agreement, also becomes illegal. Consequently, a collateral transaction is void and cannot be enforced in a Court of law. It may be noted that even if the collateral transaction is lawful in itself, but it will be treated as illegal and void.

Exceptions

The maxim, "From an illegal cause no action arises" subject to the following exceptions:

(a) Illegal purpose not carried out

Where the contract which is illegal remains executory, i.e., the illegal purpose has not been carried out in whole or in part, either party to it is allowed on opportunity for repentance and is permitted to recover money paid or goods delivered in respect of the contract. It is, however, necessary that the party seeking to recover must withdraw from the transaction before the illegal purpose is executed and the withdrawal should be genuine.

(b) Where the parties to an illegal contract the less guilty party may be able to recover money paid or properly transferred under following cases —

(i) where that plaintiff has been the victim of fraud or oppression at the hands of the defendant, he may, upon proof of such fraud or oppression, recover anything paid or delivered to the defendant under the contract.

(ii) where the contract is rendered illegal by a statute in the interests of a particular class of persons of whom the plaintiff is one.

Illegal and Void Agreements

The Contract Act draws distinction between an agreement which is only void and the one in which the consideration or object is also unlawful. An illegal agreement is one which is actually forbidden by the law (Section 23), but a void agreement may not be forbidden, "the law may merely say that if it is made, the courts will not enforce it (Section 25 to 30). Thus, every illegal agreement is also void but a void agreement is not necessarily illegal. Another similarity between an illegal and a void agreement is that in either case the main or the primary agreement is unenforceable. Nothing can be recovered under either kind of agreement and if something has been paid it cannot be recovered back. Thus, a guilty party has no right of action on an illegal contract. A person who contracted to hire a premises, unknown to the landlord, for holding a meeting for blasphemous purpose, was not allowed to sue the landlord for breach of contract when the latter, on learning the real purpose, refuse to give the premises.[149] Money lent for an illegal purpose is not recoverable.[150] A renewed promise to pay an illegal debt will be equally tainted by the illegality[151]. Money paid to procure a seat in medical college could not be recovered.[152] Where a contract is lawful in its inception, but is performed in an unlawful manner, no recovery may be allowed. Thus, in a contract of transport, the lorry was overloaded, which was an offence under the Road Traffic Act and the goods having been damaged during the journey, the consignor was not allowed to recover the loss. His manager had knowledge of the over-loading[153].

CHAPTER

30

Contingent and Quasi Contracts

Contingent contract

According to section 31 of the Indian Contract Act, contingent contract is a contract to do or not to do something, if some event, collateral to such contract, does not happen.

Examples —

(a) A contracts to pay B Rs. 10,000 if B's house is burnt. This is a contingent contract.

(b) A agrees to sell a certain piece of land to B, in case he succeeds in his litigation concerning that land. This is a contingent contract.

A contingent contract is a sort of a conditional contract and the condition is of uncertain nature. A contract which is subject to a certain or an absolute type of condition cannot be regarded as a contingent contract. When the performance of a contract is not immediately due but if becomes so only after the happening or non-happening of some contingency (i.e. some uncertain event) is known as contingent contract. All contracts of insurance, except life insurance, contract of indemnity and guarantee are the examples of contingent contract.

Essentials of a Contingent Contract

(1) The performance of a contingent contract is made dependent upon the happening or non-happening of some event.

(2) The even must be uncertain. If the event is bound to happen and the contract has got to be performed in any case it is not a contingent contract.

(3) The event must be collateral ...... i.e., incidental to the contract.

Example

There was a contract for the sale of American parachute cloth by A to B. The goods were to be delivered when they arrived. A failed to give delivery and B sued for damages for breach. A pleaded that the contract was a conditional one and as the goods had not arrived he had no obligation to give delivery. Held, the contract was an absolute one and the obligation of A was not contingent upon the arrival of the goods (*Ranchhadas v. Nathmal Mirachand and Co.*[154])

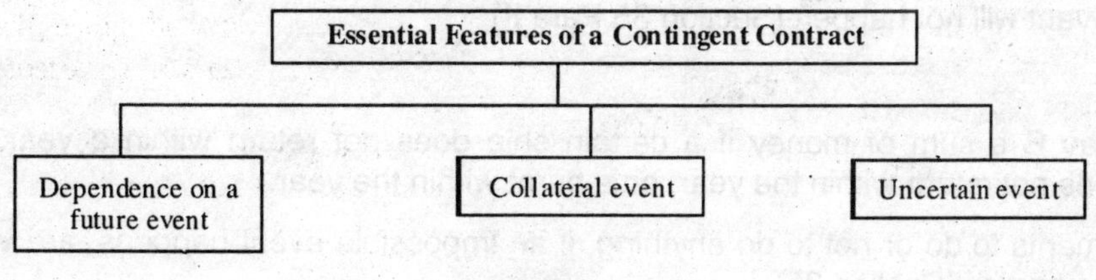

Figure No. 1

Contingency dependent on act of party

The performance of a contingent contract depends on the happening or non happening of an event collateral to such contract. The word 'event' includes an 'act' and a contract may be contingent on some act of the promisor or of a third party. But if the performance of the promise depends on the mere will and pleasure of the promisor, it is no promise at all. Thus a promise by A to pay B Rs. 100 if A so chose is no promise and, therefore, it cannot be deemed to depend on a contingency.

Similarly, if a promisor says that for a certain service he will pay whatever he himself thinks right or reasonable, there is no promise (*Roberts v. Smith*[155]). But a promise to pay what a third party shall determine is valid, e.g., a promise in an agreement between A and B to pay what C shall determine, and a promise to pay under a policy of insurance subject to the approval of directors, are valid promises.

Rules Regarding Contingent Contracts (Section 32 to 36)

The rules regarding contingent contracts are summarised here under—

1. Contingent contracts to do or not to do anything if an uncertain future event happens cannot be enforced by law unless and until that event happens. And if, the event becomes impossible such contract become void (Section 32).

Examples—

(I) A makes a contract with B to sell a horse to B at a specified price if C, to whom the horse has been offered, refuses to buy him. The contract cannot be enforced by law unless and until C refuses to buy the horse.

(II) A contracts to pay B a sum of money when B marries C, C dies without being married to B. The contract becomes void.

2. Contingent contracts to do or not to do anything if an uncertain future event does not happen can be enforced when the happening of that event becomes impossible, and not before (Section 33).

Examples—

(a) A agrees to pay B a sum of money if a certain ship does not return. The ship is Sunk. The contract can be enforced when the ship sinks.

(b) A agrees to sell his car to B if C dies. The contract cannot be enforced so long as C is alive.

3. If a contract is contingent upon as to how a person will act at an unspecified time, the event shall be considered to become impossible when such person does anything which renders it impossible that he should so act within any definite time, or otherwise than under further contingencies (Section 34).

Example—

A agrees to pay B a sum of money if B marries C. C marries D. The marriage of B to C must now be considered impossible, although it is possible that D may die and that C may afterwards marry B.

4. Contracts contingent upon the happening of a specified uncertain event within a fixed time become void if, at the expiration of the time fixed, such event has not happened or it, before the time fixed, such event becomes impossible (Section 35 Para I).

Example—

A promises to pay B a sum of money if a certain ship returns within a year. The contract may be enforced if the ship returns within the year, and becomes void if the ship is burnt within the year.

5. Contracts contingent upon the non-happening of a specified event within a fixed time may be enforced by law when the time fixed has expired and such event has not happened, or, before the time fixed expired, if it becomes certain that such event will not happen (Section 35 Para II).

Example—

A promises to pay B a sum of money if a certain ship does not return within a year. The contract may be enforced if the ship does not return within the year, or is burnt within the year.

6. Contingent agreements to do or not to do anything, if an impossible event happens, are void, whether or not the fact is known to the parties (Section 36).

Examples—

(a) A agrees to pay B Rs. 1,000 if two straight lines should enclose a space. The agreement is void.

(b) A agrees to pay B Rs. 1,00C if B will marry A's daughter, C. C was dead at the time of the agreement. The agreement is void.

Difference between Contingent Contracts and Wagering Agreements

1. Mutual Promise

A wagering agreement consists of mutual promises each of which is conditional on the happening or non happening of certain event. A contingent contract may not consist of mutual promise. If may be said that all Wager's are contingent contracts but all contingent contracts are not Wagers. For example, insurance contracts, contracts of indemnity and guarantee are contingent contract but not wagers.

2. Validity

A wagering agreement is absolutely void. It is illegal in Bombay and England. But a contingent contract is a valid contract.

3. Performance

In a Wagering agreement, neither party intends to perform the contract, but only to deal in difference. This is not so in contingent contracts.

4. Interest in the subject matter

In wagering agreement, the parties to the agreement have no other interest in the subject matter of the agreement, except for the stake. But in a contingent contract, parties do have some other interest in the subject matter. They are interested in the occurrence or non-occurrence of the event.

5. Future Event

In a wagering agreement, the future event is the sole determining factor of the contract while in a contingent contract, the future event is merely collateral or incidental to the contract.

6. All contingent contracts are not of a wagering nature, because all the contingent contracts are not void. All wagering agreements are also contingent contracts because they are dependent on uncertain event.

Wagering and Insurance Contracts Distinguished

Insurance Agreements	Wagering Agreements
1. There is insurable interest.	1. There is no insurable interest.
2. Both parties are interested in the subject-matter.	2. Neither party has any interest in the happening or non-happening of an event.
3. These are valid contracts.	3. These are void agreements as they are opposed to public policy.
4. These are contracts of indemnity except life insurance contracts, which are contingent contracts.	4. These are conditional contracts.
5. A contract is based on scientific and actuarial calculation of risks.	5. A wagering agreement is just a gamble.

QUASI-CONTRACTS (Section 68 - 72)

Certain obligations are imposed by law. These obligations are similar to those which are created by contract. When such obligations are imposed by law in the absence of any contract, if is called quasi-contract. Indian contract Act terms quasi-contract as certain relations resembling those created by law, "The quasi-contracts are based on the maxim of no man must grow rich out of another person's costs. In other words, these are based on the equitable principle that a person shall not be allowed to enrich himself at the expense of another.

According to Dr. Henks, Quasi-contract is a situation in which law imposes upon one person, on grounds of natural justice, an obligation similar to that which arises from a true contract, although no contract, express or implied, has in fact been entered into by them."

Quasi-Contracts under Indian Contract Act

The Indian contract Act refers the Quasi-contracts under the heading, certain, (Section 68 to 72).

1. Claim for necessaries supplied to a person incapable of contracting on his account.
2. Reimbursement of person paying money due by another in payment of which be is interested (section 69).
3. Obligation of person enjoying benefit of a non-gratuitous act (Section 70).
4. Rights and liabilities of the finder of lost goods. (Section 71).
5. Liability of persons to whom money is paid or things delivered, by mistake or under coercion (section72).

1. Necessaries Supplied to person Incapable of contracting

If a person, incapable of entering into a contract, or any one whom he is legally bound to support, is supplied by another person with necessaries suited to his condition in life, the person who has furnished such supplies is entitled to be reimbursed from the property of such incapable person (Section 68).

Thus, though the contracts by minors, idiots, lunatics, etc. are void, but section 68 provides that their estates are liable to reimburse the trader who supplies them with necessaries of life. This is on the basis of quasi-contract.

1. A supplies B, a lunatic, with necessaries suitable to his condition in life. A is entitled to be reimbursed from B's property.
2. A who supplies the wife and children of B, a lunatic, with necessaries suitable to their conditions in life, is entitled to be reimbursed from B's property.

2. Payment by an Interested person

A person (i) who is interested in the payment of money, (ii) which another is bound by law to pay, and (iii) who therefore pays it, is entitled to be reimbursed by the other (Section 69).

Illustration

B holds land in Bengal, on a lease granted by A, the Zamindar. The revenue payable by A to the Government being in arrears, his land is advertised for sale by the Government. Under the revenue law, the consequence of such sale will be the annulment of B's lease. B, to prevent the sale and consequent annulment of his own lease, pays to the Government the sum due from A. A is bound to make good to B the amount so paid.

In order that the section may apply, it is necessary to prove that:

(i) The payment made should be bonafide for the protection of one's interest.

(ii) The payment should not be a voluntary one.

(iii) The payment must be to another person.

(iv) The payment must be one which the other party was bound by law to pay.

3. Liability for Non-Gratuitous Act

Section 70 creates liability to pay for the benefits of an act which the doer did not intend to do gratuitously. The section in as follows:

Where a person lawfully does anything for an other person or delivers anything to him, not intending to do so gratuitously, and such other person enjoys the benefit there of, the latter is bound to make compensation to the former in respect of, or to restore, the thing so done or delivered.

Illustrations

(a) A, a tradesman, leaves goods at B's house by mistake. B treats the goods as his own. He is bound to pay for them

(b) A Saves B's property from fire. A is not entitled to compensation from B if the circumstances show that he intended to act gratuitously.

To establish a right of action under section 70, the following conditions must be fulfilled—

(1) The thing must have been done lawfully, i.e., the act must be lawful.

(2) The intention must be to do it non-gratuitously, and.

(3) The person for whom the act is done must enjoy the benefit of it.

It should be noted that the section 70 does not apply to persons incompetent to contract and as such they are under no obligation to compensate the other person for any benefit received by them. Both the parties must be competent to contract. It should also be noted that a person is not bound to pay for which he had option of refusing.

4. Responsibility of Finder of lost goods

Ordinarily speaking, a person is not bound to take care of goods belonging to another, left on a road or other public place by accident or inadvertence, but if he takes them into his custody, an agreement is implied by law.

Although, there is in fact no agreement between the owner and the finder of the goods, the finder is for certain purposes, deemed in law to be a bailee and must take as much care of the goods as a man of ordinary prudence would take of similar goods of his own. This obligation is imposed on the basis of a quasi-contract section 71, which deals with this subject, says:

"A person who finds goods belonging to another and takes them into his custody, it is subject to the same responsibility as a bailee."

Thus in respect of duties and liabilities, a finder is treated at par with bailee. The finder's position, therefore, has been considered along with bailment. The Supreme Court has ruled in *Union of India v. Amar Singh*[156] that statutory fiction by which a contract of bailment is inferred between a finder of goods and the real owner should not be enlarged by analogy or otherwise and, therefore, a railway authority which took into its custody wagons containing the plaintiff's goods and which were left across the border by Pakistan become the contractual bailees of goods and if was not necessary to regard them as finders within the meaning of Section 70.

The finder, however, can sell the gods in the following cases:

(i) Where the thing found is in danger of perishing or losing the greater part of its value,

(ii) Where the owner cannot, with reasonable diligence, be found out,

(iii) Where the owner is found out, but refuses to pay lawful charges of the finder, and

(iv) Where the lawful charges of the finder in respect of the thing found, amount to two-thirds of the value of the thing found.

5. Liability of person to whom money in paid or thing delivered by mistake or under coercion

A person to whom has been paid, or anything delivered by mistake or under coercion, must repay or return it (Section 72) mistake must be as to the existence of the obligation and not merely as to some collateral matter which may form a motive for the payment.

Illustrations

(a) A and B jointly owe 100 rupees to C. A alone pays the amount to C and B, not knowing this fact, pays 100 rupees over again to C. C is bound to repay the amount to B.

(b) A railway company refused to deliver up certain goods to the consignee, except upon the payment of an illegal charge for carriage. The consignee pays the sum charged in order to obtain the goods. He is entitled to recover so much of the charge as was illegally excessive.

Notice that the term mistake as used in "Section 72 does not make any distinction between a mistake of law or a mistake of fact. The term 'mistake' has been used without any qualification or limitation whatever .... (*Sales Tax officer, Banaras v. Kanhaiya Lal Mukund Lal Saraf*[157]).

The word 'coercion' is used in this section in its general sense and not as defined in section 15. Thus, money paid under pressure of circumstances, such as prevention of the execution of a decree on a property which the party paying is interested, may be recovered even though 'coercion' as defined in section 15 is not established (*Seth Kanhaya Lal v. National Bank of India*[158]).

Quantum Meruit

The phrase "quantum merit" means 'as much as merited' or 'as much as earned'. The general rule of law is that unless a person has performed his obligations in full, he can not claim performance from the other.[159] But in certain cases, when a person has done some work under a contract, and the other party repudiated the contract, or some event happens which makes the further performance of the contract impossible, then the party who has performed the work can claim remuneration for the work he has already done. The right to claim quantum meruit does not arise out of the contract as the right to damages does, it is a claim on the quasi-contractual obligation which the law implies in the circumstances. (*Patel Engg. Co. Ltd. v. Indian Oil Corporation Ltd.*[160])

The object of allowing a claim on quantum meruit is to recompensate the party or person for value of work which he has done. Damages are compensatory in nature while quantum meruit is restitutory. It is but reasonable compensation awarded on implication of a contract to remunerate. Where a person orders from a wine merchant 12 bottles of whiskey and he sends 10 bottles of whiskey and 2 of brandy, and the purchaser accepts them, the purchaser must pay reasonable price for the brandy.

The claim for quantum meruit arises in the following cases:

(1) When an agreement is discovered to be void, or when a contract becomes void.

Any person who has received any advantage under such agreement or contract is bound torestore it, or to make compensation for it to the person from whom he received it.

Examples —

(i) A pays B Rs.1000/- in consideration of B's promising to marry C, A's daughter. C is dead at the time of the promise. The agreement is void, but B must repay A the 1000/- rupees.

(ii) A contracts with B to deliver to him 250 kilos of rice before the first of May. A delivers 130 kilos only before that day and none after. B retains the 130 kilos after the first of May. He is bound to pay A for them.

(2) When something is done without any intention to do so gratuitously (Sec. 70)

(3) When there is an express or implied contract to render services but there is no agreement as to remuneration.

(4) When one party abandons or refuses to perform the contract.

Where there is a breach of contract, the aggrieved party is entitled to claim reasonable compensation for what he has done under the contract.

Example —

C, an owner of a magazine, engaged P to write a book to be published by installments in his magazine. After a few installments were published, the magazine was abandoned. Held, P could claim payment on quantum meruit for the part already published (*Planche v. Colburn*[161]).

(5) When a contract is divisible and the party not in default has enjoyed the benefit of the part performance.

(6) When an indivisible contract for a lump can claim the lump sum, but the other party can make a deduction for bad work.

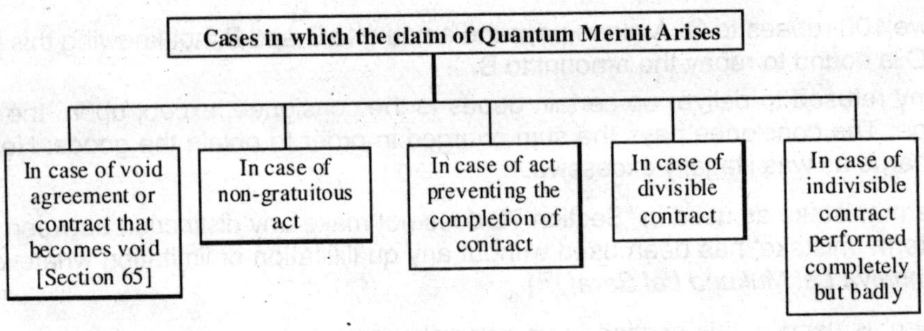

Figure No. 2

Example

A agreed to decorate B's flat for a lump sum of £750. A did the work but B complained for faulty workmanship. It cost B £204 to remedy the defect. Held, A could recover from B £750 less £204 (Hoening v. Isaces[162]).

Compensation for failure to discharge obligation created by quasi contract (Section 73, Para 3):

When an obligation created by a quasi-contract had not been discharged, the injured party is entitled to receive the same compensation from the party in default, as if sued person had contracted to discharge it and had broken his contract.

CHAPTER

31

Performance of Contract (Sections 37-67)

A contract creates obligations. 'Performance of a contract' means the carrying out of those obligations. Performance of contract takes place when the parties to the contract fulfill their obligations arising under the contract within the time and in the manner prescribed. Section 37 (Para 1) lays down that the parties to a contract must either perform, their respective promises, unless such performance is dispensed with or excused under the provisions of the Contract Act, or of any other law.

Rules Relating to Performance

Rules relating to performance of promises are summarized below:

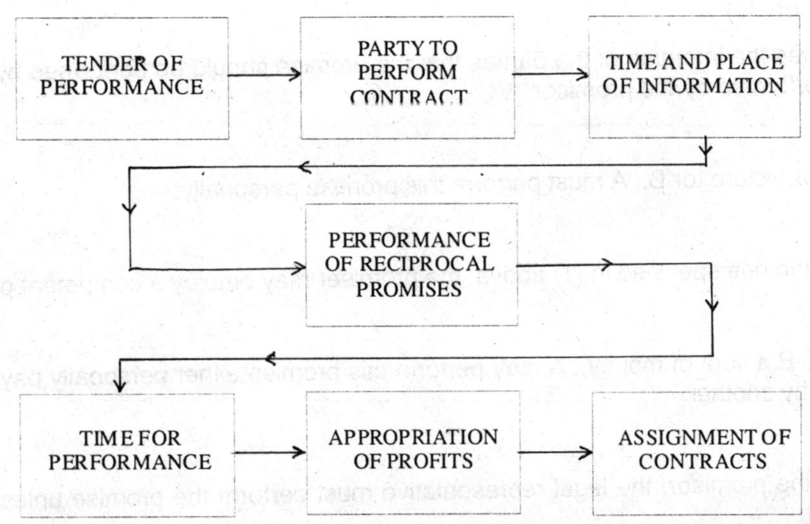

Rules Relating to Performance

Offer to Perform (Section 38)

Sometimes, it so happens that the promisor offers to perform his obligation under the contract at the proper time and place but the promisee does not accept the performance. This is called as 'Tender' or 'attempted performance'. According to Section 38, if a valid tender is made and is not accepted by the promisee, the promisor shall not be responsible for non performance nor shall be lose his right under the contract. A tender or offer of performance to be valid must satisfy the following conditions:

1. It must be unconditional

A conditional offer of performance is not valid and the promisor shall not be relieved thereby. A tender is conditional where it is not in accordance with the terms of the contract.

Examples

(a) A tender was made on a condition that a receipt for the full discharge of the contract be given. Held, the tender was invalid. (*Finch v. Miller*[163])

(b) X offers to Y the principal amount of the loan. This is not a valid tender since the whole amount of principal and interest is not offered.

2. It must be made at the proper time and place. A tender of goods after the business hours or of goods or money before the due date is not a Valid tender.

Example

A owes B Rs. 500 payable on 15th April with interest. He offers to pay on the 15th May the amount with interest upto the 15th May. It is not a valid tender as it is not made at the appointed time.

As to what is proper time and place, depends upon the intention of the parties and the provisions of Section 46 to 50.

3. It must be of the whole quantity contracted for or of the whole obligation. A tender of an installment when the contract stipulates payment in full is not a valid tender.

If, however, the deviation from the terms of the contract is 'microscopic', i.e., very negligible, the court may take a practical view of the matter by holding that the contract has been correctly performed.

Example

In a contract requiring delivery of 4,950 tons of wheat, the seller delivered 4,950 tons 55 Lbs. Held, the contract was duly performed by the seller (*Shipton, Anderson and Co. v. Well Bros. and Co.*[164])

4. It must be by a person who is in a position and is willing to perform the promise.

5. The promise may be performed by promisor himself, or his agent or by his legal representative.

Promisor Himself (Section 40)

If it appears that it was the intention of the parties that the promise should be performed by the promisor himself, such promise must be performed by the promisor.

Example

A promises to paint a picture for B. A must perform this promise personally.

Agent

In cases other than the one specified in (1) above, the promiser may employ a competent person to perform it.

Example

A promises to pay to B a sum of money. A may perform this promise either personally paying the money to B or causing it to be paid to B by another.

Legal Representative

In case of death of the promisor, the legal representative must perform the promise unless a contrary intention appears from the contract.

Where, however, a contract involves personal skill or is founded on normal considerations, it comes to an end with the death of the promisor.

Example

A promisee to paint a picture for B by a certain day. A dies before that day. The contract cannot be enforced either by A's representative or by B.

6. It may be made to one of the several joint promisees. In such a case, it has the same effect as a tender to all of them.

7. In case of tender of goods it must give a reasonable opportunity to the promisee for inspection of the goods. A tender of goods at such time when the other party cannot inspect the goods is not a valid tender. But in the following case, tender was held to be valid.

Example

The plaintiffs agreed to sell ten tons of linseed oil to the defendant to be delivered "Within last fourteen days of March". Delivery was tendered at 8.30 p.m. on March 31, a Saturday. The defendant refused to accept the goods owing to lateness of the hour. Held, though the hour was unreasonable, the defendant could still take delivery before midnight. (*Startup v. Macdonalid (1843) 6 Man G.523* [165])

8. In case of tender of money, the debtor must make a valid tender in the legal tender money. If the creditor refuses to accept it, the debtor is not discharged from making the payment. Tender, in this case, does not discharge the debt. But when the creditor files a suit against the debtor, the debtor can set up the defence of tender. If he deposits the money in the Court and proves his pleas, the creditor gets the amount originally tendered to him but without any interest, whereas the debtor gets judgement for his cost of defence.

Contracts which need not be performed

Following contracts need not be performed (Section 62 to 67):

1. If the parties mutually agree to substitute the original contract by a new one or to rescind or alter it. (Section 62).

Example

A owes money to B under a contract. It is agreed between A, B and C that B shall henceforth accept C as his debtor, instead of A. The old debt of A to B is at an end, and a new debt from C to B has been contracted.

2. If the promisee dispenses with or remits, wholly or in part the performance of the promise made to him or extends the time for such performance or accepts any satisfaction for it (Section 63).

Examples

(i) A owes B Rs. 5,000/-. C pays to B Rs. 1,000/- and B accepts them, in satisfaction of his claim on A. This payment is a discharge of the whole claim.

(ii) A promises to paint a picture for B. B afterwards him to do so. A is no longer bound to perform the promise.

3. If the person, at whose option the contract is voidable, rescides it (Section 64).

4. If the promisee neglects or refuses to afford the promisor reasonable facilities for the performance of his promise (Section 67).

Example

A contracts with B to repair B's house' B neglects or refuses to point out to A the places in which his house requires repair. A need not perform. A is excused for the non performance of contract if it is caused by such neglect or refusal.

Impossibility of Performance and Frustration

According to Section 56 an agreement to do an act impossible in itself is void. For example, A agrees with B to discover a treasure by magic. The agreement is void. Even subsequent impossibility renders a contract void. Sometimes the performance of a contract is quite possible when it is made by the parties. But some event subsequently happens which renders its performance impossible or unlawful. In either case, the contract becomes void. Where, for example, after making a contract of marriage, one of the parties goes mad, or where a contract is made for the import of goods and the import is thereafter forbidden by a Government order, or where a singer contracts to sing and becomes too ill to do so, the contract in each case becomes void. The principle of subsequent impossibility is popularly called the doctrine of frustration.

Grounds of Frustration

The principle of frustration of contract is applicable to a variety of situations. The well established grounds, however, are: (i) destruction of the subject-matter, (ii) change of circumstances, (iii) non-occurrence of contemplated event, (iv) death or incapacity of party, (v) Government or legislative intervention, and (vi) intervention of war (see fig.)

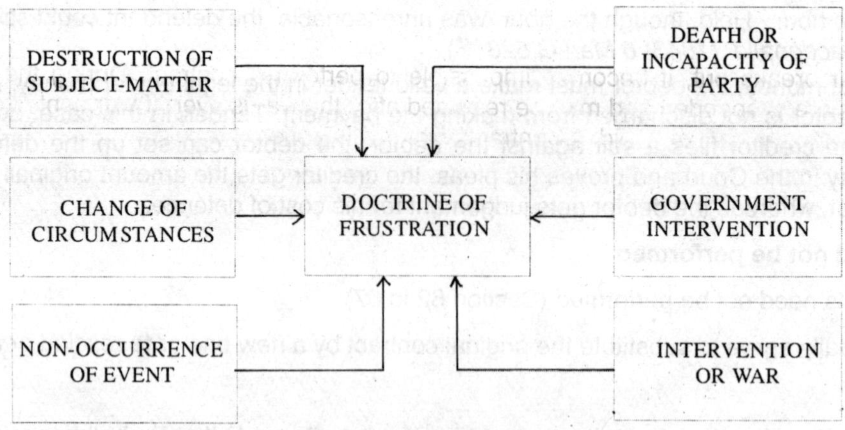

Figure No. 2 Heads of frustration

(i) Destruction of Subject-matter

The doctrine of frustration applies with full force where the actual and specific subject-matter of the contract has ceased to exist. A leading case in this context is the *Taylor v. Caldwell* (1863). In this case, the defendant had agreed to let the plaintiffs, the use of their music hall between certain dates for the purpose of holding a concert there. But before the consent was given, the hall was destroyed by fire without the fault of either party. The contract was held not to be absolute on the principle of frustration. Similarly, when a cinema hall engaged for showing a film collapsed on account of heavy rains, the contract was held to be frustrated (*V.L. Narasu v. P.S.V. Iyer*, 1953).

(ii) Change of Circumstances

A contract will frustrate when circumstances arise which make the performance of the contract impossible in the manner and at the time contemplated. The Punjab High Court observed in (P.I.) *Mehra & Sons v. Ramchand Omprakash* (1952) thus: "It is clear that if there is entirely unanticipated change of circumstances, the question will have to be considered whether this change of circumstances has affected the performance of the contract to such an extent as to make it virtually impossible or even extremely difficult or hazardous. If that be the case, the change of circumstances not having been brought about by the fault of either party, the court will not enforce the contract."

(iii) Non-Occurrence of a Contemplated Event

Sometimes, the performance of a contract is possible, but owing to the non-occurrence of an event contemplated by both the parites as the reason for the contract, the value of the performance is destroyed. The leading case to be quoted here is the *Krell v. Henry* (1903). In this case the defendant agreed to hire a flat from the plaintiff for June 26 and 27, for witnessing a coronation procession of King Edward VII. A part of the rent was paid in advance. But the procession having been cancelled owing to the king's illness, the defendant refused to pay the balance. He was freed from paying the balance because non-occurrence of the event, which was the basis for the contract, discharged the contract.

(iv) Death or Incapacity of Party

When the performance of a contract depends on the existence of a given person, the contract is discharged on the death or illness of that person. Thus, where the nature or terms of a contract require personal performance by the promisor, his death or incapacity puts an end to the contract. For example, A contracts to act at a theatre for six months in consideration of a sum paid in advance by H. On several occasions, A is too ill to act. The contract to act on those occasions becomes void.

(v) Government or Legislative Intervention

The performance of a contract may be prevented by the passing of a legislation or even by an executive decision as in the case of acquisition of property which might be the subject-matter of a contract of sale. Certain transactions may be banned and this ban will discharge the parties from contracts. Sale of agricultural land, for example, is affected by land reforms legislation. Similarly, sale of urban land is affected by the urban land ceiling law. In *Boothalinga Agencies v. V.T.C. Poraiswam Nadar* (1969), the defendant had a licence to import chicory for manufacturing coffee powder. The licence was subject to the condition that he would use it only in his factory. He agreed to sell the whole shipload. Before the arrival of the ship, the sale of such imported goods was banned. The contract to sell was held to be frustrated because of the ban.

(vi) Intervention of War

As soon as a war breaks out, it becomes impossible to perform a contract. During the continuance of war, therefore, the contracts are suspended and may be resumed after the war is over. If war continues for a longer period the inordinate delay makes the contract void. A contract with an alien enemy is void.

Exceptions to Doctrine of Frustration

Supervening impossibility or doctrine of frustration will not discharge a contract in the following cases:

(a) Difficulty of Performance

Unexpected difficulty does not excuse performance. In Karl Ettlinger v. Chagandas & Co., (1915) X promised to send certain goods from Bombay to Antwerp in September. In August, war broke out and shipping space was available at very high rates. It was held that the increase of freight rates did not excuse performance.

(b) Commercial Impossibility

A contract is not discharged merely because expectation of higher profits is not realised, or the rates of materials have gone up because of outbreak of war, or there is a sudden depreciation of currency.

(c) Default of a Third Party

Where performance of a contract is not possible because of the default by a third party, the contract is not discharged. In Harnandrai Fulchand v. Pragdas (1923), A, a wholesaler, entered into a contract with B for the sale of a certain type of cloth to be produced by C, a manufacturer of the cloth. It was held that A was liable to B for damages.

(d) Strikes, Lock-outs and Civil Disturbances

A strike by workers or a lock-out by an employer does not excuse performance unless there is a clause in the contract providing that in such cases the contract is not to be performed or that the time of performance is to be extended. Same logic applies to a civil disturbance too.

(e) Failure of One of the Objects

When there are several purposes for which a contract is entered into, failure of one of them does not discharge the contract.

In *Smt. Poornima Rani Datta v. Smt. Lakshmi Bala Das*, the Court was called upon to decide the issue relating to the frustration of a contract in the light of the facts narrated below:

The defendant entered into a agreement to sell the suit property to the plaintiff for a consideration of Rs. 5,300 and executed a registered deed of agreement on 24-11-1972. On acceptance of Rs. 500 as earnest money towards the consideration, it was agreed between the parties that within 4 months from the date of the execution of the deed of agreement, the plaintiff would pay the balance of consideration money of Rs. 4,800 and the defendant would execute the sale deed. It was further stipulated in the agreement that the defendant, within 3 months from the date of execution of the deed, would amicably evict the tenant in respect of the suit property to the plaintiff and that, in default, the defendant would refund the earnest money of Rs. 500 with interest to the plaintiff. The plaintiff was all along ready and willing to perform her part of the contract but the defendant refused to perform her part of the contract. The plaintiff accordingly brought a suit for specific performance of the contract and for possession.

The Court held:

Second part of Section 56 of the Contract Act was not attracted and did not stand in the way of enforcement of the contract for sale when the alleged impossibility of performance of the defendant's part of the contract for giving vacant possession had been resorted to by the defendant without making any bonafide and effective attempt to evict the tenants in terms of the agreement and without keeping the plaintiff informed about her such attempt and failure.

Devolution of Joint Liabilities and Rights

Devolution of Joint Liabilities (Section 42-44)

'Devolution' means passing over from one person to another.

When two or more persons have made a joint promise, they are known as joint promisors. Unless a contrary intention appears by the contract, all such persons, during their joint lives, and, after the death of any of them, his representative jointly with the survivor or survivors and, after death of the last survivor, the representatives of all, jointly must fulfill the promise.

According to this section, joint promisors must, during their joint lives, fulfill the promise. And if any of them dies, his representative must, jointly with the surviving promisors, fulfill the promise. But this is subject to any private arrangement between the parties. They may expressly or impliedly prescribe a different rule.

It would be seen that section 42 deals with voluntary discharge of obligations. If the parties do not discharge their obligations of their own volition, Section 43 comes into play. Section 43 lays down three rules as regards performance of joint promises.

(i) Any one of the joint promisors may be compelled to perform (Section 43 Para 1)

When two or more persons make a joint promise and there is no express agreement to the contrary, the promisee may compel any one or mere of the joint promisors to perform the whole of the promise. This means the liability of joint promisors is joint and several.

(ii) A joint promisor compelled to perform may claim contribution (Section 4, Para 2)

When a joint promisor has been compelled to perform the whole of the promise, he may compel the other joint promisors to contribute equally with himself to the performance of the promise, unless a contrary intention appears from the contract.

Example

A partner of the firm is a joint promisor with other partners. He is entitled to claim contribution from other partners in case he is required to pay the debt of the firm. (*Bakshi Hardatt v. The State of J and K* A.I.R. (1977) NOC 207 (J and K)[166])

(iii) Sharing of loss arising from default (Section 43 Para 3)

If any one of the joint promisors makes default in the contribution, the remaining joint promisors must bear the loss arising from such default in equal shares. The same principle applies in the case of recovery of a loan by a creditor from the heirs who by operation of law become joint promisors after the death of the single promisor. [Orissa Cement Ltd. v. Union of India A.I.R. (1967) Ori. 158 [167]]

Release of Joint Promisor (Section 44)

Where two or more persons have made a joint promise, a release of one of such joint promisors by the promisee does not discharge the other joint promisor or promisors, neither does it free him from responsibility to the other joint promisor or promisors.

In *Kirtee Chunder v. Struthers,*[168] the plaintiff sued some of the partners of a firm for damages, but then he settled his claim against one of them and agreed to withdraw his claim and suit against him. Held, that the suit could be carried on against the rest of the partners.

The position in English Law is, however, different. Under the English Law, if the promisee discharges one of the several joint promisors, such discharge acts as a discharge of all the joint promisors. Thus, under English Law suit must be brought against all the promisors jointly.

Devolution of Joint Rights (Section 45)

When a person has made a promise to two or more persons jointly, then, unless a contrary intention appears from the contract, the right to claim performance rests with all the joint promisees after the death of any of them with the representatives of such deceased promisee jointly with the survivor or survivors and after the death of the survivors also, with the representatives of jointly. Thus, unlike the case of joint promisors whose liability is joint as well as several, the right of the joint promisees is only joint and thus any of them cannot enforce performance unless so agreed.

Example

A in consideration of Rs. 5000/- lent to him by B and C, promises B and C jointly to repay them that sum with interest on a day specified, B dies. The right to claim performance rests with B's representative jointly with C during C's life, and after C's death with the representatives of B and C jointly.

In *Johar Roy v. Premji Bhimji,*[169] the Supreme Court has held that where a joint promisee refuses to join as a co-plaintiff, he should be taken on record as proforma defendant. The Court cannot compel any person to be a plaintiff if he does not want to be so.

Time and Place of Performance (Section 46 to 50 and 55)

Time and place of performance of a contract are matters to be determined by an agreement between the parties themselves. Section 46 to 50 lay down the following rules regarding to time, place and manner of performance as summed up hereunder.

1. Where no application is to be made and no time is specified (Section 46)

Where, by the contract, a promisor is to perform his promise without application by the promisee, and no time for performance is specified the engagement must be performed within a reasonable time.

The question "what is a reasonable time" is, in each particular case, a question of fact (Explanation to Sec. 46). It depends on the special circumstances of the case, the usage of trade or the intention of the parties at the time of entering into the contract.

2. Where time is specified and no application is to be made (Section 47)

When a promise is to be performed on a certain day, and the promisor has undertaking to perform it without application by the promisee, the promisor may perform it at any time during the usual hours of business on such day and at the place at which the promise ought to be performed.

Example

A promises to deliver goods to B at his warehouse on the first January. On that day, A brings the goods to B's warehouse, but after the usual hour for closing it, and they are not received. A has not performed his promise.

3. Application for performance on a certain day to be at proper time and place (Section 48)

When a promise is to be performed on a certain day and the promisor has not undertaken to perform it without application by the promisee, it is the duty of the promisee to apply for performance at a proper place and within the usual hours of business.

The question "what is a proper time and place" is in each particular case, a question of fact. (Explanation to Section 48)

4. Place for performance of promise, where no application to be made and no place fixed for performance (Section 49)

When promise is to be performed without application by the promisee, and no place is fixed for the performance of it, it is the duty of the promisor to apply to the promisee to appoint a reasonable place for the performance of the promise, and to perform it at such place.

Example

A undertakes to deliver a thousand mounds of Jute to B on a fixed day. A must apply to B to appoint a reasonable for the purpose of receiving it, and must deliver it to him at such place.

5. Performance in manner or at time prescribed or sanctioned by the promisee (Section 50)

The performance of any promise may be made in any manner, or at anytime which the promisee prescribes or sanctions.

Examples

(i) A and B are mutually indebted, A and B settle an account by setting off one item against another, and B pays A the balance found to be due from him from such settlement. This amount to payment by A and B respectively, of the sums which they owed to each other.

(ii) A owes B Rs. 2000/-. B accepts some of A's goods in reduction of the debt. The delivery of the goods operates as a part payment.

(iii) B owes A Rs.2000/-. A desires B to pay the amount to A's account with C, a banker. B, who also banks with C, orders the amount to be transferred from his account to A's credit, and this done by C. Afterwards and before A knows of the transfer, C fails. There has been a good payment by B.

(iv) A desires B, who owes him Rs.100, to send him a note for Rs.100 by post. The debt is discharged as soon as B puts into the post a letter containing the note duly addressed to A.

Reciprocal-Promises

When a Contract consists of an exchange of promisee, they are called reciprocal promises.[170]

Reciprocal promises have been classified by Lord Mansfield in *Jones v. Barkley*,[171] as follows:

1. Mutual and Dependent
2. Mutual and Independent and
3. Mutual and Concurrent

1. Mutual and Dependent

In such a case the performance of one party depends upon the prior performance of the other party. Thus, if the promisor who must perform, fails to perform it, he cannot claim the performance of the reciprocal promise. On the other hand, he must make compensation to the other party to the contract for any loss which such other party may sustain by the non-performance of the contract.

Examples

(i) A promises B to sell him 100 bales of merchandise to be delivered next day and B promises A to pay for them within a month. A does not deliver according to his promise. B's promise to pay need not be performed, and A must make compensation.

(ii) A contracts with B to execute certain builder's work for a fixed price, B supplying the necessary timber for the work. B refuses to furnish any timber and the work cannot be executed. A need not execute the work and B is bound to make compensation to A for any loss caused to him by the non-performance of the contract.

2. Mutual and Independent

In such cases, each party must perform his promise independently and irrespective of the fact whether the other party has performed, or is willing to perform, his promise or not, the promises are mutual and independent.

Example

In a contract of sale, B agrees to pay the price of goods on 10th instant, S promises to supply the goods on 20th instant. The promises are mutual and independent.

3. Mutual and Concurrent

In such cases, the promises of both the parties are to be performed simultaneously, they are said to be mutual and concurrent. The example of such promises may be sale of goods for cash.

Rules regarding performance of reciprocal promises

These are contained in Section 51 to 54 and 57, and are reproduced as below:

(A) Simultaneous performance o reciprocal promises (Section 51)

When a contract consists of reciprocal promises to be simultaneously performed, no promisor need perform his promise unless the promisee is ready and willing to perform his reciprocal promise.

Examples

(i) A and B contract that A shall deliver goods to B to be paid for by B on delivery. A need not deliver the goods, unless B is ready and willing to pay for the goods on delivery. B need not pay for the goods, unless A is ready not willing to deliver them on payment.

(ii) A and B contract that A shall deliver goods to B at a price to be paid by installments, the first installment to be paid on delivery. A need not deliver unless B is ready and willing to pay the first installment on delivery. B need not pay the first installment, unless A is ready and willing to deliver the goods on payment of the first installment.

(B) Order of Performance of reciprocal promises (Section 52)

Where the order in which reciprocal promises are to be performed is expressly fixed by the contract, they must be performed in that order, and where the order is not expressly fixed by the contract, they must be performed in that order which the naturo of transaction requires.

Example

(i) A and B contract that A shall build a house for B for a fixed price. A's promise to built the house must be performed before B's promise to pay for it.

(ii) A and B contract that A shall make over his stock-in-trade to B at a fixed price, and B promises to give security for the payment of the money. A's promise need not be performed until the security is given, for the nature of the transaction requires that A should have security before he delivers up his stock.

In a case *Hashman v. Lucknow Improvement Trust*[172], the defendant took a lease of land from the Municipality of a town on condition that he pays Rs.630 for leveling charges and possession was to be delivered after leveling. The question arose whether the sum was to be paid before or after the leveLling. The agreement was silent on the point.

And, therefore, the court held that "in the ordinary course of business work is not usually paid for before it is done. It is the custom in some cases for payment to be made in installments as the work progresses but the person for whom a work is done is not expected to pay the entire cost in advance unless there is an express agreement to that effect."

(C) Effect of one party preventing another from performing promise (Section 53)

When a contract contains reciprocal promises, it may happen that one party to the contract prevents that other from performing his promise. In such a case, the contract becomes voidable at the option of the party so prevented. Further, the party so prevented is entitled to compensation from the other party for any loss which he may sustain in consequence of the non-performance of the contract.

Example

A and B contract that B shall execute certain work for A for a thousand rupees, B is ready and wiling to execute the work accordingly, but A prevents him from doing so. The contract is voidable at the option of B, and if he elects to rescind it, he is entitled to recover from A compensation for any loss which he has incurred by its non-performance.

The same result would follow where the obstruction to performance is caused by the inadequacy of the machinery or material supplied by one of the parties. In a case before the Privy Council — *Kleinert v. Abosso Gold Mining,*[173] where in order to get his mine cleared of a rock, the defendant had a supply a crusher. The crusher supplied was too inadequate for the job. This was held to be such an obstruction to as enabled the contractor to recover his expenses and loss of profits. Similarly, in a case before the Supreme Court *Har Prasad Choubey v. Union of India*[174], a bidder to whom a coal mine was knocked down was allowed to have refund of his deposit when the Coal Commissioner refused to permit him to take the coal to U.P., and any such restriction being not present in the terms of the auction.

(D) Effect of default as to promise to be performed first (Section 54)

Where the nature of reciprocal promises is such that one of them can not be performed till the other party has performed his promise then if the other party fails to perform it, he cannot claim the performance of the reciprocal promise from the first party. In such a case, the other party must make compensation to the first party to the contract for any loss which the first party may sustain by the non-performance of the contract.

Examples

(i) A hires B's ship to take in any convey, from Calcutta to Mauritius, a Cargo to be provided by A, B receiving a certain freight for its conveyance. A does not provide any cargo for the ship. A cannot claim the performance of B's promise, and must make compensation to B for the loss which B sustains by the non-performance of the contract.

(ii) A contracts with B to execute certain builders work for a fixed prince, B supplying the scaffolding and timber necessary for the work. B refuses to furnish any scaffolding or timber, and the work cannot be executed. A need not execute the work, and B is bound to make compensation to A for any loss caused to him by non performance of the contract.

(iii) A contracts with B to deliver to him, at a specified price, certain merchandise on board a ship which cannot arrive for a month, and B engages to pay for the merchandise within a week from the date of the contract. B does not pay within the weak. A's promise to deliver need not be performed, and B must make compensation.

(iv) A promises B to sell him one hundred bales of merchandise, to be delivered next day, and B promises A to pay for them within a month. A does not deliver according to his promise. B's promise to pay need not be performed and A must make compensation.

In a case before Supreme Court — *Nathulal v. Phoolchand,*[175] the plaintiff was the owner of ginning factory constructed on agricultural land nominally held in the name of his brother. He sold the factory to the balance being payable on a fixed date. The buyer defaulted in paying upon that date and the seller rescinded the contract and brought an action for possession.

SHAH J. held that the nature of the contract required that the seller should have his own name recorded as the owner and obtain permission of the state government for transfer of the agricultural land before he could claim the final payment. So long as the seller did not carry out his part of contract, the buyer could not be called upon to pay the balance of the price.

(E) Reciprocal promise to do things legal and also other things illegal (Section 57)

Where persons reciprocally promise, firstly to do certain things which are legal, and secondly, under specified circumstances, to do certain other things which are illegal, the first set of promises is a contract, but the second is void agreement.

A and B agree that A shall sell B a house for Rs. 10,000/-, but that if B uses it as a gambling house, he shall pay A Rs. 50,000/- for it.

The first set is for reciprocal promises, namely, to sell the house and to pay Rs.10,000/- for it, is a contract.

The second set is for an unlawful object, namely, that B may use the house as a gambling house, and is a void agreement.

Time for Performance (Section 55)

Sometimes the parties of a contract specify the time for its performance. Ordinarily, it is expected that either party will perform his obligation at the stipulated time. But if one of them fails to do so, the question arises, what is the effect upon the contract. Section 55 provides the answer.

(1) A contract in which time is essential (Section 55 Para1)

If the intention of the parties was that time should be of the essence of the contract, then a failure to perform at the agreed time renders the contract voidable at the option of the opposite party. If, in such a case, the promisee accepts performance of the promise after the fixed time, he can not claim compensation for any loss occasioned by the non-performance of the promise at the agreed time.

Time is generally considered to be of the essence of the contract in the following three cases:

(i) Where the parties have expressly agreed to treat it as of the essence of the contract,

(ii) Where delay operates as an injury, and

(iii) Where the nature and necessity of the contract require it to be so construed, for example, where a party asks for extension of time for performance.

In Bhudra Chand v. Betts[176], the plaintiff stipulated with the defendant to engage his elephant for the purpose of Kheda operations (to capture wild elephants). The contract provided that the elephant would be delivered on the 1st Oct. 1910, but the defendant obtained an extension of time till the 6th October and yet did not deliver the elephant till the 11th. The plaintiff refused to accept the elephant and sued for damages for the breach.

He was held entitled to recover as the parties intended that time should be of the essence of the contract. "This conclusion is confirmed by the circumstance that the defendant obtained an extension of the time, if the time were not of the essence of the contract, he need not have asked for extension of time". Thus, the matter depends upon the intention of the parties. Even where "a specific date is mentioned for the completion of the contract, one has not to look at the letter but at the substance of the agreement in order to ascertain the real intention of the parties."

In commercial or mercantile contracts which provide for performance within a specified time, time is ordinarily of the essence of the contract.

Thus, (a) In a contract for the purchase of a chassis for a diesel truck to be supplied within two months, time was held to be of the essence of the contract. (*Hitkari Motors v. Attar Singh*[177]) (b) In a contract for the sale of purchase of goods the prices of which fluctuate rapidly in the market, the time of delivery and payment are considered to be of the essence of the contract (*Mahabir Pershad v. Durga Dutta*[178])

2. When time is not of the essence (Section 55, Para 2)

In a contract, in which time is not of the essence of the contract, failure on the part of the promisor to perform his obligation within the fixed time does not make the contract voidable, but the promisee is entitled to compensation for any loss occasioned to him by such failure.

Intention to make time as the essence of the contract, if expressed in writing must be in a language which is unambiguous and unmistakable. The mere fact that a certain time is specified in a contract for the performance of a promise does not necessarily make time as the essence of the contract. If the contract includes clauses providing for extension of time in certain contingencies or for payment of fine or penalty for every day or week the work undertaken remains unfinished on the expiry of time provided in the contract, such clauses are construed as rendering ineffective the express provision relating to the time being of the essence of the contract (*Hind Construction Contractors v. State of Maharashtra*[179]).

In cases other than commercial or mercantile contracts, the ordinary presumption is that time is not of the essence of the contract. Accordingly, "in a contract for the sale of immovable property, time would not be regarded as of the essence unless it is shown that the parties intended so."[180]

In a contract of sale of immovable property time is not of the essence unless it is shown that the intention of the parties was that time should be the essence of the contract (*Indira Kaur v. Sheo Lal Kapoor*[181]).

Subsequent Notice

Time may be made the essence of a contract by a subsequent notice. The subsequent notice, specifying time, ought to fix the longest time that could reasonably be required for the performance of acts which remain to be done (*Crawford v. Toogwood*[182]). Any subsequent notice making time as the essence of the contract ought to fix a reasonably long time requiring the other party to perform his contract.

Effect of acceptance of performance at time other than that agreed upon (Section 55 Para3)

"If, in case of a contract voidable on account of the promisor's failure to perform his promise at the time agreed, the promisee accepts performance of such promise at any time other than that agreed, the promisee cannot claim compensation for any loss occasioned by the non performance of the promise at the time agreed, unless, at the time of such acceptance, he gives notice to the promisor of his intention to do so."

Appropriation of Payments (Section 59 to 61)

Appropriation means application of payments. The question of appropriation of payment is closely connected with the question of time and place of performance as to several debts owing by one party to another. When a debtor (customer) owes several distinct debts to the same creditor (banker) and makes a payment without instruction to the creditor that may arise against which debt the payment is to be appropriated. The principles are incorporated in section 59-61 of the Indian Contact Act 1872. The provisions of these sections are summarised below:

1. Appropriation by Debtor

According to section 59, the debtor has the right to instruct expressly which debt, if he owes more than one, shall be canceled by the money he tenders to the creditor. If there is no express instruction as to the appropriation, there may be circumstances which imply that the debtor intended appropriation to a particular debt, the debtor's intention must be followed if money is accepted. If the creditor does not agree to the specific directions of the debtor as to the appropriation he must refuse to accept the payment.

Examples

(i) A owes B, among other debts Rs.1000 upon a promissory note which falls due on the 1st June. He owes B no other debt of that amount. On the 1st June, A pays B Rs.1000, the payment is to be applied to the discharge of the promissory note.

(ii) A owes B, among other debts, the sum of Rs. 567. B writes to A and demands payment of this sum. A sends to B Rs. 567. This payment is to be applied to the discharge of the debt of which B had demanded payment.

2. Appropriation by Creditor

According to Section 60 of the Indian Contract Act, where the customer has omitted to intimate and there are no other circumstances indicating to which debt the payment is to be applied, the creditor has the right to appropriate it, at his discretion to any lawful debt actually due and payable to him from the debtor. He may even apply it to liquidate either a time-barred debt or an unenforceable debt. Appropriation, under this section cannot be made towards an illegal debt.

On the question whether a part payment should be treated towards principal or interest, the general principle, subject to any contract to the contrary, is that the payment should first be applied to the interest and after the interest is fully paid off, to the principal (*Rulia Devi v. Raghunath Prasad*[183]).

3. Where neither party appropriates

Creditor can make his appropriation at any time even when he is being examined at the trail of the case. Entries in the books of account are not binding on the creditor if he has not communicated them to the debtor. Section 61 of the Indian Contract Act reads, where neither party makes any appropriation the payment shall be applied in discharge of the debts in order of time, whether they are or are not barred by the law enforce for the time being as to the limitation of suits. If the debts are of equal standing (i.e., of the same date) the payment shall be applied in discharge of each proportionately.

Rule in Clayton's case.[184] This rule is applicable where the parties have a current account, i.e., a running account between them. In such a case appropriation impliedly takes place in the order in which the receipts and payments take place and are carried into the account. It is the first item on the debit side of the account that is discharged or reduced by the first item on the credit side, the appropriation is made by the very act of setting the two items against each other. In simple words, it means that, unless there is a contrary intention, the items on the credit of an account must be appropriated against the items on the debit in order of date.

Contracts which need not be performed

Section 62 to 67 of the Indian Contract Act mention the contract which need not be performed.

(i) If the parties to a contract agree to substitute a new contract for it or to rescind or alter it, the original contract need not be performed (Section 62)

(ii) Promisee may dispense with or remit, wholly or in part, the performance of a promise made to him, or may extend the time for such performance, or may accept instead of it any satisfaction which he thinks fit (Section 63)

(iii) When a person at whose option a contract is voidable rescinds it, the other party there to need not perform any promise contained therein in which he is a promisor (Section 64)

(iv) If any promisee neglects or refuses to afford the promisor, reasonable facilities for the performance of his promise, the promisor is excused from performance of the contract thereby (Section 67)

(v) When a contract becomes void because of supervening impossibility or illegality (Section 56)

(vi) When a person has the right to rescind a contract (Section 75)

(vii) When a promisor is excused by any other law, e.g., the Limitation Act, or a company is not liable to fulfill a contract under the doctrine of *ultra vires*.

CHAPTER

32

Discharge of Contract

Discharge of contract means termination of the contractual relationship between the parties. A contract is said to be discharged when it ceases to operate, i.e., when the rights and obligations created by it come to an end. After the formation of a valid contract, the next stage is reached, namely the fulfillment of the object the parties had in mind. When the object is fulfilled the liability of either party under the contract comes to an end. The contract is then said to be discharged.

A contract may be discharged —

(1) By Performance

(2) By Agreement (Sections 62-67)

(3) By Impossibility of performance (Section 56)

(4) By Breach of Contract (Section 39)

(5) By Operation of Law

(6) By Lapse of time.

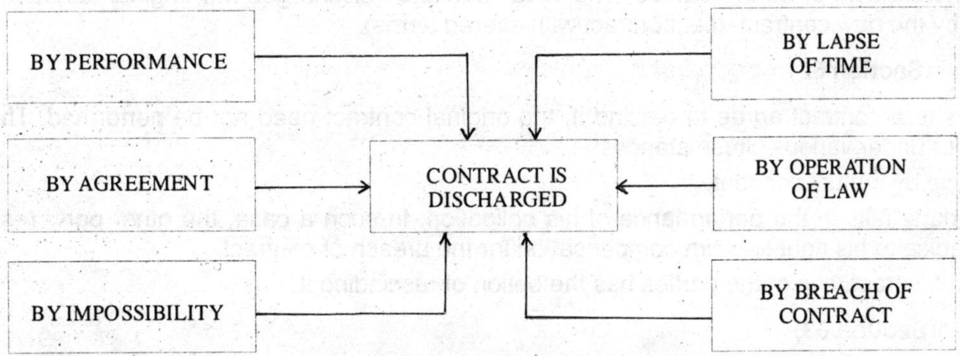

Discharge of a contract

Figure No. 1

(1) By Performance

The obvious mode of discharge of a contract is by performance. Performance means the doing of that which is required by a contract. Discharge by performance takes place when the parties to the contract fulfill their obligations arising under the contract within the time and in the manner prescribed. In such a case, the parties are discharged and the contract comes to an end. But if only one party performs the promise, he alone is discharged. Such a party gets a right of action against the other party who is guilty of breach.

Performance of a contract may be (i) actual performance or (ii) attempted performance

(i) Actual performance

When both the parties perform their promises, the contract is discharged.

Thus, where A contracts to sell his house to B for Rs.5 lakhs as soon as the house is delivered to B and B pays the agreed price for it, the contract comes to an end by actual performance.

(ii) Attempted performance or Tender

Tender is not actual performance but is only an offer to perform the obligation under the contract. The offer of performance or tender has the same effect as performance. If the promisor offers to perform his obligation, but the promisee refuses to accept the performance, the promisor stands discharged of his obligations.

2. By Agreement

The rights and obligations created by an agreement can be discharged without their performance by means of another agreement between the parties.

The various cases of discharge of a contract by mutual agreement are dealt with in sections 62 and 63 and as discussed below.

(i) Novation (Section 62)

It means that there being a contract in existence some new contract is substituted for it, either between the same parties or between different parties, the consideration mutually being the discharge of the old contract. It is transaction by which, with the consent of all the parties concerned, the old contract is revoked and substituted by a new contract. Since novation implies a fresh contract in place of original one, all the parties to the old contract must agree to it. The new agreement should be valid and made before the breach of the original promise. If the new agreement is unenforceable, then the old contract revives.

Example

An existing mortgage was discharged by the substitution of a new agreement of mortgage. The new agreement was not enforceable for want of registration. Held, the parties could fall back upon the original mortgage. (*Shanker Lal Damodar v. A. Ajaipal*[185]).

(ii) Alteration (Section 62)

The term 'alteration' may be defined as charge in one or more terms of the contract. The alteration is valid when it is made with the consent of all the parties. The valid alteration discharges the original contract, and the parties, becomes bound by the new contract (i.e. contract with altered terms).

(iii) Rescission (Section 62)

If the parties to a contract agree to rescind it, the original contract need not be performed. The rescission of a contract may occur under various circumstances:

(a) It may be done by mutual consent.

(b) Where one party fails in the performance of his obligation. In such a case, the other party rescind the contract without prejudice to his right to claim compensation for the breach of contract.

(c) In a voidable contract, one of the parties has the option of rescinding it.

(iv) Remission (Section 63)

It is the acceptance of a lesser sum than what was contracted for or a lesser fulfillment of the promise made. It is a unilateral act of the promisee discharging, at his will and pleasure, the obligation of another. A promisee may remit or give up a part of his claim and a promise to do so is binding even though there is no consideration for doing so. The effect of the provision is that the party who has the right to demand the performance of a contract may:

(a) remit or dispense with it, wholly or in part, or

(b) extend the time for performance, or

(c) accept any other satisfaction instead of performance.

(v) Waiver

It means to "dispense with" or the abandonment of a right which a person is entitled to. A party to a contract may waive his rights under the contract, whereupon the other party is released from his obligation.

(vi) Merger

When a superior right and an inferior right coincide and meet in one and the same person, the inferior right vanishes into the superior right. This is known as merger. A man holding property under lease, buys the property. His rights as a lease vanish. They are merged into the rights of ownership which he has now acquired.

Example

A is a tenant of B's flat. A purchases the flat from B. A's tenancy is inferior right to B's ownership. As the ownership (Superior right) vests in A on purchase, the tenancy of A merges and is extinguished in ownership. A becomes owner and ceases to be tenant.

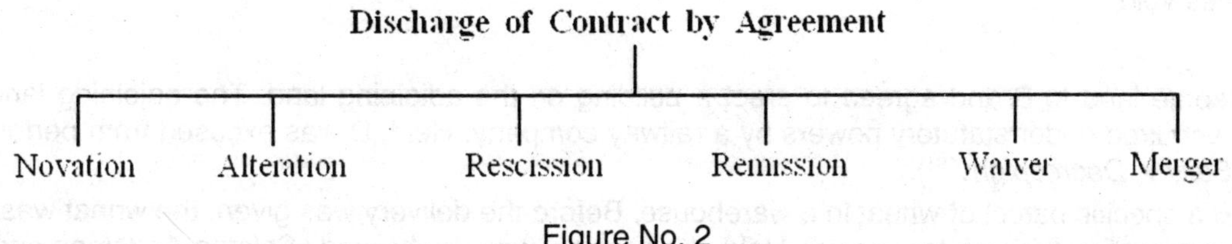

Figure No. 2

(3) By Impossibility of Performance

According to Section 56, impossibility of performance may fall into (i) impossibility existing at the time of contract known as pre contractual or initial impossibility and (ii) subsequent or supervening impossibility also known as post contractual impossibility. The agreement in the first case is void ab initio due to absolute impossibility.

Section 56 says that "an agreement to do an act impossible in itself is void." It further lays down that even though the act was not impossible, or unlawful at the moment of time the agreement was made, but becomes impossible or unlawful afterwards, the contract becomes void when the act becomes impossible or unlawful.

Discharge by Supervening impossibility

A contract is discharged by supervening impossibility in the following cases:

(i) Destruction of subject matter of contract

When the subject matter of contract, subsequent to its formation, is destroyed without any fault of the parties to the contract, the contract is discharged.

Examples

(a) A music hall was let for series of concerts on certain days. The hall was burnt down before the date of the first concert. The contract becomes void (*Taylor v. Caldwell*[186]).

(b) A person contracted to deliver a part of a specific crop of potatoes. The potatoes were destroyed by pests though no fault of the party. The contract was held to be discharged. (*Howell v. Coupland*[187])

(c) A sold to B a cargo of cotton seed to be shipped by a particular ship. Before the time for shipping arrived the ship was damaged by standing so as to render the loading of the cargo impossible according to the contract. Held, the contract was discharged (*Nickoll and Knight v. Ashton Edridge and Co.*[188]).

(ii) Non-existence or Non-occurrence of a state of things necessary performance

If a contract is made on the basis of continued existence of certain state of circumstances, the contract stands discharged if the state of things charges or ceases to exist.

Examples

(a) A and B contract to marry each other, Before the time fixed for the marriage. A goes mad. The contract becomes void.

(b) A contract was to hire a flat for witnessing a coronation procession of King Edward VII. The coronation procession was canceled due to the illness of the King. In a suit for the recovery of the rent, it was held that the contract became impossible of performance and that the hirer need not pay the rent (*Krell v. Henry*[189]).

This kind of failure of the object of a contract is often called "frustration of the contract".

(iii) Death or incapacity of Personal Service

Where the performance of a contract depends on the personal skill or qualification of a party, the contract is discharged on the illness or incapacity or death of that party.

Examples

(a) A, a singer, agrees with B to give his performance at some particular theatre on a specified date. While on his way to the theatre. A meets an accident and is rendered unconscious. The agreement becomes void.

(b) An artist undertook to perform at a concert for a certain price. Before she could do so, she was taken seriously ill. Held she was discharged due to illness (*Robinson v. Davison*[190])

(iv) Change of Law

The performance of a contract may become unlawful by a subsequent change of Law. In such cases, the original contract becomes void.

Examples

(a) D leased some land to B and agreed to erect a building on the adjoining land. The adjoining land, after some time, was acquired under statutory powers by a railway company. Held, D was excused from performance of the contract (*Baily v. Decrespigny*[191]).

(b) A sold to B a specific parcel of wheat in a warehouse. Before the delivery was given, the wheat was requisitioned by the government under statutory power. Held, the contract was discharged (*Shipton Anderson and Co. Re.* [192]).

(v) Outbreak of war

A contract entered into during war with a alien enemy is *void ab initio.* A contract entered into before the war commenced between citizens of countries subsequently at war, remains suspended during the pendency of the war. After the termination of the war, the contract revives and may be enforced.

Cases not covered by supervening impossibility

Ordinarily when a person undertakes to do something, he must do it unless its performance becomes absolutely impossible due to any of the circumstances discussed above. Therefore, in the following cases, a contract is not discharged on the ground of supervening impossibility:

(i) Difficulty of performance

A contract is not discharged by the mere fact that it has become more difficulty of performance due to some uncontemplated events or delays.

(ii) Commercial Impossibility

A party to the contract cannot be discharged from performing his part of the contract simply on the ground that it will be non-profitable for him to perform the contract.

Example

A contracts to lay gas mains is not discharged because the outbreak of war makes it expensive to procure the necessary materials (*M/s Alopi Pd. v. Union of India*[193]).

(iii) Impossibility due to the behaviour of a third party

The doctrine of supervening impossibility does not cover the cases where a contract could not be performed because of the default by a third person on whose word the promisor relied.

Example

A, a wholesaler, entered into a contract with B for the sale of a certain type of cloth to be produced by C, a manufacturer of that cloth. C did not manufacturer of that cloth. Held, A was liable to B for damages (*Harnandrai Fulchand v. Pragdas*[194])

(iv) Strikes, Lockouts and Civil Disturbances

Events like these do not terminate contracts unless there is a clause in the contract of that effect.

Examples

(a) A agreed to supply B certain goods to be produced in Algeria. The goods could not be produced because of riots and civil disturbance in that country. Held, there was no excuse for non-performance of the contract. (*Jacobs v. Credit Lyonnais*[195])

(b) The unloading of a ship was delayed beyond the date agreed with the shipowners owing to a strike of dock workers. Held, the shipowners were entitled to damages, the impossibility of performance being no excuse (Budget v. Binnington[196])

(v) Failure of one of the objects

Where a contract is made for several purposes, failure of one of the objects does not discharge the contract.

Example

A agreed to let a boat to H to (a) view the naval review at the coronation and (b) to cruise round fleet, owing to the king's illness, the naval review was canceled, but the fleet was assembled and the boat could have been used to cruise round the fleet. Held, the contract was not discharged (*Herne Bay Steamboat Co. v. Hutton*[197]).

Effects of Supervening Impossibility

(1) Section 56 provides that when the performance of a contract becomes subsequently impossible or illegal, the contract becomes void.

(2) Section 65 further provides that when a contract becomes void, any person who has received any advantage under it must restore it, or make compensation for it, to the person whom he received it.

(3) Section 65 (Para 3) provides that "where one person has promised to do something which he knew, or with reasonable diligence, might have known, and which the promisee did not know to be impossible or unlawful such promisor must make compensation to such promisee for any loss which such promisee sustains through the non-performance of the promise."

Examples

(a) A contracts to sign for B at a concert for Rs. 1000, which are paid in advance. A is too ill to sign. A must refund to B Rs. 1000/-

(b) A pays B Rs.1000 in consideration of B's promising to marry C, A's daughter, C dies before marriage. B must repay A the Rs.1000/-

(4) By Breach of Contract

Parties to a contract are expected to perform their respective promises. If a party breaks his obligation which the contract imposes, there takes place "breach of contract". It confers a right of action for damages on the injured party. Breach of contract may by

(i) Actual breach of contract or

(ii) Anticipatory or constructive breach of contract.

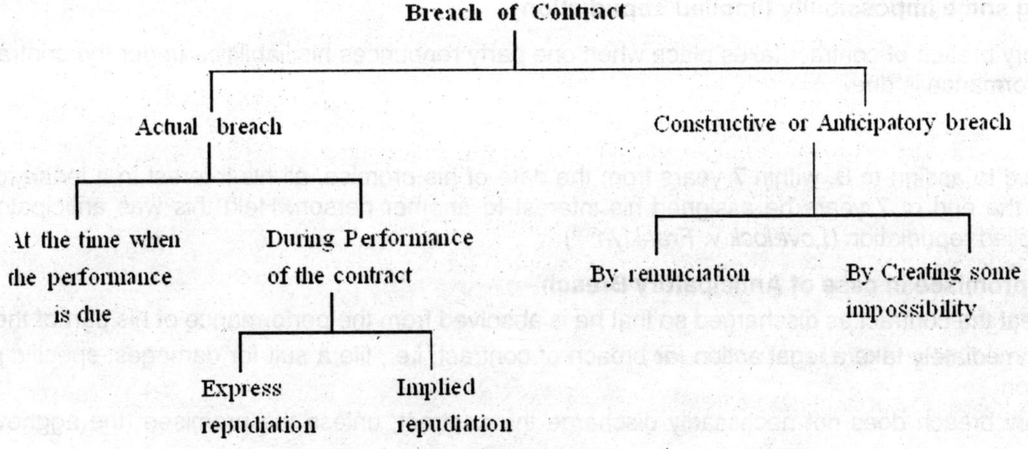

Figure No. 3

1. Actual Breach of Contract

It may take place —

(i) At the time when the performance is due

Actual breach of contract occurs when, at the time when the performance is due, one party fails or refuses to perform his obligation under the contract.

(ii) During the performance of the contract

Actual breach of contract also occurs when during the performance of the contract, one party fails or refuses to perform his obligation under the contract. This refusal to perform may be by —

(a) Express repudiation (by word or act): Where there has been some performance of the contract and one party by his word or act refuses to continue to perform his obligation in some essential respect, the other party can treat the contract as no longer binding on him and sue for breach of contract.

Example

C contracted with a railway company to supply it 3,000 tons of railway chairs at a certain price, to be delivered in installments. After 1,787 tons had been supplied, the railway company asked C to deliver no more. Held, C could bring an action for breach of contract (*Cort v. Ambergate etc Rly Co.*[198]).

(b) Implied repudiation (Impossibility created by the act of a party to the contract): If a party, during the performance, makes by his own act the complete performance of the contract impossible, the effect is as if he has breached the contract, and the other party is discharged from the further performance of the contract.

Example

P, a British subject, was engaged by the captain of a warship owned by the Japanese Government to act as a fireman. Subsequently when the Japanese Government declared war with China, P was informed that the performance of the contract would bring him under the penalties of the Foreign Enlistment Act. He consequently left the ship. Held, he was entitled to recover the wages agreed upon (*O'Neil v. Armstrong*[199]).

In both cases (a) and (b) the party not in breach can treat the contract as no longer binding on him and sue for breach of contract.

2. Anticipatory breach of contract

Anticipatory breach of contract occurs when a party repudiates his liability or obligation under the contract before the time for performance arrives. This may happen in one of the following ways —

(i) By Renunciation (Express repudiation)

Anticipatory breach of contract takes place when one party renounces his obligation under the contract expressly, before the performance is due.

(ii) By creating some impossibility (Implied repudiation)

Anticipatory breach of contract takes place when one party renounces his liabilities under the contract expressly, before the performance is due.

Example

A promised to assign to B, within 7 years from the date of his promise, all his interest in a lease for the sum of £140. Before the end of 7 years he assigned his interest to another person. Held this was anticipatory breach of contract by implied repudiation (*Lovelock v. Franklyn*[200]).

Rights of the promisee in case of Anticipatory Breach

(i) He can treat the contract as discharged so that he is absolved from the performance of his part of the promise.

(ii) He can immediately take a legal action for breach of contract, i.e., file a suit for damages, specific performance, or injunction.

Anticipatory breach does not necessarily discharge the contract, unless the promisee (the aggrieved party) so chooses.

If the promisee refuses to accept the repudiation of the contract by the promisor and treats the contract as alive, the consequences are as follows:

(i) The promisor may perform his promise when the time for its performance comes and the promisee will be bound to accept the performance.

(ii) If, while the contract is alive, an event (Say, a Supervening impossibility) happens which discharges the contract legally, the promisor may take advantage of such discharge. In such a case, the promisee loses his right to sue for damages.

Measure of damages in anticipatory breach of contract

(i) If the contract is ended at once

If the contract is ended by the promisee at once, he can sue the promisor for damages. The amount of damages will be measured by the difference between the price prevailing on the date of breach and the contract price.

(ii) If the contract is kept alive till the date of performance of the contract

If the promisee keeps the contract alive till the date of performance, the measure of damages will be the difference between the price prevailing on the date of the performance and the contract price.

The aggrieved party may, after putting an end to the contract, bring an action for damages for breach, but he will be bound under section 64 to restore to the other party the benefits he might have received under the contract.

Remedies for Breach of Contract (Section 73 -75)

As soon as either party commits a breach of the contract, the other part becomes entitled to any of the following reliefs:

(1) Rescission of the contract.

(2) Damages for the loss sustained or suffered.

(3) A decree for specific performance.

(4) An injunction.

(5) Suit on Quantum Meruit

1. Rescission of the Contract

When a breach of contract is committed by one party, the other party may sue to treat the contract as rescinded. In such a case, the aggrieved party is freed from all his obligations under the contract.

Party rightfully rescinding contract entitled to compensation (Section 75)

A person who rightfully rescinds the contract is entitled to compensation for any damage which he has sustained through the non-fulfilment of the contract.

2. Damages

'Damages' means compensation in money which the party who suffers by a breach of contract is entitled to receive from the party who has broken the contract. The fundamental principle underlying damages is not punishment but compensation. Damages are of four kinds—

(a) Ordinary Damages

(b) Special Damages

(c) Vindictive or Punitive or Exemplary damages and

(d) Nominal Damages

(a) Ordinary Damages (Section 73)

Ordinary damages are those which flow as a natural consequence in the usual course of things from the breach, i.e., damages which the parties may be deemed to have known as likely to arise on a breach, even at the time of entering into a contract.

(b) Special Damages

Special damages are those resulting from a breach of contract under special circumstances. The special circumstances must have been known to both the parties. They ought to have known the loss that is likely to result from out of the breach of the contract, by taking the special circumstances into account. In such circumstances, special damages are awarded.

(c) Exemplary Damages

These damages are awarded with a view to punish the defendant, and not solely with the idea of awarding compensation to the plaintiff. These have been awarded (a) for a breach of promise to marry (b) for wrongful dishonour of a cheque by a banker possessing adequate funds of the customer. The measure of damages in case (a) is dependent upon the severity of the shock to the sentiments of the promisee. In case (b) the rule is smaller the amount of the cheque dishonoured, larger will be the amount of damages awarded.

(d) Nominal Damages

Nominal damages are awarded in cases of breach of contract where there is only a technical violation of the legal right, but no substantial loss is caused thereby. The damages granted in such cases are called nominal because they are very small, for example, a rupee or a shilling.

Duty to mitigate damages suffered.

It is the duty of the injured party to minimise damages (*British Westinghouse and Co. v. Underground Electric etc, Co.*[201]). He can not claim to be compensated by the party in default for loss which is really not due to the breach but to his own neglect to minimise loss after the breach.

Liquidated Damages and Penalty

Sometimes, parties themselves at the time of entering into a contract agree that a particular sum will be payable by a party in case of breach of the contract by him. Such a sum may either be by way of liquidated damages, or it may be by way of "penalty".

Liquidated Damages

The term liquidated damages means the sum which has been fixed by the parties as a genuine pre-estimate of the damage likely to be caused by the breach of the contract. The parties may try to avoid the delay and the expense involved in litigation and hence decided that amount to be paid as damages also. Where such a sum is fixed by the parties, the Court never tries to interfere with it, provided it is reasonable.

Penalty

On the other hand, if the sum mentioned in the contract is so extravagant and unconscionable as to have no connection with the greatest loss that may possibly result out of the breach, it is known as Penalty. In such cases, the amount fixed hold the parties in terror.

English law recognises a distinction between liquidated damages and penalty, whereas liquidated damages are enforceable but penalty cannot be claimed. In India, there is no such distinction recognised between penalty and liquidated damages. Section 74 which contains law in this regard states.

"Where a contract has been broken, if a sum is named in the contract as the amount to be paid in case of such breach, or if the contract contains any other stipulation by way of penalty, the party complaining of the breach is entitled (whether or not actual damage or loss in proved to have been caused thereby), to receive from the party who has broken the contract, reasonable compensation not exceeding the amount as named, or, as the case may be, the penalty stipulated for." Thus, where the amount payable in case of breach is fixed in advance whether by way of liquidated damages or penalty, the party may claim only a reasonable compensation for the breach, subject to the amount so fixed.

Amendment of 1988

Section 74 was amended by the Indian Contract (Amendment) Act 1988. The amended section provides that where a party has agreed in an agreement with the Government that he shall not pay directly or indirectly any commission, perquisite, fees or other consideration of any kind to anyone for the purpose of negotiating procuring or making the said contract, the Government shall be entitled to claim damages for breach of such stipulation which may be upto double the amount of any commission, fees, perquisite or other consideration paid by him.

Payment of Interest

Several times, in bonds and other instruments standing as securities for money, provision for enhanced rates of interest in case of default will be provided. The following rules are observed with regard to payment of interest.

(i) Payment of interest in case of default

A stipulation for payment of interest in case of default is not in the nature of a penalty, if the interest is reasonable. If the court finds that the rate of interest is exorbitant and is penal in character, it may grant relief.

(ii) Payment of interest at higher rate

A stipulation for increased interest from the date of the bond, and not from the date of default, is always in the nature of a penalty, and relief is granted against it.

(iii) Payment of compound interest on default

Where compound interest is payable on default, if it is at the same rate, it is not a penalty. If it is at a higher rate it is a penalty. Therefore, whether they amount to penalty or not depends on the facts of each case.

In *Sunder Koer v. Rai Sham Krishan*,[202] the privy council observed that compound interest at the rate exceeding the rate of interest on the principal money being in excess of the ordinary and useful stipulation, may well be regarded as in the nature of a penalty.

(iv) Payment of interest at a lower rate

An agreement to pay a particular rate of interest with a stipulation that a reduced rate will be acceptable if paid punctually is not a stipulation by way of penalty.

3. A degree for specific performance

In certain cases of breach of a contract, damages are not an adequate remedy. The court may, in such cases, direct the party in breach of carry out his promise according to the terms of the contract. This is a direction by the Court for specific performance of the contract at the suit of the party not in breach.

This remedy is, however discretionary and will not be granted in the following cases.

(i) where monetary compensation is an adequate remedy,

(ii) where the court cannot supervise the execution of the contract, e.g., a building contract,

(iii) where the contract is for personal service, i.e., a contract to paint a picture, and

(iv) where one of the parties is a minor.

The remedy of specific relief unlike that of damages cannot be obtained as a matter of right but rests entirely on the discretion of the court.

The contracts which may be specifically enforced are briefly stated as follows:

(i) Agreement to sell or transfer immovable property,

(ii) Sale with a condition to purchase,

(iii) Agreement for exchange of immovable property,

(iv) Agreement to lease,

(v) Contract by limited owner to sell or lease,

(vi) Agreement to sell or divide reversionary interest,

(vii) Agreement to partition,

(viii) Compromise of family settlements and doubtful rights,

(ix) Agreement for the sale of shares having a limited market,

(x) Contracts in performance of trust.

4. An Injunction

Injunction means an order of the court restraining the wrongdoer from doing, or continuing, the wrongful act complained of where a party is in breach of a negative term of contract (i.e., where he does something which he promised not to do), the court may, by issuing an order, prohibit him from doing so.

Examples

(a) W agreed to sing at L's theatre, and during a certain period to sign nowhere else. Afterwards W made contract with Z to sing at another theatre and refused to perform the contract with L. Held, W could be restrained by injunction from singing for Z (*Lumley v. Wagner*[203]).

(b) G agreed to buy the whole of the electric energy required for his house from a certain company. He was, therefore, restrained by an injunction from buying electricity from any other person (*Metropolitan Electric Supply Company v. Ginder* [204]).

(c) N, a film actress agreed to act exclusively for W for a year and for no one else. During the year she contracted to act for Z. Held she could be restrained by injunction from doing so (*Warner Bros. v. Nelson*[205])

5. Quantum Meruit

The phrase *Quantum Meruit* means as much as is merited (earned). The normal rule of Law is that unless a party has performed his promise in its entirety, it cannot claim performance from the other. To this rule, however, there are certain exceptions on the basis of '*Quantum Meruit*'. A right to sue on a *quantum meruit* arises where a contract partly performed by one party, has become discharged by the breach of the other party. This right is founded on an implied promise by the other party arising from the acceptance of a benefit by that party.

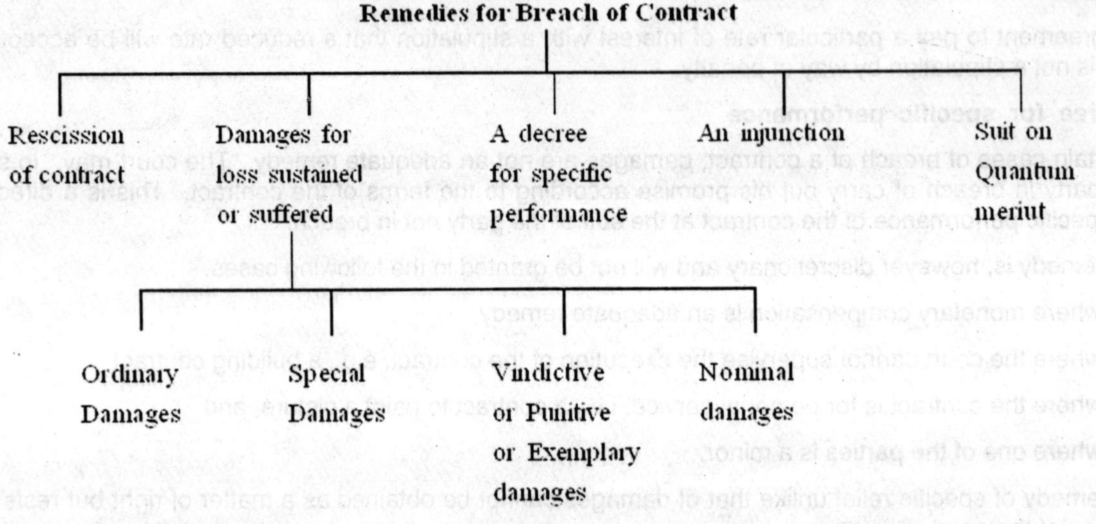

Figure No. 4

The above figures depicts in nutsheell the various remedies available to a person/party for the breach of contract. However, the law of torts provides a numerous provisions for breach and a very common phenomenon in England, unfortunately the law of torts, though, invoked in India too, but not effective in the real sense.

CHAPTER

33

Indemnity and Guarantee

Contract of Indemnity

Section 124 to 127 of the Indian Contract Act deals with contract of Indemnity. A contract by which one party promises to save the other from any loss caused to him by the conduct of the promisor himself, or by the conduct of any other person is called "Contract of Indemnity" (Sec. 124). The person who promises to make good the loss is called the indemnifier (Promisor) and the person whose loss is to be made good is called the indemnified or indemnity-holder (Promisee). A Contract of Indemnity is really a class of Contingent Contracts.

The only illustration appended to the section says that if a person promises to save another from the consequences of a proceeding which may be commenced against him, it is a Contract of Indemnity.

A contracts to indemnify B against the consequences of any proceedings which C may take against B in respect of a certain sum of 200 rupees. This is a Contact of Indemnity.

Essentials of a Contract of Indemnity

(1) There must be two parties in a contract of indemnity, viz, Indemnifier and Indemnified.

(2) A contract of indemnity may be express or implied.

(3) This contract being a specie of contract, is subject to all the rules of contract, such as free consent, legality of object, etc.

(4) A contract of Indemnity is enforceable only when the promisee suffers a loss the happening of which is unknown. The indemnity holder is entitled to enforce the contract only if he suffers the loss against which the indemnity holder was promised to be protected.

(5) Consideration in the case of contract of indemnity is essential to enable the indemnity holder to claim to be compensated.

Illustration

A agrees to indemnify B if the latter published a defamatory article in his newspaper against C. If C sues B and is fined, he cannot recover fine from A inspite of his promise to indemnify B.

Definition is not exhaustive

The definition of 'Contract of Indemnity' as given in the Indian Contract Act is not exhaustive. It includes:

(a) express promises to indemnify, and

(b) cases where the loss is caused by the conduct of the promisor himself or by the conduct of any other person.

It does not include:

(a) implied promises to indemnify, and

(b) cases where loss arises from accidents and events not depending on the conduct of the promisor or any other person.

In India, it has been held that "Section 124 and 125 of the Contract Act are not exhaustive of the law of indemnity and the courts here would apply the same equitable principles that the courts in England do." (*Gajanan Moreshwar v. Moreshwar Madan*[206]). Moreover, if Section 124 is strictly interpreted even contracts of insurance would have to be excluded from the definition. Such a strict application of the definition was not intended by the legislature.

A contract of indemnity may be express or implied. An implied contract of indemnity may be inferred from the circumstances of the case or from relationship of the parties.

Section 69 also implies a promise to indemnify. A contract of indemnity is a species of the general contract. As such it must have all essential elements of a valid contract.

Rights of Indemnified (i.e. the Indemnity- holder)

Section 125 deals with rights of indemnified (i.e. indemnity-holder) when sued. According to section 125, an indemnity holder is entitled to recover from the promisor:

(1) All damages which he may be compelled to pay in any suit in respect of any matter to which the promise to indemnify applies.

(2) All costs of suit which he may have to pay to such third party, provided in bringing or defending the suit. (a) he acted under the authority of the indemnifier or (b) he did not act in contravention of the orders of the indemnifier and in such a way as a prudent man would act in his own case.

(3) All sums which he may have paid under the terms of any compromise of any such suit, if the compromise was not contrary to the order of the indemnifier, and was one which it would have been prudent for the promisee to make.

Rights of Indemnifier

The Indian Contract Act is silent regarding the rights of the indemnifier in a contract of indemnity. By reading Section 141 which deals with the surety's rights, it may be said that the rights of the indemnifier are the same as those of the surety.

Commencement of Indemnifier's Liability

The Indian Contract Act (Section 125) does not state the time of the commencement of the indemnifier's liability under the contract of indemnity. There have been diversified views held regarding the time of commencement of the indemnifier's liability. Some High Courts (The High Courts of Lahore,[207] Nagpur[208] and Bombay[209]) have held that the indemnifier is not liable until the indemnified has incurred an actual loss. But other High Courts (The High Courts of Calcutta,[210] Allahabad[211] and Bombay[212]) have held that the indemnified may compel indemnifier to place him in a position to meet liability that may be cast upon him without waiting until the promisee (indemnified) has actually discharged it.

The latter view, which is based on equitable principles is now quite well established and the law on the point may well be taken as settled. It has been rightly observed in an English case, Liverpool Insurance Co's case,[213] "...... to indemnify does not merely mean to reimburse in respect of money's paid, but to save from loss in respect of liability against which the indemnity has been given ...... if it be held that payment is a condition precedent to recovery, the contract may be of little value to the person to be indemnified, who may be unable to meet the claim in the first instance."

Indemnity like any other contract must have all the essentials of a valid contract.

Contract of Guarantee

Definition

Section 126 of Indian Contract Act defines contract of a guarantee, surety, principal debtor and creditor.

A "Contract of guarantee" is a contract to perform the promise or discharge the liability of a third person in case of his default. The person who gives the guarantee is called the "Surety", the person in respect of whose default the guarantee is given is called the "principal debtor", and the person to whom the guarantee is given is called the "Creditor". The function of a contract of guarantee is to enable a person to get a loan, or goods on credit or an employment. In *Birkmyr v. Darnell*[214], the said: "If two come to a shop and one buys and the other to give him credit, promises the seller, 'if he does not pay you, I will.'" This type of collateral undertaking to be liable for the default of another is called a "Contract of guarantee".

Illustration of Contract of Guarantee

(a) A money bond conditioned for the performance of the contract by the contractors was held to be a contract of guarantee.[215]

(b) A undertakes personal liability on behalf of the principal debtor by merely depositing document of his property as security. It was held that A was a surety within the meaning of Section 126.[216]

(c) Where in execution of a decree there is an arrangement recorded between the decree holder, the judgment debtor and a surety, that if the debtor fails to pay within a certain stipulated time, the decree-holder can proceed against the surety, it was held that it was a contract of guarantee.[217]

(d) A says to B "you may safely do business with C as I have been helping him with finance and taking goods from him." This is not a contract of guarantee.[218]

Essentials of a Contract of Guarantee

1. Form

A contract of guarantee is just like any other contract which may be either oral or in writing (Section 126). It may be express or implied. Implied guarantee may be inferred from the course of conduct of the parties concerned.

2. Tripartite Agreement

Every contract of guarantee involves three agreements between (i) the creditor and the principal debtor, (ii) the surety and the creditor, and (iii) the surety and the principal debtor.

3. Primary Liability in some person

There must be a primary liability in some person other than the surety. The word 'liability' as used in the definition of guarantee (Section 126) means 'a liability which is enforceable at law.' If that liability does not exist, there cannot be a contract of guarantee. But a guarantee given for the debt of a minor is an exception to this rule.

The primary liability in a contract of guarantee is that of the principal debtor. The liability of the surety is secondary. It arises only when there is a default by the principal debtor.

4. The promise to pay must be conditional

In other words, the liability of the surety should arise only when the principal debtor makes a default.

5. Consideration

A contract of guarantee should also be supported by some consideration. But there need be no direct consideration between the surety and the creditor. Section 127 says:

"Anything done, or any promise made for the benefit of a principal debtor, may be a sufficient consideration to the surety for giving the guarantee."

The section says that "anything done .... for the benefit of the principal debtor" is good consideration. The legal detriment incurred by the promisee at the promisor's request is sufficient to constitute the element of consideration.

6. Competency

The principal debtor, surety and creditor must be person competent to contract. However, under certain circumstances, a surety is liable though the principal debtor is not, i.e., the original contract is void as is the case of a contract with a minor the surety is liable not only as surety but also as a principal debtor. A person of unsound mind or an undischarged insolvent cannot give a valid guarantee.

7. Consent

There must be free consent otherwise the contract of guarantee may become void or voidable. Generally, a contract of guarantee is not a contract of the utmost good faith, i.e., *uberrimae fidei*, but it is sometimes a first cousin to it. Mere nondisclosure will not effect the contract of suretyship unless there is an intentional concealment. Section 142 and 143 implement these principles.

Section 142 — Guarantee obtained by misrepresentation invalid — "Any guarantee obtained by means of misrepresentation made by the creditor, or with his knowledge and assent, concerning a material part of the transaction, is invalid".

Section 143 — Guarantee obtained by concealment, invalid — A guarantee which the creditor has obtained by means of keeping silence as to material circumstances is invalid.

Examples

(a) A engages B as clerk to collect money for him, B fails to account for some of his receipts, and A, in consequence calls upon him to furnish security for his duly accounting. C gives his guarantee for B's duly accounting. A does not acquaint C with B's previous conduct. B afterwards makes default. The guarantee is invalid.

(b) A guarantees to C payment for loan to be supplied by him to B to the amount of 2000 tons. B and C have privately agreed that B should pay five rupees per ton beyond the market price, such excess to be applied in liquidation of an old debt. This agreement is concealed from A. A is not liable as a surety.

Distinction between a Contract of Guarantee and a Contract of Indemnity

A contract by which one party promises to save the other from loss caused to him by the conduct of the promisor himself or by the conduct of any other person is called a contract of indemnity (Section 124).

A contract of guarantee is defined as a contract to perform the promise or discharge the liability of a third person in case of his default. The person who gives the guarantee is called the 'Surety', the person for whom the guarantee is given is called the Principal Debtor and the person to whom the guarantee is given is called creditor.

1. There are tow parties to the contract of indemnity, viz., the indemnifier (Promisor) and the indemnified (Promisee). And there are three parties to the contract of guarantee, viz., the creditor, the principal debtor and the surety.
2. The liability of a Promisor is primary and independent in a contract of indemnity. In a contract of guarantee, the liability is secondary, the primary liability being that of the principal debtor.

In *Punjab National Bank Ltd. v. Shri Vikran Cotton Mills and Another,*[219] the Supreme Court observed that "A promise to be primarily and independently liable for another person's conduct may amount to a contract of indemnity. A contract of guarantee requires concurrence of three persons — the principal debtor, the surety and the creditor — the surety undertaking an obligation of the surety depends substantially on the principal debtor's default. Under a contract of indemnity, liability arises from loss caused to the promisee by the conduct of the promisor himself, or by any other person."

3. In the case of contract of indemnity, there is only one contract in the case of a contract of indemnity, i.e., between the indemnifier and the indemnified.

   In the contract of guarantee, there are three contracts: one between the principal debtor and the creditor, the second between the creditor and the surety and the third between the surety and the principal debtor.
4. In the contract of indemnity, it is not necessary for the indemnifier to act at the request of the indemnified. But in contract of guarantee, it is necessary that the surety should give the guarantee at the request of the debtor.
5. In the contract of indemnity, the liability of the indemnifier arises only on the happening of a contingency. In the contract of guarantee, there is usually an existing debt or duty, the performance of which is guaranteed by the surety.
6. An indemnifier cannot sue a third party for loss in his own name, because there is no privity of contract. He can do so only if there is an assignment in his favour.

In contract of guarantee a surety, on discharging the debt due by the principal debtor, steps into the shoes of the creditor. He can proceed against the principal debtor in his own right.

Kinds of Guarantee

A contract of guarantee may be either 'Retrospective' i.e. for an existing debt or 'Prospective,' i.e., for a future debt. Guarantees are further divided into 'Specific' also known as simple or single guarantee and 'Continuing'. When the guarantee is given for a single or particular debt it is called a specific guarantee and it comes to an end when the debt guarantee has been paid. A guarantee which extends to a series of transactions is called a continuing guarantee (Section 129).

Again guarantee may be for a part of a whole debt or for the whole debt subject to limit. When the intention of the parties is not explicit, it will be presumed that where a portion of a floating balance is guaranteed it is for a part of it only. When a portion of a fixed and ascertained debt is guaranteed, the guarantee applied to the whole debt subject to the limit.

Continuing Guarantee

When a guarantee extends to a series of transactions, it is called a continuing guarantee (Section 129).

The liability of the surety in case of a continuing guarantee extends to all the transactions contemplated until the revocation of the guarantee.

Examples —

(i) A in consideration that B will employ C in collecting the rents of B's shopping complex promises B to be responsible, to the amount of 3,000 rupees, for the due collection of payments by C of those rents. This is a continuing guarantee.

(ii) A guarantees payment to B, a tea dealer to the amount of Rs. 10,000, for any tea he may from time to time supply to C for it. Afterwards B supplies C with tea to the value of Rs. 20,600. C fails to pay. The guarantee given by A was a continuing guarantee and he is accordingly liable to B to the extent of Rs. 10,000.

Whether a guarantee is a continuing guarantee or not depends on the language of the guarantee, the subject-matter and the surrounding circumstances.

Examples —

"I agree to be answerable to K for the amount of five sacks of flour, to be delivered to T, payable in one month." Held, it was a guarantee for five sacks delivered at one time, but not a continuing guarantee to cover subsequent deliveries though not exceeding in the whole five sacks (Kay v. Groves[220])

There can be a continuing guarantee for a fixed period. A continuing guarantee only speaks of continuing transactions and not the period of such transactions (*Eastern Bank Ltd. v. Parts Services of India*[221]).

Revocation of a continuing guarantee

A continuing guarantee can be revoked as to future transactions in the following ways:

1. By Notice

A continuing guarantee may at any time be revoked by the surety as to future transactions by notice to the creditor (Section 130). Notice will be applicable only for the future transactions and not those transactions which had already taken place.

2. By death of surety

The continuing guarantee is revoked by the death of the surety provided such a notice had been received by the creditor (Section 131). The liability of the surety for previous transactions however remains.

3. By variation in contract (Section 133)

If any variation has been made in the terms of contract of guarantee between the creditor and the principal debtor without the knowledge or concurrence of the surety, the contract of guarantee is revoked.

4. Creditor's act of omission

Any act or omission by the creditor which impairs the eventual remedy of the surety against debtor amounts to revocation of the contract of guarantee (Section 139).

5. By Novation

When the parties agree to substitute a new contract for the old contract or rescind or alter the old contract of guarantee, it will amount to revocation (Section 62).

Specific guarantee

When a guarantee extends to a single transaction or debt, it is called a specific or simple guarantee. It comes to an end when the guaranteed debt is duly discharged or the promise is duly performed.

Example —

A guarantees the repayment of a loan of Rs. 10,000 to B by C (a banker). The guarantee in this case is specific guarantee.

Rights of Surety

Rights of a surety may be classified under three heads:

(A) Rights against the creditor.

(B) Rights against the principal debtor and

(C) Rights against co-sureties.

A. Rights against the creditor

(i) Ask the creditor to sue the debtor

On the guaranteed debt having fallen due for payment, the surety may ask the creditor to sue the debtor to collect amount, but he cannot compel him to do so. But he must then indemnify the creditor against any risk or delay arising as a consequence.

(ii) Require the creditor to terminate the Debtor's Services

In the case of fidelity guarantee, if the principal debtor's dishonestly comes to light, the surety can require the creditor to terminate the principal debtor's services as to save him from further loss.

(iii) Claim to any set off

The surety on being called upon to pay, can claim any set-off to which the principal debtor is entitled from the creditor.

(iv) Access to the securities of the debtor with the creditor

The surety can, after paying the guaranteed debt, compel the creditor to assign to him all the securities taken by the creditor either before or at the time of the contract of guarantee, whether the security was aware of them or not.

(v) Right to share reduction

On debtor's insolvency, the surety is entitled to claim the proportionate reduction of his liability by the amount of dividend claimed by the creditor (from the official receiver of the principal debtor). Similarly, debtor's debt obligation is scaled down by subsequent legislation, the creditor is entitled to claim proportionate reduction in his liability.

B. Rights against principal debtor

(i) Right of Subrogation

After paying the guaranteed debt, the surety steps into the shoes of the creditor and acquires all the rights which the latter had against the principal debtor (i.e., he gets subrogated to all the rights and remedies available to the creditor) [Section 140]. If the creditor has the right to stop goods in transit or has a lien, the surety, on payment of all he is liable for, will be entitled to exercise these rights.

(ii) Rights as to securities with the creditor

The surety has the right to proceed against such securities of the principal debtor, as the creditor could himself proceed.

(iii) Right of Indemnity

The surety is entitled to be indemnified by the principal debtor for all payments rightfully made by him (Section 145). After the surety makes payment under the guarantee, he becomes a creditor of the principal debtor and can recover from the latter the amount he has paid with interest. If he sustains any damage beyond the amount paid, he can recover that damage also.

C. Rights against Co-Sureties

When two or more persons guarantee the same debt jointly or severally, whether under the same or different contracts, they are known as co-sureties. As the co-sureties share the liabilities, they have in equity also the right to share the means of recovery.

(i) Rights of Contribution

Where a debt has been guaranteed by more than one person, they are called as co-sureties. Section 146 provides for a right of contribution between them. When a surety has paid more than his share, he has a right of contribution from the other sureties who are equally bound to pay with him.

Where, the co-sureties have guaranteed different sums, they are bound under Section 147 to contribute equally, subject to the limit fixed by their guarantee, and not proportionately to the liability undertaken.

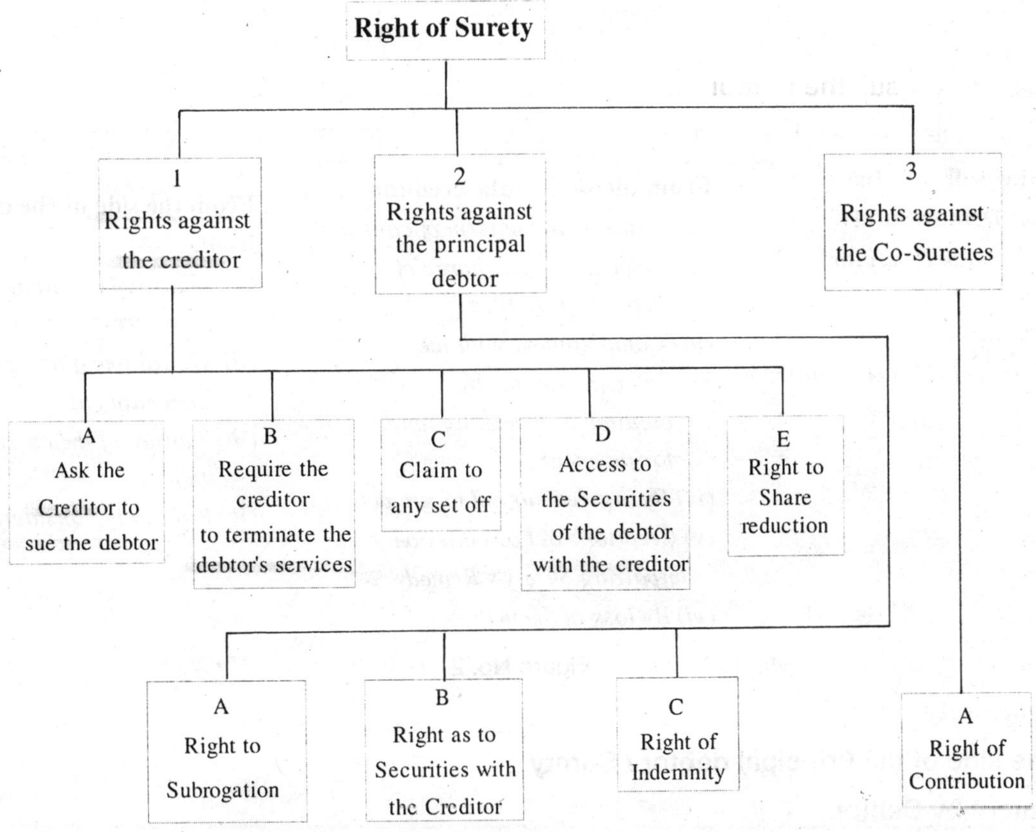

Figure No. 1

Liabilities of Co-Sureties

Unless the contract provides otherwise, the liability of the surety is co-extensive with that of the principal debtor (Section 128). In other words, the surety is liable for all those amounts, the principal debtor is liable for.

Example

A guarantees to B the payment of a bill of exchange by C, the acceptor. The bill is dishonoured by C. A is liable not only for the amount of the bill but also for any interest and charges which may have become due to it.

The liability of surety is called as secondary or contingent, as his liability arises only on default by the principal debtor. But as soon as the principal debtor defaults, the liability of the surety begins and runs co-extensive with the liability of the principal debtor, in the sense that the surety will be liable for all those sums for which the principal debtor is liable. The creditor may file a suit against the surety without suing the principal debtor. Further, where the creditor holds securities from the principal debtor for his debt, the creditor need not first exhaust his remedies against the securities before suing the surety, unless the contract specifically so provides.

The creditor is even not bound to give notice of the default to the surety, unless it is expressly provided for.

Liabilities of Surety in case of a minor principal debtor

According to the decision of the Bombay High Court in *Kashiba v. Shripat,*[222] the surety can be held liable, though a minor debtor is not liable. But the decisions of the Bombay High Court have taken a different view. The Madras High Court in a recent case of *Edavan Nambiar v. Moollaki Raman*[223] held that unless the contract otherwise provides, a guarantor for a minor cannot be held liable.

Discharge of Surety

A surety is said to be discharged when his liability comes to an end. In other words, discharge of surety means he is freed from his obligations. This can happen in various ways, either by the action of the surety himself or by the creditor or by the principal debtor or by both or by operation of Law. The various modes of his discharge are shown in the chart given below:

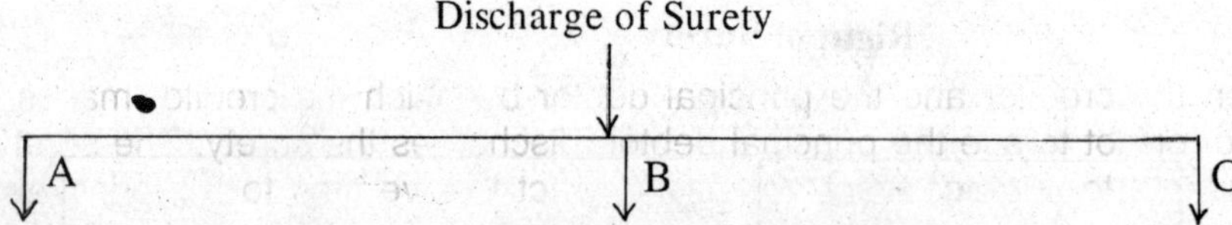

From the side of the Principal Debtor/Surety.

(i) By Payment by debtor

(ii) By Revocation

(iii) By death

(iv) By general rules of contract

From the side by the creditor

(i) Variation in the term of contract

(ii) Release or discaharge of debtor by creditor

(iii) Compounding with the Principal debtor by creditor or extending time for payment

(iv) By agreement not to sue debtor

(v) Creditor's act or omission impairing Surety's Remedy

(vi) By loss of Security

From the side of the contract itself.

(i) Guarantee obtained by misrepresentation

(ii) Guarantee obtained by concealment

(iii) Failure of the co-surety to join

(iv) Failure of consideration

Figure No. 2

Discharge of Surety

A. From the side of the Principal debtor / Surety

(i) By Payment by Debtor

Surety is also discharged from his liability when the principal debtor has paid the debt himself.

(ii) By revocation

A continuing guarantee may at any time be revoked by the surety, as to future transactions, by notice to the creditor (Section 130). But the surety remains liable for transactions already entered into.

(iii) By death of Surety

By the death of the surety the contract of guarantee comes to an end unless there is any contract to the contrary, as a revocation of a continuing guarantee, so far as regards future transactions (Section 131).

(iv) By general rules of contract

A contract of a guarantee is discharged by all the different ways as the case of contract in general and the surety is discharged as a party to the contract.

B. From the side by the creditor

(i) Variation in the term of the contract

Any variance, made without the surety's consent, in the terms of the contract between the principal debtor and the creditor, discharges the surety as to transactions subsequent to the variance (Section 133). Variation must be such which materially affects the interest of the surety. Where the guarantee is for the payment of distinct debts, a variance in the nature of one of them will not discharge the surety as to the rest.

(ii) Release or discharge of debtor by creditor

The surety is discharged by any contract between the creditor and the principal debtor, by which the principal debtor is released or by any act or omission of the creditor, the legal consequence of which is the discharge of the principal debtor. (Section 134). Thus, under this clause, the surety is discharged in the following two circumstances:

(a) If the creditor makes a fresh contract with the principal debtor by which the latter is released from his liability,

(b) If the creditor does any act or omission which has the effect of discharging the principal debtor from his liability.

(iii) By compounding with principal debtor by creditor or extending time for payment

A contract between the creditor and the principal debtor by which the creditor makes a composition with, or promises to give time to, or not to sue the principal debtor, discharges the surety. The surety shall, however, be not discharged if (a) he assents to such contract, (b) the contract to give time to the principal debtor is made by the creditor with a third person, and not with the principal debtor (Section 135). Where a contract to give time to the principal debtor is made by the creditor with a third person, and not with the principal debtor, the surety is not discharged (Section 136).

Example

P purchased a motor car from C under a hire purchase agreement on guarantee of S for the due performance of the agreement. C for valuable consideration gives P further time for payment of one of the installments. Held, the giving of time to P discharged S from any further liability under the guarantee (*Midland Motor Showrooms Ltd. v. Newman*[224]).

(iv) Agreement not to sue debtor

An agreement by the creditor not to sue the principal debtor without the consent of the surety, discharges the surety from his liability (Section 137). But if the creditor did not sue the principal debtor or did not enforce any other remedy against the debtor, the surety is not discharged unless provided otherwise in the contract of guarantee.

(v) Creditor's act or omission impairing Surety's remedy

If the creditor does any act which is inconsistent with the rights of the surety, or omits to do some act which his duty to the surety requires him to do, and the eventual remedy of the surety himself against the principal debtor is thereby impaired, the surety is discharged (Section 139).

Examples

(a) B contracts to build house for C for a given sum to be paid by installments as the work reaches certain stages. A becomes surety of B's due performance of the contract. C, without the knowledge of A, repays to B the last two installments, A is discharged by this prepayment.

(b) A puts M as apprentice to B, and gives a guarantee to B for M's fidelity. B promises on his part that he will at least once a month, see M make up the cash. B omits to see this done as promised, and M embezzles. A is not liable to B on his guarantee.

(vi) By Loss of security

If the creditor loses or without the consent of the surety, parts with any security given to him at the time of the contract of guarantee, the surety is discharged from liability to the extent of the value of security. (Section 141).

Example

C advances to B, his tenant, Rs. 2000 on the guarantee of A. C has also a further security for the Rs. 2000 by a mortgage of B's furniture. C cancels the mortgage. B becomes insolvent, and C sues A on his guarantee. A is discharged from liability to the amount of value of the furniture.

The following acts committed by the creditor will not discharge the surety:

(a) When the creditor contracts with a third party to give time to the principal debtor for the payment of the debt or the performance of the promise, surety is not discharged.

(b) When the creditor does not sue, i.e., mere forbearance or enforce any other remedy against the principal debtor for the payment of the money or the performance of the terms, the surety is not discharged from his liability to the creditor (Section 137).

(c) Release by the creditor of one co-surety does not discharge the other co-sureties from their liability to the creditor (Section 138).

(d) Release of any security/securities by the creditor which he had received from the debtor subsequent to the contract of guarantee.

C. From the side of the contract itself

The surety is liable under the guarantee only if the contract of guarantee is valid. If the contract of guarantee is valid then the surety will not be liable, i.e., he will be discharged from his liabilities. Thus, where a guarantee is obtained by coercion, undue influence, fraud etc., then it will not be valid and the surety is not liable under such a guarantee. The following are the ways in which a contract of guarantee becomes invalid.

(i) Guarantee obtained by misrepresentation

Any guarantee which has been obtained by means of misrepresentation made by the creditor, or with his knowledge and assent, concerning a material part of the transaction, is invalid (Section 142).

(ii) Guarantee obtained by concealment

Any guarantee which the creditor has obtained by means of keeping silence as to material circumstances is invalid (Section 143).

(iii) Failure of the Co-Surety to join

Where a person gives a guarantee upon a contract that a creditor shall not act upon it until another person has joined in it as co-surety, the guarantee is not valid if that other person does not join (Section 144). This means if the surety agrees to be only one of several co-sureties, he will not be liable unless the others execute the guarantee.

(iv) Failure of Consideration

Failure of consideration is a good ground for the discharge of a surety. But there must be substantial failure of consideration in order to make or operate as discharge invalid. Since there is a common consideration between the creditor and the principal debtor, makes the contract void and the surety is discharged (Section 127).

CHAPTER

34

Contract of Bailment and Pledge

Definition of Bailment

Section 148 of the Indian Contract Act 1872 defines 'bailment' as "the delivery of goods by one person to another for some purpose, upon a contract, that they shall, when the purpose is accomplished, be returned or otherwise disposed of according to the directions of the person delivering them. The person delivering the goods is called the 'bailor' and the person to whom they are delivered is called the 'bailee'."

The explanation to the above Section points out that delivery of possession is not necessary, where one person already in possession of goods, contracts to hold them as bailee.

Examples

(i) A delivers scooter to B for repair. There is a contract of bailment between A and B.

(ii) A lends a book to B to be returned after the examination. There is a contract of bailment between A and B.

(iii) Delivery of goods to a carrier for the purpose of carrying them from one place to another.

(iv) An Insurance Company places a damaged insured car of A in possession of R, a repairer. A is the bailor, the insurance company is the bailee and R is thesub bailee (*N.R. Srinivasa Iyer v. New India Ass. Co. Ltd.*[225]).

Characteristics of Bailment

From the definition of bailment, the following characteristics should be noticed.

1. Contract

A bailment is normally based upon a contract either express or implied between bailor and the bailee. However, the finder of goods is an exception to this rule, i.e., a finder of goods becomes a bailee though there is no contract between finder and true owner. A person already in possession of goods may become a bailee by a subsequent agreement, express or implied.

2. Delivery of Goods

A bailment necessarily involves delivery of goods by one person (called the bailor) to another person (bailee) for some purpose upon a contract. Delivery of goods may, however, be actual or constructive. Actual delivery may be made by handing over goods to bailee. Constructive delivery may be made by doing something which has the effect of putting the goods in the possession of the intended bailee or any person authorised to hold them on his behalf (Section 149).

3. The possession of goods must change

In bailment, the possession of goods must change, though temporarily. The change of possession for this purpose should be distinguished from a mere "custody". One who has custody without possession, like a servant or a guest using his host's goods is not a bailee. The goods must be handed over to the bailee for whatever is the purpose of bailment. Once this is done, a bailment arises, irrespective of the manner in which this happens.

Example

A lady employed a goldsmith for melting her old jewellery and making new one out of it. Every evening she received the unfinished jewellery and put it into a box kept at the goldsmith's premises. She kept the key of that box with herself. One night the jewellery was stolen from the box. Held, there was no bailment as the goldsmith had re-delivered to the lady (the bailor) the jewellery bailed with him by her (*Kaliperumal v. Visalakami*[226]).

4. For Some Purpose

The delivery of goods from bailor to bailee must be for some purpose. If goods are delivered by mistake to a person, there is no bailment. The purpose may be the lending, giving or depositing the goods for (i) safe custody or (ii) as a security for a debt or (iii) for repair, or (iv) for conversion of form etc.

5. Ownership must not change

In bailment, ownership of the goods is retained by the bailor. It is not transferred.

6. Return of Specific Goods

When the purpose for which the bailment is created, is accomplished, the goods are to be returned or disposed of according to the instructions of the bailor. The goods returned should be the same ones which were bailed. If the goods are not to be specifically returned, there is no bailment. But there is a bailment even if the goods bailed are, in the meantime, altered in form, e.g. when a piece of cloth is stitched into a suit.

7. Bailment is concerned only with goods

Bailment is possible only of goods, i.e., of movable property and chattels and not of immovable property. Moreover, in a contract of bailment it is only possession that passes from the bailor to the bailee and not ownership. Thus, if the property in goods is transferred for money consideration, it is a sale and not a bailment. Similarly, money paid into a bank to the credit of a current (or any type of) account does not constitute bailment. Money and actionable claims are not goods. However, the deposit of Government Promissory Notes. Promissory Notes, with the bank for safe custody is treated a bailment. But if they are sent for collection, it is not bailment.

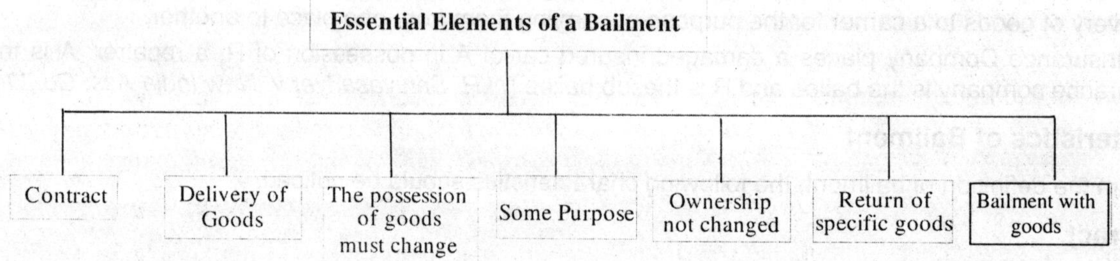

Figure No. 1

Gratuitous and Non Gratuitous Bailment

Bailments may be classified into gratuitous and non gratuitous bailment or bailment for reward.

Gratuitous bailment is a bailment where no consideration passes between the bailor and the bailee. In such type of bailment, neither the bailor not the bailee is entitled to any remuneration, e.g. lending of books to a friend on the other hand a non-gratuitous bailment is one where consideration passes between the bailor and the bailee and the bailor or the bailee gets remuneration e.g. giving of a watch or scooter for repair or cloths for stitching. It is also called as bailment for reward. Cases of bailments for reward are divided into two classes, viz., (i) those in which a reward is received by the bailor and (ii) those in respect of which the reward is to be received by the bailee.

Rights of Bailor

(1) Enforcement of Rights

The bailor can enforce by suit all the liabilities or duties of the Bailee.

(2) Restoration of Goods lent Gratuitously (Section 159)

When the goods are lent gratuitously, the bailor can demand their return whenever he please even though he lent them for a specified time or purpose. But if the bailee suffers any loss exceeding the benefit actually derived by him from the use of such goods because of premature return of goods, the bailor shall have to indemnify the bailee.

(3) Entitled to Increase or Profits to Goods Bailed (Section 163)

In the absence of any contract to the contrary, the bailee is bound to deliver to the bailor, or according to his directions, any increase or profits which may have accrued from the goods bailed.

(4) Compensation from a Wrongdoer (Section 180)

If a third person wrongfully deprives the bailee of the use or possession of the goods bailed or does them any injury, the bailor or the bailee may bring a suit against the third person for such deprivation or injury.

(5) Right of Termination (Section 153)

A Contract of bailment is voidable at the option of the bailor, if the bailee does any act with regard to the goods bailed, inconsistent with the conditions of the bailment. In such a case, the bailor can terminate the bailment.

(6) Right to Share

Right to have his share in the compensation received in any such suit.

Duties of Bailor

(1) To disclose faults in the goods (Section 150)

The bailor in gratuitous bailment, is bound to disclose to the bailee, faults in goods bailed, of which he (the bailor) is a aware and which are likely to interfere with the use of them or expose the bailee to extraordinary risks. If the bailor does not make such disclosure, he is responsible for damages arising to bailee directly from such faults.

On the other hand, if goods are bailed for reward, the bailor is responsible to the bailee for such damage arising to the bailee directly from the faults in goods bailed, even though he was aware or not of the existence of such faults in the goods bailed.

(2) To bear extraordinary expenses of bailment

The bailee is bound to bear ordinary and reasonable expenses of the bailment but for any extraordinary expenses the bailor is responsible.

Where in case of a gratuitous bailment, the goods are to be kept or to he carried or some work is to be done upon the goods by the bailee for the bailor, the bailor must repay to the bailee all the necessary expenses incurred by him for the purpose of the bailment (Section 158).

(3) To Indemnify the Bailee (Section 164)

Where the title of the bailor to the goods is defective and the bailee suffers as a consequence, the bailor is responsible to the bailee for any loss which the bailee may sustain by reason that the bailor was not entitled to make bailment or to receive back the goods, or to give directions respecting them.

(4) To Receive Back the Goods

It is a right as well as a duty of the bailor to receive back the goods when the bailee returns them after the expiry of the term of the bailment or when the purpose for which bailment was created has been accomplished. If the bailor refuses to receive back the goods, the bailee is entitled to receive compensation from the bailor for the necessary expenses of custody.

Rights of Bailee

The duties of the bailor are the rights of the bailee. As such, the bailee can, by suit, enforce the duties of the bailor. The other rights or the bailee are as follows:

(1) Right to Compensation (Sections 164 and 166)

If bailor has no right to bail the goods or to receive them back or to give directions regarding them and consequently the bailee is exposed to some loss, the bailor is responsible for the same. If the bailor has no title to the goods, and the bailee, in good faith delivers them back to or according to the directions of the Bailor, the Bailee shall not be responsible to the owner in respect of such delivery.

(2) Right to Remuneration

The bailee is entitled to lawful charges for providing services. But where the goods are bailed and work is to be carried on them by the bailee, and the bailee is to receive no remuneration, the bailee is entitled to claim the necessary expenses incurred by him. It may be noted that this right can be claimed by gratuitous bailee only. In non-gratuitous bailment, the bailee can also claim extraordinary expenses incurred by him.

(3) Lien (Section 170-171)

Lien means the right of a person to retain possession of some goods belonging to another until some debt or claim of the person in possession is satisfied. It appertains to the person who has possession of the goods which belong to another, entitling him to retain them until the debt due to him has been paid.

Possession is essential for exercising the right of lien, and in order to create a lien the possession must be (a) rightful (b) not for a particular purpose, and (c) continuous.

Example

A Company agreed to garage the motorcar of H for three years for an annual charge. H was entitled to take the car out of the Company's garage as and when she liked. The annual payment being in arrears the company detained the car at the garage and claimed a lien. Held, as H was entitled to take the car away as and when she pleased, the company had no lien (Hilton v. Car Maintenance Co. Ltd.[227]).

Right of lien may arise (a) by statute or (b) by express or implied contract or (c) by a general course of dealing between the parties in a particular trade.

Lien may be of two types

(i) General Lien
(ii) Particular Lien

(i) General Lien

A general lien is a right to retain all the goods or any property (which is in possession of the holder) of another until all the claims of the holder are satisfied. This is a right to retain the property of another for a general balance of account.

General lien, according to Section 171, is available to bankers, factors, wharfingers, attorneys of High Court and policy brokers. These persons are entitled to retain possession of the goods bailed to them as security until their claims are fully satisfied in the absence of a contract to the contrary.

(ii) Particular Lien (Section 170)

A particular lien is one which is available to the bailee against only those goods in respect of which he has rendered some service involving the exercise of labour or skill. Section 170 explains 'particular lien' as follows:

"Where the bailee has in accordance with the purpose of the bailment, rendered any service involving the exercise of labour or skill in respect of the goods bailed, he has, in the absence of a contract to the contrary, a right to retain such goods until he receives due remuneration for the services he has rendered in respect of them."

(4) Right of Action against Trespassers (Section 180)

Bailee can sue any person who has wrongfully deprived him of the use or possession of the goods bailed or has done them an injury. His remedies against wrongdoers are the same as those of the owner. An action may, therefore, be brought by the bailee or the bailor.

(5) Right to claim compensation in case of Faulty Goods (Section 150)

The bailee has a right to know the faults in the goods bailed to him, of which the bailor is aware and which materially interfere with the use of them, or expose the bailee to extraordinary risks. A bailee is entitled to receive compensation from the bailor for any loss or damages arising directly from such faults in the goods bailed.

(6) Delivery of goods to bailor without title (Section 166)

If the bailor has no title to the goods and the bailee, in good faith, delivers them back to, or according to the directions of, the bailor, the bailee is not responsible to the owner in respect of such delivery.

(7) Right to Interplead (Section 167)

If a person, other than the bailor, claims goods bailed, the bailee may apply to the Court to stop the delivery of the goods to the bailor, and to decide the title to the goods.

(8) Right to Bailment by several Joint Owners

If several joint owners of goods bail them, the bailee may deliver them back to, or according to the directions of one joint owner without the consent of all, in the absence of any agreement to the contrary. In such a case, delivery of goods to any one of the several joint bailors of goods will amount to delivery of goods to all of them, in the absence of any agreement to the contrary.

Duties of Bailee

These include:

1. Duty of Reasonable Care of Goods Bailed (Section 151 and 152)

In all cases of bailment, the bailee is bound to take as much care of the goods bailed to him as a man of ordinary prudence would, under similar circumstances, take of his own goods of the same bulk, quality and value as the goods bailed (Section 151).

In case, bailee has taken the amount of care as described above, he shall not be responsible, in the absence of any special contract, for the loss, destruction or deterioration of the thing bailed (Section 152).

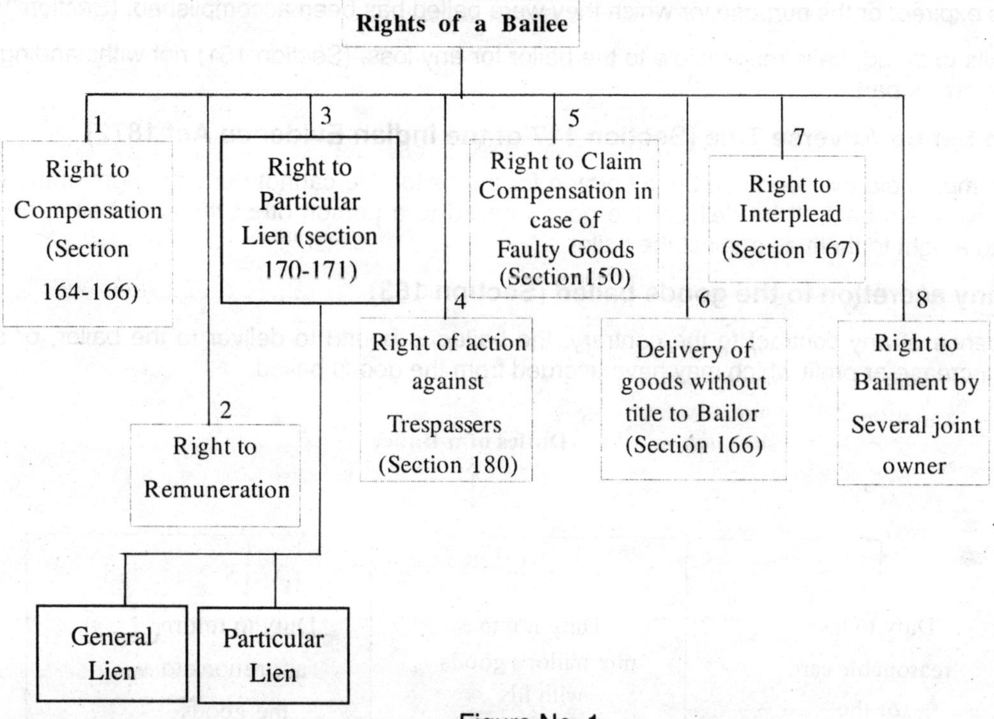

Figure No. 1

2. Not to make unauthorised use of goods bailed (Section 153 and 154)

Bailee must use the goods according to the conditions of the contract of bailment or the directions of the bailor. He must not use the goods in a manner inconsistent with the terms of bailment. If he does so, the bailor can terminate the bailment and recover any loss that might have been caused due to such unauthorised use.

Examples

(i) A lends a house to B for his won riding only. B allows C, his wife, to ride the horse. C rides with care, but the horse accidentally falls and is injured. A is liable to make compensation to B for the injury done to the horse.

(ii) A hires a horse in Calcutta from B expressly to march to Varanasi. A rides with due care, but marches to Cuttack instead. The horse accidentally falls and is injured. B is liable to make compensation to A for the injury to the horse.

3. Not to mix the goods bailed with his won goods (Section 155-157)

The bailee must not mix the goods of the bailor with his own goods, but must keep them separate from his own goods. If he mixes the bailor's goods with his own goods —

(a) with the bailor's consent

If the bailee with the consent of the bailor, mixes the goods of the bailor, mixes with his own goods, the bailor and the bailee shall have an interest, in proportion to their respective shares, in the mixture thus produced (Section 155).

(b) without the bailor's consent

If the bailee, without the consent of the bailor with his own goods, and the goods can be separated or divided, the property in the goods remains in the parties respectively, but the bailee is bound to bear the expenses of separation or division, and any damages arising from the mixture (Section 156).

(c) without bailor's consent when goods cannot be separated

If the bailee without the consent of the bailor, mixes the goods of the bailor with his own goods, in such a manner that it is impossible to separate the goods bailed from the other goods and deliver them back, the bailer is entitled to be compensated by the bailee for the loss of the goods. (Section 157)

4. Duty to Return Goods without Demand

It is the duty of the bailee to return goods bailed to the bailor without demand, as soon as the time for which they were bailed has expired, or the purpose for which they were bailed has been accomplished. (Section 160)

If bailee fails to do so, he is responsible to the bailor for any loss. (Section 161) not withstanding the exercise of reasonable care on his part.

5. Duty Not to Set up Adverse Title (Section 117 of the Indian Evidence Act 1872)

The bailee must hold the goods on behalf of and for the bailor. He cannot deny the right of the bailor to bail the goods and receive them back. If he delivers the goods bailed to a person other than the bailor, he may prove that such person had a right to them as against the bailor.

6. To return any accretion to the goods bailed (Section 163)

In the absence of any contract to the contrary, the bailee is bound to deliver to the bailor, or according to his directions, any increase or profit which may have accrued from the goods bailed.

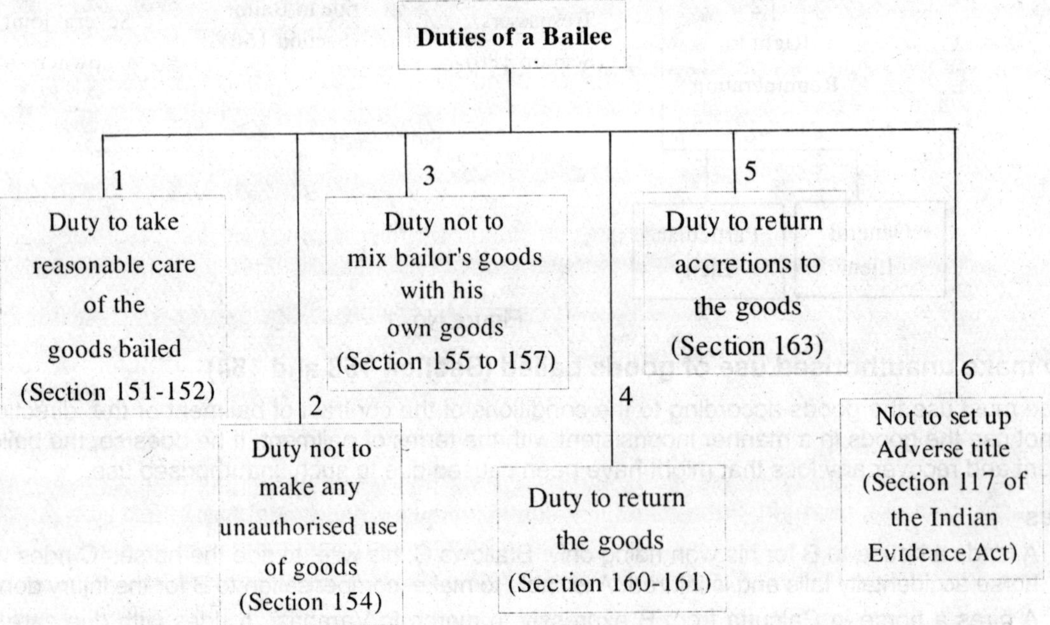

Figure No. 2

Termination of Bailment

A contract of bailment is terminated in the following cases:

1. Lapse of time

When the bailment is for a specific period, it terminates on the expiry of that period.

2. Accomplishment of the purpose

A bailment is terminated on the accomplishment of the purpose for which it was made.

3. Inconsistent use of goods

A contract of bailment may be terminated by the bailor if the bailee does any act with regard to the goods bailed, inconsistent with the conditions of bailment (Section 153).

4. Death of the bailor or bailee

A gratuitous bailment is terminated by the death of either the bailor or the bailee (Section 162).

5. Gratuitous Bailment

The lender of a thing for use may at any time terminate the bailment, even if it was lent gratuitously for a specified time or purpose. But if any loss is caused to bailee because of such premature termination, it must be made good by the bailor (Section 159).

Finder of Lost Goods

A person who comes by an article is not obliged to pick it up or take charge of it. But if he does pick it up, he becomes a bailee. Section 71 lays down that "A person who finds goods belonging to another and takes them into custody is subject to the same responsibility as a bailee." He is bound to take as much care of the goods as a man of ordinary prudence would, under similar circumstances, take of his own goods of the same bulk, quality and value as the goods found.

Rights of the Finder of Goods

The rules relating to the rights of the Finder of Goods are given below:

1. Right of Possession

The finder is entitled to retain possession of the goods against every one except the true owner.

2. Right of Lien

When the true owner is found, the finder can exercise possessory lien over the goods against the owner until he receives compensation for expenses, etc. incurred in connection with preservation of the goods found. But he cannot sue the owner for the compensation, or trouble and expenses voluntarily incurred by him to preserve the goods and to find out the owner.

3. Right to Sue for Reward

The finder can sue for any specific reward which the owner has offered for the return of the goods.

4. Right to retain the goods (Section 168)

A finder of lost goods may retain the goods until he receives the compensation for money spent in preserving the goods and/or amount spent in finding the true owner. A finder, however, cannot sue for such compensation.

5. Right to sell (Section 169)

When a thing which is commonly the subject of sale is lost, the finder may sell it when

(i) the owner cannot with reasonable diligence be found, or

(ii) If found, the owner refuses to compensate the finder for his lawful charges, or

(iii) the thing found is in danger of perishing or of losing the greater part of its value, or

(iv) the lawful charges of the finder, in respect of the thing found, amount to two-thirds of its value.

Obligations of finder of goods

The main obligation (duties and liabilities) are:

(i) He must take reasonable care of the goods and if, spite of this, the goods are destroyed, he is not responsible for any loss.

(ii) He must not use the goods for his own purpose.

(iii) He must not mix the goods with his own goods.

(iv) He must try to find out the owner of the goods. If he does not do that, he will be liable as a trespasser.

Distinction between Particular Lien and General Lien

Particular Lien	General Lien
1. Particular lien can be exercised only against those goods in respect of which the bailee has rendered some skill and labour.	1. General lien can be exercised against any goods or property of another in possession of the person exercising the right.
2. This is a right to retain the goods only for a charge for labour employed or expenses incurred upon the goods.	2. This is a right to retain any property belonging to the other party for a general balance of account.

Termination of Lien

In the following circumstances, the right of lien can be terminated:

1. The right of lien is a personal right, which continues so long as the bailee is in possession of the goods. It is lost as soon as the possession of the goods is surrendered by the bailee.
2. The right of lien is terminated as soon as the amount due to the bailee is paid to him. The tender (offer) of the amount also terminates the lien.
3. The bailee may give up his right of lien by entering into an agreement. In such cases, the lien is also terminated.

Pledge

Section 172 defines a Pledge as the bailment of goods as security for payment of debt or performance of a promise. Bailment, as per section 148, means the delivery of goods by one person to another for some purpose, under a contract that the goods shall, when the purpose is accomplished, be returned or otherwise disposed of according to the directions of the person delivering them. The person who offers the security (i.e., the bailor) is called the 'Pawnor' or 'Pledger' and the person who receives the goods as security (i.e., bailee) is called the 'Pawnee' or 'Pledgee'. From this it is clear that in the case of pledge (i) there should be bailment of goods, and (ii) the object of such bailment should be to hold the goods as a security for the payment of a debt or performance of promise and not for safe custody or any other purpose.

Since pledge is a branch of bailment it must satisfy the essential requirements of bailment, viz.,

(i) there must be delivery of goods

(ii) the delivery must be made for some specific purpose,

(iii) the delivery must be made on condition that the goods shall be returned in specific when the purpose is over, or disposed of according to the directions of the bailor, and

(iv) only possession, but not the ownership of the goods, is transferred.

A pledge is created only when the goods are delivered by the borrower to the lender or to someone on his behalf with the intention of their being treated as security against the advance. Delivery of goods may, however, be actual or constructive. If, because of the bulk of the property or for some other reason, actual delivery is impracticable, a symbolic delivery will suffice (as for example delivery of the keys to a safe deposit box).

Example

The producer of a film borrowed a sum of money from a financier-distributor and agreed to deliver the final prints of the film when ready. Held, the agreement was not a pledge, there being no actual transfer of possession (*Revenue Authority v. Sudarshan Pictures*[228]).

Rights of Pledgee or Pawnee

1. Right of retainer

The pledgee has a right to retain the possession of the goods pledged till he recovers the debt, interest and other necessary expenses incidental to possession or preservation of the goods (Section 173).

2. Right of retainer for subsequent advances

When the pledgee lends money to the same pledger after the date of the pledge, it is presumed that the right of retainer over the pledged goods extends to subsequent advances also. This presumption can be rebutted only by a contract to the contrary (Section 174).

3. To recover any extraordinary expenses

The pledge is also entitled to receive any extraordinary expenses incurred for the preservation of goods pledged. He is entitled to this right of the pledgee even if the pledger has violated some provisions of the law in respect of goods pledged (Sec. 175). For such expenses, he has no right to retain the goods, he can only sue to recover them.

4. Security for other debts

He cannot retain the goods for debts other than those for which pledge is made. Unless the parties contract that here shall be security also for any other subsequent debts.

5. To bring civil suit for amount due

In the case of default by the pledger to make payment of the debt, the pledgee has the right either (a) to bring a civil suit against the pledger for the amount due, and retain the goods pledged as collateral security, or (b) to sell the goods pledged himself after giving the pledger reasonable notice of sale, or (c) to ask the Court to put the pledged articles to sale.

6. Sale after Notice

Pledgee may sell the goods pledged after giving the pledger a reasonable notice of the sale. It is not obligatory for pledgee to sell the goods within reasonable time after the notice of sale is served. If the proceeds of such sale are insufficient to meet claim of the pledgee, the pledger is still liable to pay the balance. If the sale proceeds are greater than the amount so due, the pledgee has to return the excess or surplus to the pledger.

The pledgee may sell the goods before filing the suit in a Court of Law. If the suit is filed for the recovery of the amount then the goods can be sold through Court orders only.

7. Right to Damages

The pledgee has a right to be compensated for any damage which he suffers as a result non-disclosure of any defects or faults in the goods pledged which are within the knowledge of the pledger.

8. Right to Indemnity

The pledgee has a right to claim any damages suffered because of the defective title of the pledger.

9. Remedy against Deprivation

In case of injury to the goods or their deprivation by a third party, the pledgee would have all such remedies that the owner of the goods would have against them.

Duties of a Pledgee/Pawnee

1. To take Reasonable Care

The pledgee is required to take as much care of the goods pledged to him as a person of ordinary prudence would, under similar circumstances, take of his own goods, of a similar nature.

2. Not to make any unauthorised use

The pledgee must not make the goods to an unauthorised use. If he makes any unauthorised use, the pledger is entitled to terminate the contract and claim damages, if any.

3. Return on Repayment

The pledgee must return the goods pledged on payment of the debt. If the goods are not returned by the pledgee at the proper time, he is responsible to the pledger for any loss, destruction or deterioration of the goods pledged.

4. To Return any Increase or Profit

The pledgee must return to the pledger any increase or profit which have accrued from the goods pledged, e.g. dividends, bonus shares, etc. in respect of pledged shares.

5. Not to Set-up Adverse Title

The pledgee should not deny the pledger's title. He should not setup his own title or that of third party.

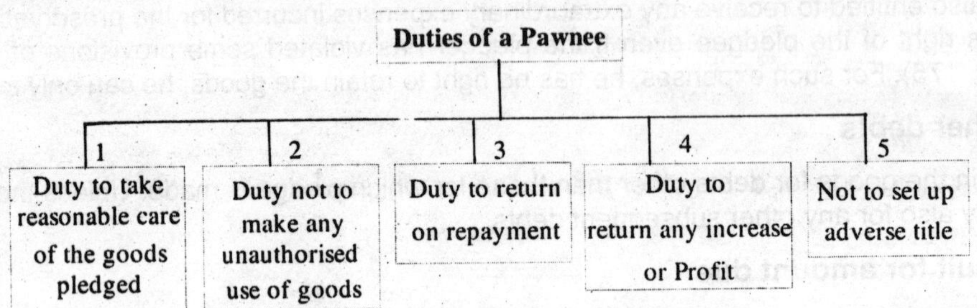

Figure No. 3

Right of a Pledger/Pawner

1. Right of Redemption

Even after the expiry of a stipulated period, or if there has been a default by the pledger, he may redeem the goods pledged at any subsequent time before the actual sale of the goods pledged. But he must pay expenses which may have been arisen from his default. The period of limitation in the case of a loan on a pledge is three years to run from the date of the loan.

2. To Receive Notice of sale

The pledger has a right to receive a reasonable notice in case of the pledgee intends to sell the goods and in case he does not receive the notice, he shall have a right to claim any loss that may result on such sale.

3. To receive the surplus

In case of sale, the pledger is entitled to receive from the pledgee any surplus that may remain with him after the debt is completely paid off.

4. To take action for conversion

If the sale is effected by the pledgee without giving a reasonable notice to the pledger, the latter has got a right to ask for damages on the ground of conversion. But he cannot sue for a declaration that the sale is contrary to law.

5. Right to Increase or Profit

The pledger has a right to receive any increase or profit which may have accrued from the goods pledged.

Duties of a Pledger/Pawnor

1. Disclose the Faults

The pledger should disclose to the pledgee, the faults in the goods pledged, of which he is aware. If he does not disclose, he will be liable for the loss resulting therefrom.

2. To meet any extraordinary expenditure

The pledger is responsible to meet any extraordinary expenditure incurred by the pledgee for the preservation of the goods.

3. To Indemnify the pledgee

If the title of the pledger to the goods pledged is defective and the pledgee suffers any loss due to this fact, the pledger should indemnify the pledgee.

Pledge by Non-owner

The general rule is that it is the owner who can ordinarily create a valid pledge. But under certain following circumstances pledge by a non owner is also valid.

1. Pledged by mercantile agent

Where a mercantile agent, is, with the consent of the owner, in possession of goods or the documents of title to goods, any pledge made by him, when acting in the ordinary course of business, shall be a valid pledge. But the pledge is valid only if the pledgee acts in good-faith and without having notice that the pledger has no authority to pledge (Section 178).

The term 'mercantile agent' is defined in Section 2(9) of Sale of Goods Act 1930, as below:

"Mercantile agent having in the customary course of business as such agent, authority, either to sell goods or to consign for the purpose of sale, or to buy goods, or to raise money on the security of goods."

2. Pledge by person in possession under a voidable contract

Where a person obtains possession of goods under a voidable contract, the pledge created by him is valid provided:

(a) the contract has not been rescinded before the contract of pledge, and

(b) the pledgee acts in good faith and without notice of the pledger's defect of title (Section 178-A).

3. Pledge by Pawnor who has a limited interest

Where a person pledges goods in which he has only a limited interest, the pledge is valid to the extent of that interest (Section 179). A person having a lien over the goods or a finder of goods may pledge them to the extent of his interest.

4. Pledge of Co-owner

A joint owner who is in sole possession of the goods, with the consent of others, can make a valid pledge.

5. Pledge by seller or buyer in possession after sale

A seller left in possession of goods after sale and a buyer who obtains possession of goods with the consent of the seller before sale, can create a valid pledge provided the pawnee acts in good faith and has no notice of the previous sale of goods to the buyer or of the lien of seller over the goods. (Section 30 of the Sale of Goods Act 1930).

CHAPTER

35

Contract of Agency

Agency is a relation between two parties created by agreement express or implied. The relationship of agency arises whenever one person called the agent has authority to act on behalf of another called the principal.

The law relating to agency is contained in chapter X (Section 182 to 238) of the Indian Contract Act 1872.

Definition of Agent and Principal

An agent is defined in Section 182 of the Indian Contract Act as "a person employed to do any act for another or to represent another in dealings with third person." In other words, an agent is a person who acts in place of another. The person for whom such act is done, or who is so represented, is called the 'Principal'. The function of an agent is to bring his principal into contractual relations with third persons. This means that an agent is merely a connecting link between the principal and third parties.

Essentials of Contract of Agency

The relationship of agency is based upon a contract. The contract may be either express or implied. The essentials of agency are as follows:

(1) There should be the appointment by the principal of an agent.

(2) The principal should confer authority on the agent to act for him.

(3) The authority conferred should be such as will make the principal answerable to third parties.

(4) The object of the appointment must be to establish relationship between principal and third parties.

(5) The relationship of agency being based on confidence between the principal and agent.

Who Can Employ An Agent?

Any person who is of the age of majority according to the Law to which he is subject, and who is of sound mind, may employ an agent (Section 183). Thus, a minor or lunatic cannot contract through an agent since they cannot contract themselves personally.

Who May Be An Agent

Since agent is a mere connecting link between the principal and third party, it is immaterial whether or not the agent is legally competent to contract. Section 184 of the Contract Act provides that any person may become an agent. In other words, even a minor can be employed as agent and the principal shall be bound by the acts of such an agent. The principal is liable to the third party for the acts of the agent. Thus as between the principal and a third person any person may become an agent. But no person who is not of the age of majority and of sound mind can become an agent so as to be responsible to his principal.

It may be noted that consideration is an essential element for the validity of every contract, but Section 185 lays down that "no consideration is necessary to create an agency".

A contract of agency is one of good faith; the agent must disclose to his principal every information coming to his knowledge which may influence the principal in the making of the contract with the third parties.

Test of Agency

The test for determining whether a person is or not an agent is this: Has that person the capacity to bind the principal and make him answerable to a third person by bringing him (the principal) into legal relations with the third person and thus establish a privity of contract between that person and the principal? If yes, he is an agent, otherwise not. This relationship of agency may be created either by express agreement or by implication.

Agent and Servant

An agent must be distinguished from servant.

(i) An agent is bound to follow all the lawful instructions of the principal but he is not subject to the direct control and supervision of the principal. A servant, on the other hand, acts under the direct control and supervision of his master and is bound to carryout all his reasonable orders given to him in course of employment.

(ii) An agent is employed to bring the principal into legal relations with third persons or to represent him in dealings with third persons. A servant does not ordinarily create legal relations between the employer and the third person.

(iii) A principal is liable for the wrongs of his agent done within the scope of his authority. A master is liable for the wrongs of the servant if they are committed in the course of his employment.

(iv) A servant usually serves only one master, but an agent may work for several principals at the same time.

Creation of Agency

An agency may be constituted in three following ways:

(i) by express agreement,

(ii) by implied agreement, and

(iii) by ratification.

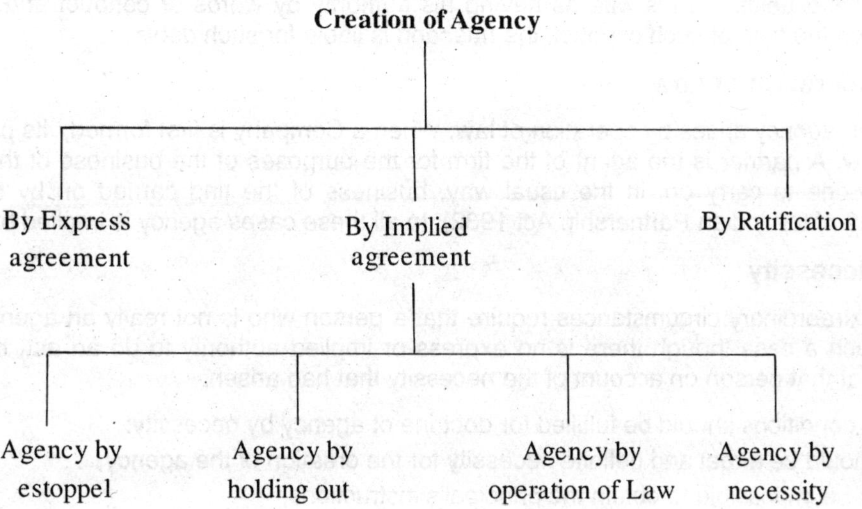

Figure No. 1

(i) Agency by Express Agreement (Section 187)

A person may be appointed as agent, either by word of mouth or by an agreement in writing. The usual form of a written contract of agency is the power of attorney on a stamped paper.

(ii) Agency by Implied Agreement (Section 187)

Implied agency arises from the conduct, situation or relationship of parties. It may be inferred from the circumstances of the case, and things spoken or written or the ordinary course of dealing, may be accounted as circumstances of the case.

Implied agency includes:

(a) Agency by estoppel

(b) Agency by holding out

(c) Agency by operation of law and

(d) Agency by necessity.

(a) Agency by estoppel (Section 237)

In many cases an agency may be implied from the conduct of the parties, though no express authority has been given. Thus, where the principal knowingly permits a person to act in a certain business in his name or on his behalf, such a principal is estopped from denying the authority of the supposed agent to bind him.

Example

If a railway company holds out that its parcel clerk can accept consignments for dispatch, it cannot afterwards say, that he had no such legal authority.

There are three possible cases of agency by estoppel:

(i) A person can be held out as an agent although he is actually not so,

(ii) person acting as agent may be held out as having more authority than he actually has,

(iii) A person may he held out as agent after he has ceased to be so.

(b) Agency by holding out

Agency by holding out is a branch of the agency by estoppel. In this case, a prior positive or affirmative conduct by the principal is necessary in creation of agency by holding out.

Example

Where a husband holds out his wife as having his authority by words or conduct and a third party advances money to the wife on the faith of such conduct, the husband is liable for such debts.

(c) Agency by Operation of Law

Sometimes, an agency arises by operation of law. When a Company is first formed, its promoters and its agents by operation of Law. A partner is the agent of the firm for the purposes of the business of the firm, and the act of a partner, which is done to carry on, in the usual way, business of the find carried on by the firm, binds the firm (Sections 18 and 19 of the Indian Partnership Act 1932). In all these cases agency is implied by operation of Law.

(d) Agency by Necessity

Sometimes extraordinary circumstances require that a person who is not really an agent for another should act as an agent. In such a case though there is no express or implied authority to do an act, the law implies such an authority in favour of that person on account of the necessity that had arisen.

The following conditions should be fulfilled for doctrine of agency by necessity:

(i) There should be a real and definite necessity for the creation of the agency,

(ii) It should be impossible to obtain the principal's instructions,

(iii) The person acting as an agent should act bonafide and in the interest of parties concerned.

Agency of Husband and Wife

Agency of husband and wife is a agency by necessity. A husband is bound to maintain (i.e. to supply necessaries of life) his wife. Where the husband and wife and living together, the wife is presumed to have implied authority to pledge the husband's credit for necessaries.

Where the wife lives apart. A wife, who is deserted by her husband for no fault of her, has authority to pledge her husband's credit for necessaries. The husband cannot escape liability by telling his wife not to pledge his credit nor even by telling the tradesman not to supply necessaries on credit. The wife enjoys this right only if her husband does not provide for her maintenance. But where she lives apart of her own will, and without any jurisdiction, she is not the agent of her husband and cannot pledge his credit even for necessaries. The husband is not bound to maintain her under such circumstances.

3. Agency by Ratification

A contract of agency may be formed either by precedent authority or by subsequent authority or ratification.

Ratification is a kind of affirmation or approval of a previous unauthorised act or acts relating to a contract. It implies the adoption by the principal of an act made by an agent in his behalf but without his authority. Section 196 of the Contract Act provides that "where acts are done by one person on behalf of another, but without his knowledge or authority, he may elect to ratify or to disown such acts. If he ratifies them, the same effects will follow as if they had been performed by his authority.

Examples

(i) Agent insures principal's goods without his authority. If principal ratifies agent's act, the policy will be as valid as if agent had been authorised to insure the goods.

(ii) A without having any authority of B acts as B's agent and enters into a contract with C. The contract will be binding on B, if he ratifies or approves of the same.

Ratification may be expressed or may be implied in the conduct of the person on whose behalf the acts are done (Section 197).

Requisites of a Valid Ratification

To make a ratification valid, the following conditions must be fulfilled.

(1) Act must have been done on behalf of the person ratifying.
(2) The principal must be in existence at the time of contract.
(3) The principal must have contractual capacity both at the time of the contract and at the time of ratification. Thus, minor on whose behalf a contract is made cannot ratify it on attaining majority.
(4) The transaction must have been subsisting at the time when it is ratified.
(5) Ratification must be made within a reasonable time. Reasonable time shall vary from case to case.
(6) The act to be ratified must be a lawful one. There can be no ratification of an illegal act or act which is *void ab-initio.*
(7) The principal should have full knowledge of the facts. Section 198 states "No valid ratification can be made by a person whose knowledge of the facts of the case is materially defective."
(8) Whole transaction must be ratified. The principal cannot reject the burdens and accept only the benefits.
(9) Ratification may be express or implied.
(10) Ratification must be communicated.
(11) Ratification must not injure a third person.
(12) The principal must be in existence at the of the act that is to be ratified.

Classification of Agents

A general classification of agents from the point of view of the extent of their authority is as follows:

1. Special Agent

A special agent is a person appointed to do some particular act or enter into some particular contract. A special agent, therefore, has only a limited authority to do the specified act. If he does anything beyond the specified act, he runs the risk of being personally liable since the principal may not ratify the same. Such an agent has a limited authority and as soon as the act is performed, his authority comes to an end.

2. General Agent

A general agent, is one who is appointed to represent the principal in all matters concerning a particular business e.g. manager of a firm or managing director of a company. Such an agent has authority to do all acts connected with a particular trade, business or employment.

3. Universal Agent

A universal agent is one whose authority to act for the principal is unlimited. He has authority to bind his principal by any act which he does, provided that act is legal and agreeable to the law of the land.

Another classification of agents from the point of view of the nature of work performed by them is as follows:

(1) Commercial or Mercantile Agents

A 'Mercantile agent', according to Section 2(9) of the Sale of Goods Act 1930, means "a mercantile agent having in the customary course of business as such agent, authority either to sell goods, or to consign goods for the purpose of sale, or to buy goods, or to raise money on the security of goods." This definition does not cover all kinds of mercantile agents which are as follows:

(a) Broker

A broker is a mercantile agent engaged to buy or sell property or to make bargains and contracts between the engager and a third party for a commission called brokerage. A broker has no possession of goods or property. He is merely a connecting link between the engager and a third party.

(b) Factor

A factor is a mercantile agent who is entrusted with the possession of goods with an authority to sell the same. He can even sell the goods on credit and in his own name. He is also authorised to raise money on their security. A factor has a general lien on the goods in possession. A factor, however, cannot barter the goods, unless expressly authorised to do so, he cannot delegate his authority.

(c) Commission Agent

A commission agent belongs to a somewhat indefinite class of agents. He is employed to buy and sell goods, or transact business generally for other persons receiving for his labour and trouble a money payment, called commission.

(d) Del Credere Agent

A del credere agent is one who, in consideration of an extra commission, guarantees his principal that the persons with whom he enters into contract on behalf of the principal, shall perform their obligations. He occupies the position of both a guarantor and an agent.

(e) Banker

The relationship between a banker and his customer is really that of debtor and creditor. But he acts as his agent when he buys or sells securities on his behalf. When he collects cheques, bills, interest, dividends etc. or when he pays insurance premium out of customer's account, as per customer's mandate, he acts as his agent.

(f) Auctioneer

An auctioneer is an agent appointed by a seller to sell his goods by public auction for a reward generally in the form of a commission. He is primarily the agent of a seller, but after the sale has taken place, he becomes the agent of the purchaser also. He has authority to receive the price of the goods sold. He can sue also for the price in his own name. The Principal is liable to the third parties for the acts of the auctioneer if the auctioneer acts within the scope of his apparent authority even though he disobeys instructions privately given to him.

Non Mercantile or Non-Commercial Agents

These include attorneys, solicitors, insurance agents, clearing and forwarding agents and wife etc.

Sub-Agent and Substituted Agent

The general rule is that an agent cannot appoint an agent. However, Section 190 deals with the circumstances as to when and how far an agent can delegate his duties. An agent may appoint an agent in the following circumstances:

(i) Where expressly permitted by the principal.
(ii) Where the ordinary custom of the trade permits delegation
(iii) The nature of agency is such that it cannot be accomplished without the appointment of a sub-agent.
(iv) Where the nature of the job assigned to the agent is purely clerical and does not involve the exercise of discretion.
(v) In an unforeseen emergency.

Definition of Sub-Agent

Section 191 defines a sub-agent as "a person employed by and acting under the control of the original agent in the business of agency."

Substituted Agent

A substituted agent is a person appointed by the agent to act for principal in the business of the agency with the knowledge and consent of the principal. In the words of Section 194, "where an agent, holding an express or implied authority to name another person to act for the principal in the business of the agency has named another person accordingly, such person is not a sub-agent but an agent of the principal for such part of the business of the agency as is entrusted to him."

A substituted agent is deemed to be the agent to the principal and not his sub-agent. A privity of contract is established between the principal and the substituted agent.The agent is not concerned about the work of the substitute. A duty, however, is implied on the original agent to choose a proper substituted agent with reasonable care.The agent selecting must use discretion and prudence. But he is not to guarantee solvency, skill or integrity of the person selected. If he fails to exercise such care, he becomes liable for damages to the principal for his negligence.

Example

A directs B, his solicitor, to sell his estate by auction, and to employ an auctioneer for the purpose. B names C, an auctioneer, to conduct the sale. C is not a sub-agent, but is A's agent for the conduct of the sale.

Difference between Sub-Agent and Substituted Agent

Both a sub-agent and substituted agent are appointed by the agent. But however, the following are the points of the distinction between the two.

Sub Agent	Substituted Agent
1. The agent not only appoints a sub-agent but also delegates to him a part of his own duties.	1. The agent does not delegate any part of his task to substituted agent.
2. A sub-agent does his work under the control of agent.	2. A substituted agent works under the instructions of the principal.
3. There is no privity contract between the principal and the sub-agent.	3. Privity of contract is established between a principal and a substituted agent.
4. The sub-agent is responsible to the agent alone and is not generally responsible to the principal.	4. But a substituted agent is responsible to the principal and not to the original agent who appointed him.
5. The agent is responsible to the principal for the acts of the sub-agent.	5. The agent is not responsible for the acts of substituted agent, provided he has taken due care in selecting him.
6. In case of sub-agent the agent remains answerable for the acts of the sub-agent as long as sub-agent continues.	6. The agent's duty ends once he has named him

Rights and Duties of an Agent

Rights of an agent

An agent has the following rights against the principal.

1. Right to Remuneration (Section 219-220)

An agent is entitled to receive agreed remuneration. In the absence of any special contract, payment for the performance of any act is not due to the agent until, the completion of such act. (Section 219). The completion of such act depends on the terms of the contract. Thus, commission becomes payable to the broker, when he has procured a party who is willing to negotiate on reasonable terms and is desirous to entering into a contract with the principal (*Sheikh Farid Baksh v. Hargulal Singh*[229]). The agent was not entitled to commission as sale had not been completed, [*Luxor (Eastbourne) Ltd. v. Cooper*[230]]. The transaction for which the agent claims remuneration should be the direct or indirect result of his services or efforts (*Green v. Barlett*[231]).

An agent who is guilty of misconduct in the business of the agency is not entitled to any remuneration in respect of that part of the business which he has misconducted (Section 220).

2. Right of Retainer (Section 217)

An agent may retain out of any sum received on account of the principal in the business of the agency, all moneys due to himself in respect of advances made or expenses properly incurred by him in conducting such business and also such remuneration as may be payable to him for acting as agent.

3. Right of Lien (Section 221)

In the absence of any contract to the contrary, agent is entitled to particular lien, i.e., right to retain goods, papers and other property, whether movable or immovable of the principal received by him, until the amount due to himself for commission, disbursements and services in respect of the same has been paid or accounted for him (Section 221). This lien of the agent is a particular lien. It is confined to claims arising in connection with the goods or property in respect of which the right is claimed. But by special contract, an agent may have a general lien extending to all claims arising out of the agency.

4. Right of Indemnification (Section 222)

The employer of an agent is bound to indemnify him against the consequences of all lawful acts done by such agent in exercise of authority conferred upon him.

Example

A, an agent, seized goods of T, a third party, at the command of P, the principal. Although the goods had been seized improperly, it was shown that A had acted bonafide. Held, A was entitled to be indemnified (*Toplis v. Crane*[232]).

The right of agent to be indemnified does not extend to acts which are known to the agent to be unlawful. Section 224 provides in this regard that where, any person employs another to do an act which is criminal, the employer is not liable to the agent, either upon an express or an implied promise, to indemnify him against the consequences of that act.

Section 223 provides that an agent shall have right to be indemnified against consequences of act done in good faith. It reads "where one person employs another to do act, and the agent does the act in good faith, the employer is liable to indemnify the agent against the consequences of that act, though it causes an injury to the rights of third person.

5. Right of Compensation (Section 225)

The principal must pay compensation to his agent in respect of injury caused to such agent by the principal's neglect or want of skill.

6. Right of stoppage in transit

Under following circumstances an agent can stop the goods in transit.

(a) Where he has bought goods for his principal by incurring a personal liability, he has a right of stoppage in transit against the principal, in respect of the money which he has paid or is liable to pay. This right of the agent is similar to that of the unpaid seller.

(b) Where he is personally liable to the principal for the price of the goods sold, he stands in the position of an unpaid seller towards the buyer and can stop the goods in transit on the solvency of buyer.

Duties of Agents

An agent owes a number of duties to his principal. These duties are as follows:

1. To conduct the business of agency according to the principal's directions (Section 211)

This duty of the agent must be literally complied with. When agent acts otherwise, if any loss be sustained, he must make it good to his principal, and, if any profit accrues, he must account for it. If the agent's disobedience is material, the principal may even terminate the agency.

Examples

(a) A, an agent was directed by his principal to warehouse the goods at a particular warehouse. He warehoused a portion of the goods at another place, equally good but cheaper. Those goods were destroyed by fire. Held, A was liable to P for the value of the goods destroyed. (*Lilley v. Doubleday*[233]).

(b) An agent, was instructed to insure goods, neglects to do so. He is liable to the principal for their value in the event of their loss (*Pannalal Jankidas v. Mohanlal*[234]).

In the absence of instructions from the principal he must follow the custom of the business at the place where it is conducted.

2. To carry out the work with reasonable care, skill and diligence (Section 212)

The agent should conduct the business with the skill and diligence that is generally possessed by persons engaged in similar business, except where the principal knows that the agent is wanting in skill. But he is not liable to his principal in respect of loss or damage which is indirectly or remotely caused by such neglect, want of skill or misconduct.

Examples

(a) A, an agent for the sale of goods, having authority to sell on credit, sells to B on credit, without making the proper and usual enquiries as to the solvency of B. B at the time to such sale, is insolvent. A must compensation to his principal in respect of any loss thereby sustained.

(b) A, an insurance broker, employed B to effect an insurance on a ship, omits to see that the usual clauses are inserted in the policy. The ship is afterwards lost. In consequence of the omission of the clauses nothing can be recovered from the underwriters. B is bound to make good the loss to A.

3. To render proper accounts to principal (Section 213)

A agent is bound to render proper accounts to his principal on demand.

4. To communicate with the principal in difficult situations (Section 214)

It is the duty of an agent, in case of difficulty to use all reasonable diligence in communicating with his principal and in seeking to obtain his instructions.

5. Not to deal on his own account

An agent should not deal on his own account without first obtaining the consent of his principal. If he does so, the principal can claim from the agent any benefit which he might have obtained.

6. Not to make secret profit from agency

An agent must not, except with the knowledge and assent of the principal, make any profit beyond the agreed commission or remuneration.

Examples

(a) An auctioneer received from the buyer commission in addition to what his principal paid him as commission. Held, he was bound to hand over the total commission to the principal (*Andrews v. Ramsay and Co.*[235]).

(b) Principal employed an agent to buy a house for him. Agent bought a house for £2,000 in the name of a nominee. He then entered into a contract with the nominee to purchase a house for £4500 which he report to principal for £5000. Held, agent was liable to account to principal not only for the immediate profit of £500 but also for £2500 profit on the transaction (*Regier v. Combell Stuart*[236]).

7. To pay all sums to his Principal (Section 218)

An agent is bound to pay to his principal all sums received on his account.

8. Not to delegate authority (Section 190)

An agent must not depute another person to do what he has himself undertaken to do.

9. Not to use agency information against Principal

An agent must not use any agency information against the interest of Principal. If he uses any such information and the principal suffers a loss he is bound to compensate the principal.

10. Agent's duty on termination of agency by principal's death or insanity

11. Not to put himself in a position where interest and duty conflict

An agent is under a duty, in all cases to act in the interest of the principal. He must not put himself in a position where his duty to the principal and his personal interest conflict unless he has made full disclosure of his interest to his principal. Specifying its exact nature and obtained his assent.

Example

Principal employed a stockbroker, to buy some shares for him. Stockbroker sold his own shares to principal without disclosing that the shares belonged to him. Held, principal could rescind the contract (*Armstrong v. Jackson*[237]).

Rights and Duties of Principal

Rights of Principal

The principal can enforce all the duties of the agent. The Principal has the following remedies against the agent.

1. To recover damages

If the principal suffers any loss due to disregard by the agent of the directions by the principal or by not following the custom of trade in the absence of directions by the principal or where the principal suffers due to lack of requisite skill, care or diligence on the part of the agent, he can recover damages accruing as a result from the agent.

2. To obtain an account of Secret Profits and recover them and resists a claim for remuneration

If the agent, without the knowledge and assent of the principal, makes any secret profits out of the agency, the principal has the right to recover them from the agent.

3. To resist agent's claim for indemnity against liability incurred

Where the principal can show that the agent has acted as principal himself and not merely as agent, he can resist the agent's claim for indemnity against liability incurred by him in such a transaction.

Duties of Principal

The rights of an agent are the duties of the principal. The principal owes the following duties to an agent:

(1) The principal is bound to indemnify the agent against the consequences of all lawful acts done by such agent in exercise of the authority conferred upon him (Section 222).

(2) Principal's liability to indemnify an agent against the consequences of an act done in good faith, though it causes an injury to the rights of third person (Section 223).

(3) The Principal is, however, not liable for acts which are criminal in nature though done by the agent at the instance of the principal (Section 224).

(4) The Principal must make compensation to his agent in respect of injury caused to such agent by the principal's neglect or want of skill (Section 225).

The rights and liabilities of Principal to Third Persons

The rights and liabilities of a Principal in relation to third persons under contracts made by his agent depend upon, whether (a) an agent contracts as agent for a named Principal (b) an agent contracts for a principal whose name he does not disclose (c) an agent contracts in his own name but in reality for a Principal whose existence he does not disclose.

(A) Agent acting for a Named Principal

The position of the named principal for the acts of his agent is as follows:

1. When the agent acts within the scope of his authority (Section 226)

Where an act is done by an agent within the scope of his authority, his acts are binding on the principal. The principal will be bound by the acts of the agent provided (a) the act is lawful and (b) it is within the scope of agent's authority.

Example

Where an agent is authorised to receive payment on behalf of the principal, a payment to the agent discharges the debtor from liability to the principal and the fact that the agent embezzled the money is immaterial.

2. When the agent exceeds his authority (Section 227 and 228)

The principal is liable for those acts of the agent which are within the scope of his authority. According to Section 227, where an agent has done more than what he is authorised to do, and it is separable the principal is bound by that a part which is within his authority.

However, where an agent exceeds his authority, the principal may repudiate the whole of the transaction if what he (the agent) does beyond the scope of his authority cannot be separated from the rest. (Section 228).

Example

Principal authorises agent to buy 10 sheep for him. A buys 10 sheeps and 20 lambs for one sum of Rs. 6000. Principal may repudiate the whole transaction.

3. Principal bound by notice given to agent (Section 229)

The principal is bound by the notice given to the agent in course of the business of the principal. Thus, the knowledge of a manager of a bank is knowledge of the bank. Similarly knowledge of one partner in a firm is knowledge of all the partners. Knowledge of the agent is the knowledge of the principal. But where knowledge is not acquired by the agent in course of his employment, it cannot be imputed to the principal.

But where the agent has committed a fraud on his principal, any notice given to him is not regarded as having been obtained.

However, the rule will apply if the agent had committed a fraud on the principal.

4. Liability of Principal by Estoppel (Section 237)

A principal is liable where he has, by words or conduct, induced a belief in the contracting party that the agent was within the scope of his authority. The liability of the principal under Section 237 is not based on any real authority, but is by estoppel.

5. Liability for misrepresentation or fraud by an agent (Section 238)

The principal is liable for the misrepresentations made or frauds committed by the agent in the course of his business for the principal whether the fraud is committed for the benefit of the principal or that of the agent.

Example

Principal instructed his agent to reinsure an overdue ship at a certain port. Agent heard that the ship had actually been lost. He did not disclose this fact to the insurer. Held, principal could not recover upon the policy (*Blackburn, Lowe Co. v. Haslam*[238]).

B. Agent acting for a Unnamed Principal

Where an agent disclosed the fact, that he is an agent, but at the same time does not disclose his principal's name, the contract made by the agent is binding on the principal. But the unnamed principal should be in existence at the time of the contract.

Example

An agent signed the contract as a broker, "to my principal's", but did not disclose the name of the principal, it was held that the broker was not personally liable.

C. Agent acting for an undisclosed principal

The doctrine of undisclosed principal comes into operation when an agent enters into a contract with a person without disclosing the name and the existence of his principal. The agent in such a case gives an impression to the third party as if he is contracting in an independent capacity.

Section 231 deals with rights of parties to a contract made by an agent for the undisclosed principal. On such contracts, agent can sue and he sued in his own name because he is then in the eyes of law real contracting party. But the agent's right to action comes to an end with the intervention of the undisclosed principal. Once the third party knows of the existence of the principal as well as of the agent, he has a right to sue both or either of them. Once he elects to sue one and not the other, it would appear he exhausts his cause of action.

Personal Liability of Agent

An agent is, however, personally liable in the following cases (Section 230).

(1) When the agent acts for a foreign principal (Section 230 Para 2)

When the contract is made by an agent for the sale or purchase of goods for a merchant residing abroad, the agent is personally liable

(2) When the agent acts for an undisclosed principal (Section 230 Para 2)
When an agent acts for an undisclosed principal, he is personally liable

(3) When the agent acts for a principal who cannot be sued (Section 230 Para 2)
Where the principal is incompetent (minor or an idiot) to enter into a contract the agent is personally liable.

(4) Where the agent's authority is coupled with interest

When an agent has an interest in the subject-matter of the contract entered into by him with a third party, his authority is coupled with interest. He has, in such a case, the right to sue or be sued, but only to the extent of his interest in the subject-matter.

5. Where an agent received or pays money by mistake or fraud

Where an agent receives money from a third party by mistake or fraud, he is personally liable to the third party. Likewise, he has the right to sue the third party for the recovery of the money where he has paid it by mistake or under fraud of third party.

6. Where the agent signs the negotiable instrument in his own name

An agent is personally liable who signs a negotiable instrument is his own name without making it clear that he is signing it as an agent only.

Example

An agent executed a hundi in favour of third person for a loan taken by him from third person. The hundi purported to be drawn by a firm. A did not sign the hundi as agent of the firm and did not disclose to third person the name of the principal who was the proprietor of the firm. Held agent was personally liable (*Trilok Chand v. Rameshwar Lal*[39]).

7. Where the agent exceeds his authority

Where an agent acts either without any authority or exceeds his authority, he is deemed to have committed breach of warranty of authority in such a case. He will be held personally liable if his acts are not ratified by the alleged principal.

8. Where an agent acts for a non existing principal

Sometimes, the promoters of a company, which is to be incorporated enter into contracts on behalf of the company, though in such a case the alleged principal (Company) has no legal existence till the time of incorporation. In such cases the promoters are held personally liable.

9. Where the contract expressly provides

A person while entering into a contract with an agent may expressly stipulate that he would hold the agent personally liable in case of breach of contract, and if the agent agrees to it, he is personally liable.

10. Where the trade usage or custom makes him personally liable

Where there is a trade usage or a custom making the agent personally liable, he is liable unless there is a contract to the contrary.

Termination of Agency

Section 201 describes the modes under which an agency terminates or comes to an end. Section 2201 lays down that "an agency is terminated by the principal revoking his authority, or by the agent renouncing the business of the agency, or by the business of the agency being completed, or by either the principal or agent dying or becoming of unsound mind, or by the principal being adjudicated an insolvent under the provisions of any act for the time being in force for the relief of insolvent debtors."

The modes of termination agency are as follows:

1. By Revocation (Section 203)

The principal may revoke the authority of the agent at any time before the agent has exercised his authority so as to bind the principal unless the agency is irrevocable (Section 203). But if the act is begun, the authority can only be revoked subject to any claim which the agent may have for breach of contract (Section 204). Where the agency is continuous notice of revocation is essential to the agent as well as to the third parties who have acted on the agency with the knowledge of the principal.

Where there is an express or implied contract that the agency should be continued for a period of time, the principal must make compensation to the agent, or the agent to the principal, as the case may be, for any previous revocation or renunciation of the agency without sufficient cause (Section 205). Reasonable notice must be given of such revocation or renunciation, otherwise the damage thereby resulting to the principal or the agent, as the case may be, must be made good to the one by the other (Section 206).

Revocation and renunciation may be expressed or may be implied in the conduct of the principal or agent respectively (Section 207).

Example

An agent was appointed to do all acts and carry on business on behalf of the principal during his absence from. Held, the power should be treated as impliedly revoked when principal returned to India (*Azam Khan v. Sattar*[240]).

2. By Completion of Business (Section 201)

An agency is automatically and by operation of law determined when its business is completed.

Example

An agent was appointed to sell goods, when the sale was completed the agency ceased to be exercisable. Agent can not afterwards alter the terms of the sale (*Venkatachalam v. Narayanan*[241]).

3. By Renunciation by Agent (Section 206)

An agent may renounce the business of agency in the same manner in which the principal has the right of renunciation. In the first place, if the agency is for a fixed period, the agent would have to compensate the principal for any previous renunciation without sufficient cause. Secondly, a reasonable notice of renunciation is necessary. If the agent renounces without proper notice, he shall have to make good any damage thereby resulting to the principal.

4. Death or Insanity (Section 201)

When the agent or the principal dies or becomes of unsound mind, the agency is terminated.

5. On Expiry of Time

When the agency is for a fixed period of time, it comes to an end on the expiry of that time, even if the work is not completed.

6. Insolvency of Principal (Section 201)

Insolvency of the principal, not of the agent, terminates the agency.

Effect of Termination (Section 208)

As between the principal and the agent, termination of agency is effective only when it becomes known to the agent, but so far a third parties are concerned, termination of agency takes effect when it is known to them.

Examples

(i) A, directs B to sell for him and agrees to give B five percent (5%) commission on the price fetched by the goods. A afterwards, by letter revokes B's authority. B, after the letter is sent, but before he receives it, sells the goods for Rs.100/-. The sale is binding on A, and B is entitled to five rupees as his commission.

(ii) A, at Madras, by letter directs B to sell for him some cotton lying in a warehouse in Bombay, and afterwards, by letter, revokes his authority to sell, and directs B to send the cotton to Madras, B, after receiving the second letter, enters into a contract with C, who knows of the first letter, but not of the second, for the sale to him of the cotton. C pays B the money, with which B absconds. C's payment is good as against A.

(iii) A directs B, his agent, to pay certain money to C. A dies, and D takes out probate to his will. B, after A's death, but before hearing of it, pays the money to C. The payment is good as against D, the executor.

Where the agency is terminated by the death of the principal, the termination is effective only when it comes to the knowledge of the agent.

Section 210 provides that the termination of an agent's authority amounts to termination of all sub agents appointed by him.

Agent's Duty on Termination (Section 209)

When the principal dies or becomes of unsound mind, the agent must take, on behalf of the representatives of his late principal, all reasonable steps for the protection and preservation of the interests entrusted to him.

Irrevocable Agency

When an agency (i.e. the relationships between the principal and agent) can not be terminated or put an end to, it is said to be an irrevocable agency.

An agency is irrevocable in the following cases:

1. Where the agency is coupled with interest

An agency is said to be coupled with an interest when the agency is created for the purpose of securing some benefit over and above his remuneration as an agent. Thus, an agency is coupled with interest when the agent has an interest in the authority granted to him or when the agent has an interest in the subject matter with which he is authorised to deal. Such an agency cannot, in the absence of any contract to the contrary, be terminated to the prejudice of such interest.

Examples

(i) A creditor is employed as an agent to collect rents due to the principal for adjusting the amount towards his debt, the authority of the agent is coupled with interest and it is irrevocable during the subsistence of the interest.

(ii) Principal consigns 1000 bales of cotton to agent who made advances to him on such cotton, and desires A to sell the cotton and to repay himself, out of the price, the amount of his own advances. Principal cannot revoke this authority, not is it terminated by his insanity or death.

The above rule applies only if the agency is created for the protection of the interest of the agent. It does not apply where the interest arises after the creation of the agency. It is important that the agency is created with the object of securing a benefit to the agent, and it is not sufficient that the agency secures a benefit to the agent incidentally.

2. Where the agent has incurred a personal liability

When an agent has incurred personal liability the agency becomes irrevocable, for the principal cannot be permitted to withdraw, leaving the agent exposed to risk or liability he has incurred.

3. Where the agent has partly exercised the authority

Section 204 of the Contract Act lays down that the principal cannot revoke the authority given to his agent after the authority has partly exercised so far as regards such acts and obligations as arise from acts already done in the agency.

Example

Principal authorises agent to buy 1000 bags of Paddy account of principal and to pay for it out of principal's money remaining in agent's hands. Agent buys 1000 bags of paddy in his own name, so as to make himself personally liable for the price. P cannot revoke A's authority so far as regards payment for the paddy.

PRACTICE QUESTIONS

1. What are the advantages of the Contract Act accruing to business perso?
2. (a) What is a contract? Why must you, as a manager, know as to what is a contract?

   (b) What tests would you apply to ascertain whether an agreement is a contract?
2. Are there any essentials of a contract so as to make it enforceable by law?
3. "All agreements are not contracts but all contracts are agreements." Comment.
4. Explain what you understand by 'void', 'voidable', 'illegal' and 'valid' contracts. Briefly refer to the rights of parties under such agreements.

5. Enumerate some of the contracts which are expressly declared to be void Indian Contract Act, 1872.
6. (a) How safe are oral contracts? (b) "There are some contracts and documents which are required to be not only in writing and signed by the parties, but in addition, required to be registered with some competent authority or the other." Discuss.
7. Define offer and distinguish between offer and invitation to offer.
8. (i) How is an offer made? (ii) Explain an implied offer, a specific offer, a general offer, a counter-offer?
9. If the special conditions forming part of an offer are contained in a document which is delivered after the contract is complete, is the other party (say a customer) bound by them?
10. What are the reasons due to which the offer lapses or is revoked? If no time is fixed by the offeror within which the offer is to be accepted does the offer remain open for an indefinite period of time?
11. (i) When is an offer said to be accepted? (ii) In which way acceptance of offer may be made?
12. Comment: (i) "Acceptance must be absolute and qualified"? (ii) "A mere mental acceptance is no acceptance", (iii) "Acceptance must be according to the mode prescribed by the offeror"? (iv) "A mere mental acceptance not evidenced by words or conduct is in the eye of law no acceptance".
13. Discuss the rules regarding communication of offer and acceptance. "A stranger to a contract cannot maintain a suit". Discuss.
14. (i) Who is competent to contract? (ii) What determines enough maturity to make a contract? (iii) Can anyone enter into a contract?
15. When does mental incompetence prohibit a valid contract? Is minor competent to contract?
16. "A minor's estate is liable for necessaries of life supplied." Comment.
17. "It is not only the consent but free consent of the parties which is necessary for raking the contract binding." Explain.
18. What is coercion? State its effect on the validity of a contract.
19. What is undue influence? When is it presumed as regards persons in particular relationships?
20. On whom does lie the burden of proving that contract (i) was, or (ii) was not induced by undue influence?
21. What is fraud? What are the essential elements or conditions necessary for its existence?
22. "An attempt to deceive which does not deceive is no fraud." Comment.
23. What is "mistake" as it affects the validity of a contract? What are the consequences of a mistake on contracts?
24. What is meant by 'unilateral mistake'?
25. "Insufficiency of consideration is immaterial but an agreement without consideration is void." Comment.
26. Consideration may be present, past or future. Illustrate.
27. Are there any exceptions to the rule "No consideration, No contract".
28. A stranger to a contract cannot maintain a suit but a stranger to consideration can do so", comment.
29. The term consideration is used in the sense of *'quid pro quo'* or 'something in return'. Does this 'something' to be necessarily in terms of money? Illustrate your answer.

Unlawful Consideration and Object

30. What are the cases in which consideration and object of an agreement are unlawful, thereby making it unenforceable?
31. What is an illegal agreement?
32. Certain agreements, which are against public policy, have been declared to be void by law. Enumerate them and illustrate.
33. Explain the following: (i) agreements for stifling prosecution; (ii) contracts in the nature of champerty and maintenance; (iii) agreements in restraint of marriage
33. What precisely is meant by a wagering agreement? Is it a contingent contract?
34. (i) "An agreement in restraint of trade is void". Examine this statement mentioning exceptions, if any. (ii) "Liberty to trade is not an asset which the law permit a person to barter except in special circumstances with well recognised limitations." Comment.
35. State the contracts expressly declared void by the Indian Contract Act. Also state whether all void agreement are illegal.
36. Explain the meaning of a contingent contract.
37. Distinguish between a wagering agreement and a contingent contract.

38. What are quasi contracts? Enumerate the quasi-contracts dealt with under Indian Contract Act, 1872.
38. Discuss the rights and obligations of a finder of goods.
39. What do you understand by *quantum meruitl?* When does the claim on *aui meruit* arise?
40. (i) What is meant by performance of contracts? (ii) What is meant by : perform? (iii) Who must perform the promise under a contract? (iv) Are the: contracts which need not be performed?
41. Summarise the rules regarding the time, place and manner of performance of contracts.
42. What is a reciprocal promise. Into how many groups reciprocal promises may be divided? Summarise the rules concerning performance of different kinds of reciprocal promises.
43. Explain (i) Novation, (ii) assignment of contracts?
44. What are the different modes of discharge of contracts? Explain the discharge of contract by performance or tender.
45. (i) Explain the concept of "subsequent impossibility" as a mode of discharge of contract, (ii) "Impossibility of performance is, as a rule, not an excuse for non-performance of a contract." Discuss.
46. Discuss the consequences of non-performance of a valid contract.
47. When does a contract discharge by operation of law?
48. What are the different ways in which a breach of contract may arise?
49. Whether time is the essence of a contract or not?
50. What are the main types of remedies for breach of a contract?
51. State the principles on which damages are awarded for breach of contracts.
52. Give some examples of ordinary damages. Can ordinary damages be claimed for any remote or indirect loss or damage by reason of the breach?
53. Give some examples of special damages. Is it that the communication of the special circumstances a prerequisite to the claim for special damages?
54. What is meant by liquidated damages and penalty?
55. What is specific performance? Under what circumstances, it is (i) granted (ii) not granted?
56. What is a penalty clause? Why is it that the court will not enforce a penalty clause?
57. Explain (i) exemplary damages (ii) *quantum meruit.*
58. "The parties to a contract, in a sense, make the law for themselves." Discuss.
59. "Freedom to contract is a myth or an illusion." Discuss.
60. What is standard form contracting? Discuss its advantages and disadvantages for traders and consumers.
61. What do you understand by the contract of guarantee?
62. "The liability of a surety is secondary and co-extensive with that of principal debtor." Comment.
63. What is a 'continuing guarantee'? When can it be revoked?
64. Described the rights of a surety against (i) co-sureties and (ii) the creditor.
65. Explain the circumstances under which a surety may be discharged from the liability by the conduct of the creditor.
66. Define the contract of Indemnity'. Describe the rights of the indemnifier and the indemnity-holder.
67. "Indemnity is not necessarily given by repayment after payment. Indemnity requires that the party to be indemnified shall never be called upon to pay." Discuss.
68. Distinguish between a contract of guarantee and a contract of indemnity.
69. Define bailment. What are the requisites of a contract of bailment? Explain.
70. Distinguish between 'gratuitous bailment' and 'bailment for hire'.
71. Comment on the following:
(i) "Bailor is liable to the bailee for loss caused by faults in the goods bailed whether the bailor was aware of the same or not."
(ii) "Bailor must compensate the bailee for all expenses."
(iii) "Bailee's right of lien is a particular lien and does not extend to other goods of the bailor in his possession."
(iv) "The finder of lost goods has no right to file a suit for recovery of expenses incurred by him for finding out the true owner." Discuss.
72. Discuss the characteristics of a pledge.

73. What are the respective rights and duties of a pawnor and a pawnee?
74. When is a pledge created by non-owners valid?
75. When a pledgor fails to redeem his pledge, what rights does the pledgee have in the pledge?
76. "Every pledge is a bailment, but every bailment is not a pledge". Discuss.

References

1. Balfour v. Balfour (1919) 2 K.B. 571
2. Rose and Frank Co. v. Crompton Bros. (1925) A.C. 445
3. Jones v. Vernon's Pools Ltd. (1938) 2 All E.R. 626.
4. Balfour v. Balfour (1919) 2 K.B. 571.
5. Could v. Could (1970) 1 Q.B. 275.
6. Fitch v. Snedker (1868) 38 N.Y. 288.
7. Lalman v. Gauri Dutt (1913) 11 All. L.J. 489.
8. Carlill v. Carbolic Smoke Ball Co. (1893) 1 Q.B. 256.
9. Olley v. Marlborough Court Ltd. (1949) K.B. 532.
10. Tinn v. Hoffman and Co. (1873) 29 LT 271.
11. Neale v. Merrett (1930) W.N. 189.
12. Heyworth v. Knight (1864) 144 E.R. 120.
13. Ramsgate Victoria Hotel Co. v. Montefiore (1886) L.R. 1 Ex 109.
14. Powel v. Lee (1908) 24 T.L.R. 606.
15. Byrne and Co. v. Van Tienhoven (1880) 5 C.P.D. 344.
16. Kanhaiyalal v. Dineshwara Chandra A.I.R. (1959) M.P. 234.
17. Entores v. Miles Far East Corporation (1955) 2 All E.R. 493.
18. Bhagwan Dass Kedia v. Girdharilal A.I.R. (1966) S.C. 543.
19. Mohiri Bibi v. Dharmodas Ghose (1903) 30 Cal. 539.
20. Raghavachariah v. Srivas (1917) 40 Mad. 30.
21. Abdul Ghaffar v. Prem Piare Lal A.I.R. (1934) Lah 480.
22. Indran Ramaswamy v. Anthiappa Chettiar (1906) 6 M.L.J. 422.
23. Smith v. King (1892) 2 Q.B. 543.
24. Sindha v. Abraham (1895) 20 Bom. 755.
25. Leslie v. Shiell (1914) 3. K.B. 607.
26. Nash v. Inman (1908) 2 K.B. 1.
27. Byrant v. Richardson (1866) 14 L.T. 24.
28. Roberts v. Gray (1913) 1 K.B. 520.
29. Martin v. Gale (1876) 4 Ch. D. 428.
30. Inder Singh v. Parmeshwardhari Singh A.I.R. 1957 Pat 491.
31. Mighell v. Sultan of Johore (1854) 1 Q.B. 149.
32. Blackstone Commentaries
33. Pollock on Contracts 13th ed., P. 113.
34. Thomas v. Thomas (1842) 2 Q.B. 851 at 859.
35. Durga Prasad v. Balden (1881) 3 All 211.
36. National Bank of Upper India v. Bansidhar (1930) 5 Luck 1.
37. Chinnayya v. Ramayya (1882) 4 Mad. 137.
38. Tweddle v. Atkinson (1861) 1 Band S 392.
39. Sindha v. Abraham (1895) 20 Bom. 755.
40. Bolton v. Madden (18730 L.R. 9 Q.B. 57.
41. Collins v. Godfrey (1831) 100 E.R. 1040.
42. Lord Loughbotough.
43. Ram Das v. Krishan Dev A.I.R. (1986) H.P. 9.
44. Venkataswamy v. Rangaswamy (19030) 13 M.L.J. 428.
45. Rajlukhy v. Bhoothnath (1900) C.W.N. 488.
46. Dunlop Pneumatic Tyre Co. v. Seefridge and Co. (1915) A.C. 847.
47. Khwaja Md. Khan v. Hussaini Begum (1910) 37 IA 152.
48. Rana Uma Nath Bakhs Singh v. Jang Bahadur A.I.R. 1938 PC 245.
49. Duropti v. Jaspat Rai (1905) P.R. 171 (Punjab Rec).
50. Shuppa Ammal v. Subramaniyam (1910) 33 Mad 2.
51. Commissioner of Wealth Tax v. Vijayaba A.I.R. (1979) S.C. 982.
52. Devaraja Urs v. Ram Krishniah A.I.R. 1951 Mys 109.
53. Smith and Snipes Hall Farm Ltd. v. River Douglas Catchment Board (1949) 2 K.B. 500.
54. Krishan lal Sadhu v. Promila Bala A.I.R. (1928) Cal. 578.
55. Foster v. Mackinnon (1869) L.R. 4 C P704.

56. Ranganayakamma v. Alwarsetty (1889) 13 Mad 214.
57. Muthian Chettiar v. Karuppan Chetti (1927) 50 Mad. 786.
58. Bansraj v. The Secretary of State (1939) A.W.R. 247.
59. Amiraju v. Seshamma (1917) 41 Mad. 33.
60. Mannu Singh v. Umadat Pandey (1890) 12 All. 523.
61. Ranee Annapurni v. Swaminath (1910) 34 Mad. 7.
62. Inche Noriah v. Shaikh Allie Bin Omar (1929) A.C. 127.
63. Sher Singh v. Pirthi Singh A.I.R. (1975) All. 259.
64. Niko Devi v. Kripa A.I.R. (1989) H.P. 51.
65. Saraswathi v. lakshmi Kantam A.I.R. (1978) Mad. 361.
66. Lakshmi Chand v. Pt. Niader Mal, A.I.R. (1961) All. 295.
67. Howes v. Bishop (1909) 2 K.B. 390.
68. Shaik Ismail v. Amir Bibi (1902) 4 Bom. L.R. 146-148.
69. Ward v. Hobbs (1878) A.C. 13.
70. Peek v. Gurney (1873) 6 HL 377.
71. Bisset v. Wilkinson (1927) A.C. 177.
72. Horsefall v. Thomas (1862) 158 E.R. 813.
73. Shri Krishan v. Kurukshetra University (1976) I Sec 311.
74. Haji Ahmad Yarkhan v. Abdul Gani A.I.R. 1937 Nag. 270.
75. Oceanic Steam Navigation Co. v. Soonderdas Dharmasey (1980) 14 ILR Bom. 241.
76. Dick Bentley Productions Ltd. v. Harold Smith Motors Ltd. (1965) 2 All E.R. 65.
77. Mohan Lal v. Sri Gungaji Cotton Mills Co. (1900) 4 Cal. WN 369.
78. Richview Construction Co. v. Raspa (1975) 11 Ontario Reports (2d) 377.
79. Oriental Banking Corporation v. John Fleming (1879) 3 Bom. 242.
80. Nursey Spinning and Weaving Co., Re. ILR (1880) 5 Bom. 92.
81. Babul v. R.A. Singh A.I.R. (1968) Pat. 190.
82. R.v. Kylsant (1932) 1 K.B. 142.
83. Galloway v. Galloway (1914) 30 T.L.R. 531.
84. Couturier v. Hastie (1856) 5 H.L.C. 673.
85. Raffles v. Wichelhaus (1864) 2 H stet C 906.
86. Nicholson and Venn v. Smith Marriott (1947) 177 L.T. 180.
87. Cox v. Prentice (1815) 3 M and S 344.
88. Cooper v. Phibbs (1867) L.R. 2 H.L. 149.
89. Webster v. Cecil (1861) 30 Bear 62.
90. Griffith v. Brymer (1903) 19 T.L.R. 434.
91. Cundy v. Lindsay and Co. (1878) 3 App Cor. 459.
92. Lake v. Simmons (1927) A.C. 487.
93. Solwer v. Potter (1940) 1 K.B. 271.
94. Ingram v. Little (1961) 1 Q.B. 31.
95. Foster v. Mackinnon (1869) L.R. 4 C.P. 704.
96. Bay v. Pollara and Morris (1930) 1 K.B. 628.
97. Solle v. Butcher. (1950) 1 K.B. 671.
98. Velu Payachi v. Siva Sooriam A.I.R. (1950) Mad. 987.
99. Napier v. National Business Agency Ltd. (1951) 2 All. E.R. 263).
100. & 101. Alexander v. Rayson (19360 1 K.B. 169.
102. Scott v. Brown Doering McNab and Co. (1892) 2 Q.B. 724.
103. Sujan Singh v. Mokham Chand A.I.R. 1983 Pand H 180.
104. W. H. Smith and Sons v. C. Clington (1908) 26 TLR 34.
105. Ram Saroop v. Bansi Mandar (1915) 42 Cal. 742.
106. Gheru Lal Parekh v. Mahadeo A.I.R. (1956) S.E. 781.
107. Baivijli v. Nansa Nagar (1885) Bom. 152.
108. Richardson v. Mellish (1824) 2 Bing 229, 252.
109. Janson v. Driefontein Consolidated Mines Ltd. (1902) A.C. 484.
110. Nagle v. Fielden (1966) 2 Q.B. 633.
111. Ratanchand Hirachand v. Asker Nawaz Jung AIR(1976)A.P. 112.
112. Gherulal v. Mahedeo Das AIR 1959 SC 781.
113. W.H. Smith and Sons v. Clinton (1908) 26 T.L.R. 34.
114. Sati Bhagwan Das Shastri v. Raja Ram AIR 1927 All. 406.
115. Ouseph Poule v. Catholic Union Bank (1964) 7 SCR 745.
116. Lowe v. Peers (1768) Burr 225.
117. Maheswar Das v. Sakhi Bei AIR (1978) Ori. 84.
118. Venkatakrishna v. Venkatachalam 32 Mad. 185.
119. Vaidyanathan v. Gangarazu (1920)17 Mad. 9.

120. Niranjan Shankar v. Century Spinning and Mfg. Co. Ltd AIR (1967) S.C. 1068.
121. Shaikh Kalu v. Ram Saran Bhagat (1909) 8 C.W. N. 388.
122. Madhav v. Raj Coomar (1874) 18 B.L.R. 76.
123. Norden feet v. Maxim Nordenfelt, etc. Co. (1893) AC 538.
124. Khemchand v. Dayal Das (1942) Sind 114.
125. Deshpande v. Arvind Mills AIR 1946 Bom. 423.
126. Brahamputra Tea Company v. Searth (1855) 1 L.R. 11 Cal. 545.
127. Krishna Murgai v. Superintendence Co. of India AIR 1979, Delhi 232.
128. Cohen v. Wilkie 16 C.W.N. 534.
129. Forster and Sons Ltd. v. Suggett, (1918) 35 TLR 87.
130. Robb v. Green (1895) 2 Q.B. 315.
131. Hiwae Ltd. v. Park Royal (1946) Ch. 169.
132. Attwood v. Lamont (1920) 3 K.B. 511.
133. S.B.Fraser and Co. v. Bombay Ice Mfg. Co. (1904) 29 Bom. L.R. 107.
134. Jai Ram v. Kahna Ram AIR (1963) H.P. 3.
135. Giddu Narayanish v. Mrs. Annie Besant (1915) 38 Mad. P.C.
136. Horwood v. Millar's Timber and Trading Co. (1917) 1 K.B. 305.
137. Saminathag v. Muthusami 30 Mad. 530.
138. Parkinson v. College of Ambulance (1925) 2 K.B. 1.
139. Guthing v. Lynn (1831) 2 B. Ad. 232.
140. Pushpabala v. LIC of India AIR 1978 Cal. 221.
141. Carlill v. Carbolic Smoke Ball Co. (1892) 2 Q.B. 484 at 490.
142. Babasaheb v. RajaRam AIR 1931 Bom. 264.
143. Narayan Ayyangar v.K. Vallachami Ambalam (1927) ILR 50 Mad. 696 F.B.
144. Sir Dorabji Tata v. Edward F Lanci (1918) ILR 42 Bom. 676.
145. H. Anroj v. Govt. of Tamil Nadu AIR 1986 S.C. 63.
146. Coleys v. Odham's Press (1936) 1 K.B. 416.
147. Babalalteb v. Rajaram (1931) 33 Bom. L.R. 260.
148. Badridas Kothari v. Meghraj Kotharl AIR 1957 Cal 125.
149. Cowan v. Milbourn, (1867) 36 LJ Ex. 24.
150. C.H.T. Ltd. v. Ward (1963) 3 All. E.R. 835.
151. Hill v. William Hills (Park Lane) Ltd. (1949) 2 All. E.R. 442 HL.
152. N.v.P. Pandian v. M.M. Roy AIR 1979 Mad. 42.
153. Ahsmore, Benson Pease and Co. Ltd. v. A.v. Dawson Ltd. (1973) 2 All. E.R. 856.
154. Ranchhadas v. Nathmal Hirachand and Co. (1949) 51 Bom. L.R. 491.
155. Roberts v. Smith (1859) 4 H and N. 315.
156. Union of India v. Amar Singh (1960) 2 SCR 75, at pp 84-85.
157. Sales Tax Officer, Banaras v. Kanhaiya Lal Mukund Lal Saraf (1957) SCR 1350.
158. Seth Kanhaya Lal v. National Bank of India (1913) 40 IA 56.
159. Cutter v. Powell (1795) T.T. 320.
160. Patel Engg. Co. Ltd. v. Indian Oil Corporation AIR (1975) Pat. 212.
161. Planche v. Colburn (1831) 8 Bing 14.
162. Hoening v. Isaacs (1952) AIR 11 E.R. 176.
163. Pinch v. Miller (1848) 5 C.B. 428.
164. Shipton, Anderson and Co. v. Weil Bros. and Co. (1912) 1 K.B. 574.
165. Startup v. Macdonald (1843) 6 Man G. 523.
166. Bakshi Hardatt v. The State of J and K AIR (1977) NOC 207 (J and K).
167. Orissa Cement Ltd. v. Union of India, AIR (1967) Ori. 158.
168. Kirtee Chunder v. Struthes (1878) 4 Cal. 336.
169. Johar Roy v. Premji Bhimji (1977) 4 SCC 562.
170. Radhakrishna S. Rai v. T. Dawoodbai AIR 1962 SC 538.
171. Jones v. Barkley, 4 Doug, 659.
172. Hashman v. Lucknow Improvement Trust (1927) 10 IC 847.
173. Kleinert v. Abosso Gold Mining Co. (1913) 58 Solicitors' Journal, 45, on appeal from the Supreme Court of Gold Coast.
174. Har Prasad Choubey v. Union of India (1973) 2 SCC 11
175. Nathulal v. Phool Chand (1963) 3 SCC 120: AIR 1970 SC 546: (1970) 2 SCR 854.
176. Bhudra Chand v. Betts (1915) 22 Cal. LJ 566: 33 IC 347.
177. Hitkari Motors v. Attar Singh AIR (1962) J and K 10
178. Mahabir Pershad v. Durga Dutta AIR 1961 SC 900.
179. Hind Contractors v. State of Maharashtra AIR (1979) S.C. 720.
180. Mulla Badruddin v. Tufail Ahmed AIR 1963 MP 31.
181. Indira Kaur v. Sheo Lal Kapoor AIR 1988 SC 1074.
182. Crawford v. Toogwood 13 Ch. 153.

183. Rulia Devi v. Raghunath Prasad AIR (1979) Pat. 115
184. Clayton's Case (1816) 1 Mer. 572.
185. Shanker Lal Damodar v. A. Ajaipal AIR 1946 Nag. 260.
186. Taylor v. Caldwell (1863) 3 B and S 826.
187. Howell v. Coupland (1867) Q.B.D. 258.
188. Nickoll and Knight v. Ashton Edridge and Co. (1901) 2 K.B. 126.
189. Krell v. Henry (1903) 2 KB 740.
190. Robinson v. Davison (1871) LR 6 Ex. 269.
191. Baily v. De Crespigny (1869) L.R. 4 Q.B. 180.
192. Shipton Anderson and Co., Re (1915) 3 K.B., 676.
193. M/s Alopi Pd. v. Union of India (1960) S.C. 589.
194. Harnandrai Fulchand v. Pragdas AIR 1923 P.C. 54.
195. Jacobs v. Credit Lyonnais (1884) 12 Q.B.D. 589.
196. Budget v. Binnington (1851) 1 Q.B. 35.
197. Herne Bay Steamboat Co. v. Hutton K.B. 740.
198. Cort v. Ambergate Etc. Ply. Co. (1815) 17 Q.B. 127.
199. O'Neil v. Armstrong (1895) 2 Q.B. 418.
200. Lovelock v. Franklyn (1846) 8 Q.B. 371.
201. British Westinghouse and Co. v. Underground Electric etc. Co. (1915) A.C. 673.
202. Sunder Koer v. Rai Sham Krishan (1907) 34 Cal 150.
203. Lumley v. Wagner (1852) 5 De G.M. and G 604.
204. Metropolitan Electric Supply Company v. Ginder (1901) 2 Ch. 799.
205. Warner Bros v. Nelson (1937) 1 K.B. 209.
206. Gajanan Moreshwar v. Moreshwar Madan AIR (1942) Bom. 302.
207. Sham Sunder v. Chandra Lal 1935 Lah. 974.
208. Ranganath v. Pachasoo 1935 Nag. 147.
209. Sanker Nimbagui v. Laxman Napu 1940 Bom. 161.
210. Kamnannath Bhattacharjee v. Nohokumar (1899) 26 Cal. 241.
211. Shiam Lal v. Abdul Salal 1931 All 754.
212. Gajnan Moreshwar v. Moreshwar Madan 1942 Bom. 302.
213. Liverpool Insurance Co's case (1914) 2 Ch 617.
214. Birkmyr v. Darnell (1704) 91 ER 27.
215. Trade I Corpn. v. W.H. and D. Co. 1937 AC I.
216. Jagjiwandas v. King Hamilton, 55 Bom. 677.
217. Karuppan v Nagappa AIR 1934 Mad. 186.
218. Shamasuddin v Show Wallace and Co. AIR 1939 Mad. 520, 522.
219. Punjab National Bank Ltd. v. Shri Vikram Cotton Mills and Another AIR 1970 S.C. 1973.
220. Kay v. Groves (1829) 6 Bing 276.
221. Eastern Bank Ltd. v. Parts Services of India Ltd. AIR 1986 Cal. 61.
222. Kashiba b. Shripat (1895) 19 ILR Bom. 697.
223. Edavan Nambiar v. Moolaki Raman AIR 1957 Mad. 164.
224. Midland Motor Showrooms Ltd. v. Newman (1929) 2 K.B. 256.
225. N.R. Srinivasa Iyer v. New India Ass. Co. Ltd. AIR 1983 SC 899.
226. Kaliperumal v. Visalakasmi AIR 1938 Mad. 32.
227. Hatton v. Car Maintenance Co. Ltd. (1915) 1 ch. 621.
228. Revenue Authority v. Sudarshan Pictures AIR (1968) Mad. 319.
229. Sheikh Farid Buksh v. Hargulal Singh AIR (1937) All. 46.
230. Luxor (Eashourne) Ltd. v. Cooper (1941) A.C. 108.
231. Green v. Barlett (1863) 14 C.B. (N.S.) 631.
232. Toplis v. Crane (1938) 5 Bing N.C. 636.
233. Lilley v. Doubleday (1881) 1 Q.B.D. 510.
234. Kankidas v. Mohanlal AIR (1951) S.C. 144.
235. Andrews v. Ramsay and Co. (1903) 2 K.B. 635.
236. Regier v. Combell Stuart (1939) Ch. 766.
237. Armstorng v. Jackson (1977) K.B. 822.
238. Blackburn, Lowe Co. v. Haslam (1888) 21 Q.b.d. 144.
239. Trilok Chand v. Rameshwar Lal AIR (1975) Pat. 196.
240. Azam Khan v. S. Sattar AIR (1978) A.P. 422.
241. Venkatachalam v. Narayanan (1914) Mad. 376.

PART L

THE COMPANIES ACT, 1956

THE COMPANIES ACT 1956

CHAPTER

36

Evolution of Company Law

In ancient Rome, a 'Corporation' could be formed either by law or by a decree of the senate or by some special constitution. A Corporation had its own fundamental charter and by laws by which it was regulated and administered. The powers and privileges of a corporation would vary according to its constitution. It could appoint 'syndics' or officers for its day to day management. All decisions were taken by members at meetings and the decision taken by two-third majority of members present at the meeting were binding. A corporation could come to an end either by expiry of fixed term, if any, or by the death of all members or by operation of law.

Development

The experience of Roman law had been fully utilised by the British people. With the growth of industry and commerce in Great Britain, large scale business become a common feature. It was no longer possible for the businessmen to take unlimited personal risks in the form of sole-proprietorship and partnership. At this stage a group of businessmen started a new form of organisation by pooling their individual capital or stock into a joint stock and made an appeal to the king or the Queen. As the case may be, to permit them to have their individual liabilities limited upto the amount of stock pooled by each of them. The king or the Queen granted this by a charter. The East India company, formed by a Royal charter of 1600 in an example.

With the decline of the powers of the King or the Queen and emergence of the supremacy of parliament. companies were being formed or incorporated by **the Act of Parliament.** The first company of this kind is the Bank of England, formed in 1694. Subsequently, formation or incorporation of companies was regularised by passing of **the Joint Stock Companies Act in 1844.** This was the first comprehensive company legislation known to the world. This Act was replaced by the Limited Liabilities Act in 1855 which was amended and renamed in 1862 as the **Companies Act.** At that time a company would mean a public company. The concept of private company was introduced by passing the **Companies Act in 1907.** In this way the foundation of Company Law with all its different aspects was laid in Great Britain to be followed in other countries including India. The British Companies Act has been amended a number of times and a major change has been brought about in 1948 according to the recommendations of **Cohen Committee.** In U.K., Companies may be formed by Royal Charter but such companies are generally non-trading ones and meant for some cultural or philanthropic purpose, e.g., the Institute of Chartered Accountants, the Institute of Cost and Management Accountants.

Company Legislation In India

It is nothing but an extension of the same in U.K. The British people for their own commercial interest introduced company legislation in this country by passing the Registration of Joint Stock Companies Act in 1850 (based on Joint Stock Companies Act of 1844 of Great Britain). The Act of 1850 was followed by two other Acts of 1860 and 1866 bringing together provisions for registration, regulation and winding up of companies (including Banking and Insurance Companies as well as Charitable or Non-Trading Concerns). The first comprehensive Act on companies, known as **the Indian Companies Act,** was passed in 1913, which was thoroughly amended in 1936. The amendment was mainly aimed at the management of a company.

After independence it was felt that the Companies Act had to be thoroughly recast in the context of the changed socio-economic environment. Some immediate amendments were made in 1951. In 1950 Government of India appointed a committee with 12 members (in the line of the Cohen Committee of D.K.) under the chairmanship of Sri C.H. Bhabha to make a report on the future company legislation in the country. The Bhabha Committee presented its report in 1952. A Draft Bill for new company legislation was prepared and placed before parliament and it took two years to get the Bill passed because of its vastness. **The Companies Act of 1956** was made effective from 1-4-56. This is perhaps the biggest legislation in the commercial field consisting of 713 Sections with innumerable sub-sections and 12 schedules.

There have been so far **20 amendments** to the Companies Act out of which the amendment of 1960 under the recommendations of the Shastri Committee, the amendment of 1969 under the recommendations of the Patel Committee and the amendment of 1974 are very significant. In 1977 the Government appointed a high powered Expert Committee under the chairmanship of justice Rajinder Sachar for a review of the company legislation. The Report submitted by the Sachar Committee in August 1978 is under consideration of the Government.

Sachar Committee Reports

On June 23, 1977 the central Government constituted a high-power committee to consider and report on the changes required to be made in the form and structure of the Act of 1956. The Committee (under the Chairmanship of Rajender Sachar) submitted its report on August 29, 1978. The report of the committee is very comprehensive and deals with all important provisions of the law. The committee has recommended significant changes with regard to the following:

(a) to make the provisions more simple and relevant to the present circumstances.

(b) to meet the needs of modern corporate management.

(c) to introduce worker's participation in the company's management.

(d) to protect the minority shareholders against mismanagement and

(e) to ensure social responsiveness by the company to the needs of the community.

Let us see how far the government takes in view the recommendations of the committee to amend the Companies Act 1956 in future.

The Companies (Amendment) Act 1988

Based on the recommendations of the High Powered Expert (Sachar) Committee Report and the experience gained by the government in the administration of the Companies Act, 1956, by the Companies (Amendment) Act of 1988. These amendments have been incorporated in the book at appropriate places.

Applicability of the Act

The Act extends to the whole of India except that—

(1) as regards Nagaland, it applies, subject to such modifications, if any, as the central government may, by modification in the Official Gazette specify [Section 1(3)],

(2) as regards Goa, Daman and Diu, such of the provisions of the Act shall not apply or shall apply with such exceptions and modifications to any existing company or my company registered under the Act on or after 26th January, 1963, and for such periods with effect from that or any periods with effect from that or any subsequent date as may be specified by the Central Government in the Official Gazette (Section 620-B), and

(3) as regards Jammu and Kashmir such of provisions of the Act shall not apply or shall apply with such exceptions and modifications or adaptations to any existing company or any company registered under the Act after the commencement of the Central Laws (Extension to Jammu and Kashmir) Act 1968 (i.e., 15th August) and for such period or periods with effect from the commencement of the central laws extention to Jammu and Kashmir) Act (Section 620-C).

The Act applies to all classes of companies that is public companies, private companies and associations not trading for profit. It all and contain certain provisions relating to companies incorporated out side India, but which have an established place of business in India.

Meaning and Nature of Company

Meaning: From the Websters dictionary we get different meanings of term 'Company' related to business, such as "(a) a chartered commercial organisation or medieval trade guild, (b) an association of persons for carrying on a commercial or industrial enterprise, (c) those members of a partnership firm whose names do not appear in the firm name (John Doe and Company)." The first meaning is understandable when we go through the evolution of the concept of company mainly through British experience. In the second case company means any form of commercial association and in the third case it is specially applicable to a partnership firm.

In fact the term Company is not a technical word as such it can be used in the name of any group of persons doing some business together. Even a sole- proprietorship concern uses the word Company in its name.

Definition

According to Section 3 (1) (i) of the Companies Act 1956, a Company means a company formed and registered under this Act or an existing company as defined in clause (ii)". Clause (ii) states that "an existing company means a company formed and registered under any previous Companies laws."

The Act provides elaborate provisions for the formation of a company including registration or incorporation, which is the primary part of formation (Section 1.12). Once the registration or incorporation is complete the Registrar of Companies issues a certificate of incorporation and once the certificate IS issued, the company becomes a body corporate (Section 34).

Therefore, a company means a registered body and a body corporation. According to the Act, there are many other types of companies also (Section 1.7).

The definition, however, leads us no where in understanding the word "Company." Another attempt has been made in Section 566 which reads, "a joint stock company means a company having a permanent paid — up or nominal share capital of a fixed amount, or held and transferable as stock, or divided and held partly in one way and partly in another. Such a company when registered with limited liability under this Act shall be deemed to be a company limited by shares."

Although this definition of Section 566 is a good attempt in defining of joint stock company, it does not bring out all its characteristics.

Lindley's definition

Perhaps the clearest and most useful description of a company has been given by Lord Lindley in his famous book — "A Treatise on the Law of Companies". According to him, "By a Company is meant an association of many persons who contribute money or money's worth to a common stock and employ it in some trade or business, and who share the profit and loss (as the case may be) arising therefrom. The common stock so contributed is denoted in money and is the capital of the company. The persons who contribute it or to whom it belongs are members. The proportion of capital to which each member is entitled in his share. Shares are always transferable although the right to transfer them is after more or less restricted".

A Company, thus, may be defined as an incorporated association, which is an artificial legal person, having an independent legal entity, with a perpetual succession, a common seal, a common capital comprising transferable shares and carrying limited liability. Some times, the term' corporation' (a word derived from the Latin word corpus which means body) is also used for a company.

Characteristics

The various above noted definitions reveal the following essential characteristics of a Company.

1. Separate Legal Entity:

Unlike partnership, Company is distinct from the persons who constitute it. (*R.D. Singh v. Secretary, Bihar State Small Industries Corpn*[1], *Kathiawar Industries Ltd. v. e.G. of Evacuee Property*[2]). A Company can hold property, can sue and can be sued in its own name. In other words, it has an independent existence. Any of its members can enter into contracts with it in the same manner as any other individual can and he cannot be held liable for the acts of the company even if he holds virtually the entire share capital. The company's money and property belong to the company and not to the Shareholders. Section 34(2) says that on registration, the association of persons becomes a body corporate by the name contained in the memorandum.

The importance of the separate entity of a company was very well brought out in the famous case of *Salomon v Salomon and Co. Ltd.*[3]. **Lord Macnanghtan** in this famous case observed that:

"The company is at law a different person altogether from the subscribers; and though it may be that after incorporation the business is precisely the same as it was before, and the same persons are managers and the same hands receive the profits, the company is not in law the agent of the subscribers or trustee for them. Nor are they subscribers or trustee for them. Nor are the subscribers as members liable, in any shape or firm, except to the extent and in the manner provided by the Act."

The facts of the famous Salomon's case were as follows:

One Salomon was boot and shoe manufacturer. His business was in sound condition and there was a substantial surplus of assets over liabilities. He incorporated a company named Salomon and Co. Ltd. for the purpose of taking over and carrying on his business. The seven subscribers to the memorandum were Salomon, his wife and daughter and four son's and they remained the only members of the company. Salomon, with his own sons, constituted board of directors of the company. The business was transferred to the company for £40,000. In payment Salomon took £20,000 shares of £2 each and debentures worth £10,000. These debentures certified that the company owed Salomon £10,000 and created a charge on the company's assets. One share was given to each remaining member of his family. The company went into liquidation within a year.

On winding up, the state of affairs was broadly something like this: Assets — £6,000, Liabilities — Salomon and debenture-holder: — £ 1 0,000 and unsecured creditors — £7,000. Thus after paying off the debenture holder, nothing would be left for the unsecured creditors.

The unsecured creditors, therefore, contended that, though incorporated under the Act, the company never had an independent existence, it was in fact Salomon under another name, he was the managing director, the other directors being his sons and under his control. His vast preponderance of shares made him absolute master. The business was solely his, conducted, solely for and by him and the company was a mere sham and fraud, in effect entirely contrary to the intent and meaning of the Companies Act.

But it was held that Salomon and Co. Ltd. was a real company fulfilling all the legal requirements. It must be treated as a company as entirely consisting of certain corporators, but a distinct and independent corporation.

In *Lee v. Lee Farming Limited* a company was formed for the purpose of manufacturing aerial top-dressing. Lee, a qualified pilot, held all but one of the shares in the company, and by the articles was appointed governing director of the company and chief pilot, Lee was killed while piloting the company's aircraft, and his widow claimed compensation for his death under the Workmen Compensation Act. The company opposed the claim on the ground that Lee was not a 'worker' as the same person could not be employer and the employee.

Held: There was a valid contract of service between Lee and the company, and Lee was, therefore, a worker. Mrs. Lee's contention was upheld.

In *Bacha F. Guzdar v. The Commissioner of Income- Tax. Promay*[5], the plaintiff (Mrs. Guzdar) received certain amounts as dividend in respect of shares held by her in a tea company, under the Indian Income-Tax Act, agricultural income is exempted from payment of income-tax. As income of a tea company is partly agricultural, only 40% of the company's income is treated as income from manufacture and sale and, therefore, liable to tax. The plaintiff claimed that the dividend income in her hands should be treated as agricultural income up to 60%, as in the case of a tea company, on the ground that dividends received by shareholders represented the income of the company. Held by the Supreme Court, that though in income in the hands of the company was partly agricultural yet the same income when received by Mrs. Guzdar as dividend could not be regarded as agricultural income.

2. Limited Liability:

The Company, being a separate person is the owner of its assets and bound by its liabilities.

Members, even as a whole, are neither the owner's of the company's undertaking, nor liable for its debts. In other words, the liability of the members is limited. No member is bound to contribute anything more than the nominal value of the shares held by him.

A Company may be a company limited by shares or a company limited by guarantee.

In a company limited by shares, the liability of members is limited to the unpaid value of the shares. For example, if the face value of a share in a company is Rs. 10 and a member has already paid Rs.7 per share, he can be called upon to pay not more than Rs.3 per share during the lifetime of the company. In a company limited by guarantee, the liability of members, is limited to such amounts as the members may undertake to contribute to the assets of the company, in the event of its being wound up.

3. Separate Property:

A Company is a legal person distinct from its members. It is, therefore, capable of owing enjoying and disposing of property in its own name. Although its capital and assets are contributed by its shareholders, they are not the private and joint owner's of its property. The company is the real person in which all its property is vested and by which it is controlled, managed and disposed of.

4. An Artificial Person:

A Company is purely a creation of law. It is invisible, intangible, immoral (Law alone can dissolve it) and exists only in the eyes of Law. It has no soul, no body, no conscience and still it is in a position to exist to enter into a contract, to appoint people as its employees and in short, it can do everything just like natural persons except, of course, it cannot take oath, cannot appear on its own person in a court (i.e., it must be represented by counsel), cannot be sent to jail, cannot practise a learned profession like Law or Medicine, nor can it marry or divorce. But a company cannot be treated as a 'fictitious' entity because it really exists.

5. Incorporated Association:

A Company to be distinct from other associations like a partnership or Joint Hindu Family, must be incorporated or registered under the Companies Act Unlike a natural person, a company seeks its existence from the law. The registration or incorporation of a body corporate as a company marks the birth of a company. Thus, registration is compulsory. It will probably be not out of place to mention that an association of more than 10 persons in the case of the banking industry and 20 persons in other trading activities, if not registered as a company, becomes an illegal association.

6. Perpetual Succession and Common Seal:

A Company being an artificial person cannot be incapacitated by illness and it does not have an allotted span of life. The death, insolvency or retirement of its members leaves the company unaffected.

In the case of a company, it may be said that "members may come and members may go but the company goes on forever: During the war, all the members of one private company while, in a general meeting, were killed by a bomb. But the company survived, not even a hydrogen bomb could have destroyed it[6].

A Company's life is determined by the terms of its memorandum of association. It may be perpetual or it may continue for a specified time to carry on a task or object as laid down in the memorandum of association. Again since the company has no physical existence, it must act through its agents (called directors) and all such contracts entered into by the agent must be under the common seal of the company.

The common seal is the official signature of a company. The name of the company is engraved on it, as a substitute for its signature. Any document not bearing the common seal of the company will not be binding on the company.

A company registered under the Act should have only one common seal for use within India.

The Department of Company Affairs clarifies that a metallic (and not a rubber stamp) seal should be used in the day-to-day working of the company.

7. Not a Citizen:

Although a company is a legal person having nationality and domicile, it is not a citizen (*State Trading Corporation of India Ltd. v. Commercial Tax officer*[7]). A company cannot, therefore, claim the protection of those fundamental rights which are expressly guaranteed to citizens only, e.g., the right of franchise. But still they are sufficiently protected under the constitution. For instance, their freedom of trade or commerce cannot be curtailed, and no unjust discrimination in any matter whatsoever can be shown against them. The company has the right to challenge a law if the la\v happens to violate fundamental rights of citizens (*Prithivi Cotton Mills v. Broack Borough Municipality*[8]).

According to the constitution of India, citizen means men and women and so a body corporate cannot be a citizen (*Jupiter General Insurance Co. v. A. Rajagopalan*[9]). All citizens are persons but all persons are not citizens.

8. Transferability of Shares:

Since business is separate from its members in a company form of organisation, it facilitates the transfer of members interests. When joint stock companies were established, the great object was that the shares should be capable of being easily transferred.[10]

Accordingly, the Companies Act in Section 82 declares; The shares or other interests of any members in a company shall be movable property, transferable in the manner provided by the articles of the company. Thus incorporation enables a members to sell his shares in the open market and to get back his investment without having to withdrawn the money from the company. This right may be restricted by articles of a private company. This provides liquidity to the investor and stability to the company.

Characteristics of a Company

- Separate legal entity (1)
- Limited liability (2)
- Separate property (3)
- An Artificial person (4)
- Incorporated Association (5)
- Perpetual succession and common seal (6)
- Not a citizen (7)
- Transferability of shares (8)

Corporation or Body Corporate

Sometimes, the term 'corporation' (a word derived from the Latin word 'corpus' which means 'body') or a 'body corporate' is used for a company in the Companies Act 1956.

According to Section 2(7), 'body corporate' or 'corporation' includes a company incorporated outside India but does not include:

(a) a corporation sole;
(b) a registered cooperative society;
(c) any other body corporate (not including a company) which the central government may specify in this behalf.

Corporations may be of the following two types:

(a) Corporations sole, and
(b) Corporations aggregate.

A corporation sole is a corporation constituted in a single person who, in right of some office or function, has corporate status. Examples of corporation sole are to be found in perpetual offices each as the president, governors crown, ministers, a public trustee.

A corporation aggregate consists of a number of persons associated together so that they form a single person, e.g. a limited company, a municipality or a municipal corporation.

Lifting The Corporate VEIL

From the juristic point of view, a company is a separate legal person distinct from its members.

This was laid down in *Salomon v. Salomon and CO.*". The courts in general consider themselves bound by this pnnciple. The effect of the principle laid down in this case is that there is a veil between the company and its members and the courts do not lift it, to look at the economic reality. The fact, however, is that a company is an association of persons who are the beneficial owners of all the corporate property. And sometimes, it may become necessary break through the corporate Veil or facade and to look at the persons behind the company. In such a case, the court may in its discretion disregard the corporate fiction to pay regard to the economic realities behind the legal facade. This is known as "lifting or piercing the corporate veil."

The human ingenuity, however, stared using this veil of corporate personality blatantly as a clock for fraud or for improper conduct. It therefore became necessary for the courts to break through or lift the corporate veil and look at the persons behind the company who are the real beneficiaries of the corporate fiction.

Exceptions

The circumstances and cases in which the corporate veil may be lifted or pierced fall under two heads:

(A) Under Express statutory provisions
(B) Under judicial interpretation.

A. Under Express Statutory Provisions

These include the following exceptions:

1- When the Number of Member is Reduced below Statutory Minimum

Some times the number of members in a company may fall below the statutory minimum (seven in the case of a Public Company and two in the case of a private company). In such a case, if the company carries on business for more than Six months, every person who is cognizant of the fact and is a member during the time, the company so carries on business after these six months, is severally liable for the whole of the debts of the company contracted during that time (Section 45).

2- Where the Relationship of Holding and Subsidiary Companies is established

Where one company controls the management of another company, the former is called the holding company and the latter the subsidiary company. In the eyes of law, the holding company and its subsidiaries are separate legal entities. However in the following cases, a subsidiary company may lose its separate identity to a certain extent.

(i) where at the end of its financial year, a company has subsidiaries, it must lay before its members in general meeting not only its own accounts, but also a set of group accounts showing the profit or loss earned or suffered by the holding company and its subsidiaries collectively and their collective state of affairs at the end of the year [Section 212 (i)].

(ii) The central government, where it feels desirable, may direct the holding and subsidiary companies to synchronize their financial years.

(iii) The court may, on the facts of a case, treat a subsidiary company as merely a branch or department of one large undertaking owned by the holding company.

3. For Investigation into Related Companies under Section 235 and 237

Section 239 of the Companies Act provides that if it is necessary for the satisfactory completion of the investigation into the affairs of a company, the inspector appointed to investigate may look into the affairs of another related company under the same management or group. For calculating the total number of companies under the same management, regard shall have to be paid to persons behind the legal facade.

4. For Investigation of the Ownership of Company

The separate legal entity may be disregarded under Section 247 of the Companies Act, 1956.

This Section authorises the central government to appoint one or more inspectors to investigate and report on the membership of any company for the purpose of determining the true persons who are financially interested in the company and who control or materially influence its policy.

5. When There is Fraudulent Trading

Sometimes in the course of the winding up of a company it may appear that some business of the company has been carried on with intent to defraud creditors. In such a case, the court may declare that any persons who were knowingly parties to the carrying on of the business in this way are personally responsible without any limitation of liability for all or any of the debts or other liabilities of the company as the court may direct [Section 542(1)]. The court may do so on the application of the official liquidator, or the liquidator or any creditor or contributory of the company.

C. Under Judicial Interpretation

There is vast scope for the court to lift the corporate veil under judicial interpretation.

It is however, difficult to count all the cases in which the courts have lifted or might lift the corporate veil. Some of the most important cases of lifting of veil under judicial decisions may be given.

1. Protection of Revenue

The courts may ignore the corporate entity of a company where it is used for tax evasion or to circumvent tax obligation (Juggilal v. I.T. Commissioner[12]). Again the tax liability of an assessee depends upon the residential status and residential status depends upon the situation of central management. Thus, the court may lift the veil for determining the residential status and tax liability of the company. The following case illustrates the point:

Sir Dinshaw Maneckjee Pelit, Re[13].

D was a rich man having dividend and interest income. He wanted to avoid surtax.

For this purpose, he formed four private companies, in all of which he was the majority shareholder. The companies made investments and whenever interest and dividend incomes were received by the companies, D. applied to the companies for loans which were immediately granted and never repaid. In a legal proceeding the companies treated as if they were of "D".

2. Avoidance of Welfare Legislation

Avoidance of welfare legislation is as common as avoidance of taxation and the approach of the court in considering problem arising out of such avoidance has necessarily to be the same as avoidance of taxation. It is the duty of the court in every case where ingenuity is expended to avoid welfare legislation to get behind the smoke-screen and discover the true state of affairs (*Workmen of Associated Rubber Industry Ltd. v. Association Rubber Industry Ltd*[14]).

3. Prevention of Fraud or improper conduct

The legal personality of a company may also be disregarded in he interest of justice where the machinery of incorporation has been used for some fraudulent purpose like defrauding creditors or defeating or circumventing Law. (*Tata Engg. and Locomotive Co. Ltd. v. State of Bihar*[15]). The following case illustrates the point: *Jones v. Lipman*[16], L agreed to sell a certain land to 1. for £5,250. He subsequently changed his mind and to avoid the specific performance of the contract, he sold it to a company (with a capital of £100) which was formed specially for the purpose. The company had L. and a clerk of his solicitors as the only members. J. brought an action for the specific performance against L and the company, and ordered that the company should transfer the land to J.

4. Where the Company is a 'Sham'

The court also lifts the veil where a company is a mere cloak or Sham. The following cases illustrates the point:

Gilford Motor Co. Ltd. v. Home[17]. Horne, a former employee of a company, had agreed with the company not to solicit its customers. He formed a company to carry on a business which, if he had done so personally, would have been a breach of the agreement. An injunction was granted against both him and the company to restrain them from carrying on the business. The company was described in this judgement as "a device, a stratagem", and as a mere cloak or Sham for the purpose of enabling the defendant to commit a breach of his covenant against solicitation.

Delhi Development Authority v. Skipper Construction Company (P) Ltd.[18]. The Skipper Construction failed to pay the full purchase price of a plot to DDA. Instead construction was started and space sold to various persons. The two sons of the directors who had businesses in their own names claimed that they had separated from the father and the companies they were running had nothing to do with the properties of their parents. But no satisfactory proof in support of their claim could be produced. Held that the transfer of Shareholding between the father and the sons must also be treated as a Sham. The fact that the director and members of his family had created several corporate bodies did not prevent the court from treating all of them as one entity belonging to and controlled by the director and his family.

5. Company Avoiding Legal Obligations

Where the use of an incorporated company is being made to avoid legal obligations, the court may disregard the legal personality of the company and proceed on the assumption as if no company existed.

6. Company acting as agent or trustee of the shareholders

Where a company is acting as agent for its shareholders, the shareholders will be liable for the acts of the company (*Smith Stone and Knight Ltd. v. Birmingham Corporation*[19]). It is a question of fact in each case whether the company is acting as agent for its shareholders. There may be an express agreement to this effect or an agreement may be implied from the circumstances of each particular case.

7. Company Formed is against public interest or public policy

Where the doctrine of corporate veil conflicts with public policy, the courts lift the corporate veil for protecting the public policy. (*Connors Ltd. v. Connors*[20]).

8. Determination of character of a company whether it is enemy

A company may assume an enemy character when persons in de facto (in actual fact, real) control of its affairs are residents in an enemy country. In such a case, the court may, in its discretion, examine the character of persons in real control of the company, disregard the corporate fiction and declare the company to be an enemy company. *Daimler Co. Ltd. v. Continental Tyre and Rubber Co.*[21]. A company was incorporated in England for the purpose of selling in England tyres made in Germany by a German company which held the bulk of shares in the English company. The remaining shareholders, except one, and all the directors were German residents. During the first world war the English company commenced an action for recovery of a trade debt. Held, the company was an alien company and the payment of debt to it would amount to trading with the enemy, and therefore the company was not allowed to proceed with the action.

Exceptions of Lifting the Corporate Veil

Under Express Statutory Provisions

1. Number of members reduced below statutory minimum.
2. Relationship of Holding and Subsidiary Companies established.
3. Investigation into Related Companies under Section 239 and 237.
4. For investigation of the ownership of company.
5. When there is Fraudulent Trading.

Under Judicial Interpretation

1. Protection of Revenue.
2. Avoidance of welfare legislation.
3. Prevention of Fraud or improper conduct.
4. Company is a 'Sham'.
5. Company avoiding legal obligations.
6. Company acting as agent on Trustee of the shareholders.
7. Company formed is against public interest or public policy.
8. Determination of character of a company whether it is enemy.

ILLEGAL ASSOCIATION

Section 11 of the Companies Act, 1956 provides that company, association or partnership carrying on banking business with more than 10 members or carrying on any other business with more than 20 members that has for its object the acquisition of gain, without being registered under the Companies Act, shall be considered an illegal association.

Exceptions

However, Section 11 does not apply in the following cases:

(i) The Stock Exchange

The stock exchange is not regarded as an illegal association as it is not formed for the purpose of carrying on any business.

In *V. V. Ruia v. Dalmia*[22], it was decided that a stock exchange is not covered by Section 11 because it is not formed for the purpose of carrying on any business.

(ii) Joint Hindu Family

A Joint Hindu Family carrying on a business as such is not an illegal association [Section 11 (3)].

Section 11 does not apply to one joint family, that is, a Joint Hindu Family may carry on any business, even for earning profits and with any number of members without being registered or formed in pursuance of any Indian laws as required by Section 11 of the Companies Act, 1956 and yet it will not be illegal association. But, where two or more joint Hindu families join hands to carry on business, the provisions of Section 11 become applicable. However, in such a case, in computing the number of persons, the minor members of such families will be excluded (*Pannaji v. Senaji*[23]).

(Hi) Associations not for profit-making

It may be noted that Section 11 shall apply only if the business is being carried on for gain or profit. It meant the Section does not apply in the following circumstances:

(a) Associations, which carry on business but whose object is not the acquisition of' gain' for its members, need not be registered under the Act.

All charitable, religious, scientific, literary, social and other associations including clubs not having as their object the acquisition of gain are excluded from the purview of the Section.

(b) Again if there is gain to members of the association without carrying on a business by virtue of pooling agreements to eliminate competition, then also the association need not be compulsorily registered under the Companies Act (*New Mofussil Co. Ltd. v. Rustomji*[24]).

Disabilities of an illegal Association

Following are the disabilities of an illegal association.

(i) An illegal association is not allowed to enter into any contract, nor can it sue any member or outsider.
(ii) It can not be sued by a member or an outsider for any debts due to it because it cannot contract any debt.
(iii) It has no existence in the eyes of the law. However, it can get itself registered any time and become a legal entity.
(iv) Every member is personally liable for all liabilities incurred in business.
(v) Every member is punishable with fine which may extend to Rs. 1000.
(vi) It is not possible to wind it up under the Act.

Relief to Members

The only relief to a member of an illegal association is that he can claim a refund of his original subscription provided that it has not already been used by such association in its business (*Greenberg v. Cooperstein*[25]). Such an association, however, is liable to assessment of income-tax on its profit. Against a subsequent reduction in the number if its members below 20 will not change the character of the association till it is registered (*Madan Lal v. Janki Prasad*[26]). Moreover, subsequent registration would not alter the position with regard to past acts too (*Gujarat Trading Co. v. Tricumji*[27])

Advantages of Incorporation

A company incorporated under the Companies Act 1956 has many advantages as compared to the partnership form a business. The principal advantages in brief are:

(i) A company has an independent legal entity, as such it is free from the hazards of personal misfortunes of its members and can embark upon its future plans with greater confidence, while a partnership has no independent legal personality and outsiders can deal with partners.
(ii) A company enjoys perpetual existence while a partnership firm is dissolved on death, lunacy or retirement of a partner unless the contract is to the contrary. Thus a company is more stable than a partnership firm with heavy investment and a long gestation period which are feasible for only a company form of organisation.
(iii) Liability of the company of a member is limited to the face value of share owned by them while that of the partners is unlimited.
(iv) A company is in a position to collect huge funds as there is no limit to the membership of a public company, while for a private company the limit is 50 which again is a good number. In a partnership, there cannot be more than 20 members in the trading business and or in the banking business.
(v) A company can be controlled by the acquisition of the majority of shares which carry voting power. The control of partnership cannot be so acquired as the shares of the partners are not freely transferable.
(vi) If a business concern is converted into a company, it permits its proprietor to realise his goodwill or to relieve himself of the actual management, if he so desires, whilst retaining the controlling interest in the business. It also enables its employees to become shareholders. This is not so in the case of a partnership.
(vii) Since a company is a legal person distinct from its members, loans between the members or between the company and its members present no difficulty. The company and its members can sue each other in the ordinary way. In a partnership, such dealings cause difficulties as the partners are not separate from the firm.

Disadvantages

They are:

(i) Incorporation of a company involves a number of formalities and expenses not only at the incorporation stage but also later too. At the time of incorporation, a member of documents have got to be published. Not only this during its existence it has to work under the strict control of the government and has to comply with the rules and regulations of the Companies Act. Moreover, in winding up too, a lot of expense is involved. On the other hand, a partnership can be form with even an oral agreement and can be dissolved informally and cheaply involving very little expense.

(ii) The other disadvantage of incorporation is that the company has to publish its accounts, etc. for the registration as well as for the shareholders, so that the privacy of business affairs is lost, while a partnership may keep all its affairs secret.

(iii) In the company form of organisation, there is a virtual divorce between ownership and management with the result wastage and inefficiency may creep into the company management. On the other hand, in partnership the partners look after the business personally and no wastage occurs and more over the effort and reward have a direct link.

On the whole, the disadvantages of the company form are not too many. Which form of a organisation should be chosen depends upon factors like the amount of capital required in the business's gestation period, risk of loss, number of persons intending to start business, etc.

Distinction Between Partnership and Company

(1). Registration of a firm is not compulsory even under the Partnership Act, whereas incorporation/ registration of a company is compulsory under the Companies Act.

(2) A minimum of two persons may constitute a partnership. The maximum membership in case of partnership doing banking business is 10 persons and for other business it is 20 persons. A minimum of two and a maximum of 50 constitute a private limited company and a minimum of seven and maximum unlimited number constitute a public limited company. However, the number of members cannot increase the number of subscribed and paid for shares. Usually it is loss than the subscribed and paid for shares.

(3) A firm has no individual legal status, while a company has a separate legal existence of its own and is considered a person separate from its members.

(4) A partner cannot contract with a firm, where as a shareholder can contract with the company.

(5) A partnership like a company has no perpetual existence.

(6) The property of the firm is the property of the partners. On the contrary, in the case of a company, the property always belongs to the company.

(7) Management in case of partnership vests in the hands of the active partners, where as in the case of a company, the management vests in the board of directors elected by the shareholders.

(8) A partnership has fewer statutory obligations, where as a company is regulated strictly under the Companies Act.

(9) Partners of a firm are liable to an unlimited extent, i.e., in partnership there is an unlimited liability, where as the liability of the shareholders is usually limited.

(10) A partner cannot transfer his interest in the firm without the consent of the other partners. A transferee becomes a partner of the firm only with the consent of the other partners, where as in the case of a company shares are easily transferable and the transferee of a share becomes a member of the company without any difficulty.

(11) Creditors of the firm are also the creditors of the partners individually, where as in the case of a company the creditors are the creditors only of the company and not of the individual shareholders.

(12) Accounts of a partnership firm need not be audited by a auditor, where as those of the company must be audited by an auditor.

(13) Every partner is an agent of the other partner. On the other hand, the shareholder of a company is not an agent of the company or of the other shareholders.

(14) Death of the partner may mean dissolution of a partnership where as the death of a shareholder or even of a director does not affect the existence of a company.

CHAPTER

37

Classification of Companies

Companies may be classified into various categories on the following basis. A classification on the Basis of Incorporation companies can be generally classified according to incorporation into the following broad groups:

1. Royal or Chartered Companies

This is the oldest form of companies in its true sense used to be formed in Great Britain by the Royal Charter, i.e., the special order of the King or Queen for the time being occupying the throne. In India, we do not find such type of companies. The East India Company is the most significant example of a chartered company formed in 1600. It may be noted that such type of East India company was also formed in other European countries following the example of Great Britain. A chartered company is governed by its charter which defines the nature of the company and at the same time incorporates it. These companies find no place in India after the country attained independence in 1947.

2. Statutory Companies

Such companies have now-a-days become very popular all over the world including India.

These are nothing but corporations formed by specific Acts of Parliament or the state legislative but these are practically national corporations formed to sender specific services to the nation with more or less monopoly in a particular industry or commerce. These are public enterprises and very often public utilities. The British Broad Casting Corporation formed in 1926 is the first example. In India, numerous statutory corporations have been formed and are being formed in the country. For example, the Reserve Bank of India, the State Bank of India, the Life Insurance Corporation, the Industrial Finance Corporation, the Unit Trust of India, the Food Corporation of India, the Industrial Development Bank of India, the State Trading Corporation, etc. These companies are mostly public undertakings and are formed with the main object of public utilities and not for profit. Any change in the working of these companies is regulated by parliament's or legislature's amendments only. The Companies Act, 1956 applies to these companies if its provisions are not inconsistent with the provisions of the special Acts under which they are formed.

3. Registered Companies

A registered company is one which is formed and registered under the Indian Companies Act, 1956 or under any earlier Companies Act in force in India. Companies registered under the Companies Act are either.

(i) Government Companies or

(ii) Ordinary Companies

(i) Government Companies (Section 617)

Any company in which not loss than 51% of the paid-up share capital is held by the Central Government or by any State Government or Government or partly by the Central Government and partly by one or more State Government is called a Government Company. A company which is subsidiary of a Government Company is also a Government Company.

The concept of government companies is enlarged by the Amendment Act, 1914.

Section 619 (B) provides that the provisions of audit of government companies shall apply to a company in which not less than 51% of the paid-up share capital is held by one or more of the following or any combination there of, as if it were a government company, namely:

(a) the Central Government and one or more government companies;
(b) any state government or governments and one or more government companies;
(c) the central government, one or more state governments and one or more government companies:
(d) the central government and one or more corporations owned or controlled by the central government;
(e) the central government, one or more state government and one or more corporations owned or controlled by the central government;
(f) one or more corporations owned or controlled by the central government or the state government;
(g) more than one government company.

Rules Applicable to Government Companies

(a) Appointment of auditor

The auditor of a government company shall be appointed or re-appointed by the central government on the advice of the comptroller and Auditor General of India [Section 619(2)]. The comptroller and Auditor General shall have the power to direct the manner in which the company's accounts shall be audited by the auditor. He shall also have the power to conduct a supplementary or test audit of the company's accounts by such person or persons as he may authorise in this behalf [Section 619(3)].

(b) Audit reports to be submitted to Comptroller and Auditor General of India

The auditor of a government company shall submit a copy of his audit report to the comptroller and Auditor general of India who shall have the right to comment upon, or supplement, the audit report [Section 619(4)]. Any such comments upon, or supplement to, the audit report shall be placed before the annual general meeting of the company [Section6l9(5)].

(c) Audit report to be placed before Parliament

Where the central government is a member of the government company, It shall cause an annual report on the working and affairs of the company to be prepared within three months of its annual general meeting before which the audit report is placed. The report shall be laid before both houses of parliament together with a copy of the audit report, and any comments upon, or supplement to, the audit, made by the comptroller and auditor general of India [Section 619-A(1)].

Where in addition to the central government, any state government is also a member of a government company, the state government shall cause a copy of the above documents to be laid before the House or both Houses of the state legislature [Section 619-A(2)]. Where the central government is not a member of a government company, the state government or every state government which is a member shall cause the above documents to be prepared within the specified time and laid before the House or both Houses of the state legislature [Section 6l9-A(3)].

(d) Provisions of Section 619 to apply to certain companies

According to Section 619-B, the provisions of Section 619 shall apply to a company in which at least 51% of the paid-up share capital is held by one or more of the following or any combination there of, as if it were a government company, namely:
(i) the central government and one or more government companies;
(ii) any state government or governments and one or more government companies;
(iii) the central government, and one or more corporations owned or controlled by the central government,
(iv) the central government, one or more state governments and one or more government companies;
(v) the central government or one or more state governments and one or more corporations owned or controlled by the central government;
(vi) one or more corporations owned or controlled by the central government or the state government; and
(vii) more than one government company.

(e) Certain Provisions of the Companies Act not to apply

The central government may, by notification in the official Gazette, direct that any of the provisions of the Companies Act (other than Sections 618, 619 and 619-A), specified in the notification —
(a) shall not apply to any government company; or

(b) shall apply to any government company, with such exceptions, modifications, and adaptations, as may be specified in the notification [Section 620(1)].

This power of the Central Government is subject to the control of Parliament [Section 620 (2)].

(ii) Ordinary Companies

These are the companies where the government does not hold 51% or more of the share capital of such a company. In this category, the companies may be

(A) Private limited companies, and

(B) Public limited companies.

(A) Private Limited Companies

Until 1913, all registered companies were public companies. The institution of a private company was introduced for the first time by the Companies Act, 1913. A private limited company means a company which by its articles:

(a) Restricts the right to transfer the shares, if any: The significance of the words' if any' used in this clause should be understood clearly. It means in case of a private company having no share capital, there need not contain restrictions regarding the right of members to transfer shares, while other restrictions (a) and (b) will apply.

(b) Limits the number of its members to 50 (minimum two) not including—

   (i) Persons who are in the employment of the company as well as shareholders.

   (ii) persons who, having been formerly in the employment of the company, were members of the company while in employment and have continued to be members after the employment ceased and

(c) Prohibits any invitation to the public to subscribe for any shares in or debentures of the company.

As against these restrictions, a private company is entitled to several privileges in the sense that quite a few provisions of the Act which apply to public companies do not apply to private companies. It is by virtue of these exemptions that a private company has been described as an incorporated partnership. Ordinary companies are like bees working in a beehive. Private companies can keep their affairs to themselves. Private companies can be classified as:

(i) Companies limited by shares;

(ii) Companies limited by guarantee (if they have a share capital);

(iii) Unlimited companies (if they have a share capital).

But there cannot be a private company with unlimited liability.

Special Privileges and Exemptions available to a Private Company

A private company enjoys certain special privileges which are not available to a public company.

It is so because in a private company the money is raised from few people and generally they belong to the same family or group or are close friends. Therefore, not much public interest is involved therein. But in case of public companies where the money is raised from general public and the number is quite large, it is necessary to safeguard their interest, hence several restrictions are imposed on public companies.

Following are the special privileges available to a private company:

(1) A private company can be formed with only two members [Section 12(1)].

(2) A private company can proceed to allot shares without waiting for the minimum subscription [Section 69]. The reason is that a private company is not required to offer shares to the public.

(3) A private company is not required to issue a prospectus. Therefore, it can allot shares without issuing a prospectus or delivering to the Registrar a statement in piece of prospectus [Section 70 (3)].

(4) A private company need not offer issue of shares to the existing shareholders, i.e., a private company is free to allot new issue to outsiders [Section 81 (3)].

(5) A private company can issue any kind of shares and allow disproportionate voting rights since Section 85 to 89 of the Act are not applicable to it [Section 90 (2)].

(6) A private company can commence business immediately after its incorporation [Section 149 (7)].

(7) It need not have an index of members [Section 151 (1)].

(8) A private company is not required to hold a statutory meeting or to file a statutory report with the Registrar of Companies [Section 165 (10)].

(9) Only two members, who are personally present at the meeting, shall form the quorum unless the articles provide for a larger number [Section 174 (1)].

(10) In case of a private company, poll can be demanded by one person present in person or by proxy, if not more than seven persons are present; if the number of members present is more than seven, two members present in person or by proxy can demand a poll [Section 179 (1) (b)].

(11) A private company need have a minimum of two directors only [Section 252 (2)].

(12) All the directors may be appointed by a single resolution.

(13) The directors of a private company need not file their written consent to act as directors or to take up their qualification shares [Section 264 and 266].

(14) The directors of a private company need not retire by rotation [Section 255].

(15) Section 266 dealing with restrictions on appointment or advertisement of directors is not applicable to a private company [Section 266 (5) (b)].

(16) Where a new director is to be appointed, a special notice of fourteen days is required. This provision is not applicable to a private company, unless it is a subsidiary of a public company [Section 251 (2)].

(17) Directors of a private company can vote on a contract in which they are interested [Section 300].

(18) A private company is exempted from restrictions regarding managerial remuneration.

Additional special exemptions and privileges of Independent private companies

In addition to the exemptions enumerated above, an independent private company (i.e., a private company which is not a subsidiary of a public company) enjoys the following privileges too:

1. Regarding managing personnel, i.e., director, managing director, etc.

It enjoys considerable freedom with regard to its directors, managing director or manager, i.e., it need not comply with those provisions and restrictions relating to the agencies of management which are applicable to public companies. For examples.

(i) All directors can be life directors and the requirement of retirement by rotation does not apply. (Section 255).

(ii) The number of directors can be increased beyond the limit fixed in the articles of association without the sanction of the Central Government (Section 259).

(iii) No Central Governments' approval is required either for appointment or reappointment of a managing director or whole time director of the company (Section 268 and 269).

(iv) No restrictions on the number of companies to be managed by a director (20 in case of public companies) or by a managing director (two companies in case of a public company) apply to such a company (Section 278 and 316).

(v) No restrictions on loans to directors apply to such a company (Section 295).

(vi) All its directors can be appointed in block by a single resolution (Section 225).

(vii) An interested director may participate in the board's proceedings and exercise his vote (Section 300).

(viii) By its article of association, it may provide special disqualifications for appointment of directors, (Section 274).

(ix) Again, the restriction on the period of appointment of the managing director/manager (five years in case of public company) does not apply to an independent private company (Sections 317).

(x) No restrictions are imposed as to the selling of whole or part of the undertaking with the powers of the board of directors (Section 293).

(xi) The rule of overall maximum managerial remuneration does not apply to a private company which is not a subsidiary of a public company. In the case of a public company or a private company which is a subsidiary of a public company, the overall managerial remuneration must not exceed 11% of the net profits, or if there are no or insufficient profits in any year, a sum not exceeding Rs. 50,000 can be paid (Section 198).

(xii) No restrictions on the payment of remuneration to directors, managing directors, etc. apply to such a company, while the overall maximum remuneration is fixed at 11% of the net profits for agencies of management in case of a public company (Section 198).

2. Provisions against purchase of shares, etc. in other companies in the same group do not apply (Section 372).

3. Restrictions on advancing loans to other companies under the same management do not apply (Section 370).
4. Section 416 requires an agent of a company who makes or contract on behalf of the company but keeps the company as an undisclosed principal to make a memorandum in writing of the terms of the contract. He must also deliver the memorandum to the company and send copies to each of the directors. Private companies are exempted from these provisions.
5. Provisions as to kinds of capital (Section 85), new issue of share capital (Section 86), voting rights (Section 87), issue of shares with disproportionate rights (Section 89) do not apply.
6. A transferor or transferee of shares has no right of appeal to the Central Government against refused by the company to register a transfer of its shares [Section 111 (3)].
7. No person other than a member of the company is entitled to inspect, or obtain copies of the profit and loss account of a private company filed with the Registrar (Section 220).
8. Provisions as to the appointment of the managing director do not apply (Section 316 and 317). There is no restriction as to the number of companies of which a person may be appointed managing director. Also a managing director may be appointed for a period exceeding five years.
9. The provisions of Sections 171 to 186 relating to general meetings if the articles otherwise provide, do not apply (Section 170).

It is to be remembered, however, that all the above exemptions and privileges are available to a private company so long as it maintains its independent character. When it becomes a subsidiary of a public company or is deemed to be a public company, it will be treated at par with a public company.

Loss of privileges by a private company

Section 43 provides that if a private company contravenes any of the three conditions included in its Articles as per Section 3 (I) (III), then it will be treated as if it is a public company and it will then result in loss of privileges and exemptions to which it is normally entitled to.

The proviso to Section 43 states that if the contravention of any of the three restrictions contained in the articles was accidental, or if the company law board is satisfied that it is just and equitable to grant relief, it may relieve the company from these consequences on the application by the company or any other interested person.

Conversion of a private company into a public company

A private company may become a public company in the following cases:

1. Conversion by default (Section 43)

Where a default in made by a private company in complying with the essential requirements of a private company (viz restriction on transfer of shares, limitation on the number of members to 50 and prohibition of invitation to the public to buy shares or debentures), the company ceases to enjoy some of the privileges of a private company and the provisions of the Companies Act apply to it as if it were not a private company. The Company Law Board may relieve the company from the consequences as aforesaid, if it is of opinion that the non-compliance was accidental or due to inadvertence or other sufficient cause. It may also grant relief if on some other grounds it is just and equitable.

2. Conversion by operation of law

The Amendment Act, 1960 introduced a new Section 43-A (which was further amended by the Amendment Act 1974) creating a new class of companies known as "deemed to be public companies" The Section deals with those private companies which employed public money to an appreciable extent and yet escaped the restrictions and limitations to disclosure and otherwise as applied to public limited companies. Under the above Section, a private company becomes a public company.

(i) A private company would be deemed to be a public company where 25% or more of its paid-up share capital (whether preference or equity) is held by one or more bodies corporate (whether public or private). But in computing the above percentage, share held by a banking company shall not be taken into account in the following two cases:
   (a) Where the shares are held as a trustee of some trust, not being a case where shares are held as a trustee for the benefit of any body corporate; or
   (b) Where the shares are held as or on behalf of an executor or administrator of a deceased person to whom such shares belonged and the shares have not been bequeathed by will to any body corporate by the deceased.

(ii) A private company having an average annual turnover of one crore of rupees or more during the 'relevant period' shall become a public company, on and from the expiry of a period of three months from the last day of the relevant period during which the private company has the said average annual turnover.

(iii) If 25% or more of the paid-up share capital (whether preference or equity) of a private company having a share capital is held by a public company, the private company shall become a public company, on and from the expiry of three months from the date of such commencement, unless within that period, the said percentage is reduced to below 25% of the paid-up share capital of the company.

For the purposes of Section 43-A(1), bodies corporate means public companies or private companies which had become public companies by virtue of Section 43-A [Explanation to Section 43-A as added by the Amendment Act of 1988].

"Turnover" of a company means the aggregate value of the realisation made from the supply or distribution of goods or on account of services rendered or both, by the company during a financial year.

(iv) Where a private company invites, accepts or renews deposits from the public, such private company becomes a deemed public company from the date on which such invitation, acceptance or renewal, as the case may be, is first made [Section 43-A(1-e) as added by the Companies (Amendment) Act, 1988]. Deposits received by a private company from its members, directors or their relatives are excluded from the meaning of the term public.

Privileges

The articles of association of a private company, which has become. Public by virtue of Section 43-A, may continue to have the essential requirements (viz., restriction on transfer of shares, limitation an the number of members to 50 and prohibition of invitation to the public to buy shares or debentures) which make it a private company. Such a company may continue to have two directors and less than 7 members.

A private company which becomes a public company by virtue of Section 43-A continues to be a public company until it has, with the approval of the Central Government and in accordance with the provisions of the Companies Act, again become a private company [Section 43-A(4)).

Exceptions

There are three exceptions, where a private company will not be deemed to be a public company:

1. A private company of which the entire paid-up share capital is held by another single private company or by one or more bodies corporate incorporates outside India.
2. A private company in which only a portion of share capital is held by one or more bodies corporate incorporated outside India, which if incorporated in India would have been private companies, provided that the Central Government, on an application made by order, so directs.
3. Any other private company, if such of the following conditions is satisfied, namely,
   (a) where the shareholding company (or companies) is/are itself/themselves a private company (or companies); and
   (b) no other company holds shares in any such shareholding company (or companies); and
   (c) The total number of shareholders in the shareholding company (or companies), together with the individual shareholders of the private company (excluding past and present employees who are members) does not exceed 50.

Information to Registrar

Within three months from the date on which a private company becomes a public company by virtue of Section 43-A the company must inform the Registrar that it has become a public company as aforesaid. Thereupon the Registrar deletes the, word 'public' before the word 'limited' in the name of the company in the register and also makes the necessary alterations in the certificate of incorporation issued to the company and in its memorandum of association [Section 43-A (2)].

If a company makes a default in complying with this provision, the company and every officer shall be punishable with fine which may extend to Rs. 500 every day during which the default continues [Section 43-A (5)].

3. Conversion by choice (Section 44)

A private company may convert itself into a public company by taking the following steps:

(i) Special Resolution

A private company desiring to become public must pass a special resolution deleting from its articles the requirements of Section 3(1) (iii) i.e., removes restrictions as to membership, transfer of shares and public subscription. From the date of alteration, it becomes a public company.

(ii) Prospectus

Within 30 days from the passing of the special resolution, a prospectus or a statement in lien of prospectus must be filed with the Registrar. It must also be accompanied by a copy of the special resolution and a copy of altered articles.

All other requirements of the Act should be complied with, such as increasing the number of shareholders to seven and directors to three, the statutory minimum. Further, the word 'private' will be deleted from the name of the company.

Conversion of a Public Company into a Private Company

A public company may be converted into a private company by passing a special resolution. The special resolution, among others, should be to charge the Articles of the company so as to include the conditions as prescribed to Section 3(1)(iii) which make a company a private company. But provision to Section 3(1) lays down that an alteration made in the Articles which has the effect of converting a public company into a private company shall have effect only when such alteration has been approved by the Central Government. Where the alteration has been approved by the Central Government, a printed copy of the Articles as altered shall be filed by the company with the Registrar within one month of the date of receipt of approval [Section 31 (2-A)).

The Central Government may permit the conversion of a public into a private company only if it is in the interest of the company itself and there is a large measure of agreement among the members to the proposed conversion.

(B) Public Limited Companies

A public company means a company which is not a private company [Section 3(1) (iii)].

Any seven or more persons can join hands to form a public company. Public limited companies may be —

(i) companies limited by shares;
(ii) companies limited by guarantee, and
(iii) unlimited companies.

(i) Companies Limited by Shares

'Where the liability of the members of a company is limited by the memorandum to the amount unpaid on the shares, such a company is known as a company limited by shares or a limited liability company [Section 12 (2) (a)]' The liability can be enforced any time during the winding up of the company. It means if the shares are fully paid, the liability of the shareholder holding such shares is nil the essential feature of this company is that it must have a share capital, as the extent of liability is determined by the face value of the share. These are the most popular types of organisation.

(II) Companies Limited by Guarantee

A company limited by guarantee may be defined as 'a company having the liability of its members limited by its memorandum to such amount as the members may respectively thereby undertake to contribute to the assets of the company in the event of its being wound up' [Section 12 (2) (6)]. The amount guaranteed by each member cannot be demanded until the company is wound up. Here, it is the nature of a "reserve capital".

It cannot be mortgaged or charged in any way before the liquidation of the company. But such amount can be called by the company for paying the cost of liquidation and the general liabilities at the time of liquidation.

Such companies are formed not for the purpose of profit but for the promotion of art, science, culture, charity, sport, commerce or some similar purpose. The chamber of commerce, trade associations and sport clubs are usually guarantee companies because they neither require a huge capital nor aim at marking profits. The articles of association of such a company must state the number of members with which the company is to be registered.

Companies limited by guarantee and having a share capital are excepting certain provisions, governed by the same provisions as are applicable to companies limited by shares.

(iii) Unlimited Companies

'A company having no limit on the liability of its members is an unlimited company [Section 12 (2) (c)].' It means the liability of members of this type of company is unlimited, i.e., it may extend to the personal property of the members. Here also it may be noted that a member continues to be liable for one year after be ceases to be a member, subject to the following two conditions.

(a) debts contracted by the company before be ceases to be a member remain unpaid and.
(b) the existing members are unable to satisfy the contributions required to be made by them [Section 426].

Every member is liable for the debts of the company, as an ordinary partnership, in proportion to his interest in the company. Such a company mayor may not have a share capital. If it has a share capital, it may be a public company or a private company.

The Act prohibits the formation of partnerships consisting of more than 20 in case of partnerships carrying on banking business). If persons in excess of this number wish to associate for some purpose without limiting their liability for the debts of their business, they have to choose the form of an unlimited company, such companies are, however, extremely rare these days.

Classification of companies can easily be shown in chart given below.

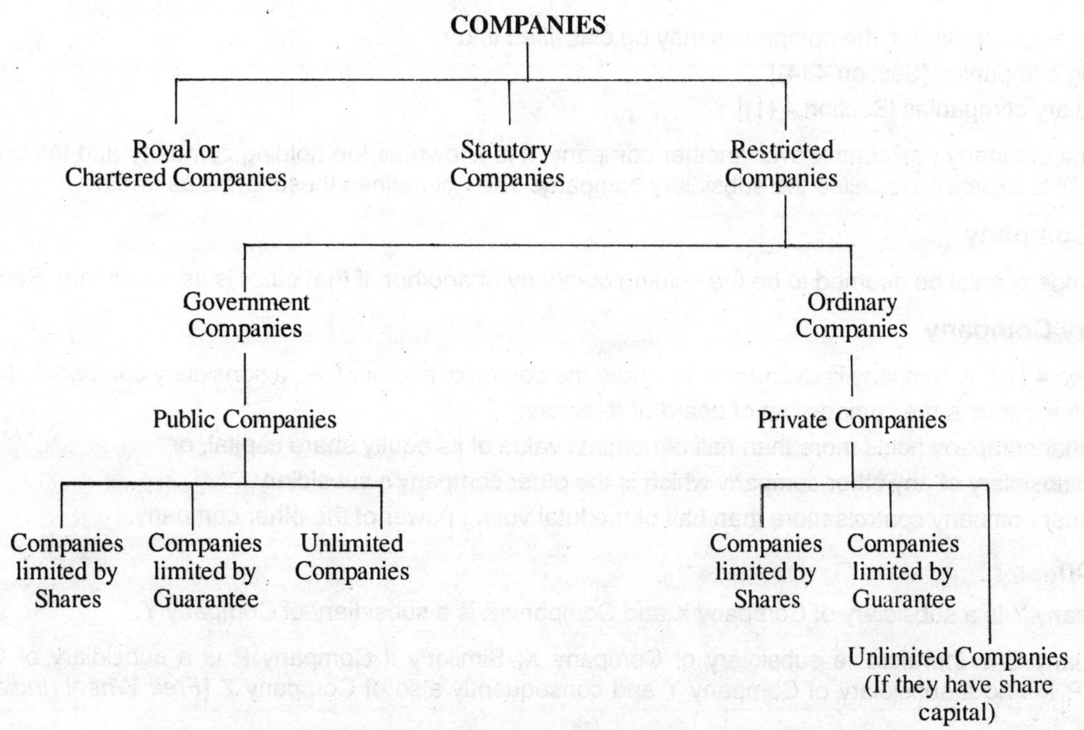

Distinction between Private and Public Company

Following are the main points of distinction between a private and a public company.

(1) In the case of a private company, minimum number of persons to form a company is two while it is seven in the case of a public company.

(2) In the case of private company, the maximum number must not exceed 50 whereas there is no such restriction on the maximum number of members in case of a public company.

(3) In private company, the right to transfer shares is restricted, whereas in case of public company the shares are freely transferable.

(4) A private company cannot issue a prospectus, while a public company may, through prospectus, invite the general public to subscribe for its shares or debentures.

(5) A private company can commence business immediately after receiving the certificate of incorporation, while a public company can commence business only when it receives a certificate to commence business from the Registrar of Companies.

(6) A private company need not hold a statutory meeting but a public company must hold a statutory meeting and file a statutory report with the Registrar.

(7) The directors of a private company are not required to file with the Registrar written consent to act as director or sign the memorandum of association or enter into a contract for his qualification shares. But the directors of a public company must file with the Registrar their written consent to act as directors must sign the memorandum and must enter into a contract for their qualification shares.

(8) Directors of a private company may be appointed by a single resolution, but it is not so in case of a public company.

(9) Directors of a private company are not required to retire by rotation, but in case of a public company, at least 2/3 of the directors must retire by rotation.

(10) The number of directors in a private company may be increased to any extent without the permission of the Central Government, but in case of a public company if the number of directors is to be more than 12 then the approval of the Central Government is necessary.

(11) Two members personally present form the quorum in a private company but in a public company this number is 5 members.

Classification on the Basis of Control

On the basis of control, the companies may be classified into:

(i) Holding companies [Section 4 (4)].

(ii) Subsidiary companies [Section 4 (1)].

When a company has control over another company, it is known as the holding company and the company over which control is exercised is called the subsidiary company. The Act defines these terms as under:

Holding Company

"A company shall be deemed to be the holding company of another, if that other is its subsidiary [Section 4 (4)]."

Subsidiary Company

[Section 4 (1)]; A company is deemed to be under the control of another (i.e., a subsidiary company), if and only if

(a) that other controls the composition of board of directors;

(b) that other company holds more than half of nominal value of its equity share capital, or

(c) it is a subsidiary of any other company which is the other company's subsidiary.

(d) that other company controls more than half of the total voting power of the other company.

Illustration

Company Y is a subsidiary of Company X and Company Z is a subsidiary of Company Y.

Company Z is therefore, a subsidiary of Company X. Similarly if Company P is a subsidiary of Company Z, Company P will be a subsidiary of Company Y and consequently also of Company X [*Free Wheel (India) Ltd v. Dr. Veda Mitra*[28]).

Shares Hold or Powers Exercisable to be Excluded

In coming to conclusion, whether one company is subsidiary of another, shares hold or powers exercisable, in the following cases shall be excluded:

(i) Where the shares are held or power is exercised by the company over the other in a fiduciary capacity;

(ii) Where shares are held and power is so exercised because of the provisions of any debentures or of a trust deed;

(iii) Where shares are held or powers are so exercised by way of security by a lending company.

Every holding company has to attach to its annual accounts, copies of the balance sheet, profit and loss account, director's report and the auditor's report, etc. in respect if each subsidiary company as per requirements of Sections 212 to 214, so that a true and fair view of the state of affairs of the group as whole may be presented to a shareholder, a creator and a potential investor in that company. Under Section 77, a subsidiary company is restricted from buying shares of its holding company.

Companies Not For Profit or Licenced Companies

According to Section 13 (1) (a), the name of a limited company must end with the word "limited" in the case of a public company, and with the words, 'private Limited' in the case of private company. Section 25 of the Act, however, permits the registration, under a licence granted by the Central Government, of associations not for profit with limited liability without using word 'Limited' or the words 'Private Limited' to their names.

The peculiarities of such companies are:

(i) On registration, it enjoys certain exemptions and privileges as compared to an ordinary limited company.

(ii) Such companies are allowed to exclude the words 'Limited' or 'Private Limited' from their names.

(iii) They are registered without paying any stamp duty in connection with their memorandum and articles of association.

(iv) These companies also need not comply with the provisions of Sections 147, I60(I)(aa), 166(2), 177(1), 209(4)(a), 257, 264(1), 285, 287, 299,301 and 302(2), of the Companies Act either wholly or in part as per the Government of India, Notification No S.O. 1578 dated July 8, 1961.

(v) Such companies may be public or private companies and may not have a share capital.

Conditions for Grant of Licence

The Central Government may grant such a licence to an association where it is proved to the satisfaction of the Central Government that it:

(a) is about to be formed as a limited company for promoting commerce, science religion charity or any other useful object; and

(b) intends to apply its profits, if any, or other income in promoting its objects, and to prohibit the payment of any dividend to its members.

The Central Government may direct that the association may be registered as a company with limited liability, without, the addition to its name of the word 'Limited' or the words private limited [Section 25 (1)]. The association may thereupon be registered accordingly. on registration it enjoys all the privileges, and is subject to all the obligation, of limited companies [Section 25 (2)]. Unless its Articles otherwise provide, it is exempt from such of the provisions of the Companies Act as may be specified by the Central Government in a general or special order [Section 25 (6)].

A licence may be granted by the Central Government on such conditions and subject to such regulations as it thinks fit. The conditions and regulations are binding on the body to which the licence is granted. These conditions shall be inserted in the Memorandum, or in the Articles, or partly in the one and partly in the other, if the Central Government so directs [Section 25 (5)].

Section 25 (4) provides that a firm may be a member of any association or company licensed under Section 25.

Revocation of Licence

The government has power to revoke the licence granted to such companies if it thinks fit on giving the company notice and after an opportunity to object [Section 25 (7)]. If a body whose licence is revoked contains the words 'Chambers of Commerce, it must, within three months from the date of revocation or such period as the Central Government may allow, change its name to a name which does not contain those words [Section 25 (a)]. Similarly, the body or company will have to write 'Limited' or 'Private Limited' at the end of its name.

ONE-MAN COMPANY OR FAMILY COMPANY

As is clear from the name itself, a "one man company or a family company" is one of which almost the whole share capital is held by a single man who takes a few dummy members simply to meet the statute's requirements regarding the minimum number of members — may be by giving only one share to each of the dummy members (*Salomon v. Salomon and Co. Ltd.*[29]). The dummy members are usually nominees of the principal shareholder who is the virtual owner of the business and who carries it on with limited liability. Example: A private company is registered with a share capital of Rs. 5,00,000 divided into 5,000 shares ofRs. 100 each. Of these shares 4,999 are held by A and one share is held by A's wife B, This is a one man company.

Such a company in fact is a true company in the eyes of law and is regarded as a separate entity distinct form its shareholders, unless otherwise proved. It is obvious from the observations made in the following case:

T. R. Pratt (Bombay) Ltd. v. E.D. Sassoon and Co. Ltd. [30].

"Under the law an incorporated company is a distinct entity, and although all the shares may be practically controlled by one person, in law a company is distinct entity and it not permissible or relevant to inquire whether directors belonged to the same family or whether it is compendiously described as "one-man company".

PUBLIC FINANCIAL INSTITUTIONS

The following financial institutions shall be regarded, for the purposes of the Companies Act, as public financial institutions, namely,

(1) The Industrial Credit and Investment Corporation of India (ICICI).
(2) The Industrial Finance Corporation of India (IFCI).
(3) The Industrial Development Bank of India (IDBI).
(4) The Life Insurance Corporation of India (LIC).
(5) The Unit Trust of India (UTI).

Sub-Section (2) of Section 4-A empowers the Central Government to specify other institutions, as it may think fit, to be a public financial institution by issuing a notification in the official Gazette.

However, no institution shall be so specified unless —

(i) It has been established or constituted by or under any Central Act. or
(ii) not less than 51% of the paid up share capital of such an institution is held or controlled by the Central Government.

Foreign Company

It means any company incorporated outside India.

(a) Which after the commencement of the Indian Companies Act established a place of business within India, and
(b) Which before the commencement of the Act had established a place of business within India and continue to have established place of business within India at the commencement of the Act.

The Act lays down certain requirements to be observed by such companies which have been incorporated in foreign countries, but which have offices and places of business in India.

Requirements Regarding Foreign Companies 1. Documents

Every foreign company within 30 days of the establishment of business shall file with the Registrar the following documents:

(i) A certified copy of the charter, statutes, memorandum and articles of the company and, if the instrument is not in English, a certified translation there of.
(ii) the full address of the registered or principal office of the company.
(iii) A list of the directors and secretary of the company.
(iv) The names and addresses of any person or persons resident in India, authorised to accept on behalf of the company service of processes and any notices required to be served on the company.
(v) The full address of the principal place of business in India [Section 592 (i)].

If any alteration is made in the above particulars, the company shall file with the Registrar a return of such alteration (Section 593).

The above documents shall be filed with the Registrar of the state where the principal place of business is situate and with the Registrar at New Delhi.

2. Accounts

The provisions of Section 209 regarding books of account to be kept by a company shall apply to a foreign company also so far as it concerns its business in India [Section 594].

According to Section 594, unless exempted by the Central Government, it is required to file with the Registrar every year three copies of the balance sheet and profit and loss account like a company under the Companies Act. The foreign company must also send, along with these documents, three copies of a list in the prescribed form of all places of business established in India.

3. Name

A foreign company shall conspicuously exhibit on the outside of every office or place where it carries on business in India the name of the company, together with the name of the country where it is incorporated in English and in one of the local languages. All bill-heads letter papers, and all other official publications of the company shall also show the name (Section 595).

4. Registration of charges

The provisions relating to the registration of charges (Sections 124 to 145), annual returns (Section 159), books of account (Sections 209 and 209-A), special audit in certain cases (Section 233-A), audit of cost accounts (Section 233-B), power of Registrar to call for information (Sections 234 to 246), in so far as they apply to its Indian business, shall apply to foreign companies also (Section 600).

5. Requirements as to prospectus (Section 603)

It enumerates the particulars to be stated in the prospectus inviting subscriptions for shares or debentures by a foreign company. These are as follows—

(i) Name of company in English.
(ii) Name of the country in which it is incorporated.
(iii) Whether the liability of the member is limited.
(iv) Particular regarding its constitution, date and country of incorporation, and the law under which it was incorporated abroad.
(v) The address of its registered office and the address of its principal place of business, and
(vi) Matters required to be included in a prospectus issued by a company incorporated under the Companies Act.

Before a prospectus is issued, circulated or distributed by a foreign company in India, a copy of it shall be registered with the Registrar of Companies. The prospectus shall be dated.

Section 598 provides a penalty for the company, for every officer or agent of the company for default in complying with any of the above requirements. The penalty is a fine which may extend to Rs. 1,000 in case the default continues, an additional fine which may extend to Rs. 100 for every day during which the default continues.

Further, a foreign company failing to comply with the foregoing provisions[31] is prohibited from enforcing any contract by way of a suit, set-off or counter claim (Section 599).

6. Requirements Regarding Winding-up

Where a foreign company, which has been carrying on business in India, ceases to carry on such business in India, it may be wound up as an unregistered company under part X (Section 582-590) of the Act. A foreign company's business in India can be wound up even in cases where the company has been dissolved or where it has ceased to exist under the law of the country in which it was incorporated (Section 584).

CHAPTER

38

Formation of Company

The formation of company is a lengthy process indeed. The whole process of formation of a company may be roughly divided into three following parts:

(i) Promotion

(ii) Registration, and

(iii) Floatation.

(i) Promotion

Promotion is in fact the first stage in the formation of a company. Promotion means "the discovery of business opportunities and the subsequent organisation of funds, property and managerial ability into a business concern for the purpose of making profits therefrom".[32]

Palmer[33] defined a 'Promoter' as "a person who originates a scheme for the formation of the company, has the Memorandum and Articles prepared, executed and registered and finds the first directors and settles the terms of the Preliminary contracts and prospectus (if any) and makes arrangements for advertising and circulating the prospectus and placing the capital, is a promoter."

A promotor is a person who does the necessary preliminary work incidented to the formation of a company.

In Whaley Bridge Calico Printing Co. v. Green and Smith[34], Bowen L.J. stated that the term 'promoter' is a term not of law, but of business, usefully summing up in a single word a number of business operations familiar to the commercial world, by which a company is generally brought into existence. It is a short and convenient way of designating those who set in motion the machinery by which the Act enables them to create on incorporated company

A person who acts in a professional capacity is not a promoter, like an advocate, solicitor or auditor.

The term promoter has not been defined under the Companies Act, although the term is used expressly in Sections 62,69,76,478 and 519. Even in English law, no general statutory definition of a promoter is available. In Section 38(1) of the English Companies Act, a promoter is indirectly described as a person engaged or interested in the formation of a company and Section 43(5) gives a definition for the purpose of that Section only, stating, the expression 'Promoter' means a promoter who was a party to the preparation of the prospectus, but does not include any person by reason of his acting in a professional capacity or persons engaged in procuring the formation of the company. Thus, the persons assisting the promoters by acting in a professional capacity do not thereby become promoters themselves.

Perhaps, the true test of whether a person is a promoter is whether he has a a desire that the company be formed, and is prepared to take some steps, which mayor may not involve other persons, to implement it.

Who Can Be A Promoter ?

A promoter may be an individual, firm, association of persons or even a limited company, whether a person is or is not a promoter depends upon the nature of the role played by him in the promotion of business.

The Role of The Promoter

The role of the promoter is vital in the formation of a company. His functions in this regard may be summarised as under:

(i) He conceives the idea of the formation of the company after a thorough study of the business world that a particular business field is still unexplored or may be explored further.

(ii) He draws up the scheme and determines the object of a future company.
(iii) He prepares the Memorandum of Association, the Articles of Association and the Prospectus. He gets together the able directors to act as such for the company.
(iv) He takes the necessary leave of the appropriate Government authorities for that purpose.
(b) He finds out suitable financiers to back up the company
(vi) He makes arrangement with vendors, legal advisers and other persons required for floating a company.
(vii) He takes pain for filing the necessary documents with the Registrar of Companies for the certificate of incorporation.
(viii) He bears all the preliminary expenses.

Legal Position of a Promoter

As to the exact legal status of the promoter, the statutory provisions are silent in most part, except for a couple of Sections in the Specific Relief Act, 1963. His legal status is incapable of precise statement.

A promoter is Neither a Trustee nor an Agent. Though a promoter acts on behalf of the company, he cannot be called truly an agent or trustee. The reason is that a person cannot act as an agent or a trustee for a person who is non-existent and the company is non-existent at the time when the promoter acts for it.

Fiduciary Relation with the Company

Though a promoter acts on behalf of the company, be is neither an agent nor a trustee of the company under incorporation but certain fiduciary (founded on trust) duties have been imposed on him under the Companies Act 1956. As such he is said to be in a fiduciary position towards the company as well as the original allottees of shares.

In *Erlanger v. New Sombrero Phosphate Co.*[35] Lord Cairns observed in this regard.

"The promoters of a company stand undoutedly in a fiduciary position. They have in their hands the creation and moulding of the company. They have a power of defining how and when and in what shape, and under what supervision it shall start into existence and beging to act as a trading corporation."

In equity, the promoters of a company stand in a fiduciary relation to it and those persons whom they induce to become shareholders in it, and cannot in equity bind the company by any contract with themselves as promoters without fully disclosing to the company all material facts which the company ought to know."

As a necessary consequence of this principle, it follows that the promoters.

(a) must make a full disclosure of all the material facts relating to formation of the company, and
(b) must not make secret profits it may thus be observed that it is not the profit made by the promoter which the law forbids but the non-disclosure of it. He is supposed to disclose any profit made out of the promotion either to the independent board of directors or to the shareholders as a body (and not a selected few).

    If any secret profit is made in violation of this rule, the company may, on discovering it, compel him to account for and surrender such profit (*Cape Breton Co., Re*[36]).
(c) After starting the act of promotion, he must give to the company the benefit of any contract which be enters into for the company,
(d) He must not make an unreasonable use of his position to earn profit as he is entitled to a reasonable remuneration.

Duties and Liabilities of Promoters

Promoters have following duties with regard to the prospectus (if issued)

(a) See that the prospectus contains the necessary particulars.
(b) See that the prospectus does not contain any untrue statement or hide any material fact.

Liabilities

He incurs following liabilities in case of non performance of above duties.

(i) Civil Liability

He makes himself liable to pay any compensation to any shareholder who buys shares on the faith of the said prospectus containing untrue statements or concealing material facts.

(ii) Criminal Liability

(a) Promoter is liable to the original allottee of shares for the mis-statements contained in the prospectus. It is clear that his liability does not extend to subsequent allottees. He may also be imprisoned for a term which may extend to 2 years or may be punished with fine upto Rs. 5,000 for such untrue statements in the prospectus (Section 62 and 63).

(b) In the course of winding up of the company, on an application made by official liquidator, the court may make a promoter liable for misfeasance or breach of trust (Section 543). The court may also order for the public examination of the promoter (Section 478 and 519).

Where there are more than one promoters, they are jointly and severally liable and if one of them is sued and pays damages, he is entitled to claim contribution from other or others.

The death of a promoter does not rlieve his estate from liability arising out of abuse of his fiduciary position.

Remuneration of Promoters

The promoter has no right to get compensation from the company for his services for promoting the company unless there is a contract to that effect. If there is no such contract, he is not entitled to get any compensation in respect of any payment made by him in connection with the formation of company. In practice, a promoter takes remuneration for his services in one of the following ways:

(1) He may sell his own property at a profit to the company for cash or fully paid shares provided he makes a disclosure to this effect.

(2) He may be given an option to buy a certain number of shares in the company at par.

(3) He may take a commission on the shares sold.

(4) He may be paid a lump-sum by the company.

Any remuneration paid to the promoters must be disclosed in the prospectus, if it is paid within a preceding two years from the date of prospectus.

Preliminary or Pre-Incorporation Contracts

The promoters of a company usually enter into contracts to acquire some property or right for the company which is yet to be incorporated. Such contracts are called preliminary or pre incorporation contracts. The promoters generally enter into such contracts as agents for the company about to be formed. The legal position is that "two consenting parties are necessary to a contract whereas the company, before incorporation, is a non entity" (*Kelner v. Baxter*[37]). As such the company is not liable for the acts of the promoters done before its incorporation.

Position of Promoters as Regards Preliminary Contracts

1. Company not Bound

A Pre-Incorporation contract never binds a company since a company can not contract before its existence, and a company before incorporation has no legal existence.

Another reason is that Promoters "are proverbially profuse in their promises and if the corporation were to be bound by them it would be subject to many unknown, unjust and heavy obligations" (*Parke v. Modem Woodmen*[38]).

In *re English and Colonial Produce Co. Ltd.*,[39] a solicitor was engaged to prepare the necessary documents and obtain the registration of a company. He paid the registration fee and incurred certain expenses incidental to registration. Held the company was not bound to pay for those services and expenses.

2. Company cannot enforce Preliminary Contract

The company cannot after incorporation enforces the contract made before its incorporation.

In *Natal Land and Colonisation Co. v. Pauline Colliery Syndicate*,[40] N. Co.' Contracted with A the nominee of the syndicate (Which was not then incorporated) to grant a lease of certain coalmining rights for three years. After the syndicate was registered, it claimed the contracted lease which the 'N. Co.' refused. In a suit for specific performance, it was held that the syndicate was not entitled to its claim as it was not in existence when the contract was made and a company cannot obtain the benefit of a pre incorporation contract.

3. Promoters Personally Liable

The promoters remain personally liable on a contract made on behalf of the company not yet in existence. Such a contract is deemed to have entered into personally by the promoters. The case of *Kelner v. Baxter* is an important case on this point.

In this case A, Band C on behalf of the proposed company entered into a contract with K for the supply of wine worth L900. The wine was supplied and consumed after the company was formed. But before the payment the company went into liquidation. It was held that A, Band C were personally liable on the contract. The ground on which such decision was based is that no one can represent a natural or an artificial person which is not in existence. The promoter cannot act as an agent of a proposed company, for the contractual capacity of a company arises only after its incorporation.

Ratification of a Preliminary Contract

It may be noted that the company cannot even adopt the pre-incorporation contract by 'ratification' after its incorporation, because of incorporation with the changed name. The change of name will be effective from the date on which the new certificate of incorporation is issued. However, the change in name will not affect the existing rights and liabilities.(Section 23).

But no approval of the Central Government is needed where the only change in the name is the addition there to or the deletion therefrom of the word 'Private' consequent on the conversion of a public company into a private company or *vice versa* (Section 21).

Specific Performance of Preliminary Contract

Until the passing of the Specific Relief Act, 1963, the promoters found it very difficult to carry out the work of incorporation, since contracts prior to incorporation were void and also could not be ratified, people hesitated to either supply any goods or work for the cause of incorporation. Promoters also felt shy of accepting personal responsibility. Thc Specific Relief Act, 1963, came as a sigh of relief to the promoters. Section 15(h) and 19(e) of this Act provide that when promoters of a company have, before its incorporation entered into a contract for the purposes of the company and such a contract is warranted by the terms and its incorporation, specific performance may be obtained by or enforced against the company; provided that the company has accepted the contract and has communicated such acceptance to the other party to the contract.

Contracts like preparation and printing of the memorandum, Articles, etc. renting of promises, hiring secretariat staff or envisaged under the Act.

Formation

According to section 3(1)(i), a company has to be 'formed and registered'. Formation of a Company is something more than mere registration of incorporation of it. **Registration is a part (most significant Part) of formation.** Some steps have to be taken by a Public Company before it can commerce business. Actually, formation is complete when the company is capable of commencing business. Generally, however no distinction is made between formation and registration or incorporation. Company promotion is still bigger issue which entails commercial activities too.

A company is formed for doing activities in order to fulfill the 'object' laid out in the memorandum of the company therefore has to commence its business. A public company has to undergo two distinct stages for this purpose:

Stage I — Getting certificate of incorporation and

Stage II — Getting the certificate for commencement of Business.

The first stage completes registration and the second stage completes formation.

Three categories of people are involved in the process of formation of a company and all of them can be called interested in the formation of the Company. They are:

(1) Promoters

They are the first members of the company and are vitally interested in the company (unless they are professional promoters as found in some western countries).

The promoters bring the other two categories of people to fulfill their plan.

(2) Experts

Advices of some experts like Lawyers, Chartered Accountants etc., are commissioned against payment of fees whose expertise is necessary in preparing documents and fulfiling other legal formalities. The promoters may even appoint a qualified secretary as this stage on monthly remuneration and his employment is ratified with retrospective basis after the company comes into existence. The expenses already made by the promoters by themselves are reimbursed in future by the company.

(3) Witness

There must be one witness who should testify the signature of the subscribers to the Memorandum. The witness must be somebody other than the subscribers (Section 15). The same rule shall apply to the articles (Section 30).

The procedure of formation of a Company

The Act presents an elaborate procedure for formation of a company, covering a number of sections and a big set of rules. These are described below step by step:

1. The Certificate of Incorporation

An application to be made to the Registrar of Companies of the State where the proposed company is going to be registered, suggesting intended name of the proposed company and wanting to know whether the suggested name is available. Generally three names, in order of priority are suggested. The suggestions shall be made carefully so that the provisions of Emblems and names (Prevention of Improper use) Act, 1950 are not violated. The application shall be made in a form vide Rule 44 of the Companies (Central Government's) General Rules and Forms, supplied by the office of the Registrar. The application shall be accompanied with prescribed fee.

The Registrar will send a reply, ordinarily within 14 days, stating whether the name is available or not. If not, a fresh application has to be made with fresh suggestion.

2. The Memorandum of Association (Sections 13 to 15) and the Articles of Association (Section 26 to 30)

The Memorandum of Association of a company is its charter which contains the fundamental conditions upon which alone the company can be incorporated. It tells as the objects of the company's formation and the utmost possible scope of its operations beyond which its actions cannot go. Thus, it defines as well as confines the powers of the company. If anything is done beyond these powers, that will be ultra vires (beyond power of) the company and so void.

The Memorandum serves a two-fold purpose. It enables shareholders creditors and all those who deal with the company to know what its power and what is the range of its activities. Thus, the intending shareholder can find out the field in, or the purpose for which his money is going to be used by the company and what risk he is taking in making the investment. Also, anyone dealing with the company, say, a supplier of goods or money, will know whether the transaction he intends to make with the company is within the objects of the company and not *ultra vires* its objects.

The articles of association of a company and its bye laws are regulations which govern the management of its internal affairs and the conduct of its business. They define the duties, rights, powers and authority of the shareholders and the directors in their respective capacities and of the company, and the mode and form in which the business of the company is to be carried out. The Articles of association of a company have a contractual force between company and its members as also between the members inter se in relation to their rights as such members. They are subordinate to and are controlled by memorandum. Articles cannot supersede the objects as set out in the memorandum of association. The Memorandum lays down the scope and powers of the company, where as the articles govern the ways in which the objects of the company are to be carried out.

The Memorandum of Association (Section 13 to 15) and the Articles of Association (Sections 26 to 30) have to be prepared. 'Prepared' means they have to printed and paragraphed with each paragraph serially numbered. Each document shall be signed with a date by at least two subscribers in case of a Private company and at least seven subscribers in case of a Public Company in the presence of a witness. Each subscriber shall write in his own hand his own name, his father's name, address, occupation and number of shares held (in case of a company having share capital) by him and similarly full description of the witness also has to be given by the witness in his own hand. While drafting the documents Table A,B,C,D and E (Section 2.1) have to be followed as they are applicable.

A public company may not prepare its own Articles but may follow Table A in full or may follow Table A in part and prepare its own Articles in part. A private company must prepare its Articles at least in part (for the restrictions).

3. One copy of the Memorandum and one copy of the Articles, which are to be filed with the Registrar, have to be stamped according to the Indian Stamp Act.

4. The following documents to be filed with the Registrar:

(a) One signed and stamped copy of the Memorandum.

(b) One signed and stamped copy of the Articles.

(c) A declaration of compliance (i.e., all the formalities of the Act and the Rules have been complied with) in the prescribed Form No.1, made by an advocate, an attorney or pleader entitled to appear before a High Court, or a Chartered Accountant practicing in India, engaged in the formation of the company or by a person named in the articles as a Director or Manager or Secretary of the Company (Section 33).

5. The following documents also may be filed:

(a) Notice of the situation of the registered office of the Company in Form No. 18 (Section 146).

This can however be filed within 30 days from the date of incorporation but generally it is filed in advance together with other documents.

(b) Particulars of the directors, manager and secretary in Form No. 32 (Section 303).

These particulars are to be filed within 30 days from appointment, but the appointment may be made from the very beginning by mentioning in the Articles.

6. The following documents also have to be filed.

(a) The written consent of each person named in the Articles as director to act as director, in Form No. 29 [Section 266(1)(a)].

(b) A written undertaking by such person to take and pay for qualification shares, if any, in Form No. 29, unless he has already taken or paid for the qualification shares or he has subscribed to the Memorandum and Articles with the sufficient number of shares covering the qualification shares [Section 266(1)(b)].

These documents need not have to be filed by a Private Company or a Public Company not having share capital.

7. Together with the above documents filing also has to be made of the following:

(a) Registrar's letter informing availability of the name.

(b) A letter of authority duly stamped and signed by the subscribers in favour of one of them or any other person for making necessary corrections in the documents, on their behalf, if wanted by the Registrar.

Filing fees have to be paid at the time of filing each document at the rate as given in Schedule X of the Act. The rate increases as the amount of authorised capital increases.

Registration fees of the Company has to be paid at the rate given in schedule X of the Act.

The rate increases as the amount of authorised capital increases.

Functions of the Registrar

(1) The Registrar (actually his office) will now scrutinise all the documents and papers filed with him. He may accept them as they are or subject to corrections suggested by him or he may reject them. He cannot reject the documents indiscriminately. The subscribers to the documents may move the High Court for a writ of mandamus.

(2) The Registrar will now register all the documents and issue a **Certificate of Incorporation** thereby certifying under his hand that the Company is limited [Section 34(1)].

The date given by the Registrar on the Certificate of Incorporation is the date on which the Company is born as a body corporate. The certificate also bears a Registration Number. The company has to use that number whenever the company wants to do any communication with the Registrar.

A private company can commence business immediately.

Issue of Certificate of Incorporation by the Registrar is conclusive evidence that the company is duly registered under this Act (Section 35).

Getting the Certificate for Commencement of Business

A public Company having share capital will now decide whether it wants to be (1) widely held i.e. it intends to invite the Public to buy shares in or debentures of it, or (2) closely held, i.e., it does not intend to invite the public to buy shares in or debentures of it.

On registration the company comes into existence as a legal person distinct from its members who constitute it from the earliest moment of the day of incorporation stated in the certificate of incorporation, with rights and liabilities similar to a natural person, competent to enter into contracts (Section 34).

Conclusiveness of Certificate of Incorporation

A certificate of incorporation given by the Registrar in respect of a Company is conclusive evidence that all the requirements of the Companies Act in respect of registration have been complied with and nothing can be inquired into as to the regularity of the prior proceedings and the certificate cannot be disputed on any grounds whatsoever (Section 35). This is known as Rule in Peel's Case (*Bamed's Banking Co., Re Peel's case*[41]).

The following cases illustrates the point:

In the case of Moos a Goolam *Ariff v. Ebrahim Gulam Ariff*[42], the Memorandum was signed by two adult persons and by a guardian of the other five members, who were minors. The Registrar, however, registered the company and issued a certificate of incorporation. The court held the certificate to be conclusive for all purposes.

Jubilee Cotton Mills Ltd v. Lewis[43], on the 6th January the necessary documents were delivered to the Registrar for registration. Two days after, he issued the certificate of incorporation but dated it 6th January instead of 8th, i.e., the day on which the certificate was issued. On 6th January, some shares were allotted to L, i.e., before the certificate of incorporation was issued. The question arose whether allotment was void. Held, the certificate of incorporation is conclusive evidence of all that it contains. Therefore, in law the company was formed on 6th January and, therefore, the allotment of shares was valid.

The certificate of incorporation has been held to be conclusive on the following points:

1. That requirements of the Act in respect of registration of matters precedent and incidental thereto have been complied with. If after the receipt of certificate of incorporation by a Company it is discovered that there were certain irregularities with regard to its registration, these will not affect the validity of the company.
2. That the association is a company authorised to be registered under the Act, and has been duly registered.
3. That the date borne by the certificate of incorporation is the date of birth of the Company, i.e., the date on which company comes into existence.

Even though the certificate of incorporation is conclusive for the purpose of incorporation, it does not make an illegal object of legal one. But the position is firmly established that if an company is born, the only method to put an end to it is by resorting to the provisions of the Act which provide for the winding up of the companies [T.v. Krishna v. Andhra Prabha (Pvt.)Ltd.[44]].

Effects of Registration (Section 34)

When a company is registered and a certificate of incorporation is issued by the Registrar, three important consequences follow:

1. The company becomes a distinct legal entity. Its life commences from the date mentioned in the certificate of incorporation.
2. It acquires a perpetual succession. The members may come and go, but it goes on forever, unless it IS wound up.
3. Its property is not the property of the shareholders. The shareholders have a right to share in the profits of the company when realised and divided. Likewise, any liability of the company is not the liability of the individual shareholders.

A private limited company can commence business immediately after its incorporation.

CHAPTER

39

Memorandum of Association

The Memorandum of Association of a company is a fundamental document of the Company.

It contains "the fundamental conditions upon which alone the company is allowed to be incorporated" (*Guinness v. Land Corpn.. Of Ireland*[45]). It is the charter of the company and defines its *raison d'etre* (i.e. reason for existence). It lays down the area of operation of the Company. It also regulates the external affairs of the company in relation to outsiders. Its purpose is to enable shareholders and those who deal with the company to know what its permitted range of enterprise is. It not only shows the object of the formation of the company but also the utmost possible scope of it. It is, as it were, the area beyond which the actions of the Company cannot go; inside that area the shareholders may make such regulations for their own governance as they think fit (*Ashbury Rly. Carriage and Iron Co. Ltd. v. Riche*[46]).

Purpose of Memorandum

The Memorandum serves a two fold purpose:

1. It enables shareholders, creditors and all those who deal with the company to know what its powers are and what is the range of its activities. Thus, the intending shareholder can find out the field in, or the purpose for which his money is going to be used by the company and what risk he is taking in making the investment.
2. The outsiders dealing with the company know with certainty as to what the objects of the company are and as to whether the contractual relation into which they contemplate to enter with the company is within the objects of the company (*Cotman v. Brougham*[47]).

Printing and Signing of Memorandum

The Memorandum of Association of a Company shall be —

(a) printed,

(b) divided into paragraphs numbered consecutively, and

(c) signed by 7(seven) [Two(2) in case of Private Company] subscribers.

Each subscriber shall sign (and add his address, description and occupation, if any) in the presence of at least one witness who shall attest the signature and shall likewise add his address, description and occupation, if any (Section 15).

Form of Memorandum (Section 14)

Section 14 requires that the Memorandum of a company shall be in such one of the Forms in Table B,C,D and E in schedule I to the Companies Act, 1956 as may be applicable in the case of the Company, or in Forms as near thereto as circumstances admit.

Table B — For a Company limited by shares.

Table C — For a Company limited by guarantee and not having share capital (The table also includes the articles).

Table D — For a Company limited by guarantee and having share capital (The table also includes the articles).

Table E — For a unlimited Company (with share capital) (The table also includes the articles)

A Company registered under the Act of 1859 shall be governed by Table B of that Act (Section 657).

Contents of Memorandum (Section 13)

The Memorandum of every Company shall contain the following clauses (described as Conditions of the Company's incorporation):

(1) The name of the company with "limited" as the last word of the name in the case of a Public Company, and "Private limited" as the last words in the case of a Private Company.
(2) The name of the State, in which the Registered Office of the Company is to be situated.
(3) The objects of the Company, stating separately "Main Objects" and "Other Objects".
(4) In the case of the companies (other than trading corporations) with objects not confined to one state, the states to whose territories the objects extend.
(5) In the case of a Company limited by shares or by guarantee, the Memorandum shall also state that the liability on its members is limited.
(6) The amount of the authorised share capital, divided into shares of fixed amounts.

These contents of the Memorandum are called compulsory clauses.

The Memorandum shall conclude with an "Association clause" which states that the subscribers desire to form company and agree to take shares in it.

The compulsory clauses are explained one by one below:

(1) The Name Clause

The first clause of a Memorandum shall state the name of the proposed company. The name of a company establishes its identity and is the symbol of its existence (*Osborn v. The Bank of U.S.*[48]). The promoters are free to choose any suitable name for the company, subject to the following rules, select any suitable name:

(i) Undesirable name to be avoided

No Company shall be registered with a name which in the opinion of the Central Government is undesirable [Section 20(1)].

According to the clarifications issued by the Deptt. of Company Affairs, a name is considered undesirable and a Company is not allowed to be registered with such a name:

(a) If the name is identical with or too nearly resembles the name by which a Company is already registered [Section 20(2)]. Names under which well known firms and other bodies are doing business are also considered undesirable for a new company.
(b) If the proposed name is identical with or too nearly resembles, a name of a Company in liquidation. Because the name of the Company in liquidation is borne on the register till it is finally dissolved, a name which is identical with or too closely resembles the name of a company dissolved as a result of liquidation proceedings should also not be allowed for a period of two years from the date of such dissolution since the dissolution of the company could be declared void within the period aforesaid by a order of the court under Section 599 of the Act.
(c) The provisions of the Emblems and Names (Prevention of Improper use) Act 1950 shall not be violated.
(d) If a company gets registered with a name which resembles the name of an existing company, the other company with whom the name resembles can apply to the court for an injunction to restrain the new company from adopting the identical name (*British Bata Shoe Co. Ltd v. Czechoslovak Bata Co. Ltd.*[49]).

An injunction will not be granted to prevent the use of a purely descriptive word with a definite meaning and in common use. Where the names of the two companies contain a word which is in common use, its use cannot be restrained and even a very trifling distinction between the two names will suffice to make it acceptable.

Asiatic Govt. Security Life Insurance Co. Ltd. v. New Asiatic Insurance Co. Ltd.[50]

In this case although the names of the two companies, Asiatic Government Security Life Insurance Co. and New Insurance Co. Ltd. resembled to a large extent, it was held by the Court that the two names were not identical, and, therefore, the defendants were not restrained from using their name.

(e) If it is intended or likely to produce a misleading impression regarding the scope of its activities which would be beyond the resources at its disposal.
(f) 'Limited' or 'Private Limited' as the last word or words of the name.

The Memorandum shall state the name of the Company with 'Limited' as the last word of the name in case of a Public limited Company, and with 'Private Limited' as the last words of the name in case of a Private limited Company. In case the company has been formed for the promotion of art, Science, religion, etc., the Central Government may permit by a licence, the omission of the word 'Limited' or the words 'Private Limited'.

Where the word 'Limited' forms part of a company's name, omission of this word shall make the name incorrect. If the Company makes a Contract without the use of the word Limited, the officers of the Company who make the contract would be deemed to be personally liable.

Atkins and Co. Ltd. v. Wardle[51]

A,B and C, directors of the South shield salt water Baths Co. Ltd, acting on behalf of the Company, accepted a bill of exchange as 'directors of South shield salt water Baths Co.'. Held, having omitted the word 'Ltd.' from the Company's name, the directors who signed the bill were personally liable.

(g) Use of some key words according to authorised capital

The department of Company Affairs vide its circular dt. 7-3-1989 has clarified that if a company uses any of the following key words in its name, it must have a minimum authorised capital mentioned against the key words:

	Keywords	**Required authorized capital (Rs.)**
(i)	Corporation	5 crores
(ii)	International, Globe universal, Continental, Inter-continental, Asiatic, Asia, being the first word of the name	1 crore
(iii)	If any of the words at (ii) above is used within the name (with or without brackets)	50 lakhs
(iv)	Hindustan, India, Bharat, being the first word of the name	50 lakhs
(v)	If any of the words at (Iv) above is used within the name (with or without brackets)	5 lakhs
(vi)	Industries/udyog	1 crore
(vii)	Enterprises, Products, Business, Manufacturing	10 lakhs

Publication of Name (Section 147)

Every company shall:

(a) Paint or affix its name and address of its registered office and keep the same painted or affixed, on the outside of every office or place of business in a conspicuous position in letters easily legible and in the language in general use in the locality.
Department of Company Affairs has clarified that exhibition of its name in English alone, without at the same time showing it in the local language will not be sufficient compliance with the requirements of the section.
The word "outside of every office' do no mean outside the premises in which the office is situate (*Dr. H.L. Batliwala sons and Co. Ltd. v. Emperor*[52]) where office is situated within a compound, the display outside the office room though inside the building is sufficient.

(b) have its name engraved in legible characters on its seal.

(c) have its name and the address of its registered office mentioned in legible characters in all business letters, bill heads, negotiable instruments, invoices, receipts, etc. of the company.

Penalty

If a company does not paint or affix its name and the address of its registered office in the prescribed manner, the company and every officer of the company who is in default shall be punishable with fine.

Besides, sub-section (4) makes an officer of a company or any person on its behalf who signs or authorises to be signed on behalf of the company any bill of exchange, hundi, promissory note or cheque etc., wherein the name of the company is not mentioned in the prescribed manner, shall be personally liable to the holder of such bill of exchange, hundi, promissory note, cheque etc. for the amount thereof unless it is paid by the company.

It is for the Registrar to take appropriate proceedings against the company, if the provisions of Section 147 are violated [*CO Hansa Koya v. Shakti Automobiles (P) Ltd.*[53]].

Personal liability will, however, be not incurred in the following cases:

(a) The holder of a negotiable instrument, on which the company's name has been incorrectly stated, will not be able to enforce the personal liability under Section 147(4) against the officer concerned if the error was due to the holder's own act [*Durham Fancy Goods Ltd. v. Michael Jackson (Fancy Goods) Ltd. and Another*[54]].

(b) The word 'Limited' is abbreviated to 'Ltd' (*P. Stacey and Co. v. Wallis*[55]).

(c) There is an accidental omission of the word 'Limited' (*Dermatine Co. v. Ashworth*[56]). In this case, a bill of exchange was accepted on behalf of a limited company. The rubber stamp of the company was longer than the paper. As a result, the word 'limited' did not appear on the instrument. Held, the directors who accepted the bill of exchange were not personally liable because omission was neither deliberate nor of negligent origin. It was a obvious error of most trifling kind and the mischief aimed at by the Act did not here exist.

2. The registered office clause

Every company shall have a registered office from the day on which it begins to carry on business, or as from the 30th day after the date of its incorporation, whichever is earlier. All communications and notices are to be addressed to that registered office [Section 146(1)]. Notice of the situation of the registered office and every change shall be given to the Registrar within 30 days after the date of incorporation of the company or after the date of change [Section 146(2)]. If default is made in complying with these requirements, the company and every officer of the company who is in default shall be punishable with fine which may extend to Rs. 50 for every day during which the default continues [Section 146(4)].

The situation of the registered office of a company determines its domicile (*Daimler Co. Ltd. v. Continental Tyre and Rubber Co.Ltd.*[57])

3. The Objects clause

The objects clause defines the objects of the company and indicates the sphere of its activities.

A company cannot do anything beyond or outside its objects and any act done beyond them will be ultra vires and void, and cannot be ratified even by the assent of the whole body of shareholders. The objects clause both defines and confines scope of the company's powers, and once registered, it can only be altered as provided by the Act. Lord Cranworth L.C. observed in *Eastern Counties Rly. v. Hawkes*[58]) that "the legal personality of a company exists only for the particular purposes of incorporation as defined in the object clause".

The objects clause in the Memorandum of every company shall state —

(a) Main objects of the Company to be pursued by the company on its incorporation,

(b) Objects incidental or ancillary to the attainment of the main objects, and

(c) Other objects of the company not included in (a) and (b) above. A company, may on receipt of certificate to commence business, pursue any business given in the 'main objects'. In the case of companies (other than trading companies) with objects not confined to one state, the Memorandum must give the name of the state/(s) to whose 'territories' the objects extend. No business given in 'other objects' can, however, be commenced unless prior approval of shareholders with regard thereto is obtained by way of special resolution passed in general meeting [Section 149(2A)]. Where special resolution is not passed, the Central Government, may on an application made by the Board of directors allow a company to commence business in the 'other objects', provided the votes cast in favour of the resolution exceed the votes cast against the resolution, if any [Section I49(2B)).

The objects of the company must not be illegal, immoral or opposed to public policy or in contravention of the Companies Act.

The narrower the objects expressed in the Memorandum, the less is the subscriber's risk, but the wider such objects the greater is the security of those transact business with the company (*Cotman v. Brougham*[59]).

A statement of objects in the Memorandum has twofold operation: It states affirmatively the ambit and extent of vitality and power which by law are given to the company, and it states, if it is necessary so to state, negatively that nothing shall be done beyond that ambit, and that no attempt shall be made to use the corporate life for any other purpose than that which is so specified (*Ashbury Rly Carriage and Iron Co. v. Riche*[60]).

4. Liability clause

This clause states the nature of liability of the members. In case of a company with limited liability, it must state that liability of members is limited, whether it by shares or by guarantee. This means that in case of a company limited by shares, a member can be called upon at any time to pay to company the amount unpaid on the shares held by him. In case of companies limited by guarantee, this clause will state the amount which every member undertakes to contribute to the assets of the company in the event of its winding-up.

In case of an unlimited company, this clause need not be given in the Memorandum of association. In fact, the absence of this clause in the Memorandum means that the liability of its member is unlimited.

5. The Capital clause

The capital in the Memorandum of a company, having a share capital, shall state the amount of the share capital with which the company is to be registered and the division thereof into shares of a fixed amount. The capital with which a company is registered is called 'registered', 'authorised' or 'nominal' capital. A company cannot issue more shares than are authorised for the time being by the Memorandum. The Shares issued by a company can only be equity shares or preference shares, but they cannot have disproportionate rights (Section 85 and 89). A private company which is not a subsidiary of a public company may continue to issue shares of any kind and with disproportionate rights (Section 90).

6. The Association clause

At the end of the Memorandum of every company there is an association or subscription clause or a declaration of association which reads something like this:

"We, the several persons whose names and addresses and occupations are subscribed, are desirous of being formed into a company in pursuance of this Memorandum 'of association, and we respectively agree to take the number of shares in the capital of the company set opposite our respective names". This is followed by the names, addresses and descriptions of the subscribers and the number of shares taken by each one of them. Each subscriber has to take at least one share.

The Memorandum has to be signed by at least 7 subscribers in the case of a Public Company, and by at least two subscribers in the case of a Private Company. The signature of each subscriber shall be attested by at least one witness who cannot be any of the other subscribers.

Alteration of Memorandum

Section 16 provides that the company cannot alter the conditions contained in Memorandum except in the cases and in the mode and to the extent express provision has been made in the Act. These provisions are explained herein below:

(1) Change of name (Section 21)

Section 21 provides that the name of a company may be changed at any time by passing a special resolution at a general meeting of the company and with the written approval of the Central

Government. (A special resolution is one which is passed by three-fourths majority of those voting at a meeting). However, no approval of the Central Government is necessary if the change of the name involves only the addition or deletion of the word "private" (i.e., when public company is converted into a private company or *vice versa*).

If through inadvertence or otherwise, a company has been registered with a name which is identical with or too closely resembles with the name of an existing company, the company may change its name by passing an ordinary resolution and by obtaining the approval of the Central Government in writing (Section 22).

Fresh Certificate of incorporation

The change of name must be communicated to the Registrar of Companies within 30 days of the change. The Registrar shall then enter the new name on the register in the place of the old name and shall issue a fresh certificate of incorporation with necessary alterations [Section 23(1)]. The change of name becomes effective on the issue of fresh certificate of incorporation. The Registrar will also make the necessary alteration in the Memorandum of Association of the Company [Section 23(2)].

However, change of name shall not effect any rights or obligations of the company or render defective any legal proceedings by or against it. Moreover, any legal proceedings which might have been continued or commenced by or against the company by its former name may be continued by or against the company by its new name [Section 23(2)].

Within 30 days of the passing of the special resolution, a printed or a type written copy of the resolution should be sent to the Registrar of Companies.

(2) Change of Registered Office

The registered office clause of a company may be altered by following the procedure given below:

A. Change of registered office in the same city, town or village

The only formality in this case is, passing of the board's resolution to that effect and inform the Registrar within 30 days of the change.

B. Change of registered office from one State to another State

Shifting of the registered office from one State to another involves alteration of the Memorandum and is a complicated affair. The change is allowed if it enables the company to meet out any of the purposes enumerated in Section 17(1) of the Act. These are:

(a) To enable the company to carry on its business more economically or more efficiently.
(b) To enable the company to attain its main purpose by new or improved means.
(c) To enlarge or change the local area of the company's operation.
(d) To carryon some business which under existing circumstances may conveniently or advantageously by combined with the business of the company
(e) To restrict or abandon any of the objects specified in the Memorandum.
(f) To sell or dispose of the whole, or any part of the undertaking of the company
(g) To amalgamate with any other company or body of persons.

The shift of the registered office from one State to another can be done by a special resolution which is required to be confirmed by the Company Law Board (CLB). The Company Law Board before confirming the resolution, will satisfy itself that sufficient notice has been given to every creditor and all other persons whose interests are likely to be affected by the alteration, including the Registrar of Companies and the Government of the State in which the registered office is situated. Also, the CLB will give an opportunity to members and creditors of the company, the Registrar and other persons interested in the company to be heard. The CLB may confirm the resolution on such terms and conditions as it think fit.

It was made clear in *Zuari Agro Chemicals Ltd. v. F.S.Wadia and others,*[61] that the Company Law Board will not substitute its own wisdom or judgement for the collective wisdom or judgement of the company expressed in special resolution. But the bonafides of the company's application for change can be screened.

Loss of revenue of State, whether relevant consideration

In *Oriental Paper Mills Ltd. v. State,*[62] it was observed that a State whose interests are affected by the change has a locus standi to oppose shift of registered office of a company. Accordingly, the Orissa High Court declined to confirm change of registered from Orissa to West Bengal, inter alia, on the ground that in a Federal Constitution every State has the right to protect its revenue and, therefore, the interest of the State must be taken into account.

But in *Minerva Mills Ltd. v. Govt. of Maharashtra*[63], justice Ray of the Bombay High Court held that the Company Law Board cannot refuse confirmation on the ground that the change would cause loss of revenue to a State or would have adverse effects on the general economics of the State. The question of loss of revenue to one State would have to be considered in the prospects of total revenues for the Republic of India and no parochial considerations should be allowed to turn the scale in regard to change of registered office from one state to another within India.

Similar view was expressed in *Rank Film Distributors of India Ltd. v. Registrar of Companies, West Bengal*[64]. A Division Bench of the Calcutta High Court observed that State has no statutory right under Section 17 to oppose the shifting of the registered office from one State to another.

A printed of a typewritten copy of the special resolution both under Section 146 and Section 17 should be sent to the Registrar of Companies within 30 days of its passing.

A certified copy of the CLB's order should be filed within three months thereof with the Registrar of Companies of each State — the old and the new State. If it is not filed within the prescribed time, then the alteration shall, at the expiry of such period, become void and inoperative.

A notice of the new location of the registered office must be given to the Registrar of the State to which the office has been shifted, within thirty days after the change of the office (Section 146).

A company is in a position to shift its registered office from one state to another for certain purposes only.

C. Change of registered office from one town to another town in the same State

If a company wants to change its office from one city, town or village to another within the same State, it has just to pass special resolution in the general meeting and to communicate the change to the registrar within 30 days.

(3) Change of Objects clause

This change is allowed to the company if it enables the company to meet out any of the purposes enumerated in Section 17(1) as given below. In addition the following procedure has to be adopted:

(i) Passing a special resolution and filing its copy with the Registrar within 30 days.

(ii) Getting confirmation of the Company Law Board. The Board before confirming has to satisfy itself that

  (a) Sufficient notice has been given to every debentureholder, Creditor and to every other person whose interests may be affected by the alteration,

  (b) Every objecting creditor has either been paid in full or his consent has been obtained,

  (c) Notice has also been given to the Registrar about the intended change so that he may appear before the Board and State his objections and suggestions, if any, and

  (d) The alteration is fair and equitable considering the interests of the members and creditors of the company. The Company Law Board may allow the alteration either wholly or in part, and on such terms and conditions as it may think proper. Lastly, a copy of the Company Law Board's confirmation order together with a printed copy of Memorandum, as altered, must be filed with the Registrar within three months of the order, who shall register the same and issue a certificate of registration within one month. The alteration will be effective only on getting this Certificate of Registration (Section 17, 18 and 19).

Grounds of alteration [Section 17(1)]

Alteration may be on any of the following grounds:

(i) To carry on its business more economically and more efficiently

The alteration which is contemplated in this clause seems to be an alteration which will leave the business of the company substantially what it was before, with only such changes in the mode of conducting it as will enable it to be carried on more economically or more efficiently. Scientific Poultry Breeder's Assn. Re[65]. A company which was formerly forbidden by its Articles of Association from paying remuneration to its managers wanted to alter its objects clause so as to acquire power to pay this remuneration to carry on its business more economically or efficiently. This alteration was allowed.

In *Dalmia Cement (Bharat) Ltd., In re*[66], the Court observed that whether a company can carry on its business more economically or more efficiently is a matter for the judgement of the directors. If the directors consider that under the existing circumstances, it will convenient and advantageous to combine the new objects with the existing objects, and if it appears that such a conclusion may be fairly arrived at, the court will not go behind it and hold an enquiry as to whether the opinion of the directors is well founded or is justified.

The true legal position observed the Delhi High Court, is that the business must remain substantially the same and additions, alterations and changes should only be steps-in-aid to improve the efficiency of the company (*Delhi Bharat Grain Merchants Assn. Ltd., In re*[67]).

(ii) To attain its main purpose by new or improved means

The emphasis here is on attaining the company's main purpose. The word 'purpose' is more restricted than 'objects'. So, the alteration must be one to carry out the main purpose of the company rather than one of the objects of the company.

For the companies registered after 10th October, 1965, there is no difficulty in ascertaining the main purpose because the Memorandum would state it. But for the companies registered earlier, one has to look not only to the Memorandum but also to what has actually been done.

(iii) To enlarge or change the local area of its operation

In *Indian Mechanical Gold Extracting Company, In Re,*[68] the company's business was confined to the 'Empire of India'. It wanted to enlarge its operations by dropping these words. It was allowed to do so on the condition that the word 'India' was also dropped from its name.

In Egyptian Delta Land and Investment Co., Re[69], a company which was formed to acquire land in Egypt wanted to alter its Memorandum to take power to acquire land in Sudan. Held, the alteration could be made provided the company inserted the words 'and Sudan' after the word 'Delta' in its name.

(iv) To carry on some business which under existing circumstances may conveniently or advantageously be combined with the objects specified in the Memorandum.

In fact, most of the amendments sought in objects clause are based on this ground. This clause enables a company to diversify. The working of the clause makes its scope very wide in as much as any activity which may either conveniently or advantageously by combined with the existing business may be allowed.

Thus, a company formed for generating power was allowed to carry on 'Cold storage and other allied business' [In *re, Ambala Electric Supply Co. Ltd.*[70]].

In Parent Tyre Co. Ltd. In re[71], a tyre company was allowed to take power to undertake financial operations. Similarly, a company formed for business in jute was allowed to add business in rubber [*Juggilal Kamlapat Jute Mills v. Registrar of Companies*[72]].

However, Punjab Distilling Industries Ltd. which was engaged in carrying on Distillery business and other allied objects was not allowed alteration of its objects so as to include a cinema business. The Punjab High Court held that it was not a business which could be conveniently or advantageously be combined with the existing business [*Punjab Distilling Industries Ltd. v. Registrar of Companies*[73]].

Likewise, Cyclists Touring Club Ltd. was not allowed to change its objects so as to admit motorists since one of the objects was to protect cyclists from motorists [*In re, Cyclists Touring Club Ltd.* [74]].

In Sipani Automobiles[75] (1993), diversification sought by the company was refused by the Company Law Board on the ground that the company had liabilities (Rs. 24 Crores) far in excess of its Current Assets (Rs. 21 Crores) besides accumulated losses and also had to pay a large number of persons who had deposited moneys for booking of its motor cars. In these circumstances, Company Law Board observed that it would not only be against Public interest but also against public policy to permit the addition of the proposed new clauses.

Confirmation of alteration of objects is not to be refused only because new business is wholly different from existing business [*New Asiatic Insurance Co. Ltd, In re*[76], *New Asarwa Mfg. Co. Ltd., In re*[77], *Motilal Padampat Sugar Mills Co. (P) Ltd., In re* [78]].

The detailed guidelines in this regard were laid down in *Straw Products Ltd. v. Registrar of Companies*[79]. These are:

(x) The language of Section 17(1)(d) permits the alteration in the Memorandum of association of a company to enable it to carry on a business which is entirely a new departure from the business already carried on provided (a) that such business is one which can conveniently or advantageously be combined with the existing business of the Company and (b) this must be so under the existing circumstances and not under hypothetical circumstances. The additional business need not be even akin to the existing business but it must not be destructive of or inconsistent with and detrimental to the existing business. It must leave the existing business substantially what it was before.

(y) The question whether any additional business in one which may be conveniently or advantageously combined with the business of the Company carried on at the time when the special resolution is passed, is essentially a business proposition and must be determined by the persons engaged in the business of the company.

(z) The Court can confirm the alteration either wholly or in part subject to such terms and conditions as it may deem fit on being satisfied that the alterations sought to be confirmed are not beyond the scope of Section 17(1) and do not adversely affect the rights and interests of the members of the Company and/or of its creditors. No hard and fast rule can be laid down as to the quantum of evidence necessary for the satisfaction of the Court.

The fact that the Company is in sound financial position and that the shareholders unanimously or by majority decision seek alterations of the Memorandum is a factum in favour of confirmation thereof.

(v) To restrict or abandon any of the objects specified in the Memorandum

Even for deleting any portion of the object clause, the procedure laid down in Section 17 has to be followed. C.L.B. has jurisdiction to confirm alteration which involves the abandonment of objects which are in their character fundamental. In *Hampstead Garden Suburb Trust Ltd., In re*[80], one of the objects of the company was that the surplus in the event of winding up was to be given or transferred to some institution or institutions having objects similar to the objects of the company, and in default to some charitable object. It was sought to be amended so as to give or transfer the said balance to H. Ltd. The company's contention was that the alteration by special resolution was within its powers as the alteration was to 'restrict or abandon any of the objects of the company'.

Held that, what was sought to be done by the alteration was, first, to exclude altogether any institution or institutions having objects similar to the objects of this company, and, secondly, to make the balance go to specific charity, i.e., one of the class beneficiaries. This virtually amounted to destruction of the objects and could in no way be regarded as restricting or abandoning any of the objects.

(vi) To sell or dispose of the whole or a part of the undertaking, or any of the undertakings, of the company, or

(vii) To amalgamate with any company or body of persons.

(4) Change in liability clause (Section 38)

A company limited by shares or guarantee cannot change its Memorandum so as to impose any additional liability on the members or to compel them to buy additional shares of the company unless all the members agree in writing to such change either before or after the change (Section 38).

However, in case where the company is a club or any other similar association and the alteration in the Memorandum requires the members to pay recurring or periodical subscriptions at a higher rate, although he does not agree in writing to be bound by the alteration, it shall be binding on him.

The change becomes effective from the date of passing the resolution. Information to be registrar must, however, be sent together with relevant papers within 30 days of passing the special resolution.

Shareholders of an unlimited liability company can make their liability limited by passing a special resolution and obtaining the court's sanction. A copy of the special resolution must be filed within 30 days of its passing and a copy of the Court's confirmation order must be filed, within three months of the order, with the Registrar. Alteration is effective from the date of registration by the Registrar.

(5) Change in the Capital clause

Section 94 provides that, if the articles authorise, a company limited by share capital may, by an ordinary resolution passed in general meeting, alter the conditions of its memorandum in regard to capital so as—

(1) to increase its authorised share capital by such amount as it thinks expedient by issuing fresh shares,

(2) to consolidate and divide all or any of its share capital into shares of larger amount than its existing shares,

(3) to convert all or any of its fully paid-up shares into stock, and reconvert the stock into fully paid-up shares of any denomination,

(4) to sub-divide its shares, or any of them, into shares of smaller amount than fixed by the memorandum, but the proportion paid and unpaid on each share must remain the same,

(5) to cancel shares which, at the date of the passing of the resolution in that behalf, have not been taken or agreed to be taken by any person.

1. Increase of Authorised Share Capital

A company, limited by shares, if the articles authorise, can increase its authorised share capital by passing an ordinary resolution. Within 30 days of the passing of the resolution, a notice of increase in the share capital must be filed with the Registrar of Companies. On receipt of the notice, the Registrar shall record the increase and also make any alterations which may be necessary in the company's memorandum or article or both.

If default is made in filing the notice, the company and every officer of the company who is in default shall be punishable with fine upto Rs. 50 per day during which the default continues (Section 97).

2 & 3. Consolidation and Sub-division of Shares

Consolidation is the process of combining shares of smaller denomination. For instance, 10 shares of Rs. 10 each may be consolidated into one share of Rs. 100.

Subdivision of shares is just the opposite of consolidation, e.g., one share of Rs. 100 may be divided into 10 shares of Rs.10 each.

Once a resolution has been passed, a copy of the resolution is required to be sent within 30 days to the Registrar of Companies.

4. Conversion of shares into stock and vice-versa

Stock is simply a set of fully paid-up shares put together and is transferable in any denomination or fraction. On the other hand, a share is transferable as a whole, it cannot be split into part. For example, a share..of Rs. 10 can be transferred as a whole, it cannot be transferred in parts. But if 10 shares of Rs. 10 each fully paid are converted into stock of Rs. 100, then the stockholder can transfer stock, say worth Rs. 5 also.

Section 94 empowers a company to convert its fully paid-up shares into stock by passing a resolution in general meeting, if its articles authorise such conversion. A notice is to be filed with the Registrar within 30 days of the passing of resolution specifying the shares so converted.

It is to be noted that stock cannot be issued in the first instance. It is necessary to first issue shares and have them fully paid-up and then convert them into stock. Also, stock can be converted into fully paid-up shares by passing a resolution in general meeting.

When shares are converted into stock, the shareholders are issued stock certificates. In the Register of members, the amount of stock is written against the name of a particular member in place of a number of shares. The stockholder is as much a member of the company as a shareholder.

5. Diminution of Share Capital

Sometimes, it so happens that shares are issued, but are not taken up by the members of the public and, therefore, by resolution in general meeting, cancel shares which, at the date of passing of the resolution in that behalf, have not been taken or agreed to be taken by any person and diminish the amount of the share capital by the amount of the shares so cancelled. This constitutes diminution of capital and should be distinguished from reduction of capital.

Restriction to Alteration of Memorandum by order of the Court (Section 404)

When an application is made to the Court under Section 397 or 398 for remedy against oppression or mismanagement the Court may make order as it thinks fit (Section 402) by which the memorandum of the company may stand as altered. The company shall not have power in future to make any alteration of its memorandum in any manner which is inconsistent with the Court's order. But such alteration may be made with the level of the Court [Section 7(2) and 7(3)].

Invalidity of Memorandum (Section 37)

In the case of a company limited by guarantee and not having a share capital, and registered on or after 1st April 1914, every provision in the memorandum (or articles or in any resolution of the company) purporting to give any person a right to participate in the divisible profits of the company otherwise than as a member shall be void.

Doctrine of Ultra Vires

The term *ultra vires* denotes some act or transactions on the part of the company which, although not unlawful or contrary to public policy or laws of the land if done by an individual, is yet beyond the legitimate powers of the corporation defined by the statute under which it is formed or the statutes which are applicable to it or by its charter or memorandum of association.

A company is to confine its area of operations within the limit set out in the object clause.

This has been done to protect the shareholders and creditors of the company. Thus, any such act which is beyond the express or implied powers of the memorandum is absolutely null and void and cannot be ratified by the shareholders even if all of them agree to it (*Ashbury Railway Carriage and Iron Company v. Riche*[81]).

Thus, a company may do any act which is:

(i) Expressly provided in the object clause;

(ii) Necessary or incidental to the attainment of the objects, provided it is not expressly prohibited.

(iii) authorised to be done by the Companies Act 1956.

Everything else is ultra vires the company. If an act is *ultra vires* the company, it does not create any legal relationship. Such an act is absolutely void and even the whole body of shareholders cannot ratify it and make it binding on the company. But there is nothing to prevent a company from protecting its property. The leading case on the point is:

National Telephone Co. v. St. Peter Port Constables[82],

In this case, a telephone company put up telephone wires in a certain area. The company had no power in the memorandum to put up wires there. The defendants cut them down. Held, the company could sue for damage to the wires.

Ashbury Railway Carriage and Iron Co. v. Riche[83],

A company with the objects, namely, (i) to make and sell or lend on hire railway carriages and wagons and all kinds of railway plant, fittings, machinery and rolling stock, (ii) to carry on business of mechanical engineers and general contractors (iii) to purchase, lease, work and sell mines, minerals, land and buildings, (iv) to purchase and sell as merchants, timber, coal, metals or other materials. The company contracted to finance the construction of a railway bridge in Belgium and there was evidence that the agreement had been ratified by all the members. Later the company repudiated the agreement and was sued for breach of contract. In its defence the company pleaded its lack of capacity to enter into a contract which was outside the scope of object clause. The other party brought an action for damages for breach of contract. His contentions were that the contract in question came well within the meanings of the words' general contractors' and, was, therefore, within the powers of the company, and secondly, that the contract was ratified by the majority of the shareholders.

Held, that the term general contractors must be taken to indicate the making generally of such contracts as were connected with the business of mechanical engineers. If the term' general contractors' was so interpreted it would authorise the making of contracts of any and every description such as, for instance, or fire and marine insurance and the memorandum in place of specifying the particular kind of business, would virtually point to the carrying on of business of any kind whatsoever and would, therefore, be altogether unmeaningful. Hence, the contract was entirely beyond the objects in the memorandum of association.

If an act is *ultra vires* the powers of the directors as defined be the articles, the shareholders can ratify it. If it is *ultra vires* the Articles, the company can ratify it by altering the Articles by passing a special resolution. Again if it is done irregularly, it can be validated by the consent of all the shareholders provided it is within the powers of the company.

Whether a particular act on the part of a company is within its powers is a question of fact and is decided on the construction of the terms of the Memorandum. But as regards an outsider dealing with the company, he can hold the directors personally liable for breach of implied warranty of authority, whether the act is *ultra vires* the company or *ultra vires* the directors.

Effects of the Ultra Vires Transactions

The effects and consequences of *ultra vires* transactions are given hereunder:

(1) Any member of the company can get an injunction from the Court restraining the company from proceeding with the *ultra vires* acts.

(2) If the directors make any contract beyond the powers of the company, it will be a breach of warranty which will make the directors personally liable. But it may be noted that the liability for a breach of warranty arises in favour of those persons only who have no notice of the powers of directors. This is because the memorandum constitutes a constructive notice to anyone dealing with the company. From the side of company, if the directors have misapplied the funds of the company, they can be compelled to refund the money.

(3) If money or property obtained under an *ultra vires* contract has been used, to pay intra vires debts of the company, the party giving the loan has the right to follow his property or money if it exists in specie. But he must act before the identity of the property is lost or the money is spent.

(4) A person borrowing money from the company under a contract which is *ultra vires* can be sued by the company to recover the amount so lent.

Ultra Vires Torts

A company is not liable for torts committed by its agents or servants during the course of ultra vires transactions. There is a lot of injustice involved in this rule. A person may, on pain oflosing the bargain, be required to acquaint himself with the company's memorandum. But that can hardly be expected of a person who has been the victim of a *ultra vires* tort. For example, a company is operating omnibuses — a venture entirely alien to its objects as described in the memorandum. The of one such bus negligently injures the plaintiff who sues the company for the tort. It can no doubt be contended against him that the driver was not a servant of the company. The company having no existence outside its corporate sphere could not have appointed him. But can it be said that the plaintiff ought to have known this fact? Doubtless the plaintiff deserves to be compensated. But the law has not yet clearly declared the justice of his demand. As the law seems to stand at present, to make a company liable for any tort it must be shown:

(i) that the activity in the course of which it has been committed falls within the scope of the memorandum, and

(ii) that the servant committed the tort within the course of his employment.

Articles of Association

The preparation of the articles of association is the next step in the formation of the company.

The articles of association may be understood as document containing regulations for the internal management of the affairs of a company. They are subordinate to and controlled by the memorandum. The memorandum lays down the scope and powers of the company, and the articles govern the ways in which the objects of the company are to be carried out and can be framed and altered without the interference of the court.

The Articles of association are the rules, regulations and bye-laws for the internal management of the affairs of a company. They are framed with the object of carrying out the aims and objects as set out in the memorandum of association. They are as such subordinate to, and controlled by, the memorandum. The Articles of Association of a company have a contractual force between company and its members as also between the members inter se in relation to their rights as such members [*Ramkrishna Industries (P) Ltd. and others v. P.R.Ramakrishna and others*[84]]. They are subordinate to and are controlled by memorandum. Articles cannot supersede the objects are set out in the memorandum of association (*Birds Investments Ltd. v. C.I.T.*[85]).

Contents of Articles

Articles usually contain provisions relating to the following matters:

(1) Share capital, rights of shareholders, variation of these rights, payments of underwriting commission.
(2) Lien on shares
(3) Calls on shares
(4) Transfer of shares
(5) Transmission of shares
(6) Forfeiture of shares
(7) Conversion of shares into stock
(8) Share warrants
(9) Alteration of Capital
(10) General meetings and proceedings there at
(11) Voting rights of members, voting and poll proxies
(12) Directors, their appointment, remuneration, qualifications, powers and proceedings of Board of directors.
(13) Manager
(14) Secretary
(15) Dividends and reserves
(16) Accounts, audit and borrowing powers
(17) Capitalisation of profits
(18) Winding up.

In framing the Articles of a company, care must be taken to see that regulations framed do not go beyond the powers of the company itself as contemplated by the Memorandum of Association. They should also not violate any of the provisions of the Companies Act. If they do, they would be *ultra vires* the Memorandum or the Act and will be null and void.

Registration of Articles (Section 26)

It is not absolutely necessary for a public company limited by shares to register the articles of association along with the memorandum of association. According to Section 26, a Public company limited by shares mayor may not register the articles of association signed by the subscribers to the memorandum. If, however, it does not register its own articles, then the articles given in Table A of Schedule I automatically becomes applicable and thus these regulations will govern the internal administration of the company's affairs.

The following companies must register the articles of association along with the memorandum (Section 26).

(1) A company limited by guarantee,

(2) A company limited, both by shares and guarantee.

(3) A private company limited by shares

(4) An unlimited company.

In any case, the articles of company must be: (i) Printed (ii) divided into paragraphs, numbered consecutively, (iii) signed by subscribers to the memorandum in the presence of at least one witness who shall attest the signatures.

The articles are to be stamped with requisite stamp and filed along with the memorandum (Section 3).

The articles of a company, not being a company limited by shares, shall be in such of the forms in Table C, D and E in schedule first as may be applicable or in a form as near thereto as circumstances admit (Section 29).

Articles of an unlimited company, a company limited by guarantee and a private company (Section 27)

1. Unlimited Company —

In the case of an unlimited company, the Articles shall state-

(a) the number of members with which the company is to be registered, and

(b) if it has a share capital, the amount of share capital with which the company is to be registered [Section 27(1)].

2. Company limited by guarantee —

In the case of a company limited by guarantee, the Articles shall state the number of members with which the company is to be registered [Section 27(2)].

3. Private Company —

In the case of a private company having share capital, the Articles shall contain provisions which —

(a) restrict the right to transfer shares,

(b) limit the number of its members to 50 (not including employee-members) and

(c) prohibit any invitation to the public to subscribe for any shares or debentures of the company [Section 27(3)].

Alteration of Articles

Companies have been given very wide powers to alter their Articles. It is a statutory power and any provision in the Articles making the Articles unalterable is regarded as bad in law.

Procedure for alteration

Section 31 (1) provides that subject to the provisions of this Act and conditions contained in its memorandum a company may be special resolution, alter its articles, provided that no alteration can be made so that a public company is converted into a private company without the approval of the Central Government.

Section 31 (2) further provides that any alteration made has the effect as if it was contained in the original document. Section 31 (2-A) said that a copy of the special resolution has to be filed with the Registrar (in Form No. 20) within 30 days and in case the approval of the Central Government is received for conversion of a Public Company into a Private Company, then a copy of that approval also has to be filed within 30 days from receiving the approval.

Once there is any alteration in the articles, then every copy of the articles of the company issued afterwards must contain the change. For violation of this rule, the company and every officer in default shall be punishable with fine which may extend to Rs. 10 per copy issued (Section 40).

In case, the shares of a company are enlisted in a stock exchange, then 6 copies of the special resolution have to be submitted to the stock exchange, one of which is a certified copy.

Significance of alteration

Alteration of articles is a right of a company which cannot be taken away or restricted by any provision in the memorandum or articles of a company (*Allen v. Gold Reefs of West Africa Ltd.*[86]). An articles seems to be stipulations of contract. By alteration some terms of the contract may be broken, even then the alteration is valid though the company may have to pay damages to a third party (*Southern Foundries Ltd. v. Shirlaw*[87]). The main point is that the alteration shall be bonafide, in the interests of the company and not in the interests of a class of members. By alteration no fraud on minority can be done (*Greenhalgh v. Arderene Cinemas Ltd.*[88]). An alteration was retrospective effect on members except when it causes to increase the liability of a member (*Sidebottom v. Kershaw Leese and Co. Ltd.*[89]). A Registrar may refuse to register an alteration which aims at an unlawful object (*The Pioneer Mutual Benefit and Friend-in-need Society Ltd. v. Assistant Registrar of Joint Stock Companies*[90]).

Alteration of the Articles by the order of the Court

Section 404 provides, when an application has been made under section 397 or 398 to the Court for remedy against oppression and mis-management, the Court may make order by which the articles of the company may stand altered.

Limitation to Alteration

However, in spite of the power to alter its articles, a company can exercise this power subject to certain limitations. These are:

1. Must not be inconsistent with the Act

The alteration must not be inconsistent with any provision of the Companies Act [Section 31 (1)].

For example, no company can purchase its own shares (Section 77) and if the articles of a company are altered so as to have the power to purchase its own shares, then such power will be void.

2. The alteration must not exceed the powers given by the memorandum or conflict with other provisions of the memorandum.

3. Must not sanction anything illegal

The alteration must not sanction anything which is illegal or opposed to public policy or unlawful. But if it is legal and it is not clearly prohibited by the memorandum it may be held to be valid even where it alters the whole structure of the company.

4. Must be for the benefit of the company

The alteration must be bonafide for the benefit of the company as a whole. The alteration will not, however, be had merely because it inflicts on an individual shareholder.

If an alteration is made not for the benefit of the company, but for the benefit of a particular class of shareholders, or if the effect of the alteration is to discriminate between the majority shareholders and minority shareholders so as to give the former an advantage over latter, the Court will restrain the company from making the alteration. Further the alteration must not constitute an oppression or a fraud on the minority.

Brown v. British Abrasive Wheel Co. Ltd.,[91] A company was in financial difficulties, the majority of the shareholders were willing to provide more capital if the remaining shareholders, amounting to about 2% of the whole, would sell them their shares. The majority then passed a special resolution altering the Articles so as to enable 98% of the shareholders to buyout any other shareholders.

Held, the alteration, of the Articles could be restrained as it was designed to allow the majority to do compulsorily what they could not do by agreement.

Allen v. Gold Reefs of West Africa Ltd.,[92]

A company had a lien on all shares 'not fully paid' for calls due to the company. There was only one shareholder. A, who owned fully paid-up shares. He also held partly-paid shares in the company. A died. The company altered its articles by striking out the words 'not fully paid up' and thus gave itself a lien on all shares — whether fully paid up or not. The legal representative of A challenged the alteration on the ground that the alteration had retrospective effect.

Held, the alteration was good, as it was done bonafide for the benefit of the company as a whole, even though the alteration had a retrospective effect.

Sidebottom v. Kershaw Leese and Co.,[93]

By alteration in the articles, a company was empowered to expropriate shares held by any member who was in business in competition with the company. At the time of alteration, there was only one member doing business in competition with the company. He challenged the alteration.

Held, the alteration was valid, although only one member was at that time within the ambit of alteration, as the alteration was bona fide and for the benefit of the company.

5. Alteration by Special Resolution only

The alteration can be made only by a special resolution as defined in the Act. Even clerical errors in the Articles should be set right by a special resolution (*Evans v. Chapman*[94]).

6. Approval of Central Government when a Public Company is converted into a Private Company (Section 31)

The alteration in the Articles which has the effect of converting a Public Company into a Private Company can be made only if it is approved by the Central Government. The power of Central Government under Section 31 has been delegated to the Regional Directors of the Company Law Board.

7. Must not cause breach of contract with third party

The alteration must not cause a breach of contract with third party (outsider). or avoid a contractual liability.

In *British Murac Syndicate Ltd. v. Alberton Rubber CO.*,[95] an agreement provided that so long as the plaintiff Syndicate should hold 5000 shares in the defendant company. A provision to the same effect was contained in article 88 of the defendant Company's Articles. The plaintiff syndicate nominated two directors whom the defendant Company refused to accept. An attempt was then made to cancel article 88, but an injunction was granted to restrain it. The learned Judge observed that "The contract clearly involved as one of its terms that article 88 was not be altered."

However, where the damage is capable of being measured in term of money, the company may alter its articles subject to being answerable in damages for breach.

8. Must not increase liability of members

The alteration must not is any way increase the liability of the existing members to contribute to the share capital of, or otherwise pay money to, the company unless they agree in writing before or after the alteration is made. But where the company is a club or association, the Articles may be altered to provide for subscription or charges at a higher rate (Section 38).

9. No Power of the Court to amend Articles

The Court has no power to amend or rectify the Articles even where there is a mistake or drafting error. It can only declare some clause to be ultra vires (Scott v. Frank Scott (London) Ltd.[96]).

10. The amended regulation in the Articles of Association cannot operate retrospectively but only from the date of amendment (*Pyare Lal Sharma v. Managing Director J and K Industries Ltd.*[97]).

Relationship of Articles and Memorandum

1. The Articles are Subordinate to Memorandum

Articles cannot give powers to the company which are not conferred by the Memorandum nor can they create rights which are inconsistent with the memorandum. This is so because the object of the memorandum is to state the purposes for which the company has been established, while the Articles provide the manner in which the internal management of the company is to be carried (*Byron v. Metropolitan Omnibus* Co.[98]).

2. The terms of the Memorandum cannot be modified or controlled by the Articles

However, if there is any ambiguity in the memorandum, the articles may be referred to for clarification. But so far as the fundamental conditions in the memorandum are concerned, they cannot be explained with the aid of the articles.

3. Memorandum must be read in conjunction with the Articles This is the case when it is necessary

(a) to explain any ambiguity in the terms of the memorandum, or

(b) to supplement the memorandum upon any matter about which it is silent except as regards matters which must by statute by provided by the memorandum. The artitles may explain or supplement the memorandum, but cannot extend or enlarge its scope.

Memorandum and Articles: A comparative study

Memorandum of Association (Memorandum) and Articles of Association (Articles) are the two documents which are prepared by the promoters at the time of incorporation of a company. The first one is the primary and the second one is the secondary documents. There are many points of similarity and many points of dissimilarity between the two documents, which are discussed below.

Points of Similarity

(1) Both are prepared at the time of incorporation of a company.

(2) Both are signed by the same persons (together with at least one witness).

(3) Both have same type of form — Printed, subdivided into paragraphs numbered consecutively and signed.

(4) Both have effects of a signed contract between the company and every member of the company be implication.

(5) Both are under the doctrine of 'constructive notice'. As both of them are public exhibits, it can be presumed that any third party entering into a contract with a company has inspected the documents.

(6) A member is entitled to get a copy of each of the documents of payment offee.

(7) The Court may alter the contents of each of the documents through an order as remedy against oppression and mismanagement.

(8) For both the documents there are models or Tables provided in the Act for drafting.

(9) Both are overridden by the Act.

Points of dissimilarity

(1) Memorandum is the fundamental document while the Articles is the subsidiary one.

(2) Memorandum must be prepared by every company but articles may not be prepared by a Public Company limited by shares.

(3) Memorandum defines the objects and their limits of a company beyond which the company cannot go but the articles prescribes the regulations for the internal affairs of the company.

(4) Memorandum has the effects on the members as well as the outsiders but the articles has the effects on the members only.

(5) Any act done by a company beyond the objects of the company is void and cannot be ratified by the members subsequently. This is known as the doctrine of ultra vires. If the company does any act which is not permitted by the Articles it can be ratified by the members subsequently. This is known as the doctrine of Indoor management.

(6) Any clause in the memorandum can not be altered easily. A special resolution by members supported with the approval by the Central Government or the Company Law Board or the Court is necessary. Any clause in the Articles can be altered easily by a special resolution of members (Subject to exceptions).

(7) Both the documents are overridden by the Act but the Articles IS subordinate to the memorandum.

(8) Sometimes the Articles may supersede the memorandum e.g. for reduction of share capital there must be provision in the Articles, provision in the memorandum will not do.

(9) If there is any dispute or discrepancy about any matter mentioned both in the Memorandum and in the Articles, then whatever is given in the Memorandum will stay and be binding.

(10) The number of clauses are far more in the Articles than those in the Memorandum.

(11) The clauses in the memorandum are sometimes classified into condition clauses and Articles clauses but there is no classification of the clauses of the Articles.

(12) The Act is specific about the clauses of memorandum but not so in case of the Articles.

Binding Force of Memorandum and Articles

Section 36 provides that the memorandum and articles, when registered, bind the company and its members to the same extent as if they had been signed and sealed by each members and contained covenants on the part of each members to observe and be bound by all the provisions of the memorandum and articles. Thus, the company is bound to the members, the members are bound to the company and the members are bound to the other members by whatever is contained in these documents. But neither a company nor its members are bound to outsiders. The binding force or the effect of the memorandum and articles may be discussed under the following heads:

1. Members bound to Company

Each member must observe the provisions of the articles and memorandum. For instance, a company has a right of lien on member's shares, or to forfeit the shares on non-payment of calls. Each member is not only bound by the covenants of memorandum and articles as originally framed but as altered from time to time in accordance with the provisions of the Companies Act. The Memorandum and articles constitute a binding contract between the members and company. The effect of this is that each member is bound to the company to conform to the memorandum and the Articles as if each member has actually signed the same.

Borland's Trustee v. Steel Bros and Co. Ltd.[99], The Articles of a company as altered provided that the shares of any member who became bankrupt should be sold to certain persons at a fair price. B, a shareholder, became bankrupt and his trustee in bankruptcy claimed that he was not bound by the altered Articles.

Held, the articles were a personal contract between B and the company, and as such B and his trustee were bound.

Shareholders cannot among themselves enter into an agreement which is contrary to or inconsistent with the articles of association of the company (*V. B. Rangaraj v. V.B. Gopalakrishnan*[100]).

2. Company bound to members

Similarly, a company is bound to members by whatever is contained in its memorandum and articles of association. The company is bound not only to the "member as a body" but also to the individual members as to their individual rights. The member can restrain a company from spending money on ultra vires transactions. An individual member can make the company fulfil its obligations to him, such as to send the notice for the meetings, to allow him to cast his vote in the meetings.

3. Members inter se

The articles bind the members *inter se*, i.e., one to another so far as rights and duties arising from the articles are concerned. The memorandum and the articles constitute a contract between them and are also binding on each member as against the other or others. Such a contract can, however, be enforced through the medium of the company.

Rayfield v. Hand,[101]

The Articles of a company provided that whenever any member wished to transfer his shares, he was under an obligation to inform the directors of his intention and the directors were under an obligation to take the said share equally between them at a fair value. The directors refused to take the shares of a particular member on the ground that the Articles did not impose an enforceable liability upon them.

Held, the directors were under an obligation to purchase the shares, as members of the company, in terms of the provisions of the Articles. There was a personal liability of members *inter se.*

4. Company or members bound to outsiders

The Articles do not constitute any binding contract between the company and an outsider.

An outsider cannot take advantage of the Articles to found a claim thereon against the company.

Eley v. Positive Government Ass. Co.[102],

The Articles of the company provided that E should be the solicitor of the company for life and could be removed from office only for misconduct. Later on he also became a member of the company. But after employing him as a solicitor for a number of years, the company discontinued his services. He, being a member, sued the company for damages for breach of contract contained in the articles of association.

Held, his suit was dismissed on the ground that, he as a solicitor was no party to the articles.

He must prove a contract independent of the articles. There was no infringement of his right as a member. The breach of contract was there but in his capacity as a non member.

Constructive Notice of Articles and Memorandum

Section 610 provides that the memorandum and articles, when registered, become public documents and then they can be inspected by anyone on payment of a nominal fee in the office of the Registrar of Companies. When it is so, every person dealing with the company whether as a shareholder or as an outsider is presumed to have known the contents of the two important public documents of the company. Imputation of knowledge as to the contents of memorandum and the articles is known as constructive notice of the public documents.

The doctrine of constructive notice operates as against an outsider but in favour of the company.

In *Kotla Venkataswamy v. Ram Murthyi*[103],

The articles provided that all deeds and documents of the company shall be signed by the Managing Director, secretary and a working director. A mortgage deed was accepted with secretary and working director's signature only. Held, the deed was invalid.

Doctrine of Indoor Management

There is, however, one limitation to the doctrine of constructive notice, namely that so far as the internal proceedings of the company are concerned, the stranger dealing with the company is entitled to assume that the provisions of the articles have been observed by the officers of the company. An outsider cannot be expected to see that the company carries out its internal regulations. In other words, they are not bound to enquire into regularity of internal proceedings. An outsider is not expected to see that the company carries out its internal regulations.

This doctrine is generally known as the doctrine of' indoor management' and was first laid down in the *Royal British Bank v. Turguand*[104]. The directors of the Bank were authorised to borrow money by issuing bonds with previous approval by the company at a general meeting. But the directors borrowed money by bonds without such approval.

It was held that issue of bonds was not invalid and Turguand, a bond holder could sue the bank for the money. It was not possible to know for the bond holder, as an outsider, whether a resolution authorising the directors had been passed by the company or not. This was a case of indoor management.

But a person dealing with an officer of a company may rely on the ostensible authority of such officer in respect of a transaction provided:

(a) the transaction is one which normally falls within the scope of authority of one in the position of such officer and
(b) the articles of association of the company contains provisions for delegation of powers of the company or its board to such officer in respect of such transaction.

The gist of the rule is that persons dealing with limited liability companies are not bound to inquire into their indoor management and will not be affected by irregularities of which they had no notice.

This Rule is based on Public Convenience and Justice.

First, the memorandum and the articles are the public documents. They are open to inspection by everybody. But the details of internal proceedings are not open to public inspection. An outsider is presumed to know the constitution of the company, but not what mayor may not have taken place within the doors that are closed to him. (*Pacific Coast Coal Mines Ltd. v. Arbuthnot*[105]).

Secondly, the lot of creditors of a limited liability company is not a particularly happy one: it would be unhappier still if the company could escape liability by denying the authority of the officers to act on its behalf.

Some Indian Courts observations on this doctrine

(1) Even where the directors exceed their powers or infringe the restrictions imposed on them, the company may be bound, for an outsider dealing with the company is only bound to see that the transaction is apparently regular and consistent with the articles (*Dewan Singh v. Minerva Films Ltd.*[106]).
(2) Though strangers to a company constructive notice of the memorandum and articles, they are entitled to assume that the provisions therein contained have been complied with by the officers of the company (*Meenakshi Mills Ltd. v. Callianjee and Sons*[107]).
(3) A third party dealing with a director or a manager in good faith is protected even if director/ manager exercises his power irregularly (*Ram Baran Singh v. Muffasil Bank Ltd.*[108]).

(4) It would hardly be conducive to facility of business if outsiders were compelled to search the register and find for themselves whether a person permitted to act as a director of the company for some length of time was also its director *de jure*. (*D. Pudumjee and Co. v. N.H. Moos*[109]).

(5) Lenders to a company should acquaint themselves with memorandum and articles, but they can not be expected to remark upon an investigation as to legality, propriety and regularity of acts of directors [*Official Liquidator, Manasube and Co. (P) Ltd. v. Commissioner of Police*[110]].

Exceptions to the doctrine of Indoor Management

The doctrine of Indoor management is subject to the following exceptions:

1. Knowledge of Irregularity

The doctrine of' indoor management' does not apply where the person dealing with the company knows about the irregularity. The *Howard v. Patent Ivory Co.*[111] is a case in point. In this case, the directors knew the extent of borrowing power of the company without the consent of the general meeting. But they themselves lent out to the company in excess of that power. It was held that the company was not liable for the excess amount ofloans.

2. Outsider's Negligence

Where an outsider is put on suspicion as to the further enquiry into the 'indoor management'. he cannot subsequently plead the indoor management rule for protection. *A.L. Underwood Ltd v. Bank of Liverpool and Marines*[112], is a case in point. The sole director of a company in this case paid into his own account cheques drawn in favour of the company.

Held, the bank was liable as it ought to have made proper inquires before crediting the account of the director.

3. Acts void ab initio and forgery

Where the acts done in the name of a company are void ab initio, the doctrine of indoor management does not apply. The doctrine applies only to irregularities that otherwise might affect a genuine transaction. It does not apply for a forgery. A company can never be held bound for forgeries committed by its officers.

Ruben v. Great Fingal Consolidated Co.[113],

In this case, a share certificate was forged by the secretary of a company. The secretary then issued it under the seal of the company in return for money advanced. The holder of the certificate claimed to be entitled to be registered as the holder of the shares. Held, the certificate did not confer any right on the shareholder.

4. Acts outside the scope of apparent authority

Where an outsider purported to act as a director in the transaction, the rule of indoor management is not available. (*Morris v. Kanssen*[114]).

In *Kreditbank Cassel v. Sehenkers Ltd.*[115] a branch manager of a company drew and endorsed bills of exchange on behalf of the company. He had no authority from the company to do so. Held, the company was not bound.

5. Special Resolution

Where the articles provide for special resolution which has not been passed, the benefit of indoor management is not available for the special resolutions are the public documents (*Irvin v. Union Bank of Australia*[116]).

CHAPTER

41

Prospectus

After the grant of the certificate of registration, the next problem of the company is to raise funds for its working. A private company is not allowed to invite the public for subscribing to any shares in or debentures of the company, [Section 3(iii)(c)]. On the other hand, a public company, which cannot arrange its capital privately, may resort to several devices. These may be:

(a) By issue of a prospectus,

(b) By an offer for sale, or

(c) By a "placing"

Definition of Prospectus

When a public company or the promoters of a public company decides that the money should be raised from the public by way of invitation to offer to the shares and debentures of the company, a document is drawn up which is known as a 'Prospectus'.

Section 2(36) defines a prospectus as "any document described or issued as a prospectus and includes any notice, circular, advertisement or other document inviting deposits from the public for the subscription or purchase of any shares in, or debentures of, a body Corporate".[117]

In simple words, any document inviting deposits from the public or inviting offers from the public for the purchasing shares or debentures of a company is a prospectus.

The main characteristic of a prospectus is that invites the public for making investment. From the definition it is very clear that the prospectus is not an offer itself from the company to the public. It is rather an invitation to offer to the public. The company is at liberty to accept the offers made by the public for the purchase of shares in and debentures of the company.

But if the document satisfies the condition of invitation to the public, it is an prospectus even though it is issued to a defined class of the public (*Nash v. Lynde*[118]). Thus, an advertisement which stated that some shares are still available for sale according to the terms of the company which may be obtained on application" was held to be a prospectus as it invited the public to purchase shares (*Pramtha Nath Sanyal v. Kali Kumar Dutt*[119]).

What is meant by the term Public

It is difficult to say exactly how many persons constitute Public. What is meant by the term Public has been clarified in Section 67. Section 67(1) states that Public includes "any section of the public whether elected as members or debenture holders, or as clients of the person issuing the prospectus or in any other manner". The word Public does not however, include a small and closely restricted group of investors which has been described by the Act as "being a domestic concern of the persons making and receiving the offer or invitation" [Section 67(3)(b)]. The invitation by a director to his near relatives or 'kith and kin' is not an invitation to the Public. (*Rattan Singh v. Moga Transport Co. Ltd.*[120]).

The words 'Subscription or Purchase' have to be clarified. Purchase means there is consideration of price but shares may be subscribed by way of adjustments or for otherwise than cash, e.g., against some service rendered.

Summing up the overall position it may, thus be stated that the material point to be considered, while deciding about what constitutes an 'offer to the Public' is not the number of persons to whom the 'offer for sale' is made, but it is the nature of offer so made. If the offer makes the shares and debentures available for subscription by persons other than those receiving the offer, it is deemed to have been made to the 'public'. On the other hand, if the offer can be accepted only by those to whom it is made or if it is made only to the friends or relatives of directors, it is not one made to the public.

To be issued by whom and when

Prospectus may be issued (a) by or on behalf of a company or (b) by or on behalf of a person who is or has been engaged or interested in the formation of a company (Section 56) (Company means here Public Company) or (c) by a private company after being converted into a Public company (Section 44).

A prospectus has to be issued by a Public Company (if it intends to be widely held) whenever it wants to invite the public to subscribe or purchase shares in or debentures of the company. Therefore, prospectus may be issued at two times — (a) after the incorporation of a Public Company is completed or (b) an existing company wanting to issue fresh shares or debentures. There is a difference with regard to the contents of these two types of prospectus. A Private Company shall file prospectus with the Registrar when it has been converted into a Public Company, within 30 days from the date of conversion.

Dating of Prospectus (Section 55)

Section 55 states that every prospectus must be dated and that date is deemed to be the date of publication of the prospectus. In case the prospectus is issued by an intended company, it has to be signed by the proposed directors of the company or by their agents authorised in writing. In case of existing companies, the prospectus has to be signed by every person who is named therein as director or proposed director of the company or by his agent authorised in writing.

Contents of a Prospectus

Section 56 of the Companies Act lays down that the matters and reports stated tin schedule II to the Companies Act must be included in a prospectus. There is no provisions in the Act itself with regard to the contents of a prospectus. But schedule II of the Act provides a model which has to be strictly followed to prepare a prospectus. This format of schedule II was revised by the government vide its notification dated 3-10-1990. The schedule contains three parts — I, II and III. A summary of the contents of the schedule II is given below:

Part I state the matters specified in Part I of schedule II, and

Part II set out the reports specified in Part II of schedule II

Part III the provisions as stated above have effect subject to the provisions contained in part III of schedule II.

Part I — State the matters specified in Part I of schedule II

(1) The **main objects** of the company and details of the signatories of the memorandum in case the prospectus is issued after two years from the date of commencement of business.

(2) **The number and classes of shares** and about redemption in case of redeemable preference shares.

(3) **Directors** — details of them, qualification shares, remuneration etc., terms of contract with the managing director if any.

(4) Deleted.

(5) **Minimum Subscription** to be raised to meet preliminary expenses, to purchase any property for working capital etc.

(6) Time of opening the subscription list.

(7) The **amount payable** on application and allotment, if any etc.

(8) Particulars of **any options to subscribe** and persons entitled thereto.

(9) Particulars of **shares and debentures** issued in the preceding two years **otherwise in cash.**

(10) The amount **paid or payable as premium** on each share issued in preceding tow years or to be issued or other shares of same class at lower premium or at par or at discount and reasons.

(11) The **names** of underwriters and directors, opinion about their capability.

(12) **Particulars of the Vendors of Property** acquired or to be acquired, amount payable and interests of directors and others in transactions in two preceding years.

(13) The amount or rate of **commission** payable on subscriptions or paid within two preceding years to promoters sub-underwriters etc.

(14) The amount or estimated amount or **preliminary expenses** and the expenses of issue.

(15) The **amount paid or benefit given** within two preceding years or **payable or to be given** to any promoter or officer.

(16) **Particulars of contracts** with managing director or manager, if any or of material contracts (not ordinary business contracts within preceding two years.

(17) The names and addresses of auditors if any.

(18) **Particulars of interests** of every promoter or director in the promotion or property of the company acquired within preceding two years or to be acquired.

(19) The **rights** attached to different classes **of shares,** if any.

(20) Restrictions to members with regard to attending meetings or transferring shares, if any.

(21) The length of time during which the business has been carried on by the company or of a business to be acquired by the company.

(22) Particulars of the capitalisation of any reserves or profits of the company or subsidiaries. Particulars about **surplus by revaluation** of the company or subsidiaries.

(23) A reasonable time and place **where** copies of balance sheets and profits and loss accounts (as under Part II) **can be inspected.**

Part II — Reports specified in Part II of schedule II

(1) A **report by the auditors** of the company with respect to

  (a) profit and losses of last five years (i.e. maximum),

  (b) rates of dividend on each class of shares during those years, and

  (c) the assets and liabilities at the last date to which the accounts were made up. If the company has subsidiaries then the accounts of the subsidiaries also.

(2) If the proceeds of the issue of shares or debentures to be used to purchase a business or more than 50% interests in it then report on the profit and loss account and assets and liabilities of that business on last date (not more than 120 days from the date of issue of prospectus).

(3) If the proceeds to be applied directly or indirectly to acquire shares in other body corporate at last date, how the profits have been deal and whether it has any subsidiaries.

Part III — Provisions applying to Parts I and II of the schedule

(1) **Clause I and 14 shall not apply** if the prospectus is issued after two years from the date of the company is entitled to commence business.

(2) The persons to be considered as **vendors to the company.**

(3) A vendor includes lessor.

(4) If the company or other business has been carrying on business for less than 5 financial years then reports on the accounts shall relate to the equal number of years.

(5) Where the five **financial years cover a period of loss** than five years then five years shall mean five financial years.

(6) If **figures** of profits and losses or assets and liabilities **require adjustments** for the purpose of the report, then indication of it in the report and the reasons thereof.

(7) Any report required in Part II shall be **by qualified accountants and not** an officer or servant or a partner or in employment of a company or its holding or subsidiary company or a subsidiary of the company's holding company.

Exemptions

The provisions do not apply to:

(1) An invitation to underwrite [Section 56(3)(a)].

(2) When shares and debentures are not offered to the public [Section 56(3)(b)].

(3) An invitation to existing shareholders or debenture holders [Section 56 (5)(a)].

(4) When the terms of issue of shares or debentures are uniform with those of previously issued ones which are dealt in a recognised stock exchange [Section 56 (5)(b)].

In fact, prospectus may not be issued in cases of (3) and (4), though in practice some document resembling a prospectus is sent out. This document draws a provisions of Section 60, i.e., it needs registration with the Registrar.

Abridged Form of Prospectus

Section 56(3) of the Companies Act, 1956 (as amended by the Act of 1988 w.e.f. 31-5-91) requires that no one shall issue any form of application for shares in or debentures of a company unless the same is accompanied by a memorandum containing such salient features of prospectus as may be prescribed. Thus, instead of appending full prospectus, now 'abridged prospectus' need only be appended to the application form.

In order to provide for greater disclosure of information to prospective investors so as to enable them to take an informed decision regarding investment in shares and debentures, Form 2-A has been prescribed as a format of abridged prospectus. It is further required that the abridged prospectus and the share-application form should bear the same printed number and the two should be separated by a perforated line. Accordingly, the investor may detach the application form before submitting the same to the company or the designated bankers.

When 'Abridged Prospectus' not necessary ?

In the following circumstances, an 'abridged prospectus' containing the prescribed particulars as per Form 2A need not accompany the application forms:

(i) In the case of a bonafide invitation to a person to enter into an underwriting agreement with respect to the shares or debentures [Section 56(3)(a)].

(ii) When shares or debentures are not offered to the public [Section 56(3)(b)].

(iii) Where offer is made only to existing members/debenture holders of the company by way or rights, whether with or without the right of renunciation [Section 56(5)(a)].

(iv) In the case of issue of shares or debentures which are in all respects similar to those previously issued and dealt in and quoted on a recognised stock exchange [Section 56(5)(b)].

Penalty

Non-compliance of the aforesaid provisions by any person shall attract punishment in terms of fine which may extend to Rs. 5000/-.

Besides, the omission from a prospectus of a matter required to be included by Section 56 may give rise to an action for damages at the instance of a subscriber for shares or debentures who has suffered loss thereby. It should be noted that the Act does not say that directors shall be liable, but this seems to be implied from Section 56(4).

Draft Prospectus to be made Public

SEBI vide its circular No. 3(95-96) dated 29-9-1995 has provided for making public the draft prospectus filed with SEBI. The Lead Merchant Bankers shall simultaneously file copies of the draft document with the stock exchanges where the issue is proposed to be listed. Lead Merchant Bankers shall also make copies available to the Public. Lead Managers/Stock Exchanges can charge an appropriate sum to the person requiring such copy(ies).

The Expert's Consent to the Issue of Prospectus

A prospectus may contain a statement purporting to be made by an expert. The term "expert" includes an engineer, a valuer, an accountant, and any other person whose profession gives authority to a statement made by him. The reports from an expert must not be included in a prospectus unless:

(i) Such expert is unconnected with the formation or management of the Company (Section 57). Where a prospectus includes a statement made by an expert, he shall not be engaged or interested in the formation, promotion or management of the company.

'Expert' includes an engineer, a valuer, an accountant and any other person whose profession gives authority to a statement made by him.

(ii) Expert's consent to issue of prospectus containing statement by him (Section 58).

A prospectus (including a statement made by an expert) shall not be issued, unless —

(a) the expert has given his written consent to the issue of the prospectus with the statement included in the form and context in which it is included, and

(b) a statement that he has given and not withdrawn his consent as aforesaid appears in the prospectus.

If the report of the expert is published in contravention of the above mentioned provisions, every person who is knowingly a party to the issue of the prospectus shall be punishable with fine upto Rs. 5000 (Section 59).

Registration of Prospectus (Section 60)

A prospectus can be issued by or on behalf of a company or in relation to an intended company only when a copy thereof has been delivered to the Registrar for registration. The registration must be made on or before the date of Publication thereof. The copy must be signed by every person who is named therein as director or proposed director of the company, or by his agent authorised in writing. Further, the prospectus must state on the face of it that a copy of it has been delivered to the Registrar for registration. It must also specify that necessary documents and consent of the experts have been attached to or endorsed on the copy so delivered.

The prospectus must be issued within 90 days of the date on which a copy thereof is delivered for registration. If a prospectus is not issued within this period, it is deemed to be a prospectus, a copy of which has not been delivered to the Registrar.

Objects of Registration

These are:

(1) to keep an authenticated record of the terms and conditions of issue of shares or debentures, and

(2) to pinpoint the responsibility of the persons issuing the prospectus for statements made by them in the prospectus.

The object of the promoters or directors in issuing a prospectus is to make it as attractive as possible. The object of the legislature is to prevent the public from being misled and defrauded.

Refusal to Register Prospectus [Section 60(3)]

The registrar must not register a prospectus unless the formalities regarding the dating of the prospectus, its contents, registration, etc., have been complied with and the prospectus is accompanied by the consent in writing of the person, if any, named therein as the auditor, legal adviser, attorney, solicitor, banker or broker of the company or intended company to act in that capacity.

Penalty for Non-Registration [Section 60(5)]

If a prospectus is issued without a copy thereof being delivered to the Registrar for registration, or without the necessary documents or the consent of the experts, the company and every person who is knowingly a party to the issue of the prospectus is punishable with fine which may extend to Rs. 5000/-.

Statement in Lieu of Prospectus (Section 70)

If a Public company makes a Private arrangement for raising its capital then it must file a statement in lieu of prospectus with the Registrar at least three days before any allotment of shares or debentures can be made. The statement is required to contain the particulars set out in Part I of Schedule III of this Act and the reports set out in Part II of the Schedule. The information and the reports required to be disclosed in the statement are almost the same as are required to be disclosed in a prospectus. The statement must be signed by every person who is named therein as a director or proposed director of the company or by his agent authorised in writing.

If allotment of shares or debentures is made without filing the statement in lieu of prospectus, the allottee may avoid it within two months after the statutory meeting, or where no such meeting is to be held, within two months of the allotment. Contravention also renders the company and every director liable to a fine upto Rs. 1000/-.

Prospectus in Terms of Newspaper Advertisement

Where a prospectus is issued as newspaper advertisement, under Section 66, it is not necessary to specify therein the contents of the memorandum or the signatories thereto, or the manner of shares subscribed by them. It means this section says, excepting these matters, all other particulars referred to must be given even in a newspaper advertisement. But then it will be a very costly exercise indeed. The Company Law Department has laid down that such an advertisement must state at the top. "This is an announcement and not a prospectus" and in addition it must contain information about the company and proposed issue under the following heads:

(1) Name of Company.

(2) Address of the registered office.

(3) Existing and proposed activities.

(4) Location of the Industry.

(5) Board of directors.

(6) Manager/Managing director(s), if any.

(7) (a) Authorised Capital

(b) Subscribed Capital

(c) proposed issue to the Public (whether at par, premium or discount).

(8) Dates of opening and closing of the subscription list.

(9) Application forms along with prospectus to be had from the registered office of the company, or from the underwriters/BrokersIBankers whose names and addresses are given below:

Underwriters

Brokers

Bankers.

Further, the Central Government feels that there is no bar to the terms of Payment being included in the announcement made in the press provided it does not offend the provisions of Section 56.

Offer for Sale-deemed Prospectus (Section 64)

The provisions relating to a prospectus (as regards registration contents and full disclosure) are very stringent and the duty of preparing and filing a prospectus in accordance with the law is extremely onerous (*Pramatha Nath Sanyal v. Kali Kumar Dutt*[121]). These requirements used to be evaded by companies in the post by allotting the whole of an issue of shares or debentures to an issuing house at a certain price. The issuing House then published an advertisement (which obviously is not a prospectus) in the nature of an offer for sale inviting the members of the public to buy the shares or debentures from it at a higher price. Section 64 has been designed to check the by-passing of the provisions of Section 56 (Section 56 requires certain information to be disclosed and certain reports to be set out in the prospectus) by making an offer of sale of shares or debentures through the medium of Issuing Houses. Section 64 provides that all documents containing offer of shares or debentures for sale shall be included within the definition of the term 'Prospectus'.

When applications are received by the issuing house, it renounces (gives up) its interest in the shares or debentures in favour of an applicant to the extent of the number of shares or debentures allotted to him. When this is done, the applicant becomes an allottee of the company. By this method of allotment, stamp duty is saved.

The provisions of Section 64 are summed up as under:

1. Prospectus by implication

All documents containing offer of shares or debentures for sale are included within the definition of the term 'prospectus' and are deemed to be prospectus by implication of law. Where a company allots or agrees to allot any shares in, or debentures of, the company to an issuing house with a view to all or any of those shares or debentures being offered for sale to the public, any document by which the offer for sale to the public is made by the issuing house is for all purposes, deemed to be a prospectus issued by the company [Section 64(1)].

2. Intention to offer shares or debentures to the public

Normally, an allotment of, or agreement to allot, shares or debentures to an Issuing House is deemed to have been made with a view to the shares or debentures being offered for sale to the public if it is shown—

(a) that the offer of shares or debentures for sale was made within 6 months after the allotment or agreement to allot, or

(b) that at the date when the offer was made, the whole consideration to be received by the company in respect of shares or debentures had not been received by it [Section 64(2)].

Additional Information

In case of a document that is deemed as prospectus, Section 64(3) requires that it must contain certain information in addition to the information required to be stated in a prospectus under Section 56. Thus, it should also state:

(a) the net amount of consideration received or to be received by the company in respect of the shares or debentures to which the offer relates, and

(b) the place and time at which the contract under which the said shares or debentures have been or are to be allotted may be inspected.

For purposes of registration of a prospectus under Section 60, the persons making the offer of sale to the public are to be deemed as directors of the company [Section 64(4)].

Where the person making the offer is a company or a firm, the documents (i.e., deemed prospectus) must be signed by at least two directors or one-half of the partners, as the case may be [Section 64(5)].

Circumstances under which a document containing an offer for sale of shares or debentures be not deemed to be a prospectus

A document containing an offer for sale of shares or debentures is a prospectus not depends upon whether it extends an invitation to the public to subscribe or not. The *prima facie* test 'Public offer' or 'Public invitation' is whether the terms of the offer or invitation are such that, despite its limited circulation, it is open to any person who so chooses to bring his money and apply for shares in response to the invitation. If the offer or invitation is so open, then it constitutes a 'Public Offer'. If, on the other hand, an offer or invitation can be accepted only by the person to whom it is made and none other, then it will not be deemed to be an offer or invitation to the public.

The word 'Public' includes any section of the public (Section 67). It may, thus, include all registered medical practitioners in Delhi, all advocates of High Court of Delhi, all Englishmen living in India.

Is the issue of prospectus compulsory? When prospectus is not required to be issued?

No, issue of prospectus by a Company is not compulsory in the following cases:

(i) A private company is not required to issue a prospectus.

(ii) Even a Public Company need not issue a prospectus if the promoters or directors feel that they can mobilise resources through personal relationship and contracts. In such cases, the company is required to file a statement called 'statement in lieu of prospectus' with the Registrar of Companies.

(iii) As per the Amendment Act, 1988, a Company may issue any forms of application for shares or debentures accompanied by a memorandum containing the prescribed salient features of a prospectus (instead of prospectus). However, in such a case, a copy of the prospectus must be made available to any person on request [Section 56(3)].

(iv) Where the application form is issued in connection with the bonafide invitation to a person to enter an underwriting agreement with respect to the shares or debentures [Section 56(3)].

(v) Where the application form is issued in relation to shares or debentures not offered to the public [Section 56(3)].

(vi) Where the shares or debentures are offered to existing holders of shares or debentures (i.e., rights issue) with or without the right of renunciation in favour of other persons [Section 56(5)].

(vii) Where the issue relates to shares or debentures which are, or to be, uniform in all respects with shares or debentures previously issued and dealt in and quoted on a recognised stock exchange [Section 56(5)].

(viii) Where invitation to the public for subscription to the shares or debentures of a company is made in the form of an advertisement, ordinarily called as "prospectus announcement" [Section 66].

The Golden rule for framing of Prospectus

A prospectus is a document which holds out to the public as to what a company is, what it purposes to do and what its prospects are. It invites deposits from the public or invites offers from the public to subscribe to the share capital and debentures of the company. It is, therefore, but reasonable that there must be full, frank and honest disclosure of all material facts with scrupulous accuracy in a prospectus and no material fact should be mis-stated or with held, mis-statements and non-disclosure of material facts in a prospectus are fatal to the contract for the purchase of shares and debentures. As such the greatest care is necessary in its preparation. The obligations imposed on those responsible for the issue of a prospectus are not only to state accurately all the relevant facts but also not to omit any fact which may be relevant. This is 'the golden rule as to framing of prospectus'.

The 'Golden Rule' for framing of a prospectus was laid down by Justice Kindersely in *New Brunswick and Canada Rly. and Land Co. v. Muggeridge*[122]. Briefly, in the following words:

"Those who issue a prospectus holding out to the public the great advantages which will accrue to persons who will take shares in a proposed undertaking and inviting them to take shares on the faith of the representations therein contained, and bound to state everything with strict and scrupulous accuracy and not only to abstain from stating as fact that which is not so, but to omit no one fact within their knowledge the existence of which might in any degree affect the nature or extent or quality of the privileges and advantages which the prospectus holds out as inducement to take shares."

In a word, the true nature of the Company's venture should be disclosed. Thus, the prospectus as a whole must not give a misleading impression, even though on analysing the statements separately, a true sense could be made out. If there is any mis-statement of a material fact in a prospectus or if the prospectus omits any material fact, there may arise civil and criminal liability.

Liability for Omissions, Mis-statement or Untrue statement

A prospectus must contain matters in conformity with the provisions in the schedule II.

No one shall issue any form of application for shares or debentures unless the form is accompanied by a prospectus which comply with the form given in the schedule II subject to some exceptions. Any person who violates this shall be punishable with fine which may go upto Rs. 5000/- [Section 56(3)]. **This is a case of omission. It has a negative character. But mis-statement or untrue statement is something of positive nature and wider in its meaning.** According to Section 65(1) of the Companies Act, 1956 —

(a) A statement included in a prospectus shall be deemed to be untrue, if the statement is misleading in the form and context in which it is included, and

(b) Where the omission from a prospectus of any matter is calculated to mislead, the prospectus shall be deemed in respect of such omission, to be a prospectus in which an untrue statement is included.

The expression "included" with reference to a prospectus means, included in the prospectus itself or contained in any report or memorandum appearing on the face thereof or by reference incorporated therein or issued therewith.

The omission under Section 65 is different from the same term omission under Section 56.

Under Section 65 the omission is "Calculated to mislead". So there is normally a bad intention but omission under Section 56 may not be calculated or with a bad intention. Omission under Section 65 tantamounts to falsification while it may not be so under Section 56. Therefore, Section 56 does not provide any remedy for the aggrieved subscriber but remedies have been suggested (Section 62) for untrue statement as a whole under Section 65. Section 56(3) refers to exemptions from liability too in certain cases but that does mean the person at fault is free from liabilities under other provisions in the Act [Section 56(6)].

Untrue or false statement means establishing something to be a fact which is actually not a fact.

This can be done directly or indirectly (Concealment).

Such omissions or mis-statements shall not be included not in the prospectus only but also not in any report or memorandum appearing in the prospectus or incorporated in it as reference or issued therewith [Section 65(2)].

There is a third category of wrong-doing, i.e., inducement to an agreement. This is definitely more deliberate and definitely with a bad intention. Inducement takes place when a person either by knowledge or recklessly making any statement promise or forecast which is false deceptive or misleading or by any dishonest concealment of material facts induces or attempts to induce another person to enter into or to offer to enter into — (a) an agreement for or with a view to acquiring or disposing of, subscribing for, or underwriting shares or debentures or (b) an agreement the purpose or pretended purpose of which is to secure a profit to any of the parties from the yield of shares or debentures or by reference to fluctuations in the value of shares or debentures (Section 68).

The latter part of the sentence refers to transfer of shares or debentures. The whole action tantamounts to fraud. The Act makes no distinction between 'induce' and attempt to 'induce'.

Effects of Omission, Mis-statement or Untrue statement or inducement

The faults or wrong-doings under three different categories (given above) are of different grades and accordingly the effects vary. The effects are of two types: **remedial** from the side of the sufferer and **penal** from the side of the wrongdoer. These are given below:

1. Effects of Omission

If any person violates the requirements of Section 56(1), i.e., making the prospectus in conformity with the schedule II, is punishable with fine which may go upto Rs. 5000/-.

Exemption

No such liability shall be incurred if the prospectus was issued either (a) in connection with a bonafide invitation to a person to enter into an underwriting agreement with respect to the shares or debentures or (b) in relation to shares or debentures which were not offered to the public [Section 56(3)].

This Section does not make any remedial provision for those who have purchased shares or debentures on the basis of such a defective prospectus.

2. Effects of Mis-statement or Untrue statement

The Act is very severe with regard to such wrong-doing. The effects are of two types remedial and penal as the liabilities are also of two types civil and criminal. Exemptions and defence are also provided. These are discussed below—

Civil Liability—

Civil liability means any person who has suffered loss or damage by subscribing shares or debentures on the faith of the prospectus, may claim compensation from the following persons:

(a) every person who is director of the Company at the time of the issue of the prospectus,

(b) every person who has authorised himself to be named and is named in the prospectus as a director, or as one having agreed to become a director, either immediately, or after an interval of time,

(c) every promoter of the company, and

(d) every person (including an expert) who has authorised the issue of the prospectus. But an expert is liable only in respect of his own untrue statements [Section 62(1),(6)].

Thus, an allottee of shares, who had applied for shares on the faith of the prospectus containing untrue statements has remedies available against the different persons, i.e., the company, directors, promoters and experts.

The onus of proof in on the aggrieved subscriber

He has to prove that he has suffered loss because there was a mis-representation on some material fact. For example, a statement in the prospectus that the company had purchased a property though there was a stage of negotiation (*Ross v. Estates Investment Co.*[123]). The directors may be held liable in tort for mis-statement in prospectus (*Hedley Byrne and Co. Ltd. v. Heller and Partners Ltd.*[124]). It has to be noted that the company cannot be held liable.

Remedies against the Company

Any person who, relying on mis-statements in or omission of material facts from a prospectus takes shares from the Company may—

(i) rescind the contract would be that the shareholder would give up the shares and get back his money with interest. he must, however, take action to rescind the contract:

  (a) within a reasonable time,

  (b) before proceedings to wind up the company have commenced, and

  (c) before he does anything (after he comes to know of the mis-statements in the prospectus), which is inconsistent with the right to repudiate, e.g. to accept dividends.

The allottee can claim relief only if he can show that the mis-statement or omission was:

(i) one of fact and not of Law, nor an expression of opinion,

(ii) material, and

(iii) acted upto by him.

The second right of the allottee against the company is to sue for damages for deceit. **In** order to succeed, the allottee must, in addition to the three facts mentioned above (in connection with the rescission of contract), prove:

(i) that those acting on behalf of the company acted fraudulently,

(ii) that those purporting to act on behalf of the company were authorised to act in its behalf; and

(iii) that he suffered a loss or damages.

It is important to remember that the allottee can not both retain the shares and get damages from the company. In actual practice, suit for damages against the company is rarely filed. The usual claim against the company is for rescission of the contract of allotment. Damages are generally claimed from the directors, promoters and other persons who had authorised the issue of the prospectus personally, or from experts, who had signed reports to in the prospectus.

Remedies Against the Directors, Promoters and Experts

A person induced to take shares on the basis of any untrue statement in the prospectus is entitled to claim from the directors or promoters or anyone else responsible for the false statement in the prospectus.

(a) damages for deceit under General Law,
(b) compensation under Section 62,
(c) damages for non compliance of the requirement of Section 56.

(a) Damages for Deceit under General Law

The allottee can claim damages if:

(i) he proves the same facts as are required to be proved for the recession of the contract, and
(ii) also proves that the mis-statement in the prospectus was fraudulent.

This remedy is available even if the allottee's right to rescind the contract to take shares is lost or even if the company goes into liquidation.

(b) Compensation under Section 62

Under this Section, the following persons will be liable to pay compensation to the person who has subscribed for any shares or debentures on the faith of the prospectus for any loss sustained by him on account of an untrue statement included therein (i.e. in the prospectus):

(i) every person who is a director of the Company at the time of the issue of the prospectus,
(ii) every person who has authorised himself to be named and is named as a director in the prospectus,
(iii) every person who is a promoter of the company, and
(iv) every person who has authorised the issue of the prospectus [Section 62(1)].

Their liability may be studied under the following heads:

(1) Liability for damages for mis-statement in prospectus (Section 62)

Every director, promoter and every person who authorises the issue of the prospectus (into matter whether he has seen it or not) is liable to pay compensation to the aggrieved party (who subscribes for any shares or debentures on the faith of the prospectus) for loss or damage he may have incurred by reason of any untrue statement in the prospectus.

Defences of directors, promoters, etc. Section 62(2) provides that a director, promoter or any person who authorises the issue of the prospectus which contains untrue statements is not liable to pay compensation to the aggrieved allottee if they prove any of the following:

(i) that having consented to become a director of the company, he withdrew his consent before the issue of the prospectus and the prospectus was issued without his consent,
(ii) that the prospectus was issued without his knowledge or consent and that on becoming aware of its issue he promptly gave reasonable public notice that it was issued without his knowledge or consent,
(iii) that after the issue of prospectus and before allotment thereunder, he on becoming aware of the untrue statement withdrew his consent thereto and gave reasonable public notice of his withdrawal and the reason therefore,
(iv) that he had reasonable ground to believe and did upto the time of allotment believe that the statement was true,
(v) that the statement, if it is made by an official person, was a correct and fair representation of the statement of the official person and if it is an extract or copy of an official document was a correct and fair copy of the document.

Right of Contribution

Every person who becomes liable to make any payment under Section 62 may recover, contribution from other guilty persons who are liable for fraudulent misrepresentations in the prospectus [Section 62(5)]125.

(2) Liability for damages for non-compliance with Section 56

The omission from the prospectus of a matter required to be included by Section 56 may give rise to an action for damages at the instance of a subscriber for shares who has suffered loss thereby, even if the omission does not make the prospectus false or misleading. The Act does not say that the directors will be liable but this seems to be implied from Section 56(4).

(3) Liability under the General Law

Under the General Law, a shareholder can hold all or any of the persons responsible for the issue of a prospectus liable for any mis-statement or fraud on their or his part if he was actually deceived by reason of his having acted on the faith of the mis-statement or fraud in the prospectus. According to Section 17 of the Indian Contract Act 1872, fraud means and included, *inter alia*, the suggestion as a fact, of that which is not true by one who does not believe it to be true and active concealment of a fact by one having knowledge or belief at the fact.

A person can only liable in fraud in a prospectus where he makes a statement to be acted upon by others, which is false and is made (a) knowingly, or (b) without belief on its truth, or (c) recklessly, not caring whether it was true or false (*Derry v. Peek*[126]).

The remedy under General Law is also available (a) where the right of rescission as against the company is lost through negligence, and (b) where the company goes into liquidation.

Criminal Liability

Where a prospectus contains any untrue statement, every person who authorised the issue of prospectus is punishable with imprisonment which may extend to two years or with fine which may extend to Rs. 5000/- or with both [Section 63(1)]. He may, however, escape liability if he proves:

(i) that the statement was immaterial, or
(ii) that he has reasonable grounds to believe, and did upto the time of the issue of the prospectus believe, that the statement was true.

An expert who has signed u/s 58 and u/s 60(3) as merely an expert shall not be deemed to have authorised that issue of the prospectus under this section [Section 63 (2)].

The punishment for issuing an application for shares or debentures that is not accompanied with the prospectus is a fine which may extend to Rs. 5000/- [Section 56(3)].

Penalty for fraudulently inducing persons to invest money (Section 68)

Section 68 provides that any person who, either knowingly or recklessly makes any statement, promise or forecast which is false, deceptive or misleading or by any dishonest concealment of material facts, induces or attempts to induce another person to enter into or to offer to into any agreement for or with a view to acquiring, disposing of, subscribing for, underwriting shares or debentures shall be punishable with imprisonment for a term which may extend to 5 years or with fine which may extend to 5 years or with fine which may extend to Rs. 10000/- or with both.

Section 68 is expected to serve as a sufficient deterrent to unscrupulous company promoters against making untrue and deceptive statements in a prospectus with a view to obtaining capital from the public.

Allotment of Shares in Fictitious Names Prohibited (Section 68-A)

Following acts are punishable with imprisonment for a term extending to five years:

(i) making any application to a Company for acquiring or subscribing for, any shares therein under a fictitious name, or
(ii) making a company to allot or register any transfer of shares therein to any other person in a fictitious name.

Also this section should be prominently reproduced both in the prospectus as well as in application forms for shares.

Minimum Subscription (Section 69)

'Minimum subscription' is the amount stated in a prospectus as the minimum amount which, in the opinion of the Board of directors, shall be raised by the issue of share capital in order to provide for the matters specified below:

(i) The purchase price of any property purchased or to be purchased which is to be defrayed in whole or in part out of the proceeds of the issue,
(ii) any preliminary expenses payable by the company, and commission so payable to any person in consideration of his agreeing to subscribe for or of his procuring or agreeing to procure subscriptions for any shares in the company,
(iii) the repayment of any moneys borrowed by the company in respect of any of the above-mentioned matters,

(iv) working capital
(v) any other expenditure stating the nature and purpose thereof and the estimated amount in each case.

The amount that would be received against shares in cash, cheque or any other instrument which has been paid is counted in the minimum subscription, shares allotted for consideration other than cash are not to be included in the minimum subscription.

All moneys received from applicants for shares shall be deposited and kept deposited in a scheduled bank until the minimum subscription has been received by the money.

Commencement of Business (Section 149)

All kinds of private companies, whether limited by shares, limited by guarantee or unlimited can commence business immediately after their incorporation whereas a public company can do so only after it obtains a certificate of commencement of business.

Public Company issuing a prospectus

Where a Company having a share capital has issued a prospectus inviting the public to subscribe for its shares, it can commence business or exercise borrowing powers if the following conditions are satisfied:

(i) the minimum subscription has been raised,
(ii) every director of the company has paid to the company, on each of the shares taken by him or agreed to be taken by him the amount payable by him on application and allotment of the shares in cash,
(iii) no money is repayable to applicants for any shares or debentures offered for public subscription by reason of any failure to apply for or to obtain stock exchange permission,
(iv) there has been filed with the Registrar a duly verified declaration by one of the directors or the secretary that the above provisions have been complied with.

Public Company not issuing a prospectus

Where a company having a share capital has not issued a prospectus inviting the public to subscribe for its shares, it can commence business or exercise borrowing powers if the following conditions are fulfilled [Section 149(1)] —

(i) there has been filed with the Registrar a Statement in lieu of prospectus,
(ii) every director of the company has paid to the company on each of the shares taken by him or agreed to be taken by him the amount payable by him on application and allotment,
(iii) there has been filed with the Registrar a duly verified declaration by one of the directors or the secretary that the above provisions have been complied with [Section 149(2)].

The Registrar shall, on the filing of a duly verified declaration in accordance with the above provisions, certify that the company is entitled that the company is so entitled [Section 149(3)].

The provisions contained in Section 149 do not apply to a private company [Section 149(7)].

CHAPTER

42

Shareholders and Members

Definition of a Member

The definition of a member of company is given in Section 41 of the Companies Act in the following words:

1. The subscribers of the memorandum of a company shall be deemed to have agreed to become members of the company and on its registration, shall be entered as members in its register of members.
2. Every other person who agrees in writing to become a member of a company and whose name is entered in its register of members shall be a member of the company.

On this basis, two pre-requisites for a person to become a member of a company are:

(i) the agreement in writing to take shares of the company, and
(ii) the registration of his name in its registration of his name in its register of members;

Thus, the test of membership is whether the name of a person appears on the company's register of members. If his name appears on the register of members, then only can he be treated as a member of the company. Thus a person cannot be a member until his name is entered in the register of members.

Member and Shareholder

The 'members' or 'Shareholders' of a company are the persons who collectively constitute the company as a corporate entity. The words 'member' and 'shareholder' are used interchangeably (*Balkrishna Gupta v. Swadeshi Polytex Ltd.*[127]). They are synonymous in the case of a company limited by shares, a company limited by guarantee and having a share capital and an unlimited company whose capital is held in definite shares. But in the case of an unlimited company or a company limited by guarantee, a member may not be a shareholder, for such a company may not have a share capital. Contrarily, the bearer of a share warrant is a shareholder, but not a member, as his name is struck off the register of members [*Sri Kanta Data v. Venkateshwara Real Estate Enterprises (P) Ltd.*[128]].

A shareholder may be distinguished from a member as follows:

1. A registered shareholder is a member but a registered member may not be a shareholder because the company may not have a share capital.
2. A person who owns a bearer share warrant is a shareholder but he is not a member as his name is struck off the register of members [Section 115(1)]. This means that a person can be a holder of shares without being a member.
3. A legal representative of a deceased member is not a member until he applies for registration. He is, however, a shareholder even though his name does not appear in the register of members.

Mode of Acquiring Membership

A person may become a member in a company in any of the following ways:

1. Membership by Subscription

"The subscribers of the memorandum of a company shall be deemed to have agreed to become members of the company, and on its registration, shall be entered as members in its register of members" [Section 41(i)]. Thus, neither an application nor allotment of shares is necessary (*Official Liquidator v. Suleman Bhai*[128]).

2. Membership by Application and Registration

Apart from the subscribers of Memorandum, "every other person, who agrees in writing to become a member and whose name is entered in the register of members, is a member of the Company [Section 41(2)]. The words 'in writing' were added by the Companies (Amendment) Act, 1960. It follows that except in the case of the subscribers to the memorandum, a person does not become member of the company, until his name is duly recorded in the register of members.

In *Shri Balaji Textiles Mills Pvt. Ltd. v. Ashok Kamble*[129], it was held that the requirement of application in writing was not an essential conditions for a member to file a petition for relief against alleged oppression and mismanagement, since other evidence was available to show that petitioner was member of the Company.

Registration of the name of a person as a member of a company may arise from anyone of the following ways:

(i) By application and allotment

An application for shares is an offer to take shares, allotment is acceptance of the offer by the company which creates a binding contract between the applicant and the company.

The application may be absolute or conditional. If it is absolute, an allotment and its notice is a sufficient acceptance. If it is conditional, the allotment must be according to the terms of the application, otherwise there will be no contract.

In *Aldborough Hotel Co., Re Simpson's case*[130],

S, a builder, wrote to a hotel Company offering to take up 300 shares on the condition that a contract for alterations to the hotel would be given to him. His offer was accepted and 300 shares were allotted to him. Such a contract was never made and the Company went into liquidation.

Held, S was not liable as a contributory for the amount unpaid on the 300 shares because his agreement to take the shares was conditional on the contract for alterations being given to him.

(ii) By Transfer

A person may purchase shares in the open market. he becomes a member when the transfer of shares is effected and his name is entered in the register of members.

(iii) By Succession

A person becomes a shareholder by transmission of shares through death, lunacy, or insolvency of member.

The official Receiver or Assignee is also entitled to be a member is place of the shareholder who has been adjudicated insolvent.

(iv) By Estoppel

If a person holds himself out in writing or allows his name to be on the register of members, he is deemed to be a member of the company. Thus, if a person's name is improperly placed on the register of the members, and he knows and assents to it, he cannot afterwards say that he is not a member. Estoppel is simply a rule of evidence which prevents a person from denying the legal implications of his conduct.

3. Membership by Qualification Shares

The Companies Act 1956 does not require directors to hold any shares at all. If Articles of Association of a company require a person to hold qualification shares then he can be appointed as a director only if he takes or signs an undertaking to take and pay for the qualification shares. He, thus, becomes a member and is in the same position as a subscriber to the memorandum of the Company is.

How May Become a Member?

The Act does not prescribe any qualifications for becoming a member of a Company. But however, since the membership involves an agreement to become a member, he must be a person competent to contract as per the Indian Contract Act 1872. Thus any person who is competent to contract (Section 11 of the Indian Contract Act, 1872) may become a member of a company. This is subject to the provisions of the memorandum and the Articles of the Company. The Articles may provide that certain persons cannot become members of the company. The position of certain persons in this regard is given below:

(a) Minor

The position of a minor as a member of a company is summarised as under:

(i) A minor is incompetent to become the member of a company because an agreement with a minor is absolutely void (*Mohari Bibi v. Dharamadas Ghose*[131]).

If an application for shares is made by a father as guardian of his minor child, company registers the shares in the name of the child describing him as a minor, neither the minor nor the guardian can be placed on the list of contributories at the time of winding up.

In *Palaniappa Mudaliar v. Official Liquidator, Pasupathi Bank Ltd.*[132], an application for shares in a company was made by a father on behalf of his minor daughter. The company registered the shares in the name of the daughter described as minor. Subsequently it went into liquidation.

Held, the agreement with minor was void and the father, who signed the application, could not be deemed to have contracted for the shares, and thus could not be placed on the list of contributories.

(ii) If shares are allotted to a minor in response to his application and his name entered on the Register of members, in ignorance of the fact of minority, the company can repudiate the allotment and remove his name from the Register on coming to know of the minority of the member. The company must repay all moneys received from him in respect of the allotted shares.

The minor can also repudiate the allotment during his minority and he shall be returned the amount he paid towards the allotment of shares.

(iii) If the name of the minor continues on the Register of members and neither party repudiates the allotment, the minor does not incur any liability on the shares during minority and he cannot be held a contributory at the time of winding up (*Fazabhoy Jaffar v. The Credit Bank of India*[133]).

(iv) An agreement in writing for a minor to become a member may be signed on behalf of the minor by his lawful guardian and the registration of a transfer of shares in the name of the minor, acting through his or her guardian, specially where the shares are fully paid, cannot be refused on the ground of the transferee being a minor (*Nandita Jain v. Bennet Coleman and Co. Ltd.* [134]).

(b) Company

A company, being an artificial person and a separate legal entity may become a member of another company, if it is so authorised by its memorandum to purchase shares. (Section 391 and 494). But a company cannot become a member of itself, i.e., it cannot purchase its own shares [Section 77(1)].

In *Trevor v. Whitworth,*[135] a company was authorised by its Articles to purchase its own shares.

W sold his shares to company. Before the full price of the shares was paid, the company went into liquidation. W claimed to prove in the liquidation for the balance of the price of the shares. Held, the transaction was *ultra vires* the company as the company had no power to purchase its own shares, and hence the claim of W failed.

A company cannot lend money to anyone for the purpose of purchasing its own shares [Section 77(2)].

(c) Insolvent

An insolvent may be a member of a company. So long as his name appears in the register of members, he is entitled to vote even though his shares vest in the official Assignee or Receiver.

(d) Partnership firm

Since a partnership firm has no legal personality, it cannot purchase shares in a company in its own name. However, partners, either individually or in their joint names (as joint members) may hold shares in a company as a part of the partnership property.

(e) Joint Hindu Family

It can have shares in the name of its Karta.

(f) Foreigner

A foreigner may become a member of a company, but if at any time he becomes an alien enemy, his right as a member of the company are suspended.

(g) Joint Holders

The shares of a company may also be held jointly by two or more persons. In a Public Company, even joint shareholders are counted as separate members but in a Private Company joint holders are treated as a single member.

Cessation of Membership

A person may cease to be a member of a company.

(1) By an act of parties

(2) By operation of Law.

1. By an act of the parties

A person may cease to be a member of a company —

(a) if he transfers his shares to another person.

(b) by the sale of his shares by the company in exercise of right of lien over his shares.

(c) by forfeiture of his shares

(d) by a valid surrender of his shares.

(e) if redeemable preference shares are redeemed.

(f) if he rescinds the contract to take shares on the ground of misrepresentation in the prospectus or on the ground of irregular allotment.

(g) if share warrants are issued to him in exchange of fully paid shares.

2. By operation of Law

(a) The shares of an insolvent vest in the Official Receiver or Assignee. When the official Receiver or Assignee transfers his shares to another person, the insolvent ceases to be a member on the registration of the transferee as a member. But the insolvent remains a member as long as his name appears in the register of the company (*Wise v. Lansdell*)[136].

(b) By the death of a member, the estate of the deceased remains liable until the shares are registered in the name of his legal representative.

(c) During the winding up of a company a member continues to be liable as a contributory and is also entitled to share in the surplus assets, if any.

Duties, Liabilities and Rights

Duties

Followings are the duties of a shareholder —

(a) as a subscriber of the memorandum to take the shares written opposite his name direct from the company and pay for it,

(b) to take shares when they are duly allotted to him and pay for them according to the terms of issue of shares,

(c) to pay all valid calls as and when they are made,

(d) to abide by the decisions of the majority of members unless the majority act vindictively, oppressively, malafide or fraudulently,

(e) to contribute to the assets of the company when it goes into liquidation.

Liability of Members

Liability of members of a company depends upon the nature of the company.

(a) Unlimited Company

Each member is liable in full for all debts contracted by the company during the period he was a member.

(b) Company Limited by Guarantee

Each member is liable to contribute the amount guaranteed by him to be paid.

(c) Company Limited by Shares

In the case of such companies, the liability of a member is limited to the amount unpaid on the shares held by him. Thus, a member is not required to pay more than the value of his shares or so much amount on his shares as remains unpaid.

Rights of Members

The rights of members of a company can be classified under following three heads:

(A) Statutory Rights

These rights are given to the members by the Companies Act. These rights can not be taken away or modified by any provision in the memorandum or the articles of association. Such rights, for example, are:

(a) right of priority to have shares offered in case of increase of capital (Section 81)
(b) right to transfer shares (Section 82).
(c) right to receive notice of meetings, attend and vote at the meeting (Section 172).
(d) right to receive a share certificate (Section 113).
(e) right to participate in the appointment of auditors and directors, etc. at the annual general meeting (Section 224-225).
(f) right to receive copies of annual accounts of the company (Section 210 and 219).
(g) right to make an application to the Company Law Board for ordering an investigation into the affairs of the company (Section 235).
(h) right to present a petition to the Company Law Board for relief in case of oppression and mismanagement (Section 399).
(i) right to petition to the High Court for the winding up of the Company (Section 439).

(B) Documentary Rights

These rights are given to the members by the memorandum of association and articles of association.

(C) Legal rights

These rights are given to members under General Law, for example, in case of any mis-statement or concealment of a material fact in a prospectus, a person who has applied on the faith of such prospectus and has been allotted shares or debentures, can avoid the contract and claim damages under the General Law.

Right of Shareholders in the property of a Company

An incorporated company's assets are the property of the company and not that of its shareholders (*George Newman and Co., Re*[137]). No shareholder, therefore, has any right to any item of property owned by the Company for he has no legal or equitable interest therein. He is entitled to a share in the profits while the company continues to carry on business and a share in the distribution of the surplus assets when the company is wound up (*Bacha F. Guzdar v. Commissioner of Income Tax, Bombay*). [138] In *R.C. Cooper v. Union of India* following observation made.

"A Company registered under the Companies Act is a legal person separate and distinct from its individual members. Property of the company is not that of the shareholders. A shareholder has merely an interest in the Company arising under its Articles of Association."

Register and Index of Members

Register of Members

It is the statutory obligation of every company to maintain a register of its members containing the following particulars:

(a) Name and address and the occupation of each member,
(b) Number of shares held by each member, the amount paid or agreed to be considered as paid,
(c) The date of which each person was entered in the register as a member.
(d) The date at which any person ceased to be a member.

If the company has converted any of its shares into stock and given notice of the conversion to the Registrar, the register shall show the amount of stock held by each member instead of shares.

No notice of any trust, express, implied or constructive, is allowed to be entered on the register.

Declaration is also to be made to the public trustee in certain cases.

If any fault is made in maintaining the register in the above manner, the company and every officer of the company, who is in default, is punishable with the fine which may extend to Rs. 50 for every day during which the default continues (Section 150).

Index of Members (Section 150)

Every company having more than fifty members must keep an index of members, unless the register is already in the form of an index. Any alteration in the register of members must be noted in the index within 14 days alteration. The index must, in respect of each member, containing a sufficient indication to enable the entries relating to that member in the register to be readily found. The index must always be kept at the same place as the register of members.

If default is made in complying with the provisions of Section 151, the company and every officer of the company, who is in default, shall be punishable with fine which may extend to Rs. 50.

Place of Keeping of Register

The register and index of members shall be kept at the registered office of the company. These may, however, be kept at any other place within the city town or village in which the registered office of the company is situate provided—

(a) that place has been approved by a special resolution passed by the company in general meeting, and

(b) the Registrar has been given in advance a copy of the proposed special resolution.

Inspection of Register and Index

A company's register of members and index is a public document and open to inspection except when closed index the provisions of the Act, by members and debenture holders free and by other persons on payment of such sum as may be prescribed for each inspection, for at least two hours a day during business hours.

The right to inspect also includes the right to make extracts from the register (*British India Corporation Ltd. v. Robert Menzies*) [139]. The company is also sound to supply on demand a copy of the register on a payment of such sum as may be prescribed for every 100 words or fractional part thereof. The company shall send any copy required by any person within a period of 10 working days.

Power to close register (Section 154)

A company may close the register of members for a total period of 45 days in a year and not exceeding 30 days at anyone time. The company shall give at least 7 days previous notice of the closure of the register by advertisement in some newspaper circulating in the district in which the registered office of the company is situate. During the period of closure, no transfer of shares can take place and therefore, the company may determine its membership and may send notices of general meetings and calls made and also the dividend warrants to is members.

Rectification of register of members (Section 111)

The register of members is *prima facie* evidence of any matters which the Act directs or authorises to be inserted in but application for ratification of the register may be made to the Company Law Board by any person aggrieved or any member of the company itself, if—

(a) the name of any person is without sufficient cause entered or omitted in the register of members of a company or

(b) default is made, or unnecessary delay takes place, in entering in the register the fact of any person having become, or ceased to be, a member.

The company Law Board may, after hearing the parties, either reject the application or direct rectification of the register and also direct the company to pay damages, if any, sustained by any party aggrieved.

If default is made in giving effect to the orders of the Company Law Board under Section 111, the company and every officer of the company, who is in default, shall be punishable with fine which may extend to Rs. 1000 and with a further fine which may extend to Rs. 100 for every day after the first day after which the default continues.

Annual Returns (Section 159-161)

Every company shall file with the Registrar an annual return containing certain particulars.

1. Annual return by company having share capital (Section 159)

Every company having a share capital shall within 60 days from the date of the annual general meeting prepare and file every year with the Registrar a return known as 'annual return', containing following particulars specified in part I and II of schedule V.

(1) Registered office,
(2) Register of members,
(3) Register of debenture holders,
(4) Shares and debentures,
(5) Indebtedness,
(6) Members and debenture holders, past and present, and
(7) Its directors, managing directors, managers and secretary, past and present,
(8) Name and addresses of and number of equity shares held by each of the following namely:
    (a) Foreign holdings,
    (b) Government-sponsored financial institutions,
    (c) Bodies corporates [not covered under (a) and (b) above],
    (d) Directors and their relatives, their shareholdings and directorships,
    (e) Other top 50 shareholders.

The copy of the annual return filed with the Registrar shall be signed by a director and by the manager or secretary, if any or by 2 directors.

The return shall be accompanied with a certificate signed likewise stating, that the return states facts as they stood on the day of annual general meeting.

Where the annual general meeting for any year has not been held, any reference to day on which any annual general meeting is construed as a reference to the latest day on or before which that meeting should have been held in accordance with the provisions of the Act.

The fact that no general meeting was held is no justification for not complying with the requirements of Section 159 (*State of Bombay v. Bhandan Ram Bhandari*).[140]

II. Annual return by company not having a share capital (Section 160)

Every company not having a share capital shall within 60 days from the day on which each of the annual general meetings is held, prepare and file with the registrar a return stating the following particulars as they stood on that day.

(a) Registered office,
(b) Name of members and respective dates on which they became members,
(c) Names of persons who ceased to be members since the date of annual general meeting of the immediately preceding year, and the dates on which they so ceased.
(d) Particulars regarding its directors, managers and its secretary.
(e) A statement containing the particulars of the total amount of indebtedness of the company in respect of charges which are to be registered with the Registrar.

The return shall be annexed the following certificates to the returns:

(i) that the returns state the facts as they stood on the day of the annual general meeting.
(ii) that since the date of the lost annual return the transfer of all shares and debentures and the issue of all further certificates of shares and debentures have been recorded on the books maintained for the purpose,
(iii) In the case of a Private Company:
    (a) That the company has not issued any invitation to the public to subscribe for any shares or debentures of the company.
    (b) That irrespective of its paid-up share capital the company did not have during the relevant period an average turnover of rupees one crore or more,
    (c) That since the date of the annual general meeting, the company did not held 25% or more of the paid-up share capital of one or more public companies.

The copy of the annual return filed with the Registrar shall be singed by a director and by the manager or secretary, if any or by two directors.

CHAPTER

43

Share Capital

Meaning of Capital

Capital in ordinary sense denotes the value of some accumulated goods. In the business world, capital means finance or that part of money which is invested for earnings. Such money comes out of savings. A body corporate needs such finance or capital to carry out its activities. This is contributed by the members who join the body corporate whether at the time of incorporation or afterwards.

Definition of Capital

The Act does not define capital from Section 12.We may deduce that capital of a company comes either in the form of share capital or guarantee capital. There are companies where both types of capital simultaneously exist.

Share Capital

The common form of capital of a company is the 'Share Capital'. Share capital means the capital raised by a company by the issue of shares. The Act has not defined the term' Share Capital'. Section 13 (4) (a) states that unless the company is an unlimited company, the memorandum shall also state the amount of share capital with which the company is to be registered and the division thereof into shares of a fixed amount.

Types of Share Capital

The share capital is of different types and the classification is primarily based on time sequence.

They are:

(1) Nominal Authorised or Registered Capital

The is the capital with which a company is registered. In fact, authorised capital is no capital in real sense. It is the limit upto which the company can raise capital. This is the maximum capital which the company will have during its lifetime. When the original amount of the authorised capital is exhausted by issue of shares, it can be increased by passing an ordinary resolution.

(2) Issued Capital

Issued capital is the nominal value of the shares which are offered to the public for subscription.

A company does not normally issue all its capital at once, so that issued capital in such a case is less than the nominal capital. The issued capital an never exceed the nominal capital; it can at the most be equal to the nominal capital.

(3) Subscribed Capital

This is that part of issued capital which is taken up by subscribers for consideration of cash.

The amount of subscribed capital is either equal to or less than the issued capital. The subscribed capital can never be more than the issued capital.

(4) Called up Capital

The company may not call up full amount of the face value of the shares. Thus, the called-up capital represents the total amount called-up on the shares subscribed. The amount of called-up capital can be either equal to or less than the subscribed capital.

Thus uncalled capital represents the total amount not called up on shares subscribed, and the shareholders continue to be liable to pay the amounts as and when called. However, the company may reserve all or part of the uncalled capital, which can then be called in the event of the company being wound up. For this purpose, a special resolution is required to be passed, and then it known as Reserve Capital or Reserve Liability (Section 99).

Paid-up Capital

It is the total amount of capital paid up or credited as paid-up on shares issued, including premium on shares.

Kinds of Shares Capital

According to Section 86, the capital of a company may be of two kinds:

(i) Preference shares capital.

(ii) Ordinary shares (Equity share capital)

(i) Preference Shares Capital

Preference shares capital means, in the case of a company limited by shares, that part of the capital of the company which carries a preferential rights as to—

(a) Payment of dividend during the lifetime of the company, and

(b) Return of capital on winding up [Section 85 (1)].

Preference shares may be

(i) Cumulative and non-cumulative,

(ii) Participating and

(iii) Redeemable.

2. Ordinary Shares (Equity Share Capital)

Equity shares capital means all share capital which is not preference share capital [Section 85 (2)].

Alteration of Share Capital (Section 94)

Section 94 provides that, if the articles authorise, a company limited by share capital may, by an ordinary resolution passed in general meeting, alter the conditions of its memorandum in regard to capital so as:

(1) to increase its authorised share capital by such amount as its thinks expedient by issuing fresh shares;

(2) to consolidate and divide all or any of its share capital into shares of large amount than its existing shares,

(3) to convert all or any of its fully paid-up shares into stock, and reconvert the stock into fully paid-up shares of any denomination,

(4) to sub-divide its shares, or any of them, into shares of smaller amount than fixed by the memorandum, but the proportion paid and unpaid on each share must remain the same,

(5) to cancel shares which, at the date of the passing of the resolution in that behalf, have not been taken or agreed to be taken by any person.

A cancellation of shares, is not deemed to be a reduction of share capital within the meaning of the companies Act, 1956. The company must give notice of the above alteration to the registrar within 30 days after doing so (Section 95 and 97).

Reduction of Share Capital

The capital of the company is the primary consolation to the creditors. Reduction of capital without sanction of the court or without the approval of the creditor is a deceit. The depletion of fund out of which the creditors of the company are paid means betrayal of the trust of the creditors. So, Company Law which is designed to protect the interest of the creditors and the public provides strict procedures for reduction of capital.

Section 100-105 provide for the reduction of share capital. Under Section 100, a company limited by guarantee and having a share capital may reduce its share capital if so authorised by its articles by a special resolution, in any way by:

(i) extinguishing or reducing the liability on any of its shares, [Section 100 (1) (a)) or

(ii) cancelling any paid-up capital which is lost or is unrepresented by any available assets, [Section 100 (1) (b)] or

(iii) Paying off any paid-up share capital which is in excess of the wants of the company, [Section 100 (1) (c)].

Procedure for reduction of share capital (Section 100-103)

1. Special Resolution

(a) The reduction of share capital must be authorised by the articles. If the articles do not contain any such provision, they must first be changed by a special resolution to that effect.

(b) The reduction of share capital must be passed by a special resolution at the general meeting of the company.

2. Application to the Court

The company shall then apply to the court by petition for an order confirming the reduction of capital [Section 101 (1)]. The main duty of the court is to look after the interests of the creditors and different classes of shareholders. The court may fulfill this duty towards them in the following manner:

(a) where reduction of capital involves either diminution of liability or return of paid-up share capital, or repayment of amount already paid on any share [Section 101 (2) (a)]. The court shall direct that it will take effect subject to the following conditions,

(b) Every creditor on a fixed day shall, by entitled to object to the proposed reduction.

(c) The court there after shall settle a list of bonafide creditors. It may also extend the time by issue of notice within which the creditors not entered on the list may file objections or may excluded from right of objection (5) [Section 101 (2) (b)].

(d) Where a creditor entered on the list does not consent to reduction and his debt is not discharged or determined by the company, the court may either have his interest secured or, if it thinks fit, dispense with his consent [Section 101 (2) c and (3)].

The court on being satisfied that every creditor of the company who has objected to the reduction has been paid of his debt or claim may make an order confirming the reduction of such terms and conditions as it deems fit and proper [Section 102 (1)].

In ordering the reduction the court may also direct that the company will have to observe the following conditions:

(a) That the company will add to its name "and reduced" as the last words for a specified period. The company may also be directed to publish reasons for the reduction for public information [Section 102 (2)].

The addition of the words 'and reduced' is required in order to give warning to the public financial position of the company (*Pinkney and Sons Steamship Co. Ltd. Re.*).[141]

(b) That the company will publish the reason for reduction or such other information as the court thinks fit.

The court shall also see, before confirming reduction of capital, that the reduction is fair and equitable as between different classes of shareholders in the company. The scheme for reduction of capital is obviously fair if it involves proportionate reduction of share capital in respect of all classes of shares.

3. Registration of Order of Court with Registrar

The order of the court confirming the reduction shall be produced before the Registrar along with following documents.

(a) a certified copy of the order and

(b) a minutes approved by the board showing the following information:

- (i) The amount of share capital.
- (ii) The number of shares into which it is to be divided.
- (iii) The amount of each share.
- (iv) The amount, if any, at the date of the registration deemed to be paid upon each share.

The Registrar shall then certify under his hand that the order and the minutes have been duly registered. This certificate shall be the conclusive evidence that all the statutory requirements for reduction of capital have been complied with by the company [Section 103 (4)].

The resolution for reducing capital as confirmed by the order of court shall take effect on its registration by the Registrar [Section 103 (2)]. Notice of the registration shall be published in such manner as the court may direct [Section 103 (3)].

Penalty

Section 105 provides for punishment with imprisonment extending to one year or with fine or both, if any officer of the company knowingly conceals the name of any creditor entitled to object to the reduction or misrepresents the nature or amount of claim or debts (i.e., enables) such concealment or misrepresentation.

Reduction of Share Capital without the Sanction of The Court

There are some cases in which there is reduction of share capital and no confirmation by the court is necessary. These are:

(i) Where shares are forfeited for non-payment of calls.

(ii) When capital is paid off out of accumulated profits.

(iii) When shares are cancelled by ordinary resolution under Section 94 (1) (e).

(iv) Where shares are surrendered on grounds similar to forfeiture.

Reduction of Capital and Diminution of Capital

Reduction of capital involves working off past losses against capital cancellation of the uncalled capital or repayment of surplus capital. It may involve reduction of issued capital, subscribed or paid up share capital. Diminution of capital denotes cancellation of the authorised or issued capital (but not subscribed). Diminution of capital does not constitute a reduction of capital within the meaning of the Companies Act.

Distinction

(1) Diminution of capital is the reduction of the issued capital. Reduction of capital involves reduction of subscribed or paid up capital, there is no reduction of issued capital.

(2) Both require authorisation by Articles but whereas 'diminution' can be effected by an ordinary resolution (if so authorised by Articles), reduction of capital cannot be effected without passing a special resolution.

(3) 'Reduction' requires confirmation by court (Section 100) but 'diminution' needs no confirmation by the court (Section 94).

(4) In case of 'reduction', court may order the company to add the words' and reduced' after its name [Section 102 (3)] but no such order can be passed in case of diminution (Section 94).

(5) In case of 'diminution', notice is to be given to Registrar within 30 days from the date of cancellation where upon the Registrar shall record the notice and make the necessary alteration in the memorandum of Association and Articles of Association. In case of reduction more detailed procedure has been prescribed though there is no time limit as in case of diminution'.

Liability of Members After Reduction (Section 104)

A member of the company, past or present, cannot be held liable for an amount exceeding the difference between the amount deemed to have been paid on his shares and the nominal value of the reduced shares. However, in one circumstance, a shareholder who was a member of the company at the time of registration of the order for reduction, may be called upon to pay the original nominal value of the shares instead of the reduced value. Where a creditor having the right to object to a reduction may have been lift out of the list of creditors and subsequently the company has become unable to pay its debts, the court may in such a case, order the number to that amount on their shares which they would have been liable to pay before the reduction, so as to meet the claim of such a creditor.

Shareholder's Pre Emptive Right

If a company limited by shares proposes its subscribed share capital by allotment of further shares after the expiry of two years from the formation of the company or after the expiry of one year from the first allotment of shares, which ever is earlier, it must offer these new shares to the existing equity shareholders in the ratio of shares held by them. This right of shareholders to 'be offered new shares to them before they are offered to the public is known as shareholders right of pre-emption. Section 81 deals with this point. The object of this Section is to prevent—

(a) discrimination among shareholders by ensuring equitable distribution of shares among them, and

(b) directors from offering shares to outsiders before they are offered to the shareholders, Section 81 days down the following procedure in regard to further allotment of shares:

(1) Offer to the Existing Shareholders

Such further shares shall be offered to the existing equity shareholders of the company in proportion, as nearly by an circumstances admit, to the capital paid up on those shares at that date.

In *Gas Meter Co. Ltd. v. Diaphragm and General Leather Co. Ltd.*[142], the articles of Diaphragm Company provided that the new shares, should first be offered to the existing shareholders.

The company offered new shares to all shareholders excepting Gas Meter Company which held its controlling shares. Held Diaphragm Company could be restrained from doing.

(2) Notice of Offer

The offer shall be made by notice specifying the number of shares offered. The notice shall give at least 15 days from the date of the offer within which the offer may be accepted. If the offer is not accepted within this period, it shall be deemed to have been declined.

(3) Shareholder's right of Renunciation

Unless the articles of the company otherwise provide, the notice should also inform the shareholders that they have the right to renounce (give up) all or any of the shares offered to them in favour of the nominees.

(4) Refusal by Shareholder

After the expiry of the time specified in the notice or on receipt of earlier intimation from the person to whom such notice is given that he declines to accept the shares offered, the Board of directors may dispose them of in such manner as they think most beneficial to the company.

Offer of New Shares to Outsiders

The new share of the company may be offered to outsiders or any persons (including the equity shareholders): —

(a) If a special resolution to that effect is passed is passed by the company in general meeting authorising the Board to allot shares to outsiders,

(b) Where no such special resolution is passed, if the company at the general meeting passes an ordinary resolution to that effect and the approval of the Central Government is obtained. The Central Government will accord its approval if it is satisfied on an application by the Board of directors that the proposal is most beneficial to the company,

(c) If any shareholder to whom the shares are offered declines to accept the shares. In such a case the Board of directors may dispose of the shares in such manner as they think most beneficial to the company.

(d) If the new shares are issued within two years from the formation of the company or one year of the allotment made for the first time, whichever is earlier.

The above provisions do not apply to a private company.

Conversion of Loans and Debentures into Shares

The power of conversion has been granted to the Central Government by the Companies Amendment Act 1963. Under this power, where a company has taken any loans from the Central Government by issuing any debentures or otherwise, the Government may, in the public interest, convert such debentures or loans into shares in the company. The terms and conditions of such conversion should be such as appear reasonable to the Central Government in the circumstances of the case.

In determining the terms and conditions of the conversion of loans and debentures into shares.

The Central Government must have due regard to: —

(a) The financial position of the company,

(b) The original terms of issue,

(c) The rate of interest on loans and debentures,

(d) The capital of the company, its liabilities, reserves and profits during the preceding five years and

(e) The current market value of company's shares [Section 81 (5)].

It may be noted that an order for conversion can be passed by the Central Government even if the terms of issue of such debentures or terms of such loan do not include a term providing for an option for such conversion.

A copy of every order proposed to be issued by the Central Government under sub-section 4 must be laid in draft before each House of Parliament [Section 81 (6)].

If the terms and conditions of conversion are not acceptable to the company, the company may prefer an appeal to the court within 30 days in regard to such terms and conditions. Subject to the decision of the court, the order of the Central Government shall be final and conclusive [Section 81 (4) to (7)].

Section 94-A (The Amendment Act of 1974) provides that where the Government or a public financial institution has converted its debentures into shares the capital of the company shall thereby stand increased by an equal amount and memorandum accordingly. The Central Government has to send a copy of the order to the Registrar so that he may effect the necessary alterations in the memorandum of the company.

Reorganisation of Share Capital

Reorganisation of share capital of a company can take place in following three ways:—

(1) by the consolidation of shares of different classes, or

(2) by the division of shares of one class into shares of different classes, or

(3) by both these methods [Section 390 (b)].

Where the reorganisation of share capital is proposed:

(a) between a company and its creditors, or

(b) between a company and its members,

The court in such a case can order a meeting of the creditors or members of the company [Section 391 (1)].

A majority of 3/4th is in value of the creditors or members present and voting either in person or by proxy at the meeting, should also agree to the re-organisation of share capital. The re-organisation should also be sanctioned by the court. If these conditions are satisfied, the re-organisation is binding on all the creditors or all the members and also on the company, or, in the case of a company which is being wound up, on the liquidator and contributories of the company, [Section 391 (2)].

The order of the court has no effect until a certified copy of the order has been filed with the Registrar [Section 391 (2)].

Variation of Rights of Shareholder's Rights (Section 106)

Where the share capital of a company is divided into different classes, of shares the rights attached to the shares of any class may be varied.

(i) with the consent in writing of the holders of not less then 3/4th of the issued shares of that class, or

(ii) with the sanction of a special resolution passed at a separate meeting of the holders of the issued shares of that class,

(iii) if permitted by memorandum and articles of the company, or

(iv) if such variation is not prohibited by the terms of issue of the shares of that class. Any such alteration of memorandum must be filed with the Registrar.

Rights of Dissentient Shareholders (Section 107)

The holders of not less than 10% of the issued shares of a class, who did not consent to or vote in favour of the resolution for the variation, may apply to the court for cancellation of such variation. Where such application is made, the variation shall have effect only if it is confirmed by the court. Application to the court should be made within 21 days after the date on which the consent was given or the resolution was passed. On any such application, the court grants a hearing to the applicants any other persons who apply to the court to be heard and appear to the court to be interested in the application. The court may, if it is satisfied, having regard to all the circumstances of the case, that the variation would unfairly prejudice the shareholders of the class represented by the applicants, disallow the variation, and shall, if not so satisfied, confirm the variation. The decision of the court on any such application is final. The company must, within 30 days, forward a copy of the order to the Registrar. If default is made, the company and every officer of the company, who is in default, are publishable with fine which may extend to Rs. 50 (Section 107).

Voting Rights (Section 87)

There are voting rights for all classes of shareholders. They are: —

Voting Rights of Equity Shareholders

Every member of a company limited by shares and holding any equity shares shall have a right to vote in respect of such capital on every resolution placed before the company his voting right on a poll shall be in proportion to his share of the paid-up equity capital of the company [Section 87 (1)].

Voting Rights of Preference Shareholders

Every member of a company limited by shares and holding any preference shares therein, shall in respect of such capital, have a right to vote only on resolutions place before the company which directly affect the rights attached to his preference shares, e.g., any resolution for winding up the company or for the repayment or reduction of its share capital.

However, the preference shareholder shall be entitled to vote on every resolution placed before the company at any meeting, if the dividend due on such capital or any part of dividend has remained unpaid.

(i) in the case of cumulative preference shares for a period of not less than two years preceding the date of commencement of the meeting, and

(ii) in the case of non-cumulative preference shares, either in respect of a period of not less than two years ending with the expiry of the financial year immediately preceding the commencement of the meeting or in respect of a period of not less than three years comprised in the six years ending with the expiry of the financial year preceding the meeting. The voting rights of the preference shareholders must be in the same proportion which the capital paid-up in respect of the preference shares bears to the total equity capital of the company [Section 87 (2)].

The articles of the company may provide that no member shall exercise any voting right in respect of any shares registered in his name on which any calls or other sums presently payable by him have not been paid, or in regard to which the company has exercised any right of lien.

The above rules do not apply to a private company which is not a subsidiary of a public company [Section 90 (2)].

Prohibition of Issue of Shares with disproportionate Rights (Section 88)

A company cannot issue fresh equity shares which carry voting rights or rights in the company as to dividend, capital or otherwise which are disproportionate to the rights attaching to the holders of existing equity shares.

SHARES

The capital of a company is divided into certain indivisible unit of a fixed amount. These units are called shares.

Definition

Section 2(46) of the Companies Act defines a 'Share' as under:

"A Share means Share in the share capital of a company. It includes stock except where a distinction between stock and shares is expressed or implied." The share capital of the company is divided into shares of different company is divided into shares of different denominations. These denominations are called 'Shares' which are issued by the company to the public for subscription to enable the company to raise its share capital.

(i) A share signifies the following:

It is the interest of a Shareholder in the company measured by a sum of money for the purpose of liability in the first place, and of interest of the shareholder in the company in the second (*Borland's Trustee v. Steel Broz Co. Ltd.*[143]).

(ii) It carries with it certain right and liabilities while the company is a going concern or while the company is being wound up. In this sense it may be defined as a bundle of rights and obligations (*Vishwanath v. East India Distilleries*).[144]

(iii) A share is not negotiable instrument. (*C.I.T. v. Associated Industrial Dev Co.*).[145]

A share is a personal estate capable of being transferred in the manner laid down in the articles of association. It is a movable property which can either be mortgaged or pledged. Share is included in the definition of goods under the provisions of the Sale of Goods Act 1930. Every Share issued by a company must be numbered so that one share may be distinguished from another share. A certificate of share issued by a company under its common seal specifies the shares held by any member. The Share certificate is the prima facie evidence of the title of the member to such shares [Section 84 (l)]. The Share certificate is not a negotiable instrument.

Each Share in a company having a share capital must be distinguished by its appropriate number [Section 83]. In the case of a company having a share capital, the memorandum must state the amount of share capital with which the company is to be registered and the division thereof into shares of a fixed amount [Section 13 (4)].

Stock and Shares

A limited company having a share capital may, if so authorised by its articles, convert all or any of its fully paid-up shares into stock and reconvert that stock into fully paid-up shares of any denomination [Section 94(1)(c)].

Shares can therefore be converted into stock when they are fully paid-up. The sum total of fully paid-up shares is stock. Fully paid-up shares may be converted into stock for purposes of convenience, as stock can be divided into fractions of any amount, irrespective of the original value of the shares. By the conversion of fully paid-up shares into stock, the company recognises the fact of the complete payment of the shares.

If the company has converted any shares into stock, the company shall, within 30 days after doing so, give notice thereof to the registrar (Section 95). all the provisions applicable to shares shall thereupon cease to apply to such stock (Section 96). The registrar of members shall show the amount of stock held by each of the members concerned instead of the shares so converted which were previously held by him (proviso to section 150).

Distinction Between Share and Stock

The principal difference between shares and stock has been stated by *Lord Cairns L.C. in Morrice v. Aylmer*,[146] as stated below:

1. Fully Paid-up

Shares mayor may not be fully paid-up where as the stock is always fully paid-up.

2. Nominal Value

Shares have a fixed nominal value. But stocks have no fixed nominal value.

3. Division into Fraction

Shares are described as indivisible units, whereas stock is a sum total of holding, shares cannot be divided into fractions, but it is possible to divide stock into a many fractions as the company deems fit.

4. Issued Originally

Shares can be issued originally direct to the public, whereas the stock cannot be directly offered by the company to the public in the first instance. The company can only convert the fully paid-up shares into stocks.

5. Formality for issue

Shares may be issued on the decision of the Board, but the issue of stock cannot be effected except by ordinary of the company where such power is conferred by the articles.

6. Numbering

Shares are numbered, but there is no necessity of numbering stock when the stock is of different denominations.

7. Registration

Registration of share capital with the Registrar is compulsory before issuing shares whereas stock can be issued only after passing an ordinary resolution, if articles permit, and after passing a special resolution in case the article do not permit, and filing a notice of conversion with the Registrar.

8. Member

A holder of share is the member of the company and the share certificate is a *prima facie* evidence of title, on the other hand, the stock holder is not necessarily a member.

Types of Shares

Before the companies Act, 1956 a company could issue the following kinds of shares:

(i) preference shares

(ii) ordinary shares

(iii) deferred shares or founder's shares

After the Companies Act 1956, according to section 86, a Company can issue only two kinds of shares:

(i) preference shares, and

(ii) ordinary shares

(i) Preference Shares

Preference Shares with reference to any company limited by shares are those which carries the following two conditions:

(a) a right to be paid a fixed amount of dividend or the amount of dividend calculated at a fixed rate and also.

(b) a right to be paid the amount of capital paid-up on such shares in the event of winding up of the company.

The articles of the company may provide some other preference too to the preference shareholders. Preference share capital is the sum total of preference shares [Section 85 (1)].

Kinds of Preference Shares

Following are the various kinds of preference shares:

(a) Cumulative Preference Shares

These shares are entitled to a fixed dividend whether there are profits or no profits. If the profits are not sufficient to pay dividends in a particular year, than the dividends are accumulated and paid in a succeeding year out of the profits along with the fixed dividends for that year. These shares are entitled to dividends only when there are sufficient profits available for distribution. As the dividends can be accumulated, they are called 'Cumulative Preference Shares'. It may be noted that if the company goes into liquidation, no arrears of dividend are payable, unless declared.

(b) Non Cumulative Preference Shares

These are the shares on which the dividend does not go on accumulating. If there are no profits or there are inadequate profits in any year, these shares will get no dividend or a partial dividend as they cannot claim arrears of dividends for any year out of the profits of the subsequent.

Preference Shares are presumed to be cumulative unless otherwise stated.

(c) Participating Preference Shares

These are preference shares which receive their fixed dividend e.g. 9% in the normal way, but which then participate further in the undistributed profits along with the equity shares after a certain fixed percentage has been paid on them as well. The holders of such shares may also be entitled to get a share in the surplus assets to the company on its winding up if a specific provision exists to that effect in the articles.

(d) Non-Participating Preference Shares

These shares are entitled to only a fixed rate of dividend and no participate further in the surplus profits, irrespective of the magnitude of such profit. If the articles are silent, all preference shares are deemed to be non-participating unless stated otherwise in the terms of issue.

(e) Convertible Preference Shares

The holders of these have a right to convert them into equity shares within a certain period.

(f) Non-Convertible Preference Shares

The preference shares without a right of conversion into equity shares are called non-convertible preference shares.

(g) Redeemable Preference Shares

Shares which can be purchased back by the company are called 'redeemable preference shares'.

The company reserves its right to call back or purchase the shares at any time subject to the provisions of its articles. A company limited by shares may issue "redeemable preference shares" if so authorised by its articles must authorise the redemption of the preference shares at the option of the company. The shares can be redeemed by the company subject to the following conditions only:

(i) The shares shall be redeemed only
   (a) out of the profits of the company, or
   (b) out of the proceeds of a fresh issue of shares made for purpose of redemption;

(ii) only such shares shall be redeemed which are fully paid-up.

(iii) The premium, if any, payable on redemption shall be provided for out of the profits of the company or out of the company's 'Shares premium account' before the shares are redeemed;

(iv) Where the shares are redeemed otherwise than out of the proceeds of fresh issue, then out of the profits which would otherwise have been available for dividend, there shall be transferred to a 'reserve fund' a sum equal to the nominal amount of the shares redeemed. Such 'reserve fund' shall be called 'the capital redemption reserve account'.

The capital redemption reserve account may be applied by the company in paying up unissued shares of the company to members of the company as fully paid-up bonus shares.

Subject to the above conditions, the redemption of preference shares may be effected on such terms and in such manner as may be provided by the articles of the company.

The redemption of preference shares shall not be taken as reducing the amount of the authorised capital of the company.

The communication of any redemption of redeemable preference shares must be sent to the registrar within 30 days of the date of redemption.

Further new section 80-A introduced by the Amendment Act 1988 makes provision for redemption of irredeemable preference shares already issued by companies within a period of 5 years.

Non-compliance with the provisions of section 80 will render the company and every officer of the company who is in default liable to a fine upto Rs. 1000 [Section 80 (b)].

Equity Shares

All shares which are not preference shares are equity shares. Equity shareholders have the residual rights of the company. They may get higher dividend than preference share holders if the company is prosperous or get nothing if

Comparative Study of Preference Shares and Equity Shares

Points of Differences	Preference Shares	Equity Shares
1. Right of receiving dividend	They enjoy first Preference to receive dividend	They rank next to Preference Shares in receiving dividend.
2. Right of receiving back their capital.	They enjoy first right of priority even in this respect.	They rank next to Preference Shares in the return of capital
3. Rate and Magnitude of dividend	Divident fixed by Articles, e.g. 13.5% per annum,. It is usually subject to income tax. No rise in the dividend when the company is prosperous except when shares are participating preference shares. Unpaid dividends can accumulate if they are cumulative preference shares.	Dividend fluctuating according to asset value, earning power and stability of the company. Rising dividends when the company is prosperous. Equity Shares have no sub-divisions. They are always non-cumulative. But they can share the fruits of prosperity.
4. Voting Rights	They are entitled to enjoy voting right only under exceptional circumstances, e.g. dividends unpaid for two years or resolution affecting their rights to be passed.	They enjoy normal voting rights. They are the real risk bearers. Voting rights shall be in proportion to the paid up amount in shares.
5. Face Value	Relatively higher usually Rs. 200.	Neither too high nor too low. Usually Rs. 10 or 100.
6. Nature of Capital	It is called rentier Capital as it gets income like rent	It is called Risk Capital or Venture Capital as income is not fixed.
7. Capital Appreciation	It is called rentier Capital as it gets income like rent.	It is called Risk Capital or Venture Capital as income is not fixed.
8. Appeal to investors	In absence of any share in the prosperity of the Company. Shares have no Capital appreciation.	With rising dividends equity shares enjoy capital appreciation.
8. Appeal to investors	They involve a Small risk. Their rights are secured and stable. The Cumulative type has practically no risk. Hence, they appeal to cautious investors, who prefer stable and regular dividend. Banks, Life Insurance prefer these shares.	The equity share capital in absence of deffered shares, is called the risk-capital of the company. They have to bear the risk of loss in the expectations of higher and rising dividends. Hence, they appeal to ordinary investors, who prefer rising though unstable income.
9. Redeemability during life time of the company	They can be redeemable at the end of a certain period (i.e. 10 years). They are very useful for raising temporary additional finance for further expansion.	Equity Shares are always irredeemable and they constitute a permanent share capital of the company, not subject to redemption during the lifetime of the company.

Application and Allotment of Shares

A prospectus issued by a company inviting the public to subscribe to the shares of a company is a mere invitation. An application for shares is an offer by a prospective shareholder to take shares. When an application is accepted it is an allotment. Allotment creates a binding contract between the parties (Prospective Shareholders).

Allotment as such has not been defined in the Companies Act. It is an appropriation by the directors out of the previously unappropriated capital of a company of a certain number of shares to a person. Till such allotment is made, shares as such do not exist. It is only by an allotment in thus sense that shares come into existence. Where forfeited shares are reissued, it is not an allotment but a sale (*Sri Gopal Jalan and Co. v. Calcutta Stock Exchange Association Ltd.*).[147]

Communication of Allotment

As a general rule, the allotment must be communicated to the person making the application so that it is legally complete.

Communication need not be in a particular form unless the articles of the company provide otherwise. Whatever is the mode of communication, it must be made to the applicant or his agent who is duly authorised to receive it. In case of postal communication, allotment is complete as soon as the letter of allotment is posted even though it is never received (*Household Fire Insurance Co. v. Grant*). [148]

Time Limit of Allotment

The allotment must be made within a reasonable time after the receipt of the application.

Otherwise the applicant shall not be bound to accept it (*Ramasgate Hotel Co. v. Montefiore*[149]). Here, M applied for shares in June but the allotment was not made till November. Held, M was not bound to take the shares.

In *Karachi Oil Products Ltd. v. v. Kumar Shree Narendra Singhji,*[150] it was held that an allotment of shares made almost a year after the date of application was ineffective. In this case, an application for shares was made on 11-7-1941 and allotment was made on 15-6-42. The court, observed that an allotment to be valid should be made within reasonable time and the applicant is not bound to accept the allotment if made after the lapse of reasonable time.

However, if there is unreasonable delay in allotment of shares but shares are accepted by applicant and are not repudiated he cannot plead that his offer had lapsed because of delay. Thus, where the applications shares certificates were sent to the defendants on 20-10-47 which were received by them but when the company made demands on 31-8-48 for the share amounts, the defendants repudiated and denied liability for the amount of the shares allotted to them, it was held that there was an offer and acceptance sufficient to constitute a concluded contrast — *St. M.R. v. R. Murugappa Chettiar v. Pudukothai Ceramics Ltd.*[151].

Absolute and Unconditional Allotment

The allotment must be absolute and unconditional, i.e. must be made on the same terms as stated in the application. Thus, where a person applied for 500 shares, he is not bound to accept an allotment of, say, 100 shares.

Similarly, the applicant applied for shares in a company on the condition that be should be appointed a branch manager of the company. Shares were allotted to him but he was not appointed the branch manager. Held, he was not bound by the allotment — *Ramanbhai v. Ghasi Ram*[152].

Likewise, no condition should be attached to the acceptance of an offer to purchase shares.

If the acceptance introduced a new term, it will be a new offer by a company and it shall not be effective unless it is accepted by the applicant *Gackson v. Turquand*[1S3].

Allotment not to be in Contravention of any other Law

If shares are issued in a manner prohibited by foreign exchange regulations, the issue would be invalid and void and confer on the allottee no title whatsoever to the shares — *re Trans Atlantic Life Assurance Co. Ltd.*[154].

Similarly, an allotment of shares made for any improper motive is bad and can be struck down — *Unit Trust India v. Om Prakash Berlia*[155].

Statutory Provision Regarding Allotment

A valid allotment has to comply with the requirements of the Act. The various provisions are discussed as under:

1. Minimum Subscription

No shares which are offered to the public for subscription can be allotted until the minimum subscription stated in the prospectus has been subscribed, and the amount payable on application has been received in cash by the company [Section 69 (1)]. The amount stated in the prospectus shall be reckoned exclusively of any amount payable otherwise then cash [Section 69 (2)].

2. Application Money

The money payable on application for each share shall not be less than 5% of the nominal value of the shares [Section 69 (3)]. All money received from applicants for shares must be deposited and kept deposited in a scheduled bank —

(a) Until the certificate to commence business is obtained, or

(b) Where such certificate has already been obtained until the entire amount payable on application for shares in respect of the minimum subscription has been received [Section 69 (4)].

If the minimum subscription is not subscribed within 120 days after the issue of the prospectus, the money paid by the shareholder must be returned immediately. If such money is not repaid within 130 days after the issue of the prospectus, the directors are jointly and severally liable to repay the money with interest at 6% per annum from the expiry of the 130 days [Section 69 (5)].

A condition requiring an applicant for shares to waive a breach of the above requirements is void. The provisions prohibiting allotment until the minimum subscription is received do not apply to any allotment of shares to the first allotment of shares [Section 69 (7)].

3. Statement in lien of prospectus (Section 70)

Where a company having a share capital does not issue a prospectus, it can allot any shares or debentures only when at least 3 days before the first allotment of the shares or debentures, these has been delivered to the Registrar for registration a statement in lien of prospectus. This does not apply to a private company.

4. Effect of irregular allotment (Section 71)

An allotment of shares is irregular when it has been made by company —

(a) Without receiving the minimum subscription, or

(b) Where it has not issued a prospectus without filing with the Registrar for registration a statement in lien of prospectus at least 3 days before the first allotment of shares.

Irregular allotment of shares made by a company is voidable at the instance of the applicant.

This is so even if the company is being wound up. The effect of irregular allotment is that it may be set aside by the allottee of shares —

(a) Within 2 months of the holding of the statutory meeting of the company, or

(b) Where the company is not required to hold a statutory, or where the allotment is made after the holding of the statutory meeting, within 2 months after the date of allotment [Section 71 (1)].

Any director, who has knowledge of the fact of the irregular allotment of shares is liable to compensate the company and the allottee respectively for any loss, damages or costs. Proceedings to recover any such loss, damages or costs can be commenced within 2 years from the date of the allotment.

In this connection, provisions of section 69 regarding the effect of not receiving minimum subscription should also be noted. If the company is unable to receive minimum subscription within 120 days after the first issue of prospectus [According to SEBI guidelines, within 120 days from the date of opening of the issue], it must refund within 130 days of the issue of the prospectus all moneys received from the applicants. If the money is not refunded within the said 130 days, then the directors of the company shall be jointly and severally liable to reply that money with interest at the rate of six per cent annum [According to SEBI guidelines @ 15% per annum] from the expiry of the both day.

Effect of Allotment of Shares in Contravention of Section 72

The validity of an allotment is not affected by non compliance of the provisions of section 72. the allotment is valid. However, the company and every officer who is in default is liable to be fined upto Rs. 5000/-.

Effect of Allotment in Contravention of Section 73

The allotment, if made shall be void, and money becomes refundable to the allottee. Irregular Allotment and its effects may be summarised as below:

Name of irregularity	Legal effects on Allotment	Liability of company of directors etc.
1. Where conditions as to minimum subscription are not fulfilled (Section 69).	Allotment is voidable [Section 71 (1)].	Director responsible for contravention liable for damages to allottee as well as the company [Section 71 (3)].
2. Where a statement in lien of prospectus is required to be delivered to the Registrar and requirements are not observed, (Section 71).	Allotment is voidable [Section 71 (1)].	Company and every director, responsible for contravention punishable with fine upto Rs. 1000 [Section 70 (4)].
3. Where time limit regarding the opening of the subscription list is not observed (Section 72).	Allotment is valid [Section 73 (1)].	Company and every officer who is in default liable for fine upto Rs. 5000/- [Section 72 (3)].
4. Requirements of law as regards obtaining permission to deal the issue on deal the issue on stock exchange are my passed (Section 73).	Allotment is void (Section 73).	If money become due to be refunded and the company does not reply in 8 days, directors to repay it with interest at such rate which shall not be less than 4% and not more than 15% as may be prescribed having regard to the length of the period of delay in making prepayment (As per the amendment of 1988).

5. Opening of the subscription list (Section 72)

Where shares are offered by a prospectus no allotment shall be made until the beginning of the fifth day after the date on which the prospectus is first issued or on such later day as may be specified in the prospectus. This date is known as the 'opening of the subscription list.' The object of this is to give time for consideration before submission of applications. Where after the issue of the prospectus a public notice is given by some responsible person, disclaiming his responsibility for the issue of the prospectus, no allotment shall be made until the beginning of the fifth day after that on which such public notice is first given. The allotment of shares in contravention of this provision is valid. But the Company and every officer who is in default shall be liable to a fine upto Rs. 5000 [Section 72(3)]. An application for shares for shares shall not be revocable until after the expiry of the fifth day after the opening of the subscription list [Section 72(5)].

6. Shares to be dealt in on Stock Exchange (Section 73)

Where a prospectus states that application has been or will be made for permission for shares to be dealt in on one or more recognised stock exchanges, such prospectus shall state the names of the stock exchanges. Any allotment made on an application under the prospectus shall be void —

(i) if permission has not been applied for before the tenth day of the issue of the prospectus.

or

(ii) if permission is refused before the expiry of 10 weeks from the closing date of the subscription list.

Such permission has to be granted by each of the stock exchanges in which application for permission has been made. A company can appeal both against the decision of the stock exchange refusing permission and its failure to dispose of the application list. Such allotment shall not be void until the disposal of the appeal [Section 73 (1)].

If a prospectus states that application has been or will be made for permission to deal in the shares on a recognised stock exchange, the money received from applicants must be paid into a separate bank account maintained with a scheduled bank. On failure to apply for permission or where permission has not been granted, the company has to return all moneys received from the applicants within 8 days after the company becomes liable to pay. If the application money is not repaid within 8 days, the directors are jointly and severally liable to repay the money with interest not less than 4% and not exceeding 15% per annum from the expiry of the 8th day. A director will not be liable if he proves that the default was not due to any misconduct or negligence on his part [Section 72 (2)]. F or failure to return the money within the time, the company and every officer who is in default shall be liable upto a fine to Rs. 5000 and where repayment is not made within 6 months from the expiry of the eighth day. [Section 73 (5)].

Moneys standing to the credit of the separate bank account referred to in sub-section (3) shall not be utilised for purpose other than either of the following purposes namely—

(a) Adjustment against allotment of shares, where the shares have been permitted to be dealt in on the stock exchange or specified in the prospectus,

(b) repayment of money received from applicants in pursuance of the prospectus, where shares have been permitted to be dealt in on the stock exchange or each stock exchange specified in the prospectus as the case may be, or where the company is for any other reason unable to make the allotment of share [Section 3 (A)].

If shall be deemed that permission has not been granted if the application for permission, where made, has not been disposed of within the time specified in sub-section (1) above [sub-section (5)].

7. Return as to allotments (Section 75)

Within 30 days of allotment of shares by a company, the company, shall file with the registrar a statement known as 'return as to allotment'. The return shall contain—

(a) particulars about the number and nominal amount of the shares allotted for cash, the names, addresses, and occupations of the allottees and the amount paid on each share.

(b) particulars about the shares (not being bonus shares) allotted as fully or partly paid-up, for any consideration other than cash.

(c) particulars about the number and nominal amount of bonus shares and their allottees.

(d) A copy of the resolution passed by the company authorising issue of the shares at a discount and a copy of the Company Law Board order sanctioning the issue.

There is no need to file a return of the issue and allotment of shares forfeited for non-payment of calls. On default every officer of the company shall be liable to a fine upto Rs. 500 for every day during which the default continues.

8. Retention of Over-Subscription

In case the issue is over-subscripted then shares etc. are allotted as per the scheme of allotment framed in consultation with the stock exchange(s) and passed by a Board resolution.

As per the latest guidelines of controller of capital issues [vide press release dated 8.4.1988, (Now SEBI)] a company raising equity capital, (not being bonus shares) may retain over-subscribed equity to the extent of 15% of the amount sanctioned. But the intention to avail of this option is to be stated in the application of the controller of capital issue and approval is be obtained, and this fact is also to be mentioned in prospectus or statement in lien of prospectus.

Additional Guidelines in case of under-subscribed capital issues

In case of capital issues made after 8th April, 1990, the following additional guideline [issued by the mimstry of Finance, Department of Economic Affairs, vide No. F2/14/CCI/90 dated 6.4.1990] will apply if, any how, the issue remain under-subscribed.

1. A company making any rights/public issue of securities would not be allowed to make the allotment of the shares/debentures etc., unless it has received a minimum of 90% subscription against the entire issue.

   If the subscription to this extent is not received, the entire amount collected with applications would have to be refunded to the applicant at the end of 90 days from the closure of issue.

2. If cases where a composite approval has been obtained for rights and public issues from C.C.I/ SEBI the above limit of 90% will apply to the total amount, irrespective of whether the issue are made simultaneously or not.

3. For issues made against such composite approvals, the gap between the closure dates of various issues (e.g. rights, Indian public, NRIs etc.). Should not exceed 30 days.

4. Rights issues would not be allowed to kept open for more than 60 days.

5. If there is a development on underwriters subscription from them will have to be obtained within 90 days from the closure of the issue to achieve the minimum 90% level.

6. If would be essential for the promoters to made their subscription in advance before the public issue opens, and give a certificate to this effect to the regional stock exchange concerned.

7. Subscription received against rights/public issues will be kept in specific bank accounts and companies would not have access to such funds unless they have received an approval from the concerned regional stock

exchange(s) for allotment. Where listing has been proposed on more than one exchange no allotment or utilization shall be allowed till listing approval is available from each of the exchanges concerned.

8. Companies will be required to submit certificates to the regional stock exchange, with copy to SEBI and the CCI, signed by the merchant banker and the chief executive/company secretary of the company to the effect that the issue has been subscribed upto 90% of the total for getting approval of the stock exchange for allotment.
9. Companies will make adequate disclosures in the prospectus letters of offer, advertisement, publicity literature, investors/brokers conferences, etc. in this context and also undertake to refund the amounts at the end of 90 days from the closure of the issue, if not subscribed upto 90%, and to pay interest at 15% per annum if refunds are delayed by more than ten days after this period.

These guidelines/conditions will apply to all public/rights made here after, except those for which prospectuses/letters of offer have been filed/issued upto 8th April, 1990.

CALLS ON SHARES

A call may be defined as a demand by the company on the shareholders to pay whole or part of the balance remaining unpaid on each share made at any time during the lifetime of the company or during its winding up. It is, thus, an intimation to the shareholder to discharge his obligation by paying the whole or part of the amount which remains unpaid on the shares. All money payable by any member to the company under the memorandum or articles is a debt due from him to the company. But he is not bound to pay unless a call has been made.

According to Lord Lindly, the word 'call' is used to denote both demand for money and also the sum demanded.

Legal Provisions Relating to Call

A valid call must be made in accordance with the provisions of the Companies Act and the articles of association of the company, followings are the requisites of a valid call.

1. Resolution of the Board [Section 292 (1) (a)]

The call must be made by the directors, such directors must be dully appointed and qualified.

A call must be made under a proper resolution of the Board of Directors. The resolution must be passed at a duly authorised meeting. The meeting of the directors must be duly convened and proper quorum must be present.

2. For the benefit of the company

The power to make a call is in the nature of a trust and must be exercised for the benefit of the company and not for their own benefit. If it is exercised malafide, i.e., for the benefit of directors, the call may be prevented by a injunction.

3. Uniform Basis (Section 91)

The calls must be made on a uniform basis on all shares falling under the same class.

4. In Accordance with Articles

The case must be made strictly in accordance with the provisions of the Articles, and must specify the amount of the call and the time and the place of payment. If this is not done, the call will be invalid.

Call in Advance

Section 92 provides that a company, if authorised by its articles can accept advance payment that is calls in advance from any shareholder in respect of the shares held by him. For such payment he becomes a creditor of the company and is entitled to interest, not exceeding 6% per annum or the company may also pay larger, dividends in proportion to such amount if so authorised by the Articles (vide section 93 of the Companies Act 1956). But because of such payment the shareholder cannot claim any extra voting rights (Section 92).

Purchase By Company of its Own Shares

No company limited by shares and no company limited by guarantee and having a share capital shall have power to buy its own shares, unless the consequent reduction of capital is effected and sanctioned by the court.

No public company and no private company which is a subsidiary of a public company, shall give any financial assistance for the purchase of any shares in the company or in its holding companies.

Purchase by a company of its own shares amounts to reduction of capital, and therefore is prohibited under the Act. The right course for the company would be to follow the procedure of reduction of capital.

Following transactions are not prohibited:

(i) where provision of money is made under a scheme (e.g. a pension schemes to enable trustees to buy fully paid shares in the company to be held for the benefits of the employees of the company including salaried directors.

(ii) where a loan is made by a banking company in the ordinary course of its business.

(iii) where loans are made by a company to employees other then directors to enable them to buy fully paid shares in the company to be held by them as beneficial owners. The amount of loan cannot exceed the employee's salary for a period of 6 months.

A company and its every officer contravening the above provisions shall be punishable with a fine which may extend to Rs. 1000/-.

Issue of Shares For Consideration Other Than Cash

Shares may be issued either for cash or for consideration. Where no cash is received by the company against allotment of shares, the shares are issued for consideration. Consideration may be property, goods or services received by the company in lien of which the company issues shares in its share capital. Shares may be issued for consideration as partly or fully paid-up shares.

Where shares are allotted for consideration other than cash, the company shall within 30 days thereafter produce for the inspection and examination of the Registrar a contract in writing constituting the title of the allottee to the allotment, together with any contract of sale or a contract of services or other consideration in respect of which that allotment was made. Such contract shall be duly stamped and filed with the Registrar with a return stating the number and nominal amount of shares so allotted, the extent to which they are to be treated as paid-up and the consideration for which they have been allotted.

But in case of such a contract, if there be any fraud or the consideration is illusory or colourable, the person to whom such fully or partly paid-up shares are allotted will be held liable in spite of the fact that the contract is filed with the Registrar. In a case of *Estate v. Hiralal,*[156] the Supreme Court observed.

The consideration for the allotment of shares may be money or money's worth e.g. the transfer to the company of property. If a valid contract is made for the acceptance by the company of specified property in payment of shares, the court will not, whilst the contract stands, inquire into the value of the consideration even at the instance of the liquidator. Where, however, the contract is fraudulent or shows on the fact of it that the consideration given to the company is illusory or is clearly not equivalent to the nominal value of the shares, the shares cannot, to this extent, be treated as fully paid and the shareholder may be held liable to pay for them in full.

Remember, a company cannot allot fully or partly paid-up shares in consideration of promissory notes.

Issue of Shares at premium (Section 78)

A company may issue its shares at a premium, i.e., at the price higher than their face (nominal) value. Although there is no restriction on the issue of shares at a premium, the companies Act regulates the disbursement of the amount of premium so collected. First of all, the premium must be transferred to the "Share premium account" if used for any purpose other than those specified in section 78 and listed below shall be deemed as reduction of share capital.

The share premium may be applied by a company only for any of the following purposes:

(a) in paying up unissued shares of the company to be issued to members as fully paid-up bonus shares,

(b) in writing off the preliminary expenses incurred by the company,

(c) in writing of the expenses of or the commission or discounts allowed on any insure of shares or debentures, or

(d) in providing for any premium payable on the redemption of redeemable preference share or debentures.

The provisions of Section 78 apply with retrospective effect as such any premium received before the commencement of the Companies Act 1956, is also governed by these provisions.

Issue of Shares at Discount (Section 79)

Issue of shares at discount means the issue of shares on payment of less than the nominal or face value of such shares at a discount can be issued by the company if the following conditions are fulfilled.

(1) Shares to be issued must be of a class already issued.
(2) The issue of the shares at a discount is authorized by a resolution passed by the company in a general meeting and sanctioned by the Company Law Board.
(3) The resolution must specify the rate of discount which must not exceed 10% unless the Company Law Board is of the opinion that a higher percentage of discount may be allowed in the special circumstances of the case.
(4) The company must have been working for at least a year from the date it was entitled to commence business before it can issue shares at a discount.
(5) The shares must be issued with two months of the sanction by the Company Law Board or within such extended time as the Company Law Board may permit.

Every prospectus relating to the issue of the shares must contain particulars of the discount allowed on the issue of the shares or of so much of that discount as has not been written off at the date of the issue of the prospectus. If default is made in complying with this provision the company and every officer of the company who is in default, shall be punishable with fine which may extend to Rs. 50/-.

SHARE CERTIFICATES (Section 84 and 113)

Every person whose name is entered as a member in the register of members shall be entitled to receive one certificate for all his shares without payment. If he requires more than one certificate for his shares, he will pay Rs. 1 for every additional certificate after the first. In respect of any share or shares held jointly by several persons, the company shall not bound to issue more than one certificate, and delivery of certificate for a share to one of the several joint holders shall be sufficient to all such holders. The company shall deliver certificates of shares within three months of the allotment of shares, or within two months after the application for registration of the transfer of any such shares. The same provisions also apply to debentures and debenture stock the company Law Board may on being satisfied; extend the above periods to a further period not exceeding 9 months [Section 113(1)].

Penalty And Remedy For Default

According to section 113, of the Act, every company shall complete and have ready for delivery such certificate within three months after the allotment and within of shares unless the conditions of the registration of the transfer of shares unless the conditions of issue of the shares otherwise provide. In case of default, a notice may be served on the company to make good the default. If the company fails to comply with the notice within 10 days after the service of notice, the court may on the application of such person order the company and every other officer there of to make good the default. The court may order the company or any other officer of the company who is in the default shall be punishable with fine which may extend to Rs. 500 for every day of default. The section applies in relation to debentures and debenture stock as well.

The share certificate must be under the common seal of the company and specify the shares to which it relates, the amount paid there on and the name, address and occupation of the holder of the shares. If shall be signed by at least 2 directors and the secretary.

Objects And Advantages of Shares Certificate

A share certificate under the seal of a company, specifying the shares held by a member is, prima facia evidence of the title of the member to such shares [Section 84 (1)]. Thus, it is very easy to for a shareholder to sell his shares in the market by producing a share certificate showing his title to these shares. Besides, it would be very easy for a lender to lend money to the shareholder taking the possession of his share certificate by way of security.

A share certificate of a company creates two kinds of estoppel against the company —

1. Estoppel as to Title

If a company authorises the issue of a certificate stating that' A' is the registered holder of certain shares, it cannot afterwards allege that A is not entitled to those shares. But if an officer of the company who has no authority to issue certificates issues a forged certificate, there is no estoppel.

2. Estoppel as to Payment

If the certificate states that the shares are fully paid, the company cannot afterwards allege that they are not fully paid. But such a statement in the certificate would not help a person who know that the shares were not paid for in full in cash.

Lost Or Defaced Certificates

A share certificate may be renewed or its duplicate be issued if such certificate —

(a) is proved to have been lost or destroyed or

(b) having been defaced or mutilated or tom is surrendered to the company [Section 84 (2)].

If a company with intent to defraud renews a certificate or issues a duplicate certificate, the company shall be punishable with fine which may extend to Rs. 10,000 and every defaulting officer shall be punishable with imprisonment upto 6 months or fine upto Rs. 10,000 or with both [Section 84 (3)].

SHARE WARRANT (Section 114 and 115)

A share warrant is a document issued under the common seal of the company which shows that the bearer of the warrant is entitled to the shares specified there in. It is a substitute for the share certificate. A share warrant is a bearer document and is transferable by mere delivery. Such share warrants are negotiable instruments.

A public company limited by shares may issue share warrants under a common seal in the following circumstances:

(i) If it is authorised by its articles,

(ii) Shares are fully paid-up,

(iii) Previous approval of the central government is obtained.

Share warrants should contain the number of shares in respect of which they have been issued.

A share warrant may have coupons attached to it, for the payment of future dividends on the shares specified in the warrant (Section 114).

The bearer of a share warrant is not a member of the company, [Section 2(27)]. On issue of a share warrant, the name of the member is struck-off the register of members and enter in that register the following particulars —

(a) the fact of the issue of the warrant,

(b) a statement of the shares specified in the warrant distinguishing each share by its number, and

(c) the date of the issue of the warrant [Section 115 (1)].

The bearer of a share warrant shall subject to the Articles of the company, be entitled, on surrendering the warrant for cancellation to have his name entered as a member in the register of members. He shall have to pay such fee to the company as the Board of directors may from time to time determine [Section 115(2)]. He may, if the Articles of the company so provide, be deemed to be a member of the company for any purpose defined in the Articles [Section 115 (5)].

Distinction Between 'Share Certificate' And 'Share Warrant'

The points of distinction are stated below:

Points of Distinction	Share Certificate	Share Warrant
1. Issue	Both Public as well as private companies issue a share certificate.	It is issued by a Public Company only.
2. Members	It is to be issued where the shares are partly paid-up.	It can be issued only with respect to fully paid-up shares.
3. Original	The holder of a share certificate is a member of the company.	Its holder is not a member unless the articles otherwise provide.
4. Negotiable Instrument	A share certificate can be issued 'in original'.	It can not be issued originally. Share Certificates can be cancelled and in lieu thereof share warrants are issued.
5. Fully paid up	It is not a 'negotiable instrument'.	It is by mercantile usage a negotiable instrument.
6. Transferability	A Share Certificate can be issued when shares are fully paid up or even partly paid-up.	A Share Warrant can be issued only when shares are fully paid-up.

Points of Distinction	Share Certificate	Share Warrant
7. Stamp duty	Transfer of a share certificate requires registration of transfer with the company.	Transfer of a share warrant is complete just by delivery. No registration of transfer is required.
8. Ownership	Stamp duty is payable on transfer of shares specified in a share certificate.	No stamp duty is payable on transfer of shares specified in a share certificate.
	A Share Certificate entitles the person named their in to a specified number of shares.	A Share Warrant entitles its 'bearer' to a specified number of shares.
9. Petition	The holder of share certificate can present a petition for the winding up of the company.	The holder of a share warrant cannot do so.
10. Dividend	Dividend is paid to the holder of a share certificate by the issue of a dividend warrant in his favour.	Dividend due on a share warrant is advertised in newspapers and is payable to the holder of the dividend warrant on presentation of the relevant coupon attached to the share warrant.
11. Qualification	Shares evidenced by a Share Certificate can be included in the qualification shares of a director.	Share evidenced by a share warrant can not be included in the qualification share of a director.
12. Document	A Share Certificate is a document showing prima facie title to the shares represented thereby.	A share warrant is the share security itself, transformed for the purpose of negotiation into a different character.

Transfer of Shares (Section 108-122)

A share in a company is a movable property, transferable in the manner provided by the articles of the company (Section 82) shares are the personal property of the shareholder and he has power to transfer his shares. It is an absolute right which cannot be taken away by any provision in the articles.

Section 82 empowers every shareholder to transfer his shares in the manner laid down in the Articles and in accordance with the various provisions of law. Thus, a private company is statutorily obliged to place certain restrictions on the right of its members to transfer shares. One of the most common restrictions on transfer of shares in a private company is the "pre-emption clause", which states that the intending transferor must offer his shares to existing members of the company, before offering them to non-members, so long as a member can be found to purchase them at a fair price to be determined in accordance with the articles.

In the case of public companies also, there may be some restrictions on the right of members to transfer shares. Regulation 21 (Table A) provides that the Board of directors may refuse to register the transfer of any share on which the company has lien. Regulation 22 also envisages certain conditions which may be introduced by a company in its Articles restrict transfer of shares. If provides that the Board may also decline to recognise any instrument of transfer unless: (a) the instrument of transfer is accompanied by the certificate of the shares to which it relates and such other evidence as the Board may reasonably require to show the right of the transferor to make the transfer; and (b) the instrument of transfer is in respect of only one class of shares.

Right of a shareholder to transfer his share is always subject to provisions in Articles of association (*Mathrubhumi Printing and Publishing Co. Ltd. v. Vardhaman Publishers Ltd.*).[157]

Power of the Board of Directors to Refuse Registration of Transfer of Shares

Where the Articles of association of a company give power to the Board to refuse registration of a transfer of shares, such power must be exercised by a resolution of the Board. The Board may refuse to register the transfer as long as they are acting in the interests of the company, but it they exercise their discretion to refuse male fide, i.e., they act oppressively, or corruptly, Company Law Board or the court will interfere and order registration. The Articles may, of course be specific and empower the Board of directors to refuse to register transfers on certain specific grounds. As per section 111, as amended by the Act of 1988, if a company refuses to register the transfer of shares, it shall, within 2 months from the date of lodging the instrument of transfer, send notice of refusal to the transferor of transferee giving reasons for such refusal. The Company Law Board, on appeal, may direct the registration of the transfer.

Procedure of Transfer

The provisions relating to transfer are laid down in sections 108 to111. The provisions of these sections are as following:

1. Instrument of Transfer (Section 108)

A proper instrument of transfer duly stamped executed and signed by both the transferor and the transferee is delivered to the company. The instrument of transfer must contain the name address and occupation, if any of the transferee. The instrument is so executed must be delivered to the company along with the certificate of shares or the seller of allotment as the case may be [Section 108 (1)].

Every instrument of transfer of shares must be in the prescribed form and before it is signed by the transferor and any entry is made therein, it shall be presented to the prescribed authority who shall stamp thereon the date of presentation. This form will then be executed by the transferor and the transferee and completed in all other respect and delivered to the company for registration. Where the shares are quoted on or dealt in a recognised stock exchange, such form shall be delivered to the company within two months from the date put on the form or before the register of members of the company is closed for the first time after the date of presentation, whichever is later. Where the shares are not so dealt in on a recognised stock exchange, it must be delivered within two months from the date put on the form [Section 108 (1)].

The Transferee becomes a member of the company only when the transfer is registered by the company.

2. Transfer by Legal Representative (Section 109)

A transfer executed by the legal representative of a deceased member, who is not himself a member, is valid.

3. Application for Transfer (Section 110)

The application for the registration of transfer may either be made by the transferor or the transferee. Where it is made by the transferor and relates to partly paid-up shares, the company must give notice of application by prepaid registered post to the transferee. If the transferee does not object to the transfer within two weeks from the receipt of the notice, then his name may be entered on the Register of members. With regard to an application by the transferee or by the transferor relating to fully paid-up shares, no such notice is required.

The transferee becomes a member of the company only when the transfer is registered by the company. The transferor continues to be the holder of the shares until his name is cancelled from the register of members and the name of the transferee entered in his place. When this is done, a new share certificate or the old certificate duly endorsed in the name of the transferee is issued to the transferee.

4. Refusal to Register Transfer

Though a member has an absolute right to transfer shares, a company may, if authorised by its articles, refuse to register the transfer of shares. Where a company refuses to register a transfer, whether in pursuance of any power of the company under its Articles or otherwise it shall, within two months from the date on which the instrument of transfer was delivered to the company, send notice of refusal to the transferee and the transferor, giving reasons for such refusal [Section111 (1)].

Refusal by the company on the ground that the registration of transfer will create share certificates of less then marketable lot and would be in contravention of Articles of association shall not be valid. Company Law Board in *Dipak Kumar Jayantilal Shah v. The Atul Products Ltd.*[158] held that there is no prohibition under the companies Act or any other Act for holding share certificates below marketable lots. The provisions of Law will override the provisions of Articles of association.

Appeal

If a company refuses to register a transfer of shares, it shall notify within two months of its refusal to the transferor and the transferee. The transferor or transferee may appeal to the company Law Board against any refusal of the company to register the transfer. The appeal shall be made within 2 months of the notice of such refusal or where no notice has been sent by the company, within four months from the date on which the instrument of transfer was delivered to the company. The Company Law Board shall give an opportunity to the company, the transferor and the transferee, to explain their case. It may, if it kinks that refusal is not justified, order the company to register the transfer. If registration is directed, it shall be done within 10 days of the receipt of the order.

These provisions in respect of appeals are applicable in case of a private company if it refuses to register any transmission of shares sold by a court or other public authority. In such a case, the company law Board may give an option to the company either to accept the purchaser as a member or get the shares purchased by a member of the company at a price and within the time specified in the order.

In *Dr. Jitendra Nath Seha and Another v. Shymal Mondal,*[159] it was observed that after the amendment of section III in 1988 all the provisions of section 111 are applicable to a private company except to the extent provided in sub-section (13). Section 111 before its amendment was not applicable to a private limited company so long as it was not a subsidiary of the public company.

Power of Directors to Reject Transfer

This may be discussed under two heads:

(1) Where the articles do not contain any clause, allowing the directors to reject the transfer, the shareholder may freely transfer his shares and can compel the directors for registering of shares.

(2) Where the Articles contains a clause empowering the directors to reject the transfer. If the Articles contain a clause empowering the directors to reject the transfer, the directors can reject such transfer but subject to the following conditions.

   (i) The power to refuse, however must be exercised bonafide and in a just manner in the best interests of the company. The directors cannot exercise this power for ulterior purposes, such power is usually exercised if the shares are partly paid-up, the calls on shares are unpaid, or the company has lien on the shares or the directors do not approve the transferee. They may likewise refuse to register a transfer to an infant, a bankrupt or a person of unsound mind. The directors may also refuse to register a transfer where to their knowledge the stated consideration is less than the real consideration.

   (ii) for rejection, the conditions given in the articles must be followed.

   (iii) refusal must be exercised within a reasonable time.

   (iv) refusal must be exercised by the Board and not by one of the directors.

Where the refusal is reasonable and bonafide and is done according to the provisions of the articles, the refusal is valid and the directors need not state their reasons. The court will not interfere with the discretionary powers of the directors nor will compel them to state their reasons. But such discretion cannot take away the character of free transferability of shares in the absence of cogent material or other factors restricting transferability.

Certificate of Transfer (Section 112)

In practice, a company issues only one certificate in respect of a number of shares purchased by a person. If he wants to sell only a part of the shares, he is required to produce before the company his certificate of shares alongwith the instrument of transfer for the purpose of certification. Certification is an act of endorsement on the instrument of transfer by an officer of the company that the share certificate relating to the shares to be transferred has been lodged with the company. The officer writes on the instrument of transfer the words' certificate lodged' and mentions the number of shares for which it is lodged. The seller than delivers the certified instrument of transfer to the purchaser who can take certification as tantamount to delivery to himself of the share certificate. In due course, the company cancels the old certificate and prepares two new share certificates, one for the shares sold to the purchaser and the other for the seller for the balance of shares which remain unsold. When these certificates are issued to the transferee and the transferor, both of them become members of the company.

The 'certification of transfer' to be valid should satisfy the following requirements:

(i) the instrument of transfer should be certificated with the words 'certificate lodged' or words to the like effect,

(ii) the person issuing the certification instrument must be a person authorised to issue such instruments of transfer on the company's behalf,

(iii) the certification must be signed by any officer or servant of the company or any other person, authorised to certificate transfers on company's behalf. Where a body corporate has been so authorised, it may be signed by any officer or servant of that body corporate.

It may be noted that there is no statutory obligation cast on the company to certify transfers.

Forged Transfer

An instrument of transfer of shares on which the signature of the transferor is forged is called a forged instrument any transfer of shares effected on such instrument is called a 'forged transfer'. A forged document never has any legal effect. The first thing that a company should do when an instrument of transfer is tendered to it is to inquire into its validity. The company should send a notice to the transferor at his address and inform him that such a transfer has been lodged and that if no objection is made before a specified day, it would be registered.

Consequences of a Forged Transfer

The consequences of a forged transfer are as follows:

(i) A forged transfer is a nullity and it does not confer any legal title to the transferee.

The true owner can have his name resorted in the register of members and he continues to be the owner of the shares.

(ii) If the company has issued a share certificate to the transferee on a forged transfer and he has sold these shares to an innocent buyer, the buyer gets no right to be registered as a shareholder. In such a case, he can claim damages from the company on the ground that he acted on the share certificate of the company. (*Balkis Consolidated Co. Ltd. v. Tomkinson*).[160]

(iii) If the company has been put to a loss by reason of the forged transfer, it may recover the loss from the person who procured registration, even though he might have acted in good faith.

In, *Sheffield Corporation v. Barelay*[161] B lodged with company for registration a forged transfer of some shares with stood in the name of T. and H. T having forged H's signature effected the transfer. B was ignorant of this. The company registered the transfer in the name of B. B transferred the shares to C to whom certificates were issued. H subsequently discovered the forgery and compelled the company to issue him new shares. Held, B was bound to indemnify the company which in turn was bound to indemnify C.

Blank Transfer

Blank Transfer is an instrument of transfer of shares signed by the transferor in which the name of the transferee is not filed.

Since the name of the transferee is not filed the shares in such cases may further be transferred merely by delivering the blank instrument of transfer of shares. The date of sale and the name of the transferee are left blank in transfer deed. The idea of a blank transfer of shares is that the buyer or pledgee gets equitable interest in the shares and he may sell them on failure of the pledger to discharge the debt after giving him a reasonable time (*Arjun Prasad v. Central Bank of India*).[162]

Thus stamp duty and registration fee is saved. The process of purchase and sale can be repeated any number of times with the blank transfer deed and ultimately when it reaches the hands of last transferee who wants to retain the shares can file in his name and date and get it registered in the company's books. On such registration, the last buyer is recognised as a shareholder by the company.

Transmission of Shares

A company cannot register a transfer of shares without a duly executed instrument of transfer, but this does not affect the right of a company to register another person's name where a right to such person has been devolved by Law. The transmission of shares means transfer of title in shares by operation of law. In other words, the transmission of shares signifies involuntary assignment of shares because in this case the property in shares passes not by the act of the parties, but by operation of law. Transmission of shares takes place:

(i) on the insolvency of a shareholder, property in shares passes to his official receiver — who shall become entitled to the shares owned by the insolvent.

(ii) on the death of a shareholder, the property in shares passes to his legal representatives who shall become entitled to shares owned by the deceased,

(iii) on the lunacy of a shareholder, the property in shares passes to the administrator appointed by the court.

This, it is abundantly clear that in all the above mentioned instances, i.e., on the insolvency, or the death or lunacy of a member the transmission of shares takes place by operation of Law. In case of transmission of shares, no instrument of transfer is necessary. The person to whom the shares are transmitted should make an application to the company for registration of shares in his name.

The Articles of a company usually contain provisions relating to transmission of shares.

As regards the transmission of shares, the legal representative has two options. He may get himself registered as a member of the company or he may transfer shares to some other person.

Distinction between transfer and transmission of shares

(i) Transmission of shares takes place by operation oflaw while transfer of shares in effected by a deliberate act of the share holder.

(ii) The transmission requires an evidence showing the entitlement such as succession certificate etc. whereas transfer of shares requires an execution of an instrument of transfer.

(iii) Stamp duty is payable for the 'execution of transfer' while no stamp duty is payable in case of transmission.

(iv) In case of transfer of shares, as soon as the transfer is complete, the liability of the transfer or ceases. But in case of transmission of shares, the shares continue to be subject to the original liabilities.

LIEN ON SHARES

A lien is the right to retain possession of some property of another until some claim attaching to it is settled or discharged. In the case of a company lien on a share means that a member would not be permitted to transfer his shares unless he pays his debt to the company. The right of lien on shares is not conferred on a company by the statute. The articles of a company generally provide that the company shall have a first lien of the shares of each member for all moneys payable. The right of lien does not exist on fully paid-up shares. The articles may give the right of lien over shares either for unpaid calls or for any other debt due by the member to the company. Lien also extends to the dividends payable on the shares.

Right of lien is lost if the shareholder mortgages or pledges his shares to a third party before incurring any liability to the company. The death of a shareholder does not destroy the lien. The right of lien can be exercised even though the claim has become barred by law of limitation.

SURRENDER OF SHARES

Surrender of shares means voluntary return of shares by the shareholder to the company for cancellation. There is no provision for the surrender of shares either in the Companies Act or in Table A but the articles of some companies may allow it as a short-cut to the long procedure of forfeiture, where their forfeiture is justified. In any other circumstance, surrender of shares cannot be accepted without sanction of the court, as this would amount to a reduction of capital. A surrender and a forfeiture have practically the same effect, the only difference being that the former is done with the assent of the shareholder while the latter is done at the instance of the company.

A surrender of shares will be void if it amount to a purchase of shares by the company or if it is accepted for the purpose of relieving a member of this liabilities.

A person ceases to be a member of the company on a valid surrender of shares. But he shall be liable as a contributory as a past member of the company if it is wound up within 12 months of his surrendering his shares. Shares which have been validly surrendered can be reissued in the same way as forfeited shares.

Forfeiture of Shares

It is the duty of every shareholder to pay the amount of call. If he does pay the call on him, the company may bring on action against him and the action taken is forfeiting the shares of such shareholder. Thus forfeiture of shares means confiscation of the shares of a shareholder by way of penalty for non-payment of any call made in respect thereof. A company has no inherent power to forfeit shares. The power to forfeit shares must be contained in the Articles. Shares can only be forfeited for non-payment of calls. An attempt to forfeit shares for other reasons is illegal. A forfeiture is valid if and only if the following conditions are satisfied.

(a) Where the Articles of the company must confer such powers on the board of directors.

(b) A notice under the authority of the Board of directors must be given to the defaulting shareholder. The notice shall specify a date, not being earlier than the expiry of 14 days from the date of service of notice on or before which the payment is to be made and must also state that in the event of non-payment within that date will made the shares liable for forfeiture.

(c) There must be a proper resolution of the Board.

(d) The power of forfeiture must be exercised bonafide and for the benefit of the company.

Effect of forfeiture

(i) Forfeited shares become the property of the company. The company can dispose of these forfeited shares in any manner it likes. If the company sells them to some person he is registered as the holder of these shares.

(ii) A person, whose shares have been forfeited, cases to be a member of the company. But he shall remain liable to pay to the company all moneys which at the date of forfeiture were payable by him to the company in respect of the shares. The liability of such a person shall cease as and when the company receives payment in full in respect of the shares.

(iii) The company must specify the total number of shares forfeited in every annual return submitted to the Registrar under section 159.

Distinction Between Lien and Forfeiture

The main points of distinction between the forfeiture and lien are stated below:

Points	Lien on Shares	Forfeiture of Shares
1. Reason	Lien on shares may take place both in respect of debt Enforceability due on other transactions.	Forfeiture of shares may take place for non-payment of any call made in respect thereof.
2. Enforcement	Lien is enforced by sale.	Forfeiture is enforced by depriving the member of his shares.
3. Action	Lien is a form of security for the debt.	Forfeiture is a penal action for non payment.
4. Refund	In lien on the sale of shares, the former owner gets the difference between the amount received for them and the amount of his debt. In other words, surplus money (if any) is refunded to the shareholder.	On forfeiture, the shares become the property of the company and the shareholder receives nothing. Even he loses his claim to the paid-up amount on such forfeited shares.
5. Reduction of Capital	In lien since the shares are necessary sold the question of reduction of capital does not.	Forfeiture of shares results into a reduction of capital unless those shares are re-issued.

DIVIDENDS

The Companies Act does not define the term' dividend'. In general, the dividends is the portion of the profits of company which is distributed among its shareholders in proportion of their shares and in accordance with their rights as a shareholders. In other words, a dividend is a proportion of the distributed profits of a company. It need not be expressly provided in its memorandum or articles. Subject to certain statutory requirements and the provisions of the Articles, the amount to be distributed as dividend is a matter of internal management and the courts do not interfere with the discretion of the directors and shareholders in this regard.

Provisions regarding dividends

These provisions are contained in Section 93 and 205 to 207.

1. Resolution at the annual general meeting

The dividend is declared by the shareholders at the annual general meeting by a resolution. The Board determines the rate of dividend to be declared. The rate determined by the Board has to be sanctioned by the members of the company in annual general meeting. The shareholders may reduce the rate of dividend recommended by the Board but cannot increase it.

2. Payment of dividend in proportion to paid-up capital

A company may, if authorised by its Articles, pay dividends in proportion to the amount paid-up on each share (Section 93). Where unequal amounts have been paid on shares, the dividends may be unequal as among different shareholders. In the absence of such a clause in the Articles, members are entitled to dividend in proportion to the nominal value of the shares, and not in proportion to the amount paid thereon.

3. Dividend to be paid only out of profit

A company may declare and pay dividends out of current or previous years profit or out of both or out of money provided by the central or state government for payment of the dividend in pursuance of a guarantee given by such government. In the public interest the central government may allow a company to declare dividend out of profits of the current year without requiring the company to provide for depreciation. [Section 20 (1)].

4. Transfer to the reserves upto 10% of profits

Before declaring any dividend certain percentage of profit as prescribed by the central government, but not exceeding 10 per cent will have to be transferred to the reserves of the company. The company, if authorised by its Articles may voluntarily create greater reserves [Section 205 (2A)].

5. Compliance with Provisions of Section 80-A

A company which fails to comply with the provisions of section 80-A (which deals with redemption of redeemable preference shares) shall not, so long as such failure continues, declare any dividend on its equity shares [Section 205 (2-B)].

6. Dividend payable only in cash

The dividend is payable only in cash. But the capitalisation of profits or reserves of the company for the purpose of issuing fully paid bonus shares or paying up any amount for the time being unpaid on any shares held by the members of the company is not prohibited [Section 205(3)].

7. Dividend to be paid out of current year's profits

Dividend can be paid only out of current year's profits. In the event of inadequacy or absence of profits in any year, the company can declare dividends out of past years profits transferred to reserves in accordance with the rules framed by the central government or the company has to obtain previous approval of central government [Section 205-A(3)].

8. Unpaid Dividend Account

Where a dividend is not paid within 42 days of its declarations, the company shall within 7 days from the date of expiry of the 42 days, transfers the unpaid dividend to a special account of .... company limited company (Private) Limited [Section 205-A(l)].

9. Transfer to General Account of the Central Government

Any money transferred to the unpaid Dividend Account which remains unpaid or unclaimed for a period of three years shall be transferred by the company to the general revenue account of the Central Government [Section 205-A(5)].

10. Payment of Unpaid or Unclaimed Dividend

Any person claiming to be entitled to any money transferred to the general revenue account of the Central Government may apply to the Central Government for an order for payment of money claimed [Section 205 -B].

11. Dividend to be Paid to Registered Shareholder

The dividend must be paid only to the registered shareholder or to his order or to his bankers, or to the bearer of share warrants [Section 206].

12. Dividend a debt from the date of declaration

The dividend becomes a debt from the date on which it is declared.

13. Penalty

Where the dividend has been declared by the company but has not been paid or the warrant in respect there has not been posted within 42 days from the date of entitled to payment of the dividend, every director, who is knowingly a party to the default, is punishable with imprisonment upto 7 days and with fine (Section 207).

INTERIM DIVIDEND

An interim dividend is a dividend paid between two ordinary general meetings of the shareholders and can be paid if the directors are authorised by the articles. The Board may from time to time pay the members such interim dividends as a justified by the profit of the company. (Articles 86 of Table A). But before declaring an interim dividend, the directors must satisfy themselves that the financial position of the company warrants the payment of such dividend out of profits available for distribution. An interim dividend, if authorised by the Articles is not a debt. It is settled law that in case of an interim dividend which the directors have resolved to pay, they have an option at any time before payment to review their decision and resolve not to pay. The Supreme Court in *J. Dalmia v. Commr. Of Income Tax*[163], held that the interim dividend is not a debt and, therefore not an enforceable obligation. Comparing and contracting final dividend with interim dividend.

DIVIDEND WARRANT

A dividend warrant is an instrument containing an order on a company banker directing it to pay the stated amount to or to the order of the shareholder named therein who is entitled to claim divided. It is in two parts — one part is a notice of the dividend to the shareholder as well as certificate of deduction of income tax, and the other part is the dividend warrant. The notice and certificate part give particulars as to the meeting which declared the dividend the rate of dividend declared and the period to which it relates, the gross amount of dividend due on shares, the amount of income tax and surcharge deducted and the net amount due. This part also includes a declaration form to be filed in and signed by the shareholder to be submitted to income tax authorities. It certifies that the dividend relates to shares which were his own property.

Payment of Interest out of Capital (Section 208)

Sometimes, shares in a company may be issued for the purpose of raising money to defray the expenses of the construction of any work or building or the provision of any plant, which cannot be made profitable for a lengthy period, the company may pay interest on paid-up share capital under certain conditions provided such payment is bonafide and in the interests of the company. The conditions are:

(i) Such payment is authorised by the articles or a special resolution.

(ii) Previous approval of the Central Government is obtained.

(iii) Before sanctioning any such payment the Central Government may appoint a person to inquire into and report to it on the circumstances of the case. The expense of inquiry will have to be borne by the company.

(iv) The payment of interest must be made only for such period as may be determined by the Central Government. The period should in no case extend beyond the close of the half year next after the half year during which the work or building has been actually completed or the plant provided.

(v) The rate of interest shall in no case exceed 4% per annum or such other rate as the Central Government shall direct.

The payment of interest shall not operate as a reduction of the amount paid-up on the shares in respect of which it is paid.

CHAPTER

44

Borrowing Powers

The Companies Act does not expressly give to the company any power to borrow money. Every trading company needs money to finance its activities. A part of this requirement is met by the issue of shares, for the rest the company has to resort to public borrowings. Every trading company, unless prohibited by its memorandum or articles, has implied power to borrow money for the purposes of its business, and to give security for the loan by creating a mortgage or charge of its property. On the other hand, non-trading companies have no implied power to borrow unless the memorandum of association gives them the power to do so. A public company having a share capital cannot exercise the borrowing power unless a certificate of commencement of business has been obtained by it (Section 149). A private company can, however, exercise borrowing powers soon after its incorporation.

Exercise of Borrowing Powers

The borrowing power is exercised by the Board of directors subject to provisions in the memorandum and the articles of the company. The Companies Act 1956 prescribes, however, a statutory limit upon the borrowing powers of directors. Section 293(1)(d) provides that the directors of a public company, or a subsidiary thereof, shall not, except with the consent of such company in general meeting, borrow moneys which together with those already borrowed will exceed the aggregate of the paid-up capital of the company and its free reserves. This limit will not include temporary loans obtained from the company's bankers in the ordinary course of business.

Thus, the power of the directors to borrow is subject to two main limitations:

(a) Limitations enumerated in the articles and memorandum, and

(b) Statutory limitations.

Ultra Vires Borrowing and Intra Vires Borrowing

Borrowing by a company may be a borrowing which is:

1. *ultra vires* the company, or
2. *intra vires* the company but *ultra vires* the directors.

Borrowing ultra vires the company

Borrowing by a company shall be deemed to be *ultra vires* where the company borrows inspite of no power to borrow or borrows beyond the limit fixed by the memorandum or Articles. In such a case, the contract is void and the lender cannot sue the company for the return of the loan. The securities given for such *ultra-vires* borrowing are also void and inoperative.

Remedies of Lender's

In ultra vires borrowing the lender has the following remedies:

(a) Injunction and Recovery

If the money, assets, property, etc. purchased with such money is identifiable and are still in the possession of the company, the lender can obtain an injunction to restrain the company from parting with them and seek a tracing order to trace and recover them.

(b) Subrogation

If the money borrowed has been used to pay-off debts which could have been enforced against the company, the lender may sue the company being subrogated to the rights of the creditors who were paid-off. This is based upon the principle that a company which borrows to pay-off existing debts, does not thereby, increase its liabilities. In *Neath Building Society v. Luce*,[164] a building society became indebted to some of its members for principal and interest due on mortgage. It borrowed money *ultra vires* to pay-off principal and interest. It was held that the lenders were subrogated to the rights of the creditors paid-off.

The right of subrogation does not entitle the lender to any security held by the original creditor or to any priority that the original creditors may have had over the other creditors of the company.

(c) Identification and Tracing

If the lender can identify his money or any property purchased with it, he can obtain a tracing order and follow the property, i.e., he can claim the money or the property purchased with the money borrowed. The company in such a case is regarded as holding the money lent on trust for the lender.

(d) Recovery of Damages

The lender in certain conditions may sue the directors for damages for the breach of an implied warranty of authority unless the *ultra vires* borrowing could have been discovered from the two important documents of the company, i.e., the memorandum and the articles.

Firbank v. Humphreys and other.[165] F did construction work for a company and agreed to accept debentures in payment instead of cash. F did not know that all the debentures which the directors could issue were already issued. As the company has no assets to satisfy F's claim on the debentures, he sued the directors. Held, the issue of debentures was *ultra vires* and void and the directors were liable for breach of implied warranty of authority. They were ordered to pay F the par value of the debentures he ought to have received. Weeks v. Propert:[166] A railway company had fully exercised its borrowing powers. The directors advertised for money to be lent on the security of debentures. W lent L 500 and received a debenture. The debenture was declared void. It was held that W could sue the directors for breach of warranty implied from the prospectus.

2. Borrowing Intra Vires the Company but Ultra Vires the Directors

If the borrowing is in excess merely of the powers of the directors but not of the company, it can be ratified and rendered valid by the company. The legal position of this case is very simple. *Intra vires* acts can be ratified by the members of a company and thereupon such acts become valid. Thus borrowing by directors in excess of their powers can be ratified by the company and rendered valid. Even if the company refuses to ratify the acts of the directors, the doctrine of indoor management shall protect the lender, provided that he is in a position to establish that he advanced the money in good faith. In such a case, the company has the right of subrogation against the directors.

Security for Borrowing

The company may borrow by creating a security in the form of a mortgage, hypothecation, or a charge or through issuance of a bill of exchange, hundi etc. However, no company can create a charge on its reserve capital.

Registration of Charges

A company having power to borrow money is empowered also to charge its assets, subject however to any limitations in its memorandum or articles. Even uncalled capital may be charged but for this purpose the company's articles must give the power and there must be nothing in the memorandum to the contrary.

Section 125 requires the following charges must be registered with Registrar within 30 days of their creation:

(1) a charge for the purpose of securing any issue of debentures,
(2) a charge on uncalled share capital of the company,
(3) a charge on any immovable property,
(4) a charge on any book debts of the company,
(5) a charge not being a pledge on any movable property of the company,
(6) a floating charge on the undertaking or any property of the company including stock in trade,
(7) a charge on calls made but not paid,
(8) a charge on a ship or any share in a ship,
(9) a charge on goodwill, on a patent of a licence under a patent, on a trade mark, or on a copyright or a licence under a copyright.

It is the duty of the company to send the above particulars to the Registrar within 30 days of charge or extended period which cannot be more than 7 days, but registration may also be effected on the application of the creditor. The creditor may in such a case recover the registration fee from the company (Section 134).

Effect of Non-Registration

(1) In case a registrable charge is not registered within the prescribed time, it becomes void
(i) against the liquidator, and
(ii) any creditor of the company [Section I25(i)]
(2) However, the debt, in respect of which the charge was given remains valid, that is, it can always be recovered as an unsecured debt [Section 125(2)]
(3) Another effect of non-registration of a charge is that the money secured thereby becomes immediately payable [Section 125(3)].
(4) The company and every officer may be subjected to a penalty upto Rs. 500 for every day during which the default continues [Section 142(1)].
(5) Where any charge on any property of a company required to be registered under section 125 has been so registered, any person acquiring such property or any part thereof, or any share of interest therein, shall be deemed to have notice of the charge as and from the date of such registration (Section 126).

Register of Charges to be kept by the Registrar (Section 130)

The Registrar shall, in respect to each company, cause to be kept a register containing the particulars of all the charges requiring registration. Every company shall forward to the Registrar for being entered in the register the particulars of all the charges requiring registration in such form and manner, and after payment of, such fees as may be prescribed. The particulars of the charge shall relate to:

(1) The date of the creation of the charge,
(2) The amount secured by the charge,
(3) The short particulars of the property charged, and
(4) The person entitled to the charge.

The pages of the register shall be consecutively numbered and the registrar (a) cause to be kept in such register in the prescribed form the documents of charges filed in such form and manner as may be prescribed, and (b) sign or initial every page of such register.

Index to Register of charges (Section 131)

The Registrar is required to keep a chronological index, in the prescribed form and with the prescribed particulars of the charges registered with him.

Certificate of Registration (Section 132)

On registration the Registrar gives a certificate of registration starting the amount secured by the charge. Such certificate is a conclusive evidence that the requirement of the Act as to registration have been complied with (section 132).

Modification of Charges (Section 135)

Section 135 of the companies Act 1956 provides that whenever the terms or conditions, or the extent and operation, of any charge registered are modified, it shall be the duty of the company to send to the Registrar the particulars of such modification within 30 days. The particulars of modification shall be filed in form no 8.

The Company's Register of Charge (Section 143)

Every company has to keep at its registered office a register of charges and enter there in all charges specifically affecting property of the company and all the floating charges on the undertaking or on any property of the company, giving in each case:

(a) a short description of the property charged,
(b) the amount of charge, and
(c) the names of persons entitled to charge.

If any officer of the company knowingly omits or willfully authorises or permits the omission of any of the above entries, he shall be punishable with fine which may extend to Rs. 500.

Under section 136, every company must kept at its registered office a copy of every instrument creating any charge requiring registration. But in the case of a series of uniform debentures, a copy of only one debenture of the series is sufficient. The register of charges and the documents must be open for inspection by any person.

DEBENTURES

The most usual form of borrowing by a company is by issue of debentures. The definition of debenture' as contained in Section 2(12) of the Companies Act does not explain the term. According to Section 2(12), "debenture includes debenture stock, bonds and any other securities of a company whether constituting a charge on the company's assets or not." The nature of debenture is thus not described by this definition. A debenture is a document given by a company as evidence of a debt to the holder usually arising out of loan and most commonly secured by a charge. Debentures are commonly issued in a manner similar to the issue of shares by means of a prospectus inviting applications. The money might be payable by installments on application, allotment and calls. But usually the amount is payable in one lump-sum.

According to Chitty, J. "debenture means a document which either creates a debt or acknowledges it, and any document which fulfills either of those conditions is a debenture."

According to Gower, L.C.B. "debenture is a name applied to certain types of documents evidencing an indebtedness which is normally, but not necessarily secured by a charge over property."

According to Palmer, the word, "debenture' signifies "any instrument under seal evidencing a deed, the essence of it being the admission of indebtedness."

Thus debenture is a document creating or acknowledging an indebtedness of the company which mayor may not be secured.

Characteristics of Debentures

The usual characteristics of a debenture are:

(1) It is issued by a company and is usually in the form of a certificate which is an acknowledgement of indebtedness.

(2) It is issued under a company's seal but it is not necessary for the validity of a debenture. A certificate signed by two directors of a company is valid.

(3) It usually specifies a particular period or date as the date of repayment. It also provides for the payment of a specified principal and interest at the specified date. But a company is not debarred from issuing perpetual or irredeemable debenture.

(4) It is generally secured by a charge, fixed or floating on any part of the company's property or undertaking. But this is, however, not an essential conditions because section 2(12) provides that the debentures mayor may constitute a charge on the assets of the company.

(5) It is usually one of the series of like debentures. But a single debenture may be issued to one man.

(6) A debenture holder does not have any right to vote in the company meetings (Section 117).

(7) Debentures can be issued on right basis to the existing shareholders of the company.

(8) They can enforce the sale of security in case of default.

(9) Debentures can be issued on right basis to the existing shareholders of the company.

Kinds of Debentures

Debentures may be of following kinds:

1. Dearer Debentures

Such debentures are payable to bearers, and such debentures possess the characteristics of a negotiable instruments and are transferable by delivery. Notice of the transfer of such debenture is not required to be given to the company. Interest on a bearer debenture is paid by means of coupons allowed to it and it must be presented for payment of the company's bankers when the date of payment arrives.

2. Registered Debentures

Registered debenture is one which is registered in the name of a holder in the books of the company. It is transferable in the same way as a share. These are not negotiable instruments. Interest on such a debenture is payable to the registered holder or to the order of the registered holder. Such debenture-holders debenture holders can transfer their debentures in the open market in the same way as shares are transferred. The transfer of the registered debentures is required to be registered with the company.

3. Secured Debentures

When some assets or property of the company are charged in favour of the debenture holders, the debentures are deemed to be secure. The charge which a company may create on its assets may be a fixed charge or a floating charge or both specific and a floating charge.

4. Unsecured or Naked Debentures

Debentures which do not carry any charge on the assets of the company are naked or unsecured debentures. In such a case the debenture-holder is an ordinary unsecured creditor of the company. Unsecured debentures are mere acknowledgements of a debt due from the company, creating no rights beyond those of ordinary unsecured creditors.

5. Redeemable Debentures

A redeemable debenture is one under which the principal money is paid-off to the debenture-holder on the expiry of the fixed term. The company may redeem a certain number of debentures each year or option may be given to the company to redeem all of them by a specific date. Redeemed debentures can be reissued by the company by reissuing the same debenture or by issuing the other debentures in their place.

6. Perpetual Debentures or Irredeemable Debentures

Perpetual debentures are also known as irredeemable debentures. Such debenture as payable only in the event of a winding-up or on some serious default by the company or payable at a remote period. There is no time limit within which the company is bound to pay the amount due on such debentures. Section 120 provides, "A condition contained in any debenture or in any deed for securing any debentures, whether issued or executed before or after the commencement of this Act, shall not be invalid by reason only that thereby, the debentures are made irredeemable or redeemable only on the happening of a contingency, however remote, or on the expiration of a period however long."

Thus, A perpetual mortgage in the nature of a debenture issued by a company is valid under section 120 of the Companies Act, though It will be invalid under transter of property act. *Knights bridge Estates Trust Ltd. v. Byme.*[168]

A company mortgaged 75 houses and other properties to secure L 3,10,000 repayable by 80 half-yearly instalments. There was no right of redemption before 40 years expired. The company claimed to redeem the mortgage. The house of lords held that the mortgage was debenture and it could be made irredeemable under the law.

7. Convertible Debentures

Such debentures contains a clause entitling the holder thereof to convert his debt into equity or preference shares of the company at a specified rate of exchange. The rate of exchange of debentures for the shares however, must not be less than the per value of the shares unless the requirements of the Act as to the issue of shares at a discount are complied with. In the case of such debentures, the holder may exercise his option and convert them into shares at times specified in the debentures.

According to convertibility, debentures are further classified into three categories:

(i) Fully convertible debentures
(ii) Non-convertible debentures
(iii) Partly convertible debentures

(i) Fully Convertible Debentures

Such debentures are those debentures that are converted into equity shares of the company on the expiry of a specified period.

(ii) Non-Convertible Debentures

Such debentures do not confer any option on the holder to convert the debentures into equity shares and are redeemed at the expiry of a specified period.

(iii) Partly Convertible Debentures

Such debentures consist of two parts (a) convertible and (b) non-convertible. The convertible portion is convertible into equity shares a the expiry of specified period. Non-convertible portion, on other hand, is redeemed at the expiry of a certain period.

Difference Between Debenture and Debenture Stock

The difference between debenture and debenture stock is same as that between share and share stock.

Debenture	Debenture Stock
(i) A debenture is the description of an instrument.	(i) A debenture stock is the description of the borrowed capital consolidated into one mass for the sake of convenience by an instrument.
(ii) It is always for a fixed and transferable only in its entirely.	(ii) It may be created for any amount of money by consolidation of several debenture amounts and a single certificate is issued covering several debentures. It is transferable in fragments subject to the provisions of the articles.

Issue of Debentures

Debentures are commonly issued in a similar manner as shares by means of a prospectus inviting applications the money being usually payable by installments on application, allotment and on specified dates. The authority to issue debentures rests with the board of directors (Section 292). Debentures may be issued at par, at a premium or at a discount,[169] unless the articles specifically forbid issue of debentures at a discount.

Debenture certificate must be complete and ready within three months of allotment, unless the terms of the issue provide a longer period (Section 113). Section 117 provides that no company shall, after the commencement of the Act issue debentures carrying voting rights at any meeting of the company.

Debentures with Pari Passu Clause

Debentures are usually issued in a series with *Pari Passu* clause, i.e., a clause whereby all debentures of a particular series though issued at different and varying times are to rank together, as regards the security created by them. The effect of a *Pari-Passu* clause is that all the debentures of a series are to be paid rateably, and if there are insufficient assets to pay all the debenture-holders in full, the amount is distributed in proportion to the amounts owing to each of them. If there is no *Pari Passu* clause in the terms of issue, the debentures would be payable according to the date of issue and if they are issued on the same date and serially numbered, they would rank in numerical order.

Reissue of Redeemed Debentures (Section 121)

Section 121 authorises the companies to keep alive and re-issue debentures which have been first redeemed by the company unless there is provision to the contrary, express or implied, in the Articles, or in the conditions of issue, or in any other contract entered into by the company or the company has shown an intention to cancel the debentures. Such reissue may be of the same redeemed debentures or new debentures in place of the redeemed ones.

On such reissue of redeemed debentures the holders of debenture has the same rights and priorities as if debentures had never been redeemed. Re-issued debentures are treated as new debentures for the purpose of stamp duty.

The Company's Balance Sheet must give particular of any redeemed debentures which the company has power the issue. A contract to subscribe for debentures can be specifically enforced. (Section 122).

Debenture Trust Deed

When debentures are issued for public subscription, involving a considerable number of debenture-holders, it is not feasible to create a separate charge in favour of thousands of debenture-holders. Therefore the most common and convenient form of securing them is to execute a Trust deed conveying the property of the company to the trustees and declaring a trust in favour of the debenture-holders. A trust deed normally grants the trustees a fixed charge over the companies freeholds and leaseholds and a floating charge over the rest of the property.

The trust deed contains provisions about the respective rights of the company and the debenture holders.

Advantages

The following are the advantages of having a trust deed.

(1) In case of default by the company, the trustees are there to take the necessary steps instead of leaving to the initiative of individual debenture-holders.

(2) The trustees will have a legal mortgage of the property and will also hold the title deeds. So that the person who subsequently lend money to the company cannot gain priority over the debenture-holders.
(3) The debenture-holders can through the trustee sell the property charged, and thus, realise the security without the aid of the court.
(4) The trustees are empowered to see that the property is kept insured and properly maintained.
(5) The trustees are authorised to appoint a receiver out of the court or to enter into the possession of the property and carry on the business of the company in case of urgency.

Powers

A trust deed normally contains clauses giving the trustees the following powers.

(1) To take a mortgage over the company's property in which case the title deeds are transferred to them and the company is thereafter prevented from creating further charges ranking in priority to debentures.
(2) To sell or lease the property and to renew leases.
(3) To exchange the mortgaged property for other suitable property.
(4) To modify subsisting contracts applying to any part of the property.
(5) To compromise claims.
(6) To commence and defend actions.
(7) To appoint a receiver on the security becoming enforceable.

Right and Remedies of Debenture-Holders Rights

Rights

The debenture-holders following rights:

(1) They can inspect trust deeds [Section 118 (4)], the register and index of debenture-holders, and
(2) Require the company to furnish a copy thereof after the payment of the requisite fees.

Remedies

The remedies of a debenture-holder vary according to whether he is secured or unsecured.

Unsecured Debentures

An unsecured debenture-holder is in exactly the same position as a creditor and he has the same remedies thus:

(a) he may sue the company for recovery of the money secured by the debenture and execute the degree against the property of the company, or
(b) he may present a petition for winding up the company under section 433(e) on the ground that company is unable to pay its debts, or
(c) if there be winding up in progress, he can prove in such winding up the amount due to him.

Secured Debentures

Secured debenture-holder has above three remedies, but in addition he has also recourse to any of the following remedies:

(a) Sale

He may sell the property through trustees if such power is given by the debenture trust deed.

(b) Debenture-Holder's Action

When the company defaults in making payment, he may sue the company on behalf of himself and other debenture-holders of the same class to obtain payment and enforce his security by sale.

(c) Appointment of Receiver

The trustees may appoint a receiver if the conditions which give him power to do so are fulfilled or apply to the court in a debenture-holder's action to appoint one.

(d) Foreclosure

The trustees may apply to the court for foreclosure of the right of the company to redeem the debenture but in such case all the debenture-holders of every class as well as the company should be joined as parties to the action.

(e) Proof of Balance

If the company is insolvent and his security is insufficient, he may value his security and prove for the balance. In the alternative, he may surrender his security and prove for the whole amount of his debt.

Register of Debenture-Holder (Section 152)

Every company must keep in one or more books a register of the holders of its debentures.

It must enter there in the following particulars namely:

(i) The name, address and occupation of each debenture-holder.

(ii) The debentures held by each holder with their distinctive numbers, amount paid or considered as paid on them.

(iii) The date on which each person was entered in the register as a debenture-holder.

(iv) The date on which any person ceased to be a debenture-holder.

The company is also required to keep an index of the debenture holders when their number exceeds fifty. It should make necessary alterations in the index with 14 days of any alteration made in the register of debenture holders.

The above provisions do not apply with respect to debentures which, *ex facie*, are payable to bearer thereof (Section 152).

Mortgages and Charges

A company can issue secured and unsecured debentures. If the debentures are not secured by the assets of the company, the debenture-holders position is that of an unsecured creditor. Secured debentures are issued by creating a charge on the assets of the company. The term 'Charge' means generally an interest. The word 'charge' is defined in section 124 of the Act as including a mortgage. It also includes a lien or other equitable charge, However, a mortgage is different from a lien and a charge.

Section 58(1) of the transfer of Property Act, 1882 defines a mortgage as follows:

"A mortgage is the transfer of an interest in specific immovable property for the purpose of securing the payment of money advanced or to be advanced by way of loan an existing or future debt or the performance of an engagement which may give rise to a pecuniary liability."

Section 100 of the transfer of Property Act, 1882 states "where immovable property of one person is by act of parties or operation of law made security for payment of money to another and the transaction does not amount to mortgage, the latter person is said to have a charge on the property."

Fixed and Floating Charges

The charge on the assets of a company given by a debenture or a trust may be a fixed (specific) charge or a floating charge.

Fixed or specific Charge

A fixed or specific charge is one which is created on some ascertained and definite property of the company, e.g., a charge on land and building. It prevents the company from dealing in that property without the consent of the holder of charge. The company can, if it wants to deal in that property, do so subject to the charge.

Floating Charge

The term 'floating charge' has not been defined anywhere in the Companies Act. A floating charge is an equitable charge which does not faster on any ascertained or definite property and as such the company can deal with any of its assets in the ordinary course of business. The consent of the debenture-holders is not necessary for the company to deal with its assets.

Lord Power has defined the term floating charge as, "it is a charge which floats like a cloud over the whole assets from time to time falling within a generic description."

The essence of a floating charge is that the security remains dormant until it is fixed or crystallizes.

Characteristics of a Floating Charge

The characteristics of a floating charge have been very clearly stated by *Romer L.J. in Re. Yorkshire Wool Combers Association Ltd.* [170], as follows:

(1) It is a charge on a class of assets of the company, both present and future.
(2) That class is one which, in the ordinary course of business of the company, would be changing from time to time.
(3) It is contemplated that until some stops are taken by or on behalf of those interested in the charge, the company may carry on its business in the usual way.

Tests as to whether a charge is a floating charge

The principal tests as laid down in *Imperial Bank of India v. Bengal National Bank Ltd.*[171], as to whether a charge is floating charge or not, are:

(1) It is a charge upon all classes of assets present or future.
(2) Would the assets charged in the ordinary course of business be charged from time to time.
(3) Has the company power until some steps is taken by the charge holder to carry on the business of the company in ordinary way.

If the answer of these questions is in the affirmative, the charge is a floating charge.

Crystallisation of a Floating Charge

Crystallisation is the conversion of a floating charge into a fixed charge on the assets in the class charged at the moment of crystallisation.

(1) When the company ceases to carry on business, or
(2) When the company goes into liquidation, or
(3) When default is made in the payment of any principal money or interest and the debenture-holder brings an action to enforce this security, or
(4) When a receiver is appointed.

Government stock investment Co. Ltd. v. Manila Railway Co. Ltd.,[172]. The debentures created a floating charge. After three months interest become due, but the debenture-holders took no steps. The company then made a mortgage of a specific part of its property. The house of Lords hold that the mortgage has priority. It was observed, "It is of the essence of floating charge that it remains dormant until the undertaking charged ceases to be a going concern, or until the person in whose favour the charge is created intervenes. As long as he does not intervene the business will be carried on, not as of right, but by the sufferance of the debenture-holders and at their money."

Consequences of a Floating Charge

The company can —

(1) deal in the property on which a floating charge is created, till the charge crystallises;
(2) not with standing the floating charge, create specific mortgages of its property having priority over the floating charge; and
(3) sell the whole of its undertaking if that is one of its objects specified in the memorandum, in spite of the floating charge on the undertaking (*Borax Co. Re Foster v. Borax Co.*[173]).

Invalidity of Floating Charge

A floating charge created within 12 months of the commencement of the winding-up of a company will be invalid unless it is proved that the company immediately after the creation of the charge was solvent. Even a charge created within twelve months of the commencement of the winding-up of the company is valid to the extend of the cash paid or to be paid to the company in consideration for such charge, together with interest on that amount at the rate of 5% per annum or such other rate as may for the time being be notified by the Central Government in this behalf in the Official Gazette (Section 534).

Distinction between fixed and Floating Charges

In *Illingworth v. Houldsworth,*[174] Lord Macnaghten distinguished the two types of charges as follows:

"A specific charge ....is one that without more fastens on ascertained and definite property or property capable of being ascertained and defined; a floating charge, on the other hand, is ambulatory and shifting in its nature, hovering over and, so to speak, floating with the property which it is intended to affect. until some event occurs or some act is done which causes it to settle and fasten on the subject of the charge within its reach and grasp."

Registration of Charges

Where a company creates a charge over its property, section 125 requires that the following charges are void against the liquidator or creditors unless registered with the Registrar of companies. The prescribed particulars of the charge, together with the instrument, if any by which the charge is created or evidenced or a copy there of must be filed with the within 30 days of their creation. The Registrar may extend the time for filing of the particulars and instrument creating the charge by seven days provided the company had sufficient cause for not filing the particulars within the specified.

(a) A charge for the purpose of securing any issue of debentures,
(b) A charge on uncalled share capital,
(c) A charge on any immovable property wherever situated or any interest therein.
(d) A charge on any book debts of the company,
(e) A charge not being a pledge on any movable property of the company,
(f) A floating charge on the undertaking or any property of the company including stock in trade,
(g) A charge on calls made but not paid,
(h) A charge on a ship or any share in a ship,
(i) A charge on goodwill or a patent or licence under a patent, on a trade mark or copy right.

Effects of non-registration of a Charge

1. The Charge is Void

If any charge required to be registered is not so registered, it shall be void as against the subsequent encumbrances as well as against the liquidator and the creditors [Section 125 (1)].

2. The money Secured Becomes Immediately Payable

When a charge becomes void under section 125, the money secured thereby shall become immediately payable [Section 125(3)].

3. No Right of Lien on the Documents of Title

When a charge becomes void for non-registration, no right of lien can be claimed on the documents of title as they are only ancillary to, and were delivered pursuant to, the charge (*Molton Finance Ltd., Re*).[175]

4. Penalties

If default is made in filing with the Registrar for registration the particulars:

(a) of any charge created by the company, or
(b) of the payment or satisfaction or a debt in respect of which a charge has been registered or
(c) of the issue of debentures of a series, requiring registration with the Registrar, then, unless the registration has been effected on the application of some other person, the company and every officer of the company or other person who is in default, are punishable with fine which may extend to Rs. 500 for every day during which the default continues.

If a company makes a default in complying with any other requirements as to the registration with the Registrar of any charge created by the company or of any fact connected therewith, the company and every officer of the company who is in default, is punishable with fine which may extend to Rs. 1000/-.

Company's Register of Charges (Section 143)

Every company shall keep at its registered officer a register of charges and enter therein all charges specifically affecting property of the company and all floating charges on the undertaking or any other property of the company, giving in each case.

(a) short description of the property charged;
(b) the amount of the charge,
(c) except in the case of securities payable to the bearer, the names of the persons untitled to the charge.

If any officer of the company knowingly omits or willfully authorises cr permits the omission of any entry in the register of charges he is liable to a fine upto Rs. 500/-.

Section 144 provides that the copies of the instrument creating charges and the register of charges maintained by the company shall be open to inspection by a creditor or member of the company.

Register of Charges Kept by the Registrar (Section 130)

The Registrar shall, in respect to each company cause to be kept a register containing the particulars of all the charges requiring registration. Every company shall forward to the Registrar for being entered in the register the particulars of all the charges requiring registration in such form and manner, and after payment of, such fees as may be prescribed.

The particulars of the charge shall relate to:

(1) the date of the creation of the charge,
(2) the amount secured by the charge,
(3) the short particulars of the property charged, and
(4) the person entitled to the charge.

The page of the register shall be consecutively numbered and the registrar shall:

(a) cause to be kept in such register in the prescribed form the documents of charges filed in such form and manner as may be prescribed, and
(b) sign or initial every page of such register.

Index to Register of Charges (Section 131)

The Registrar is required to keep a chronological index, in the prescribed form and with the prescribed particulars, of the charges registered with him.

Certificate of Registration (Section 132)

On registration, the Registrar shall issue a certificate of registration stating therein the amount thereby secured. Such a certificate will be conclusive evidence that the requirements as to registration have been complied with.

A copy of the certificate shall be endorsed on every debenture issued by the company after such registration. Any person who contravenes these provisions shall be punishable with the fine upto Rs. 1,000/- (Section 133).

Distinction Between Mortgage And Charge

1. Mode of Creation

A charge may be created either by act of parties or by operation of law, while a mortgage is created by act of the parties.

2. Transfer of interests

In a charge, there is no transfer of an interest or right in property but merely the creation of a right of payment out of property specified. A mortgage is a transfer of interest in specific movable property.

3. Specified Property

A mortgage presupposes specific property existing at the date of transfer but a charge may relate to unspecified property it may be a floating security.

4. Personnel Liability

There is no personal liability to pay in a charge while in a simple mortgage which requires registration, there is a personal liability to pay.

5. Registration

A simple mortgage requires registration where as a charge created by operation of law does not require registration.

Comparison Between Shareholders and Debenture-holders

	Share/Share holders		Debenture/Debenture holders
1.	A shareholder is the owner of the company, a registered member.	1.	Debenture-holder is the secured or unsecured creditor of the company.
2.	Shares issued without security or charge on the assets of the company.	2.	Debenture, generally issued secured and carry a charge on the assets of the company.
3.	Share capital is the owned capital, an important source of getting the capital, generally non-repayable during the lifetime of the company. It is a permanent capital.	3.	Debenture capital is a loan capital, an external source of raising the capital usually repayable during the lifetime of the company, having a fixed period of maturity.
4.	Share-holder may get dividend fixed or variable. Dividends shall be payable only out of annual or undistributed profits.	4.	Debenture is a fixed rate of interest, lower than the normal rate of dividend.
5.	They stand last as claimants for the return of capital at the position of winding up.	5.	Debenture-holders have a prior claim for the return of capital. If they are secured creditors, they can realise their security and prove for the balance at the time company's liquidation.
6.	Dividends are taxable before declaration, i.e, paid out of net profit after tax.	6.	Interest is an element of cost not subject to corporation tax.
7.	They are Governed by the articles of association, and have rights and privileges. Members are entitled to receive notices, annual accounts and report, attend general meetings, exercise their right of vote.	7.	Debenture-holders have no such right and privileges enjoyed by shareholders. As per trust deed they may be entitled to get copies of annual accounts and appoint one or two directors as their representatives on the Board.
8.	No repayment possible except (i) under winding up, (ii) when reduction of capital is approved by special resolution and confirmed by court (iii) when shares are redeemable preference shares.	8.	Debentures can become repayable automatically at the time of winding up or when the company makes a default.

CHAPTER

45

Management of Companies - I

(Management and Administration)

Directors

A company is an artificial person with a legal entity lacking both body and mind. It cannot act in its own person. It can do so only through some human agents. The persons by whom the business of the company is carried on are known as directors. They are in fact the brain of a company. speaking about the importance of directors, Nevile J. observed that "the Board of directors, are the brain and the only brain of the company which is the body and the company can and does act only through them". (in *Bath v. Standard L and Co.*)[176].

Definition [Section 2(13)]

Section 2(13) defines a 'director' as any person occupying the position of a director by whatever name called. Only an individual can be appointed a director (Section 253). The important factor to determine whether a person is or not a director is to refer to the nature of the office and its duties. It does not matter by what name he is called. A director may, therefore, be defined as a person having control over the direction, conduct, management or superintendence of the affairs of a company. It does not matter whether they are designated as directors, trustees or governors so long as they are charged with the responsibility of management. A body corporate, association or a firm cannot be appointed a director of a company, only an individual shall be appointed as a director.

Number of Directors

Every public company other than a public company which has become such by virtue of Section 43-A of the Act must have at least three directors and every private company must have at least 2 directors [Section 252(2)], subject to the minimum number of directors, the articles of a company may prescribed the maximum and the minimum number of directors for its Board of directors. The number so fixed may be increased or reduced within the limits prescribed by the articles by an ordinary resolution of the company in general meeting (Section 258). Any increase beyond the maximum permitted by the Articles must be approved by the Central Government. But where the increase in number does not make the total number of directors more than 13, no approval of the Central Government is needed (Section 259).

Appointment of Directors

Directors may be appointed in the following ways:

(1) By the articles as regards first directors (Section 245)
(2) By the company in general meeting (Section 255 to 257,263,264)
(3) By the directors (Section 260,262,313)
(4) By third parties (Section 255)
(5) By the principle of proportional representation (Section 265)
(6) By the Central Government (Section 408)

1. First Directors

Usually the first directors, are named in the articles of association of the company. The appointment of such directors will be valid only if each of them, before the registration of the article.

(a) signed and filed with the Registrar a consent in writing to act as such director, and
(b) (i) signed the memorandum for his qualification share, if any, or
    (ii) taken his qualification shares from the company, or

(iii) signed and filed with the Registrar an undertaking in writing to take and pay for his qualification shares, or
(iv) delivered to the Registrar an affidavit to the effect that the qualification shares are registered in his name.

If the articles of the company are not registered because Table A has been adopted by the company or if the directors are not named in the articles of the company, the subscribers of the memorandum may appoint the directors and if they do not appoint any directors, all the subscribers who are individuals will be deemed to be the directors of the company until the first annual general meeting of the shareholders appoints new directors (Section 254).

2. Appointment by Company

Appointment of subsequent directors is made at every annual general meeting of the company.

Section 255 provides that not less than two thirds of the total number of directors of a public company must be subject to retirement by rotation. The remaining directors of such a company must also be appointed by the company in general meeting.

At every subsequent annual general meeting, one-third of the directors of a public company or a liable to retire by rotation. If the number is not three or a multiple of three, then the number nearest to one-third must retire from office. The directors to retire by rotation at every annual general meeting must by those who have been longest in office since their last appointment. As between persons who become directors on the same day, those who are to retire will, subject to any agreement among themselves, be determined by lot.

At the annual general meeting at which a director retires, the company may fill up the vacancy by appointing the retiring director or some other person thereto. If the place of the retiring director is not so filled, and the meeting has not expressly resolved not to fill the vacancy, the meeting shall stand adjourned. If at the adjourned meeting also the vacancy is not filled, and the meeting has not expressly resolved not to fill the vacancy, the retiring director shall be deemed to have been reappointed at the adjourned meeting unless:

(1) at the meeting or at the previous meeting a resolution for the reappointment of such directors has been put to the meeting and lost;
(2) he has, by a notice in writing, addressed to the company or its Board, expressed his unwillingness to be reappointed;
(3) he is not qualified or disqualified for appointment;
(4) a special or ordinary resolution is necessary for his appointment or reappointment (Section 256).

A person other than a retiring director is also eligible for appointment to the office of director subject to his necessary qualifications. A notice in writing signifying his candidatures must be left at the office of the company at least fourteen days before the date of meeting. The notice may be given either by the candidate himself or by his proposer. The company shall inform the members as necessary for the company to serve individual notices upon the members if the company such candidature not less than 7 days before the meeting, in at least two newspapers. One of the newspapers must be in English language and the other in the regional language of the place where the registered office of the company is located. These provisions do not apply to a private company, unless it is a subsidiary of a public company.

A person who is being proposed as a candidate for the office of a director must sign and file with the company his consent in writing to act as a director if appointed. The requirement does not apply to a director retiring by rotation (Section 264).

3. Appointment by Directors

The board of directors may appoint

(i) Additional directors
(ii) Alternative directors
(iii) Directors filling causal vacancy.

(i) Additional Directors (Section 260)

The board of directors of a company may, if authorised by the articles, appoint additional directors without consulting the shareholders in a general meeting. Such additional directors hold office only up to the date of next annual meeting of the company. The number of directors and the additional directors must not exceed the maximum strength fixed for the board by the articles.

(ii) Alternate Directors (Section 313)

The board of directors may appoint an alternate director if authorised by the articles or by a resolution of the company in a general meeting. An alternate director acts in the place of a director who is absent for more then three months from the state in which Board meetings are held. He cannot hold office for a period longer than that permissible to the original director in whose place he has been appointed. He must vacate office on return of the original director.

(iii) Causal Vacancy (Section 262)

In the case of a public company, or a private company which is a subsidiary of a public company, the office of any director appointed by the company in general meeting may be vacated before his term of office expires in the normal course. In such a case, the resulting casual vacancy may be filled by the board of directors at a meeting of the board. This power of the board is subject to any regulations in the articles of the company. A vacancy caused by the retirement of a director by rotation is not a causal vacancy will hold office only upto the date upto which the director in whose place he is appointed would have held office.

4. Appointment of Directors by Third Parties (Section 255)

The articles under certain circumstances give power to the debenture-holders or other creditors, e.g., a banking company or a financial corporation, who have advanced loans to the company to appoint their nominees to the board. The number of directors so appointed must not exceed 1/3rd of the total number of directors, and they are not liable to retire by rotation.

5. Appointment by Proportional Representation

The articles of a company may provide that the appointment of not less then 2/3 of the total number of directors of a public company (or of a private company which is a subsidiary of a public company) shall be according to the principle of proportional representation, either by the single transferable vote or by a system of cumulative voting or otherwise, such appointments shall be made once in three years and interim causal vacancies may be filled up according to Section 262 (Section 265).

6. Appointment by The Central Government (Section 408)

The Central Government may appoint such manner of directors on the board of a company as the Company Law Board may specify as being necessary to effectively safeguard the interest of the company, its shareholders or the public interest. The period of appointment shall not exceed 3 years on anyone occasion. The purpose of this appointment is to prevent the affairs of the company from being conducted either:

(a) in a manner which is oppressive to any members of the company, or
(b) in a manner which is prejudicial to the interest of the company or to public interest.

The directors so appointed are not required to hold any qualification shares. Further, they are required to keep the company law board informed of the affairs to the company to enable it to take such timely action as may be required by the exigencies of the circumstances.

Restriction on number of Directorships

No person can be a director in more than twenty companies. The following companies. The following companies shall be excluded in calculating the number of companies of which a person may be a director:

(a) a private company which is neither a subsidiary nor a holding company of a public company,
(b) an unlimited company,
(c) an association not carrying on business for profit or which prohibits the payment of a dividend,
(d) a company in which such person is only an alternate director.

Where a person already holding the office of director in 20 companies is appointed as a director of any company, the appointment will not take effect unless such person has within fifteen days thereof, effectively vacated his office as a director in any of the companies in which he was already a director, his new appointment will become void if he does not make a choice within 15 days as aforesaid. Any person who holds office or acts as a director of more than 20 companies in contravention of the above provisions shall be punishable with fine which may extend to Rs. 5000 in respect of each of those companies after the first 20 (Section 279).

Restrictions on Appointment of Directors (Section 266)

A person shall not be capable of being appointed director of a company by the articles and shall also not be named as a director or proposed director in prospectus unless before the registration of the articles, or the publication of the prospectus or the filling of the statement in lien of prospectus, as the case may be, he has:

(1) Signed and filed with the Registrar a consent in writing to act as such director and has,

(2) (i) Signed the memorandum for his qualification shares, if any, or

(ii) taken his qualification shares, if any, from the company and paid or agreed to pay for them, or

(iii) Signed and filed with the Registrar an undertaking in writing to take from the company his qualification shares, if any, and pay for them, or

(iv) made and filed with the Registrar an affidavit to the effect that his qualification shares are registered in his name.

Section 266 does not apply to a private company.

Share Qualification of Directors (Section 270)

The act does not make it obligatory on any director to hold shares in the company. The articles of association generally require that the qualification of a director shall be the holding of a specified number of shares known as qualification shares. Unless he is already qualified, he must obtain the qualification shares within two months after his appointment as a director. Any provision in the articles of a company is so for as it requires a person to hold the qualification shares before his appointment as a director or to obtain them within a shorter time than two months will be void. The nominal value of these shares must not exceed Rs. 5000 or the nominal value of one share where it exceeds Rs. 5000. The holding of share warrant shall not be deemed to be the holding of qualification shares.

It is not essential for the director to buy his shares directly from the company. The director must also hold these shares in his own right. Shares held by a director jointly with any other person may be a sufficient qualification. Again if a director holds the shares as a trustee, he is duly qualified provided that it does not appear on the register of members that he is a trustee. But if a director takes his qualification shares from a promoter, it amounts to a breach of trust.

If a person acts as a director of a company without holding the qualification shares he will be punishable with fine which may extend to Rs. 50 for every day between such expiry and the last day on which be acted as a director. Moreover by virtue of section 283, if a person fails to obtain the qualification shares as prescribed by the articles within the period specified, he automatically vacates office and cannot act as a director after the expiry of that period. The above provisions do not apply to a private company, unless it is a subsidiary of the public company (Section 273) nor do they apply to directors appointed by the Central Government under section 408.

Disqualifications of Directors

The act provides various disqualifications for directorship. Such disqualifications are either permanent or temporary or consequential or revocable. The following persons are disqualified for appointment as a directors of a company.

(1) According to Section 274, a person cannot be appointed as a director of a company:

(a) who has been found to be of unsound mind by a court of competent jurisdiction.

(b) who is an undischarged insolvent.

(c) who has applied to be adjudicated as an insolvent and whose application is pending.

(d) who has been convicted of an offence involving moral turpitude and sentenced to imprisonment for not less than 6 months and a period of 5 years had not elapsed since the expiry of his sentence.

(e) who has not paid any call on shares in respect of shares of the company held by him for a period of six months from the last day fixed for the payment.

(f) who has been disqualified by an order of the court under section 203, of an offence in relation to promotion, formation or management of the company or fraud or misfeasance in relation to the company.

(2) According to section 203, the court may make an order that a person shall not, without the leave of the court, be a director of, or in any way, whether, directly or indirectly, be concerned or take a part in the promotion, formation or management of a company for such period as specified in the order but not exceeding 5 years, who

(a) is convicted of any offence in connection with the promotion, formation or management of a company.

(b) has been found, in the course of winding up of a company, (i) guilty for any offence for which he is punishable under section 542 or (ii) guilty as an officer of the company of any fraud or misfeasance or any breach of duty in relation to the company.

A person who acts as a director in contravention of such an order is punishable with imprisonment for term not exceeding 2 years or with fine not exceeding Rs. 5000 or with both.

(3) According to Section 209A, a director is bound to produce for inspection books of account by the registrar or an authorised officer of the Central Government and if he violates this rule shall be disqualified to become director of any company for a period of 5 years.

(4) According to Section 388E, the Central Government shall, by an order, remove a director of a company from his office if the High Court finds him to be unfit for directorship and by that order he becomes disqualified to be a director of any company for a period of 5 years unless the Central Government in concurrence with the High Court lifts that ban before the expiry of 5 years.

(5) According to Section 407, where the agreement with a director has been terminated under Section 402, such a director is disqualified for a period of 5 years from the date of order of termination of agreement, to be a director of that company. Any such director contravening this rule or any other director who is a party to such contravention shall be punishable with imprisonment for a period not exceeding one year or with fine not exceeding Rs. 5000 or both.

(6) According to Section 226, the auditor of a company cannot be director of the company.

A private company which is not a subsidiary of a public company may provide in its articles, further grounds of disqualifications for a director of that company.

Legal Position of Directors

The act does not make any specific provision with regard to the exact legal position of directors. It is very difficult to define the exact legal position of the directors of a company, and sometimes as managing partners of a company. They arc commorcial mon, said *M.R. Jessel in Forest of Dean Coal Mining Co. Re case,*[177] "managing a trading concern for the benefit of themselves and of all the shareholders in it. They stand in a fiduciary position towards the company in respect of their powers and capital under their control." Justice L. Bowen commented in the case *Imperial Hydropathic Hotel Co., Blackpool v. Hampson*[178] "Directors are described sometimes as agents, sometimes as trustees and sometimes as managing partners." However, no definite position can be ascribed to directors in view of their diversified roles.

1. Directors as Agents

The First characteristic of directors is that they are agents of the company. A company is an artificial person and it cannot act itself. It must, therefore function through directors as its human agents: Acts of the directors for and on behalf of the company exclude directors from personal liability, provided they are within the scope of their authority or if the shareholders ratify their acts, if they are within the powers of the company. The relationship between the company and directors is that of principal and agent.[179]

The important functions of the directors as agent of the company are to enter into contracts, to create negotiable instruments and to borrow money on behalf of the company.

It is, however, not true to say that the directors are nothing more than agent of company. They have in certain matter independent powers. They are not bound to consult the shareholders in all matter (*Allen v. Hyalt*[180]).

Directors are not agents of the members of the company[181]. The members at a general meeting cannot override the powers of the directors by passing a resolution[182] (even unanimously). On the other hand, directors may not carry out the decisions taken by members if the directors think that such decision is not proper in the interest of the company [*Pother v. Hindustan Trading Corporation (P) Ltd.*[183]].

The position of directors as agents is superior to that of ordinary agents and so they are called more an agent. An ordinary agent derives his authority from his principal but the directors as agents derive their authority not only from their principal, i.e., the company by virtue of its articles but the directors also derive their authority from the act it self. Such authority cannot be overridden.

2. Directors as Trustees

The directors are not only agents of the company but in some sense and to some extent they are also trustees for the company. They are selected to manage the affairs of the company for the benefit of the shareholders. It is an office of trust.

They are trustees of the company's money and property in the sense that they must account for all the company's money and property over which they exercise control. They have also to refund to the company any of its money or property which they have improperly paid away or transferred. They are, however, not trustees in the real sense of the word because they are not vested with the ownership of the company's property. It is only as regards some of their obligations to the company and certain powers that they are regarded as trustees of the company.

Directors are trustees of the powers entrusted to them and they must exercise their powers honestly and in good faith and in the interest of the company.

Alexander v. Automatic Telephone.[184] The directors of a company paid up nothing on their own shares. They, however, made all the other share holders pay 356d on each share. They did not tell the other share holders of the difference held, this was breach of trust and the directors must pay to the company 356d on each of their shares.

The directors are trustees for the company and not for the shareholders, in their individual capacity (*Percival v. Wright*).[185]

However, it is to be noted that the directors are not trustees in the strict sense of the term. The distinction between a director and trustees has been very clearly made by *James L.J. in Smith v. Anderson*[186] in the following words.

The distinction between a director and a trustee is an essential distinction founded on the very nature of things. A trustee is a man who is the owner of property and deals with it as principal, as owner and as master, subject only to an equitable obligation to account to some persons to whom he stands in the relation of a trustee, who are his '*Cestui que trust*' (beneficiaries). The office of director is that of a paid servant of the company. A director never enters into a contract for himself, but he enters into contract for his principal, that is for the company of which he is a director, or for whom he is acting.

3. Directors as Managing Partner

Directors are elected representatives of the shareholders and therefore they are in a position of managing partners but they are not exactly partners in the legal sense as the liability of a director is limited to the value of shares held by him and he has no authority to bind the other directors and shareholders.

Under the partnership law, one individual partner is the agent of the firm, i.e., all the partners taken together and the business of the firm can be carried on by anyone partner acting for all. In partnership firm, having a good number of partners, sometimes specially authority is "delegated on a particular partner for various reasons and such a partner is called managing partner. In a company, the management is in the hands of plural executives. And so, the directors are managing partners. Even though substantial powers may be entrusted upon a director or to an outsider manager such a person has to act under the superintendence, control and direction of the Board of Directors. Therefore, unlike in a partnership firm, no power can be delegated on a single director as a managing partner. The principle of delegatus non postest degegare, i.e., power once delegated cannot be further delegated, is applicable to company management.

4. Directors as Officers

For certain matters, directors are treated as officers of a company. As such they are liable to certain penalties if the provisions of the Companies Act are not strictly complied with.

5. Directors as Organs of the Company

The company is artificial person and it acts through the persons known as directors. Therefore, they are known as organs of the company. The board of directors are the brain and the only brain of the company which is the body and the company can and does not act only through them. [87] When the brain functions, the corporation is said to function.

In nutshell, we can say that the directors are neither agents nor trustees, nor managing partner in full sense of the term. In fact, the directors combine in themselves all these positions. Thus, the best way to sum up their position is to described it as fiduciary relationship to the company. They may also be held as officers of the company and as such may be held responsible for their faults and omissions.

Vacation of Office by Directors (Section 283)

Section 283 says that the office of a director shall become vacant, if:

(a) he fails to obtain or ceases to hold at any time thereafter, his share qualification, if any,

(b) he is found to be of unsound mind by a competent court,

(c) he applies to be adjudicated an insolvent,

(d) he is adjudged in insolvent,

(e) he is convicted by a court of an offence involving moral turpitude and sentenced to imprisonment for not less then 6 months,

(f) he fails to pay any calls on the shares held by him within six months from the date fixed for payment, unless the central government has by notification in the Official Gazette removed his disqualification;

(g) he absents himself from three consecutive meetings of the Board of directors or from all the meetings of board for a continuous period of three months whichever is longer without obtaining lean of absence from the Board,

(h) he (whether by himself or by any person for his benefit or on his account) or any firm in which he is a partner or any private company of which he is a director, accepts a loan or any guarantee or security for a loan from the company in contravention of Section 295,

(i) he does not disclose to the Board of directors of his interest in any contract or proposed contract with the company,

(j) he is restrained by courts from being a director for committing fraud or misfeasance in relation to the company under Section 203,

(k) he is removed by the company in general meeting in pursuance of Section 284,

(l) having been appointed a director by virtue of his holding any office or the other employment in the company, he cases to hold such office or other employment in the company.

Of the above grounds the first six are similar to those which disqualify a director from holding the office under Section 274 of the act. The grounds stated in (d) and (f) above shall not disqualify a director from holding his office immediately until 30 days have elapsed from the date of the adjudication, sentence or order where no appeal is preferred. But in case of an appeal the specified disqualifications shall take effect on the expiry of the 7 seven days from the date on which such appeal is finally disposed off.

A person who acts as a director knowing fully well of his disqualification is subject to a penalty which may extend to Rs. 500/- for each day on which he so acts as a director.

A private company which is not a subsidiary of a public company can be removed by (a) shareholders, (b) central government, or (c) the court.

Removal of Directors

A director of a company may be removed by:

(i) by shareholders

(ii) by Central Government

(iii) by the Court

(i) By Shareholders (Section 284)

A company may, by an ordinary resolution, remove a director before the expiry of his period of office. But a company can not remove in following cases:

(a) a director appointed by the central government under Section 408,

(b) a director in the case of private company, holding office for life on the 1st April, 1952, or

(c) directors appointed in accordance with the principle of proportional representation, under Section 265.

Special notice is required of any resolution to remove a director. Where some of the shareholders wants to remove a director or to appoint someone in his place, they must give a notice to the company at least 14 days before the meeting, specifying the intention to move the resolution. On receipt of such notice, the company will immediately send a copy thereof to the director concerned. He may make any representation in writing and the copy of such representation may be sent by the company to every member. Where the copy of the representation is not sent because it is received too late or because of the company's default, the director may (without prejudice to his to be heard orally) require that the representation shall be read out at the meeting.

The vacancy created by the removal of a director may be filled up in the same meeting provided special notice of the proposed appointment was also given. The successor can hold office until the date up to which his predecessor would have held office if he had not been removed. If the vacancy is not filled at the meeting, the Board may fill it as a casual vacancy provided the director who has been removed is not appointed.

(ii) By Central Government (Sections 388-B to 388-E)

A director can also be removed at the initiative of the central government. The central government may, by order, remove from office any director against whom an adverse judgement has been given by a High Court, on a reference made by the government, for an alleged fraud, misfeasance, gross negligence or breach of trust, etc., in carrying out his legal obligations.

The effects will be:

(a) The person so removed shall not hold the office of a director or any other office connected with the conduct and management of the affairs of the company for a period of five years, unless the period is remitted,

(b) No compensation is payable to him for the termination of office. The company may, with the previous approval of the central government, appoint another person to that office.

(iii) By Court

On an application to the court under Section 397 or 398 for the prevention of oppression and mismanagement the court may terminate, or set aside or modify any agreement between the company and the managing director, or any other director or manager. On such termination, the director cannot serve the company in a managerial capacity for a period of five years from the date of the order of termination, without the permission of the court. The director on removal cannot sue the company for damages or compensation for loss of office.

CHAPTER

46

Management of Companies - II
(Directors: Power, Duties and Liabilities)

Powers of Directors

As the company is an artificial person, it acts through its directors. Powers of directors means powers of the board of directors, functioning through meetings or otherwise. Except where specific provisions are made in the act that the power of a company shall be exercised in general meetings with regard to certain power, in all other cases the powers shall be exercised by the board of directors of the company. Section 291 to 293-A contain the powers of the board and the restriction thereon. The powers of directors are discussed under the following heads:

A. General Powers of The Board (Section 291)

Section 291 (1) of the act defines "Subject to the provisions of the act, the Board of Directors of a company shall be entitled to exercise all such powers and to do all such acts and things as the company is authorised to exercise and do."

The effect of this Section is that subject to restrictions contained in the act, memorandum and articles, the powers of directors are co-extensive with those of the company itself. There are, however, subject to two conditions.

(i) The board of directors are not entitled to exercise the powers reserved for the shareholders in general meetings and

(ii) In the exercise of their powers, the directors are subject to the provisions of the act, memorandum and the articles and other regulations not inconsistent therewith passed by the company in general meetings.

Further Section 291(2) states that no regulation made by the company in general meeting shall invalidate any prior act of the board which would have been valid if that regulation had not been made.

It is clear from the provisions that the general powers of the board are ultimately bound by what 'the company is authorised to do and that by. Its memorandum and articles and contrary provisions anywhere else. A general meeting can not interfere with the day-to-day functions of the board. (*Suburban Bank Private Ltd., Trichur v. Tharaith*).[188] Similarly, the board also cannot do anything beyond its powers (*East Coast Transport and Shipping Company. Private Ltd., v. Official Liquidator*).[189] The director cannot defend their irregular acts on the plea of ignorance of law (*Louis Steen v. Charles Allen Law*). [190]

B. Powers to be exercised by Board only at meeting (Section 292)

1. According to Section 292(1) the board of directors of a company (public as well as private) shall exercise following powers only by means of resolution passed at the board meetings.
   (a) the power to make calls on share holders in respect of money due on their shares,
   (b) the power to issue debentures,
   (c) the power to borrow moneys other than on debentures,
   (d) the power to invest the funds of the company in any shares of debentures of any other companies the same group, within the prescribed limits.
   (e) the power to make loans.

The board may, by a resolution passed in its meeting, delegate its powers to borrow money, to make investments and to make loans, to any committee of directors, the managing director, the manager or any other principal officer of the company to such extent (as given below) on such conditions as the board may prescribed.

Provided further that this Section does not apply to the board of a banking company which in ordinary course of business accepts deposits, make payments and borrow from other banks.

Clause (c) shall mean arrangement between a company and its bankers with regard to overdraft, cash credit or otherwise.

(2) Every resolution delegating the power referred to in clause (c) shall specify the total amount outstanding at anyone time upto which moneys may be borrowed by the delegate.

(3) Every resolution delegating the power referred to in clause (d) shall specify the total amount upto which the funds may be invested, and the nature of the investments which may be made, by the delegate.

(4) Every resolution delegating the power referred to in clause (e) shall specify the total amount upto which loans may be made by the delegate, the purpose for which the loans may be made and the maximum amount ofloans which may be made for each such purpose in individual cases.

(5) The company in general meeting may impose restrictions and conditions on exercising of above powers by the board.

It may be noted that in this Section a new term 'Principal Officer of the company' has been referred to. But the act now where has defined the term.

There are some other provisions in the act where directors are required to exercise the following powers at the meeting of the board:

(i) the power to fill the causal vacancies of directors [Section 262(1)],

(ii) the power to give consent to contracts in which a director or his relative or a firm in which the director or his relative is interested [Section 297 (4)],

(iii) the power to receive notice of disclosure of director's interest in contracts [Section 299(3)(C)],

(iv) the power to receive director's disclosure of shareholdings. [Section 308(2)],

(v) the power to provide loans or guarantees for loans to other bodies Corporate (Section 370),

(vi) the power to invest in the shares of other companies [Section 372 (5)],

(vii) the power to appoint a person as managing director or manager who is already a managing director or manager of another company [Sections 316 (2) and 386 (2)],

(viii) the power to make a declaration of solvency for members voluntary winding up [Section 488],

(ix) the power to recommend rates of dividend on equity shares, declaring interim dividend, recommending rates of depreciation or creation of reserve.

The term investment means laying out funds for profit[91]. Where the board has delegated any power or not, the onus of proof lies on the board. 192

C. Restrictions on powers of the board (Section 293)

According to Section 293, the board of directors of a company (public or private) which is a subsidiary of a public company, shall exercise the following powers only with the consent of shareholders in general meeting:

(1) To sell, lease or otherwise dispose of the whole, or substantially the whole undertaking, of the company.

(2) To remit or give time for repayment of any debt due by the director of the company, except in the case of an advance made by banking companies to its directors in the ordinary course of business.

(3) To invest the amount of compensation received by the company in respect of compulsory acquisition of company's property or business, other than trust securities.

(4) To borrow money in excess of the aggregate of the paid up capital of the company,

(5) To contribute to charitable or other funds not directly relating to the business of the company, or welfare of its employees, any amount the aggregate of which in any financial year exceeds Rs. *5000/-* or 5 per cent of its overage net profits during the last three years immediately preceding, which ever is greater (Section 239).

(6) To appoint sole selling agents for a period of 5 years at a time (Section 294).

(7) To make loans or to stand security to the extent of 10% of the aggregate of the subscribed capital of the company (Section 370).

(8) To invest in upto 10% of the subscribed capital to any other body corporate (Section 372).

However, the aggregate of the investment made in all companies shall not exceed 30% of the subscribed capital of the investing company (This does not apply to a company whose principal business is to make such investments). It all the other companies are in the same group, however, the aggregate should not exceed 20% of the subscribed capital of the investing company [Section 370 (I-B) and Section 372 (II)].

Restriction on Political Contribution

(1) With a view to permitting the corporate sector to playa legitimate role within the defined norms in the functioning of our democracy, Section 293 A (as per amendment act of 1985) allows companies to make contributions to political parties or for political purposes to any person, directly or indirectly, out of their profits.

According to Section 293A(1) the board of directors can not contribute any amount or amounts of the company (a) to any political party or (b) for any political purpose to any individual or body.

Not only the board of directors but even any company in general meeting cannot make such contribution.

(2) If the company contravenes this provision, it shall be punishable with fine which may go upto Rs. 5,000/- and every officer in default shall be punishable with imprisonment for a term upto 3 years and with fine.

(3) The company shall disclose in its profit and loss account the amount or amounts of such contributions during the financial year to which that account relates, giving (a) particulars of the total amount contributed, and (b) the name of the party or person to which or to whom such amount has been contributed [Section 293-A(4)].

Abuse of Powers by The Directors

There are many cases of abuse of powers by directors which were held invalid for example P

(a) Directors issued fresh shares to destroy the majority of a group of shareholders though the company really needed additional capital (*Howard Smith Ltd. v. Ampol Petroleum Ltd.*).[193]

(b) Directors of a company forfeited the shares of one shareholder to save him from his liability (Esparto Trading Co. case[194]).

(c) Directors of a company made a call shares of some selected shareholders only to put them into difficulty (Galloway v. Halle Concerts Society[195]).

Duties of directors

As directors hold a key position, they are bound to comply with the provisions of the Companies Act. The directors have two kinds of duties.

(A) Duties under the provisions of the act or statutory duties.

(B) Duties of general nature or general duties.

A. Duties under the provisions of the act or statutory duties

The duties of directors begin with incorporation of a company and ends with its liquidation.

The various duties of directors are given below:

(1) to see that all moneys received for shares from applicants of shares are deposited in a scheduled bank.

(2) to repay the application money to the applicants or shares if the company fails to obtain the certificate to commence business within the prescribed time [Section 6(4 and 5)].

(3) to see that each member of the company gets a copy of the statutory reports at least 21 days before the statutory meeting (Section 165).

(4) to place before the members at the annual general meeting the profit and loss account and the balance sheet of the company [Section 210 (I)].

(5) to check the accuracy of the prospectus before its issue to public (Section 56).

(6) to sign by every person who is named in the prospectus as a director of the company (Section 60).

(7) to file a certified declaration before the registrar of companies to obtain certificate of commencement of business.

(8) to sign on annual returns by at least one director and manager or secretary (Section 161).

(9) to call the annual general meeting in time (it must be held within an interval of 15 months, except in the case of first annual general meeting, where the time interval may be for 18 months.

(10) to get the directors reports ready to lay before annual general meetings (Section 217).

(11) declaration of dividends and payment of dividends [Section 206 and 207].

(12) to file copies of final accounts with the registrar within 30 days after an annual general meeting (Section 220).

(13) to produce all books and papers of the company before the investigator, in case the central government has appointed him for investigating the affairs of the company (Section 240).

(14) to help the central government in case of an inquiry is being instituted against anyone in the company (Section 242).

(15) to call the meeting of the board of directors at least once in every three months (at least 4 such meetings shall be held in every year) (Section 285).

(16) to submit a report by each director within 20 days of his appointment, regarding holding, of any position in any other bodies corporate (Section 305).

(17) to disclose before the company about the share holding by each director, in other, bodies (Section 328).

(18) to present the statement of affairs to the liquidator, before commencing the winding up process (Section 454).

(19) to take and pay for the qualification shares within 2 months from the date of appointment (Section 270).

(20) to disclose their interest in any of the contracts entered into by the company. The disclosure must be made at the first meeting of the board held after become so interested (Section 299).

B. Duties of General nature or General duties

The general duties of the directors vary according to circumstances, size and nature of the company's business. The general duties may be classified as

(1) Duty to act honestly
(2) Duty of reasonable care
(3) Act personally
(4) Duty of disclosure
(5) Duty to attend meetings

1. Duty to act honestly

The first and the most obvious obligation of directors is to act with honestly in the discharge of their duties and not to make secret profits.

2. Duty of Reasonable Care

Directors should carryout their duties with such care, skill and diligence as is reasonably expected from persons of their knowledge and status. They are not expected to display an extraordinary care. The directors are not liable for mere errors of judgement[196].

3. Act Personally

The directors must perform their duties personally and not to delegate power to other person.

The maxim "*delegatus non-potest delegate*" (a delegatee cannot delegate further) applies to them like all against.

4. Duty of Disclosure

Section 297 provides that except with the consent of the board of directors, a director of the company, or his relative, a firm in which such a director or relative is a partner, any other partner in such a firm or a private company of which the director is a member or director, shall not enter into any contract with the company.

(i) for the sale, purchase or supply of any goods, materials or services, or

(ii) for underwriting the subscription of any shares in or debentures of the company. Further, in the case of a company having a paid up share capital of not less than Rs. 1 crore, no contract in which the directors are interested shall be entered into except with the approval of the central government.

Exceptions

The consent of the board of directors is not necessary in the following cases:

(1) sale or purchase of goods for cash at prevailing market prices.

(2) contracts entered into in the regular course of business involving Rs. 5000/- in the aggregate in any year.

(3) any transaction of a banking or insurance company in the ordinary course of business.

In the circumstances of urgent necessity, a director, relative, firm, partner, or private company referred to above may enter into any contract for the sale, purchase or into any contract for the sale, purchase or supply of goods, without obtaining the consent of the board. The consent of the board must, however, be obtained within 3 months of the date on which the contract was entered into the consent must be given by a reasonable passed at the meeting of the board. If the board does not give consent to any contract, anything done in pursuance of the contract shall be voidable at the option of the board.

It is the duty of every director to disclose to the board the nature of his concern or interest in any contract or arrangement entered into by or on behalf of the company. The disclosure must be made at the meeting of board of directors. An interested director cannot take part in the discussion of or vote on each contract. His presence at the board's meeting shall not be taken into account for the purpose of forming a quorum nor will his vote be counted. In default of disclosure, the director is punishable with a fine of Rs. 5000/- besides vacating office.

5. Duty to attend meeting

It is the duty of directors to attend meetings unless physically impossible. Directors are not bound to attend all the meetings of the board, although they are under an obligation to attend whenever in the circumstances in which they are reasonably able to do so.

Liabilities of Directors

A public company may make the liability of any or all of its directors unlimited if sufficient provision exists in the company's memorandum. In case no such provision exists in the company original memorandum, the company may if authorised by articles and by a special resolution passed at its meeting, alter the memorandum so as to render unlimited liability to directors. But any such new provision will become effective against any director only when he has consented to it [Section 323(2)].

In case the company proposes a person for appointment to the office of a director with unlimited liability, a notice in writing shall be given to him before he accepts the office or act therein [Section 322 (2) and (3)].

The directors of a company incur three types of liability:

(1) Liability towards the company
(2) Liability towards outsiders or third parties
(3) Criminal liability

1. Liability towards the Company

The directors are liable to the company in the following ways:

(i) Liability for ultra-vires acts

Directors are personally liable to the company if they act in contravention to memorandum or articles of association. It is not necessary to prove fraud in such cases. For example, when they pay dividends in the any profits and when they dissipate the funds of the company in *ultra vires* transactions.

(ii) Liability for negligence

Directors are liable for negligence in performing statutory duties. There is no statutory definition of negligence as such each case has to be decided after due consideration of the particular facts thereof. But they will not be liable where they have acted bonafide and for the benefit of the company. If the directors are guilty of negligence they will be liable, even if the articles otherwise provide (Section 201).

(iii) Liability for Breach of Trust

Directors being the trustees of the company, they should discharge their duties in the best interest of the company. They are liable to the company for any loss resulting from breach of trust. They are also accountable to the company for any secret profits they might have made in transactions on behalf of the company.

(iv) Liability for acting fraudulently

The debts or the liabilities of the company in the event of its winding up are due to any act done fraudulently during the period of promotion or in managing the affairs of the company, they are personally liable to the company.

(v) Liability for Misfeasance

Directors are liable to the company for misfeasance. The word misfeasance covers willful misconduct or willful negligence. Mere failure on the part of the director to take necessary steps for recovery of debts due to the company does not constitute misfeasance. If the company is in the course of winding up, the court may, on the application of the liquidator, creditor or contributory examine into the conduct of a director for any misfeasance or breach of trust in relation to the company.

2. Liability Towards Outsider or Third Parties

Directors act as agents of the company. Therefore, where the directors enter into contracts in the name and on behalf of the company, they will not be personally liable for these contracts. It is the company which will be liable to third parties for such contracts. However the directors will be personally liable to third parties of contract in the following cases:

(i) liability for contracts entered into their own names rather than in the name of the company.

(ii) liability in case of misstatement in prospectus as per Section 62 of the act.

(iii) liability in case of failure to repay the application money to the applicants of shares within the prescribed time limit.

(iv) liability for non-refund of application money in case of refusal by stock exchange to enlist company's shares (refund of money within 8 days of refusal otherwise 12% interest.

(v) liability for acting beyond the powers of directors but, at the same time, acting within the powers of the company.

(vi) liability for ultra-vires acts which can not be ratified even by the unanimous consent of shareholders.

(vii) liability for breach of implied warranty: when the directors take loans from third parties, there is an implied warranty that they have complied with the requirements under the provisions of the article of the company. In case of breach of such provision, they are personally liable to third parties for breach of implied warranty.

(viii) liability due to irregular allotment of shares by avoiding the provisions of Sections 69, 70 and 71 (3).

(ix) liability when limited liability is made to unlimited (Section 322 and 323).

(x) liability at the time of winding up of the company: If any fraud was committed either at the time of promotion or for fraudulently managing the company, they will be liable to the company.

3. Criminal Liability

Inspite of civil liabilities of directors, there are numerous provisions of the companies act relating to maintenance of proper accounts, filing of returns or observance of certain statutory formalities. If they fail to perform these statutory duties, the Act provides penalties by way of fine or punishment or both, in addition to criminal liability under the common law of the country or under I.P.C. The following are some of the criminal liabilities of directors:

(i) liability for making misstatement in prospectus — 2 years imprisonment or a fine which may extend to Rs. 5000/- or with both (Section 63).

(ii) liability for inducing persons to invest fraudulently in a company — 5 years imprisonment or fine of Rs. 10,000/- or with both (Section 68).

(iii) when failed to file with registrar the statement of allotment of shares in the prescribed form within 30 days of allotment, fine exceeding to Rs. 500/- per day till default continues [Section 75(4)].

(iv) when failed to issue the share certificates within the prescribed time limit - fine extending to Rs. 500/- per day till the default continues.

(v) when failed to file annual returns with the registrar — fine extending to Rs. 501/- per day till the default continues (Section 162).

(vi) when failed to call the statutory meeting within the prescribed time limit a fine extending to Rs. 500/- per day till the default continues (Section 165).

(vii) when failed to call annual general meeting of the company fine of Rs. 5001/- for default and if the default continues a further fine of Rs. 250/- per day (Section 168).

(viii) when continued in the office as undischarged insolvent — an imprisonment for term extending 2 years or Rs. 5000/- as fine or with both (Section 202).

(ix) when failed to make payment of dividend to the shareholders within 42 days of declaration — simple imprisonment for a term of 7 days and fine (Section 207).

(x) when failed to present the final account before the annual general meeting — imprisonment for a term extending to 6 months, or a fine upto Rs. 1000/- or with both (Section 209).

(xi) when failed to provide requisite information to auditors — imprisonment for a term extending to 6 months or a fine up to Rs. 5000/- or with both.

(xii) when failed to carryout the restrictions imposed by the central government in regard to transfer of shares, voting rights, future issue of shares dividends, etc — imprisonment for term extending to 6 months or a fine up to the amount of Rs. 5000/- or with both (Section 250).

(xiii) for lending of money to directors against the restrictions under the act — imprisonment for a term extending to 6 months or fine upto Rs. 5000/- or with both (Section 295).

(xiv) to hold office of a director in more than 20 companies at a time-fine extending to Rs. 5000/- per month (Section 279).

(xv) when failed to disclose about the share holding in different companies — imprisonment for a term extending to 2 years or a fine upto Rs. 5000/- or with both (Section 308).

(xvi) for continuing in the office of director even after its vacation by order of the court imprisonment for a term extending to one year or a fine upto Rs. 5000/- or with both (Section 407).

(xvii) for making solvency declaration (in the case of members voluntary winding up) without having reasonable grounds - imprisonment for a term extending to 2 years or a fine or Rs. 500/- or with both (Section 542).

(xviii) if the business of the company has been carried on with the intention to defraud creditors or for any fraudulent purpose, imprisonment for a term extending to 2 years or a fine of Rs. 500/- or with both (Section 542).

(xix) in case of falsification of books of the company with the intention to deceive any person (falsification may include destroy, mutilation, alteration, falsification etc) — imprisonment for term extending to 7 years and fine (Section 539).

(xx) if wrongfully obtains possession of a company's property or wrongfully refuses to deliver it to the company — imprisonment for a term upto 2 years.

Relief from liability

According to Section 633, where it appears to the court that a director has acted honestly, reasonably and having regard to all the circumstances, the court may relieve him either wholly or partly from his liability on such terms as it may think proper.

CHAPTER

47

Management of Companies - III

(Managing Director, Manager and Managerial Remuneration, Sole Selling Agents)

Managing Director

According to Section 197 A, a company, in addition to directors may appoint managing director.

Section 2(26) of the act clearly defines a managing director. According to Section 2 (26), "Managing Director means a director who, by virtue of an agreement with the company or resolution passed by the company in general meeting or by virtue of its memorandum or articles of association is entrusted with special powers of management which would not otherwise be exercisable by him, and includes a director occupying the position of managing director by whatever name called." He is however subject to the control 0 the board of directors. A managing director has a special status but he has no special status as understood by Section 42 of the Specific Relief Act of 1963. He is a whole-time director and is the chief executive of the company.

Characteristics

Above definition makes clear the following characteristics of managing directors:

(1) He is one of the directors of a company.

(2) He exercises the functions of supervision, control and direction.

(3) He is entrusted with substantial powers of management.

(4) This substantial powers would not have been exercised in the absence of an agreement or any resolution passed at a general meeting or by virtue of memorandum or articles.

(5) There may be more than one managing director in a company.

(6) He is also eligible to be reappointed.

(7) When a director is either removed from his office or his term of appointment expires, his term of office as managing director also automatically expires.

Appointment of Managing Directors

On analysing the definition of managing director as given in Section 2(26) of the act, a managing director can be appointed in anyone of the following ways:

(1) By agreement with the company, or

(2) By a resolution passed by the company in general meeting, or

(3) By a resolution of the board of directors, or

(4) By a clause in the memorandum of association or articles of association of the company.

The companies (Amendment) act 1988 has brought out major changes in the provisions relating to process of appointment of managing director/whole-time director/manager. The existing provisions are as under:

(1) A public company or a private company which is a subsidiary of a public company, having a paid up share capital of such sum as may be prescribed shall have a managing or whole-time director or a manager [Section 269(1)].

The sum prescribed (effective from 18th September, 1990) is rupees 5 crores or more.

(2) Such appointment can be made without the prior approval of the central government if such appointment is made in accordance with the conditions specified in Schedule XIII and a return in the prescribed form is filed within 90 days from the date of such appointment [Section 269(2)].

(3) If a company intends to introduce more conditions other than those stated in schedule XIII for appointment of a managing director/whole time director/manager, it must obtain permission of the central government in this behalf within 90 days from the date of such appointment [Section 269 (2 and 3)].

(4) The central government shall not accord its approval to such an application unless it is satisfied that:
   (a) it is in the interest of the company to have a managing or whole-time director,
   (b) the proposed managing or whole-time director of the company is, in the opinion, fit and proper person to be appointed as such and that the appointment of such person as managing or whole time director is not against the public interest, and
   (c) the terms and conditions of appointment are fair and reasonable [Section 269 (4)].

(5) The central government has powers to reduce the term of appointment proposed by the company [Section 269 (9)].

(6) If the approval is not accorded by the central government, the person occupying the office of managing or whole-time director shall vacate on the date when the decision of the central government has been communicated to the company, failing which he shall be punishable with fine which may go upto Rs. 500/- for every day during which he omits or fails to vacate [Section 269 (6)].

(7) If the appointment is not approved by the central government, it may refer the matter to the company law board for is final decision [Section 269 (7)].

(8) On receipt of such a complaint, company law board will issue a show cause notice to the company or to any officer who is responsible for effective compliance of Schedule XIII [Section 269 (8)].

(9) If it is proved to the satisfaction of the company law board that a breach of conditions of Schedule XIII was committed in appointing the managing director/whole-time director/manager, it will notify the breach on the part of the company [Section 269 (9)].

'Appointment' includes re appointment and 'whole-time director' includes a director in the whole-time employment of the company.

Disqualifications of Managing Director (Section 267)

Following persons cannot be appointed as a managing director:

(a) A person who is an undischarged insolvent or who has at any time been adjudged as insolvent.
(b) A person who suspends or has at any time suspended payment to his creditors or who makes or has at any time made a composition with them.
(c) A person who is or has been convicted by the court for an offense involving moral turpitude.
(d) A person who is not a director of a company (only a director can be appointed as a managing director).

Conditions of Appointment

According to Schedule XIII of companies (Amendment) act 1988 only following persons shall be appointed as managing director/whole-time director/manager of a company.

(1) Persons who have not been subjected to imprisonment or fined to a sum of Rs. 1000/- or more under the following Acts (as amended from time to time).
   (i) Import and Export (Control) Act 1947.
   (ii) Essential Commodity Act 1955.
   (iii) Income Tax Act 1961.
   (iv) Excise Duty Act 1962.
   (v) Gold (Control) Act 1968.
   (vi) Wealth Tax Act 1957.
   (vii) Central Excise and Salt Act 1944.
   (viii) Indian Stamp Act 1899.
   (ix) Industrial (Development and Regulation) Act 1951.
   (x) M.R.T.P. Act 1969.
   (xi) Foreign Exchange Regulation Act 1973.
   (xii) Food Adulteration Prevention Act 1954.

(2) A person who has completed 25 years of age but have not been completed 70 years or the maximum age limit set by the company, whichever is earlier.

(3) A person who has not been detained under foreign exchange regulation and smuggling activities prevention act 1974.
(4) A person who has not been a managing partner of a firm.
(5) A person who is an Indian citizen and resident of India.
(6) A person who has nct been a managing partner of a firm.
(7) A person who has not been holding the office of managing director or whole-time director or manager in any other company.

Managing Director for more than one company

Ordinarily one person can be a managing director of not more than two companies at a time. But according to Section 316, a public company or a private company which is a subsidiary of a public company may appoint or employ as its managing director, if he is the managing director or manager of one and of not more than one (including a private company which is not a subsidiary of a public company) provided that such employment is made or approved by a resolution at a meeting of the board with the consent of all the directors present at the meeting and a specific notice of the meeting mentioning the resolution to be passed has been issued to all the directors then in India.

The central government may, be order, permit any person to be appointed as a managing director of more than two companies if the central government is satisfied that it is necessary that the companies should, for their proper working, function as a single unit and have a common managing director.

Term of office of Managing Director (Section 317)

The maximum term of appointment of a managing director is five years. But, there is nothing to prohibit re-appointment, re-employment or the extension of the term of office. A managing director may be re-appointed or re-employment or his term of office may be extended for a further period not exceeding 5 years for each occasion provided that any such re-appointment, re-employment or extension shall not be sanctioned earlier than 2 years from the date on which it come into force.

Section 317 does not apply to a private company which is not a subsidiary of a public company.

Removal of Services of Managing Director

The act provides no specific section with regard to the removal of a managing director.

A managing director can not continue in his office if he ceases to be director *Smt. Jain v. Delhi Flour Mills Co. Ltd.*[197]

A managing director is entitled to compensation if his appointment is prematurely removed even if the article of the company is clearly provided for such removal. Similarly, where the removal is brought about by alteration of the articles in a manner inconsistent with the terms of appointment, he will be entitled for compensation. Whatever compensation is paid shall be disclosed and also shall be approved by the company in general meeting (*Kaye v. Croydon Tramways Co.*[198]). Where the appointment is not for a fixed period removal at any time may cause no liability in damages.

MANAGER

Who is a Manager ?

According to Section 197 A, a company, in addition to director, may appoint manager (in place of managing director) and Section 2(24) of the companies act, 1956 defines the term manager as "an individual who, subject to the superintendence, control and direction of the board of directors, has the management of the whole, or substantially the whole of the affairs of a company, and includes a director or any other person occupying the position of a manager by whatever name called, whether under a contract of service or not." The approval of the central government is essential for such an appointment.

'Manager' is a person who has management of the whole of the affairs of the company, not an agent who is to do a particular thing, or a servant who is to obey orders, but a person who is entrusted with power to transact the whole of the affairs of the company.

On the true construction of Section 2(24), it is clear that the word 'Manager' does not include 'Director'. In other words, a plain reading of the definition of 'Manager' as embodied in Section 2(24) of the act clearly indicates that 'every manager cannot be a director and every director cannot be a manager.' Also, the duties attached to the managers are quite different from those of directors. To put it in one sentence, a 'director' cannot be said to be a 'manager' unless he is appointed as such.

Characteristics

The above definition of term 'manager' clarifies the following characteristics of manager:

(i) Manager acts under the control and superintendence of the board of directors.

(ii) He possess the management of the whole or substantially the whole of the affairs of a company.

(iii) He takes important decisions related with execution of policies determined by the board of directors and supervise the work of office of the company.

(iv) It is not necessary that he should to enter into any agreement with the company for holding the position of a manager.

(v) Manager is a paid servant of a company.

(vi) It is not necessary that a manager must be a director of the company.

(vii) An individual only may be appointed as manager, not any firm body corporate or association (Section 384).

Appointment of Manager (Section 386)

No person can appoint any person as 'manager' if he is either the manager or managing director of any other company. Even then, if the company wants to employ him, then:

(a) it must be approved by a resolution passed at the meeting,

(b) specific notice of such appointment must be given to every director present in India,

(c) it is approved by central government who will approve only if a common manager is necessary for the proper working of more than two companies.

Provisions of Schedule XIII as applicable to managing director and whole time director are equally applicable to the appointment of manager. These provisions have already been discussed above.

Disqualifications of a Manager (Section 385)

Following persons are disqualified for appointment of manager:

(i) A person who is an undischarged insolvent or who has been adjudged insolvent within the preceding five years (Section...........).

(ii) A person who suspends or has within the preceding five years suspended payment to his creditors or makes or has made within the above period a composition with them.

(iii) A person who has, within the proceeding 5 years, been convicted by a court in India of an offence involving moral turpitude [Section 385(1)].

(iv) An individual only may be appointed as manager not any firm, body corporate or association.

The Central Government, however, reserves the right of removing the above disqualifications either generally or in relation to any company.

Period of Appointment

The rules are same with regard to period of appointment as they are for a managing director. Therefore Section 317 applies.

Remuneration

The position of a manager is the same as that of a managing director with regard to remuneration.

Remuneration payable to manager has been laid down in part II of schedule XIII. In case the remuneration of manager is fixed beyond the limit prescribed by the schedule XIII, the approval of the central government is essential in this regard.

The remuneration payable to a manager may be made on the basis of monthly salary or on the basis of certain fixed percentage of net profits of the company or by both these methods, however, the total remuneration payable to a manager, shall not exceed 5% of the net profits of the company (Section 387).

The above provision is not applicable to a private company, which is not a subsidiary of a public company (Section 388-A).

Liability of Manager

The liability of a manager may be made unlimited in a limited liability company (Section 322).

If authorised by articles, the liability of a manager may subsequently be made unlimited by altering the memorandum (Section 323). The position of a manager is the same as that of a director as understood by Section 322 and 323.

Difference Between Manager and Managing Director

Profits of difference	**Managing Director**	Manager
1. Positions	A managing director must be a director of a company [Section 2(26)].	A manager may be a director or an outsider [Sec. 2(24)].
2. Contract of Service	He always serves under a formal contract of service with the company. He is manager as well as Director.	The manager need not be under a formal contract of service.
3. Extensiveness of Power	He has only substantial powers of management [Sec.2 (26)]. His power is comparatively limited.	He has management of the whole or substantially the whole of the affairs of the company [Section 2(24)].
4. Number	A company may have two or more managing directors at a time and different activities may be entrusted on them	A company may have only one manager and the whole affairs of the company may be entrusted on him.
5. Qualification shares	Being a member of the Board of Directors, he is required to take and pay for the qualification shares under the provisions of the Act.	He is not required to purchase qualification shares to become a manager of a company.
6. Relationship with Board of directors	The relationship of a managing director with directors of board is like co-directors.	The relationship of a manager with the directors or the board is as that of master and servant.
7. Appointment	Managing director is appointed either on the basis of a provision in the articles or by the Board of directors or by a resolution passed in the general meeting of the company.	A manager is appointed by the Board of directors.
	Appointment of managing director requires approval by the Central Government. (Section 309)	Section 269 IS applicable to a manager.
8. Membership of the board	He is one of the members of the Board.	He is not a member of the Board.
9. Disqualification	A managing director may be disqualified who has made legal defaults any time in his life (Section 267).	A manager may be disqualified who has made legal defaults within preceding 5 years from appointment. (Section 385).
10. Waiver of disqualification	There is no povision for waiver by the Central Government of his disqualification (Section 267).	His disqualification may be waived by the Central Government either generally or for any company or companies (Section 385).
11. Attendance in the meeting	The managing director being a member of the board is authorised to take part in the company meetings and can tender his votes.	He is not authorised to participate in the company meetings and to tender his vote at the meetings.
12. Nature of job	Managing director is the representative of the officers of the company and a member of the board. His position, therefore, is not like an employee of the company.	Manager is an employee of the company.
13. Remuneration	In case more than one managing director is appointed, their remuneration cannot be exceeded the limit of 10% of the net profit of the company.	If the company appoints only one manager, his remuneration cannot be more than 5% of the net profits of the company.

Difference between Directors and Managing Director

Director	Managing Director
1. Directors are elected by shareholders.	1. He is elected by directors.
2. They are appointed for three years.	2. He is appointed for five years.
3. They retire by rotation at the end of 3 years.	3. He is exempted from the provisions of retirement by rotation.
4. His office is not Salaried office. He receives only honorarium.	4. Regular office of profit or salary.
5. The power of management is not in the hand of individual director. They exercise power collectively through Board meeting.	5. Managing director is entrusted with substantial powers of management as per Board resolution or agreement. These are delegated to him by Directors.
6. They mayor even may not be a shareholder.	6. He is first a director and then can act as Managing director.
7. Director act only as a guide, consultant or adviser.	7. He is chief executive and head of the company.
8. They are considered as agent of the shareholders or company.	8. He is considered as agent of the Board of directors.
9. In absence of M. director or manager, all directors may have 3% of annual net profits as their remuneration. Other wise they would have only 1%.	9. For one managing director managerial remuneration is 5% and for two or more it is 10% of annual net profits.
10. Directors are incharge of overall supervision and control of company's business and act as the brain of the company. They are policy-making and decision-making authority.	10. Managing Director is in charge of executive and administrative work and acts as the hands, eyes and ears of the executive arm of the board of directors.

Whole-Time Director

A 'whole-time director' includes 'a director in the whole-time employment of the company'.

The provisions applicable to the appointment of a managing director are also applicable to the appointment of a whole-time director.

Disqualification of a whole-time director

No company (Public or Private) can appoint or employ or continue the appointment or employment of any person as its whole-time director:

(a) who is an undischarged insolvent or has, at any time, been adjudged an insolvent,

(b) who suspends or has, at any time, suspended payment to his creditors, or markes or has made composition with them, or

(c) who is or has been convicted by the court of an offence involving moral turpitude.

'Whole-Time Director' and 'Managing Director' — A Comparison

Similarities: It is noteworthy that many salient features of whole-time director are similar to managing director, for instance:

1. Both whole-time director and managing director must be directors.
2. Section 267 of the Act applies to both, viz., whole-time director as well as managing director cannot be appointed or employed if they are undischarged insolvent, or if they are convicted by a court of an offence involving moral turpitude, etc.
3. Section 283 of the Act is applicable to whole-time director as well as managing director, namely: the office of a whole-time director and the managing director shall become vacant if they are found to be of unsound mind, if they fail to obtain the share qualification (if any) required of them by the articles of the company, if they fail to pay any call in respect of shares held by them, etc.
4. Section 274 of the Act also applies to both the whole-time director and the managing director, i.e., laying down the circumstances under which a person cannot be appointed as whole-time director or managing director of a company

Distinctions: Yet, there are many points of differences between a whole-time director and a managing director, which are discussed hereunder:

1. ***Appointment:*** The appointment of a whole-time director requires the consent of shareholders by a special resolution.

   The appointment of a managing director need not necessarily be made with the consent of shareholder.

2. ***Term of appointment:*** The term of appointment of a whole-time director is not fixed and as such the appointment can be for any number of years.

   The managing director can be appointed for a maximum period of 5 years at a time.

3. ***Managerial Personnel:*** Whole-time director can be appointed along with a manager or a managing director. That is, whole-time director and managing director can work at the same time and thus, can co-exist.

   A managing director cannot be appointed along with a manager. That is, managing director and a manager cannot work together and thus, cannot co-exist.

4. **Whole-time directorships:** Whole-time director cannot be a whole-time director for more than one company, thus cannot have more than one whole-time directorship.

   Managing director can be a managing director of more than one company and performs important administrative functions. He does not exercise substantial powers of management such as introduction of new products, adoption of new techniques trade discount structure, etc.

   The managing director exercises 'substantial power of management' .

Managing Agents Secretaries and Treasurers

By Companies (Amendment) Act of 1969, the system of managing agency or of secretaries and treasurers has been abolished and the companies have been prohibited to employ managing agents, secretaries and treasurers after 3rd of April 1970.

Managerial Remuneration

The remuneration payable to directors is usually determined by the articles of association or a resolution passed by the company in its general meeting. However, this will be subject to the provisions of Section 198 and 309 of the act.

According to Section 198, total managerial remuneration payable to directors, managing director(s) or manager and whole-time director, in respect of any financial year should not exceed 11 % of the net profits of the Company for the financial year. In years of inadequate profits, a sum not exceeding Rs. 50,000 per annum may be paid to all managerial personnel with the prior approval of the Central Government. In this context, however, the Central Government has been empowered to sanction greater sum by way of minimum remuneration provided:

(i) It is satisfied about bonafides of the case, and

(ii) a monthly payment is being made or is proposed to be made to any managing or whole- time director or the manager or to anyone or more of them.

Note that, this provision with regard to managerial remuneration does not apply to an independent private company (i.e. a private company not being a subsidiary of a public company).

The term 'remuneration' includes payment of any obligation of the director by the company, expenditure by the company or rent free accommodation, any expenditure on amenities provided free of cost or at concessional rate and payment of life insurance premium on the life of director by the company. But the term 'remuneration' shall not include:

1. Any amount paid to director for services, if

   (i) services are of a professional nature, and

   (ii) in the opinion of the Central Government, the director possesses the requisite qualification for the practice of the profession [Section 309 (i)].

2. Any fees payable to the director for attending each meeting of the Board or a Committee there of [Section 198 (2)].

As regards the part time directors, ordinarily they should be paid only sitting fees and traveling and halting allowances. But where company wishes to pay more, it must satisfy the government that in specific cases such directors rendered some specific service to the company beyond merely attending Board meetings.

Remuneration received by a director in any other capacity (for example, for services of professional nature for which the director had requisite qualifications) shall not be included in overall limit.

Section 637AA inserted by Companies (Amendment) Act 1974, provides that while fixing remuneration, the government is bound to take into account:

(a) the financial position of the company,
(b) the remuneration or commission drawn by him in any other company,
(c) professional qualifications and experience of the individual concerned,
(d) public policy relating to removal of disparities in income.

For determining the maximum remuneration of managerial personnel, net profits are to be calculated in the manner laid down in Sections 349 to 351. The overall limits may be shown in the following table:

Remuneration Receivers	Maximum of Annual net profits
1. All directors, while they are assisted by managing director(s) or manager and or whole-time director(s).	1%
2. All directors, when not assisted by managing director(s) or manager and/or whole-time director(s).	3%
3. Managing director (when there is one managing director).	5%
4. Manager (there cannot be more than one manager).	5%
5. Whole-time director (when there is one such director).	5%
6. The managing directors or whole time director (when there are more than one of either category or of both categories.	10%
7. Total managerial remuneration to all directors, managing director(s), or manager and/or whole-time director(s).	11% (in case of inadequate profits Rs. 50,000 per annum with the prior approve of the Central Government) .

Companies (Amendment) Act 1988 had earlier made major changes in remuneration payable to managerial personnel. The schedule of remuneration to managerial persons has again changed by a notification issued by the Department of Company Affairs, Government of India, New Delhi in July 1993. The revised provision are as follows:

1. The overall maximum managerial remuneration which may be paid by a public company or its subsidiary in respect of a financial year shall not exceed 11% of the net profits of the company [Section 198(1)].
2. If the company earns no profits or earns inadequate profits in any financial year, no remuneration is payable to directors, managing director, or whole-time director unless approved by the Central Government [Section 198(4)].
3. The mode of remuneration payable to managing director or the manager may be on any of the following basis:
   (i) on monthly basis, or
   (ii) as a specified percentage of the net profits of the company, or
   (iii) by both.
4. When a company makes payment of remuneration to the managerial personnel, according to schedule XIII part II, and within the provisions of Sections 198 and 309, there shall be no need to obtain the permission of the Central Government in this regard.
5. The maximum remuneration (Personal and aggregate) payable to whole-time director or managing director shall not exceed 5% of the net profits in favour of one such director. If there are more than one director, it shall not exceed 10% for all them put together [Section 303 (2)].
6. In following cases, extra remuneration is paid for the services rendered in any other capacity:
   (i) Where the services of a professional nature have been rendered, and
   (ii) In the opinion of the Central Government, the director possesses the requisite qualifications for the practice of that profession.
7. While computing the total remuneration payable to the managing director or whole-time director, the following expenditures incurred by the company are also taken into consideration.
   (i) any expenditure incurred in providing free accommodation and other amenities,
   (ii) any expenditure incurred in providing any other amenity either absolutely free or at concessional rate,

(iii) any expenditure incurred in providing life insurance, pension, annuity or gratuity for any such person, his spouse or child.

(iv) any expenditure incurred in providing any obligation or service which, in the absence of provisions by the company, would have been incurred by that person, [Section 198].

8. If a managing director was paid excess amount than the prescribed limit, he shall hold the excess amount in trust for the company and shall be bound to refund it to the company [Section 309(5A)].
9. The condition of returning the excess amount held by a managing director cannot be waived unless permitted by the Central Government.
10. If a managing director receives commission as his remuneration from a company, he shall not be permitted to accept commission or other such benefits from its subsidiary company [Section 309 (6)].

    These restrictions shall not be applicable to an independent private company [Section 309 (9)].
11. No company can make a tax-free remuneration to its employees or officers [Section 200].

Remuneration of part time directors

The provisions regarding remuneration to part time directors are as under:

(1) The mode of remuneration payable to part-time directors may be either on monthly, quarterly or yearly basis as approved by the Central Government, or a commission as authorised by a special resolution passed at the general meeting of the company.

(2) The maximum limit of remuneration payable may be:

(i) where manager, or managing director or whole-time director is holding office in a company, the maximum remuneration payable to part-time director(s) shall not exceed 1% of the net profits.

(ii) where there is no manager or managing director or whole-time director holding office, the remuneration payable to part time (directors) shall be to the extent of not more than 3% of the net profits [Section 309(4)].

(3) The Central Government vide its notification dated 10th June 1988, has fixed the fees to part-time directors for attending even board meetings at a minimum rate of Rs. 250/- and maximum of Rs. 1000/- based on the authorised capital of the company.

Managerial Remuneration Norms Liberalised in January 1994 and in February 1994

The Central Government by the two notifications issued by the Department of Company Affairs in January 1994 and February 1994 revised and liberalised the provisions governing the ceiling on the salary commission and perks of company managers in the private sector. 'Adequate' profit making companies have been given full freedom to work out a suitable remuneration package for them.

Notification Issued in January 1994

According to notification of January 1994 full freedom has been given to a company having adequate net profits to work out a suitable remuneration package for its managerial personnel within the limit of below 5 per cent of its net profits for one and below 10 per cent of the net profits if there are more than one managerial personnel. In case of absence of 'adequate' net profits (where managerial remuneration exceeds 5 or 10 percent of net profits or the company is loss making), limits have been fixed ranging from Rs. 40,000 per months for capital upto Rs. 1 crore to Rs. 87,500 per month for capital of over Rs. 15 crores.

In case the company's capital is between Rs. 1 crore and Rs. 5 crores, the ceiling is Rs. 57, 000 per month and for capital between Rs. 5 crores and Rs. 15 crores, the limit has been fixed at Rs. 72,000 per month. The government has also done away with the provision of breaking up the total remuneration package into salary, perks and commissions. Now a profit making company can restructure the total salary package at it wants without seeking the government permission.

The condition that a sick company needs the government's permission for appointment of managerial personnel has been withdrawn. Approval is no longer required for a managing director or manager of a company to become remuneration from only one of the two companies. In case this is not done, government permission will be mandatory.

Ceilings on salaries and requisite were last raised on July 14 of 1993 to Rs. 6 lakhs and Rs. 4.50 1akhs respectively, from the earlier limits of Rs. 1.80 1akhs and Rs. 1.35 1akhs. But these were considered cumbersome in light of the general climate of liberalisation.

Notification issued in February 1994

Managerial pay norms further liberalised in February 1994. The Department of Company Affairs (DCA) has further revised schedule 13 of the Companies Act 1956, dealing with managerial remuneration. The revision provides total flexibility to the companies in paying their whole-time or managing director within an overall ceiling of 10%.

In other words, there will be no restriction on the nature of quantum of remuneration paid by a company to its managerial personnel as long as the remuneration paid during any financial year is within five to ten percent of the net profits, as the case may be, of that financial year. The department has suggested that all restrictions on managerial remuneration be removed and it be left totally to the companies to decide the remuneration packages for its managers, as is the case all over the world. It should be done in a phased manner, there is a good chance that even the 10% overall ceiling may be done away with. However, this revision marks the second step in the process if liberalising the remuneration clause.

In the case of loss-making units, the companies would have full freedom the work out a suitable remuneration package for its managerial personnel within the limit on remuneration as specified in para 2 of section II of part II.

The provision for 10% reduction in the salary of managerial personnel in the event of inadequacy of profits has also been deleted if a managerial person has been appointed on a specified salary with a provision for 10% reduction in the event of loss of net profits, the company can delete the said condition without obtaining the union governments approval, in accordance with Section 310. This enables the company to take a decision without the approval of centre.

Further, it has become mandatory for companies to seek the approval of shareholders for the remuneration payable to the managing director or whole-time directors through a specific resolution.

This following an observation that companies have in the past got the power to revise or fix a remuneration delegated to the board of director through a general resolution. It has been emphasised the powers are not delegatable, and the specific remuneration being paid to each one of the directors has to be approved by the shareholders in a general body meeting.

Although there is no specific penalty provided in case of violation of this provision, yet it will be governed by Section 629 (A) of the companies act, which provides for a fine of Rs. 500 and Rs. 50 per day in case of continuing offence.

Perquisites

The ceiling on the manageriai perks has been raised from Rs. 1.15 to Rs. 4.50 lakh per annum.

Perks will comprise house rent allowances, leave and travel concession, medical reimbursement, fees on club and personal accidental insurance, etc.

The most impact making change is that the ceiling on total perquisites has now been fixed at a uniform maximum limit of Rs. 4.5 lakh per annum as against the previously existing perquisite ceiling of Rs. 1.15 lakh in case the appointee is stationed in a smaller city and Rs. 1.35 lakh in case of metropolitan cities.

The distinction, which so far existed on the basis of the station of the managers, has now been removed and the amount fixed at Rs. 4.5 lakh or an amount equal to the salary, whichever is less.

This in effect means that in case of the lower slabs, the perks will be equal to the salary and in case of the higher slab it will amount to 75% of the salary.

The ceiling on gratuity which was hitherto upto rupees one lakh has also been abolished.

In case of housing also, certáin important changes have been brought about. While under the old dispensation, the allowed house rent allowance for the managing directors was 60% of the salary, and in case of other managers 50%, the order of the government has fixed the limit at uniform rate of 60%, the upper limit of the salary now being Rs. 50,000.

Earlier, there was also no provision for furnished accommodation, but now, furnished accommodation can be provided to the managerial personnel as the company thinks fit.

Another concession made in the perks of the managers is that the premium on the personal accident insurance has been raised from Rs. 1000 to Rs. 4000.

The new dispensation also permits the encasement of leave at the end of tenure, something that did not exist in the Act or the bill.

In addition to these, the perks accruing to the expatriate managing director whole-time director or manager shall not be included in the computation of the ceiling on perquisites.

For instance, in case of children education allowance, the admissible limit is Rs. 5000 per month per child or actual expenses incurred whichever is less. This allowance is admissible upto a maximum of two children.

Secretary

A company secretary means "a person who is a member of the institute of company secretaries of India"[Section 2(1) (c) of the Company Secretaries Act 1980]. According to Section 2(45) of the companies act as amended in 1988 'Secretary means a company secretary within the meaning of Section 2(1)(c) of the Company Secretaries Act 1980, and includes any individual possessing the prescribed qualifications appointed to perform the duties which may be performed by a secretary under this Act and any other ministerial or administrative duties which may be performed by a secretary under this Act and any other ministerial or administrative duties.

Secretary in whole-time practice

'Secretary in whole time practice' means a secretary who shall be deemed to be in practice and who is not in full-time employment [Section 2(45-A)]. Now the small companies which cannot employ a whole-time company secretary will be in position to avail of the services of the company secretaries in whole-time practice for complying with various statutory requirements.

Status of Company Secretary

The status of a company secretary has altered a great deal now. He is now the chief administrative officer of a company. Section 2(30) also says that an 'officer' includes 'secretary'. The courts have also recognised the improvement in the status of the secretary. 199

Thus whereas the directors are the brain of a company (as they lay down the general policy of the company and direct its affairs), the secretary is the companies eyes, ears and hands (as he carries out the policies of the management, follows directions and executes many a decision taken by the directors on the authority delegated to him).

Appointment

A company secretary is generally appointed by directors at their meeting. He may also be appointed by the articles in which case his appointment shall be confirmed by a resolution of the directors passed in their first meeting after his appointment. A copy of the resolution appointing a person as secretary shall be forwarded to the Registrar of companies.

Qualifications

The qualifications of a person to be eligible for appointment as secretary are as follows:

(i) Every company having a paid-up share capital of not less than Rs. 25 lakhs shall have a whole-time secretary.

(ii) No person shall be appointed as a whole-time secretary unless he is a member of the institute of company secretaries of India.

(iii) A company having a paid-up share capital of less than Rs. 25 1akhs may appoint any individual as its whole-time secretary to perform the duties of a secretary under the Companies Act 1956 and any other ministerial or administrative duties. But no individual shall be eligible to be so appointed unless he possesses one or more of the following qualifications, namely:

   (i) Membership of the Institute of Company Secretaries of India,

   (ii) Pass in Intermediate examination conducted by the Institute of Company Secretaries of India,

   (iii) Post-graduate degree in Commerce or Corporate Secretaryship granted by any University in India,

   (iv) Degree in Law granted by any University,

   (v) Membership of the Institute of Chartered Accountants of India,

   (vi) Membership of the Institute of Cost and Works Accountants of India,

   (vii) Post graduate degree or diploma in Management Sciences, granted by any University or the Institutes of Management, Ahmedabad, Calcutta, Bangalore or Lucknow,

(viii) Post graduate diploma in Company Secretaryship granted by the Institute of Commercial Practice under the Delhi Administration or Diploma in Corporate Laws and Management granted by the Indian Law Institute, New Delhi,

(ix) Post graduate diploma in Company Law and Secretarial Practice granted by the University of Udaipur, or

(x) Membership of the Association of Secretaries and Managers, Calcutta.

Where the paid-up share capital of a company is increased to Rs. 25 lakhs or more, the company shall, within a period of 1 year from such increase, appoint a whole-time secretary who is a member of the Institute of company secretaries of India.

Certain Companies to have Secretaries (Section 383-A)

Every company having paid-up share capital of Rs. 25 lakhs or more shall have a whole-time secretary. Where the Board of directors of any such company or companies have only two directors, neither of them shall be the secretary.

Penalty

Ifa company fails to comply with the provision of Section 383-A, the company and every officer of the company who is in default, shall be punishable with fine which may extend to Rs. 50 for every day during which the default continues. When any proceedings against a person in respect of this offence are taken, he may defend himself by proving that all reasonable efforts to comply with the provisions of Section 383-A were taken or that the financial position of the company was such that it was beyond its capacity to engage a whole-time secretary.

CHAPTER

48

Company Meetings and Proceedings

A meeting is an assembly, gathering or coming together of more than one person for transaction of some lawful purpose.

In every organisation, its members may meet and discuss the matters of their common interests and take decisions. In companies, a large part of its affairs is decided at meetings. The shareholders discuss the affairs of the company in their meeting and exercise their ultimate control over the management. The directors frame the policies and programme for the company and exercise their powers in board meetings. The company management is carried on through various kinds of meetings. Such as meetings of shareholders, directors, creditors, etc.

Purpose of Meetings

The purpose of a meeting is to as certain the opinions of the persons concerned. It helps discussions and exchange of views among the persons concerned and then decision comes out. The Act, therefore, makes holding of meetings compulsory and makes provisions for them. The Regulations 47 to 63 of the Table A and the Regulations 73 to 81 show the model rules which are generally followed by companies limited by shares.

Importance of Meetings

The members exercise control over the company through meetings. The Board of directors also functions through holding of meetings. The Act specifically mentions powers of the Board to be exercised at the board meetings as well as powers subject to approval by the members by resolutions passed at company meetings. Shares are classified according to the voting rights of the members at the meetings.

Procedure of Meeting

Holding of a meeting has a procedure which has three stages —

Before the meeting (notice), at the meeting (resolutions) and after the meeting (minutes). The entire procedure is a part of secretarial practice. Every association needs a secretary for all types of secretarial work including holding of meetings. A company being or association needs the services of the secretary. The company secretary as an officer of the company has many statutory duties to perform and is responsible for holding of meetings. According to Act, some types of companies must appoint qualified secretary. When there is no such secretary, any director may do the job.

If there is any irregularity at any stage of the procedure, the meeting becomes invalid and decisions taken at such a meeting becomes ineffective.

The above provisions does not apply to a private company unless it is a subsidiary of a public company (Section 90). A member shall not have excess voting right on call money paid by him in advance (Section 92).

A person is a member whose name appears in the register of members and he has voting right. A representative as understood under Sections 187 and 187 A shall have the right to vote. The voting right of a members cannot be taken away except when call money has not been paid by him or when the company has lien or his shares (Section 182).

A member who has a number of votes at the time of poll, may, either himself or by proxy, use the votes differently (Section 183). An alien enemy member, however, cannot vote.

How To Vote?

At any general meeting, unless a poll is demanded, the decision shall be taken on a show of hands. (Section 177). It may be construed therefore that there are two methods of voting (a) by show of hands and (b) by poll. Poll is effected by using ballot papers. A proxy can vote by poll only.

A non trading company may provide be the item to be considered at the meeting with the permission of the chair.

Types of Meetings

The meetings of a company may be classified as follows:

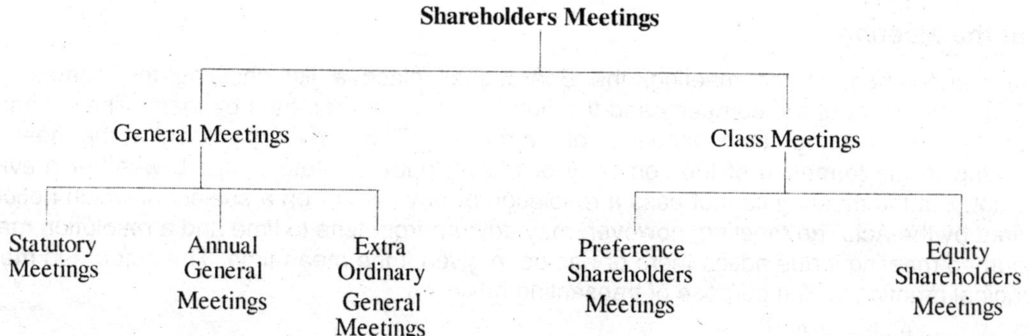

General Meetings of Share holders

These meetings may be (a) statutory meeting (b) annual general meetings and (c) extra ordinary meetings.

(a) Statutory Meeting (Section 165)

The first meeting of the shareholders of a public company after obtaining the certificate of commencement of business is known as statutory meeting. This meeting is hold only once in the life time of a company. At this meeting of shareholders, the directors give a complete idea about the general affairs of the company after its registration. At this meeting, the directors present an informal report about the method adopted for allotment of shares, money received by the company by application and allotment, preliminary expenses incurred by the company till the date of incorporation, the preliminary contracts, if any, approved by the company, and the importance of such contracts in the life of the company, etc. The directors also present the statutory report of the company at this meeting.

Under Section 165(1) of the act, "every company limited by shares and every company limited by guarantee and having a share capital shall, within a period of not less than one month and not more than six months from the date on which the company is entitled to commence business hold a general meeting of the company, which shall be called the statutory meeting." A private company and a company limited by guarantee and not having a share capital need not hold such a meeting.

Notice of Meeting

The board of directors are required to give a notice of the meeting to all shareholders at least 21 days before the date of the meeting, specifying therein that it would be the statutory meeting of the company. A notice with less than 21 days may be valid if members holding 95% paid-up share capital have consented to it [Section 165(2)].

Statutory Report

The board of directors shall send a report called the statutory report to every members of the company at least 21 days before the meeting duly certified as correct by at least two directors, one of whom must be the managing director, if there is one [Section 165(4)]. A copy of the duly certified report shall be filed with the Registrar for registration [Section 165(5)].

The statutory report shall contain the following particulars:

(a) The total number of shares allotted distinguishing those allotted as fully or partly paid-up otherwise than in cash, and stating in the case of shares partly paid-up the extent to which they are so paid-up and in either case the consideration for which they have been allotted.

(b) The total amount of cash received by the company in respect of all the shares allotted.

(c) An abstract of receipts and payments made there at upto a date within seven days of the date of the report and an account or estimate of the preliminary expenses.

(d) Names, addresses and occupations of its directors and auditors and also of its manager and secretary, if any, and the changes which have occurred since the date of the incorporation.

(e) The particulars of any contract and the modification or the proposed modification of any contract which is to be submitted for the approval of the members at the meeting.

(f) The extent to which the under writing contracts have not been carried out and the reasons therefore.
(g) The arrears, if any, due on calls from any director and the manager.
(h) The particulars of any commission or brokerage paid or to be paid to any director or to the manager in connection with the issue or sale of shares or debentures of the company,

Procedure at the Meeting

At the commencement of the meeting, the Board shall place a list showing the names, addresses and occupations of the members of the company and the number of the shares held by them. The list shall remain open for inspection by members during, the continuance of the meeting. The members present at the meeting may discuss any matter relating to the formation of the company or arising out of statutory report, whether previous notice has been given or not. But the meeting cannot pass a resolution or any item or on a subject of which notice has not been given as required by the Act. The meeting, however, may adjourn from time to time and a resolution may be passed at any such adjourned meeting if due notice there of has been given it the mean time. The adjourned meeting is treated as if it is an original meeting for the purpose of transacting business.

Effect of non-compliance

If any default is made either in delivering the statutory report to the Registrar or in holding the statutory meeting, every director and officer of the company who is in default will be liable to a fine which may extend to Rs. 500. Failure to company with the provisions of Section 165 of the Act will be a ground for winding up of the company by the court under Section 433 of the Act. The court may, however, give directions for the statutory report to be filed or a meeting to be held, as the case may be and refuse to order the winding up of the company (Section 433).

Annual General Meeting (Section 166 and 167)

Every company must in each year (calendar year) hold, in addition to any other meetings, a general meeting as its annual general meeting and must specify the meeting and must specify the meeting as such in the notices calling it.

The first annual general meeting must be held within 18 months from the date of incorporation.

In that case, the company is not required to hold an annual general meeting in the year of incorporation or in the following year. There after it must be held in each year and there shall not be a gap of more than fifteen months between two annual general meetings. However, the Registrar has the power to extend the time for holding the annual general meeting (except the first annual general meeting) by a period not exceeding three months [Section 166(1)]. The annual general meeting of a company shall be held within 6 months from the date of ending of the financial year [Section 210 (3)].

The annual general meeting must be held on a working day and during business hours. It should be either held at the registered office of the company or at some other place within the city, town or the village in which the registered office of the company is situated. The Central Government may exempt a class of companies from these provisions and subject to conditions imposed. A public company, a private company which is a subsidiary of a public company, may be its articles fix its time for annual general meetings and also may by resolution passed in one annual general meeting fix time for its subsequent annual general meetings. A private company which is not subsidiary of a public company may be virtue of articles and also by a resolution agreed to by all the members fix the time as well as the place for its annual general meeting [Section 166(2)].

The Board of Directors has the responsibility to lay before the annual general meeting the profit and loss account and the balance sheet (Section 210) and a Board's report (Section 217). In the case of first annual general meeting, the account shall cover the period from the date of incorporation to a date not earlier than the date of the meeting by more than 9 months. In the case of any other annual general meeting, the account shall cover a period from the date of the preceding account and not earlier than the date of the meeting by more than 6 months. From this, it can be construed that the annual general meeting shall be held within 6 months from the date of ending of the financial years. If also appears from the section that a company may hold a number of general meetings in a year.

Importance of Meeting

It is only at the annual general meeting of a company that the shareholders can exercise any control over its affairs. The shareholders also get an opportunity to discuss the affairs and review the working of the company. They can also take the necessary steps for the protection of their interests. Appointment of auditors is also made at the annual general meeting. Annual accounts are presented for consideration of the shareholders and dividends are declared in this meeting. The shareholders can take up any other business relating to the affairs of the company for discussion.

Consequences of Default

If default is made in holding of the meeting of the company in accordance with Section 166, or in complying with any directions of the Central Government, the company and every other officer of the company who is in default shall be punishable with fine which may extend to Rs. 5,000 and in the case of a continuing default with a further fine which may extend to Rs. 250 for every day after the first during which the default continues (Section 168).

The company is liable for mere default but for the prosecution of a director or an officer of the company, it must be shown that he was knowingly a party to the default. Further, the company, would not be liable for the default, if it is due to a cause beyond its control. *In re Bank of Deacon Ltd.*,[200] the books of the company had been seized by the police and produced in the criminal court, the Kerala High Court held that the company would not be punished because the default was beyond the control of the company.

Powers of the Company Law Board to call Annual General Meeting (Section 167)

If default is made in holding annual general meeting in accordance with Section 166, the Company Law Board may call, or direct the calling of, a general meeting of the company. It shall also give such ancillary or consequential directions as it thinks fit in relation to the calling, holding and conducting of the meeting. A general meeting so held shall, subject to any directions of the Company Law Board, be deemed to be an annual general meeting of the company.

Extraordinary General Meeting (Section 169)

Under article 47 of Schedule 1, all general meetings other than Annual General meeting shall be called extraordinary general meeting. But a statutory meeting of the company is not treated as an extraordinary general meeting.

Extraordinary meetings are called in emergencies or on special occasions, when it is found necessary to transact certain business which cannot be postponed until the next general meeting of the company. The extraordinary general meeting may be convened.

(1) By the Board of Directors

The regulation 48 of Table 'A' of Schedule 1 provides that directors may, by their own motion, convene an extraordinary general meeting.

(2) By the directors on the requisition of members

Section 169(1) provides that it becomes essential for the director to call an extraordinary general meeting on the requisition signed by members holding one-tenth of the total voting rights or holders of at least one-tenth of the paid-up share capital.

Rules regarding holding, of extraordinary general meeting (on the requisition on members)

(1) The propose or the matter for consideration shall be set out in the requisition for meeting [Section 169(2)].
(2) It should be signed by the requisitionists in each of the requisition [Section 169(2)].
(3) The requisition may be presented at the registered office of the company [Section 169(2)].
(4) The directors may within 21 days from the date of receipt of requisition, take steps to call an extra-ordinary general meeting and it should be held within 45 days from the date of requisition [Section 169(6)].

3. By the Requisitionists

(1) If the directors have failed to call the meeting within 45 days from the date of requisition by the members, the requisitionists may themselves proceed to call the meeting.
(2) The expenses for holding the meeting is the liability of the company and the company may recover the same out of the remuneration payable to the directors in default.
(3) Such a meeting may be called before the end of three months from the date of requisition. But an adjourned meeting can be held even after 3 months [Section 169(7)].
(4) The requisitionists may hold the meeting at any suitable place if the registered office is not made available to them for holding the extraordinary meeting.

4. By one director and two members

In case the total number of directors required to form the quorum is not available in India, any one director and two members together can convene the extraordinary general meeting [the will be the same as contained in Rule 48 (2) of Table 'A'].

5. By the order of the Company Law Board (Section 186)

If for any reason it is impracticable for a company to call, hold or conduct a general meeting (other than annual general meeting) in the manner as required by the Act or the articles of the company. The company law board may call such a meeting either:

(i) on its motion, or
(ii) on the application of a director of the company, or
(iii) by any member of the company who is entitled to vote at the meeting.

In such a case, the Company Law Board may,

(i) dictate the method of calling or holding or conducting the meeting, or
(ii) pass any ancillary or consequential orders which may lead to any change in the Act or in the articles of the company.
(iii) direct that even one member of the company present in person or by proxy shall be deemed to constitute a meeting.

The word' impracticable' means impracticable from the reasonable point of view. The Company Law Board should take a common sense view of the matter and act as a prudent person of business.

The power of the Company Law Board to call meeting was earlier vested in the court, has after the passing of the companies (Amendment) act 1974, been transferred to the Company Law Board.

Notice of the meeting

A 21 days notice for an extraordinary general meeting is necessary. But a short notice may be accepted if the members holding 95% voting rights have consented to it [Section 172 (2)].

Such notice shall specify the special business to be transacted and shall be accompanied by the agenda and an explanatory statement.

Class Meeting

Under the Companies Act, class meeting of various kinds of shareholders and creditors are required to be held under different circumstances. Under Section 106, class meetings of the holders of different classes of shares are to be held if the rights attaching to these shares are to be varied. Similarly under Section 394, where a scheme of arrangement is proposed, meetings of the several classes of shareholders and creditors are required to be held. Also at the time of winding up, the meetings of creditors and members, for certain purposes, are held.

Objective of class meeting

(1) To make variation in the rights attached with shares.
(2) To discuss any scheme of arrangement.
(3) To wind up the company voluntarily
(4) To wind up the company compulsorily by the orders of the court.

The variation in the rights attached with the shares can only be made where there is sufficient provision in the memorandum and the articles of the company. The variation in the rights may be made by a special resolution. passed at the meeting of that particular class of shareholders. But, if the holders of at least 10 percent shares ofthat particular class disagrees to the variation, the may appeal to the court to restrain from the execution of the resolution so passed by the class meeting. Such an appeal may be made to the court within 21 days of passing the resolution, for variation of rights, by the members who have neither given the consent on the resolution nor the voting was taken place in their favour.

The Court may arrange to hear the parties concerned and give its decision either on resolution or restraining from its implementation.

Unless otherwise provided in the articles, the rules regard to notice, quorum, proxy, voting, etc. applicable to general meetings shall apply to class meetings as well.

Requisites of a valid meeting

1. Proper Authority

The board of directors is the proper authority to convene a general meeting of a company and for this purpose the board should pass a resolution at a duly convened meeting of the board. However, if the board fails to call a general meeting of the company, the members of the Company Law Board may call such a meeting.

If there is some defect in appointment or qualification of the directors present at the board meeting, and this comes to light after the board has acted bonafide, such a defect is not necessarily fatal to the validity of their resolution.

2. Notice of meeting (Section 171)

A general meeting of a company may be called by giving not less than 21 days"notice in writing to the members of the company. [Section 171(1)]. 'Not less than 21 days means that both the date of the meeting and the date on which it is served are to be excluded. 21 days must be 21 clear days. Where the notice is sent by the post, it shall be deemed to have been received at the expiration of forty-eight hours after the posting[201] (Section 53). Any accidental omission to give notice to some member or not receipt of notice does not invalidate the meeting [Section 172(3)]. Accidental act means an act done not intentionally but it causes loss.[202]

The requirement of' 21 days notice of the meetings' overrides any provision in the articles for a shorter period. But the articles can validly provide for longer notice than the statutory 21 days minimum period.

A notice advertised in a newspaper circulating in the neighbourhood of registered office of the company shall deemed to be duly served on the day on which the advertisement appears on every members of the company who has no registered address in India and has not given to the company his address within India for serving the notice to him (Section 53).

The meeting can, however, be called by giving a shorter notice in the following cases:

(a) In the case of an annual general meeting, by the consent of all the members entitled to attend and vote.
(b) In the case of any other meeting, by the consent of the members holding not less than 95% paid-up share capital of the company, or holding not less than 95% of the total voting power of the company (when the company does not have a share capital).

Contents of Notice

The following matters are included in a notice of the meeting:

(1) The date, time and place of meeting.
(2) The type of meeting, whether statutory, annual general meeting and so on.
(3) The Section of the Act, giving rights to call the meeting.
(4) The purpose of the meeting (The agenda of the meeting may be enclosed).
(5) Resolutions proposed to be passed at the meeting (Special mention about special resolution, if any, to be passed at the proposed meeting must be indicated).
(6) Important contract, if any, to be accepted in the meeting (a draft copy of such contract may also be sent).
(7) Proxy forms are to be enclosed.

Notice to whom

Notice of every meeting of the company must be given to:

(i) Every member of the company entitled to vote upon the matters which are proposed to be dealt with the meeting.
(ii) Legal representatives of deceased members.
(iii) Administrator appointed by Government or to the official Receiver, in case of insolvency of a member.
(iv) The auditor or auditors of the company [Section 172(2)].
(v) The board of directors.

If the notice of a meeting is not given to every person entitled to notice, any resolution passed at the meeting will be ineffective.

Ordinary and Special Business

Notice of meeting must contain a statement of nature of business to be transacted in the meeting.

Section 173 classifies the business into ordinary business and special business.

Ordinary Business

The following business which is transacted at every annual general meeting is considered as ordinary business.

(i) The consideration of accounts, balance sheet and the report of the board of directors and auditors.
(ii) The declaration of a dividend.

(iii) The appointment of directors in place of those of retiring.
(iv) The appointment of and fixing the remuneration of auditors.

Special Business

Any business other than ordinary business transacted at an annual general meeting and all business transacted at the statutory meeting and at any extra ordinary general meeting is deemed as special business. In case of any items of special business to be transacted in the general meeting, an explanatory statement shall be annexed to the notice of the meeting. That statement must set out all material facts concerning each such item of the business including in particular the nature of the concern or the interest if any, therein of any director and the manager. Where any item of such business relates to or affects any other company, the statement must set out the extent of share holding interest in such other company, of every director and the manager if any, of the company, if such interest is not less than 20% of the paid up share capital of such other company. Where the item of such business relates to the according of approval to any document by the meeting, the statement annexed to the notice must specify the time and the place where the document can be inspected. The purpose of the statement is to enable the members to understand and appreciate the nature of the business or items of business proposed to be considered at the meeting and make up their mind whether to go to attend and vote at the meeting or abstain from voting.

3. Quorum of meeting (Section 174)

The word, quorum means the minimum number of persons who must be present to make a meeting valid. If the quorum is not present, there is no meeting and the proceedings held there at are invalid. The quorum is generally fixed by the articles.

According to Section 174 — unless otherwise provided in the articles of the company, any five members in case of a public company (not a public company *uls* 43A) and any two members in case of a private company personally present shall make the quorum.

The representative of a body corporate appointed under Section 187 or the representative of the President of India or the Governor of a state under Section 187A is a member personally present for the propose of determining a quorum.

If the articles do not otherwise provide, the following provisions shall apply with respect to the quorum at meeting of a public or private company:

(i) In case the quorum is not present within half an hour from the time fixed for holding the meeting, the meeting shall stand dissolved, if it is called upon the requisition of members. In other cases, the meeting shall stand adjourned to the same day in the next week, at the same time and place or to such other day and other time and place, as may be determined by board.
(ii) If at the adjourned meeting also the quorum is not present within half an hour from the time fixed for holding the meeting, the members present at the meeting shall constitute the quorum.

It has been held in *Re Hartley Baird Ltd.*[203] that the quorum required is the quorum to be present at the time of beginning to consider the business and it need not be present through out or at the time of taking the vote on any resolution. Where the total number of members of a company becomes reduced below the quorum fixed for a meeting, it would appear that the rule as to quorum would be satisfied, if all the members of the company, though less than the quorum are present. But, where only one person is present, he cannot form a quorum as a single member cannot constitute a meeting.

It is also necessary that the quorum fixed for the meeting must be present throughout the meeting proxies are not counted for the directors meeting is fixed by the articles. If the articles are silent, one-third of the total number of directors shall constitute the quorum.

Exception to the rule of quorum

However, the Company Law recognises certain exceptions to the rule of quorum. In certain circumstances where even a single member present in the meeting may constitute the quorum, such circumstances are:

One-Man Quorum

(i) When a meeting is adjourned for want of quorum, if only one person is present at the adjourned meeting, then he alone shall make the quorum.
(ii) When the annual general meeting is convened by the Central Government or convened by the order of the Central Government, it may direct that even one member present in person or proxy shall constitute a valid quorum (Section 167).

(iii) When the Company Law Board orders for holding a meeting (other than annual general meeting), it may direct that one member personally present or proxy shall form a valid quorum (Section 186).

(iv) When, the board of directors appoints a one man committee for any specific purpose, then that person shall make the quorum of the meeting of that committee.

(v) At a class meeting, where one person holds all the shares of that class, he shall make the quorum.

4. Chairman of the Meeting

A chairman is necessary to conduct a meeting. According to Section 175 —

(i) unless the articles of the company otherwise provide, the members personally present at a meeting shall elect a chairman from among themselves by show of hands.

(ii) If poll is demanded for the election of the chairman, the poll shall be taken immediately.

In such a case, the chairman elected on a show of hands must exercise all the powers of the chairman.

(iii) If any other person is elected as chairman, as a result of the poll, he shall be the chairman for the rest of the meeting. It may be noted that the provisions of Section 175 are applicable only when the articles do not provide otherwise. Articles may make provision for a Deputy Chairman who will preside in case the chairman does not arrive. A Chairman need not be a member of a company.

Articles of the company may adopt Regulations 50-52 of Table 'A' regarding appointment of a Chairman. The regulations 50-52 are as follows:

1. The Chairman, if any, of the Board shall preside as Chairman at every meeting of the Company.
2. If there is no chairman or if he is not present within 15 minutes of the time fixed for holding the meeting or is unwilling to act as Chairman of the meeting, the Directors present shall elect one of them as chairman.
3. If at any meeting, no Director is willing to act as a Chairman, or if no Director is present within 15 minutes of the time appointed for holding the meeting, the members present shall elect one among them as Chairman.

Power and Duties of a Chairman

Power:

The Act, however, makes no elaborate provisions with regard to the powers of chairman the main powers of chairman are as follows:

(i) A chairman has prima facie authority to decide all the questions.

(ii) He can adjourn the meeting when it is not possible, by reason of disorder etc, to conduct the meeting and complete business.

(iii) He has right to decide priority amongst the speakers to demand poll, to exercise casting vote, to expel unruly member and he can, with the support of a majority, apply closure to the discussion after it has been reasonably debated.

Duties:

(i) He must act at all times bonafide and in the interest of the company as a whole. A chair man who presides over a meeting of a company is neither wholly a ministerial officer nor wholly a judicial officer, his duties are of mixed nature. He is not liable for damages, if acting bonafide according to the best of his judgement and without malice.

(ii) It is his duty to preserve order, and to see that the business is properly conducted.

(iii) He must ensure that the sense of the meeting is properly ascertained in regard to any question before it.

(iv) He must ensure that the provisions of the Companies Act and the articles of association are observed, and that the business is taken in the order set out in the agenda, and that the business is taken in the order set out in the agenda, and that business is within the scope of the meeting.

(vi) He must exercise his casting vote bonafide in the interest of the company.

(v) He must ensure that proper opportunity is given to the members to express their views, that the voting is fair.

(vii) He must decide questions arising for decision during the meeting, and must see to it. That the majority do not refuse to bear the minority.

(viii) He must ensure that proceedings of the meeting are correctly and properly recorded in the minutes book.

5. Minutes of Meeting's Proceedings

According to the Webster dictionary, the word 'proceedings' means "an official record of things said or done" and the word 'minutes' means "an official record of proceedings of a meeting". Actually, minutes refers to the summary of proceedings. Proceedings as a record contains the description of the meeting, the decision taken as well as details of the discussions taking place at the meeting while minutes contains the description of the meeting and the decisions taken at the meeting and does not contain the details of the discussions. The first part is called "the minutes of narration" and the second part "the minutes of decision".

According to Section 193, every company shall keep minutes of all proceedings of every general meeting (statutory meeting, annual general meeting or extraordinary general meeting) and of proceedings of every meeting of its Board of directors and of every Committee of the Board.

This is done by making within 30 days of the conclusion of every such meeting concerned, entries of the proceedings in the minute book kept for that purpose.

The provisions regarding the minutes, minute book and the method of keeping the minute book are as follows:

Keeping:

(i) Each page of the minute book must be initialed or signed by the chairman of the same meeting or the next succeeding meeting. The last page of the record of proceedings of each meeting in a minute book must be dated and signed. Every company must cause entries in the minutes of proceedings of every meeting within 30 days of the conclusion of every such meeting concerned.

(ii) The minutes must contain a fair and correct summary of the proceedings.

(iii) All appointments of officers made at the meeting must be included in the minutes.

(iv) In no case the minutes of proceedings of a meeting must be attached to the minute book by pasting or otherwise.

(v) It is the absolute discretion of the chairman of the meeting not to include in the minutes any matter which, in his opinion — (a) is or could reasonably be regarded as defamatory of a person, (b) is irrelevant or immaterial to the proceedings, or (c) is detrimental to the interest of the company.

If default is made, the company and every officer in default shall be punishable with fine which may extend to Rs. 50.

Evidence

(i) According to Section 194, minutes of meetings kept in according with the provisions shall be evidence of the proceedings recorded there in.

(ii) According to Section 195, until the contrary is proved, the meeting shall be deemed to have been duly called and held, and all the proceedings at these meetings shall be deemed to have duly taken place, and in particular, all appointments of directors or liquidators made at the meeting shall be deemed to be valid.

Inspection

(i) According to Section 196 (l), the minutes books of the general meetings of a company must be kept at the registered office of the company and be open during business hours for the inspection of any member without charge for at least two hours a day.

(ii) A member is entitled to be furnished within 7 days, after he has made a request in that behalf to the company, with a copy of any minutes on payment of 37 paise for every one hundred words or a fractional part there of, required to be copied.

(iii) If inspection is refused or if any copy is not furnished within the specified time, the company and every other officer of the company who is in default shall be punishable with fine which may extend to Rs. 500 for each offence.

(iv) On receiving complaint on refusal of inspection or non furnishing of copy, the court may order for immediate inspection and furnishing of copy.

Publication

(i) According to Section 197, (1) no document purporting to be a report of the proceedings of a general meeting of a company can be circulated or advertised at the expense of the company unless it includes all matters required by Section 193, to be contained in the minutes of the proceedings of such meeting.

(ii) If there contravention of the above rule, the company and every officer in default shall be punishable with fine which may go upto Rs. 500.

6. Voting and Poll

The resolutions proposed in a general meeting of a company are decided on the votes of the members of company. Every member whose name appears in the register of members has a right to vote at a general meeting. A shareholder's vote is a right of property. He may use it in manner he likes. He is not bound to exercise it in the best interests of the company. In the case of a company which has no share capital, each member is entitled to one vote only. But, where a company has a share capital, if the articles are silent every shareholder has one vote in respect of each share.

A company is authorised to make provisions in its articles restricting the voting rights of a member on the ground that (i) calls on his shares or any other sum presently payable have not been paid, or (ii) the company has exercised right of lien in respect of those shares where the articles of a company do not contain such provisions, a member cannot be prevented from voting even though calls payable by him have not been paid (Section 181). A public company shall not put any restrictions on voting except the one mentioned in Section 181. Any other restriction put on the right of voting will be void even though such provisions are contained in the articles (Section 182). A member entitled to more than one vote is free to split his votes in favour of and against the same resolution. Such use of votes is possible only on a vote by poll, for on a show of hands no member can register more than one (Section 183).

Methods of Voting

The voting may be by

(i) show of hands, or

(ii) by taking a poll

(1) Voting by a show of hands

At any general meeting, resolutions put to vote are first decided by a show of hands (Section 177). But, where a poll is demanded it is not necessary that the resolution should be put to vote by show of hands. On a show of hands each member has one vote and a proxy cannot vote unless the articles otherwise provide. The declaration by the chairman that a resolution on a show of hands has or has not been carried and an entry to that effect in the minutes book shall be conclusive evidence of that fact (Section 178).

(2) Voting by poll

A vote by a show of hands is only a rough and ready method of taking the sense of a meeting.

Voting by poll is an improvement to other methods of voting. This method differs from that of' shows of hands for two reasons. Firstly, each member is entitled to cast a number of votes according to the number of shares hold by him. Secondly, absentee members can also exercise their right of voting through proxies when poll is demanded and granted by the chairman. A poll may be demanded before or on the declaration of the result of the voting on any resolution on a show of hands. Such a poll cannot be demanded after the declaration of result and after the chairman has taken up any other item from the agenda for consideration of the meeting. A poll may be taken either by the chairman of his own motion or on a demand of the members. The chairman is bound to order a poll if demand is made by the following persons.

(i) In case of a public company having share capital, any number of members personally present or by proxy and holding at least one-tenth of the total voting rights or have already paid at least Rs. 50,000 against the shares held by him or by them.

(ii) In the case of a private company, anyone member having right to vote on the resolution and present in person or by proxy, (when less than seven members are personally present), or two members or by their proxies when more than seven members are personally present.

(iii) In case of any other kind of companies, poll may be demanded by a member or members present in persons or by proxy, and having at least 1/10th the total voting power in respect of the resolution. The demand of poll may be withdrawn at any time by the person or persons who made the demand (Section 179).

A poll demanded on a question of adjournment or the appointment of a chairman must be taken immediately. In any other case, it must be taken within 48 hours of the demand for poll (Section 180). It is complete when the result is ascertained, and not on an earlier day when the votes are cast. Where a poll is taken, the meeting is regarded as continuing until the ascertainment of the result of the poll. Jackson v. Hamlyn[204]

A poll was demanded on a question of adjournment and taken, but the scrutinizers informed the chairman that the result could not be announced within the time during which the meeting hall was available. Held, the meeting subsequently convened to hear the result was a continuation of the original meeting has power to regulate the manner in which a poll is to be taken.

The chairman of the meeting has power to regulate the manner to which a poll is to be taken.

Restrictions on voting power

The articles may provide that a member shall not exercise any voting in respect of any shares registered in his name on which a call or any other sum due to the company has not been paid (Section 181). Excepting this restriction, a public company or a private company which is a subsidiary of a public company must not impose any other restriction on the voting right of a member (Section 182).

Rights of member to use his votes differently

On a poll taken at a meeting of a company, a member entitled to more than one vote or his proxy need not use all his votes or cast in the same way all the votes he uses (Section 183).

7. Proxy

Proxy is a person authorised to attend and vote for another at a meeting. According to Lord Hanworth M.R., proxy is a personal representative of the shareholder who may be described as his agent to carryout a course which the shareholder himself has decided upon. It also refers to the instrument by which the appointment is made. A proxy need not be a member of the company. Section 176 (1) of the Act lays down that any member who is entitled to attend and vote at the meeting is entitled to appoint another person as his proxy to attend and vote on his behalf. A proxy mayor may not be a member of the company and a proxy is not entitled to speak at the meeting unless the articles otherwise provided for.

The instrument appointing a proxy must be in writing and signed by the appointer or by his authorised agent. If the appointer, is a body corporate, it shall be under its seal or be signed by its officer or attorney duly authorised by it. A proxy cannot be appointed by a company which has no share capital, unless the articles provide otherwise [Section 176 (1)].

A member of a private company is not entitled to appoint more than one proxy to attend on the same occasion, but a member of proxies according to his voting rights [Section 176 (1)]. A proxy is not entitled to vote except on a poll. A proxy appointed by a member of private company can take part in the debate, if its articles so provided for. A proxy may be lodged at the company's office at least 48 hrs. before the commencement of the meeting.

Any member who is entitled to vote at a meeting can inspect the proxies lodged within 24 hrs. of the time fixed for the meeting or after the conclusion of the meeting, provided a clear three day's notice in writing is given to the company to the effect [Section 176 (7)].

No invitation to appoint to any person as proxy shall be sent at the expense of the company, and if any such invitation is sent, it is an offence liable to a fine extending to Rs. 1000 [Section 176 (4)].

Proxy appointed is revocable at any time by giving a notice of revocation to the company before the proxy has acted. Where a shareholder who has appointed a proxy, and there after he personally attends and votes at the meeting, the proxy appointed by him stands revoked (*Cousins v. International Brick Co.*[205]). Again in case of death of a shareholder after he has appointed a proxy, revokes the authority of the proxy, but not until the company receives notice of his death.

Where the President or the Governor holds shares in a company, his duly appointed representative shall enjoy all the rights of a member. The representative in such cases shall not be considered as a proxy. He can take part in discussions, can vote by show of hands and demand for a poll. He can appoint a proxy to attend and vote at a meeting instead of presenting himself at the meeting [Section 187].

A proxy has following, rights

(i) To attend and vote at a company meeting.
(ii) To demand for holding a poll.
(iii) Right to vote on polling only or otherwise stated by articles.
(iv) A specially appointed proxy is entitled to vote on a particular resolution only for which he was appointed, where as a general proxy is entitled to vote on all the resolutions.

8. Motions and Resolution Motion

A motion is a proposal put before a meeting for consideration and adoption. A motion is liable to amendment or alteration before it is adopted by the meeting. It is treated as a dropped when it is not seconded by another member.

To present a motion and initiate discussion the following rules should be complied.

(1) It must be in writing and signed by the proposer and must be within the scope of notice of the meeting and related with the business in hand.
(2) It must comply with the provisions of the Act and the articles of the company.
(3) Only the members are entitled to move a motion.
(4) All the motions must be seconded by another member.
(5) Once the motion is duly proposed and seconded, it becomes the property of the meeting. The mover cannot withdraw it unless the meeting unanimously permits for withdrawal.
(6) Before the original motion is put to vote, amendments may be offered on it. Amendment may be made on a motion presented to meeting for consideration and discussion, if the majority of them members present at the meeting consented to it. The amendment must be affirmative form and in writing and duly signed. If there are a number of amendments to the same motion, the chairman will give them a priority order in which they may be taken up.

Resolution

An accepted motion is a resolution. According to the Webster dictionary, the word resolution means "a formal expression of opinion, will or intent voted by an official body or assembled group." "Resolution" therefore means a majority decision or opinion. A motion when seconded becomes a proposal and a proposal when passed becomes a resolution.

Kinds of Resolution

Three kinds of resolutions are recognised by Companies Act.

(a) Ordinary Resolutions
(b) Special Resolutions
(c) Resolutions requiring a special notice

(a) Ordinary Resolutions

An ordinary Resolution is one which is passed at a general meeting by a simple majority of members entitled to vote therein. Simple majority means that the vote cast either by show of hands or on a poll in favour of a particular proposal including the casting vote of the chairman exceeds the votes cast against it. Section 189 (1) provides that a resolution shall be an ordinary resolution when the votes at the general meeting casted by members in its favour are more than those caste of against it. In an ordinary resolution there is no importance to the total number of persons voting in favour of the proposal or against it. Usually, ordinary resolution can be passed in any general meeting for which 21 days notice is given. All resolutions which are not special or which do not require special notice are ordinary resolutions. A ordinary resolution is required for the following purposes:

(i) Declaration of dividends
(ii) Appointment of directors (Section 255)
(iii) Appointment of auditors and fixing their remuneration (Section 224).
(iv) Authorising voluntary winding up under specified circumstances by members (Section 484).
(v) Adoption of statutory report (Section 165).
(vi) Issue of shares at discount (Section 79).
(vii) To increase or decrease the number of directors within the limit set by the articles.
(viii) To change the conditions contained in the contracts stated in the prospectus or statement in lien of prospectus.
(ix) To empower the directors for further issue of capital.
(x) To increase or recognition of capital under Section 94.
(xi) To appoint any officer in the company.
(xii) To give donation to charitable purpose at a limit of 5% of the preceding three years average profits.

(B) Special Resolutions

Under Section 189 (2) of the act, a resolution is called a special resolution when: (i) the notice of the general meeting specifies that a particular proposal will be accepted by a special resolution, (ii) when 21 days clear notice is given for calling the meeting, and (iii) where the resolution is passed with 3/4 majority.

The votes may be cast either on a show of hands or by poll. A special resolution is a most useful part of the mechanism of a company. It is by and through the instrument of a special resolution that the companies carries importance executive and administrative acts which are, or may be necessary for the company's benefit. The aim of passing a special resolution is to ensure that every importance change shall be made only after due deliberation and with the sanction of the greater body of shareholders of the company. The articles of association may provide that certain types of business shall be approved by a special resolution. The act also provides that in certain specified cases, a company must pass a special resolution. A special resolution is required for the following purposes:

(1) To alter the name clause, objects clause and registered office clause of the memorandum of association (Section 146).
(2) To alter the articles of the company (Section 31)
(3) To offer further issue of subscribed capital when shares are offered to outsiders (Section 81).
(4) To create reserve capital (Section 99).
(5) To reduce the share capital of the company (Section 100).
(6) To authorise payment of interest out of capital (Section 208).
(7) To request the Central Government to appoint inspectors for investigation of the affairs of the company (Section 237).
(8) To authorise payment of remuneration to directors who are not in the whole time employment of the company (Section 309)
(9) To make the liability of directors unlimited (Section 323).
(10) To have the company wound up by the court (Section 433).
(11) To wind up the company voluntarily (Section 484).
(12) To appoint a director or his relative to a place of profit in the company (Section 314).
(13) To providing loan or standing guarantee against loans to the companies under the same management (Section 370).
(14) To reconstitute the basic structure of the company.

C. Resolution requiring special notice

This is a new kind of resolution. It was introduced by the Companies Act, 1956, under Section 190 what is required in case of such a resolution is that a special notice of the intention to move the resolution has to be given to the company. Resolution requiring special notice is proposal for which at least 14 days notice is required to be given to the company, before the meeting at which it is to be moved. The company, on receipt of such special notice will give a notice of information to its members at least 7 days before the meeting, in the same manner the notice for a meeting is sent. If such a notice is not practicable, the company may by an advertisement or in any other method, notify the information to its members.

Resolution requiring special notices

Special notice is required in the following cases.

(1) For the appointment of an auditor other than the retiring auditor (Section 225).
(2) For express resolution that the retiring auditor shall not be re-appointed (Section 225).
(3) For appointment of a director other than a retiring director (Section 257).
(4) For removing a director before the expiry of his term (Section 284).
(5) For appointing another person as director in place of the director removed (Section 284).

Circulation of Resolutions

Section 188 provides a method by which members desirous of moving a resolution at the annual general meeting can give notice and explanation in advance to the other members of what they intend to do. A company is bound on requisition in writing by a specified member of members (a) to give notice to the members of any resolution which is intended to be moved at the next annual general meeting, (b) to circulate to the members any statement of not more than one thousand words with respect to the proposed resolution or any business to be dealt with at the meeting. The expenses of any such notice and circulation will be born by the requisitionists. The requisition for circulating resolution shall be deposited with the company at its registered office not less than six weeks and any other requisition not less than two weeks before the next annual general meeting. The requisition must be signed by the required for requisition must either be (1) one hundred or more members having the right to vote on the resolution and holding shares on which a total amount of not less than 1/20th of the total voting power of all the members having the right to vote on the resolution.

On receipt of the requisition the company shall give notice of the proposed resolution to all members of the company entitled to receive notice of the next annual general meeting. The company shall also circulate the statement among its members entitled to notice of the general meeting. The company is not bound to circulate the resolution or statement if the Court finds, on application by the company or an aggrieved person, the same to be defamatory or abuse of the provisions of the Section. The cost of such application may be recovered from the requisitionists.

Registration of Resolutions and agreements

Section 192 provides that certain resolutions and agreements shall be registered with the Registrar so that he can maintain a complete record of the important transactions of the company. It affords an opportunity to the members of the public to ascertain the position of the company in certain respects. The following are the resolutions and agreements which are to be registered.

(i) Special resolutions.

(ii) Any resolution of the Board of Directors of a company or agreement executed by a company relating to the appointment or variation of the terms of appointment of a managing director.

(iii) Resolutions which have been agreed to by all members on a subject, which otherwise required a special resolution.

(iv) All resolutions and agreements which effectively bind members of any class of shareholders even though not agreed upon by those members.

(v) Resolutions or agreements which have been agreed to by all the members of any class of shareholders on a subject which required to be passed by a resolution of a particular majority in a particular manner.

(vi) Resolutions authorising the directors of a company to:

- (a) sell, lease or otherwise dispose of the whole or any part of the company's undertaking.
- (b) borrow money beyond the limits of the paid-up capital and free reserves.
- (c) contribute to charitable or other funds exceeding Rs. 50,000 or 5% of the average of the net profits of the last three years which every is greater.

(vii) Resolution approving the appointment of sole-selling agents.

(viii) Resolutions requiring a company to be wound up voluntarily.

Certified copies of above resolutions and agreement, duly signed by an officer of the company shall be filed within 30 days of the passing of the resolution or the making of the agreement. In case of non-compliance, the company and every officer of the company who is in default shall be fined upto Rs. 20 for every day during which the default continues.

Difference between Motion and Resolution

	Motion		Resolution
1.	It is a proposal put before the meeting for adoption.	1.	It is a decision to adopt the proposal.
2.	It is proposed resolution for acceptance by the meeting of the company.	2.	It is a motion accepted by the meeting.
3.	It may be amended.	3.	It cannot be amended.
4.	It may be moved duly amended.	4.	No such formalities are possible on a resolution.
5.	It initiates debate in a company meeting.	5.	It is the result of the debate.
6.	It is not the sense of the meeting.	6.	It is the will or sense of the meeting.
7.	It may be withdrawn from the meeting with the unanimous consent of the meeting.	7.	It is a part of the minutes and hence can not be withdrawn.
8.	It mayor may not be accepted by members.	8.	A motion, if accepted, becomes a resolution and thereafter, it cannot be rejected.
9.	It begins with the words "To resolve".	9.	It begins with the word 'Resolved'.

CHAPTER

49

Power of Majority and Protection of Minority

The General Principle of Company law is that questions relating to management are decided by majority. Majority may be a simple majority or special majority of the shareholders. This rule of majority is often referred to as the rule in *Foss v. Harbottle*.[206] The rule of supremacy of majority got legal recognition in this famous case. The court will not interfere to protect the minority against the consequences of the resolution.

In this case, the directors were guilty of fraudulent acts causing losses to the company. Two members started proceedings against the directors. But the Company in general meeting, by majority, resolved not to take any action against the directors. The court held that the actions of the directors could be confirmed by majority shareholders. The basis of the rule in this case in that the will of the majority should prevail. On becoming a member of a Company, the shareholder agrees to submit to the will of the majority of the members expressed in a general meeting and in accordance with the law, memorandum and articles.

The decision in this case is really the logical result of the principle that a Company is a separate legal person, it follows that if a wrong is done to it, the Company is the proper person to bring an action. This is a simple rule of procedure which applies to all wrongs that only the injured party may sue.

Advantages of rule in Foss v. Harbottle

1. Recognition of the separate legal personality of Company

If a Company has suffered some injury and not the individual member. It is the Company itself which can seek redress.

2. Need to preserve right of majority to decide

The principle in *Foss v. Harbottle* preserves the right of majority to decide how the affairs of the Company shall be conducted. It is but fair that the wish of the majority should prevail.

3. Multiplicity of futile suits avoided

If the individual shareholders were permitted to sue anyone who had injured the Company through a breach of duty, there could be as many actions as there are shareholders. Legal position proceedings would never cease and there would be enormous wastage of time and money.

Litigation at the suit of a minority futile if majority do not wish it

If the irregularity complained of is one which can be subsequently ratified by the majority it is futile to have litigation about it except with the consent of the majority in general meeting.

Exception to the rule in Foss v. Harbottle (Protection of Minority)

1. Where the act done is illegal or ultra vires of the company

Any shareholder can bring an action against the Company and if its affairs in respect of matters which are illegal or *ultra vires* of the Company because even unanimous approval by shareholders cannot approve such acts.

2. Breach of Judiciary Duty

Where the wrongs done are obvious but the majority does not allow any action to be brought against the directors and members there can be an action against them.

3. Fraud on Minority

Where the majority shareholders use their strength to gain an advantage by defrauding the minority, their conduct is liable to be impeached. The fraud or oppression must involve an unconscionable use of the majority, power resulting in loss or gross unfairness to the minority.

Menier v. Hooper's Telegraph Works Ltd.[207]

In this case, two companies A and B were in rivalry. The majority of the members of Company A were also the members of Company B. Company A had commenced an action against Company B. At a meeting of Company A, the majority passed a resolution to compromise the action in a manner favourable to Company Band unfavourable to A. Thus, they attempted to deprive the Company of the benefits which could have been recovered from Company B. Consequently, in an action by the minority, the resolution was held invalid. "It would be a shocking thing", the court observed, "If that could be done, because the majority have put something into their pockets at the expenses of the minority".

3. Where the act is supported by insufficient majority

Where the matter is one which must be decided by a special resolution, it can not be validly done or sanctioned by a simple majority.

4. Where the personal rights of an individual member have been infringed

Every share holder has certain rights against the Company. Some of those rights have been conferred by the Companies Act itself, some arise out of articles or general law, e.g., right to vote, right to notice, right of inspection of documents etc. Such rights cannot be curbed by a majority.

5. Oppression and Mismanagement

When the decisions of the majority oppresses the minority, (i.e., they are unduly harsh on the minority) or lead to mismanagement (i.e., they adversely affect the interest of the Company) under Section 397 and 398, the court or Central Government as the case may be redress the grievances of the minority.

Prevention of Oppression and Mismanagement

The term oppression means unjust or unfair conduct which results in some harsh or wrongful burden upon certain shareholders. It is not just the difference of opinion between two group of shareholders or negligence or inefficiency but an abuse of power by the group in control, having an element of lack of a fair dealing'.

When the affairs of a Company are being conducted in a manner prejudicial to public interest or the interest of the Company or when a material change has been taken place in the management of the Company which is likely to be prejudicial to public interest or the interest of the Company the affairs of the Company are said to be mismanaged.

With a view to preventing oppression and mismanagement, the Companies Act, 1956 lays down the following specific provisions:

According to Sections 397 and 398, any member of a Company may make an application to the court for appropriate relief.

The prevention of oppression and mismanagement may be discussed under the following two heads:

(1) Prevention of oppression and mismanagement by court and

(2) Prevention of oppression and mismanagement by the Central Government.

Prevention of Oppression and Mismanagement by Court

According to Section 397

(1) Any members of a Company who complain that the affairs of the Company are being conducted in a manner prejudicial to public interest or in a manner oppressive to any member or members (including anyone or more of themselves) may apply to the court for an order, provided they have a right to apply by virtue of Section 399.

(2) If, on the basis of the application, the court is of the opinion that the compliant is right and the winding up of the Company should be the just and equitable consequence but that shall be unfair to the members, the court may make order to bring an end to the complaints.

The application shall contain sufficient material which may be reasons for winding up (*Maharani Lalita v. Indian Motor Company*)[208]. The application shall contain what relief is exactly sought and no vague prayer (*Re Antigen Laboratories Ltd.*[209])

It has to be noted that in the Section preference has been given to an allegation of prejudicial to public interest.' The management of a Company must consider the impact of its policies on the society. That is called public interest (*Thomas v. Bradbury, Agrees and Co.*)[210].

Who can make application

According to Section 399 the following members shall have the right to apply

(a) In case of a Company having a share capital (i) 100 members or 1/10th of the members whichever is less or (ii) members holding not less than 1/10th of the issued share capital.

The applicants should have paid all calls and other sums due on their share, it means that no call money remains unpaid by the applicants;

(b) In case of a Company not having share capital - at least 1/10th of the total number - members must apply.

However, the Central Government may permit a lesser number of members than above to apply to the court for relief.

(c) The Central Government may itself apply under Section 401.

(d) The Central Government may require any member or members, so authorised, to give reasonable security to meet the cost as may be ordered by the court.

A member means a person whose name appears in the Register of Members. A person whose name has been ordered by the Central Government or the court to be entered in the Register but the Company has not done it, is entitled to make application[211]. The issued capital must be also subscribed to that extent[212].

The Central Government itself may make an application to the court (Section 401). The court shall give notice to the Central Government for representation before making order on any application made to the Court (Section 400).

Powers of Court

Powers of the Court under Section 402 to prevent oppression and mismanagement are wide.

This Section empowers the court to make the following orders for relief against oppression.

(i) The regulation of conduct of Company's affair in future,

(ii) The purchase of the shares or interests of any members of the Company by other members of the Company, by other members thereof or by the Company,

(iii) In case of purchase of its shares by the Company, the consequent reduction of its share capital,

(iv) The termination, setting aside or modification of any agreement between the Company and the managing director, any other director or the manager, upon such terms and conditions as the court thinks fit,

(v) Termination, setting aside or modification of any agreement between the Company and its managing director, or any other director and the manager upon such terms and conditions as may in the opinion of the court, be just and equitable in all circumstances of the case,

(vi) The setting aside of any transfer, delivery of goods, payment, execution or other act relating to property of the Company made within three months before the date of application it would make such order only if the circumstances are such that the transaction would have been deemed to be a fraudulent preference in an insolvency proceeding against an individual,

(vii) Any other matter for which in the opinion of the court it is just and equitable that provision should be made.

If necessary the court may appoint an administrator or special officer.[213] The court may order for an enquiry before making order for relief[214].

The court may make any interim order before making the final order (Section 403).

Any order by the court may effect alteration of the memorandum or articles of the Company.

Such alteration shall be deemed as if duly done under the provisions of the act. In future, the Company cannot alter its memorandum or articles in a manner inconsistent with the order of the court, without taking leave of the court. A certified copy of every order of alteration or giving leave to alter by the court shall be filed with the Registrar within 30 days from making the order and if default is made, the Company and every officer in default shall be punishable with fine upto Rs. 5000/- (Section 404).

A managing director, a director or a manager or any other person who has not been made a respondent may apply to the court to be a respondent and the court if satisfied may direct that he may be added as a respondent.

On the death of a respondent, his legal representative cannot be proceeded against.[215]

If any officer or member of a Company in respect of which an application has been made under Section 397, falsifies, destroys or omits to keep proper accounts or does any fraudulent act with an intention of deceiving or defrauding any person, the court may declare that such person would be personally liable to compensate the person concerned and also liable to compensate the Company (Section 406).

If the court makes an order Section 402 of termination, setting aside or modification of any agreement with any person,

(a) Such person shall not be entitled to any claims against the Company for damages or for compensation for loss of office or in any other respect;

(b) No managing or other director or manager whose agreement has been terminated or set aside shall be re-appointed within 5 years of time without the leave of the court.

Any person who acts as managing or other director or manager of the Company in violation of (b) above and any other director or every director who is a party to such violation shall be punishable with imprisonment for a terms upto one year or with fine which may go upto Rs. 5000 or with both.

The court shall grant leave provided a notice of the intention of applying to the court for leave is served on the Central Government and it is given opportunity of being heard.

Powers of the Central Government

The Act vests wide powers in the Central Government to take steps against oppression which may be (a) either of its own or (b) on receiving application or (c) even apprehending some undesirable situation to come.

Power to appoint directors (Section 408)

Where there is oppression or mismanagement within the meaning of Sections 397 or 398, the shareholders can apply to the Central Government for relief under Section 408. This the Central Government can do of its own or on the application of 100 or more members of the Company or by members holding 10% or more members of the Company.

If the Central Government is satisfied about oppression or mismanagement, it may appoint two persons as directors of the Company to prevent such oppression or mismanagement. The appointment can be for a period not exceeding three years at a time. The directors so appointed shall not be required to hold any qualification shares nor shall be liable to retire by rotation. they may, however, be removed by the Central Government from office at any time and other persons may be in their place. After such appointment, no change in the constitution of the Board of directors can be made without the consent of the Central Government.

When Central Government appoints a person as a director or additional director, it has the right to issue such directions to the Company as it may consider necessary or appropriate in regard to its affairs, the government can also require such person to report to the government from time to time with regard to the affairs. The government can also require such person to report to the government from time to time with regard to the affairs of the Company.

Power to prevent change in Board of Director (Section 409)

Where a complaint is made to the Central Government by the managing director or any other director or the manager of a Company that as a result of a change which has taken place or is likely to take place in the ownership on any shares a change in the Board of directors is likely to take place which if allowed would affect prejudicially the affairs of the Company, the Central Government, may, if satisfied after such enquiry as it thinks fit, by order direct that non resolution passed or to be passed or no action taken or to be taken bringing a change in the Board of directors, shall be effective unless confirmed by the Central Government, nothing in the act or in the memorandum or articles or resolution of the Company can prevent it.

The Central Government may make an interim order before making the final order. The Section does not apply to a Private Company unless it is subsidiary of a Public Company. An application under these Sections to be made in plain paper but the provisions of Section 604 B shall apply.

CHAPTER

50

Accounts and Audit

A Company has to keep its accounts in proper books of account. An accountant is in charge of 'Accounts' of the Company. He is responsible to maintain proper books of account. The accountant is the chief executive officer of the Company's account office. The Companies Act, 1956 contains a number of provisions relating to accounts and audit designed to ensure that the members of a Company are furnished with all the necessary information relating to its affairs.

Books of Account (Section 209)

As required by Section 209, every Company must keep at its registered office proper books of account in respect to—

(a) all sums of money received and expended by the Company and the matter in respect of which the receipt and expenditure take place,

(b) all sales and purchases of goods by the Company,

(c) the assets and liabilities of the Company, and

(d) in the case of Company engaged in production, processing, manufacturing or mining activities, such particulars relating to utilisation of material or labour or to other items of cost as may be prescribed, if such class of companies are required by the Central Government to include particulars in the books of account.

All such books of account may be kept either at the Company's registered office or at such other place in India as the Board of directors may decide with the condition that within 7 days of taking such decision a notice in writing is filed with the Registrar giving the full address of that other place.

Where a Company has branch offices whether in India or outside India, it would be enough if the branch offices maintain the accounts relating to their respective accounts. But the branches have to submit to the registered office or at the other place where the books of accounts of the Company are kept proper summarised returns of their respective accounts at an interval of not more than 3 months [Section 209 (2)].

The books of accounts shall be considered as 'proper' if they give a 'true and fair view' of the state of affairs of the Company and its branch offices explaining their transactions [Section 209 (3)].

Preservation of Books

The books of accounts of every Company relating to a period of not less them 8 years immediately preceding the current year or, the period between the incorporation of the Company and immediately preceding the current year, whichever is shorter, together with the voucher relevant to any entry in such books of account shall be preserved in good manner [Section 209 (4-A)].

Inspection of Books

The books of accounts and other books and papers shall be open to inspection by any director during business hours [Section 209 (4)]. The Registrar of companies and any other officer of the government authorised by the Central Government may inspect the books and records, such inspection can be made without giving previous notice to the Company or any of its officers. The Company must produce the books and records before them and furnish them with any other information that they may desire. The Company shall also give all reasonable assistance. The inspecting officer may make copies or make marks of identification on the books of account. The person making inspection has been vested with the powers of Civil Court.

Responsibility for Keeping the Books of Account

The primary duty for the proper maintenance of the books of account is that of the managing director or manager. Where a Company has neither a managing director nor a manager, it is the responsibility of every director of the Company. These persons may charge any other competent and reliable person with the responsibility of seeing that proper books of account are maintained. For failure to take reasonable steps to maintain them are liable to imprisonment which may extend to six months or with fine upto Rs. 1,000, or both. However, no person shall be sentenced to imprisonment for any such offence unless it was committed willfully.

If at the time of winding-up it is disclosed that proper books of account have not been maintained by the Company throughout the period of 2 years immediately preceding the commencement of winding up or from the incorporation to the commencement of winding up, whichever is shorter, every office of the Company in default shall be punishable with imprisonment for a term upto one year (Section 514).

Statutory Books

In addition to the books of accounts required to be maintained by a Company under Section 209, a Company is also required to maintain some other books with a view to safe-guarding the interests of the shareholders. Such books are called statutory books and are as follows:

(1) Membership register
(2) Index of members
(3) Register of debenture holders
(4) Foreign register of members
(5) Register of charges
(6) Register of directors
(7) Register of directors share holding
(8) Minutes book
(9) Books of accounts
(10) Register of investment
(11) Register of contracts etc.
(12) Register of loans granted to companies under the same management.

Non-Statutory or Statistical Books

In addition to statutory books, there are many other books which are required to be maintained for the proper and efficient running of Company. These books are not only found to be desirable but often indispensable in practice. Some of important statistical or non-statutory books are as follows:

(1) Balance ticket book
(2) Certified transfer register
(3) Dividend book
(4) Share transfer register
(5) Share certificates book
(6) Forfeiture of shares register
(7) Register of documents scaled
(8) Director's attendance book
(9) Log book
(10) Register showing the account of documents submitted to the registrar
(11) Share application and allotment book
(12) Agenda book
(13) Calls book
(14) Share transmission book
(15) Register of probates and letters of administration, etc.

Annual Accounts and Balance Sheet

The annual accounts of a Company consists of a balance sheet at the end of a financial year and a profit and loss account. In the case of a non-trading company, an income and expenditure account is prepared instead of a profit and loss account for the financial year.

Report to the annual general meeting

At every annual general meeting of a Company, the board of directors must lay before the meeting —

(i) A balance sheet for the year,

(ii) A profit and loss account for that period [Section 210 (1)] and

(iii) Director's report (Section 217)

In the case of a Company not carrying on business for profit, an income and expenditure account must be laid before the Company at its annual general meeting instead of a profit and loss account [Section 210 (2)]. the profit and loss account or income and expenditure account must relate the period —

(a) in the case of first annual general meeting, from the date of incorporation of the Company to date not more than nine months before the date of meeting, and

(b) in the case of any subsequent annual general meeting, from the date immediately after the period for which account was loss submitted to, not more than six months before the date of meeting.

The period, for which the accounts are prepared is called 'financial year'. It may be less or more than a calendar year. But it shall not exceed fifteen months. It may, however, be extended to eighteen months with the permission of the Registrar. In case of non-compliance with the above provisions, every director is liable for each offence to imprisonment for a term which may extend to six months or with fine which may extend to Rs. 1,000 or with both.

Authentication

Every balance sheet and every profit and loss account of a Company must be duly signed on behalf of the board of directors by the manager or secretary, if any, and not less than two directors of the Company, one of the directors who sign must be a managing director where there is one (Section 215).

Annexures

The profit and loss account must be annexed to the balance sheet and the auditor's report including the auditor's separate, special or supplementary report, if any must also be attached there to (Section 216).

Form and contents of balance sheet and profit and loss account (Section 211)

Every balance sheet and profit and loss account of a Company must give a true and fair view of the state of affairs of the Company as at the end of the financial year. It must be prepared according to the part I (for balance sheet) and the part II (for profit and loss account) of the schedule VI attached to the Act or in such other form as may be approved by the Central Government. The schedule VI does not apply to any insurance, or banking or electricity generation Company because specific forms have been provided in the respective Acts for such companies.

The Central Government may, by notification in the Official Gazette and subject to any conditions mentioned in the notification or not, exempt any class of companies from compliance with any requirements in the schedule VI. The Central Government, may, on the application or with the consent of the board of directors of the Company, by order, modify any of the requirements of this act as to the matters to be stated in the Company's balance sheet or profit and loss account for the purpose of adopting them to the circumstances of the Company.

Non-compliance with these provisions is punishable with imprisonment upto the six months or fine upto Rs. 1,000 or with both (Section 211).

Circulation of Annual Account (Section 219)

Section 219 makes the following provisions:

A copy of every balance sheet, including the profit and loss account, the auditor's report and every other document required by the act to be annexed or attached thereto and to be laid before the Company in the general meeting must be sent, not less than 21 days before the date of meeting, to every member, every debenture holder, every trustee for debenture holders (whether they are entitled to receive general notice or not) and to every other person entitled to receive notice of general meetings. If the copies are sent less than 21 days before the date of the meeting, they shall be deemed to be duly sent if it is so agreed by all the members entitled to vote at the meeting. If any default is made in complying with above provisions of Section 219, the Company and every officer of the Company who is in default are punishable with fine which may extend to Rs. 500.

Any member or debenture holder, whether he is or is not entitled to have the Company's balance sheet sent to him, shall, on demand, without charge and any person from whom the Company has received deposit, on demand with the prescribed fee of Rs. 1, be entitled to be furnished with a copy of the last balance sheet together with other annexed and attached documents including profit and loss account and auditor's report.

If the above made demand is not complied with within 7 days, the Company and every officer in default shall be punishable with fine which may extend to Rs. 5000. This Section is applicable to both public and private companies.

Boards Report (Section 217)

There must be attached to every balance sheet laid before a Company in general meeting, a report by its board of directors. The report shall deal with the following:

(a) the statement of Company' s affairs,

(b) the amounts, if any, which it proposes to carry to any reserves in the balance sheet,

(c) the amount which it recommends for payment as dividend.

(d) Material charges and commitments, if any, affecting the financial position of the

Company which have occurred between the end of the financial year to which the balance-sheet relates and the date of the report [Section 217 (1)].

The board's report shall also deal with any changes which have occurred during the financial year

(a) in the nature of Company's business,

(b) in the Company's subsidiaries or in the nature of the business carried on by them and

(c) generally in the classes of business in which the Company has interest [Section 217 (2)].

The boards' report shall also include a statement showing the name of every employee of the Company who (a) if employed throughout the financial year was in receipt of remuneration for that year, in the aggregate, was not less than Rs. 1,44,000, or (b) if employed for a part of the financial year, was in receipt of remuneration for any part of that year at a rate which, if the aggregate was not less than Rs. 12,000 per month (with effect from 18-9-90).

The statement shall also indicate whether any such employee is a relative of any director or manager of the Company, and if so, the name of such director [Section 217 (2-A)].

Companies (Disclosure of Particulars in the Report of Board of directors)

In exercise of the powers conferred by Section 642 read with this clause, the Central Government made the following rules which came into force from the 1st day of April, 1989. Every Company shall, in the report of its Board of directors, disclose,

A. Conservation of energy

(i) energy conservation measures taken;

(ii) additional investments and proposals, if any, being implemented for reduction of consumption of energy;

(iii) impact of the measures at (i) and (ii) above for reduction of energy consumption and consequent impact on the cost of production of goods;

(iv) total energy consumption and energy consumption per unit of production in respect of industries specified in this regard.

B. Technology absorption

(v) efforts made in technology absorption in the prescribed form,

C. Foreign Exchange Earnings

(vi) activities relating to exports, initiatives to increase exports, development of new export markets for products and services, and export items,

(vii) total foreign exchange used and earned.

The Board is also bound to give fullest information, and explanations in its report on every reservation, qualification or adverse remark contained in the auditors report [Section 217 (3)]. The Board's report is to be signed by its chairman if he is authorised in that behalf by the Board. Where he is not so authorised, it shall be signed by such number of directors as are required to sign the balance sheet and profit and loss account [Section 217 (4)] and profit and loss account are laid before the general meeting.

Filing of Accounts with the Registrar (Section 220)

Within 30 days from the date when the balance sheet and profit and loss account has been laid before the Company at an annual general meeting three copies of the balance sheet and of the profit and loss account signed by the managing director, manager or secretary of the Company or if there is none of these, by a director of the Company, together with three copies all the annexed or attached documents, shall be filed with the Registrar. But in case of a private Company, the copies of balance sheet and of the profit and loss account shall be filed separately (Section 610).

If the annual general meeting does not adopt the balance sheet, the statement of that fact and the reasons thereto shall also be attached to the copies of balance sheet filed with the Registrar.

The Companies (Amendment) Act 1971 has amended Section 220 which provides that even where the annual general meeting of a Company for any year is not held its balance sheet and profit and loss account shall be filed with the Registrar within 30 days from the latest day on or before which that meeting should have been hold in accordance with the provisions of the Act. In case of non-compliance, the Company and every officer who is in default shall be punishable with fine upto Rs. 50 for every day during which the default continues.

Auditors

The members of the Company are virtually the owners of the Company. The members have monetary interest and stake in the Company. They depend on the directors for the management of the Company and for safeguarding of the assets. The directors are responsible and authorised to prepare the annual accounts to be presented before the members at the annual general meeting for consideration and adoption if found acceptable. The others have to depend upon the doings of these directors or superior officers. In such circumstances, some independent agency is required to check accounts of the Company. It is for this reason that the audit of the books of account of a Company has been made compulsory by the Act. The Act makes provision for auditing or checking the accounts primarily in the interest of the members and indirectly in the interests of the public at large. The importance of audit is supreme.

Appointment of Auditors (Section 224A and 225)

The Act makes elaborate provisions with regard to the first and subsequent appointments of auditors of a Company.

First Auditors

The first auditors of a Company shall be appointed by the Board of directors within one month of the incorporation of the Company. The auditors so appointed shall hold office until the conclusion of the first annual general meeting of the Company. If the Board fails to appoint such auditors, the Company may in the general meeting appoint the first auditors. The Company may at general meeting remove the auditors appointed by the Board and appoint in their place any other person as auditors who have been nominated for appointment by any member of the Company, and of whose nomination notice has been given to the members of the Company not less than 14 days before the date of the meeting.

Subsequent Auditors

Subsequent auditors must be appointed at each annual general meeting of the Company, and the auditor so appointed shall hold office from the conclusion of that meeting until the conclusion of next annual general meeting. Every Company shall, within 7 days of the appointment of an auditor at its annual general meeting, give intimation thereof to the auditor so appointed. Every auditor so appointed shall inform the Registrar within 30 days of the receipt of the intimation of his appointment, whether he has accepted the appointment or not.

The Amendment Act, 1974 requires every Company while appointing or reappointing an auditor, to obtain a certificate from the auditor that the appointment or reappointment if made will be within the specified number means:

(a) In the case of a person or firm, holding appointment as auditor of a number of companies, each of which has a paid-up share capital of less than Rs. 25,00,000 — twenty such companies.

(b) In any other case, twenty companies, out of which not more than ten should have paid-up share capital of Rs. 25,00,000 or more.

In the case of a firm of audiotrs, a specified number of companies shall be construed as a 'specified number of companies' per partner of the firm. Where any partner of a firm of auditors is also a partner in any other firm or firms of auditors, the number of companies which may be taken shall not exceed the specified number in the aggregate.

Where a person or a firm is an auditor of a number of companies, exceeding the specified number, immediately before the Commencement of the Companies (Amendment) Act 1974, he or it shall intimate within 60 days from such commencement, to the Company or companies whose appointment he or it would not like to accept from the commencement of the next financial year. He or it shall also intimate to the Registrar the names of the companies of which he or it is willing to be reappointed as the auditor, and forward a copy of the intimation to each of the companies referred to therein.

Re appointment of Retiring Auditors

An auditor appointed at any annual general meeting, should ordinarily be reappointed.

A retiring auditor is reappointed except in the following cases:

(a) He is not qualified for reappointment.

(b) He has given the notice to the Company in writing of his unwillingness to be reappointed.

(c) A resolution has been passed at that meeting appointing somebody instead of him or providing expressly that he shall not be reappointed, or

(d) Where notice has been given of an intended resolution to appoint some person or person the place of a retiring auditor and by reason of the death, incapacity or disqualification of that person or persons, the resolution cannot be proceeded with [Section 224(2)].

Where at an annual general meeting no auditors are appointed or reappointed, the Central Government may appoint a person to fill the vacancy. The Central Government may appoint a person to fill the vacancy. The Company shall inform the Central Government within 7 days of it fails to appoint or reappoint the auditors at an annual general meeting. If the Company fails to give notice, the Company and every officer of the Company who is in default shall be punishable with a fine which may extend to Rs. 500 [Section 224(4)].

Casual Vacancy

The Board may fill any causal vacancy in the office of an auditor. While any such vacancy continues, the remaining auditor or auditors, if any, may act. But where such vacancy is caused by the resignation of an auditor, the vacancy can only be filled by the Company in general meeting. Any auditor appointed in a causal vacancy holds office until the conclusion of the next annual general meeting [Section 224(6)].

Appointment of Auditor by Special Resolution

Section 224-A has been introduced by the Amendment Act, 1974. This Section specified the cases in which an auditor can be appointed or reappointed only by special resolution. According to new Section 224-A, in the case of a Company in which at least 25% of the subscribed share capital is held or jointly by a public financial institution, a Government Company, a nationalised bank or an Insurance Company carrying on general insurance business, the appointment or re-appointment of an auditor shall be by a special resolution of the annual general meeting. This provision also applies where 25% or more of the subscribed capital is held by the Central Government or State Government or by any institution established by a State Act, in which the State Government holds not less than 51% of the subscribed share capital.

Where any Company referred to above, omits or fails to pass at its annual general meeting a special resolution appointing or reappointing an auditor it shall be deemed that no auditor has been appointed. In such an event the Company shall within 7 days, give notice of that fact to the Central Government and the Central Government will appoint a person to fill the vacancy [Section 224-A(2)].

Removal of an Auditor

The Act some provisions for removal of an auditor or auditors which are as below:

(i) The Company may at a general meeting remove an auditor or all or any of all auditors, first appointed by the Board [Section 224(5)]. For such removal, no special notice for the intended resolution is necessary [Section 225(4)].

(ii) Any auditor (Other than the first auditor appointed by the Board may be removed from office before the expiry of his term by the Company in general meeting after obtaining the previous approval of the Central Government [Section 224(7)]. No special notice for the intended resolution is necessary [Section 225(4)].

(iii) A special notice is required for a resolution at an annual meeting to appoint a person other than the retiring auditor or to provide that the retiring auditor shall not be reappointed [Section 224(1)]. On receipt of the special notice the Company shall send a copy thereof to the retiring auditor [Section 225(2)]. The retiring auditor has a right to make written representation (not exceeding a reasonable length to the Company). At the request of the auditor, the Company shall send a copy of the representation to the members. If a copy of the representation cannot be sent to the members because it was received too late or because of the Company's default, the auditor may require that the representation shall be read out at the meeting. The court may direct that the representation need not be circulated or read out at the meeting if it is satisfied that the right of making representation is being misused by the auditor for making needless publicity for defamatory matters [Section 225(3)].

Remuneration

The remuneration of the auditor of a Company shall be fixed by the Company in the general meeting or in such manner as the Company in general meeting may determine. If the auditors are appointed by the Board of directors or by the Central Government, their remuneration may be fixed by the Board or by the Central Government as the case may be. Any sums paid by the Company in respect of auditors expenses shall be deemed to be included in the expression 'remuneration' [Section 224(8)].

Qualifications and disqualifications [Section 226]

A person is qualified for appointment as auditor of a Company only if he is a Chartered Accountant within the meaning of the Chartered Accountants Act, 1949. A firm of auditors of which all the partners practising in India are qualified for appointment may be appointed by its firm name to the auditor of a Company. In such case, any partner may act as auditor in the name of the firm.

Disqualifications

The following persons are disqualified from being appointed as auditors of a Company—

(a) A body corporate

(b) An officer or employee of the Company

(c) A person who is a partner, or who is in the employment of an officer or employee of the Company.

(d) A person who is indebted to the Company for an amount exceeding Rs. 1000 or who has given any guarantee of any third person to the Company for an amount exceeding Rs. 1000.

(e) A person who is disqualified for appointment as auditor of any other body corporate which is (i) that Company's subsidiary or (ii) its holding company, or (iii) a subsidiary of its holding company.

If an auditor becomes subject, after his appointment, to any of the disqualifications specified above, he is deemed to have vacated his office as such.

Power and Duties of Auditor

The various rights and powers enjoyed by the auditors under the Companies Act, 1956 are as follows:

(1) Every auditor has a right of access at all times to the books of accounts and vouchers of the Company whether kept at the head office or elsewhere and is entitled to require from the officers of the Company such information and explanations as the auditor thinks necessary to perform his duties [Section 227(1)].

(2) Where the accounts of any branch office is audited by another auditor then the Company's auditor—

  (a) is entitled to visit the branch office if necessary to perform his duties and

  (b) has a right of access at all times to the books of accounts and vouchers maintained at the branch office [Section 228(2)].

(3) An auditor has the right to receive all notices and other communications relating to any general meeting of the Company which are sent to any member. The auditor is entitled to attend any general meeting and to be heard there on any business matter in which he is concerned (Section 231).

(4) If an auditor is acquitted by the Court from any allegation brought against him by any shareholder and the allegation is proved to be false, then the court may direct the complainant to pay compensation to the auditor in addition to his other liability. An auditor in this respect has the right to enjoy the privilege of an officer of the Company as provided in Section 6.25.

Duties of Auditors

The auditors have the following statutory duties in addition to any other duties which may be imposed upon them by the articles of the Company.

1. **The auditor has the duty to enquire (Section 227(I-A)].**
   (a) Whether loans and advances made by the Company on the basis of security have been properly secured and whether the terms on which they have been made are not prejudicial to the interests of the Company or its members;
   (b) Whether the transactions of the Company which are represented merely by book entries are not prejudicial to the interests of the Company;
   (c) Whether the Company is not an investment Company (within the meaning of Section 372) or a banking Company, whether so much of the assets of the Company as consist of shares, debentures and other securities have been sold at a price less than at which they were purchased by the Company;
   (d) Whether loans and advances made by the Company have been shown as deposits;
   (e) Whether personal expenses have been charged to revenue account;
   (f) Where it is stated in the books and papers of the Company that any shares have been allotted for cash, whether cash has actually been received in respect of such allotment and if no cash has actually been so received, whether the position as stated in the account books and the balance sheet is correct, regular and not misleading.

The duties of auditors have been exhaustively reviewed by the Court of Appeal *in re*: City Equitable Fire Insurance Co.[216]. The following points were made in this case:

(i) The extent of an auditors responsibility depends upon the terms of his engagement, either by a special contract or as contained in the articles.

(ii) The duty imposed on the auditor by the Act is not defined as regards its nature or extent, but it depends on the information and explanations furnishod to him.

(iii) The auditor should not be content with a certificate that the securities of the Company are with a particular person or firm unless such person or firm is trustworthy and is one who or which in the ordinary course of business keeps securities for his or its customers. The auditor must also see that the securities of the Company actually exist by making a personal inspection of them. If they are in the safe custody of a banker in the ordinary course of business, he may rely upon the certificate of the bankers.

2. Duty to Assist Investigators

An auditor is bound to assist the inspectors in every possible way when the affairs of the Company are being investigated (Section 240).

3. Auditor's Report

It is a duty of the auditor to make a report to the members of the Company on:

(a) the accounts examined by him,

(b) balance sheet and profit and loss account, and

(c) every document annexed to the balance sheet and profit and loss accouont laid before the company in general meeting during his tenure of office.

The words "the members" mean 'the assembled in a general meeting.'[217]

Obligation to make an inquiry [Section 227(1-A))

Section 227(1-A) imposes an obligation on an auditor to inquire in particular —

(a) Whether loans and advances made by the Company, on the basis of security, have been properly secured and whether the terms on which they have been made are not prejudicial to the interests of the Company or its members;

(b) Whether transactions of the Company which are presented merely by book entries are not prejudicial to the interests of the Company;

(c) Where the Company is not an investment Company or a banking Company, whether so much of the assets of the Company as consist of shares, debentures and other securities have been sold at a price less than that at which they were purchased by the Company;

(d) Whether loans and advances made by the Company have been shown as deposits;

(e) Whether personal expenses have been charged to revenue account;

(f) Where any shares have been allotted for cash, whether cash has actually been received in respect of such allotment and if no cash has been received, whether the position shown in the books and balance sheet is correct, regular and not misleading.

This duty of inquiry has been cast on the auditors to safeguard the public money from being indirectly drained for the personal benefit of the persons, directly or indirectly, in control of the affairs of a Company.

Principles governing report and its contents

The principles governing an auditor's report and his duty in respect thereof have been laid down in a number of decided cases.

Deputy Secretary to the Govt. of India, Ministry of Finance v. S.N. Das Gupta.[218] The actual cash in hand was much less than was shown in the books of a banking Company. The auditor failed to verify this cash balance. Held he was guilty of neglect of duty.

In London and General Bank, Re (No. 2)[219], Lindley L.J. observed as follows:

"A person whose duty it is to convey information to others does not discharge that duty by simply giving them so much information as is calculated to induce them or some of them to ask for more an auditor who gives shareholders means of information, instead of information, in respect of a Company's financial position does so at his peril and runs the serious risk of being held judicially to have failed to discharge his duty."

Matters to be stated in Auditor's Report

The auditor's report shall also state —

(a) Whether he has obtained all the information and explanations which to the best of his knowledge and belief were necessary for the purposes of his audit;

(b) Whether proper books of accounts as required by law have been kept by the Company, and proper returns adequate for the purposes of his audit have been received from branches not visited by him;

(c) Whether the report of the accounts of any branch office audited by some person other than the Company's auditor has been forwarded to him and how he has dealt with it in preparing his report;

(d) Whether the Company's balance sheet and profit and loss account dealt with by the report are in agreement with the Company's books of account and returns [Section 227(3)] ; and

(e) Whether the accounts examined by him, in his opinion give the information required by the Act and whether the balance sheet and profit and loss account laid before the Company in general meeting render a true and fair view of the state of affairs of the Company and of its profits or losses for the financial year for which they have been prepared.

Where any of these matters is answered in the negative or with a qualifications, the report shall state the reason for it [Section 227(4)].

(f) Further, the Central Government may, by general or special order, direct, that in the case of certain specific companies, the auditor's report shall also include a statement of such matters as may be specified in the order. Before making such an order the Central Government consult the Institute of Chartered Accountants of India in regard to the class or description of Companies and other ancillary matters proposed to be specified in the order [Section 227(4-A)]. For instance, the Central Government, in consultation with the Institute of Chartered Accountants of India, issued an order on 10th November, 1975, called "The Manufacturing and Other Companies (Auditor's) Report order, 1975" whereby audit report shall have to contain additional information on the working of a Company. This audit has been given the nomenclature of "social audit". The order applies to every Company which is engaged in one or more of the following activities, namely:

(a) manufacturing, mining or processing,

(b) supplying and rendering services,

(c) trading, and

(d) the business of financing, investment, chit fund, nidhi or mutual benefit societies.

The order does not apply to a banking Company as defined in Section 5(c) of the Banking Regulation Act 1949.

(g) The accounts of a Company shall not be deemed as not having been properly drawn up and the auditor cannot make such remark merely that the Company has not disclosed certain matters if (i) those matters are such as the

Company is not required to disclosed by virtue of this or any other Act and (ii) those provisions are specified the balance sheet and profit and loss account of Company [Section 227(5)].

(h) The auditor has to sign his report. Only the person appointed as auditor of the Company, or where a firm is so appointed, only a partner of the firm practising in India, may sign the auditor's report or sign or authenticate any other document of the Company required by law to be signed or authenticated by the auditor (Section 229).

The auditor in his report states that the balance sheet and profit and loss account show a true and fair view of the Company's affairs but he does not guarantee that the balance sheet is accurate.[220] He must verify that assets and shall not rely on the figures in the last balance sheet or on the words of persons in management of the Company.[221] But he may rely on directors in respect of the bad debts.[222]

It is not enough for an auditor to state that the balance sheet in not correct. He has to point out what is wrong.[223] An auditor is responsible to the member's but not to any individual member.[234]

Penalty (Section 232 and 233)

If default is made by a Company in complying with any of the provisions contained in Section 227, the Company, and every officer of the Company who is in default shall be punishable with fine which may extend to Rs. 500 (Section 232). Further if any auditor's report is not in conformity with the provisions of Section 227, the auditor concerned and the person, if any, other than the auditor who signs the report shall be punishable with fine which may extend to Rs. 1,000. The fine shall however be levied if the default is wilful (Section 233).

Signatures of audit report (Section 229)

Only the person appointed as the auditor, only a partner in the firm practising in India, may sign the auditor's report, or sign or auditor's report, or sign or authenticate any other document of the Company required by law be signed or authenticated by the auditor.

If default is made by a Company in complying with any of the Company who is in default, shall be punishable with fine which may extend to Rs. 500 (Section 232). Further, if any document is signed or authenticated, otherwise than in conformity with the requirements of Section 229, the auditor concerned and the person who signs or authenticates the document, if the default is willful, shall be punishable with fine which may extend to Rs. 1,000 (Section 233).

Reading and Inspection of auditor's report (Section 230)

The auditor's report shall be read before the Company in general meeting and shall be open to inspection by any member of the Company, and every officer of the Company who is in default, shall be punishable with fine which may extend to Rs. 500 (Section 232).

Further duties

In addition to the duties of an auditor discussed above, he has also to perform to following duties:

1. Statutory report

After the statutory report has been certified as correct by not less than 2 directors of a Company, the auditor of the Company must certify the report as correct, so far as it relates to (a) the shares alloted by the Company, (b) the cash received in respect of shares and (c) the receipts and payments of the Company [Section 165(4)].

This provision does not apply to private companies as they are not required to hold a statutory meeting [Section 165(10)].

2. Prospectus

Section 56(1) requires a report by the auditor of the Company with respect to profits and losses, assets and liabilities and the rates of dividends, if any, paid by the Company to be included in a prospectus (Part II of Schedule II). The auditor has to certify these as correct.

3. Assistance in investigation

According to Section 240, it is the duty of all the officers and other employees and agents (and for Section 240, the expression 'agent' includes 'auditor') of a Company:

(a) to preserve and to produce to an inspector (appointed under Section 235 to investigate the affairs of the Company) or any person authorised by him in this behalf with the previous approval of the Central Government all books and papers of, or relating to, the Company, which are in their custody and power, and

(b) otherwise to give to the inspector all assistance in connection with the investigation which they are reasonably able to give.

Types of Audit

There are following different types of Audit as envisaged in the Act.

(i) Statutory Audit
(ii) Special Audit
(iii) Audit of Cost Accounts (Section 233-B)
(iv) Branch Audit

(i) Statutory Audit

This is the main type of audit which is of routine character and is commonly known as statutory audit. Every Company shall at annual general meeting, appoint an auditor or auditors to audit its accounts (Section 224). The auditor's report shall be attached to the balance sheet (Section 216).

N on compliance of any provision in sections 225 to 231 the Company and every officer shall be punishable with fine which may go upto Rs. 500/-.

(ii) Special Audit

The Central Government under Section 233-A may at any time direct by order that a special audit of the Company's account for such period or periods as specified in the order shall conducted by a chartered accountant (whether practicing or not) appointed by the Central Government by order or by the auditor of the Company, when the Central Government is of the opinion —

(a) that the affairs of the Company are not being managed in accordance with sound business principles or prudent commercial practices, or

(b) that the Company is being managed in a manner likely to cause serious injury or damage to the interests of the trade, industry or business to which it pertains, or

(c) that the financial position of the Company is such as to endanger its solvency.

The said chartered accountant or the Company's auditor shall be called special auditor.

The special auditor shall have the same powers and duties as those of the Company's auditor provided that he shall make the report to the Central Government. The report of the special auditor shall mostly contain the same matters as understood by auditor's report but shall also include a statement on any other matters as understood by auditor's report. But shall also include a statement or any other matter if the Central Government so directs. The Central Government may be specified order direct any person to furnish such information or additional information and that within such a time as specified, as may be required by the special auditor. For non compliance of such order, such person shall be punishable with fine may go upto Rs. 500/-.

On the receipt of the report of the special auditor, the Central Government may take action as it considers necessary under law and if the Central Government does not take any action within four months from the date of receipt of report, that Government shall send to the Company either a copy of or extracts from the report to the Company to be circulated among the members or to be read at the next general meeting.

The expenses of special audit including the remuneration of the special auditor shall be determined by the Central Government which is final and paid by the Company and in default of such payment, it shall be recovered from the Company as an arrear of land revenue.

(iii) Audit of Cost Accounts (Section 233-B)

The Central Government may issue necessary direction under Section 233-B for conducting cost audit of companies engaged in production, processing, manufacturing or mining activities. The companies shall maintain books according to rules framed by the Central Government and must include particulars relating to utilisation of material, labour or other items of cost.

The Central Government may, by order, direct that an audit of the Cost accounts of those companies shall be conducted by an auditor who shall be a cost accountant within the meaning of the Cost and Works Accountants Act 1959. But where the Central Government is of the opinion that sufficient number of Cost Accountants are not available for conducting the audit of Cost accounts of companies, the Central Government may be notify in the Official Gazette, and direct that for a specified period the chartered accountants possessing the prescribed qualifications may also conduct such audit of Cost Accounts. The Cost auditor shall be appointed by the Board of directors with the previous approval of the Central Government. An audit, conducted under this Section, will be in addition to an audit conducted under Section 224.

Cost auditor shall have the same powers and duties in relation to an audit conducted by him as an auditor under Section 227(1). He shall make his report to the Central Government in the prescribed form and forward a copy of the same to the Company. An auditor appointed under Section 224 and a person who is disqualified under Section 226(3) and (4) shall not be appointed as Cost auditor. If a cost auditor becomes disqualified after his appointment, he shall cease to audit the Cost accounts of the Company.

The Company is under a duty to give all facilities and assistance to the person appointed for conducting the audit of the Cost accounts. The Company shall within 30 days from the date of receipt of the Cost auditors report, furnish the Central Government full information and explanations on every reservation or qualification contained in such report. After considering the report of the cost auditor and the information and explanation furnished by the Company, the Central Government may, if it considers necessary, demand further information. The Central Government may then take such action on the report as it considers necessary. It may direct the Company to circulate the report to its members along with the notice of the next annual general meeting.

In the case of non-compliance with the provision of this Section, the Company shall be liable to a fine upto Rs. 5,000/-. Every officer, who is in default, is also liable to imprisonment for a term which may extend to three years or to a fine upto Rs. 5000/- or with both.

(iv) Branch Audit (Section 228)

Where a Company has a branch office, the accounts of that office shall be audited by the Company's auditor or where the branch office situates in a country outside India, either by the company's auditor or by a person who is qualified to be an auditor according to the laws of that Country.

Where the branch office is audited by a person other than the Company's auditor, the Company's auditor shall have the following rights;

(a) shall be entitled to visit the branch office if he thinks it necessary for his duties and

(b) shall have right of access at all times to the books and accounts and vouchers maintained at the branch office. But in case of Banking Company having a branch outside India, it shall be enough if the auditor is allowed access to the report submitted by the branch office.

Where a Company in general meeting decides that an auditor other than the Company's auditor shall be appointed for its branch office or a person qualified according to the laws of that country where the branch office is situated outside India.

Powers, Duties and Remuneration of Branch Auditor

The branch auditor shall have the same powers and duties as the Company's auditor. He shall prepare a report on the accounts of the branch office examined by him and forward the same to the Company's auditor who shall deal with it in preparing his report. He shall receive such remuneration and hold his appointment subject to such terms and conditions as may be fixed by the Company in general meeting or by the Board of directors if so authorised by the Company in general meeting.

Exemption from audit

The Central Government may make rules providing for the exemption of any branch office from the provisions of Section 228 and may make rules having regard to all of any of the following matters, namely—

(a) the arrangement made by a Company for the audit of accounts of the branch office by a person who is otherwise qualified to be a branch auditor even though he is an officer of employee of the Company;

(b) the nature and quantum of activity carried on at the branch office during a period of 3 years immediately preceding the date on which the branch office is exempted from the provisions of this Section;

(c) the availability at the reasonable cost of a branch auditor for the audit of accounts of the branch office;

(d) any other matter which in the opinion of the Central Government justifies that grant of exemption to the branch office from the provisions of Section 228.

Penalty (Section 232)

If default is made in complying with any of the provisions of Section 228, the Company, and every officer of the Company who is in default, shall be punishable with fine which may extend to Rs. 500/-.

Power of Registrar to Call for Information (Section 234)

Where on per suing any document which a Company is required to submit under the Companies Act, the Registrar is of opinion that some further information or explanation is necessay, he may require the Company to furnish the same within a specified period. On receipt by the Company of the order from the Registrar, it is the duty of the Company and of all persons who are or have been officers of the Company, to furnish the required information or exemption to the best of their power.

If the Company does not supply the required information or explanation, or supplies inadequate information, the Registrar may require the Company to produce before him for his inspection the necessary books and papers within the specified period. In such a case, it is the duty of the Company, and of all persons, who are officers of the Company, to produce such books and papers. The Company and the officers in default are punishable with fine which may extend to Rs. 500, and in the case of a continuing default with an additional fine which may extend to Rs. 50/- per day. The Court trying the offence may, on the application of the Registrar and after notice to the Company order the Company to produce before the Registrar for its inspection the necessary books and papers.

Siezure of Documents by Registrar (Section 234-A)

Where, upon information in his possession or otherwise, the Registrar has reasonable ground to believe that the books of account and papers of or relating to, a Company or its managerial personnel, may be destroyed, mutilated, altered, falsified or secreted, he may make an application to the magistrate of the first class or, as the case may be, the presidency magistrate, for an order for the seizure of such books and papers.

After considering the application and hearing the registrar, the magistrate may authorise the Registrar —

(a) to enter the place or places where such books and papers are kept,

(b) to search that place or those places in the manner specified in the order, and

(c) to seize such books and papers as he considers necessary.

The Registrar shall return the books and papers seized within 30 days of the seizure to the Company or the managing director or the manager or any other persons from whose custody or power they were seized and inform the magistrate of such return. But he may, before returning such books and papers, take copies of or extracts from them or place identification marks on them or any part thereof.

CHAPTER

51

Winding up of Companies

A Company is an artificial person, created by Law, having perpetual succession. It carries out its affairs under the provisions of law, throughout its life. The process through which the life of a Company comes to an end is know as winding up, under this process an administrator called 'liquidator' is appointed, he takes control of the Company, collects its assets, pays its debts and finally distributes surplus if any to the members in proportion to their holding in the Company.

Characteristics of Winding up

(1) Winding up is a process.

(2) Under the process, the life of the Company is ended and its property is administered for the benefits of its members and creditors.

(3) A liquidator is appointed to realise the assets and properties of the Company.

(4) After payments of debts, if any surplus of assets is left out, they will be distributed among the members according to their rights.

(5) Winding up does not necessarily means that the Company is insolvent. A perfectly solvent company may be wound up by the approval of members in a general meeting.

(6) There are differences between winding up and dissolution.

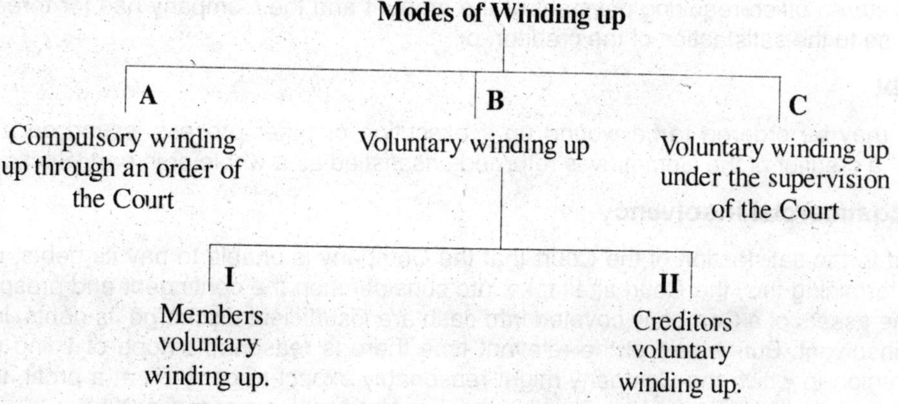

Modes of winding up:

There are three modes of winding up of a Company. These are:

(a) Compulsory winding up by the Court.

(b) Voluntary winding up, which is itself of two kinds:

  (i) Members voluntary winding up,

  (ii) Creditors voluntary winding up,

(c) Winding up under the supervision of the Court.

A. Compulsory winding up by the Court [Section 433]

A Company may be wound up by an order of the Court. Section 433 lays down the following grounds upon which a Company may be wound up by the Court.

1. Special resolution of the Company [Section 433 (a)

A Company may, by a special resolution passed at its general meeting, be wound up by the orders of the Court. The Court is, however, not bound to order for winding up simply because the Company has not resolved. the power is discretionary. The Court may refuse to order winding up where it is opposed to public or Company's interest.

2. Default in holding statutory meeting or in delivering statutory report to the Registrar [Section 433 (b)

If a Company makes a default in delivering statutory report to the Registrar or in holding the statutory meeting in time, the Court may order winding up of the Company. The petition for winding up can be given either by the Registrar or by a contributory. If it is brought by a creditor, it must be filed before the expiry of 14 days from the last date on which the statutory meeting ought to have been held. The power of the Court is discretionary and it may, instead of making a winding up order, direct that the statutory report be delivered or that a meeting be held.

3. Failure to commence business within a year of incorporation [Section 433 (c)

If a Company does not commence its business with in a year of its registration or has suspended business for a year, the Court may order for winding up. Here also the power of the Court is discretionary and will be exercised only when there is a clear indication that there is no intention to carry on business. Where the failure to commence business or suspension of business was due to gloomy business prospectus, the Court may refuse to pass a winding up order.

4. Reduction in membership [Section 433 (d)

The Court may order for the winding up of a Company if it is unable to pay its debts. The basis of an order for winding up under this clause is that the Company has ceased to be commercially solvent, i.e., it is unable to meet its current demands, although the assets when realised may exceed its liabilities. According to Section 434 of the Act a Company shall be deemed to be unable to pay its debts in the following cases:

(i) When a statutory notice was served

If a creditor to whom the Company is indebted a sum above Rs. 500/- has served on the Company with a demand at its registered office requiring payment of the amount and the Company has for three weeks either fails to payor a compromise to the satisfaction of the creditor, or

(ii) Decreed debt

A Company may be ordered to be wound up if execution or other process issued on a decree (order of the Court) in favour of a creditor of the Company is returned unsatisfied as a whole or in part [Section 434 (b)].

(iii) In case of commercial insolvency

If it is proved to the satisfaction of the Court that the Company is unable to pay its debts, it may pass orders for winding up. In determining this, the Court shall take into consideration the contingent and prospective liabilities of the Company. If all the assets of a Company coveted into cash are insufficient discharge its debts, in a commercial sense the Company is insolvent. But "where at the relevant time there is reasonable hope of tiding over the difficulty and emerging into a region In which the Company might reasonably expect to carry on at a profit, the Company may not be ordered to be wound up on this ground" (Sudhiya v. Bihar National Insurance Co.225).

6. Just and equitable reasons [Section 433 (1)]

The last ground on which the Court can order the winding up of a Company is when the Court is of the opinion that is just and equitable that the Company should be wound up. This clause gives the Court a very wide power to order winding up wherever the Court considers it just and equitable to do. But the Court may give due weight to the interest of the Company, its employees, creditors, shareholders and the general public. Moreover, the Court may refuse to order for winding up, if it is of the opinion that some other remedy is available to the petitioner. What is 'just and equitable' cause depends upon the facts of each particular case.

The following are the instances where the Courts have exercised their discretion under this clause

(i) Deadlock Management

Where there is a deadlock in the management of the Company in the sense that it is not possible for the Company to carry out its objects for which it was formed.

Yenidjije Tobacoo Co. Ltd., Re.[226] Wand R were the sole shareholders and directors of a Company with equal rights of management and voting power. After a time, they became bitterly hostile to each other and disagreed about the appointment of important servants of the Company. All communications between them were made through the secretary as they were not on speaking terms with each other. The Company made large profits in spite of the disagreement. Held, there was a complete deadlock in the management and the Company should be wound up.

(ii) Loss of Substratum

When the main objects of the Company have failed to materialise or the Company has lost its substratum, it is just and equitable to wind up the Company.

German Date Coffee Co., Re[227]. The object clause of a Company stated that it was formed for the working of a German patent which would be granted for making coffee from dates and also for the acquisition of inventions incidental thereto, and to acquire other inventions for similar purposes. The German patent was never granted but the Company did acquire and work a Swedish patent and carried on business at Hamburg where coffee was made from dates, but not under the protection of a patent. Held, on a petition by two shareholders, that the main object could not be achieved and, therefore, it was just and equitable that the Company should be wound up.

(iii) Oppression of Minority

When the majority of the shareholders are using their powers unfairly or have adopted, an oppressive policy towards the minority or the management is carried on in such a way that the minority is disregarded.

(iv) Illegal or fraudulent purposes

Where the Company has ceased to carry on its authorised business and is engaged in fraudulent or illegal purposes it is just and equitable to wind up the Company.

(v) Where the members of the Company have lost their confidence with the Company it will be just and equitable to wind up a Company on this ground.

(vi) When the Company is a mere bubble and it does not carry on any business or does not have any property.

Who may Petition [Section 439]

Section 439 of the Companies Act enumerates the persons who can file a petition to the Court for the winding up of a Company—

1. By the Company itself

The Company may by a special resolution passed at its general meeting, may request the Court for its order for compulsory winding up of the Company [Section 439(1) (a)].

2. By the creditors [Section 439 (1) (b)]

A creditor may appeal to the Court for getting a winding up order. The term creditor includes a secured creditor, debenture holder and the trustee for debenture holders.

A secured creditor or an unsecured creditor is equally eligible to obtain a winding up order.

Moreover a foreign creditor can also file a petition for winding up order. If a Company did not pay to its foreign commission agent, he has the right to file an application for winding up order.

The Court will not order the winding up of the Company where the debt is bonafidely disputed.

Where a creditor's petition is opposed by other creditors, the Court may ascertain the wishes of the majority of the creditors before making any order for winding up.

Where a petition is brought by a contingent or prospective creditor or creditors, it shall not be admitted before the leave of the Court is obtained. Such leave shall be granted only when the Court is satisfied that there is prima facie case for winding up the Company and reasonable security for costs has been given.

3. By any contributory [Section 439 (a) (c)]

The present and past members who are liable to contribute to the assets of the Company in winding up, are called contributions. Any contributor may present a petition for compulsory winding up of the Company. A contributory is entitled to present a petition for winding up only—

(a) When the number of members is reduced to below 7 in the case of a public Company and below 2 in the case of a private Company, or
(b) When he holds shares which were originally allotted to him, or
(c) When he has held his shares for any 6 out of the previous 18 months, or
(d) When the shares have devolved on him through the death of a former holder [Section 439 (4)].

A contributory shall be entitled to present a petition for winding up, not with standing that he may be the holder of fully paid-up shares or that the Company may have no asset at all, or may have no surplus assets left among the shareholder's after the payment of its liabilities.

But, a contributory against whom call money is due may be prevented to file a petition to the Court for winding up. However, if he agrees to the satisfaction of the Court that he is ready to pay the dues, the Court may permit him to do so.

4.By Registrar of Companies [Section 439 (1) (e)]

The registrar is empowered to file a petition for the winding up of a Company on any of the following grounds:

(a) Where the default is made by the Company to hold its statutory meeting or to file statutory report,
(b) Where the Company fails to commence its business within one year of its corporation or suspends business for a whole year,
(c) Where the number of members are reduced below the statutory minimum, and
(d) Where the Company is unable to pay its debts. The Registrar is not entitled to make a petition on the ground that the Company is unable to pay its debts unless it so appears to him from the financial condition of the Company as disclosed in its balance sheet or from the report of a special auditor appointed under Section 233 A or an inspection appointed under Section 235 or 237.

In all the above cases, the Registrar must obtain the previous sanction of the Central Government before making petition for winding up. The Central Government shall not give such permission unless opportunity has been given to the Company to make its representations.

5. By The Central Government or Any Person Authorised by it [Section 439 (1) (f)]

The Central Government is also authorised by the Companies Act to present a petition for winding up. This can be done on the basis of report of inspectors appointed to investigate the affairs of the Company, to the effect that the Company has been conducting its business fraudulently or unlawfully. The government may authorise any person to present petition for winding up in a case falling within this Section.

6. By The Liquidator

Where the member's voluntary winding up or winding up under the supervision of the Court is in progress, if the liquidator finds that the compulsory winding up would be more better to safeguard the interests of the creditors and shareholders, he may file a petition to the Court for compulsory winding up.

COMMENCEMENT OF WINDING UP (Section 441)

Where before the presentation of the petition for the winding up of a Company by the Court a resolution has been passed by the Company for voluntary winding up, the winding up is deemed to commence from the date of the resolution. In all other cases (i.e. where the Company has not previously passed a resolution for voluntary winding up), the winding up of the Company by the Court is deemed to commence from the time of the presentation of the petition for the winding up.

Advertisement of petition

Every petition for winding up a Company shall be advertised 14 days before the hearing, stating the date on which the petition was presented and the names and addresses of petitioners.

Commencement of winding up

The winding up of a Company by the Court is deemed to commence at the time of the presentation of the petition for winding up. But where, before the presentation of the petition, a resolution has been passed by the Company for voluntary winding up, the winding up shall be deemed to have commenced at the time of the passing of resolution (Section 441).

Power of Court

Power of Court to stay or restrain proceedings against Company (Section 442)

At any time after the presentation of a winding of petition and before a winding up order has been made the Company, or any creditor or contributory, may apply to the Court for a stay of, or restraint of further proceedings in the Court.

Power of the Court on hearing petition (Section 443)

On hearing a winding up petition, the Court may—

(a) dismiss it with or without cost, or (b) adjourn the hearing conditionally or unconditionally, or (c) make any interim order as it thinks fit, or (d) make an order for winding up of the Company with or without costs or any other orders as it thinks fit.

The Court cannot, however, refuse to make a winding-up order on the ground only that the assets of the Company have only been mortgaged to an amount equal to or in excess of those assets or that the Company has no assets.

Order for convening the statutory meeting

In case the winding up petition was filed on the ground of default in holding the statutory meeting or filing the statutory report to Registrar, the Court has the discretion to direct the Company to hold the meeting and deliver the report, instead of passing a winding up order [Section 433 (3)].

1. Consequences of winding up order

In case the Court order for winding up of the Company, it may also order to appoint a liquidator.

Thereafter, communication of appointment is given to the person to be appointed as liquidator and also to the registrar of Companies (Section 444).

2. Certified copy of winding up order to the Registrar

A certified copy of the winding up order is filed with registrar by the Company as well as by the petitioner, within 30 days of issue of such order by the Court. The registrar shall notify in the official gazette that such an order has been made (Section 445).

3. Submission of statement of affairs by the Company

Within 21 days from the date of winding up order, or from the date of the appointment of liquidator, a statement as to affairs of the Company has to be presented before the liquidator duly certified by a Director/Manager/Secretary or any other officer of the Company subject to the direction of the Court. The statement must show complete details about cash in hand, debts and liabilities, details about the creditors, etc. [Section 445 (1)].

4. Settlement of the list of contributors

The Court shall also settle the list of contributories, make calls and determine any other questions arising in winding up on the application of the liquidator (Section 467).

5. Preliminary report by the liquidator

The liquidator shall present a preliminary report to the Court after the receipt of statement of affairs, within 6 months from the date of winding up order. He should state in this report all details about:

(a) Cash and negotiable securities.
(b) Debts due from contributories.
(c) Debts due to Company.
(d) Movable and immovable properties belonging to the Company.
(e) Unpaid calls.

If the Company has failed, the causes of failure, and whether in his opinion, further inquiry is desirable as to any matter concerning to the promotion, formation or failure of the Company or its management [Section 455 (7) (a)].

6. Dissolution

The Court may issue dissolution order when it finds and is convicted that:

(a) it is difficult for the liquidator to proceed with the winding up for want of funds, or

(b) the affairs of the Company are completely wound up (Section 481).

7. Notice of Dissolution to the Registrar

A copy of dissolution order is filed with registrar within 30 days of such order by the Court, failing which a fine upto Rs. 50/- per day shall be payable till the default continues (Section 481).

Effect of Winding up order

1. Notice to government liquidator and registrar

Notice of the winding up order passed by the Court is delivered to government liquidator and the registrar within 30 days of the winding up order (Section 444).

2. A certified copy of the order to the registrar

On the making of a winding up order, it is the duty of the petitioner in the winding up proceedings and of the Company to file with the registrar a certified copy of the order within 30 days from the date of the making of the order [Section 445(1)].

For calculating the period of 30 days from the making of a winding up order, time required for obtaining a certified copy of the order is excluded.

3. Modification by the Registrar

On the filing of a certified copy of the winding up order, the registrar must make a minute thereof in his book relating to the Company. He shall also notify in the Official Gazette that such an order has been made [Section 445(2)].

4. Notice of discharge to officers and employees

Such order shall be deemed to be notice of discharge of the officers and employees of the Company, except when the business of the Company is continued [Section 445 (3)].

5. Prevention of legal proceedings [Section 446 (1)]

When a winding up order has been made and the official liquidator is appointed, no suit or other legal proceedings shall be commenced except with the permission of the Court, subject to such terms as the Court may decide (*Smt. Tarubala Saha v. North Bank Ltd.*[228]). If a suit is instituted impleading a Company after it is ordered to be wound up, without obtaining permission of the Court as required under Section 446 of the Companies Act, 1956, the suit is incompetent and the permission of the Court cannot be granted with retrospective effect to enable the continuation of the suit (*S .R. Mathuswami Gounder and other v. Official Liquidator*[229]). However, in *Kondaskar v. 1.1.0. Companies Circle Bombay,*[230] it has been held by the Supreme Court that an income-tax officer can commence assessment proceeding without leave of the Court.

6. Rights of the Court to settle certain matters

The Court has the rights to settle:

(a) any suit or proceeding pending at the date of the winding up order in favour or against the Company, or

(b) any claim pending in favour or against the Company, or

(c) any application pending for a settlement of disputes between the Company's creditors and members under Section 391, or

(d) any question of priority or legal matters arising out of the winding up process [Section 446 (1)].

7. Operation of winding up order in favour of all

An order of winding up a Company operates in favour of all the creditors and of all the contributories of the Company as if had been made on the joint petition of a creditor and of a contributory (Section 447).

8. Official Liquidator as Company's liquidator

On a winding up order being made in respect of a Company, the official liquidator, shall by virtue of his office become the liquidator of the Company (Section 449).

9. Sale or Transfer of property void

Sale or transfer of Company's property shall be treated as void after a winding up order is issued.

10. Transfer of properties before the winding up order

Any property transferred or sold prior to six months of the winding up order shall be treated as void, on the basis of fraudulent preferences.

11. Cession of director's powers

Power of the directors ceased to exist as soon as the liquidator takes charge of the winding up process.

Powers of the Court on winding up order

Some of the powers exercised by the Court on a winding up order are stated below:

1. Powers to stay winding up order

On receipt of an application either from the liquidator or from any creditor or contributory, the Court may stay the proceedings of the winding up either altogether or for a limited time, on such terms and conditions as may think fit (Section 466).

2. To settle the list of contributories

The Court may settle the list of contributories and can get the assets of the Company for discharging the liabilities of the Company. For this purpose, the Court has the power to prepare a list of such shareholders (called contributories) as are liable to contribute to the assets of the Company (Section 467).

3. To order for delivery of property to liquidator

The Court may ask any person (contributory, trustee, banker, agent, etc.) who is in possession of any money, property, books etc. that belongs to the Company to hand over the same to the liquidator (Section 468).

4. Right to call from a contributory to clear dues

Apart from his liability as a shareholder, where any other money is due from a contributory to the Company, the Court may order for the payment of the same (Section 469).

5. To make calls

The Court may ask the contributories to pay the uncalled money on shares when it finds that assets are inadequate to meet the liabilities and the expenses of winding up (Section 470).

6. To call for money from debtors

If the Company owes any sum from a person, the Court may ask to debtor to pay the same to the Company (Section 471). Such amount is deposited in the 'public account' of the Reserve Bank of India.

7. Power to exclude creditors

Those creditors who have failed to prove their claims within stipulated period may be excluded by the Court from the list of creditors [Section 474].

8. To summon any person known or suspected to have in possession of Company's property.

The Court may also summon before it any officer of the Company or person known or suspected to have in his possession any such property of the Company. Any such person may be examined on oath [Section 477 (2)].

9. To order for the public examination of promoters, directors etc.

If the official liquidator has made a report to the Court that, in his opinion a fraud has been committed by any person or officer to appear before it for public examination [Section 478].

10. To order for arrest of the absconding shareholder, if any

If the Court came to know about the possibility of absconding of any shareholder from India or he is winding any property of the Company, it has power to order for the arrest of that shareholder [Section 479).

11. To order for dissolution of the Company

Dissolution order is issued by the Court when it is convinced that (1) it is difficult for the liquidator to proceed with the winding up for want of funds or (2) the affairs of the Company are completely wound up. Within 30 days of the dissolution order the liquidator should file a copy of the order with the Registrar [Section 481].

Power to declare dissolution (or annulment of dissolution)

If the liquidator of the dissolved Company or any other person interested (a person entitled to claim damage for negligence of the Company is a person "interested" for this purpose), applies to the Court within 2 years from the date of the dissolution, the Court may order the dissolution as void. The applicant at whose initiative the dissolution has been declared void should file a copy of the Court order with the Registrar within 30 days of such order (Section 559).

Liquidator in winding up by the Court

Under the present Act, the only person who is competent to Act as the liquidator in a winding up is the official liquidator. A liquidator is a person who is appointed by the Court to conduct the proceeding in winding up the Company and perform such duties in reference thereto as the Court may impose [Section 451(1)]. For the purpose of winding up, there shall be attached to each High Court an official liquidator appointed by the Central Government. Who may be either a whole time or part time officer. In District Court the official receiver will be the official liquidator. The Central Government may appoint one or more deputy or assistant official liquidators to assist the official liquidator. On a winding up order being made the official liquidator by virtue of his office, becomes the liquidator of the Company. A body corporate cannot be appointed a liquidator in any form of winding up. Where the official liquidator becomes or acts as liquidator, he shall be paid by the Central Government out of the assets of the Company such fees as may be prescribed [Section 415(1)).

A liquidator is described by the style of the official liquidator of the particular Company in respect of which be acts and not by his individual name (Section 452).

Provisional Liquidator [Section 450]

At any time after the presentation of a winding up petition and before the making of a winding up order, the Court may appoint the official liquidator, to be a liquidator, provisionally.

Before appointing a provisional liquidator, the Court must give notice to the Company and give a reasonable opportunity to it to make its representations, if any, if the Court thinks fit, it may dispense with such notice, but in that case, it must record the special reasons for not giving the notice in writing.

On a winding up order being made by the Court, the official liquidator ceases to hold office as provisional liquidator and becomes the liquidator of the Company.

Statement of Affairs [Section 454]

The Company must make out and submit to the official liquidator a statement as to the affairs of the Company in the prescribed form verified by an affidavit and containing the following particulars:

(a) The assest of the Company stating separately the cash, balance in hand and at the bank and the negotiable securities held by the Company.

(b) Its debts and liabilities.

(c) Names, residences and occupation of its creditors stating separately the amount of secured and unsecured debts.

(d) In the case of secured debts, particulars of securities given, their value and the dates on which they were given.

(e) The debts due to the Company and the names, residences and occupations of the persons from whom they are due and the amount likely to be realised on account thereof.

(f) Such further or other information as may be prescribed or as the official liquidator may require.

The statement must be submitted and verified by one or more of the directors and by the manager, secretary or other chief officer of the Company and it must be submitted within 21 days from the relevant date or within such extended time not exceeding three months [Section 454 (3)].

Duties of the liquidator

The liquidator of a Company in compulsory winding up must perform such duties in reference thereto as the Court may impose. These are as under.

(l) He must conduct equitably and impartially all proceedings in the winding up according to the provision of the law.

(2) He must submit a preliminary report to the Court. The report shall contain particulars —

  (a) as to the amount of capital issued, subscribed, and paid up, and the estimated amount of assets and liabilities,

  (b) if the Company has failed, the cause of the failure, and

  (c) whether, in his opinion, further inquiry is desirable as to any matter relating to the promotion, formation, or failure of the Company, or the conduct of the business thereof [Section 455 (1)].

(3) Additional reports

The official liquidator may, if he thinks fit make further reports stating the manner in which the Company was promoted or formed. He may further state if any fraud has been committed by any person in his promotion or formation, or since the formation thereof. He may also state any other matters which it is desirable to bring to the notice of the Court [Section 455 (2)].

(4) Custody of Company's property

Where a winding up order has been made or provisional liquidator has been appointed, the liquidator or the provisional liquidator, as the case may be, shall take into his custody all the property, effects and actionable claims to which the Company is entitled. So long as there is no liquidator, all the property and effects of the Company shall be deemed to be in the custody of the Court [Section 456].

(5) Control of Powers

The liquidator shall, in the administration of the assets of the Company and the distribution there of among creditors, have regard to any directions which may be given by resolution of the creditors or contributories at any general meeting or by the committee of inspection. Any directions given by the creditors or contributories at any general meeting shall override any directions given by the committee of inspection [Section 460 (1) and (2)].

(6) Meetings of creditors and contributories

The liquidator may summon general meetings of the creditors and contributories, whenever he thinks fit, for the purpose of ascertaining their wishes. He shall summon such meetings at such times as the creditors or contributories may, by resolution, direct or whenever requested in writing to do so by not less than $1/10^{th}$ in value of the creditors or contributories as the case may be [Section 460 (3)].

(7) Directions from the Court

The liquidator may apply to the Court for directions in relation to any particular matter arising in the winding up. He shall also use his own discretion in the administration of the assets of the Company and in the distribution thereof among the creditors [Section 460 (4) (5)].

(8) Proper Books

The liquidator shall keep proper books for making entries or recording minutes of the proceedings at meetings and such other matters as may be prescribed. Any creditor or contributory may, subject to the control of the Court, inspect any such books, personally or by his agents [Section 461].

(9) Audit and Accounts

The liquidator shall at such times as may be prescribed but at least twice each year during his tenure of office present to the Court an account of his receipts and payments as liquidator. The Court shall cause the account to be audited. For the purpose of the audit, the liquidator shall furnish the Court with such vouchers, information and the books as the Court may require. One copy of the audited accounts thereof shall be filed and kept by the Court. The other copy of the account shall be delivered to the Registrar for filing. Each copy shall be open to the inspection of any creditor, contributory or person interested. Where an account relates to a Government Company in liquidation, the liquidator shall forward a copy thereof to the Central and or State government(s), as the case may be [Section 462].

(10) Appointment of committee of inspection

The liquidator shall within 2 months from the date of winding up order convene a meeting of the Company's creditors, to determine whether or not a committee of inspection should be appointed to act with the liquidator [Section 464].

(11) Pending Liquidation

The liquidator shall within 2 months of the expiry of each year from the commencement of winding up, file a statement duly audited by a qualified auditor of the Company, with respect to the position of the liquidation.

The statement shall be filed —

(a) in the case of a winding up by or subject to the supervision of the Court, in the Court, and

(b) in the case of a voluntary winding up, with the Registrar.

When the statement is filed in the Court, a copy shall simultaneously be filed with the Registrar and shall be kept by him along with the other records of the Company [Section 551].

Powers of liquidator

A liquidator has two types of powers under the Act:

(I) Powers to be exercised with the sanction of the Court

(II) Powers to be exercised without the sanction of the Court.

I. Powers to be exercised with the sanction of the Court

(1) To institute or defend any suit, prosecution or other legal proceedings (civil or criminal) in the name of the Company or on behalf of the Company.

(2) To carry on business so far it may be necessary for the beneficial winding of the Company.

(3) To sell the immovable and movable property of the Company by the public auction.

(4) To raise on the security of the assets of the Company.

(5) To sell the immovable and movable property of the Company under the private contract of sale.

(6) To secure loan by mortgaging the property of the Company.

(7) To enter into necessary compromise or arrangement with regard to payment to creditors.

(8) To enter into any compromise or accept suitable security in connection with payment to debtors and calls outstanding on shareholders.

(9) To appoint any advocate or legal advisor to assist him in connection with the discharge of his duties.

(10) To do all such things as may be necessary for winding up the affairs of a Company and distribution of its assets.

II. Powers to be exercised without the sanction of the Court

(1) To execute all deeds and other documents in the name and on behalf of the Company and to use the Company's common seal.

(2) To prove and claim from an insolvent contributory for any balance against his estate.

(3) To draw, accept and endorse any negotiable instrument on behalf of the Company.

(4) To obtain letters of administration to any deceased contributory and take necessary steps for obtaining payment of any money due from the contributory of his estate.

(5) To appoint an agent to do any business which the liquidator is unable to do himself.

(6) To check the records and returns of the Company.

(7) To extend the date of final payments by the buyers in an auction sale of Company' s property.

(8) To call the meetings of the creditors and contributories to discuss the matters related to winding up process.

It is to be noted that all these powers are exercised by the liquidator within the control of the Court [Section 457].

Contributory

Section 428 defines the term 'Contributory'. It means every person who is liable to contribute to the assets of the Company in the event of its being wound up and includes the holders of fully paid up shares. A debtor to the Company is not a contributory nor a person who guarantees such debts. When a Company goes into liquidation every member whether past or present has to contribute to the assets of the Company. The list of contributories is made out in two parts A and B list those of past members, who have ceased to be members within one year preceding the winding up. The' A' contributories, i.e., those in the list of present members are primarily liable for everything and must be first individually exhausted before any 'B' contributory can be called upon.

A past member is not required to contribute in the following cases:

(a) where he had ceased to be a member for a period of one year or upward before the commencement of winding up.

(b) where the debt or liability of the Company was incurred after he ceased to be a member.

(c) where the present members are able to satisfy the contributions required to be made to them under the Act.

Voluntary Winding up

Companies are usually wound up by this method as it is an easier process of winding up. It is altogether different from a compulsory winding up. In this form of winding up, the Company and its creditors are left to settle their affairs by themselves, without going to the Court, but the parties can request the Court for general direction or orders, wherever necessary. This form of winding up is by far the most common and the most popular form.

Circumstances for Voluntary winding up

A Company may be wound up voluntarily when —

(a) The period fixed by the articles for the tenure of the Company has expired or an event upon which the Company is to be wound up has happened and the Company in general meeting has passed a special resolution.

(b) The Company has for any cause whatever passed a special resolution to wind up voluntarily [Section 484]. The Company may be wound up by special resolution even if it is prosperous.

A resolution for voluntary winding up must be advertised in the Official Gazette and also in some newspaper, circulating in the district where the registered office of the Company is situated, within 14 days of the passing of the resolution. If default is made in complying with this provision, the Company and every defaulting officer shall be punishable with fine which may extend to Rs. 50/- per day for every day during which default continues [Section 485]. Officer herein includes the liquidator also.

A voluntary winding up commences from the date of the passing of the resolution [Section 486].

From the commencement of the winding up, the Company cease to carry on its business except so far as may be required for the beneficial winding up of such business. But the corporate status and powers continue until it is dissolved.

Kinds of voluntary winding up [Section 488]

Section 488 of the Act, provides for two kinds of voluntary winding up:

(A) Members voluntary winding up, and

(B) Creditors voluntary winding up.

A. Members Voluntary Winding up Declaration of Solvency

Section 488 provides that where it is proposed to wind up a Company voluntarily the directors or a majority of them are required to make a declaration of solvency stating that in their opinion the Company, within a period of not exceeding three years, from the date of commencement of winding up, will be able to pay its debts in full [Section 488(91)).

Such declaration shall be made within five weeks immediately preceding the date of the passing of the resolution for winding up and shall be delivered to the Registrar before that date. It should also be accompanied by copies of the report of the auditors on the profit and loss account and the Balance sheet of the Company prepared upto the date of declaration and should include a statement of the Company's asset and liabilities as on the date [Section 488(2)).

Where such a declaration is duly made and delivered, the winding up following shall be called members voluntary winding up. Where the same is not duly made, it shall be called creditors voluntary winding up.

Provisions Applicable to Member's Voluntary Winding up

Section 490-98 of the Act deal with provisions applicable to members voluntary winding up.

They are as follow:

1. Appointment of Liquidator [Section 490]

The Company in general meeting shall appoint one or more liquidators for winding up the affairs of a Company and for distributing the assets. The Company shall also fix his remuneration and unless his remuneration is not fixed, he will not take charge of his office. The remuneration so fixed by the shareholders shall not be increased in any circumstances whatsoever, without sanction of the Court [Section 490(1) and (2)].

2. Boards Powers to Cease [Section 491]

On the appointment of liquidator, all powers of the Board of directors, managing director(s) and manager, shall cease to exist except when the Company or the liquidator may sanction their continuance.

3. Power to fill the vacancy of the liquidator [Section 492]

If any vacancy occurs in the office of the liquidator, the Company may, in general meetings fill the vacancy subject to any arrangement with its creditors. The vacancy may arise due to the death, resignation or otherwise.

4. Notice of appointment of liquidator to Registrar [Section 493]

Within 10 days from the date of appointment of a liquidator, a notice of information may be given to registrar of the event.

In case of default the Company and every officer of the Company who is in default shall be punishable with a fine, extending to Rs. 100/- for every day of default.

5. Disposal of property [Section 494]

The liquidator may, with the sanction of a special resolution of the Company, sell all or part of the Company's business or property or shares or like interest in another Company to be distributed among the members.

6. Meeting of the Creditors (Section 495)

If, at any time, the liquidator is of the opinion that the Company will not be able to pay its debts in full within the period mentioned in the declaration of solvency, he must call a meeting of the creditors and lay down before them a statement of the assets and liabilities.

On default the penalty is a fine which may extend to Rs. 500/- where a liquidator has called a creditors meeting under Section 495, the winding up, then, would proceed as if it was creditors voluntary winding up [Section 498].

7. Annual general meeting at the end of first year and subsequent years [Section 496]

If the winding up continues for more than one year, the liquidator must call a general meeting of the Company and a meeting of the creditors at the end of the first year of the commencement of winding up and at the end of each of the subsequent years and may lay before them an account of the acts or the dealings.

8. Final meeting and dissolution [Section 497]

As soon as the affairs of the Company are fully wound up, the liquidator shall perform the following duties:

(i) He shall make up an account of the winding up, showing how the same has been conducted and how the property has been disposed of.

(ii) He shall call a general meeting of the Company for laying before it the said accounts. The meeting shall be called by advertisement specifying the time, place and object thereof. The advertisement shall be made not less than one month before the meeting in the Official Gazette and also in some local newspaper where the registered office of the Company is situated. Failure to call meeting is punishable with fine upto Rs. 500.

(iii) Within one week after the meeting, the liquidator shall send a copy of the account to the registrar and the official liquidator and also a return of the holding of the meeting and the date thereof.

The registrar on receiving the account and either of the returns shall forthwith register the same.

The official liquidator on receipt of the account and the return is required to make a scrutiny of the books and papers of the Company. The liquidator of the Company its past and present officers shall afford an opportunity to the official liquidator for this purpose. The official liquidator shall send a report, the Court may order either further investigation of the affairs of the Company or dissolution of the Company with effect from the date specified in the order.

B. Creditor's voluntary winding up

If the directors make no declaration of solvency before the members pass a winding up resolution, the winding up shall be a creditor's voluntary winding up. Since an insolvency is unable to pay its debts in full, the law gives rights to the creditors of the Company to have dominating role in it.

The provisions for creditor's voluntary winding up are similar to those applicable to the members voluntary winding up except that in the former, it is the creditors who appoint the liquidator, fix his remuneration and generally conduct the winding up. Section 500 to 509 deal with creditors voluntary winding up. They are discussed as under

Provisions applicable to Creditors voluntary winding up

1. Meeting of Creditors (Section 500)

If a voluntary winding up is proposed and no declaration of solvency has been made, then the Board must call a meeting of the creditors either on the same day or the next day of the general meeting in which the resolution is passed. Notice of the meeting should be advertised in the official gazette as well as in two newspapers. The meeting must lay before the creditors a statement of Company's position and whatever resolution is passed in that meeting a copy of that should be filed with the registrar.

2. Notice to Registrar [Section 501]

Notice of any resolution passed at a creditors meeting shall be given by the Company to the registrar within 10 days of the passing thereof.

3. Appointment of liquidator [Section 502]

The creditors and the members at their respective meetings may nominate a liquidator for the purpose of winding up the affairs and distributing the assets of the Company. If the creditors and the members nominate different persons, the creditors nominee is the liquidator. But any director, member or creditor of the Company may within 7 days after the date on which the nomination was made by the creditors, apply to the Court for an order that the person nominated as liquidator by the Company or any other person shall be the liquidator.

If no person is nominated by the creditors, the person nominated by the members shall be the liquidator. Likewise, if no person is nominated by the Company, the person nominated by the creditors shall be the liquidator.

4. Appointment of committee of inspection [Section 503]

Creditors in their meeting, may appoint a committee of inspection of not more than 5 members.

Company may also appoint members on this committee. In case of dispute matter will be referred to the Court. This committee will fix the remuneration of the liquidator and in the absence of this committee, creditors will fix the remuneration.

The powers and proceedings of such committee of inspection are the same as those of a committee of inspection appointed in a winding up by Court, as provided in Section 465.

5. Fixing of Liquidator's remuneration [Section 504]

The committee of inspection, or where there is no such committee the creditors shall fix the remuneration of the liquidator. Where the remuneration is not fixed, it shall be determined by the Court. The remuneration once fixed cannot be increased in any case.

6. Board's powers to cease [Section 505]

On the appointment of a liquidator, all the powers of the Board of directors shall cease, except in so far as the committee of inspection, or if there is no such committee, the creditors in a general meeting, may sanction.

7. Vacancy in office of liquidator [Section 506]

If a vacancy occurs by death, resignation or otherwise in the office of the liquidator (other than a liquidator appointed by or by the direction of the Court), the creditors in a general meeting may fill the vacancy.

8. Meeting at the end of each year [Section 508]

If the winding up continues for more than one year, the liquidator must call a general meeting of the Company and a meeting of the creditors at the end of the first year of the commencement of winding up and at the end of each of the subsequent years and an account of the acts or the dealings.

9. Final Meeting and Dissolution [Section 509]

As soon as the affairs of the Company are wound up, the liquidator shall make up the account of the winding up showing how the winding up has been conducted and property of the Company has been disposed of. He shall call a general meeting of the Company and a meeting of the creditor for the purpose of laying the accounts before the meetings. Each such meeting shall be advertised in the official gazette and also in some newspaper circulating in the district where the registered office of the Company is situated. Within a week after the meeting the liquidator shall send to the registrar a copy of the account and a return which will be registered. There after the procedure is the same as in members voluntary winding up.

Voluntary Winding up [Section 488]

Members voluntary winding up Provisions voluntary winding up	Creditors voluntary winding up Provisions of creditors winding up
(1) Appointment of liquidator Section 490.	(1) Meeting of creditors Section 500.
(2) Board's power to cease Section 491.	(2) Notice to registrar Section 501.
(3) Power to file the vacancy of the liquidator Section 492.	(3) Appointment of liquidator Section 502.
(4) Notice of appointment of liquidator to registrar Section 493.	(4) Appointment of committee of inspection Section 503.
(5) Disposal of property Section 494.	(5) Fixing of liquidators remuneration Section 504.
(6) Meeting of the creditors Section 495.	(6) Boards power to cease Section 505.
(7) Annual general meeting at the end of first year and subsequent years Section 496.	(7) Vacancy in office of liquidator Section 506.
(8) Final meeting and dissolution Section 497.	(8) Meeting at the end of each year 508.
	(9) Final meeting and dissolution Section 509

Distinction between members and creditors voluntary winding up

Basis of difference	Members voluntary winding up	Creditors voluntary winding up
1. Declaration of Solvency	The member's voluntary winding up may take place only when directors make a solvency declaration of the Company before the registrar.	In the case of creditor's voluntary winding up the question of solvency declaration does not arise as it is undertaken by an insolvent Company.
2. Meeting's	In the case of member's voluntary winding up, meetings of the creditors are not required to be called.	But in the case of creditors voluntary winding up, meetings of the creditors as well as of members both are called.
3. Appointment of liquidator	In members voluntary winding up, the liquidator is appointed by the members by passing a resolution in the meeting of the Company.	In creditors voluntary winding up, creditors and members may nominate a liquidator in their respective meetings. In case they nominate different persons, the creditors nominee shall be appointed as liquidator.

Basis of difference	Members voluntary winding up	Creditors voluntary winding up
4. Liquidator's remuneration	In members voluntary winding up, the liquidator's remuneration, is fixed at the general meeting of the Company.	In creditors voluntary winding up, it is either fixed by the committee of inspection or by the Court in the absence of such a committee.
5. Committee of inspection	In members voluntary winding up, no committee of inspection is usually constituted.	In creditors voluntary winding up, a committee of inspection consisting nominees of creditors and members is constituted to supervise the process of winding up.
6. Control on winding up process	In the case of members voluntary winding up, the Company plays dominating role in the winding up process.	In the case of creditor's voluntary winding up, the creditors play dominating role in the winding up process.
7. Resolution for winding up	An ordinary or a special resolution (as the cake may be) is passed at the general meeting of the Company.	An ordinary or a special resolution is passed at the general meeting of the Company as well as at the meeting of the creditors.
8. Number of liquidator	One or more liquidators can be appointed in the case of members voluntary winding up.	Only one liquidator shall be appointed.
9. The vacancy of liquidator	In case any vacancy occurs in the office of the liquidator, It shall be filled at the general meeting of the Company, by passing a resolution.	In case any vacancy occurs in the office of the liquidator, it shall be filled by the creditors in general meetings, or by committee of inspection, or by the Court.
10. Special power to liquidator	Special powers may be given to the liquidator by a special resolution passed at the meeting of the company.	Special powers may be given to the liquidator either by a special resolution passed at creditor's meeting or on the basis of powers delegated by committee of inspection, duly sanctioned by Court.

C. Winding up Subject to Supervision of Court

At any time after a Company has passed a resolution for voluntary winding up, the Court may make an order that the voluntary winding up shall continue, but subject to such liberty to creditors, contributories or others to apply to the Court and generally on such terms and conditions as the Court thinks just [Section 522].

A petition for the continuance of a voluntary winding up subject to the supervision of the Court shall be deemed to be a petition for winding-up by the Court [Section 523].

The Court will not in general make a supervision order on the petition of a contributory, unless it is satisfied that the resolution for winding up voluntarily was so obtained that the minority of members were overborne by fraud or improper or corrupt influence. Where the Company is insolvent, the wishes of the creditors only are regarded or where investigation is required.

Where a Company is being wound up voluntarily or subject to the supervision of the Court may be presented by—

(a) any person authorised to do so under Section 439 (which deals with provisions as to application for winding up), or

(b) the official liquidator [Section 440 (1)].

The Court shall not make a winding up order on the petition presented to it unless it is satisfied that the voluntary winding up or winding up subject to the supervision of the Court cannot be continued with due regard to the interest of the creditors or contributors or both [Section 440 (2)].

Power of Court to appoint or remove liquidators

When an order for winding up is made by the Court, it may appoint an additional liquidator or liquidators. The Court is also empowered to remove any liquidator so appointed and fill the vacancy created, either by removal or by death or resignation [Section 524 (1 and 2)].

The liquidator appointed subject to the supervision by the Court shall have the same power and duties in all matter, as the liquidator appointed under voluntary winding up [Section 526].

While the winding up remains basically a voluntary winding up, a supervision order shall be considered to be an order for compulsory winding up for all purposes including stay of suits and other proceedings.

The Court can supersede a supervision order by passing a compulsory winding up order. If this happens, the Court has the powers to appoint the voluntary liquidator as the official liquidator [Section 527].

Reasons for the voluntary winding up under the supervision of the Court

The reasons may be:

(i) When the rules relating to the winding up are not being strictly adhered to, or

(ii) When the majority is playing a fraud on the minority,

(iii) When the resolution for voluntary winding up was obtained by fraud,

(iv) When the liquidator is negligent in collecting the assets of a Company, or

(v) When the liquidator is prejudiced or partial, etc. However, the Court had wide discretion in the matter of either to grant or refuse the supervision order.

Consequences of winding up

Consequences of winding up may be discussed under the following heads:

1. Consequences as to shareholders

A shareholder is liable to pay the full amount upto the face value of the shares held by him. Not only the present members but past members are also liable in the event of winding up of the Company. The liabilities of present member is the amount remaining unpaid on the shares held by him while a past member can be called upon to pay if the contributions made by the present members are not adequate.

2. Consequences as to creditors

A Company, whether solvent or insolvent, can be wound up under the Act. In case of solvent Company, all claims of its creditors when proved are fully met. But in case of insolvent Company, the rules under the law of insolvency shall apply.

As regards the secured creditor, he need not prove his claim against the Company. He may realise his security and satisfy the debts. For deficiency (if any), he may put up his claim before the liquidator. The secured creditor has also the option to relinquish his security and to prove the amount as if he was an unsecured creditor.

Order of Payment

As soon as the assets are realised and the list of claimants is finalized, the liquidator has to commence making payment. From the provisions of Section 511,520 and 530, it appears that:

First comes the claims of the secured creditors, second comes costs, charges and expenses of the winding up including liquidators remunerations, Third comes preferential creditors, fourth comes the creditors secured by floating charge, fifth comes unsecured or ordinary creditors, and at the end comes members or contributories.

As regards members, if any of them has paid in excess of the amount of call made on him, that will be returned to him first and thereafter the shareholders are given their capital and thereafter, if any surplus is found, that will be distributed among the member shareholders if the articles of the Company so provide.

Preferential payments [Section 530]

Preferential payments are the payments made to certain unsecured creditors in priority to all other debts on winding up of the Company. The preferential payments are:

(a) All revenues, taxes, cesses and rates due to Central or State governments or to a local authority the amount should have become due and payable within 12 months of winding up.

(b) All wages or salary of an employee in respect of services rendered to the Company and due for a period not exceeding 4 months within 12 months before the above relevant date and any compensation payable to any workman under any of the provisions of the Industrial Disputes Act, 1947. The total amount must not exceed Rs. 1000 in the case of anyone claimant.

(c) All accrued holding remuneration becoming payable to any employee on account of winding up.

(d) All amount due in respect of contributions payable during 12 months next before the relevant date, by the Company as the employee of any persons under the Employee's State Insurance Act, 1948, or any other law for the time in force. But this is not payable if the Company is being wound up voluntarily for the purpose of reconstruction and amalgamation with another Company.

(e) All amounts due in respect of any compensation or liability under Workmen's Compensation Act 1923, in respect of death or disablement of any employee of the Company. But this is not payable if the Company is being wound up voluntarily for reconstruction or amalgamation.

(f) All seems due to any employee from a provident fund, a pension fund, a gratuity fund, or any other fund for the welfare of the employees maintained by the Company.

(g) The expenses of any investigation held in pursuance of Section 235 or 237, in so far as they are payable by the Company.

Overriding preferential payments [Section 529-A]

Section 529-A [introduced by Companies (Amendment) Act 1985] seeks to protect the interest of workmen in case of winding up. According to it, a Company shall, on its winding up, pay in priority all other debts (a) workmen's dues, and (b) debts due to secured creditors.

It is to be noted that the above preferential creditors will rank equally amongst themselves. They have to be paid in full, unless the assets are insufficient in which case they shall abate in proportion to the total amount [Section 529-A(2)].

3. Consequence as to servants and officers [Section 445 (3)]

A winding up order is deemed as a notice of discharge to the officers and employees of the Company, except when the business of the Company is continued.

4. Consequence as to proceedings against the Company

When a winding up order is passed,

(a) no suit or other legal proceeding against the Company can be commenced except by the leave of the Court.

(b) All existing suits can not be proceeded with except with the leave of the Court [Section 446 (1)].

(c) Even in voluntary winding up, the Court may restrain proceedings against the Company if it thinks fit.

Effect of winding up on antecedent and other transactions fraudulent preference [Section 531]

Any transfer of property, movable or immovable, delivery of goods, payment, execution of other act relating to property made by or against a Company within 6 months before the commencement of its winding up which had it been made, be deemed a fraudulent preference of its creditors and be invalid accordingly.

Fraudulent preference here relates similarly to fraudulent preference under Insolvency Law, where any individual transfers any property or makes any payment within 3 months before the presentation of an insolvency petition, shall be deemed a fraudulent preference in his insolvency, under Companies Act, 1950, the period is 6 months instead 00 months.

Avoidance of Voluntary Transfer

Section 531 A introduced the Amendment Act, 1960, lays down that any transfer of property, movable or immovable, or any delivery of goods made by a Company within a period of one year before the commencement of its winding up shall be void against the liquidator unless such transfer or delivery is made in the ordinary course of business or in favour of a purchaser or encumbrance in good faith and for valuable consideration.

Further, any transfer or assignment by a Company of all its property to trustees for the benefit of all its creditors is void [Section 532].

Effect of Floating Charge [Section 534]

A floating charge on the property of the Company shall be invalid if the Company goes into liquidation within 12 months from the date of such charge. However, a floating charge will be valid in the following cases:

(a) If the Company immediately after the creation of charge was solvent, or

(b) If the Company had received any cash in consideration thereof at the time of or after the creation of such charge.

Disclaimer of onerous property [Section 535]

'Disclaimer' means abandoning. Where any part of the property of a Company which is being wound up consists of:

(a) land of any tenure, burdened with onerous covenants,

(b) shares or stock in Companies,

(c) any other property which is unsalable by reason of its binding the possessor thereof either to the performance of any onerous act or to the payment of any sum of money, or

(d) unprofitable contracts,

The liquidator of the Company may, with the leave of the Court, by a writing signed by him, at any time within 12 months after the commencement of the winding up, disclaim the property.

The disclaimer shall release the Company and the property from the rights, interests and liabilities from the disclaimer of any other person.

The Court before or on granting leave to disclaim may require such notices to be given to persons interested.

OFFENCES BY OFFICERS IN LIQUIDATION (Section 538)

Any officer of the company, whether past or present, in the winding up the Company is punishable with fine and imprisonment in connection with certain offences. He is punishable, for instance,

(i) if he does not, to the best of his knowledge and belief, fully and truly disclose to the liquidator all the property of the property of the Company;

(ii) if he does not deliver upto the liquidator, or as he directs, all such part of the Company as is in his custody or under his control and which he is required by law to deliver upon;

(iii) if he does not deliver upto the liquidator, or as he directs, all such books and paper of the Company as are in his custody or under his control and which he is required by law to delivery up;

(iv) if he conceals any part of the property of the Company to the value of Rs 100 or more, or conceals any debt due to or from the Company;

(v) if he fraudulently removes any part of the property to the value of Rs. 100 or more within 12 months next before the commencement of the winding up or at any time thereafter;

(vi) if he makes any material omission in any statement relating to the affairs of the Company;

(vii) if he knowingly or believing that a false debt has been proved, by any person under the winding up, fails for a period of one month to inform the liquidator thereof;

(viii) if he, after the commencement of the winding up, prevents the proportion of any book or paper affecting or relating to the property or affairs of the Company;

(ix) if he makes, or is privy to the making of any false entry in any book or paper affecting or relating to the property or affairs of the Company;

(x) if he, by false representation or other fraud, obtains on credit for or on behalf of the Company and property which the Company does not subsequently pay for;

(xi) if he attempts to account for any part of the Company by fictitious losses or expenses;

(xii) if he pledges or disposes of any property of the Company which has been obtained on credit and has not been paid for, unless such pledge or disposal is in the ordinary course of business of the Company;

In the case of any of the offences mentioned in (x) and (xii) the defaulting officer shall be punishable with imprisonment for a term which may extend to 5 years, or with fine, or with both and in case of any other offence with imprisonment for a term which may extend to 2 years or with fine or with both.

Falsification and Improper Books Maintenance (Section 539 and 541)

If with intent to defraud or deceive any person, any officer or contributory of a Company which is being wound-up, destroys, mutilates, alters, falsifies or secretes any books or papers or securities, or makes any false or fraudulent entry, in any register, books of account or documents of Company, he shall be punishable with imprisonment and fine.

Where proper books of account are not kept for a period of two years immediately preceding the commencement of the winding up, every officer of the Company who is in default shall be punishable with imprisonment.

Section 543 of the Act gives powers to the Court to assess damages against such delinquent directors, officers, etc. The Court has also powers under Section 545 of the Act to prosecute the offender or to refer the matter to the Registrar.

Final Disposal of the Books and Other Documents of the Company (Section 550)

When the affairs of the Company have been completely wound up and it is about to be dissolved, its books and papers and those of the liquidator may be disposed of as follows:

(a) in the case of winding up by or subject to the supervision of the Court, in such manner as the Court directs,

(b) in the case of member's voluntary winding up, in such manner as the Company by special resolution directs, and

(c) in the case of creditor's voluntary winding up, in such a manner as the committee of inspection or, if there is no such committee, as the creditors of the Company may direct.

After the expiry of 5 years from the dissolution of the Company, no responsibility shall rest on the Company, the liquidator, or any person to whom the custody of the books and papers has been committed, if any book or paper could not be produced to any person interested therein.

Committee of Inspection (Section 465)

In the case of creditors voluntary winding up, the Court may order the appointment of a Committee which shall consist of not more than 12 members. The members drawn from the creditors and contributors constitute the committee. The liquidator, within two months, is required to summon a meeting of the creditors for determining the membership of the committee. Within 14 days of the creditors meeting, he shall call a meeting of tho contributories to consider the creditor's suggestions with respect to the membership of the Committee. In case there is any difference of opinion, the liquidator may request to the Court for final decision in the matter of membership.

The Committee shall have powers to inspect the liquidators accounts. The quorum for a meeting of the committee shall be one-third of the total members of its members or two members personally present, whichever is higher. The Committee acts by a majority of its members. A member may resign by notice in writing given to the liquidator. His office shall be deemed vacant if he is adjudged as an insolvent or compounds or arranges with his creditors or is absent from attending five consecutive meetings of the Committee without leave of absence. A member may also be removed at a meeting of the creditors, if he represents them or a meeting of the contributories if he represents contributories. The removal is effected by an ordinary resolution of which 7 days notice shall be given. The vacancy is then filled at a meeting of the creditors or contributories as the case may be.

The committee may meet at such times as, it may from time to time, appoint. The liquidator or any member of the Committee may call a meeting as and when he thinks necessary.

Dissolution of a Company (Section 481)

The Court makes an order for the dissolution of a Company on any of the grounds stated below—

(i) when affairs of the Company have been completely wound up, or

(ii) when the Court is of opinion that the liquidator cannot proceed with the winding up of a Company for want of funds or assets, or

(iii) when it is just and reasonable in the circumstances of the case that an order of dissolution of the Company should be made, or

(iv) for any other reason whatsoever.

The Company is dissolved from the date of order of the Court. Within 30 days of the order of the Court, the liquidator must send a copy of the order to the registrar, failing which he is punishable with fine which may extend to Rs. 50 for every day of default.

Where a Company has been dissolved by process of winding up, or by order of Court under Section 481 or for facilitating reconstruction and amalgamation or otherwise, the Court may at any time within 2 years of the date of dissolution make an order declaring the dissolution to have been void. A certified copy of such an order shall be filed with the registrar within 30 days after making of such order.

DEFUNCT COMPANY (Section 560)

A defunct Company is one which is not carrying on business or which is not in operation.

Section 560 deals with such Companies. According to Section 560, where the Registrar has reasonable cause to believe that a Company has become defunct he shall send a letter to the Company inquiring whether it is carrying on business or is in operation. If he does not receive any answer within one month of the sending of the letter, he shall within 14 days after the expiry of the month send to the Company by post a registered letter referring to the first letter, and stating that no answer thereto has been received. He shall further mention in the letter that if no reply is received to the second letter within one month, a notice will be published in the Official Gazette with a view to striking the name of the Company from the Companies register. If the Registrar either receives an answer that the Company is not carrying on business or does not receive any answer within one month of the sending of second letter, he may inform that the Company and publish in the Official Gazette that, at expiration of 3 months from the date of that notice, the name of the Company will be struck of from the register and the Company will be dissolved. The Company may, within 3 months show cause why it should not be dissolved.

Restoration

If the Company, or any member or creditor of the Company, feels aggrieved by the Company having been struck off the register, he may within 20 years, apply to the Court. The Court may order that the name of the Company be restored to the registrar if it is satisfied that the Company was, at the time of the striking off, carrying on business or was in operation or otherwise that it is just that the Company be restored to the register, upon a certified copy of the order of the Court being delivered to the Registrar for registration, the Company is deemed to have continued in existence as if its name had not been struck off. This means restoration operates retrospectively. When the name of a Company is restored, it is deemed to have in existence all through with the same rights and liabilities. *In re Boxco Ltd.* 231, where a Company, not knowing that it had been struck off, mortgaged its assets, a subsequent order of restoration validated the mortgage.

Winding up of an Unregistered Company (Section 465)

An unregistered Company includes any partnership association or Company consisting of more than 7 members at the time of petition, but does not include:

(1) a Railway Company incorporated by an Act of Parliament or other Indian Laws,

(2) a Company registered under the Companies Act 1956,

(3) a Company registered under any previous Companies Act.

Procedure of winding up (Section 582) (Section 583)

An unregistered Company may be wound up under the Act and with few exceptions all the provisions of the Act relating to winding up process. Such a Company can be wound up only by the order of the Court, not voluntarily, nor under supervision of the Court.

The circumstances or the grounds for winding up of unregistered Company may be:

(a) where the Company has been dissolved, or has ceased to carry on business, or

(b) where the Company is unable to pay its debts, or

(c) where the Court is of the opinion that it is just and equitable to wind up the Company.

Winding up of Foreign Companies (Section 584)

A foreign Company may be wound up like an unregistered Company under Part X of this Act.

Section 584 states that "where a body corporate incorporated outside, which has been carrying on business in India, ceases to carry on business in India, it may be wound up as an unregistered Company under the part (i.e., Part X), notwithstanding that a body corporate has been dissolved or otherwise ceased to exist as such under or by virtue of the laws of the country under which it was incorporated."

In other words, where a foreign Company having had a place of business in India, ceased to carry on its business, it may be ordered to be wound-up as an unregistered Company, even if it has already been dissolved in its mother Company.

CHAPTER

52

Amendments to Companies Act

SALIENT FEATURES OF THE IMPORTANT PROVISIONS OF THE COMPANIES (AMENDMENT) ACT, 1988

Section 2 (45) ***& 2*** **(45A) — Secretary.** The definition of the term 'Secretary" has been amended to mean a company secretary within the meaning of Section 2(1) *(c)* of the Company Secretaries Act, 1980 and shall include any other individual possessing the prescribed qualifications and appointed to perform the duties which may be performed by a secretary under this Act and any other ministerial and administrative duties.

Section *2(45A)* defines the concept of 'Secretary in whole time practice' to mean a secretary who shall be deemed to be in practice within the meaning of Section 2 (2) of the Company Secretaries Act, 1950 and who is not in full time-employment.

Section 5. — Officer in Default. A specific meaning has been assigned to the expression 'Officer in default'. The expression is defined to mean all the following officers of the company, namely:

(a) the managing director or managing directors;

(b) the whole-time director or whole-time directors;

(c) the manager;

(d) the secretary;

(e) any person in accordance with whose directions or instructions the Board of directors of the company is accustomed to-tie;*

(f) any person cnarged by the Board with the responsibility of complying with that provision:

Provided that the person so charged has given his consent in this behalf to the Board.

(g) where any company does not have any of the officers specified in clauses *(a)* to *(c)*, any director or directors who may be specified by the Board in this behalf or where no director is so specified, all the directors.

However, where the Board exercises any power under clause *(f)* or clause *(g),* it shall, within thirty days of the exercise of such powers, file with the Registrar a return in the 'prescribed form'.

The changed definition of 'officer who is in default' has omitted the words "who is knowingly guilty of the default' and the words "who knowingly or wilfully authorises or permits such default...", which, according to some, means that presence of guilty mind in the commission of an offence or the concept of *'Mens-Rea'* need not be imputed while prosecuting the officials specified in the amended Section 5. Others, however, feel that the Government's intention is not and cannot be to take away the right of a person to seek exonerance in situations he is not really guilty.

Further, an apprehension is being expressed in certain quarters that under pressure a person may give his consent to take responsibility contemplated under clause *(f)* of the amended section.

This amendment has been made operative w.e.f. 15th July, 1988.

Section I0E & 10F — Constitution of an independent Company Law Board, This Section contemplates the constitution of an independent Board to be called the Board of Company Law Administration with powers spanned over a number of provisions of the Companies Act. In fact, some of the powers which earlier vested with the Central Government or the Court shall now vest in this Board. The following is the list of Sections under which the stated substitution has been done or certain additional powers have been conferred on the Board:

Sections 58-A, 8O-A, 111, 113, 235, 236, 237, 241, 248, 250, 251, 269, 408, 610,621-A, 640-A

The members of the Board shall be appointed by Central Government and shall have qualifications to be once again prescribed by the Government. Since it has not been so for done, most of the aforesaid provisions including the amended provisions of Sections 10E and 10F have not yet been made operational. **Section 33**

Under this Section, for signing the declaration, 'a chartered accountant in whole-time practice in India' has been substituted for 'a chartered accountant practising in India' and the expression is defined to mean a chartered accountant who is not in full time employment. Besides, a Secretary who has been engaged in the formation of a company has also been empowered to sign the declaration.

Section 43A. Deemed Public Company. Significant amendments have been made in this Section.

Section 43A (1). A private company shall, by virtue of 25 per cent or more of its paid-up share capital being held by other body or bodies corporate, be deemed as public company only if the body corporate so holding is a 'public company' or a 'deemed public company'. In other words, if 25 per cent or more of the paid up share capital is held by a private company or a foreign company, it shall not be so deemed. Besides, as per the already existing provision, *i.e.,* where the specified percentage is held by a banking company as a trustee or executor for any individual, or individuals, the private company shall not be deemed as a public company. However, general exceptions as contained in Section 43 (6) and (7) have been withdrawn by deleting these sub-sections. This has been rightly done to prevent their misuse.

Section 43A (1-A). The limit of Rupees one crore under the turnover criterion has been substituted by the words "to be prescribed by the Central Government" and the Central Government has prescribed this limit as 5 crores.

Section 43A (1-B). Besides the aforesaid criterion, a private company shall also be deemed as a public company where it holds 25% or more of the paid-up share capital of a public company. This is as per the existing provision of Section 43 A (1-B).

Section 43A (1-C). This section is a new addition and contemplates a new criterion of accepting deposits by an advertisement or renewing such deposits for deeming a private company as public.

Thus the position under Sec. 43-A may be summarised as follows:

A private company shall be deemed as a public company in the following cases:

(a) Where it accepts, after an invitation by an advertisement, or renews deposits from the public other than its members, directors or their relatives.

(b) it holds 25% or more of the paid-up share capital of a public company.

(c) it has public company(ies) or deemed public company(ies) as its shareholders holding 25% or more of its paid-up share capital, subject, however, to certain exceptions,

(d) its average annual turnover for the last three consecutive financial years is Rs. 5 crores or more.

Section 56 — Prospectus. This section requires a company to deliver a document containing salient features of a prospectus, in place of Prospectus, along with the application form. However, company shall have to provide a copy of the prospectus to anyone who may so demand.

Section 58A — Repayment of Deposits, Sub-section (9) has been added to safeguard the interest of the depositors in view of certain companies failing tf meet their obligation as per the terms and conditions of deposits. The Company Law Board may in such cases of failure, either on its own or on an application by the depositor, direct the company to pay the deposit within the specified time and subject to the specified conditions.

Section 73 makes *listing of all public issues* of shares or debentures compulsory and where the permission has not been applied for or refused, the money must be repaid within 5 days. Failure to pay within 8 days will make the company and every director in default to repay with interest @ *4%* to 15% (to be prescribed, depending on the length of delay period).

Section 80 *prohibits issue of irredeemable preference shares* or preference shares redeemable beyond 10 years.

Section 80A. This newly inducted section requires the companies to redeem irredeemable preference shares, if any, within 5 years. The shares may be redeemed even by issue of redeemable preference shares. In case of failure, penal consequences include fine up to Rs. 1,000 for every day during which default continues. Further, no dividends or transfer of profits to reserves shall be permitted [Section 205]

Section 108. The currency of transfer forms has been extended from 2 months to 12 months.

Sections 108A to 108H. These sections have been omitted since these were transferred to MRTP Act way back in 1984.

Section 111—Refusal to register a transfer. In case of refusal to register a transfer, an appeal can be made to the Company Law Board within 2 months from the date of the receipt of the notice of such refusal.

CLB has been empowered to even award compensation as an alternate remedy.

Section 125—Registration of a charge. A charge may now be registered within 30 days (in place of 7 days) after the expiry of the initial period of 30 days on payment of additional fee.

Section 179—Demand for poll. The amendment now provides that a demand for poll can only be made by the shareholders having some minimum interest—not being less than 1/10th of total voting power or paid-up value of shares held to be not less than Rs. 50,000,

Section 205—Delinking of Depreciation under the Companies Act from that under the Income Tax Act

The omission of the words "the Indian Income-tax Act or the rules made thereunder" from Sections 205(2)(d) and 350 shall have the effect of permitting companies to provide depreciation as per Schedule XIV appended to the Act. Since the rates under Schedule XIV are much lower than under Income-tax Act, larger book profits shall be available to the companies.

Section 205A—Unclaimed Dividend. The total amount of dividend remaining unclaimed or unpaid within 42 days of declaration must be deposited in the unpaid dividend account.

Section 209—Books of accounts. Section 209(3) now makes it obligatory on companies to maintain accounts on accrual basis and according to double entry system of accounting.

Section 217—Report of the Board to contain certain information. The amended Section requires the report of the Board of directors to contain information with respect to the conservation of energy, technology absorption, foreign exchange earnings and outgo, in such manner as may be prescribed.

Further, sub-section 2A and the subsequent notification issued thereunder now require information about only those employees whose salary is Rs. 6,000 p.m. or Rs. 72,000 p.a. or more.

Section 219—Abridged version of Balance Sheet and Profit and Loss Account. Section 219, as amended, gives a choice to the listed companies either to send detailed accounts to its shareholders or a statement containing the salient features only (salient features to be prescribed).

However, if a company has sent only the salient features of accounts to its shareholders, it must send a copy of detailed accounts free of cost to a shareholder, who demands the same, within 21 days before the meeting.

The accounts and documents need not be sent to debenture holders except to the trustees of the debenture holders unless specifically demanded. However, these shall be required to be sent to the trustees of the debenture holders.

Section 220—Adoption of Accounts. If the accounts are not adopted in any annual general meeting or the meeting is adjourned without adopting the accounts, it will be obligatory to report to the Registrar the reasons for the same.

Section 224 (IB)—Appointment of Auditors. The amended section prohibits the appointment of any person who is in full time employment elsewhere. Similarly, for counting number of audits per partner in case of a firm of auditors, a partner who is in full time employment elsewhere is not to be counted.

Section 269—Compulsory appointment of Managing/Whole-time Director or Manager

(1) The amendment in this Section and the notification issued thereunder now provide that every public limited company or a subsidiary of a public limited company having a paid-up capital of Rs. 1 crore or more must have a managing or whole-time director or manager.

(2) For appointment of a managing/whole-time director or a manager, approval of the Central Government will not be necessary if the following conditions are satisfied:

(a) he had not been sentenced to imprisonment for any period or to a fine exceeding one thousand rupees for conviction of an offence under fourteen Acts mentioned in Schedule XIII; *(b)* he had not been detained for any period under the conversation of Foreign Exchange and Prevention of Smuggling Activities Act, 1974; (c) he has completed the age of 30 years but has not attained the age of 65 years; *(d)* he is not a managing or whole-time director or manager or in any way in whole-time employment elsewhere; (e) he is a citizen of India and is a resident in India; *(f)* the Company had not suffered loss or had inadequacy of profits during the preceding financial year immediate to the financial year in which appointment is made or in, any of the three financial years in the four financial years immediately preceding.

3. In case any of the above conditions are not complied with, an application must be made to the Central Government within 90 days of appointment. If the appointment is not approved by the Central Government, the appointee shall vacate the office immediately on communication of the decision by Central Government. If the Central

Government has once given its approval to the appointment of a person convicted or detained as per para, *(a)* or *(b)* above, no subsequent approval on those grounds would be required.

Section 314—Ceiling for Appointment of Relatives of Directors. The Section is amended to omit the absolute monetary ceiling of monthly remuneration of Rs. 500 and Rs. 3,000 and the words 'to be prescribed by the Central Government' have been substituted. The Government by its notification of 10th June, 1988 has provided as follows:

(1) The total monthly remuneration, for the purposes of clause *(b)* of sub-section (1) of Section 314, shall be not less than rupees three thousand or more; and

(2) The total monthly remuneration, for the purposes of sub-section (IB) of Section 314, shall be not less than rupees six thousand.

Section 310, 311 and Schedule XIII—Managerial Remuneration. Salary (including Dearness Allowance) and Commission can be paid calculated on the basis of effective capital which includes paid-up share capital, reserves and surplus (including capital reserve, revaluation reserve, debenture redemption reserve), long-term loans and deposits as reduced by investments, accumulated losses and preliminary expenses not written off. Schedule XIII gives the following rates of remuneration that may be payable as per the effective capital of the company.

Effective Capital	Minimum Monthly Salary	Maximum Annual Commission in addition to Salary subject to a ceiling of 1% of Profits, 50% of Salary	Maximum Annual Commission where Salary is not Paid
Rs.	Rs.	Rs.	Rs.
Less than 20 Lakhs	6,000/-	26,000/-	1,08,000/-
20 Lakhs or more but less than 50 Lakhs	7,500/-	45,000/-	1,35,000/-
50 Lakhs or more but less than 1 Crore	9,000/-	54,000/-	1,62,000/-
1 Crore or more but less than 3 Crores	11,000/-	66,000/-	1,98,000/-
3 Crore or more but less than 5 Crores	13,000/-	78,000/-	2,34,000/-
5 Crore or more	15,000/-	90,000/-	2,70,000/-

Perquisites

In addition to salary and commission as above, perquisites like housing, medical reimbursement, level travel concession, club fee, etc., may also be allowed to managerial personnel equal to annual salary or Rs. 1.35 lakhs per annum whichever is less in case the person has been posted at Delhi, Bombay, Calcutta or Madras and in other cases Rs. 1.15 lakhs per annum whichever is less. Perquisites have been classified into three categories and the new Schedule XIII clearly specifies the limits of the value of perquisites.

Increase in Managerial Remuneration

Sections 310 and 311 have been amended to the effect: *(a)* that for any increase in the remuneration, Central Government approval shall not be required so long as the increase is within the prescribed ceilings provided under Schedule XIII. Unde. Section 310 the sitting fee payable to a director for each meeting of the Board of Directors or a Committee thereof shall not exceed .

Companies having paid-up Share capital	Maximum Sitting Fee Rs.
Upto Rs. 50 Lakhs	250
More than Rs. 50 Lakhs and upto Rs. 5 Crore	500
More than Rs, 5 Crore and upto Rs. 30 Crores	750
Above Rs. 10 Crores	1,000

Payment of Gratuity (Amendment) Act, 1987 Salient Features

(1) The coverage of the Act is extended to persons drawing wages up to Rs. 2500 per month.

(2) Provision is made for depositing the amount of gratuity payable to a minor with the controlling authority who shall invest the money in a bank or a financial institution for the benefit of minor.

(3) The existing ceiling of 20 months' wages for payment of gratuity is replaced by a monetary ceiling of Rs. 50,000.

(4) Provision is made for compulsory insurance of employers' liability to pay gratuity under the Act or in the alternative for the setting up of a gratuity fund under the provisions of the Act in relation to establishments employing five hundred or more employees.

(5) Provision is made for payment of simple interest at a specified rate, if the amount of gratuity is not paid within 30 days from the date it becomes payable.

6. Penalties are made moré stringent.

NEXT AMENDMENT

On 22nd October 1999, a committee was constituted under Justice v. Balakrishna Eradi to examine the existing laws relating to winding up of Companies, revival of sick companies along with Laws relating to recovery of debts, securities contracts, insolvency of companies and to suggest recuperative measures for the ailing corporate sector on these issues.

National Company Law Tribunal

The Bill proposes to set up a National Company Law Tribunal (NCLT) which would encompass the power and jurisdiction of Company Law Board, Board for Industrial and Financial Reconstruction Appellate Authority for Industrial and Financial Reconstruction and of the High Court relating to company law matters. The cases pending with the company law Board and the winding up cases that are before various High Courts will stand transferred to proposed NCLT. The matters pending in BIFR/AAIFR would abate, however, such companies would file fresh reference to NCLT. NCLT will have principal seat in Delhi with atloast ten special benches at principal seats of High Courts. NCLT will consist of President and not mire than 62 judicial and technical members. An Appellate Tribunal in Delhi has also been proposed where the appeals against NCLT has to be filed within forty-five days from the receipt of the orders from the NCLT. An appeal against the order of Appellate Tribunal would lie before Supreme Court.

Revival Of A 'Sick Company'

Under the proposed Sec 2(46 AA) of the proposed bill, a 'Sick Company' is defined as one whose accumulated losses in any financial year are equal to or more than fifty percent of its average networth during our financial year immediately preceding such financial year or a company who fails to repay its debt within any three consecutive quarters on demand, for its repayment by a creditor or creditors. This is a marked change from the provisions of Sec 3 (1) (o) of The sick companies (Special Provisions) Act, 1985 (SICA) where a sick industrial company has at the end of any financial year accumulated losses equal to or exceeding its entire net worth and is registered for not less than five years. This change in definition will result in a Sick Company getting the attention earlier thereby improving the chances of its revival. The provision regarding the default in payments by the company for three consecutive quarters will not only allow the Board of directors of company but also Banks and Financial institution to refer the company to the Tribunal for its revival even it the company is registered for less than 5 years. This provision will even bring the companies registered for less than five years under the ambit of 'Sick Company'.

In the proposed dispensation the time period within which a company can be referred to NCLT been increased from 60 days (time period given in SICA) to 180 which is further extendable by 90 days, thus giving the sufficient time period to refer the company to the Tribunal for the revival or rehabilitation. The application to the tribunal is proposed to be accompanied by a certified copy of accounts audited by the body of auditors prépared by the Tribunal and not by the Board of Directors (as provided in SICA), thus removing the scope for manipulation of accounts by the directors of the company and there by preventing them from misusing the provisions of SICA. It would however be seen that the professionals that are being appointed by the Tribunal are of clean background and are well experienced in their fields. While referring the company to the Tribunal the company is required to submit a scheme of revival and rehabilitation to the Tribunal under section 424 A of the proposed bill. The bill also stipulates that the permission of the Central or State Government shall be taken before a government company can be referred to the tribunal.

On receiving a reference the Tribunal will conduct an inquiry and if the Tribunal finds that it is impracticable for sick company to make its net worth exceed the accumulated losses or cannot repay its debt, it can order the winding up of the company itself against the earlier proviso in SICA where in the BIFR used to refer the winding up of the company concerned to the High Court which was a time consuming process. In the new desperation time period of one year has been stipulated for the completion of winding up proceedings after the passing of the winding up order. The Tribunal needs to work carefully and vigilantly to ensure that the winding up proceedings are completed within the prescribed time frame.

Under Section 424 D (11), creditors of a sick company may also prepare and submit a scheme for revival or rehabilitation of a sick company provided it meets them approval of the two third creditors of the company. The provision is silent on the fact that whether this criterion of 2/3rd is related to numerical aspect or to the total amount expenses of the creditors.

An amendment has also been proposed in Sec. 434(1) of The Companies Act, 1956 where the amount or Rupees five hundred has been raised to Rupees One lakh, i.e., now a creditor can file a suit for winding up of the company only if the company is unable to repay the amount of Rs.1, 00,000/- or more. This is an encouraging step as the amount of Rs.500/- is very meager, for which a company should be wound up.

Problems In Winding Up Of A Company

The problems that are being highlighted regarding winding up of a company in justice Eradi Committee Report relates to delay in filing of statement of Affairs, delay in handing over updated books of account and records, delay in finalization of list of creditors and debtors, inadequate power and staff given to Official Liquidator (OL), non availability of funds etc. In the proposed bill, steps are being taken to solve and minimize these problems. Section 493(1) of the proposed Bill says that every company has to file its statement of affairs synchronous with the petition for winding up or while opposing a petition for its winding up. The statement shall be filed along with the names and addresses of the directors, creditors and debtors of the company and the location of assets and their values and such other information as ordered by the Tribunal. This provision will reduce the delay, which used to occur in making a statement of affairs of the company. Under section 457 C (a) of the proposed Bill, the Official Liquidator has been entrusted with wide powers such as he can appoint Chartered Surveyors, Chartered Accountants to value the assets of the company. In this Bill, earlier provisions of OL requiring to take courts permission for even small decisions has been done away with For example now he can appoint security guards to protect the property of the company and other helping staff required.

Establishment of A Fund

To tackle the paucity of funds the proposed Bill envisages to put in place Revival and Rehabilitation Fund funded by the collection of cess which will be levied at the rate of .005% -1% on the annual turnover or the gross receipts of the company. This proposed fund will take care of the interim payment of wages to the workers protection of assets and for other rehabilitation works. The fund is not free from the clutches of the Government as the Bill proposes to transfer the collected amount to the consolidated fund of India. The parliament may, by way of delegation create a body, which will release funds to Tribunal from time to time. This procedure may result in avoidable delays, as the Tribunal will have to interact with agency created for managing the funds. Another flaw which is apparent in this provision, is the levying of cess on the annual turnover of the company instead on the Profit of the company, i.e., even the company that is incurring losses has to contribute to the fund.

Power To Review

In the new dispensation NCLT has been bestowed with inherent powers to review its own decisions, which has been provided as per Sec. 10 FN of the proposed bill.

The establishment of NCLT may prove to be a great help to the corporate world as now there will be special benches at principal seats of the High Court and the companies don't have to come to Delhi every time for the revival and rehabilitation proceedings. Furthermore with the change in definition of a sick company, a lot more companies can come under the ambit of a Sick Company and thereby can get the needful attention on time. With the establishment of fund and change in definition of Sick Company and winding up procedures, the time period for revival and winding up will reduce. In all efforts are being made by the central government to achieve its proposed objectives through this bill, i.e., to avoid multiplicity of suits, protection of rights of the workers and to reduce the time period for winding up of a Sick Company. Now what is required is to see that the provisions of this bill are strictly implemented and the objectives of this bill are achieved.

The year 2001 has seen some major changes in the corporate sector. Increasing liberalisation has forced companies to become more competitive and adopt different strategies to survive. The Government has also responded by continuing with its liberalisation policy and further simplifying the laws and procedures.

Significant changes have been made in the field of corporate laws in the last couple of years in areas such as capital market regulations, corporate governance, simplification of tax laws, rationalisation of excise and customs duty etc. We also understand that more such progressive measures such as introduction of VAT, introduction of a new Competition Act to replace the existing MRTP Act etc. are in store in the near future.

Significant changes in Company Law Amendment Act, 2000

Company Law in India has been left largely undisturbed since the enactment of the Companies Act, 1956. Periodically, certain amendments have been carried out, to keep in tune with the changing circumstances. The Government has planned to overhaul the entire Companies Act, 1956 and replace it with an entirely new Act. However, as this has been delayed, some of the major items were introduced by way of an amendment to the Companies Act by the enactment of the Companies Amendment Act, 2000.

Further changes by way of changes in deposit acceptance, notification of rules for new provisions introduced in the Amendment Act, 2000 have also been made during the year 2001.

The major changes can be summarised as under:

- Introduction of the Companies Amendment Act, 2000
- Amendments to Deposit Acceptance Regulations
- Rules regarding passing of resolutions by Postal Ballot
- Rules regarding issue of shares with differential voting rights
- Rules regarding appointment of directors by small shareholders
- Companies (Amendment) Bill, 2001
- Companies (Second Amendment) Bill, 2001
- Companies (Amendment) Ordinance, 2001

Companies Amendment Act, 2000

The major amendment to the Companies Act, 1956 were carried out by enacting the Companies (Amendment) Act 2000, which came into force with effect from 14th December 2000. This Act fulfilled some of the long standing demands of the corporate sector.

The major highlights of the Act are:

- New definitions added
- Concept of deemed public companies abolished
- Depositor protection measures introduced
- Introduction of postal ballot for listed companies
- Directors responsibilities/disqualifications increased
- Right of small share holders to appoint directors — made optional
- Constitution of audit committee made mandatory for certain companies
- Secretarial compliance audit introduced

An analysis of some of the major changes in the Act is given under.

New Definitions

Securities

As per Section 2 (45AA) a new term "Securities" has been defined in the Companies Act. It states that Securities shall mean securities as defined in Section 2(h) of the Securities Contract (Regulation) Act, 1956. As per the definition in the Securities Contract (Regulation) Act, securities include marketable shares, debentures etc.

As marketable shares, debentures etc have been held to mean only listed shares and debentures, it leads to the conclusion that all references in the Companies Act to "securities" would only mean listed securities. This would imply that the provisions of Section 372 A etc will not have any applicability in case an investment is made in the shares of an unlisted company.

Interim Dividend

As per the newly inserted Section 2 (14A), Dividend has been defined to include Interim Dividend. Also, the Directors have been empowered to declare interim dividend.

This amendment seems to have been prompted by the fact that in a number of cases the Board of Directors declared interim dividend, but did not pay the same, contending that interim dividend is not a debt which was enforceable against the company.

This amendment seeks to confer on interim dividend the same legal status as a final dividend declared by the shareholders. The move, though a welcome measure, casts certain obligations on the company before declaring interim dividend. The Company is now bound to comply with the provisions of the Companies Act such as providing for depreciation and transferring certain percentage of profits to reserves, before the declaration of interim dividend.

Minimum Capitalisation Norms

The Act has now made it mandatory for all companies to have a minimum paid up share capital. This welcome step will ensure that "shell companies" are slowly weeded out.

The Minimum capitalisation has been fixed at Rs. 1 lakh for Private Companies and Rs. 5 lakhs for Public Companies. A two year time frame has been given for existing companies to achieve this limit. In case of companies which are incorporated after this Act, then, such companies need to comply with the limits at the time of incorporation.

The section also provides that in case companies do not fulfill the capitalisation norms, then, the Registrar of Companies "shall" strike off such a company as being a "defunct company" under Section 560 of the Companies Act. As this is a mandatory provision, this would offer an easy exit to companies which are not active, without going through the formalities of applying to the Registrar of Companies for striking off their name as a defunct company.

Depositor Protection Measures introduced

The Amendment Act has sought to ensure protection of small depositors by the introduction of two new sections 58AA & 58AAA in the Act. Small Depositors have been defined as persons who have deposited upto Rs.20,000 in a financial year with a company.

Defaults made by a company on small deposits is required to be intitmated to the Company Law Board. The Company is also restrained from accepting further deposits from small depositors. It is however, permitted to accept deposits from other depositors.

Section 58 AA (7) provides that where a company accepts deposits from small depositors and then obtains any bank loan, the bank loan shall be first used for repayment of the deposit made by the "small depositor." This seems to be applicable even when a company is not defaulting on the repayment of any deposit.

This clause seems to be erroneously drafted and should be made applicable only when the company has defaulted on repayment of deposits. However, in spite of several representations, the section continues to remain as it is, thereby creating a great deal of confusion to the corporate sector.

Non Voting Shares permitted to be Issued - Sec 86

Section 86 of the Act permits a company to issue equity shares with differential voting rights. The Government has on 9th March 2001, framed the rules for issue of shares with differential voting rights.

Issue of Debentures – Sec 117

Major changes have been made with regard to issue of debentures by companies by the introduction of Section 117 A, 117 B & 117 C.

Section 117 A requires that a Debenture Trust Deed shall be executed in respect of any issue of debentures made by a company.

Section 117B makes appointment of Independent Debenture Trustees mandatory in the case of any public issue of debentures. The section also casts an obligation upon the Trustees to monitor the quality and value of assets of the Company and to file a petition before the Company Law Board, if they are of the opinion that the assets are inadequate to meet the redemption of the debentures.

Section 117 C is a far reaching provision as it makes it mandatory for all companies to create a Debenture Redemption Reserve in respect of debentures issued after this Act, from out of the profits every year. However, the quantum of reserve to be created has not been specified.

Under the SEBI Guidelines, Financial Institutions are exempt from creation of DRR. However, under the Companies Act, they would be liable to create DRR in respect of the debentures issued by them. This seems to be an apparent contradiction. It is expected that some clarification would be issued in this matter.

It is also important to note that it is impossible for financial institutions to create a DRR for the whole amount of the debentures borrowed. This is because, such financial institutions raise large amounts by way of debentures — usually 2-3 times their networth. In such cases, the profits will simply not be adequate to provide for a Debenture Redemption Reserve.

Introduction of Postal Ballot – Sec 192 A

A new Section 192 A has been introduced which requires listed companies to transact certain items of business only through a postal ballot. This is to ensure that equal representation is provided to all shareholders to vote on important matters. The Central Government has, on 10th May, 2001, laid down the rules relating to postal ballot, which are dealt with later on in this Article.

Appointment of Auditors – Sec 224

Section 224 (1-B) of the Act has been amended. The intention of the amendment seems to be to exclude private companies in computing the number of companies for which a person can be appointed as an auditor. However, the intention of the legislature has not been reflected in the language of the Section. The Fourth Proviso to Section 224 (1-B) states that "the provisions of this sub-section does not apply to a private company."

This would mean that in case a private company wishes to appoint an Auditor, then, it can appoint as its Auditor:

(i) A person who is holding the post of an Auditor in excess of the specified number of companies, and/or,

(ii) Also a person who is in full time employment elsewhere.

But a public limited company, if it wishes to appoint a person as its auditor, will still have to ensure that the Auditor who is proposed to be appointed is within the limits specified in Section 224 (1-B).

Modifications to the Auditors Report – Sec 227

The Act has amended the format of the Auditor's Report. The Auditor is now required to state in his report any adverse remarks on the functioning of the company in "Thick Type" or in "Italics". The Auditor is also required to report on the Disqualification of any Director under the newly introduced Sec 274 (1) (g).

Appointment of Director by Small Shareholders – Sec 252

This is another step towards ensuring participation of all shareholders in the decision-making process of the Companies. This provision is applicable to all public limited companies with a paid-up capital exceeding Rs.5 Crs and having more than 1000 "small share holders". "Small Shareholders" have been defined as persons whose nominal value of share holding is less than Rs.20,000.

The Central Govt has on 9th March, 2001, prescribed the rules for the appointment of Director by Small Shareholders.

Additional Disqualifications for a Director – Sec 274 (1) (g)

Section 274 of the Companies Act has now been amended to provide for an additional disqualification for a person being appointed as a Director of a company.

As per the newly inserted Section 274 (1) (g), if a person is already a Director of a Public Company, and that public company fails to

- File Balance Sheet and Annual Return for 3 consecutive years from 1.4.99, or;
- Defaults in payment of Dividend or repayment of Deposit/Debentures for more than 1 year;

then, for a period of 5 years from the date of default, such a person cannot be appointed as a Director of another Public Company.

The section makes it clear that the disqualification will only be at the appointment stage. Hence, a Director of a defaulting company will not be liable to vacate office. The onus on reporting such disqualifications has been placed on the Auditor of the Company.

Constitution of Audit Committee — Sec 292A

A new provision making constitution of an Audit Committee has been made mandatory. This applies to all public companies (listed or unlisted) having paid-up capital of Rs.5 crores & above.

Under this Section, an Audit Committee of the Board has to be formed with a minimum of 3 Directors. Two thirds of the total strength of the Committee shall be Directors other than managing or whole time directors. Terms of reference to be specified by Board.

It may be noted that the Listing Agreement of the Stock Exchanges also require Listed Companies to constitute an Audit Committee. As per the provisions of the Listing Agreement, the Audit Committee should have a minimum 3 Directors. The committee should consist only of Non-Executive Directors with majority being Independent. However, in the Companies Act, the Audit Committee is permitted to have a maximum of one thirds as Executive/Whole-Time Directors. The Listing Agreement also prescribes the scope of Audit Committee.

Introduction of Secretarial Audit – Sec 383 A

A new provision has been introduced for Companies having a paid up capital above Rs.10 lakhs and less than Rs.50 lakhs. Such companies are required to file a Compliance Certificate certified by a Practicing Company Secretary with the Registrar of Companies. The copy of the certificate is also to be attached with Board Report u/Sec 217.

Companies (Compliance Certificate) Rules, 2001 — Dated 31st January 2001

The Companies Amendment Act, 2000, had made it mandatory for companies not required to appoint a whole-time secretary and having a paid up capital exceeding Rs. 10 lakhs, to file a certificate from a company secretary in whole time practice. These rules lay down the format of the said certificate.

As per the Rules, this certificate shall also be appended along with the report of the Board of Directors and circulated to the shareholders.

Companies (Appointment of Small Shareholders' Director) Rules 2001 — Dated 9th March , 2001

The Companies Amendment Act, 2000 has introduced a new provision which enables small shareholders to appoint their nominees as Directors on certain Companies. This is applicable only to public limited companies having a paid up capital above Rs. 5 Crores and having 1000 or more small shareholders. Small shareholder has been defined as a person holding shares of the nominal value of Rs. 20,000 or less.

However, this is not a mandatory provision and the company has the discretion to appoint a nominee of the small shareholder on its Board.

The Government has laid down these rules, which are to be observed in such an appointment.

As per the said Rules, the Company may suo moto nominate a small shareholder for the post of a Director. Alternatively, the small shareholders also have the right to nominate a person. However, such person should also be a small shareholder.

The election of such a director shall, in the case of a listed company, be conducted through postal ballot. In the case of an unlisted company, it may be passed at a general meeting.

The person so appointed shall hold office for a period of 3 years, during which time, he shall not be liable to retire by rotation. Also, such a director cannot be appointed as the Managing Director or whole time director of the Company.

It is important to note that a director who is nominated by small shareholders has no special rights. In the absence of any specific authority, a single director may not be able to make any difference to the management. Also, such a director may not have any say in the day to day running of the business, but would nevertheless, be liable for any default committed by the Company.

Companies (Issue of Share Capital with Differential Voting Rights), Rules 2001 — Dated March 9th 2001

The Companies Amendment Act, 2000, has vide Section 86, permitted public companies to issue shares with differential voting rights. Consequently, Section 88 which prohibited issue of such shares, now stands deleted.

It may be borne in mind that the prohibition on issue of shares with differential voting rights was only on public companies. Private companies, were, all along permitted to issue shares with differential/nil voting rights.

After the enabling provision, the Government has, on 9th March 2001, notified the Rules relating to issue of shares with differential voting rights.

As per the said Rules, only a company which has a track record of profitability as per Section 205 and has not defaulted in filing annual accounts and annual returns for three immediately preceding financial years and has not defaulted on repayment of its deposits/debentures, is eligible to issue such shares.

It is necessary that the Articles of Association of the company authorises the issue of shares with differential voting rights. Hence, existing companies which do not have this provision in their Articles, have to amend their Articles. Consequently, it also becomes necessary to amend the Capital Clause of the Memorandum of Association of the company.

At the time of seeking shareholders approval for such an issue, the Company is to disclose the variation in voting rights which is proposed to be brought about by such an issue.

It may be noted that companies are not permitted to convert their equity shares into shares with differential voting rights and *vice versa*. It should also be ensured that the shares with differential voting rights which are issued do not exceed 25% of the total share capital issued (including both equity and preference capital).

Companies (Passing of Resolution by Postal Ballot) Rules, 2001 — Dated 10.5.2001

The Companies (Amendment) Act, 2000, requires every listed company to transact certain items of business only through a postal ballot. These Rules have been laid down to specify the items for which postal ballot is necessary and the mode of conducting the postal ballot. These rules permit a shareholder to vote by postal or electronic mode.

As per the said Rules, the following items of business shall be passed only through a postal ballot:

i.Alteration of object clause of MOA

(i) Alteration of AOA in relation to insertion of provisions defining company

(ii) Buyback of own shares u/s 77A

(iii) Issue of shares with differential voting rights u/s 86

(iv) Change in registered office outside the local limits of the present place

(v) Sale of undertaking u/s 293 (1) (a)

(vi) Granting of loans/guarantees / security in excess of the limits specified u/s 372 A

(vii) Election of a director u/ proviso to Sec 252 (1)

(viii) Variation in the rights attached to a class of shares or debentures u/s 106.

However, it is open for a company to transact any other item of business, other than the above mentioned items, through postal ballot.

The Company is required to give notice to all shareholders either by registered post ack due or under Certificate of Posting along with an advertisement in a leading English Newspaper and one vernacular newspaper in the area.

The shareholder is to give his consent within 30 days of the date of notice. Replies received after this date will be considered invalid.

The Company would appoint an independent person to act as the scrutinizer, who would scrutinize all the ballots received and submit a report to the Chairman.

The Chairman would declare the result at the General Meeting.

It is important to note that transacting the items of business mentioned aforesaid, does not absolve the company from holding a general meeting. Under the Rules, the Company is required to hold a General Meeting to declare the result of the postal ballot.

Also, it is pertinent to observe that the matters for which notice has been given by postal ballot, cannot be amended or withdrawn. In other words, the inherent power of the shareholders to amend the resolution or withdraw the resolution, is removed in a scheme of postal ballot.

Amendments in Deposit Acceptance Regulations

The Government has amended the Companies (Acceptance of Deposits) Rules, to provide for the following:

- The maximum rate of interest has been reduced from 15% to 14%.
- Amounts received by a private company from its director, relative of such director, or member are exempt from the definition of a deposit.
- Companies with Net Owned Fund of less than Rs. 1 Crore are not permitted to invite public deposits.
- In case of default in repayment of deposits, the Company shall pay a penal rate of 18% p.a to the depositor for the period of delay. In case the depositor is a small depositor, then, the rate shall be 20% p.a.
- The Company shall state the following in the advertisement:
  - The total number of small depositors and amount due to them in respect of which default has been made.
  - The fact of waiver of interest accrued on deposits of small depositors

The introduction of a minimum networth criteria to accept public deposits is a welcome measure and will ensure that companies which are not financially sound, do not misuse the public deposits route to cheat investors.

However, the introduction of the penal interest clause is surprising. When the Company is unable to repay a matured deposit, how will it be able to pay the same along with the penal interest. The clause seems to have been inserted only to instill a sense of fear among companies.

Establishment of the Investor Education Protection Fund

As per Section 205 C of the Companies Act, every company is required to transfer certain sums to the Investor Education & Protection Fund. The Central Government, has by a notification on 1st October 2001, constituted the Investor Education & Protection Fund and has also framed rules for the same.

Accordingly, the Companies which are required to credit amounts to the Fund , shall do so within 30 days from the due date and shall also file with the concerned ROC a copy of the challan evidencing deposit to the Fund along with a Statement in Form 1.

The Fund may use the moneys so collected for the purposes of investor awareness programmes and may release funds to such organisations, which are engaged in these activities.

However, the following points need to be clarified:

- The treatment of the balance lying in the Unpaid Dividend Account of Companies as on 31.10.1998 (the date when the amendment proposing the Fund came into effect) has not been specified. Will such balances also be liable for transfer to the Fund after a period of 7 years. This may not be appropriate as transfer of such amounts to the Fund will deprive the shareholder to claim the amount back. Hence, the requirement of transfer to the Fund should apply only in case of dividends declared by Companies after 31.10.1998.
- The periodicity of transfer of the amount of unclaimed matured deposits has also not been specified. However, it can be safely assumed that it would be sufficient if companies transfer such amounts at the end of every year and not as and when the 7 year period is completed in respect of each deposit.

Companies (Amendment Bill) 2001

The Companies (Amendment Bill) 2001 was introduced in Parliament on 30th August 2001. The salient features of the Bill are:

- Consolidating the powers relating to Companies with the proposed National Company Law Tribunal, which are presently vested with various authorities such as High Courts, Company Law Board, BIFR, AAIFR. Orders passed by the Tribunal can be appealed before the Appellate Tribunal. On orders passed by the Appellate Tribunal, an appeal can be preferred before the Supreme Court only. Hence, the jurisdiction of the High Courts on all matters relating to Companies Act is proposed to be removed.

- A New Part VI A is proposed to be inserted in the Companies Act to provide for matters relating to revival, rehabilitation and winding up of sick industrial Companies. This would result in the repeal of the Sick Industrial Companies (Special Provisions) Act.
- The definition of a "sick company" is proposed to be changed to include a company which has 50% erosion of net worth also as a sick company.
- Also, a company which fails to repay any amount to its creditor for any 3 consecutive quarters, shall also be treated as a sick company. It is interesting to observe that there is no minimum limit which has been prescribed here. Failure to repay even Rs. 100 for the specified time period would result in the company being categorised as a sick company. Also, the onus has been cast upon the Auditors to certify that the company is a sick company under this clause.
- A new fund is to be formed for the rehabilitation of sick companies and a levy is proposed to be made from all companies for contribution to the Fund. The levy is a percentage of the turnover of the Company. This is irrespective of whether the company is a profit making company or not. From the section, it also appears that even sick companies are liable to contribute to the Fund.
- Default in filing of Balance Sheet and Annual Return by companies for 5 consecutive years, has also been made as a ground for winding up the Company.
- All pending cases against Companies in any Forum under the Companies Act are proposed to be transferred to the High Court.

Companies (Second Amendment Bill) 2001

This Bill enables co-operatives to convert themselves as companies under the Companies Act. However, it is proposed to retain the salient features of a cooperative even after their conversion as companies.

This is proposed to be done by introduction of a new Part IX A under the Companies Act to deal with such companies. This conversion can be done only if two-thirds of the of the members agree. The converted company would be designated as "producer company" to indicate that ownership and transfer of shares of such companies are restricted.

Companies (Amendment) Ordinance, 2001 – Dated 23.10.2001

The Ordinance empowers Companies to buy back their own shares without seeking approval of the shareholders.

Such companies can pass a board resolution and buy back upto 10% of the total paid up equity capital and free reserves of the Company

Once such a buy back offer has been made, the Company is prohibited from making another buy back for another 1 year.

Companies are now permitted to come out with a further issue of shares after 6 months from the date of buy back. Earlier, companies were prohibited from coming out with a further issue of shares for a period of 24 months from the date of the buy back.

Amendments to Foreign Exchange Management Act, 2000

The Foreign Exchange Management Act (FEMA) came into force with effect from 1st June 2000, thereby replacing the earlier enactment – the Foreign Exchange Regulation Act, 1973.

The introduction of FEMA has been welcomed by all sections of people – both the industry and the professionals. FEMA has led to considerable liberalisation of the foreign exchange regime in India, coinciding with the comfortable foreign exchange reserves of India. The object behind introduction of FEMA is to free all current account transactions, while capital account transactions would continue to be regulated by the RBI. However, the process of approvals has been made simpler.

FEMA is broadly divided into 7 Chapters and 49 Sections. Under FEMA, there are the Rules which are notified by the Government of India relating to Current Account Transactions. With regard to Capital Account Transactions, the RBI has issued notifications and circulars permitting certain capital account transactions.

After the enactment of FEMA, some major amendments have been carried out in FEMA.

These relate to:

- Automatic Approval for External Commercial Borrowings
- Amendments relating to Inbound Investments
- Amendments relating to Outbound Investments
- Other Amendments

Automatic Approval for External Commercial Borrowings

The RBI has vide A.P.D.I.R Circular Number 10, dated 5th September 2000, considerably liberalised the procedure for making External Commercial Borrowings.

Accordingly, now it is possible to borrow amounts upto US $ 50 Million without taking prior approval of the Ministry of Finance/RBI, subject to the following conditions:

(i) The loan is raised from internationally acceptable and recognized lenders

(ii) The average maturity of the loan is not less than 3 years

(iii) The loan should be organised through a reputed merchant banker registered with the regulatory authorities of the host country.

Amendments relating to Inbound Investments

Registered Foreign Venture Capital Investors permitted to invest in Indian Venture Capital Companies. Vide A.P.D.I.R Circular Number 24, dated 6th January 2001, the RBI has now permitted foreign venture capital investors to invest in India Venture capital undertakings.

However, this does not come under the automatic route, and the foreign investor must seek approval before making such investment.

It is necessary that the Foreign Venture Capital Investor (FVCI) must be registered with the SEBI and must apply to the RBI through SEBI to invest in an Indian Venture Capital Undertaking.

The FVCI may purchase or sell the securities held by it in the Indian Venture Capital Undertaking at any price and shall also adhere to the relevant SEBI Guidelines.

Foreign Investment prohibited in Print Media

Earlier, foreign investment was permitted in the print media sector. However, the RBI has vide, A.P.D.I.R Circular Number 24, dated 6th January 2001, prohibited any foreign investment in the print media sector under both the Direct Investment Route and under the Portfolio Investment Route.

Prohibition on Overseas Corporate Bodies to make further investments in Indian Companies under the Portfolio Investment Scheme

Foreign Investment was permitted under the Portfolio Investment Scheme (PIS) route for all categories of investors – FIIs, OCBs, NRIs etc, subject to certain sectoral caps.

Overseas Corporate Bodies (OCBs) – are entities that are incorporated abroad where the beneficial ownership by Non Resident Indians exceeds 60% or more.

OCBs were permitted to invest in the Indian Companies, both under the Foreign Direct Investment Scheme and also under the Portfolio Investment Scheme. However, the OCBs were not registered with any regulatory agency in India such as SEBI or RBI.

Considering the recent trends in the stock markets and the role played by OCBs, the Government has decided to prohibit OCBs from making any further investments in Indian Companies under the PIS Route. They are permitted to retain their existing investments till such time they are sold. However, they are permitted to invest in Indian

Companies under the Foreign Direct Investment Route – vide A.P.D.I.R Circular Number 13 (2001-02), dated 29th November, 2001.

Amendments relating to Outbound Investments

Rules for direct investments outside India liberalised

The RBI has vide A.P.D.I.R Circular Number 13 (2001-02), dated 29th November, 2001 further liberalised the rules for foreign direct investments outside India by Indian Companies. Accordingly,

- o Indian Companies can now freely invest upto US $ 50 Million in a financial year in JV/Wholly Owned Subsidiaries outside India, provided the entity is engaged in the similar line of business. The requirement that the Indian Entity should have a 3 year profitability track record, has also been dispensed with.
- o Indian Companies, which have issued ADR/GDR, can also use 100% of such proceeds for overseas investments as against the limit of 50% earlier.
- o Registered Partnership Firms in India are now permitted to invest upto USD 1 Million in a financial year, in foreign concerns which are engaged in the similar line of business. However, such firms should be members of Indian Professional bodies such as ICAI, Bar Council, ICSI etc.
- o Employees of Indian Branches/Indian Subsidiaries of Foreign Companies, are now permitted to acquire the shares offered by the parent foreign company upto a limit of USD 20,000 in a calender year. This has been increased from the earlier limit of USD 10,000 in a block of five years.

Other Amendments

- o Endorsement of the foreign exchange drawn on the passport, has now been made optional.
- o An Indian party can make a payment to a foreign company/entity, which has paid the guarantee amount on behalf of the Indian party.
- o Authorised Dealers have been permitted to grant loans to Non Residents in India in Indian Rupees for their official/personal purposes.
- o Foreign Nationals resident in India are now permitted to open foreign currency accounts outside India, without any approval from the RBI.
- o Indian companies are now permitted to payment in Rupees to its non whole time director, who is a non resident and who visits India, towards sitting fees, commission etc.

Companies Bill builds tough amendments for investors' protection The Companies (Amendment) Bill 2003 tabled in the Rajya Sabha by Finance Minister, Jaswant Singh has proposed tough amendments to the Companies Act, 1956 to improve corporate governance and reinforce investors' rights.

The Central Government can, for instance, attach the Bank accounts of persons associated with the securities market and their intermediaries for one month for violations of the Act. The Bill proposes to cap circular trading by entities engaged in share-broking – as seen in the last stock scam – by introducing restrictions on inter-corporate loans to be made and received by share-broking companies.

GETTING TOUGH

- Penalty for fraudulently including investors, including imprisonment.
- Reserves from revaluation of assets not to be used for issue of bonus shares. Interim dividends can't be revoked.
- Holding companies required to prepare consolidated financial statements. Net worth threshold lowered to Rs. 5 Crore for norms on board size and constitution of audit panel to apply.
- Promoters/directors must be identified at the time of incorporation.
- Number of investment firms an individual can float to be capped.
- Minimum holding to be prescribed to prevent proliferation of shall cos.
- To prevent recurrence of vanishing companies, the Bill mandates identification of promoters/directors at the time of incorporation.

- The Bill has also introduced provision that would enable the Central Government to prescribe a cap on the number of investment companies an individual can float and minimum shareholding to prevent proliferation of shell companies.
- An amendment to Section 372A of the Act proposes that a company should route all investments through a single investment company.
- To enable larger number of shareholders to attend AGMs, the Bill has said AGMs and other general meetings can be held on Sundays.
- Other provisions to protect investor interest include penalty for fraudulently inducing persons to investment money, including imprisonment. Such acts can fetch directors and officers of a company imprisonment for a term of six months to five years and a fine upto Rs. 1 lakh.
- Similarly, penalties have been introduced to bar allotment of shares if a minimum subscription is not received. Promoters and officers of such companies can be fined up to Rs. 50,000 and even imprisoned for upto two years if application money is not refunded within six months.
- Companies Bill limits voting rights to sectoral cap
- The Government is set to place restrictions on foreign investors seeking voting rights on preference share holdings in lieu of dividend in case of companies where sectoral caps for foreign equity participation apply. A provision to this effect has been included in the Companies Amendment Bill 2003.
- The provision has been introduced to ensure that the preference share route is not used by foreigners to gain control of a corporate entity.
- The existing provisions of the Companies Act, 1956 allow holders of cumulative preference shares to seek voting rights on all resolutions placed before the board of a company if they have not been paid dividend for two years.
- Similarly, the holders of non-cumulative preference shares are entitled to seek voting rights if the dividend remains unpaid for three years.

NO TROJAN HORSES

- Foreign investors in preference shares cannot vote if the Sectoral cap is topped.
- In all other cases differential voting will be allowed.
- Bill to let Government change rules to keep pace with FDI policy.

Once the new provisions come into force, foreign investors in preference shares of Indian companies would be entitled to voting rights on par with their holding only if the voting rights so acquired are within the Sectoral cap level. In all other cases, the holders would be entitled to differential voting rights.

More importantly, if the foreign equity participation is at the maximum permissible level in a Company the preference shareholder may not be allowed any voting rights. The amendment Bill will have provisions enabling the Government to place restrictions and make changes in accordance with changing FDI policy. The issue of restricting voting rights on preference shares if it leads to breach of Sectoral cap has been under consideration for almost two years now, ever since foreign investors in BPL Telecom sought voting rights on their preference shares.

That the amendment of the Companies Act, 1956 which came into existence in May 2006 envisages fewer sections, instead of more, is welcome in itself. In all other areas too, the new Act should reflect the spirit of the times — a liberalised regime and voluntary compliance consistent with sufficient safeguards to protect public interest.

The Government proposed to amend the present Companies Act, 1956 and simplify it by reducing the number of sections. Simultaneously, certain new provisions may be introduced. In the past, amendments to the Act were done piecemeal, such as the provision relating to inter-corporate borrowings, managerial remuneration, and so on. A holistic view needs to be taken of the entire Act and changes brought about in tune with the changing global conditions.

In the past five decades, the Companies Act has been amended more than 20 times, the last one being in 2002 based on the recommendations of the Sachar Committee. Instead of reducing, the changes have only increased the number of sections.

The Concept Paper, prepared by the Department of Company Affairs, indicates that the number of sections will be brought down from the present 658 to 289. If carried out faithfully, this is to be welcomed.

Besides the substantive Act, the Government has issued a large number of rules to administer the law. Yet, quite often, there is a conflict in interpretation by different authorities including the Benches at the appellate level.

No doubt, any law, more so that relating to taxation and company affairs, needs to be supported by rules issued under the rule-making power of the government. As they say, the devil lies in the detail! Therefore, rules must be framed with least ambiguity or scope for multiple interpretations.

In today's globalising economy, it is necessary that corporate managements are treated with a certain degree of trust and, towards that end, the law must provide for flexibility in management decisions, of course, with safeguards in the form of guidelines to be voluntarily complied.

Already, the statutory meeting, which is a mere formality and the first milestone after incorporation essentially to inform shareholders that all legal formalities have been completed and that the company has had a trouble-free birth, has been dispensed with.

Restrictions on the conduct of annual general meetings on Sundays and public holidays may also go and this will ensure better attendance by members. There is also a suggestion in the Concept Paper to expand the scope for postal ballot. This is to be welcomed. Section 285 stipulates that the board meeting should be held at least once in three months.

In keeping with advances in technology, it is proposed to allow video-conferencing for board meetings with valid minutes being kept as stipulated. However, the government may specify powers that cannot be exercised in meetings held through video-conferencing. These are new provisions dictated by the advances in communication technology that help in speedy decision-making.

However, in certain other areas crucial to the functioning of corporate institutions in a fast changing global environment where they have to plan for mergers and acquisitions or restructuring and expansion of business, there may be certain limitations. The proposed restriction on the subsidiary structure is one such.

For example, the Concept Paper stipulates that a subsidiary of a parent company cannot have a subsidiary of its own. In other words, a multi-layered subsidiary structure is ruled out. The reason is not clear. If it is feared that this may lead to concentration of power through interlocking directorships, that can easily be taken care of by restricting the numbers.

Similarly, any fear that funds from one entity may be diverted to another is also unwarranted since this will be subject to provisions of the Act and shareholder's approval. In today's business environment, corporates must enjoy the freedom to alter the structure in line with profit expectations and specialisation.

Then, there is the question of independent directors. Their role has been the subject of discussion for quite some time now.

Essentially, independent directors on the boards of companies receiving loans from financial institutions has been the conventional practice. Such directors, appointed by the financial institutions, are supposed to act as the custodians of the FIs' interests in the company.

It is proposed that while the number of directors for a public limited company be kept at a minimum of three, a public company with paid-up capital or turnover of a prescribed level (to be specified), this number may be fixed at seven of whom not less than three, or nearly 50 per cent of the board strength, shall be independent directors. They do not function in an executive capacity and receive only director's remuneration and no other pecuniary benefits.

The problem in India is the absence of an adequate number of qualified and experienced senior executives who can function effectively as independent directors without becoming captive to managements interests. Not being an organic part of the company, such independent directors have to depend on their intuition and business acumen to deal with tricky situations.

Merely prescribing that 50 per cent of the board may consist of independent directors will only open the floodgates to several persons not adequately equipped to do that function. Per contra, several board-managed public companies have a good track record of ethical standards. Therefore, the need of the hour is to induct greater professionalism and accountability.

New compulsions such as compliance with environment standards, quality of products or services, global competition, and so on, call for specialised knowledge and skill at the board level.

It is worth considering if a training institution, under the aegis of financial institutions, can be set up to create a cadre of independent directors who may be professionally well equipped. As recommended by the Naresh Chandra Committee, the Concept Paper proposes to introduce an audit committee in public companies with a prescribed level of paid-up capital.

Independent directors may have a role in such audit committees. Also, accepting the Naresh Chandra Committee recommendation, a special audit concept will be introduced. The present Section 79 of the Companies Act governs "related party transactions". The scope of this Section may be amplified to cover provision of services, loans, leasing, underwriting, and appointment of agents.

A proposal has also been mooted to levy and collect cess on turnover or gross receipts of companies to using such money for the rehabilitation or revival or protection of assets of sick industrial companies. Such levy may not be less than 0.005 per cent and not more than 0.1 per cent on the value of annual turnover or gross receipt, whichever happens to be more. This is a proposal in the Companies Amendment Act 2000, which has so far not been implemented. The moot point here is not so much about the levy of cess as how it will be administered.

How will one decide whether the assets of sick companies can be rehabilitated? Is the bureaucracy well-equipped to handle this job? Would it not be better to ensure such a revival to market forces to be brought about by healthy companies taking them over or inducting better management on mutually acceptable terms? In extreme cases, it might even be better to let chronically sick units to die rather than throw good money after bad in the hope of revival.

Obviously, there has been opposition to the proposal from the corporate sector and chambers of commerce on the ground that it is unfair to penalise healthy companies for the cause of removing sickness in industry without a *quid pro quo*. No such system seems to exist in other countries. The bureaucracy's extended arm of patronage at somebody's cost cannot be the right approach. This provision, therefore, needs to be carefully examined.

There is a proposal to make defaults in repayment of public deposits a cognisable offence, resulting in arrests of such defaulting managements. In recent times, there have been not only cases of even the so called reputed companies defaulting in their obligations to repay fixed deposits but companies were formed with misleading names essentially to defraud innocent public depositors and disappear with their cash.

There is no doubt a need for power in government hands to take appropriate action in cases of wilful fraud or reckless management action. Such a provision has to be built into the Act. But in times of business uncertainty caused by market failures, technological limitations or product obsolescence there has to be some flexibility to allow managements to reschedule payments within reasonable time under Government scrutiny.

Prosecutions as a first step may not be warranted though tightened supervisory mechanism as in the banking sector may be justified to prevent fraud or misappropriation of public deposits. Here, the institutions may be too large and widespread.

One way to simplify the Act is, wherever feasible, prescribing guidelines for company managements to adopt and comply with. In such cases, experience will lead to the evolution of right procedures. The Concept Paper has indicated that, as per Section 52 of the Act, a holding company shall have the option to prepare consolidated accounts, including balance sheets and profit and loss accounts for its subsidiaries and for itself.

This shall be in sufficient compliance with the Act. But, elsewhere, under Section 53, the directors are obliged to prepare separate annual accounts for the holding company and its subsidiaries.

There seems to be an apparent contradiction between the two sections and needs to be resolved. A consolidated accounts with highlights of financial results, in brief, of its subsidiaries in a prescribed format, can be an alternative.

There are several other provisions of the Act such as appointment of managerial personnel and fixing their remuneration, passing of resolution, and so on, where there are no major discrepancies to warrant detailed discussion.

Suffice it to state that a stage has been reached when the new Act should reflect the spirit of the times — liberalised regime and voluntary compliance consistent with sufficient safeguards to protect public interest.

Good corporate governance should, in major part, take care of these requirements. The Government should quickly come out with the draft Bill and open it for public debate before passing the law.

The Companies (Amendment) Act, 2006 providing for obtaining Director Identification Number by directors, electronic filing of returns with the Registrar of Companies has come into effect to give statutory sanction to the e-governance initiatives. The text of the Companies (Amendment) Act, 2006 is given below:

Companies (Amendment) Act, 2006

[Act No. 23 of 2006, dated 29-5-2006]

An Act further to amend the Companies Act, 1956.

BE it enacted by Parliament in the Fifty-seventh Year of the Republic of India as follows:

Short title and commencement.

1. (1) This Act may be called the Companies (Amendment) Act, 2006.

(2) It shall come into force on such date as the Central Government may, by notification, appoint and different dates may be appointed for different provisions of this Act.

Amendment of section 253

2. In section 253 of the Companies Act, 1956 (1 of 1956) (hereinafter referred to as the principal Act), the following proviso shall be inserted, namely:

Provided that no company shall appoint or re-appoint any individual as director of the company unless he has been allotted a Director Identification Number under section 266B..

Insertion of new sections 266A, 266B, 266C, 266D, 266E, 266F and 266G

3. After section 266 of the principal Act, the following sections shall be inserted, namely:

Director Identification Number

266A. Application for allotment of Director Identification Number. Every

(a) individual, intending to be appointed as director of a company; or

(b) director of a company appointed before the commencement of the Companies (Amendment) Act, 2006, shall make an application for allotment of Director Identification Number to the Central Government in such form, and manner (including electronic form) alongwith such fee, as may be prescribed:

Provided that every director, appointed before the commencement of the Companies (Amendment) Act, 2006, shall make, within sixty days of the commencement of the said Act, such application to the Central Government:

Provided further that every applicant, who has made an application under this section for allotment of Director Identification Number, may be appointed as a director in a company, or, hold office as director in a company till such time such applicant has been allotted Director Identification Number.

266B. Allotment of Director Identification Number. The Central Government shall, within one month from the receipt of the application under section 266A, allot a Director Identification Number to an applicant, in such manner as may be prescribed.

266C. Prohibition to obtain more than one Director Identification Number. No individual, who had already been allotted a Director Identification Number under section 266B, shall apply, obtain or possess another Director Identification Number.

266D.Obligation of director to intimate Director Identification Number to concerned company or companies. Every existing director shall, within one month of the receipt of Director Identification Number from the Central Government, intimate his Director Identification Number to the company or all companies wherein he is a director.

266E. Obligation of company to inform Director Identification Number to Registrar. (1) Every company shall, within one week of the receipt of intimation under section 266D, furnish the Director Identification Number of all its directors to the Registrar or any other officer or authority as may be specified by the Central Government.

(2) Every intimation under sub-section (1) shall be furnished in such form and manner as may be prescribed.

266F. Obligation to indicate Director Identification Number. Every person or company, while furnishing any return, information or particulars as are required to be furnished under this Act, shall quote the Director Identification Number in such return, information or particulars in case such return, information or particulars relate to the director or contain any reference of the director.

266G. Penalty for contravention of provisions of section 266A or section 266C or section 266D or section 266E. If any individual or director, referred to in section 266A or section 266C or section 266D or a company referred to in section 266E, contravenes any of the provisions of those sections, every such individual or director or the company, as the case may be, who or which, is in default, shall be punishable with fine which may extend to five thousand rupees and where the contravention is a continuing one, with a further fine which may extend to five hundred rupees for every day after the first during which the contravention continues.

Explanation. For the purposes of sections 266A, 266B, 266C, 266D, 266E and 266F, the Director Identification Number means an identification number which the Central Government may allot to any individual, intending to be appointed as director or to any existing directors of a company, for the purpose of his identification as such.

Insertion of new sections 610B, 610C, 610D and 610E

4. After section 610A of the principal Act, the following sections shall be inserted, namely:

610B. Provisions relating to filing of applications, documents inspection, etc. through electronic form.(1) Notwithstanding anything contained in this Act, and without prejudice to the provisions contained in section 6 of the Information Technology Act, 2000 (21 of 2000), the Central Government may, by notification in the Official Gazette, make rules so as to require from such date as may be specified in the rules, that —

(a) such applications, balance sheet, prospectus, return, declaration, memorandum of association, articles of association, particulars of charges, or any other particulars or document as may be required to be filed or delivered under this Act or rules made thereunder, shall be filed, through the electronic form and authenticated in such manner as may be specified in the rules;

(b) such document, notice, any communication or intimation, required to be served or delivered under this Act, shall be served or delivered under this Act through the electronic form and authenticated in such manner as may be specified in the rules;

(c) such applications, balance sheet, prospectus, return, register, memorandum of association, articles of association, particulars of charges, or any other document and return filed under this Act or rules made thereunder shall be maintained by the Registrar in the electronic form and registered or authenticated, as the case may be, in such manner as may be specified in the rules;

(d) such inspections of the memorandum of association, articles of association, register, index, balance sheet, return or any other document maintained in the electronic form, which is otherwise available for such inspection under this Act or rules made thereunder, may be made by any person through the electronic form as may be specified in the rules;

(e) such fees, charges or other sums payable under this Act or rules made thereunder shall be paid through the electronic form and in such manner as may be specified in the rules;

(f) the Registrar shall, register change of registered office, alteration of memorandum of association or articles of association, prospectus, issue certificate of incorporation or certificate of commencement of business, register such document, issue such certificate, record notice, receive such communication as may be required to be registered or issued or recorded or received, as the case may be, under this Act or rules made thereunder or perform duties or discharge functions or exercise powers under this Act or rules made thereunder or do any act which is by this Act directed to be performed or discharged or exercised or done by the Registrar, by the electronic form, in such manner as may be specified in the rules.

(2) The Central Government may, by notification in the Official Gazette, frame a scheme to carry out the provisions specified under sub-section (1) through the electronic form:

Provided that the Central Government may appoint different dates in respect of different Registrar of Companies or Regional Directors from which such scheme shall come into force.

610C. Power to modify Act in relation to electronic records (including the manner and form in which electronic records shall be filed). (1) The Central Government may, by notification in the Official Gazette, direct that any of the provisions of this Act, so far as it is required for the purpose of electronic record specified under section 610B in the electronic form,

(a) shall not apply, in relation to the matters specified under clauses (a) to (f) of sub-section (1) of section 610B, as may be specified in the notification; or

(b) shall apply, in relation to the matters specified under clauses (a) to (f) of sub-section (1) of section 610B only with such consequential exceptions, modifications or adoptions as may be specified in the notification:

Provided that no such notification which relates to imposition of fines or other pecuniary penalties or demand or payment of fees or contravention of any of the provisions of this Act or offence shall be issued under this sub-section.

(2) A copy of every notification proposed to be issued under sub-section (1), shall be laid in draft before each House of Parliament, while it is in session, for a total period of thirty days which may be comprised in one session or in two or more successive sessions, and if, before the expiry of the session immediately following the session or the successive sessions aforesaid, both Houses agree in disapproving the issue of the notification or both Houses agree in making any modification in the notification, the notification shall not be issued or, as tho case may be, shall be issued only in such modified form as may be agreed upon by both the Houses. 610D. Providing of value added services through electronic form. The Central Government may provide such value added services through the electronic form and levy such fees as may be prescribed.

610E. Application of provision of Act 21 of 2000. All the provisions of the Information Technology Act, 2000 relating to the electronic records (including the manner and format in which the electronic records shall be filed), in so far as they are not inconsistent with this Act, shall apply, or in relation, to the records in electronic form under section 610B.

Some of the major changes envisaged through the proposed Amendment Bill are as follows:

- Allotment of Director Identification Number (DIN) to any individual, intending to be appointed as director in a company or for any existing director of a company, for the purpose of his identification as such, through electronic mode;
- Ensuring secure e filing and authentication of documents consistent with Information Technology Act, 2000 through Digital Signature Certificates. This modality would prevent any tempering of e-documents subsequent to filing. The e-documents shall be registered, maintained and inspected through electronic mode;
- Provision of such value added services by the Government through electronic forms from the electronic database created in the data process.
- Enabling powers to the Government to prescribe rules where necessary to facilitate e filing by corporate entities and access to corporate data statutorily placed in the public domain.

PRACTICE QUESTIONS

1. What are the characteristics of a company?
2. State the principles of law laid down in *Salomon v. Salomon & Co.* What are the statutory exceptions to the decision in *Salomon's case?*
3. "The legal personality of a company is distinct and different from its members individually and collectively." Comment and point out the circumstances when the separate of a company is disregarded by the courts.
4. Distinguish between a public limited company and private limited company.
5. What are the provisions of the Companies Act, 1956 for the conversion of (i) a private company into a public company; and (ii) a public company into a private company.
6. Explain (i) a company limited by guarantee (ii) a one-man company and (iii) an association not for profit, (iv) holding company and its subsidiary.
7. Write notes on the following: (i) minimum members of a company (ii) maximum members of a company, and (iii) illegal association.
8. Who is a promoter? Explain duties and liabilities of promoters.
9. Write notes on (i) certificate of incorporation, (ii) commencement of business.
10. State the usual steps to be taken in the formation of a company under the Companies Act, 1956.

11. Is a contract made before incorporation of a proposed company binding on it?
12. Write a short note on 'consequences of incorporation of a company'.
13. Define memorandum of association. What does it contain?
14. How are alterations made in a memorandum of association?
15. Define articles of association. Can articles of association be altered?
16. State the relation of a memorandum of association with the articles of association.
17. Explain the doctrine of *ultra vires* in the context of joint stock companies.
18. Explain the interrelationship of Doctrine of Constructive Notice with the Doctrine -of Indoor Management. State the exceptions, if any, to the Doctrine of Indoor management.

What is a prospectus? Who are liable for misstatements in a prospectus? Explain the extent of civil and criminal liability for such misstatements.

20. Write a short note on statement in lieu of prospectus.
21. State the restrictions and limitations on inviting and accepting deposits by companies.
22. (a) What is a misstatement in a prospectus? (b) What are the defences available to a director for any misstatement in a prospectus?
23. Discuss the remedies available to an allottee who had applied for shares on the faith of a false prospectus.
24. Define 'share' and 'stock' and distinguish between the two.
25. Write notes on the following: (i) Issue of shares at premium (ii) Issue of shares at discount.
26. Describe the procedure for alteration of share capital.
27. Describe the procedure for reduction of share capital.
28. Write short notes on: (i) Right shares (ii) Bonus shares
29. A company limited by shares intends to buy some of its own shares. Advise.
30. Explain the provisions regarding the increase of the subscribed capital by a public company by allotment of further shares.
31. What is meant by allotment of shares? State the statutory requirements in this respect.
32. What are the consequences cf an irregular allotment of shares?
33. "A share certificate is prima facie evidence of the title of the person whose name is entered on it." Comment.
34. Write short note on: (i) Listing of shares, (ii) Opening and closing the subscription list, (iii) Return of allotment (iv) Duplicate share certificate.
35. How is membership of a company acquired? Distinguish between a member and a shareholder.
36. How does one cease to be a member of a company?
37. Write short notes on: (i) Annual Return (ii) Reissue of forfeited shares. *Transfer and* 1.
38. The Articles of association of a public limited company empower the Board of Directors to refuse registration of transfer of its shares without assigning any reasons. Is it valid?
39. Explain the provisions regarding refusal to transfer shares.
40. Distinguish between transfer and transmission of shares.
41. What are the legal requirements which a company must comply with while borrowing?
42. What is *ultra vires* borrowing? What remedies are available to a lender if a company resorts to *ultra vires* borrowing.
43. What is a debenture? What are the different kinds of debentures that may be issued by a company? Distinguish between a share and a debenture.
44. What is a floating charge? Explain the circumstances in which a 'floating charge' becomes fixed.
45. Distinguish between floating and fixed charge.
46. What charges are registered under the Companies Act, 1956?
47. What is the effect of non-registration of a registrable charge?
48. "All investments made by a company must be held by it in its own name." *General* 1.
49. What are the different kinds of general meetings of a company?
50. Define statutory meeting of a public company.
51. Summarise the provisions as regards annual general meeting.
52. What are the provisions of the Companies Act, 1956 in respect of an extraordinary general meeting to be held on requisition?

53. Write a short note on the powers of the Tribunal to call meetings.
54. Write short notes on: (i) Notice of a meeting (ii) Proxy (iii) Voting by poll (iv) Resolutions (v) Explanatory statement (vi) Quorum
55. What books of account is a company bound to maintain?
56. Give the provisions relating to the preparation authentication, circulation, adoption and filing of the annual accounts of a company.
57. How is an auditor appointed? What are the matters to be stated in his report?
58. Write a short note on qualifications and disqualification of auditors.
59. State briefly the provisions relating to the appointment of the first auditor of a company.
60. State the law relating to appointment and remuneration of auditors.
61. (a) What is dividend? (b) What are the conditions to be fulfilled before a company may declare and pay dividend? (c) To whom should such a dividend be paid.
62. Are company directors trustees or agents of the company? Explain.
63. How is a dirçctor (i) appointed and (ii) removed from office?
64. What are the disqualifications of a person for appointment as the director of a company?
65. State in relation to a public company: (i) When additional directors can be appointed and for what period? (ii) When an alternate director can be appointed and for what period? (iii) How the office of a director is filled in case of a casual vacancy and for what period?
66. When can Board of Directors appoint directors?
67. State the circumstances under which a director would vacate office.
68. Total strength of the Board of Directors of a company is ten. How many directors are liable to retire by rotation at the next annual general meeting?
69. When can directors be appointed by the principle of proportional representation under s.265? (a) What do you understand by an office or place of profit held by a director in a company? (b) What restrictions have been imposed in respect of holding an office or place of profit by a director.
70. State the requirements of the Companies Act with respect to contracts in which particular directors are interested.
71. How many meetings of a Board of Directors of a company must be held in a year and at what intervals?
72. Define Managing Director and state the statutory provisions regarding his appointment and remuneration.
73. What are the powers of directors that cannot be exercised without the approval of members given in a general meeting?
74. Distinguish between a managing director and a whole-time director.
75. Can a director be paid compensation for loss of office?
76. Write short notes on: (i) alternate director, (ii) managerial remuneration, and *Inter-Corporate*
77. Explain the term 'secretary' Describe the provisions regarding compulsory appointment of a secretary.
78. Describe the qualifications which a person must possess for appointment as a company secretary.
79. Explain the true scope of the rule in *Foss v. Harbottle* on the majority rule and minority rights state the exception to the rule.
80. State the provisions of the Companies Act on prevention of oppression and mismanagement.
82. Explain the powers of the Central Government to appoint directors on the Board of a company to prevent oppression and mismanagement.
83. Explain the term 'compromise', 'arrangement', 'reconstruction' and 'amalgamation'. Who can apply to court for compromise or arrangement?
83. Who is a dissenting shareholder in case of 'amalgamation' of companies? What are the provisions with regard to the acquisition of shares of dissenting shareholders?
84. Summarise the provisions of s.395 relating to takeover of a company by acquisition of its shares.
86. What are the duties of the Board of directors of a company which has become a sick industrial company?
87. Describe the procedure to be followed for an inquiry into the working of a sick industrial company.
88. What measures can be taken in respect of a company where orders have been made by the Tribunal after the completion of an inquiry into its working?
89. Write explanatory notes on the following: (a) Industrial company; (b) Net worth (c) Sick industrial company, (d) Rehabilitation of a sick industrial company by giving financial assistance, (e) Winding up of a sick industrial company (f) misfeasance proceedings.

90. What is winding up? Discuss the circumstances in which a company may be wound up by the Tribunal.
91. What is the effect of a winding up order passed by the Tribunal?
92. Define the term 'contributory'. Discuss the liability of members of a company in the event of its being wound up.
93. Explain the procedure to wind up a company voluntarily.
94. What is a defunct company? What procedure is followed to dissolve it?
95. What is the difference between winding up and dissolution?
    (a) Primary Produce (c) Producer Company (d) Withheld Price

References

1. R.D. Singh v. Secretary, Bihar State Small Industries Corpn, (1975) 45 Comp cas 527.
2. Kathiawar Industries Ltd. v. c.G. of Evacerce Property (1967) AIR Punj 337.
3. Salomon v. Salomon and Co. Ltd. (1897) AC 22.
4. Lee v. Lee Air Farming Limited (1960) 3 All ER 420 PC.
5. Bacha F. Guzdar v. The Commissioner of Income-Tax, Bombay AIR (1955) SC 74.
6. Gower L.C.B., The Principles of Modern Company Law 3rd Ed. (1976) Footnote P.76.
7. State Trading Corporation of India Ltd. v. Commercial Tax Officer. (1963) 2 Comp L.J. 234 (S.c.).
8. Prithivi Cotton Mills v. Broach Borough Municipality AIR 1968, Gujarat 235.
9. Jupiter General Insurance Co. v. A; Rajagopalan (1952) Punj 11.
10. Lord Blackburn in Rre Bhhia and San Franciso Rly. Company (1865) 3 Q.B. 515.
11. Salomon v. Salomon and Co. (1897) AC. 22.
12. Juggilal v. I.T. Commissioner Al.R. (1969) S.C. 982.
13. Sir Dinshaw Maneekjee Petit, Re AIR (1927) Born. 371.
14. Workmen of Associated Rubber Industry Ltd. v. Associated Rubber Industry Ltd. (1986) 59 Compo Cas. 134 (S.C.).
15. Tata Engg. and Locomotive Co. Ltd. v. State of Bihar AIR (1965) S.c. 40.
16. Jones v. Lipman (1962) All E.R. 342.
17. Gilford Motor Co. Ltd. v. Home (1933) Ch 935 C.A
18. Delhi Development Authority v. Skipper Construction Company (P) Ltd. (1996) 4 SC ALE 202.
19. Smith Stone and Knight Ltd. v. Birmingham Corporation (1939) All E.R. 116.
20. Connors Ltd. v. Connors (1940) 4 All E.R. 174.
21. Daimler Co. Ltd. v. Continental Tyre and Rubber Co. (1916) 2 AC 307.
22. v.v. Ruia v. Dalmia (1930) P.c. 300.
23. Pannaji v. Senaji AIR (1968) Born. 347.
24. New Mofussil Co. Ltd. v. Rustomji 38 Born. L.R. 408.
25. Greenberg v. Cooperstein (1926) 2 Ch 667.
26. Madan Lal v. Janki Prasad 49 All 319.
27. Gujarat Trading Co. v. Tricumji (1954).
28. Free Wheel (India) Ltd. v. Dr. Veda Mitra (1969) A.I.R. Delhi 258.
29. Saloman v. Saloman and Co. Ltd. (1897) AC. 22.
30. T.R. Pratt (Bombay) Ltd. v. E.D. Sassoon and Co. Ltd., AIR (1936) Born. 62.
31. Excepting the provisions of Section 603 regarding the prospectus.
32. Quotations ofG.W. Gerstenberg, Financial organisation and Management of Business, P.-189.
33. C.M. Schmitihoff, Palmer's Company Law, 20th Edition.
34. Whaley Bridge Calico Printing Co. v. Green and Smith (1880) 5 Q.B.D. 109.
35. Erianger v. New Sombrero Phosphate Co. (1878) 3 App Cas, 1218.
36. Cape Breton Co., Re (1885) 29 Ch. D. 795.
37. Kelnerv.Baxter(1866)L.R.2C.P.174.
38. Park v. Modem Woodmen 181 All 214-234.
39. Re English and Colonial Produce Co. (1906) 2 Ch 435.
40. Natal Land and Colonisation Co. v. Pauline Colliery Syndicate (1904) AC 120.
41. Peel's case [Barned's Banking Co., Re Peel's case], (1867) L.R. 2 Ch 674.
42. Moosa Goolam Ariffv. Ebrahim Gulam Ariff.
43. Jubilee Cotton Mills Ltd. v. Lewis (1924) AC. 958.
44. T.v. Krishna v. Andhra Prabha (Pvt.) Ltd. Al.R. (1960) A.P. 123.
45. Guinness v. Land Corpn. oflreland. (1882) 22 Ch. d. 349.
46. Ashbury Ply, Carriage and Iron Co. Ltd. v. Riche, (1875) L.R. 7 H.L. 653.
47. Cotman v. Brougham (1918) AC. 514.
48. Osborn v. The Bank of U.S., 9 Wheat (22 U.S.) 733.
49. British Bata Shoe Co. Ltd. v. Czechoslovak Bata Co. Ltd. (1964) 64 R.P.C. 72.
50. Asiatic Govt. Security Life Insurance Co. Ltd. v. New Asiatic Insurance Co. Ltd. (1939) 9 Camp. Cas.208.
51. Atkins and Co. Ltd. v. Wardle (1889) 61 L.T. 23.
52. Dr. H.L. Batliwally Sons and Co. Ltd. v. Emperor (1941) 11 Compo Cas. 154 (Born).
53. C. Hansa v. Shakti Automobiles (P) Ltd. (1992) 73 Compo Cas 74 (Mad).

54. Durham Fancy Goods Ltd. v. Michael Jackson (Fancy Goods) Ltd. and Another (1968) 2 Q.B.
55. P Stacey and CO. v. Wallis (1912) 28 T.L.R. 219.
56. Dermatine CO. v. Ashworth (1905) 21 AT.L.R. 510.
57. Daimler Co. Ltd. v. continental Tyre and Rubber Co. Ltd. (1916) 2 AC. 307.
58. Daimler Co. Ltd. v. continental Tyre and Rubber Co. Ltd. (1916) 2 AC. 307.
59. Cotman v. Brougham (1918) A.C. 514.
60. Ashbury Ply, Carriage and Iron Co. Ltd. v. Riche, (1875) L.R. 7 H.L. 653.
61. Zuari Agro Chemicals Ltd. v. F.S. Wadia and others (1974) 44 Comp Cas 465.
62. Oriental Paper Mills Ltd. v. State AIR (1957) Ori 232.
63. Minerva Mills Ltd. v. GOVt. of Maharashtra (1975) 45 Compo Cas. 1 (Born).
64. Rank Film Distributors of India Ltd. v. Registrar of Companies, West Bengal AIR (1969) Cal. 32.
65. Scientific Poultry Breeder's Assn., Re (1933) Ch. 337.
66. Dalmia Cement (Bharat) Ltd. In re (1964) 34 Compo Cas. 729 (Mad.).
67. Delhi Bharat Grain Merchants Assn. Ltd., In re (1974) 44 Comp Cas 214 (Delhi).
68. Indian Mechanical Gold Extracting Company, In Re (1891) 3 Ch. 538.
69. Egyptian Delta Land and Investment Co. Re (1907) W.N. 16.
70. In re Ambala Electric Supply Co. Ltd (1963) 33 Comp Cas 585 (Punjab).
71. Parent Tyre Co. Ltd. In re (1922) 2 Ch 222.
72. Juggilal Kamlapati Jute Mills v. Registrar of Companies (1966) 1 Comp L.J. 292.
73. Punjab Distilling Industries Ltd. v. Registrar of Companies (1963) 83 Compo Cas. 811 (Punj).
74. In re, Cyclists Touring Club Ltd. (1907) 1 Ch 269.
75. In Sipani Automobiles v. Chartered Secretary L.W.: 179: 10.93.
76. New Asiatic Insurance Co. Ltd., In re (1967) 37 Compo Cas 331 (Punj).
77. New Asarwa Mfg. Co. Ltd., In re (1975) 45 Comp Cas 151 (Guj.)
78. Motilal Padampati Sugar Mills Co. (P) Ltd. In re (1964) 34 Compo Cas 86 (All).
79. Straw Products Ltd. v. Registrar of Companies (1969) 30 Compo Cas. 974 (Ori.).
80. Hampstead Garden Suburb Trust Ltd., In re (19360 33 Compo Cas. 166.
81. Ashbury Ply, Carriage and Iron Co. Ltd. v. Riche, (1875) L.R. 7 H.L. 653.
82. National Telephone CO. v. St. Peter Port Constables (1900) A.c. 317.
83. Ashbury Ply, Carriage and Iron Co. Ltd. v. Riche, (1875) L.R. 7 H.L. 653.
84. Ramakrishna Industries (P) Ltd. and others v. P.R. Ramkrishna and others (1988) 64 Compo Cas.
85. Birds Investments Ltd. v. C.LT. (1965) 35 Comp Cas. 147 Cal.
86. Allen v. Gold Reef of West Africa (1900) 1 Ch. 656.
87. Southern Foundries (1926) Ltd. v. Shirlaw (1940) 2 All E.R. 445.
88. Greenhalgh v. Amerence Cinemas Ltd. (1950) 2 All E.R. 1120.
89. Sidebottom v. Kershaw Leese and Company Ltd. (1920) 1 Ch. 154.
90. The Pioneer Mutual Benefit and Friend-in-need Society Ltd. v. Assistant Registrar of Joint Stock Companies A 1933 Mad. 129.
91. Brown v. British Abrasive Wheel Co. Ltd. (1919) 1 Ch. 290.
92. Allen v. Gold Reefs of West Africa Ltd. 19001 Ch. 656.
93. Sidebottom v. Kershaw Leese and Co. (1920) Ch. 154 (C.A.).
94. Evans v. Chapman, (1902) 18 L.T. 506.
95. British Murace Syndicate Ltd. v. Alberton Rubber Co. (1915) 2 Ch. 186.
96. Scott v. Frank Scott (London) Ltd. 1940 Ch.794.
97. Pyare Lal Sharma v. Managing Director, J and K Industries Ltd. (1989) 3 Compo L.J. (S.c.) 70.
98. Byorn v. Metropolitan Omnibus Co. (1885) 27 L.J. Ch. 685.
99. Borland's Trustee v. Steel Bros and Co. Ltd. (1901) 1 Ch. 279.
100. v.B. Ramgaraj v. v.B. Gopalakrishanan (1992) 73 Compo Cas. 201 (S.c.).
101. Rayfield v. Hand (1960) Ch 1.
102. E1ey v. Positive Government Ass Co., (1876) 1 Ex. D. 88.
103. Kotla Venkataswamy v. Ram Murthy AIR (1934) Mad. 579.
104. Royal British Bank v. Turguand (1856) 6 E and B 327.
105. Pacific Coast Coal Mines Ltd. v. Arbuthnot (1917) AC. 607.
106. Dewan Singh v. Minerva Films Ltd. (1959) 29 Compo Cas. 263 (Punj)
107. Meenakshi Mills Ltd. v. Callianjee and Sons (1935) 5 Compo Cas. 103 (Mad.).
108. Ram Baran Singh v. Muffasi1 Bank Ltd. AIR (1925) All 206.
109. D. Pudamjee and Co. v.N.H. Moos AIR 1976 Born. 28.
110. Official Liquidator, Manasube and Co. (P) Ltd. v. Commissioner of Police (1968) 38 Compo 884 (Mad.).
111. Howard v. Patent Ivory Co. (1888) 38 Ch. 156.
112. A.L. Underwood v. Bank of Liverpool and Marines (1924) 1 K.B. 775
113. Ruben v. Great Fingal Consolidated Co. (19060 AC. 439.
114. Morris v. Kanssen (1946) AC. 459.
115. Kreditbank Cassel v. Schenkers Ltd. (1927) 1 K.B. 826.

116. Irvin v. Union Bank of Australia (1877) 2 App Cas 336. (P.c.).
117. The words 'inviting deposits' from the Public have been inserted by the Companies (Amendment) Act 1974.
118. Nash v. Lynde (1929) AC. 158.
119. Pramtha Nath Sanya1 v. Kali Kumar Dutt AIR (1925) Cal 714.
120. Rattan Singh v. Moga Transport Co. Ltd. AIR 1939 Punj 196.
121. Pramtha Nath Sanya1 v. Kali Kumar Dutt AIR (1925) Cal 714.
122. New Brunswick and Canada R1y. and Land CO. v. Muggeridge (1860) 3 L.T. 651.
123. Ross v. Estates Investment Co. (1868) 3 Ch. App. 682.
124. Hedley Byrne and Co. Ltd. v. Heller and Partners Ltd. (1964) AC. 465.
125. Stevens v. Hoare (1904) 20 T.R.R.407.
126. Derry v. Peak (1889) 14 App. Cas 337.
127. Balkrishna Gupta v. Swadeshi Polytex Ltd. [(1985) 58 Compo Cas. 563 (S.C.)]
128. Official Liquidator v. Su1eman Bhai AIR (1955) M.B. 116 S.
129. Sri Balaji Textiles Mills Pvt. Ltd. v. Shok Kamble (1989) Compo L.J. (Karn.) 322.
130. Aldborough Hotel Co.; Re Simpson's case (1896) 4 Ch. App. 184.
131. Mohari Bibi v. Dharmadas Ghose (1903) ILR 30 Cal. 539.
132. Palaniappi Mudaliar v. Official Liquidator, Pasupathi Bank Ltd. AIR (1942) Mad. 470.
133. Fazalbhoy Jaffar v. The Credit Bank of India (1914) 39 Born. 331.
134. Nandita Jain v. Bennet Coleman and Co. Ltd. Appeal No. 27 of 1972, Company News and Notes. Feb. 1973.
135. Trevor v. Whitworth (1887) 12 App. Cas. 409.
136. Wise v. Lansdell (1921) 1 Ch. 420 (Ch. D).
137. George Newman and Co. , Re (1895) 1 Ch. 674.
138. Bacha F. Guzdar v. Commissinor ofIncome Tax Bombay AIR (1955 S.c.) 74.
139. British India Corporation v. Robert Menzies AIR (1936) All. 468.
140. State of Bombay v. Bhandan Ram Bhandari AIR (1961) S.c. 186.
141. Pinkney and Sons Steamship Co. Ltd., Re (1892) 3 Ch. 125.
142. Gas Meter Co. Ltd. v. Diaphram and General Leather Co. Ltd. (1925) 41 T.L.R.342.
143. Borland's Trustee v. Steel Bros. and Co. Ltd. (1901) 1 Ch. 279.
144. Vishwanath v. East India Distilleries (1957) 27 Compo Cas. 175.
145. c.I.T. v. Associated Industrial Dev. Co. (1969) 2 Comp L.J. 19.
146. Morrice v. Aylmer (1974) 10 Ch App. 148, 154.
147. Sri Gopal Jalan and Co. v. Calcutta Stock Exchange Association Ltd. AIR 1964 SC 250.
148. House hold Fire Insurance Co. v. Grant (1879), 4 Ex. D. 216.
149. Ramagate Hotel CO. v. Monte fiore (1866) L.R. Ex. 109.
150. In Karachi Oil Products Ltd. v. Kamar Shree Narendra Singhji (1948) 18 Compo Cas. 215 (Born).
151. St. Mr. v.R.Murugappa Chettiar v. Pudukottai Creemics Ltd. (1955) 25 Compo cas 78 (Mad).
152. Ramanbhai v. Ghasi Ram (1918) Born L.R. 595.
153. Gackson v. Turquand (1869) L.R. 4 HL 305.
154. Re. Trans Atlantic Life Assurance Co. Ltd. (1979) 3 All E.R. 352.
155. Unit Trust of India v. Om Prakash Bertia (1983) 54 Compo Cas 723 (Born).
156. Estate v. Hira1a1, AIR 171 S.c. 920.
157. Ma1hrubhumi Printing and Publishing Co. Ltd. v. Vardhaman Publishers Ltd. (1992) 73 Camp. Cas. 150 (Ker).
158. Dipak Kumar Jayanti1a1 Shah v. The Atul Products Ltd. [Decided on 18-9-1992, Reported in Chartered Secretary , February 195 3 issue)
159. Dr. Jitendra Nath Saha and Another v. Shymal Montal (decided by Company Law Board on 25-8-92.
160. Balkis Consolidated Co. Ltd. v. Tomkinson (1893) A.c. 396.
161. Sheffield Corporation v. Barelay (1905) A.c. 392.
162. Arjun Prasad v. Central Bank of India AIR (1956) Pat. 32.
163. J. Dalmia v. Commr. ofIncome Tax (1964) 34 Compo Cas 668.
164. Neath Building Society v. Luce (1889) 43: Ch. D. 158.
165. Fir bank v. Humphreys and Others 91816) 18 Q.B.D. 54.
166. Weeks v. Propert (1873) L.R. 8 C.P.427.
167. State Bank of India v. Vishwanirayat (P) Ltd. (1987) 3 Compo L.J. 171.
168. Knightsbridge Estates Trust Ltd. v. Byrne (1940) A.C. 613.
169. Issue of debentures at a discount shall, however, be void and will be restrained if the issue is coupled with an option to the debenture holders to take fully paid shares of the company for the nominal amount of debentures at this would amount to issue of shares at a discount. [Moseley v. Koffyfontein Mines (1904) 2 Ch 108].
170. Re Yorkshire Wool Combers Association Ltd. (1903) 2 ch. 284.
171. Imperial Bank of India v. Bengal National Bank Ltd. (1931) 1 Compo Cas. 159.
172. Government Stock Investment Co. Ltd. v. Manila Railway Co. Ltd. (1897) A.C. 81.
173. Boray Co. Re. Foster v. Boray Co. (1901) 1 ch 326.
174. Illingworth v. Hou1dsworth (1904) A.C. 355.
175. Molton Finance Ltd., Re. (1968) Ch. 328.

176. Bath v. Standard Land Co. (1910) 2 Ch 408.
177. Forest of Dean Coal Mining Co. Re 91878) 10 Ch. D. 450.
178. Imperial Hydropathic Hotel Co., Black pool v. Hampson (1882) 23 Ch. D. 1.
179. Ferguson v. Wilson (1866) LR 2 Ch. App. 77.
180. Allen v. Hyalt (1914) 30 T.L.R. 444.
181. Gramophone and typewriter Ltd. v. Stanley (1908) 2 K.B. 89.
182. Queen and Axtens Ltd. v. Salmon (1908) A.c. 442 H.L.
183. Pothen v. Hindusthan Trading Corporation (P) Ltd. (1967) 37 Compo Cas. 266.
184. Alexander v. Automatic Telephone Co. (1900) 2 Ch. 56.
185. Pereiva1 v. Wright (1902) 2 Ch. 421.
186. Smith v. Anderson (1925) Ch 407.
187. Neville J. Bath v. Standard Land Co. (1910) 2 Ch. 408.
188. Suburban Bank Private Ltd., Trichur v. Thariath, A (1968) Ker. 206.
189. East Coast Transport and Shipping Co. Private Ltd. v. Official Liquidator (1962) 32 Comp cas 197.
190. Louis Steen v. Charles Allen Law (1964) 34 Comp Cas. 195.
191. Waman1a1 v. Scindia Steam Navigation Co. A (1944) Born. 131.
192. Sri Krishna Rathi v. Monda1 Bros. and Co. (P) Ltd. (1966) 1 Comp L.J. 10.
193. Howard Smith Ltd. v. Ampol Petroleum Ltd. (1974) All E.R. 1126.
194. Esparto Trading Co. Case (1879) 12 Ch D 291.
195. Gallow v. Halle Concerts Society (1915) 2 Ch 233.
196. City Equitable Fire Ins. Co., Re (1925) Ch 437.
197. Smt. Jain v. Delhi Flour Mills Co. Ltd. (1974) 44 Comp Cas 228.
198. Kaye v. Croydon Tramways Co. (1898) 1 Ch 358.
199. Panarama Developments (Guildford) Ltd. v. Furnishing Febries Ltd. (1971) 3 All E.R. 16-B.
200. In re Bank of Deacon Ltd AIR 1960 Kerala - 15.
201. Bharat Kumar Diwali v. Bharat Carbon and Ribbon Manufacturing Company Ltd. (1973) 43 Compo Cas. 19.
202. Fenton v. Thoriey and Co. Ltd. (1903) AC. 443.
203. Re Hart1ay Baird Ltd. (1954) 2 AFR 695.
204. Jackson v. Hamlyn (1953) All E.R. 887.
205. Cousins v. International Brick Co. (1931) 2 Ch. 90.
206. Foss v. Harbottle (1843) 2 Hare 461.
207. Menier v. Hooper's Telegraph Works Ltd. (1874) 9 Ch. App 350.
208. Maharani Lalita v. Indian Motor Co. 32 Comp Cas 207.
209. Re Antigen Laboratories Ltd. (1951) 1 All E.R. 110.
210. Thomas v. Bradbury Agrew and Co. (1906) 2 K.B. 627.
211. Stadmed Pr. Ltd v. Kshetra Mohan Shah A 1968 Cal. 572.
212. Re Abert David Ltd. 68 ewn 163, 170.
213. Richardson Eruddas Ltd. v. Haridas Mundra 63 C.W.N. 439.
214. Syed Mohamed v. R.s Sundaramoorthy A 2958 Mad 587.
215. J.K. Investment Trust Ltd. v. Muir Mills Co. Ltd. A 1961 All 413.
216. re: City Equitable Fire Insurance Co. (1925) Ch. 407.
217. Allen Craig and Co. (London) Ltd. Re (1934) W.N. 68.
218. Deputy Secretary to the Govt. of India, Ministry of Finance v. S.N. Das Gupta AI.R. (1955) Cal.
219. London and General Bank, Re (No.2) (1895) 2 Ch 573.
220. Union Bank of Allahabad Re A 1925 All 519.
221. Council of the Institute of Chartered Accountants of India v. Rajaram (1962) 32 Comp Cas 1153.
222. Official liquidator, Karachi Bank Ltd. v. S. Dewanmal (1933) 3 Comp Cas 23.
223. Newton v. Birmingham Small Arms Co. (1906) 2 Ch. (378).
224. Allen Craig and Co. (London) Re; 1934 All ER Rep 301.
225. Sudhiya v. Bihar National Insurance Co. AIR 1941.
226. Yenidjeje Tobacco Co., Ltd, Re (1916) 2 Ch 426.
227. German Date Coffee Co., Re (1882) 20 Ch. D 169.
228. Smt. Tarubala Sahu v. North Bank Ltd. (1972) 42 Compo Cas. 588 Cal.
229. S.R. Mathuswami Gounder and Others v. Official Liquidator (1970) 40 Compo Cas. 77.
230. Kondaskar v. I.T.O. (Companies circle), Bombay AIR (1972) SC 878.
231. Re Boxco Ltd. (1970) 2 WLR 959.

176. Salil v. Standard Land Co. (1910) 2 Ch 468.
177. Forest of Dean Coal Mining Co., Re (1878) 10 Ch. D. 450.
178. Imperial Hydropathic Hotel Co., Blackpool v. Hampson (1882) 23 Ch D 1.
179. Ferguson v. Wilson (1866) L.R. 2 Ch. App. 77.
180. Allen v. Hyatt (1914) 30 T.L.R. 444.
181. Gramophone and Typewriter Ltd. v. Stanley (1908) 2 K.B. 89.
182. Queen and Aeltas Ltd. v. Salmon (1909) A.C. 442 H.L.
183. Pothan v. Hindusthan Trading Corporation (P) Ltd. (1967) 37 Comp. Cas. 226.
184. Alexander v. Automatic Telephone Co. (1900) 2 Ch 56.
185. Bersel Mfg. v. Wright (1902) 2 Ch 442.
186. Smith v. Anderson (1823) Ch 401.
187. Neville J. Gash v. Standard Land Co. (1910) 2 Ch 468.
188. Subhash Bank Private Ltd., Trichur v. Thankam, A (1963) Ker. 205.
189. East Coast Transport and Shipping Co. Private Ltd. v. Official Liquidator (1966) 32 Comp. Cas. 15.
190. Louis Stein v. Claudee Allen Law (1954) 24 Comp. Cas. 166.
191. Wamgirrat v. Scindia Steam Navigation Co. A (1944) Bom. 131.
192. Shankar Prasad v. Munnal Brasama Co. (P) Ltd. (1961) 1 Comp. L.J. 105.
193. Howard Smith Ltd. v. Ampol Petroleum Ltd. (1974) All E.R. 1126.
194. Leopold Trading Co., Case (1875) 19 Ch D 291.
195. Garlov v. Nelle Qualeena Society (1945) 2 Ch 255.
196. City Equitable Fire Ins. Co., Re (1925) Ch 407.
197. Smt. Rani v. Delhi Flour Mills Co. Ltd. (1974) 44 Comp. Cas. 238.
198. Fyle v. Croydon Tramways Co. (1895) 1 Ch 358.
199. Langham Developments (Guildford) Ltd. v. Furnishing Fabrics Ltd. (1974) 3 All E.R. 1058.
200. In re Bank of Deccan Ltd. AIR 1960 Kerala 15.
201. Bharat Kumar Shah v. Thermal Carbon and Ribbon Manufacturing Company (1979) 49 Comp. Cas. [illegible]
202. Fenton v. Toohey and Co. Ltd. (1903) A.C. 443.
203. Re Hartley Baird Ltd. (1954) 2 All E.R. 695.
204. Jackson v. Hamlyn (1953) All E.R. 887.
205. Cousins v. International Brick Co. (1931) 2 Ch 90.
206. Ross v. Harbottle (1843) 2 Hare 461.
207. Musselwhite v. Musselwhite [illegible] Ltd. (1874) 9 Ch. App. 350.
208. Wadeerani Lalta v. Indian Motor Co. 32 Comp. Cas. 207.
209. Re [illegible] Laboratories Ltd. (1954) 1 All E.R. 1.
210. Thomas v. Bradbury Agnew and Co. (1906) 2 K.B. 627.
211. Maharajaj R. Ltd. v. Sukhra Nonali Bros. A 1958 Cal. 572.
212. Re Albert David Ltd. 68 C.W.N. 140.
213. Richardson Cruddas Ltd. v. Haridas Mundra 66 C.W.N. 438.
214. Syed Mohamed v. M.S. Sundaramoorthy A 2956 Mad 697.
215. J.K. Investment Trust Ltd. v. Mill Mills Co. Ltd. A 1961 All 413.
216. Re City Equitable Fire Insurance Co. (1925) Ch. 407.
217. Allen Craig and Co. (London) Ltd. Re (1934) Ch. 483.
218. Deputy Secretary to the Govt. of India, Ministry of Finance v. S.N. Das Gupta AIR (1956) Cal.
219. London and General Bank Ltd. (No. 2) (1895) 2 Ch 673.
220. Union Bank of Allahabad Re A 1925 All 119.
221. Council of the Institute of Chartered Accountants of India v. Rathnam (1963) 32 Comp. Cas. 1153.
222. Official Liquidator, Karachi Bank Ltd. v. S. Dewarmal (1958) 28 Comp. Cas. 29.
223. Newton v. Birmingham Small Arms Co. (1906) 2 Ch. 378.
224. Allen Craig and Co. (London) Re. 1934 All E.R. Rep. 38.
225. Sudhir v. Bharat National Insurance Co. AIR 1943.
226. Vandane Tobacco Co. Ltd. Re (1918) 2 Ch 426.
227. German Date Coffee Co., Re (1882) 20 Ch D 169.
228. Smt. Tarkash Sahu v. North Bank Ltd. (1972) 42 Comp. Cas. 368 Cal.
229. S.E. Mathuswami Gounder and Others v. Official Liquidator (1970) 40 Comp. Cas. 772.
230. Kontacker v. T.C. (Companies circle), Bombay AIR (1972) SC 876.
231. Re Bexendale (1970) 2 W.L.R. 469.

PART M

RIGHT TO INFORMATION ACT, 2005

CHAPTER

53

Right to Information Act, 2005

INTRODUCTION

Information is oxygen for the democratic society. In a foreword by the Director of General of UNESCO to the Mac Bride Report titled "Many Voices, One World", the distinguished statesman emphasizes that communication is at the heart of all social intercourse.

Liberty of thought is the basis of freedom of speech and expression under Article 19(1)(a) which is essential component of democratic governance. As the information will be at the genesis of thought and expression, the right to information is vital not only for life of society but also for the life of individual, the Article 21 guaranteeing Right to live includes the basic right to be informed.

At this point, a review of existing legislation on information right is relevant. International, national and state level laws, regulations, executive orders, judicial pronouncements and practices show that every democratic set up has more scope to reveal and much more obligation to reduce the secrecy.

The United Nations, in its Universal Declaration of Human Rights 1948 included freedom of expression and free flow of information as a Human Right essential In the pursuit of peace and progress: "Article 19 – Everyone has a right to freedom of opinion and expression, this right includes freedom to hold opinions without interferences and to seek, receive and impart information and ideas through any media and regardless of frontiers."

In International Covenant on Civil and Political Rights reinforced this provision. "Article 19(2) – Everyone shall have the right to freedom of Expression, this right shall include freedom to seek, receive and import information and ideas of all kinds, regardless of frontiers, either orally, in writing or in print, in the form of art, or through and other of his choice."

The declaration of the Principles of International Cultural Cooperation adopted by the General Conference of UNESCO (1966) states that "broad dissemination of ideas and knowledge, based on the freest exchange and discussion is essential to creative activity, the pursuit of truth and the development of the personality."

In the most recent Declaration on Fundamental principles concerning the contribution of the Mass Media to strengthening Peace and International understanding, to the Promotion of Human Rights and to countering Racialism. Apartheid and Incitement to war (UNESCO) (Adopted on November 28, 1978) it is stated that "The exercise of freedom of opinion, expression and information recognized as an integral part of human rights and fundamentals of peace and international understanding."

DEMOCRATIC REQUIREMENT

Information is not private property. It is the national property. The government and public officers who are supposed to serve the people and hence the people as ultimate beneficiaries or sovereign, are entitled to know and benefit from it. Thus, the government and public officers who are supposed to serve the people on the payment from public purse, are none else than the trustees of this national resource information. Besides moral and legal obligation, it is their constitutional obligation also based on the philosophical foundation of freedom of speech and expression under Article 19(1)(a) of the Constitution.

The development of the right to information as a part of the constitutional law of the country started with petitions of the press to the Supreme Court for enforcement of certain logistical implications of the right to freedom of speech and expression such as challenging governmental orders for control of newsprint, bans or distribution of papers, etc. It was through the following cases that the concept of the public's right to know developed.

The landmark case in freedom of the press in India was *Bennett Coleman & Co. vs. Union of India* (AIR SC 783) in which the petitioners, a publishing house bringing out one of the leading dailies challenged in the government's newsprint policy which put restrictions on acquisition, sale and consumption of newsprint. This was challenged as restricting the petitioner's right to freedom of speech and expression. The court struck down the newsprint control order saying that it directly affected the petitioners right to freely publish and circulate their paper.

In a later case – *Indian Express Newspaper (Bombay) Pvt. Ltd. vs. Union of India* (1995 1 SSC 641), the court remarked "The basic purpose of freedom of speech and expression is that all members should be able to form their beliefs and communicate them freely to others. In sum the fundamental principle involved here is the people's right to know."

A subsequent case – *Manubhai D. Shah vs. Life Insurance Corporation* (AIR 1981 Guj. 15), in which it was held that if an official media or channel was made available to one party to express its views or criticism the same should also be made available to another contradictory view.

In *Prabha Dutt vs. Union of India* (AIR 1982 SC 6) the court held that there accepting clear evidence that the prisoners had refused to be interviewed, there could be no reason for refusing permission to the media to interview prisoners in death row:

Right to Know Cause of Arrest

The most recent judgment enumerating in detail the procedural safeguards for arrest and custody were given in cases *O. K. Basu vs. State of West Bengal* (AIR 1997 SC 610) and *Joginder Kumar vs. State of U.P.* (1994 4 SCC 260). Most of these directions translate into the right of the accused or his kin to have access to information regarding his arrest and detention such as preparation of a memo of arrest to be countersigned by the arrestee and a relative or neighbour, preparation of a report of the physical condition of the arrestee, regarding of the place of detention in appropriate registers at the police station, display of details of detained persons at a prominent place at the police station and at the district headquarters, etc.

Principles of Administrative Law

Developments in administrative law further strengthened the right. In *State of UP vs. Raj Narain* (AIR 1975 SC 865) the respondent has summoned documents pertaining to the security arrangements and the expenses thereof of the then Prime Minister. The Supreme Court in examining a claim for privilege of certain documents summoned, kept to itself the power to decide whether disclosure of certain privileged documents was in the public interest or not.

There have been numerous cases favouring disclosure of governmental information and transparency, but this was easily one of the strongest formulations of the right in all its manifestations. As a result of a lack of clear legislation on this, people continue to knock at the doors of the court every time they want to enforce this right. The common citizen neither has the means nor the time and inclination to get into convoluted legal processes and even public interest litigation is a tool which can reach only a few. Advocacy on this issue, using the legal process has become more focused with citizens petitions for directly enforcing the right to information being filed more and more frequently. Environmental groups have sought the right to know from government crucial concerning the environmental details of development projects.

Major victory for right to information is the great judgment of the Supreme Court on 2nd May, 2002 and 13 March, 2003, whereby the voter's right to know the antecedents of candidates was vindicated in a very effective manner. These developments have won half the battle for the right to information. The legal developments also indicate how the right to information and transparency for a verity of governmental actions.

Openness and Accessibility for Democracy

Now it has been widely recognized that openness and accessibility of people to information about the government's functioning is a vital component of democracy. It is wrong to consider democracy as a form of the government where the participation of people is restricted merely to periodical exercise of the right to franchise. Citizens need not retire to passivity between two elections.

The United Nations

Recognizing the importance of freedom of information at individual, organizational, national and international levels, the United Nations has declared "freedom of information as a fundamental human right". In 1946, during its first session, the UN General Assembly adopted Resolution.

The International Convention on civil and potential rights, a legally binding treaty was adopted by the UN General Assembly in 1966. In 1993, the UN Commission on Human Rights established the office of the UN Special Rapporteur on Freedom of opinion and expression. The UN has also recognized the Fundamental right to access information held by the State.

The Commonwealth

The Commonwealth, a voluntary association of 54 countries based on historical colonial links has taken concrete steps during the last few decades to recognize the Right to Information. More recently, the commonwealth has taken a number of significant steps to elaborate on the concept of that right.

Organization of American States

In 1985 an Advisory opinion, the Inter-American Court of Human Rights interpreting Article 13(1) recognized freedom of information as a fundamental human right. In 1994, the Inter-American Press Association (NGO) organized the Hemisphere conference on Free speech which adopted a set of principles on freedom of expression. In October 2000, the Inter-American Declaration of Principles on Freedom of Expression was approved which is most comprehensive official document of freedom of information in Inter-American System.

The Council of Europe

The Council of Europe is an inter-governmental organization, composed of 43 member states One of its foundational documents in the European Convention of Human Rights, which guarantees, in Article 10, the freedom of expression and information as a fundamental human right.

Transparency of American States

Sweden was the first to enforce the policy of openness in administration. There, all the governmental information is public unless certain matters are specifically listed as exempted from general rule. They have provided for a system of appeal against the wrongful withholding of information by public officials since 1766.

The freedom of information has been recognized in the constitutional framework. Documents dealing with national security, foreign policy and foreign affairs can be withheld from public scrutiny but the government is bound to give a written statement quoting legal authority for withholding the documents.

New Zealand

The Article 2.71 of the New Zealand Constitution provides "the government has a responsibility to keep the public informed about important issues of the day. New Zealand has also adopted a new Freedom of Information Act."

Australia

In December 1982, Australia enacted freedom of information legislation. Main features of this Act are the creation of public right to access to documents, the right to amend or update incorrect government records, the right to appeal against administrative decisions.

Finland

Finland has a law on the Public Charter of Official Documents in 1951. Norway and Denmark have also authorised Public access to official information sources. Canada and Australia also made legislation of this subject. French Constitution recognizes the free communication of thoughts and opinions.

Britain

In Britain the campaign for reduction of secrecy was going on. In 2000, the Freedom of Information Act came into existence.

South Africa

The South African Law on this right is a unique example of principle of open governance. The South African Open Democracy Bill empowers the public to effectively scrutinize and participate in governmental decision making that affects them.

Government in Sunshine Act in USA

In America there are three Acts which upheld the freedom of press and information.

Freedom of Information Act was made in 1966 which was amended in 1974 to make it more effective.

The Private Act of 1974 protected individual Privacy against the misuse of federal records while granting access to records concerning them which are maintained by federal agencies and,

The government in the Sunshine Act 1976 provided that meetings of government agencies shall be open to the public.

The policy behind the Freedom of Information Act is to make disclosure a general rule and not the exception, to provide equal rights of access to all individuals, to place burden on the government to justify the withholding of a document, not on the person who requests it, to provide right to seek injunctive relief in the court if individuals are denied access improperly. Under the Information Act any person, nor merely an affected individual or group, is eligible to ask for information because what is aimed at is not merely redressal of grievances but encouragement of an informed citizenry.

Judicial Activism in other Countries

The best example to explain this preposition is that the Supreme Court, on March 13, 2003 directed the Election Commission to make it mandatory for contesting candidates to disclose their antecedents in an affidavit along with nomination form, so that the voter may think over and make a right choice. This was recognized as part of right to freedom of speech and expression under Article 19(1)(a), which is held to be basis structure of constitution and hence inviolable. Similarly, in D.K. Basu and Joginder Kumar cases the Supreme Court held that the detainees had right to know the grounds of their arrest and also right to know the grounds of their arrest and also right to know that such right exists in them. This expression is preferred over 'Freedom of Information'.

Evolution of Access Law of State Level

State Legislation on Information: In India also, at the State level, Tamil Nadu and Goa passed their own Acts on the right to information in 1997. In Rajasthan, the Act was made in 2000. The State of Karnataka has also promulgated the Karnataka Information ordinance, 2000, before the Centre came up with a Bill to ensure Public access to information. Delhi passed the similar law in 2001. Madhya Pradesh and Maharashtra passed Right to Information Act in 1998 and 2000 respectively.

A comparative overview of these State laws shows that the various models adopted have different kinds of pros and cons. Some State laws have a long list of exceptions and few have adequate provisions for imposing liability for not providing information.

EVOLUTION OF ACCESS LAW AT CENTRE

Obstruction to Information

There are various factors obstructing this right. India have still a large section of illiterate people. Earlier compulsory primary education to the children was Directive principle of state policy. Now it is a fundamental right after the 86th Amendment to the Constitution. An enlightened people make democracy.

Confidentiality

Another problem is the code of confidentially of civil services who maintain an ethic of silence in public services who maintain an ethic of silence in public affairs. Government and civil servants must be under a duty to discloser to their citizens the truth of things.

The Press Council of India has scrutinized parallel legislations in countries like USA, Canada and New Zealand and proposed a draft on Right to Information. The draft proposes to amend the Official Secrets Act and Civil Service Conduct Rules (1964).

Need to Punish Denial of Information

There should be a large provision to punish any official who denies access to information. When citizens expose cases of corruption, the administration must act immediately to process the case and prosecute the guilty. The information is the weapon to fight the corruption. The government, which talks about the transparency, fears to be transparent.

The law providing Right to Information will definitcly entitle the activities and make them effective and innovative to check the corruption and to see the proper utilization of public money.

Enlightenment and Entitlement

Thus, access to government records provide much needed enlightenment and entitlement to the people to fight the corruption and bring the peaceful progress. More than sixty per cent of the public money meant for a government scheme and only a little amount trickles to a real work.

The Law of Right to Information should consist of such provisions to compel the authorities to come out with details of working of their schemes with the list of beneficiaries.

The heads of department and banks or other official bodies implementing the welfare schemes should announce the lists of proposed beneficiaries and criterion for their selection along with the process adopted for selecting them. There should be sufficient protection for the personal privacy and information not connected with governance.

Press Commission's Criticism

Senior Advocate and Jurist, Mr. A. G. Noorani summarizes his critique of the Official Secrets Act, 1923 to say that it is in breach of the fundamental Right to Freedom of Speech and Expression (Article 19(1)(a) of the Constitution of India) as well as of the Right to Life and Liberty (Article 21).

An allegation of an offence under the Act must be put to strict proof and the defense of public interest must be available.

Section 3 of Official Secret Act defines spying, while Section 5 makes the possession of information which relates to a prohibited place an offence. This section is used in Narmada Valley project case to prevent activities and journalists from visiting dam site. This is a blatant example of misuse of the Act for a different purpose which defeats the object of transparency and ridicules the need to information. The Central Civil Services Conduct Rules prohibit government servants from revealing any information, oath of secrecy to be administered to any person elected to public officer under the constitution are some of the examples of culture of secrecy. Section 123 Evidence Act, also prohibits the giving of evidence from unpublished official records. Section 124 says that no officer shall be compelled to disclose communications made to him in official confidence.

The battle for appropriate legislation for the right to information has been fought on two main planks. The first is a demand for amendment of the Draconian Colonial Official Secrets Act, 1923 and the second is the campaign for any early and effective law on the Right to Information.

Section 5 of the Official Secrets Act, 1923 makes it an offence to part with any information received in the course of official duty, to non-officials.

Objection to this provision have been raised ever since 1948 but the position has not changed much.

Sardar Sarovar Project

The imposition of the Official Secrets Act being used to prohibit entry of journalists into an area where massive displacement is taking place due to construction of a large dam, one of the world's largest dams, the Sardar Sarovar Project. A strong movement against the construction of the dam has raised. Public debate and dissent was sought to be suppressed by the use of Official Secrets Act. Whenever activities tried to educate people on this issue the local administration came down heavily on them. Besides using the Official Secrets Act, illegal arrests, false cases the physical threats became the order of the day. Judicial intervention from time-to-time have become the last recourse to activists working in this area.

Killer MIC and Secrecy

A dramatic instance which has been in the eye of international attention during the last few years is the Bhopal Gas Tragedy, in which leakage of Methyl Isocynate gas from the Union Carbide factory in Bhopal claimed several thousand lives and maimed and handicapped at least the next three generations. Not only did the government refuse to make public details of the monetary settlement between the government and the Union Carbide, at a workshop on the medical aspects of the victims were arrested for Official Secrets Act.

In the Bhopal Gas Tragedy case, are strong seeds for the demand for mandatory provisions to be made in a law, binding government as well as private companies to give information voluntarily on issues affecting the health and environment.

A working group was formed by the Government of India in 1977 to look into requirements to the Official Secrecy Act to enable the greater dissemination of information to the Public. But the position has not changed.

In 1989 another committee was set up, which recommended restriction of the area where the governmental information could be hidden and opening up of all other spheres of information. No legislation followed these recommendations.

The First Bill Prepared by the Press Council

The first major draft legislation on Right to Information in the country was circulated by Press Council of India in 1996, one important feature of his draft legislation was that it affirmed in its preamble the constitutional position that the Right to Information already exists under the constitution as the natural corollary to the fundamental right to free speech and expression under Article 19(1) of the Constitution. It stated that the legislation merely seeks to make explicit provisions for securing to the citizen this right to information.

The draft legislation affirmed the right to every citizen to information from any public body. Information was defined as any fact relating to the affairs of the public body and included any of the records relating to its affairs. The right to information include inspection, taking notes and extracts and receiving certified copies of the documents.

The Alternative Bills

Another draft legislation drafted by the Consumer Education Research Council (CERC). The draft legislation extends those rights to any person, except 'alian enemies' on the assumption that there is nothing to prevent citizens from sharing information with non-citizens. It requires public agencies at the federal and state levels to maintain their records in good order provide a directory of all records under its control, promote the computerization of records in interconnected networks and publish all laws, regulations, guidelines and circulars related to or issued by government department. The CERE requires government authorities to respond to any request for information within ten days. The CERE contains a class exception for cabinet documents but other documents relating to security, defense, international relations, and economic and commercial affairs and subject to a "grave and significant damage" test. There are other exemptions for personal information in the interest of privacy.

Another virtue of the CERE is that it provides for an independent appeal against negative decisions to release information to a network of information commissioners at the national, state and district levels and later to an information tribunal.

Shaping the National Legislation

The election manifestos of most of the major political parties in the last decade have promised transparency and administrative reforms. These promises were given impetus at the 24th May, 1997 conference of chief ministers of Indian states. The Prime Minister favoured a Right to Information and the idea of social audit as an instrument of greater accountability was emphasized.

The conference resolved that the Central and State governments would work together on transparency and the Right to Information. The conference recognized that secrecy and lack of openness is responsible for corruption in official dealings.

The Government of India agreed to take immediate steps, in consultation with states to introduce freedom of information legislation, along with amendments to the Official Secrets Act and the Indian Evidence Act, before the end of 1997.

The Government of India appointed a working Group which drafted the Freedom of Information Bill, 1997.

The Shourie Committee

The working group appointed by the government in 1997 was known as "Shourie Committee" since it was headed by former bureaucrat Late H.D. Shourie.

The Shourie Committee's draft freedom of information law failed to provide for penalties for groundless refusals to disclose. Appeals were allowed to consumer courts providing a simple remedy to consumers. The draft excluded the private sector and non-governmental organization. Unfortunately, the legitimacy and effectiveness of the work of this committee was undermined by lack of public consultation.

Freedom of Information Bill, 2000

The Shourie draft was never introduced into the parliament. However, it was revived with some changes in July 2000, when it was introduced as the Freedom of Information Bill, 2000. The weakness of the Bill reflects the lack of political will to implement a good information disclosure system. It fails to provide for an independent review of refusals to disclose information either by an independent administrative body or by the courts. The lack of public interest override for those exclusions and exemptions further undermines the Bill. The Bill was not altered before it was passed as it was, in the last quarter of 2002.

Working Group on Promotion of Open and Transport Government

The government of India appointed a working group on Right to Information and promotion of open and transparent government. In its report the working group explained the significance of the transparency as follows:

"........... Meaningful participation of people in major issues affecting their lives is now a vital component of the democratic governance and such participation can hardly be effective unless people have information about the way government business is transacted. Democracy means choice and sound, and informed choice is possible only on the basis of knowledge."

Ambiguous Non-obstante Clause

The working group has submitted a draft of such legislation. There are two reservations on that draft. The draft Bill provides for a non-obstante clause in order to let the Right to Information Legislation prevail over other existing clause in order to let the Right to Information Legislation prevail over other existing laws. If the courts read the provision harmonious with the existing provisions in Section 123 of the Evidence Act or, Section 5 of the Official Secrets Act, the Right to Information will be substantially restricted. If the courts interpret the non-obstiante clause literally, those sections will stand repealed by implication. However, normally repeal by implication is against the principles to statutory interpretation. Therefore, there is a need that the new legislation on Right to Information should comprehend all those restrictions, which are legitimate and repeal all other Acts which are contrary to it.

The Right to Information Act, 2005 should have repealed Sections 123 and 126 of Indian Evidence Act, and Section 5 of the Official Secrets Act and also the relevant provisions of the Atomic Energy Act. Information, which would breach privacy of the persons except when such a matter is connected with the discharge of a public function, could be protected through appropriate provisions.

Adjudication of Disputes

The second reservation is the mechanism for adjudication of disputes arising out of not allowing the information to get communicated.

The District Forums or State Commissions set up under the Consumer Protection Act.

Disputes regarding refusal of information would raise questions of constitutional law in turn are attended by professional adjudicators.

FOI Act has got few disputes that Consumer Protection Act. The committee report had got no detailed analysis.

However, the Act 2002 provided powers to states to make detailed rules to enforce the law. Further, it is explained that each and every department or organization also can make detailed set of rules and forms depending upon the information available for dissemination at their level, on request from the people and such rules should be formally notified by the State concerned.

Campaigns and Struggles to Achieve the Access Right

There is no concrete plan to sensitize or orient bureaucrats and public servants at all levels to the new regime of transparency. There ought to be immediate and forceful introduction of the issue of right to information at all orientation and training programmes carried out by the state academy for administration which conducts programmes for government officials.

The second drawback detected was the lack of accountability mechanism for enforcement of the orders. While many of the orders stipulate mandatory putting up of noticeboards and periodical mandatory release of information, reports from different parts of State suggest that this has not been done. While the government in the State Capital has devised a system of monitoring the implementation reporting is poor.

Civil society groups brought by Commonwealth Human Right Initiative (CHRI) have initiated a campaign to educate people about the operation of the right and to activate the orders by filing applications for information. The campaign however, aims at increasing interaction between civil society members, media and government and these experiences are now being highlighted through frequent workshops at various levels including State Capital and villages.

Environmental activities could identify strongly with the need for information on environment issues, which are directly concerned with sheer survival.

Constant networking and a continuous flow of information on issues were very important. Authentic and updated information on any subject is not easily available to people. Though continuous and constant communication, their interest in the issues can be kept alive.

Frequent interactions at workshops helped to bring the issues in focus. It also helped to reach the ground level experiences of the people to government and the media. This feedback is simultaneously complied and fed to the policymaker.

Purpose and Suggestions

Change in the Title

In fact, the Right to Information has already been recognized as a fundamental right by Supreme Court of India in several decisions and has been seen to be the obverse side of the Freedom of Speech and Expression guaranteed under Article 19(1)(a) of the Constitution of India. Moreover, it is also inherent in the guarantees of the right to life and personal liberty and the right to equal protection of the law contained in the Constitution of India.

The introductory statement of the new Act (Right to Information Act, 2005) suggests that the freedom to access is being given in the interest of administrative reform – "in order to promote openness, transparency and accountability in administration and in relation to matters connected herewith or incidental thereto".

It recommended: The Act must be entitled 'The Right to Information Act'.

The introduction to the Act must be read as "An Act to enforce the fundamental right to information".

The Act must contain a detailed statement of objects and reasons, with recitals as to the nature of the problem the law seeks to address, the importance of the right in terms of shifting the equation between the State and citizen through transparency, participation and accountability and a clear directive in all its actions in providing information to people.

Section 3 must be rewarded to read as under:

"Every public authority shall be under a duty to provide information to people in accordance with the provisions of this Act. The Union Government did not consider it necessary to state it so emphatically or it might have hesitated to grant such a right to the citizen."

Recommendations of Parliamentary Committee

The Parliamentary Committee stated that the union has power to legislate saying, 'as the Subject Right to Information is not specifically provided for in the Seventh Schedule to the Constitution, the union through the residuary Clause (97) of List 1, has the right to legislation on the subject.'

These suggested changes were not adopted. Well considered recommendations were totally ignored and the parliament accepted the unchanged Bill as introduced by the government after the gap of three years.

Purpose of Act

The model legislation developed by Article 19 organization suggested that the right to access to information held by private bodies where this is necessary for purpose of the Act should be as follows:

To provide right to information held by the public bodies in accordance with the principles that such information should be available to the public.

Necessary exceptions to the right to access should be limited and specific.

Decision on the disclosure of such information should be reviewed independently of the government.

To provide the exercise or protection on any right, subject only to limited and specific exceptions.

The law would be more effective if the exceptions are limited and specific which was not so in this legislation.

A New Access Law 2005

After years of struggle for the Central Legislation on Right to Information the Civil Society Groups emerged into the National Campaign for People's Right to Information (NCPRI) in 1966. Justice P.B. Sawant then chairman of Press Council of India and other prominent persons drafted the Bill for NCPRI which is known as Press Council draft. In response to Supreme Court's directive, the National Democratic Alliance Government passed Freedom of Information Act, 2002 which was not effective and never notified.

The United Progressive Alliance Government's Common Minimum Programme made a solemn pledge to provide a government that is corruption free, transport and accountable at all times .... and to make the Right to Information Act "more progressive, participatory and meaningful Alliance Government has set up a National Advisory Council to see the common minimum programme is implemented."

Bureaucracy was resisting the law and knowing this, activities increased pressure on the government to make comprehensive access law leading to passing of Right to Information Act, 2005 with significant improvements.

However, this Bill, as introduced in Parliament had many weaknesses. The Bill was referred to a standing committee of the Parliament and to group of ministers. In the next session the Bill was passed after over a hundred amendments introduced by the government to accommodate the recommendations of the parliamentary committee and the group of ministers. Finally, it was enacted by the Parliament and received the assent of the President on 15 June, 2005 and promulgated throughout the country on 13 October 2005.

EARLIER PROVISIONS

The concept of democracy in India is enshrined in the Preamble to the Constitution of India, wherein opening words provide that "We, the People of India," and in the end it lays down "give to ourselves this Constitution". The citizens have the fundamental right to know what the government is doing in its name. Freedom of speech is the lifeblood of democracy. The free flow of information and ideas informs political debate. It is a safety valve; people are more ready to accept decisions that go against them if they can in principle seek to influence them. It acts as a brake on the abuse of power by public officials. It facilitates the exposure of errors in the governance and administration of justice in the country (*K. vs. Secretary of State for the Home Department* Ex. *P. Simms,* (2000) 2 LR 115 (AC)).

After independence, India adopted democratic form of government, which implies the government of the people, by the people and for the people. Where a society has chosen to accept democracy as its creedal faith, it is elementary that the citizens ought to know what their government is doing. The citizens have a right to decide by whom and by what rules they shall be governed and they are entitled to call on those who can survive without accountability and the basic postulate of accountability is that the people should have information about the functioning of government. It is only if people know how government is functioning that they can fulfil the role which democracy assigns to them and make democracy a really effective participatory democracy. "Knowledge", said James Madison, "will for ever govern ignorance and a people who meant to be their own governors must arm themselves with the power knowledge gives. A popular government without popular information or the means for obtaining, it is but a prologue to force or tragedy or perhaps both." The citizens' right to know the facts, the true facts, about the administration of the country is, thus, one of the pillars of a democratic State. And that is why the demand for openness in the government is increasingly growing in different parts of the world (*S.R Gupta vs. Union of India,* AIR 1982 SC 149: (1981) Supp. SCC 87).

With the globalization of trade and industry and well knit world today, the disclosure of information – may be of the purity, potency and price of commodities in the market or the functioning of the government is necessary and for this purpose various Conventions have been held at National and International levels, which suggested imparting of the information on the working of the government to its citizens subject to some restrictions being imposed by the law in the interest of security of the country, etc.

The demand for openness in the government is based principally on two reasons. It is now widely accepted that democracy does not consist merely in people exercising their franchise once in five years to choose their rulers and, once the vote is cast, then retiring in passivity and not taking any interest in the government. Today it is common ground that democracy has a more positive content and its orchestration has to be continuous and pervasive. This means inter *alia that* people should not only cast intelligent and rational votes but should also exercise sound judgement on the conduct of the government and the merits of public policies, so that democracy does not remain merely a sporadic exercise in voting but becomes a continuous process of government – an attitude and habit of mind. But this important role people can fulfil in a democracy only if it is an open government where there is full access to information in regard to the functioning of the government.

For a long period the working of the government had been shrouded in secrecy and the poor citizens had to run from pillar to post even to get small information about his application to get copies of record-of-rights or his representation made to the government functionaries and instances are not lacking where he had not received reply to his genuine request for years together. The Supreme Court of India, while interpreting Article 19(1) of the Constitution of India clearly laid down in a number of decisions that the fundamental right of freedom of speech and expression includes right to acquire information and to disseminate it which is necessary for self-expression enabling the people to contribute to debate on social and moral issues.

In view of this provisions were made in various Acts passed by the legislature for imparting information to the citizens from time-to-time. Sections 74 to 78 of the Indian Evidence Act, give right to the person to know about the contents of the public documents and in this connection Section 70 of the Indian Evidence Act lays down that the public officials shall provide copies of public documents to any person, who has the right to inspect them. Under the Factories Act, compulsory disclosure of information has to be provided to factory workers regarding dangers including health hazards arising from their exposure to dangerous materials and the measures to overcome such hazards. Under Section 25(6) of the Water (Prevention and Control of Pollution) Act, every state is required to maintain a register of information on water pollution and it is further provided that so much of the register as relates to any outlet or any effluent from any land or premises shall be open to inspection at all reasonable hours by any person interested in or affected by such outlet, land or premises. Under Section 33A of the Representation of the People Act, a candidate contesting elections is required to furnish in his nomination paper the information in the form of an affidavit concerning: (i) accusation of any offence punishable with two or more years of imprisonment in any case including the framing of charges in pending cases; and (ii) conviction of an offence and sentence of one or more than one year imprisonment.

Before the enactment of the Freedom of Information Act, 2002, a little could be achieved in the field of in the Right to Information through the following enactments/rules/regulations:

(1) The Constitution of India;
(2) The Indian Penal Code (45 of 1860);
(3) The Indian Evidence Act, 1872;
(4) The Representation of the People Act, 1951;
(5) The Companies Act, 1956;
(6) The Atomic Energy Act, 1962;
(7) The Code of Criminal Procedure, 1973;
(8) The Bureau of Indian Standards Act, 1986;
(9) The Geographical Indications of Goods (Registration and Protection) Act, 1999;
(10) The Trademarks Act, 1999 and 2000;

(11) The Design Act, 2000;
(12) The Semi-conductor Integrated Circuits Layout Design Act, 2000;
(13) The Information Technology Act, 2000;
(14) The Protection of Plant Varieties and Farmers' Right Act, 2001;
(15) The Competition Act, 2002;
(16) The Delimitation Act, 2002;
(17) The Medical Termination of Pregnancy Regulations, 2003;
(18) The Central Civil Services (Conduct) Rules, 1964;
(19) The All India Services (Conduct) Rules, 1968.

Former judge of Supreme Court of India Hon'ble Mr. Justice V.R. Krishna Iyer, took up the matter regarding Right to Information to the citizens with the then Prime Minister of India in his open letter dated 26th December, 1989, in which it was categorically highlighted that "the right to know and the freedom of information are inalienable components of the freedom of expression and participation in public affairs, which Constitution confers on every citizen of the country............. It is heartening that, in the very first broadcast to the nation you made as Prime Minister, you emphasized the importance of the freedom of information and the annihilation of secrecy as a crafty art of government............. Accepting this postulate, some things require to be done immediately so that, the credibility of the Indian community in the changed ethos of open government may be created".

During the last decade, the right to information has got a momentum as never before and on the civil societies side also some organizations; social activists and individuals did excellent work in this field. The Mazdoor Kissan Shakti Sangathan (MKSS) (established in 1990) has done a great job in the field of right to information in rural India and its struggle for minimum wages and to get the information regarding Muster Rolls being maintained compelled the Government of Rajasthan to enact Right to Information Act and then various other State Governments enacted the Right to Information Acts, viz:

(1) The Tamil Nadu Right to Information Act, 1997
(2) The Goa Right to Information Act, 1997
(3) The Karnataka Right to Information Act, 2000
(4) The Rajasthan Right to Information Act, 2000
(5) The Assam Right to Information Act, 2001
(6) The Delhi Right to Information Act, 2001
(7) The Odisha Right to Information Act, 2002
(8) The Maharashtra Right to Information Act, 2003, and
(9) The Jammu and Kashmir Right to Information Act, 2004

The Freedom of Information Act, 2002 (5 of 2003) was enacted by the Government of India to provide for freedom to every citizen to secure access to information under the control of public authorities, consistent with public interest, in order to promote openness, transparency and accountability in administration and in relation to matters connected therewith or incidental thereto. The Statement of Objects and Reasons appended to the Freedom of Information Act, 2002 laid down that the Freedom of Information Bill seeks to achieve the following objects:

(1) The need to enact a law on Right to Information was recognized unanimously by the Chief Ministers Conference on 'Effective and Responsive Government' held on 24th May, 1997 at New Delhi. In its 38th Report relating to Demands for Grants of the Ministry of Personnel, Public Grievances and Pension, the Parliamentary Standing Committee on Home Affairs recommended that the government should take measures for enactment of such legislation.

(2) In order to make the government more transparent, and accountable to the public, the Government of India appointed a Working Group on Right to information and Promotion of Open and Transparent Government under the Chairmanship of Shri H.D. Shourie. The working group was asked to examine the feasibility and need for either full-fledged Right to Information Act or its introduction in a phased manner to meet the needs of open and responsive governance and also to examine the framework of rules with reference to the Civil Services (Conduct) Rules and Manual of Office Procedure. The said Working Group submitted its report in May 1997 along with a draft Freedom of Information Bill to the Government. The Working croup also recommended suitable amendments to the Civil Services (Conduct) Rules and the Manual of Departmental Security instructions with a view to bring them in harmony with the proposed Bill.

(3) The draft Bill submitted by the Working Group was subsequently deliberated by the Group of Ministers constituted by the Central Government to ensure that free flow of information was available to the public,

while *inter alia*, protecting the national interest, sovereignty and integrity of India, and friendly relations with foreign states.

(4) The proposed Bill is in accord with both Article 19 of the Constitution as well as Article 19 of the Universal Declaration of Human Rights, 1948.

(5) In our present democratic framework, free flow of information for the citizens and non-government institutions suffers from several bottlenecks including the existing legal framework, lack of infrastructure at the grass root levels and an attitude of secrecy within the Civil Service as a result of the old framework of rules. The government proposes to deal with all these aspects in a phased manner so that the Freedom of Information Act becomes a reality consistent with the objective of having a stable, honest, transparent and efficient government.

(6) The proposed Bill will enable the citizens to have an access to information on a statutory basis. With a view to further this objective, Clause 3 of the proposed Bill specifies that subject to the provisions of this Act, every citizen shall have right to freedom of information. Obligation is cast upon every public authority under Clause 4 to provide information and to maintain all records consistent with its operational requirements duly catalogued, indexed and published at such intervals as may be prescribed by the appropriate government or the competent authority.

With the passage of time, it was felt that even this Act failed to fulfil the aspiration of the citizens of India in the field of right to know and to get information since this Act was never enforced. In order to ensure greater and more effective access to information, it was thought that the Freedom of Information Act, 2002 must be made more progressive, participatory and meaningful.

On this issue Nation; Advisory Council suggested certain important changes to be incorporated into the said Act to ensure smoother and greater access to information. After examiner the suggestions of the National Advisory Council and others, the government decided to make a number of changes in the law. In view of the significant changes proposed by the National Advisory Council and others, it was decided to repeal the Freedom of Information Act, 2002 and enact another law for providing an effective framework for effectuating the right of information recognized under Article 19 of the Constitution of India. To achieve this object, The Right to Information Bill was introduced in the Parliament in December 2004. The important changes proposed to be incorporated, *inter alia*, include establishment of an appellate machinery with investigating powers to review decisions of the Public Information Officers; penal provisions for failure to provide information as per law; provisions to ensure maximum disclosure and minimum exemptions consistent with the constitutional provisions, and effective mechanism for access to information and disclosure by authorities, etc.

In view of the significant changes proposed in the existing Act, the government decided to repeal the Freedom of Information Act and in the proposed legislation to provide an effective framework for effectuating the right to information. Indian Parliament passed the Right to Information Act, 2005, which came into force on 15.06.2005. This enactment set out its objectives in the Preamble, which aims to promote transparency and accountability in the working of every public authority. This Act was brought into Statute book on the premise that informed citizenry and transparencies of information are vital to the vibrant democracy.

Thus, the Right to Information Act, 2005, which came into force in India in totality with effect from 12th October, 2005 is regarded as a milestone in the history of social legislation to impart information to citizens of India regarding working of the government and its corporations, etc., to make them more transparent as a result of which corruption, if not eliminated at all, would be checked to a greater extent. The Right to Information Act thus provides an effective framework for effectuating the right of information, a fundamental right, recognized under Article 19 of the Constitution of India.

The Preamble to the Right to Information Act, 2005 lays down that, whereas the Constitution of India has established democratic Republic; and whereas democracy requires an informed citizenry and transparency of information which are vital to its functioning and also to contain corruption and to hold governments and their instrumentalities accountable to the governed; and whereas revelation of information in actual practice is likely to conflict with other public interests including efficient operations of the governments, optimum use of limited fiscal resources and the preservation of confidentiality of sensitive information and whereas it is necessary to harmonise these conflicting interests while preserving the paramountcy of the democratic ideal and, therefore, it is expedient to provide for furnishing certain information to citizens who desire to have it. It is not out of place to mention here that most of the problems today are the result of non-observance of moral values by the younger generations after the independence that have prompted them to make money by fair or foul means. The absence of availability of information on the working of the government generally generate corruption and nepotism and, therefore, the enactment of this Act is an important milestone in furtherance of the democratic process whereby it shall be possible for the citizens to get information on all important issues and decisions affecting them and thereafter to adjudge the performance of the government, which they elected, for themselves.

OVERALL OBSERVATIONS

Taking the judicial verdict in a right perception, Indian Parliament passed the Right to Information Act, 2005, which came into force on 15.06.2005. This enactment set out its objectives in the Preamble, which aims to promote transparency and accountability in the working of every public authority. This Act was brought into Statute Book on the premise that informed citizenry and transparencies of information are vital to the vibrant democracy.

The Right to Information Bill was introduced in the Lok Sabha in December 2004. Both Houses of Parliament passed it with major amendments in May 2005. The assent of the President was received on June 15 and the Act was notified in the Gazette of India on June 21, 2005. As per Section 1(3) of the Act the provisions of sub-Section (1) of Section 4, sub-Sections (1) and (2) of Section 5, Sections 12, 13,15, 16, 24, 27 and 28 shall come into force at once, and the remaining provisions of this Act shall come into force on the one hundred and twentieth day of its enactment which means that these provisions have come into force w.e.f. 12th October, 2005. This Act has repealed the Freedom of Information Act, 2002. The Act extends to the whole of India except the State of Jammu & Kashmir. However, Jammu & Kashmir has its own "the Jammu and Kashmir Right to Information Act, 2004".

The Right to Information Act basically has two Parts: (a) Substantive law, and (b) Procedural law. Section 3 could coupled with some other provisions like Sections 8, 9, 18, 19 and 20 of the Act deal with substantive law while Section 6 along with some other provisions like Section 7 of the Act deal with procedural law. Thus, the Act is a completed Code in itself.

Before we go to the discussion about the real content of this Act, it would be better at the beginning itself to notice the mechanism, which this Act has created for the purpose of securing information by the citizens from public authorities.

The core of the enactment is that the citizen can obtain such information he needed from public authorities. It is the mandate of Sections 3 and 4 of the Act to provide information to the citizens.

"Public authorities" means all the government departments and all Institutions set up under any law either of the Union or the State or by or under any notification issued in exercise of executive power. They also include all institutions under the management or control of the governments or receiving State aid. All industrial establishments set up or controlled under the Union or the State and all local authorities and also all research institutions and institutions set up for the promotion of art, culture, and literature are all public authorities for the purposes of this Act.

To ensure the free flow of information to the public from public authorities promptly, the Act provides for appointment of Public Information Officer in each of the public authority institutions at different levels. Similarly, Assistant Public Information Officer has to be designated in every division and subdivision of the administrative units. The most unique feature of this enactment is that all the aforesaid appointments may be by designation, must be made by the concerned authorities within a timeframe of one hundred days of the coming into force of the Act, i.e., on 15.06.2005 as per the mandate of sub-clause (1) of Sec 5. Unfortunately, even after a lapse of stipulated time as mandated in the Act, the concerned authorities have not yet completed the process of designating the hierarchy of Public Information Officer in various departments.

All these institutions are liable to make available the information they have on the mere call of the citizen. In order to render this service with utmost promptitude, the Act provides for appointment of Public Information Officers in each of the public authorities at different levels. They are appointed by designation of their existing staff. Assistant Public Information Officers are also similarly designated in every division and subdivision of the administrative units.

The first step to be taken by the citizen seeking information is that he may send the application for information to the Assistant Public Information Officers who will transmit it within 5 days to the Public Information Officer. The application so transmitted shall be attended to and disposed of by the Public Information Officer within 30 days of its receipt by him. Here disposal of application means a real and substantial disposal. He should make available the full information in the form it is requested. If the entire material is not available he must make available so much of information as is available with him in the first instance and transmit within 5 days, the rest of the application to the concerned Public Information Officer for disposal who should in his turn shall comply with the request within 30 days as originally fixed. If the information is partly made available and the rest is rejected, the Information Officer shall state the reasons thereof.

The information under this Act includes any mode of information in any form of record, document, e-mail, circular, press release samples, samples of electronic data, etc. The most welcoming feature of this enactment is that the information can be obtained within a fixed timeframe of 30 days and if the information relates to life or personal liberty, then it can be obtain within 48 hours. No such timeframe provision has been made in any Act or code till this date. There are certain limitations or exemption under Sec.8 of the Act, which precludes the citizen getting such information. Subject to the limitation narrated under Sec.8, every public authority is under an obligation to provide the information on request both written and oral.

The Act made provisions for the Constitution of Central Information and State Information Commissions for the respective States as the appellate authorities and for monitoring the proper working of this Act.

The next stage is that if the Public Information Officer refuses to make the information either partly or fully or fails to respond or respond in an unsatisfactory manner, the applicant for information may file an appeal before the officer higher in status over the Public Information Officer. This appeal before the higher officer is called the First Appeal.

Second Appeal is the third stage. The authority to entertain the Second appeal is the Central/State Information Commission. The powers of Information Commission are very extensive. If the appeal is allowed the Commission may direct the Information Officer to furnish the information in the manner asked for. If the Commission finds the Information Officer to be at fault, the Commission may levy on him heavy penalties and may also direct initiation of disciplinary proceedings against him to the original Appointing Authority. The mechanism thus created for making the information available to the citizen is four-tired commencing from Assistant Public Information Officer, above him, the Public Information Officer, then Senior Officer who is the Appellate Officer and finally the Information Commission which is the Second Appellate Authority.

In addition to making the application for information, the Citizen has another right to file a complaint to the Central/State Information Commission direct if the services being provided under the above chain of officers are found to be wanting in any respect. The Commission while disposing of the complaint may in addition to granting the reliefs as applied for, may further issue General Orders for rectifying the deficiencies in the system complained against by the citizens.

While that much is the procedure to be followed by the citizens in obtaining the information from public authorities, the Central/State Commissions, which are independent statutory bodies, have overall control over the whole system. The Commission have power to supervise the work of Information Officers and call from them the reports. The Commission will prepare an Annual Statement of the work done, the number of applications for information received and the method of their disposal. The Commission while submitting its own report containing the above particulars to the government may also include the action taken by the Commissions against erring officers.

Now comes the crucial question. What is the meaning of the word 'information'? To what extent the citizen can claim to be informed from the public authorities? To what extent of information the Public Information Officer is competent to make it available? If all that which is classified as 'Secret' is not to be disclosed to the citizens, what exactly is the advantage gained by reason of the right to information guaranteed under the Act.

'Information' means only that information which is recorded in a material form, not oral. Opinions are information if they are reduced into writing. Therefore it is implied that the Act does not concern itself with any oral communications. Notwithstanding their right to information, the citizens are not entitled to all information available with the public authorities. The citizens' entitlement to information is limited to the extent of information recorded and published and to the extent of information recorded but unpublished and if non-publication is due to any secrecy provisions, the Public Information Officer is given the powers to decide whether the revealing of information will serve a larger public interest, than that served by retaining the information as secret.

The Right to Information Act by Sections 4 and 5 directs that all public authorities shall collect, document and computerise all the information they have and publish the same in all media possible including the Web. At first look it may appear as though only that information which is recorded and published only will be made available to the citizens. But this is not the real purpose of the Act. The Public Information Officer is bound to find out the source and availability of the information asked for and if it is one already published, the Information Officer will straight away makes available to the applicant all the information. If the information exists, but it is marked secret, the Public Information Officer will decide a comparative public interest involved and releases the same if he finds that the public interest served by releasing to the public overweighs the public interest for which it is kept in secret.

Now the next question arises in this context is as to what type of information the Public Information Officer may not reveal. Sections 8 and 9 are the sections which enumerate as many as 18 exceptions in relation to which the Public Information Officer is not competent to release it to the public straight away. They are the information likely to prejudice the Sovereignty, Integrity and Security of State. Information, which is likely to disturb peace and international relations, also cannot be released. The Public Information Officer shall not release the information forbidden by any Court or information, which amounts to contempt of the Court or contempt of legislatures. The Public Information Officer will not be able to disclose information relating to commercial confidence, trade secrets or any intellectual property the disclosure of which would harm the competitive position of any third party. Information relating to any fiduciary relationships, information relating to which if released might endanger the lives of others, information which is likely to impede the processes of investigation cannot be released by the Public Information Officer. Information relating to personal matters of any individual shall not be released unless they form an integral part of the individual's public life.

After excluding all the exemptions what appears to be the real and substantial matter to be made available to the citizens is all which relates to the administration only. That also seems to be the real purpose of the Right to Information Act because the information intended to be provided is aimed at enlightening the people tc make them participate more actively in the affairs of the administration and prevent corruption. It is to this extent the citizen is helped by providing instant information. Whatever be the limitations which appear to be otherwise legitimate the citizen is certainly exposed to everything he wants to know on what the government does. In this view it may be said that with the coming into force of the Right to Information Act the government will sure becomes open government.

Before concluding this introduction, it will not be out of place to mention a few errors in the drafting of the Act. The very first doubt, which arises, is whether the definition of public authority includes the government departments. This is so because the expression 'public authorities' does not spell out clearly that all government departments are public authorities and the same has to be inferred from the language used as one constituted or established under the Constitution or any State law. The definition reads as follows:

Section 2(1)(b): Public authority means any authority or body or institution of self-government established or constituted:

(a) by or under the Constitution;

(b) by any other law made by Parliament;

(c) by any other law made by State Legislature;

(d) by notification issued or order made by the appropriate Government and includes any,-

   (i) body owned, controlled or substantially financed;

   (ii) non-government organisation substantially financed directly or indirectly by funds provided by the appropriate government.

It is only by deduction from the several Clauses set out above, it is inferred that the government departments are included in the expression public authorities. Hence, it is suggested that the government departments may be specified in the definition at the very commencement of the definition. The next trouble is that there is a mixture of ideas in Sections 18 and 19 of the Act whereas while enumerating the reliefs, the Information Commission can give, as Appellate Authority, the reliefs it can give, as the authority to dispose of the complaints by citizens are included. They should have been separately dealt with under separate sections.

Another anomaly that is noticeable is the omission in the statute that the rule making power of the Competent Authority may be subject to the approval or ratification by the government. Here the power to make rules is vested in the Supreme Court, High Court, Speaker or Chairman of the Parliament/Legislatures. While the rules made by the government are subject to the rule of laying them on the Table of Legislature, the rules made by the Competent Authority are not required under this Act to be laid before the Legislature nor are they made subject to the supervisory control of the Central or State Governments or the Legislature. It is possible that the rules made by Competent Authorities may sometimes conflict with those of others made by the Central or State Governments. Hence, it is suggested that the rules that may be made by the Competent Authority shall be subject to either prior permission or subsequent ratification by the concerned governments.

Another feature of this Act is that judicial intervention is prohibited, i.e., the Court has no power to entertain any suit or application or other proceedings in respect of any order made under this Act. The Act provides for rule making power to both Central and State Governments and such rules that were framed shall be laid before Parliament in case of Central Govt. and State Legislature in case of State Govt.

In the case of Civil Procedure Code that is to be operative throughout India, the rules made for the purposes of the Code form part of the Code itself. It means, the legislature itself has made orders and rules. They are appended to act itself as a schedule. The power to make rules, the Civil Procedure being a subject mentioned in a concurrent list, is conferred on the Parliament and the State Legislatures. However, the power given to the High Court to make rules for themselves and for subordinate courts is restricted. There shall be appointed a Rules Committee by the High Court consisting of three High Court Judges, one Dist. Judge, and one Legal Practitioner. Committee shall frame the rules and it is only after the committee recommends their adoption, the High Court can issue the rules. Even then, the rules thus made by the High Court are subject to the approval of the Government of the State within the territory of which the High Court is located. Thus, three things are apparent here.

(1) Making of rules, amendments or annulments can be done by the Parliament or State Legislatures;

(2) There is no power either with the Central or State Governments to make rules in CPC;

(3) The High Court as delegated authority can make rules only after observing the formalities required therefore and after obtaining the approval of the State Government. In the absence of any control by the Centre over the rules that may be made by the State Government in the case of Right to Information Act may create some difficulties in future. Similarly, in the absence of any control over the rules that may be made by the competent authorities may create difficulties in future, if the later run counter to the Central Rules, or to the Central and State Rules as the case may be.

There is one more difficulty that requires to be solved at the earliest. Rule making power is conferred on the Central Government and State Government simultaneously and independently. The Right to Information Act is a Central legislation and it has to be enforced uniformly throughout India. When such be the case, the rule making authority granted to the State Governments should have been made subject to the rules which may be made by the Centre and any rule when made by the State if it conflicts with the Central rule shall have a prior approval of the Central Government. Otherwise what is required by Central Government to be kept confidential may be directed by another government to be disseminated to the public. Therefore, the dichotomy created in the field of rule making power shall be removed by making the power of the State Government to make the rules subject to Central approval either prior to making the rule or thereafter seeking ratification.

Finally there remains one more question about the power of the Parliament to enact this Act. Article 19(1) of the Constitution of India states that all citizens shall have the right to freedom of expression and the Courts have held that the right to freedom of information forms part of this fundamental right of free expression. Article 19(2) states that "nothing in sub-clause (a) of Clause (1) shall affect the operation of any existing law, or prevent the State from making any law, in so far as such law imposes reasonable restrictions on the exercise of the right conferred by the said sub-clause in the interest of the sovereignty and integrity of India, security of State, friendly relations with foreign States, Public order, decency or morality or in relation to contempt of Court, defamation or incitement to an offence". Since the expression State mentioned in this sub-article includes the Centre and State Governments, it means that, the Parliament as well as the State Governments have power to enact the law on Right to Information, which in substance declares on one hand that all citizens shall have a Right to Information and yet imposes on the other hand several restrictions on this right.

What happened now as a matter of fact is that several States have already either enacted the law on this subject, or have enacted the law and brought it into force. Some States have introduced Bills in their Legislatures awaiting enactment. Some States have enacted them and have not brought them into force. For instance, in the States of Andhra Pradesh, Kerala, Madhya Pradesh and Uttar Pradesh Bills are published and in the States of Assam, Delhi, Goa, Jammu and Kashmir, Karnataka, Maharashtra and Tamilnadu, the Bills were passed by their respective Legislatures and became Acts. Delhi and Tamilnadu have published the rules also. The question now is whether the Parliamentary Act, which has, since come into force on 15.06.2005 overrides all the State legislations and whether all those States shall hereafter implement the Central law only and not the State law. The answer can only be that the Central law only should be enforced and that all other enactments will become ineffective for the reason that the law passed by the Parliament in exercise of its jurisdiction to enact it under a Constitutional provision like Article 19(2), shall necessarily prevail over any other enactment made by the State in exercise of the same power. This question shall not be looked at from the point of view of the separation of powers envisaged under Articles 245 and 246 read with 7th Schedule, but is governed by the expression "subject to the provisions of Constitution" contained in Section 245, which in this case should be read as contained in Article 19(2). In view of this matter it can be concluded that the Right to Information Act, 2005 made by the Parliament will render all other enactments made by the States exercising the same power under Article 19(2) ineffective. A question of conformity and repugnance between the Centre and State Acts does not arise.

By and large the Right to Information Act is well conceived. It is seen to be of great assistance to the people in the present context of administrative deficiencies and deviations coming up for open debate, discussion or condemnation.

The Act is complete Code in itself as it is having penalty clause Sec.20 of the Act authorized the Central/States information commission to impose penalty of Rs. 250/-up to Rs. 25,000/-, on erring officials, by giving an opportunity to them. More so the commissions are also authorized to recommend for disciplinary action against the erring public authorities as well as for non-complying the provisions of the Act, under the service rules applicable to them.

In at nutshell it can be said that this piece of legislation is unique in many accepts. It entitled the citizen to know the details of governance subject to certain limitations. It will further reduce the gap between the rulers and ruled. By enforcing the Right of Information, every citizen can become a watchdog for the attainment of rule of law, the dynamic concept. Every country in the world regardless of forms of governments claims to be a Welfare State, thereby claiming that it exists for the welfare and social good of the people. The purpose of an ideal government is to ensure that there will be liberty, peace, justice and equality, for the free development of all.

Right to information is a product of fundamental rights as interpreted by the Supreme Court of India. This enactment is not only furtherance of the political equality but also social and economic equality. Our constitution is a majestic instrument and if implemented in letter and spirit, the present generation would be placed a happy administration. Every body at the helm has to respect the human rights. It is worthwhile to recall the words of S.W. Philippines "Human rights are more than legal concepts, they are the essence of man. They are what make man human......deny them and you deny men's humanity" ....It is further necessary to recall the words of M. C. Chagla, while he was our Ambassador in America, "But the lawyer must be interested in the rules of law. The meaning of this expression had considerable extension in our modern times. At one time it means the supremacy of law and the equality of every person before the law. But as society developed it was realized that this was too narrow an interpretation of that expression. It is now accepted that rule of law can only be effective in a country provided the conditions are such that the dignity of the human personality and the liberty of the individual are respected. Law cannot function in a vacuum. If sections of the society are deprived the benefit of law and are treated as second class citizen as if the law does not protect the liberty of the individual, then it would be meaningless to say that the rule of law prevails."

It is worthwhile to recall the words of Ved Prakash Marwah, the former Governor of Jharkand while delivering lecture on transparency and accountability in public governance in 2004 we may say that the target group for good governance "the people of this country", but it is really pressure groups – be they industrialists or the business houses or regional outfits or trade unions, even media – who keep exerting pressure on the public administration. It would be wrong to see Right to Information as an end in itself. Nor can it be analyzed in isolation. A right momentum has to be generated through which the public at large has to be educated about this enactment and of their entitlement to know everything relating to public transaction. The NGOs: has to play the vital role in this regard like, M.K.S.S, Rajastan. I would like to share an apocryphal story doing the rounds why corrupt public servants are scared of the Right to Information Act, with the readers. It is just like R.K. Laxman brand of common men humour.

This Act is designed to facilitate and further its end, i.e., empowerment of public to know what is going on under the guise of administration and should not be treated as an enactment providing penalties and punishments.

Without any hesitation it can be said that this Act should be the voice of so-called voiceless in our society. Lastly, remind everybody that one should not be crazy about rights only and one should also be mindful about ones duties. Rights and duties are the two sides of a coin.

India with all its thousand years of cultural heritage and vedic vintage has not been able to assure to its people even a pretence of the Preamble's grand undertaking of Justice, liberty, dignity and fraternity to every citizen. Let everyone of us strive hard to make India a social justice nature.

IMPORTANCE OF THE ACT

In a democracy like ours, people and not the government is supreme. It is in these circumstances that every citizen of country has a right to know what the government is doing in its name to adjudge the performance of the government by getting information on each and every decision being taken by the government. This Right of Information is, however, subject to certain limitations and conditions, which can be imposed by the government under law in the interest of the security and integrity of the country. The voice of the public to get information from the government got momentum during the last decade and various State Governments enacted Right to Information Acts in the years 2000-2002, which were applicable in the respective States. Then came the Freedom of Information Act 2002. However, with the passage of time, it was found that even this Act did not fulfil the aspiration of the citizens of India. In order to ensure greater and more effective access to information, it was thought that the Freedom of Information Act, 2002 must be made more progressive, participatory and meaningful and accordingly National Advisory Council suggested certain important changes to be incorporated in the Act to ensure greater access to information and after examining the suggestions of National Advisory Council and the public, the Government of India decided that in view of the significant changes proposed by the National Advisory Council and others, the Freedom of Information Act, 2002 should be repealed and to enact another law for providing effective freedom and the right to information and thus, the Right to Information Act, 2005 has been enacted by the Parliament, which is considered as a landmark step in the field of fundamental right of life and liberty guaranteed under Article 19 of the Constitution of India.

The Right to Information Bill was passed by Lok Sabha on 11th May, 2005 and by Rajya Sabha on 12th May, 2005 and it received assent of the President of India on 15th June, 2005 and has come on the Statue book as the Right to Information Act, 2005 (22 of 2005). This Act, therefore, is the outcome of efforts of Civil Social Organizations, Peoples' Movements and the suggestions of the National Advisory Council set up to monitor the promises made by the UPA Government in its Common Minimum Programme because one of the promises of the UPA Government was to make the right to information more participatory, progressive and meaningful. This Act is applicable to the whole of

India except Jammu & Kashmir. However, Jammu & Kashmir has passed the Jammu and Kashmir Right to Information Act, 2004. As per Section 1(3) of the Right to Information Act, the provisions of sub-section (1) of Section 4, sub-sections (1) and (2) of Section 5, Sections 12, 13, 15,16, 24, 27 and 28 shall come into force at once, and the remaining provisions of this Act shall come into force on the one hundred and twentieth day of its enactment. Therefore, the entire Act came into force w.e.f. 12th day of October, 2005.

The Preamble to the Right to Information Act, 2005 lays down that, whereas the Constitution of India has established democratic Republic; and whereas democracy requires an informed citizenry and transparency of information which are vital to its functioning and also to contain corruption and to hold governments and their instrumentalities accountable to the governed; and whereas revelation of information in actual practice is likely to conflict with other public interests including efficient operations of the governments, optimum use of limited fiscal resources and the preservation of confidentiality of sensitive information and whereas it is necessary to harmonise these conflicting interests while preserving the paramountcy of the democratic ideal and, therefore, it is expedient to provide for certain information to citizens who desire to have it. It sets out the following objectives to be achieved through the Right to Information Act.:

(a) to provide for setting out the practical regime of right to information for citizens to secure access to information under the control of public authorities;

(b) in order to promote transparency and accountability in the working of every public authority;

(c) the Constitution of a Central Information Commission and State Information Commissions; and

(d) for matters connected therewith or incidental thereto.

The importance of Right to Information can be judged from the report of National Commission to Review the Working of Constitution under the Chairmanship of Justice M.N. Venkatachaliah, wherein it was pointed out as under:

"Major assumption behind a new style of governance is the citizen's access to information. Much of the common man's distress and helplessness could be traced to his lack of access to information and lack of knowledge of decision making processes. He remains ignorant and unaware of the process, which vitally affect his interest. Government procedures and regulations shrouded in veil of secrecy do not allow the clients to know how their cases are being handled. They shy away from questioning officers handling their cases because of the latter's snobbish attitude and bow-wow style. Right to information should be guaranteed and needs to be given real substance. In this regard government must assume a major responsibility and mobilize skills to ensure flow of information to citizens. The traditional insistence on secrecy should be discarded. In fact, we should have an oath of transparency in place of an oath of secrecy. Administration should become transparent and participatory. Right to minimizing manipulative and dilatory tactics of the babudom, and, last but most importantly putting a considerable check on graft and corruption".

Democracy means government of the people, by the people and for the people. However, if the citizens are ignorant of the decisions taken by the government and reasons advanced for the same, there can be no government by the people. The public has a fundamental right to know what the government has been doing in its name (*Regina vs. Shayiler* (2003) 1 AC 247: 2002 UKHL 11; also refer to *R. vs. Secretary of State for the Rome Deptt. Ex. P. Mc-Quillan* (1995) 4 All ER 400; *Tinnely & Sons vs. United Kingdom,* (1988) 27 EHRR 249). Freedom of expression constitutes one of the essential foundations of society (*Ashdown vs. Telegraph Group Ltd.*, 2001 LR 685 (Ch D); Also refer to *Handyside vs. United Kingdom* (1976) 1 EHRR). The fundamental right to free of expression and imparting information have been recognized as common law (of England) for many years (737*Regina vs. Shayiler* (2003) 1 AC 247: 2002 UKHL 11; *Also refer to Attorney Genral vs. Guardian Newspapers Ltd.* (1990) 1 AC 109). The freedom of expression constitutes one of the essential foundations of a democratic society and one of the basic conditions for its progress and each individual's self-fulfilment. Subject to Article 10(2) of Rome Convention it is applicable not only to "information" or "ideas" that are favourably received or regarded as inoffensive or as a matter of difference, but also to these that offend shock or disturb. Such are demands of that pluralism, tolerance and broadmindedness without which there is no democratic society (*Yogi vs. Germany.* (1995) 21 EHRR 205).

(a) Thus, Right to Information would lead to openness in the administration as the citizens would get information about various issues and would, thus, promote transparency in the government, increasing the efficiency of the government by making officers accountable and ultimately reducing the corruption, if not eliminating the same totally. The freedom of speech and expression is a right given to every citizen of this country and not merely to a few. Freedom of speech and expression is basic to and indivisible from a democratic polity. It encompasses freedom of press. It includes right to impart and receive information. The right of free speech and expression includes the right to receive and impart information. For ensuring the free speech right of the citizens of this country, it is necessary that the citizens have the benefit of plurality of views and a range of opinions on all public issues. A successful democracy posits an 'aware' citizenry. Diversity of opinions, views, ideas and ideologies is essential to enable the citizens to arrive at informed judgement on all issues touching them (*Secretary, Ministry of Information and Broadcasting Government of India vs. Cricket Association of Bengal* AIR 1995 SC 1236: (1995) 2 SCC 171: AIR 1995 SCW 1856).

STATEMENT OF OBJECTS AND REASONS

"Statement of Objects and Reasons for introducing a Bill in the Legislature is not admissible as an aid to construction of the Statute as enacted: far less can it control the meaning of the actual words used in this Act. It can only be referred to for the limited purpose of ascertaining the circumstances that actuated the sponsor of the Bill to introduce it and the purpose for doing so. The Preamble of a Statute which is often described as a key to the understanding of it may legitimately be consulted to solve an ambiguity or to ascertain and fix the meaning of words in their context which otherwise bear more meanings than one. It may afford useful assistance as to what the Statute intends to reach, but if the enactment is clear and unambiguous in itself then no Preamble can vary its meaning. While constructing a Statute one has also to bear in mind the presumptions that the Legislature does not intend to make any substantial alteration in the existing law beyond what it expressly declares or beyond the immediate scope and object of the Statute…. (*A.C. Sharma vs. Delhi Administration* (1973) 1 SCC 726.

No doubt the Statement of Objects and Reasons cannot be treated as part of the legislation, yet it must be borne in mind by those connected with the administration of the law, as to what is the intention and purpose of the legislation as understood by the mover of the Bill. The Statement of Objects and Reasons to the Right to Information Bill reads as under:

"In order to ensure greater and more effective access to information, the government resolved that the Freedom of Information Act, 2002 enacted by the Parliament needs to be made more progressive, participatory and meaningful. The National Advisory Council deliberated on the issue and suggested certain important changes to be incorporated in the existing Act to ensure smoother and greater access to information. The government examined the suggestions made by the National Advisory Council and others and decided to make a number of changes in the law. "The important changes proposed lo be incorporated, *inter alia,* include establishment of an appellate machinery with investigating powers lo review decisions of the Public Information Officers; penal provisions for failure to provide information as per law; provisions to ensure maximum disclosure and minimum exemptions, consistent with the constitutional provisions; and effective mechanism for access to information and disclosure by authorities, etc. In view of significant changes proposed in the existing Act, the government also decided to repeal the Freedom of Information Act, 2002. The proposed legislation will provide an effective framework for effectuating the right of information recognized under Article 19 of the Constitution of India."

The statement of objects and reasons, seeks only to explain what reasons induced the mover to introduce the Bill in the House and what objects he sought to achieve. But those objects and reasons may or may not correspond to the objectives that the majority of members had in view when they passed it into law. The Bill may have undergone radical changes during its passage through the House or Houses, and there is no guarantee that the reasons which led to its introduction and the objects thereby sought to be achieved have remained the same throughout till the Bill emerges from the House as an Act of the legislature, for they do not form part of the Bill and are not voted upon by the members. The statement of objects and reasons appended to the Bill should be ruled out as an aid to the construction of Statute (*Ashwani Kumar Ghose vs. Arabinda Bose,* AIR 1952 SC 369: *Kavalappara Kottarathil Kochuni vs. State of Madras and Kerala,* AIR 1960 SC 1080). The statement of objects and reasons is not admissible as an aid to the construction of a Statute. But it can be referred to for the limited purpose of ascertaining the conditions prevailing at the time which actuated the sponsor of the Bill to introduce the same and the extent and urgency of the evil which he sought to remedy (*State of West Bengal vs. Subodh Gopal Bose AIR* 1954 SC 92: *Commissioner of Income Tax. Madhya Pradcsh vs. Sodra Devi (Smt.)* AIR 1957 SC 832).

It is a recognized rule of interpretation of Statutes that the expressions used therein should ordinarily be understood in a sense in which they best harmonize with the object of the Statute and which effectuate the object of the Legislature. If an expression is susceptible of a narrow or technical meaning, as well as a popular meaning, the Court would be justified in assuming that the Legislature used the expression in the sense which would carry-out its object and reject that which renders the exercise of its powers invalid. In interpreting a Statute the Court cannot ignore its aim and object (*New India Sugar Mills Ltd. vs. Commissioner of Sales Tax, Bihar,* AIR 1963 SC 1207). It is indeed true that the statement of objects and reasons for introducing a particular piece of legislation cannot be used for interpreting the legislation if the words used therein are clear enough.

But the statement of objects and reasons can be referred to for the purpose of ascertaining the circumstances, which led to the legislation in order to find out what was the mischief, which the legislation aimed at (*S.C. Prashar vs. Vasantsen Dwarkadas,* AIR 1963 SC 1356). The Court cannot construe a provision of the Constitution on the basis of the statement of objects and reasons (*P. Vajravelu Mudaliar vs. Special Deputy Collector for Land Acquisition,* AIR 1965 SC 1017).

Statement of objects and reasons for introducing a Bill in the legislature is not admissible as an aid to the construction of the Statue as enacted; far less can it control the meaning of the actual words used in the Act. It can only be referred to for the limited purpose of ascertaining the circumstances, which actuated the sponsor of the Bill to introduce it and the purpose for doing so (*A. C. Sharma vs. Delhi Administration* AIR 1973 SC 913). The statement of objects and reasons cannot be taken into account for the purpose of interpreting the plain words of the section. But it gives an indication as to what the Legislature wanted to achieve (*Workmen of F.T. & R. Co. vs. Management AIR* 1973 SC 1227). The statement of objects and reasons is relevant when the object or purpose of an enactment is in dispute or uncertain. They can never override the effect, which follows logically from the explicit and unmistakable language of its substantive provisions. Such effect is the best evidence of intention. A statement of objects and reasons is not a part of the Statute and, therefore, not even relevant in a case in which the language of the operative parts of the Act leaves no room, whatsoever, to doubt (*State of Haryana vs. Chunan Mal AIR* 1976 SC 1654).

The address of Prime Minister, Dr. Manmohan Singh in the Lok Sabha, on the Right to Information Bill on 10th May, 2005 is important and the excerpts of the same are given below:

"In the modern world, we are dealing with very complex societies, and these complex societies require extensive interference of governments in day-to-day activities. In our own country total government expenditure – Centre, States and local bodies combined-accounts for nearly 33 per cent of our gross national product. In addition, because of various compulsions of the situation, governments have lo interfere by way of regulatory bodies in the normal processes of how an economy functions.

Now, it is, therefore, of utmost importance that when governments account of such a large proportion of total national expenditure, when governments interfere extensively with the way ordinary citizens of the country go by doing their business, these powers should be exercised with utmost caution and utmost concern for public welfare in the widest sense of the term.

Civilized governments everywhere have been searching for ways and means to deal with problems of corruption, problems of ineffectiveness of governments at various levels. We have the judiciary; we have the representative institutions of parliamentary system of government to check both corruption and to ensure that money that is voted for truly subserve the public purpose. But, it has been found that it is not enough that governments should go to the people once in five years.

It is necessary to find other means of empowering our citizens to feel that processes of governance truly serve the public purpose. The Right to Information is a quest for that sort of mechanism, which will empower our citizens with information, which enables them to judge for themselves whether or not governments are functioning in accordance with what can be considered as 'public interest' in the widest possible sense of the term. It goes without saying that all information can be misused also. Therefore, much will depend upon how information seekers approach their tasks. People should recognize the dangers that are inherent in such a situation because in our society information is power. But one way of ensuring that this power is a widely distributed as possible is to ensure that access to information is not a monopoly of the few.

The Bill lays down architecture for accessing information, which is simple, easy, time-bound, and, in my view, inexpensive. It has stringent penalties for failing to provide information or affecting information flow in any way. In fact, it imposes obligation on agencies to disclose information, *suo moto*, thus reducing the cost.

We all know that in development and their relinkages. We all know that the benefit meant for the poorer sections of the people do not reach them. We all know that the public funds meant for serving the causes of the poor and the downtrodden are, in fact, eaten up by more influential sets of people. The Right to Information Bill, hope, give our public-spirited people another instrument through which they will be able to prevent this patent misuse of public fund or public patronage. Therefore, this Bill is a Historic Bill. What it seeks to do is to strength the foundations of our democracy. It seeks to promote the cause of a transparent humans administration. It seeks to make our administration more accountable than ever before.

Therefore, the passage of this Bill, we see the dawn of a new ear in governance processes – an era of performance and efficiency, an era which will ensure that benefits of growth flow of all sections or society, an era which will eliminate the scourge of corruption, an era which will bring the common man's concerns to the heart of all the process of governance, an era which will truly fulfil the hopes of the founding fathers of our republic.

Great responsibility will rest on the shoulders of those who seek information, and also those who will administer this Act. It is hoped that we have, in this country, men and women who know how to draw a right balance. We need a strong and purposeful government. We need government processes, which rise to the challenges of our time, which would enable us to ensure that this country moves forward to realize its chosen destiny. At the same time, one can also be convinced that the future of this country is to strengthen the foundations of democracy and the Bill is an important step forward in promoting a culture of transparency, a culture of accountability, and to ensure that

Governments do work to promote the public good in the widest possible sense of the term. "That was the ambition of the foundation fathers of our republic."

The Statement of the Minister who had moved the Bill in Parliament can be looked at to ascertain mischief sought to be remedied by the legislation and the object and purpose for which the legislation is enacted. The statement of the Minister who had moved the Bill in Parliament is not taken into account for the purpose of interpreting the provisions of the enactment (*P. V. Narasimha Rao vs. State (CBI/SPE)*, AIR 1998 SC 2120 p.2158)). No one may speak for the Parliament and Parliament is never before the Court. After Parliament has said what it intends to say, only the Court may say what the Parliament meant to say. None else. Once a Statute leaves Parliament House, the Court is the only authentic voice which may echo (interpret) the Parliament. This, the Court will do, with reference to the language of the Statute and other permissible aids (*Sanjeev Coke Manufacturing Co. Ltd., vs. Bharat Coking Coal Ltd.* AIR 1983 SC 239 (251): (1983) 1 SCR 1000 p.1029).

The speeches made by the members of the Legislature on the floor of the House, when a Bill for enacting a statutory provision is being debated, are inadmissible for the purpose of interpreting the statutory provision but the speech made by the mover of the Bill explaining the reason for the introduction of the Bill can certainly be referred to for the purpose of ascertaining the mischief sought to be remedied by the legislation and the object and purpose for which the legislation is enacted. This is in accordance with the recent trend in juristic thought not only in Western countries but also in India that interpretation of a Statute being an exercise in the ascertainment of meaning, everything which is logically relevant should be admissible (*K.P. Varghese vs. Income Tax Officer, Ernakulam,* AIR 1981 SC 1922: (1982) 1 SCR 629). The primary and foremost task of a Court in interpreting a Statute is to ascertain the intention of the Legislature, actual or imputed. Having ascertained the intention the Court must then strive to so interpret the Statute as to promote and advance the object and purpose of the enactment. For this purpose, where necessary, the Court may even depart from the rule that plain words should be interpreted according to their plain meaning. There need be no meek and mute submission to the plainness of the language. To avoid patent injustice, anomaly or absurdity or to avoid invalidation of a law, the Court would be well justified in departing from the so-called golden rule of construction so as to give effect to the object and the purpose of the enactment by supplementing the written word, if necessary (*Girdhari Lal & Sons vs. Balbir Nath Mathur* AIR 1986 SC 1499).

(a) In order to interpret a particular provision and to infer the intention of the legislature, the objects and reasons stated in the Bill, when it is presented to the legislature, could be used (*Rib Tapes, (India) Pvt. Ltd. vs. Union of India* AIR 1986 SC 2014). A Statute is best understood if one knows the reason for it. The reason for a Statute is the safest guide lo its interpretation. The words of a Statute take their colour from the reason for it. There are external and internal aids to discover the reason for a Statute. The external aids are statement of objects and reasons when the Bill is presented to Parliament, the reports of parliamentary committees.....Occasional excursions into the debates of Parliament are permitted. Internal aids are the Preamble, the Scheme and the provisions of the Act. No provision in the Statute and no word of the Statute may be construed in isolation (*Utkal Contractors & Joinery Pvt. Ltd. vs. State of Odisha* AIR 1987 SC 1454). Though the Statement of Objects and Reasons accompanying a legislation could not be used to determine the true meaning and effect of the substantive provisions of a Statute, it was permissible to refer to the same for the purpose of understanding the background, the antecedent state of affairs, the surrounding circumstances in relation to the Statute, and the evil which the Statute sought to remedy (*Narain Khamman vs. Parguman Kumar Jain* AIR 1985 SC 4: (1985) 1 SCC 1 (8) as referred to in *Devadoss vs. Veera Makali Amman Koil Athalur,* AIR 1998 SC 750 p. 756).

PREAMBLE AS AN AID

It is not necessary that every Act passed by the legislature must have the Preamble. However, when Preamble is added to an Act, it is a part of the Act itself and can serve as a key to the interpretation of the Act as it denotes the policy and the object behind the Statute and the mischief sought to be remedied.

The Preamble of a Statute is not an enactment but a mere recital of the intent of its framers and the mischiefs to be remedied and it may be considered as a key to the construction of the Statute whenever the enacting part is open to doubt: but it cannot restrict or extend the enacting part when the latter is free from doubt.

Lord Tenterden, CJ in Halton vs. Cove 1 B & Ad 538 said, Although the enacting words of a Statute are not necessarily to be limited or controlled by the words of the Preamble but in many instances go beyond it, yet, a sound construction of every Act of Parliament, the words in the enacting part must be confined to that which was the plain object and general intention of the Legislature in passing the Act; and the Preamble affords a good clue for discovering what was that object was.

The Preamble of a Statute has been said to be a good means of finding out its meaning as it were a key to the understanding of it (*A. Thangal Kunju Musaliar vs. M. Venkatachalam Potti* AIR 1956 SC 246). The object and purpose of a Preamble is well settled. A Preamble is a key to open the mind of the Legislature but it cannot be used to control or qualify precise and unambiguous language of the enactment. The Preamble and title, whatever their value might be as aids to the construction of a Statute, undoubtedly throw light on the intent and design of the legislature and indicate the scope and purpose of the legislation itself (*Pappatlal Shah vs. State of Madras,* AIR 1953 SC 274). The petitioner cannot dispute the correctness of the recitals in the Preamble to the Statute (*S. Inder Singh vs. State of Rajasthan* AIR 1957 SC 510). Preamble bears the same relationship to the operative part of a Statute as to the recitals to the operative part of a document. Hence, where the operative part of a Statute is ambiguous, but not otherwise, the Preamble may be resorted to, to explain or to show the scope and intention of the Legislature. It is only when it conveys a clear and definite meaning in comparison with relatively obscure and indefinite enacting words that the Preamble may legitimately prevail (*Attorney General vs. H.R.H. Prince Earnest Augustus of Hanover* (1957) 1 AIR ER 49: 1957 AC 436).

The Preamble of a Statute is "a key to the understanding of it" and it may legitimately be consulted to solve any ambiguity, or to fix the meaning of the words which may have more than one or to keep the effect of the Statute within its real scope, whenever the enacting part is in any of these respects open to doubt (*Kavalappara Kottarathil Kochuni vs. State of Madras and Kerala* AIR 1960 SC 1080). It is one of the cardinal principles of construction that where the language of Act is clear, the Preamble must be disregarded though, where the object or meaning of an enactment is not clear the Preamble may be resorted to, to explain it. Again, where very general language is used in an enactment, which, it is clear, must be intended to have a limited application, the Preamble may be used to indicate to what particular instances the enactment is intended to apply. We cannot, therefore, start with the Preamble for construing the provisions of an Act, though we would be justified in resorting to it, nay, we will be required to do so, if we find that the language used by Parliament is ambiguous or is too general though in point of fact Parliament intended that it should have a limited application (*Burrakur Coal Co. Ltd. vs. Union of India* AIR 1961 SC 954). The Preamble of an Act cannot limit or change the meaning of the plain words (*Motipur Zamidari Co. (Pvt.) Ltd. vs. State of Bihar* AIR 1962 SC 660). No resort to the Preamble would be justified in interpreting the provisions in the Act when the words used in it are clear and unambiguous. A Preamble is a key to the interpretation of a Statute but is not ordinarily an independent enactment conferring rights or taking them away and cannot restrict or widen the enacting part, which is clear and unambiguous. The motive for the legislation is often recited in the Preamble but the remedy may extend beyond the cure of the evil intended to be removed (*R. Venkataswami Naidu vs. Narasram Naraindas* AIR 1966 SC 361).

A Preamble is a key to open the mind of the Legislature but it cannot be used to control or qualify precise and unambiguous language of the enactment. It is only when there is a doubt as to the meaning of a provision that recourse may be had to the Preamble to ascertain the reasons for the enactment and hence the intention of the Parliament. If the language of the enactment is capable of more than one meaning then that one is to be preferred which comes nearest to the purpose and scope of the Preamble. In other words, Preamble may assist in ascertaining the meaning but it does not affect clear words in a Statute. The Courts are thus not expected to start with the Preamble for construing a statutory provision nor does the mere fact that a clear and unambiguous statutory provision goes beyond the Preamble give rise itself to a doubt on its meaning (*Tribhuban Parkash Nayyar vs. Union of India* AIR 1970 SC 540: (1969) 3 SCC 99). A Preamble though a key to open the mind of the Legislature cannot be used to control or qualify the precise and unambiguous language of the enactment. It is only in case of doubt or ambiguity that recourse may be had to the Preamble to ascertain the reason for the enactment in order to discover the true legislative intendment (*Y.A. Mamarde vs. Authority* under the Minimum Wages Act, AIR 1972 SC 1721: (1972) 2 SCC 108).

Therefore, it can be said that the Preamble of a Statute which is often described as a key to the understanding of it may legitimately be consulted to solve an ambiguity or to ascertain and fix the meaning of words in their context which otherwise bear more meanings than one. It may afford useful assistance as to what the Statute intends to reach but if the enactment is clear and unambiguous in itself then no Preamble can vary its meaning (*A.C. Sharma vs. Delhi Administration* AIR 1973 SC 913). The general purpose or object of the Act given in the Preamble may not show the specific purpose of the classification made. The Court has, therefore, to ascribe a purpose to the statutory classification and coordinate the purpose with the more general purpose or the Act and with other relevant Acts and public policies (*Supdt. & Remembrancer, L. A. vs. Girish Kumar* AIR 1975 SC 1030). The Preamble is an aid in construing the provisions of the Act.... When there is a Preamble it is generally in its recitals that the mischief to be remedied and the scope of the Act are described. It is, therefore, permissible to have recourse to it as an aid in construing the enacting provisions (*All Saints High School vs. Government of Andhra Pradesh* AIR 1980 SC 1042). The Preamble embodies and expresses the hopes and aspirations of the people (*Atam Prakash vs. State of Haryana* AIR 1986 SC 859).

The significance of the Preamble in gathering the legislative intent was stated in *Arnit Das vs. State of Bihar* (2000) 5 SCC 488: 2000 SCC (Cri) 962 in the following words; "The Preamble suggests what the Act was intended to deal with. If the language used by Parliament is ambiguous the Court is permitted to look into the Preamble for constructing the provisions of an Act. The Preamble is a key to unlock the legislative intent. If the words employed in an enactment may spell a doubt as to their meaning it would be useful to so interpret the enactment as to harmonise it with the object which the Legislature had in its views".

The only rule for the construction of Acts of Parliament is, that they should be constructed according to the intent of Parliament which passé the Act. If the words of the Statute are in themselves precise and unambiguous, then no more can be necessary than to expound the words in their natural and ordinary sense. The words themselves alone, in such cases, best declare the intention of the lawgiver. But if any doubt arises from the terms employed by the Legislature, it has always been held a safe means of collecting the intention, to call in aid the ground and cause of making the Statute and to have recourse to the Preamble, which according to Dyer CJ. Is a key to open the minds of the makers of the Act, and the mischiefs, which they intended to redress. (Per Tindal CJ. In Sussex Peerage case 11 Cl & Fin 85). It was also held that the Preamble of the Constitution was not part of the Constitution, In re, Berubari Union Exchange of Enclaves AIR 1960 SC 845. This view was however, overruled in *Keshavananda Bharti vs. State of Kerala* (1973) 4 SCC 225, wherein it was held that the Preamble is a part of the Constitution.

The Preamble of the Act states that to have been the object of the Statute and it was held in *Nga Hoon vs. R.* (1857-59) 7 MIA 72: 4 WR (PC) 109 that, "That there can be no doubt that the Court must construe the Preamble as a key to the construction of the Statute though, it would not, of course, control every provision because, very often, subsequent provisions of a Statute extend beyond the limits of the Preamble".

In *Commissioner for Special Purposes of Income Tax vs. Pemsel* (1891) AC 531 it was held, "The purpose for which resort may be had to the Preamble of a Statute has been stated in a well known passage: 'If any doubt arises from the terms employed but the Legislature, it has always been held a safe means of collecting the intention to call in aid the ground and cause of making the Statute, and to have recourse to the Preamble, which according to Dyer CJ', is a key to open the minds of the makers of the Act, and mischiefs they intended to redress".

In *State of West Bengal vs. Anwar Ali Sarkar* AIR 1952 SC 75: 1952 SCR 284, it was held, "The express provision of an enactment, if it is clear and unambiguous, cannot be curtailed or extended with the aid of the Preamble to the Act. It is only when the object or meaning of the enactment is not clear that recourse can be had to the Preamble to explain it." The Preamble and the body of the sections sufficiently formulate the Legislative policy and the ambit and character of the Act is such that the details of that policy can only be worked out by delegating them to a subordinate authority within framework of that policy. (*Hari Shanker Bagla vs. State of M.P.* AIR 1954 SC 465: 1955 1 SCR 380).

It is one of the cardinal principles of construction that where the language of an Act is clear, the Preamble may be resorted to explain it. Again, where very general language is used in an enactment, which, it is clear, must be intended to have a limited application, the Preamble may be used to indicate to what particular instances the enactment is intended to apply. We cannot, therefore, start with the Preamble for constructing the provisions of an Act, though we would be justified in resorting to it, nay, we will be required to do so, if we find that the language used by Parliament is ambiguous or is too general, though, in point of fact, Parliament intended that it should have a limited application. (*Burrakur Coal Co. vs. Union of India* AIR 1961 SC 954: (1962) 1 SCR 44: *Irani vs. State of Madras* AIR 1961 SC 1731: (1962) 2 SCR 169).

Therefore, the Preamble may, no doubt, be used to solve any ambiguity or to fix the meaning of the words, which may have more than one meaning, but it cannot be used to eliminate as redundant or unintended, the operative provisions of a Statute.

Although the Preamble and the provisions of a Statute assist the Court in finding out the object and policy, the object and policy need not always be strictly confined to the Preamble and the provisions contained therein. (See *Registrar, Cooperative Societies vs. K. Kunjabmu* (1980) 1 SCC 340: *Bhim Singhji vs. Union of India* (1981) 1 SCC 166: *Punjab Tin Supply Company vs. Central Government* (1984) 1 SCC 206: *Rathi Khandsary Udyog vs. State of U.P.* (1985) 2 SCC 485: *Modi Industries Ltd. vs. State of U.P.* (1994) 1 SCC 282: *Lucknow Development Authority vs. M.K. Gupta* (1994) 1 SCC 243: *Sita Devi vs. State of Bihar* 1995 Supp (1) SCC 670)

Maxwell 11th Edn. P.45 states "A Preamble is a key to the interpretation of a Statute but is not ordinarily an independent enactment conferring rights or taking them away and cannot restrict or widen the enacting part which is clear and unambiguous. The motive of Legislation is often recited in the Preamble but the remedy may extend beyond the cure of the evil intended to be removed."

In this Act, Preamble has to be necessarily read as a part of the Act. The Preamble gives clear guidelines on the extent of information that could be made available and the extent to which it can be withheld. The Preamble unequivocally states that "confidentiality of sensitive information" shall be preserved and what all that could be supplied only is "certain" information and that too which is under the control of public authorities. The Preamble touches the core issue that the dissemination of information is fundamental to the functioning of the government and also to its transparency, some others such as to contain corruption and for holding the government and its instrumentalities accountable to the governed. These purposes permeate all the 31 Sections of the Act hence is the importance of the Preamble.

In the above context, the question whether Preamble forms part of the Act or outside it is academic.

Occasions may arise when the provisions of an enactment shall have to be interpreted in the context of what was said by several committees appointed to study the Act and several persons including the ministers have said in Parliament during the debates on the Bill. It is held by Courts that in all such circumstances that such utterances will only help in appreciating the mind of the Parliament in one way or the other and they shall not be binding on the Court (*State of Kerala Industrial Development Corporation Ltd vs. C.I.T.* (2003) 259 ITR 5 1 (SC): *Sole Trustee Shikshan Trust vs. C.I.T.* (1975) 101 ITR 234 (SC)).

The precise role of the Preamble in the Right to Information Act is that the Preamble broods over the entire Act whether one is interpreting the word "information" in its restrictive sense defined in Section 2(e) or is fixing the scope of the rule making powers of the government notwithstanding its freedom it shall be governed by the paramountcy of public interest.

SCHEME OF THE ACT

The Right to Information Act consists of six Chapters arranged as under:

Chapter I Preliminary
Chapter II Right to Information and Obligations of Public Authorities
Chapter III The Central Information Commission
Chapter IV The State Information Commission
Chapter V Powers and Functions of the Information Commissions, Appeal and Penalties
Chapter VI Miscellaneous

As per the Scheme of the Act, Chapter I is Preliminary chapter dealing with short title, extent, commencement and definitions of certain words used in the Act. As per Section 1(3) of the Act, the Right to Information Act extends to whole of India except the State of Jammu & Kashmir and provisions of sub-Section (1) of Section 4, sub-Sections (1) and (2) of Section 5, Sections 12,13,15,16, 24, 27 and 28 shall come into force at once, and the remaining provisions of this Act shall come into force on the one hundred and twentieth day of its enactment. According to Section 2(f) of the Act, "information" means any material in any form, including records, documents, memos, e-mails, opinions, advices, press releases, circulars, orders, logbooks, contracts, reports, papers, samples, models, data material held in any electronic form and information relating to any private body which can be accessed by a public authority under any other law for the time being in force. Moreover, as per Section 2(j) of the Act, "Right to Information" means the Right to Information accessible under this Act which is held by or under the control of any public authority and includes the right to:

(i) inspection of work, documents, records;
(ii) taking notes, extracts, or certified copies of documents or records; (iii) taking certified samples of material;
(iv) obtaining information in the form of diskettes, floppies, tapes, video cassettes or in any other electronic "mode or through printouts where such information is stored in a computer or in any other device.

Chapter II of the Act deals with right to information and obligations of public authorities. Section 3 of the Act provides that subject to provisions of this Act, all citizens shall have the right to information. The words used in Section 3 are "all citizens" and not "all persons", which is important. Thus, right to information is conferred only on all citizens of India and not the foreigners visiting India. Section 4 of the Act provides for obligations of the public authorities to maintain its records duly catalogued and to publish the particulars of its organization, functions and duties, etc., within the prescribed period; Section 5 deals with designation of Public Information Officers and Section 6 deals with the request of the citizens for obtaining information while Section 7 deals with the disposal of such request. Section 8 of the Act provides for exemption from disclosure of information in cases provided therein; whereas Section 9 lays down that request for information shall be rejected where such access would involve an infringement of copyright subsisting in a person other than the State.

Chapter III deals with Central Information Commission wherein Constitution of the Central Information Commission, terms of office and conditions of service and the procedure for removal of Chief Information Commissioner or the Central Information Commissioner are laid down. Likewise, Chapter IV deals with the State

Information Commission regarding Constitution of the State Information Commission, term of office and conditions of service and procedure for removal of State Chief Information Commissioner or State Information Commissioner, etc. Chapter V of the Act provides for power and functions of the Information Commission; the procedure for appeal against the order of Central Public Information Officer or State Public Information Officer and the penalties for refusing to receive an application for information without any reasonable cause, etc.

Chapter VI of the Act, like many other Statutes, deals with miscellaneous matters. Section 21 of the Act provides for protection of action taken in good faith; whereas Section 22 lays down that this Act shall have overriding effect and Section 23 bars the jurisdiction of Courts to entertain any suit, application and other proceedings in respect of any order made under this Act. Section 24 lays down that the Act shall not apply to certain organisation specified in the Second Schedule; while Section 25 deals with monitoring and reporting of the implementation of the provisions of this Act and Section 26 lays down that appropriate government may, to the extent of availability of finances or other resources, prepare the programmes. Sections 27 and 28 of the Act empower the appropriate government and the competent authority to make rules to carry-out the functions of this Act; while Section 29 of the Act provides for laying of the rules and Section 30 empowers the Central Government to remove difficulties.

Section 31 has repealed the Freedom of Information Act, 2002. In exercise of the powers conferred by Sections 27 and 28 of the Act, the appropriate governments and the Competent Authorities have framed Right to Information Rules 2005.

The title of Statute is an important part of the Act and may be referred to for the purpose of ascertaining its general scope and of throwing light on its construction although it cannot override the clear meaning of the enactment (*Ashwini Kumar Ghose vs. Arabinda Bose* AIR 1952 SC 369). The title of a chapter cannot legitimately be used to restrict the plain terms of an enactment *(Commissioner of Income-tax, Bombay vs. Ahmedbhai Umarbhai & Co.* Bombay AIR 1950 SC 134). The true nature of a law has to be determined not on the label given to it in the Statute but on its substance (*M.P.V. Sundararamier & Co. vs. State of Andhra Pradesh,* AIR 1958 SC 468). The policy and purpose of a given measure may be deduced from the long title and the preamble thereof........Where the general policy of the Bill as laid down in its title and elaborated in the preamble is "to provide for the better organization and development of educational institutions providing a varied and comprehensive educational service throughout the Stale", it was held that each and every one of the clauses in the Bill has to be interpreted and read in the light of this policy (*Kerala Education Bill 1957 (in re:)* AIR 1958 SC 956).

RIGHT TO INFORMATION ACT 2005
I. OBJECTS AND REASONS OF RIGHT TO INFORMATION

Vision and policies which result into enactment of legislations in various countries vary considerably as to their subject matter and content. Yet there is a common thread line running through to promote access to information held by public bodies. Article 19 Society based in London has published a set of principles, documenting the best practice standards on Right to Information legislation. *(T N Report of the Special Rapporteur. Promotion and Protection of the Right to Freedom of Opinion and Expression, DOC. EICN.4/2000/63, 18 January, 2000; para 44)*. UN Special Report on Freedom of Expression detailed the standards to which Right to Information should conform (UN Standards). *(Report of the UN Special Rapporteur on Freedom of Expression, 1998 UN Doc. E/CN.4/1990/40, January 28)*.

UN Human Rights Committee has resolved that restrictions must meet a three part test, (*UN Human Right Committee on 21 July, 1994, No. 458/191, para 9.7)* as follows: (i) Law should be formulated with sufficient precision with regard to restrictions; (ii) Restrictions must pursue a legitimate aim, such as respect of the rights or reputation of others and, also for the protection of national security or of public order, or of public health or morals; (iii) There must be a pressing social need for the restriction. The reasons given by the State to justify the restriction must be "relevant and sufficient" and the restrictions must be proportionate to the aim pursued. *(The Sunday Times vs. United Kingdom, European Court of Human Rights, Application No. 9815/82, 8 EHRR 407, paras 39-40)*.

In the area of Right to Information this three part test implies that the law to the principle of maximum disclosure. The principle of maximum disclosure establishes a presumption that all informations held by the public bodies should be subject to disclosure and that this presumption may be overcome only where there is an overriding risk of harm to a legitimate interest. It also implies that systems and processes should be established ensure that members of the public can access information and the public bodies should make all reasonable efforts to facilitate this access. *(UN Principles on Freedom of information, 2000 UN Doc.E/CH4/2000/63)*.

(i) Basic Principles

The following nine principles are set out, on which the Public's Rights to Information is based: (UNESCO Mendal Toby, Freedom of Information, A Comparative Legal Survey (London, 2001), page 2).

Principle 1: Maximum Disclosure

"Right to Information legislation should be guided by the Principle of maximum disclosure."

Bureaucracy today is not willing to shed its power, unless through appropriate legislation, it is compelled to accept the principles of 'maximum disclosure'. FOI legislation must be onus of proof upon bureaucracy, in case where it seeks to deny access to information. Scope of the law should be wide enough to include that requester is not to demonstrate purpose, for which the information is required. Information or records should be broadly defined to include all information, held by the body in question, regardless of formed date of creation, which created it and whether or not it has been classified. (*Ibid*, at 26).

The principle also requires that no public bodies including courts, legislature, and offices of governors, Prime Minister, President or security outfits should be excluded from the scope of legislation.

There legitimate 'public interests' can be safeguarded through narrowly specified regime of exceptions. Public corporations and private organizations of autonomous bodies like Chartered Accountants, University Grant Commission or Medical Council of India and others which carry-out public functions or are substantially publicity funded or services provides like contractors handling governments jobs or multinationals or large national corporations should be included within the ambit of law. In South African legislation, private entities are required to disclose certain information.

Principle 2: Suo Moto Publication

"Public bodies should under an obligation to publish key information." It is not sufficient that law imposes duty on public bodies to accede to requests for information. Law should impose an obligation upon them to actively publish and disseminate key categories of information, even in the absence of a request. Certainly this obligation is easier to prescribe than to implement because of resources crunch. Government and large bodies find no buyers for their publications. But at least important information may be put on website. Computer technologies are making it cheaper to publish and disseminate information.

Principle 3: Open and Transparent Governance

"Public bodies must be actively promote open government." Where there is secrecy, there is suspicion. If administration is clean and clear, then why to hide under the carpet. Why claim privilege? In most situations, public interest lies towards the side of openness, and not towards secrecy. Openness cannot be forced even through most progressive legislations. But, if law provides for openness, something starts happening somewhere, and some day Pandora box opens suddenly. Public movements have demonstrated this.

The best approach is orientation programmes by Secretary level official. The messages percolate down easily through provisions of incentives for good performers and exporting poor performers. It requires setting up institutions like Information Commissions, Human Right Commissions, Public Grievance Commissions, Vigilance Commissions or Ombudsman. Legislation should provide for such over seeking mechanism and also for publication of their own annual reports.

Prosecutions for defaulting or delaying are rare throughout the world. Government servants are not criminal upon whom penalties can be imposed in such cases. But agencies are busy elsewhere on matters they consider as important. A provision for possible sanction is necessary test of any legislation, in any appellate body, particularly in those cases where access to information is wilfully or culpably being obstructed.

It is useful to make the general public aware about the right. Broadcast media goes well with the illiterate or even with busy people like executives. Newspapers all another important source of information. Publication of guides or people's charters go a long way for the needy or common people.

Effective public management of records is key element for right to information. In the absence of proper record maintenance by public bodies, even the officials do not know what information they have or where it can be located.

Principle 4: Limited Exemptions

Exceptions should be clearly and narrowly drawn and subject to strict and public interest, test.

Balancing between Right to Information and legitimate secrecy claims is most problematic feature of most information laws. Effectiveness of the information law is easily undermined through excessively broad or open regime of exceptions.

The Council of Europe has recommended the following grounds for exemptions:

1. Member states may limit the right of access to official documents. Limitations should be set down precisely in law, be necessary in a democratic society and be proportionate to the aim of protecting.

i. national security, defence and international relations;

ii. public society;

iii. the prevention, investigation and prosecution of criminal activities;
iv. privacy and other legitimate private interests;
v. commercial and other economic interests, be they private or public;
vi. the equality of parties concerning Court proceedings;
vii. nature;
viii. inspection, control and supervision by public authorities;
ix. the economic, monetary and exchange rate policies of the State;
x. the confidentiality of deliberations within or between public authorities during the internal preparation of a matter. *(Aarhus Convention, Article 3).*

The Article 19 society principles set out a three-part test for exceptions: (1) the information must be related to a legitimate aim specified in the law, (ii) disclosure must threaten to cause substantial harm to that aim, and (iii) the harm to the aim must be greater than the public interest in having the information. *(Article 19 Society, London Principle 3).*

First part of the test relates to justifications for holding information with reference to purpose of aims.

Second part of the test shows that it is not sufficient that there is a nexus between exempted field and purpose or aim. It should go a step further; the disclosure must pose a serious threat to the interest.

Imminent danger test permits withholding information where substantial harm would be done to the cause. There may be a legitimate case to keep secrecy as to why a particular weapon system was opted by armed forces, but it would be of no use to deny the information that is tangential to their operations, i.e., whether any illegitimate commission was paid or not during the deal.

Harm test cannot be applied in cases where the information is already publicly available or access is being denied or supplied with consent. Most of the students applying for admissions to US University sign on the waiver form, which deny them access to information, submitted about them, in their recommendation letters.

Harm test is excluded in cases, where exemptions are applied in whole sale, to the whole organization. These are known as 'class exemptions'. Indian law is a classic example where 18 security related organizations are included in Schedule II of the Right To Information Act, 2005 under exempt category, with provisions for inclusion or deletion of the list.

Third part of the test implies that disclosure may mean a harm to a particular aim but overall public interest is served by disclosure. When corruption is exposed in a defence deal, temporarily it may weaken the defence, but ultimately in the long run it will actually strengthen it. This overriding public interest is recognized by European Council:

"Access to a document may be refused if the disclosure of the information contained in the official document would or would likely to harm any of the interests mentioned in paragraph I, unless there is an overriding public interest in disclosure." *[UNESCO Aarhus Convention, Article 4(4)].*

Indian and English Courts have always upheld the principles under Section 123 and 124 of the Evidence Act, 1872 dealing with affairs of the State and privileged communication, the principles that where part of a record is exempt, the rest of the record should be disclosed where it may reasonably be separated for the whole.

Toby Mendal draws attention to another aspect, although not belonging to three-part test, that time limits on withholding information creates a presumption that information which has been withheld will eventually become subject to disclosure. However, time limit system usually also allows for extensions but only where the authorities can demonstrate an ongoing risk to a legitimate aim. (*Mendal Toby, Freedom of Information, A Comparative, Legal Survey (London 2000) page 31).*

Principle 5: Processes to Facilitate Access

"Request for information should be processed rapidly and fairly and an independent review of any refusals should be available."

Right to Information Laws stipulate the process for taking a decision upon a request to provide information. They also provide for independent review of refusals.

Public bodies usually appoint or designate among existing officials, a Public Information Officer, who is responsible for proper implementation of the Act, in his department or under his jurisdiction. Requests are usually made in writing or even sometimes orally.

The requester is usually required to specify the form of access in which the information is to be provided, e.g., inspection of records, or noting down from it, or a photo copy of it. Sometimes it depends upon the condition of the record, i.e., it is in deteriorated form or it is available in the electronic form.

Assistance should be provided where a request is deficient, either too wide in scope or it is not specific or clear. Acknowledgement is made or a receipt is issued to the requester.

Requester should be responded, by sending him a notice stating the fee to be paid, the form in which the request will be provided, likely time to be taken and, where the request is rejected or part of the information is denied, reasons for denial are provided along with information about any right of appeal. Where the public body in question does not hold the information requested, it should provide reasonable assistance to the requester to locate it.

According to international standards most of the countries have two appeals system. *(Aarhus Convention Article 9; African Principle IV(2) Commonwealth Principle CDE Recommendation IX and the UN Standards, 2000).* First appeal lies to the higher authorities of the same public body. It helps in correcting mistakes and ensuring internal consistency. Second appeal usually lies to an independent appellate authority to review decisions made by public bodies. Review is usually not limited to the question of disclosure of information, but usually covers delays, fees, form of access, etc. Second appellate body is usually protected against political interference. Appellate procedure should be quick, fair and cost-effective. It should have full powers to inspect the document, in camera if necessary, to investigate the matter, to compel witness to appear before it and the like. Its decisions should be binding and enforceable Courts where necessary.

Finally, the law should provide for the right to appeal against administrative decisions to Courts. The provisions are essential to set standard of disclosure in controversial areas and to develop the law through seasoned judgments. In many legislations this right is restricted where public bodies abuse their powers, delay the matters or deter all but the most determined and well of requesters.

Principle 6: Costs

"Individuals should not be deterred for making requests for information by excessive costs".

Charging fee is a controversial matter and requires a balanced, uniform and consistent approach. Several steps are required before information can be provided such as, search for documents, preparing them, reviewing whether they are exempted or not, and actual cost or providing access. Providing information occupies a certain amount of time. Law should clearly provide: How much cost should be borne out by the public exchequer or how much of the total cost should be apportioned to the requester? Sometimes issue of cost-determination is resolved by looking at the purpose for which information is being asked, e.g., public interest or personal reasons.

Different laws take different approaches to fees. Some limit charges to the cost of duplication, along with a set fee for making a request. Some charge different fees for public and private purpose. Still others allow requesters to occupy a certain amount of public time, say two hours as fee and beyond that fee is charged on different scale. Usually fee structure and schedules are set in the rules framed under delegated legislation.

Principle 7: Open Meetings

"Meetings of public bodies should be open to public."

Right to information applies usually not only to records and documents but also to meetings of public bodies. Usually this matter is covered under separate laws. US Sunshine Act, 1974 provide for public meetings. In India proceedings of Parliament and State Legislatures is shown live on televisions, and passes are issued (for safety reasons) to the intending public to witness the proceedings from public galleries. However, this provision has not yet trickled down to meetings of local bodies and other public bodies.

Principle 8: Disclosure Takes Precedence

"Laws which are inconsistent with the principle of maximum disclosures should be amended or repealed."

Survive without keeping certain secrets near its chest. Some system of conflict resolution need to be evolved, so that civil servants are not put in a double jeopardy. They may be prohibited from divulging information under a secrecy law and yet required to divulge it under Right to Information Act. Inconsistency needs resolution and is possible by constructing these laws in a manner as to avoid inconsistency. However, where inconsistency cannot be resolved through interpretation, two provisions of Right to Information Act, should override secrecy laws. Specific provisions are necessary for the purpose. Over time a period of it is necessary to review all laws, civil servant rules and classification of document norms, which restrict the disclosure of information, in order to bring them in conformity with the Right to Information law.

Principle 9: Whistleblower's Protection

"Whistleblowers acting who release information on wrong doing - Whistleblowers must be protected."

Whistleblowers acting in good faith and in the reasonable belief that the information being released by them is substantially true and disclosed evidence *of wrongdoing.* Whistleblowers get protection against any legal, administrative or employment related sanctions for releasing wrongs done by their colleagues/superiors. Wrong doings cover commission of a criminal offence, failure to comply with a legal obligation, a miscarriage of justice, corruption, dishonesty, serious lapses or mismanagement of a public body. Serious threats to health, safety or environment whether linked to individual wrongdoing or not are also protected. Normal rule is that Whistleblower should first approach Chief Vigilance Commission or other appropriate forum, but its effectiveness is marred due to various factors like corruption, red-tapism, etc.

In most of the countries this protection is granted through a separate law. However, till such a separate enactment is made some sort of protection under RTI Act, 2005 is required to be specifically provided, in India too.

Salient Features of RTI Act, 2005

The need for the legal status to the Right to Information is cause and concern today. India observed the judicial pronouncement and democratic need of such right during the post years. The law commission of India's 179th Report and reports of number of committees and councils working on this subject sensitized the Government of India to enact a specific law on the right to information.

Central Government enacted freedom of Information Act, 2002. This Act never came into force as it was never notified. In order to ensure greater and more effective access to information the government resolved that Freedom of Information Act, 2002 enacted by Parliament needs to be more progressive, participatory and meaningful.

The important changes proposed to be incorporated, *inter alia*, include establishment of an appellate machinery with investigating powers to review the decisions of public information officers; penal provisions for failure to provide information as per law; provision to encases maximum disclosure and minimum exemptions, consistent with the constitutional provisions and effective mechanism for access to information and disclosures by authorities, etc. In view of significant changes proposed in the existing Act, the government also decided to repeal the Freedom of Information Act, 2002. The salient features of Right to Information Act are as follows:

1. Enforcement Date

It comes into force on 12th October, 2005, (120th day of its enactment on 15th June, 2005). Some provisions have come into force with immediate effect, viz.:

1. Obligation of publication authorities.
2. Designation of Public Information Officers and Assistant Public Information Officers.
3. Constitution of Central Information Commission.
4. Constitution of State Information Commission.
5. Non-applicability of the Act to Intelligence and Security Organizations.
6. Power to make rules to carry out the provisions of the Act.

2. Extension of the Act

The Act extends to the whole of India except the State of Jammu & Kashmir. *(Sec. 1(2) of Right To Information Act, 2005).*

3. Information: Meaning

Information means any material in any form inducing records, documents, memos, e-mails, opinions, advices, press releases, circulars, orders, logbooks, contracts, reports, papers, samples, models, data material held in any electronic form and information relating to any private body which can be accessed by a Public Authority under any other law for the time being in force. *(Sec. 2(f) of Right To Information Act, 2005).*

4. Right to Information: Meaning

It includes the right to:

i. Inspect works, documents, and records.
ii. Take notes, extracts or certified copies of documents or records.
iii. Take certified samples of material.
iv. Obtain information in the form of printouts, diskettes, floppies, tapes, video cassettes or in any other electronic mode or through printouts. *(Sec. 2(j) of Right To Information Act, 2005).*

Subject to provisions of this Act, all citizens shall have Right to Information *(Sec. 3 of Right To Information Act, 2005).*

The Right to Information is a right conferred on the citizens of India only that too to the individuals. Corporates and Associations can avail the Right to Information through an individual who constitutes their management.

Section 3 of the Act unequivocally declares that all citizens shall have the Right to Information. This right is an integral part of Right to Freedom of Speech and Expression, which is fundamental right. Non-observance of this Act will lead to certain penalties on the erring officials.

The citizen can request the concerned public authority orally or in writing to furnish information and he can also seek for supplementaries and also can seek clarifications.

The application for information was filed by an Association and not in the name of any person. It was held that an Association as Appellant would not come under the definition of citizen. *(Karnataka Indian Medical Manufacturing Association vs. CAO Indian Systems of Medicines, KIC 72 APL06, Karnataka State Information Commission).*

In the Preamble of the RTI Act, the words 'citizen' and 'citizenry' are used in a plural sense. Similarly, in Section 3 of the RTI Act, the word 'Citizens' has been used in a plural sense and not in singular sense. Therefore, a group of citizens are also entitled to apply and seek information under the Right To Information Act 2005.

5. Application Procedure for Requesting Information ***(Sec. 6 of Right To Information Act, 2005)***

i. Apply in writing or through electronic means in English or Hindi or in the official language of the area to the PIO, specifying the particulars of the information sought.
ii. Reason for seeking information is not required to be given. This is an enabling provision as no one will be asked and 'whys' for obtaining information.
iii. Pay fees as may be prescribed (if not belonging to the below poverty line category).

6. The Limit to get the Information ***(Sec. 7 of Right To Information Act, 2005)***

i. 30 days from the date of application.
ii. 48 hours for information concerning the life and liberty of a person.
iii. 5 days shall be added to the above response time, in case the application for information is given to Assistant Public Information Officer.

7. Fees ***(Sec. 7 of Right To Information Act, 2005)***

i. A request for obtaining information shall be accompanied by an application fee of Rs. 10 by way of cash against proper receipt or by demand draft or bankers cheque payable to Account Officer of Public Authority.
ii. If further fees are required, then the same must be intimated in writing with calculated details of how the figure was arrived at.
iii. Application fee to be prescribed must be reasonable.
iv. Applicant can seek review of the decision on fees charged by the PIO by applying to the appropriate appellate authority.
v. No fees will be charged from people living below the poverty line.
vi. Applicant must be provided information free of cost if the PIO fails to comply with the prescribed time limit.

8. Ground for Rejection of Applications

i. If it is covered by exemption from disclosure (Sec.8).
ii. If it infringes copyright of any person others than State (Sec. 9).

9. Obligation of Public Authority ***(Sec. 4 of Right To Information Act, 2005)***

Every public authority shall:

a. Maintain all its records duly catalogued and indexed in a manner and the form which facilitates the Right of Information under the Act and ensure that all records that are appropriate to be computerized are within reasonable time and subject to availability of resources, computerized and connected through a network of all over the country on different systems so that access to records is facilitated.
b. It shall publish within one hundred and twenty days of enactment.
    i. the particulars of its originations, functions and duties;
    ii. the powers and duties of its officers and employees;
    iii. the procedure followed in decision making process, including channels of supervision and accountability;
    iv. the norms set by for the discharge of its functions;

v. the rules, regulations, instructions manuals and records used by its employees for discharging of its functions.

vi. A statement of the categories of the document held by it or under its control.

vii. the particulars of any arrangements that exists for consultation with, or representation by the members of the public, in relation to the formulation of policy or implementation thereof;

viii. a statement of the boards, councils, committees and other bodies consisting of two or more persons constituted by it. Additionally, information as to whether the meetings of these are open to the public or the minutes of such meetings accessible to the public.

ix. A directory of its officers and employees;

x. The monthly remuneration received by each of its officers and employees, including the system of compensation as provided in its regulations;

xi. The budget allocated to each of its agency, indicating the particulars of all plans, proposed expenditures and reports on disbursements made;

xii. The manner of execution of subsidy programmes, including the amounts allocated and the details and beneficiaries of such programmes;

xiii. Particulars of recipients of concessions, permits or authorizations granted by it;

xiv. Details of the information available to, or held by it, reduced in an electronic form;

xv. The particulars of facilities available to citizens for obtaining information, including the working hours of a library or reading room, if maintained for public use;

xvi. The names, designations and other particulars of the Public Information Officers. [Sec. 4(l)(b)]

c. *Suo moto* Publication: It shall be constant endeavours of public authority to provide much information to public at regular interval. The provision is an enabling one and if implemented will prove to be citizen-friendly as they will get most of the information from government initiatives only.

10. Public Authority *(Sec. 2(h) of Right To Information Act, 2005)*

It means any authority or body or institution of self-government established or constituted: [Sec. 2(h)]

- by or under the Constitution;
- by any other law made by Parliament;
- by any other law made by State Legislature;
- by notification issued or order made by the appropriate government and includes any:
  (a) body owned, controlled or substantially financed;
  (b) non-government organisations substantially financed directly or indirectly by the appropriate government.

The definition at first instances seems to be broad which to some extent is true also but bodies are still excluded which are directly in business with common citizen. For instance a private sugar mill or cotton mill. Will the Act be applicable to them? It is often seen that there nature of work is similar to the government mill, so their bodies must also come within the purview of the Act.

11. Public Information Officers (PIOs) *(Sec. 5 of Right To Information Act, 2005)*

PIOs are officers designated by the public authorities in all administrative units or offices under it to provide information to the citizens requesting for information under the Act. Any officer, whose assistance has been sought by the PIO for the proper discharge of his or her duties, shall render all assistance and for the purpose of contraventions of the provisions of this Act, such other officer shall be treated as a PIO.

12. Duties of a PIO

- PIO shall deal with request from persons seeking information and where the request cannot be made in writing, to render reasonable assistance to the person to reduce the same in writing. *(Sec. 6(1)(b) of Right To Information Act, 2005).*
- If the information requested for is held by or its subject matter is closely connected with the function of another public authority, the PIO shall transfer, within 5 days, the request to that other public authority and inform the applicant immediately. *(Sec. 6(3) of Right To Information Act, 2005).*
- PIO may seek the assistance of any other officer for the proper discharge of his/her duties. *(Sec. 5(4) of Right To Information Act, 2005).*

- PIO, on receipt of a request, shall as expeditiously as possible, and in any case within 30 days of the receipt of the request, either provide the information on payment of such fee as may be prescribed or reject the request for any of the reasons specified in Sec. 8 on Sec. 9. *(Sec. 7(1) of Right To Information Act, 2005).*
- Where the information requested for concern the life or liberty of a person, the same shall be provided within forty-eight hours of the receipt of the request.
- If the PIO fails to give decision on the request within the period specified, he shall be deemed to have refused the request. *(Sec. 7(2) of Right To Information Act, 2005).*
- Where a request has been rejected, the PIO shall communicate to the requester: (i) the reasons for such rejection, (ii) the period within which an appeal against such rejection may be preferred, and (iii) the particulars of the Appellate Authority. *(Sec. 7(8) of Right To Information Act, 2005).*
- PIO shall provide information in the form in which it is sought unless it would disproportionately divert the resources of the Public Authority or would be detrimental to the safety or preservation of the record in question. *(Sec. 9 of Right To Information Act, 2005).*
- If allowing partial access, the PIO shall give a notice to the applicant, informing. *(Sec. 10(2) of Right To Information Act, 2005).*
  - (a) that only part of the record requested, after severance of the record containing information which is exempt from disclosure, is being provided; *(Sec. 10(2)(a) of Right To Information Act, 2005).*
  - (b) the reasons for the decision, including any findings on any material question of fact, referring to the material on which those findings were based; *(Sec. 10(2)(b) of Right To Information Act, 2005).*
  - (c) the name and designation of the person giving the decision; *(Sec. 10(2)(c) of Right To Information Act, 2005).*
  - (d) the details of the fees calculated by him or her and the amount of fee which the applicant is required to deposit; *(Sec. 10(2)(d) of Right To Information Act, 2005),* and
  - (e) his or her rights with respect to review of the decision regarding non-disclosure of part of the information, the amount of fee charged or the form of access provided. *(Sec. 10(2)(e) of Right To Information Act, 2005).*
- If information sought has been supplied by third party or is treated as confidential by that third party, the PIO shall give a written notice to the third party within 5 days from the receipt of the request and take its representation into consideration. *(Sec. 11(1) of Right To Information Act, 2005).*
- Third party must be given a chance to make a representation before the PIO within 10 days from the date of receipt of such notice. *(Sec. 11(2) of Right To Information Act, 2005).*

13. Central Information Commission: Constitution *(Sec. 12 of Right to Information Act, 2005)*

1. Central Information Commission to be constituted by the Central Government through a Gazette Notification.
2. Commission includes one Chief Information Commissioner (CIC) and not more than 10 Information Commissioners (IC) who will be appointed by the President of India.
3. Oath of Office will be administered by the President of India according to the form set out in the First Schedule.
4. Commission shall have its Headquarter in Delhi. Other offices may be established in other parts of the country with the approval of the Central Govt.
5. Commission will exercise its powers without being subjected to direction by any other authority.

14. Eligibility criteria and what is the process of Appointment of CIC/IC?

1. Candidates for CIC/IC must be persons of eminence in public life with wide knowledge and experience in law, science and technology, social service, management, journalism, mass media or administration and governance. *(Sec. 12(5) of Right To Information Act, 2005).*
2. CIC/IC shall not be a Member of Parliament or Member of the Legislature of any State or Union Territory. He shall not hold any other office of profit or connected with any political party or carrying on any business or pursuing any profession. *(Sec. 12(6) of Right To Information Act, 2005).*
3. Appointment Committee includes Prime Minister (Chair), Leader of the Opposition in the Lok Sabha and one Union Cabinet Minister to be nominated by the Prime Minister. *(Sec. 12(3) of Right To Information Act, 2005).*

15. Term of office and other service-conditions of CIC *(In case of Central Information Commission it is Sec. 13 and in case of State Information Commission the provisions are in Sec. 16)*

1. CIC shall be appointed for a term of 5 years from date on which he enters upon his office or till he attains the age of 65 years, whichever is earlier. *(Sec. 13(2) of Right To Information Act, 2005).*
2. CIC is not eligible for reappointment.
3. Salary will be the same as that Chief Election Commissioner. This will not be varied to their disadvantage during their service period.
4. IC shall hold office for a term of five years from the date on which he enters upon his office or till he attains the age of sixty-five years, whichever is earlier and shall not be eligible for reappointment as IC. *(Sec. 13(2) of Right To Information Act, 2005).*
5. Salary will be the same as that of the Election Commissioner. This will not be varied to the disadvantage of the IC during service. *(Sec. 13(5)(b) of Right To Information Act, 2005).*
6. IC is eligible for appointment as CIC but will not hold office for more than a total of five years including his/her term as IC. *(Sec. 13(2) of Right To Information Act, 2005).*

16. The State Information Commission: Constitution *(Sec. 15 of Right To Information Act, 2005)*

1. The State Information Commission will be constituted by the State Government through a Gazette notification. It will have one State Chief Information Commissioner (SCIC) and not more than 10 State Information Commissioners (SICs) to be appointed by the Governor.
2. Oath of office will be administered by the Governor according to the form set out in the First Schedule.
3. The headquarters of the State Information Commission shall be at such place as the State Government may specify. Other offices may be established in other parts of the State with the approval of the State Government.
4. The Commission will exercise its powers without being subjected to any other authority.

17. The eligibility criterion and the process of appointment of State Chief Information Commissioner/State Information Commissioners *(Sec. 15 of Right To Information Act, 2005)*

The Appointment Committee will be headed by the Chief Minister. Other members include the Leader of the Opposition in the Legislative Assembly and one Cabinet Minister nominated by the Chief Minister. *(Sec. 15(3) of Right To Information Act, 2005).*

The qualifications for appointment as SCIC/SICs shall be the same as that for Central Commissioners.

The salary of the State Chief Information Commissioner will be the same as of an Election Commissioner. The salary of the State Information Commissioner will be the same as that of the Chief Secretary of the State Government.

18. Powers and Functions of Information Commissions *(Secs. 18 and 19 of Right To Information Act, 2005)*

The Central Information Commission/State Information Commission has a duty to receive complaints from any person who has not been able to submit an information request because a PIO has not been appointed;

(a) who has been refused information that was requested;
(b) who has received no response to his/her information request within the specified time limits; (Complaint case against the PIO can be filed under this Section of the Act)
(c) who thinks the fees charged are unreasonable;
(d) who thinks information given is incomplete or false or misleading; and
(e) any other matter relating to obtaining information under this law.

A. Power to order inquiry if there are reasonable grounds *(Sec. 18(2) of Right To Information Act, 2005)*

CIC/SCIC will have powers of Civil Court such as:

(a) summoning and enforcing attendance of persons, compelling them to give oral or written evidence on oath and to produce documents or things;
(b) requiring the discovery and inspection of documents;
(c) receiving evidence on affidavit;
(d) requisitioning public records or copies from any court or office;
(e) issuing summons for examination of witnesses or documents;
(f) any other matter which may be prescribed.

All records covered by this law (including those covered by exemptions) must be given to CIC/SCIC during inquiry for examination.

B. Power to secure compliance of its decisions from the Public Authority includes *(Sec. 19(8)(a) of Right To Information Act, 2005)*

(a) providing access to information in a particular form;

(b) directing the public authority to appoint a PIO/APIO where none exists;

(c) publishing information or categories of information;

(d) making necessary changes to the practices relating to management, maintenance and destruction of records;

(e) enhancing training provision for officials on RTI;

(f) seeking an annual report from the public authority on compliance with this law;

(g) require it to compensate for any loss or other detriment suffered by the applicant *(Sec. 19(8)(b) of Right To Information Act, 2005)*.;

(h) impose penalties under this law *(Sec. 19(8)(c) of Right To Information Act, 2005)*.; or

(i) reject the application *(Sec. 19(8)(d) of Right To Information Act, 2005)*.

19. Appeal *(Sec. 19 of Right To Information Act, 2005)*

The applicant can move an Appeal under following conditions:

1. Does not receive decision written time specified in the Act.
2. Is aggrieved by the decision by the PIO.
3. The time limit is 30 days and appeal may be preferred to senior officer. The appeal may be admitted even after the expiry of 30 days if the officer is satisfied that the appellant was prevented by sufficient cause from filing the appeal in time.
4. There is also provision of second Appeal and it shall lie within 90 days from the date on which decision should have been made or actually received with Central or State Commission as the case be.
5. The onus to prove that a denial of a request was justified shall be on the Public Information Officer, who denied the request. The appeal shall be disposed within 30 days and not extending more than 45 days. The decision of commission shall be binding.

20. Penalties *(Sec. 20 of Right To Information Act, 2005)*

The Central or State Commission when deciding any complaint or appeal is of opinion that PIO, has without any reasonable cause refused to receive an application for information or has not furnished information within time or *mala-fidely* denied the request or knowingly gives incorrect, incomplete or misleading information or destroyed information, it shall impose penalty of Rs. 250 each day till application is received or information is furnished, so however the total amount of such penalty shall not exceed Rs. 25,000.

It is to be noted that Act does not provide anywhere whether the penalty will be charged personally or department will pay. But the anomaly is settled now and Central Information Commission has declared that officer is personally liable.

21. Reporting Procedure *(Sec. 25 of Right To Information Act, 2005)*

1. Central Information Commission will send an annual report to the Central Government on the implementation of the provisions of this law at the end of the year. The State Information Commission will send a report to the State Government.
2. Each Ministry has a duty to compile report from its Public Authorities and send them to the Central Information Commission or State Information Commission, as the case may be.
3. Each report will contain details of number of requests received by each Public Authority, number of rejections and appeals, particulars of any disciplinary action taken, amount of fees and charges collected, etc.
4. Central Government will table the Central Information Commission report before Parliament after the end of each year. The concerned State Government will table the report of the State Information Commission before the Vidhan Sabha (and the Vidhan Parishad wherever applicable). *(Sec. 25 of Right To Information Act, 2005)*.

22. Not Open to Disclosure *(Sec. 8 of Right To Information Act, 2005)*

The following is exempt from disclosure (Sec. 8 of Right To Information Act, 2005).

(i) Information, disclosure of which would prejudicially affect the sovereignty and integrity of India, the security, strategic, scientific or economic interests of the State, relation with foreign State or lead to incitement of an offence;

(ii) Information which has been expressly forbidden to be published by any court of law or tribunal or the disclosure of which may constitute contempt of court;

(iii) Information, the disclosure of which would cause a breach of privilege of Parliament or the State Legislature;

(iv) Information including commercial confidence, trade secrets or intellectual property, the disclosure of which would harm the competitive position of a third party, unless the competent authority is satisfied that larger public interest warrants the disclosure of such information;

(v) Information available to a person in his fiduciary relationship, unless the competent authority is satisfied that larger public interest warrants the disclosure of such information;

(vi) Information received in confidence from foreign Government;

(vii) Information, the disclosure of which would endanger the life or physical safety of any person or identify the source of information or assistance given in confidence for law enforcement or security purposes;

(viii) Information which would impede the process of investigation or apprehension or prosecution of offenders;

(ix) Cabinet papers including records of deliberations of the Council of Ministers, Secretaries and other officers;

(x) Information which relates to personal information the disclosure of which has no relationship to any public activity or interest, or which would cause unwarranted invasion of the privacy of the individual;

(xi) Notwithstanding any of the exemption listed above, a public authority may allow access to information, if public interest in disclosure outweighs the harm to the protected interests.

23. Partial Disclosure Allowed *(Sec. 10 of Right To Information Act, 2005)*

Only that part of the record which does not contain any information which is exempt from disclosure and which can reasonably be severed from any part that contains exempt information, may be provided. *(Sec. 10 of Right To Information Act, 2005).*

24. Act not Applicable to *(Sec. 24 of Right To Information Act, 2005).*

Central Intelligence and Security agencies specified in the Second Schedule like IB, RAW, Directorate of Revenue Intelligence, Central Economic Intelligence Bureau, Directorate of Enforcement,

Narcotics Control Bureau, Aviation Research Centre, Special Frontier Force, BSF, DRPF, ITBP, CISF, NSG, Assam Rifles, Special Service Bureau, Special Branch (CID), Andaman and Nicobar, the Crime Branch-CID-CB, Dadra and Nagar Haveli and Special Branch, Lakshadweep Police.

Agencies specified by the State Governments through a Notification will also be excluded. *The exclusion, however, is not absolute and these organisations have an obligation to provide information pertaining to allegations of corruption and human rights violations.* Further, information relating to allegations of human rights violations could be given but only with the approval of the Central or State Information Commission, as the case may be. (Sec. 24)

25. The Role of Central/State Governments *(Sec. 26 of Right To Information Act, 2005)*

1. Develop educational programmes for the public especially disadvantaged communities on RTI.
2. Encourage Public Authorities to participate in the development and organisation of such programmes.
3. Promote timely dissemination of accurate information to the public.
4. Train officers and develop training materials.
5. Compile and disseminate a User Guide for the public in the respective official language.
6. Publish names, designation, postal addresses and contact details of PIOs and other information such as notices regarding fees to be paid, remedies available in law if request is rejected, etc. (Sec. 26)

26. The Rule making power *(Sec. 27 and 28 of Right To Information Act, 2005)*

Central Government, State Governments and the Competent Authority as defined in S. 2(e) are vested with powers to make rules to carry-out the provisions of the Right To Information Act, 2005 (S. 27 and S. 28)

27. The power to deal with the difficulties while implementing this Act *(Sec. 30 of Right To Information Act, 2005).*

If any difficulty arises in giving effect to the provisions in the Act, the Central Government may, by Order published in the Official Gazette, make provisions necessary/expedient for removing the difficulty. (Sec. 30)

SCHEDULE

In *Aphali Pharmaceuticals Ltd. vs. State of Maharashtra* (1989) 4 SCC 378: AIR 1989 SC 2227, it was held:

"A Schedule in an Act of Parliament is mere question of drafting. The Schedule may be used in construing provisions in the body of the Act. It is as much an Act of Legislature as the Act itself and it must be read together with the Act for all-purpose of construction. Expression in the schedule cannot control or prevail against the express enactment and in case of any inconsistency between the Schedule and the enactment is to prevail and if any part of the Schedule cannot be made to correspond it must yield to the Act. It is the legislative intent that is material.

Schedules appended to the Statutes form part of the Statute. Schedules are added in the end in order to avoid encumbering the Sections in the Statute with matters of excessive detail. Schedules generally contain details and various forms to facilitate the working of the policy underlying the Sections of the Statute itself. Schedules occasionally contain such rules and forms that can be suitably amended according to local or changing conditions by process simpler than normal one required for amending other parts of a Statute.

The division of a Statute into sections and Schedules is a mere matter of convenience and a Schedule therefore may contain substantive enactment. (*A.G vs. Lamplough* (1878) 3 Ex D 214: 38 LT 87: 47 LJ QB 555 (BRETT, LJ): *Ujagar Prints vs. Union of India* AIR 1989 SC 516: 1989 (3) SCC 488. They may go even beyond the scope of the Section to which the Schedule may appear to be connected by its heading. In such a situation the clear positive provision in the Schedule may be held to prevail over the *prima facie* indication furnished by its heading and the purpose of the Schedule contained in the Act. (*Ujagar Prints vs. Union of India* AIR 1989 SC 516: 1989 (3) SCC 488; *Aphali Pharmaceuticals Ltd. vs. State of Maharashtra* (1989) 4 SCC 378: AIR 1989 SC 2227). In case the language is not clear, the provision of the Schedule may be construed as confined to the purpose indicated by its heading and the Section in the Statute to which it appears to be connected. In case of any conflict between the body of the Act and the Schedule the former shall prevail. (*Aphali Pharmaceuticals Ltd. vs. State of Maharashtra* (1989) 4 SCC 378: AIR 1989 SC 2227).

RIGHT TO INFORMATION – AN OVERVIEW

- When you pay for things you buy at a shop, do you not ask for an account and a receipt?
- Then why do you not seek an account from your government?
- The Government spends your money. You have a right to hold it to account.
- The right to seek and receive information is Your basic HUMAN RIGHT.
- Tell your government you have the RIGHT TO KNOW.

Right to Information Act, 2005

Right to information is more or less a universal concept. The concept of Right to Know and Right to Information, and right to make a demand for certain documents with the public authorities had been dealt with, and have been appraised. The idea that governments withhold information for the public's benefit has become outdated. During the last decade, many countries have enacted legislations on Freedom of Information, giving their citizens access to governmental information, and thus, opening way to democracy in the real perspective.

In India, the Official Secrets Act, 1923 was enacted to protect the official secrets. The new information law intend to disclose information, replacing the 'culture of secrecy' in administration to 'culture of openness and transparency'. It promote public accountability which is a part of governance. Where the accountability is exposed, the malpractice, mismanagement, abuse of discretion, bribery, etc., are trimmed down to their size.

The right to know flows directly from the guarantee of free speech and expression in Article 19(1)a of the Constitution of India. Yet, it requires fair and efficient procedures to make the Freedom of Information work.

The first and most well known Right to Information movement in India was by the Mazdoor Kisan Shakti Sangathan (MKSS) in Rajasthan during the early 1990s. MKSS's struggle for the access to village accounts and transparency in administration is widely credited and sparked off the right to information movement in India. The Right to Information Act, 2005 provides the procedure by which the public can make requests for information held by the public authorities. It also provides for the set up of Information Commissions to deal with complaints and appeals arising in the information system. The Act provides for the openness of the governmental activities and to publish regular information. The Act also provides minimal exceptions to the right to information where national security, public order, privacy, etc., are concerned.

The basic object of the Act is to provide access to information for the common man. And in order to exercise the freedom of speech and expression, a citizen should be informed. Informed citizenry which is the essence of RTI Act is the curator of democracy. The Act is also beneficial to the governments themselves as openness and transparency in the decision making process assist in developing citizens' trust in government actions and maintaining a civil and democratic society. The transparency and accountability in the public authority shall contain corruption and thus, the government and its various instrumentalities become accountable to the governed, i.e., the citizens.

Principles of the Right to Information

The three key principles on which the Right to Information is based are:

1. The right of every citizen to request access to information from the government about its decisions and activities.
2. The duty on all government bodies to provide information, unless releasing it would genuinely cause serious harm to public interest.
3. The additional duty on the government to routinely publish key information even in the absence of a request.

SIX reasons why citizens should have the Right to Information

1. Promotes democratic governance

Democracy only truly works when: (1) informed citizens are able to thoughtfully choose their representatives on the basis of the strength of their record and performance, rather than on rumours or ethnic/geographic, religious affiliations; and (2) Citizens can hold their elected representatives and officials to account for their policies, decisions and other actions while in power. The right to information enables citizens to check whether government acts according to democratic values and constitutional norms.

2. Supports participatory development

Often governments design and implement development strategies in a closed environment. However, if governments are obliged to provide information, citizens can participate in the planning, implementation, monitoring and evaluation of development programme.

3. Improves quality of service delivery

Proactive publication of information by the government can be used to promote more effective service delivery. Such disclosure supports more informed participation of communities in the operation and oversight of public services. Information should be regularly published at all levels about how much public money is being spent, what the money is being spent on, over what period of time, and by which departments and to what norms of service delivery are citizens entitled. Citizens can use the information to demand more effective service delivery from the various levels of governments.

4. Promotes national stability

Democracy and national stability are enhanced by policies of openness which promote greater public trust in government. Information seeking and sharing establishes a two-way dialogue between citizens and the state which can combat feelings of alienation and powerlessness. Open government addresses issues of exclusion or unfair advantage of one group over another

5. Exposes corruption

Access to Information or Right to Information is an effective tool for curbing corruption. When citizens can access information about government activities and decisions, it is much harder for officials to cover up their corrupt practices and hide poor policymaking. The right to information improves public administration by acting as a powerful deterrent to corruption in government .

6. Supports equitable economic development

Access to information presupposes a transparent licensing and regulatory requirements. The benefits of economic development have often not been equitably enjoyed by all citizens. Simple and cheap access to information will empower smaller stakeholders to more effectively participate in the economy, ensuring equitable economic growth.

Basic Principles of Right to Information

To be successful, any law that intends to promote free access to information should have the following principles. These principles have evolved over time, which have been consistently endorsed by the UN. These should be incorporated into all information access law:

Maximum Disclosure:

All arms of government for example, the legislature, the executive, the courts, police and the armed services should be covered by the law. Even the private sector should be covered, at least where it is spending public money and/or performing public functions. All bodies should be required to release as much information as possible.

Minimum Exceptions:

Exceptions should be included only to protect and promote the public interest and should be kept to a minimum. The law should not permit non-disclosure to protect government from embarrassment or the exposure of wrongdoing. Exemptions should ALL be subject to a harm test and blanket 'public interest override' whereby a document which could be exempt should still be disclosed if the public interest in the specific case requires it.

Simple Access Procedures:

The law should include clear and uncomplicated access procedures so that people can obtain information quickly and simply. Application processes should be user-friendly for the illiterate and the poor. Any fees for access should be kept to an absolute minimum because the tax payer already funds the information creation and maintain process.

Independent Appeals Mechanisms:

A powerful independent, impartial body such as an Information Commission, Ombudsman or Human Rights Commission must be given the power to review refusals to disclose information and compel release. The fear of independent scrutiny ensures that exemption clauses are interpreted responsibly and citizens' requests are not unduly obstructed.

Penalties:

The powers of oversight bodies should include a power to impose penalties for non-compliance with the law. Without sanctions, such as fines for delay or imprisonment for wilful destruction of documents, there is little compulsion on government officials to comply with the law.

Monitoring Reporting and Training

The law should mandate a body to monitor and support the implementation of the Act by developing codes of practice and submitting annual reports to Parliament. The law should also require training for officials and public education programmes to be held.

Different ways in which access to information is provided under RTI Act: The main object of the Act is to provide information. And the Act provides the ways in which the information can be accessed. The Sec. 3 states that, subject to the provisions of this Act, all citizens shall have the Right to Information. The Act enforces a duty upon the public authorities to disclose all information starting from the particulars of its organisation, functions, and duties, to budget allocated to each of its agency. It shall also publish relevant facts while formatting important policies which affect public and to give reasons for its administrative or quasi-judicial decisions to affected person. Thus, the Act imposes an obligation upon the public authorities to disclose information. Also, it is stated under Sec. 4 (2) that every public authority shall take constant steps to provide information *suo moto* to the public. Thus, the authorities have to give information voluntarily so that the public have minimum resort to use this Act.

The public authorities also have to disseminate information widely in any form which is easily accessible to the public. The word 'dissemination' has been defined in the Act. Disseminated means making known or communicated the information to the public through noticeboards, newspapers, public announcements, media broadcasts, the internet or any other means, including, inspection of offices of any public authority. Thus the dissemination of information by public authorities has been made mandatory by the Act.

Finally, the Information can be obtained by request in writing or through electronic means in English or Hindi or in the official language of the area in which the applications is being made (Sec. 6). Here, the person has to give payment of fees. And where the request cannot be made in writing, the Central PIO and State PIO shall render all assistance to the person to reduce the oral request into writing.

Where the information has not been provided correctly or within time, access to information is made available by means of appeal or complaint to the Information Commission. (Sec. 8(a)1).

Right to Information Act, 2005, what should you know?

The Right to Information (RTI) Act, 2005 has come into effect from 12th October, 2005. It is applicable to the whole of India except the State of Jammu & Kashmir. The objective of RTI Act is to promote transparency, contain corruption, facilitate easy access to information for the public and ensure citizens participation in administration. In other words RTI Act seeks to improve the quality of Governance. For a common man RTI Act is another tool to obtain information about the services available, the eligibility conditions and the status of his complaint/grievance.

What is covered?

The RTI Act is applicable to all bodies or institutions of self-government established or set up by or under the Constitution or under other Acts made by Parliament or by a State Legislature of by notification or order issued by the appropriate government. In other words the RTI Act covers all departments of State and Central Government, Union Territories, local bodies like City Municipal Councils, Corporations, Jilla Panchayat, Tatuk Panchayat and Gram Panchayat.

Government schools, colleges and aided institutions, government hospitals, police stations, nationalized banks and Non-governmental Organisations (NGOs) which are substantially financed by the government also come under the purview of RTI Act. Those bodies covered under the RTI Act are called PUBLIC AUTHORITIES.

What is information?

Information is any material in any form, (t includes records, documents, memos, e-mails, advices, press releases, circulars, orders, logbooks, contracts, reports, papers, samples, models, data material held in any electronic form. It also includes information relating to any private body which can be accessed by the public authority under any law for the time-being in force.

Whom to ask for information?

Every public authority will have designated Public Information Officers (PIOs). You have to apply to the respective PIO for information. As per the government directives, the names and address of the PIOs in a public authority as well as their contact information should be provided at the authority's website. It shall also be displayed in the notice-boards.

Who can seek information?

Every Indian citizen has the right to seek information. However, if an application is made by an employee or office bearer of any corporation, association, company, NGO, etc., who is also a citizen of India, information shall be supplied to him/her, provided the applicant gives his/her full name. In such cases, it will be presumed that a citizen has sought information at the address of the corporation, NGO, etc.

When you can ask?

You can ask if you need information on government activity, government's reasons for certain decisions, information on suspected corruption and to suggest certain improvements. You can also ask when your complaint or grievance is not resolved within a reasonable time.

What you can ask?

Apart from information you can also ask for inspection of works, documents and records. You can take notes, extracts, certified copies of documents/records. You have the right to take certified samples of materials, information on discs, floppies, tapes, video cassettes or any other electronic mode. You have the right to take computer printouts of information.

However the Public Authority is not supposed to create information or to interpret information or solve the problems raised by the applicant or to furnish replies to hypothetical questions. Only such information can be had under the RTI Act which already exists with the public authority.

How to ask?

You can ask information either in writing to the Public Information Officer (PIO) of a department or through e-mail. Though each of the States may have prescribed a format of the application, it is not compulsory. Application can be made on a plain paper in writing in English or Hindi or in the official language of the area in which the application is made.

What should the application contain?

Your application should be addressed to the concerned PIO and contain your name, address, telephone number and e-mail (if available) and the information you require. The year to which the information pertains should be included. The application should also give the details of the application fee paid. Finally it should have your signature, date and place.

Should you indicate the reason for request?

No. You need not reveal why you require the information.

Does it cost money to obtain information?

Yes. Depending on the rules framed by your State Government you will have to pay the application fee and additional fee for the information. In Karnataka the application fee is Rs. 10 and Rs. 2 per page of A3/A4 size for the information. The PIO will decide the amount for larger size papers and for samples and models. Wherever information can be provided on a floppy or a disc the charge will be Rs. 50 per disc or floppy. Similarly, separate fee is prescribed for inspection of files. However, no charge be paid for the 1^{s} hour of inspection.

Is there any exemption from payment of fees?

Yes. If you are belonging to Below the Poverty Line (BPL) you need not pay the application fee. If the information you are seeking is up to 100 pages, it will be provided free of cost. In excess of 100 pages will be charged at rates applicable to other category of applicants. In case information is provided beyond the time limits specified in the RTI Act all applicants are eligible to get the information free of cost

When will I get the information?

The information you seek from the PIO has to be provided or refused within 30 days from the date of application, 48 hours for information concerning the life and liberty of a person. Five days shall be added to this time, in case the application for information is given to Assistant Public Information Officer. If the interest of a third party is involved the time limit is 40 days.

Is appeal against PIO allowed?

In case you fail to get information within the prescribed time limit or is not satisfied with the information furnished you may prefer an appeal to the First Appellate Authority who is an officer senior in rand to the PIO. The appeal should be filed within 30 days from the date on which the limit of 30 days of supply of information is expired or from the date on which the information or decision of the PIO is received. No money is required for preferring an appeal. If the First Appellate Authority fails or pass an order or if you are dissatisfied with the order of the first appellate authority you may prefer a Second Appeal with the Central or State Information Commission as the case may be, within 90 days from the date on which the decision should have been made or was actually received.

What should the Appeal Application contain?

The Appeal can be on a plain paper containing your name, address, number given to your earlier application, name and address of the PIO, particulars of the decision against which information was denied, date of application and reasons for appeal. It may also contain the relief sought and a verification statement by the appellant.

When can the PIO refuse information?

You may not be given the information if: (a) it affects the sovereignty, integrity, security, scientific or economic interest of a state, etc., (b) it is expressly forbidden by the law or a tribunal (c) it may cause breach of privilege of Parliament or State Legislature (d) includes commercial confidence, trade secrets or intellectual property (e) available to a person in his fiduciary relationship (f) received in confidence from a foreign government (g) it impedes investigation procedures (h) cabinet papers (i) personal information.

However, the PIO may provide the above information if public interest in disclosure outweighs the harm to the protected interests.

What are the other reasons for refusal of information?

In addition to the above a PIO may refuse information: (a) if it is too general in nature. In such a case the PIO has to assist you in reframing the question (b) if the volume of information required that it is to be retrieved or processed would involve an unreasonable diversion of the resources of a public authority and would adversely interfere with the functioning of such authority (c) relates to information that is contained in published material available to public or is likely to be published within 30 days of the receipt of such an application (d) relates to information which would cause unwarranted invasion of the privacy of any persons, or (f) if it infringes the copyright of any person other than the State.

Will the defaulting PIO penalised?

Yes. If a PIO fails to furnish the information or fails to communicate the rejection order within the time specified or does not give the particulars of the appellate authority, the PIO shall be liable to pay a penalty of Rs. 250 per day for each day of delay, subject to a maximum of Rs. 25,000. The Information Commission may also recommend disciplinary action against the PIO concerned.

Information Commission

The Act gives State Information Commission or Central Information Commission, as the case may be, an important role in developing the system and mechanism for the disclosure and dissemination of information by considering the public interest and the necessity of right to know. They are given wide discretion and they are expected to ensure the transparency and to be liberal in interpreting the provisions of the Act in favour of disclosure than concealment. It is their duty to pursue the bureaucratic mindset and to guide them towards dissemination of information. The State Information Commission or Central Information Commission, as the case may be, are autonomous bodies without being subjected to directions by any other authority.

The Act states that the Information Commissioners shall be persons of eminence in public life with wide knowledge and experience in law, science and technology, social service, management, journalism, mass media or administration and governance. The Act does not restrict a former or serving civil servant from becoming a commissioner. But various advocacy groups like National Campaign for People's Right to Information (NCPRI) expresses that a person who has served in a particular ministry should not be made the Information Commissioner responsible for that ministry because there might be a conflict of interest.

Therefore, it is important to have a transparent process of selecting the information commissioners to ensure independence and competence and they are truly eminent, suited to the position.

The Information Commissioner has wide powers to secure compliance of its decisions from the public authority like,

- Directing the public authority to appoint PIO if they are not designated in a public authority
- Publishing information or categories of information
- Enhancing training provision for officials on right to information
- Impose penalties under the Act
- Direct the Public authority to take departmental actions under service rules
- Providing access to information, if requested, in a particular form
- To seek an annual report from the public authority in compliance with the Act.
- Require the public authority to compensate the complainant for any detriment suffered
- Reject the application .

Appeals: Sec. 19 of the Act provides two-tier system of appeals – First Appeal and Second Appeal.

First Appeal: Any person who is aggrieved by the decision of the Central PIO or State PIO, as the case may be, or not receiving the requested information within 30 days, can prefer a first appeal before the First Appellate Authority.

The Appellate Authority shall be an officer who is senior in rank to the Central PIO or State PIO, in each public authority. And the appeal is to be filed within 30 days from the expiry of time period specified for receiving a decision or from receipt of a decision. But this limitation period shall be relaxed if the appellate authority is satisfied that there is sufficient cause that prevented the filing of appeal within the time limit.

An appeal can be preferred also by the third party in case of third party information. [Sec.19 (2)] and third party means a person other than the citizen making a request for information and includes public authority.

Second Appeal: The second appeal lies before the State or Central Information Commission against the decision of the first appellate authority. The second appeal has to be filed within 90 days from the date of receipt of the decision, which can be condoned, in case the commission is satisfied that there are sufficient reasons for the delay.

As per Section 19(7), the decision of Central or State Information Commission, as the case may be, shall be binding. The Information Commission can review their own decisions, if there is a technical error in the decision or if there was an omission to consider relevant material facts in a particular case.

Also it is to be noted that, it is the requester who appeal under the Act. There is no provision in the RTI Act to consider appeals or complaints by the PIO himself against the order of an Appellate Authority. This is because the PIO is the information provider and hence, there is no question of denial of information by the PIO.

Is RTI Act successful?

The RTI Act has paved way for informed citizenry which would strengthen the democratic Government of India. With the enactment of Information Act, we can use our right to speech and expressions and control the governmental activities effectively. Since the Act requires information regarding the pendency of application, the reasons as to why they are not disposed of, etc., now, there is improvement in the efficiency of the departments. There is always the risk of a designated official calling for the relevant information at the instance of a citizen which will act as a check on the inefficiency of officers. Thus, the government becomes accountable to the citizens. The idea of open government is becoming a reality with the implementation of RTI Act.

One of the important after effects of the Act is changing the mindset of the bureaucracy. The RTI Act can be called a success only if the bureaucracy accepts that they have constitutional obligation to serve information, at the instance of request. There is always a wide disparity between the legislation in theory and legislation in practice. Several of the legislations have met failure in practical implementation. And this adds to the 'social cause' of Right to Information, which shall maintain transparency in administration, to restrain corruption to greater extent. And it has to be noted that several legislations have been enacted after the independence, but very few of them have been successfully implemented and having such a massive social impact.

Perhaps there is no other law like RTI Act, which touches the day-to-day life of a common man.

HOW TO FILE AN APPLICATION

Submitting an application under the Right to Information (RTI) Act, 2005 is not a difficult proposition. All it requires is to identify a subject and the body from which you need the information. For example, you may like to know the total amount allocated for various developmental works for your ward or gram panchayat. Or if you want to know how your MP or MLA is spending his/her MP/MLA Local Area Development Fund you may get such information by using the RTI Act. In case you are interested in knowing the fate of your application for a ration card, electricity supply connection, water connection, building plan sanction or any other grievance with the public authorities, you may know it through the RTI Act.

Here are the steps you need to follow for filing an application under the RTI Act Section 6.

Step 1: Identifying the Public Authority

The first step in seeking information under the RTI Act, 2005 is to identify the Public Authority who holds the information you want. In case you are not sure of the public authority, you can consider the one most likely to have that information. Even if you submit the application to an office which does not have the information that you want, it doesn't matter. The law requires that the public authority cannot return the application, but has to transfer it to the correct public authority who has the information and inform you about the transfer. You need not pay the application again to this public authority.

Step 2: Identify the Public Information Officer

After identifying the public authority, the next step is to identify the exact person known as the Public Information Officer (PIO) or Assistant Public Information Officer (APIO) who has the information that you require. In some public authorities there may be more than one PIO. In such a case you may have to identify the correct PIO. The public authorities are supposed to display the details of the PIOs in the noticeboards. In case you submit the application to an APIO the time limits for a response to your application will increase from 30 to 35 days.

Step 3: Preparing the Application

Drafting the application is the most important step in exercising your right to information. Your application should be clear and concise. The RTI Act allows you to write or draft the application in English, Hindi or in the official language of your area. The application can also be sent by e-mail. It is important to draft your application in specific terms so that the PIO cannot return it on the grounds that it was too vague or difficult to understand.

Though some of the State Governments have prescribed a format in which the application is to be made, it is not compulsory. You can draft the application on your own, provided it contains essential information like (a) your name and address (b) name and address of the PIO (c) the information that you need (d) the year to which the information relates to. It should also contain your signature and date.

The application should be accompanied by the application fee. In Karnataka the application fee is Rs.10. This may be remitted in the form of cash, DD, bankers' cheque, Indian Postal Order or in other form as specified in the relevant Rules. Remember that you need not give any reason for requesting information or any other personal details except those that may be necessary for contacting the PIO.

In case you belong to the Below the Poverty Line (BPL) you need not pay the application fee. However you need to prove by way of documentary evidence that you belong to BPL category.

If you are submitting the application via email, you will have to pay the fees within seven days from the date of application. If you fail to do so then your application will be treated as withdrawn.

Step 4: Submission of the Application

You can submit the application to the PIO or the APIO as the case may be. If you send the application by post you should send it by registered post or under certificate of posting so that you have proof of postage and the PIO cannot claim that he/she never received the application. If you submit the application in person, always make sure to get an acknowledgement.

Processing the Application

After having completed the above exercise, it is the turn of the PIO to process your application and either provide you the information or transfer it or reject it as the case may be. In case the PIO accepts your application, he/she will inform you the number of pages in which the information is contained and the amount to be paid for the information. The PIO will also provide you the name and address of the Appellate Authority in case you want to appeal against the decision of the PIO.

In case the required information is not available with the PIO to whom the application is sent, the PIO will identify the person or PIO with whom the information is likely to be available and transfer it to him/her. The applicant will be informed about the transfer. The transfer should be done within 5 days after receipt of the application.

The PIO can reject the application if the information you have requested falls under one of the exemptions in the RTI Act and the PIO additionally decides that there is no overriding public interest in releasing the information. In case of rejection the PIO has to give you written notice within 30 days. The decision to reject must also state the reasons for rejection, the period within which you can appeal and the name and contact details of the Appellate Authority.

If the PIO fails to give you a decision notice, then this is regarded as a 'deemed refusal'. You may then appeal to the departmental Appellate Authority or send a complaint to the Central or State Information Commission of the State concerned.

Step 5: First Appeal

In every public authority, an officer senior in rank to the PIO has been designated to hear appeals. He/she is referred to as the Appellate Authority (AA). You can make an appeal to the AA if: (a) you are aggrieved by the decision made (b) no decision was made within the proper time limits (c) you are a third party consulted during the application process and you are unhappy with the decision made by the PIO.

The appeal should be sent in writing within 30 days on which you received the decision or you should have received the decision from the PIO. Some State Governments have prescribed a format for the appeal and also the details to be included in the appeal.

The AA should take a decision within 30 days of filing the appeal. However, the time limit can be extended to 45 days. Any delay after this has to be recorded. If you are not satisfied with the decision of the AA you have the right to make a Second Appeal.

Step 5: Second Appeal

The Second Appeal against the AA can be made to the Central or State Information Commission as the case may be. The appeal should be filed within 90 days from the date on which the decision should have been made or from the date a decision was actually received. However, the Information Commission has the discretion to allow appeals after this period has expired.

The procedure for Second Appeal, the information to be provided, fee to be paid, if any, are prescribed by the Central or State Government. The procedure is similar to that of First Appeal.

Making a Complaint

Instead of making an appeal to the AA and then to the Information Commission you also have the option of approaching the Information Commission directly and submitting a complaint under Section 18(1) of the Act. You can file a complaint if: (a) you have not been able to submit an application to the PIO for various reasons (b) you have been refused access to any information requested (c) you do not get a response to your request within the prescribed time limits (d) you have been asked to pay fees which you think are unreasonable (e) you believe the information you have been given is incomplete, misleading or false (f) you face any other problem related to accessing information under the RTI Act.

Step 6: Appeal to the Courts

In case you are not satisfied with the decision of the Central or State Information Commission, as the case may be, you can file an appeal in the State High Court or the Supreme Court.

How to make RTI Act More Effective?

1. It is strongly felt that even after four years of implementation of the Act; most of the Public Information Officers take this Act carelessly and have the least knowledge of the Act. The Commissions have powers to enhance training provision for officials on Right to Information and ask them to give guidance on how to use the Act. It can be suggested that, a mandatory provision to establish a system of education on the RTI Act to be given, to promote the freedom of information.

2. It is highly recommended that the appellate authority should also be included within the penalizing provisions and not to put the PIO alone in the frame. In a case, CIC/EB/C/2006/0040, the same question arose, i.e., whether an appellate authority can be penalised under this Act? The Appellate authority is not covered under the penalizing

provisions of the Act. But in this case, it was proved that he clearly failed to uphold the Act in the public interest. This decision of the CIC asked the public authority to consider disciplinary action under their service rules.

3. Most of the information cases deals with seeking the personal information. Information sought on public interest is rarely seen. Hence, it is necessary to set up a public education campaign on 'how to access information and its application' at Panchayat, school level, etc., in order to make them feel empowered.

4. In order to reduce the pendency of information cases, there should be speedy disposal of petitions. One of the drawbacks of having governmental officers as PIO was that most of them did not know the procedures of working of commissions. Repeated hearings were required, since the PIOs' were unable to bring explanations/affidavits giving reasons for the delay in disposing request. So, it is suggested that manual for public authorities should include the 'procedures for appearing for hearings before the Information Commissions' while dealing with information cases.

5. The Act does not confer any power on SIC or CIC to invalidate or strike down Rules issued by the appropriate Government or the Competent Authorities. But should it be specifically mentioned in the RTI Act, when the Rules are made for the effective implementation of the Act. And such a situation shall arise only when Rules issued are detrimental to the object of the Act. The rules made by the Central Government or State Government, shall be laid before each House of Parliament or before the State legislature, as the case may be. Hence, it is suggested that each Rule made by the competent authority, based on RTI Act should also be put to scrutiny by Information Commissions or a superior body.

Shortcoming and Challenges of Act

We must recognise that in every country there are laws other than the State law, which is the law practised in the courts. There are innumerable unwritten laws, living laws or customary laws that have been in use but have not been recognised. These are laws of the land and the common man uses them," says Christoph Eberhard, associate researcher at the French Institute of Pondicherry for the project 'Societies and Medicines in South Asia'.

The Law Commission of India's 179th Report and Reports of number of Committees and Council working on this subject sensitized the Government of India to enact a specific law on Right to Information. Likewise in May 2005 the Right to Information Act, (22 of 2005) was passed by Indian Parliament, which came into effect from 12 October, 2005.

The Act in its preamble says to provide for setting up the practical regime of Right to Information for all citizens to secure access to information under control of public authorities in order to promote transparency and accountability in administration. Thus, adhering to the principles of democracy. The Preamble to the Act is very promising but how far the promise is kept is the real question? It is evident fact that real test of any machine is assessed in its working conditions rather than on ideal conditions. Our bureaucratic system functions under the shield of "Official Secrets Act" and most of the officials are averse to part with any information. Even the legislatures, the elected representatives of the people at times are deprived of getting information in reply to the question they put in the House fourteen days in advance. The concerned Ministers being guided by their respective bureaucratic machinery prefer to shift responsibility by simply saying *"information are being collected"*. The Assurance Committee in more than one occasion has expressed their concern over the apathetic attitude of the official set up. But we don't find any substantial change in the attitude. The grievance cells functioning in different departments have also miserably failed to redress miseries of common mass. Then how can we expect good response from the same apparatus? How far the old system would be able to handle the new Act is a million dollar question*? (Basanta Das, "Right To Information: A Step Towards Accountability" Teb. (2006) Orissa Review,60*-61 at 60).

If we look S.2(j) which *inter alia* say "Right to Information means" the Right to Information accessible under the Act which is held by or under the control of any public authority. The Act provides Right to Information only from public authority, which is not at par with the principles of UDHR 1948. Art. 19 of UDHR provide Right to Information through any media and regardless of frontiers, i.e., both private and public bodies.

Another noteworthy provision in the definition clause is the definition of Information. It means any material in any form. It includes records, document, memos e-mail, etc. S. 2(i) defines records which *inter alia* includes File'. Thus, the combined reading of S. 2(f),(i),0) would indicate that a citizen has right to access to a file of which the file notings are an integral parts. Recently the term "File Noting" was in news due to a controversy. Before going into the controversy let us discuss what does a 'File Noting means? File Noting are comment made on pages that are inserted in every "current file" containing official document made on green pages that are inserted in every "current file" containing correspondence such as minutes of meeting, or orders, when a file is put up to an officer, he writes his comments or decision on the green pages called 'Note file' and forward it along with 'current file'. "The 'Note file' is key to understand the rationale behind a decision", says AK Venkatasubramanyam, a former civil servant and founder of Chennai based NGO Catalyst Trust. Now let us see what was the controversy attached to it. Department of personnel (DoPT) decided to use frequently asked Question (FAQ) on its website. *(www.persmin.nic.in)* In response to the question, "what does information mean? The website quotes the whole Section 2(f) and then arbitrarily adds the words "but does not include File notings' [S.2(f)]". Objections and reminder from citizens group to the DoPT fell on deaf ears, and the matter was brought before the Central Information Commission in the form of an appeal. In its decision of January 31, 2006 in *Satyapal vs. TCIL (ICPB/A1/2006)* held that "no file would be complete without note sheets having file noting'. In other words file noting are integral part of a file". And further held….. "Therefore, we are of the firm view that, in terms of the existing provision of RTI Act, a citizen has the right to seek information contained in 'file noting' unless the same relates to matters covered under S.8 of the Act." Thus, the relevance of the CPIO, TC/LO on the website clarification of the Department of Personnel to deny the information on the basis that 'file notings' are exempted is misplaced. The Central information Commission had ordered in *Pyare Lal vs. Ministry of Railway* to the DoPT to remove the phrase "but does not include file notings".

It is unfortunate that till date DoPT has not complied with the order passed by Central Information Commission. Moreover, Union Government was trying to remove 'file noting' from arena of information through amendment. This created ripples in the country and social activists like Aruna Roy, Anna Hazare, Arvind Kejriwal and many more protested against the government decision. Currently due to fear of mass agitation government withdrew its initiation on the issue.

Section 4 of the Act *prima facie* looks a starry provision. However, only those stars shine like the sun which are nearer to ground. The Section 4 of the Act casts an obligation on every "Public Authority" as defined by the Act to make voluntary disclosure on seventeen items and publish the same for general information. These information need to be computerized and connected through network all over the country. The Act stipulates one hundred and 120 days from the enactment of this Act, i.e., by 12th October, 2005 for publication of the information by Public Authority. More than eighteen months have passed but the provision is not yet implemented. Except few most of the department have adopted slothful approach towards the implementation of section. The section is also not backed by any sanction provision. This makes it impotent.

Section 5 of the Act makes it mandatory that every public authority shall within one hundred days of the enactment of this Act designate as many officer as Central Public Information Officers or State Public Information Officers in all Administrative Units and at each subdivisional level or other subdistrict level as a Control Assistant Public Information Officer or a State Assistant Public Information Officer. The Act nowhere mention about the qualification of these officers. Therefore, the appointment of these officers depends upon the whims and fancies of the concerned department.

Provision to Section 7 Subclause (5) provides that person living below the poverty line (BPL) has been exempted from the fees to file application. However, both the Acts and the rules are silent whether they would be required to deposit required amount of fees to receive information in shape of printout copies, floppy diskette, CD, or maps and plans. In country like India more than 26% of population is falling under the BPL category. What will be the fate of their Right to Information is not even imaginable.

S. 8 and S.9 provides grounds for reason of rejection of an Application for Information. Right to Information finds its root embedded in Art. 19(c) of the Indian Constitution. The reasonable restriction provided under Art. 19(2) is understandable and same should be the ground for rejecting the application form. But Section 8 and S.9 of the RTI Act has much wider impact than Art. 19(2) of the Indian Constitution.

'Another vital aspect of the Act which is to be scrutinized is Central Information Commission (CIC). CIC is constituted for the purpose of safeguarding the aim of the Right to Information Act, i.e., Free flow of Information and punishing those who are coming in the way of implementation of the Act. The approach adopted by CIC is disheartening. An analysis of the orders passed by the CIC has revealed that in 71 per cent of the total appeals received, the CIC "disposed of appeals" without calling the appellants. It also did not adhere to the principal of natural justice, which requires hearing the appellants to ensure that denial of information is in accordance with exemptions listed in the law.' *(Save "Right To Information Act, Kalam Urged". The Hindu,30/10/06, New Delhi Ed.)*

Similarly, the CIC has not penalized even a single official guilty of denial of information during the first year, which amount to serious violations of the RTI Act. The Act explicitly provides for penalty in such cases. (*Ibid.*)

Penalty was imposed in only two cases of about 15,000 cases decided by CIC so far. One has already been withdrawn and other is in the process of being withdrawn. (*Ibid.*)

The CIC had issued notices in 59 cases without result or penalty. At the same time pendency of cases at the CIC is increasing daily with an average 2,000 cases reported every month. Since penalty is not being imposed as stipulated in the Act, the number of appeals is on rise. The CIC has displayed a lack of knowledge of principles and procedures of justice.

Rights can become reality only when they are achievable by every common citizen of the nation. In country like India, awareness towards one's right is minimal. Most of the Indians and specifically those residing in villages are

ignorant about any such Act. If, however, they know about the Act, they don't know where to go and file the application. All the common man of Indian society is totally ignorant about the functioning of the government to which he has voted to rule. Unless he or she has the basic knowledge regarding the budgetary provisions, funds allotted for different projects and schemes or other welfare measures for which government decisions have already been taken how can he seek for information? (*Supra* note 79).

Contrary to the scheme of the RTI Act, a lot of departments are asking applicants to explain the reason for seeking information. The application form issued by Delhi Development Authority for instance requires the applicant to specify his "interest in obtaining information". This fly in the face of S.6 of the RTI Act which says "An applicant making request for information shall not be required to give any reason for requesting the information or any other personal details except those that may be necessary for contacting him. *(Manoj Mittal. Information Act Faces First Test", Times of India, 23/12/2005 New Delhi Ed.)*

S.23 of the RTI Act bars the jurisdiction of the Courts otherwise than by way of appeal under the Act. Non-interference of Court does not seem to be reasonable more over when CIC has shown cold response towards the implementation of the Act. This is surely leading to miscarriage of justice.

Another major shortcoming of the Act is that there is no provision relating to safeguard of whistleblowers. Whistleblowing means telling in advance of a danger arising out of a stamp or treachery. *(S.P. Sathe, "Right To Information" First Ed.(New Delhi: Butterworths Publication: 2006) p.26).* This may be done either by a citizen or by a person who is part of the government. Late Satyendra Dubey, a brave engineer blew the whistle on the rampant corruption in the Golden Quadrilateral Project Construction. He had written a letter to then Prime Minister requesting that his anonymity be maintained. Since his anonymity was not sustained, he was killed by those who would have been adversely affected by the disclosure. In fact, it is not enough to merely pass the law giving information. The Act should contain provision for safeguarding the whistleblowers.

There is no doubt that Right to Information has raised new hopes to promote transparency and accountability in government. In order to make it more potent the legislature has to make effort to remove the shortcomings. Moreover, public and public authorities have to go in hand in hand in order to make corruption free society.

RTI ACT IN NUTSHELL

- SECTION 2 OF THE ACT. PROVIDES: Definitions
- Subject Matter: Central/State Information Commission, Information, Right to Information, Central/State Chief Information Commissioner, third party and competent authority, etc., defined
- SECTION 3 OF THE ACT. PROVIDES: Right to Information
- Subject Matter: All citizens shall have such right.
- SECTION 4 OF THE ACT. PROVIDES: Obligations of public authorities
- Subject Matter: Strict provisions for providing information
- SECTION 5 OF THE ACT. PROVIDES: Public Information Officers
- Subject Matter: Designation of Central and State Public Information Officers, etc.
- SECTION 6 OF THE ACT. PROVIDES: Request for obtaining Information
- Subject Matter: Written request or through electronic means with fee as may be prescribed.
- SECTION 7 OF THE ACT. PROVIDES:Disposal of request
- Subject Matter: Within 30 days from date of request in normal cases but if the information matters for the life or liberty of a person it can be obtained within 48 hours from or request.
- SECTION 8 OF THE ACT. PROVIDES: Exemption from disclosure to access
- Subject Matter: Information affecting sovereignty of India, security, strategic, scientific of economic interest of State, forbidden informations, secret information and cabinet information, etc., cannot be obtained.
- SECTION 9 OF THE ACT. PROVIDES: Grounds for rejection to access
- Subject Matter: Information not to be provided if it involves the infringement of copyright of an individual.
- SECTION 10 OF THE ACT. PROVIDES: Severability
- Subject Matter: If some part of record is exempt from disclosure, then information of other part can be obtained.
- SECTION 11 OF THE ACT. PROVIDES: Third Party Information
- Subject Matter: Submission of third party to be considered.
- SECTION 12 OF THE ACT. PROVIDES: Constitution of Central Information Commission
- Subject Matter Power conferred on the Central Government.

- SECTION 15 OF THE ACT. PROVIDES: Constitution of State Information Commission
- Subject Matter: Power conferred on the State Government.
- SECTION 18 OF THE ACT, PROVIDES: Complaints.
- Subject Matter: In case of non compliance by CP10/P10 for providing information, making delay, providing ambiguous or false information, information sector can directly approach commission instead of Appeal u/s 19 of the Act.
- SECTION 19 OF THE ACT. PROVIDES: Appeal
- Subject Matter: Any person who is aggrieved by a decision of the Central/State Public Information Officer within 30 days after expiry of specified time for decision or within 30 days from the date or decision.
- SECTION 20 OF THE ACT. PROVIDES: Penalties
- Subject Matter: Rs. 250 per day till application is received or information is furnished in the Central Information Commission or State Information Commission as the case may be, subject to maximum limit of Rs. 25,000. Disciplinary action can also be taken under the service rule.
- SECTION 23 OF THE ACT. PROVIDES: Bar of Jurisdiction of Courts
- Subject Matter: No Court has jurisdiction to deal with complaint made under this Act, and
- SECTION 24 OF THE ACT. PROVIDES: Act not to apply to certain organisations
- Subject Matter: Information in relation to certain organisations established by the Central Government cannot be obtained.

IMPORTANT MILESTONES

Aritcle 19 (2) of the 'International Covenant on Civil and Political Rights'.

(ICCPR), A United Nations General Assembly Resolution 2200A (XXI) of 1996 states:

"Everyone shall have the right to Freedom of Expression; this right shall include freedom to seek, receive and impart information and ideas of all kinds, regardless of frontiers, either orally, in writing or in print, in the form of art, or through any other media of his choice."

Article 10 of the UN Convention against Corruption 2005 states: "... to combat corruption each (member State) shall, in accordance with the fundamental principles of its domestic law, take such measures as may be necessary to enhance transparency in its public administration.

The Word Conference on Human Rights, held in Vienna in 1993 has declared that the Right to Development adopted by United Nations General Assembly in 1986 is a universal and inalienable right and an integral part of fundamental human rights. Right to freedom of expression is regarded as closely linked to the right to development.

Over the years, the Supreme Court has consistently ruled in favour or the citizen's right to know.

In Bennett Coleman, the right to information was held to be included within the right to freedom of speech and expression guaranteed by Art. 19 (1) (a).

Bennett Coleman vs. Union of India, AIR 1973 SC 60.

In Raj Narain, Mr. Justice Mathew Explicitly stated:

It is not in the interest of the public to cover with a veil of secrecy the common routine business ... "the responsibility of officials to explain and to justify their acts is the chief safeguard against oppression and corruption." (*State of UP vs. Raj Narain,* (1975) 4 SCC 428).

The Supreme Court in Secretary, Ministry of I&B, Government of India vs. Cricket Association of Bengal held that:

the right to impart and receive information from electronic media was included in the freedom of speech.(1995) 2 SCC 161.

In S.P Gupta, the right of the people to know about every public act, and the details of every public transaction undertaken by public functionaries was described. (*S.P Gupta vs. UOI,* AIR 1982 SC 149).

In P.U.C.L., the right to information was further elevated to the status of human right, necessary for make governance transparent and accountable. It was also emphasized that governance must be participatory. (*People's Union for Civil Liberties vs. UOL,* 2004 (2) SCC 476).

A mass-based organisation called the Mazdoor Kisan Shakti Sangathan (MKSS) took an initiative to lead the people in a very backward region of Rajasthan – Bhim Tehsil – to assert their right to information by asking for copies of bills and vouchers and names of persons who have been shown in the muster rolls.

MKSS succeeded in getting photocopies of certain relevant documents.

MKKS has organized several public hearings (Jan Sunwai). People's anger made one Engineer of the State Electricity Board to return, in public, an amount or Rs. 15,000 he had extracted from a poor farmer.

The Rajasthan experience on demanding right to information was echoed in other Status.

The need to enact a law on Right to Information was recognised unanimously by the Chief Ministers Conference on "Effective and Responsive Government", held on 24th May, 1997 at New Delhi.

The Government of India, Department of Personnel, decided to Information and Promotion of Open and Transparent Government) in January 1997 under the chairmanship of Mr. H.D Shouri, which submitted its comprehensive and detailed report and the draft Bill on Freedom of Information in May 1997.

The Press Council of India, the Press Institute of India, the National Campaign for People's Right to Information unanimously submitted a resolution to the Government of India to amend the proposed Bill in February, 2000.

The Government of India introduced the Freedom of Information Bill, 2000 (Bill No. 98 of 2000) in the Lok Sabha on 25th July, 2000.

The Bill, which cast as obligation upon public authorities to furnish such information wherever asked for, was passed by the Parliament as the Freedom of Information Act, 2002.

However, the Act could not be brought into force because the date from which the Act could come into force, was not notified in the Official Gazette.

The United Progressive Alliance (UPA) Government at the Centre, which came into power in 2004, set up a National Advisory Council (NAC).

The Council suggested important changes to be incorporated in the FOI Act. These suggestions were examined the FOI Act more progressive, participatory and meaningful.

Later, however, the UPA Government decided to repeal the FOI Act, and enacted a new legislation the Right to Information Act, 2005 effectuating the right of information recognised under Article 19 (1) (a) of the Constitution of India.

Chronology of RTI Laws in India

- Tramilnadu, Goa 1997
- Rajasthan, Karnataka 2000
- Delhi 2001
- Maharashtra, Assam 2001
- Madhya Pradesh 2002
- Madhya Pradesh 2003
- Jammu and Kashmir 2004

IMPORTANT DATES

- 06.01.2003 Parliament enacted FOIA 2002
- 23.12.2004 The RTI Bill introduced in the Lok Shaba
- 11.05.2005 Lok Sabha passed the RTI Bill
- 12.05.2005 Rajya Sabha passed the RTI Bill
- 15.06.2005 The President gave assent to the Act; few Provisions came into force
- 21.06.2005 RTIA published in the Gazette of India, Part II, Sec. 1 Ext. No. 25
- 12.10.2005 RITIA came fully into force

GIST OF RIGHT TO INFORMATION ACT, 2005

An applicant making request for information shall not be required to give any reason for such request.

It would indeed be timely to discuss the Right to Information Act, 2005 The object of the Act. is:

(1) To set out the practical regime for furnishing information to the citizens, and

(2) To promote transparency and accountability in government and semi-government offices.

The Act is applicable to the whole of India except the State of Jammu & Kashmir. Assent of the President of India was received on this Act on 15th June, 2005 and it was published in the Gazette of India on June 21st, 2005.

Like so many other Acts, Sec. 2 of this contains various definitions which are also subject to the context required. Some major definitions are that of information, record 'the Right to Information and third party'. Section 3 of this Act provides statutorily the Right to Information to all the citizens. Some major obligations are:

- To maintain all its records duly catalogued and indexed and make them available on computer as soon as and as far as possible.
- Publish within 120 days the details of the organization, its functions, the duties and power of its officers and empolyees, the procedures, norms, rules, regulations, instructions, manuals and records to be followed, the process of consultation with the representatives of the public and committees constituted for it, a directory or its officers and employees, their monthly remunerations and other compensations, etc., the budget allotted to each of its agencies, the subsidy programmes, the details of the public information officers, etc.
- To update the above information every year.
- To publish all the relevant facts while formulating or taking any important policy decisions.
- To give clear reasons for every administrative or quasi-judicial decision, affecting any person.
- To disseminate widely and endeavour in such a manner as to give easiest access of information to the citizens.

Section 5 provides that every department should designate an officer as Central or State public information officer and in every administrative unit or office, an officer as assistant pubic information. Sec. 5 may seek assistance of any officer whose assistance is necessary for the disposal of the application for informatin.

- The application for information may be furnished either in writing in English or Hindi or the other official language or through electronic media.
- According to Sec. 6(2), making request for information shall not to be required to give any reason for such request.
- The time for disposal of applications for information, according to Sec. 7 is 30 days of the receipt of the request.
- But where the request is made through other officers a further period of 5 days is also to be added.
- If the information is not furnished within such period, the request shall be deemed to be rejected.
- In case the cost is required for furnishing the information, the person below the poverty line shall be exempted from that. Certain informations are exempted from disclosure. Their details are given in Sec. 8.

Understanding Sec. 20

Question:

Is it true that penalty for delay/denial is mandatory? Or is it a discretionary power of SIC/CIC? Answer

The RTI Act is clear that penalty for delay/denial is mandatory. The PIO may however lawfully avoid penalty or disciplinary action based on some conditions.

Detailed Explanation:

Sections 20(1) and 20(2) – Penalties and Disciplinary Action respectively -- are the teeth of the RTI Act, 2005. Information seekers all over India feel that this section gives them leverage over unresponsive administrative officials. However, Information Commissioners are bent on showing that Penalty and Disciplinary Action depends more on their "discretionary powers".

To understand the correct legal position, let us carefully read this section:

Section 20 Penalties Etc.

20(1) Where the Information Commission at the time of deciding any complaint or appeal is of the opinion that the PIO has, without any reasonable cause, refused to receive an application for information or has not furnished information within the time specified under Sub-section (1) of Section 7 or *malafidely* denied the request for information or knowingly given incorrect, incomplete or misleading information or destroyed information which was the subject of the request or obstructed in any manner in furnishing the information, it shall impose a penalty of two hundred and fifty rupees each day till application is received or information is furnished, so however, the total amount of such penalty shall not exceed twenty-five thousand rupees:

The PIO shall be given a reasonable opportunity of being heard before any penalty is imposed on him:

The burden of proving that he acted reasonably and diligently shall be on the Public Information Officer

20(2) Where the Information Commission at the time of deciding any complaint or appeal is of the opinion that the PIO has, without any reasonable cause and persistently, failed to receive an application for information or has not furnished information within the time specified under Sub-section (1) of Section 7 or *malafidely* denied the request for information or knowingly given incorrect, incomplete or misleading information or destroyed information which was the subject of the request or obstructed in any manner in furnishing the information, it shall recommend for disciplinary action against the PIO under the service rules applicable to him.

The word "shall" means that if some conditions are fulfilled, Information Commissioner MUST impose penalties and/or recommend disciplinary action against PIOs. What are these conditions? They are:

(1) PIO has, without any reasonable cause, refused to receive an application for information or has not furnished information within the time specified under Section 7(1)

(2) *malafidely* denied the request for information

(3) knowingly given incorrect, incomplete or misleading information or destroyed information which was the subject of the request

(4) obstructed in any manner in furnishing the information

For the law to be effective, the Information Commissioner is required to record his opinion in his Order, stating whether or not one or more of the above points are true. If his Order indicates that he believes one of these above to be true, then he cannot legally avoid imposing penalty or recommending disciplinary action. (If he fails to do so, one may file a writ petition with the High Court, asking for a writ of *mandamus* directing him to impose suitable penalty and/or recommend disciplinary action.)

Meanings and Interpretations of important terms:

- "Any reasonable cause" means reasonable causes under RTI Act, namely:
  (a) Exemptions mentioned in Sections 8 and 9
  (b) Denial u/s 11, i.e., information requested is of a third-party "confidential" nature, and the PIO, being expressly requested by the third party not to disclose it, decides not to disclose, especially as disclosure is not in public interest.
  (c) The item requested is not "information" as defined under Section 2(f)
  (d) The authority from whom the information is demanded is not "public authority" as defined under Section 2(h).

  To a small extent, extraneous reasons of delay (but not outright denial) that are not mentioned in the RTI Act may also be considered. For example:

  (e) The file is lost, and all due attempts have been made, or are being made, to recover the contents of the file from other relevant files stored with other government departments.
  (f) The public authority was busy for some days or weeks coping with the fallout of a *force majeure* event such as 26/7 or 26/11, or other events like elections, Ganesh festival, etc.

However, as the list of extraneous reasons expands, the RTI Act gets diluted. The Act is diluted when PIOs are allowed to escape with excuses such as "I accompanied the minister on a foreign tour, and so I couldn't reply to the RTI applications", "I went to my native place for two weeks" or "I was on election duty". Many Information Commissioners are routinely accepting such excuses for failure to comply with the deadlines of Section 7(1). Some are noting these reasons in their Orders. Others are not recording the reasons, but are giving clean chits by stating, "I am of the opinion that the PIO had genuine reasons for not providing information on time."

RED ALERT! Even if such extraneous reasons are allowed as reasons for delay, they must never be accepted as valid reasons for denial of information, otherwise it amounts to creating new exemption clauses, over and above the one listed in the RTI Act! Citizens must resist Information Commissioners' tendencies to create new exemptions!

- "*Malafidely*" literally means "in bad faith". However, in practise, it means "without reasonable cause" under RTI Act, as detailed in the earlier section. Negligence, repetitive delays/denial etc are also to be deemed as being in bad faith. Many Information Commissioners allow even repeated non-compliance by the same PIO to go unpunished. They say, "*Kya karega bechara*? The poor fellow is overworked by his department! He is really a sincere fellow, and whatever his lapses are, his intentions are not bad." Some Information Commissioners argue that even habitual offenders are not *malafidely* denying the information, as they bear no personal malice towards the appellant, or have no intention to hide the facts!
- Knowingly giving incorrect, incomplete or misleading information or destroying information which was the subject of the request is punishable under the RTI Act. Please note, the Section also says, "the burden of proving that he acted reasonably and diligently shall be on the Public Information Officer". Therefore, it is to be automatically assumed by the Information Commissioner that the PIO "knowingly" committed his actions of omission or commission, and it is for the PIO to produce evidence that he did so unknowingly.

QUESTIONS

1. What are the Six reasons why citizens should have the Right to Information? Explain.
2. Elaborate in detail the procedure to file an application under RTI Act, 2005.
3. What are the various shortcomings and challenges of RTI Act, 2005?
4. Explain the nine principles on which the Public's Rights to Information is based.
5. Mention various types of information which have been exempted from disclosure under Section 8 of RTI 2005.
6. What is the role of Information Commission in developing the system and mechanism for disclosure and dissemination of information?
7. Sec. 19 of RTI Act, 2005, provides two-tier system of appeals. Discuss?
8. Mention the various sections of RTI Act, 2005 and summarize their contents?
9. Do you consider that RTI Act, 2005 still needs some stringent provisions? Enumerate them.
10. Write a critical note on the RTI Act, 2005.
11. The concept of democracy in India is enshrined in the Preamble to the Constitution of India wherein opening words provide that "We, the People of India", and in the end it lays down "give to ourselves this Constitution". Comment.
12. "For a long period the working of the government had been shrouded in secrecy and the poor citizens had to run from pillar to post even to get small information about his application to get copies of record-of-rights or his representation made to the government functionaries and instances are not lacking where he had not received reply to his genuine request for years together." Discuss how far the RTI Act, 2005 has succeeded in this respect.

Write Short Notes on the following:

1. Why Bennett Coleman & Co. versus Union of India is known as landmark case in Freedom of Press in India?
2. Why Freedom of Information is considered as Fundamental Human Right?
3. According to Right to Information Act, 2005, Sec. 2(1)(B), what is public authority?
4. Under what exceptions the public information officer is not competent to release information to the public?
5. What does "information" mean in RTI Act, 2005?
6. What is the application procedure for requesting information in RTI 2005?
7. Mention at least three duties of a Public Information Officer.
8. What are three key principles on which RTI is based?
9. Mention the three Acts which upheld the Freedom of Press and Information in America?
10. What is the relevance of Shourie Committee in enactment of Right to Information?